YEARBOOK OF EUROPEAN LAW

Editorial Statement

The *Yearbook of European Law* seeks to promote the dissemination of ideas and provide a forum for legal discourse in the wider area of European law. It is committed to the highest academic standards and to providing informative and critical analysis of topical issues accessible to all those interested in legal studies. It reflects diverse theoretical approaches towards the study of law. The *Yearbook* publishes contributions in the following broad areas: the law of the European Union, the European Convention for the Protection of Human Rights, related aspects of international law, and comparative laws of Europe.

Contributions for publication in the articles section should be sent to the following address:

Professor Takis Tridimas
Co-editor
Yearbook of European Law
Centre for Commercial Law Studies
Queen Mary College, University of London
13–14 Charterhouse Square
London
EC1M 6AX

Tel.: +44(0)20 7882 6056
Fax: +44(0)20 7882 5791
Email: t.tridimas@qmul.ac.uk

YEARBOOK OF EUROPEAN LAW

25

2006

EDITORS

P. EECKHOUT
Professor of European Law
King's College London

T. TRIDIMAS
Sir John Lubbock Professor of Banking Law
Queen Mary College, University of London

BOOK REVIEW EDITOR

G. DE BÚRCA

OXFORD
UNIVERSITY PRESS

OXFORD

UNIVERSITY PRESS

Great Clarendon Street, Oxford OX2 6DP

Oxford University Press is a department of the University of Oxford.
It furthers the University's objective of excellence in research, scholarship,
and education by publishing worldwide in

Oxford New York

Auckland Cape Town Dar es Salaam Hong Kong Karachi
Kuala Lumpur Madrid Melbourne Mexico City Nairobi
New Delhi Shanghai Taipei Toronto

With offices in

Argentina Austria Brazil Chile Czech Republic France Greece
Guatemala Hungary Italy Japan Poland Portugal Singapore
South Korea Switzerland Thailand Turkey Ukraine Vietnam

Oxford is a registered trade mark of Oxford University Press
in the UK and in certain other countries

Published in the United States
by Oxford University Press Inc., New York

British Library Cataloguing in Publication Data

Data available

Library of Congress Cataloging in Publication Data

Data available

Typeset by Newgen Imaging Systems (P) Ltd, Chennai, India
Printed in Great Britain
on acid-free paper by
Biddles Ltd, King's Lynn

ISBN 978–0–19–921137–1

1 3 5 7 9 10 8 6 4 2

Editorial Committee

Contents

ARTICLES

SURVEY

REVIEWS OF BOOKS

Abbreviations

AC	Appeal Cases
AETR	Accord européen relative au travail des equipages des véhicules effectuant des transport, internationaux par route (also ERTA)
AG	Advocate General
A-G	Attorney General
AJCL	*American Journal of Comparative Law*
All ER	All England Law Reports
AöR	*Archiv des öffentlichen Rechts*
Art.	Article
BVertfG	Bundesverfassungsgericht
BYIL	*British Yearbook of International Law*
CA	Court of Appeal
CAP	Common Agricultural Policy
CBI	Confederation of Business Industry
CDE	*Cahiers de droit europeen*
CEN	European Committee for (technical) Standardization
CFI	Court of First Instance of the European Communities
CFiLR	*Corporate and Financial Law Review*
CFSP	Common Foreign and Security Policy
CLJ	*Cambridge Law Journal*
CLP	*Current Legal Problems*
CM/Cmnd	Command Paper
CML Rev.	*Common Market Law Review*
CMLR	Common Market Law Reports
DÖV	*Die Öffentliche Verwaltung*
DVBI	*Deutsches Verwaltungsblatt*
EAEC	European Atomic Energy Community
ECB	European Central Bank
ECHR	European Convention on Human Rights
ECJ	European Court of Justice
ECLR	European Competition Law Review
ECrtHR	European Court of Human Rights
ECR	European Court Reports

ECSC	European Coal and Steel Community
EEA	European Environmental Agency
EFSA	European Food and Safety Authority
EIB	European Investment Bank
EIPA	European Institute of Public Administration
EFTA	European Free Trade Area
EJML	*European Journal of Migration and Law*
EL Rev.	*European Law Review*
ELJ	*European Law Journal*
EMU	*European Monetary Union*
EPL	*European Public Law*
ERPL	*European Review of Private Law*
ERTA	European agreement concerning the work of crews of vehicles engaged in international road transport (also AETR)
ESCB	European System of Central Banks
EU	European Union
EuGRZ	*Europäische Grundrechte-Zeitschrift*
EUI	European University Institute
Eu LR	European Law Reports
EuR	*Europarecht*
Euratom	European Atomic Energy Community
EuZW	*Europäische Zeitschrift für Wirtschaftsrecht*
GATS	General Agreement on Trade and Services
GATT	General Agreement on Tariffs and Trade
GG	Grundgesetz
GYIL	*German Yearbook of International Law*
Harv LR	*Harvard Law Review*
HC	House of Commons
HL	House of Lords
IANL	Immigration Asylum and Nationality Law
ICLQ	*International and Comparative Law Quarterly*
IGC	Intergovernmental Conference
ILM	International Legal Materials
ILO	International Labour Organization
IMF	International Monetary Fund
JBL	*Journal of Business Law*
JCMS	*Journal of Common Market Studies*
JEPP	*Journal of European Public Policy*

JZ	*Juristenzeitung*
KB	King's Bench
LIEI	Legal Issues of European/Economic Integration
Lloyd's Rep	Lloyd's Law Reports
LQR	*Law Quarterly Review*
MEP	Member of the European Parliament
MJ	*Maastrict Journal of European and Comparative Law*
MLR	*Modern Law Review*
MP	Member of Parliament
n.	Footnote
NJW	*Neue Juristische Wochenschrift*
OECD	Organization for Economic Co-operation and Development
OFT	Office of Fair Trading
OJ	Official Journal of the European Community
OJLS	*Oxford Journal of Legal Studies*
OSCE	Organization for Security and Co-operation in Europe
PL	*Public Law*
QB	Queen's Bench
QBD	Queen's Bench Division of the High Court
QMV	Qualified Majority Voting
RIDC	*Revue Internationale de droit comparé*
RIDPC	*Rivista Italiana di Diritto Pubblico Communitario*
RMCUE	*Revue du Marché commun et de l'Union européenne*
RMUE	*Revue du Marché unique européen*
RTDE	*Revue trimestrielle de droit européen*
SEA	Single European Act
SLT	*Scots Law Times*
TEC	Treaty Establishing the European Community
TEPSA	Trans European Policy Studies Association
TRIPS	Agreement on Trade-Related Intellectual Property Rights
UCLA Law Rev.	*University of California at Los Angeles (Law Review)*
UN	United Nations Organization
UNTS	United Nations Treaty Series

WLR Weekly Law Reports
WTO World Trade Organization

Ybk Yearbook
YEL *Yearbook of European Law*
YLJ *Yale Law Journal*

ZaöRV *Zeitschrift für ausländisches öffentliches Recht und Völkerrecht*

Recent Developments in the Law of the European Central Bank

Chiara Zilioli and Martin Selmayr[*]

It is now more than eight years since the European Central Bank (ECB) was established in Frankfurt am Main. The creation of this new supranational organization by the EC Treaty has enriched European Community law with many new, and some quite unique, features of institutional and substantive law. As a consequence, the law of the ECB has evolved into a specialized field of Community law that is today covered intensively in legal writings[1] and even taught as its own subject for post graduates at a number of universities.[2]

The law of the ECB first of all results directly from the Treaty establishing the European Community (the EC Treaty) and the Statute of the European System of Central Banks and of the European Central Bank (the Statute), which is attached to the EC Treaty as a Protocol. These provisions can be called, for the purposes of this article, 'primary ECB law'. In addition, the ECB itself has contributed to

---

[*] Dr Chiara Zilioli is Head of the Legal Advice Division in the Directorate-General Legal Services of the European Central Bank, Frankfurt am Main. Dr Martin Selmayr, at the ECB in 1998 and 1999 is today Spokesman of the European Commission responsible for Information Society and Media and also Director of the Centre for European Law at the University of Passau. The reflections made in this article are to be attributed solely to its authors.

[1] Examples are: Smits, *The European Central Bank. Institutional Aspects*, The Hague/London/Boston (1997); Endler, *Europäische Zentralbank und Preisstabilität. Eine juristische und ökonomische Untersuchung der institutionellen Vorkehrungen des Vertrags von Maastricht zur Gewährleistung der Preisstabilität*, Stuttgart (1998); Weinbörner, *Die Stellung der Europäischen Zentralbank (EZB) und der nationalen Zentralbanken in der Wirtschafts- und Währungsunion nach dem Vertrag von Maastricht*, Frankfurt am Main (1998); Reumann, *Die Europäische Zentralbank: Zwischen Selbstbestimmung und vertragsmäßiger Zusammenarbeit mit der Gemeinschaft*, Herbolzheim (2001); Scheller, *The European Central Bank. History, Role and Functions*, Frankfurt am Main (2nd end, 2006). Also the most comprehensive book on monetary law by F.A.Mann includes today, in its 6th edition, a detailed chapter on EMU and the ECB; see Proctor, *Mann on the Legal Aspect of Money*, Oxford (2005), p. 329 *et seq.* See also Zilioli and Selmayr, *The Law of the European Central Bank*, Oxford (2001) and—in the updated Italian version *La Banca centrale europea*—Milan (2007); Selmayr, *Das Recht der Wirtschafts- und Währungsunion I*, Baden-Baden (2002); and ECB (Ed.), *Legal Aspects of the European System of Central Banks. Liber Amicorum Paolo Zamboni Garavelli*, Frankfurt am Main (2005), with many contributions from lawyers of the ECB and national central banks. Since February 2006, the ECB publishes a Legal Working Paper series to disseminate the results of research and reflection on the law of the ECB; see <http://www.ecb.de/pub/scientific/lps/date/html/lpsall.en.html>.

[2] Examples are: the course on 'Economic and Monetary Union' taught by *Giovanni Graziani* and the seminar 'The European Central Bank: tasks and inter-institutional relations' tought by

the development of this specialized field of Community law by adopting, in accordance with Article 110 EC and Article 34 of the Statute, several regulations, decisions, recommendations, opinions, as well as guidelines and instructions (Articles 12.1 and 14.3 of the Statute). This body of ECB-made law can also be called 'secondary ECB law'.[3]

With eight years, the ECB is still a relatively young organization that counts today about 1,360 employees. However, the law of the ECB has shown a remarkable stability and continuity over this first period of supranational central banking, thereby proving that the draftsmen of the Treaty of Maastricht[4] made many wise choices and laid solid legal foundations for the new organization responsible for the single currency. While the EU as a whole has witnessed stormy times over the past years, which included sharp disputes over the 'Stability and Growth Pact', the arrival of altogether 15 new Member States since Maastricht, the debate about the financing of the EU as well as a substantial legitimacy crisis in 2005 following the negative outcome of referenda in France and in the Netherlands on the 'Treaty establishing a Constitution for Europe' (the Constitutional Treaty),[5] the ECB itself remained relatively unaffected by these developments.[6] Steadily, the ECB has conducted the monetary policy for initially 11, then (with the accession of Greece to the euro on 1 January 2001) 12 and today—following the

Chiara Zilioli in the context of the Advanced Diploma in European Studies (ADES) at the Fondazione Collegio Europeo di Parma <http://www.europeancollege.it/allegati_upload/dase/15_allegato1_FILE.pdf>; the course 'Law of Central Banks' taught by several ECB and Bundesbank lawyers in the curriculum of the LL.M. Finance at the Institut for Law and Finance at the Johann Wolfgang Goethe-University, Frankfurt am Main, <http://www.ilf-frankfurt.de/ILF_Curriculum.10.0.html>; the course 'Law of Economic and Monetary Union' taught by *Martin Selmayr* in the curriculum of the LL.M. at the Europe-Institute of the University of Saarbrücken, <http://www.europainstitut.de/euin/llm/index_vorl.html>; the course unit 'Economic and Monetary Union' taught in the second semester of the Master of European Legal Studies at The European Centre for Judges and Lawyers, the Luxembourg Antenna of the European Institute of Public Administration (EIPA), <http://www.eipa.nl/cms/repository/product/InformationMELS_0652701_en.doc>; the course 'Economic and Monetary Union' taught by *Bart van Riel* in the second semester of the Master in European Union Studies at the University of Leiden, <http://www.ma-eus.leidenuniv.nl/index.php3?c=23>; the course 'European and international law of financial markets, money and central banks' taught by *Martin Selmayr* in the curriculum of the LL.M. for European and International Economic Law at Schloss Hofen (Austria), <http://www.vobs.at/schlosshofen/EUROPA/EURLehrgänge/Europ-Int-Wirtschaftsrecht/Wirtschaftsrecht.htm>; the course 'European Monetary Union and Banking Law' taught by *Roger J. Goebel* at Fordham Law School, Center on European Union Law, <http://law.fordham.edu/ihtml/ce-2europeanunion.ihtml?id=650>; the course 'Law of Economic and Monetary Union' taught by *René Smits* at the Amsterdam Law School of the University of Amsterdam, <http://studiegids.uva.nl/web/sgs/en/c/501.html>.

[3] On the different types of secondary ECB law (ECB regulations, ECB decisions, ECB recommendations, ECB opinions, ECB guidelines, ECB instructions) and their legal effects, see Zilioli and Selmayr, *The Law of the European Central Bank*, Oxford (2001), p. 91 *et seq.*

[4] Cf. Van den Berg, *The Making of the Statute of the European System of Central Banks: An Application of Checks and Balances*, Amsterdam (2005).

[5] Treaty establishing a Constitution for Europe [2003] OJ C310/1.

[6] Cf. Selmayr, 'Europäische Zentralbank', in: Weidenfeld and Wessels (Eds.), *Jahrbuch der Europäischen Integration 2005*, Baden-Baden (2006), p. 123.

introduction of the euro in Slovenia as from 1 January 2007[7]—13 Member States. The ECB has ensured thereby that the euro has become a stable currency with a low inflation rate of close to 2 per cent on average. The ECB also could contribute, with its policy and expertise, to the convergence of European financial law and prudential supervision standards as well as to the progressive integration of Europe's financial markets.[8] One factor promoting continuity and stability of the ECB's policy was certainly that its legal foundations remained untouched in these first years. The Treaty reforms of Amsterdam and Nice, which amended many provisions of primary Community law, did not lead to any major changes with regard to the provisions of primary ECB law.[9]

Also successions at the top of the ECB, as regards its President and the Members of its Executive Board, took place smoothly and in line with the rules established in Maastricht, in spite of many sceptical voices at the time when the ECB was set up. *Otmar Issing* was the last member of the first Executive Board to leave the ECB when his eight-year-term ended in May 2006[10]—a moment that also marked the end of the first cycle in terms of personalities at the top of the ECB. The first President of the ECB, *Willem F. Duisenberg*, appointed (under great controversy) in 1998 for a mandate of eight years[11] as foreseen in Article 11.2 subparagraph 2 of the Statute, had remained in office for five and a half years until he decided, in view of his age, to retire voluntarily[12]—just 19 months before his premature death which was tremendously regretted among central

---

[7] Council Decision 2006/495/EC of 11 July 2006 in accordance with Article 122(2) of the Treaty on the adoption by Slovenia of the single currency on 1 January 2007 [2006] OJ L195/25.

[8] See ECB, 'The contribution of the ECB and the Eurosystem to European financial integration', Monthly Bulletin, May 2006, p. 62. See also Sáinz de Vicuña, 'Optional instruments for the integration of European financial markets', in: ECB (Ed.), *Legal Aspects of the European System of Central Banks, supra* note 1, p. 397.

[9] Cf. De Witte, 'The Pillar Structure and the Nature of the European Union.: Greek Temple or French Gothic Cathedral?', in: Heukels, Blokker and Brus (Eds.), *The European Union After Amsterdam. A Legal Analysis*, The Hague/London/Boston (1998), p. 53, who said that the whole EMU chapter 'although inserted in the EC Treaty, is really a pillar itself, solitary and untouched by recent intergovernmental conferences.'

[10] *Issing*, who had shaped considerably the monetary strategy of the ECB, was replaced by *Jürgen Stark*, formerly Vice-President of Deutsche Bundesbank, who was appointed as member of the Executive Board of the ECB as from 1 June 2006, cf. Decision 2006/371/EC taken by common accord of the Governments of the Member States having the euro as their currency at the level of Heads of State or Government of 19 May 2006 appointing a member of the Executive Board of the European Central Bank [2006] OJ L136/41. See also *Missing Issing? How the loss of an ECB pivot will be felt*, Financial Times, 16 March 2006, p.11.

[11] See Art. 1.1 of Decision 98/345/EC taken by common accord of the Governments of the Member States adopting the single currency at the level of Heads of State or Government of 26 May 1998 appointing the President, the Vice-President and the other members of the Executive Board of the European Central Bank [1998] OJ L154/33.

[12] On 7 February 2002, at the occasion of the tenth anniversary of the Treaty of Maastricht, *Duisenberg* had informed the Presidency of the Council about his intention to step down on 9 July 2003, his 68th birthday. On this, see <http://www.ecb.de/press/pr/date/2002/html/pr020207.en.html>. To ensure a smooth succession, *Duisenberg* in the end remained in office until 31 October 2003 when the decision to appoint his successor took effect.

bankers and many others worldwide. As ECB President, he was followed by *Jean-Claude Trichet*, formerly the President of the Banque de France, who was appointed for eight years,[13] as required by the Statute, thus demonstrating to all sceptics that the often-told story of an (illegal) agreement to divide the first mandate of the President of the ECB in two consecutive four years terms between the two biggest Member States[14] was nothing else than a myth firmly defeated by both the independent characters of *Duisenberg* and *Trichet* and the clear foundations of their personal independence in primary ECB law that has allowed them to resist against all signs of potential political pressure.

In spite of the stability and continuity of the ECB, of its policy and of its law, legal practice has evolved substantially under the legal provisions in place. It has developed, implemented and fine-tuned primary and secondary ECB law, has filled up the spaces and added many examples and illustrations to what originally had been an untested field of law. On the basis of the practical experience with the law of the ECB, and of a first important ruling of the European Court of Justice (ECJ) on it, we will in the following pages give an update[15] (as of January 2007) on the most relevant questions that the law of the ECB needs to address today. We will start with analysing, once again and in the light of recent developments, the legal nature of the ECB, the scope of its independence and the ECB's relationship with the Community institutions, in particular with the Community legislature. We will then have a close look at the evolution of the relationship between the ECB and the national central banks of the EU Member States within the European System of Central Banks (ESCB) to assess in particular whether the legal provisions of the EC Treaty and the Statute, which subordinate national central banks to the governance of the ECB, have been properly implemented and observed in practice. We will finally dedicate some attention to the ECB's recent international activities, which are evidence of the growing international importance of the euro and are on the way to make the ECB an as important central bank on the world stage as the US Federal Reserve System is today.

I. The Legal Status of the ECB: the Debate Continues

Already at the Intergovernmental Conference leading to the Treaty of Maastricht, the legal status of the ECB was the subject of many controversies. Worth remembering are initial ideas to submit the ECB to policy guidelines of the

---

[13] Decision 2003/767/EC taken by common accord, at the level of Heads of State or Government, by the Governments of the Member States having the euro as their currency of 16 October 2003 appointing the President of the European Central Bank [2003] OJ L277/16.

[14] On this, see Selmayr, 'Gefahr für die Europäische Zentralbank?' [1998] Europablätter 39.

[15] On our earlier writings on the law of the ECB, see Zilioli and Selmayr, 'The External Relations of the Euro Area: Legal Aspects' [1999] CML Rev. 273; 'The European Central Bank, its System and

European Council[16] as well as the proposal to make the EC and/or the Member States the shareholders of the ECB.[17] Neither proposal was retained in the final version of the Maastricht Treaty. The EC Treaty provides on the one hand, in Article 108 EC, for the independence of the ECB, of the national central banks and of the members of their decision-making bodies from all instructions of the Community institutions and bodies as well as from the governments of the Member States. The Statute grants on the other hand to the ECB its own financial resources, stemming from the capital and the foreign reserves that its shareholders, which are the national central banks, have to transfer to it (in accordance with Articles 28, 29 and 30 of the Statute), and also from monetary policy operations (Articles 32 and 33 of the Statute).[18] However, in spite of these clear rules in primary ECB law, the debate on the scope of the ECB's independence continued after Maastricht and even sharpened with the advent of the euro and thus of the practical reality of EMU on 1 January 1999.

A. More than just an Academic Debate

Since Maastricht, the debate on the status of the ECB has continued first of all in legal writing. Being the first ones to express a more detailed analysis of this

---

its Law' [1999] Euredia 187 and 307, re-published in [1999–2000] YEL 348; 'The European Central Bank: An Independent Specialized Organization of Community Law' [2000] CML Rev. 591; *The Law of the European Central Bank*, Oxford (2001); and 'The Constitutional Status of the European Central Bank' [2007] CML Rev. (in print).

[16] This idea was still present when then President of France *François Mitterrand* described the status of the ECB, in a TV debate on 3 September 1992, prior to the French referendum on the Treaty of Maastricht, as follows: 'La Banque Centrale, la future Banque Centrale [. . .] elle ne décide pas [. . .]. Les techniciens de la Banque Centrale sont chargés d'appliquer dans le domaine monétaire les décisions du Conseil européen, prises par les douze Chefs d'Etat et de Gouvernement, c'est-à-dire par les politiques qui représentent leurs peuple [. . .]. Or, j'entends dire partout [. . .] que cette Banque Centrale Européenne sera maîtresse des décisions! Ce n'est pas vrai! La politique monétaire appartient au Conseil Européen, et l'application de la politique monétaire appartient à la Banque Centrale, dans le cadre des décisions du Conseil Européen.' Quoted according to Issing, *Unabhängigkeit der Notenbank und Geldwertstabilität*, Mainz (1993), 31, footnote 48.

[17] Cf. Bailleix Banerjee, *La France et la Banque Centrale européenne*, Paris (1999), pp. 102, 103, 130 and 311.

[18] Two types of monetary income need to be distinguished: firstly, monetary income accruing to the national central banks of the euro area Member States in the performance of ESCB activities, and secondly, monetary income accruing directly to the ECB itself. As regards the monetary income accruing to the national central banks, Article 32.5 of the Statute provides that it is first pooled and then allocated to the national central banks in accordance with their paid-up shares in the capital of the ECB. However, before that it serves as back-up to cover possible losses incurred by the ECB according to Article 33.2 of the Statute. So far, the Governing Council of the ECB decided twice—on 16 March 2000 and 11 March 2005—to make use of the monetary income of the national central banks in this way. On the monetary income accruing directly to the ECB (which is the result of the ECB's capacity to issue euro banknotes itself under Article 106(1) EC), the Statute does not provide for a specific distribution mechanism; this income thus counts as direct profit of the ECB under Article 33 of the Statute which is primarily to be transferred to the general reserve fund of the ECB, with any surplus to be distributed to its shareholders in proportion to their paid-up shares. Today, the ECB issues 8% of the euro banknotes itself and thereby generates directly monetary income; see the

important issue for the proper functioning of Economic and Monetary Union,[19] we took as starting point the rules of the EC Treaty and of the Statute itself. We therefore emphasized in our contributions not only the independence the ECB enjoys under Article 108 EC from all instructions, but also pointed to the many further elements in the EC Treaty and in the Statute that strengthen the ECB's special and independent status: the ECB's own legal personality, that is worded in Article 107(2) EC in identical terms as the legal personality of the EC (Article 281 EC) and of the European Atomic Energy Community (Article 184 Euratom)[20]; its own decision-making bodies and their far-reaching personal independence; the own law-making powers of the ECB under Article 110 EC Treaty and Articles 12.1, 14.3 and 34 of the Statute, which allow the ECB to adopt regulations, decisions, recommendations, opinions, guidelines and instructions; as well as the own budgetary and financial resources of the ECB. We have concluded from all these legal features of the ECB's independence that the ECB should be classified not alongside the classical Community institutions in the sense of Article 7 EC, from which the ECB is legally clearly distinct, but as *an independent specialized organization of Community law*,[21] which in many instances has features similar to the legal persons EC and Euratom. The special status of the ECB is, in our view, not an end in itself but serves its primary objective to maintain, in accordance with Article 105(1), first sentence EC and Article 2 of the Statute, price stability for Europe's single currency. This requires that decisions affecting the euro must, in principle, be taken and implemented by an organization solely committed to this objective and legally protected against political pressure.[22]

The foundation of the ECB on primary Community law, as entrenched in the EC Treaty and the Statute, has been always a key feature of our analysis. Unlike some writers,[23] we never placed the ECB or ECB law *outside* the framework of Community law, but always emphasized that the ECB, following the decision

---

banknote allocation key in the Annex to Decision ECB/2001/15 on the issue of euro banknotes [2001] OJ L337/52, as last amended by Decision ECB/2006/25 [2007] OJ L24/13.

[19] See the articles quoted *supra* note 15.

[20] This is also stressed by Smulders, in: von der Groeben and Schwarze (Eds.), *Kommentar zum EU- und EG-Vertrag*, Baden-Baden (2004), Art. 107 EG, para. 6 *et seq.*

[21] See Zilioli and Selmayr, 'The European Central Bank: An Independent Specialized Organization of Community Law' [2000] CML Rev. 591, in particular at p. 621 *et seq.* See already Selmayr, 'Die Wirtschafts- und Währungsunion als Rechtsgemeinschaft' [1999] Archiv des öffentlichen Rechts 357, at p. 372: 'selbständige Sonderorganisation'; and Selmayr, 'Die EZB als Neue Gemeinschaft—ein Fall für den EuGH?' [1999] Europablätter 170, at p. 177: 'selbständige Sonderorganisation des Gemeinschaftsrechts'.

[22] Zilioli and Selmayr, *supra* note 21, p. 629: 'the independent nature of the ECB is not an end in itself, but has been created by the authors of the Treaties in order to secure freedom from inflation within the European Union'. See also Selmayr, 'Die Wirtschafts- und Währungsunion als Rechtsgemeinschaft', *supra* note 21, p. 372: 'nicht Selbstzweck, sondern dient der Realisierung ihrer vorrangigen Verpflichtung auf das Ziel der Preisstabilität'.

[23] Cf. Wolf, 'Die Revision des Grundgesetzes durch Maastricht' [1993] Juristenzeitung 594, at p. 595. See also the initial terminology of Hahn, *Der Vertrag von Maastricht als völkerrechtliche*

taken at the Intergovernmental Conference at Maastricht *not* to create an inter-governmental 'fourth pillar' for Economic and Monetary Union,[24] is deliberately a creation of the EC Treaty, subject to the rules of primary Community law and to the control of the ECJ.[25] For us, ECB law is thus an integral part of Community law. We have therefore always stressed that the ECB is an organization *of Community law*. For us, the strength of Community law, and the monopoly of the ECJ to rule, in the last instance, on disputes surrounding primary and secondary ECB law, has always been the best guarantee for a solid legal entrenchment of the ECB's independence.[26] As we wrote in 2000 already: '*To view the ECB as an independent specialized organization of Community law therefore expresses its subordination not to the political process, but to the rule of Community law*'.[27]

To provoke an academic debate about the institutional novelties of the ECB, we illustrated the special status of the ECB as a new organization responsible for Europe's single currency with the term '*new Community*'[28] to show that the ECB could be seen, in view of its striking organizational features, as a legal person akin to EC and Euratom as it has, in its fields of competence, legal personality and is

---

Übereinkunft und Verfassung, Baden-Baden (1992), according to whom the Treaty of Maastricht integrated the ECB as 'eigenständigen Handlungsträger' (= 'independent actor') into the EU (p. 42) and disconnected it at the same time from the 'Ämterverfassung' (= organisational structure) both of the Community and of the Member States (p. 73). This terminology was later revised by Hahn and Häde, 'Die Zentralbank vor Gericht. Rechtsschutz und Haftung in der Europäischen Wirtschafts- und Währungsunion', [2001] Zeitschrift für Handelsrecht 30, at p. 33 *et seq.*, where the ECB is now qualified as 'Gemeinschaftsinstitution mit organähnlicher Stellung' (Community organ with institution-like status).

[24] On the rejection of the 'fourth pillar' proposal, see Zilioli and Selmayr, *supra* note 21, p. 601 *et seq.*; and Selmayr, *supra* note 1, p. 182 *et seq.* with many further references. See also Zilioli and Selmayr, *The Law of the European Central Bank*, Oxford (2001), p. 9 *et seq.* In spite of our explicit position against the 'fourth pillar' proposal and our clear view that the ECB is a supranational creation of Community law, one author has misunderstood our arguments and made the attempt to wrongly associate us with the 'fourth pillar' proposal; see Dutzler, 'OLAF or the Question of Applicability of Secondary Community Law to the ECB', European Integration Online Papers 2001, N° 1, <http://eiop.or.at/eiop/texte/2001-001a.htm> (meanwhile removed). On this, see our comment 'A Matter of Academic Propriety', posted at <http://eiop.or.at/eiop/comment/2001-001c.htm>. The clearly misleading interpretation of our view by Dutzler was later corrected, without however changing the personal opposition of the author to our view; see Dutzler, *The European System of Central Banks: An Autonomous Actor? The Quest for an Institutional Balance of EMU*, Wien (2003), p. 70 *et seq.*

[25] Zilioli and Selmayr, *supra* note 21, p. 623: '[A]n understanding of the ECB as an independent specialized organization *of Community law* rather than a separate pillar [. . .] emphasizes that despite its independence, the ECB undoubtedly forms part of the Community legal order by which it has been established; that it is an organization within the European Union's first and central pillar; and that it is therefore fully subject to the principles of primary Community law and to the jurisdiction of the ECJ.'

[26] Zilioli and Selmayr, *supra* note 21, p, 642 *et seq.* See also Selmayr, 'Die Wirtschafts- und Währungsunion als Rechtsgemeinschaft', *supra* note 21, p. 391. This view is followed by Schütz, 'Die Legitimation der Europäischen Zentralbank zur Rechtsetzung', Europarecht 2001, p. 291, at p. 302.

[27] Zilioli and Selmayr, *supra* note 21, p. 624.

[28] Zilioli and Selmayr, *supra* note 21, p. 622: 'While ECSC and EAEC and are, from their origin, specialized organizations for coal and steel and atomic energy policy, the ECB has been established by

therefore particularly supranational and independent from national politics. In addition, this emphasis on the legal personality of the ECB also made clear why, in our view, it would be the ECB itself, and not the legal person Community, which would be legally liable under Article 288(3) EC for the acts and omissions of the ECB's decision-making bodies and of ECB employees; because the ECB is certainly a Community organization, but not an organization owned by or under the control *of* the Community.[29] With this understanding of the special status of the legal person ECB, we followed an approach already chosen since the 1960s by academics who have written about the legal status of the European Investment Bank (EIB),[30] and also by the EIB itself. These writers initially emphasised that in many respects, the EIB would be a '*third party in relation to the Communities*'[31]— a certainly provocative description that nevertheless helped considerably to achieve, following several legal disputes, in 1988 a formal recognition of the autonomy of the EIB in the case law of the ECJ,[32] as well as a judicial affirmation that the EIB is not an institution of the Community, but a '*Community body established and endowed with legal personality by the Treaty*',[33] a legal personality which is, in the words of the ECJ, '*distinct from that of the Community*'.[34] Being on the one hand '*a Community body intended to contribute towards the attainment of the Community's objectives*' which '*by virtue of the Treaty forms part of the framework of the Community*',[35] while being on the other hand distinct from the legal person EC, gives the EIB an '*ambivalent nature*'[36] which makes it, in the view of Advocate-General *Mancini*, '*a specific and autonomous segment of the organizational machinery of the Community*'[37] that, as autonomous legal person, stands in

---

primary Community law as the specialized organisation for monetary policy. In this sense, one can even qualify the ECB, from a functional perspective, as a 'new Community' within the European Union's central pillar which stands on equal footing with the original three Communities.' See also the illustration at p. 624. See also, identically, Selmayr, 'Die EZB als Neue Gemeinschaft—ein Fall für den EuGH?' [1999] Europablätter 170, at p. 177.

[29] On this, see Zilioli and Selmayr, *supra* note 21, p. 637 *et seq.*

[30] See, eg, Käser, 'The European Investment Bank: its Role and Place within the European Community system' [1984] YEL 303; Dunnett, 'The European Investment Bank: Autonomous Instrument of Common Policy?' [1994] CML Rev. 721.

[31] A good summary of the doctrine on the EIB was made by AG *Mancini* in para 5 *et seq.* of his conclusions on Case 85/86, *Commission v Board of Governors of the European Investment Bank* [1988] ECR 1281.

[32] In Case 85/86, *supra* note 31, the ECJ recognized that the EIB must be able to act in 'complete independence on the financial markets' (para. 28) and therefore has been granted by the EC Treaty a considerable degree of 'operational and institutional autonomy' (para. 29).

[33] ECJ, Case 85/86, *supra* note 31, para. 24; cf. already Case 110/75, *John Mills v EIB* [1976] ECR 955, para. 14. See also Case C-370/89, *Société Générale d'Entreprises Electro-Mécaniques SA (SGEEM) and Roland Etroy v European Investment Bank* [1992] ECR I-6211, para. 13.

[34] Case 85/86, *supra* note 31, para. 28.   [35] Case C-370/89, *supra* note 33, para. 13.

[36] Case 85/86, *supra* note 31, para. 30. On the ambivalent nature of the EIB see also Ohler, in: Streinz (Ed.), *Kommentar zum EU- und EG-Vertrag*, München (2003), Art. 266 EGV, para. 5 *et seq.*

[37] Para. 13 of AG *Mancini's* conclusions on Case 85/86, *supra* note 31. Today, the EIB is classified as 'selbständige Sondereinrichtung im Rahmen des institutionellen Gefüges der Gemeinschaft' (= 'independent specialized body within the institutional framework of the Community') by

many respects '*on a footing of absolute equality*' with the Community,[38] or, as the ECJ put it in an earlier case, is '*associated*' to the Community in a situation of '*operational unity*'.[39] In view of the special features of the ECB, which give it an even stronger independent status than the EIB,[40] we have considered that these statements are certainly also true for the ECB itself.

Our view on the special legal status of the ECB as an independent specialized organization of Community law, even though supported by a number of academics,[41] has been considered to be similarly provocative by many writers as earlier views on the status of the EIB. *Häde*,[42] who essentially shares our view of the strong independence of the ECB and draws similar practical conclusions as we do, nevertheless criticises our classification from a formal legal perspective: in his view, as there is no separate 'ECB Treaty' next to the EC Treaty, the ECB must be considered as an integral part of the legal person EC. *Smits*,[43] and similarly

Müller-Borle and Balke in: von der Groeben and Schwarze (Eds.), *Kommentar zum EU-und EG-Vertrag*, Baden-Baden (2004), Art. 266 EG, para. 3.

[38] Para. 8 of AG *Mancini's* conclusions on Case 85/86, *supra* note 31.

[39] Joined Cases 27/59 and 39/59, *Alberto Campolongo v High Authority of the ECSC* [1960] ECR 391, at p. 404.

[40] Cf. CFI, T-460/93, *Etienne Tête v European Investment Bank* [1993] ECR II-1257, para 19: '[I]t should further be considered that the future European Central Bank will be substantially different from the EIB.' Even though we have referred to the example of the EIB, we always have stated that an analogy between ECB and EIB is not appropriate; see Zilioli and Selmayr, *supra* note 21, p. 617 *et seq.*, where we set out the different features of the independence of the ECB and of the EIB; see already Selmayr, *supra* note 28, p. 175.

[41] See, eg, Scheller, *supra* note 1, p. 43 *et seq.*, under the heading: 'The ECB as specialised organisation of Community law'; Smulders, in: von der Groeben and Schwarze (Eds.), *Kommentar zum EU- und EG-Vertrag*, Baden-Baden (2004), Art. 8 EG, para. 3: 'Man kann der Meinung sein, die EZB bilde eine unabhängige Organisation im Rahmen des ersten (und zentralen) Pfeilers der Union, die gleichzeitig unabhängig von den beiden doch eng mit ihnen verbunden ist.' See also Schweitzer, in: Grabitz and Hilf (Eds.), *Das Recht der Europäischen Union. Kommentar*, München (last update: August 2006), Art. 290 EGV, para. 14: 'Die EZB ist nicht Gemeinschaftsorgan, sondern eine selbständige Sonderorganisation des Gemeinschaftsrechts'. Pernice, 'Das Ende der währungspolitischen Souveränität Deutschlands und das Maastricht-Urteil des BverfG,' in: Due *et al.* (Eds.), Festschrift für Ulrich Everling, Band II, Baden-Baden (1995), p. 1057, called the ECB at p. 1059 a 'Gemeinschaft in der Gemeinschaft' (= 'Community within the Community'). Even Dutzler, *The European System of Central Banks: An Autonomous Actor? The Quest for an Institutional Balance of EMU*, Wien (2003), p. 88, has to admit: 'It cannot be denied that from a formalistic point of view, a number of Treaty provisions seem to support those calling the ECB a 'new Community'. The model seems convincing, as it is able to draw on the sheer number of specific provisions and institutional particularities, assigning to the ECB full decision-making powers for a key aspect of macroeconomic policy, and an extremely high degree of independence from the other Community institutions.'

[42] Häde 'Zur rechtlichen Stellung der Europäischen Zentralbank' [2006] Wertpapiermitteilungen 1605, in particular at p. 1607 *et seq.*

[43] Smits, *The European Central Bank in the European Constitutional Order* (2003), published at <http://www.ejlr.org/App_Content/PDF/90-77596-01-1.pdf>, especially at p. 11 *et seq.* and 23 *et seq.*, who points to the fact that at national level, also independent agencies and central banks 'certainly form part of the overall State structure'; cf. also Gaitanides, *Das Recht der Europäischen Zentralbank*, Tübingen (2005) p. 51 *et seq.* with book review by Selmayr [2006] CML Rev. 886. We take the view that the system of governance at EU level at present has not yet reached a stage where one may compare it to that of a state, even though the entry into force of the Constitutional Treaty could facilitate such comparisons.

Dutzler,[44] take the view that the far-reaching independence of the ECB which we see enshrined in Community law would represent an institutional result unintended by the draftsmen of the Treaty. According to *Torrent*, common sense would command to consider a central bank established by the EC Treaty as the 'central bank of the Community',[45] and not as an independent legal person only associated to the Community. Finally, *Amtenbrinck* and *de Haan* take a political approach; the question they discuss is less what the Treaty actually says but rather 'whether the ECB *should* be an independent specialized organization of Community law'.[46] For them, an understanding of the ECB as independent specialized organization of Community law is incompatible with the (allegedly subordinate) role to be played by the ECB in macroeconomic policies and, more fundamentally, with the principle of democracy.

Here, the circle appears to close between the academic debate and the *rationale* behind the political attempts to question, already since the start of Economic and Monetary Union, the legitimacy of the independent status of the ECB, reaching from the political attacks on the independence of the ECB by the former German Finance Minister *Oskar Lafontaine*[47] via Italy's former Prime Minister *Silvio Berlusconi's* urging for replacing the ECB's primary objective of price stability by a triple objective of growth, stability and employment[48] to recent proposals by the then Minister of the Interior of France (and now presidential candidate of the UMP), *Nicolas Sarkozy*, to change the status and the objectives of the ECB to clarify its subordination to the political process,[49] echoed in the pleading by the presidential candidate of the French Socialist Party *Ségolène Royal* for submitting the ECB to the decisions of the Eurogroup and of the European Council.[50] All this shows that, as regards the independence of the ECB, there is in the end no such thing as a mere academic debate.[51]

---

[44] Cf. Dutzler, *The European System of Central Banks, supra* note 24, p. 72: 'It is not easy to imagine a more revolutionary thesis of the Community's institutional structure'.

[45] Cf. Torrent, 'Whom is the European Central Bank the Central Bank of? Reaction to Zilioli and Selmayr' [1999] CML Rev. 1229.

[46] Cf. Amtenbrinck and de Haan, 'The European Central Bank: An Independent Specialized Organization of Community Law—A Comment' [2002] CML Rev. 65, p. 65.

[47] See Süddeutsche Zeitung N° 254 of 4 November 1998, p. 4, which wrote in this context even about a 'Krieg um die EZB' ('a war takes place about the ECB'); see also Süddeutsche Zeitung N° 31 of 8 February 1999, p. 6 and N° 32 of 9 February 1999, p. 21.

[48] In an interview with 'Gente', quoted by DowJones VWD-News No 110 of 9 June 2004, p. 6.

[49] In his speech 'Pour la France du travail' in Agen of 22 June 2006, published at <http://www.sarkozynicolas.com/index.php?option=com_content&task=view&id=91&Itemid=1>, where he said: 'Il est urgent que soit créé un véritable gouvernement économique de la zone Euro et que soient rediscutés le statut et les objectifs de la BCE.'

[50] In her speech '*Remettre l'Europe en mouvement*' in Oporto on 8 December 2006, published at <http://www.desirsdavenir.org>, in which she stressed: 'Ce n'est plus à M. Trichet de décider de l'avenir de nos économies, c'est aux dirigeants démocratiquement élus. Remettre l'Europe sur les rails, cela suppose que la Banque centrale européenne soit soumise à des décisions politiques, celles de l'Eurogroupe, mais aussi celles du Conseil européen'.

[51] The political answer to the most recent attacks on the independent status of the ECB was already given by ECB President *Jean-Claude Trichet* in his hearing in the European Parliament's

B. First Judicial Clarifications of the Status of ECB and the Scope of its Independence

Against the background of academic and political controversy on the status of the ECB, it can only be welcomed that it fell eventually to the ECJ to clarify, on 10 July 2003, the relationship between the ECB and the institutions and bodies of the Community in a landmark judgment,[52] just as the ECJ had done this already decades ago with regard to the EIB.[53]

(i) The OLAF Dispute

The legal dispute concerned the fight against fraud and the scope of the investigative competences of the European Anti-Fraud Office (OLAF)[54] to protect the financial interests of the Community. By means of a Regulation, based on Article 280 EC,[55] adopted on 25 May 1999 following a proposal from the Commission by the European Parliament and the Council (the OLAF regulation), OLAF had been given the authority to conduct anti-fraud investigations within 'the institutions, bodies, offices and agencies established by, or on the basis of, the Treaties'[56] to combat fraud, corruption and any other illegal activity 'affecting the financial interests of the European Community'.[57] It was the clear political intention of the

---

Economic and Monetary Committee on 20 December 2006, <http://www.ecb.de/press/key/date/2006/html/sp061220.en.html>: 'Had we not had a highly credible monetary policy, we would not have been able to anchor solidly medium and long-term inflationary expectations in the euro area and we would have had to pay a significant price in terms of growth and job creation'; by Commission President *Jose Manuel Barroso* on 19 December 2006 in the plenary of the European Parliament: 'La position de la Commission européenne est bien connue: nous respectons totalement l'indépendance de la BCE.'; and by German Chancellor *Angela Merkel* in Le Monde of 13 January 2007, p. 3: 'Si nous voulons conserver la confiance dans l'euro, nous devons le laisser hors du débat politique. [. . .] Laisser à la banque centrale son indépendance, c'est la position allemande très ferme.' See also Pisany-Ferry, 'L'indépendance de la BCE, un faux débat', La Tribune, 19 December 2006, p.32.

[52] Case C-11/00, *Commission of the European Communities v European Central Bank* [2003] ECR I-7147. The analysis of this judgment is drawn from Zilioli and Selmayr, 'The Constitutional Status of the European Central Bank' [2007] CML Rev. 355.

[53] Case 85/86, *supra* note 31.

[54] Established by Commission Decision 1999/352/EC, ECSC, Euratom of 28 April 1999, [1999] OJ L136/20.

[55] Regulation (EC) No 1073/1999 of the European Parliament and of the Council of 25 May 1999 concerning investigations conducted by the European Anti-Fraud Office (OLAF) [1999] OJ L136/1. On OLAF, see Kuhl and Spitzer, 'Das Europäische Amt für Betrugsbekämpfung (OLAF)' [2000] EuR 671; Mager, 'Das Europäische Amt für Betrugsbekämpfung (OLAF)—Rechtsgrundlagen seiner Errichtung und Grenzen seiner Befugnisse' [2000] ZEuS 177; Gless, 'Das Europäische Amt für Betrugsbekämpfung (OLAF)' [1999] EuZW 618; Pujas, 'The European Anti-Fraud Office (OLAF): a European policy to fight against economic and financial fraud?' [2003] Journal of European Public Policy 778.

[56] Article 1 (3) of Regulation (EC) No 1073/1999, *supra* note 55.

[57] Article 1 (1) of Regulation (EC) No 1073/1999, *supra* note 55.

Community legislature, supported by the European Council,[58] to cover with this broad wording also the ECB.[59]

The ECB agreed entirely with the Community institutions about the need to fight against fraud also with regard to the financial resources under the control of the ECB, namely its capital, foreign reserves and monetary income. However, the ECB had a number of institutional concerns with regard to the way in which the Community legislature intended to subject it to the control of OLAF. The ECB felt that the EC Treaty had deliberately not integrated its financial resources into the budget of the Community, but had left them solely under the control of the ECB to bolster its financial independence. The protection of the ECB's financial interests should thus, in the view of the ECB, not be ensured by the Community legislature under Article 280 EC (a provision following the Treaty articles on the Community budget[60]), but by the ECB itself.[61] The ECB also feared for its independence. It considered OLAF not to be entirely independent from the Commission, as it had remained in organizational terms a service of the Commission. In order to participate in the fight of the Community against fraud, the ECB therefore decided to set up, by means of an ECB decision of 7 October 1999,[62] an own mechanism to combat fraud and other illegal activities 'detrimental to the financial interests of the ECB'.[63] This mechanism consisted of enhanced powers for the ECB's Directorate Internal Audit and the creation of an independent external Anti-Fraud Committee to which the ECB's Directorate Internal Audit would be accountable. As legal basis for this decision, the ECB chose Article 12.3 of the Statute, which entitles the ECB to adopt its own Rules of Procedure.

On 14 January 2000, the Commission challenged, by means of an action for annulment under Article 230 EC, this decision of the ECB. The Commission

---

[58] See para. 35 of the Presidency Conclusions of the European Council of Cologne of 3 and 4 June 1999, published at <http://www.consilium.europa.eu/ueDocs/cms_Data/docs/pressData/en/ec/57886.pdf>, which states: 'It is in the view of the European Council eminently desirable that all Community bodies should join this interinstitutional initiative [= OLAF], and it therefore invites the European Court of Justice, the European Court of Auditors, the European Central Bank and the European Investment Bank to consider as soon as possible the terms under which the Office may carry out internal investigations in those bodies too and also what form cooperation with the Office might take'.

[59] See recital 7 of Regulation (EC) No 1073/1999, *supra* note 55: 'Whereas, given the need to step up the fight against fraud, corruption and any other illegal activities detrimental to the Communities' financial interests, the Office must be able to conduct internal investigations in all the institutions, bodies, offices and agencies established by or on the basis of the EC and Euratom Treaties (hereinafter "the institutions, bodies, offices and agencies")'.

[60] Case C-11/00, *supra* note 52, para. 82.

[61] The ECB suggested that the OLAF Regulation should be 'construed as not applying to bodies whose financial interests are different from those of the European Community and are not linked to the latter's budget.' See Case C-11/00, *supra* note 52, para. 60.

[62] Decision ECB/1999/5 of the ECB of 7 October 1999 on Fraud Prevention [1999] OJ L291/36.

[63] Article 1.1 of Decision ECB/1999/5, *supra* note 62. See also Recital 3: 'Whereas the ECB attaches great importance to the protection of its own financial interests and to efforts to combat fraud and other illegal activities detrimental to its financial interests.'

argued that the ECB's decision infringed the OLAF regulation adopted by the Community legislature which in its view clearly provided that the OLAF regime was applicable also to the ECB. In the view of the Commission, the ECB had thus no right and no legal basis to set up its own anti-fraud mechanism, but was obliged to cooperate with OLAF.

The ECB lost the OLAF case. In its judgment, the ECJ denied the ECB an own competence to adopt its own anti-fraud measures in competition with the Community legislature. The main reason for this was a broad interpretation given by the ECJ to the notion of 'financial interests of the Community' in Article 280 EC. The ECJ held that this notion must be interpreted in a broad sense '*as encompassing not only revenue and expenditure covered by the Community budget but also, in principle, revenue and expenditure covered by the budget of other bodies, offices and agencies established by the EC Treaty*'.[64] The ECJ recognized that the financial resources of the ECB are indeed separate from the Community budget,[65] but decided that this did not matter in view of the broad meaning of 'financial interests of the Community' in Article 280 EC: '*The fact that a body, office or agency owes its existence to the EC Treaty suggests that it was intended to contribute towards the attainment of the European Community's objectives and places it within the framework of the Community, so that the resources which it has at its disposal by virtue of the Treaty have by their nature a particular and direct financial interest for the Community*'.[66] In order to protect the financial interests of the Community defined thus broadly, it was, according to the ECJ, within the powers of the Community legislature to decide that the investigative function in the fight against fraud had to be centralized in a single specialized and independent body.[67] The ECJ consequently annulled the ECB decision establishing its own anti-fraud regime, thereby requiring the ECB to implement the OLAF regulation and cooperate with OLAF in fighting against fraud and other illegal activities detrimental to the financial resources of the ECB. As a follow-up to the judgment, the ECB adopted, on 3 June 2004, a decision that provides for a duty of all ECB employees (including the members of its decision-making bodies) to fully cooperate with OLAF.[68]

(ii) The Legal Nature of the ECB

The importance of the OLAF decision goes well beyond its immediate results. Even though the ECB lost the OLAF case, the ruling of 10 July 2003 can be considered a positive one also from the ECB's perspective as it reaffirms and

---

[64] Case C-11/00, *supra* note 52, para. 89.   [65] *ibid.*, para. 97.   [66] *ibid.*, para. 91.
[67] *ibid.*, para. 160.
[68] Decision ECB/2004/11 of the European Central Bank of 3 June 2004 concerning the terms and conditions for European Anti-Fraud Office investigation of the European Central Bank, in relation to the prevention of fraud, corruption and any other illegal activities detrimental to the European Communities' financial interests and amending the Conditions of Employment for Staff of the European Central Bank [2004] OJ L230/56.

clarifies the many remarkable features of the independent status granted to the ECB by the EC Treaty and the Statute. Indeed, a closer look at the judgment reveals that the ECJ made use of this first decision on the institutional framework of the ECB to make far-reaching legal statements on the law of the ECB in general which could become an immense support for a solid independence of the ECB in case of future legal and/or political battles.

With regard to the legal nature of the ECB, the ECJ declares, first of all, that '*the ECB was established and given legal personality by the EC Treaty*',[69] and thus is a creature of primary Community law. The ECJ thereby dismisses the argument of all those who still prefer to assimilate the ECB to the many Community offices and agencies—such as the Office for Harmonization in the Internal Market in Alicante or the European Medicines Agency in London—which are created not by primary, but by secondary Community law, and therefore by definition are dependent on the Community institutions as their creators.[70] In contrast to this, the ECB owes its existence not to the Community legislature, but directly to primary Community law.

The ECJ further concludes that the ECB '*falls squarely within the Community framework*',[71] thereby confirming the view, repeatedly defended by us, that the ECB, in spite of its strong independence, is not a solitary EU pillar of its own, but an integral part of the first, supranational pillar of the EU and therefore based on, and subject to, primary Community law.[72] The ECJ mentions three links between the ECB and the Community framework: the ECB's task to contribute to the achievement of the objectives of the Community as laid down in Article 2 EC, notably an Economic and Monetary Union and the promotion of sustainable and non-inflationary growth[73]; the right (and duty) attributed by the Statute to the Council to take some decisions related to the financial resources of the ECB, namely to approve the external auditors responsible for examining the books and accounts of the ECB (Article 27.1 of the Statute) and to determine the limits and conditions for an increase of the capital of the ECB and for further calls of foreign reserve assets (Articles 28.1, 30.4 of the Statute); and finally, the possibility for the Council to amend certain provisions of the Statute in accordance with Article 107(5) EC. For the ECJ, all this is a confirmation that there are, between the ECB and the Community, links in terms of objectives, financial interests and also institutionally.

---

[69] Case C-11/00, *supra* note 52, para. 92; already para. 64.

[70] This has been the position of Torrent, *supra* note 45, p. 1233 and footnote 11. Against this already Zilioli and Selmayr, *supra* note 21, p. 608 *et seq.*; cf. also Häde, *supra* note 42, p. 1607. See however Lavranos, 'The limited, functional independence of the ECB' [2004] EL Rev. 115, at p. 120, who, by following Torrent on this, obviously misses this point in the judgment. However, even AG *Jacobs* clearly states in para. 60 of his conclusions on Case C-11/00, *supra* note 52, that the particular position of the ECB within the framework of the Community 'distinguishes it from, on the one hand, the institutions, and on the other hand, the agencies and offices created by secondary Community law.'   [71] Case C-11/00, *supra* note 52, para. 92.

[72] See *supra* notes 25 and 27.   [73] Case C-11/00, *supra* note 52, paras 91 and 92.

The ECJ however disappoints all those who now would have expected a clear statement about what the position of the ECB is *within* the Community framework, more precisely about the legal relationship between the legal persons EC and ECB. Is it one of subordination or one of equal footing? Is there an organic or even a proprietary link between the Community and the ECB which would make the acts of the latter imputable on the former? Carefully, the ECJ avoids all pronouncements on this, even though Advocate-General *Jacobs* had concluded that the ECB should be seen as organically dependent on the Community.[74] The ECJ follows this proposal neither explicitly nor implicitly, but instead appears to deliberately not use any word[75] which could be understood as taking sides in the academic debate.[76] The reluctance of the ECJ to use this possibility to clarify judicially once and for all the legal nature of the ECB is even more interesting in view of the fact that in the parallel case on the relationship between OLAF and the EIB (decided on the same day), the ECJ did not shy away from classifying the EIB, in unequivocal terms and altogether three times in the text of the judgment, as 'Community body'[77] a notion not used in the OLAF judgment for the ECB. It seems that the ECJ wanted, in judicial self-restraint, to leave the legal classification

---

[74] See para. 60 of the conclusions of AG Jacobs on Case C-11/00, *supra* note 52: 'The particular position of the ECB *within* that framework—which distinguishes it from, on the one hand, the institutions and, on the other hand, the agencies and offices created by secondary law—cannot, in my view, lead to the conclusion that the ECB is not body forming *part* of the Community. The ECB [...] may therefore be described as the Central Bank *of the European Community*; it would be inaccurate to characterise it, as have some legal writers, as an organisation which is "independent of the European Community", a "Community within the Community", a "new Community" or, indeed, as something falling outside the notion of a body established by, or on the basis of, the EC Treaty in Regulation No 1073/1999'.

[75] See in particular paras. 65, 89, 91 *et seq.* of Case C-11/00, *supra* note 52, where the ECJ visibly avoids the word 'institution' in connection with the ECB.

[76] This is also observed by Elderson and Weenink, 'The European Central Bank redefined? A landmark judgement of the European Court of Justice' [2003] Euredia 273, at p. 282: 'The Court did not actually express a view on the exact nature of the ECB. [...] As the ECB had argued that it is not an "institution", the Court could have been more explicit on this issue.' Even Lavranos, *supra* note 70, at p. 117, who in his analysis relies mainly on the conclusions of AG *Jacobs*, has to admit that 'the Court did not explicitly state that the ECB is part of the Community.' See also Sucamelli in his Note a sentenza 'L'indipendenza della Banca centrale europea fra separazione ed equilibrio istituzionale' [2004] Rivista italiana di diritto pubblico comunitario 694, at p. 704: 'È curioso che la Corte sia ben più prudente, astenendosi invece dal prendere una posizione precisa sul merito.' Only Häde, *supra* note 42, p. 1607 (at p. 1610 *et seq.*), wants to see the judgment as a very clear positioning of the ECJ in favour of classifying the ECB as 'Einrichtung der EG' ('body of the EC') and as 'Zentralbank der EG' ('central bank of the Community'), even though these proprietary terms are (in our view deliberately) not used by the ECJ in the OLAF judgment.

[77] See Case 15/00, *Commission of the European Communities v. European Investment Bank* [2003] ECR I-7281, para. 75: 'It is appropriate to bear in mind in that regard that although it is not a Community institution, the EIB none the less is a Community body established and endowed with legal personality by the EC Treaty [...].' Para 98: '[T]he EIB is a Community body established and endowed with legal personality by the EC Treaty.' Para 123: '[I]t may be noted that it [=the EIB] was established by the EC Treaty and is a Community body [...].' This different treatment of the EIB by the ECJ shows that it is justified not to draw automatically an analogy between the law of the EIB and the law of the ECB; see *supra* note 40.

of the ECB for the time being to further academic debate. In this, the ECJ may have been influenced by the fact that the Constitutional Treaty, was, at the time of the OLAF judgment, just eight days away from being presented by Convention President *Valéry Giscard d'Estaing* to the Intergovernmental Conference for final deliberations.

(iii)   The Main Features of the ECB's Independence

The ECJ dedicates a considerable part of the OLAF judgment to describing the main features of, and the ratio behind, the independence of the ECB. In clear words, which may in the future serve as succinct summary of the ECB's independence, the ECJ recognizes in its judgment '*the distinctive features of its [the ECB's] status within the Community legal order*'.[78] The ECJ considers it to be appropriate '*to state at the outset that the draftsmen of the EC Treaty clearly intended to ensure that the ECB should be in a position to carry out independently the tasks conferred upon it by the Treaty*'.[79] The ECJ then points to two kinds of evidence for this intention: firstly,[80] Article 108 EC, which protects the ECB against instructions both at Community level and at national level (and which one may henceforth call 'independence in the narrow sense'); secondly,[81] a number of factors which are '*conducive to strengthening the independence thus enshrined in Article 108 EC*'. The ECJ here appears to develop a broader Community law principle of central bank independence for which Article 108 EC is only a minimum requirement and that elsewhere in the EC Treaty finds much more far-reaching expressions.[82]

While the ECB's independence granted by Article 108 EC itself resembles, as the ECJ underlines, in many respects the independence prescribed by the EC Treaty for some Community institutions, notably the European Parliament, the Commission[83] or the Court of Justice, this is not the case with the other factors mentioned by the ECJ (independence in the broader sense), namely: the legal personality of the ECB[84]; its '*own resources distinct from those of the Community budget*'[85]; its own decision-making bodies; the enjoyment of privileges and immunities by the ECB; the fact that only the ECJ, on an application by the Governing Council or the Executive Board of the ECB, may retire a member of the ECB's Executive Board, on the conditions laid down in Article 11.4 of the

---

[78] Case C-11/00, *supra* note 52, para. 64.   [79] *ibid.*, para. 131.   [80] *ibid.*, para. 132.
[81] *ibid.*, para. 133.

[82] This is also noted by Elderson and Weenink, 'The European Central Bank redefined? A landmark judgement of the European Court of Justice' [2003] Euredia 273, p. 294: 'It seems as if the Court considered Article 108 of the EC Treaty—already a very explicit and strong expression of central bank independence in its own right—as merely guaranteeing *a minimum level of independence*, which level is then *enhanced by the additional factors* cited by the Court'.

[83] See Article 213(2) EC.

[84] This legal personality is 'distinct from that of the Community', as AG Jacobs rightly notes in para. 152 of his conclusions on Case C-11/00, *supra* note 52.

[85] Case C-11/00, *supra* note 52, para. 97.

Statute. One may add that the latter contrasts in particular with the independence of the Commission, the individual members of which can be retired by the ECJ also on an application by the Council (Article 216 EC); and where the college of Commissioners must resign collectively in case of a motion of censure in the European Parliament (Article 201 EC)—two important external influences which are absent in the case of the ECB. The ECJ also explains why the ECB enjoys such a far-reaching independence: '*Article 108 EC seeks, in essence, to shield the ECB from all*[86] *political pressure in order to enable it effectively to pursue the objectives attributed to its tasks, through the independent exercise of the specific powers conferred on it for that purpose by the EC Treaty and the ESCB Statute.*'[87]

This is a welcome clarification which will help considerably to further develop a uniform legal concept of supranational central bank independence in Community law in the future. It is bound to influence in particular the ECB and the European Commission when they, in their regular Convergence reports, assess the degree of central bank independence in new Member States which join the European Union, as well as the progress made in this respect in Member States which endeavour to meet the criterion of legal convergence provided for in Article 122(2) in conjunction with Article 121(1), first subparagraph second sentence of the EC Treaty. In both cases, both independence from instructions as required under Article 108 EC and central bank independence as a broader principle of Community law that serves the primary objective of price stability have to be carefully observed, in line with the criteria established now by the ECJ in the OLAF judgment.

(iv) The ECB and Secondary Community Law: the ECJ's Solomonic Solution

In what is perhaps the most important part of the OLAF judgment, the ECJ clarifies the relationship between the ECB and secondary Community law. The legal question to be decided was: is secondary Community law, such as the OLAF regulation, applicable to the ECB?

In legal doctrine, there are, in essence, two opinions on this issue. On the one hand, some writers have argued that the ECB, just like every national central bank, would (or should[88]) be hierarchically subordinated to the Community legislature and therefore would have to follow, as a matter of principle, all secondary Community law.[89] Behind this opinion is in one way or another the understanding that in a democracy it is only logical that general legislation is

---

[86] Here, the ECJ goes further than AG *Jacobs* which only saw a need to protect the ECB 'from short-term political pressure'; see para. 150 of the AG's conclusions on Case C-11/00, *supra* note 52.

[87] Case C-11/00, *supra* note 52, para. 134.

[88] Amtenbrinck and de Haan, *supra* note 46, p. 65.

[89] See Dutzler, 'OLAF or the Question of Applicability of Secondary Community Law to the ECB', European Integration Online Papers 2001, N° 1, <http://eiop.or.at/eiop/texte/2001-001a.htm> (meanwhile removed); and Dutzler *The European System of Central Banks: An Autonomous Actor? The Quest for an Institutional Balance of EMU*, Wien (2003), p. 84 *et seq*. Also

always adopted by the legislator and applies by definition to all 'organs' of the State; and that also central banks in the Member States were always, even in cases of pronounced central bank independence, subject to law adopted by the legislature.

On the other hand, we have argued[90] that the ECB, unlike national central banks traditionally, owes its existence not to legislation, but to the EC Treaty itself and thus to 'the constitutional charter of a Community based on the rule of law'.[91] While it is clear that even one of the most independent central banks such as the Deutsche Bundesbank was always subject to the German legislature (which had created the central bank statute in 1957 in the form of a normal act of Parliament and was thus at liberty to amend it at any time by simple majority either explicitly or through other legislation[92]), the ECB's status is particularly entrenched against amendments by the Community legislature. The ECB's tasks and competences as well as its independence can be modified only by constitutional change, namely by an amendment of primary Community law agreed by common accord by the representatives of all 27 Member States and then ratified by all 27 EU Member States in accordance with Article 48 EU. In addition, we observed that, as independent specialized organization of Community law, the ECB is endowed by primary Community law itself, namely by Article 110 EC and by Article 34 of the Statute, with own law-making powers (such as the power to adopt regulations or decisions with the same normative value as secondary Copmmunity law under Article 249 EC) in its fields of competence the exercise of which is protected by Article 108 EC also against the Community legislature. From this, we have concluded that, as a rule, the ECB is itself both the regulator of the ESCB and the primary Community legislator in the field of monetary policy,[93] and that only by way of exception, where the EC Treaty or the Statute so explicitly provide (as it is for example the case with complementary legislation by the Council required under Article 107(6) EC), the general Community legislature could lay down rules which would apply to the ECB.[94]

AG *Jacobs*, in his conclusions on Case C-11/00, *supra* note 52, appears to be in favour of a complete submission of the ECB to secondary Community law when he stresses, in para. 159, that the ECB is 'subject to [. . .] Community law', without making a distinction between primary and secondary Community law.

[90] Zilioli and Selmayr, *supra* note 21, p. 629 *et seq.*, under the heading 'ECB law and its relationship with secondary law adopted by the Community institutions'. See also Zilioli and Selmayr, *The Law of the European Central Bank*, Oxford (2001), p. 37 *et seq.*

[91] Cf. ECJ, Opinion 1/91, *European Economic Area* [1991] ECR I-6079, para. 21.

[92] The German Basic Law guarantees in its Article 88, first sentence only the existence of a federal bank of issue, and neither the independence nor the organizational form of the central bank. See the decision of the highest German administrative court on this matter in BVerwGE 41, 334.

[93] Zilioli and Selmayr, *supra* note 21, p. 632. See also von Bogdandy, Bast and Arndt, 'Handlungsformen im Unionsrecht: Empirische Analysen und dogmatische Strukturen in einem vermeintlichen Dschungel' [2002] Zeitschrift für ausländisches Recht und Rechtsvergleichung 77, at p. 142, who use the term 'sektoraler Sondergesetzgeber' for the ECB.

[94] Zilioli and Selmayr, *supra* note 21, p. 632 *et seq.*

The ECJ settled this important academic controversy in its OLAF judgment in a Solomonic way. Taking the far-reaching independence of the ECB as point of departure, the ECJ states in the judgment that '*recognition that the ECB has such independence does not have as consequence of separating it <u>entirely</u> from the European Community and exempting it from <u>every</u> rule of Community law.*'[95] The ECJ says here two important things: first of all, that it is true that the legal person ECB is institutionally distinct from the Community and therefore not subject to *all* rules of Community law; secondly, that as the ECB nevertheless falls '*squarely within the Community framework*',[96] certain rules of Community law apply also to the ECB.

What are now these rules of Community law that apply to the ECB? The ECJ explains this in some detail. First of all, all *primary* Community law (the provisions of the EC Treaty and of the Statute) are capable of applying to the ECB as creation of the EC Treaty, and the ECJ mentions as examples the ECB's obligation to contribute to the objectives of the European Community (Article 105(1) EC) and to act within the limits of the powers conferred upon it by the EC Treaty and the Statute (Article 8 EC).[97] It also follows from the ECB's integration into the Community framework that it is subject to '*various kinds of Community controls*' foreseen in the EC Treaty and in the Statute, namely to the judicial control by the ECJ and, within the limits described in Article 27.2 of the Statute, to the control by the Court of Auditors.[98]

With regard to *secondary* Community law, the ECJ states that '*it is evident that it was not the intention of the Treaty draftsmen to shield the ECB from <u>any</u> kind of legislative action taken by the Community legislature*'.[99] In other words: *Some* kind of legislative action on the ECB is allowed under the EC Treaty. As proof, the ECJ refers to the provisions of the EC Treaty which explicitly allow the Council to adopt complementary legislation on the ECB, such as Article 107(6) EC. The ECJ, however, does not restrict the competence to legislate on the ECB *a priori* to cases explicitly mentioned in the EC Treaty and in the Statute, but develops general conditions under which the Community legislature has an (implicit) power to exceptionally adopt legislative measures—such as the OLAF regulation— capable of applying to the ECB.

For legislative action on the ECB to be legal, first of all a *positive* condition must be met according to the ECJ's reasoning[100]: such powers must have been '*conferred*' on the Community legislature '*by the EC Treaty*'[101] and the Community legislature must have adopted the legislative measures in question '*under the conditions*'

---

[95] Quoting from the earlier part of the judgment in Case C-11/00, *supra* note 52, para. 135, with emphasis added.   [96] Case C-11/00, *supra* note 52, para. 92.
[97] *ibid.*, para. 135.   [98] *ibid.*, para. 135.   [99] *ibid.*, para. 135. Emphasis added.
[100] *ibid.*, para. 136.
[101] The importance of this condition is also stressed by Elderson and Weenink, 'The European Central Bank redefined? A landmark judgement of the European Court of Justice' [2003] Euredia 273, p. 287, 'as it recognises that the legislator can only adopt legislation of relevance to the ECB in so far as the Treaty allows for this'.

laid down in the EC Treaty. One could also call this the condition of a legal basis, and it is interesting to note that here, the ECJ uses wording inspired by the principle of conferred powers of Article 5(1) EC that normally must be complied with to justify the existence of Community competences with regard to competences of the Member States. Here, the ECJ clearly takes into account that the Community and the ECB are both legal persons with their own law-making powers, and that therefore a legal basis is necessary for the former to legislate on the latter.

As a second and *negative* condition, the ECJ adds to this[102] that the submission of the ECB to such legislative measures must not 'undermine its ability to perform independently the tasks conferred on it by the EC Treaty'. This condition seems to have been taken by the ECJ from Article 108 EC directly, which it here clearly interprets with the intention of ensuring the practical effect ('effet utile') of this provision. Even though Article 108 EC, by prohibiting that instructions are given to the ECB, does not prevent the Community legislature to adopt general rules capable of applying to the ECB (provided that there is a legal basis for such general rules), it nevertheless excludes that such general rules could undermine or circumvent the prohibition of instructions.

As far as the OLAF regulation was concerned, the first condition was met following the broad meaning given by the ECJ to the notion of 'financial interests of the Community' in Article 280 EC.[103] The ECJ also found that the second condition was met, as the OLAF regulation *per se* did not undermine the ECB's ability to independently perform its tasks. The ECJ considered OLAF to enjoy 'complete independence' from the Community institutions,[104] an institutional guarantee which eliminated, according to the ECJ, the risk of a circumvention of Article 108 EC via OLAF feared by the ECB. In the view of the ECJ, OLAF is furthermore limited to the specific task of anti-fraud investigations and subject to judicial scrutiny, so that 'any defects in which the provisions of the regulation are applied cannot entail its illegality'[105]; the ECJ thus refers the ECB to the court action in case of an abusive application of the OLAF regulation. Finally, adding a further element to ensure that the ability of the ECB to perform its statutory tasks is not jeopardized, the ECJ underlines that the OLAF regulation leaves room to ensure that 'matters specific to the performance of its task',[106] such as the need to protect sensitive information linked to monetary policy matters also in the context of an OLAF investigation. By thereby acknowledging that the ECB retains a *'margin of autonomy of organisation [...] for the purpose of combating fraud'*,[107] the ECJ allows the ECB to specify itself, in an ECB decision, the details of its cooperative links with OLAF to take this need into account.[108] The ECJ could therefore

---

[102] Case C-11/00, *supra* note 52, para. 137 *et seq.*   [103] *ibid.*, para. 89.
[104] *ibid.*, para. 139.   [105] *ibid.*, para. 142.   [106] *ibid.*, para. 143.
[107] *ibid.*, para. 182.
[108] The ECB has made use of this possibility in its Decision ECB/2004/11, *supra* note 68, where it provides, in Article 4, for a special procedure with regard to sensitive information. A special decision of the ECB's Executive Board is required to grant OLAF access to information or to transmit

conclude that the OLAF regulation itself did not undermine the independence of the ECB.

(v) Practical Consequences of the OLAF Judgment for the Relationship between Secondary ECB Law and Other Secondary Community Law

For the future development of the ECB, of ECB law in particular and of Community law in general, the two conditions established by the ECJ in the OLAF case for the application of secondary Community law to the ECB have important practical implications. From the OLAF judgment, one may first of all conclude that the ECB remains clearly the primary legislator in the fields of its own competence, as here, legislative powers have, as a rule, *not* been conferred by the EC Treaty on the Community legislature, but on the ECB itself, so that already the first condition mentioned in the OLAF case will not be met for potential concurrent initiatives by the Community legislature. It is thus the ECB, and not Parliament, Council or Commission, that have the power to adopt regulations in the field of monetary policy under Article 34.1 in conjunction with Article 3.1, first indent of the Statute; to enact regulations for ensuring efficient and sound clearing and payment systems within the Community and with other countries, as provided for in Article 22 of the Statute[109]; or to determine the Conditions of Employment for the members of the ECB's Executive Board under Article 11.3 of the Statute and for the staff of the ECB under Article 36.1 of the Statute. If in one of these cases, the Community legislature were to adopt legislation with the intention of applying it to the ECB—take, as a theoretical example, a regulation of the European Parliament and of the Council setting a maximum level of 2 per cent for central bank interest rates in the Community—such legislation would be void *ab initio* as it would violate both conditions of the OLAF judgment: such a legislative measure of the Community legislature would both lack a legal basis (none has been conferred on the Community legislature by the EC Treaty or the Statute with regard to monetary policy matters), and it would also clearly undermine, in violation of Article 108 EC, the ECB's ability to perform independently its monetary policy functions.

---

information in 'exceptional cases, in which the circulation of certain information outside the ECB could seriously undermine the ECB's functioning'. This applies to 'information concerning monetary policy decisions, or operations related to the management of foreign reserves and interventions on foreign exchange markets, provided that such information is less than a year old, data received by the ECB from prudential supervisors regarding the stability of the financial system or individual credit institutions or information concerning the euro banknotes' security features and technical specifications.'

109 Too narrow is the view of Keller, 'Regulation of Payment Systems—Some Reflections on Article 22 of the Statute of the ESCB' [2001–2002] Euredia 455, which essentially wants to limit the ECB to technical legislation in this respect, excluding any legislation with regard to private law matters. Against this, see Smits and Gruber, in: *von der Groeben and Schwarze (Eds.), Kommentar zum EU-und EG-Vertrag*, Baden-Baden (2004), Art. 22 ESZB-Satzung, paras 12 and 13.

In addition, it follows from the OLAF judgment that there are cases outside the field of the tasks conferred to the ECB where primary Community law exceptionally allows the Community legislature to adopt general legislation capable of applying also to the ECB where the two conditions established by the ECJ in the OLAF judgment are met. The adoption of measures to fight against fraud on the basis of Article 280 EC is one such example, as we know from the OLAF case itself. As a further example, one could point to Article 286 EC, under which the European Parliament and the Council are entitled to extend the application of the general data protection legislation addressed to the Member States[110] also 'to the institutions and bodies set up by, or on the basis of, this Treaty'. As there is, with Article 286(2) EC, a clear legal basis for such legislative measures, and as their application to the ECB would not undermine the ECB's ability to perform independently its tasks—data protection legislation is, in principle, 'neutral' seen from the perspective of the tasks of the ECB—such general data protection legislation for the entire Community framework[111] could also be applied to the ECB provided that the procedural conditions of the legal basis are respected.

According to the OLAF judgment, one could also argue that there is no reason why the general language regime of the Community, as laid down on the basis of Article 290 EC in Regulation No 1,[112] should be excluded *a priori* from application to the ECB.[113] In this respect, the ECB has already anticipated the spirit of

---

[110] Cf. Directive 95/46/EC of the European Parliament and of the Council of 24 October 1995 on the protection of individuals with regard to the processing of personal data and on the free movement of such data [1995] OJ L281/31. This Directive is based on Article 95 EC and addressed, as all Directives, to the Member States only. It therefore cannot bind directly institutions, bodies, offices and agencies at Community level. Therefore, a specific legal basis is required to extend and adapt Community data protection legislation also at Community level. This is why Article 286 EC was added to the EC Treaty by the Treaty of Amsterdam.

[111] Regulation (EC) No 45/2001 of the European Parliament and of the Council of 18 December 2000 on the protection of individuals with regard to the processing of personal data by the Community institutions and bodies and on the free movement of such data [2000] OJ L8/1. It should be noted that the ECB has applied this regulation since that date, and also appointed a Data Protection Officer.

[112] Regulation No 1 determining the languages to be used by the European Economic Community [1958] OJ 17/385, as amended for so far the last time by Article 1(1), 15th indent of Council Regulation (EC) No 1791/2006 of 20 November 2006, adapting certain Regulations and Decisions in the fields of free movement of goods, freedom of movement of persons, company law, competition policy, agriculture (including veterinary and phytosanitary legislation), transport policy, taxation, statistics, energy, environment, cooperation in the fields of justice and home affairs, customs union, external relations, common foreign and security policy and institutions, by reason of the accession of Bulgaria and Romania [2006] OJ L363/1, adding, as of 1 January 2007, Bulgarian and Rumanian as 22nd and 23rd official and working language 'of the institutions of the Union'.

[113] We have so far argued against a direct application of Regulation No 1 to the ECB; see Zilioli and Selmayr, *supra* note 21, p. 631. After the OLAF judgment, one could argue, on the one hand, that Regulation No 1 could apply to the ECB as it does not undermine the ECB's ability to independently perform its tasks. On the other hand, Article 290 EC allows the Council only to determine the rules governing the languages 'of the *institutions* of the Community', which raises the question whether the first condition of the OLAF judgment is met, namely whether this is a sufficient legal basis for legislating also on the ECB. Even though the OLAF judgment avoids a clear statement on the legal nature of the ECB, one can certainly read from the judgment a clear reluctance to classify the

the OLAF judgment in its Rules of Procedure, which explicitly provide for the application of the 'principles of the Council Regulation (EC) No 1 to determine the languages to be used by the European Economic Community' to the legal acts of the ECB specified in Article 34 of the Statute.[114] This appears to be a wise legal choice, as it implements in substance the general language regime of the Community institutions,[115] but also leaves the ECB the possibility to issue, in its special relationship with the national central banks, ECB guidelines and instructions only in one language version[116] when necessary to ensuring the speedy and efficient functioning of the ESCB. Here, the priority for the ECB to deal with 'matters specific to the performance of its task', as recognised in the OLAF judgment,[117] legally supports an adapted application of secondary Community law.

The Community tax on salaries, wages and emoluments of Community officials and other servants, which is laid down in a Regulation of the Council,[118] is a further case where secondary Community law is capable of applying to the ECB. In practice, it is already applied to the ECB since its establishment.[119] The legal basis for this tax—which is the other side of the coin of the exemption of the salaries of Community officials and other servants from national taxes—is Article 13(1) of the Protocol of 8 April 1965 on the privileges and immunities of

---

ECB, in view of its distinctive features within the Community legal order, as 'Community institution'; see in particular paras. 65, 89, 91 *et seq.* of Case C-11/00, *supra* note 52, where the ECJ always visibly avoids the use of the word 'institution' in connection with the ECB; cf. also para. 60 of AG *Jacob's* conclusions on Case C-11/00, *supra* note 52, where he acknowledges that the particular position of the ECB within the framework of the Community 'distinguishes it from [. . .] the institutions'. This could indicate that Article 290 EC is not a sufficient legal basis for legislating directly on the ECB.

[114] Article 17.8 of Decision ECB/2004/2 of the ECB of 19 February 2004 adopting the Rules of Procedure of the ECB [2004] OJ L80/33. Emphasis added.

[115] On the language regime of the ECB, see already Schweitzer, in: Grabitz and Hilf (Eds.), *Das Recht der Europäischen Union. Kommentar*, München (last update: August 2006), Art. 290 EGV, para. 14; and Athanassiou, *The Application of Multilingualism in the European Union Context*, ECB Legal Working Paper Series, No 2, February 2006, <http://www.ecb.int/pub/pdf/scplps/ecblwp2.pdf>.

[116] See Articles 17.2 and 17.6 of Decision ECB/2004/2, *supra* note 114.

[117] Cf. *supra* note 106.

[118] Regulation (Euratom, ECSC, EEC) No 549/69 of the Council of 25 March 1969 determining the categories of officials and other servants of the European Communities to whom the provisions of Article 12, the second subparagraph of Article 13 and Article 14 of the Protocol on the privileges and immunities of the Communities apply [1969] OJ L74/1, English special edition: Series I Chapter 1969(I), p. 119.

[119] Article 2 of Council Regulation (EC, ECSC, EURATOM) No 1198/98 of 5 June 1998, amending Regulation (Euratom, ECSC, EEC) No 549/69, determining the categories of officials and other servants of the European Communities to whom the provisions of Article 12, the second subparagraph of Article 13 and Article 14 of the Protocol on the privileges and immunities of the Communities apply [1998] OJ L166/3, and Article 4c of the amended Regulation. Already the staff of the EMI (the ECB's predecessor) was subject to the Community tax; see Article 1 of Council Regulation (ECSC, EC, Euratom) No 3607/93 of 13 November 1993, amending Regulation (Euratom, ECSC, EEC) No 549/69, determining the categories of officials and other servants of the European Communities to whom the provisions of Article 12, the second paragraph of Article 13 and Article 14 of the Protocol on the privileges and immunities of the Communities apply [1993] OJ L332/11, and Article 4a of the amended Regulation (meanwhile repealed).

the European Communities, which originally was attached to the second Merger Treaty and is today incorporated into primary Community law by Article 9(4) and (5) of the Amsterdam Treaty. While Article 13(1) of this Protocol gives a legal basis for taxing officials and other servants of the Communities, Article 23 of the Protocol, added by the Treaty of Maastricht, states that the entire Protocol shall also apply 'to the European Central Bank, to the members of its organs and to its staff, without prejudice to the provisions of the Protocol on the Statute of the European System of Central Banks and the European Central Bank'. This means that, in line with the first condition of the OLAF judgment, the Council has the power to apply, on a proposal by the Commission and acting by simple majority under Articles 13(1), 23 of the Protocol on the privileges and immunities of the European Communities, the Community tax also to the employees of the ECB. However, the Council has this power only if it observes also the second condition of the OLAF judgment, namely that the application of the Community tax to the ECB does not undermine the independent performance of its tasks. It would thus be a clear violation of the second condition if the Community tax on ECB employees was raised as a consequence of a decision of the ECB to raise interest rates; or if the Community legislature were to decide in such a context that ECB salaries would be taxed at a higher rate than those of Commission or Council officials.

More difficult is the application of secondary Community law on public procurement to the ECB. The Community legislature so far took the decision to apply the general principles of the Community Directives on public procurement[120]—which, as directives, by definition only apply to the Member States—also at Community level. By means of the Financial Regulation applicable to the general budget of the Community, based on Article 279 EC, the Community institutions and bodies covered by the Community budget are also subject to certain procurement obligations.[121] Following the OLAF judgment, the financial resources of the ECB are, however, clearly distinct from the Community budget,[122] so that this Regulation at the moment cannot apply to the ECB.[123] The question is whether the Community legislature could extend the

---

[120] See Directive 97/52/EC of the European Parliament and of the Council of 13 October 1997, amending Directives 92/50/EEC, 93/36/EEC and 93/37/EEC concerning the coordination of procedures for the award of public service contracts, public supply contracts and public works contracts [1997] OJ L328/1.

[121] See Title V, 'Procurement', of Council Regulation (EC, Euratom) No 1605/2002 of 25 June 2002 on the Financial Regulation applicable to the general budget of the European Communities [2002] OJ L248/1, as amended by Council Regulation (EC, Euratom) No 1995/2006 of 13 December 2006 [2006] OJ L390/1, which applies, according to Article 88, to public contracts where payment is made 'in whole or in part from the budget', and where the contracting authority is one of the 'Community institutions' (Article 104).

[122] Case C-11/00, *supra* note 52, paras 89 and 97.

[123] This is also noted by the Commission in its reply of 25 July 2002 to a Written Question E-1687/02 from Member of Parliament *Herbert Boesch* [2002] OJ C301 E 210: 'it should be pointed out to the honourable Member that the ECB and the EIB are not subject to the provisions of the above-mentioned Financial Regulation'.

scope of the Financial Regulation also to the ECB. Unlike Article 280 EC, which is broadly worded to cover measures to protect the financial interests of the Community, Article 279 EC is a legal basis which clearly relates to the establishment and the implementation of the Community budget only. Article 279 EC thus fails to meet the first condition of the OLAF judgment and therefore does not confer on the Community legislature the power to adopt measures capable of applying also to the ECB. This does, however, not mean that the ECB is free to deal with public procurement as it pleases. The ECB is bound by primary Community law, and in particular by Article 105(1), third sentence EC according to which the entire ESCB must act 'in accordance with the principle of an open market economy with free competition favouring an efficient allocation of resources'. Primary Community law thus requires the ECB to adopt, in a way transparent to the general public, a public procurement policy which, while taking into account the specificities of certain of its tasks such as monetary policy, is clearly coined by market and competition principles. This should lead, in practice, to results very comparable to the application of the Financial Regulation of the Community,[124] even though it allows again account to be taken of the specific requirements of public procurment by a central bank.[125]

There remains one scenario that has not been specifically addressed in the OLAF case: that both the ECB and the Community legislature have been given by primary Community law a (partly overlapping) competence to legislate on a particular issue.[126] In view of the broad interpretation given by the ECJ to some legal basis in the EC Treaty, the possibility of this scenario arising cannot be excluded. In such a case, a truly horizontal conflict of legislative powers therefore would need to be settled on the basis of general principles of primary Community law. As a theoretical example, one could take a hypothetical Council regulation that would provide that all euro banknotes would have the denominations 1, 2, 5, 10, 50, 100, 200, 500, and that their design should include in the future, say, the images of the past Presidents of the European Parliament, of the European Commission and of the Eurogroup. For the time being, it is legally undisputed

---

[124] See the Commission's reply to Written Question E-1687/02, *supra* note 123: '[A]ccording to the information at its disposal, the Commission would like to point out that these two institutions [= ECB and EIB] have adopted their own contract-award regulations which, whilst taking account of the specific nature and objective of their tasks, draw heavily on Community legislation on public procurement and the above-mentioned Financial Regulation'.

[125] A practical example for this is the new regime established by the ECB for the public procurement of euro banknotes; cf. Guideline ECB/2004/18 of the ECB of 16 September 2004 on the procurement of euro banknotes [2004] OJ L320/21, the context of which is further explained *infra*, at p. 70 *et seq.*

[126] Such an overlap of competences should be a relatively rare case as in most cases the EC Treaty and the Statute are clear in delimitating the competences of the Community institutions and of the ECB. See already Zilioli and Selmayr, *supra* note 21, p. 635. Too narrow, however, is the view of Keller, *supra* note 109, at p. 467, who sees the two areas of secondary legislative powers as mutually exclusive and—in order to avoid any conflict—interprets the regulatory powers of the ECB much narrower than warranted by the EC Treaty and the Statute and the principle of 'effet utile'.

that to take such a legislative measure on the denominations and the design of the euro banknotes would be the competence of the ECB, which so far has decided on these issues under Article 106(1) EC.[127] Even though the wording of Article 106(1) EC only mentions the exclusive power to authorize the issue of banknotes, the ECB (with the support of legal doctrine) has taken this to include also the power to decide about the denominations and specifications of the euro banknotes. But let us imagine for a moment that at some point in the future, the Council, on a proposal of the Commission and after consultation of the European Parliament and the European Central Bank, would adopt such a regulation[128] on the basis of Article 123(4), (5) EC—which is the legal basis for all measures that help to introduce rapidly the euro—or, alternatively, on the basis of Article 308 EC, the general competence for the Community legislature to legislate in fields where it does not have in another provision of the EC Treaty a more specific competence to ensure that the objectives of the Community are met.

Those who have argued—and continue to argue even after the OLAF judgment[129]—that the ECB is fully subject to all secondary Community law, will in such a case probably take the view that secondary law adopted by the Community legislature (even if not adopted in co-decision with the European Parliament) generally has a 'higher democratic value' than secondary law adopted by the ECB. Following this argument, the hypothetical Council regulation would take precedence over the legal act of the ECB on euro banknotes. We, however, believe that from the EC Treaty and from the Statute, one cannot derive a normative hierarchy between legal acts of the Community institutions and of the ECB.[130] This can be seen, *inter alia*, from the fact that both Article 249(2) EC and Article 110(2), first subparagraph EC define a regulation, regardless of whether adopted by a Community institution or by the ECB, in identical terms as a legal act that has 'general application', is 'binding in its entirety' and 'directly applicable in all Member States'. We would also like to point to the case law of the ECJ according to which the decision about the proper legal basis is, in the system of the

---

[127] See Decision ECB/2003/4 of the ECB of 20 March 2003 on the denominations, specifications, reproduction, exchange and withdrawal of euro banknotes [2003] OJ L78/16, which is based on Article 106(1) EC and on Article 16 of the Statute. At present, the smallest denomination of euro banknotes is 5. The design of the euro banknotes depicts the abstract theme 'Ages and style of Europe'.

[128] Politically, such a legislative measure has already been requested a number of times by Members of the European Parliament; see, as an example, the Written Questions by *Georges Berthu* No. E-3990/97, E-3988/97 and E-3989/97 of 15 January 1998, published in [1998] OJ C187/107, where he requested that the 'eminently political decision' on the design of euro banknotes needed to be taken by the Council on the basis of Article 109l(4), third sentence (now Article 123(4), third sentence EC), as such a 'serious matter of principle' could not be left to the decision by a 'non-democratic body' such as the ECB.   [129] See Lavranos, *supra* note 70, at p. 121.

[130] On this, see Zilioli and Kroppenstedt, in: *von der Groeben and Schwarze (Eds.), Kommentar zum EU- und EG-Vertrag*, Baden-Baden (2004), Art. 110 EG, para. 2: 'besteht kein Zweifel, dass die von der EZB erlassenen Rechtsakte die gleiche Rechtsqualität haben wie die vom Rat, vom Rat gemeinsam mit dem Europäischen Parlament sowie von der Kommission erlassenen Rechtsakte'. See also para. 3: 'So kann auch nicht davon ausgegangen werden, dass unter den jeweils erlassenen Rechtsakten ein Rangverhältnis besteht'.

EC Treaty, not an issue about which of several competing Treaty articles provides for the more democratic procedure, but which of them is closer to the subject-matter concerned.[131] Interestingly, also in the OLAF judgment, the ECJ did not recur to the principle of democracy to decide about the conditions under which secondary Community law could apply to the ECB,[132] but chose a substantive legal approach by examining in particular whether the legal basis chosen (in the OLAF case: Article 280 EC) was sufficient as legal basis for the matter in question.

We would therefore argue that the relationship between a Council regulation and an ECB legal act cannot be determined by virtue of its author or following a normative hierarchy not foreseen by the EC Treaty. Instead, we propose to decide such horizontal conflicts of competence, as always in Community law, on the basis of the 'centre of gravity' of the subject-matter to be regulated, and thus in line with the principle *lex specialis derogat legi generali*. Where the ECB is, within the system of the EC Treaty, closer to the subject-matter (and this will have to be evaluated in the light of the contents and the objectives of the legal act in question[133]), the measures adopted by the ECB would take precedence. Where the Community legislature is closer (as it was the case also with the OLAF regulation), its measures would prime the measures adopted by the ECB. Following this logic, one would have to argue that the ECB is, as supranational 'bank of issue' under Article 106(1) EC, closer to the subject-matter of euro banknote issuance and therefore also entitled to decide about their denominations and specifications.[134] This argument would be supported by the fact that Article 106(1) EC is, by virtue of Article 122(3) EC, limited in its application to the EU Member States having adopted the euro, and also for this reason the more appropriate legal basis for legislative measures on euro banknotes. If the Community legislature wanted

---

[131] See ECJ, Case C-70/88, *Parliament v Council* [1991] ECR I-4529, para. 17; Case C-155/91, *Commission v Council* [1993] ECR I-939, para. 7–21; Case C-269/97, *Commission v Council* [2000] I-2257, para. 44. Very telling in this respect is the recent Case C-178/03, *Commission v Parliament and Council* [2006] ECR I-107, in which AG *Kokott*, in para. 59 *et seq.* of her conclusions, had pleaded to prefer Article 175 EC over Article 133 EC as it would, in line with the principle of democracy, give the European Parliament a stronger say in the adoption of the measure in question. The ECJ, however, did not follow her reasoning; see para. 56 *et seq.* of the judgment.

[132] Even AG *Jacobs* notes in footnote 147 of his conclusions on Case C-11/00, *supra* note 52: 'Whether the accountability of the ECB envisaged by the Treaty is adequate is not at issue in the present case.'   [133] Cf. the case law quoted *supra* note 131.

[134] This is also the legal view of the Council; see the reply by the Council of 19 February 1998, [1998] OJ C187/107: 'It ensues from the allocation of powers provided for under the Treaty that the European Central Bank *alone* is empowered to authorize the issue of banknotes in euro, also as regards aspects relating to their presentation (Article 105(a) of the Treaty and Article 16 of the Protocol to the Statute of the European System of Central Banks and of the European Central Bank).' Emphasis added. This view is widely shared in legal doctrine; see Smits, *supra* note 1, p. 206; Weenink, 'The Legal Nature of Euro Banknotes' [2003] Journal of International Banking Law and Regulation 433, at p. 434 and at p. 435 *et seq.*; Selmayr, *supra* note 1, p. 429 *et seq.*; Zilioli and Selmayr, 'The European Central Bank, its System and its Law' (second and third part) [1999] Euredia 307, at p. 359 *et seq.*; Zilioli and Preso in: von der Groeben and Schwarze (Eds.), *Kommentar zum EU- und EG-Vertrag*, Baden-Baden (2004), Art. 106 EG, paras 6, 9 and 16, where the ECB is called 'Banknoten-Gesetzgeber'.

to base its measures on banknotes on Article 308 EC, one could in addition argue that this provision requires the achievement of Community measures 'in the course of the operation of the common market', while rules on euro banknotes are closer to the proper functioning of Economic and Monetary Union, which, under Article 2 EC, is an objective to be legally distinguished from that of achieving the common market. In our theoretical case of a horizontal conflict of legislative competence, we would therefore rule in favour of the competence of the ECB, which, as the specialized organization of Community law for monetary policy, is the appropriate specialized legislator for deciding on the denominations and the design of euro banknotes.

(vi) The Scope of the ECB's Right to be Consulted

In a so far less noted part of the judgment of 10 July 2003,[135] the ECJ for the first time gives an indication about the interpretation of Article 105(4), first indent EC. The reason for this is that in the OLAF case, the question had been raised whether the ECB should have been consulted prior to the adoption of the OLAF regulation, in view of the fact that this regulation was deemed applicable also to the ECB. The answer to this question is of great practical importance as the consultation procedure foreseen in Article 105(4), first indent EC could prevent horizontal conflicts of regulatory competence between the ECB and the Community legislature from arising in the first place.

According to Article 105(4), first indent EC, the ECB must be consulted by the Community institutions 'on any proposed Community act in its fields of competence'. In a similar way, Article 105(4), second indent EC requires national authorities to consult the ECB 'regarding any draft legislative provision in its fields of competence'. The scope of the ECB's right to be consulted both at Community level and at national level thus depends on the interpretation given to the terms *'in its fields of competence.'* The correct interpretation is very important as, under Community law, the duty to consult the ECB is to be regarded as an essential procedural requirement, non-respect of which leads to the illegality of the Community legal act[136] or the national provision in question.[137]

---

[135] Case C-11/00, *supra* note 52, para. 106 *et seq.*

[136] Cf. (as regards the failure to consult the European Parliament) Case 138/79, *Roquette Frères v Council* [1980] ECR 3333, para. 33; and (as regards the failure to consult the Economic and Social Committee) Joined Cases 281, 283, 284, 285 u. 287/85, *Germany and others v Commission* [1987] ECR 3203, para. 38 *et seq.* This case law is generally applied also to the duty to consult the ECB; cf. Kempen, in: Streinz (Ed), *Kommentar zum EU- und EG-Vertrag,* München (2003), Art. 105 EGV, para. 23; Gaiser, 'Gerichtliche Kontrolle im Europäischen System der Zentralbanken' [2002] Europarecht 517 (at p. 519); see already Zilioli and Selmayr, 'The external relations of the euro area: legal aspects', [1999] CML Rev. 273, at p. 344, footnote 251. See also AG *Jacobs* in para. 131 of his conclusions on Case C-11/00, *supra* note 52.

[137] See already Zilioli and Selmayr, *The Law of the European Central Bank,* Oxford (2001), p. 100 *et seq.* See also ECB, *Guide to Consultation of the European Central Bank by National Authorities Regarding Draft Legislative Provisions,* Frankfurt am Main (2005), p. 25.

There are essentially three possible understandings of what the fields of competence of the ECB are. First, a restrictive interpretation would be to say that the ECB should only be consulted whenever its core functions as a central bank, namely the definition and implementation of monetary policy in the sense of Article 105(2), first indent EC, are directly affected. One could argue that such a restrictive interpretation is to a certain extent supported by the scheme of the EC Treaty, which mentions the compulsory consultation of the ECB not in a general provision, but only in the fourth paragraph of Article 105(4) EC. From this, some conclude that the duty to consult the ECB does apply only to the 'basic tasks' of the ESCB, as defined in Article 105(2) EC (monetary policy in the narrow sense), but not to the further tasks referred to in the subsequent paragraphs of Article 105 and also not to the tasks mentioned in the other provisions of the EC Treaty or the Statute.[138]

A second, broad interpretation would require consultation of the ECB whenever the ECB is affected by the proposed legal act in question, whether in a substantive manner in the context of the exercise of its tasks, or institutionally in the way the ECB, its decision-making bodies and the ESCB as a whole operate.[139] According to this broad interpretation, the ECB would also have to be consulted on general Community legislation capable of applying to it, such as the OLAF regulation or a Community regulation laying down data protection rules for all institutions, bodies, offices and agencies established by, or under, the EC Treaty.

A third, more balanced understanding of Article 105(4) EC would be to say that the ECB must be consulted whenever it has, in view of the specialized tasks entrusted to it by the EC Treaty and the Statute, a specialized knowledge that needs to be taken into account to ensure the quality of Community and national legislation. This would mean that the ECB would have to be consulted whenever one of its tasks under the EC Treaty or the Statute are concerned. The notion of 'fields of competence' of the ECB in Article 105(4) EC would thus be identical with the tasks given to the ECB in the EC Treaty and in the Statute. This view is to a certain extent supported by the (non-exhaustive) list already laid down in Article 2 of Council Decision 98/415/EC of 29 June 1998 on the consultation of the European Central Bank by national authorities regarding draft legislative provisions.[140] According to this decision, national authorities must consult the ECB 'in particular' on the following: currency matters; means of payment; national central banks[141]; the collection, compilation and distribution of

---

[138] This appears to have been the view of the Commission in Case C-11/00, *supra* note 52, para. 109.

[139] Cf. the plea of the ECB in Case C-11/00, *supra* note 52, para. 107, where the ECB considered the OLAF regulation to be void for failure to consult the ECB on an act that 'encroaches upon its powers of internal organisation'. See also para. 108: 'The ECB argues that its power to organise its internal affairs is one of the fields of competence under Article 105(4) EC'.

[140] [1998] OJ L189/42. See also ECB, *Guide to Consultation of the European Central Bank by National Authorities Regarding Draft legislative, supra* note 137.

[141] This particular clause seems to include any institutional change proposed by the legislator that has to do with the structure of the national central bank, and thus supports a broad understanding of the duty to consult the ECB.

monetary, financial, banking, payment systems and balance of payments statistics; payment and settlement systems; rules applicable to financial institutions insofar as they materially influence the stability of financial institutions and markets; and 'on any draft legislative provisions on the instruments of monetary policy' by the national authorities of those Member States which have not yet adopted the euro.

In the OLAF case, AG *Jacobs* indicated a certain preference for the third, balanced understanding of Article 106(4) EC. Starting with a systematic interpretation of the EC Treaty, he noted that it is the opening article of Chapter 2 (Monetary Policy) of Part Three, Title VII of the EC Treaty that provides, in its fourth paragraph, for consultation of the ECB.[142] He therefrom concluded:

The notion of measures 'in its fields of competence' in the fourth paragraph must be understood in the light of the enumeration of tasks in Article 105(2) EC, and of the fact that Article 105 EC is placed in Chapter 2 under the heading 'Monetary Policy' rather than in Chapter 3 which lays down 'Institutional provisions' for the ECB. It follows, in my view, that Article 105(4) EC must be interpreted as applying to proposed measures which are concerned with the issues covered by Article 105(2) EC (monetary policy, foreign exchange operations, management of foreign reserves and payment systems) and, *perhaps*, by Article 105(5) and (6) EC (prudential supervision) and Article 106 EC (issue of banknotes and coins). Article 105(4) EC does not, however, apply to measures falling within, or overlapping with, the specific competences which the ECB has been granted under Articles 12 and 36 of the Statute.[143]

While AG *Jacobs* apparently still had some doubts, as indicated by the use of the word 'perhaps', whether there was not also a case for a more restrictive interpretation of Article 105(4) EC, the ECJ is remarkably unequivocal in this respect. Even though the ECJ rejects the broad interpretation according to which the ECB must always be consulted when simply affected by legislative proposals,[144] the ECJ also observes '*that Article 105(4) EC is placed in Chapter 2, devoted to monetary policy, of Title VII of Part Three of the EC Treaty*'.[145] Already from the scheme of the EC Treaty, the ECJ considers the fields of competence of the ECB in the sense of Article 105(4) EC to extend beyond the 'basic tasks' as defined in Article 105(2) EC to all the tasks mentioned in Chapter 2, which includes, as monetary policy in the wider sense, all tasks assigned to the ECB by Community law, including prudential supervision (Article 105(5) and (6) EC), banknotes (Article 106(1) EC) and also external monetary relations and foreign exchange matters (Article 111 EC). The ECJ supports this interpretation with a teleological argument by stating that the purpose of the duty to consult the ECB is '*essentially to ensure that the legislature adopts the act only when the body has been heard, which,*

---

[142] Para. 136 of AG *Jacob's* conclusions on Case C-11/00, *supra* note 52.

[143] Para. 137 of AG *Jacob's* conclusions on Case C-11/00, *supra* note 52. Emphasis added.

[144] Case C-11/00, *supra* note 52, para. 111, where the ECJ denied a duty to consult the ECB on the OLAF regulation which is a measure to prevent fraud detrimental to the financial interests of the Community and thus 'an area in which the ECB has not been assigned any specific tasks.'

[145] Emphasis added.

by virtue of the specific functions that it exercises in the Community framework in the area concerned and by virtue of the high degree of expertise that it enjoys, is particularly well placed to play a useful role in the legislative process envisaged.'[146]

The interpretation given in the OLAF case to Article 105(4) EC shows that the ECB is not an omnicompetent entity that must always, by definition, be involved in the legislative process at Community and national level, regardless of the subject-matter concerned. The ECB is instead an organization with specialized tasks in the field of monetary policy in the large sense of Chapter 2 of Title VII of Part Three of the EC Treaty. The ECB can thus be truly said to be an independent *specialized* organization of Community law that, with its independent expertise, is meant to contribute to the quality of the law-making process both at Community and at national level. It is in line with the specialization of the ECB that its consultation is compulsory whenever legislation with regard to the monetary law of the euro is adopted by the Council[147]; whenever the European Parliament and the Council legislate, in the context of the internal market, on financial instruments which are relevant for the ECB's operations[148]; whenever the Commission adapts the Harmonised Consumer Price Index, according to which the inflation rate is measured in the EU[149]; and whenever international agreements are negotiated by the Community which require amendments to secondary Community law related to the fields of competence of the ECB.[150] In contrast to this, an obligation to consult the ECB with regard to institutional matters can only be said to result in cases which would have a direct bearing on the proper functioning of the ECB or the ESCB.[151] Not to consult the ECB in such a case could amount to a violation of the

---

[146] Case C-11/00, *supra* note 52, para. 110.

[147] Cf., as one example, Opinion CON/2006/36 of the ECB of 6 July 2006 at the request of the Council of the European Union on a proposal for a Council Regulation amending Regulation (EC) No 974/98 on the introduction of the euro and on a proposal for a Council Regulation amending Regulation (EC) No 2866/98 on the conversion rates between the euro and the currencies of the Member States adopting the euro [2006] OJ C163/10.

[148] Cf., as one example, Opinion CON/2005/53 of the ECB of 9 December 2005 at the request of the Council of the European Union on a proposal for a directive of the European Parliament and of the Council amending Directive 2004/39/EC on markets in financial instruments, as regards certain deadlines [2005] OJ C323/31.

[149] Cf., as one example, Opinion CON/2005/33 of the ECB of 4 October 2005 at the request of the Commission of the European Communities on a draft Commission regulation implementing Council Regulation (EC) No 2494/95 as regards the common index reference period for the harmonised index of consumer prices [2005] OJ C 254/4.

[150] Cf., as a first example, Opinion CON/2005/7 of the ECB of 17 March 2005 at the request of the Council of the European Union on a proposal for a Council decision concerning the signing of the Hague Convention on the Law applicable to certain rights in respect of securities held with an intermediary (COM(2003) 783 final) [2005] OJ C81/10. In this case, the useful effect of Article 105(4) EC required that consultation of the ECB took place already *before* the international agreement was entered into by the Community, and thus at a moment where there was still time to change the substance of the international obligations to be accepted by the Community.

[151] Such a consultation of the ECB is explicitly foreseen in Article 105(6) EC, which allows the Council, with the assent of the European Parliament, to confer upon the ECB specific tasks related to prudential supervision; in Article 105(5) EC, which allows the Council to modify a limited number of technical provisions of the Statute; and in Article 105(6) EC, which requires the Council to adopt

duty of sincere cooperation applicable also at Community level,[152] and it is in line with this duty that the ECB so far always has been consulted on such matters.[153] In addition, in one case which is particularly important for the proper functioning of Economic and Monetary Union as a whole, a duty to consult the ECB on institutional matters is explicitly foreseen in Article 48(2), second sentence EU Treaty: in the case of proposed Treaty amendments which include 'institutional changes in the monetary area'.[154] This is why consultation of the ECB was compulsory when the Constitutional Treaty was drafted,[155] as this Treaty, even though in large parts based on the *acquis communautaire*, is meant to replace, at least formally, the legal foundations of the ECB by a new set of constitutional rules.

C. Towards a Constitutional Change?

The status of the ECB was certainly not the main focus of the historical process that in the end led to the Constitutional Treaty signed in Rome on 29 October 2004. Much broader was the task of the European Convention which drafted the Constitutional Treaty from 28 February 2002 to 10 July 2003, namely how to ensure that the enlarged European Union, in the context of continuing globalization, will become more transparent, more democratic and more efficient. The result of this historic work is a constitutional design for a European Union with a single legal personality, based on a single Treaty; a more supranational decision-making process in the Council based, as a rule, on qualified majority voting; enhanced parliamentary powers both at EU and at national level; a more direct participation of

so-called complementary legislation under specific provisions of the Statute, such as determining the limits and conditions for the ECB's powers to impose sanctions on natural and legal persons not complying with secondary ECB law.

[152] As the specialized organization of Community law in charge of monetary policy, the ECB should be regarded as an integral part of the institutional balance established by the EC Treaty for the purposes of EMU. The institutional balance thus is clearly distinct in the context of EMU than in the case of other Community policies—such as agriculture or telecom policy—where the ECB is not part of the institutional balance.

[153] For example, see the Opinion CON/98/16 of the EMI at the request of the Council of the European Union under Articles 106(6) and 109f(8) of the Treaty establishing the European Community (the Treaty) and Article 42 of the Statute of the ESCB on a proposal from the Commission for a Council Regulation (EC, Euratom, ECSC) amending Regulation (EEC, Euratom, ECSC) No 260/68, which lays down the conditions and procedure for applying the tax for the benefit of the European Communities [1998] OJ C190/8.

[154] A variation of this is Article 10.6 of the Statute which allows, even though without convening an Intergovernmental Conference, a Treaty amendment to change the voting rules in the ECB's Governing Council. Instead of being consulted only, the ECB here also has the right to initiate itself the Treaty amendment procedures; for such a case, cf. Recommendation ECB/2003/1 of the European Central Bank of 3 February 2003 under Article 10.6 of the Statute of the European System of Central Banks and of the European Central Bank, for a Council Decision on an amendment to Article 10.2 of the Statute of the European System of Central Banks and of the European Central Bank [2003] OJ C29/6.

[155] See the Opinion CON/2003/20 of the ECB of 19 September 2003 at the request of the Council of the European Union on the draft Treaty establishing a Constitution for Europe [2003] OJ C229/7.

citizens in the EU's decision-making process, including in the form of a citizen's initiative asking for specific EU legislation; a Charter of Fundamental Rights as integral part of the Union's constitutional law; and the Union's enhanced capability to express a single voice in foreign affairs through a European foreign minister who at the same time would be Vice-President of the European Commission. At present, the Constitutional Treaty still awaits ratification by all EU Member States to enter into force,[156] but it is certain that its main elements will strongly influence the future development of the European Union.

Even though the ECB is not the main subject of the Constitutional Treaty, and even though this new Treaty is not yet in force, the planned constitutional changes have already triggered a quite intense academic debate about their possible impact on the ECB. While some authors either fear[157] or welcome[158] that the Constitutional Treaty would modify the special legal status of the ECB, other commentators, including the ECB itself,[159] have taken the view that the Constitutional Treaty would not lead to substantive changes[160] and rather see in the provisions of the Constitutional Treaty many welcome clarifying nuances

[156] As we finish this article, 17 EU Member States have ratified the Constitutional Treaty. In addition, Germany has completed the national ratification procedure but is still waiting for a judgment of its Federal Constitutional Court that would allow the German President to sign the national ratification law.

[157] Very critical Deutsche Bundesbank, 'Zur Währungsverfassung nach dem Entwurf einer Verfassung für die Europäische Union', *Monatsbericht, November 2003*, p. 67, at p. 69, according to which the Constitutional Treaty would abrogate the special status of the ECB: 'Diese Sonderstellung ist bisher eine zusätzliche Absicherung der Unabhängigkeit der EZB. Demgegenüber enthält der Konventsentwurf die Neuerung, dass die EZB explizit als Organ der EU eingestuft wird (Art. I-29 Abs. 3). Damit wird die im Vertrag von Maastricht verankerte Sonderstellung der EZB aufgegeben'. This view is shared by Gramlich and Manger-Nestler, 'Währungsrechtliche Defizite der Verfassung für Europa', [2005] Europäische Zeitschrift für Wirtschaftsrecht 193; and by Vaubel, in: Frankfurter Allgemeine Zeitung. No 141 of 21 June 2004, p. 13, 'Ökonomen zur Europäischen Verfassung', who criticizes the loss of autonomy of the ECB ('Autonomieverlust der EZB'). See also Smits, *The European Central Bank in the European Constitutional Order* (*supra* note 43), p. 37 *et seq.*, who criticizes the proposal of the Convention to make the ECB an institution.

[158] See Gaitanides, *supra* note 43, p. 54: 'Mit Inkrafttreten des 'Vertrages über eine Verfassung für Europa' wird sich die institutionelle Unabhängigkeit der EZB daher nicht mehr aus der 'organisatorischen, Sonderstellung' der Notenbank herleiten lassen'. See also Lavranos, *supra* note 70, p. 123: 'Indeed, the current intentions of the Masters of the Treaties as illustrated by the Draft Constitutional Treaty and the ongoing negotiations within the IGC indicate that the ECB will have to settle with the concept of limited, functional independence.'

[159] Cf. the ECB's Opinion CON/2003/20 (*supra* note 155), para. 5: 'The ECB understands that the transfer of the provisions on the ECB and the ESCB from the EC Treaty to the Constitution will not entail any changes to the substance, and that the tasks, mandate, status and legal regime of the ECB and of the ESCB remain substantially unchanged'. See also ECB 'The European Constitution and the ECB', *Monthly Bulletin, August 2004*, p. 51, at p. 61: 'Overall, it is clear that the special features of the ECB and the ESCB are preserved by the European Constitution. [. . .] [T]he European Constitution fully confirms and further clarifies the sui generis nature of the ECB, which sets the ECB apart from the core EU institutions'.

[160] See Duhamel, *Pour l'Europe. Le texte intégral de la Constitution expliqué et commenté*, Paris (2003), p. 196 (comment on Article I-29 of the Convention draft of the Constitutional Treaty): 'Les choses sont dites autrement, mais ce sont les mêmes.' Cf. also Kapteyn, 'EMU and Central Bank: Chances Missed', [2005] European Constitutional Law Review 123, at p. 127 *et seq.*, who apparently regrets that the ECB was not made more subject to the political process: 'Concrete legal instruments

either with regard to the special status of the ECB[161] or its integration into the EU's institutional framework.[162]

(i) Main Novelties of the Constitutional Treaty for the ECB

The 448 Articles of the Constitutional Treaty also deal with the ECB, as they encompass not only new provisions in Part I of the Constitutional Treaty, including a specific provision on the ECB in Article I-30, but also incorporate, in Part III, the entire *acquis communautaire* of primary Community law, including the substantive and institutional provisions on monetary policy (Articles III-177, III-185 to III-202, III-382 to III-383) and the provisions of the Statute, which is annexed as Protocol No. 4 to the Constitutional Treaty.[163] A closer look reveals

to hold the ECB accountable are lacking'. Critical also Mazier, 'Les politiques macroéconomiques en Europe : enlisement ou croissance', in: Raveaud, Saïdi and Sauze (Eds.), *Douze économistes contre le projet de Constitution européenne*, Paris (2005), p. 127, at p. 130: 'L'indépendance de la BCE est confortée par le Traité constitutionnel.' Similar, even though argued from a different starting point, is the view of Seidel, *Die Stellung der Europäischen Zentralbank nach dem Verfassungsvertrag*, ZEI Policy Paper B 19/2004, p. 5 *et seq.*

[161] Cf. Brok and Selmayr, 'La Constitution européenne et le cadre de la politique économique, monétaire et financière' [2004] Le Forum Franco-Allemand 57, at p. 62: 'Le texte finalement adopté confirme au contraire le statut de la BCE comme organe specialisé soumis à l'objectif prioritaire du maintien de la stabilité des prix'. Similar Brok and Selmayr, 'Constitución de la Unión europea y conferencia intergubernemental: el fracaso del "método Metternich"', in: Vidal-Beneyto (Ed.), *El reto constitucional de Europa*, p. 127, at p. 141. See also Selmayr, 'Die Europäische Zentralbank', Weidenfeld and Wessels (Eds.), *Jahrbuch der Europäischen Integration 2002/2003*, Berlin (2003), p. 117, at p. 120: '[Der Verfassungsvertrag] bestätigt, dass die EZB ein Sonderorgan ist, dass durch seine Rechtspersönlichkeit und seine Unabhängigkeit auch gegenüber den Unionsorganen charakterisiert ist und im Unterschied zu diesen vorrangig auf die Preisstabilität verpflichtet ist.' Cf. also Zilioli and Selmayr, 'The Constitutional Status of the European Central Bank' [2007] CML Rev. (in print); and Zilioli, 'The Constitution for Europe and its Impact on the Governance of the Euro', in: Torres, Verdun, Zimmermann (Eds.), *EMU Rules: The Political and Economic consequences of European Monetary Integration*, Baden-Baden (2006), p. 49.

[162] This is the view of Louis, 'The Economic and Monetary Union: Law and Institutions' [2004] CML Rev. 575 (at p. 603): 'We are of the opinion that since nothing has changed in the Statute of the ESCB and the ECB concerning its independence and its functioning, the new qualification of the ECB has the merit of enshrining in the Constitutional Treaty the reality of the ECB as being part of the Union's institutional order'. Cf. also Louis, 'L'Union économique et monétaire et la gouvernance économique', in : Dony and Bribosia (Eds.), *Commentaire de la Constitution de l'Union européenne*, Brussels (2005), p. 261, at p. 277: '[O]n notera une certaine clarification du statut de la Banque centrale européenne'. Similar de Poncins, *Vers une Constitution européenne. Texte commenté du projet de traité constitutionnel établi par la Convention europénne*, Paris (2003), p. 177 (comment on Article I-29): 'Point à relever: définition plus claire du rôle et du fonctionnement de la Banque centrale européenne qui prend place parmi les institutions sans figurer dans la liste établie à l'article I-18.' See also Tohidipur, 'The Emperor's New Clothes: The ECB and the New Institutional Concept', [2005] German Law Journal <http://www.germanlawjournal.com/> 1575, at p. 1592: 'One could conclude that the Constitutional Treaty does not lead to substantial changes to the current monetary constitution. [. . .] But the gap between the self-conception of the ECB and the institutional surrounding has been heightened by the normative inclusion of the ECB in the institutional structure of the European Union through the Constitutional Treaty, which may signify the explicit end of the self-conception as an 'independent specialized organization of Community Law.'

[163] Under Article IV-442 of the Constitutional Treaty, the Protocols to this Treaty 'shall form an integral part thereof' and are thus as much Union constitutional law as the provisions of the Constitutional Treaty themselves.

that these constitutional provisions, taken together, have ambivalent consequences for the ECB: on the one hand, following the general logic of the Constitutional Treaty to enhance the consistency and transparency of the new single institutional framework of the European Union, the ECB becomes more visibly anchored within the European Union's organizational structure than it is today. On the other hand, the unique character of the ECB as both an independent and specialized organization remarkably appears even strengthened by the Constitutional Treaty.

Unlike the Maastricht Treaty, the Constitutional Treaty makes an attempt to classify the ECB. In Article I-30(3), first sentence of the Constitutional Treaty says: '*The European Central Bank is an institution*'. The consequence of this is, first of all, a simplified drafting of many provisions of the Constitutional Treaty which need no longer to distinguish, as today they have to, between institutions on the one hand and the ECB on the other.[164] Provisions on the ECB in Part III of the Constitutional Treaty are therefore placed in Section I 'The Institutions' of Chapter 1 'Provisions Governing the Institutions' of Title VI 'The Functioning of the Union'.[165] This change in terminology will undoubtedly strengthen the link of the ECB with the Union's institutional framework as soon as the Constitutional Treaty will enter into force. It should however be noted that the ECB is not, as proposed in initial drafts of the Convention Praesidium,[166] included in the list of the five core institutions which are, according to Article I-19, the component parts of the Union's institutional framework (European Parliament, European Council, Council of Ministers, European Commission and Court of Justice), which is defined further in Chapter I of Title IV of Part I of the Constitutional Treaty. Instead, the Constitutional Treaty places the ECB in Chapter II of this Title under the heading 'The Other Union Institutions and Advisory Bodies',[167] underlining thereby both the special status of the ECB compared to the core institutions and its specialized competences.

---

[164] Today, Article 111(3), second subparagraph, Article 233(3) and Article 234(1)(b) EC need to distinguish between the Community institutions and the ECB. Under the Constitutional Treaty, Article III-323(2), III-368 and III-369(1)(b) only refer to 'institution' or 'institutions of the Union', without having to mention the ECB separately.

[165] This was decided not in the Convention, but on the advice of legal experts during the Intergovernmental Conference; see 'Editorial and Legal Comments on the draft Treaty establishing a Constitution for Europe' of the Working Group of IGC Legal Experts, CIG 4/03 of 6 October 2003, published at <http://www.consilium.europa.eu/igcpdf/en/03/cg00/cg00004.en03.pdf>, p. 239.

[166] Cf. draft Article 14(2) in CONV 691/03 of 23 April 2003. The inclusion of the ECB in the list of core Union institutions was criticized in an amendment proposed by Brok and 30 other Convention members of the EPP group in the Convention; cf. CONV 709/03 of 9 May 2003, published at <http://european-convention.eu.int/docs/treaty/pdf/414/14Brok%20EN.pdf>, where the following justification is given for treating the ECB in a provision apart: 'Concerning the ECB (European Central Bank), there is no doubt that it is one of the important bodies of the EU. But it is less an organ and more an instrument for administering the Euro and doing so by strictly following the principle of price stability. Due to its specific character as an organisation of the Union it is dealt with in Article 14 b.'

[167] According to Louis, *supra* note 162, p. 601, the final provisions of the Constitutional Treaty 'draw a line between the "institutional framework", which includes the four classic institutions before Maastricht, together with the European Council, on the one hand, and "other institutions and

The wording used by the Constitutional Treaty also confirms the special characteristics of the ECB. Article I-30(2), second sentence stresses, in the same way as does today Article 105(1), first sentence EC, that '*[t]he primary objective of the European System of Central Banks shall be to maintain price stability*', which shows that the ECB remains[168] the specialized Union institution the main responsibility of which is to ensure that the Union's general objective of 'price stability', provided for in Article I-3(3) of the Constitutional Treaty,[169] is met. Article I-30 of the Constitutional Treaty reaffirms that the ECB '*shall have legal personality*' (Article I-30(3), second sentence), which makes the ECB the only Union institution referred to in Part I[170] which has legal personality next to the Union's own legal personality as laid down in Article I-7.[171] At the same time, Article I-30(3), third sentence of the Constitutional Treaty provides that the ECB '*shall be independent in the exercise of its powers and in the management of its finances*'. Article I-30(3), fourth sentence finally requires that '*Union institutions, bodies, offices and agencies and the governments of the Member States shall respect that independence*'. With this wording, the Constitutional Treaty even appears to strengthen the independence of the ECB. Indeed, so far the word 'independence' as such is nowhere to be found in the EC Treaty as explicit legal feature of the ECB which would go beyond its freedom from instructions.[172] In contrast with this, the

bodies", among which the ECB and the Court of auditors, which are labelled "institutions" and consultative organs.' See also p. 603: 'By distinguishing on the one hand, the institutional framework, that corresponds to the basic Governmental functions within the Union and the "other institutions", in the field of money and public accounting, the Constitution would introduce an element of clarity.'

[168] Proposals to amend the objectives of the ECB by the objectives of growth and employment were accepted neither in the Convention nor in the Intergovernmental Conference; see the proposed amendment by *Pervenche Berès, Olivier Duhamel, Ben Fayot, Caspar Einem, Elena Paciotti, Sylvia Kaufmann, Anne Van Lancker, Emilio Gabaglio, Roger Briesch, Helle Thorning-Schmidt, Luis Marinho, Carlos Carnero—Gonzalez, Linda Mc Avan, Maria Berger, Elio Di Rupo, Vytenis Andriukaitis, Adrian Severin, Claudio Martini, Proinsias De Rossa, Robert Badinter* with regard to (what was then) Article III-74, published at <http://european-convention.eu.int/Docs/Treaty/pdf/831/Art%20III%2074%20Beres%20FR.pdf>.

[169] Price stability was inserted among the general objectives of the Union only in the final stage of the Intergovernmental Conference; see the document of the Irish presidency CIG 76/04 of 13 May 2004, published at <http://www.consilium.europa.eu/igcpdf/de/04/cg00/cg00076.de04.pdf>. The ECB had explicitly asked for this in para. 8 of its CON/2003/20, *supra* note 155.

[170] The EIB appears to be considerably downgraded by the Constitutional Treaty. It is not mentioned in Part I of the Constitutional Treaty, but only in Article III-393 and in the Protocol No. 5 on the Statute of the European Investment Bank.

[171] Next to the Union, the Constitutional Treaty only preserves the legal personality of Euratom; see Protocol No. 36 annexed to the Constitutional Treaty amending the Treaty establishing the European Atomic Energy Community, which does not abrogate the legal personality of Euratom provided for in Article 184 EAEC, which thus continues to apply. In contrast with this, the legal personality of the EC was merged with, and replaced by the new legal personality of the Union; see Article IV-438(1) of the Constitutional Treaty.

[172] The word 'independence' is currently only used in Article 116(5) EC, and therein only with regard to the duty of the Member States to start, during the second stage of Economic and Monetary Union, 'the process leading to the independence of its central bank'. In addition, Article 7 of the Statute use the word 'independence' as title of the provision which defines the ECB's freedom from instructions in accordance with the wording of Article 108 EC.

Constitutional Treaty introduces the concept of central bank independence as a general and broad concept that extends to the entire exercise of the ECB's powers as well as to the management of 'its'[173] finances, thereby underlining that the finances of the ECB are not part of the Union's budget and making explicit that the ECB also enjoys financial independence. Finally, the Constitutional Treaty also strengthens, at least verbally, the independence of the ECB against instructions as it does not simply incorporate Article 108 EC as its stands in Part III, but clarifies, in the wording both of Article I-30(3), fourth sentence and of Article III-188, that the ECB is also independent from instructions of all 'Union institutions, bodies, offices or agencies' and that they all must not seek to influence the decision-making bodies of the ECB. This clarifies that also the European Council, which will become a Union institution by virtue of Article I-19(1), second subparagraph, second indent of the Constitutional Treaty may neither give instructions to the ECB[174] nor seek to influence its decision-making bodies[175]; the same applies to other Union bodies such as the informal Eurogroup[176] which is meant to become more visible under the Constitutional Treaty.[177] The risk, seen by some,[178] that the European Council or the Eurogroup could, under the Constitutional Treaty, issue policy guidelines for the ECB, is therefore constitutionally excluded.

The Constitutional Treaty finally preserves the special nature of the ECB as an organization that derives its legal personality, its independence and its powers directly from primary Community law (in future: constitutional Union law) which can only be amended if all Member States agree. Proposals which would have allowed to amend crucial provisions of the Statute through a simplified amendment procedure, as they were considered temporarily during the Intergovernmental

[173] Note the use of the possessive pronoun.

[174] Today, in view of the unclear status of the European Council under the EC Treaty, one must qualify it either as 'Community institution' *by analogy* or as 'any other body' to apply Article 108, first sentence EC also to potential instructions of the European Council.

[175] Today, the duty not to seek to influence the members of the decision-making bodies of the ECB and of the national central banks applies directly only to the 'Community institutions and bodies' and to 'the governments of the Member States'. If the European Council is qualified as 'any other body', it is thus directly covered only by Article 108, first sentence EC. Article 108, second sentence EC would then only apply indirectly to the European Council as all its members would be bound by it already: the Heads of State or government as 'governments of the Member States', and the President of the Commission via the Commission's duty as 'Community institution' to observe Article 108, second sentence EC. On this problem, see Reumann, *supra* note 1, p. 31 *et seq.* In contrast to this, Article III-188, second sentence of the Constitutional Treaty directly applies to the European Council as Union institution.

[176] Today, the Eurogroup is, as any other body, directly covered only by Article 108, first sentence EC, but not by Article 108, second sentence EC, which would apply directly only to the national Finance Ministers in their capacity as members of the governments of the Member States. On the Eurogroup more generally, cf. Louis, 'The Eurogroup and Economic Policy Co-ordination' [2001–2002] Euredia 19. See also the detailed analysis by Puetter, *The Eurogroup: How a Secretive Circle of Finance Ministers Shape European Economic Governance*, Manchester (2006).

[177] On this, Servais and Ruggeri, 'The EU Constitution: Its Impact on Economic and Monetary Union and Economic Governance', in: ECB (Ed.), *Legal Aspects of the European System of Central Banks*, *supra* note 1, p. 43, at p. 62 *et seq.*

[178] See Gramlich and Manger-Nestler, *supra* note 157.

Conference,[179] were in the end not included in the Constitutional Treaty.[180] The incorporation of the main features of the ECB and of its independence in Part I of the Constitutional Treaty also entrenches them even against the slightly simplified amendment procedure of Article IV-445 of the Constitutional Treaty which allows amendments of Part III of the Constitutional Treaty (which may not increase the competences of the Union) without convening a new Convention.[181]

(ii) Practical Implications of the Constitutional Treaty for the Law of the ECB

If the Constitutional Treaty entered into force today, a number of practical implications could be anticipated for the ECB. Firstly, whenever the Constitutional Treaty refers to the notion 'institution', the ECB will in the future normally be meant, unless a specific rule dealing with the ECB exists in the Treaty and prevails over the general one. This clarifies, for example, that the ECB is subject to examinations into maladministration by the European Ombudsman under Article I-49[182] with whom the ECB so far cooperates on a voluntary basis[183]; and

[179] Such a proposal had been made by the Commission; see CIG 37/03 of 24 October 2003, p. 8 and COG 52/03 ADD 1 of 25 November 2003, Annex 9. It would have introduced a new Article III-79(7) into the Constitution which would have read as follows: 'Article III-84(1) and 2(a) of the Constitution and Articles 10 to 12 and 43 of the Statute of the European System of Central Banks and the European Central Bank may be amended by a law of the Council, acting unanimously, either on a proposal from the Commission and after consultation of the European Parliament and the European Central Bank, or on a recommendation from the European Central Bank and after consultation of the European Parliament and the Commission.' The ECB expressed its opposition to this idea by letter of President *Trichet* of 26 November 2001 to *Franco Frattini*, then President of the Council of the European Union, published at <http://www.ecb.eu/press/pr/date/2003/html/pr031127.en.html>.

[180] This sharply contrasts with the legal situation of the EIB. Under Article III-393(3) of the Constitutional Treaty, *all* provisions of the EIB's Statute (which is attached to the Constitutional Treaty as a Protocol) may in the future be amended by a European law of the Council, adopted unanimously by the Council either at the request of the EIB and after consultation of the European Parliament and the Commission, or on a proposal from the Commission and after consulting the European Parliament and the EIB. Ratification by all Member States is not required. Under the EC Treaty, to which the EIB Statute is attached as a Protocol, the EIB Statute as a whole can be changed only by following the general procedure for Treaty amendments under Article 48 EU, namely common accord among the representatives of all Member States and ratification by all Member States. Since the Nice Treaty, Article 266(3) EC in addition provides for a simplified amendment procedure of Articles 4, 11, 12 and 18(5) of the EIB Statute by unanimous Council decision; critical on this from the perspective of the EIB's independence Müller-Borle and Balke, *supra* note 37, Art. 266 EG, para. 2.

[181] Convening a new Convention is normally required under Article IV-443 for amendments to the Constitutional Treaty. However, also in the case of the simplified amendment procedure under Article IV-445, a unanimous decision of the European Council, consultation of the ECB and ratification in all Member States is required, which is in practice as difficult as is today an amendment of the EC Treaty and of the Statute under Article 48 EU. On the amendment procedures under the Constitutional Treaty, see Servais and Ruggeri, *supra* note 177, p. 86 *et seq.*

[182] See 'Editorial and Legal Comments on the draft Treaty establishing a Constitution for Europe' (*supra* note 165), p. 111: 'Since the European Council and the European Central Bank now become Institutions of the Union (Article I-18), the European Ombudsman will be competent to investigate any cases of maladministration by those Institutions.'

[183] Under Article 195 EC, the European Ombudsman is today responsible only for complaints concerning cases of maladministration 'in the activities of the Community institutions and bodies',

also to the citizen right to good administration, which is incorporated in Article II-101 as part of the Charter of Fundamental Rights of the Union. The ECB would also be clearly subject to the *duty of sincere cooperation* with the other Union institutions, which applies under Article I-19(2), second sentence of the Constitutional Treaty to all Union institutions.[184] Some argue that this duty could endanger the independence of the ECB.[185] We take the view that this is an unjustified fear.[186] We have always believed that already today the ECB, as an organization established by the EC Treaty, has a duty to cooperate sincerely with the Community institutions and bodies and that the Community institutions and bodies must reciprocate with similarly sincere cooperation with the ECB.[187] This results in our view from an analogical application of Article 10 EC, read in conjunction with the case law of the ECJ.[188] The duty of sincere cooperation is thus nothing new for the ECB, but already is required under Community law as it stands today. It should, however, be noted that this duty of sincere cooperation, as it applies today and would continue to apply under the Constitutional Treaty, can influence only the ways and means the powers of the institutional actors are

which makes it questionable whether this applies also to the ECB. The ECB, however, decided to adopt a broad interpretation and cooperate voluntarily with the Ombudsman; see the Ombudsman's Press Release 6/1999 of 17 May 1999, 'European Central Bank responds positively to Ombudsman's inquiry into public access to documents', published at <http://www.euro-ombudsman.eu.int/release/en/ecb1.htm>. On this already Zilioli and Selmayr, *The Law of the European Central Bank*, Oxford (2001), p. 49. So far, the Ombudsman looked into 11 cases of alleged maladministration at the ECB; see <http://www.euro-ombudsman.eu.int/decision/en/ecb.htm>.

[184] See 'Editorial and Legal Comments on the draft Treaty establishing a Constitution for Europe' (*supra* note 165), p. 55: 'The fact that the European Council and the ECB will be institutions within the legal meaning of the term will have implications: loyal cooperation between institutions [...].'

[185] See Deutsche Bundesbank, *supra* note 157, p. 69: 'Aus einer Organstellung der EZB folgt, dass sie der Pflicht zur "loyalen Zusammenarbeit" (Art. I-18 Abs. 3) mit den anderen Organen unterliegt. Welche Auswirkungen dies haben wird, bleibt abzuwarten. So ist etwa die Frage, ob die Pflicht zur loyalen Zusammenarbeit zur Forderung nach einer Ex-ante-Koordinierung der Geldpolitik mit anderen Politikbereichen, etwa mit der Finanzpolitik, führt, von besonderer Brisanz'. This view is shared by Gramlich and Manger-Nestler, *supra* note 157, p. 193.

[186] Similar Louis, in : Dony and Bribosia, *supra* note 162, p. 277: '[N]ous voyons mal comment la BCE pourrait se soustraire à cette obligation de loyauté, un principe constitutionnel, et comment celle-ci pourrait mettre en danger le statut particulier de la BCE'.

[187] See already Zilioli and Selmayr, *supra* note 136, p. 338 and footnote 230, where we argued that the duty of loyal cooperation in external relations, as regards the external representation of Community policies, must also be extended to the ECB.

[188] Cf. Case 204/86, *Greece v Council* [1988] ECR 5323, para. 16; Case 65/93, *European Parliament v Council* [1995] ECR I-643, para. 23 *et seq*. See also Declaration No 3 on Article 10 of the EC Treaty, annexed to the Final Act of the Nice Treaty: 'The Conference recalls that the duty of sincere cooperation which derives from Article 10 of the Treaty establishing the European Community and governs relations between the Member States and the Community institutions also governs relations between the Community institutions themselves. In relations between those institutions, when it proves necessary, in the context of that duty of sincere cooperation, to facilitate the application of the provisions of the Treaty establishing the European Community, the European Parliament, the Council and the Commission may conclude interinstitutional agreements. Such agreements may not amend or supplement the provisions of the Treaty and may be concluded only with the agreement of these three institutions.'

exercised, but never alter or supplement the distribution of powers itself.[189] The ECB thus can certainly be expected, on the basis of the duty of sincere cooperation, to continue its regular dialogue with the European Parliament, the Council and the Commission on matters relevant for the exercise of its monetary policy competences, and also to conduct the modalities of this dialogue in a cooperative way, but certainly not to abstain from, or change a particular decision on, say, interest rates when such a decision is, in the view of the ECB, necessary to meet the ECB's objectives under the Treaty. We see nothing in the Constitutional Treaty that would change this legal situation.[190]

Secondly, the new terminology used for the ECB ('institution') means that under the Constitutional Treaty, it could, in principle, become slightly easier for secondary Union legislation to comply with the conditions established in the OLAF judgment and thus to be capable of applying also to the ECB. Whenever a legal basis in the Constitutional Treaty says that Union legislation adopted by the European Parliament and/or the Council applies to the 'institutions'—as do, for example, Article I-51 concerning European laws or framework laws on 'the protection of individuals with regard to the processing of data by Union institutions, bodies, offices and agencies'[191] and Article III-433 for 'the rules governing the languages of the Union's institutions'—the ECB will now be clearly meant. The practical implications of this will, however, be rather limited as in most of these cases the ECB already complies today with such general secondary Community law,[192] while in a few cases, specific provisions in the Constitutional Treaty exclude the ECB either directly[193] or indirectly[194] from their scope to preserve its special nature.

---

[189] Cf. Streinz, in: Streinz (Ed.), *Kommentar zum EU- und EG-Vertrag*, München (2003), Art. 7 EGV, para. 22, who also uses the term 'Organtreue' for the inter-institutional duty of sincere cooperation: 'Dieses Gebot der Rücksichtsnahme schränkt nicht den politischen Gestaltungsspielraum der Organe ein, sondern verbietet die missbräuchliche (und erfordert die zweckgerichtete) Ausübung von Verfahrensrechten'.

[190] One could even argue that under the Constitutional Treaty, the duty of sincere cooperation applies to a lesser extent to the ECB than among the core institutions of the Union's institutional framework. As Article I-19(2), second sentence of the Constitutional Treaty is placed in the opening provision of Chapter 1 'The Institutional Framework' of Titel IV of Part I, to which the ECB as 'other institution' does not belong, the duty of sincere cooperation can be only applied to the ECB by analogy, and by taking into account the specific independent responsibilities of the ECB. Similar Louis, in: Dony and Bribosia *supra* note 162, p. 277.

[191] Cf. 'Editorial and Legal Comments on the draft Treaty establishing a Constitution for Europe' (*supra* note 165), p. 113: 'With the disappearance of the "pillars", the rules on data protection will apply in the areas of CFSP and JHA, as well as to the European Council and the European Central Bank, which will be Institutions (see comments on Article I-18(2).'

[192] This is, for example, the case with regard to the language regime (see *supra* note 114).

[193] Such an explicit exclusion is provided for in Article III-399(1) second sentence of the Constitutional Treaty, for European laws adopted on the basis of Article I-50(3), subpara. 2 to guarantee public access to documents of the Union institutions. This will allow the ECB to continue its present regime on public access as laid down in Decision ECB/2004/3 of 4 March 2004 on public access to European Central Bank documents [2004] OJ L80/42.

[194] This is the case with regard to Article III-427 of the Constitutional Treaty according to which a European law shall lay down the staff regulations of officials and the Conditions of Employment of

A third practical change compared to today's legal situation could occur if secondary Union law and secondary ECB law on the same subject-mater were to come into conflict under the Constitutional Treaty, a possibility that we have illustrated already above with the example of legislation on the design of euro banknotes.[195] We have shown that under the present EC Treaty, there is no hierarchical relationship between a regulation adopted by the Council or jointly by the European Parliament and the Council on the one hand and an ECB regulation on the other hand, as both stand today normatively on equal footing. Under the Constitutional Treaty, regulations adopted jointly by the European Parliament and the Council would become 'European laws' which are qualified as 'legislative acts' (Article I-33(1), second subparagraph, Article I-34(1) of the Constitutional Treaty). In contrast to this, ECB regulations would remain 'regulations' and would be qualified, in Article I-35(2), as 'non-legislative acts', as would be Council and Commission regulations adopted to implement European laws or European framework laws. There are two possible interpretations of this new terminology in case of a possible normative conflict between a European law and an ECB regulation: one could argue that both continue to stand on equal footing as their legal effects are defined, in Article I-33(1), subparagraphs 2 and 3, in identical terms, and as the regulatory power to adopt them stems in both cases directly from the Constitutional Treaty; this would plead in favour of continuing to distinguish between these powers in case of conflict according to the subject matter concerned.[196] One could, however, also argue that in the case of a conflict between a

---

other servants of the Union. At the same time, Article 36(1) of Statute, in the version annexed to the Constitutional Treaty as Protocol No. 4, continues to give the Governing Council of the ECB, on a proposal from the Executive Board, the competence to lay down the Conditions of Employment for the staff of the ECB. Under this scheme, the general EU Staff Regulations could thus, if at all, only be said to apply to ECB staff if the Conditions of Employment have not already settled the matter. Cf. the Order of 30 March 2000 of the CFI in Case T-33/99, *Pinedo v ECB* [2000] ECR IA-63, II-273, para. 33, where the CFI applied by analogy Articles 90 and 91 of the Staff Regulations (see <http://ec. europa.eu/civil_service/docs/toc100_en.pdf>) for identifying the procedural conditions under which a potential applicant for a position at the ECB could challenge the way in which a competition for a certain post had been organised. The reason for this was that at the time of the dispute, the Conditions of Employment of the ECB had not yet been published. The ECB's Conditions of Employment (Decision ECB/1998/4 of 9 June 1998 on the adoption of the Conditions of Employment for Staff of the European Central Bank, as amended on 31 March 1999 [1999] OJ L125/32, as amended by Decision ECB/2001/6 of 5 July 2001 [2001] OJ L201/25, with the full text published at <http://www.ecb.int/ecb/jobs/pdf/conditions_of_employment.pdf> state themselves, under Point 9(c): 'In interpreting the rights and obligations under the present Conditions of Employment, due regard shall be shown for the authoritative principles of the regulations, rules and case law which apply to the staff of the EC institutions'. See also CFI, Joined Cases T-94/01, T-152/01 and T-286/01, *Hirsch, Nicastro and Priesemann v ECB* [2003] ECR II-27 paras. 53 and 54, where the CFI drew on the objectives of the scheme of education allowances according to the case law applicable to staff of the Community institutions to interpret the rules on the education allowance for ECB staff.

[195] *Supra* p. 40 *et seq.*

[196] Cf. Zilioli, *supra*, note 161, p. 63 *et seq.* This view is also favoured by Louis, 'Monetary Policy and Central Banking in the Constitution', in: ECB (Ed.), *Legal Aspects of the European System of Central Banks, supra* note 1, p. 27, at p. 39 *et seq.*

legislative act and a non-legislative act, the legislative act will always prevail. This line of reasoning would be supported by the principle of democracy which, even though at present still in a state of adolescence in Community law, would become a much more prominent principle in the constitutional legal order of the Union with the entry into force of the Constitutional Treaty.[197]

A final practical change resulting from the institutional novelties of the Constitutional Treaty concerns the liability regime of the ECB. Under Community law as it stands at present, the wording of Article 288(3) EC[198] is open to interpretation. While many—and in particular those who contest vehemently our view of the ECB's special legal nature[199]—argue that acts or omissions of the ECB must be imputed to the legal person Community which thus would be liable for the ECB, we have always taken the view that, as a legal consequence of the ECB's separate legal personality, its pronounced independence and its own financial resources, it would be unjustified to make the legal person Community liable for the ECB's acts or omissions. As there is no hierarchical or proprietary relationship between the legal person ECB and the Community, we always have seen it as a logical consequence of the special status of the ECB that the ECB is liable itself in such cases and must pay for damages caused by its decision-making bodies and its staff from its own financial resources.[200] One would assume that the Constitutional Treaty, which makes the ECB an 'institution', would have settled this debate in favour of our opponents and would now

---

[197] See Article I-2 of the Constitutional Treaty, according to which democracy becomes a cornerstone of the Union which can be taken into account by the ECJ in the interpretation of all provisions of the Constitutional Treaty (see Article I-29), including the provisions on the ECB and on economic and monetary policy. This is confirmed by Title VI, which includes under the heading 'The Democratic Life of the Union' a number of provisions on representative democracy and on participatory democracy which are applicable to all Union institutions, and thus also to the ECB.

[198] Article 288(3) EC reads as follows: 'The preceding paragraph [which provides for the non-contractual liability of the Community for damage caused by its institutions and its servants] shall apply under the same conditions to damage caused by the ECB or by its servants in the performance of their duties'.

[199] See, in particular, Dutzler, *supra* note 24, p. 81 *et seq.* who comes to the telling conclusion that the Community is the bearer of liability and that ECB act would have to be imputed to the Community, even though the ECB would have to pay the damage from its own funds. 'That the ECB by virtue of Article 108 EC conducts the monetary policy without being subject to instructions, is a sign of its independence, but does not prevent that the actions of the ECB can ultimately be imputed to the Community.' A liability of the Community for the ECB is also favoured by Weber, 'Das Europäische System der Zentralbanken' [1998] Wertpapiermitteilungen 1465, at p. 1470; by Gellermann, in: Streinz (Ed.), *Kommentar zum EU- und EG-Vertrag*, München (2003), Art. 288 EGV, para. 33; and by Ehricke, *ibid.*, Art. 235 EGV, para. 8.

[200] Zilioli and Selmayr, *The Law of the European Central Bank*, Oxford (2001), p. 44 *et seq.* Already Selmayr, 'Die Wirtschafts- und Währungsunion als Rechtsgemeinschaft', *supra* note 21, p. 371, footnote 62. Our view is shared by Hahn and Häde, *supra* note 23, p. 55; Häde, *supra* note 42, p. 1609; Gaiser, *supra* note 136, p. 531; La Marca, 'Il controllo giurisdizionale sulla Banca Centrale Europea e sull'Istituto Monetario Europeo', in: *Il diritto dell'Unione europea*, Milan (1996), p. 773, at p. 789 *et seq.*; Baur, *Die Haftung der Europäischen Zentralbank*, Frankfurt am Main (2001), p. 16. Even Gaitanides, *supra* note 43, p. 255 follows our view in this respect.

clearly state that it must be for the Union to bear the liability for all its institutions, including the independent institution ECB.[201] However, this is not the case, on the contrary. In the important context of legal liability, where legal responsibilities need to be clearly attributed, not the terminology but the special legal nature of the independent legal person ECB is seen as decisive by the Constitutional Treaty. The Constitutional Treaty therefore clarifies in Article III-431(3) that notwithstanding the liability of the Union for its institutions, '*the European Central Bank shall, in accordance with the general principles common to the laws of the Member States, make good any damage caused by it or its servants in the performance of their duties.*'

For us, this confirms that under the Constitutional Treaty, the balance tips rather more than less towards an understanding of the ECB as *independent specialized organization of constitutional Union law*. In this capacity, the ECB has become a Union institution, but not the property of the Union. It can thus be truly said that the ECB, similar to a young tree, has been successfully transplanted from the EC Treaty to the Constitutional Treaty, without its Maastricht roots having been affected, while the branches of its independence have even grown stronger in their new and prosperous constitutional environment.[202] This being said, we need of course insert a word of caution and recall that according to the European Court of Justice, '*[i]t would be contrary to the principle of legal certainty if [. . .] account were to be taken of an alleged development in relations between institutions which does not yet find confirmation in any provisions of the Treaties currently in force or in the provisions of a Treaty which has not yet entered into force*'.[203] A final word on the legal nature of the ECB can thus be only said once the Constitutional Treaty will have been ratified by all EU Member States—which we sincerely hope. Because the Constitutional Treaty would make the Union more democratic, its institutional structure more transparent and its functioning more efficient, and a strong Union is essential for a strong euro.[204]

---

[201] This had indeed been proposed by legal experts at the Intergovernmental Conference; see 'Editorial and Legal Comments on the draft Treaty establishing a Constitution for Europe' (*supra* note 165), p. 488, which had proposed the deletion of the specific paragraph on the liability of the ECB and justified this as follows (p. 489): 'The third paragraph is no longer necessary as the ECB is an Institution and is therefore covered by the second paragraph'.

[202] Cf. Padoa-Schioppa, *The ECB and the Constitution*, Wall Street Journal of 26 September 2003, p. A8, who uses the metaphor of the ECB, the euro and the monetary policy framework to be a young tree which needs to be transplanted from the Rome-Maastricht ground to that of the new Constitution, preserving its roots and leaving its main branches intact.

[203] Case C-269/97, *Commission v Council* [2000] ECR I-2257, para. 45.

[204] Cf. Duisenberg 'The first lustrum of the ECB', Speech at the International Frankfurt Banking Event on 16 June 2003, published at <http://www.ecb.int/press/key/date/2003/html/sp030616.en.html>: 'The ECB welcomes all efforts to further the construction of a united Europe. [. . .] Throughout the five years of its existence, the ECB has stated that a strong euro is good for a strong Europe. I would now like to add that a strong Europe is good for a strong euro.'

II. The Relationship between the ECB and the National Central Banks: E Pluribus Unum?

An issue that has also been widely discussed in academic doctrine and in legal practice in the first eight years after the establishment of the ECB is its relationship with the national central banks with whom it is institutionally integrated into the European System of Central Banks (ESCB). For this relationship, it is crucial to understand that Monetary Union, as it has been implemented under the EC Treaty, is nothing less than the introduction of a *single* currency[205] that irrevocably replaces legally[206] and physically[207] the previous national currencies. This Monetary Union requires further a *single* monetary policy and a *single* exchange-rate policy for the single currency, as is recognized explicitly by Article 4(2) EC. Such a single policy can only be successfully defined and implemented by a *single* organization which is able to ensure the uniform application of its decisions throughout the single currency area.[208]

This is the reason why, as we have argued in all our writings, the ESCB, even though made up of both the ECB and the national central banks (Article 107(1) EC), is, in its legal construction, a clearly centralized system,[209] governed solely by the decision-making bodies of the ECB (Article 107(3) EC and Article 8 of the Statute) and able to take decisions by simple majority[210] (Articles 10.2, third subparagraph, second sentence, and 11.5, second sentence of the Statute). We have also shown that it is exclusively the ECB which, under the general rule of Article 9.2 of the Statute, may decide to implement ESCB tasks either itself or 'through the national central banks',[211] whatever is deemed more appropriate by

---

[205] Articles 4(2); 121(4), second sentence; 123(4), third sentence; 123(5) EC.

[206] Articles 1, sixth indent, 2, 3, 5 and 6 of Council Regulation (EC) No 974/98 of 3 May 1998 on the introduction of the euro [1998] OJ 139/1.

[207] Article 10 of Council Regulation (EC) No 974/98, *supra* note 206.

[208] Cf. Padoa-Schioppa (then Deputy Director General of the Bank of Italy), 'The Genesis of EMU: A Retrospective View', European University Institute, Jean Monnet Chair Paper RSC Bo 96/40 (Florence 1996) published at <http://www.iue.it/RSCAS/WP-Texts/JM96_40.html>, p. 3: 'The essence of a monetary union is institutional, not economic. It is the fact that the responsibility for monetary decisions is shifted to one single institution instead of being entrusted to a plurality of central banks, whether or not they are tied by an exchange-rate mechanism. In other words, creating a monetary union means moving from a plurality of decision-making centres to just one.'

[209] Cf. Zilioli and Selmayr, *The Law of the European Central Bank*, Oxford (2001), p. 57 *et seq*. See also Scheller, *supra* note 1, p. 50: 'Centralised decision-making through the ECB's decision-making bodies is not limited to the formulation of policies, such as changes in the ECB's key interest rates. It extends to the implementation of policies through the ECB and the NCBs.'

[210] According to Padoa-Schioppa, *The Euro and its Central Bank. Getting United after the Union*, Cambridge, Massachusetts (2004), p. 29, '[t]he majority principle marks the divide between a true union and occasional agreements, between a domestic and an international order.'

[211] We have qualified national central banks acting in this capacity as 'agents of the ECB', cf. Zilioli and Selmayr, *supra* note 209, at p. 73 *et seq*. See also Eichengreen, 'Designing a central bank for Europe: a cautionary tale from the early years of the Federal Reserve System', in: Canzoneri (Ed.), *Establishing a Central Bank: Issues in Europe and Lessons from the US*, Cambridge (1992), p. 13 (at p. 13): 'Once the ECB comes into operation, national central banks will forsake their remaining

the ECB,[212] while specific provisions such as Article 5.2,[213] 12.1[214] or 36.2[215] of the Statute give guidance for the discretion of the ECB in this respect. We have also explained that legally, the principle of subsidiarity does not apply inside the ESCB in view of the exclusive nature of the competences related to monetary policy.[216] We have finally assumed that in its first years of existence, it is likely that the ECB, in view of its limited personnel,[217] its young reputation and the need to keep a direct contact with the market participants in a still fragmented European financial market, will often make use of the national central banks for carrying out ESCB tasks, but that this could change over time.[218]

autonomy and become mere branch offices of the new institution.' Amtenbrink, *The Democratic Accountability of Central Banks: A Comparative Study of the European Central Bank*, Oxford (1999), comes to the same conclusion (at p. 120): 'Since the ESCB is governed by decision-making bodies of the ECB and the central banks are obliged to act in accordance with the guidelines and instructions of the ECB, the ESCB may better be viewed as a single-tier system. In fact, the national central banks function as an executive arm of the ECB.' Acting as agents of the ECB, the national central banks engage the liability of the ECB under Article 288(3)EC, cf. Zilioli and Selmayr, *supra* note 209, at p. 129 *et seq.* Cf. also *Fernández Martín/Texieira*, 'The imposition of sanctions by the European Central Bank' [2000] ELR 391 (at p. 397), who stress that '[t]he existence of a prior empowering [European Central] Bank act constitutes a prerequisite for any NCB action covered by ESCB tasks', and that therefore, 'any infringement of rights alleged by third parties must be referred to the enabling act of the Bank, and not to the NCB implementing act, which is merely an executive act. In other words, NCB acts that correctly implement acts of the Bank can ultimately be imputable to the Bank, and not to the relevant NCB.'

212 Cf. Zilioli and Selmayr, *supra* note 209, at p. 114 *et seq.*: '[. . .] Article 9.2 of the Statute shows that even in the context of the implementation of ECB law, there is no room for a presumption ruling in favour of indirect implementation through the national central banks, as this provision explicitly attributes the competence to decide between direct and indirect implementation to the ECB. The allocation of implementing powers is thus not decided by general principles or by presumptions, but is in each individual case up to the discretion of the ECB's decision-making bodies. In an extreme case, it would thus be legally possible to imagine that all ECB law is implemented exclusively by the ECB's own activities.'

213 Cf. Zilioli and Selmayr, *supra* note 209, at p. 119 *et seq.*: the statistical tasks of the ESCB shall be carried out, 'to the extent possible', by the national central banks.

214 Cf. Zilioli and Selmayr, *supra* note 209, at p. 116 *et seq.*: for carrying out monetary policy operations, the ECB shall have recourse to the national central banks '[t]o the extent deemed possible and appropriate' by the ECB.

215 Cf. Zilioli and Selmayr, *supra* note 209, at p. 120 *et seq.*: only direct implementation by the ECB is allowed in the context of the clearing and settlement of balances arising from the allocation of monetary income.   216 Cf. Zilioli and Selmayr, *supra* note 209, at p. 70 *et seq.*

217 It is estimated that the national central banks of the Member States that have adopted the euro have a combined total of more than 50,000 employees, of which at least 50% are involved in carrying out ESCB tasks, while the ECB has fewer than 1,500 staff members. See Scheller, *supra* note 1, p. 50.

218 Cf. Zilioli and Selmayr, *supra* note 209, at p. 121: 'Direct implementation of ECB law is, at the present stage, still the exception. This is not due to legal restraints, but merely a factual situation.' And at p. 126: 'For the moment, indirect implementation, i.e. implementation of ECB law through the national central banks, represents the rule within the ESCB.' See also, Bini Smaghi and Gros, *Open Issues in European Central Banking*, London (2000), p. 21: 'the main reason for decentralization is the desire to protect the employment of specialised staff in the NCBs'. They envisage a progressive *de facto* centralization over time. Even some authors from national central banks acknowledge that the ESCB 'could become more centralized'; see Hochreiter, 'The Role of National Central Banks (NCBs) in the Eurosystem—Current State of Play' [2000] Atlantic Economic Journal 300 (at p. 300).

For years, many national central banks were independent national institutions that had built a strong reputation in their Member States. The decision of the drafters of the Maastricht Treaty to transfer all monetary policy competences to the Community level therefore came as a radical change of position: while national central banks enjoy under the EC Treaty an even greater independence from political power than in their national constitutional systems, they are—if their country participates in the single currency—subject to the instructions of the ECB and lost the power to decide individually the monetary policy for their respective country. Against this background, some legal experts have contested, and still contest, the emphasis on the centre in our analysis of the ESCB. These authors take the view that national central banks still have their own, reserved, competences in parallel to the competences of the ECB; that the ECB would have no right to deprive national central banks of their 'domaine réservé'[219]; or that the 'European preference for subsidiarity' would reinforce the tendency to decentralization.[220] A few writers even resorted to sociological explanations and thereby tried to show that the Governing Council of the ECB is in reality nothing else than the group in which national central bank governors meet and where they jointly and in a quasi-intergovernmental manner decide the monetary policy for the euro area.[221]

It is probably normal that, in the first years of a Monetary Union, conflicts between the 'centre' and the 'periphery' arise, at least in the form of academic disputes. We note, however, the encouraging statement made by the ECJ in the

---

[219] Cf. Priego and Conlledo (both Banco de España), 'The role of the decentralisation principle in the legal construction of the European System of Central Banks', in: ECB (Ed.), *Legal Aspects of the European System of Central Banks, supra* note 1, p. 189, at p. 193, where they stress that national central banks would have 'the legitimacy to carry out tasks not only by virtue of a legal instrument of the ECB, but from their status as national central banks within the legal framework of the ESCB' and conclude (at p. 194) that certain tasks concerning monetary policy and operations in the payment systems 'are performed by the NCBs in their own right and in their own name', which would be 'not entirely compatible with a view of the NCBs as agents, which has no explicit support in any legal text'. They also take the view (at p. 196) that '[n]ot all ESCB tasks may potentially be centralised'.

[220] Cf. Wellink, Chapple and Maier, *The role of national central banks within the European System of Central Banks: The example of De Nederlandsche Bank*, No. 2002–13 of the Monetary and Economic Policy series of the Netherlands Central Bank, <http://www.dnb.nl/dnb/bin/doc/ms2002-13_tcm13-36225.pdf>, p. 18. On the perspective of Oesterreichische Nationalbank, the central bank of Austria, cf. Hochreiter, *supra* note 218, p. 300: 'The institutional design of the European System of Central Banks (ESCB) follows the principle of subsidiarity.'

[221] Cf. Seidel, 'Im Kompetenzkonflikt: Europäisches System der Zentralbanken (ESZB) versus Europäische Zentralbank' [2000] Europäische Zeitschrift für Wirtschaftsrecht 552, who considers the ESCB as a loose, confederate, intergovernmental or multilateral structure only ('Verbund', p. 552) in which the ECB would be at the same time agent and supervisory organ ('Ausführungs- und Aufsichtsorgan', p. 552) of the national central banks and which would by governed by the 'Governing Council of the ESCB' (p. 552); this would institutionally reflect that monetary sovereignty would be shared between the Member States and the Community ('Folge der auf die Gemeinschaft und ihre Mitgliedstaaten aufgeteilten Währungssouveränität', p. 553). See in detail Seidel, *Die Weisungs- und Herrschaftsmacht der Europäischen Zentralbank im Europäischen System der Zentralbanken—eine rechtliche Analyse*, ZEI Policy Paper B 111/2003. This view is to a certain extent reflected on the website of the Deutsche Bundesbank, which stresses that decisions for the Eurosystem are not taken by the ECB, but by the Governing Council; see the description at <http://www.bundesbank.de/aufgaben/aufgaben_aufgaben.php>.

OLAF judgment, where it mentioned the ESCB only in passing, while emphasizing that 'the heart' of the ESCB 'is the ECB'.[222] This metaphor in our view underlines accurately that it is, legally, the ECB that makes the System run, while the national central banks follow the rhythm given by the decisions, guidelines and instructions of the ECB. We also observe that the Constitutional Treaty, which is meant to present the future institutional design of the Union, includes, in its Part I, a specific Article I-30 with the heading 'The European Central Bank', which focuses on the ECB, while provisions on the national central banks are found only in Part III and in the Statute—a fact criticized heavily by some[223] as it confirms that the ECB is constitutionally more visible than they feel appropriate. We, however, believe that both the statement in the OLAF judgment and the emphasis of the Constitutional Treaty on the ECB reflect properly the institutional reality as it has evolved during the first eight years of Monetary Union.

A. The Evolution of a Supranational Decision-Making Culture in Monetary Policy

It is a remarkable success of the institutional set-up of Monetary Union that the transition from initially 11, then 12 and now 13 national monetary policies to the single monetary policy of the ECB took place smoothly and without any disruptive effects. This is particularly due to the fact that as of 1 January 1999, all members of the Governing Council of the ECB—both the six members of the ECB's Executive Board and the initially 11, as of 1 January 2001 12 and, as of 1 January 2007, 13 governors of the central banks of the Member States which participate in the single currency—have acted as truly supranational central bankers, with their views clearly focused on price stability in the euro area as a whole. It was a good sign that it was *Hans Tietmeyer*, then the governor of the Deutsche Bundesbank, who from the first meeting of the ECB's Governing Council onwards insisted on the need for all governors to act in a supranational manner.[224] Truly symbolic for this was *Tietmeyer's* request to replace, on the name

---

[222] Case 11/00, *supra* note 52, para. 92.

[223] Cf. Deutsche Bundesbank, 'Zur Währungsverfassung nach dem Entwurf einer Verfassung für die Europäische Union', *Monatsbericht, November 2003* (Frankfurt am Main), p. 67, at p. 70, which criticized this change of wording: 'Denn nach der Währungsverfassung von Maastricht werden das ESZB und die EZB gleichgeordnet geregelt (Art. 8 EG-Vertrag). Ein Auseinanderziehen der Regelungen zur EZB in Teil I und zum ESZB in Teil III könnte als Änderung des bislang zwischen EZB und nationalen Zentralbanken bestehenden engen Beziehungsgeflechts und als (weitere) Änderung des Maastricht-Vertrages verstanden werden.' See also Seidel, *Die Stellung der Europäischen Zentralbank nach dem Verfassungsvertrag*, ZEI Policy Paper B 19/2004, p. 6 *et seq.*, who would have preferred that Part I of the Constitution had dealt with the 'Governing Council *of the ESCB*' (sic!) only, which in his view should have become an institution of the Union.

[224] Cf. Tietmeyer, 'Ein dezentrales Umsetzen der gemeinsamen Geldpolitik sichert nahtlosen Übergang auf europäische Ebene', Frankfurter Rundschau of 9 October 1998, p. 13. See also Wellink, Chapple and Maier, *supra* note 220, p. 5: 'NCB members of the Governing Council do not consider themselves as representatives of their home country.'

tags around the table of the ECB's Governing Council, the names of the national central banks with the names of the individual governors[225] to underline the participation of the governors *ad personam* and not as representatives of their countries or national central banks. This is fully in line with our understanding that Article 108 EC, the EC Treaty's core provision on central bank independence, also rules out instructions of the national central banks, or of their decision-making bodies, addressed to their governor as member of a decision-making body of the ECB.[226] The monetary decisions taken by the ECB since 1999 have shown clearly that this supranational spirit prevailed in the discussions on monetary policy decisions, even though in the first months some encouragement from the side of the first ECB President *Duisenberg* and the other members of the ECB's Executive Board may well have been necessary.[227]

A supranational decision-making culture can thus be observed to develop inside the ESCB, which emphasizes much more the Community function and Community responsibility of the national central bank governors and of the national central banks than an understanding of them as national legal persons, which they formally have remained even though the EC Treaty and the Statute harmonized in several ways the institutional principles governing national central banks and in particular their independence. Of course, this transformation of the understanding of national central banks into bodies carrying out, under the authority of the ECB, Community tasks, which in case of conflict will prevail even over any additional tasks that national law may assign to them

---

[225] On this, see Padoa-Schioppa, *supra* note 210, p. 30, who also mentions that members of the Governing Council of the ECB sit at the table by the alphabetical order of their names, 'with no distinction between national governors and Board members'.

[226] Zilioli and Selmayr, *supra* note 209, at p. 89 *et seq.*; and Selmayr, *Das Recht der Wirtschafts- und Währungsunion I*, *supra* note 1, p. 312. This view is shared by Häde, in: Calliess and Ruffert (Eds.), *Kommentar zu EU-Vertrag und EG-Vertrag*, 2nd edition, Neuwied (2002), Art. 108 EGV, para. 8. Against this, see the view of the former President of the (as it then was) Land Central Bank of Bavaria *Zeitler*, 'Die Europäische Währungsunion als Stabilitätsgemeinschaft' [1995] Wertpapiermitteilungen 1609, at p. 1614. The ECB confirmed in the 'Code of Conduct for the members of the Governing Council' of 16 May 2002 [2002] OJ C123/9, under point 3.1, that the members of the Governing Council are also independent from instructions from 'any decision-making body that they belong to'.

[227] See the anecdote reported by *Duisenberg*, in: ECB (Ed), *The Eurosystem, the Union and Beyond. The Single Currency and Implications for Governance. An ECB colloquium held in honour of Tommaso Padoa-Schioppa*, 27 April 2005, Franfurt am Main (2005), p. 10, at p. 11: 'I remember—and I am allowed to quote this incident—the first time that the Governing Council took a monetary policy decision to lower interest rates back in April 1999. A couple of days before we actually met, I used to call my colleagues in the Governing Council to announce that it was likely that they would be confronted with a proposal to change interest rates at our forthcoming meeting. I spoke, amongst others, to Matti Vanhalla, our much missed late colleague of Finland. When I told him of the inclination to lower interest rates he shouted to me down the telephone: "Oh no, not for Finland". When I started muttering, he said: "Stop, Wim, I know what you are going to say. I have to take a euro area perspective". I said: "Precisely, Matti". He replied: "Well, I have reflected on it already. You have my support"'.

(Article 14.4 of the Statute), is still ongoing and will certainly need further time to be completed.[228]

A very important laboratory in this respect are the so-called 'ESCB Committees', which have been established by the ECB under Article 9 of the ECB's Rules of Procedure.[229] The purpose of these committees is to 'assist in the work of the decision-making bodies of the ECB', for example as regards monetary policy, banknotes or statistics, and to 'report to the Governing Council via the Executive Board'.[230] ESCB committees are composed of up to two members from each of the national central banks of the Member States which have adopted the euro,[231] and from the European Central Bank.[232] They are, as a rule, chaired by a staff member of the ECB,[233] and the ECB always provides secretarial assistance.[234] At present, there are 12 such committees with a mandate given to them by the ECB's Governing Council under Article 9 of the ECB's Rules of Procedure.[235] In the initial years of the ECB, some considered these ESCB Committees as bodies which would allow the national central banks to bring the ECB under their control in its daily operations[236] and even have compared the ESCB Committees with the possibility of Member States to influence the decision-making of the Commission via the Comitology procedure[237] or with the

---

[228] On this challenge, see Padoa-Schioppa, *supra* note 210, p. 127: 'Given their dual profile, however, national central banks themselves are caught in this tangle. While the ECB Council is mandated to optimize the single overall system of euroland, and national central banks, as components of the Eurosystem, are 'governed' by the ECB Council, as national institutions they tend to be defenders of the status quo. All this makes their position awkward.'

[229] Decision ECB/2004/2 of 19 February 2004 adopting the Rules of Procedure of the European Central Bank [2004] OJ L80/33.

[230] Article 9(1), second sentence of Decision ECB/2004/2, *supra* note 229.

[231] Staff members from the central banks outside the euro area may participate in ESCB committee meetings only when they deal with matters falling within the field of competence of the General Council of the ECB and whenever the chairperson and the Executive Board of the ECB deem this appropriate; see Article 9(3) of Decision ECB/2004/2, *supra* note 229.

[232] Article 9(2), first sentence of Decision ECB/2004/2, *supra* note 229.

[233] Article 9(2), third sentence of Decision ECB/2004/2, *supra* note 229.

[234] Article 9(2), fifth sentence of Decision ECB/2004/2, *supra* note 229.

[235] Cf. ECB, *Annual Report 2005*, Frankfurt am Main (2006), p. 171: Accounting and Monetary Income Committee (AMICO), Banking Supervision Committee (BSC), Banknote Committee (BANCO), Eurosystem/ESCB Communications Committee (ECCO), Information Technology Committee (ITC), Internal Auditors Committee (IAC), International Relations Committee (IRC), Legal Committee (LEGCO), Market Operations Committee (MOC), Monetary Policy Committee (MPC), Payment and Settlement Systems Committee (PSSC) and Statistics Committee (STC). In addition, there is Human Resources Conference (HRC), an ad hoc committee for the purpose of developing and implementing a new HR strategy, established under Article 9a of Decision ECB/2004/2, *supra* note 229; and the Budget Committee (BUCOM), established under Article 15(2) of Decision ECB/2004/2, *supra* note 229, which has the special role to assist the Governing Council of the ECB in matters related to the budget of the ECB.

[236] See Seidel, 'Im Kompetenzkonflikt: Europäisches System der Zentralbanken (ESZB) versus Europäische Zentralbank', *supra* note 221, p. 553, who believes that the staff members of national central banks on the ESCB Committees are bound by instructions of their national central banks.

[237] The Comitology procedure allows committees made up of representatives of the Member States to control the implementation of powers delegated by the Council to the Commission. It is

role played by COREPER[238] in preparing the meetings of the Council of Ministers.[239] In this understanding, staff members of the national central banks on the ESCB Committees could have operated as 'Trojan horses' of national influence or as defenders of the interests of their respective national central bank.[240] In the daily work of the ECB, such fears so far fortunately have been proven to be unjustified. Instead, the supranational spirit already present at the level of the Governing Council of the ECB is also being transmitted to the ESCB Committees which progressively are developing the *esprit de corps* of ECB bodies entrusted with the mandate to contribute, with their advice in their field of expertise, to the proper functioning of the ECB, even though it is understandably more difficult for individual staff members of a national central bank to live this independence with regard to their employers than for the central bank governors themselves.

To eliminate all doubts about the status of the ESCB Committees, the ECB's Rules of Procedure, as amended by the Governing Council of the ECB in February 2004, deleted the initial sentence according to which staff members of the national central banks serving on an ESCB Committee were 'representatives' of the national central banks.[241] Under the new version of the ECB's Rules of Procedure, they are now to be qualified as experts, sit in Committee meetings behind tags bearing their own name instead of that of a national central bank, and must now be appointed directly by the respective Governor of the national central bank,[242] who will certainly do this by having his own role as supranational decision-maker in mind. This amendment to the ECB's Rules of Procedure

governed by Council Decision 2006/512/EC of 17 July 2006, amending Decision 1999/468/EC laying down the procedures for the exercise of implementing powers conferred on the Commission [2006] OJ L200/11. Comitology is compared to ESCB committees by Seidel, *supra* note 236, p. 553 *et seq.*

[238] Under Article 19 of the Rules of Procedure of the Council (as laid down by Council Decision 2004/338/EC, Euratom of 22 March 2004 [2004] OJ L319/15, as amended by Council Decision 2006/34/EC, Euratom of 23 January 2006 [2006] OJ L22/32), COREPER (the Committee of the Permanent Representatives of the Member States) is responsible for preparing the work of the Council. Article 19(4) provides that COREPER shall be chaired by the Permanent Representative or Deputy Permanent Representative of the Member State which holds the Presidency of the Council. Participation of Commission representatives in COREPER meetings is not foreseen in the Council's Rules of Procedure. Already in terms of composition and chairmanship, COREPER thus differs considerably from the ESCB Committees.

[239] Louis, *supra* note 162, p. 588 writes that ESCB Committees play 'gross modo' a role similar to that of COREPER

[240] Seidel, *supra* note 236, p. 554, considers the ESCB Committees as a constitutional weakness of Monetary Union. Cf. also Hochreiter, *supra* note 218, p. 300 (at p. 300), where he envisages the possibility that the ESCB Committees could become 'the nucleus for a different, decentralized evolution in the longer term'. Critical on the initial design of the ESCB Committees also Selmayr, 'Wie unabhängig ist die Europäische Zentralbank? Eine Analyse anhand der ersten geldpolitischen Entscheidungen der EZB' [1999] Wertpapiermitteilungen 2429, at p. 2441 *et seq.*

[241] Article 9(1) of the Rules of Procedure of the European Central Bank as amended on 22 April 1999 [1999] OJ L125/34, now replaced by Decision ECB/2004/2, *supra* note 229.

[242] Article 9(2), first sentence of Decision ECB/2004/2, *supra* note 229.

clarified that staff members cannot be bound by instructions of the national central banks in their work as members of an ESCB Committee,[243] but serve on these Committees to promote solely the Community interest. Unlike committees of national representatives in the Comitology procedure, and also unlike COREPER,[244] ESCB Committees are therefore not the place for inserting national (or national central bank) influence into the ECB's decision-making process. They have only an advisory and not a decision-making function and are therefore an instrument for the ECB to draw on the high expertise of the staff of the national central banks and to activate it in the Community interest. Staff of national central banks serving on ESCB Committees will therefore always have to look at the supranational interest of the ECB even though this may often mean to move from the status quo to new and more efficiency-oriented supranational solutions. Without any doubt, this will continue to be seen as a challenge for quite some time also in the future.

B. A New Decision-Making Model to Prepare the ECB for Enlargement

Recent institutional developments have further strengthened the supranational features of the decision-making process in the ECB. The driver for these changes has been the enlargement of the European Union. Since the entry into force of the Treaty of Maastricht, the number of EU Member States has more than doubled, from 12 to today 27 countries. With the introduction of the euro in Slovenia, the euro area comprises since 1 January 2007 13 Members States, and since then, the Governing Council of the ECB counts 19 members: the six members of the Executive Board of the ECB and 13 national central bank governors. Further enlargements both of the EU[245] and of the euro area[246] can be expected in the not too distant future. For the ECB, this prospect of further enlargement has made

---

[243] See already Selmayr, *supra* note 240, p. 2442; and Zilioli and Selmayr, *supra* note 209, p. 89, footnote 28.

[244] It is important to note that COREPER can take many decisions on behalf of the Council, while ESCB Committees have always only an advisory role. They are not entitled to take decisions on behalf of the ECB.

[245] Currently, Croatia, the former Yugoslav Republic of Macedonia and Turkey have the status of candidate countries.

[246] In February 2007, Cyprus and Malta applied for an abrogation of their present derogation under Article 122(2) EC. Under Article 4(2) in conjunction with Article 10 EC, all EU Member States (with the exception of the UK, see number 5 of the UK Protocol) shall endeavour to meet the legal and economic requirements to introduce the single currency as soon as possible; on this obligation, which is particularly relevant in the case of Sweden, but could also become relevant for Poland, see Zilioli and Selmayr, *supra* note 209, p. 135 *et seq.* See also Louis, *supra* note 162, p. 603 *et seq.*, who qualifies, at p. 605, the Swedish position as an 'infringement', even though 'not one that could possibly be settled by an infringement action before the Court of Justice.' We would view this as a more political than a legal statement as we see nothing in Article 226 EC that could prevent the Commission from starting infringement proceedings in such a case, especially where a country, in spite of the clear obligations in Articles 108, 109 EC, does not comply with the requirement of central bank independence at national level.

amendments to its decision-making procedures inevitable. The ECB is particularly dependent on a speedy and efficient decision-making process and therefore could not maintain its present way of supranational decision-making if the membership of its Governing Council—already today 'by far the most numerous body in charge of monetary policy in any central bank of the World'[247]—would continue to increase without limitations.

This is why the Nice Treaty opened, with an 'enabling clause' inserted in the new Article 10.6 of the Statute, the possibility to reform the decision-making process in the Governing Council of the ECB, currently foreseen in Article 10.2 of the Statute, by way of a slightly simplified[248] Treaty amendment procedure. On this basis, the Council, meeting in the composition of Heads of States or Government, adopted unanimously on 21 March 2003[249] a new version of Article 10.2 of the Statute on the basis of a recommendation of the ECB[250] and after consulting the European Parliament[251] and the Commission.[252] Following ratification by all Member States,[253] the new voting rules for the Governing Council of the ECB entered into force on 1 June 2004.[254] The new rules could not change the composition of the Governing Council, which continues to be foreseen in Article 10.1 of the Statute and which can only be changed by the ordinary Treaty amendment procedure under Article 48 EU. This means that also in the future, each central bank governor of the Member States introducing the

---

[247] Louis, *supra* note 162, p. 597.

[248] In contrast to Article 48 EU, Article 10.6 of the Statute does not require that an Intergovernmental Conference is convened.

[249] Decision 2003/223/EC of the Council meeting in the composition of the Heads of State or Government of 21 March 2003 on an amendment to Article 10.2 of the Statute of the European System of Central Banks and of the European Central Bank [2003] OJ L83/66.

[250] Recommendation ECB/2003/1 of the European Central Bank of 3 February 2003 under Article 10.6 of the Statute of the European System of Central Banks and of the European Central Bank, for a Council Decision on an amendment to Article 10.2 of the Statute of the European System of Central Banks and of the European Central Bank [2003] OJ C29/6. In Declaration No 19, annexed to the Nice Treaty, on Article 10.6 of the Statute of the European System of Central Banks and of the European Central Bank, the Intergovernmental Conference voiced its expectation 'that a recommendation within the meaning of Article 10.6 of the Statute of the European System of Central Banks and of the European Central Bank will be presented as soon as possible.' The ECB presented such a recommendation two days after the entry into force of the Nice Treaty on 1 February 2003. For this recommendation, Article 10.6, subpara. 2 of the Statute required a unanimous decision of the Governing Council of the ECB.

[251] The European Parliament had strongly criticized the proposed reform which it considered excessively complex (Report A5-0063/2003 of 10 March 2003, Rapporteur: *Ingo Friedrich*) and had instead asked the Constitutional Convention to identify a better solution. The European Parliament would have preferred in particular to increase the number of Executive Board members from six to nine. The Constitutional Convention, however, did not make any proposals in this respect.

[252] The Commission, in its Opinion of 19 February 2003, COM(2003) 81, supported the ECB's reform proposals in principle, but also made clear that it would have wished for a more efficient and more transparent system.

[253] Cf., for example, the German 'Gesetz über die Zustimmung zur Änderung der Satzung des Europäischen Systems der Zentralbanken und der Europäischen Zentralbank' of 6 January 2004, Bundesgesetzblatt 2004 II/2.   [254] Cf. ECB, *Annual Report 2004*, p. 164.

euro will be able to participate in the meetings and deliberations of the Governing Council of the ECB, which could thus grow to up to 33 members if all of the current 27 Member States introduced the euro.[255] However, under the amended version of Article 10.2 of the Statute, no more than 21 members of the Governing Council will be entitled to vote in the future: the six members of the Executive Board and no more than 15 national central bank governors.

On the day the sixteenth EU Member State will introduce the euro,[256] the 15 voting rights of the national central bank governors will start to rotate while the six voting rights of the members of the ECB's Executive Board will remain permanently attributed to them. The rotation system[257] provided for in Article 10.2 of the Statute means that central bank governors are divided initially in two,[258] later in three groups[259] in accordance with the relative size of the economy[260] and of the financial sector[261] of their respective Member State. To each of these groups, a number of voting rights is assigned which rotate amongst its members. The group of the central bank governors from the economically and financially strongest Member States include less members, while the members of the other groups are more numerous. As a result, the central bank governors from the economically and financially stronger Member States will be more frequently entitled to vote than the other central bank governors.[262]

---

[255] This is, with some justification, criticized by Wagner and Grum, 'Adjusting ECB Decision-Making to an Enlarged Union', in: ECB (Ed.), *Legal Aspects of the European System of Central Banks*, *supra* note 1, p. 73, at p.84 *et seq.*

[256] According to Article 10.2, subpara. 1, sixth indent of the Statute, the Governing Council of the ECB, acting by a two-thirds majority of all its members, with and without a voting right, may decide to postpone the start of the rotation system until the date on which the number of governors exceeds 18. This option for delay is criticised in Commission Opinion of 19 February 2003, *supra*, note 252, points 2 and 4.

[257] A detailed explanation can be found in Scheller, *The European Central Bank, supra* note 1, p. 55 *et seq.*, who illustrates the new rotation system with a number of helpful diagrams. See also the article 'The adjustment of voting modalities in the Governing Council', in: ECB, *Monthly Bulletin, May 2003*, p. 73; and the Speech of Yves Mersch, President of the Central Bank of Luxembourg of 25 March 2003, 'The reform of the Governing Council of the ECB', BIS Review 16/2003, p. 14, published at <http://www.bis.org/review/r030331c.pdf>. Further implementing provisions with regard to the rotation system still need to be adopted by the Governing Council of the ECB under Article 10.2, subpara. 1 sixth indent of the Statute. See also the detailed analysis by Servais, 'The Future Voting Modalities of the ECB Governing Council', in: Oesterreichische Nationalbank, Workshops No. 7/2006, *The European Integration Process: A Changing Environment for National Central Banks*, Vienna (2006), p. 246. See also Berger, *The ECB and Euro-Area Enlargement*, IMF Working Paper No. 02/175, October 2002, p. 28.

[258] Article 10.2, subpara. 1, third sentence, first indent of the Statute.

[259] As from the date of the introduction of the euro in the 22nd EU Member State; cf. Article 10.2, subpara. 1, third sentence, second indent of the Statute.

[260] Measured by the share of the respective Member State in the aggregate gross domestic product at market prizes, multiplied by 5/6th; cf. Article 10.2, subpara. 1, third sentence, first indent, sentences 1 and 2 of the Statute.

[261] Measured by the share of the respective Member State in the total aggregate balance sheet of the monetary financial institutions, multiplied by 1/6th; cf. Article 10.2, subpara. 1, third sentence, first indent, sentences 1 and 2 of the Statute.

[262] With 27 Member States participating in the single currency, the first group would include five central bank governors which would have four rotating voting rights; the second group would

The new voting rules for the Governing Council of the ECB are careful not to revolutionize the still young institutional set-up of the ECB,[263] but are nevertheless remarkable in at least three respects. First, the new voting rules represent a considerable departure in primary Community law from the principle of equality of the Member States as they favour economic and financial strength. Apparently, the efficiency of the decision-making process was in the particular case of the ECB's Governing Council more important for the economically and financially weaker Member States than their national interest in equal representation. This can be understood at the same time as a strong commitment to the supranational nature of the ECB in which national interests are less relevant than elsewhere in the EU.[264] Secondly, the new rules are remarkable as in spite of the differentiation now introduced according to the economic and financial strength of their respective Member States among central bank governors, they still do not become representatives of their Member State, of their national central bank or of their group[265] in the future, but continue to participate in the Governing Council 'in a personal and independent capacity'.[266] One can even say that they will in the future have to bear much more the European interest in mind than today as then,

include 14 central bank governors with eight rotating voting rights; and the third group would include eight central bank governors with three rotating voting rights.

[263] See Allemand, 'L'audace raisonnée de la réforme de la Banque centrale européenne' [2003] Revue du Marché Commun 301.

[264] This exceptional situation, which distinguishes the ECB from the EU institutions, is confirmed by the declaration annexed to the minutes of the meeting of the Council of 21 March 2003, published at <http://www.consilium.europa.eu/ueDocs/cms_Data/docs/pressData/en/ecofin/75135.pdf>, which reads as follows: 'The Council confirms that the model established in its Decision on voting modalities in the Governing Council of the European Central Bank should not be seen as a precedent for the future composition and decision-making process of other Community Institutions'. It should be noted that the Treaty of Nice, in Article 4 of the Protocol on the enlargement of the European Union, provides also for a rotation system for the composition of the Commission. 'When the Union consists of 27 Member States'—this is the case as of 1 January 2007—, Article 214(1) EC will read as follows: The number of Members of the Commission shall be less than the number of Member States. The Members of the Commission shall be chosen according to a rotation system based on the principle of equality, the implementing arrangements for which shall be adopted by the Council, acting unanimously. The number of Members of the Commission shall be set by the Council, acting unanimously.' This amendment, however, applies only 'as from the date on which the first Commission following the date of accession of the twenty-seventh Member State of the Union takes up its duties'. So far, the Council has decided neither on the number of Commissioners nor on the modalities of the rotation system, even though Article 4(3) of the Protocol on the enlargement of the European Union requires the Council to do this 'acting unanimously after signing the treaty of accession of the twenty-seventh Member State of the Union.' The Treaty concerning the accession of the Republic of Bulgaria and Romania to the European Union [2005] OJ L157/1, was signed in Luxembourg on 25 April 2005.

[265] This is noted positively by Wagner and Grum, *supra* note 255, p. 85, who also point to the different situation in the IMF where each Executive Director represents the countries allocated to his/her constituency.

[266] Cf. recital 4 of Council Decision 2003/223/EC, *supra* note 249: 'All members of the Governing Council continue to participate in its meetings in a personal and independent capacity, irrespective of whether they have a voting right or not.' This is welcomed by Allemand, *supra* note 263, at p. 397.

the situation will occur more and more often that certain nationalities will not at all be represented with a voting right in the ECB's Governing Council and will therefore depend on an unbiased supranational assessment of the situation by their colleagues with voting rights. Finally, the new voting rules are remarkable because they maintain and strengthen the position of the ECB's Executive Board which will keep six *permanent* voting rights also in the case of an enlargement of the euro area to up to 27 Member States, while those of all central bank governors will rotate. By virtue of their permanent voting right, the members of the Executive Board will thus have a particularly important and stable role in the enlarged Governing Council of the ECB, the decisions of which they will be able to shape in a continued manner, in particular in view of the responsibility of the Executive Board to prepare the meetings of the Governing Council (Article 12.2 of the Statute). Altogether, the new voting rights can thus be expected to encourage an even more pronounced supranational decision-making in the Governing Council of the ECB as is already the case today.

Under the Constitutional Treaty, a further change is foreseen for the appointment of the six members of the ECB's Executive Board. To appoint one of the six members of the Executive Board, Article 112(2)(b) of the EC Treaty and Article 11.2 of the Statute today require a decision by common accord among the Heads of State or Government of the 13 Member States which have adopted the single currency. The more the euro area grows, the more the requirement of common accord (which already represented a political challenge at the occasion of the appointment of the first Executive Board in 1998[267]) could complicate such an appointment. In the interests of the proper functioning of the ECB, it thus has to be welcomed that Article III-382(2), second subparagraph of the Constitutional Treaty provides that in the future, the members of the ECB's Executive Board shall be appointed '*by the European Council, acting by a qualified majority*'.[268]

C. The Enhanced Visibility of the Eurosystem

At the time of the Maastricht Treaty, non-adoption of the euro was certainly considered to be an exceptional and certainly only transitory situation. Today, following three consecutive EU enlargements since Maastricht and with further accessions ahead, it can well be expected that the differentiation of the EU with regard to monetary integration will last for at least a further decade. This development has made it more and more necessary for the ECB to explain to the financial markets and to the public at large that it is not the central bank of the whole EU, but only for the euro area; and that it has much closer institutional ties with the

---

[267] Cf. Selmayr, 'Gefahr für die Europäische Zentralbank?' [1998] Europablätter 39.

[268] Article III-197(2)(h) and (4) of the Constitutional Treaty provides that the voting rights of the members of the European Council representing Member States outside the euro area shall be suspended in this case.

(today 13) central banks of the Member States that already have adopted the euro than with the (today 14) central banks of Member States outside the euro area. While the former are instruments for the ECB to carry out its core functions, and in particular its monetary policy decisions in the euro area, the latter are not much more than observers—via the ECB's General Council—in this process, while retaining, for the time being, their powers in the field of monetary policy according to national law (Article 43.2 of the Statute). In other words: market participants who borrow central bank money, for example, from the Banca d'Italia, the Deutsche Bundesbank or the Banka Slovenije, in legal reality thereby experience directly the supranational decisions of the ECB which are implemented through these national central banks on the basis of Community law. In contrast to this, market participants who borrow central bank money from, for example, the Bank of England, Sveriges Riksbank or Narodowy Bank Polski still do this under the terms set by these national central banks alone, in line with national law. This also means that borrowing central bank money takes place under identical conditions in Rome, Frankfurt and Ljubljana, but can still take place under considerably different conditions in London, Stockholm or Warsaw.

To underline that the central banks of the Member States that have already adopted the euro are legally part of a closely integrated system that is responsible for carrying out the decisions of the ECB in a uniform manner throughout the euro area, the ECB decided soon after its establishment to use the trade name *'Eurosystem'* for the ECB and these national central banks in its communications to the public.[269] This new terminology has been accompanied by the development of a supranational corporate identity of the Eurosystem: in the past years, the ECB's Governing Council formulated a 'mission statement' of the Eurosystem[270] as well as strategic intents[271] and organizational principles[272] for the Eurosystem, which have been published since 5 January 2005 on the websites of the ECB and of the national central banks of the Member States that have adopted the euro.[273] Today, the term 'Eurosystem' is regularly used by the ECB in

---

[269] ECB, *Monthly Bulletin, January 1999*, p. 7: 'To enhance transparency and enable the public to grasp more easily the very complex structure of European central banking, the Governing Council of the ECB has decided to adopt the term 'Eurosystem' as a user-friendly expression denoting the composition in which the ESCB performs its basic tasks.'

[270] 'Mission statement of the Eurosystem', <http://www.ecb.de/ecb/orga/escb/html/mission_eurosys.en.html>. See also ECB, *Annual Report 2004*, p. 163 *et seq.*, Box 15.

[271] 'Strategic intents of the Eurosystem', <http://www.ecb.de/ecb/orga/escb/html/intents.en.html>.

[272] 'Organisational principles for the fulfilment of Eurosystem functions by all members of the Eurosystem', <http://www.ecb.de/ecb/orga/escb/html/principles.en.html>. They include: 1. Participation, 2. Cooperation, 3. Transparency and accountability, 4. Distinguishing Eurosystem activities, 5. Cohesion and unity, 6. Exchange of resources, 7. Effectiveness and efficiency in decision-making, 8. Cost efficiency, measurement and methodology, 9. Exploit synergies and avoid duplications.

[273] See, eg, the mission statement of the Eurosystem on the website of Banca d'Italia, <http://www.bancaditalia.it/pubblicazioni/bce/varie/eurosistema.pdf>; and of that of Deutsche

its publications[274] and also in many of its legal instruments.[275] According to the ECB itself, the term Eurosystem 'underlines the shared identity, teamwork and cooperation of all of its members'.[276]

As a lawyer, one may initially have some hesitations to accept the term 'Eurosystem' as it does stem neither from the EC Treaty nor from the Statute and is so far also not recognized by the ECJ.[277] However, one cannot deny that it represents a welcome linguistic simplification to say 'Eurosystem' instead of 'the ECB and the national central banks of the Member States that have adopted the euro'. In addition, the especially close institutional relationship between the ECB and these national central banks[278] is clearly wanted by Community law. Article 14.3, first sentence of the Statute states: '*The national central banks are an integral part of the ESCB and shall act in accordance with the guidelines and instructions of the ECB*', while Article 43.1 of the Statute and paragraph 8 of the UK Protocol explicitly exempt the Member States that have not adopted the euro from the rights conferred and the obligations imposed by Article 14.3 of the Statute. The same applies to Article 9.2 of the Statute acording to which the ECB has the responsibility to carry out ESCB tasks either itself or through the national central banks, which, in line with Article 43.1 of the Statute, does not lead to rights or obligations for the Member States outside the euro area. One can therefore see in Articles 9.2, 14.3 and 43.1 of the Statute the legal roots of the existence of the Eurosystem. All national central banks are part of the ESCB, but the 13 central banks of the Member States that have adopted the euro are in addition an integral part of the Eurosystem, where they act under the guidelines and instructions of the ECB, and where the ECB, which bears the overall political and legal responsibility, may use these 13 central banks to carry out Eurosystem tasks through them.

The only problem that could result from the use of the term Eurosystem is one of perception. It could be interpreted as shifting the decision-making responsibility from the single authority of the ECB to a form of joint decision-making by the ECB and the 13 central banks of the Member States that have adopted the

---

Bundesbank, <http://www.bundesbank.de/download/ezb/publikationen/eszb_leitbild_broschuere. pdf#search=%22Bundesbank%20Leitbild%22>.

[274] See, eg, the ECB's Press Release 'Publication of the indicative calendar for the Eurosystem's tender operations in 2007' of 28 July 2006, <http://www.ecb.de/press/pr/date/2006/html/ pr060728.en.html>.

[275] Cf. Guideline ECB/2000/7 of the ECB of 31 August 2000 on monetary policy instruments and procedures of the Eurosystem [2000] OJ L310/1, as last amended by Guideline ECB/2005/17 of the ECB of 30 December 2005 [2006] OJ L30/26.   [276] ECB, *Annual Report 2004*, p. 162.

[277] On the legal limitations of the notion 'Eurosystem', cf. Zilioli and Selmayr, *supra* note 209, p.166 *et seq*.

[278] This especially close relationship is also underlined in the strategic intents of the Eurosystem (*supra* note 271) where the Eurosystem is even qualified as 'the central banking system of the euro area', and thus as a more closely integrated structure than a mere system of central banks.

euro.[279] Such 'cooperative teamwork' in monetary policy matters[280] would not only be a step backwards from the idea of a single monetary policy conducted by a single central banking organization for the euro, but would also be clearly incompatible with the EC Treaty and the Statute which require that the ESCB (which includes all national central banks, including those of the Member States that have adopted the euro) is governed not by the national central banks, but only by the decision-making bodies of the ECB (Article 107(3) EC, Article 8 of the Statute)—a general principle of primary Community law from which neither the ECB itself nor the national central banks together could lawfully depart. It is therefore to be welcomed that in its publications, the ECB has always made clear that '[t]he Eurosystem and the ESCB are governed by the decision-making bodies of the ECB: the Governing Council and the Executive Board', and that '[d]ecision-making within the Eurosystem and the ESCB is centralised.'[281] Particularly clear in this respect is the metaphor used by ECB President *Jean-Claude Trichet* when he says, with regard to the Eurosystem, that 'we operate like a sports team, with a captain—the European Central Bank—and other players, which are the 12 [today: 13] national central banks'.[282] This legally accurate understanding of the ECB as 'captain of the team' in the Eurosystem[283] has important practical implications. Legally, the use of the term Eurosystem for a central bank activity means that it takes place under the responsibility of the ECB, which

---

[279] On this, see the discussion on whether the Eurosystem could be seen as 'a team of 13 central banks' in session I at the ECB colloquium in honour of Tommaso Padoa Schioppa, reported in: ECB (Ed), *The Eurosystem, the Union and Beyond. The Single Currency and Implications for Governance. An ECB colloquium held in honour of Tommaso Padoa-Schioppa*, 27 April 2005, Frankfurt am Main (2005), p. 9 *et seq*. See also the qualification of the Eurosystem as 'the monetary authority of the euro area' in the Eurosystem's mission statement (*supra* note 270). Legally problematic appears to us the interpretation by de Lhonneux, 'The Eurosystem', in: ECB (Ed.), *Legal Aspects of the European System of Central Banks (supra* note 1), p. 161, who claims (at p. 164) that the Eurosystem 'has its own existence and its own functioning which have enabled it to assume its role and set up its organisation', refers (at p. 167) to the 'coexistence of 13 legal personalities inside the system' and even states (at p. 167) that '[t]he Eurosystem has one supreme authority, the ECB Governing Council', while omitting the role of the ECB's Executive Board.

[280] Also here, we understand monetary policy in a broad sense, covering all ESCB tasks as defined by the EC Treaty and the Statute. There would only be scope for 'cooperative teamwork' where the EC Treaty and the Statute still leave scope for autonomous action by national central banks, as it is the case for the time being in the field of banking supervision; here, it results from the close institutional relationship between the ECB and the national central banks of the Member States that have adopted the euro that a 'teaming up' with the ECB can be desirable.

[281] ECB, *Annual Report 2004*, p. 163.

[282] Interview with L'Express, published in the edition 2780 of L'Express dated 11–17 October 2004 and—in an English translation—at <http://www.ecb.int/press/key/date/2004/html/sp041009.en.html>. For further elaborating on this metaphora, see already Trichet (then still Governor of the Banque de France), 'ECB Can Boost European Growth by Keeping Inflation Down', European Affairs, Summer 2001, published at <http://www.europeanaffairs.org/archive/2001_summer/2001_summer_12.php4>: 'It is a team, a European monetary team, composed of the European Central Bank and the national central banks of the twelve euro-area countries. The ECB acts as coach and captain, and the national central banks as the players on the field, in daily contact with market participants. We all share the same team spirit, which is one of the priceless assets of the euro area.'

[283] See also Padoa-Schioppa, *supra* note 210, p. 24: 'The ECB is not another central bank operating alongside the NCBs, nor a competitor of them. Rather, it is the head of the system.' For Louis,

ultimately is liable for acts or omissions taking place under the headline Eurosystem.[284]

It could very well be that the debate surrounding the use of the term Eurosystem will continue to be limited to specialists and all in all remain of a more philosophical than legal importance. So far, neither the media nor the general public appear to have accepted the term Eurosystem in a widespread manner. The media, including financial news agencies, normally talk of the ECB whenever they refer to monetary policy decisions.[285] Understandably, also the European Convention, made up mostly of European and national Parliamentarians, did not follow suggestions to use, in the Constitutional Treaty, the term Eurosystem in the title of the Article on the European Central Bank. It was only on a formal proposal from the ECB[286] that the Intergovernmental Conference in the end inserted at least a reference to the Eurosystem in the text of Article I-30(1), second sentence of the Constitutional Treaty.[287] Therefore, when the Constitutional Treaty will enter into force, the term Eurosystem will become a legal term.[288] Behind this is

---

supra note 162, p. 589, the ECB is 'at the centre of the System', even though he recognises (at p. 588) that 'the System has taken on a dimension of its own.'

[284] See also ECB, *Monthly Bulletin, July 1999*, p. 61: 'As integral parts of the Eurosystem, the national central banks act as operative arms of the ESCB, carrying-out the tasks conferred upon the Eurosystem in accordance with the rules established by the ECB.'

[285] We made a full-text search in the database Factiva (operated by Dow Jones and Reuters and including almost all agency, newspaper and specialized media reports from all over the world) on 16 September 2006, covering a six-month-period. This led to the following results in the English text version: 547 articles with 'Eurosystem', 16 with 'ESCB', 25,199 with 'ECB' and 22,062 with 'European Central Bank'; in German: 130 articles with 'Eurosystem', 207 with 'ESZB', 8,505 with 'EZB' and 4,138 with 'Europäische Zentralbank'; in French: 41 articles with 'Eurosystème', 10 with 'SEBC', 4,115 with 'BCE' and 3,711 with 'Banque centrale européenne'; in Italian: 124 articles with 'Eurosistema', 135 with 'SEBC', 8,565 with 'BCE' and 2,400 with 'Banca centrale europea'; in Spanish: 80 articles with 'Eurosistema', 4 with 'SECB', 5,937 with 'BCE' and 6,869 with 'Banco central europeo'.

[286] Cf. the ECB's Opinion CON/2003/20 (*supra* note 155), para. 11, and in particular para. 14: 'Under the acronym "ESCB" two realities coexist. On the one hand, ESCB refers to the ECB and the NCBs of all the EU Member States. On the other hand, and by the effect of other provisions, "ESCB" also refers to the ECB and the central banks of only those EU Member States which have adopted the euro. This second concept is different from the first one, since it embodies the exclusive competence for defining and conducting monetary policy, including the issue and the overall management of the euro, the management of the official foreign reserves of the Member States that have adopted the euro, and promoting the smooth operation of payment systems. The actions necessary to carry out this competence require a high degree of harmonisation of procedures, instruments and infrastructure, and a single decision-making body with regulatory capacity.'

[287] 'The European Central Bank, together with the national central banks of Member States whose currency is the euro, which constitute the Eurosystem, shall conduct the monetary policy of the Union.' Article 1, second sentence of the Statute has also been amended by the Constitutional Treaty and reads as follows: 'The European Central Bank and the national central banks of those Member States whose currency is the euro shall constitute the Eurosystem.' No other provision of the Constitutional Treaty makes a reference to the Eurosystem.

[288] This will end '[t]he paradox [. . .] that the Eurosystem is systematically referred to in official European, especially central banking, publications without a legal basis', correctly noted by de Lhonneux, 'The Eurosystem', in: ECB (Ed.), *Legal Aspects of the European System of Central Banks* (*supra* note 1), p. 161 (at p. 162).

the political recognition that, for the years to come, the situation of Member States which do not yet participate in the single currency will continue to be a relatively normal situation. It will therefore be in most cases more accurate to talk of the Eurosystem than of the ESCB, even though the general public will probably continue to refer solely to the European Central Bank—the only term thus rightly retained in the title of Article I-30 of the Constitutional Treaty.

D. Progressive Integration within the Eurosystem

Monetary policy is a field of policy where, in view of the sensitivity of financial markets, evolution and smooth transition are generally to be preferred over revolution or disruption. It was therefore a wise choice for the ECB to build in its initial years the reputation of Europe's young currency first of all on the experience and practice of the national central banks. 'Decentralization' has therefore been the guiding policy principle[289] in the first eight years of the ECB's existence. While the ECB took all decisions centrally, as required by the EC Treaty and the Statute, it made broad use of Article 9.2 of the Statute to carry out its tasks, as a rule, through the national central banks of the Eurosystem. In particular, the vast majority of monetary policy decisions have thus been carried out in this way via the national central banks. However, progressively the day-to-day operation of Monetary Union has been triggering further integration of the EU's financial sector. This in turn has started to require the ECB to focus more and more on two essential economic and political needs when developing the way in which the Eurosystem operates: the need for uniformity in monetary policy to strengthen the level-playing field of Europe's financial actors; and the need for efficiency, that requires the ECB, as an accountable public organization, to move away from national central bank traditions towards an efficient use of its financial and personnel resources in the Community interest.

(i) The Need for Uniformity in the Implementation of Monetary Policy

An indirect, 'decentralized' implementation of a single monetary policy can only work if it is ensured that the many actors involved at the implementation level are

---

[289] In our view, 'decentralization'—which, as already explained in Zilioli and Selmayr, *supra* note 209, at p. 118 *et seq.*, should be better called 'deconcentration', in view of the overall responsibility which the ECB retains over the execution of all ESCB tasks—is more a legally possible policy choice than an imperative legal principle. There is in our view no legal presumption in the EC Treaty or in the Statute in favour of an execution of ESCB tasks through the national central banks. It is rather the discretion of the ECB whether it deems it 'possible and appropriate' to make use of the national central banks. In view of the wide discretion the ECJ normally allows with regard to complex decisions of economic policy, it is difficult to imagine a situation in which the ECJ would annul a decision of the ECB to execute certain tasks itself where the ECB deemed decentralized execution 'inappropriate' in a particular case. This is even acknowledged by the defenders of decentralization as a justitiable legal principle; see Priego and Conlledo (*supra* note 219), which state at p. 195 that Article 12.1 of the Statute

acting simultaneously and in an equally efficient manner. Otherwise, 'decentralized' implementation would inevitably lead to distortions of competition: central bank money would be easier or cheaper to access in country A than in country B. Making use of the national central banks of the Eurosystem thus enhances the responsibility of the ECB to steer the implementation process in order to ensure a uniform application of all ECB decisions in the market.[290] Article 12.1, second subparagraph of the Statute confers this responsibility to the ECB's Executive Board, which 'shall give the necessary instructions to national central banks' when implementing the ECB's monetary policy. In practice, this means that no operational activity can take place in the dealing room of a national central bank of the Eurosystem if not under the direct instructions from the ECB's Executive Board in Frankfurt.[291]

The need for uniformity in the implementation of the ECB's monetary policy decisions has had interesting spill-over effects into fields where it was initially thought that they could be left (at least partly) to the discretion of individual national central banks. Article 18.1, second indent of the Statute requires that the ECB and the national central banks of the Eurosystem base lending of central bank money on 'adequate collateral'; they thus provide liquidity to the banking system only against certain secure assets. In September 1998, the Governing Council of the ECB decided that for central bank money operations of the Eurosystem, *a two-tier-system of collateral* should be used[292]: tier one comprised only debt instruments that complied with euro area-wide eligibility criteria; tier two comprised assets deemed of particular importance for certain financial markets and banking systems and fulfilled only national eligibility criteria, even though based on minimum eligibility criteria established by the ECB.[293]

---

has 'deliberately ambiguous wording' that 'tends to empty it of concrete legal content' and 'approximates it de facto to what is known generically as "soft law"'. Very clear in this respect Louis, *supra* note 162, p. 591: 'the judge usually leaves an important margin of appreciation to the institution in charge.'

[290] Cf. Padoa-Schioppa, *supra* note 210, p. 26: 'Since so many central banks conduct, in different countries, monetary policy operations that are part of the same single policy, a strong direction from the center is imperative.'

[291] This is why we believe that instead of the notion 'decentralized implementation', one should better use the term 'indirect implementation', as also implementation through the national central banks represents a form of centralized management of a Community task; cf. Zilioli and Selmayr, *supra* note 209, p. 118 *et seq.*, with reference to ECJ, Case C-478/93, *Netherlands v Commission* [1995] ECR I-3081, para 32 *et seq.*

[292] The details of this 'two-tier-system' were laid down in Guideline ECB/2000/7 of the ECB of 31 August 2000 on monetary policy instruments and procedures of the Eurosystem [2000] OJ L210/1, Annex I, Chapter 6, sections 6.1.–6.3.

[293] Cf. Guideline ECB/2000/7 (*supra* note 292), Chapter 6, section 6.3., 'Tier two assets': 'In addition to debt instruments fulfilling the eligibility criteria for tier one, National Central Banks may consider as eligible other assets, tier two assets, which are of particular importance to their national financial markets and banking systems. Eligibility criteria for tier two assets are established by the National Central Banks in accordance with the minimum eligibility criteria stated below. The specific national eligibility criteria for tier two assets are subject to approval by the ECB. The National Central Banks establish and maintain national lists of eligible tier two assets. These lists are available to the public.'

The second tier thus allowed national central banks of the Eurosystem to maintain, in the first years following the introduction of the euro, certain national preferences for collateral in line with the traditions of the national financial markets. Market participants thus could use in some countries collateral for borrowing central bank money that was not eligible in other countries of the euro area.[294] In a single currency area with an increasing degree of financial market integration—at the end of 2005, almost 50 per cent of collateral was already used on a cross-border basis in the EU[295]—this two-tier system could of course only be of a transitory nature as it risked undermining the level playing field in the euro area.[296]

Following a public consultation launched in June 2003, the Governing Council of the ECB decided on 10 May 2004 that the two-tier system in force since the start of the final stage of Economic and Monetary Union should be gradually replaced by a modernised *Single List of collateral based on uniform eligibility criteria for the entire Eurosystem*.[297] This means on the one hand that some assets accepted so far as collateral for central bank money by individual national central banks (such as equities[298] and assets listed, quoted or traded on certain non-regulated markets) were progressively phased out—a process completed at the end of May 2007. On the other hand, certain assets so far eligible as collateral only in a few countries (in particular credit claims[299]) have now become

---

[294] This is only attenuated, but not remedied by the existence of the 'Correspondent Central Banking Model' (CCBM) that allows Eurosystem counterparties to use eligible assets (including in principle tier two assets) on a cross-border basis. This means that they may obtain central bank money from the national central bank of the Member State in which they are established by making use of assets located in another Member State.

[295] ECB, *Monthly Bulletin, May 2006*, p. 78, Chart 2.

[296] In particular, the inclusion of credit claims into tier two in a few countries (such as Germany) led to potential distortions of competition. The use of credit claims as collateral is connected to low opportunity cost (they are rarely traded and counterparties have limited alternative uses for them), but as they are primarily held by domestic counterparties, they are not readily available on a cross-border basis. There was thus the risk that the two-tier system gave a particular category of counterparties privileged access to the Eurosystem's credit operations through the use of (relatively low-cost) collateral not available to other counterparties. This is why the ECB has moved, under the Single List, to accepting credit claims as collateral throughout the euro area to create a level playing field in this respect.

[297] The legal basis for this Single List is Guideline ECB/2006/12 of 31 August 2006 amending Guideline ECB/2000/7 on monetary policy instruments and procedures of the Eurosystem [2006] OJ L352/1, which establishes the new rules governing eligible assets in Chapter 6 of its Annex. On this, cf. the article 'The Single List in the Collateral Framework of the Eurosystem', in: ECB, *Monthly Bulletin, May 2006*, p. 75. See also Löber, 'Die Neufassung der geldpolitischen Leitlinie der EZB und die Überarbeitung der Regelungen für notenbankfähige Sicherheiten' [2005] Zeitschrift für Bank- und Kapitalmarktrecht, p. 353.

[298] Equities were accepted as tier two collateral in Spain, Portugal and the Netherlands. They are intrinsically more risky than debt instruments and therefore did not meet the high credit standards introduced together with the Single List. Equities were therefore withdrawn from the tier two lists of eligible assets of these central banks as of 30 April 2005; cf. ECB Press Release of 21 February 2005, published at <http://www.ecb.de/press/pr/date/2005/html/pr050221.en.html>.

[299] By accepting credit claims as eligible collateral for Eurosystem operations, the ECB reinforces the principle of granting access to monetary policy operations and intraday credit operations to a broad range of counterparties. By thereby increasing the liquidity of an entire asset class with low

eligible collateral throughout the euro area.[300] In addition, *a uniform Eurosystem credit assessment framework (ECAF)* was created that defines the procedures, rules and techniques which ensure that the Eurosystem requirement of high credit standards for all eligible assets (marketable and non-marketable) is met.[301] The move by the ECB to the Single List of collateral eligible for Eurosystem operations is an important practical step for ensuring, through a uniform implementation of the ECB's monetary policy, equal treatment of market participants in the euro area as well as operational efficiency, while at the same time promoting the further integration of financial markets in the EU.

(ii) The Need for Efficiency and the Potential of Specialization

The need for efficiency is a further important driver of closer integration within the Eurosystem. In its mission statement and its organizational principles of January 2005,[302] the Eurosystem, even though describing the political 'principle of decentralization' as being at the root of the system, makes a strong commitment to promoting 'effective and cost-efficient solutions in all parts of the Eurosystem' as well as to identifying and exploiting, to the extent feasible, '[p]otential synergies and economies of scale', while avoiding '[u]nnecessary duplication of work and resources at functional levels and over-extensive and inefficient coordination'. Even '[t]he outsourcing of Eurosystem support functions and activities'—this means the transfer of such tasks to private bodies outside the Eurosystem—'shall be considered against the same criteria', while taking security aspects into account. Politically, it is remarkable that, here, the ECB and the national central banks of the Eurosystem explicitly recognize that a 'decentralized' implementation of Eurosystems tasks by each of the national central banks will not always lead to efficient solutions.[303]

The legal question that arises from this is: what options does the ECB have under Community law in order to achieve a more efficient implementation of Eurosystem tasks and to avoid inefficient duplication? The core provision of

opportunity cost, the ECB in addition fosters the smooth functioning of the euro area financial system.

[300] Between 1 January 2007 (the date on which the new Guideline ECB/2006/12 entered into force, cf. *supra* note 297) and 31 December 2011, an intermediate regime will be in place for credit claims, allowing each national central bank to choose the minimum threshold for the size of credit claims eligible for collateral purposes (apart from cross-border use) and whether a handling fee should be applied. As from 1 January 2012, a completely unified regime will be in place.

[301] Cf. section 6.3 of the Annex to Guideline ECB/2006/12 (*supra* note 297).

[302] *Supra* notes 270 and 272.

[303] Very critical of the present decentralized system is Padoa-Schioppa, *supra* note 210, p. 170: 'The structure of national central banks, historically designed to perform the full range of central bank functions, underwent only modest changes when they became integrated in the Eurosystem. Self-sufficiency is still the style. We would call this 'one-to-one-correspondence' between member countries and central banking infrastructures. Seen from the angle of the Eurosystem, this situation generates simultaneously insufficiency and redundancy.'

Article 9.2 of the Statute directly mentions only two solutions: the ECB shall implement Eurosystem tasks either 'by its own activities pursuant to this Statute' or 'through the national central banks pursuant to Articles 12.1 and 14'. The provision thereby offers to the ECB a true alternative to implement Eurosystem tasks either directly by using ECB staff and resources or in an indirect way by making use of the staff and resources of the national central banks. Conceptually, this allows both for complete 'decentralization' and for complete 'centralization' of Eurosystem tasks, even though the latter would currently be very difficult to achieve in practice in all cases in view of the still limited staff and resources of the ECB[304] and the need, in several fields of operation, to interact with counterparties at national level. One can certainly also read Article 9.2 of the Statute in the sense that with regard to a particular task, the ECB may partly implement this task itself and partly leave it to implementation at the level of the national central banks.[305]

But can the ECB also decide that, in the interest of efficiency, a certain task shall be implemented only by the ECB and, say, two or three central banks of the Eurosystem, while the other central banks are not involved at all in this case at the implementation level[306]? The wording of Article 9.2 of the Statute is open to such 'selective decentralization' or *specialization*, as it says that indirect implementation shall take place 'through the national central banks', and not 'through *all* national

---

[304] One could however imagine that in the case of urgent need—eg a natural disaster or a terrorist attack in a euro area Member State that affects the functioning of the national central bank—the ECB would be legally entitled and even required to take over monetary policy operations for this country or entrust it to one or several other national central banks of the Eurosystem.

[305] Monetary policy is such a case. The monetary policy laid down centrally by the ECB is implemented as a rule by the national central banks of the Eurosystem. Some measures, however, can be executed, under exceptional circumstances, by the ECB itself, such as bilateral fine-tuning reverse operations, fine-tuning outright operations, bilateral foreign exchange swaps or the bilateral collection of fixed-term deposits; on this, see Guideline ECB/2006/12 (*supra* note 297), sections 3.1.4.(d), sixth indent; 3.2.(d), fourth indent; 3.4.(d), fifth indent and 3.5.(d), fourth indent. A further example is the issuance of euro banknotes. For issuance, euro banknotes require authorization by the ECB under Article 106(1), first sentence EC. As regards implementation, Article 106(1), second sentence EC allows for a system in which both the ECB and the national central banks of the Eurosystem may implement this exclusive competence of the ECB by bringing euro banknotes into circulation. According to Decision ECB/2001/15 of the ECB of 6 December 2001 on the issue of euro banknotes [2001] OJ L337/52, as last amended by Decision ECB/2006/25 of 15 December 2006 [2007] OJ L24/13, 8% of the banknotes are thus directly issued by the ECB, while 92% are issued by the national central banks of the Eurosystem. This is financially important for the ECB as thereby seigniorage becomes a source of own income for the ECB, next to the monetary income accruing to the national central banks. The physical acts related to putting euro banknotes issued by the ECB into circulation are tasks entrusted to the national central banks of the Eurosystem by Article 3(1) of Decision ECB/2001/15, as amended.

[306] Former ECB President Duisenberg said in an interview with Il Sole 24 Ore of 12 October 2003, p. 3, that 'ogni BCN dovrà specializzarsi in un ambito pur continuando a fare altro. La specializzazione potrà esserci nel campo della ricerca economica, della stampa delle banconote, anche degli interventi sul mercato delle valute [. . .] l'idea é affascinante e consentirebbe ai paesi di continuare ad avere una banca centrale nazionale e all'Eurosistema di gestire in modo forse più razionale il rapporto tra centro e periferia'.

central banks'. The Statute also nowhere reserves a certain field of implementing competences to every single national central bank. Some may want to argue that the notion 'national central bank' implies that certain central bank competences must by definition be reserved for each of the national central banks in the Eurosystem. This is, however, not a very compelling way of reasoning. It should be noted that the core competence of every central bank, which is the setting of interest rates, is already since 1 January 1999 no longer in the hands of the central banks of the Member States which have adopted the euro.[307] Furthermore, the EC Treaty and the Statute only recognize legally that national central banks *can* be implementing bodies which are used by the ECB when it deems so possible and appropriate to carry out Eurosystem tasks, but neither the EC Treaty nor the Statute *require* the ECB to always make use of each and every national central bank for this purpose. Guidance in this respect is certainly provided by the provisions in Article 12.1 of the Statute, according to which 'to the extent deemed possible and appropriate, the ECB shall have recourse to the national central banks to carry out operations which form part of the tasks of the ESCB', but this still leaves substantial discretion to the ECB.[308]

Legally, the ECB may therefore use its discretion under Article 9.2 of the Statute to also opt for specialization in the implementation of Eurosystem tasks and thus

---

[307] Selmayr, 'Wie unabhängig ist die Europäische Zentralbank?' [1999] Wertpapiermitteilungen 2429, at p. 2430, draws the following conclusion as regards the status of national central banks: 'Seit 1. Januar 1999 sind sie daher nicht mehr selbst Zentralbanken, sondern vielmehr die operativen Arme der EZB. Vor diesem Hintergrund muss bezweifelt werden, ob die nationalen Zentralbanken innerhalb des ESZB überhaupt noch als nationale Behörden angesehen werden können.' (= 'Since 1 January, they are no longer central banks themselves, but rather the operating arms of the ECB. Against this background, it must be questioned whether national central banks, in view of their integration into the ESCB, can still be regarded as national authorities.') To a certain extent, the notion of 'national central banks' in the EC Treaty and in the Statute is comparable to the notion of 'Landeszentralbank' which was used until 2002 for the first eleven, then nine entities operating under the authority of the Deutsche Bundesbank despite the fact that they had no longer a legal personality of their own. These entities—such as the central bank of Bavaria—had a proud tradition and had, in the initial years of the Federal Republic of Germany, indeed performed central bank tasks themselves until they were merged, in 1957, with the 'Bank Deutscher Länder' into the Deutsche Bundesbank. Nevertheless, they were still referred to as 'Landeszentralbanken' until 2002 when a reform of the law of the German Bundesbank brought the terminology in line with legal reality. Since then, the former 'Landeszentralbanken' are called 'Hauptverwaltungen' (main offices); see § 8(1) Gesetz über die Deutsche Bundesbank, as amended by the 7th law of 23 March 2002 amending the law of the Deutsche Bundesbank [2002] Bundesgesetzblatt I, 1159, in force since 30 April 2002.

[308] This is also the view of *van den Berg*, Checks and Balances for the European Central Bank and the National Central Banks, OeNB-Workshops No. 7/2006 p. 156 (165): 'The fact that Article 12.1c introduces a bias towards recourse to the NCBs does not take away that there is hardly any operational task of the Systen reserved for the NCBs.' Referring to the decision of the drafters of the Statute (the Committee of Governors) to replace, in view of the lack of legal personality of the ESCB, 'ESCB' by 'ECB and NCBs' throughout the text of the Statute, *van den Berg* adds (165): 'One of the persons involved in writing the Statute for the CoG later said that changing 'ESCB' into 'ECB and NCBs' was a *coup* in favour of the future ECB, as it opened all kinds of possibilities for the centre, including in theory full centralization.' Cf. also Zilioli and Selmayr, *supra* note 212.

entrust the carrying out of certain implementation functions only to selected national central banks in the interests of efficiency.[309] Of course, the general principles of Community law apply to such decisions of the ECB. The ECB may therefore not decide in favour of specialization in an arbitrary manner or out of bias towards particular national central banks, but must always justify its decision to specialize by objective considerations of efficiency and demonstrated specialized competence. The ECB was therefore entitled to entrust the task of conducting a survey on the use of the euro in central, south-east and eastern Europe to the Oesterreichische Nationalbank,[310] in view of its geographic location and special expertise in this field. The ECB could also decide to make use of the German, French and/or Italian central bank for a specific foreign exchange operation in view of the assets available for this specific operation in the portfolio of these national central banks[311]; and to assign, in the context of the uniform Eurosystem credit assessment framework,[312] the task of in-house credit assessment for the collateral eligible for Eurosystem monetary policy operations to Deutsche Bundesbank, Banco de España, Banque de France and Oesterreichische Nationalbank.[313]

When opting for specialization, the ECB must always take into account the principle of equal treatment of market participants, as equal treatment is a fundmental right under Community law.[314] Therefore, a decision of the ECB to entrust a particular task to one or several specialized national central banks when implementing Eurosystem tasks may not lead to a situation in which market participants in different geographic parts of the euro area are treated differently when they want to access central bank money or other central bank services.[315] It should be noted, however, that *within* the Eurosystem, equal treatment cannot

---

[309] This would apply *a fortiori* in case of emergency which would prevent (temporarily or for a longer time) a particular national central bank from functioning. In such a case, the ECB would be even obliged to take over during the time of such emergency the tasks of those national central banks that are required to continue for the sake of the proper functioning of Monetary Union; and/or also to request other national central banks of the Eurosystem to implement monetary policy also towards the counterparties of this (temporarily non-functioning) national central bank.

[310] This was done in the context of the preparation of the ECB's fifth *Review of the International Role of the Euro*, Frankfurt am Main (2005); cf. pp. 11, 59 *et seq.* of this report.

[311] Cf. de Lhonneux, 'The Eurosystem', in: ECB (Ed.), *Legal Aspects of the European System of Central Banks* (*supra* note 1), p. 161, who points (at p. 176) to the fact that already today, in the field of management of foreign reserve assets, six central banks are offering to the whole Eurosystem standardized services decided by the ECB's Governing Council.

[312] Cf. *supra* note 301.

[313] Cf. section 6.3.4 of the Annex to Guideline ECB/2006/12 (*supra* note 297).

[314] This is recognized and reaffirmed in Article 20 of the Charter of Fundamental Rights of the EU, integrated as Article II-80 in the Constitutional Treaty. See already Case 283/83, *Racke v Hauptzollamt Mainz* [1984] ECR 3791, para. 7–12; Case C-15/95 *EARL de Kerlast v Unicopa and Coopérative du Trieux* [1997] ECR I-1961, para. 35; Case C-292/97, *Karlsson* [2000] ECR 2737, para 39. *et seq.*

[315] It would thus be a violation of the principle of equal treatment to select the German Bundesbank for carrying out all monetary policy operations of the ECB while allowing only German nationals access to central bank liquidity.

apply in the same way. In fact, equal treatment is, in Community law, a fundamental right reserved for natural and legal persons, but not a compulsory legal principle capable of applying in the inter- or intra-institutional relationships of public bodies, where principles of efficiency and of the discretionality of the administration, together with the principles of proportionality and transparency, determine the way in which decisions are made.[316] Equality of treatment can therefore not be invoked as organizational principle inside the Eurosystem, where considerations of efficiency even take precedence as regards the distribution of voting rights in the Governing Council of the ECB, as already explained above.[317] In the carrying out of Eurosystem operations, a complete equivalence of tasks could even prove to be sub-optimal to achieve the aims set by the Treaty. We therefore take the view that an individual national central bank could not invoke the principle of equal treatment to protect its traditional field of action and to claim that the ECB would be obliged to make use in an equal manner of this national central bank's staff and resources for carrying out specific Eurosystem tasks, as long as the decision of the ECB to make instead use of another national central bank of the Eurosystem is motivated and not arbitrary and does not lead to a discriminatory treatment of market participants.

(iii) Practical Illustrations for the Move of the Eurosystem towards Uniformity and Efficiency

A good practical illustration of a Eurosystem task where the need for uniformity and efficiency increasingly has become more important for the ECB is the production of euro banknotes.[318] On 1 January 1999, the right to authorize the issuance of euro banknotes became an exclusive competence of the ECB under Article 106(1), first sentence EC, and thereby entitled the ECB also to decide how

---

[316] This is not seen by Priego and Conlledo (*supra* note 219), at p. 197, who claim that the principle of 'equality before the law' would be a right of central banks that would have to be observed by the ECB when deciding on 'centralization', 'decentralization' or 'selective decentralization'. Also the Recommendation No R (80) 2 of the Committee of Ministers of the Council of Europe, from which Priego and Conlledo quote, concerns *not* inter- or intra-institutional relations, but the exercise of administrative authority towards individuals; see the full text of this Recommendation, which is published at <http://www.coe.int/t/e/legal_affairs/legal_co-operation/administrative_law_and_justice/texts_&_documents/Conv_Rec_Res/Recommendation(80)2.asp>. A theory according to which national central banks would become, just like citizens, holders of fundamental rights vis-à-vis the ECB finds neither support in Community law nor in national legal systems. This is, however, the view taken by de Lhonneux, 'The Eurosystem', in: ECB (Ed.), *Legal Aspects of the European System of Central Banks (supra* note 1), p. 161 (at p. 174): 'All the NCBs within the Eurosystem are to be treated without discrimination or preference'. He even claims that 'formal differentiation requirements need support in primary law [. . .] or unanimous support at the level of the Governing Council'. It is unclear from which provision of the EC Treaty or the Statute de Lhonneux draws in particular the second claim, which would seriously undermine the supranational power of the ECB's Governing Council to take decisions, as a rule, by simple majority under Article 10.2 third subparagraph, second sentence of the Statute. [317] *Supra*, p. 52 *et seq.*

[318] On this, see the article 'The euro banknotes: developments and future challenges', in: ECB, *Monthly Bulletin, August 2005*, p. 85.

to organize the production of banknotes. The decisions taken since then by the ECB in this respect can be described in four stages of progressive harmonization

- *Stage 1:* In the transitional phase between 1 January 1999 and 31 December 2001, the euro existed only in law and national banknotes continued to circulate, even though they had become non-decimal 'subdivisions' of the euro.[319] For this transitional period, the ECB authorized, by means of ECB Guidelines,[320] each national central bank of the Eurosystem to continue[321] to produce the whole series of its old banknotes.

- *Stage 2:* To be able to physically introduce the euro on 1 January 2002, a first series of euro banknotes of uniform quality had to be produced. For carrying out this truly Herculean task (around 15 billion new banknotes were needed), the ECB decided in 1998 to build on the experience and the production capacities of the national central banks and therefore to delegate, in accordance with Article 9.2 of the Statute, the task of printing euro banknotes to the national central banks of the Eurosystem.[322] There were thus 12 central banks entrusted with the task of ensuring the printing of all seven denominations of the new euro banknotes for the territory of their respective Member States, in accordance with the quantitative requirements laid down by the Governing Council of the ECB for each Member States.[323] It was for each national central bank of the Eurosystem to decide whether to produce euro banknotes in-house or whether to achieve this via a public

---

[319] Cf. Article 6(1) of Council Regulation (EC) No 974/98, *supra* note 206.

[320] See Guideline ECB/1999/NP11 of the ECB of 22 April 1999 on the authorization to issue national banknotes during the transitional period [2001] OJ L55/71, which allowed to continue the traditional way of banknote issuance in the transitional period between 1 January 1999 and 31 December 2001. It may be assumed that the ECB followed in this period this 'decentralized' approach also with regard to the production of euro banknotes, on which no specific legal instruments were made public. As justification for the decision to choose indirect implementation of this task in the initial years of the euro, the ECB could point to Article 16(2) of the Statute, which reads as follows: 'The ECB shall respect as far as possible existing practices regarding the issue and design of banknotes.'

[321] Prior to Monetary Union, all EU countries printed their national banknotes via domestic printing works (either as part of the central bank, public or commercial printing work), with the only exception of Portugal and Luxembourg (which at the time had a monetary union with Belgium) which used to buy their banknotes from commercial security printers established abroad (De La Rue/UK and Oberthur/France). Further details are given in the EMI's press release of 2 July 1997 'The production and issue of banknotes in the EU member states', published at <http://www.ecb.de/press/pr/date/1997/html/pr970702_4.en.html>.

[322] This decision is reflected in Guidelines of the ECB which, in view of their sensitive nature, are not public. Their content can, however, be understood from the official publications of the ECB; cf. ECB, *Annual Report 2001*, p. 117: 'Each NCB was responsible for procuring euro banknotes to meet its national requirements for the launch.'

[323] Cf. the ECB's press release of 5 October 2001 'Euro banknotes to be produced until 31 December 2001', published at <http://www.ecb.de/press/pr/date/2001/html/pr011005.en.html>. Under the Governing Council decision referred to therein, the German Bundesbank, for example, had to ensure the printing of 362,9 million of the total of 1,23 billion of €100 banknotes needed for the entire euro area, while the Banca d'Italia was tasked with the production of 361 million of these.

printing work or a commercial company, provided that the ECB rules on the material, the design and the security features of the euro banknotes as well as the ECB's standards of quality and safety were entirely met.[324] As a result, the first series of euro banknotes was produced in this phase at 15[325] different printing works across the EU, which enabled the Eurosystem to accomplish the production of the required euro banknotes in time for the euro cash changeover, but also required intensive coordination and quality controls.

- Stage 3: For the sake of an efficient banknote production in the time after the cash changeover—when substantially less euro banknotes needed to be produced[326]—,and to better monitor quality and ensure uniform appearance and security features for all euro banknotes, the ECB decided in April 2001 to move towards a *system of decentralized production of euro banknotes with pooling*.[327] In this pooled system, each national central bank is entrusted by a decision of the ECB's Governing Council with the production of only one, two or three of the seven banknote denominations.[328] For the banknotes

---

[324] Laid down at the time inter alia in Decision ECB/1998/6 of 7 July 1998 [1999] OJ L8/36, as amended, and meanwhile replaced by Decision ECB/2003/4 of the ECB of 20 March 2003 on the denominations, specifications, reproduction, exchange and withdrawal of euro banknotes [2003] OJ L78/16.

[325] Cf. the article 'Euro banknote preparations: from cash changeover to post-launch activities', in: ECB, *Monthly Bulletin, January 2002*, p. 55 *et seq*. Most printing works were part of, or belonged to, one of the national central banks, while only a few external ones (some of them public, some commercial) were chosen. As a consequence, there was thus one printing work chosen in each of the 12 euro area Member States, with the exception of Luxembourg (no printing work), while there were 3 in Germany and 2 in France. In addition, the printing work De La Rue in the UK was used.

[326] In the peak time of 2001, approximately 1 billion euro banknotes had to be produced per month. Afterwards, production requirements dropped to approximately 3 to 4 billion banknotes per year; cf. the article 'Euro banknotes: first years of experience', in: ECB, *Monthly Bulletin, August 2004*, p. 79 (at p. 82). Today, the yearly requirement is around 7 billion euro banknotes; cf. the article 'The euro banknotes: developments and future challenges' (*supra* note 318), 88.

[327] Cf. ECB *Annual Report 2002*, p. 132: 'In April 2001 the Governing Council decided that, in the following years, production of euro banknotes would take place in accordance with a decentralised production scenario with pooling. This means that each euro area NCB is responsible for the procurement of an allocated share of the total euro banknote supply for only a small number of denominations. This pooling arrangement helps to ensure a supply of consistent quality banknotes by reducing the number of production sites for each denomination and enables the Eurosystem to benefit from economies of scale in banknote production.'

[328] Against the background of this system of pooled euro banknote production, one can also explain the 'country code prefix' which precedes the serial number on the reverse of each banknote (on the top right and bottom left hand sides). This 'country code prefix' (eg S for Italy, X for Germany and L for Finland—see <http://www.ecb.int/bc/faqbc/design/html/index.en.html#q10>) indicates the national central bank which, in implementing the decisons of the ECB's Governing Council, originally commissioned the production of the banknote. Thus, we will find the 'country code prefix' S on many €50-banknotes that will be produced in 2007 because these will be in part commissioned by the Banca d'Italia. From the 'country code prefix' on each euro banknote, one can therefore only identify which central bank commissioned its production, but not which national central bank originally put the banknote physically into circulation. See, however, Seidel, 'Euro-Banknoten ohne Angaben der emittierenden Banken' [2003] Europäische Zeitschrift für Wirtschaftsrecht, p. 353, who claims that euro banknotes would not be legally issued by the ECB, but by the 12 national central banks of the euro area. Proof of this would be the 'national code' on each of the euro banknotes (X for Germany). However, Seidel ignores that the 'country code prefix' only refers to the place of production, and does not allow for any conclusions of where a banknote was put into circulation.

printed for the year 2007, for example, the Banca d'Italia has had to commission only parts of the production of €100-banknotes, while the German Bundesbank has been entrusted with commissioning the production of €500-banknotes and parts of the production of €5, €10 and €50-banknotes, and the Finnish Central Bank with commissioning parts of the production of €20-banknotes.[329]

- Stage 4: A system under which more than a dozen different public and commercial printing works across the EU are entrusted with the production of banknotes of the same currency requires a dense network of essentially parallel contractual agreements and ECB guidelines to ensure both a uniform quality of production and strict respect of confidentiality. In such a complex system, the objective of cost efficiency cannot always be accommodated, which is why even defenders of the role of national central banks have recognized that 'the production of banknotes is an area where further rationalisation is possible and where considerable efficiency gains can be achieved for the system as a whole'.[330] This explains why on 16 July 2004, the ECB adopted a new Guideline[331] according to which at the latest from 1 January 2012 (and possibly already earlier[332]), a single Eurosystem tender procedure will apply to the procurement of each euro banknotes denomination.[333] The move towards a *single Eurosystem tender procedure* means that the euro banknotes required by the Eurosystem—in 2006, this requirement was 7 billion banknotes[334]—will

---

Thus, for example, in 2007 €500-banknotes will certainly be physically issued also in Italy, even though will they will bear the 'German' country code prefix X.

[329] On this, see 'Latest figures on the banknotes and coins', published by the ECB at <http://www.ecb.int/bc/faqbc/figures/html/index.en.html>.

[330] Cf. Wellink, Chapple and Maier, *supra* note 220, p. 12, who state that this 'can be seen by a comparison between the number of staff involved in this task in Europe and the number involved in the US.'

[331] Guideline ECB/2004/18 of the ECB of 16 September 2004 on the procurement of euro banknotes [2004] OJ L320/21.

[332] The legal technique chosen for the transition to the single tender procedure resembles the method of Article 121 EC for the transition to the single currency itself, as it combines qualitative criteria with the establishment of a firm deadline. According to Article 2(1) of Guideline ECB/2004/18 (*supra* note 331), the single tender procedure starts at the latest on 1 January 2012, regardless of the number of participating national central banks or of the banknote production volume concerned. Before that and at the earliest on 1 January 2008, the ECB's Governing Council, acting on a proposal from the Executive Board, may decide to start with the single tender procedure on a transitory basis once it has ascertained that the production of at least half of the total annual Eurosystem banknote requirement will be tendered and at least half of all national central banks of the Eurosystem will tender the production of euro banknotes allocated to them; cf. Article 1 point 12 and Article 5(1) of Guideline ECB/2004/18 (*supra* note 331). The beginning of the transitory period would mean that the single tender procedure would already apply before 2012 to those national central banks that tender the production of euro banknotes allocated to them; cf. Article 18(1) of Guideline ECB/2004/18 (*supra* note 331).

[333] The two main characteristics of the single tender procedure are: (1) the decision to which printing works production orders for euro banknotes are awarded is taken centrally by the ECB's Governing Council; cf. Article 14(2) of Guideline ECB/2004/18 (*supra* note 331); and (2) the Governing Council must always choose the economically most advantageous tender; cf. Article 13 (1) of Guideline ECB/2004/18 (*supra* note 331).   [334] Cf. *supra* note 326.

in future be printed by the most efficient printing works in the EU,[335] whether they are in-house printing works of a national central bank, public or commercial printing works. The contracting parties of these printing works will be designated by the ECB's Governing Council among the Eurosystem members.[336] As the number of these printing works is very likely to be inferior to the number of Eurosystem central banks participating in the single Eurosystem tender procedure[337] and as it seems unlikely that all these central banks will conclude supply agreements as designated contracting authorities with each selected printing works, the ECB's Governing Council may take a decision in favour of specialization in this respect and/or may choose to make the ECB itself the contracting partner. This decision will be taken by a simple majority, in accordance with Article 10.2, third subparagraph, second sentence of the Statute. Together with the general requirement of efficiency, as expressed in the Eurosystem's mission statement and organizational principles, this will certainly help ensure that efficient solutions will be found in this respect. Even though national central banks have retained a right to 'opt out' of the new scheme,[338] the single Eurosystem tender procedure paves the way towards more efficiency in the production of euro banknotes. It can be expected that at the latest in 2012, economies of scale and effective competition will unfold as regards the production of euro banknotes, in line with the Treaty objective of an open market economy with free competition favouring an efficient allocation of resources (Articles 4(2) and 105(1), third sentence EC).[339]

Payment systems are a further example where the need for uniformity and efficiency has triggered a reform of the implementing structures chosen initially by the ECB. Traditionally, central banks have provided, in their capacity as 'banker to banks', facilities whereby banks can settle debt amongst themselves in central bank money. Such

---

[335] According to Article 7 (1) (a) of Guideline ECB/2004/18, *supra* note 331, legal establishment in the EU and physical location of production facilities in a Member State are eligibility requirements under the single Eurosystem tender procedure. Therefore, also printing works established outside the euro area but within the EU are allowed to bid for contracts to produce euro banknotes.

[336] Article 5(4) of Guideline ECB/2004/18, *supra* note 331.

[337] See Padoa-Schioppa, *The Euro and its Central Bank. Getting United after the Union*, Cambridge, Massachusetts (2004), p. 172, who pleads for 'reducing, successively, the number of factories where euro banknotes can be printed'.

[338] According to Article 6(2) of Guideline ECB/2004/18, *supra* note 331, 'NCBs that have an in-house printing works and NCBs using public printing works may choose not to participate in the single Eurosystem tender procedure. In such cases these inhouse or public printing works shall be excluded from the single Eurosystem tender procedure and they shall produce the euro banknotes allocated to their NCBs in accordance with the capital key. They may, however, decide to participate in the single Eurosystem tender procedure at a later date. Such a decision shall be irreversible.' An incentive for participating in the single tender procedure results from Article 18(2), as it allows the in-house printing works of euro area NCBs or the public printining works used by them to bid for contracts to produce euro banknotes allocated by the ECB only when their respective NCB decides to participate in the single tender procedure.

[339] This is welcome in view of the justified criticism by Padoa-Schioppa, *supra* note 337, p. 170 that '[t]oday's Eurosystem is [. . .] an archipelago of monopolies'. On the application of Community competition law to the ECB and the national central banks, cf. Fernández-Martin 'The Competition Rules on the E.C. Treaty and the European System of Central Banks' [2001] ECLR p. 51.

payment systems are of crucial importance for channelling, in a stable and reliable way, liquidity into the banking system of a currency area. With the advent of the euro and a single currency area, it became necessary to establish an efficient and robust large-value payment system for the euro area as a whole, in particular to ensure that the single monetary policy signals given by the ECB are smoothly transmitted to the banking system. This is why Article 105(2), fourth indent EC and Article 3.1, fourth indent of the Statute make it a Eurosystem task to promote the smooth operation of payment systems. On this basis, the ECB created in November 1998, by means of a Guideline, TARGET, the Trans-European Automated Real-time Gross Settlement Express Transfer system,[340] which since then has provided, in a secure and continuous way, settlement in central bank money with immediate intraday finality for credit transfers in euro, both interbank and customer payments. In its legal construction, the initial TARGET was a decentralized system, based on 16[341] national payment systems and a newly created ECB payment mechanism, which were interlinked. This allowed the ECB to start also with regard to payment systems on the basis of the tested practical arrangements already in place in the Member States. For individual transactions, TARGET always made use of the national payment infrastructures which were adapted only to comply with certain minimum common performance features, interlinking and security requirements. Thus, TARGET had from the beginning common daily operating hours (starting at 7 a.m. and ending at 6 p.m. C.E.T.[342]), as well as common closing days, while other aspects—such as the details of the pricing structure of the national payment systems—were left to national rules and practice.[343]

Even though in the first years of the euro, TARGET contributed substantially to the smooth operation of the single monetary policy, the daily practice of

---

[340] Guideline ECB/1998/NP13 of 16 November 1998, as amended, repealed and replaced by Guideline ECB/2000/NP9 of 3 October 2000 (both not published), replaced by Guideline ECB/2001/3 of 26 April 2001 on a Trans-European Automated Real-time Gross Settlement Express Transfer system (Target) [2001] OJ L140/72, replaced by Guideline ECB/2005/16 of 30 December 2005 [2006] OJ L18/1, as amended by Guideline ECB/2006/11 of 3 August 2006 [2006] OJ L221/17. On the initial TARGET, cf. Löber and Petersen, 'The Target System' [2001–2002] Euredia 157.

[341] The national central banks of the Member States which were EU Members at the start of Stage III of EMU, but which had not yet adopted the single currency, were allowed connection to TARGET; see Article 2(2) of Guideline ECB/2001/3 (*supra* note 340). Article 2(2) of Guideline ECB/2005/16 (*supra*, note 340) has extended this right to the central banks of all non-participating Member States. In 2004, Narodowy Bank Polski decided to connect its own national euro RTGS system (SORBNET-EURO) to TARGET via a bilateral link established with the Banca d'Italia; this connection went live on 7 March 2005. In addition, Slovenian banks can also be reached via TARGET, participating since July 2005 by means of remote access to the German TARGET component; on these enlargements of TARGET, see ECB, *TARGET Annual Report 2005*, p. 26. On 20 November 2006, also Eesti Pank, the central bank of Estonia, was connected with TARGET via a bilateral link established with the Banca d'Italia; see ECB, *TARGET Annual Report 2006* (in print).

[342] This results legally from Article 3(d) and Annex IV of Guideline ECB/2001/3 and of Guideline ECB/2005/16 (*supra* note 340).

[343] Louis, *supra* note 162, p. 591, therefore qualifies the initial TARGET as 'an approach geared towards minimum harmonization'.

TARGET also revealed the shortcomings of this decentralized and heterogeneous infrastructure.[344] It did not comply fully with the need for uniformity, as different national modalities with regard to the access to payment systems may distort the effects of the single monetary policy. In addition, with one payment platform per EU country plus the ECB's platform, TARGET generated cost-related efficiency problems: for example, each software modification has to be implemented in currently 17 platforms in 17 different ways.[345] For these reasons, and pressed by the prospect of future enlargements of the EU and of the euro area, the ECB decided on 24 October 2002, on the basis of the outcome of a public consultation, to replace TARGET with TARGET2. Under TARGET2, national central banks will no longer need to maintain their own payment processing platform. Instead, all national central banks will be able to share one technical platform, called the *Single Shared Platform*, which will support the real-time gross settlement services that they offer to their banks through a fully consolidated IT infrastructure. This sharing of technical infrastructure will reduce, for the benefit of the users of TARGET2, the costs per transaction through economies of scale. It will also allow to offer, throughout the euro area, a harmonized level of services with a single pricing structure. All national central banks (except the Bank of England and Sveriges Riksbank) and their customers will migrate to TARGET2 between 19 November 2007 and 19 May 2008.[346]

According to the organizational design of TARGET2, its Single Shared Platform is developed and will be operated by Deutsche Bundesbank, the Banque de France and Banca d'Italia for the benefit of the whole Eurosystem.[347] TARGET2 is thus a first concrete case of specialization in the implementation of Eurosystem tasks. The exact legal construction for TARGET2 is still under discussion. The legal architecture of TARGET2 needs to be established through ECB legal instruments (ECB Guidelines and/or ECB Regulations based on Articles 12.1 and 22 of the Statute) in which the ECB, by exercising its discretion

---

[344] See the article 'Future Developments in the TARGET system', in: ECB, *Monthly Bulletin, April 2004*, p. 59, at p. 62: 'The economic logic behind such a fragmented infrastructure, as well as its overall operational reliability, are highly debatable.' Cf. also Duisenberg in an interview with Il Sole 24 Ore (*supra* note 306): '[I]l sistema attuale, chiamato TARGET, é una specie di rete che collega i vari sistemi nazionali l'uno all'altro [. . .] un mosaico che comprende 13 sistemi diversi, 12 nazionali e uno della BCE collegati fra di loro. Non si può continuare così: le prime crepe stanno già emergendo. Abbiamo quindi deciso di creare nel giro di 5–6 anni una nuova piattaforma utilizzabile in più paesi ...'.

[345] Cf. Wellink, Chapple and Maier, *supra* note 220, p. 11, who consider it 'likely that, in the long term, the efficiency argument would imply a further consolidation in the area of wholesale payment systems. An important determinant of the speed of this process is trends in the banking and finance system. To the extent that there is a significant consolidation of banks, and increasing numbers of banks operating across the euro area, there may be less demand for national differences in payment systems. Integration of stock markets and other exchanges also increases the demand for harmonisation. These factors could eventually lead to some or all NCBs ceasing to offer payment systems.'

[346] The migration to TARGET2 is explained in detail in ECB, *Third Progress Report on TARGET2* (November 2006), published at <http://www.ecb.de/pub/pdf/other/3rd_progress_report_target2en.pdf>.

[347] Cf. 'Future Developments in the TARGET system', *supra* note 344, p. 63.

under Articles 9.2 and 12.1, subparagraph 3 of the Statute, will entrust the operation of the Single Shared Platform to Deutsche Bundesbank, the Banque de France and Banca d'Italia. At the same time, a rule on cost-sharing within the Eurosystem appears to be necessary: the three central banks will have to be compensated for the cost incurred for maintaining the Single Shared Platform by those central banks making use of it. The ECB will finally have to make clear in its legal instruments that market participants throughout the euro area must have equal access to TARGET2 under harmonized terms and conditions. TARGET2 is a test case for specialization within the Eurosystem. If it meets both the demands of payment system customers and the needs for uniformity and efficiency, TARGET2 could become an important catalyst of further financial integration in Europe.[348]

(iv) Two Competing Levels of Governance within the Eurosystem?

Not always have the needs for uniformity and efficiency been able to ensure a consistent approach by the Eurosystem. In a few instances, the informed observer can still detect a certain competition between the still young central level of decision-making (ECB) and the older 'decentralized' level with the once powerful national central banks. It is noteworthy that an opinion given by the ECB on a particular matter in the exercise of its advisory role under Article 105(4) EC and Article 4 of the Statute has not always prevented national central banks from issuing their own opinions on the same matter. Thus, Deutsche Bundesbank felt entitled to voice its own opinion on the draft of the Constitutional Treaty[349] even though the ECB had already formally adopted an Opinion on this on the request of the Council of the European Union.[350] Of course, a local communication by national central banks of the policies, decisions and opinions of the ECB can be desirable,[351] provided that it is in line with the position taken by the ECB. One may also accept that in the exceptional context of a Constitutional Treaty, a national central bank may feel entitled to make known its own views outside the ESCB. However, the integrity and credibility of the Eurosystem could be jeopardised if concurrent national central bank opinions on issues on which the ECB already took a public position would become a rule.

---

[348] Already today, an extension of TARGET2 to securities transactions is envisaged, which would again be based on a single platform and common procedures for the whole euro area. A final decision on 'TARGET2 securities' is expected for 2007; cf. ECB Press Release of 7 July 2006 'The Eurosystem is evaluating opportunities to provide settlement services for securities transactions', published at <http://www.ecb.de/press/pr/date/2006/html/pr060707.en.html>.

[349] Cf. Deutsche Bundesbank, 'Zur Währungsverfassung nach dem Entwurf einer Verfassung für die Europäische Union', *supra* note 157.

[350] Cf. ECB Opinion CON/2003/20, *supra* note 155.

[351] Wellink, Chapple and Maier, *supra* note 220, p. 4 stress that 'NCBs are important channels for ESCB communication, as they are more closely linked to their national audiences.'

In some cases, competition between the ECB and the national central banks of the Eurosystem may also contribute to a healthy discovery process aimed at the best and most precise result. This can be said to be the case with regard to the Macroeconomic Projections Exercises which take place since December 2000.[352] Following a decision of the Governing Council of the ECB, macroeconomic projections with regard to inflation and growth of real GDP over a two-year horizon are published always in the June and December issues of the ECB's Monthly Bulletin as well as on the ECB's website.[353] These projections, which play an important role in advising the monetary policy decisions of the Governing Council of the ECB, are carried out under the responsibility of the ECB's Monetary Policy Committee (one of the ESCB Committees[354]) by a team of experts from the national central banks of the Eurosystem and from the ECB. It is a unique element of these Eurosystem Macroeconomic Projections that they combine both national and euro area-wide perspectives. Both ECB staff and the staff at the national central banks of the Eurosystem first prepare their initial projections figures—the ECB for the individual countries as well as for the euro area as whole, the national central banks each for their own country— following identical underlying assumptions and a standardized reporting format. These initial projections are then submitted for a detailed discussion and 'peer review' in the ECB's Monetary Policy Committee, which may lead to revisions of the country projections. The final Macroeconomic Projections, as they are submitted in a report for the Governing Council of the ECB via the ECB's Executive Board, are the aggregation of the agreed revised country projections. Of course, this report is treated in the same way as all advice given by ESCB Committee and does not bind the decision-making bodies of the ECB. To ensure that the own projections of the ECB staff with regard to inflation and growth are transparent for all market participants, the ECB is publishing, since September 2004, 'ECB staff macroeconomic projections for the euro area' always in March and August/September.[355] This allows the ECB's decision-making bodies to have at their disposal now four times a year expert projections with

---

[352] Cf. ECB, *A Guide to Eurosystem Staff Macroeconomic Projection Exercises*, June 2001, Frankfurt am Main (2001).

[353] At <http://www.ecb.de/pub/pub/mopo/html/index.en.html?skey=staff+macroeconomic+projections>. See, eg, the 'Eurosystem staff macroeconomic projections for the euro area' of 8 June 2006 which project for the euro area average annual real GDP growth between 1.8% and 2.4% in 2006 and between 1.3% and 2.3% in 2007 as well as an average rate increase in the overall Harmonised Index of Consumer Prices between 2.1% and 2.5% in 2006 and between 1.6% and 2.8% in 2007.   [354] On ESCB Committees, cf. *supra* p. 49 *et seq.*

[355] See also <http://www.ecb.de/pub/pub/mopo/html/index.en.html?skey=staff+macroeconomic+projections>. See, eg, the 'ECB staff macroeconomic projections for the euro area' published on 31 August 2006 which forecast for the euro area average annual real GDP growth between 2.2% and 2.8% in 2006 and between 1.6% and 2.6% in 2007 as well as an average rate increase in the overall Harmonised Index of Consumer Prices between 2.3% and 2.5% in 2006 and between 1.9% and 2.9% in 2007.

regard to inflation and growth (twice from ECB staff and twice from Eurosystem staff). However, potentially varying nuances in the projections of ECB staff and Eurosystem staff could be interpreted by informed observers of the ECB as different economic assessments by the 'centre' and the 'periphery' within the Eurosystem, thereby calling into question its uniform appearance.[356]

(v) The Double Meaning of e pluribus unum

Is the Eurosystem becoming increasingly *one* supranational central banking entity instead of a conglomerate of a supranational entity and 13 competing national bodies? The need for ensuring uniformity and efficiency in the implementation of Eurosystem tasks appears to have created some pressure to move into this direction, even though the process towards efficiency-based centralization is still far from being completed. Legal practice and academic literature will therefore continue to have for still some time to reflect on interpreting and developing further the intra-institutional relations within the Eurosystem. In this context, it is telling that *Padoa-Schioppa*, when thinking about the appropriate title for his book that he later called 'The Euro and Its Central Bank', first took *e pluribus unum* into consideration, but then rejected it after consultation with his publisher.[357] *E pluribus unum* is the motto of the United States of America that was included in 1782 in their Great Seal on the suggestion of *Pierre Eugene DuSimitière* to symbolize the integration of 13 independent colonies into one united country. However, the meaning and origins of this Latin saying are not entirely clear.[358] In classical Latin, *e pluribus unum* probably meant 'one among many', which would, if applied to the Eurosystem, show that the ECB still shares many central banking functions with the national central banks. However, *e pluribus unum* was later also used in *Moretum*, a poem attributed to Virgil. This poem deals with the subject of a cheese, garlic and herb recipe. When describing the process by which the different ingredients used in the recipe blend into one, the poem says: 'color est e pluribus unus'. This meaning 'out of many, one' is the one said to be behind the Great Seal of the United States of America and could also serve as inspiration for the future development of the Eurosystem into a modern and efficient single monetary authority for the euro. The jury is, however, still out to decide whether it will be justified to use *e pluribus unum* as the title of a future legal analysis of the Eurosystem. At present, for an

---

[356] The need for more uniformity in this respect is acknowledged by Wellink, Chapple and Maier, *supra* note 220, p. 8: 'In the long run, as European integration proceeds, European interests will increasingly replace national interests [. . .]. That is likely to mean that the ECB, and therefore its president, would have an increasing role as the public face of the ESCB.'

[357] On the meaning of 'e pluribus unum', see also the Preface in Padoa-Schioppa, *supra* note 210, p. xiv *et seq.*

[358] This is observed by Trichet, in: ECB (Ed), *The Eurosystem, the Union and Beyond. The Single Currency and Implications for Governance. An ECB colloquium held in honour of Tommaso Padoa-Schioppa*, 27 April 2005, Frankfurt am Main (2005), p. 5, at p. 7.

experienced 'gourmet' of ECB law, the tastes of herbs and cheese are still sometimes identifiable.

III. The External Action of the ECB

Since its establishment, the ECB, as Europe's supranational monetary authority, has exercised its tasks not only through its monetary policy inside the euro area, but has progressively assumed its role also in international relations. This has been paralleled by the increasing international role played by the euro in line with the economic and financial size of the euro area.[359] With its international activities, the ECB could follow the tradition according to which central banks have since long participated actively in the shaping of international monetary, financial and economic decisions, be it through international organizations such as the International Monetary Fund (IMF) or via their participation in informal fora such as the Group of Seven/Eight (G7/G8).[360] The law of the ECB has proved to be a good starting point for the international role of the ECB.[361] It gives, first of all, legal personality to the ECB in Article 107(2) EC and Article 9.1 of the Statute, which is the pre-condition for participating with own rights and obligations in international relations. In addition, the law of the ECB clearly outlines the external dimension of the ECB tasks. It has even dedicated, with Article 6 of the Statute, a particular provision to the institutional issues of the ECB's international activities and to its leadership with regard to the national central banks also in this respect. The law of the ECB has also spelled out that to establish relations with central banks and financial institutions in other countries and with international organizations (Article 23, first indent of the Statute) is as much an integral part of the Eurosystem tasks as is the acquisition and the selling of all types of foreign exchange and precious metals (Article 23, second indent of the

---

[359] On the present situation, cf. ECB, *Review of the International Role of the Euro*, Frankfurt am Main (2005). The increasing international importance of the euro is reflected in the decision of the IMF to enhance, with effect from 1 January 2006, the share of the euro in the basket of the Special Drawing Right (SDR) from 29% to 34%. Other currencies are represented in the SDR basket with the following shares: 44% US Dollar, 11% Japanese Yen, 11% British Pound Sterling; cf. IMF Press Release No. 05/265, <http://www.imf.org/external/np/sec/pr/2005/pr05265.htm>. The weights assigned to the currencies in the SDR basket are based on the value of the exports of goods and services and the amount of reserves denominated in the respective currencies which are held by other members of the IMF.

[360] Cf. Rey, 'The European Monetary System' [1980] CML Rev. 7 (at p. 11): 'In international matters, central banks usually act on their own or as agents for the implementation of international obligations entered into by their governments.' See already Kramer, *Die Rechtsnatur der Geschäfte des Internationalen Währungsfonds*, Berlin (1967), in particular at p. 35 *et seq.*; Zehetner, 'Völkerrechtliche Außenvertretungsbefugnisse der Oesterreichischen Nationalbank?' in: Flume, Hahn, Kegel, Simmond (Eds.), *Internationales Recht und Wirtschaftsordnung, Festschrift für F. A. Mann zum 70. Geburtstag*, München (1977), p. 465; and Selmayr, *Das Recht der Wirtschafts- und Währungsunion I*, p. 148 *et seq.*; p. 164 *et seq.*; p. 386 *et seq.*

[361] On this, see in detail the Chapter 'The European Central Bank in International Relations' in Zilioli and Selmayr, *supra* note 209, p. 171 *et seq.*

Statute) and the conduct of all types of banking transactions in relations with third countries and international organizations, including borrowing and lending operations (Article 23, fourth indent of the Statute). We will explore in the following pages in which way the ECB has made use of these provisions of ECB law during its first eight years and which challenges it has encountered in its international activities.

A. Growing Recognition of the International Legal Personality of the ECB

In international law, international legal personality of legal persons (other than States, which are 'born' international legal persons) depends on formal or implicit recognition by other international legal persons. It is therefore not sufficient that within the ECB's 'domestic' legal order, which is European Community law, its capability to have international legal personality is largely undisputed.[362] The

---

[362] The following authors have recognized with us the international legal personality of the ECB: Kempen, in: Streinz (Ed.), *Kommentar zum EU- und EG-Vertrag*, München (2003), Art. 107 EGV, para. 9; Smulders, in: von der Groeben and Schwarze (Eds.), *Kommentar zum EU- und EG-Vertrag*, Baden-Baden (2004), Art. 107 EG, para. 6, 16 ff.; Pernice, in: Grabitz and Hilf (Eds.), *Das Recht der Europäischen Union. Kommentar*, München (last update: August 2006), Art. 4a EGV, Randnr. 11; Timmermans, 'Editorial Comment: Executive Agencies within the EC: The European Central Bank—a model?' [1996] CML Rev. 623 (at p. 629); Stadler, *Der rechtliche Handlungsspielraum des Europäischen Systems der Zentralbanken*, Baden-Baden (1996), p. 92; Louis, 'Les relations internationales de l'Union économique et monétaire', EUI Working Paper LAW No. 99/10, 17 f.; Louis, 'Les relations extérieures de l'Union économique et monétaire', in: Cannizzaro (Ed.), The European Union as an Actor in International Relations, The Hague (2002), p. 77 (at p. 80 *et seq.*); Scheller, *supra* note 1, p. 47; von Borries, 'Die Europäische Zentralbank als Gemeinschaftsinstitution' [1999] ZEUS 281 (at p. 293); Stumpf, 'Die auswärtigen Beziehungen der Europäischen Währungsunion' [2003] ZaöRV 1075 (at p. 1078 and p. 1082 *et seq.*); Horng, 'The European Central Bank's External Relations with Third Countries and the IMF' [2004] European Foreign Affairs Review 323 (at p. 325 *et seq.*); Horng, 'The ECB's Membership in the IMF: Legal Approaches to Constitutional Challenges' [2005] European Law Journal 802 (at p. 806 *et seq.*); Proctor, *supra* note 1, p. 674; see already Bognar, *Europäische Währungsintegration und Außenwirtschaftsbeziehungen. Eine Analyse des gemeinschafts- und völkerrechtlichen Rahmens der europäischen Außenwährungsbeziehungen*, Baden-Baden (1997), p. 100 (with regard to the international legal personality of the EMI); Hahn, *Der Vertrag von Maastricht als völkerrechtliche Übereinkunft und Verfassung*, Baden-Baden (1992), p. 58 (international legal personality of the EMI) and p. 66 (international legal personality of the ECB); and Weinbörner, *Die Stellung der Europäischen Zentralbank (EZB) und der nationalen Zentralbanken in der Wirtschafts- und Währungsunion nach dem Vertrag von Maastricht*, Frankfurt (1998), p. 385, in particular footnote 1348 with reference to the international legal personality of the EIB. Cf. also ECB, *Annual Report 2004*, p. 162: 'The ECB has legal personality under international law'. The international legal personality of the ECB is denied only by Weber, 'Das Europäische System der Zentralbanken' [1998] Wertpapiermitteilungen 1465 (at p. 1471), who wants to accept only an external communication function of the ECB; by Tizzano, 'La personnalité internationale de l'Union européenne' [1998] RMUE 11 (at p. 37 *et seq.* and footnote 45), who believes in an absorption of all legal persons created by the Treaties by the EU; by Häde, in: Calliess and Ruffert (Eds.), *Kommentar zu EU-Vertrag und EG-Vertrag*, 2nd edition, Neuwied (2002), Art. 8 EGV, para. 4, who considers the ECB to be a Community body which therefore could not be seen at the same time as independent international organization; and *Cafaro* 'La rappresentanza dell'Europa dell'euro nelle organizzazioni monetarie e finanziarie internazionali' [1999] Il Diritto dell'Unione Europea 737 (at p. 769), who takes the view (which is however refuted by international practice) that central banks may never have international

scope of the international activities of the ECB rather depends on whether central banks in third countries, third countries themselves, international organizations and financial institutions accept to deal directly with the legal person ECB by entering into contracts or agreements with it or by starting other forms of cooperative relations with the ECB.

Initially, some may have thought that the fact that the euro is 'a currency without a state'[363] would make it difficult for the ECB to achieve legal recognition around the world. However, international monetary, financial and economic relations are based to a large extent on pragmatism. The ECB is therefore the natural and sole counterpart for all those who want to deal, whether operationally or politically, with those responsible for Europe's single currency, which is presently the second most important currency in the world. This explains why very quickly, the ECB has become a party to international agreements with central banks of third countries[364] and has assumed the role as contact point and cooperation partner for many third countries and their central banks, with which the ECB interacts in the form of reciprocal visits of Board members, joint workshops, regular meetings or high-level policy dialogues.[365] The ECB also has sent its own representatives on missions to third countries for the purpose of training (Russia[366]) and technical assistance (Egypt[367]), and is advising on the technical

---

legal personality. This view by Tizzano and Cafaro is rightly criticized by Louis, 'Les relations extérieures de l'Union économique et monétaire', in: Cannizzaro (see above), at p. 81.

[363] This concept and its viability are explained further in the speech 'The euro—a currency without a state' given by former ECB Executive Board member Issing in Helsinki on 24 March 2006, published at <http://www.ecb.int/press/key/date/2006/html/sp060324.en.html>.

[364] The ECB entered, for example, into a new swap agreement with Norges Bank amounting to €1,535 million, which came into effect on 1 January 1999; cf. ECB, *Annual Report 1998*, p. 93.

[365] Cf. ECB, *Annual Report 1999*, p. 84; *Annual Report 2000*, p. 108 *et seq.*; *Annual Report 2001*, p. 111; *Annual Report 2002*, p. 111 *et seq.*; *Annual Report 2003*, p. 136 *et seq.*; *Annual Report 2004*, p. 138 *et seq.*; *Annual Report 2005*, p. 146 *et seq.*

[366] From November 2003 to October 2005, an ECB representative was sent to Moscow to implement a Central Bank Training Protocol signed jointly by the President of the ECB, the Head of the Delegation of the European Commission in Russia and the Chairman of the Central Bank of Russia; cf. ECB Press Release of 13 October 2003 published at <http://www.ecb.int/press/pr/date/2003/html/pr031013.en.html>. The project, which was financed by the European Commission under the TACIS programme, was coordinated by the ECB and involved experts from Deutsche Bundesbank, Banco de España, Banque de France, the Central Bank and Financial Services Authority of Ireland, the Banca d'Italia, De Nederlandsche Bank, the Oesterreichische Nationalbank, the Banco de Portugal, Suomen Pankki—Finlands Bank, Rahoitustarkastus—Finansinspektionen (the Finnish financial supervision authority), Finansinspektionen (the Swedish financial supervision authority) and the Financial Services Authority (the UK financial supervision authority). On the results of the project, cf. ECB Press Release of 13 October 2005, published at <http://www.ecb.int/press/pr/date/2005/html/pr051013.en.html>. The close cooperation with Russia may be explained by the fact that the euro area is Russia's most important trading partner, accounting for about 35% of Russia's total trade in goods. On the role of the euro in Russia, see ECB, *Review of the International Role of the Euro*, Frankfurt am Main (2005), p. 55 *et seq.*, Box 6.

[367] Since the end of 2005, two ECB representatives have been based at the Central Bank of Egypt in Cairo to accompany the 'Eurosystem Technical Assistance Programme on Banking Supervision'. On 13 October 2005, a Protocol on this programme was signed by the President of the ECB, the Head of the Delegation of the European Commission in Egypt and the Governor of the Central Bank

and economic aspects of Monetary Union (the countries of the Gulf Cooperation Council[368]). Most remarkably perhaps, the ECB entered in September 2002 into a Memorandum of Understanding with the People's Bank of China to promote bilateral cooperation.[369] This led, in December 2002, to the opening of a representation of the People's Bank of China at the seat of the ECB in Frankfurt am Main.[370] During 2005, the ECB could in addition welcome to Frankfurt the official delegations from a number of Latin American economies.[371]

Well developed is the recognition of the international legal personality of the ECB in the United States of America, where the ECB has since 1998 a permanent representation in Washington D.C. to maintain contacts with the US authorities, in particular the Federal Reserve System, and also with the IMF.[372] In 2000 the Board of Governors of the US Federal Reserve System formally amended an interpretation of its regulations to confer on the ECB the status of a 'supranational entity', such that US depository institutions receiving deposits from the ECB do not need to hold reserves against those deposits.[373] The most significant development with respect to the recognition of the ECB as an international legal person by the US authorities came on 29 May 2003 when the US President issued an Executive Order which grants to the ECB the privileges, exemptions, and immunities provided

of Egypt; cf. ECB Press Release of, published at <http://www.ecb.int/press/pr/date/2005/html/pr051113.en.html>. The programme, which is financed by the European Commission under the MEDA programme, is implemented by the ECB in partnership with Deutsche Bundesbank, Bank of Greece, Banque de France, and Banca d'Italia.

[368] The six member states of the GCC are Bahrain, Kuwait, Oman, Qatar, Saudi Arabia and the United Arab Emirates. They plan to introduce a single currency by 2010 and have sought the advice of the ECB for this; cf. Sturm and Siegfried, 'Regional Monetary Integration in the Member States of the Gulf Cooperation Council', ECB Occasional Paper Series No. 31, June 2005. Cf. also the ECB's *Annual Report 2005*, p. 147.

[369] Cf. ECB, *Annual Report 2002*, p. 113. This cooperation is particularly important since the decisions of the Chinese authorities in July 2005 to shift from a strict peg of the Yuan to the US Dollar to a new managed floating exchange rate—a decision which was welcomed by the ECB; cf. <http://www.ecb.de/press/pr/date/2005/html/pr050721.en.html>.

[370] Cf. ECB, *Annual Report 2002*, p. 113.

[371] Cf. ECB, *Annual Report 2005*, p. 148. The most important delegations were sent by Brazil, Chile and Uruguay.

[372] On the function and activities of the ECB's permanent representation in Washington D.C., cf. ECB, *Annual Report 1999*, p. 82, Box 6.

[373] Cf. Reserve Requirements of Depository Institutions, 65 Fed. Reg. 12,916 (2000), 12 C.F.R. § 204.125 (interpretation adopted 6 March 2000). Under Regulation D (Reserve Requirements of Depository Institutions) there are three categories of entities to which this special status may be granted: (1) foreign commercial banks; (2) foreign governments, their agencies or instrumentalities; and (3) foreign international or supranational entities specifically designated by the Board of Governors of the Federal Reserve System. The Board of Governors of the Federal Reserve System decided with regard to the ECB: 'The Board is amending its interpretation of Regulation D (Reserve Requirements of Depository Institutions) to include the European Central Bank among the institutions that have been specifically designated by the Board as "supranational" entities for the purposes of certain time deposits under Regulation D.' Prior to this, the Board of Governors had already granted this status to the European Community, the (as it then was) European Coal and Steal Community and to the EIB.

to public international organizations in accordance with the International Organizations Immunities Act of 1945.[374] This had been made possible by a law adopted by the US Congress in November 2002[375] that allowed for the application of this Act to the ECB.[376]

Also, in international organizations and fora, the international legal personality of the ECB has been recognized. The ECB has, since December 1998, an observer status at the IMF, based on Article X of the IMF Articles of Agreement ('Relations with Other International Organizations')[377] and also participates since February 1999 in the relevant works of the Organization for Economic Cooperation and Development (OECD) on the basis of an agreement under Protocol No. 1 of the OECD Agreement.[378] Since December 1999, the ECB is also a full member of the Bank for International Settlements.[379] The President of the ECB moreover participates today regularly, on the basis of informal agreements, in G7/8[380] and

---

[374] Cf. <http://www.whitehouse.gov/news/releases/2003/05/20030529-7.html>: 'By the authority vested in me as President by the Constitution and the laws of the United States of America, including sections 1 and 15 of the International Organizations Immunities Act (22 U.S.C. 288 and 288f-5), I hereby extend to the European Central Bank the privileges, exemptions, and immunities provided to public international organizations designated by the President under the International Organizations Immunities Act. This extension of such privileges, exemptions, and immunities is not intended to abridge in any respect privileges, exemptions, or immunities that the European Central Bank otherwise may have acquired or may acquire by international agreements or by law. George W. Bush. The White House. May 29, 2003.'   [375] 22 U.S.C. § 288, 288 f-5.

[376] There had been some doubts as to whether the ECB qualified already for the immunities accorded under the Foreign Sovereign Immunity Act 1976, 28 U.S.C. § 1603, which grants immunities to 'foreign states' or 'an agency or instrumentality of a foreign state', or 'the property of a foreign state' held by 'a foreign central bank or monetary authority'. An amendment of US immunity legislation was therefore required in order to clarify this matter. On this reasoning behind the amendment, cf. the statement by Representative *Tom Lantos* at the occasion of the mark-up of the bill on 20 March 2002 before the Committee on International Relations of the House of Representatives, published at <http://commdocs.house.gov/committees/intlrel/hfa78321.000/hfa78321_0.HTM>: 'Unfortunately, since the ECB is a new type of central bank, it does not fit the definition of a foreign central bank under the Foreign Sovereign Immunities Act (FSIA), and is therefore not granted the Immunities provided by that act'. On the issue of central bank immunity in the US, cf. Patrikis, 'Sovereign Immunity and Central Bank Immunity in the United States' in: *Effros* (Ed.), Current Legal Issues Affecting Central Banks, Volume 1, Washington (1992), p. 159. Cf. also the presentation of central bank immunity from the perspective of German law by Krauskopf and Steven 'Immunität ausländischer Zentralbanken im deutschen Recht' [2000] Wertpapiermitteilungen, 269, who show by means of comparative law that today, independent central banks with own legal personality are generally accepted as independent bearers of immunity rights.

[377] Cf. the IMF's Executive Board's Decision No. 11875-(99/1) of 22 December 1998, replaced by Decision No. 12925-(03/1) of 27 December 2002, amended by Decision No. 13414-(05/01) of 22 December 2004, published at <http://www.imf.org/external/pubs/ft/sd/index.asp?decision= 12925-(03/1)>. Para. 4 of this Decision reads: 'At Executive Board meetings, the representative of the ECB shall have the status of observer and, as such, will be able to address the Board with the permission of the Chairman on matters within the responsibility of the ECB.'

[378] Cf. ECB, *Annual Report 1998*, p. 93 and *Annual Report 1999*, p. 84.

[379] Cf. BIS Press Release No. 40/1999E of 8 November 1999, <http://www.bis.org/press/ p991108.htm>.

[380] G7 includes Canada, France, Germany, Italy, Japan, United Kingdom and United States. With the participation of Russia, G7 has meanwhile become G8. On the ECB in G7, cf. ECB,

G10[381] as well as G20[382] meetings of finance ministers and central bank governors. In April 2005, the ECB participated, with observer status, in the Annual Meeting of the Inter-American Development Bank in Okinawa.[383]

B. The Quest for 'Mr. Euro'

The recognition of the ECB as international legal person assures that Europe's supranational monetary authority is able to participate in international monetary relations without being dependent on the EU Member States and their foreign ministries. It thus gives the ECB's independence also an external dimension. The legal possibility of the ECB to act independently at international level has triggered a political debate about who has the right to represent the euro area internationally, in short: who is 'Mr. Euro' who would, to paraphrase the famous sentence of *Henry Kissinger*, receive a phone call from the monetary authorities of third countries,[384] for example to coordinate interventions on the foreign exchange markets in response to an international crisis?

The institutional set-up provided for by the EC Treaty and the Statute appears to privilege the ECB and its President for this role. Not only has the ECB international legal personality, with tasks assigned to it by the EC Treaty and the Statute in the field of monetary policy in the broad sense.[385] More important, it is also exclusively the ECB that has under its control the operational instruments for conducting a 'foreign policy in the monetary fields', namely foreign exchange

---

Annual Report 1998, p. 93. Cf. also the 'Report to the European Council on the state of preparation for Stage 3 of EMU, in particular the external representation of the Community', submitted by the Ecofin Council to the European Council of Vienna on 11/12 December 1998, Annex II to the conclusions of the Presidency, published at <http://www.consilium.europa.eu/ueDocs/cms_Data/docs/pressData/en/ec/00300-R1.EN8.htm>. 'Regarding the European Central Bank's participation in the representation of the Community at the G7 Finance Ministers' and Governors' Group, non-European partners have already accepted that the President of the ECB attends meetings of the Group for the discussions which relate to EMU, eg multilateral surveillance, exchange-rate issues, and for agreement of the relevant sections of the published Statement.'

[381] G10 includes Belgium, Canada, France, Germany, Italy, Japan, Netherlands, Sweden, United Kingdom, United States, and—since 1983—also Switzerland. The informal arrangements found for G7/8 participation (*supra* note 380) are presently also applied to G10; cf. ECB, Annual Report 1998, p. 93.

[382] Cf. ECB, *Annual Report 1999*, p. 83. G20 includes all G8 members plus Argentina, Australia, Brazil, China, India, Indonesia, Mexico, Saudi Arabia, South Africa, South Korea and Turkey as well as—as ex officio members—the World Bank President, the IMF Managing Director and the Chairmen of the IMFC and the Development Committee.

[383] Cf. ECB, *Annual Report 2005*, p. 148.

[384] Cf., eg, the article 'Künstler und Handwerker: Regierungschef Jean-Claude Juncker und Zentralbankchef Jean-Claude Trichet streiten darüber, wie eng ihr Kontakt sein soll', Süddeutsche Zeitung No. 152 of 5 July 2006, p. 18; or 'Jean-Claude gegen Jean-Claude', Financial Times Deutschland of 6 July 2006, p. 20.

[385] ECB President Trichet founds on this his argument that the ECB is perfectly able and entitled to act in external monetary matters: 'This is consistent with the principle of "parallelism" according to which the community or national authority responsible for a given policy within the Union assumes such responsibility also at the international level.' Cf. Committee on Economic and Monetary Affairs

reserves.[386] Foreign exchange currently worth more than €40 billion[387] is directly held by the ECB (Article 30.1, first sentence of the Statute[388]) which may call, in case of need, for the transfer of foreign exchange worth a further €50 billion (Article 30.4 of the Statute[389]). In addition, the ECB may activate the foreign exchange reserves controlled by the national central banks of the Eurosystem (currently worth more than €285 billion[390]), as since 1 January 1999, the holding and management of these reserves became an exclusive Eurosystem task by virtue of Article 105(2), second indent EC. To implement the policy objectives entrusted to the ECB by the EC Treaty and the Statute, the ECB may therefore intervene on the foreign exchange markets either itself with its own reserves or through the national central banks of the Eurosystem which may make use of their foreign exchange (above a certain limit) only subject to the approval of the ECB and in line with its guidelines (Article 31.2 and 3. of the Statute).

Only under special circumstances gives Article 111 EC the Council a say on the foreign exchange operations of the ECB. This would be the case if the Community decided to enter into a 'Bretton Woods No. 2'-type formal agreement on an exchange-rate system between the euro and the currencies of third counties. Such an agreement, that would also be binding on the ECB (Article 111(3) second subparagraph EC), represents for the time being a very unlikely scenario, both in view of the severe doubts in mainstream economic theory about the benefits of such a system of fixed exchange rates and, institutionally, because of the unanimity requirement in Article 111(1) EC.[391] This leaves only the option for the Council to intervene in the ECB's foreign exchange policy by means of so-called '*general orientations*' under Article 111(2) EC. Even though such general orientations may be adopted by the Council with qualified majority, they leave, by virtue of their very nature as 'general orientations' only,[392] a substantial discretion

of the European Parliament, Notice to members No 12/30 'Confirmation hearing of the candidate for the ECB Presidency', published at <http://europavl.europa.eu/hearings/20030911/econ/qa_en.pdf>.

[386] On this, cf. Selmayr, 'Darf die EZB den Wechselkurs des Euro stützen?' [2000] Europablätter 2000, p. 209; and 'Interventionen zwecks Preisstabilität. Die europarechtlichen Leitplanken für die EZB', Neue Zürcher Zeitung No 237 of 11 October 2000, p. 11.

[387] Status: February 2007; cf. also the article 'Portfolio Management at the ECB', in: ECB, *Monthly Report, April 2006*, p. 75.

[388] Cf. Decision ECB/2006/24 of the ECB of 5 December 2006 laying down the measures necessary for the contribution to the ECB's accumulated equity value for adjusting the national central banks claims equivalent to the transferred foreign reserve assets [2007] OJ L24/9.

[389] Cf. Article 2(1) of Council Regulation (EC) No 1010/2000 of 8 May 2000 concerning further calls of foreign reserve assets by the European Central Bank [2000] OJ L115/2.

[390] The market value of the foreign exchange of the ECB and of the national central banks of the Eurosystem can always be identified from the ECB's Monthly Bulletin, which publishes, since 2000, in its Part S 'Euro Area Statistics', the net value of the foreign exchange of the Eurosystem; cf., eg, ECB, *Monthly Bulletin, September 2006*, p. S 9. Cf. also the article 'Foreign exchange reserves and operations of the Eurosystems', in: ECB, *Monthly Bulletin, January 2000*, p. 51 (at p. 57).

[391] This unanimity requirement would be maintained by Article III-326(1) of the Constitutional Treaty.

[392] Cf. Zilioli and Selmayr, *supra* note 209, p. 204 *et seq.*, where we qualify these general orientations as non-binding recommendations only; cf. also Endler, *supra* note 1, p. 473 *et seq.*; Smits, *supra*

to the ECB and may under no circumstances prejudice its primary objective, which is price stability. In addition, the European Council itself made clear, in its Luxembourg Resolution adopted on 13 December 1997,[393] that in general exchange rates should be seen as the outcome of all other economic policies, and that only '*in exceptional circumstances, for example in the case of a clear misalignment*', the Council may formulate general orientations for exchange-rate policy in accordance with Article 111(2) EC. As a rule, both the definition and the implementation of the foreign exchange policy for the euro is thus entirely in the hands of the ECB.[394] Also on 22 September 2000, when the euro was at below 0.85 US dollar and it became for the first time necessary for the ECB to intervene, together with the central banks of other G7 countries, in the foreign exchange markets, these interventions took place on the sole initiative of the ECB.[395]

note 1, p. 398 f.; and Hahn, '"Allgemeine Orientierungen" oder ,allgemeine Leitlinien' für die Wechselkurspolitik der Europäischen Währungsunion?—Zur juristischen Beschaffenheit der Beschlussbefugnis des Rates gemäß Art. 111 Abs. 2 EGV (-ex-Art. 109 II)—, [1999] BayVBl. 741 (at p. 744 *et seq.*).

[393] Resolution of the European Council on economic policy coordination in Stage 3 of EMU and on Treaty Articles 109 and 109b [1997] OJ C95/1. Outdated seems today the call of the former German and French Finance ministers for 'target zones' for the euro; cf. Lafontaine and Strauss-Kahn, 'Europa—sozial und stark. Märkte brauchen die ordnende Hand des Staates', DIE ZEIT No 3 of 14 January 1999, p. 17, and the reply by former Bundesbank President Schlesinger 'Falsche Interpretation', DIE ZEIT No 8 of 18 February 1999, p. 26.

[394] Cf. the transcript of the ECB press conference of 5 October 2000 published at <http://www.ecb.int/key/00/sp001005.htm>, p. 7: Question: 'According to a very strict interpretation of the Maastricht Treaty, there would be a need for exchange rate orientations before interventions take place. Please, have there been any developments in this direction so far?' ECB President Duisenberg: 'No, that is a wrong interpretation of the Maastricht Treaty. The Maastricht Treaty provides for the possibility of the Council of Ministers giving so-called general orientations for exchange rate policy. As long as the Council has not done so, the sole body to decide on the "if" and the "when" and the "level of interventions" is the European Central Bank. In addition, the Council of Ministers—at its summit in Luxembourg in December 1997—decided and made it public that so-called general orientations would only be issued in very exceptional circumstances. Well, such exceptional circumstances have not arisen and therefore, you might justifiably conclude that both the initiative for the interventions and the action itself were fully in the hands of the Governing Council of the ECB.'

[395] This is underlined by the G7 statement adopted a day after the interventions took place, published <http://www.library.utoronto.ca/g7/finance/fm20000923.htm>, where it says in para 4 under 'Exchange Rates': '[. . .] At the initiative of the European Central Bank, the monetary authorities of the United States, Japan, United Kingdom and Canada joined with the European Central Bank on Friday, September 22, in concerted intervention in exchange markets [. . .].' It is interesting to note that the initiative of the ECB is underlined, while for the other G7 countries, reference is made to the 'monetary authorities', which demonstrates that in these countries, foreign exchange policy is at least a shared responsibility of central banks and finance ministries, if not entirely decided by the latter. In the US, the intervention was therefore made known in the form of a 'Statement of the United States Department of the Treasury'; cf. <http://www.ustreas.gov/press/ releases/ls901.htm>. Also in Japan, the Treasury claimed responsibility for the intervention; cf. <http://www.mof.go .jp/daijin/1e087.htm>. In contrast to this, in Europe the intervention was announced on the website of the ECB, thereby demonstrating also in communication terms the different and stronger role played by the ECB as Europe's monetary authority; cf. <http://www.ecb.int/press/pr/date/2000/ html/pr000922.en.html>.

Operationally, and in terms of foreign exchange policy, it is therefore certainly the ECB and its President which so far has served as 'Mr. Euro' in the international relations of the euro area, and this is likely to remain unchanged as long as no 'Bretton Woods No 2' is established. As it was properly said by ECB President *Trichet* when asked, in the hearing by the European Parliament on 12 September 2003 prior to his appointment, about 'Mr. Euro': 'Our partners know the ECB President's telephone number'.[396]

The external representation of the euro area becomes more complex when the participation in international organizations is concerned which cover not only monetary and exchange rate matters, but also general issues of macroeconomic policy. Here, in view of the different Community tasks involved, the existence of the international legal personality of the ECB raises the question of its relationship with the international legal personality of the Community. Community law already knows the phenomenon that two international legal persons established by the EC Treaty may become parallel members of the same international organization, as this is the case of the EC and the EIB (which also enjoys international legal personality[397]) in the European Bank for Reconstruction and Development (EBRD).[398] This precedent appears to make a similarly parallel membership of the EC and the ECB in an international organization such as the IMF legally possible. However, not always will such a parallel exercise of external competences be politically desirable or effective. Externally, Europe will only have a strong voice if, at least in the long run, it will be able to speak with a single voice. A good precedent in this sense can be seen in the practical arrangements found for the OECD, where the ECB participates as a separate member alongside the Commission in a joint Community delegation. This respects both the independence of the ECB in its field of competence and the need for an efficient, uniform European representation at international level.

---

[396] Cf. the report A5-0307/2003 by Randzio-Plath, which includes in Annex II the 'Answers provided by Mr. Jean-Claude Trichet to the questionnaire drawn up by the Committee on Economic and Monetary Affairs', published at <http://www.europarl.europa.eu/omk/sipade3?L=EN&OBJID=30599&MODE=SIP&NAV=X&LSTDOC=N>.

[397] Cf. Hilf, *Die Organisationsstruktur der Europäischen Gemeinschaften. Rechtliche Gestaltungsmöglichkeiten und Grenzen*, Berlin (1982), p. 42 *et seq.*; Dunnett, 'The European Investment Bank: Autonomous Instrument of Common Policy?' [1994] CML Rev. 721 (at p. 732); Müller-Borle and Balke, in: von der Groeben and Schwarze (Eds.), *Kommentar zum EU- und EG-Vertrag*, Baden-Baden (2004), Art. 266 EG, Randnr. 7; Hütz, in: Grabitz and Hilf (Eds.), *Das Recht der Europäischen Union. Kommentar*, München (last update: August 2006), Art. 9 EGV, Randnr. 4; Rossi, in: Calliess and Ruffert (Eds.), *Kommentar zu EU-Vertrag und EG-Vertrag*, 2nd edition, Neuwied (2002), Art. 266 EGV, Randnr. 4.

[398] Cf. the Agreement establishing the European Bank for Reconstruction and Development [1990] OJ L372/4. On EC membership in the EBRD, cf. Council Decision 90/674/EEC of 19 November 1990 on the conclusion of the Agreement establishing the European Bank for Reconstruction and Development [1990] OJ L372/1. On EIB membership, cf. Decision of the Board of Governors of 11 June 1990 on the membership of the European Investment Bank in the European Bank for Reconstruction and Development [1990] OJ L377/3.

So far, Article 111(4) EC, which would allow the Council, on a proposal from the Commission and after consulting the ECB, to decide on the position of the Community at international level as regards economic and monetary union, and also to decide on its representation, has not been used, even though the Commission made a proposal under this article already on 9 November 1998,[399] and even though the Nice Treaty moved the entire provision to qualified majority voting; the Council so far appears to prefer the *status quo* to the solutions proposed by the Commission to achieve a more efficient external representation in economic and monetary matters. However, in the long run, political decisions on the external representation of the euro will become necessary if the euro area wants to become a strong and active player in international monetary, financial and economic organisations.[400] The often-heard argument against such a consolidation of euro area representation, namely that the necessary adaptation of the relevant international agreements would be a serious hurdle almost impossible to overcome, appears to be a false argument in view of the combined economic and political force of the 13 Member States of the euro area. The interest of several Member States to keep the status quo, which conveniently leaves more room for individual national interests, could be a much better explanation for the present inertia in this respect.[401]

The Constitutional Treaty will, with its Article III-196, facilitate further the Community decision-making process 'in order to secure the euro's place in the international monetary system' and 'to ensure a unified representation within the international financial institutions and conferences',[402] thereby hopefully triggering new efforts to find a satisfactory solution to this almost typical dilemma of Europe's external action.[403] In this respect, the duty of sincere cooperation that

---

[399] COM(1998) 637.

[400] Cf. Bini Smaghi, 'A Single EU Seat in the IMF' [2004] JCMS 229, at p. 245 *et seq.* Cf. also his interview with FT of 29 March 2006 'Eurozone "needs bigger IMF role"', p. 3, where he considers a single EU seat at the IMF to be a 'long-term goal'. Cf. also Selmayr, 'Unabhängigkeit gegenüber Finanzministern sichern. Die Europäische Zentralbank muss im Internationalen Währungsfonds für den Euro sprechen', Financial Times Deutschland of 16 October 2000, p. 29.

[401] Cf. Padoa-Schioppa, *supra* note 210, p. 177 *et seq.*, where he notes critically: 'It is somewhat paradoxical that, in the process of stipulating ad hoc arrangements on who should speak or act on behalf of euroland, the main avocates of a minimalized role were the Europeans themselves. [. . .]. Formal representation was clearly preferred to actual influence.'

[402] See, however, Louis, in: Dony and Bribosia, *supra* note 162, p. 261 (at p. 273), who regrets that Article III-196 of the Constitutional Treaty only enables the Council to take a decision on unified external representation, but does not require it to do so.

[403] Cf. the article 'A single voice for Europe'?, International Herald Tribune of 15 September 2006, available at <http://www.iht.com/articles/2006/09/15/business/euro.php>, which quotes ECB Executive Board member Bini Smaghi as follows: 'When Europe is not a giant, it becomes many little dwarves'. Cf. also Bini Smaghi, 'Powerless Europe: Why is the Euro Area Still a Political Dwarf?' [2006] International Finance 9:2. Cf. also Louis, *supra* note 162, p. 607: 'It is necessary to tackle the question of international representation because it is not acceptable that Euro area Member States continue to express their voice in fields where they are either not competent or they are under commitments to coordinate their policy within the Union.' Cf. also the European Parliament

applies between the Community institutions, the ECB and the Member States and has usefully been reaffirmed by the Constitutional Treaty[404] should become the yardstick of all future arrangements.

C. Involvement of the ECB Prior to the Ratification of Community Agreements

The expertise of the ECB as Europe's monetary authority, combined with its growing international experience, makes it desirable that the ECB is also involved when the Community institutions, in their field of competence, negotiate international agreements which may have an impact on monetary policy in the broad sense. It would, for example, make a lot of sense to involve the ECB at an early stage when an international agreement such as the Hague Convention on the law applicable to certain rights in respect of securities held with an intermediary (agreed on 13 December 2002) is negotiated. The Hague Convention is an international multilateral treaty intended to remove, at a global scale, legal uncertainties for cross-border securities transactions.[405] As soon as the Community and its Member States will have ratified the Hague Convention,[406] its provisions will become an integral part of the Community legal order by virtue of Article 300(7) EC and will have to be implemented in new Community legislation on securities which, in turn, may have a direct impact on the monetary policy instruments of the ECB.[407]

However, it must be noted that an involvement of the ECB is explicitly only foreseen in the internal legal order of the Community where Article 105(4), first indent EC and Article 4(a), first indent of the Statute require consultation of the ECB '*on any proposed Community act in its field of competence*'. From a formalistic point of view, one could therefore argue that the ECB would only need to be

resolution P6_TA(2006)0076 on the strategic review of the International Monetary Fund (2005/2121(INI)) of 14 March 2006, point 9, where the European Parliament 'insists that the European positions in the EU representation within the IMF must be better coordinated; calls on the Member States to work towards a single voting constituency—possibly starting as a euro constituency, with a view, in the longer term, to securing consistent European representation, involving the Ecofin Council Presidency and the Commission, subject to the European Parliament's scrutiny.'

[404] On this, cf. *supra* p. 39.

[405] The heart of the Hague Convention's regime is laid down in Article 4(1), according to which the law applicable to the issues covered by the Convention is the law in force in the State that the relevant intermediary and the account holder have expressly agreed as governing their account agreement. This differs from the regime which is currently applied in the European Community, under which the law applicable to holdings of securities is determined by the location of the account.

[406] Cf. the Commission's Proposal COM(2003) 783 of 15 December 2003 for a Council Decision concerning the signing of the Hague Convention on the Law applicable to certain rights in respect of securities held with an intermediary.

[407] Cf. Devos, 'The Hague Convention on the law applicable to book-entry securities—the relevance for the European System of Central Banks', in: ECB (Ed.), *Legal Aspects of the European System of Central Banks (supra* note 1), p. 377.

consulted once Community legislation intended to implement the Hague Convention will be proposed. However, a consultation at such a late stage, where the substantive issues in such Community legislation will already be pre-determined by the binding international agreement previously agreed upon, would hardly do justice to the 'effet utile' of the requirement to consult the ECB which, as stated by the ECJ, is meant '*to ensure that the legislature adopts the act only when the body has been heard, which, by virtue of the specific functions that it exercises in the Community framework in the area concerned and by virtue of the high degree of expertise that it enjoys, is particularly well placed to play a useful role in the legislative process envisaged*'.[408] If consultation of the ECB took place only after the conclusion of the international agreement in question, the Community legislature could not take the expert advice of the ECB into account as its hands would already be bound by international law. This is why it must be concluded that consultation of the ECB in such a case must already take place *before* the international agreement is entered into by the Community, and thus at a moment where there is still time to change the substance of the international obligations to be accepted by the Community. It should be remembered that non-consultation of the ECB for acts in its field of competence legally constitutes the violation of an essential procedural requirement.[409] In the case of international agreement, this could lead to the problematic situation where the ratification act is annulled by the ECJ, while the Community remains bound to the agreement under international law.

The Hague Convention has been the first example where the Council accepted this 'effet utile'-inspired interpretation of Article 105(4), first indent EC and Article 4(a), first indent of the Statute. On 31 January 2005, the ECB received a request from the Council for an opinion on the Commission proposal to sign the Hague Convention. The ECB delivered its opinion on 17 March 2005[410] and thus at a time when it was still possible to influence the political process. The ECB opinion in particular supported the call for a detailed assessment of the Hague Convention prior to its signing by the Community to clarify a number of legal issues. Such a legal assessment was completed by the Commission on 5 July 2006.[411] For the sake of the consistency of Community law itself and to avoid a discrepancy between the international obligations of the Community and its internal legal order, the case of the Hague Convention will hopefully serve as precedent for an early consultation of the ECB in the case of future international agreements in its field of competence.

---

[408] Case C-11/00, *supra* note 52, para. 110.   [409] Cf. *supra* note 136.

[410] Opinion CON/2005/7 of the ECB of 17 March 2005 at the request of the Council of the European Union on a proposal for a Council decision concerning the signing of the Hague Convention on the Law applicable to certain rights in respect of securities held with an intermediary (COM(2003) 783 final), [2005] OJ C81/10.

[411] Cf. the Commission Press Release IP/06/930 of 5 July 2006 'Securities markets: Commission calls upon Member States to sign Hague Securities Convention'.

IV. Conclusions

Even though its 'pioneer phase' is clearly over, the law of the ECB remains a fascinating field of Community law that continues to evolve further, even though it has meanwhile clearly achieved cruising speed. In many respects, the open and sometimes controversial issues in the law of the ECB reflect the broader issues currently at stake in the constitutional law of the European Union: the need for defining properly the relationship between independent supranational governance and political accountability; the need for finding the right balance in the relations between the Union and its Member States, between national and regional differences, and the need to offer both citizens and economic actors a level-playing field of European dimension, governed by the principle of non-discrimination; and the need for moving towards a more coordinated and thus stronger external action of the Union as a whole. The further development of the law of the ECB will therefore need to be closely watched. In some cases, it may well generate solutions for questions which will remain open in the broader constitutional debate for still some time to come.

The Morphology of Legislative Power in the European Community: Legal Instruments and the Federal Division of Powers

*Robert Schütze**

I. Introduction: The European Community and the Indeterminate Province of Legislation

Each society needs common rules and mechanisms for their production. The concept of legislation is central to all modern societies. Legislation refers to the making of laws (*legis*).[1] 'But what, after all, is a law? As long as we remain satisfied with attaching purely metaphysical ideas to the word, we shall go on arguing without arriving at an understanding; and when we have defined a law of nature, we shall be no nearer the definition of a law of the State.'[2] Rousseau's critique of the indeterminate and metaphysical understandings of the concept of 'a law', expressed in 1762, was not immediately heard. When a few years later, the constitution of the United States of America was adopted, it simply stated that '[a]ll legislative Powers herein granted shall be vested in a Congress of the United States'.[3] The provision only tells us *that* Congress is endowed with legislative power but not *what* legislative power is. The newly born constitutional order of the United States—as many other modern constitutional orders—thus continued to rely on a pre-positivist constitutional conception of legislation with a 'metaphysical' dimension.

So, 'what, after all, is a law?' The concept of 'legislation' is, like all law, an offspring of history. Or more precise: the concept of legislation has been shaped by various national histor*ies*. Two competing conceptions of legislation have emerged in the modern era. The *parliamentary* or *procedural* conception of legislation is tied to our modern understanding of who should be in charge of the legislative function. Legislation is positively defined as every legal act adopted according to the *parliamentary legislative procedur*e. This procedural conception of

* Lecturer in Law, Durham University. I am grateful to A. Antoniadis, D. Chalmers, G. de Búrca and B. de Witte for their comments and suggestions.

[1] Shorter Oxford English Dictionary.
[2] J. J. Rousseau, *The Social Contract* (1762), Book 2, Chapter 6 (translated by G.D.H. Cole) (Dent & Sons, 1955), 29.   [3] Article I, section 1 U.S. Constitution.

legislation has traditionally shaped British and French constitutional thought.[4] In materially defining legislation as legal rules with general application, the *functional* conception of legislation also appeals to our historical precepts. Indeed, the thought that a legislative act represents a *general legal norm* runs through legal history.[5]

Which of these traditions has informed the European Community's constitutionalism? The European Community—born in 1958 with the genetic code of an international organization—could hardly be viewed to reproduce the *trias politica* of a nation state. Article 4 of the EEC Treaty modestly provided: 'The tasks entrusted to the Community shall be carried out by the following institutions: an Assembly, a Council, a Commission, a Court of Justice. Each institution shall act within the limits of the powers conferred upon it by this Treaty.'[6] When the European Community was established, its 'regulatory' competences were not immediately conceived of as of a 'legislative' quality. The nature of the Community in general, and its *decision*-making procedures in particular, defied the parliamentary conception of legislation: the law-making function was until the Single European Act (almost) exclusively in the hands of the Council with the European Parliament having, at most, a consultative function. From the viewpoint of national democracies, it seemed that all decision-making powers of the European Community were 'executive' in character.[7]

As an organic understanding of the separation of powers doctrine had been marred with difficulties, a functional conception of the separation of powers doctrine emerged early on. The three EC governmental branches have, consequently, been defined in the following terms: '[T]he *legislative* power relates to the function of enacting rules with a general and abstractly defined scope of application (this is what a Continental European lawyer would call the "lois matérielles"); the *executive* power relates to the function of applying the said legislative rules to individual cases or specific categories of cases; finally, the *judicial* power relates to the function of settling litigation that arises on the occasion of the application of the legislative rules to individual cases or specific categories of cases[.]'[8] In tandem with a functional understanding of the separation of powers a functional conception of legislative power entered the Community legal order. The procedural variety characterizing Community law-making reinforced the functional perspective brought to the concept of Community legislation.[9]

---

[4] For the British parliamentary definition of legislation, see: A.V. Dicey, *Introduction to the Study of the Law of the Constitution* (Macmillan & Co Ltd, 1961), especially Chapters I and II.

[5] H. Schneider, *Gesetzgebung* (C.F. Müller, 1982), 19.   [6] Article 4(1) EEC.

[7] Early commentators, therefore, spoke of the 'Beschlußrecht' of the Community (cf. H. Wagner, Grundbegriffe des Beschlußrechts der EG (Köln, 1965) as well as R.W. Lauwaars, *Lawfulness and Legal Force of Community Decisions* (A.W. Sijthoff, 1973)). More modern is the characterization of Community legislation as 'executive legislation', see: H.P. Ipsen, Zur Exekutiv-Rechtsetzung in der Europäischen Gemeinschaft, in: P. Badura & R. Scholz (eds.), *Wege und Verfahren des Verfassungslebens. Festschrift für Peter Lerche zum 65. Geburtstag* (Beck, 1993).

[8] K. Lenaerts, 'Some Reflections on the Separation of Powers in the European Community', [1991] 28 C.M.L. Rev. 11–35 at 13.

[9] What happened to the parliamentary or procedural conception of legislation in the Community legal order? Only the slow ascendancy of the European Parliament to become co-legislator with the

So, what, after all, is a *Community* law? Which types of laws does the Community have? What is the 'morphology' of the European Community's legislative instruments? How and to what extent do these legislative acts restrict the autonomy of the Member States? Can the Community choose from among its legislative instruments?

In order to respond to these questions, we shall first revisit the functional concept of Community legislation before presenting the various perspectives from which the legislative instruments have traditionally been examined. Choosing the federal division of legislative power as our privileged viewpoint, the subsequent sections will investigate the legislative and preemptive quality of the various legal acts emanating from the Community. While regulations, directives and State-addressed decisions will be analyzed as forms of 'internal legislation', directly effective international agreements concluded by the Community will be conceptualized as 'external legislation'. We shall briefly enquire when and under what conditions the Community legislator can choose among the various legislative instruments that Article 249 EC provides. The conclusion argues that the introduction of the instrument of a 'framework law' would (re-)federalize and sharpen the morphology of legislative power in the EC.

II. 'Community Legislation': The Nature of Legislation and the (Complex) Principles of Community Authorship

The EC Treaty did not positively define what 'legislative power' is. What then is 'Community legislation'? The question has obviously two dimensions: First, what characterizes a 'legislative' act in the EC legal order? Second, when will this legislative act be attributable to the 'Community'? The first dimension concerns the nature of a legislative norm. The second dimension concerns the question as to when the Community can be considered its author.

A. The First Dimension: The Functional Conception of Legislation in the Community Legal Order

The 'purest' functional conception of legislation emerges in the first half of the twentieth century and is closely associated with *Hans Kelsen* and the Vienna

---

Council under the co-decision procedure—today applicable to the majority of legal competences of the European Community—has cleared the way for the gradual emergence of a parliamentary definition of legislation in the Community legal order. The procedural conception of legislation had, to a large extent, informed the Constitutional Treaty (2004). For a discussion of the conception of legislative power underlying the Constitutional Treaty (2004), see: K. Lenaerts & M. Desomer, 'Towards a Hierarchy of Legal Acts in the European Union? Simplification of Legal Instruments and Procedures', [2005] 11 European Law Journal 744–54 and R. Schütze, *Sharpening the Separation of Powers through a Hierarchy of Norms?* EIPA Working Paper 1/2005=<http://www.eipa.nl/Publications/Summaries/05/FC0501e.pdf>.

School of Pure Law. The pure theory of law started from the premise that *all* public decision-making involved a normative dimension and that there was no ontological distinction between legislative, executive and judicial activities. The tripartite organizational structure of the State was seen as a historical contingency and not as the result of a natural physiological 'constitution' of the State. The Pure Theory of Law, therefore, rejects all 'institutional' or 'ontological' classifications of public acts into *a priori* legislative-executive-judicial. The classification of an act as 'legislative' or 'executive' can only be determined *in relation to* the totality of all legal norms within the legal order. The only recognized distinction in the management of the State was the *functional* dichotomy of 'law-creation' and 'law-application'. This view led to a 'relativistic turn' of the concept of legislation: the function of a normative act is *relative* to the state of development of the legal order.

'But what, after all, is a law?' The Pure Theory of Law distinguishes between 'general' and 'individual' norms that both form part of the legal order and thus constitute 'law'.[10] While the creation of any norm—whether general or individual—could be described as legislation 'in the broad sense', the concept of legislation is ultimately confined to the creation of general norms. Even with this limitation in mind, the activity of legislation will cut across all governmental activities:

By legislative power or legislation one does not understand the entire function of creating law, but a special aspect of this function, the creation of general norms. 'A law'—a product of the legislative process—is essentially a general norm, or a complex of such norms. ('The law' is used as a designation for the totality of legal norms only because we are apt to identify 'the law' with the general form of law and erroneously ignore the existence of individual legal norms.) (...) It never occurs in political reality that all the general norms of a national legal order have to be created exclusively by one organ designated as legislator. *There is no legal order of a modern State according to which the courts and administrative authorities are excluded from creating general legal norms, that is, from legislating, and legislating not only on the basis of statutes and customary law, but also directly on the basis of the constitution.* (...) The general norms created by these organs are called ordinances or

---

[10] H. Kelsen, *General Theory of Law and State* (Russell & Russell, 1945), 38. The passage on which Kelsen relies on comes from the first lecture of Austin's classic study of 'The Province of Jurisprudence Determined' and reads as follows: 'Commands are of two species. Some are *laws* or *rules*. The others have not acquired an appropriate name, nor does language afford an expression which will make them briefly and precisely. I must, therefore, name them as well as I can by the ambiguous and inexpressive name of '*occasional* or *particular* commands'. The term *laws* or *rules* being not infrequently applied to occasional or particular commands, it is hardly possible to describe a line of separation which shall consist in every respect with established forms of speech. (...) By every command, the party to whom it is directed is obliged to do or to forbear. Now where it obliges *generally* to acts or forbearances of a *class*, a command is a law or rule. But where it obliges a *specific* act or forbearance, or to acts or forbearance, which it determines *specifically* or *individually*, a command is occasional or particular.' (J. Austin, *The Province of Jurisprudence Determined* (CUP, 1995) at 25).

regulations or have specific designations; but *functionally* they have the same character as statutes enacted by an organ called legislator.[11]

The legislative function is, according to Kelsen, never allocated to only one governmental branch. The nature of a public act is not determined by the institution emitting it or by the legal instrument used. 'Laws', 'regulations' or 'judgments' are not automatically of a (respectively) 'legislative', 'executive' or 'judicial' nature. Rather, it is their effects within the legal order—are they creating general norms or only individual ones—that determine if they are 'legislative' or merely 'executive' acts. The Vienna School can, consequently, refer to *parliamentary* legislation, *executive* legislation and *judicial* legislation without running into linguistic contradictions.[12] Judicial acts may create general legal norms, where they assume the character of a precedent.[13] 'Legislation' is *functionally* defined as that part of law-creation that produces *generally applicable* legal norms in a legal order.

What is a general norm and what is an individual norm? Kelsen defines the latter as 'norms which determine the behaviour of *one individual in one non-recurring situation and which therefore are valid only for one particular case and may be obeyed or applied only once*' and gives the example of a court judgment whose binding force is limited to the particular situation it decides.[14] The criterion of an act's 'generality' and 'individuality' is therefore identified with its scope of application: general norms apply generally; individual norms only apply to their specified addressee(s).

From this functional perspective, what are legislative acts in the Community legal order? Legislative power means legal power. A legislative rule must be an objectively binding rule. Contracts are also binding. Yet, they are not 'law' as their binding nature is conditional.[15] The breach of contract by one party may serve as justification for not adhering to the terms of the contract by the other party. This normative *reciprocity* will not be found in legislation: a legislative rule will be

---

[11] H. Kelsen, above n.10 at 256, 269–70 (emphasis added).

[12] Kelsen points out that our thinking of legislation as 'parliamentary legislation' has been conditioned by a habit of linguistic simplification. In everyday language, we tend to speak only of one legislator—that is in democracies: parliament—and label only its acts as 'legislation': 'Thus one can hardly speak of any separation of legislation from the other functions of the State in the sense of the so-called 'legislative' organ to the exclusion of the so-called 'executive' and 'judicial' organs—would alone be competent to exercise this function. The appearance of such a separation exists because only those general norms that are created by the 'legislative' organ are designated as 'laws' (leges). (. . .) This organ never has a monopoly on the creation of general norms, but at most a certain favoured position such as was previously characterized. Its designation as legislative organ is the more justified the greater the part it has in the creation of general norms' (*ibid.*, 272–3).

[13] Courts 'exercise a legislative function when their decision in a concrete case becomes a precedent for the decision of other similar cases. A court with this competence creates by its decision a general norm which is on a level with statutes originating with the so-called legislative organ' (*ibid.*, 272). [14] Kelsen, *ibid.*, 38 (emphasis added).

[15] Contracts are typically reciprocal in nature: the primary obligation to fulfil the contract is contingent on the fulfilment of the norms by the other party. A breach of contract by one party typically releases the other party from its (primary) obligation under the contract. According to

enforceable against all the persons to whom it applies—regardless of whether it has been violated by some of its subjects.

Is the EC Treaty a treaty or institutional law? In *Commission v Luxembourg & Belgium*,[16] the defendants had argued that 'since international law allows a party, injured by the failure of another party to perform its obligations, to withhold performance of its own, the Commission has lost the right to plead infringement of the Treaty'. The Court did not accept this contractual reading of the EC Treaty as the latter was 'not limited to creating reciprocal obligations between the different natural and legal persons to whom it is applicable, but establishes a new legal order, which governs the powers, rights and obligations of the said persons, as well as the necessary procedures for taking cognizance of and penalizing any breach of it'.[17]

In *Commission v Italy*,[18] the European Court of Justice extended that line of argument to secondary law adopted on the basis of the EC Treaty. Italy had failed to implement a Community directive in time and the Court held that 'any delays there may have been on the part of the other Member States in performing obligations imposed by a Directive may not be invoked by a Member State in order to justify its own, even temporary, failure to perform its obligations'.[19] The non-reciprocal binding effect evidenced that the Community's legal instruments under Article 249 EC were indeed 'a law of an institutional and not of a contractual nature'.[20]

What about international agreements concluded by the Community? Will their normative character fall on the contractual side, or will their legislative side prevail? The constitutional possibility of 'external legislation' has been explored for more than 200 years in the US American constitutional order. Section 2 of Article VI of the US Constitution states: 'This Constitution, and the Laws of the United States which shall be made in Pursuance thereof; and *all treaties made, or which shall be made, under the Authority of the United States, shall be the supreme Law of the Land*; and the Judges in every State shall be bound thereby[.]'[21] The supremacy clause was

---

O.W. Holmes, '[t]he only universal consequence of a legally binding promise is, that the law makes the promisor pay damages if the promised event does not come to pass. In every case it leaves him free from Interference until the time for fulfilment has gone by, and therefore free to break his contract if he chooses' (O.W. Holmes Jr., *The Common Law* (Little, Brown & Company, 1881), 301). In this point, we depart from H. Kelsen as for him the concept of legislation may include public and private law creation: 'The legal transaction is an act by which the individuals authorized by the legal order regulate certain relations legally. It is a law-creating act, for it produces legal duties and rights of the parties who enter the transaction. (...) By the legal transaction, individual and sometimes even general norms are created regulating the mutual behaviour of the parties' (H. Kelsen, above n.10 at 137).

[16] *Commission v Luxemburg and Belgium*, Case 90, 91/63, [1964] E.C.R. 625.
[17] *Ibid.*, 631.   [18] *Commission v Italy*, Case 52/75, [1976] E.C.R. 277.
[19] *Ibid.*, para. 11.
[20] P. Pescatore, *The law of Integration: emergence of a new phenomenon in international relations, based on the experience of the European Communities* (Sijthoff, 1974), 67 and 69.
[21] Emphasis added.

a clear choice in favour of monism that allows international treaties to be regarded as 'external legislation'. In *Foster v Neilson*, we read:

A treaty is in its nature a contract between two nations, not a legislative act. It does not generally effect, of itself, the object to be accomplished, especially so far as its operation is infra-territorial; but is carried into execution by the sovereign power of the respective parties to the instrument.

In the United States a different principle is established. Our constitution declares a treaty to be the law of the land. It is, consequently, to be regarded in courts of justice as *equivalent to an act of the legislature, whenever it operates of itself without the aid of any legislative provision*. But when the terms of the stipulation import a contact, when either of the parties engages to perform a particular act, the treaty addresses itself to the political, not the judicial department; and the legislature must execute the contract before it can become a rule for the Court.[22]

An international treaty will be 'equivalent' to a legislative act, where the treaty 'operates of itself'. Self-executing international treaties will have a 'two-fold effect': 'It is an international agreement of the United States and, to the extent that it is intended to have domestic effects and consequences, the treaty is also a law of the United States, as much as an act of Congress.'[23]

In the EC constitutional order, a similar approach has been adopted. The Community legal order has signalled its 'monist' stance towards international treaties: Community agreements enter the Community legal order without the need for an additional act of transposition or incorporation.[24] International treaties 'form an integral part of the Community legal system' from the date of their entry into force.[25] Furthermore, Community agreements are treated like 'unilateral' acts of the Community institutions: 'As far as the Community is concerned, an agreement concluded by the Council with a non-member country in accordance with the provisions of the EC Treaty is an act of a Community institution, and the provisions of such an agreement form an integral part of Community law.'[26] Community treaties are, consequently, 'external' Community

---

[22] *Foster v Neilson*, [1829] 27 U.S. (2 Pet.) 253 at 314 (emphasis added).

[23] L. Henkin, 'The treaty makers and the law-makers: the law of the land and foreign relations', [1958–9] 107 University of Pennsylvania Law Review 903–36 at 906.

[24] The constitutional practice of concluding international agreements through decisions *sui generis* shows that international treaties themselves constitute the direct source of legal rights and obligations within the Community legal order.

[25] *Haegemann v Belgium*, Case 181/73, [1974] E.C.R. 449, para.5.

[26] *A. Racke GmbH & Co v Hauptzollamt Mainz*, C-162/96, [1998] E.C.R. 3655, para.41. A more 'dualist' position underlies *Commission v France*, Case 327/91, [1994] E.C.R. 3641 in which the ECJ insisted that the 'act' under review was not the agreement itself, but the 'treaty law' adopted to conclude the treaty. This interpretation has received academic support from T. Hartley. Hartley has claimed that the argument that the agreement itself is a Community act 'falls down since it confuses a unilateral act—which is surely what the drafters of [Article 234] must have had in mind—with a bilateral act.' (T. Hartley, 'International Agreements and the Community legal system: Some recent Developments', [1983] 8 E.L. Rev. 383–92 at 391). International agreements are accordingly considered an 'anomalous source of *Community* law' as they have their 'origin outside the Community legal

law.[27] They are equivalent to 'internal' Community legislation and part of 'the law of the land'.

Let us now turn to the 'legislative' quality of internally or externally produced Community law. In accord with the functional conception of legislation, the Community legal order has identified the legislative quality of a norm with its general application: 'The essential characteristic of a decision arises from the limitation of persons to whom it is addressed, whereas a regulation, being essentially of a *legislative nature, is applicable not to a limited number of persons, named or identifiable, but to categories of persons viewed in the abstract and in their entirety.*'[28] The functional distinction between normative acts of general application and individual normative acts has thus shaped the concept of legislation in the Community legal order. Only the former are regarded as Community legislation.

In the light of the mutual autonomy of the Community and the national legal orders, normative rules that only bind the Community institutions or the Member States will represent individual 'decisions'. They lack generality to be legislative acts. (From a functional perspective, a directive addressed to all Member States and without direct effect for third parties will constitute an individual act addressed to 25 identifiable addressees.) We shall see in the fifth part of this chapter, how the general effect of a Community norm is intimately tied to its direct effect in the national legal order. The direct and general effect of a Community norm constitute the basis for the concept of Community legislation. They are not the 'consequences' of EC legislation; they are its preconditions.[29]

B. The Second Dimension: Community Authorship— In Search for a 'Rule of Recognition'

In *whom* does the EC Treaty vest legislative power? What constitutional principles attest the Community authorship of a legal rule?[30] Will all acts adopted within the

---

order and are, in part, the acts of non-member states' (T.C. Hartley, *The foundations of European Community law: an introduction to the constitutional and administrative law of the European Community* (OUP, 2003), 159).

[27] The term 'external Community law' seems to have been first employed by J.H.J. Bourgeois, 'Effects of International Agreements in European Community Law: Are the Dice Cast?', [1983–4] 82 Michigan Law Review 1250–1273 at 1272.

[28] *Union de Federaciones Agrarias de Espana (UFADE) v Council*, Case 117/86, [1986] E.C.R. 3255, para.9 (emphasis added).

[29] *Contra*, J.A. Usher, *EC Institutions and Legislation* (Longman, 1998) 144.

[30] On the concept of authorship, see: A. von Bogdandy, F. Arndt & J. Bast, 'Legal Instruments in European Union Law and their Reform: A Systematic Approach on an Empirical Basis', [2004] 23 Y.E.L. 91–136 at 121. The attribution of legal acts to the EU is portrayed as a two-step process: 'a legal act is first attributed to an authoring institution (Council, Commission, etc.). (. . .) Mediated by the adopting institution an act is then attributed to the legal personality of the organization (the Communities and/or the European Union, depending on its legal basis and the general understanding of the Union's organizational structure.)' It is then claimed that '[i]n general, by focusing on the

institutional framework of the European Community be considered *Community rules?* In what situations, if any, are the Member States viewed as the collective authors of a legal rule? In theoretical terms, these practical questions could be bundled into the quest for an ultimate 'rule of recognition' for the EC legal order. The latter has been defined in the following terms:

> Whenever a rule of recognition is accepted, both private persons and officials are provided with authoritative criteria for identifying primary rules of obligation (...) In a very simple system like the world of Rex I (...), where only what he enacts is law and no legal limitations upon his legislative power are imposed by customary rule or constitutional document, the sole criterion for identifying the law will be a simple reference to the fact of enactment by Rex I. The existence of this simple form of rule of recognition will be manifest in the general practice, on the part of officials or private persons, of identifying the rules by this criterion. In a modern legal system where there are a variety of 'sources' of law, the rule of recognition is correspondingly more complex[.] (...) For the most part the rule of recognition is not stated, but its existence is *shown* in the way in which particular rules are identified, either by courts or other officials or private persons or their advisors.[31]

When will a rule belong to the Community legal order? Can we identify a rule (or various rules) of recognition in the EC legal order? Uncertainty about the Community authorship of a rule has existed in relation to at least four decision-making aspects: rules adopted by unanimity in the Council, mixed acts, decisions of international bodies and, finally, the EC Treaty itself. The ways in which the

decision which ultimately determines the wording of an act, Union law has developed a convincing criterion for designating both the legal and political responsibility' (*ibid.*,123). However, this abstract definition evades the very essence of the problem of Community authorship. When is 'the decision that ultimately determines the wording of the act' a *Community* decision? When does the 'Council' act as a Community institution, and when do the Member States act within the Council? Is a mixed act a Community act? These questions are not at all as easy as the authors want us to believe. Indeed, even in the rather mundane context of access to documents, the 'authorship rule' has been the source of constant disputes (S. Peers, 'The New Regulation on Access to Documents: A Critical Analysis', [2001–2] 21 Y.E.L. 385–442 at 392–3). More controversial still has been the discussion about the paternity of legal acts adopted within the Second and Third Pillar: while some commentators see them as acts of the European Union, others have argued that they ought to be attributed to the Member States (e.g. M. Pechstein & C. Koenig, *Die Europäische Union* (Mohr Siebeck, 2000), 80: 'Zurechnungsendsubjekte der Handlungen der Unionsorgane im Rahmen der GASP und der PJZS [können] nur die Vertragsstaaten des Unionsvertrages selbst sein'). Finally, the question of the (institutional) paternity of an act is different from the question of whether the Community legal order chooses to integrate legal norms generated in *non*-Community legal sources, such as customary international law. These legal acts—while created outside the Community legal order—could be given the *same legal effects* as Community law. That, however, does not turn them into 'natural' Community law.

[31] H.L.A. Hart, *The Concept of Law* (Clarendon, 1994) 100–1 (emphasis in original). For the international legal order, Hart accepted, however, that 'international law simply consists of a *set* of separate primary rules of obligation' which are not united into a single rule of recognition (*ibid.*, 233). 'It is, therefore, a mistake to suppose that a basic rule of recognition is a generally necessary condition of the existence of rules of obligation or 'binding' rules. *This is not a necessity, but a luxury,* found in advanced social systems' (*ibid.*, 235 (emphasis added)).

European Court of Justice has 'shown' the existence of a particular rule of recognition will be discussed for each of them in the following section.

(i) Unanimous Decision-making in the Council

The parallelism between unanimously agreed unilateral acts and international treaties 'has its basis in the undisputed fact that the consent of all the participating countries is a requirement which the two kinds of instruments share in common'.[32] '[A] general norm adopted by unanimous decision of an international organ composed of representatives of all parties to the treaty establishing the organ is not different from a norm created by a treaty entered into by States upon which the norm is binding'.[33] The difficulty in clearly distinguishing between unilateral and multilateral instruments originates in the double capacity in which States can act within the framework of an international organization:

A State that votes for the adoption of a law-making resolution by an international organ acts in a double capacity. On the one hand, it expresses its assent to the rights and duties formulated in the enactment, and, on the other, it contributes to the creation of what now becomes the *voluntas* of the organization, i.e. an act the authorship of which must be attributed to the organization as a corporate body and not to individual consenting members nor to the members collectively. In unanimous decisions these two elements are so well balanced that it is not possible to regard either of them as being preponderant with respect to the other. *But the undeniable analogies between a unanimous law-making resolution and a treaty come to an end when the former has been definitely adopted and becomes part of the law of the organization.* From that moment the validity, binding force, application and termination of the regulative act of the international organization, whether unanimous or not, is governed not by the law of treaties but solely by the law of the international organization which is the author of the act. Instruments which are not subject of the law of treaties are not treaties.[34]

In relation to the Community legal order, when should unanimously agreed acts be conceptualized as *unilateral* acts of the Council and when ought they to be viewed as *multilateral* contractual engagements between the Member States? The unilateral or multilateral character of unanimously agreed acts adopted in the Council was at stake in *Commission v Italy*.[35] The Italian government had invoked a 'treaty' reservation to deny the binding force of a decision taken on the basis of Article 308 EC. The Italians had referred to the negotiations within the Council 'during which the parties retained the independence which they enjoyed by virtue of their sovereignty'. This was taken to mean that 'in spite of its form, the nature of this decision is that of an *international agreement*' with the effect that 'statements made

---

[32] K. Skubiszewski, 'Enactment of Law by International Organizations', [1965–6] 41 British Yearbook of International law, 198–274 at 221.

[33] H. Kelsen, *Principles of International Law* (New York, 1952) 366.

[34] K. Skubiszewski, above n. 32 (emphasis added).

[35] *Commission v Italy*, Case 38/69, [1970] E.C.R. 47.

by a contracting party at the conclusion of such negotiations form an integral part of the agreement reached'.³⁶ The European Court of Justice was not pleased with this argument:

> The power to take the measures envisaged by this article [i.e. Article 308 EC] is conferred, *not on the Member States acting together, but on the Council in its capacity as a Community institution.* Under [Article 308] the Council acts on a proposal from the Commission and after consulting the [Parliament]. Although the effect of the measures taken in this manner by the Council is in some respects to supplement the treaty, they are adopted within the context of the objectives of the Community. In these circumstances, *a measure which is in the nature of a Community decision on the basis of its objective and of the institutional framework within which it has been drawn up cannot be described as an 'international agreement'.*³⁷

Measures adopted under Article 308 EC are *Community* acts and not multilateral international agreements. Community authorship was assumed for the Council acted 'in its capacity as a Community institution' within the institutional framework of the Community.

But can the 'Council' choose *not* to act in its capacity as a Community institution? Put differently, are the Member States free to decide when they want to act 'as' the Council and when only 'within' the Council? In *ERTA*, the European Court of Justice had to tackle the issue.³⁸ Here, the Member States—unhappy with a Commission proposal—had simply adopted 'proceedings' in order to coordinate their position for the negotiation of an international agreement. The Commission disliked being side-tracked and went to Court. The Council questioned the very admissibility of the annulment action, for it disputed the 'Community nature' of the act. The proceedings were, after all, 'nothing more than a coordination of policies among the Member States within the framework of the Council'.³⁹

The Court admitted that the legal effect of the proceedings would differ 'according to whether they are regarded as constituting the exercise of powers conferred on the Community, or as acknowledging the coordination by the Member States of the exercises of powers which remained vested in them'.⁴⁰ It then referred to Article 230 which permitted the review of the legality of Council acts other than recommendations and opinions, finding that the Article covered all 'measures *adopted by the institutions* which are intended to have legal force'.⁴¹ The fundamental question, however, remained: were these proceedings an act of the Council?

---

³⁶ *Ibid.*, para.9 (emphasis added).   ³⁷ *Ibid.*, paras.10–11 (emphasis added).
³⁸ *Commission v Council (ERTA)*, Case 22–70, [1971] E.C.R. 263.   ³⁹ *Ibid.*, para.36.
⁴⁰ *Ibid.*, para.4.
⁴¹ *Ibid.*, para.39 (emphasis added). And a little later we read: 'It would be inconsistent with this objective to interpret the conditions under which the action is admissible so restrictively as to limit the availability of this procedure merely to the categories of measures referred to by [Article 249]. An action for annulment must therefore be available in the case of all measures adopted by the institutions, whatever their nature or form, which are intended to have legal effects' (*ibid.*, paras.41–2).

In a Byzantine reasoning, the Court simply cut through the question of authorship. The 'Council' was simply equated with the 'Member States acting within the Council': '[T]he *Council's* proceedings dealt with a matter falling within the power of the Community' and therefore the proceedings 'could not have been simply the expression or recognition of a voluntary coordination, but were designed to lay down a course of action binding on both the institutions and the Member States, and destined ultimately to be reflected in the tenor of the [Community] regulation.'[42] The proceedings were thus treated as an act of the Community—irrespective of the absence of a Commission proposal—because the matter fell within the power of the Community. The Court hastened to add that while it was for the Council to 'decide in each case whether it is expedient to enter into an agreement with third countries, it does not enjoy a discretion to decide whether to proceed through inter-governmental or Community channels'.[43] The Court's conclusion smacked of a contradiction in terms, for '[t]he Council is but a Community organ. It has no intergovernmental double.'[44]

Will this mean that all rules adopted within the institutional framework or competence of the Community are *Community* rules? No, it will not. While the *ERTA* Court treated an *inter se* agreement between all Member States as an act of the Council, subsequent jurisprudence clarified that not all such *inter se* agreements would be assimilated to Community acts. In *Hurd*,[45] the Statute and the First Protocol of the European School was the subject of a national preliminary reference.[46] The Court pointed out that both were *international* agreements concluded by the Member States and that the 'mere fact that those agreements are linked to the Community and to the functioning of the institutions does not mean that they must be regarded as an integral part of Community law'.[47] Member States can, therefore, act *through* the Council as well as *within* the Council.

Indeed *inter se* co-ordination within the Council had become an established constitutional practice by the early 1970s. Among these, 'decisions of the Member States meeting in the Council' reflect the most popular and controversial category. The mouthful name is a misnomer: they are not unilateral acts—as the concept of

---

[42] *Ibid.*, para.53 (emphasis added).

[43] *Ibid.*, para.70. Would it not have been clearer to state that it was not for the *Member States* to freely choose whether to pursue a given project through international or Community channels? To add to the legal fictitiousness, the Court later admitted that is was not really the Council but the Member States acting 'in the interest and on behalf of the Community in accordance with their obligations under [Article 10] of the Treaty' (ERTA, para.90).

[44] 'Der Rat ist rechtlich nur Gemeinschaftsorgan. Er hat keinen intergouvernementalen Doppelgänger.' (C. Sasse, 'Zur Auswärtigen Gewalt der Europäischen Wirtschaftsgemeinschaft', [1971] 6 Europarecht. 208–241 at 215).

[45] *Derrick Guy Edmund Hurd v Kenneth Jones (Her Majesty's Inspector of Taxes)*, Case 44/84, [1986] E.C.R. 29.

[46] Statute of the European School of 12 April 1957 (United Nations Treaty Series, Volume 443, 129) and First Protocol of 13 April 1962 (United Nations Treaty Series, Volume 752, 267).

[47] *Derrick Guy Edmund Hurd*, para.20.

'decision' wrongly suggests, but international agreements.[48] 'En réalité, elles ne relèvent pas du droit interne des Communautés, mais bien du droit international. Ceci a pour conséquence notamment que de telles décisions ne peuvent pas être prises autrement que par accord mutuel des Etats membres, conformément au principe de 'égalité souveraine des Etats.' 'Il s'agit, somme toute, d'accords internationaux «en forme simplifiée», conclus dans le cadre offert par le Conseil des Communautés.'[49] Legal authorship ought to be attributed to the Member States, not the Community: They are 'complementary' to, but not itself, Community law.

So, when do the Member States act 'through' the Council and when 'within' the Council? Are there solid constitutional principles that determine when the Council as a Community institution authors a norm? Will all measures adopted according to a Community decision-making procedure be regarded as unilateral Community acts? In *European Parliament v Council and Commission*,[50] the Parliament cleverly argued that it was the Commission proposal, which would show that the act was adopted by the Council and not the collectivity of the Member States. The Court 'clarified' that according to Article 230 EC 'acts adopted by representatives of the Member States acting not in their capacity as members of the Council, but as representatives of their governments, and thus collectively exercising the powers of the Member States, are not subject to judicial review by the Court'.[51] The Commission proposal—this quintessential characteristic of Community law-making—was, however, not conclusive for assuming Community paternity for a legal rule: 'Not all proposals from the Commission necessarily constitute proposals within the meaning of Article 249 of the Treaty. *Their legal character must be assessed in the light of all the circumstances in which they were made.* They may just as well constitute mere initiatives taken in the form of informal proposals.'[52] Commission involvement will, consequently, be no DNA-proof for the *Community* paternity of an act adopted *within* the Council. (Nor, we should assume, will the involvement of the European Parliament represent an infallible proof of the Community authorship of a legal rule.) The Court preferred a flexible contextual approach.

(ii) Mixed Legal Acts

What is the EC's constitutional position as regards the paternity for 'mixed acts'? Are they considered Community acts or international acts authored by the

---

[48] B. de Witte, *Chameleonic Member States: Differentiation by means of Partial and Parallel International Agreements*, in: B. de Witte, D. Hanf, E. Vos (eds.), *The Many Faces of Differentiation in EU Law* (Intersentia, 2001), at 251–2. This is not uncontested. For the opposite view, see: H.P. Ipsen, *Europäisches Gemeinschaftsrecht* (J.C.B. Mohr, 1972) at 472: 'Da uneigentliche Ratsbeschlüsse ihrem *Gegenstande* und ihrer *Intention* nach *gemeinschaftsbezogen* sind, zählen sie insoweit zum Handlungsinstrumentarium des *Gemeinschaftsrechts*. Aus demselben Grunde sind sie auch im Entstehungsverfahren und hinsichtlich ihrer Kontrolle *tunlichts* dem Gemeinschaftsrecht zuzuordnen.'

[49] P. Pescatore, *L'ordre juridique des Communautés Européennes* (Presse universitaire de Liège, 1971), 140.

[50] *European Parliament v Council and Commission*, Case 181/91 and 248/91, [1993] E.C.R. 3685.   [51] *Ibid.*, para.12.

[52] *Ibid.*, para.18 (emphasis added). The Commission proposal was not regarded as essential to adopt *Community* legislation for measures under Article 67 EC during the transitional period of five years.

Member States, or both? The concept of mixity has long been part of the Community legal order— both in its internal and its external spheres. Internally, mixed acts have been employed as a form of co-operation in areas such as education and culture. They are adopted by the 'Council *and* the national Ministers meeting in the Council'. The decision-making body constitutes a 'legal hybrid'. Its acts have been characterized as 'communitarised' intergovernmental acts'.[53] Is this supposed to mean that the Community is not the natural father, but has nonetheless 'adopted' these intergovernmental acts into the Community legal family? A less metaphysical answer has been given by the Court in the external sphere: 'mixed agreements concluded by the Community, its Member States and non-member countries have the same status in the Community legal order as purely Community agreements, as these are provisions coming within the scope of Community competence'.[54] To the extent that norms within mixed agreements fall within the Community sphere, they are regarded as (external) *Community* legislation.

(iii) Decisions of External International Bodies

The absence of a clear 'rule of recognition' for the paternity of a legal rule emerges again in relation to decisions of international bodies set up by a Community agreement. These decisions, the Court of Justice found, may form an integral part of the Community legal order 'in the same way as the Agreement itself' where 'they are directly connected with the Agreement to which they give effect'.[55] Opinion 1/76, on the other hand, qualifies that statement. There, the Court had been asked to review the establishment of an international organ endowed with legislative powers to implement the objectives of the envisaged draft agreement. The body consisted—with the exception of Ireland—of a delegate from each Member State and Switzerland as well as a Commission representative. Decisions were to be taken by majority. The Commission had no vote. The marginal influence of the Community institutions had raised doubts as to the constitutionality of the arrangement for 'the decisions which are taken by the organs of the draft Agreement *cannot be considered as the action of the Community institutions*'.[56] For the Council, the international body was an 'external organ'.[57] Its decisions ought, consequently, not be considered as Community legislation.

The Court agreed. The role of the Community institutions was 'extremely limited': the 'determinate functions in the operation of the fund are performed by

---

[53] B. de Witte, 'The Scope of Community Powers in Education and Culture in the Light of Subsequent Practice', in: R. Bieber and G. Ress (eds.), *Die Dynamik des Europäischen Gemeinschaftsrechts* (Nomos, 1987) 261 at 274 and 276.

[54] *Commission v Ireland*, case 13/00, [2002] E.C.R. 2943, para.14.

[55] *Sevince*, Case 192/89 [1990] E.C.R. 3461, para.9.

[56] Opinion 1/76 (Inland Waterways), [1977] E.C.R. 741 (emphasis added), Council Submissions, 750 (emphasis added).   [57] *Ibid.*

the States' in such a way that the Member States would act 'in place of the Community'.[58] Decisions of the Fund could consequently not be classified as Community action. Furthermore, the Court specified three negative criteria that would, *ipso facto*, be incompatible with the concept of 'common action': (a) the complete exclusion, even if voluntary, of a Member State from the decision-making process, (b) the power of certain Member States to 'opt-out' from an activity, and (c) the existence of special prerogatives for certain Member States at variance with the constitutional principles governing the relations between the Member States of the Community.[59]

In sum, not all decisions of international bodies that are directly connected with the agreement to which they give effect will pass the Opinion 1/76 test. The Court will presumably apply a contextual approach and weigh, in each specific case, the respective importance of the Community and the Member State elements in the decision-making process. Only where the Community element prevails *and* where the decision-making process adheres to the three constitutional guidelines will the directly and generally effective decisions of international bodies represent *Community* legislation.

(iv) The EC Treaty as Primary Community Legislation?

Let us discuss one final point. Should the EC Treaty itself be characterized as Community legislation? In *Van Gend & Loos*, the European Court had found that an article of the EC Treaty could have 'direct application in national law in the sense that nationals of member States may on the basis of this article lay claim to rights which the national court must protect'.[60] Directly effective Treaty articles may even be enforced against other individuals.[61] Directly effective Treaty provisions of a general character, therefore, fall within the functional concept of legislation. Should these provisions, consequently, be regarded as 'constitutional legislation'? The classification of constitutional provisions as a special form of legislation is not unknown.[62]

Should the EC Treaty thus be conceptualized as the Community's 'constitutional legislation' or 'primary' Community legislation? That will depend on whether we can attribute these constitutional norms to the Community. The creation and/or amendment of a constitutional norm are governed by Article 48 TEU. New constitutional legislation requires the ratification by all the Member States in accordance with their respective constitutional requirements. The legislative procedure principally leaves the Member States as '*Herren der*

---

[58] *Ibid.*, paras.9, 11.   [59] *Ibid.*
[60] *Van Gend en Loos*, Case 26/62, [1963] E.C.R. 1 at 11.
[61] *Defrenne v Sabena*, Case 43/75, [1976] E.C.R. 455 in relation to Article 141 EC.
[62] It can be found in the German constitutional order. Here, constitutional provisions can be amended by means of parliamentary legislation in a qualified legislative procedure, see: Article 79 Basic Law.

Verträge': '[T]he member States as a collective whole retain an essential capacity, that of the "constituent power". It is the States which made the Community's constitution ... It is true that some attempt has been made to "domesticate" the exercise of that power by making it subject to a Community procedure which involves action in the Commission, the [Parliament] and the Council, and sometimes even the Court of Justice. But in the last analysis revision of the constitution is carried out by means of treaties signed and ratified by the member States.'[63] The collectivity of the Member States—not the Community—thus constitutes the author of the constitutional norm. In the Community legal order of today, constitutional legislation is, therefore, not *Community* legislation.[64] Technically speaking, it is therefore wrong to refer to Community acts adopted on the basis of the EC Treaty as 'secondary *legislation*' of the Community. Community secondary law is *primary* Community legislation.[65]

III. Choosing Perspectives: The System of Legal Instruments and The Federal Division of Powers

Morphology is the science of forms and structures.[66] The morphology of legal power will, thus, investigate the forms and structures of legal instruments. A system of legal instruments should offer distinct normative formats for legal action.[67] Forcing public actions into pre-defined formats will, thereby, increase

[63] P. Pescatore, 'International law and Community Law', [1970] 7 C.M.L. Rev. 167–83 at 179.

[64] This statement would need to be qualified only once the doctrine of judicial precedent was to become formally accepted in the Community legal order. Today, however, judgments of the ECJ—while certainly 'acts of an institution'—are only binding *inter partes* and do thus not produce legal effects *erga omnes*. ECJ judgments 'cannot, therefore, create rights and obligations in a *general way*' and it 'may therefore be concluded that the judgments of the European Court are *not sources* but *authoritative evidences* of Community law' (A.G. Toth, 'The Authority of Judgements of the European Court of Justice: Binding Force and Legal Effects' [1984] Y.E.L. 1–77 at 69–70). Only the formal recognition of a doctrine of precedent would transform the ECJ's judgments from individual norms into judicial *legislation*. This judicial legislation would then even assume constitutional quality in so far as the Court of Justice interprets primary law.

[65] The terms 'secondary law' and 'secondary legislation' have, unfortunately, been employed indiscriminately by the European Court (cf. *Commission v Germany*, Case 61/94, para.52: 'When the wording of secondary Community legislation [*sic!*] is open to more than one interpretation (. . .) the primacy of international agreements concluded by the Community over provisions of secondary legislation means that such provisions must, so far as possible, be interpreted in manner that is consistent with those agreements.') as well as academics (cf. N. Foster, *EC Legislation (Blackstone's Statute Book)* (OUP, 2006), 1, referring to the EC Treaty as 'Primary legislation', J.A. Usher, *EC Institutions and Legislation* (Longman, 1998) 128, referring to the Article 249 EC instruments as 'Community secondary legislation' and P.M. Raworth, *The legislative Process in the European Community* (Kluwer, 1993), 112, referring to the 'tertiary legislation of the Commission' under Article 211 EC). Since the EC Treaty is not *Community* legislation, it is terminologically cleaner to refer to the EC Treaty as primary or constitutional law, to Community secondary law as ('primary') legislation and to delegated legislation as 'secondary' legislation or, if need be, 'tertiary' Community law.

[66] The Chambers Dictionary (Chambers Harrap, 2000).

[67] E. Schmidt-Aßmann, *Das allgemeine Verwaltungsrecht als Ordnungsidee* (Springer, 2004), 298–301.

the rationality of a legal system. The disciplining effect of a legal morphology reinforces the rule of law. The assumption that each Community instrument represents a particular format of normative characteristics has been as old as the Community itself. The 'formality principle' has been said to require the Community legislator to choose the *adequate* instrumental form depending on the material content of the legal act.[68]

The EC legal order envisages a variety of legal instruments for Community action. The 'typical' Community instruments are listed in Article 249 EC.[69] The provision states:

In order to carry out their task and in accordance with the provisions of this Treaty, the European Parliament acting jointly with the Council, the Council and the Commission shall make regulations and issue directives, take decisions, make recommendations or deliver opinions.

A regulation shall have general application. It shall be binding in its entirety and directly applicable in all Member States.

A directive shall be binding, as to the result to be achieved, upon each Member State to which it is addressed, but shall leave to the national authorities the choice of form and methods.

A decision shall be binding in its entirety upon those to whom it is addressed.

Recommendations and opinions shall have no binding force.

In 1958, each instrument enumerated in Article 249 seemed characterized by a distinct normative format. The 'regulation' appeared as the Community's legislative instrument. The 'directive' seemed an intergovernmental instrument that could only bind States. The 'decision' was only legally binding for those to whom it was addressed. 'Recommendations' and 'opinions' lacked the quintessential element of 'hard law' as they were not legally binding at all.[70]

---

[68] For the Community this argument has been made by E. Fuß: 'Schließlich gilt für den Erlaß von Organakten das *Prinzip des sachgerechten Formengebrauchs.* Dieser Grundsatz gebietet, daß die Form bzw. die Bezeichnung eines Gemeinschaftsakts stets seinem materiellen Gehalt entspricht. Mangelt es einem Organakt an der Kongruenz von Form und Inhalt, so ist dies ein Fehler, welcher die Nichtigkeit des betreffenden Organaktes im Sinne der Art. 33 EGKSV, 173 f. EWGV und 146 f. EAGV begründet. (E. Fuß, 'Rechtssatz und Einzelakt im Europäischen Gemeinschaftsrecht', [1964] 8 Neue Juristische Wochenschrift, 327–331, at 330).

[69] The institutional practice of Community decision-making has created a number of 'atypical' acts. The most prominent example of this category is the decision *sui generis.* Atypical acts will not be discussed here. For a discussion of atypical acts, see: U. Everling, 'Probleme atypischer Rechts- und Handlungsformen', in R. Bieber & G. Ress (eds.), *Die Dynamik des Europäischen Gemeinschaftsrechts* (Nomos, 1987) 417.

[70] Logic would dictate that non-binding acts lack a 'legal character' (H.P. Ipsen, Richtlinien-Ergebnisse, in: W. Hallstein (ed.), *Zur Integration Europas: Festschrift für Carl Friedrich Ophüls aus Anlaß seines siebzigsten Geburtstages* (C.F. Müller, 1965) 67–84 at p. 68 Fn.4: 'wegen mangelnder Verbindlichkeit nicht Rechtsakte'). Yet, the European Court has accepted the possibility of their having some 'indirect' legal effect. In *S. Grimaldi v Fonds des maladies professionelles*, Case 322/88, [1989] E.C.R. 4407, para.18, the Court held that recommendations 'cannot be regarded as having no legal effect' as they 'supplement binding Community provisions'. 'Non-binding' Community acts may, therefore, have legal 'side effects'. The present study will, however, not take them into account. For an interesting overview, see L. Senden, *Soft Law in European Community law: Its Relationship to Legislation* (Hart, 2004).

The legal instruments enumerated in Article 249 EC are *internal* to the Community legal order. They unfold their legal effects within Europe's geographical scope. International agreements were not expressly mentioned in the list of Article 249 EC. This was not surprising. In 1958, the power of the Community to conclude international treaties was very limited and the status of these Community agreements was still unclear. However, the evolution of the doctrine of parallel powers has meant that the Community will be entitled to conclude international treaties wherever it has the power to adopt internal legislation.[71] International treaties should, accordingly, be viewed as an additional implied legal instrument which runs 'in parallel' to the internal legal instruments of the Community.

What was the constitutional rationale behind Article 249 EC? Three (partly overlapping) explanatory models were available in 1958 to justify the diversity of legal instruments for Community action. First, the variety of legal instruments could theoretically structure the horizontal division of powers between the Community institutions.[72] National constitutions typically vest decision-making authorities with their specific legal instrument. A legal hierarchy structures the national legal system into a pyramid of layers thereby providing a mechanism for solving legal conflicts. This theory of legal instruments—and the hierarchical relationships among them—is thus intrinsically connected with the separation of powers doctrine. Unlike national constitutional orders, however, the Community legal order did not correlate its instruments with a specific Community organ or a particular legislative procedure. The Council could act by means of regulations, directives or decisions under a single procedure.[73] The absence of a hierarchical stratification among the Community's legal instruments has thus created an

---

[71]　This is not uncontroversial. For a discussion of the 'instrument thesis' of the doctrine of parallel external powers, see: R. Schütze, 'Parallel External Powers in the European Community: From 'Cubist' Perspectives towards 'Naturalist' Constitutional Principles?', [2004] 23 Y.E.L. 225–74, at 235–6.

[72]　'Das von den Vertragsschöpfern eingeführte System der Organakte muß, um sinnvoll zu sein, auch durch eine entsprechende Hierarchie der Gemeinschaftsakte ergänzt werden. Diese Rangordnung wird in den Römischen Verträgen durch die Reihenfolge ihrer Aufführung in Art. 189 EWGV und Art. 161 EAGV deutlich zum Ausdruck gebracht. Danach kann kein Zweifel bestehen, daß die Verordnungen (und allgemeine Entscheidungen) den individuellen Entscheidungen im Rang vorgehen und selbst nur durch einen Rechtssatz abgeändert werden können.' (E. Fuß, 'Rechtssatz und Einzelakt im Europäischen Gemeinschaftsrecht', [1964] 8 Neue Juristische Wochenschrift 327–331, at 330). This position has received judicial support from the Court of First Instance in *Scholler Lebensmittel GmbH & Co. KG v Commission of the European Communities*, Case T-9/93, [1995] E.C.R. II-1611, where the CFI suggested a hierarchical relationship between legislative measures and individual decisions: 'According to the hierarchy of legal rules, the Commission is not empowered, by means of an individual decision, to restrict or limit the legal effects of such a legislative measure, unless the latter expressly provides a legal basis for that purpose' (*ibid.*, para.162). T. Hartley has consequently suggested the existence of a hierarchy between the legal instruments in Article 249 EC (T.C. Hartley, *The Foundations of European Community Law: An Introduction to the constitutional and administrative law of the European Community* (OUP, 2003), 104).

[73]　E.g. Article 308 EC. This point has been expressly made by the ECJ: '[T]he distinction between a regulation and a decision may be based only on the nature of the measure itself and the

amorphous body of secondary law.[74] The variety of legal instruments of the Community, therefore, cannot be justified by means of a *horizontal* separation of powers rationale.[75]

There was a second possible reason behind the system of legal instruments established by Article 249 EC: 'the niceties of the system of legal protection in the Treaty'.[76] The central provision for the judicial review of Community measures is Article 230 EC. Its fourth paragraph provides that '[a]ny natural or legal person may [on the grounds mentioned] institute proceedings against a decision addressed to that person or against a decision which, although in the form of a regulation or a decision addressed to another person, is of direct and individual concern to the former.' The judicial review perspective has, traditionally, been the 'dominant paradigm for the discussion about instruments'.[77] The 'battle of forms' has indeed for a long time been fought in relation to the ability of private litigants to challenge Community acts.

The European Court had originally placed Article 230 and Article 249 EC on parallel tracks. In *Confédération nationale des producteurs de fruits et légumes and others v Council*,[78] the Court found that '[Article 249] makes a clear distinction between the concept of a 'decision' and that of a 'regulation' and that it was therefore 'inconceivable that the term 'decision' would be used in [Article 230] in a different sense from the technical sense as defined in [Article 249]'. Hence, a measure was a decision and *not a regulation* where the Community act was of individual concern to specific individuals.[79]

Yet, in the course of the last two decades, the Court has 'by and large decoupled the system of legal review from the type of act at issue'.[80] In *Cordorniu*,[81] the Court found that although 'the contested provision is, by nature and by virtue of its sphere of application, of a legislative nature in that it applies to the traders concerned in general, that *does not prevent it from being of individual concern to*

---

legal effects which it produces and not on the procedure for its adoption' (*Alusuisse Italia SpA v Council & Commission*, Case 307/81, [1982] E.C.R. 3463, para.13).

[74] Bast speaks of the 'unity of secondary law', see: J. Bast, *On the Grammer of EU Law: Legal Instruments*, Jean Monnet Working Paper 9/03 <http://www.jeanmonnetprogram.org/papers/03/030901-05.html 19>.

[75] The amorphous equality governing the European Community's secondary law has been the subject of repeated criticism for some time. The European Parliament has continuously demanded the recognition of a superior layer of Community parliamentary legislation above 'normal' secondary law. Declaration No 16 annexed to the TEU even gave a mandate to the 1996 IGC to 'examine to what extent it might be possible to review the classification of Community acts with a view to establishing an appropriate hierarchy between the different categories of acts'. These reform proposals had been taken up by the Constitutional Treaty (2004). For references, see above n.9.

[76] *Advocate General Roemer, Sgarlata and others v Commission*, Case 40/64, [1965] E.C.R. 215 at 234. [77] Bast, above n.74 at 27.

[78] *Confédération nationale des producteurs de fruits et légumes and others v Council*, Case 16–17/62, [1962] E.C.R. 471. [79] *Ibid.*, at 478.

[80] Bast, above n.74 at 13.

[81] *Codorníu S.A. v Council*, Case C-309/89, [1994] E.C.R. 1853, para.19 (emphasis added).

some of them'. This new approach has been extended to directives.[82] The *déforma-tion morphologique*, brought about by the 'niceties' of the Treaty's original system of judicial review, has thus come to an end.[83] Today, the issue of legal standing can safely be put aside in a discussion of the system of legal instruments. The second explanatory rationale has, therefore, lost its power.

Let us proceed to a third reason possibly underlying the morphology of legal power in the EC. The various legal instruments could, finally, be taken to structure the vertical division of power between the European and the national level. The morphology of legal power would then have a *federal* dimension. Some early commentators argued that for each policy field the Treaty had fixed a specific format of regulatory intervention.[84] The constitutional nexus between the type of instrument and the Community competence in those early days is expressed in the following passage:

To obtain a precise view on the sharing out of legislative competence between the Community and its Member States, one must, however take account, apart from the factors determining substantive attributions, of how the various legislative instruments placed at the Community's disposal are allotted between these subject matters. The means available are not shared out equally. Far from it: the allotment depends closely upon the objective sought to be achieved in each sphere. This needs to be explained in more detail. The grant of the Community of a power to make a regulation is an indication that there is a 'transferred legislative competence'. Here the Community itself fixes the legal rules which are binding in the Member States without any intervention of the legislative or even the

---

[82] Directives have equally been found to be reviewable acts under Article 230(4) EC. In *UEAPME v Council*, T-135/96, [1998] E.C.R. II-2335, the Court of First Instance found that '[a]lthough [Article 230], fourth paragraph, of the Treaty makes no express provision regarding the admissibility of actions brought by legal persons for annulment of a directive, it is clear from the case law of the Court of Justice that the mere fact that the contested measure is a directive is not sufficient to render such an action inadmissible. (. . .) In that respect, it must be observed that the Community institutions cannot, merely through their choice of legal instrument, deprive individuals of the judicial protection offered by that provision of the Treaty. (. . .) [T]he mere fact that the chosen form of instrument was that of a directive cannot in this case enable the Council to prevent individuals from availing themselves of the remedies accorded to them under the Treaty' (*ibid.*, para.63). The jurisdictional scope of Article 230(4) EC will, of course, include decisions addressed to Member States (cf. *Plaumann & Co v Commission*, Case 25/62, [1963] E.C.R. 95).

[83] There will, however, remain differences as regards the burden of proof: 'Die Qualifikation des Rechtsaktes ist in diesem Zusammenhang nur noch insofern von Bedeutung, als ein Kläger bei an ihn adressierten Entscheidungen im Gegensatz zu Verordnungen oder Richtlinien des Nachweises einer unmittelbaren und unmittelbaren Betroffenheit enthoben ist.' (H. Chr. Röhl, 'Die anfechtbare Entscheidung nach Art. 230 Abs. 4 EGV', [2000] 60 Zeitschrift für ausländisches öffentliches Recht und Völkerrecht, 331–66 at 354)

[84] M. Zuleeg, 'Die Kompetenzen der Europäischen Gemeinschaften gegenüber den Mitgliedstaaten', [1971] 20 Jahrbuch des öffentlichen Rechts (1971), 1–64 at 6: 'Kompetenzabstufungen nach Rechtsakten' and V. Constantinsesco, *Compétences et pouvoirs dans les Communautés européennes: Contribution à l'étude de la nature juridique des Communautés* (Pichon & Durand-Auzias, 1974) 85 (emphasis added)): '[L]es organes ne sont pas libres, *sauf exception*, de choisir entre les actes énumérés à l'[article 249]. Chaque disposition du Traité énonce au contraire les actes que tel organe est habilité à édicter en fonction d'une manière déterminée. A chaque type de compétence semble donc correspondre un acte donné.'

executive national authority. (...) On the other hand, resort to the medium of the directive and the decision is an indication of a 'retained legislative competence' on the part of the Member States. (...) Yet even this retention of competence is merely formal, since we have seen that in these cases the decisions on legislative policy are taken at the Community level, so that the legislative competence exercised in this case by the States is merely a 'tied competence', i.e. an executive authority.[85]

This competence reading of the various legal instruments has occasionally been expressed by the European Court of Justice. In *Faccini Dori*,[86] the Court denied the horizontal direct effect of directives on the ground that '[t]he effect of extending that case law to the sphere of relations between individuals would be to recognize a power in the Community to enact obligations for individuals with immediate effect, whereas it has *competence* to do so only where it is empowered to adopt regulations'.[87]

In the following pages, we shall investigate the explanatory potential of this third rationale for the various legal instruments in the Community legal order. Is the morphology of legislative power in the European Community structured according to a federal rationale? In order to answer the question, we shall trace the broad lines of development of the Community's principal legal instruments— regulations, directives and state-addressed decisions as well as international agreements—alongside two dimensions. The instrument's *legislative* character will be defined as the extent to which the legal act unfolds a generally binding effect. It will be seen that the Court's jurisprudence has led to a situation whereby 'the concept of legislative measure within the meaning of the case law may apply to all the measures referred to by [Article 249] and not only to regulations'.[88] We shall thereby distinguish between three principal forms of legislation: direct, indirect and external legislation.

The second dimension represents an instrument's *pre-emptive* quality,[89] that is, the degree of legislative exclusion inherent in the use of one of the four legal instruments. The quest for the pre-emptive quality of Community measures concerns, in the final analysis, the question whether and how far the national legislator retains the ability to co-legislate with the Community in a policy field. This second dimension will, therefore, particularly relate to the *federal* division of legislative power between the Community and the national level.

---

[85] P. Pescatore, *The Law of Integration: Emergence of a New Phenomenon in International Relations, Based on the Experience of the European Communities* (Sijthoff, 1974), 62–3.

[86] *Faccini Dori v Recreb*, Case 91/92, [1994] E.C.R. 3325.

[87] *Ibid.*, para.24 (emphasis added).

[88] *Schröder and Thamann v Commission*, Case T-390/94, [1997] E.C.R. II-501, para.54. It is hard to believe that the Court of First Instance wished to include non-binding acts in this enthusiastic statement.

[89] On the concept of pre-emption in the Community legal order, see: R. Schütze, 'Supremacy without Pre-emption? The very slowly emergent Doctrine of Community Pre-emption', [2006] 43 C.M.L. Rev. 1023–1048.

IV. Direct Community Legislation: The Regulation

A. The Legislative Character of Regulations: Direct and General Applicability

Regulations shall have direct and general application in all Member States. They are the standard instrument of the European Community.[90]

By making regulations directly applicable, the Treaty recognized a monistic connection between that Community instrument and the national legal orders. Regulations would be automatically binding *within* the Member States—a characteristic that distinguished them from ordinary international law that would only be binding *on* States. In 1958, this was extraordinary for an international organization: 'L'attribution au Conseil et à la Commission du pouvoir d'adopter des actes de portée générale applicable sans interposition des autorités nationales sur le territoire de la Communauté est, sans conteste, un fait d'une importance exceptionnelle dans le développement de la société internationale'.[91]

Would the direct application of regulations imply their direct effect? The relationship between direct applicability and direct effect has been obscured by the early jurisprudence of the European Court of Justice.[92] Direct applicability should be taken to refer to the *normative* validity of a regulation within the national legal orders. The concept means that no 'validating' national act is needed to give regulations legal effects within national legal orders: 'The direct application of a Regulation means that its entry into force and its application in

---

[90] A. von Bogdandy, F. Arndt & J. Bast, 'Legal Instruments in European Union Law and their Reform: A Systematic Approach on an Empirical Basis', [2004] 23 Y.E.L. 91–136 at 98. The dominance of the regulation vis-à-vis the other legal instruments of the Community results, to a great extent, from its being the Community's principal 'executive' instrument. 69% of all regulations are 'delegated legislation', representing more than 90% of all secondary Community legislation (*ibid.*, 99).

[91] J.-V. Louis, *Les Règlement de la Communauté économique européenne* (Presses universitaires des Bruxelles, 1969) at 16. See also M. Zuleeg, 'Die Kompetenzen der Europäischen Gemeinschaften gegenüber den Mitgliedstaaten', [1971] 20 Jahrbuch des öffentlichen Rechts, 1–64, 8: 'Da die Völkerrechtslehre nach wie vor auf dem Standpunkt steht, daß die innerstaatliche Geltung einer völkerrechtlichen Norm eines staatlichen Anwendungsbefehls bedarf, erschien es den Verfassern der römischen Verträge geboten, ausdrücklich klarzustellen, daß bei Verordnungen keine besondere Geltungsanordnung mehr erforderlich ist.'

[92] In its early jurisprudence the Court often conflated the concepts of direct applicability and direct effect: 'According to [Article 249] and [Article 254] of the Treaty, regulations are, as such, *directly applicable* in all Member States[.] (…) Consequently, all methods of implementation are contrary to the *direct effect* of Community regulations and of jeopardizing their simultaneous and uniform application in the whole Community' (*Commission v Italy*, Case 39/72, [1973] E.C.R. 101, para.17). In *Amsterdam Bulb BV v Produktschap voor siergewassen*, Case 50/76, [1977] E.C.R. 137, paras.4–5 (emphasis added), we read that 'the direct effect of a Community regulation means that its coming into force and its application in favour of or against those subject to it are independent of any measure of reception into national law. By virtue of the obligations arising from the Treaty the Member States are under a duty not to obstruct the *direct effect inherent in regulations throughout the Community*'. This early jurisprudence led an early commentator to identify the concept of direct

favour of those subject to it are independent of any measure of reception into national law.'[93] Direct effect, on the other hand, refers to the ability of a norm to execute itself. It concerns the real effects of a norm in a legal order. Direct applicability makes direct effect *possible*.[94] The direct application of a norm is a condition for its direct effect. The direct application of regulations will, however, 'leave open the question whether a particular provision of a regulation has direct effect or not'.[95] In fact, as an early commentator noted:

Many provisions of regulations are liable to have direct effects and can be enforced by the courts. Other provisions, although they have become part of the domestic legal order as a result of the regulation's direct applicability, are binding for the national authorities only, without granting private persons the right to complain in the courts that the authorities have failed to fulfil these binding Community obligations. This is by no means an unrealistic con-clusion. In every member State there exists quite a bit of law which is not enforceable in the courts, because these rules were not meant to give the private individual enforceable rights or because they are too vague or too incomplete to admit of judicial application.[96]

The face that not all provisions of a regulation will be self-executing has been judi-cially acknowledged.[97] In *Azienda Agricola Monte Arcosa Srl*, the Court clearly re-affirmed the distinction between direct applicability and direct effect:

[A]lthough, by virtue of the very nature of regulations and of their function in the system of sources of Community law, the provisions of those regulations generally have immediate effect in the national legal systems without its being necessary for the national authorities to adopt measures of application, some of their provisions may none the less necessitate, for their implementation, the adoption of measures of application by the Member States. (...) In the light of the discretion enjoyed by the Member States in respect of the implementation of those provisions, it cannot be held that individuals may derive rights from those provi-sions in the absence of measures of application adopted by the Member States.[98]

---

effect of regulations with the concept of 'invocability': '[T]he Court takes the view that all regulations at all times possess *direct effect*, that is to say that—irrespective of whether they explicitly embody rights and/or obligations with regard to individuals—they in any case entitle them to invoke their provisions in the courts' (R.W. Lauwaars, *Lawfulness and Legal Force of Community Decisions*, (A.W. Sijthoff, 1973) 14).

[93] *Fratelli Variola Spa v Amministrazione delle finanze dello Stato*, Case 34/73, [1973] E.C.R. 981, para.10.

[94] The Court has, ultimately, accepted this subtle distinction between 'direct applicability' and 'direct effect'. In *Van Duyn*, para.12 (emphasis added) we find that 'by virtue of the provisions of [Article 249] regulations are directly applicable and, consequently, *may* by their very nature have direct effect'.

[95] P. Pescatore, above n.85 at 164.

[96] G. Winter, 'Direct Applicability and Direct Effect. Two distinct and different concepts in Community law', [1972] C.M.L. Rev. 425–438 at 436.

[97] See *SpA Eridania-Zuccherifici nazionali and SpA Societa Italiana per l'Industria degli Zuccheri v Minister of Agriculture and Forestry, Minister for Industry, Trade and Craft Trades and SpA Zuccherifici Meridionali*, Case 230/78, [1979] E.C.R. 2749; *Commission v Belgium*, Case 137/80, [1981] E.C.R. 653 and *Commission v The Netherlands*, Case 72/85, [1986] E.C.R. 1219.

[98] *Azienda Agricola Monte Arcosa Srl*, Case 403/98, [2001] E.C.R. 103, paras.26, 28. Article 2(5) of Regulation 797/85 and Article 5(5) of Regulation 2328/91 stated: 'Member States shall, for the

The degree of legislative discretion left to the national level prevented the provisions from being 'relied on before a national court', 'where the legislature of a Member State has not adopted the provisions necessary for their implementation in the national legal system'.[99] Regulations may, therefore, explicitly or even implicitly call for the adoption of 'implementing measures' by national authorities 'each time the implementation of norms worked out by means of regulation cannot be carried out in practice unless the Member States resort to *complementary* measures'.[100] In the event of a non-directly effective norm in a regulation, the ECJ will 'transpose' the constitutional doctrines developed in the context of directives.[101] (Yet, unlike directives, regulations can have vertical *and* horizontal direct effects. Regulations 'are therefore a *direct source of rights and duties* for all those affected thereby, whether Member States or individuals, who are parties to legal relationships under Community law.'[102])

Regulations were originally the sole legislative instrument of the young Community.[103] Their general character distinguished them from individual decisions. In *Zuckerfabrik Watenstedt GmbH v Council*,[104] the ECJ defined

purposes of this Regulation, define what is meant by the expression 'farmer practicing farming as his main occupation'. This definition shall, in the case of a natural person, include at least the condition that the proportion of income derived from the agricultural holding must be 50% or more of the farmer's total income and that the working time devoted to work unconnected with the holding must be less than half the farmer's total working time. On the basis of the criteria referred to in the foregoing subparagraph, the Member States shall define what is meant by this same expression in the case of persons other than natural persons.' For another illustration of a provision in a regulation calling for national implementing measures, see: Article 35(1) of Regulation 1/2003 (O.J. L1/1): 'The Member States shall designate the competition authority or authorities responsible for the application of Articles 81 and 82 of the Treaty in such a way that the provisions of this regulation are effectively complied with. The measures necessary to empower those authorities to apply those Articles shall be taken before 1 May 2004. The authorities designated may include court.'

    [99] *Ibid.*, para.29.
    [100] F. Capotorti, 'Legal Problems of Directives, Regulations and their Implementation', in H. Siedentopf and J. Ziller (eds), *Making European Policies Work: The Implementation of Community Legislation in the Member States, Vol.I* (SAGE Publications, 1989). The legislative practice has attracted academic criticism: If 'the Community legislator intends to require implementing legislation on the part of the Member States, it would be clearer for anybody concerned with applying Community law if the part of the Regulation, which certainly requires such [implementing] legislation were to be separated and to take the form of a *directive*' (G. Gaja, P. Hay & R. D. Rotunda, 'Instruments for Legal Integration in the European Community—A Review', in: M. Cappelletti, M. Seccombe, J. Weiler, *Integration through law : Europe and the American federal Experience Vol.I Methods, Tools and Institutions*, 113–60 at 125 (emphasis added)).
    [101] *Criminal proceedings against X*, Case 60/02, [2004] E.C.R. 651, paras.61–63, esp. para.62 (emphasis added): 'Even though in the case at issue in the main proceedings the Community rule in question is a regulation, which by its very nature does not require any national implementing measures, and not a directive, Article 11 of Regulation No 3295/94 empowers Member States to adopt penalties for infringements of Article 2 of that regulation, thereby making it possible to *transpose to the present case the Court's reasoning in respect of directives*.'
    [102] *Amministrazione delle Finanze dello Stato v Simmenthal SpA*, Case 106/77, [1978] E.C.R. 629, para.14–15 (emphasis added).
    [103] *Confédération Nationale des Producteurs de Fruit et de Légumes v Council*, Case 16–17/62, [1962] E.C.R. 471, para.2.
    [104] *Zuckerfabrik Watenstedt GmbH v Council*, Case 6/68, [1968] E.C.R. 409.

'general applicability' as 'applicable to objectively determined situations and involv[ing] legal consequences for categories of persons viewed in a general and abstract manner'. An act will not lose its general nature 'because it may be possible to ascertain with a greater or lesser degree of accuracy the number or even the identity of the persons to which it applies at any given time as long as there is no doubt that the measure is applicable as a result of an objective situation of law or of fact which it specifies'.[105] The crucial legislative characteristic of a regulation is then the 'openness' of the group of persons to whom it applies: where the group of persons is 'fixed in time', the Community measure will constitute a bundle of individual decisions addressed to each member of the group.[106]

Just as not all norms of a regulation need to be directly effective, not all provisions of a regulation must have a general character. Some provisions may have the character of individual decisions 'without prejudice to the question whether that measure considered in its entirety can be correctly called a regulation'.[107] However, one should presume that in order for a measure to be considered as a regulation the majority of its provisions should be directly and generally effective.

In relation to the geographical scope of regulations, the European Court—paying only partial tribute to the unambiguous wording of Article 249(2) EC—has confirmed that '[as] institutional acts adopted on the basis of the Treaty, (...) regulations apply *in principle* to the same geographical area as the Treaty itself'.[108] The Court has thus invited us to perceive a regulation's Community-wide applicability from an abstract normative perspective. Its normative validity across the entire territory of the European Community is constitutionally guaranteed. In actual fact, its concrete application can be confined to a limited number of Member States.[109]

B. The Pre-emptive Effect of Regulations: The Regulation as the Instrument of Legal Uniformity?

Regulations are binding in their entirety. They have been characterized as the 'most integrated form of Community secondary [*sic!*] legislation'[110] and as the 'source

---

[105] *Ibid.* at 415.

[106] *International Fruit Company and others v Commission*, Case 41–44/70, [1971] E.C.R. 411, esp. para.17.

[107] *Confédération nationale des producteurs de fruits et légumes and others v Council*, Case 16–17/62, [1962] E.C.R. 471, para.2.

[108] *Commission v Ireland*, Case 61/77, [1978] E.C.R. 417, para. 46 (emphasis added).

[109] A Regulation may only apply to one Member State without losing its character as a Regulation, see: *Compagnie française commerciale and financière v Commission*, Case 64/69, [1970] E.C.R. 221.

[110] G. Gaja, P. Hay & R.D. Rotunda, above n.100 at 124.

directe d' unification des législations'.[111] Considered as the instrument of legislative uniformity, will a regulation, thus, always totally preempt the national level within its scope of application? Is there, in other words, a fixed pre-emptive standard attached to the very instrumental format of a regulation?

The early jurisprudence of the European Court of Justice indeed emphasized the vigilantly pre-emptive nature of regulations. In order to protect the normative autonomy and uniform application of regulations within the national legal orders, the Court employed a strong pre-emption criterion. This initial approach is best illustrated in the *Bollmann* case.[112] Discussing the effect of a regulation on the legislative powers of the Member States, the ECJ found that since a regulation 'is directly applicable in all Member States, the latter, unless otherwise expressly provided, are precluded from taking steps, for the purposes of applying the regulation, which are *intended to alter its scope or supplement its provisions*'.[113] It seemed that '[l]'intervention d'un règlement prive en principe l'Etat membre du pouvoir d'arrêter des mesures normatives complémentaire à ce règlement. De telles mesures ne pourront être adoptées au niveau national qu'en vertu du règlement lui-même. Faute d'une habilitation expresse, dont la Cour s'attache généralement à restreindre la portée, elles se limitent aux règles nécessaires à l'exécution, lorsque le règlement ne contient pas l'ensemble des dispostions à ce sujet.'[114]

Early jurisprudence, consequently, suggested that all national rules that fell within the scope of a regulation or which somehow 'affected' its uniform application were automatically pre-empted.[115] Any supplementary national action would be prohibited. The Court seemed worried that any additional national action would undermine the normative autonomy of regulations: 'By virtue of the obligations arising from the Treaty and assumed on ratification, Member States are under a duty not to obstruct the direct applicability inherent in regulations and other rules of Community law.'[116] Provisions within regulations that permitted national action were, consequently, conceptualized as a re-delegation of legislative power to the national level.[117]

It was this early jurisprudence that created the myth that regulations would automatically engender occupation of the field pre-emption. Their capacity to field pre-emption came to be (wrongly) associated with their direct

---

[111] This is the title of an article by J.-V. Louis: 'Le Règlement, source directe d'unification des législation,' in D. de Ripainsel-Landy, *et al.* (eds), *Les instrumnets du rapprochement des législations dans la communauté économique européenne* (Bruxelles, 1976) 15–35.

[112] *Hauptzollamt Hamburg Oberelbe v Bollmann*, Case 40/69, [1970] E.C.R. 69.

[113] *Ibid.*, para.4 (emphasis added).   [114] J.-V. Louis, above n. 111 at 31.

[115] *Granaria v Produktschap voor Veevoeder*, Case 18/72, [1972] E.C.R. 1163, para. 16.

[116] *Fratelli Variola Spa v Amministrazione delle finanze dello Stato*, Case 34/73, [1973] E.C.R. 981, para.10.

[117] An analysis of the academic discourse concerning the pre-emptive nature of regulations in the 1970s is instructive. J.-V. Louis refers to Kovar and Pescatore, both of whom conceptualized the relationship between a regulation and national measures falling within its ambit under the lens of delegated legislation. The former author thus claimed that, 'la Cour a examiné la conformité des

applicability.[118] It was during this initial phase in the gradually emerging doctrine of Community pre-emption in which 'the Court did not base its decisions on the pre-emption doctrine as such, but on the *exclusionary effect of the type of legal acts employed, i.e. regulations.*'[119]

Subsequent jurisprudence, however, quickly disapproved of the simplistic correlation between regulations and field pre-emption. In *Bussone*, the Court found that the 'direct applicability of a regulation requires that its entry into force and its application in favour of or against those subject to it must be independent of any measure of reception into national law. Proper compliance with that duty precludes the application of any legislative measure, even one adopted subsequently, *which is incompatible with the provisions of that regulation*'.[120] But what was meant by the phrase 'incompatible with the provisions of that regulation'? In *Maris v Rijksdienst voor Werknemerspensioenen*,[121] the Court employed a weaker conflict criterion. Recalling that it was 'impossible for the authority of Community law to vary from one Member State to the other as a result of domestic laws, whatever their purpose, if the efficacy of that law and the necessary uniformity of its application in all Member States and to all those persons covered by the provisions at issue are not to be jeopardized', the regulation at issue would, however, only preclude 'the application of any provisions of national law to a *different or contrary effect*'.[122] Regulations therefore impose an obligation on national authorities to refrain from enacting national measures *contradicting* the letter or spirit of the regulation. A regulation may, thus, be placed anywhere on

mesures nationales à l'habilitation selon une démarche similaire à celles des juridictions administratives vérifiant le respect des limites d'une délégation de compétences', while the second author suggested that 'il s'agit, dans ce cas, de l'exercice par le législateur national d'une compétence 'liée'; en d'autres termes, nous sommes bien en présence d'une législation déléguée' (J.-V. Louis, above n.111 at 32–3).

[118] For example 'This capacity to pre-empt or preclude national measures can be regarded as a characteristic peculiar to a Regulation (as opposed to any other form of Community legislation) and may shed some light on the nature of direct applicability under [Article 249] of the Treaty' (M. Blumental, 'Implementing the Common Agricultural Policy: Aspects of the Limitations on the Powers of the Member States', [1984] 35 Northern Ireland Legal Quarterly, 28–51 at 39). Advocate General Warner expressed the same belief in *Zerbone v Amministrazione delle finance dello Stato*, Case 94/77, [1978] E.C.R. 99 at 126): 'Whilst a Member State may lay down rules of an administrative or procedural character in order to give effect in its territory to the provisions of a Community Regulation, and may also prescribe sanctions for any breach of such provisions where Community Law itself does not do so, a Member State may not legislate either so as to duplicate a Community Regulation or so as to purport to alter it. Nor, in the absence of a specific and valid authority conferred on a Member State, either expressly or by necessary implication, by Community legislation, may that State by its own legislation purport to supplement a Community Regulation under the guise of interpretation or otherwise'.

[119] M. Waelbroeck, 'The Emergent Doctrine of Community Pre-emption—Consent and Re-delegation', in T. Sandalow and E. Stein, *Courts and Free Markets: Perspectives from the United States and Europe, Vol. II* (OUP, 1982) 548–580 at 555 (emphasis added).

[120] *Bussone v Ministere italien de l'agriculture*, Case 31/78, [1978] 2429, paras.28–31 (emphasis added).

[121] *M. Maris, wife of R. Reboulet v Rijksdienst voor Werknemerspensioenen*, Case 55/77, [1977] E.C.R. 2327.   [122] *Ibid.*, paras.17–18 (emphasis added).

the pre-emptive spectrum. Its pre-emptive ambit depends purely on the intention of the Community legislator.

Regulations do, consequently, not automatically establish total legislative uniformity. They will not *ipso facto* exclude all national legislation falling within their scope. Regulations will not always achieve 'complete' or 'exhaustive' legislation. On the contrary, a regulation may confine itself to laying down minimum standards.[123] Regulations may replace directives, thereby assuming their predecessors' pre-emptive degree like twin brothers.[124] It is, therefore, misleading to classify regulations as instruments of strict uniformity. Member States are, naturally, precluded from unilateral 'amendment' or 'selective application', whether by means of adding exceptions or unspecified conditions.[125] However, these constitutional obligations apply to *all* Community acts and do not specifically characterize the format of regulations.

In sum, regulations will not automatically eliminate all national legislative autonomy within their respective field of operation. The 'so-called exclusive effect of a regulation, i.e. that the Member States are not allowed to take any measure in the field covered by the regulation is not *absolute*'.[126] They may be binding in their entirety, but not pre-emptive in their entirety.

V. Indirect Community Legislation: The Directive and State-addressed Decision

A. From Individual Decision to Legislative Norm: The Doctrine of Direct Effect

The directive shall be binding 'upon' each Member State 'to which it is addressed'.[127] This formulation theoretically suggested two things. First, directives

---

[123] Council Regulation No 259/93 on the supervision and control of shipments of waste within, into and out of the European Community (OJ 1993 L 30, p. 1) provides such an example of a 'minimum harmonization' regulation. The regulation has been described as 'far from providing for a complete harmonization of the rules governing the transfer of waste, and might in part even be regarded (in the words of one commentator) as an 'organized renationalization' of the subject.' (Advocate General F. Jacobs, *Parliament v Council*, Case C-187/93, [1994] E.C.R. 2857, para.22 referring to D. Geradin, 'The legal basis of the waste Directive', [1993] 18 E.L. Rev. 418–27 at 426.

[124] 'Si ce n'est que ces nouveaux règlements qui se substituent souvent à d'anciennes directives leur ressemblent comme des frères jumeaux. La substance des textes demeure très proche, et il suffit pour s'en convaincre de comparer la directive cessation de l'activité agricole (n° 72/160 du 17 avril 1972) avec le règlement no 1096/88 du 25 avril 1988. Le contenu de ces règlements semble parfois si laconique qu'on peut se demander si l'on en frôle pas le détournement de procédure' (C. Blumann, *Politique Agricole Commune* (Litec, 1996) at 81).

[125] *Commission v Italy*, Case 39/72, [1973] E.C.R. 101, para. 20.

[126] R.H. Lauwaarrs, 'Implementation of Regulations by national Measures', [1983] 1 Legal Issues of Economic Integration 41–52 at 45. *Contra*, J.A. Usher, *EC Institutions and Legislation* (Longman, 1998) at 130: 'In effect Regulations could be said simply, if inelegantly, to amount to a 'keep out' sign to national legislation.'   [127] Article 249(3) EC.

were binding *on* States, not *within* States. On the basis of a 'dualist' understanding of the relationship between Community and national law, directives would have no validity in the national legal orders. In order to operate on individuals, the Community command would need to be 'incorporated' or 'transformed' into national law. The absence of their 'direct application' and the freedom of the Member States to choose how to implement them made directives appear to be a classic instrument of international law.[128]

Second, binding on the States, directives lacked *general* application: Their legal norms applied only to those States to which they were addressed.[129] Directives were individual decisions and not legislative measures. General application could only be achieved indirectly *via* the national legislator that would transform the Community 'decision' into a national act with general legal effects. Directives were, thus, not themselves Community legislation, but the source of co-ordinated national legislation. Directives have, consequently, been described as 'indirect legislation'.[130]

The gradual promotion of the directive from an instrument of indirect to an instrument of *direct* Community legislation required a fundamental change in its normative make-up:

Seulement si on lui [la directive] reconnaît un effet direct dans les Etats membres, elle peut développer un effet identique ou similaire à celui de la loi, au sens que les particuliers peuvent l'invoquer et que ses dispositions peuvent servir de fondement aux décisions des tribunaux et des autorités administratives nationales. (...) En effet, l'applicabilité directe est d'une importance cruciale pour la question de savoir si la directive peut être qualifiée de 'loi' au sens matériel[.][131]

Only once the possibility of a directive's direct effects within the national legal orders was accepted could directives become a source of generally applicable norms. In a courageous jurisprudential line, the European Court of Justice did indeed inject these 'legislative' elements into the normative matrix of directives and substantially cured the 'infant disease' of the new legal order.[132] The medical

---

[128] For this view, see L.-J. Constantinesco, *Das Recht der Europäischen Gemeinschaften* (Nomos, 1977) at 614: 'Die Richtlinie ist im Hinblick auf das durch sie veranlaßte Verfahren in den Mitgliedsstaaten ein typisches zwischenstaatliches Instrument. Ihre Adressaten sind immer die Mitgliedstaaten; sie erlangen innerstaatliche Wirkung nur durch die nationale Ausführungsmaßnahme der Mitgliedstaaten.'

[129] The majority of directives apply to all Member Sates of the Community. These 'general directives' (G. Schmidt, *Artikel 189 Rn. 36*, in: H. von der Groeben, J. Thiesing, C.-D. Ehlermann (eds.), *Kommentar zum EU-/EG-Vertrag* (Nomos, 1999)) have received some explicit recognition in Article 254(2) EC, requiring the publication 'general directives' in the Official Journal of the European Union.

[130] P. Pescatore, 'The Doctrine of "Direct Effect": An Infant Disease of Community Law', [1983] E.L. Rev. 155–177 at 177.

[131] D. Triantafyllou, *Des compétences d'attribution au domaine de la loi : étude sur les fondements juridiques de l'action administrative en droit communautaire* (Bruylant, 1997), 93.

[132] P. Pescatore, above n. 130 at 155. The activist jurisprudence was the target of heavy judicial and academic attack. Some national judiciaries originally refused to accept it. The national defiance is

record of the judicial treatment is well documented and we can limit ourselves to a stenographic recapitulation.

The doctrine of the direct effect of Community directives was accepted in *Van Duyn v Home Office*.[133] Introducing a distinction between direct applicability and direct effect, the Court found that even if by virtue of Article 249(2) EC:

regulations are directly applicable and, consequently, may by their very nature have direct effects, it does not follow from this that other categories of acts mentioned in that Article can never have similar effects. It would be incompatible with the binding effect attributed to a directive by [Article 249] to exclude, in principle, the possibility that the obligation which it imposes may be invoked by those concerned. In particular, where the Community authorities have by directive, imposed on Member States the obligation to pursue a particular course of conduct, the useful effect of such an act would be weakened if the individuals were prevented from relying on it before their national courts and if the latter were prevented from taking it into consideration as an element of Community law.[134]

Directives could, therefore, have direct effects within national law. But would these directly effective provisions also be directly applicable? The distinction made by the Court suggested that the two concepts of direct applicability and direct effect were different; but did one exclude the other? The answer will depend on the definition given to either concept: direct applicability has been defined as the automatic 'reception of provisions of regulations into the municipal legal orders of the member States',[135] while direct effect would refer to the possibility of a norm to 'be invoked by those concerned'.[136]

The former concept concerns the abstract question of the normative validity of an 'external' legal instrument in the domestic legal order.[137] The direct effect of a norm, on the other hand, is determined by its capacity to be 'operational' or self-executing, i.e. without need of further legislative specification. The question of direct effect thus concerns the capacity of a legislative norm *to be applied in a specific case*. As national courts will typically raise the direct effect question, the concept of direct effect has come to be equated with the concept of

---

illustrated in the *Conseil d'État's* 'Cohn-Bendit' judgment. For an analysis of the judgment and the French doctrine at the time, see: J. Boulouis, 'L' applicabilité direct des Directives. À propos d'un arrêt Cohn-Bendit du Conseil d'État', [1979] 225 Revue du Marché commun, 104–110.

[133] *Yvonne van Duyn v Home Office*, Case 41–74, [1974] E.C.R. 1337.

[134] *Ibid.*, para.12.

[135] G. Winter, 'Direct Applicability and Direct Effect. Two distinct and different concepts in Community law', [1972] C.M.L. Rev. 425–38 at 431.

[136] *Yvonne van Duyn*, para.12. In a later passage the Court lapses back into confusing direct effect with direct applicability when it states that 'legal certainty for the persons concerned requires that they should be able to rely on this obligation even though it has been laid down in a legislative act which has *no automatic direct effect in its entirety*' (*ibid.*, para.13, emphasis added). The Court thus identifies direct applicability of a measure with its 'automatic direct effect in its entirety'.

[137] For a similar definition, see: K. Lenaerts & P. van Nuffel, *Constitutional Law of the European Union* (Sweet & Maxwell, 2005) 703: direct applicability is defined as 'whether a provision requires implementation *as a legal instrument*'.

justiciability.[138] Since, however, the doctrine of direct effect also address the executive branch,[139] this definition is too narrow. Direct effect should be taken to refer to the justiciability and *executability* of legislative norms. Why should the recognition of an 'administrative direct effect' represent a 'constitutional enormity'?[140] Direct effect refers to the capacity of a *legislative norm* to be the basis of an *individual decision*.[141] If a legislative norm has the capacity to execute itself, that is, apply without the need for concretizing legislation, this should be so in a judicial as well as administrative context. The recognition of administrative direct effect should, thus, be seen as a constitutional normality.

On the basis of these definitions, directly effective provisions of directives will also be directly applicable, for '[h]ow can a law be enforceable by individuals with a member-state if it is not regarded as incorporated in that State'?[142] The direct

[138] E.g. P. Pescatore, above n.130 at 176: direct effect 'boil[s] down to a question of justiciability', and A. Peters, 'The Position of International Law within the European Community Legal Order', [1997] 40 German Yearbook of International Law, 9–77 at 76: 'direct effect is best understood as an objective prerequisite for application of international rules by courts'.

[139] The executive branch will also be bound by a directive. In *Fratelli Costanzo SpA v Comune di Milano*, Case 103/88, [1989] E.C.R. 1839, para.31, the Court found it 'contradictory to rule that an individual may rely upon the provisions of a directive which fulfil the conditions defined above in proceedings before the national courts seeking an order against the administrative authorities, and yet to hold that those authorities are under no obligation to apply the provisions of the directive and refrain from applying provisions of national law which conflict with them. It follows that when the conditions under which the Court has held that individuals may rely on the provisions of a directive before the national courts are met, all organs of the administration (. . .) are obliged to apply those provisions.' For the duty of national competition authorities to disapply national legislation that contravenes Article 81 EC, see: *Consorzio Industrie Fiammiferi (CIF) v Autorita Garante della Concorrenza e del Mercato*, Case C-198/01, [2003] E.C.R. 8055, para.50: 'Since a national competition authority such as the Authority is responsible for ensuring, *inter alia*, that Article 81 EC is observed and that provision, in conjunction with Article 10 EC, imposes a duty on Member States to refrain from introducing measures contrary to the Community competition rules, those rules would be rendered less effective if, in the course of an investigation under Article 81 EC into the conduct of undertakings, the authority were not able to declare a national measure contrary to the combined provisions of Articles 10 EC and 81 EC and if, consequently, it failed to disapply it.'

[140] In this sense, see however: B. de Witte, 'Direct Effect, Supremacy and the Nature of the Legal Order', in: P. Craig and G. de Búrca (eds), *The Evolution of EU Law* (OUP, 1999), 177–213 at 193. The answer suggested by S. Prechal (*Directves in EC Law* (OUP, 2005) at 72) is the following: 'In my opinion, it should be taken into account that the position of administrative bodies is fundamentally different from that of national courts, which have, in the majority of Member States, the power to review and, where necessary, set aside national law and to refer preliminary questions to the European Court of Justice.' This explanation is arguably unconvincing: once we accept that national courts have the power to set aside national law—and for some Member States this did represented a 'constitutional enormity' when they entered the EC—it makes, in my opinion, no qualitative difference to extend that effect to national administrations.

[141] Even if direct effect is defined as the *capacity* or an *attribute* of a norm, this does not suggest that direct effect is an inherent *legal* quality of a norm. As the discussion of the doctrine of direct effect of international treaties will demonstrate, the executive or the judiciary may refuse *attributing* direct effect to a norm for political reasons. See, section VI. A below.

[142] J. Steiner, 'Direct Applicability in EEC Law—A Chameleon Concept', [1982] 98 The Law Quarterly Review, 229–48 at 234.

effect of a directive implies its direct application.[143] This proposition, however, will not work the other way: directly applicable norms are not necessarily directly effective. They are only *capable* of producing direct effects in national legal orders.[144] Finally, what about those provisions of a directive that are not directly effective? Are they nonetheless directly applicable? The answer must be in the affirmative:

The fundamental choice made by the Court of Justice in *Van Gend en Loos* and *Costa v. ENEL* as to the relationship between Community law and national law in general also determines the place of directives within the legal orders of the Member States. The Community's own legal system is an integral part of the legal systems of the Member States. This means that the whole body of Community law (including directives, which are a component of this law) is as such incorporated within the national legal orders, without measures of transformation, incorporation—or whatever else the terminology might be— being necessary. (...) Thus, if the term 'directly applicable' in Article 249(2) is understood to refer to the automatic incorporation of regulations into the domestic legal order, directives are also directly applicable in this sense.[145]

While *Van Gend en Loos* had thus pierced the dualist veil also for directives, the doctrine of direct effect would allow individuals to rely on directives even where the technical prerogative of a national act completing the 'two-stage' legislative process had not been used. As the Court would point out: '[W]henever the provisions of a directive appear, as far as their subject-matter is concerned, to be unconditional and sufficiently precise, those provisions may, in the absence of implementing measures adopted within the prescribed period, be relied upon as against any national provision which is incompatible with the directive'.[146] Directives can directly endow an indeterminate class of individuals with rights. The directive must, therefore, be regarded as 'a Community measure of general application' and as such a 'legislative measure' in its own right.[147]

Has the Court, then, turned directives from an instrument of indirect legislation to an instrument of direct legislation? The answer escapes a simple black-and-white logic: Yes, directives could contain directly and generally effective norms and, as such, were direct Community legislation. However, individuals could only rely directly on directives, where the Member States had failed to

[143] The logical relation between directly effective provisions of directives and their direct application contrasts with the position of Treaty provisions. The EC Treaty has been ratified according to the constitutional traditions of the Member States and, consequently, gained legal validity in the dualist national legal orders through the national transformation act. When the ECJ therefore established the direct effect of Article 25 EC in *Van Gend en Loos*, the validity of the provision in all national legal orders was already settled. Its direct effect could not (retrospectively) imply its direct applicability.

[144] See the discussion on regulations, section IV. A.

[145] S. Prechal, *Directives in EC Law* (OUP, 2005), 92 and 229. For the same conclusion, see C. Timmermans, 'Community Directives Revisited', [1997] 17 Y.E.L. 1–28 at 11–2.

[146] *U. Becker v Finanzamt Münster-Innenstadt*, Case 8/81, [1982] E.C.R. 53, para.12.

[147] *Laboratoires pharmaceutiques Bergaderm and Goupil v Commission*, Case T-199/96, [1998] E.C.R. II-2805.

implement the directive correctly: '[W]herever a directive is correctly implemented, its effects extend to individuals *through the medium of the implementing
measures adopted*'.[148] The Court has insisted on national implementing measures
even for those parts of a directive that are directly effective.[149] The Community
legal order thus favours the mediated *indirect* legislative effect of directives over
their direct legislative effects. The indirect effect of directives thereby never stops:
directives will always remain in the background as a form of 'fall-back' legislation
even where the national authorities have correctly implemented the directive.[150]
There is thus a permanent symbiosis between a Community directive and the
national implementing legislation.

More importantly however, the direct legislative character of directives is
constitutionally trimmed: '[T]he binding nature of a directive, which constitutes
the basis for the possibility of relying on the directive before a national court,
exists only in relation to 'each Member State to which it is addressed'. It follows
that a directive may not of itself impose obligations on an individual and that a
provision of a directive may not be relied upon as such against such a person.'[151]

---

[148]   *U. Becker v Finanzamt Münster-Innenstadt*, para.19 (emphasis added).

[149]   In *Commission v Belgium*, Case 102/79, [1980] E.C.R. 1473, para.12, we therefore read: 'The
effect of the third paragraph of [Article 249] is that Community directives must be implemented by
appropriate implementing measures carried out by the Member States. Only in specific circumstances, in particular where a Member State has failed to take the implementing measures required or
has adopted measures which do not conform to a directive, has the Court of Justice recognized the
right of persons affected thereby to rely in law on a directive as against a defaulting Member State
(. . .) This minimum guarantee arising from the binding nature of the obligation imposed on the
Member States by the effect of the directives under the third paragraph of [Article 249] cannot justify
a Member State's absolving itself from taking in due time implementing measures sufficient to meet
the purpose of each directive.'

[150]   Even after its 'correct implementation', a Directive will remain a permanent standard of review
and a potential source of direct rights, see: *Marks & Spencer plc. v Commissioners of Customs & Excise*,
Case 62/00, [2002] E.C.R. I-6325, paras.27–8.: '[T]he adoption of national measures correctly
implementing a directive does not exhaust the effects of the directive. Member States remain bound
actually to ensure full application of the directive even after the adoption of those measures.
Individuals are therefore entitled to rely before national courts, against the State, on the provisions of
a directive which appear, so far as their subject-matter is concerned, to be unconditional and
sufficiently precise whenever the full application of the directive is not in fact secured, that is to say,
not only where the directive has not been implemented or has been implemented incorrectly, but also
where the national measures correctly implementing the directive are not being applied in such a way
as to achieve the result sought by it.' The Court continued by saying that 'it would be inconsistent
with the Community legal order for individuals to be able to rely on a directive where it has been
implemented incorrectly but not to be able to do so where the national [executive!] authorities apply
the national measures implementing the directive in a manner incompatible with it.'

[151]   *M. H. Marshall v Southampton and South-West Hampshire Area Health Authority*, Case 152/84
[1986] E.C.R. 723, para.48. The principal reason for the denial of horizontal direct effect in
Marshall was thus still the 'dualist' nature of directives: their binding effect was only operative 'upon'
States. In later jurisprudence the emphasis changed as the ECJ interpreted *Marshall* in the following
manner: '[T]he case law on the possibility of relying on directives against State entities is based on the
fact that under [Article 249] a directive is binding only in relation to 'each Member State to which it
is addressed'. That case law seeks to prevent '*the State from taking advantage of its own failure to comply
with Community law*' (*Faccini Dori v Recreb*, Case 91/92, [1994] E.C.R. I-3325, para.22 (emphasis
added).

Directives cannot *directly* impose obligations on individuals. Directives lack horizontal direct effect.[152] This controversial constitutional view, taken by the ECJ 30 years ago, has overshadowed the legislative format of directives ever since. Directives could only have vertical direct effect. They were, to take this one step further, only a vertical form of direct legislation and could, moreover, only grant rights against public authorities of a State.[153] The normative character of directives as instruments of *direct* Community legislation is 'incomplete'.[154] Directives cannot, in themselves, constitute fully-fledged Community legislation.

In order to minimize this legislative defect, the Court has developed the doctrine of 'indirect effect'. National authorities are as far as possible 'required to interpret their national law in the light of the wording and the purpose of the

---

[152] In some cases the Court has allowed directives to adversely affect individuals. This phenomenon has been referred to as the 'incidental' horizontal effect of directives (P. Craig and G. de Búrca, *EU Law* (OUP, 2003), 220–27), 'horizontal side effects of direct effect' (S. Prechal, above n.145 at 261–70), the 'disguised' vertical effect of directives (M. Dougan, 'The "disguised" vertical direct effect of Directives', [2000] 59 Cambridge Law Journal, 586–612). In *Unilever Italia v Central Food*, Case C-443/98, for example, the Court found in paras.50 and 51 that while it remained true 'that a directive cannot of itself impose obligations on an individual and cannot therefore be relied on as such against an individual (see Case C-91/92 *Faccini Dori* 1994 ECR I-3325, paragraph 20), that case law does not apply where non-compliance with Article 8 or Article 9 of Directive 83/189, which constitutes a substantial procedural defect, renders a technical regulation adopted in breach of either of those articles inapplicable. In such circumstances, and unlike the case of non-transposition of directives with which the case law cited by those two Governments is concerned, Directive 83/189 does not in any way define the substantive scope of the legal rule on the basis of which the national court must decide the case before it. It creates neither rights nor obligations for individuals.'

On the other hand, the Court has set constitutional limits on the vertical effect of directives where it would indirectly impose an obligation on individuals. In *The Queen, on the application of Delena Wells v Secretary of State for Transport, Local Government and the Regions*, Case 201/02, [2004] E.C.R. I-723, the Court held that 'an individual may not rely on a directive against a Member State where it is a matter of a State obligation directly linked to the performance of another obligation falling, pursuant to that directive, on a third party [.] (...) On the other hand, mere adverse repercussions on the rights of third parties, even if the repercussions are certain, do not justify preventing an individual from invoking the provisions of a directive against the Member State concerned' (paras.55–7).

The incidental horizontal effect of directives remains a 'grey zone' in EC law—or better: a zone with various 'shades of grey' (cf. T. Tridimas, 'Black, White, and Shades of Grey: Horizontality of Directives Revisited', [2001–2] 21 Y.E.L. 327–54). The conceptual categories that have been developed to justify when a directive can adversely affect a private party and when not have degenerated into 'a form of sophistry which provide no convincing explanation for apparently contradictory lines of case law' (P. Craig and G. de Búrca, *ibid.*, at 226).

[153] Directives can only be 'beneficial' direct legislation as they can change the relationship between the State and a general class of individuals only to the benefit of the latter: directives lack 'inverse vertical direct effect' (cf. *Criminal proceedings against Kolpinghuis Nijmegen BV*, Case 80/86, [1987] E.C.R. 3969, para.10: '[A] national authority may not rely, as against an individual, upon a provision of a directive whose necessary implementation in national law has not yet taken place.').

[154] M. Dougan, above n.152 at 586.

[155] *Von Colson & Kamann v Land Nordrhein-Westfalen*, Case 14/83, [1984] E.C.R. 1891, para.26. The parameters of the duty of consistent interpretation have been defined in the following way: '[I]f the

directive'.[155] This obligation of 'consistent interpretation' applies to all national law—whether passed before or after the directive.[156] '[T]he obligation to interpret national law in conformity with the directive at issue may result in imposing a new obligation on individuals or otherwise affect their position.'[157] Within certain constitutional limits,[158] the doctrine of indirect effect, therefore, comes close to '*de facto* (horizontal) direct effect of the directive'.[159] The national courts are, however, not obliged to interpret a national provision *contra legem*. The duty of consistent interpretation is, therefore, a milder incursion on the legislative powers of the Member States than the doctrine of (horizontal) direct effect.[160] Under the latter doctrine, the national courts would be obliged to

---

application of interpretative methods recognised by national law enables, in certain circumstances, a provision of domestic law to be construed in such a way as to avoid conflict with another rule of domestic law or the scope of that provision to be restricted to that end by applying it only in so far as it is compatible with the rule concerned, the national court is bound to use those methods in order to achieve the result sought by the directive' (*Bernhard Pfeiffer (C-397/01) et al. v Deutsches Rotes Kreuz, Kreisverband Waldshut eV*, Joined Cases C-397/01 to C-403/01, [2004] E.C.R. 8835, para.116.) This passage has been taken to mean that '[n]ational courts are not obliged to invent new methods or to stain existing ones; those at their disposal, however, must be applied to full effect' (M. Klamert, 'Judicial Implementation of Directives and Anticipatory Indirect Effect: Connecting the Dots', [2006] 43 C.M.L. Rev. 1251–1275 at 1259). For the opposite view, see: S. Prechal, above n.157, 213.

156 *Marleasing SA v La Comercial Internacional de Alimentacion SA*, Case C-106/89, [1990] E.C.R. 4135, para.8: '[I]n applying national law, whether the provisions in question were adopted before or after the directive, the national court called upon to interpret it is required to do so, as far as possible, in the light of the wording and the purpose of the directive in order to achieve the result pursued by the latter and thereby comply with the third paragraph of [Article 249] of the Treaty.'

157 S. Prechal, above n.145 at 308.

158 The duty of consistent interpretation imposed on national courts finds a constitutional limit in the 'general principles of law and in particular the principles of legal certainty and non-retroactivity' (*Criminal proceedings against Kolpinghuis Nijmegen BV*, para.13). In *Criminal proceedings against Arcaro*, Case 168/95, [1996] E.C.R. 4705, the Court even claimed that '[the] obligation of the national court to refer to the content of the directive when interpreting the relevant rules of its own national law reaches a limit where such an interpretation leads to the imposition on an individual of an obligation laid down by a directive which has not been transposed' (para. 42). This ruling should, however, be interpreted restrictively. Indeed, P. Craig ('Directives: Direct Effect, Indirect Effect and the Construction of National Legislation', [1997] 22 E.L. Rev. 519–538 at 527) has sceptically pointed out: 'If this is indeed so then it casts the whole doctrine of indirect effect into doubt.' In fact '[t]his was the whole point of engaging in the interpretive exercise'. 'Greater rights for the plaintiff will almost always mean commensurately greater obligations of the defendant.' The post-Arcaro jurisprudence appears to recognize this logical necessity (cf. S. Drake, 'Twenty Years after *Von Colson*: the impact of 'indirect effect' on the protection of the individual's Community rights', [2005] 30 E.L. Rev. 329–48 at 338).

159 S. Prechal, above n.145, 211. Nevertheless, it goes too far to claim that indirect effect is 'horizontal direct effect under another name' (T.C. Hartley, above n.72 at 221).

160 The question is, of course, *how much* milder! According to S. Prechal (above n.145 at 180) (emphasis added), '[t]he interpretation of national law in conformity with the directive constitutes, in general, a *relatively mild incursion* into the national legal system. In the ultimate analysis, it is then still national law which applies, although its content may be adjusted in the light of the directive'. The opposite view has been taken by Advocate General Jacobs: 'Because the existing case law already requires national courts in effect to enforce directives against individuals, by construing all provisions

disapply conflicting national law via the principle of supremacy.[161] While the doctrine of consistent interpretation is a method to avoid conflicts, the doctrine of supremacy is a method to *solve*—unavoidable—conflicts.[162] The *de facto* horizontal direct effect of directives will, thus, not only be *indirect*, but also *limited*, since it has to operate through the medium of national law. The doctrine of indirect effect thus further reinforces the character of directives as *indirect* Community legislation.

In sum, the legislative matrix of directives is structured in the following way. Directives are directly applicable. They are incorporated in the national legal orders from the moment they enter into force. They can also be directly effective—and thus a direct legislative source—once the deadline for implementation has passed.[163] However, directives can only be vertically directly effective. Their horizontal effects will typically be indirect, that is, transmitted *via* the medium of national law. The Court moreover favours the indirect legislative nature of directives—even for those parts that are directly effective: a directive's legislative substance will thus normally reach individuals through the medium of national legislation. The directive constitutes, therefore, a form of 'background legislation'. It only comes to the fore as (vertical) direct legislation, where the interpretation of national law fails to achieve the desired Community result. While the directive has thus elements of direct legislation, 'it is normally a form of *indirect regulatory or legislative measure*'.[164]

---

of national law, whether or not adopted for the purpose of implementing a directive and whether prior or subsequent to the directive, so as to give effect to the provisions of directives, it would not be a radical departure from the existing state of the law, in terms of its practical consequences, to assign horizontal direct effect to directives; such direct effect will arise only when it is impossible so to construe any provision of national law' (*Vaneetveld v Le Foyer*, Case 316/93, [1994] E.C.R. 763, para.32).

[161] I am grateful to M. Dougan for his thoughts on this issue presented at the DELI Seminar 'Competing visions on the effect of Community law: direct effect versus supremacy' (Durham, 1 November 2006).

[162] On the definition of the supremacy principle as a 'conflict-solving' mechanism, see: R. Schütze, *Supremacy without Pre-emption? The very slowly emergent Doctrine of Community Pre-emption*, [2006] 43 C.M.L. Rev. 1023–1048.

[163] Once a directive has been adopted, a Member State will, however, be under the constitutional obligation to 'refrain from taking any measures liable seriously to compromise the result prescribed' in the directive, see: *Inter-Environnement Wallonie ASBL v Region wallonne*, C-129/96, [1997] E.C.R. 7411, para.45. This obligation follows from Article 10 (2) in combination with Article 249 (3) EC and has nothing to do with the doctrine of direct effect. However, apart from the prohibition to frustrate the very objective of the directive, there is no anticipatory indirect effect: the national authorities are not required to interpret their national law in the light of Community law before the expiry of the deadline for transposition. After *Konstantinos Adeneler and Others v Ellinikos Organismos Galaktos (ELOG)*, Case C-212/04 (nyr), there is no longer room for speculation on this issue: '[W]here a directive is transposed belatedly, the general obligation owed by national courts to interpret domestic law in conformity with the directive exists only once the period for its transposition has expired' (*ibid.*, para.115).

[164] *Gibraltar v Council*, Case 298/89, [1993] E.C.R. 3605, para.16 (emphasis added).

B. The Regulatory Intensity of Directives: Constitutional Limits to Legislative Pre-emption?

Directives shall be binding 'as to the result to be achieved' and 'leave to the national authorities the choice of form and methods'.[165] The freedom to choose form and method of implementation conformed to the ordinary canon of international law.[166] Binding as to the result to be achieved, the instrument promised to respect the national level's power to autonomously select the legislative path that would lead towards the obligatory Community end. The 'two-stage legislation' had, it seemed, been specifically designed to protect the national sovereignty of the Member States.[167] The very term 'directive' suggested an instrument that would confine itself to 'directions' or 'guidelines'. The instrument's use for the harmonization of *national* law reinforced that vision.

Do directives embody broad-stroked 'directions' that will guarantee a degree of legislative autonomy to the national level? An early academic school has indeed argued that the instrumental format 'directive' will, *ipso facto*, protect a degree of national legislative autonomy.[168] These voices championed a constitutional framework limiting the directive's degree of pre-emption. To be a 'true' directive, a Community measure would have to leave a minimum degree of material legislative freedom to the national authorities. It could never field pre-empt national legislators within its scope of application, for:

[d]ie Zuerkennung einer durchgängigen Verbindlichkeit bei gleichzeitiger vollständiger oder nahezu vollständiger Detaillierbarkeit würde bedeuten, daß die Richtlinien damit in Rechtsinstrumente verwandelt wären, die sich von den an die Mitgliedstaaten gerichteten Entscheidungen letzten Endes nur noch durch ihre Bezeichnung unterscheiden.

---

[165] Article 249(3) EC.

[166] See the discussion on the direct effect of international agreements below: see section VI.A.

[167] A. Bleckmann, *Europarecht: Das Recht der Europäischen Union und der Europäischen Gemeinschaften* (Heymanns, 1997) at 163: 'Die Einführung dieses zweistufigen Gesetzgebungsverfahrens hatte drei Gründe. Einmal sollte die Souveränität der Mitgliedstaaten und ihrer Parlamente geschützt werden. Die Gesetzgebungsbefugnis sollte weiterhin in der Hand des Staates bleiben, das nationale Parlament sollte in seiner Regelungsbefugnis nicht allzu stark eingeengt werden. Für diese Regelung sprach zweitens, daß der Gedanke der Supranationalität bei der Abfassung des EWGV schon verblaßt war. Und drittens sollte den Mitgliedstaaten mit der Richtlinie ein Raum für eigene Entscheidungen belassen werden'.

[168] The following authors can be marshalled in favour of this position: M. Zuleeg, above n.84, 10: 'Die Wahl der Mittel muß einen materiellen Entscheidungsspielraum gewähren, sie kann sich nicht lediglich auf die Wahl der Form des Umsetzungsaktes beziehen. Ohne materielle Regelungsbefugnis wäre die Einschaltung des nationalen Normsetzers sinnlos.'; G. Gaja, P. Hay, R.D. Rotunda, above n.110 at 133: 'The detailed character of many provisions may be inconsistent with the *concept of directive* as defined in the EEC Treaty [.]'; M. Pechstein, *Die Mitgliedstaaten der EG als 'Sachwalter des gemeinsamen Interesses'* (Nomos, 1987) 47: 'Im folgenden wird die Richtlinienbefugnis jedoch typologisch als Rahmenzuständigkeit verstanden.'; P.E. Herzog, Article 189, in D. Campbell *et al.* (eds.), *The law of the European Community: a commentary on the EEC Treaty* (Matthew Bender, 1995), 613: 'The view that the definition of a directive given in [Article 249(3) EC], has a limiting effect on the various grants of powers in substantive Treaty provisions authorizing the issuance of directives

Damit würde aber dem Instrument der 'Richtlinie' im Grunde genommen die Existenzberechtigung entzogen. (...) Den Mitgliedstaaten soll grundsätzlich ein Mindestmaß an Autonomie in dem von der Richtlinie jeweils geregelten Sachbereich belassen werden; sie sollen nicht auf ein in alle Einzelheiten bindend vorgeschriebenes Verhalten festgelegt werden. Hierin liegt der besondere Charakter des Rechtsinstruments 'Richtlinie', der ihm erhalten bleiben muß, wenn es nicht seinen eigentlichen Sinn verlieren soll.[169]

The directive as a specific legislative format would lose its reason for being, so the argument goes, if its preemptive character approaches that of State-addressed decisions or regulations. This position interprets the directive in competence terms: 'The constitutional definition given in Article 249 (3) EC to the directive constitutes a *competence limit*.'[170] The Community legislator would act *ultra vires*, if it went beyond the constitutional frame set by the format of the directive. When precisely the pre-emptive Rubicon was crossed remained, however, shrouded in linguistic mist: a 'substantial' or 'reasonably necessary' degree of legislative autonomy was claimed for the Member States.[171]

The argument in favour of an inherent constitutional limit to the pre-emptive effect of directives has been criticized.[172] The Treaty would refer to a choice as regards *form* and *methods* of implementation and does not expressly refer to a degree of *material* policy choice that the national level is entitled to retain. Indeed, the constitutional reality of the Community legal order has never endorsed a constitutional maximum standard for the pre-emptive effect of directives. On the contrary, in *Enka* the Court of Justice expressly recognized a directive's ability to be 'exhaustive' or 'complete' harmonization, wherever strict legislative uniformity

---

seems correct.'; D. Triantafyllou, *Vom Vertrags-zum Gesetzesvorbehalt: Beitrag zum positiven Rechtmäßigkeitsprinzip in der EG* (Nomos, 1996), 47 and 82: 'Konkurrierende Zuständigkeiten begründen insbesondere die Ermächtigungen zum Erlaß von Richtlinien. Dabei regelt— definitionsgemäß—der Gemeinschaftsgesetzgeber nur das Grundsätzliche (den Zweck), was den nationalen Gesetzgebern erheblichen Gestaltungsspielraum bei der Wahl der Mittel beläßt auch wenn sich die Regelungsdichte der Richtlinie im Laufe der Zeit erhöht hat.'; A. Furrer, *Die Sperrwirkung des sekundären Gemeinschaftsrechts auf die nationalen Rechtsordnungen: Die Grenzen des nationalen Gestaltungsspielraums durch sekundärrechtliche Vorgaben unter besonderer Berücksichtigung des 'nationalen Alleingangs'*, (Nomos, 1994), 65: 'ihr [Richtlinie] zurückhaltender, den nationalen Handlungsspielraum grundsätzlich wahrender Ansatz'.

[169] D. Oldekop, 'Die Richtlinien der Europäischen Wirtschaftsgemeinschaft' [1972] 21 Jahrbuch des öffentlichen Rechts 55–106 at 92–3.

[170] '[D]ie Legaldefinition der Richtlinie [bildet] eine Kompetenzschranke': M. Zuleeg, above n.84 at 11 (emphasis added).

[171] D. Oldekop, above n.169 at 93: 'zulässige Maximum der Detaillierung ist dann überschritten, wenn dem Richtlinienadressaten keine beachetenswerte eigene, auf die Sache selbst bezogene Gestaltungsmöglichkeit verbleibt'; P.E. Herzog, above n.168 at 614: 'reasonably necessary'.

[172] The following commentators have been critical of the view: H-J. Rabe, *Das Verordnungsrechts der Europäischen Wirtschaftsgemeinschaft* (Appel, 1963), 41: 'Die Richtlinie selbst ist frei in ihrer "Regelungsintensität".'; H.P. Ipsen, Richtlinien-Ergebnisse, in: W. Hallstein (ed.), *Zur Integration Europas*: Festschrift für Carl Friedrich Ophüls aus Anlaß seines siebzigsten Geburtstages (C.F. Müller, 1965) 67–84 at 71: '[Es] besteht nahezu ausnahmslose Einhelligkeit darüber, daß die Richtlinie im

was necessary.[173] Directives can, therefore, occupy a regulatory field and have the capacity to totally pre-empt national legislators. This is, by no means, a singular phenomenon.[174]

The Community legislator has 'used the directive as a *loi uniforme* as needed, which can impose detailed instructions on the Member States as to the legal state of affairs to be created'.[175] The national choice, referred to in Article 249(3) EC, guarantees today only the power of Member States to implement the Community *content* into national *form*: '[T]he choice is limited to the *kind* of measures to be taken; their *content* is entirely determined by the directive at issue. Thus the discretion as far as form and methods are concerned does not mean that Member States necessarily have a margin in terms of policy making.'[176] The constitutional formula of 'choice of form and methods' only safeguards the formal freedom to translate the Community norm into the legal vernacular of the national legal order. The comparison of the Community instrument 'directive' with the (German) constitutional concept of *Rahmengesetzgebung* is, consequently, misleading. The pre-emptive capacity of directives is—like that of regulations and decisions—unlimited.

C. Excursus: The Instrumental Format of State-addressed Decisions

Decisions are directly applicable and may, as individual decisions, be directly effective *vis-à-vis* their addressees. From a functional perspective brought to the concept of legislation, the Treaty had clearly denied their legislative character: decisions shall only be binding in their entirety upon those to whom they are

Interesse ihrer Funktionsfähigkeit erforderlichenfalls die abschließende Rechtsgestaltung selbst enthalten darf, so daß die mitgliedstaatliche Form- und Mittel-Bereitstellung sich darin erschöpfen muß, dem Richtliniengehalt unverändert innerstaatliche Wirksamkeit zu verschaffen.', and, E. Fuss, 'Die 'Richtlinie' des Europäischen Gemeinschaftsrechts', [1965] 80 Deutsches Verwaltungsblatt 378–84 at 380: 'daß eine Richtlinie auch eine sehr detaillierte Regelung enthalten kann, wenn und soweit dies zur Errichung eines Vertragszieles als unumgänglich erscheint'.

173 *Enka BV v Inspecteur der invoerrechten en accijnzen*, Case 38/77, [1977] E.C.R. 2203, paras. 11–12: 'It emerges from the third paragraph of [Article 249] of the Treaty that the choice left to the Member States as regards the form of the measures and the methods used in their adoption by the national authorities depends upon the result which the Council or the Commission wishes to see achieved. As regards the harmonization of the provisions relating to customs matters laid down in the Member States by law, regulation or administrative action, in order to bring about the uniform application of the common customs tariff it may prove necessary to ensure the *absolute identity of those provisions*' (*ibid.*, paras.11–12).

174 E.g. *Criminal Proceedings against T. Ratti*, Case 148/78, [1979] E.C.R. 1629.

175 J. Bast, above n.74 at 11. Again, for an early criticism, see: R.W. Lauwaars, *Lawfulness and Legal Force of Community Decisions*, (A.W. Sijthoff, 1973) 30–31: 'But can this be carried so far that no freedom at all is left to the member States? In my opinion it follows from [Article 249] that the directive *as a whole* must allow member States the possibility of carrying out the rules embodied in the directive in their own way. A directive that constitutes a uniform law is not compatible with this requirement because, by definition, it places a duty on the member States to take over the uniform text and does not allow any freedom as to choice of form and method.'

176 S. Prechal, above n.145 at 73.

addressed.[177] Decisions can be addressed to private persons. Decisions can also be addressed to Member States.[178] The normative format of this second group of decisions has evolved alongside that of directives. While in 1962 the Court had still identified the essential characteristic of a decision by reference to the fact that it applied only to a limited number of persons,[179] State-addressed decisions were soon announced to be able to create rights for a general category of 'third parties'.

In *F. Grad v Finanzamt Traunstein*,[180] the Court was asked to look at the effect of a Council decision addressed to all Member States. The German government had insisted on a textual reading of Article 249(4) EC: State-addressed decisions cannot create rights for private persons; rights or obligations within the national legal order could only emanate from the national implementing legislation. The response of the European Court was a clear no: 'Although the effects of a decision may not be identical with those of a provision contained in a regulation, this difference does not exclude the possibility that the end result, namely the right of the individual to invoke the measures before the courts, may be the same as that of a directly applicable provision of a regulation.'[181] State-addressed decisions will, consequently, be capable of creating rights for a general class of private citizens. They can be legislative acts.[182]

Yet will they be capable of imposing obligations on individuals? This is doubtlessly an inherent feature of 'private' decisions. Should this normative characteristic be extended to State-addressed decisions? Giving them horizontal direct effect would render them into a form of direct Community legislation. Some have indeed referred to the structural similarity between private decisions and State-addressed decisions to affirm the horizontal direct effect of the latter.[183]

---

[177] Article 249(4) EC. Decisions without any addressee—decisions *sui generis* (atypical acts, because of the obvious derivation from the constitutional definition offered in Article 249(4) EC)— have emerged as a new legal instrument and have been characterized as follows: 'A distinctive feature can be found in their specific operating mode: while regulations are directly applicable in all Member States and thus can directly oblige each legal subject, addresseeless decisions lack this capacity. The obligatory force of addresseeless decisions is limited. Obligatory effects are only created within the institutional sphere of the Union: they are binding upon the institutions and bodies set up by, or on the basis of, the Treaties, and their respective personnel.' (A. von Bogdandy, F. Arndt & J. Bast, 'Legal Instruments in European Union Law and their Reform: A Systematic Approach on an Empirical Basis', [2004] 23 Y.E.L. 91–136 at 104).

[178] State-addressed decisions are 'binding on all the organs of the State to which they are addressed, including the courts of that State' (*Albako Margarinefabrik Maria von der Linde GmbH & Co. KG v Bundesanstalt für landwirtschaftliche Marktordnung*, Case 249/85, [1987] E.C.R. 2345, para.17).

[179] *Confédération nationale des producteurs de fruits and légumes and others v Council*, Case 16–17/62, [1962] 471, para.2.

[180] *Grad v Finanzamt Traunstein*, Case 9/70, [1970] E.C.R. 825.   [181] *Ibid.*, para.5.

[182] R. Greaves is more cautious when referring to the 'quasi-legislative' character of state-addressed decisions (R. Greaves, 'The Nature and Binding Effect of Decisions under Article 189 EC', (1996) 21 E.L. Rev. 3–16 at 11).

[183] A. von Bogdandy, J. Bast & F. Arndt, 'Handlungsformen im Unionsrecht: Empirische Analysen und dogmatische Strukturen in einem vermeintlichen Dschungel', [2002] 62 Zeitschrift

The better view, however, is to transpose the constitutional bar to horizontal direct effects—developed in the context of directives—to state-addressed decisions.[184] State-addressed decisions should only be vertically directly effective. State-addressed decisions, therefore, constitute a second form of indirect Community legislation.

VI. External Community Legislation: International Agreements

A. International Agreements—A Direct or an Indirect Form of Community Legislation?

In the 'globalized' world of today, international agreements have become an important legal instrument. Many legal orders have 'opened-up' to a monist position: under monism, international treaties are *constitutionally* recognized as an autonomous legal source of domestic law. The European Court of Justice has, early on, chosen a monist road: international agreements concluded by the Community enter the Community legal order without the need for additional transposition or incorporation. International treaties 'form an integral part of the Community legal system' from the date of their entry into force.[185] Community agreements are, therefore, directly applicable in the Community legal order.[186] The *capacity* of international treaties to directly and generally affect the lives of European citizens renders them into a form of external Community legislation.

Yet, even in a monist legal order, not all international treaties will be directly effective. Particular treaties may lack direct effect for 'when the terms of the

für ausländisches öffentliches Recht und Völkerrecht 77–161 at 98–99: 'Als privategerichtete Entscheidung ist sie dazu gerade prädestiniert, individuelle Verpflichtungen aufzuerlegen. Es bestehen deshalb auch keine Bedenken, eine staatengerichtete Entscheidung als Ermächtigungsnorm für einen Verwaltungsakt anzuerkennen. (...) Das spezifische Profil, daß die Richtlinie der staatengerichteten Entscheidung (...) voraus hat, liegt in einem Leistungs*un*vermögen zur unmittelbaren Verpflichtung Privater.'

[184] In this sense; T.C. Hartley, *The foundations of European Community law: an introduction to the constitutional and administrative law of the European Community* (OUP, 2003) 224 and already M. Zuleeg, above n. 84 at 9. The normative similarity of directives and that of State-addressed decisions has led some authors to view directives and State-addressed decisions as expressions of a broader generic instrumental form (A. Scherzberg, 'Verordnung—Richtlinie—Entscheidung', in H. Siedentopf (ed), *Europäische Integration und nationale Verwaltung* (Steiner, 1991), 17–42 at 42: 'Richtlinie und staatengerichtete Entscheidung stellen sich dagegen als Ausprägungen einer einheitlichen Handlungsform dar.').

[185] *Haegemann v Belgium*, Case 181/73, [1974] E.C.R. 449, para.5.

[186] The following section draws on the conceptual distinction between direct application and direct effect developed in the context of internal Community legislation, see: sections IV. A and V. A.

stipulation import a contract, when either of the parties engages to perform a particular act, the treaty addresses itself to the political, not to the judicial department; and the legislature must execute the contract before it can become a rule for the Court'.[187] Where a treaty addresses the legislative branch, it will not be self-executing as its norms will not be operational for the executive or the judiciary.

The doctrine of self-execution or direct effect is still a 'monist' doctrine. Dualist systems deny the legal validity of an international treaty within the domestic legal order *a priori*. Dualism insists on a validating domestic act. International agreements are not direct instruments of domestic legislation. Monist legal systems, on the other hand, recognize the legal validity of (properly concluded) international treaties in the national legal order. However, the *effectiveness* of a particular international treaty in the national legal order will depend on the extent to which it has been given direct effect.[188] The doctrine of direct effect represents, therefore, a yardstick for the actual openness of a legal system: it is a *chiffre* for the intensity— and concrete proof—of its monist creed.

Are Community agreements instruments of direct Community legislation or indirect legislative instruments; or, perhaps, both? The key to the direct or indirect legislative nature of international treaties in the Community legal order lies again in the doctrine of 'direct effect'. The question whether a Community agreement has direct effect has—just as for internal legislation—been monopolized by the European Court of Justice.[189] Let us investigate three aspects of the doctrine of direct effect for international agreements: the conditions for direct effect, the dimensions of direct effect and, finally, the constitutional nature of the direct effect doctrine for international agreements.

---

[187] *Foster v Neilson*, [1829] 27 U.S. (2 Pet.) 253 at 314.

[188] The direct effect of an international treaty within the domestic legal order is, ultimately, a domestic decision. See: Y. Iwasawa, 'The Doctrine of Self-Executing Treaties in the United States: A Critical Analysis', [1985–6] 26 Virginia Journal of International Law 627–92 at 651: 'States determine how to implement their international legal obligations on the municipal level. It is well recognized that domestic law determines the 'validity' and 'rank' of treaties in domestic law. If this is so, domestic law should also determine the 'direct applicability' of treaties in domestic law. (...) The determination of whether the terms of a treaty are so precise that it could be considered directly applicable can vary from one state to another depending on various factors.' This is not uncontroversial, but corresponds to the position of the European Court of Justice: 'Although each contracting party is responsible for executing fully the commitments which it has undertaken it is nevertheless free to determine the legal means appropriate for attaining that end in its legal system, unless the agreement, interpreted in the light of its subject-matter and purpose, itself specifies those means' (*Portugal v Council*, 149/96, [1999] E.C.R. 8395, para.35).

[189] The Court has justified the 'centralization' of the direct effect question by reference to the uniformity of the Community legal order. The effects of the Community's international agreements 'may not be allowed to vary . . . according to the effects in the internal legal order of each Member State which the law of that State assigns to international agreements concluded by it. Therefore it is for the Court, within the framework of its jurisdiction in interpreting the provisions of agreements,

(i) Conditions for Direct Effect

When will an international treaty have direct effect in the Community legal order? The Court has devised a two-stage test.[190] In the first stage, the Court will examine whether the agreement *as a whole* is capable of containing directly effective provisions. The signatory parties to the agreement may have positively settled this issue themselves.[191] If this is not the case, the Court will employ a 'policy test' that will look at the nature, aim, purpose, spirit or general scheme of the treaty.[192] This evaluation is inherently political in nature as it will have political effects: the recognition of direct effect by the Community judicature will 'deprive the legislative or executive organs of the Community of the scope for manoeuvre [for implementation] enjoyed by their counterparts in the Community's trading partners'.[193] Direct effect is, thus, a 'political question'; and the first part of the doctrine of direct effect, therefore, a facet of a political question doctrine. Here, the Court's approach to the direct effect of external Community law differs from its approach to direct effect in the internal sphere: internal law is today *presumed* to be capable of direct effect.[194]

Where the 'political question' hurdle has been crossed, the Court will turn to examining the direct effect of a specific provision of the agreement.[195] The second stage of the test constitutes a classic direct effect analysis: individual provisions must represent a 'clear and precise obligation which is not subject, in its implementation or effects, to the adoption of any subsequent measures'.[196] While the formulation of the test is thus identical to that for internal legislation, the actual results may vary. Identically worded provisions in internal and external legislation may not necessarily be given the same effect.[197]

---

to ensure the uniform application throughout the Community' (*Hauptzollamt Mainz v Kupferberg & Cie.*, Case 104/81, [1982] E.C.R. 3641, para.14).

[190] For an excellent analysis, see: A. Peters, 'The Position of International Law within the European Community Legal Order', [1997] 40 German Yearbook of International Law 9–77 at 53–4 and 58–66.   [191] Kupferberg, para.17.

[192] Cf. *International Fruit Company and others v Produktschap voor Groenten en Fruit*, Case 21–24/72, [1972] E.C.R. 1219, para.20 as well as *Germany v Council*, Case 280/93, [1993] E.C.R. 3667, para.105.   [193] *Portugal v Council*, Case 149/96, [1999] E.C.R. 8395, para.46.

[194] A. Peters, above n.190 at 55. This difference between the doctrine of direct effect in the internal and the external sphere has been criticized by the author: '[G]iven the communitarization of international agreements, which makes them an integral part of Community law with Community nature, pure theoretical consistency would rather suggest granting direct effect to external Community law on the same footing as to internal Community law' (*ibid.*, 57).

[195] The two prongs of the test can be well seen in *Hauptzollamt Mainz v Kupferberg & Cie.*, Case 104/81 [1982] E.C.R. 3641: in paras.18–22, the Court undertook the global policy test, while in paras.23–27 it looked at the conditions for direct effect of a specific provision.

[196] *Demirel v Stadt Schwäbisch Gmünd*, Case 12/86, [1987] E.C.R. 3719, para.14.

[197] J.H.J. Bourgeois, 'Effects of International Agreements in European Community Law: Are the Dice Cast?', [1983–4] 82 Michigan Law Review 1250–1273 at 1261. See also the discussion on the pre-emptive effect of international treaties in section VI. B below. The reasoning of the Court will apply, *mutatis mutandis*, to the question of direct effect.

(ii) The Dimensions of Direct Effect

What are the dimensions of the doctrine of direct effect? Will a directly effective treaty unfold this effect vertically *and* horizontally? Two constitutional options exist. First, international treaties can have horizontal direct effect. Then international treaties would come close to being 'external regulations'.[198] Alternatively, the Community legal order could treat international agreements as 'external directives' and limit their direct effect to the vertical dimension. Community citizens could then only invoke a directly effective provision of a Community agreement against the Community and the Member States. The Court has not expressly decided the matter. Its analysis in *Polydor* seemed, however, tacitly based on the possible horizontal direct effect of the international agreement at issue.[199] There, the Court held that 'the *enforcement by the proprietor or by persons entitled under him* of copyrights (...) is justified on the ground of the protection of industrial and commercial property within the meaning of Article 23 of the Agreement and therefore does not constitute a restriction on trade between the Community and Portugal such as is prohibited by Article 14(2) of the Agreement. Such enforcement does not constitute a means of arbitrary discrimination or a disguised restriction on trade between the Community and Portugal.'[200] We should assume, contrariwise, that if the exercise of the proprietor's copyright had not been *justified* under Article 23 of the international treaty, the enforcement of his private right would have been prohibited under Article 14(2) of the international agreement. The treaty would then have imposed an obligation on an individual and would thus have had horizontal direct effect.

---

[198] It is not very helpful to approach the question of the possible horizontal direct effect of international treaties through a comparison with the EC Treaty. Yet, this has been the dominant perspective in European constitutional circles: 'Many provisions of the EC Treaty have been held to be directly effective both vertically and horizontally. The fact of their being addressed to states has been no bar to their horizontal effects. The same argument can be applied to international agreements' (D. McGoldrick, *International Relations Law of the European Union* (Longman, 1997) 133). This argument has rightly been questioned: 'On the other hand, it could be argued that a distinction should be made between the provisions of the Treaties and the provisions of international agreements concluded by the Communities. The underlying justification for the principle that certain provisions of the Treaties have direct effect is based on the nature of the Community legal order: a Community pursuing economic and social objectives and comprising not only the Member States but also their nationals. Those considerations do not apply to agreements with third countries and there is therefore no reason to construe the provisions of such agreements, in the absence of express provision, in such a way as to impose obligations on persons other than the parties to them' (I. MacLeod, I.D. Hendry & S. Hyett, *The external relations of the European communities: a manual of law and practice* (OUP, 1996) 137). The authors' warning note about the special nature of the EC Treaty as the constitutional charter of the Community must be taken seriously. However, it does not specifically provide an argument against horizontal direct effect of international agreements, but rather an argument against the direct effect of these treaties in general. In view of the 'secondary' legal nature of Community agreements, I therefore prefer to compare them to the legislative instruments under Article 249 EC.

[199] *Polydor and others v Harlequin and others*, Case 270/80, [1982] E.C.R. 329. For a discussion of the facts and the decision of the ECJ, see section VI. B below.   [200] *Ibid.*, para.22.

Doubts remained.[201] The Court did not dispel them in *Sevince*.[202] Dealing with a decision of an Association Council, the Court somewhat ambivalently held that '[a]lthough non-publication of those decisions *may* prevent their being applied to a private individual, a private individual is not thereby deprived of the power to invoke, in the dealings with a public authority, the rights which those decisions confer on him'.[203] Did this mean, contrariwise, that if these decisions— being assimilated to the international treaty that formed its base—had been published they could have had horizontal direct effect? If so, the great majority of international agreements that are directly effective will be so along the vertical and horizontal dimension.[204]

That reading has indeed gained ground. In *Deutscher Handballbund eV v Kolpak*[205] the Court was asked whether rules drawn up by the German Handball Federation 'within the framework of the autonomy which associations are recognised as having' would be discriminatory on grounds of nationality. The private sports association had refused to grant Kolpak—a Slovakian national employed by a German handball club—the same rights as German players. This seemed to violate Article 38 of the Association Agreement between the Community and Slovakia stipulating that 'workers of Slovak Republic nationality legally employed in the territory of a Member State shall be free from any discrimination based on nationality, as regards working conditions, remuneration or dismissal, as compared to its own nationals'. The question, therefore, arose whether this article 'also has effects *vis-à-vis third parties inasmuch as it does not apply solely to measures taken by the authorities but also extends to rules applying to employees that are collective in nature*'.[206]

The Court thought that this could indeed be the case. Referring to its case law on Article 39(2) EC, it recalled that 'working conditions in the different Member States are governed sometimes by provisions laid down by law or regulation and sometimes by agreements and other acts concluded or adopted by private persons'. This reasoning could be fully transposed to the equivalent provision in

---

[201] These doubts inevitably gave rise to a good degree of academic speculation. In 1985, the following questions were put to H.J. Glaesner—who was then the Director General of the Legal Service of the Council—by the House of Lords Select Committee on the European Communities: 'You are well acquainted with the direct effect doctrine of internal provisions of the Treaty of Rome. As regards external provisions, Community case law only supports direct effects which can be invoked against Member States. Is there any likelihood of it being extended to relations between private individuals...?' 'Would the distinction be likely to be that the Court would be more ready to grant an individual's right arising out of an external treaty...but would [it] hesitate to impose obligations on individuals arising out of those external treaties?' The Director-General could only answer: 'That is my feeling; it is not a philosophical consideration but a *feeling* of mine' (Select Committee on the European Communities: External Competence of the European Communities, [1984–5] Sixteenth Report (Her Majesty's Stationary Office, 1985), 154 (emphasis added)).

[202] *Sevince v Staatssecretaris van Justitie*, Case 192/89, [1990] E.C.R. 3461.

[203] *Ibid.*, para.24 (emphasis added).

[204] International agreements concluded by the Community will normally be published in the Directory of Community legislation in force.

[205] *Deutscher Handballbund eV v Maros Kolpak*, Case C-438/00, [2003] E.C.R. 4135.

[206] *Ibid.*, para.19 (emphasis added).

the Association Agreement. Consequently, 'Article 38(1) of the Association Agreement with Slovakia applies to a rule drawn up by a sports federation such as the DHB which determines the conditions under which professional sportsmen engage in gainful employment'.[207] This implicit recognition of the horizontal direct effect of international agreements has been confirmed outside the context of association agreements.[208]

In the absence of any mandatory constitutional reason to the contrary, this choice in favour of horizontal direct effect seems preferable. Like US American constitutionalism, the European legal order should not exclude the horizontal direct effect of international treaties. The problems encountered in the context of Community directives would be reproduced—if not multiplied—if the European Court were to split the direct effect of international treaties into two halves. Self-executing treaties should be able 'to establish rights *and duties* of individuals directly enforceable in domestic courts'.[209]

(iii) The Constitutional Nature of Direct Effect

Is the nature of the doctrine of direct effect in the external sphere the same as in the internal sphere of Community law? The constitutional meaning of the doctrine of direct effect has evolved over time. In the early days of the Community, the European Court of Justice appeared to conceive the doctrine of direct effect in terms of 'conferring rights on citizens of the Community which they can invoke before the courts'.[210] Premised on the assumption that the Community agreement was an 'integral part of Community law', the doctrine of direct effect seemed to concern the issue of whether an individual could invoke the international treaty to challenge the validity of Community or national legislation.

This 'subjective rights' reading of the doctrine has, however, been qualified in the Banana ruling. In *Germany v Council*,[211] the European Court of Justice was asked—for the first time—to review the legality of internal Community legislation against an international treaty under Article 230 EC. Not a Community citizen, but a Member State had questioned the validity of the EC's banana regulation. Germany argued that compliance with GATT rules was an objective condition for the lawfulness of Community acts and, therefore, had nothing to do with the question of direct effect.[212] The Court did *not* adopt this line of reasoning. 'Those

---

[207] *Ibid.*, paras.32 and 37.

[208] See: *Igor Simutenkov v Ministerio de Educacion y Cultura and Real Federacion Espanola de Futbol*, Case C-265/03, [2005] E.C.R. 2579, where the Court confirmed *Deutscher Handballbund* in the context of the Partnership and Cooperation Agreement between the EC and the Russian Federation.

[209] S.A. Riesenfeld, 'International Agreements', [1989] 14 Yale Journal of International Law 455–467 at 463 (emphasis added).

[210] *International Fruit Company and others v Produktschap voor Groenten en Fruit*, Case 21–24/72, [1972] E.C.R. 1219, para.8.   [211] *Germany v Council*, Case 280/93, [1994] E.C.R. 4973.

[212] *Ibid.*, para.103. The argument was repeated in *Portugal v Council*, Case 149/96, [1999] E.C.R. 8395, para.32.

features of GATT, from which the Court concluded that an individual within the Community can invoke it in a court to challenge the lawfulness of a Community act', the Court of Justice argued, 'also preclude the Court from taking provisions of GATT into consideration to assess the lawfulness of a regulation in an action brought by a Member State under the first paragraph of [Article 230] of the Treaty'.[213]

Did the *Bananas* ruling significantly change the nature and function of the doctrine of direct effect for international treaties? Did Europe 'slip on bananas'?[214] Under a minimalist reading, the Court simply extended the conditions for review from *private* applicants to one class of privileged applicants: the Member States. Solid constitutional reasons will justify such an extension.[215] The maximalist reading would go further and claim that nobody, not even the Community institutions, could invoke an international treaty that lacks direct effect to challenge the legality of Community or national legislation.[216] Regardless which reading will ultimately prevail, the ruling progressed to a more 'objective' meaning of the doctrine of direct effect of international agreements.[217] The Court came closer to characterizing direct effect as a function of the nature of the legal norm at issue.

---

[213] *Germany v Council*, Case 280/93, [1994] E.C.R. 4973, para.109 (emphasis added).

[214] U. Everling, 'Will Europe slip on Bananas? The Bananas Judgment of the Court of Justice and National Courts', [1996] 33 C.M.L. Rev. 401–437.

[215] These reasons are extensively discussed by A. Peters, above n.190 at 67–68.

[216] Has the maximalist reading been ruled out by subsequent jurisprudence? In *Commission v Germany (IDA)*, Case 61/94, [1996] E.C.R. 3989, the Court allowed the Commission to bring an infringement action under Article 226 EC on the basis that Germany had failed to fulfil its obligations under the International Diary Agreement (IDA), which—forming part of the WTO family—would presumably lack direct effect. The Court, however, suprisingly found that Germany had failed its obligations under the IDA. If that decision has been a conscious one, the Court will allow non-directly effective international agreements to serve as a standard of review for national measures, while it will not allow such a review for Community measures. The application of such a double standard would have the flavour of legal hypocrisy. For the opposite view, see: C. Timmermans, 'The EU and Public International Law', [1999] 4 European Foreign Affairs Review 181–94 at 192.

A second ruling could also be taken to signal a mellowing of the *Banana* ruling. In *Kingdom of the Netherlands v European Parliament and Council*, Case 377/98, [2001] E.C.R. 6229, the European Court stated in relation to the Convention on Biological Diversity (CBD): 'Even if, as the Council maintains, the CBD contains *provisions which do not have direct effect*, in the sense that they do not create rights which individuals can rely on directly before the courts, that fact does not preclude review by the courts of compliance with the obligations incumbent on the Community as a party to that agreement' (*ibid.*, para.54). However, this passage should be interpreted restrictively. The existence of a number of specific provisions without direct effect will not imply that the *agreement as a whole* lacks direct effect. The general direct effect of the CBD was not in principle excluded. It passed the general 'policy test' because the agreement 'unlike the WTO agreement, is not strictly based on reciprocal and mutually advantageous arrangements' (*ibid.*, para.53). Once the agreement passes the general policy test, the agreement as a whole can, arguably, be used as a standard of review.

[217] Instead of identifying direct effect with the existence of 'subjective rights' of individuals, the Court will rather ask whether the rule was 'among the rules applicable by their judicial organs' (*Portugal v Council*, para.43). 'This is a classic direct-effect analysis, which is geared towards establishing whether a provision is sufficiently operational for judicial application' (P. Eeckhout, *External Relations of the European Union: legal and constitutional Foundations* (OUP, 2004) 314).

The more objective notion of direct effect thus parallels the evolution of the doc-trine of direct effect in the context of internal Community legislation.

The maximalist view, however, raises an important theoretical question. If an international treaty—like the GATT Agreement—cannot legally be enforced within the Community legal order, can we seriously argue that the agreement is an integral part of the Community *legal* order? Echoes of legal realism emerge: can a rule that is not enforceable in a legal order be considered a *legal* rule? Is there, in other words, not a link between legal validity and direct effect? The argument has indeed been made in the form of an elegant metaphor. The doctrine of direct effect would constitute the 'bridge between monism and dualism':

> The notion of direct effect is eminently suitable to serve as a seeming bridge between monism and dualism. This may sound counter-intuitive, for usually direct effect is associated with monism, so much so that in strict dualism, there is no place for a direct effect doctrine. Closer scrutiny reveals, however, that direct effect functions like a double-edged sword or, perhaps more accurately, as both a sword and a shield. On the one hand, the notion of direct effect does indeed allow international norms to be applied in domestic settings; here then, it works as a sword, opening up the domestic legal order. Yet, because direct effect is only granted to some norms and not to others, it also protects the national legal order from international law. The idea of direct effect thus functions as a gatekeeper: some norms may enter, others may not. (...) Put briefly, if a treaty provision is directly effective, then it can enter the Community legal order; if it is not directly effective, then the Community legal order remains closed.[218]

The idea that the doctrine of direct effect 'introduces' international agreements into the Community legal order, however, goes too far. It would overstretch the doctrine of direct effect and blur the conceptual border with the adjacent concept of direct application. This is debatable, for one might still object that '[i]f it is not operative, it is not a rule of law'.[219] However, the question is: when is a legal rule operative in a legal order?

Norms may have direct or indirect legal effects. An international treaty lacking direct effect may still enjoy an indirect effect in the Community legal order.[220] From this perspective, a Community agreement lacking direct effect can still be seen as an integral part of Community *law*. It has normative validity within the Community legal order and is directly applicable. The lack of direct effect simply means exactly that: an agreement that has no *direct* effect. It cannot be *directly*

---

[218] J. Klabbers, 'International Law in Community Law: The Law and Politics of Direct Effect', [2002] 21 Y.E.L. 263–98 at 295 and 297.

[219] P. Pescatore, 'The Doctrine of "Direct Effect": An Infant Disease of Community Law', [1983] E.L. Rev. 155–77 at 155.

[220] These indirect effects pose serious difficulties regarding the identification of direct effect with 'incorporation'. Klabbers is, therefore, forced to admit that despite the lack of direct effect of the international norms in *Fediol III* and *Nakajima*, 'international law is somehow already incorporated in Community law' (J. Klabbers, above n.218 at 298).

relied upon as a source of rights or a standard of review in the Community legal order. A treaty without direct effect requires a medium—an internal Community measure—to unfold its full effect in the Community legal order.

What are the indirect effects which a Community agreement can unfold? Is there a doctrine of indirect effects similar to the one the Court of Justice developed for internal Community law? Two constitutional principles spring to mind in this context.[221] First, there is the principle of 'consistent interpretation'.[222] In *Commission v Germany (IDA)*,[223] the ECJ defined the principle in the following terms: '*When the wording of secondary Community legislation [sic!] is open to more than one interpretation* (...) the primacy of international agreements concluded by the Community over provisions of secondary legislation means that such provisions must, *so far as possible, be interpreted in a manner that is consistent with those agreements.*'[224] The duty of the ECJ and national courts to interpret Community legislation 'as far as possible' in line with the Community's international treaties constitutes an extension of the doctrine of indirect effects into the external hemisphere of Community law.[225]

Secondly, there is the 'principle of implementation'.[226] In two exceptional circumstances an international agreement that lacks direct effect—typically: an agreement related to the WTO—will provide an *indirect* standard of review for the legality of a Community measure. This indirect review occurs 'where the Community *intended to implement a particular obligation* assumed in the context of the WTO, or where the *Community measure refers expressly to the precise provisions* of the WTO agreements'.[227] The legality of the internal Community measure is reviewed 'in the light of'[228] the international treaty.

According to the first prong of the implementation principle, established in *Nakajima*,[229] a WTO agreement will prevail over inconsistent Community legislation, where the latter intends to implement the former. In that case, the Anti-Dumping Code of the GATT was at stake. The Court pointed out that the applicant was 'not relying on the direct effect of those provisions' but on Article 230 EC, i.e. on an '*infringement of the Treaty or any rule of law relating to its*

---

[221] It would constitute a digression to discuss the—truly 'cubist'—constitutional principles governing the interpretation of mixed agreements. For an analysis of this complex area, see: J. Heliskoski, 'The Jurisdiction of the European Court of Justice to give Preliminary Rulings on the Interpretation of Mixed Agreements', [2000] 69 Nordic Journal of International Law, 395–412, and P. Koutrakos, 'The Interpretation of Mixed Agreements under the Preliminary Reference Procedure', [2002] 7 European Foreign Affairs Review, 25–52.

[222] For a discussion of the principle, see P. Eeckhout, *External relations of the European Union: legal and constitutional foundations* (OUP, 2004) 314–16.

[223] *Commission v Germany (IDA)*, Case 61/94, [1996] E.C.R. 3989.

[224] *Ibid.*, para.52 (emphasis added).

[225] See section VA above.   [226] P. Eeckhout, above n.222 at 316.

[227] *Portugal v Council*, Case 149/96, [1999] E.C.R. 8395, para. 49 (emphasis added).

[228] *Ibid.* In *Germany v Council*, Case 280/93, [1994] E.C.R. 4973, para.111, the Court uses the phrase 'from the point of view of'.

[229] *Nakajima All Precision Co. Ltd v Council*, Case 69/89, [1991] E.C.R. 2069.

application'.[230] The Community measure had been adopted in order to comply with the international obligations of the Community, and therefore it was apparently 'necessary to examine whether the Council went beyond the legal framework thus laid down'.

We encounter a variation on that theme in *Fediol*.[231] Regulation No 2641/84 had been adopted in the aftermath of 'the conclusions of the European Council of June 1982, which considered that it was of the highest importance to defend vigorously the legitimate interests of the Community in the appropriate bodies, in particular GATT'.[232] Its Article 2(1) prohibited all 'illicit commercial practices' as 'any international trade practices attributable to third countries which are incompatible with international law or with the generally accepted rules'. The specific reference to international law, in particular GATT, in the Community measure, so the Court claimed, did entitle it to review the actions of the Commission in the light of the GATT rules. As the Community legislator had instructed the Commission to let its action be guided by the international norms, judicial review of these actions would also involve the interpretation and indirect application of GATT.[233]

What is the constitutional rationale behind these cases? What is clear is that it was not the international agreements *themselves* that provided the direct basis for review. The international treaties were only the *indirect* standard, for the Community measures were only reviewed 'in the light of' these treaties. The international norms had been mediated through a Community measure. Could one not, therefore, argue that *through the act of implementation* the EC institutions have 'used and forfeited the international scope of manoeuvre'?[234] According to this view, it is the self-binding of the Community institutions—manifested in a specific domestic act by the Community—that provides the intellectual basis for the judicial review of Community actions.[235] The indirect effect of international rules will be determined by the *intention* of the Community legislator to implement international norms. Only *'because of that intention*, the international rule can be directly invoked to control the validity of the implementing legislation'. This approach is thus somewhat *'midway* between a monist and a dualist system of integrating international law'.[236] It is, arguably, closer to the monist than the dualist end of the spectrum.[237]

---

[230] *Ibid.*, para.28.   [231] *FEDIOL v Commission*, Case 70/87, [1989] E.C.R. 1781.

[232] Preample of the Regulation.

[233] *FEDIOL v Commission*, para.20.

[234] Eeckhout, above n.222 at 319.

[235] The constitutional concept of 'self-binding', albeit in the context of the executive branch, is well known in German public law.

[236] C. Timmermans, 'The EU and Public International Law', [1999] 4 European Foreign Affairs Review, 181–94 at 190 (emphasis added). Eeckhout neatly refers to the 'dualist streak' of the Court's approach: 'Whether one calls that type of effect direct or indirect, it is clear that, in theory at least, it involves more than mere consistent interpretation' (P. Eeckhout, 'The domestic legal status of the WTO Agreement: Interconnecting legal systems', [1997] 37 C.M.L. Rev. 11–58 at 44 and 42).

[237] From the viewpoint of our definitions of, respectively, direct applicability and direct effect, it is, strictly speaking, wrong to consider that the *Nakajima* doctrine 'envisages that international

(iv) Conclusion: International Agreements as a Direct Source of (External) Community Legislation

We can now return to the question we posed at the beginning of this section. Should international treaties concluded by the Community be seen as instruments of direct Community legislation or rather as indirect legislative instruments? In contrast to the Court's preference for the mediated effect of directives, the Court's approach to international treaties favours their direct effects over their indirect effects. Only where an international agreement lacks direct effect will the Court proceed to look for its indirect effects in the Community legal order.[238] Moreover, the Court has made clear that this indirect effect of international agreements represents an exception and, as such, will be interpreted restrictively.[239] Finally, as we saw above, the Court implicitly accepts the horizontal direct effect of Community agreements. Community agreements are, therefore, predominantly a form of direct legislation. They are best conceptualized as 'external regulations'—albeit placed on a higher hierarchical rank than internal regulations.

B. Double Pre-emption: International Agreements in the Community Legal Order

International treaties that are directly effective will be capable of legislative pre-emption in the domestic legal order. The pre-emptive effect of a Community

---

obligations have been *transposed* into EC law' which (G. A. Zonnekeyn, 'The ECJ's *Petrotup* Judgement, a Revival of the 'Nakajima Doctrine?', [2003] 30 Legal Issues of Economic Integration, 249–266 at 263 (emphasis added). The Community's international obligations need no 'transposition' in the sense of giving them legal validity in the Community legal order.

[238] This result has prompted F. Snyder to argue that there is a different relationship between the doctrines of direct effect and indirect effect in the external sphere. In the internal sphere the indirect effect doctrine would be 'a complement to, not a replacement of, direct effect', whereas in the external sphere it would be 'a replacement of direct effect, not merely a complement to it' (F. Snyder, 'The Gatekeepers: The European Courts and WTO Law', [2003] 40 C.M.L. Rev. 313–67 at 356). This is, with all respect, not quite a watertight statement: the doctrine of consistent interpretation—part and parcel of the doctrine of indirect effect—always operates in parallel to the doctrine of direct effect. It, therefore, complements the doctrine of direct effect in the internal and the external spheres.

[239] *Chiquita Brands and others v Commission*, Case T-19/01, [2005] E.C.R. II-315, para.117 (emphasis added): 'The rule arising from the Nakajima judgment is designed, *exceptionally*, to allow individuals, in an indirect manner, to plead infringement by the Community or its institutions, of GATT rules or WTO agreements. *As an exception to the principle that individuals may not directly rely on WTO provisions before the Community judicature, that rule must be interpreted restrictively.*' The restrictive interpretation of the *Fediol* principle, on the other hand, follows from the fact that the Court has not often applied it. The regulation challenged in *Germany v Council (Banana)* made a reference to the Community's obligations under international law in its preamble ('Whereas, so that the Community can respect Community Preference and its various international obligations, that common organization of the market should permit bananas produced in the Community and those from the ACP States which are traditional suppliers to be disposed of on the Community market providing an adequate income for producers and at fair prices for consumers without undermining imports of bananas from other third countries suppliers')—and yet the Court did not apply the *Fediol* principle to the facts of the case.

agreement may even be felt in two ways. First, directly effective Community agreements will pre-empt inconsistent *national* law.[240] Moreover, self-executing international obligations of the Community will pre-empt internal *Community* legislation that is in conflict with the international treaty. The pre-emptive potential of external over internal Community legislation follows from the 'primacy' of international agreements over the internal legal instruments of the Community.[241] Let us address the two dimensions of this double pre-emption in turn.

The first dimension of the pre-emptive ability of Community agreements relates to conflicting *national* measures. Will the pre-emptive scope of an international norm be the same as that of an identically worded provision of a regulation? We are forced to approach this question in an indirect manner, for the typical constellation reaching the Court involves a comparison between the pre-emptive effect of an agreement and the EC Treaty. In *Polydor*,[242] the Court was asked to rule on the compatibility of the 1956 British copyright act with the agreement between the European Community and Portugal. The bilateral free trade agreement envisaged that quantitative restrictions on imports and all measures having an equivalent effect to quantitative restriction should be abolished, but exempted all those restrictions justified on the grounds of the protection of intellectual property. Two importers of pop music had been charged with infringement of Polydor's copyrights and had invoked the directly effective provisions of the Community agreement as a sword against the British law.

Would the Community agreement pre-empt the national measure? If the Court had projected the 'internal' Community standard established by its jurisprudence in relation to Articles 28 EC *et seq.*, the national measure would have been pre-empted. But the Court did not. It chose to interpret the identically worded provision in the Community agreement more restrictively.[243] Identical text will, therefore, not guarantee identical interpretation: 'The fact that the provisions of an agreement and the corresponding Community provisions are identically worded does not mean that they must necessarily be interpreted identically. An international treaty is to be interpreted not only on the basis of its wording, but also in the light of its objectives'.[244] Context will thus prevail over

---

[240] E.g. *Commission v Germany (IDA)*, Case 61/94, [1998] E.C.R. 3989, where the European Court did find a national measure pre-empted by an international agreement. The agreement at stake was the international diary agreement and the Court found 'that Article 6 of the annexes precluded the Federal Republic of Germany from authorizing imports of dairy products, including those effected under inward processing relief arrangements, at prices lower than the minimum' (para.39).
[241] *Ibid.*, para.52.
[242] *Polydor and others v Harlequin and others*, Case 270/80, [1982] E.C.R. 329.
[243] *Ibid.*, paras.15, 18–19.
[244] *Opinion 1/91 (EFTA Draft Agreement)*, [1991] E.C.R. 6079, para.14. In relation to the EEA, the Court found that it was 'established on the basis of an international treaty which, essentially, *merely creates rights and obligations as between the Contracting Parties* and provides for no transfer of sovereign rights to the inter-governmental institutions which it sets up' (*ibid.*, para.20, emphasis added). The EC Treaty, by way of contrast, constituted 'the constitutional charter of a Community

text. In interpreting the pre-emptive depth of an international treaty, the Court will take the 'function' of the agreement into account. Only where an international norm fulfils the 'same function' as the internal Community norm, will the Court project the 'internal' pre-emptive effect to the international treaty.[245] It is, therefore, not correct to assume that international treaties are fully assimilated to 'internal' Community regulations, because they form an 'integral part' of the Community legal order.[246] While the Court may apply a milder form of pre-emption to international agreements, it has not announced any constitutional limits to the pre-emptive capacity of international agreements. They could, theoretically, field pre-empt the Community as well as the national legislators within their scope of application.

Let us turn to the second dimension of the pre-emptive effect of Community agreements. The capacity of international agreements to pre-empt inconsistent internal Community legislation follows from the primacy of the former over the latter. The contours of this second pre-emption analysis can be evidenced in *Kingdom of The Netherlands v Parliament and Council*.[247] The dispute concerned the annulment of Directive 98/44 EC on the legal protection of biotechnological inventions. The Netherlands had, *inter alia*, argued that the Community legislation violated Article 27(3)(b) of the TRIPS Agreement. The directive prohibits Member States to grant patents for plants and animals other than micro-organisms, while the international treaty provides for such a legal option. The Dutch government claimed that Article 27(3)(b) of the TRIPS agreement 'pre-empted' the higher Community standard.

The Court, while admitting that 'the Directive does deprive the Member States of the choice which the TRIPS Agreement offers to the parties to that agreement as regards the patentability of plants and animals', found that the Directive was 'in itself compatible with the Agreement'. The agreement would 'not prevent certain party States adopting a common position with a view to its application. The joint

based on the rule of law', one of whose particular characteristics would be 'the direct effect of a whole series of provisions which are applicable to their nationals' (*ibid.*, para.21).

[245] An illustration can be found in *Pabst & Richarz KG v Hauptzollamt Oldenburg*, Case 17/81, [1982] E.C.R. 1331, where the ECJ was asked to compare Article 53(1) of the association agreement between the Community and Greece: 'That provision, the wording of which is similar to that of [Article 90] of the Treaty, fulfils, within the framework of the association between the Community and Greece, the same function as that of [Article 90]. (. . .) It accordingly follows from the wording of Article 53(1), cited above, and from the objective and nature of the association agreement of which it forms part that that provision precludes a national system of relief from providing more favourable tax treatment for domestic spirits than for those imported from Greece' (*ibid.*, paras.26–27). This case law has more recently been confirmed in *The Queen v Secretary of State for the Home Department, ex parte Wieslaw Gloszczuk and Elzbieta Gloszczuk*, Case C-63/99, [2001] E.C.R. 6369 and *Land Nordrhein-Westfalen v Beata Pokrzeptowicz-Meyer*, Case C-162/00, [2002] E.C.R. 1049. While the ECJ had still found that the EC Treaty and EEA had different purposes and functions, the Court of First Instance seems now to favour a parallel interpretation of the EEA Agreement with identically worded provisions of the EC Treaty and secondary law in *Opel Austria GmbH v Council*, Case T-115/94, [1997] E.C.R. II-39.   [246] Eeckhout, above n.222 at 256.

[247] *Kingdom of the Netherlands v Parliament and Council*, Case 377/98, [200] E.C.R. 6229.

selection of an option offered by an international instrument to which the Member States are parties is an act that falls within the approximation of laws provided for by [Article 95] of the Treaty'.[248] The TRIPS agreement only represented an international 'minimum harmonization' vis-à-vis the Community legal order and could, as such, not constitute an exhaustive maximum standard. The ECJ, therefore, applied a rule pre-emption criterion to determine whether a legislative conflict between the international treaty and the Community directive existed.[249]

In sum, Community agreements have the capacity of double pre-emption: they can pre-empt inconsistent national and Community legislation. The pre-emptive potential of international agreements appears to be milder: only where the agreement has the same function as an internal Community norm will the Court accept the same pre-emptive effect that would be triggered by identically worded internal Community law.

VII. The Choice of Legal Instrument: From Strict Enumeration to Subsidiarity Control

The constitutional status quo under the 1957 Treaty has been described as follows: 'As a rule', wrote E. Grabitz in 1982, 'the Treaties establishing the European Communities leave the Community institutions with *no choice as regards the legal form which their acts take*; on the contrary, for each enabling rule they prescribe the form in which the required provisions must appear.'[250] In the early Community law literature, the debate on Community instruments was conducted in terms of legal *competence* and, consequently, embedded in discussions of the enumeration principle: 'Le principe de l'attribution des compétences (*'Prinzip der begrenzten Einzelzuständigkeit'*) a pour corollaire qu'il n'est pas permis aux institutions communautaires de recourir à un acte 'plus fort' si le traité ne leur donne que le pouvoir d'adopter un acte de portée 'plus faible', par. ex., une directive et non un règlement. Il n'est pas possible de faire la même chose par une voie détournée, c'est-à-dire de recourir à des 'directives' qui ne seraient, en fait, que des règlements déguisés. D'où, l'intérêt de respecter les frontières entre ces actes.'[251] The Community will act *ultra vires*—beyond its legislative *competence*—if it adopts a regulation on a legal basis that only granted power to pass directives.

---

[248] *Ibid.*, para.58.
[249] On the various types of pre-emption in the Community legal order, see: Schütze, above n.89.
[250] E. Grabitz, 'The Sources of Community law: Acts of the Community Institutions', in: EC Commission (ed.), *Thirty Years of Community Law* (EC Commission, 1981), 81–108 at 88 (emphasis added).
[251] J.-V. Louis, *Les Règlement de la Communauté économique européenne* (Presses universitaires des Bruxelles, 1969) 276.

This competence reading of the morphology of legal instruments was, as we saw above, shared by the European Court.[252] Yet could the Community legislator avail itself of an instrument *less intense* than the one envisaged in a legal competence? Would it be constitutionally problematic, where the Community legislator would prefer the indirect legislative instrument of a directive over the direct legislative instrument of a regulation? The power to adopt a 'strong' legal instrument could theoretically be seen as implying the power to adopt less interfering legal instruments.[253] Such 'downward flexibility' seemed to leave the sovereignty-protecting rationale of the enumeration principle unaffected. Downward flexibility was accepted in the ECSC Treaty in the form of the 'principle of minimum intervention' that would guide the choice of legislative instruments.[254]

However, the principle of minimum intervention has not been extended to the EC Treaty.[255] Three main objections were invoked. First and foremost, downward instrumental flexibility would distort the federal division of legislative powers.[256] This argument is based on a competence reading of the instrument question and removes any discretion of the Community legislator to act through an instrument other than that enumerated in the EC Treaty. Secondly, there is a problem of relativism. Even if we assume that there is a scale of normative intensity across the Community's instruments, the principle of minimum intervetion begs the question: minimum intervention *for whom*? Might not a generally applicable regulation sometimes be less 'intense' than a more situation-specific decision? Finally, implied downward flexibility may create constitutional tensions in relation to the horizontal separation of powers and, more generally, with the rule of law principle. Not all constitutional orders allow its legislative branch to adopt individual decisions. For all these reasons, the implied powers doctrine had not been extended to embrace the internal (!) instruments of the Community.[257]

---

252 See section III above.

253 M. Zuleeg, above n.84 at 14: 'Die Beschlußform der Verordnung gewährt die weitestgehenden Kompetenzen. Daher können die Gemeinschaftsorgane bei Verordnungsbefugnis alle anderen Rechtsakte erlassen.'

254 Article 14(5) ECSC read: 'In cases where the High Authority is empowered to take a decision, it may confine itself to making a recommendation.' (The terminology for the ECSC differed from the Article 249 EC terminology: the term 'decision' in the ECSC corresponded to 'regulations' and 'decisions' in the EC Treaty. ECSC 'recommendations' were similar to EC directives.)

255 G. Schmidt. 'Artikel 189 Rn. 20', in: H. von der Groeben, J. Thiesing, C.-D. Ehlermann (eds.), *Kommentar zum EU-/EG-Vertrag* (Nomos, 1999).

256 D. Triantafyllou, *Vom Vertrags- zum Gesetzesvorbehalt: Beitrag zum positiven Rechtmäßigkeitsprinzip in der EG* (Nomos, 1996), 61.

257 To select an internal legal instrument other than the one provided in the legal competence, the Community legislator would need to fall back on Article 308 EC. On this issue, see: R. Schütze, 'Organized change towards an "ever closer union": Article 308 EC and the limits to the Community's legislative competence', [2003] 22 Yearbook of European Law 79–115, at 95–99. 'The Two Dimensions of Power: Regulatory Instruments and Article 308 EC'.

While the original Treaty of Rome only exceptionally knew competences that provided the Community with a choice between alternative legal instruments,[258] this phenomenon has today become the constitutional 'rule'. Successive Treaty reforms have gradually 'decoupled'[259] the two dimensions of power: the morphological question of what instrument is appropriate in a given situation has increasingly been separated from the material dimension of competence. The neutrality of many legislative competences towards the choice of legal instrument is today manifested in all those legal bases that entitle the Community simply to adopt the necessary 'measures'.[260] The choice of legal instrument has become a question of legislative discretion for the Community legislator. The discourse on the Community's instruments has, consequently, shifted from the *existence* aspect to the *exercise* aspect of the Community's legislative powers—from the enumeration to the subsidiarity principle.

The subsidiarity principle thereby influences the Community's choice of instrument *qua* the principle of proportionality. According to Article 5(3) EC, the Community must exercise its powers only to the extent necessary to achieve the objective of the Community action. The *federal* aspect of the principle of proportionality was acknowledged in the Edinburgh Guidelines and has, more recently, been consolidated in the Amsterdam Protocol on Subsidiarity and Proportionality. Unlike the Edinburgh Guidelines, the Subsidiarity Protocol seems to focus exclusively on the preemptive differences of the Community's legislative instruments.[261] The relevant articles read:

The Community shall legislate only to the extent necessary. Other things being equal, directives should be preferred to regulations and framework directives to detailed measures. (...) Regarding the nature and the extent of Community action, Community measures should leave as much scope for national decision as possible, consistent with securing the aim of the measure and observing the requirements of the Treaty. While respecting Community law, care should be taken to respect well established national

---

[258] E.g. Article 43(2) EEC.   [259] Bast, above n.74 at 13.

[260] The most prominent example of a legal competence whose nature has been identified through the legal instrument is Article 94 EC. The method of 'harmonization' or 'approximation' was identified with the instrument of the directive. Yet, ever since the SEA this view is untenable as the concept of harmonization has been severed from the specific instrument of the directive. Article 95 EC generally allows for 'measures for the approximation', including regulations, decisions and international agreements.

[261] The Edinburgh Guidelines read: 'The form of action should be as simple as possible, consistent with the satisfactory achievement of the objective of the measure and the need for effective enforcement. The Community should legislate only to the extent necessary. Other things being equal, directives should be preferred to regulations and framework directives to *detailed measures*. Non-binding measures such as recommendations should be preferred where appropriate. Consideration should also be given where appropriate to the use of voluntary codes of conduct' (EC Bulletin 10–1992 at 15). While the reference to 'detailed measures' captures the pre-emptive dimension of the choice of instrument debate, the second part of the quote suggests a subsidiary review for the choice between legally-binding and non-binding measures. One could, therefore, argue that there is a subsidiarity perspective in choosing the directive as a form of *indirect* legislation to regulations as a form of *direct* legislation.

arrangements and the organisation and working of Member States' legal systems. Where appropriate and subject to the need for proper enforcement, Community measures should provide Member States with alternative ways to achieve the objectives of the measures.[262]

There is still little jurisprudence on the application of the subsidiarity principle, especially as regards the constitutional control of the Community's choice of legal instrument. In *Portuguese Republic v Commission*,[263] we find a partial break to this silence. A Portuguese decree had provided that certain airport charges were to be determined by a public undertaking on the basis of maximum take-off weight. The discriminatory pricing policy amounted to a state measure within the meaning of Article 86 EC and the Commission had issued a decision condemning the Portuguese system. Article 86(3) EC entitles the Commission to a choice between directives and decisions. Portugal brought an action for annulment of the State-addressed decision, alleging a violation of the principle of subsidiarity-proportionality: 'The Portuguese Republic contends that the Commission infringed the principle of proportionality laid down in the third paragraph of Article 3b of the EC Treaty (now the third paragraph of Article 5 EC) by choosing from among the courses of action open to it that which was the least appropriate and the most onerous' it added: 'Since the majority of Member States differentiate between domestic and international flights when calculating their airport charges', the directive was claimed to be 'the only instrument that could have brought about the necessary simultaneous harmonization of the relevant national laws.'[264]

The Court was not swayed. The Commission would enjoy a wide discretion in matters covered by Article 86 'as regards both the action which it considers necessary to take and the *means* appropriate for that purpose'.[265] Yet, the following constitutional guidelines were given for the choice between a directive and a decision:

With regard to the powers which [Article 86(3)] authorises the Commission to exercise by means of decisions, the Court of Justice also held that they differ from those which it may exercise by means of directives. A decision is adopted in respect of *a specific situation in one or more Member States and necessarily involves an appreciation of that situation in the light of Community law*; it specifies the consequences arising for the Member State concerned[.] (...) [T]he choice offered by [Article 86(3)] of the Treaty between a directive and a decision is not determined, as the Portuguese Republic contends, by the number of Member States which may be concerned. The choice depends on whether the Commission's objective is to specify in general terms the obligations arising under the Treaty, or to assess a specific

---

[262] Articles 6 and 7 Amsterdam Protocol. For a discussion of the Protocol, see G. de Búrca, 'Re-appraising Subsidiarity's Significance after Amsterdam', Harvard Jean Monnet Working Paper, no. 7/1999=<http://www.jeanmonnetprogram.org/papers/99/990701.html>.
[263] *Portugese Republic v Commission*, Case 163/99, [2001] E.C.R. 2613.
[264] *Ibid.*, paras.16–17.   [265] *Ibid.*, para.20.

situation in one or more Member States in the light of Community law and determine the consequences arising for the Member State or States concerned.[266]

A directive should, consequently, be employed to set out in *general terms* the obligations arising for Member States under the Treaty, while a decision was to be prefered 'in respect of a specific situation in one or more Member States'. The choice of legal instrument was not determined by the number of Member States implicated, but depended on the Commission's intentions: where it did not wish to adopt generally applicable rules it could select a decision over a directive. These are not very clear constitutional guidelines on the application of the subsidiarity principle for the choice of legal instrument. We shall have to wait until the Court develops clearer criteria in future jurisprudence.

VIII. Conclusion: Rationality Lost—Rationality Regained? Re-Federalizing the Morphology of Legislative Power

'But what, after all, is a law?' '[W]hen we have defined a law of nature, we shall be no nearer the definition of a law of the State'.[267] And, even when we have defined a law of the State, we shall not necessarily be nearer the definition of a law of the European Community. In the hope of going beyond the 'Law is The Law' tautology,[268] this chapter has tried to clarify the nature of Community legislation and to analyse its various formats from the perspective of the federal division of powers.

Drawing on a functional conception of legislation, we defined legislative power as the power to adopt directly and generally effective norms. This definition covered internal and external law-making. Yet when, after all, are legislative norms *Community* norms? The question of legal authorship turned out to be complex. The Community legal order has not 'shown' one single rule of recognition, but has rather developed a number of rules of recognition. The existing constitutional principles will not unequivocally determine the normative paternity of a legislative norm. The Court appears to favour a 'contextual' approach: the involvement of the Community institutions in the rule-making process is *not* in itself a sufficient reason to assume the Community authorship of a legislative norm.

The remainder of this chapter moved to examine the morphology of the Community's legal instruments from the perspective of the federal division of

---

[266] *Ibid.*, paras.27–28 (emphasis added).   [267] J. J. Rousseau, above n.2.

[268] Nothing against tautologies, especially witty ones: 'Law, says the judge as he looks down his nose/ Speaking clearly and most severely/ Law is as I've told you before/ Law is as you know I suppose/ Law is but let me explain it once more/ Law is The Law'. The full version of the poem can be found in W.H. Auden, *Selected Poems* (E. Mendelson (ed.)) (Vintage Books, 1979), Poem 48.

power. The normative format of each instrument was analysed alongside two dimensions. The first dimension was the instrument's legislative character, that is, the extent to which a legal act unfolds directly and generally binding effects. The second dimension concerned each instrument's pre-emptive nature, that is, to what extent national legislators remain entitled to co-legislate within the scope of the Community measure.

In 1958, the regulation constituted the only legislative instrument of the Community. Directives and decisions were, originally, supranational 'executive' acts: they were binding on their addressees and could not be said to have general effects. The doctrine of direct effect of directives and State-addressed decisions injected a legislative dimension to these measures. This legislative dimension was, however, only vertical: their direct effect was limited to granting rights to individuals. Moreover, both instruments will predominantly operate *qua* national legislation—thence their character as *indirect* legislation: their legislative effect will typically 'extend to individuals *through the medium of the implementing measures*'.[269] External Community legislation had been made possible thanks to the monistic stance of the Community legal order towards international agreements concluded by the Community. In the absence of constitutional reasons to the contrary, we assumed that Community agreements can have vertical and horizontal direct effects and, therefore, classified them as direct legislation. More precisely, we argued that Community agreements could be seen as 'external regulations'.

To what extent differ the pre-emptive identities of these legislative instruments? Regulations have traditionally been seen as instruments of strict uniformity. Yet, we saw that regulations will not automatically field-pre-empt the national legislators within their scope of application. Directives, by way of contrast, have been thought of as instruments of harmonization leaving some legislative discretion to Member States. The freedom, referred to in Article 249(3) EC, however, only entitles Member States to implement the Community *content* into national *form*. Today, Community directives cannot be pressed into the constitutional mould of framework legislation. There simply is no constitutional limit on the pre-emptive effect of directives that would (p)reserve legislative power to national legislators. Nor are there any *a priori* constitutional limits on the pre-emptive capacity of State-addressed decisions or international agreements. Thus, with regard to the pre-emptive capacity of these four legislative instruments of the Community, any differentiating constitutional typology—if it were ever designed—has been glossed over by constitutional practice. In this respect, the federal reason behind the morphology of legislative power in the EC has been 'lost'.

However, when we are told that the Community must choose the least restrictive instrument so as to 'leave as much scope for national decision as possible',[270] '[c]ette controverse suppose au départ une opposition entre moyen d'intervention

---

[269] *U. Becker v Finanzamt Münster-Innenstadt*, Case 8/81, [1982] E.C.R. 53, para.19 (emphasis added). [270] Article 7 Amsterdam Protocol.

'forts', dont le type serait le règlement, et moyen d'intervention 'faibles' que seraient notamment, les directives'.[271] A subsidiarity perspective for the choice of instrument makes little sense as long as the respective pre-emptive identities of the Community's legal instruments have not been sharpened.

The desire to (re-)federalize the system of Community instruments has been apparent since the 1990s: '[P]artly as a reaction to the detailed character of many directives, a new term became fashionable: the framework directive.'[272] The introduction of the constitutional concept of 'framework law' would reinforce the constitutionalization of the philosophy of cooperative federalism that began with the introduction of complementary competences in the Community legal order.[273] If modeled on the constitutional format of a German 'framework law', the latter's pre-emptive effect should be constitutionally limited and guarantee a substantive degree of legislative choice to the national level. The framework law is the legislative instrument *par exellence* for the constitutional philosophy of cooperative federalism and the principle of subsidiarity. More than a decade ago, the EC Commission argued its case in the following words:

If legislative action is necessary, the subsidiarity principle dictates that Community legislation and national measures each be given its own respective role: Community legislation forms the framework into which national action must be fitted. For this purpose, the Treaty of Rome devised an original instrument, which typifies subsidiarity: the directive sets the result to be achieved but leaves it to the Member States to choose the most appropriate means of doing so. (...) In practice, of course, the distinction between directive and regulation has become blurred[.] (...) If the subsidiarity exercise is to produce any overall tangible results, then it must unquestionably be by systematically reverting to the original concept of the directive as a framework of general rules, or even simply of objectives, for the attainment of which the Member States have sole responsibility.[274]

Thus, instead of adding the new instrument of 'framework law' to Article 249 EC's catalogue of legal instruments, a judicial operation could equally achieve

---

[271] D. de Ripainsel-Landy & A. Gerard, 'La Notion juridique de la Directive utilisée comme instrument de rapprochement des législations dans la CEE', in : D. de Ripainsel-Landy *et al.* (eds.), *Les instruments du rapprochement des législations dans la commnauté économique européenne* (Bruylant, 1976) 37–94 at 41.

[272] S. Prechal, *Directives in EC Law* (OUP, 2005) 15, explains further: 'This is an unknown instrument in the typology of the EC Treaty and it is, in fact, not clear what it exactly refers to.' In its jurisprudence, the ECJ uses the concept in a different context. It uses the term 'framework directive' to refer to a directive that lays down general principles, which will subsequently be developed by a series of specific *Community* directives (cf. Pfeiffer above n.155 at para.4). This appears also to be the understanding brought to the concept by the Community legislator, see: for example, Directive 2002/21 on a common regulatory framework for electronic communications networks and services (Framework Directive), [2002] OJ L 108, 33–50.

[273] R. Schütze, 'Cooperative Federalism Constitutionalised: The Emergence of Complementary Competences in the EC legal order', [2006] 31 E.L. Rev. 167–84.

[274] *Commission Communication on the Principle of Subsidiarity*, Bulletin EC 10–1992, 116–26 at 123.

the desired constitutional surgery. That would require the Court of Justice to constitutionally trim the pre-emptive dimension of directives. This 'return' to the 'original concept of the directive as a framework of general rules' would preserve a degree of material legislative autonomy for the Member States. The distinct constitutional identity of the directive *vis-à-vis* the regulation could then be anchored in the former's constitutionally limited pre-emptive effect. The morphological specificity of the directive would, therefore, not be lost—even if the Court were (eventually) to accept the horizontal direct effect of directives. (The advantages of having an instrument of *indirect* legislation within the system of legal instruments could be preserved in the instrument of the State-addressed decision.) It is to be hoped that the European Court of Justice—or: *future* Constitution-makers—[275] will capitalize on the constitutional advantages of framework legislation for a clearer division of power between the Community and the Member States. The morphology of legislative power in the European Community would benefit from a regained federal rationale.

---

[275] The Constitutional Treaty (2004) would not have satisfied this constitutional wish. Article I-33(1) of the Constitutional Treaty introduced the concept of 'framework law' in the following terms: 'A European framework law shall be a legislative act binding, as to the result to be achieved, upon each Member State to which it is addressed, but shall leave to the national authorities the choice of form and methods.' From a functional perspective, 'framework laws' would have been identical to directives. (According to Article I-33 CT, the instrumental format of the directive would not be reserved to 'framework laws' but also be available for 'European regulations'.) Focusing on a better *horizontal* separation of powers, the Constitution-makers regrettably overlooked the instrumental reforms for the *vertical* separation of powers. The Constitutional Treaty would thus have hardly modified the morphology of legislative power. The only exception seems to be the recognition of decisions without addressees in Article I-33 CT.

Remembrance of Principles Lost: On Fundamental Rights, the Third Pillar and the Scope of Union Law

Eleanor Spaventa[*]

This article[1] analyses the interplay between fundamental rights and instruments adopted in the field of police and judicial co-operation in criminal matters. It argues that the limited jurisdiction of the European Court of Justice in relation to third pillar matters is problematic in relation to the Member States' obligations under the European Convention on Human Rights, and that therefore the European Court of Human Rights should assert full jurisdiction over Member States' acts adopted pursuant to third pillar instruments. Furthermore, it also argues that, even though third pillar instruments are not capable of having direct effect, national courts are under a Union law obligation to scrutinize, and if necessary set aside, national implementing measures which are inconsistent with fundamental rights as general principles of Union law.

I. Introduction

The inadequacy of the third pillar framework was acknowledged and acted upon in the Constitutional Treaty, which had introduced significant and progressive changes for the protection of fundamental rights in the European Union. Besides incorporating the Charter of Fundamental Rights in its second part, therefore making it legally binding upon the Union institutions and the Member States when implementing Union law, the Constitution also eliminated the pillar

[*] Reader and Director of the Durham European Law Institute, Department of Law, Durham University.
[1] This is an elaborated version of a paper presented at the conference 'The Enlarged European Union and its Institutions: "Looking out and Looking in" under the new Constitutional framework' held in Cambridge on 8 July 2005, and organized by the Centre of International Studies together with the Centre for European Legal Studies. I am grateful to the organizers and to the participants of the conference. I am very grateful to Tony Arnull, Catherine Barnard, Michael Dougan, and Francesco De Cecco for their helpful comments on a previous draft of this paper. The usual disclaimer applies.

structure,[2] giving almost full jurisdiction[3] to the Court of Justice in relation to instruments adopted under the Police and Judicial Co-operation Title.[4] Furthermore, the Constitution extended the co-decision procedure to third pillar matters, therefore strengthening democratic control over police and judicial co-operation.[5] This was a much needed step, given that, more than any other, those measures might affect individual rights, including the right to liberty, of those subject to the jurisdiction of any of the Member States.[6]

Following the terrorist attacks in the US in September 2001, the attacks in Madrid in March 2004, as well as now the attacks in London in July 2005, the legislative activity of the Union in matters falling within the scope of criminal law has greatly increased and will continue to do so.[7] In this respect, the Brussels European Council adopted in November 2004 the 'Hague Programme', which set out an extensive legislative agenda in the criminal sphere.[8] The Hague Programme was adopted with the expectation that the Constitution and the guarantees of fundamental rights protection, democratic and judicial scrutiny would have come into force before the formal adoption of the plethora of legislation provided for in the programme.[9] The lack of ratification of the Constitution, together with the further likely increase in legislative activity as a reaction to the London bombings,[10] poses important questions for fundamental rights

---

[2] Even though some peculiarities remained; e.g. the possibility for a member of the Council to request that a draft framework law be referred to the European Council on the grounds that it would affect fundamental aspects of its criminal justice system (Art. III-270(3) CT); possibility for a quarter of the Member States to initiate legislation in relation to definition of criminal offences/sanctions (Art. III-271 CT).

[3] But maintaining the exclusion of jurisdiction in relation to the review of the validity and proportionality of operations carried out by police, etc (Art. III-377 CT).

[4] Article III-369 CT also provides that if a question of interpretation of Union law 'is raised in a case pending before a court or tribunal of a member State with regard to a person in custody, the Court shall act with the minimum delay'. The Constitution also introduced the Court's jurisdiction to review the validity *in proceedings brought by individuals in relation to CFSP* decisions providing for 'restrictive measures against natural and legal persons' (Art. III-376 CT).

[5] For a general overview of the development of the third pillar, see P. J. Kuijper, 'The Evolution of the Third Pillar from Maastricht to the European Constitution: Institutional Aspects' (2004) 41 CML Rev 609; S. Peers, *EU Justice and Home Affairs Law* (Longman 2000); N. Walker (ed.), *Europe's Area of Freedom, Security and Justice* (OUP, 2004).

[6] See generally, S. Peers, 'Human Rights and the Third Pillar' in P. Alston (ed.), *The EU and Human Rights* (OUP, 1999), 175; S. Douglas-Scott, 'The Rule of Law in the European Union—Putting the Security into the Area of Freedom, security and Justice' (2004) 29 EL Rev 23.

[7] Cf. the Presidency's note on 'JHA Council Declaration: Follow-up', document 11330/05, of 19 July 2005, available on <http://www.statewatch.org/news/2005/aug/jha-declaration-follow-up.pdf>.

[8] Brussels European Council, 4 and 5 November 2004, Presidency Conclusions, 14292/1/04 REV 1, CONCL 3.

[9] Cf. Brussels European Council, 4 and 5 November 2004, Presidency Conclusions, 14292/1/04 REV 1, CONCL 3, points 14 and 15, and Hague Programme therein annexed.

[10] Cf. the press release of the Extraordinary Justice and Home Affairs Council Meeting held on the 13 July 2005, C/05/187, 111106/05 (Presse 187); the Commission Memo on Commission Activities in the Fight against Terrorism, 29/07/05, Memo/05/272; the Paper by the UK Presidency of the European Union *Liberty and Security—Striking the Right Balance*, presented to the European Parliament on 7 September 2005, <http://www.eu2005.gov.uk/servlet/

protection in the Union.[11] In particular, the reduced jurisdiction of the Court of Justice in relation to those acts might translate into a significant gap in fundamental rights protection, and in the denial of an effective judicial remedy as guaranteed by the European Convention on Human Rights.

This article examines the problems arising from the failure of the Constitution's ratification process in relation to fundamental rights protection in areas covered by police and judicial co-operation in criminal matters. In particular, it focuses on two problems: first, the possibility that a framework decision might conflict with fundamental rights; and secondly, the possibility that the national implementing legislation might be in breach of fundamental rights. In relation to the first issue, it will be argued that, especially when the European Court of Justice has no jurisdiction, the European Court of Human Rights has jurisdiction to ensure that Member States do not breach their Convention obligations when adopting third pillar instruments. In relation to the second issue, the article looks at the scope of application of fundamental rights as general principles of Community law in relation to legislation adopted pursuant to a framework decision. It will be argued that Member States have a justiciable obligation when implementing third pillar instruments to exercise their discretion in a manner compatible with fundamental rights. Both solutions are far from ideal in ensuring that fundamental rights are respected and protected; however, they are the only means to provide at least some guarantees whilst awaiting a much needed, if for the time being politically unlikely, Treaty amendment.

II. Jurisdiction of the European Court of Justice in Relation to Title VI

Under Title VI TEU, the Council may adopt common positions, framework decisions, decisions and conventions. Common positions are adopted without any participation of the European Parliament and the Court's jurisdiction is excluded, save for the possibility to adjudicate on disputes between Member States when the matter cannot be settled in Council.[12] Framework decisions, similarly to directives, are intended to approximate national legislation, binding the Member States as to the result to be achieved but leaving discretion as to the means to achieve such result. They are adopted, like decisions and conventions, using the consultation procedure.[13] Both framework decisions and decisions cannot have direct effect.[14]

Front?pagename=OpenMarket/Xcelerate/ShowPage&c=Page&cid=1107293561746&a=KArticle&aid=1125560449884&date=2005-09-07>.

[11] Cf. e.g. Case T-338/02, *Segi et al. v. Council*, order of 7/06/04, appeal pending (Case C-355/04 P).
[12] Article 35(7) TEU.   [13] Article 39 TEU.   [14] Article 34 TEU.

The Court has jurisdiction to give preliminary rulings in relation to the validity and interpretation of framework decisions and decisions and in relation to the interpretation of conventions.[15] However, such jurisdiction is voluntary.[16] Thus, the Member States, if they so wish, have to make a declaration accepting the Court's jurisdiction and specifying whether only courts of last instance can make a preliminary reference or whether *all* courts can refer a question of interpretation to the Court of Justice. Even when the Member State has accepted the full jurisdiction of the Court, there is no obligation under the Treaty for a court of last instance to refer the matter to the Court of Justice. At the time of writing all EU 15, except Denmark, Ireland and the UK, have made a declaration accepting the Court's jurisdiction; of the EU 10, only the Czech Republic and Hungary have made such a declaration.[17] Thus, in 11 of the Member States,[18] individuals charged of a criminal offence following the implementation of a framework decision might be unable, at least from a Union law perspective, to attack the validity of the Union act as well as the incompatibility between the national rule and the framework decision.[19]

Furthermore, only the Member States and the Commission can bring proceedings in front of the ECJ to challenge the validity of a framework decision, including its compatibility with fundamental rights.[20] Thus, not even

---

[15] In any event the Court does not have any jurisdiction 'to review the validity or proportionality of operations carried out by the police or other law enforcement services of a Member Sate or the exercise of the responsibilities incumbent upon Member States with regard to the maintenance of law and order and the safeguarding of internal security' (Art. 35(5) TEU); this was unchanged in the CT (Art. III-377).

[16] For a comprehensive and critical analysis of the Court's jurisdiction post-Amsterdam in relation to both Title IV TEC and Title VI TEU, see S. Peers, 'Who's Judging the Watchmen? The Judicial System of the "Area of Freedom Security and Justice"', (1998) 18 YEL 337.

[17] Information concerning the declarations by the French Republic and the Republic of Hungary on their acceptance of the jurisdiction of the Court of Justice to give preliminary rulings on the acts referred to in Art. 35 of the Treaty on European Union [2005] OJ L 327/19. Spain and Hungary have restricted the possibility to make preliminary references to their courts of last instance, whilst the other Member States have allowed all of their courts to make preliminary references. Belgium, the Czech Republic, France, Germany, Spain, Italy, Luxembourg, the Netherlands and Austria have reserved the right to make it compulsory for their courts of last instance to refer the matter to the ECJ.

[18] And possibly in 13 Member States, if Romania and Bulgaria fail to make the declaration pursuant to Art. 35 TEU.

[19] Even though framework decisions cannot have direct effect, they have legal effects which can be invoked by individuals (indirect effect), see the discussion on *Pupino* below. For a different view on the matter, see A. Arnull, 'Taming the Beast? The Treaty of Amsterdam and the Court of Justice' in D. O'Keeffe and P. Twomey, *Legal Issues of the Amsterdam Treaty* (Hart Publishing, 1999), 109, esp. pp. 117–20; and 'The Rule of Law in the European Union' in A. Arnull and D. Wincott, *Accountability and Legitimacy in the European Union* (OUP, 2002), 239, esp 249–51.

[20] It is true that in most cases individuals would not have standing even should Title IV TEU provide for a provision equivalent to Article 230 TEC; however, in some cases, such as when a framework decision or a decision identifies legal or natural persons, judicial review would have been available under the current Community rules. Cp the problems for judicial protection arising from Common Position 2001/930/CFSP on combating terrorism, [2001] O.J. L344/90; and Common Position 2001/931/CFSP on the application of specific measures on combating terrorism, [2001] O.J. L344/93 in Case T-338/02, *Segi et al. v. Council*, order of 7/06/04, appeal pending (Case C-355/04 P).

Parliament—let aside individuals—has standing in relation to measures adopted without its consent.[21]

We shall now examine the possible implications for fundamental rights protection of this framework. Two different situations should be analysed: first, the possibility that the framework decision is inconsistent with fundamental rights; and secondly, the possibility that, whilst the framework decision is consistent with fundamental rights, the implementing national law is not.

III. First Problem: The Framework Decision Breaches Fundamental Rights

According to Article 6 TEU, the Union shall respect fundamental rights; failure to do so entails the nullity of the act.[22] In the case of framework decisions, annulment proceedings might be brought by any of the Member States as well as by the Commission. Individuals can question the validity of a framework decision only incidentally through a preliminary ruling, and only when the relevant Member State has accepted the Court's jurisdiction pursuant to Article 35 TEU. When this is not the case, the individual whose legal situation is worsened by a national rule which implements a framework decision might well see her right to effective judicial protection significantly curtailed, since she will not be able to challenge the validity of the framework decision through a preliminary ruling. Nor would the national court be competent to assess the validity of the framework decision with fundamental rights of its own accord, since, even leaving aside the question as to whether the Community *Foto Frost* principle is applicable in this context,[23] an act of international law cannot be declared unilaterally unlawful by a national court.

Furthermore, even though it might be open to the applicant to challenge the implementing national rule in relation to national fundamental rights, this might not always be possible, at least from a Union law perspective. It is clear that if the framework decision leaves a discretion to the Member States, the national courts

[21] Parliament would only be able to challenge a third pillar instrument under the EC Treaty arguing that it should have been adopted under that Treaty rather than the EU Treaty, cf Case C-170/96, *Commission v. Council* (Airport Transit Visas) [1998] ECR I-2763. It is likely that litigation as to the correct legal basis is on the increase; see e.g. Case C-176/03, *Commission v. Council*, judgment of 13/09/05, nyr, on the correct legal basis for a framework decision imposing criminal liability for environmental damage. On competence see M. Wasmeier, 'The "Battle of the Pillars": Does the European Community Have the Power to Approximate National Criminal Laws' (2004) EL Rev 1.

[22] Although of course not necessarily such nullity would be judicially cognisable (e.g. in relation to second pillar matters).

[23] See Case 314/85, *Foto-Frost* [1987] ECR 4199; it has been argued that the ruling in *Foto-Frost* might not apply to those courts which cannot make a preliminary reference, see A. Arnull, A. Dashwood. M. Ross, D. Wyatt, *Wyatt and Dashwood's EU Law* (Sweet and Maxwell, 4th ed, 2000) at 281 and ff.

are entitled (and possibly obliged by national constitutional law) to review how that discretion has been exercised in relation to their national and Union fundamental rights. This is the route taken by the German Constitutional Court, which has declared the German legislation implementing the Framework decision on the European Arrest Warrant[24] unconstitutional because the national legislature had exercised its discretion in a way incompatible with fundamental rights as guaranteed by the Basic Law.[25]

However, things are considerably more complicated if the national implementing legislation reproduces *verbatim* the offending provision of the framework decision.[26] Here, whether the applicant could see her right effectively protected will depend very much on the national constitutional system,[27] and on the stance taken by the reviewing court. Thus, for instance, in the United Kingdom, even if the domestic court were to be prepared to scrutinize the rule *verbatim* implementing a framework decision, that would not necessarily help the applicant. According to British Constitutional law and the Human Rights Act 1998, the courts' power in relation to a statutory instrument is limited to a declaration of incompatibility between it and the ECHR,[28] with the exclusion of the possibility to set aside the offending instrument. Since, at least for the time being, Union acts are implemented through statutes, and since the UK has not made the declaration pursuant to Article 35 TEU, a person affected by a framework decision in the United Kingdom jurisdiction, might well be left without any effective judicial remedy.[29]

But even in those jurisdictions which allow for conclusive judicial scrutiny of national legislation, whether the applicant will see her fundamental rights

---

[24] Council Framework Decision 2002/584/JHA on the European arrest warrant and the surrender procedure between Member States, [2002] O.J. L190/1. For an analysis of the human rights issues concerning the European Arrest Warrant, see S. Peers, 'Proposed Framework Decision on European Arrest Warrant', in Statewatch post-September 11, 2001 analyses: No. 3, available on <www.statewatch.org/news/2001/oct/ewarrant.pdf>.

[25] *Bundesverfassungsgeright*, 18/7/05, 2 BvR 2236/04; the summary of the ruling in English is available on <www.bundesverfassungsgericht.de/bverfg_cgi/pressemitteilungen/frames/bvg05-064e.html>. A reference on the compatibility of the European Arrest Warrant with fundamental rights, and in particular with Article 6(1) ECHR, is currently pending in front of the ECJ, Case C-303/05 *Advocaten voor de wereld v Council* (Referred by the Belgian Court of Arbitration).

[26] For sake of simplicity and in order to avoid repetitions, by *verbatim* I mean both the case when the national rule reproduces the provision contained in the framework decision word by word, and the case when the framework decision leaves no discretion as to the action to be taken, even though the national rule does not reproduce the piece of Union law word by word.

[27] E.g. in Italy where the Constitutional Court has interpreted Art. 11 of the Italian Constitution (which provides for the possibility of entering in international agreements) as the basis for limiting its own review jurisdiction, see ruling *Frontini v. Ministero delle Finanze* (27/12/73, n.183), [1974] 2 CMLR 372, although it also left open the possibility of reasserting jurisdiction to declare the law which ratified the EEC unconstitutional should the Community use its powers to breach fundamental rights (see esp para 9 of the ruling).

[28] Human Rights Act 1998 s. 4; see for instance *A and Others v. Secretary of State for the Home Department* [2005] 2 AC 68.

[29] Cf. European Communities Act 1972 (as amended), s 2(2) read together with Section 1(1)(k). On this point cf J. Spencer 'The European Arrest Warrant' (2003–4) 6 CYELS 201, 207.

effectively protected will depend very much on the stance taken by the national (constitutional) court. Thus, it could be that the national court in a State which has not accepted the ECJ's jurisdiction, would perceive it as its duty under national law to scrutinize closely fundamental rights compliance of the rule implementing *verbatim* a framework decision.[30] But it could also be that the national court would feel that its obligations under Union law prevent it from carrying out such an assessment. It could in fact be argued that the principle of loyal co-operation precludes a national court from declaring the unconstitutionality of a national rule implementing *verbatim* a framework decision,[31] since to do so would go against the obligation to ensure, at least insofar as possible, that Union law is given full effect. Otherwise, the uniformity of Union law would be compromised as national courts might well reach different conclusions as to the compatibility of the national provision, and indirectly of the framework decision, with fundamental rights; and introduce a fracture in the system not dissimilar from that created in the 1970s by the German and Italian Constitutional courts as regards Community law.[32] This problem has been recently evidenced by a ruling of the Polish Constitutional Court, again in relation to the European Arrest warrant.[33] Here, the Polish Court accepted to scrutinize the Polish implementing legislation and declared it unconstitutional pursuant to Article 51 of the Polish Constitution which prohibits the extradition of Polish citizens. However, conscious of the obligations arising from EU membership as well as from the rule *pacta sunt servanda* incorporated in the Polish Constitution, the Constitutional Court delayed the effect of the ruling by 18 months to afford the legislature the time to amend the Constitution so as to be able to comply with EU law.[34] It is clear that in this case the Constitutional guarantee was *de facto*, if not *de iure*, suspended in favour of compliance with EU law, and the applicant found no redress in the ruling declaring the unconstitutionality of the national legislation. It is impossible to second-guess whether the balance would have been struck in favour of EU law if the clash had involved the protection of other national fundamental rights: however, it is plausible that, especially if the fundamental rights breach is not blatant, the national courts might give precedence to Union law obligations.

---

[30] Or even under Union law, on this point see A. Arnull *The European Union and its Court of Justice* (OUP, 2006), Ch 4.

[31] Cf. also Judge Gerherdt's dissenting opinion in the German Arrest Warrant Case, *Bundesverfassungsgericht*, 18 July 2005, 2 BvR 2236/04; as reported on <www.bundesverfassungsgericht.de/bverfg_cgi/pressemitteilungen/frames/bvg05-064e.html>.

[32] See the German Constitutional Court rulings in *Internationale Handelsgesellschaft* . . . [1974] 2 CMLR 540 (*Solange I*); *Steinike und Weinlig* . . . [1980] 2 CMLR 531; and the (Italian Constitutional Court rulings *Sentenza*, 7/3/64, n.14) (in F. Sorrentino, *Profili Costituzionali dell'Integrazione Comunitaria*, 2nd edn, Giappichelli Editore 1996, p. 61 and ss) and *Societá Acciaierie San Michele v. High Authority* (27 December 1965, n. 98), [1967] CMLR 160.

[33] Council Framework Decision 2002/584/JHA on the European arrest warrant and the surrender procedure between Member States, [2002] O.J. L190/1.

[34] *Trybunal Konstytucyjny, arrêt du 27.04.05, P 1/05, Dziennik Ustaw 2005.77.680*, as reported by *Réflets—Informations rapides sur les développements juridiques présentant un intérêt communautaire*, no. 2/2005, p. 16, also available on <http://curia.eu.int/en/coopju/apercu_reflets/lang/index.htm>.

Furthermore, the danger that the use of Union law might result in a significant gap in effective judicial protection should not be underestimated. Take by way of example what has happened in relation to the adoption of anti-terrorism measures. Here, before the framework decision on terrorism had been adopted,[35] the Council adopted Common Position 2001/931/CFSP,[36] using a mixed pillar two and pillar three legal basis. The Common Position provided a definition of terrorist acts (now reproduced in the framework decision), as well as a list of individuals and organizations which should be considered as terrorist. The measure, and especially the list provided as an annex, was adopted without any participation of the European Parliament, and was not amenable to any type of judicial review since the European courts have no jurisdiction over Common Positions, even when they are adopted using third pillar competence. Furthermore, scrutiny by national parliaments of the content of the annex was equally excluded (the national authorities not having the possibility of amending the list). Inclusion in the list did not necessarily produce effects which would require any implementing measure; nonetheless, it is clear that being defined as a terrorist organization is not without consequences for those concerned. When *Segi*, one such organization, complained about its inclusion in the annex, it found that neither the European Court of Human Rights nor the Court of First Instance had jurisdiction. The former refused to hear the case because there had been only a *potential* rather than actual breach of the Convention.[37] The Court of First Instance had to refuse the case since it has no jurisdiction to review Common Positions. As a result, and as acknowledged by the CFI itself, the claimant was left without any judicial remedy.[38]

It should be noted also that the Community has subsequently adopted a Regulation which provides for the freezing of assets of some of the individuals and organizations alleged to be linked to terrorism activities. The names of those individuals/organizations are contained in an annex to the Regulation and replicate those contained in the Common Position as updated every six months.[39]

[35] Council Framework Decision on Combating Terrorism (2002/475/JHA), [2002] O.J. L164/3.
[36] Council Common Position 2001/931/CFSP on the application of specific measures to combat terrorism [2001] O.J. L344/93.
[37] Decision declaring the inadmissibility of the case *Segi and Gestoras pro-Amnistia v. 15 States of the European Union*, (Appl. no 6422/02, and 9916/02), 23 May 2002. The ECtHR decision seems also to have been driven by the mistaken certainty that in any case the Community courts would have jurisdiction.
[38] Case T-338/02, *Segi et al. v. Council*, order of 7 June 2004, appeal pending (Case C-355/04 P), para 39. There are a number of cases currently pending in front of the Community judiciary in relation to the Common Position and the Community implementing Regulation; e.g. Case T-299/04, *Selmani v. Council and Commission* in relation to the freezing of assets of the applicant, case pending; Case T-206/02, *Kurdistan National Kongress v. Council*, order of 15 February 2005, where the CFI found that the applicant lacked standing to act on behalf of the Kurdistan Workers' Party, identified by the Regulation as one of the terrorist organizations the assets of which should be frozen.
[39] Community Regulation 2580/2001 on specific restrictive measures directed against certain persons and entities with a view to combating terrorism [2001] O.J. L344/70. Article 2(3) of the

The European Parliament is not involved in either the review of the list attached to the Common Position, or in the review of the list attached to the Regulation. In this way, even though inclusion in the list annexed to the Common Position and to the Regulation might produce adverse legal effects, Parliamentary scrutiny has been excluded, and judicial scrutiny might be very limited if present at all.[40] As much as one would like to believe in the Council's good faith in choosing the legal basis and the type of instrument for its actions, it is difficult not to share the European Parliament's view that Council acted improperly (if not altogether maliciously) with the intent to exclude any possible democratic and judicial accountability.[41] Whilst we are concerned with framework decisions, where Parliament and the courts have a role, the case illustrates well the problems which might arise when Union competence expands into the criminal domain without the appropriate guarantees having been put in place. Thus, for all these reasons, and given that, as said above, 11 of the Member States have failed to make the declaration accepting the jurisdiction of the European Court of Justice, the problem is not merely academic. It is therefore necessary to examine this framework in relation to the European Convention on Human Rights to assess whether: (i) the European Court of Human Rights would have jurisdiction; and (ii) whether the system of voluntary jurisdiction in relation to Title VI is not in itself a breach of the Convention, at least for those States which have failed to make the declaration.

IV. Between a Rock and a Hard Place: National Courts' Obligations in Relation to Union and Convention Law

As said above, from a Union law viewpoint it is doubtful whether a national court could legitimately assess the compatibility with fundamental rights of a national rule which reproduces *verbatim* a provision contained in a framework decision.

Regulation provides that the list of individuals and organizations whose assets are to be frozen shall 'be established (...) in accordance with the provisions laid down' in the Common Position. Accordingly, the list is adopted using CFSP competence (it is reviewed every six months, see e.g. Council Decision 2005/428/CFSP implementing Art. 2(3) of Regulation 2580/2001, [2005] O.J. L144/59).

[40] See also Case T-306/01, *Yusuf and Al Barakaat International Foundation* [2005] ECR II-3533, which raises similar problems in relation to measures adopted pursuant to UN resolutions. In this case the applicants complained about Council Regulation 467/2001, which imposed on Member States an obligation to freeze their assets. The Regulation had been adopted as a result of a UN Resolution, and indeed the list of those whose assets should be frozen was drafted by the UN Sanctions Committee, a committee of the UN Security Council. Whilst the CFI accepted to scrutinize whether the applicants' fundamental rights as mandatory principles of international law had been respected, the Court did not (and maybe could not) look at the substance of the matter, i.e. at whether the applicants were indeed linked with the Taliban regime, and whether there was any evidence justifying the freezing of their assets.

[41] European Parliament Resolution of 7 February 2002, P5_TA(2002)0055; cf especially point 4, '[The Parliament] [d]eplores the choice of a legal basis which falls under the third pillar for the definition of the list of terrorist organisations, thereby excluding all consultation and effective scrutiny

Should the national court do so, it might place itself and its Member State in breach of the obligations contained in the TEU.[42] But should the national court take the view that its Union obligations prevent it from scrutinizing the matter, it could be, indirectly, responsible for a breach of the European Convention of Human Rights. Thus, it would be open to the applicant to seek a remedy in front of the European Court of Human Rights.

Whilst the European Court of Human Rights does not have jurisdiction as such over Union acts, in several cases private parties have sought to establish indirect jurisdiction by challenging national measures implementing or giving effect to Community law, rather than Community law itself.[43] In the first of such cases,[44] the European Commission of Human Rights gave a rather restrictive view of its own and the European Court of Human Right's jurisdiction in relation to indirect challenges to Community law. The Commission found that even though the Convention does not preclude Member States from transferring powers to international bodies, such transfer of powers does not exclude the State's responsibility under the Convention. However, if the international organization affords 'equivalent protection' to fundamental rights as guaranteed by the Convention, then the transfer of power would be deemed compatible with the European Convention of Human Rights without the need for further scrutiny. In the view of the Human Rights Commission, the European Communities did afford such equivalent protection: its institutions considered themselves bound by fundamental rights and the ECJ controlled compliance.[45] For this reason, the European Commission of Human Rights refused jurisdiction and the case was declared inadmissible.

The doctrine of 'equivalent protection' is still valid; however, subsequent judgments of the European Court of Human Rights have significantly curtailed its scope. In *Matthews*,[46] the European Court of Human Rights held that when

---

both by the national parliaments and by the European Parliament, and also evading the jurisdiction of the Court of Justice'.

[42] Admittedly, since there is no possibility for the Commission to bring infringement proceedings against a Member State for failure to comply with a framework decision, that breach would merely create a constitutional fracture at Union level.

[43] E.g. *M & Co v. Germany* (Appl. No 13258/87), Commission decision of 9 February 1990, Decisions and Reports 64, p. 138; *Procola v. Luxembourg* (Appl. No. 14570/89), judgment of 28 September 1995, Series A no. 288; *Cantoni v. France* (Appl. No. 17862/91), judgment of 15 November 1996, Reports 1996-V.

[44] *M & Co v. Germany*, (Appl. No 13258/87), Commission decision of 9 February 1990, Decisions and Reports 64, p. 138.

[45] The decision of the Commission was by no means unanimous; Judge Schermers (who was a member of the Commission in the case at issue) ascribes this rather restrictive view of the ECtHR jurisdiction also to the fact that some members believed that the Community would soon accede to the Convention and did not want 'to interfere in the Community system' at that stage; cp. *The Human Rights Opinion of the ECJ and its Constitutional Implications*, CELS Occasional Paper No.1, at 16.

[46] *Matthews v. United Kingdom* (Appl. No. 24833/94), 18 February 1999; cp also *Cantoni v. France* (Appl. No. 17862/91), judgment of 15 November 1996, Reports 1996-V, where the ECtHR

powers are transferred to an international organization, the Convention rights need in any event to be 'secured'. The European Court of Human Rights then considered that since in the case at issue the European Court of Justice lacked jurisdiction,[47] the responsibility to 'secure' Convention rights fell upon the Member States (collectively as well as severally).[48] For this reason, the European Court of Human Rights was competent to determine whether in adopting the Community act, the United Kingdom (together with the other Member States) had failed to comply with its Convention obligations. The ruling in *Matthews* therefore suggests that when the European Court of Justice does not have jurisdiction, the European Court of Human Rights is ready to scrutinize the matter and, if need be, review Community law in relation to the Convention (albeit to establish the responsibility of the Member States rather than the responsibility of the Community).

In a more recent case, *Bosphorus*,[49] the Strasbourg Court elaborated further upon the concept of 'equivalent protection'. Here, the complaint related to a Community Regulation implementing a UN Resolution imposing sanctions against the Federal Republic of Yugoslavia (FRY, Serbia and Montenegro) during the Balkan war.[50] As a result of the Regulation, the claimant's aircraft had been impounded by the Irish authorities on the grounds that it was owned by a company based in the FRY. However, the impoundment affected a Turkish company (Bosphorus) which had leased the aircraft from the owner before the UN sanctions had been imposed. For this reason, Bosphorus complained that the impoundment of its aircraft was an undue interference with its right to peaceful enjoyment of its property. On a preliminary reference from the Irish Supreme Court, the ECJ found that given the importance of the public interest at stake, i.e. the attempt to put an end to the war in the Balkans and to the human rights violations perpetrated by the FRY in Bosnia, the interference with the applicant's right to property was justified.[51] Consequently, the Irish Supreme Court found against the claimants, who then sought redress in front of the European Court of Human Rights.

---

declared that the fact that a provision of national law reproduced almost word for word the provision of a Community directive did not remove the national rule from the scope of the Convention (see esp para 30).

[47] The act challenged had Treaty status and therefore the ECJ was not competent to assess its validity.

[48] *Matthews v. United Kingdom* (Appl. No. 24833/94), 18 February 1999, esp. para 33, 'The United Kingdom, together with all other parties to the Maastricht Treaty, is responsible (...) for the consequences of that Treaty'.

[49] *Bosphorus etc v. Ireland* (Appl. No. 45036/98), judgment of 30 June 2005, noted J.P. Jaqué (2005) 41 *Revue Trimestrielle de Droit Européen* 756.

[50] Regulation 990/93/EC concerning trade between the European Economic Community and the Federal Republic of Yugoslavia (Serbia and Montenegro), [1993] O.J. L102/14, implementing UN Security Council Resolution 820 (1993).

[51] Case C-84/95, *Boshporus* [1996] ECR I-3953.

The first question for the Strasbourg Court was whether it had jurisdiction; the impoundment was a direct result of the Community Regulation, and the Irish authorities had no discretion on the matter. In examining the issue, the Human Rights Court restated the doctrine of equivalent protection. However, it added an important *caveat*. Whilst it is to be presumed that the Community affords protection of fundamental rights that is equivalent (i.e. comparable) to that afforded by the European Convention and European Court of Human Rights, such presumption is open to rebuttal. Thus, the European Court of Human Rights held that '(...) any such finding of equivalence could not be final and would be susceptible to review in the light of any relevant change in fundamental rights' protection'.[52] It then continued '(...) any such presumption can be rebutted if, in the circumstances of a *particular case*, it is considered that the protection of Convention rights was *manifestly deficient*. In such cases, the interest of international co-operation would be outweighed by the Convention's role as a "constitutional instrument of European public order" in the field of human rights'.[53] The European Court of Human Rights then turned to the question as to whether there was a presumption of compliance between the Community system and the Convention, and found that such presumption existed. In order to justify its findings, the Strasbourg Court relied on the fact that the Community system contained fundamental rights guarantees, including the not 'fully' binding Charter of fundamental rights. However, the European Court of Human Rights also stated that the effectiveness of such guarantees depended on the mechanisms of control to ensure such rights; it then identified such guarantees in the possibility for individuals (however restricted) and for the institutions and the Member States to bring review proceedings; in the possibility for individuals to obtain damages for the Community's non-contractual liability; and in the complementary protection afforded by national courts through the preliminary reference procedure.[54] It next found that the presumption of compliance had not been rebutted in the case at issue.

A. Title VI and the European Convention on Human Rights

It is now time to consider the significance of those rulings in relation to framework decisions which are implemented *verbatim* in national law.[55] In particular, it should be considered whether the more limited judicial protection afforded by the third pillar is sufficient to trigger the presumption of compatibility; and, in any

---

[52] Para 155.

[53] Para 156, quotation marks in the original, emphasis added. It is interesting to note that the Court distinguished all its previous case law from the case at issue, and in particular the *Matthews* case (see para 157).

[54] Cf. the joint concurrent opinion of Judges Rozakis, Tulkens, Botoucharova, Zagrebelski and Garlicki for a reasoned (and reasonable in the writer's opinion) critique of the presumption of equivalence.

[55] If the national authorities are exercising a discretion, then the ruling in *Cantoni* applies, and the ECtHR has jurisdiction over the national implementing rules.

event, whether the exclusion of the jurisdiction of the European Court of Justice in some of the Member States is sufficient to rebut any such presumption so as to establish the jurisdiction of the European Court of Human Rights.

As to the first issue, one of the primary considerations for the Strasbourg Court in order to establish the presumption of equivalent protection was the role of the Court of Justice in ensuring that fundamental rights are observed. In particular, the Human Rights Court focused on the possibility: (i) of bringing judicial review proceedings; (ii) of obtaining damages for non-contractual liability; and (iii) on the preliminary ruling system. Now it is clear that the third pillar system of judicial protection falls short of each one of these criteria. The possibility of bringing review proceedings is limited to the Commission and the Member States; there is no possibility of obtaining damages from the Union[56]; and, even in those Member States which have accepted the Court's jurisdiction, there is no obligation for the national court to make a reference to the European Court of Justice. It could be argued then that the presumption of equivalent protection should not apply to third pillar instruments,[57] and that therefore a party bringing a case in front of the European Court of Human Rights would be under no obligation to rebut the presumption.[58] More importantly, given the fact that framework decisions are not 'normal' international law instruments, since they do not need to be ratified but are merely implemented and are capable of producing some autonomous legal effects,[59] it could be argued that the Member States are under a Convention obligation to reform the system, so as to afford individuals effective judicial protection. After all, the European Court of Human Rights has recognized that the European Union is a unique international legal order and that its political and legal consequences go far beyond those usual in international law. The Strasbourg Court has also made clear that the Contracting Parties cannot use international law to escape their fundamental rights obligations; and it has laid down the conditions that it considers necessary for the system to afford a protection compatible with the Convention. But if the system fails to afford such protection, if individuals see their fundamental

---

[56] Cf. Case T-338/02, *Segi et al. v. Council*, order of 7 June 2004, appeal pending (Case C-355/04 P).

[57] Not to speak about second pillar instruments, where there is no participation of the Parliament, no jurisdiction of the ECJ and no possibility for damages.

[58] Furthermore, it could be argued that if a national supreme court were to consider itself not competent to assess the constitutionality of national implementing rules, then individuals would not be required to 'exhaust' their national remedies before applying to the ECtHR. It is established case law that remedies are exhausted when the existing (not 'exhausted' ones) are inadequate and ineffective. See e.g. Case of *Assanidze v. Georgia* (Appl. No. 71503/01), judgment of 8 April 2004; Case of *Akdivar and Others v. Turkey*, judgment of 16 September 1996, *Reports of Judgments and Decisions* 1996-IV, p. 1210, para 67; and *Andronicou and Constantinou v. Cyprus*, judgment of 9 October 1997, *Reports* 1997-VI, pp. 2094–95, para 159; Case of *Johnston and others v. Ireland* (Appl. No. 9697/82), judgment of 18 December 1986. Clearly, if the national courts considered themselves incompetent to assess the compatibility of national implementing legislation with fundamental rights, the existing remedies would be ineffective and therefore there would be no need to exhaust them.

[59] Cf. C. Fijnaut, 'Police Co-operation and the Area of Freedom, Security and Justice' in N. Walker (ed.), *Europe's Area of Freedom, Security and Justice* (OUP, 2004), 241.

rights guarantees endemically reduced, then the system *as a whole* becomes problematic in relation to the Convention. Thus, it could be argued, the Member States have a positive obligation to amend the TEU so as to ensure that full and effective judicial protection is available also in relation to third pillar matters.[60] After all, the *Matthews* ruling also imposed a positive obligation on the Member States to amend the Council decision so as to allow Gibraltar residents to vote in the European Parliament's election.

In any event, even if the European Court of Human Rights took a more lenient view of the Contracting Parties' obligations under the Convention, it is clear that in those cases in which the national court cannot make the reference lacking its Member State's declaration, the presumption of compatibility would be easily rebutted.[61] Unless the national court were willing to breach its own obligation of loyal co-operation imposed by Union law, and declare the national law invalid even when there was no discretion, the protection afforded to individuals would be 'manifestly defective', since no court would be competent to assess fundamental rights compliance in the concrete case. Thus, the European Court of Human Rights would have jurisdiction to assess the compatibility of the national implementing rule with the Convention (and thus indirectly of the third pillar instrument). Moreover, and even more forcefully than before, it could be argued that the Member States are under a Convention obligation to make the declaration pursuant Article 35 TEU so as to ensure at least a minimum guarantee of judicial protection to those who are in their jurisdiction.

V. Second Problem: The Member State Exercises its Discretion in Breach of Fundamental Rights as General Principles of Union Law

We will now consider the possibility that the Member State, in implementing a framework decision, exercises its discretion in a manner inconsistent with fundamental rights as guaranteed by the European Court of Justice. Given the lack of direct effect of framework decisions this might lead to a gap in the protection of fundamental rights. In this case, it would be of course open to a national court to enforce its own national fundamental rights standards in relation to the national rule.[62] This said, this might not be particularly effective: first, because the application of domestic fundamental rights might not help the claimant (such would be the case in the United Kingdom where the courts cannot set aside a provision of primary legislation that conflicts with fundamental rights); secondly, because the national rule might be detrimental to the rights of the claimant, in that it falls

---

[60] As well as second pillar when those affect individuals.

[61] The same is true, in the writer's opinion, in all cases (including first pillar cases) in which the national court would refuse to make a reference on the compatibility of a Union law instrument with fundamental rights.

[62] And of course the European Court of Human Rights would have jurisdiction; cp e.g. *Cantoni* as well as *Bosphorus* para 157.

short of the guarantees provided by the framework decision, but still not conflict with the domestic fundamental rights standard. But, just as importantly, following the Court's ruling in *Pupino*,[63] an analysis of this scenario is necessary in order to attempt a more precise definition of the scope of Union law.

A. The Ruling in *Pupino*

In the *Pupino* case,[64] the European Court of Justice held that national courts are under a Union law obligation to interpret their domestic legislation insofar as possible consistently with framework decisions. It based its findings on a literal as well as a teleological reasoning.

First, the Court noted that Article 34 TEU is phrased in a very similar way to Article 249 EC; as in the case of directives, framework decisions bind the Member States, and consequently their courts. To reinforce this argument, the Court resorted to the familiar notion of *effet utile*: the (limited) jurisdiction of the European Court of Justice would be deprived of 'most of its useful effect' if individuals could not rely on the duty of consistent interpretation in front of national courts.

Secondly, dealing with some of the intervening Governments' objection that the TEU does not provide for the principle of loyal co-operation enshrined in Article 10 EC (the legal basis for indirect effect), the Court held that such principle applies equally to the TEU,[65] despite it not being expressly provided for. In order to justify its findings, the Court relied again on the notion of effectiveness: it would be difficult for the Union to carry out the objectives set out in Article 1 TEU if the Member States were not bound by the principle of loyal co-operation. Thus, the Court held, the principle of consistent interpretation applies also in relation to framework decisions.

The scope of the principle of indirect effect of Union law seems to be identical to its scope in Community law.[66] Thus, the national court has to interpret the national rules consistently with the framework decision only insofar as possible, i.e. without the need to give an interpretation *contra legem*,[67] and subject to the general principles of Community law (which by implication now apply also to Union law) and in particular subject to the principle of non-retroactivity of criminal sanctions and legal certainty.[68] And the obligation imposed by the ECJ is the broad *Pfeiffer* obligation— i.e. it includes an obligation to look at the legal system as a whole to attempt a consistent interpretation.[69] The reasoning of the Court suggests that the interpretative obligation binds *all* national courts, regardless of whether the Member State has

---

[63] Case C-105/03, *Pupino*, [2005] ECR I-5285.   [64] *ibid.*

[65] Cf. also D. Curtin and I. Dekker, 'The Constitutional Structure of the European Union: Some Reflections on Vertical Unity-in-Diversity' in P. Beaumont, C. Lyons and N. Walker (eds.), *Convergence and Divergence in European Public Law* (Hart, 2001), esp at 68–69.

[66] Case 14/83, *Von Colson* [1984] ECR 1891.

[67] Case C-168/95, *Arcaro* [1996] ECR I-4705; Case C-397/01, *Pfeiffer* [2004] ECR I-8835.

[68] Case 80/86, *Kolpinghuis* [1987] ECR 3969, Case C-169/95, *Arcaro* [1996] ECR I-4705.

[69] Cf. Case C-397/01, *Pfeiffer*, [2004] ECR I-8835 esp para 119.

accepted the jurisdiction of the Court. Indirect effect is based on the duty of loyal co-operation, a duty which cannot depend upon whether the Member State has made a declaration pursuant to Article 35 TEU; furthermore, there is no legal or logical reason to exclude some of the national courts from this obligation.[70] Rather, to make the application of indirect effect conditional upon a voluntary act of the Member State would be inconsistent with the principle of uniform interpretation of Union law.[71]

B. *Pupino* and Fundamental Rights

The ruling in *Pupino* might well be a useful tool in relation to fundamental rights protection in those cases in which the framework decision does not in itself conflict with fundamental rights but the national rule does.[72] According to established Community case law, Member States and their national courts are bound by fundamental rights when acting within the scope of Community law. By applying the principle of indirect effect to framework decisions, the Court has made clear that national law falling within the scope *ratione materiae* of framework decisions falls within the scope of Union law. It is also clear from the ruling in *Pupino* that fundamental rights as general principles of Union law apply as a limit to the duty of consistent interpretation; the question is thus whether they also apply as a (judicially enforceable) limit to the exercise of the Member States' discretion. In order to answer this question, it is necessary to look at the scope of application of fundamental rights as general principles in Community law.

VI. Fundamental Rights and National Rules Implementing Community Law[73]

As said above, Member States have to respect fundamental rights when implementing, or acting within the field, of Community law.[74] Thus, if a national rule implementing Community/Union law can be interpreted consistently with

---

[70] It could be argued that the Treaty drafters had foreseen that the Court's interpretation might have effects which would bind all the Member States when they provided for the possibility of all Member States to intervene in the preliminary rulings, regardless of whether they had made a declaration pursuant to Article 35 TEU; see also para 37 of the *Pupino* ruling.

[71] The fact that the principle of consistent interpretation binds also the courts of Member States which have failed to accept the Court's jurisdiction makes it all the more urgent for those States to make the Article 35 TEU declaration so as to allow their courts to ascertain the scope of Union law and of their obligations therein.

[72] It is immaterial whether the national rule was adopted with the view of implementing the framework decision, since, as in *Pupino* (and consistently with the indirect effect doctrine in Community law) the duty of consistent interpretation applies regardless to whether the national rule pre or post-dates the decision.

[73] I gratefully acknowledge some comments made by Damian Chalmers on this section on a previous draft of this article.

[74] On general principles see T. Tridimas, *The General principles of EU law* (OUP 2006), esp. chap. 1.

fundamental rights, it should be so interpreted.[75] Moreover, if the Community rule is directly effective, the national court will be under a Community law duty to set aside the national rule which breaches fundamental rights as general principles of Community law (and apply instead the Community rule which does not breach fundamental rights).[76] However, it is not clear whether the same applies if the Community rule is not directly effective. In other words, if the Community rule wrongly implemented is not directly effective (and thus cannot in itself be used to set aside the national rule), can a claimant rely on fundamental rights as general principles of Community law to set aside the offending rule? This question is crucial to our investigation since third pillar instruments are not capable of having direct effect.

Unfortunately, even in relation to Community law, there is little case law on the scope of application of the general principles in relation to non-directly effective provisions. One could well argue that *Borsana*[77] and *Booker Aquaculture*[78] are in themselves authorities for such a claim—however, if it is true that in both cases the Court accepted to scrutinize national rules implementing directives in relation to the general principles, it should be noted that since the Court found the national rule to be compatible with the principle of proportionality and fundamental rights respectively, it did not have to declare explicitly what would be the exact effect of a declaration of inconsistency. However, in *Caballero*,[79] a case concerning an employment directive, the Court found that in a semi-vertical situation, the general principles of equality and proportionality (in the Court's view, fundamental rights) are directly effective and demand that conflicting legislation be set aside.[80] But the strongest authority to hold that general principles are directly effective even when the provision that brings the situation within the scope of Community law is not in itself directly effective stems from the recent ruling in *Mangold*.[81] Here, the Court held that the principle of non-discrimination on grounds of age had to be regarded as a general principle of Community law and that the national court was under an obligation to set aside the national rules conflicting with such principle. The situation in *Mangold* fell within the scope of Community law by virtue of

[75] E.g. Case C-101/01, *Lindqvist* [2003] ECR I-12971.

[76] Take for instance all the cases concerning Treaty provisions and in particular Case C-60/00, *Carpenter* [2002] ECR I-6279.

[77] Case C-2/97, *Borsana Srl* [1998] ECR I-8597, although the Court excluded from its scrutiny measures which went beyond what was required by Community law in relation to minimum harmonization; see also Joined Cases C-286/94, C-340-95, C-401/95 and C-47/96, *Garage Molenheide BVBA et al.* [1997] ECR I-7281.

[78] Case C-20/00, *Booker Aquaculture* [2003] ECR I-7411.

[79] Case C-442/00, *Caballero* [2002] ECR I-11915.

[80] The case related to a semi-vertical situation and arguably it could have been also dealt with by imposing the vertical direct effect of the directive. However, the Court does not rely on the direct effect of the directive, but on the direct effect of the general principles.

[81] Case C-144/04, *Mangold*, [2005] ECR I-9981; for a critique of the ruling see editorials in the 2006 February issues of the CML Rev and the EL Rev.

Directive 1999/70,[82] which, however, could not produce directly enforceable rights since the situation was horizontal. Furthermore, one could also have regard to the general principle of effective judicial protection which has always been directly effective, quite independently from the directive or the provision of Community law at issue,[83] and to the general principles of equivalence and effectiveness in relation to national procedural rules,[84] which again are directly effective regardless of the type of Community measure at issue.[85] It could be of course that only *some* general principles (equality, judicial protection and maybe proportionality) are directly effective. But it could also be argued that there is some, however slim, authority to argue that, even if framework decisions cannot be directly effective, they can constitute a medium through which general principles (and especially fundamental rights) can become directly effective also in relation to criminal law.

A. General Principles and National Laws Implementing (Non-directly Effective) Framework Decisions

We have seen above that there is some (not entirely conclusive) evidence to argue that fundamental rights as general principles of Community law can be invoked to set aside a national rule implementing a directive even when the latter is not capable of having direct effect. It could therefore be argued that the same applies in relation to Union law, and in particular in relation to national rules implementing a framework decision. Thus, even though the Union law act in itself is not directly effective, the Member States are not only under a duty to respect fundamental rights when acting within the scope of Union law, but, it could be argued, such duty is judicially enforceable. In other words, if the national rule implementing the framework decision breaches fundamental rights as general

---

[82] Directive 1999/70 concerning the framework agreement on fixed-term work concluded by ETUC, UNICE and CEEP [1999] O.J. L175/43.

[83] The Court has held that when the principle of judicial protection is codified in a directive it is an expression of a general principle of Community law; see e.g. Case 222/84, *Johnston* [1986] ECR 1651. See also Case C-97/91, *Oleificio Borelli v. Commission* [1992] ECR I-6313, where the Court held that national courts are under a Community law duty to afford judicial protection allowing for review proceedings of an act that whilst being merely part of a procedure might produce adverse legal effects; and Case C-459/99, *MRAX* [2002] ECR I-6591, where the Court relied on the principle of effective judicial protection to extend the personal scope of application of Article 9 Directive 64/221 on the co-ordination of special measures concerning the movement and residence of foreign nationals which are justified on grounds of public policy, public security or public health [Sp. Ed. 1964] O.J. No. 864, 117 (now repealed by Directive 2004/38 on the right of citizens of the Union and their family members to move and reside freely within the territory of the Member States, [2004] O.J. L158/77).   [84] E.g. Case 33/76, *Rewe-Zentralfinanz* [1976] ECR 1989.

[85] This said, one could argue that the very effectiveness of the entire system would be compromised should judicial protection, equality and effectiveness not apply and that therefore these principles are 'inherent' in the Treaty. Cp the reasoning in Case C-6/90, *Francovich* [1991] ECR I-5357. If that were true, then it would be a matter of debate as to whether police and judicial co-operation in criminal matters can 'effectively' work without fundamental rights guarantees.

principles of Union law, then the national court would be under a Union law duty to set aside the offending legislation. This view seems to find support in several legal and policy considerations.

First, this view seems to be consistent with the Member States' understanding of their own fundamental rights obligations as codified in the Charter of Fundamental Rights. The Charter (once given legal status) would bind Member States whenever they implement Union law, regardless of the effect (direct or otherwise) of the provisions of Union law concerned.[86]

Secondly, there is no reason why, once the matter is brought within the scope of Union law through indirect effect, the principles governing fundamental rights protection should differ according to whether the matter is a Community or third pillar one.[87]

Thirdly, Article 35(5) TEU explicitly excludes the jurisdiction of the Court in relation to the scrutiny of the validity or proportionality of operations carried out by the police or other enforcement services as well as actions carried out in relation to maintenance of law and order and internal security. The explicit exclusion of a power of review in relation 'only' to those fields, rather than a more general exclusion, might therefore suggest that the Member States accepted that general principles, including proportionality and fundamental rights, could/should be available to scrutinize the compatibility with Union law of Member States' acts in other fields affected by the third pillar.[88]

Fourthly, and maybe much more importantly, a different result would be problematic to the point of risking a fracture in the system. When the Member States decide to act through the Union rather than through national law alone, they should accept all the consequences of so doing. If the Union is a community based on the principles of democracy, rule of law and fundamental rights, it cannot tolerate that its laws might be used as an excuse to curtail individual rights beyond what is acceptable having regard to fundamental rights principles. Otherwise, Governments might be all too tempted to adopt framework decisions, where the European Parliament's role is limited to consultation,[89] and then force legislation

---

[86] Article 51 (II-111) of the Charter.

[87] Consider also that in some cases second pillar instruments require the Community to act (e.g. Common Position 2001/931/CFSP which required the Community to enact a Regulation freezing the assets of those individuals and associations listed in the Common Position, see above section II). It would be odd were national law to be subject to the general principles when implementing the Community (derived) act, but not when implementing the Union (parent) act.

[88] A similar argument has been made in relation to the direct applicability of framework decisions and decisions by D. Curtin and I. Dekker, 'The Constitutional Structure of the European Union: Some Reflections on Vertical Unity-in-Diversity' in P. Beaumont, C. Lyons and N. Walker (eds), *Convergence and Divergence in European Public Law* (Hart, 2001), esp at 68–69; they argued that since the Treaty drafters explicitly excluded direct effect then it follows that they must have expected the other 'Community' constitutional principles (supremacy and direct applicability) to apply. A not entirely dissimilar reasoning can be found in para 37 of the *Pupino* ruling in order to establish the principle of consistent interpretation in relation to Union law.   [89] Cf. Article 39 TEU.

through national Parliaments claiming their obligations arising from Union law and limiting the possibility for a full democratic discussion.[90] And after all, it is exactly out of a concern for similar dynamics, as well as out of a desire of creating a community truly based on fundamental rights, that the Court has developed its case law in relation to directives and regulations. Those concerns are all the more pressing when the Union is reaching out to embrace the criminal law sphere. Furthermore, the need to impose a fundamental rights compliance obligation is made more urgent by the fact that it is not unusual for a framework decision to use undefined and vague terms: take for instance the framework decision on attacks on information systems. Here the Member States are requested to impose maximum penalties on such crimes, 'at least for cases which are not minor'.[91] The measure is not a minimum harmonization measure; rather, the reference to minor incidents (such as, for instance, teenage hackers) seems to suggest that more leniency is accepted, and indeed might be appropriate in some circumstances. It seems to be consistent with EU law that the way those 'minor cases' are dealt with should comply with the general principles of Community law, including fundamental rights and proportionality.[92]

Fifthly, there is no cogent reason to refrain from allowing the direct effect of fundamental rights in relation to framework decisions. This seems to have been acknowledged at the highest political level in the Constitution: should the Constitution have come into force, fundamental rights would have applied in relation to rules implementing framework decisions. If the desire to be watchful against the indirect expansion of Union law is more than legitimate, one cannot but welcome the possibility that Member States might be reminded of obligations that arise not only from Articles 6 and 7 of the TEU, but also from membership of the Council of Europe. After all it would be very peculiar if, whilst respect for fundamental rights is a pre-condition for Union membership, the Member States were to be allowed to shelter behind Union law in order to breach those very rights. It seems therefore that legal and policy reasons concur in allowing the possibility of diffuse fundamental rights scrutiny in relation to national rules implementing framework decisions.[93]

---

[90] On the UK Parliament scrutiny of EU Measures, see C.S. Kerse, 'Parliamentary Scrutiny of the Third Pillar' (2000) 6 EPL 81.

[91] Framework Decision 2005/222/JHA on attacks against information systems, [2005] O.J. L69/67. See also Framework Decision 2003/80/JHA on the protection of the environment through criminal law, [2003] O.J. L29/55 which provides for criminalization of pollution arising from negligence, or at least 'serious negligence' (Art. 3).

[92] Some framework decisions also contain a fundamental rights 'assurance' in their preamble (e.g. Framework Decision 2005/222/JHA on attacks against information systems, [2005] O.J. L69/67, *whereas* 18); this would further reinforce the Member State obligation to respect fundamental rights when implementing Union law.

[93] Diffuse judicial scrutiny occurs when all courts can assess the compatibility of a rule vis-à-vis a hierarchically superior norm (usually constitutional); such diffuse scrutiny is common in relation to executive rules, but it is usually not allowed in relation to legislation, where such scrutiny is reserved to a specific court (e.g. the Constitutional courts in Italy, Germany, Poland, Spain etc; the *Conseil d'Etat* in France; the ECJ in relation to Community measures).

VII. The Applicability of General Principles to Framework Decisions Establishing Minimum Rules

So far I have argued that fundamental rights should be directly applicable against Member States implementing framework decisions. There are, in my opinion, legal and policy reasons why this should be the case. However, there is one further problem which deserves to be mentioned: in relation to rules relating to the constituent elements of criminal acts and in relation to penalties for organized crime, terrorism and illicit trafficking, Article 31(e) TEU provides for the adoption of 'minimum measures' only. Now, the European Court of Justice has held that the general principles do not apply to national legislation in a field covered by a minimum harmonization directive, when that legislation goes beyond the minimum measures required by Community law.[94] Thus, it could be argued that even were fundamental rights to apply in relation to national rules implementing some framework decisions, they would not in relation to national legislation implementing those listed in Article 31(e) TEU.

Again however the situation is rather more complicated than it seems at first sight. First, there is the problem of whether the 'further measures' allowed are those intended to establish an even stricter definition of, or more stringent penalty for, the relevant offence,[95] or whether the further measures allowed are those intended to provide more extensive guarantees for the individual. More to the point, one could argue that the language of minimum harmonization, and its regime, cannot be so easily transposed in the field of criminal law, where the measure is not necessarily intended to provide a minimum floor of protection upon which Member States can build. Take for instance the framework decision on combating terrorism.[96] That framework decision does not suggest that it concerns minimum measures only; rather it seems to bind the Member States into defining as terrorist offences those

---

[94] Case C-2/97, *Borsana* [1998] ECR I-8597. It could be argued that in Case C-442/00, *Caballero* [2002] ECR I-11915, the Court disregarded this principle since it applied the general principles of Community law to part of a directive which was minimum harmonization only. However, as the Court did not discuss the point about level of harmonization, it would be hasty to conclude too much from this ruling. In any case, the principle has been clearly re-established in Case C-6/03, *Deponiezweckverband Eiterköpfe*, judgment of 14 April 2005, nyr, para 63 and operative part of the judgment. On these issues, suggesting that fundamental rights might apply even in cases relating to minimum harmonization, see F. De Cecco, 'Room to Move? Minimum Harmonization and Fundamental Rights' (2006) CML Rev 9.

[95] Cf. P. Asp, 'Harmonisation and cooperation within the third pillar—Built in risks' (2001) 4 CYELS 15; Asp notes that if the Union action involves minimum harmonization only, i.e. the Union measure provides for a minimum amount of repression, then the effect of harmonizing will lead to an increased level of repression, i.e. a level of repression higher than that provided in the most lenient Member State (otherwise there would be no need to harmonize). He also queries whether this approach is not inconsistent with the principle of proportionality.

[96] Council Framework Decision on Combating Terrorism (20002/475/JHA), [2002] O.J. L164/3.

listed in the decision itself. It might be that, whilst the Member State could not curtail the very broad scope of the framework decision, they could add crimes to the list of offences to be defined as terrorist crimes; and that those crimes could be subject to heavier penalties as required by Article 5 of the framework decision. Now, assuming fundamental rights can be invoked in relation to those offences listed in the framework decision (this time also by virtue of the fundamental right guarantee contained in Article 1(2) of the decision), it is not clear that given the Court's case law, Union fundamental rights would be available in relation to 'further measures'. In enacting further measures, the Member State would not in fact be exercising a 'delegated' power—rather it would be exercising its full sovereignty in the field of criminal law. As the (Community) case law stands at present then, those would fall outside the scope of Union law, and would therefore not be amenable to judicial scrutiny as to their compliance with the general principles of Union law.

More difficult, however, is the case of framework decisions which impose 'minimum harmonization' by imposing minimum penalties. Take, for instance, the framework decision on money laundering[97] which provides for a maximum penalty of at least four years: is it really convincing to argue that fundamental rights guarantees would apply to those individuals in jurisdictions which have implemented the framework decision in a more lenient way, but not in those Member States which have chosen a more repressive route?[98]

VIII. Conclusions

In the wake of the terrorist attacks against the US, a series of measures was passed at Union level, including a Common Position with an annex listing individuals and organizations believed to be involved in terrorist activities. In that circumstance, the choice of legal basis effectively sheltered the measure from any democratic and judicial scrutiny. In the wake of the London bombings, the UK Government is seeking to introduce restrictive measures at the expenses of civil liberties, not only at home,[99] but also at Union level.[100] In advocating the

---

[97] Framework Decision 2001/500/JHA on money laundering, the identification, tracing, freezing, seizing and confiscation of instrumentalities and the proceeds of crime [2001] O.J. L182/1.

[98] On those issues, see F. De Cecco, 'Room to Move? Minimum Harmonization and Fundamental Rights' (2006) CML Rev 9.

[99] Cf. the measures proposed by the Blair Government in the aftermath of the London terrorist attacks <http://www.homeoffice.gov.uk/n_story.asp?item_id=1346>; cp in particular the consultation document on 'Exclusion or deportation from the UK on non-conducive grounds' <http://www.homeoffice.gov.uk/docs4/deportation.pdf>. and the press release of the home office on 24 August 2005 'Tackling Terrorism—Behaviour Unacceptable in the UK' <http://www.homeoffice.gov.uk/n_story.asp?item_id=1351>; and the Prime Minister Speech of 5 August 2005, outlining new anti-terrorism measures to be adopted in Autumn 2005 <http://www.number-10.gov.uk/output/Page8041.asp>.

[100] Paper by the UK Presidency of the European Union, *Liberty and Security—Striking the Right Balance*, presented to the European Parliament on 7 September 2005, <http://

adoption of those measures before the European Parliament, Mr Clarke, the UK Home Secretary, launched an attack on the existing European Convention balance between individual rights and the 'protection of democratic values such as safety and security under the law'. Mr Clarke also rejected one of the tenets of human rights law (and a foundation of any democratic and 'civilized' country), by advocating that the right not to be subject to ill-treatment and torture 'must be considered side by side with the right to be protected' from terrorist attacks.[101] If it is tempting for Governments to rush measures through in the aftermath of dramatic events, it is even more tempting to do so collectively through the adoption of framework decisions, so as to limit the possibility of parliamentary and public scrutiny.[102] And after all, it would not be the first time in which Governments shelter themselves behind the screen of Union obligations to introduce measures which are politically sensitive.[103]

If the Constitution had entered into force, the introduction of restrictive measures through framework decisions would have not been much more problematic than the introduction of similar measures at purely domestic level. However, lacking ratification of the Constitution, the situation is not only unsatisfactory, but also worrying. Framework decisions are adopted without full participation of the European Parliament, with all the consequences that this implies (scarce representation of non-majority opinion, less effective debate, etc). Equally, the very adoption of instruments at Union level reduces, if not altogether eliminates, the chances of a full and meaningful debate in front of national parliaments. Furthermore, the jurisdiction of the European Court of Justice is subject to voluntary acceptance, thus raising very serious issues about the availability of effective judicial protection. This is particularly the case in relation to the reduced possibility to challenge the validity of framework decisions and decisions, even when those affect individual rights.

---

www.eu2005.gov.uk/servlet/Front?pagename=OpenMarket/Xcelerate/ShowPage&c=Page&cid=1107293561746&a=KArticle&aid=1125560449884&date=2005-09-07>.

[101] Speech by Charles Clarke, UK Home Secretary, to the European Parliament on 7 September 2005, <http://www.eu2005.gov.uk/servlet/Front?pagename=OpenMarket/Xcelerate/ShowPage&c=Page&cid=1107293561746&a=KArticle&aid=1125559979691&date=2005-09-07>. The right not to be subject to torture or ill treatment is provided by Art. 3 of the ECHR, and is an 'absolute' right contained in the Convention, i.e. a right which can never be derogated from.

[102] This said, the EU policy on Fundamental Rights seems to be rather schizophrenic; see Commission Proposal for a Council Regulation establishing a European Union Agency for Fundamental Rights (COM(2005)280 final) and Proposal for a Council Decision empowering the European Union Agency for Fundamental Rights to pursue its activities in areas referred to in Title IV of the European Union (SEC(2005)849). See generally P. Alston and O. de Schutter (eds.), *Monitoring Fundamental Rights in the EU* (Hart Publishing, Oxford, 2005).

[103] An obvious, if positive example, is that of the measures introduced by the Italian Government in the wake of the euro to reduce the deficit and reform the budget; those were measures which were very much needed regardless of euro membership, and would have had to be introduced in any case. However, they became politically more acceptable because of the public support for joining the euro. It is interesting that Mr Clarke links the adoption of restrictive measures at Union level, with the possibility of enhancing citizens' support for the project.

Lacking an adequate system of protection under Title VI, the presumption of compatibility between the Union system and the European Convention of Human Rights, the dogma upon which the European Court of Human Rights has based its restraint, cannot be convincingly maintained. Thus, not only the European Court of Human Rights should assert full jurisdiction over instruments adopted under the third pillar, but it could be argued that the Member States are under a Convention obligation to amend the system so as to provide effective judicial guarantees. This is particularly the case for those Member States which have failed to make the declaration accepting the jurisdiction of the European Court of Justice.

This said, it is possible that at least some degree of protection to those subject to the Member States' jurisdiction is afforded by a broad understanding of the consequences of the ruling in *Pupino*. It could be argued that, at least in some cases, once a provision of national law falls within the scope of Union law, fundamental rights as general principles of Union law not only bind the Member States, but also become judicially enforceable in front of the national courts. There is no doubt that this would represent a considerable expansion of the scope of Union law: after all, framework decisions are not meant to produce legally enforceable consequences. This said, it is open to the Member States to act purely through national law, and afford all the guarantees that should accompany any action in the criminal law sphere. If they decide to act at Union level instead, they should accept to be subject to the Union constitutional principles, and especially to judicially enforceable Union fundamental rights. It is to be hoped that European and national courts alike will be more than vigilant to ensure that the Union is truly based on the principles of democracy, fundamental rights and the rule of law.

Two Sides of the Same Coin?
Framework Decisions and Directives Compared

Bartłomiej Kurcz * and Adam Łazowski* **

I. Introduction

Being the most important legal instrument in the third pillar, framework decisions so far have not been very successful in attracting attention of academic writers. This fact comes to a surprise bearing in mind a number of theoretical and practical problems they lead to. Since entry into force of the Treaty of Amsterdam on 1 May 1999, the European Union has been equipped with powers to adopt framework decisions in the third pillar. Their introduction was part of much broader reform tailored to strengthen the Justice and Home Affairs area.[1] In practice, framework decisions have proved to be very useful and a commonly used tool for approximation of laws of the Member States.[2] Nevertheless, this practice has also shown a variety of drawbacks undermining considerably the effectiveness of EU law. This phenomenon is not new. Numerous challenges of a similar type have been experienced for many years in the first pillar when it comes to EC directives. A mere similarity of definitions of both instruments and adequacy of purposes they serve draws attention. It also leads to numerous theoretical and practical questions. It boils down to the question: are framework decisions and directives two sides of the same coin? The leitmotif and the main argument of this article is that despite formal belonging to different 'species', framework decisions and directives are in process of a step-by-step merger. Such growing

---

* Ph.D, Administrator, European Commission, DG Competition, Brussels. Opinions of the Author are his own and shall not be attributed to the European Commission.

** Ph.D, Senior Lecturer, School of Law, University of Westminster, London. The authors would like to thank Professor Alan Dashwood and Professor Norbert Reich for their comments to the earlier drafts of this text. The usual disclaimer applies.

[1] See, *inter alia*, D. O'Keeffe, P. Twomey (eds.), *Legal Issues of the Amsterdam Treaty* (Hart Publishing, Oxford-Portland Oregon, 1999).

[2] The recent examples include Council Framework Decision 2005/214/JHA of 24 February 2005 on the application of the principle of mutual recognition to financial penalties [2005] O.J. L76/16; Council Framework Decision 2005/222/JHA of 24 February 2005 on attacks against information systems [2005] O.J. L69/67; Council Framework Decision 2005/212/JHA of 24 February 2005 on Confiscation of Crime-Related Proceeds, Instrumentalities and Property [2005] O.J. L68/49.

synergy is visible not only in the practice of the European Commission but also in the jurisprudence of the European Court of Justice. It is significant that the Member States themselves envisaged a unification of both legal instruments in the Treaty establishing a Constitution for Europe creating framework laws.[3] In order to support the main argument of this article and develop a comprehensive answer to the question whether they are really two sides of the same coin we propose to take a number of factors into account. In this article we look at law-making procedures, implementation requirements as well as the application of both instruments at the domestic level. They are analysed in turn and the starting point is the comparison of their definitions and aims.

II. Definitions and Aims of Framework Decisions and Directives

Directives are well established legal instruments of the first pillar. Both, EC and EAEC Treaty envisage adoption of directives, which are binding on the Member States as to the result to be achieved and require implementation to national legal orders.[4] Framework decisions were invented less than a decade ago as a new legal instrument for the third pillar. Article 34 (2)(b) EU reads that *framework decisions shall be binding upon the Member States as to the result to be achieved but shall leave to the national authorities the choice of form and methods. They shall not entail direct effect.* Similarity between both definitions is very striking. The lack of direct effect of framework decisions is the only key difference. Does it mean that the Treaty drafters planned simultaneous functioning of basically equal legal acts in the first and the third pillars of the European Union? It seems that such conclusion based on the literal reading of Article 34 (2)(b) EU is bit far-fetched, though it is not far from reality. The key difference between framework decisions and directives lies in the specificity of EU pillars—supranational first pillar and inter-governmental Police and Judicial Co-operation in Criminal Matters. Although the latter is slowly getting supranational elements it is still generally acknowledged as the intergovernmental area of co-operation.

Similarities between the definitions of framework decisions and directives drew an attention of the European Court of Justice in Case C-105/03 *Criminal Proceedings against Maria Pupino.*[5] The Court acknowledged that the wording of Article 34 (2)(b) EU was clearly inspired by the EC Treaty. It added that *binding character of framework decisions, formulated in terms identical to those of the third*

---

[3] See, *inter alia*, S. Prechal, *Adieu à la Directive?*, 1 EuConst (2005) p. 481; B. Kurcz, *Europejskie ustawy ramowe i ich implementacja* [European Framework Laws and their Implementation] in: S. Dudzik (eds.), *Konstytucja dla Europy. Przyszły fundament Unii Europejskiej* [A Constitution for Europe. The Future Foundation of the European Union] (Kraków, Kantor Wydawniczy Zakamycze, 2005) p. 179.   [4] Article 249 EC, Article 161 EAEC.
[5] Case C-105/03 *Criminal Proceedings against Maria Pupino* [2005] E.C.R. I-5285; [2005] 2 C.M.L.R. 63.

paragraph of Article 249 EC, places on national authorities, and particularly national courts, an obligation to interpret national law in conformity with Community law.[6] The European Court of Justice extended the application of the well established first pillar principle of indirect effect to the third pillar legislation.[7] The lack of direct effect of framework decisions proved to be irrelevant and did not stop the European Court of Justice from reaching such conclusion. Certainly this judicial development brings framework decisions closer to directives, without, at the same time, undermining their pivotal differences resulting from the natures of the EU pillars in question.

The closeness of framework decisions and directives becomes even more obvious when their aims are compared. In case of framework decisions it is spelled out very clearly in Article 34 (2)(b) EU that the goal should be the 'approximation of the laws and the regulations of the Member States'.[8] Equally, directives are tools for approximation of national legislation.[9] This is clear, for example, from Article 94 EC. It must be remembered that the terms 'approximation' and 'harmonization' are used interchangeably. It is argued that there are no substantive differences between the two as compared to unification or co-ordination, which have a different meaning. The approximation is understood here as the creation of certain common denominators for national legal systems in selected areas of law falling within the competences of the European Communities and European Union. When contrasted with unification, approximation presents itself as a much softer and flexible tool, leaving in principle, a degree of discretion to the Member States.[10] Looking at the objectives of the first and third pillars one may conclude that framework decisions and directives despite having the same aim serve different purposes. Truly so, directives are used as the indispensable tool for creation of the internal market. Framework decisions are on the other hand used to facilitate implementation of the area of freedom, security and justice. Bearing this in mind it is submitted that such factors do not make those legal acts very different from each other. Notwithstanding the different objectives they serve they still remain the tools for approximation of laws. Moreover, practice proves that the purposes they serve may be complimentary. In order to analyse this very aspect we have to take a closer look at the formal relations between both instruments.

Prima facie one may conclude that framework decisions and directives are two independent types of legal acts operating in the different areas of EU law. In general terms such conclusion reflects the reality; however, there are examples of

---

[6] Para. 34.

[7] See, *inter alia*, S. Drake, 'Twenty years after Von Colson: the impact of 'indirect effect' on the protection of the individual's Community rights' (2005) 30 E.L. Rev. 329.

[8] This, as a matter of fact, is one the key elements differentiating framework decisions from third pillar decisions.

[9] See, *inter alia*, B. Kurcz, 'Harmonisation by means of Directives—never-ending story?', European Business Law Review (2001) p. 287.

[10] This has not always been the case in the first pillar. For example, the old approach directives on harmonizaton of technical standards.

framework decisions and directives bound by an important formal and substantive chain. This may be the case when a particular issue cannot be regulated in one of those acts due to the division of powers between the EC and EU. In order to have comprehensive regulatory framework a model has been developed where legislation is split between a directive and framework decision.[11] For example, such unique set of legal acts appeared in 2002 when Council adopted the Directive 2002/90/EC defining the facilitation of unauthorized entry, transit and residence[12] and the Framework Decision 2002/946/JHA on strengthening of the penal framework in this respect.[13] Another good example is the legislation on ship-source pollution adopted in late 2005.[14] In both cases, directives and framework decisions are complementary and serve similar purposes. There are no valid legal reasons to prevent their implementation in a single piece of a national legislation (unless justified by reasons of domestic law). Having proved its usefulness one can easily expect this model to be followed in future.[15] Especially that this kind of arrangements seem to have won a tacit approval of the European Court of Justice in Case C-176/03 *Commission v. Council.*[16]

The picture emerging from this part of the analysis is rather clear. The definitions and aims of framework decisions and directives are very similar. Although adopted in different pillars of the European Union both in principle serve a different purpose, however, under certain circumstances they may play a complimentary role.

III. Law-making Procedures and Practices

Comparison of the law-making procedures and practices gives yet another opportunity to proceed with a comparative analysis of framework decisions and directives. It does not come to a surprise that the legislative procedures in the first and in the third pillar of the European Union differ substantially. They reflect

[11] An earlier example involved a Council regulation and Council framework decision. See: Council Regulation (EC) 974/98 of 3 May 1998 on the introduction of the euro [1998] O.J. L139/1; supplemented by Council Framework Decision 2000/383/JHA of 29 May 2000 on increasing protection by criminal penalties and other sanctions against counterfeiting in connection with the introduction of the euro [2000] O.J. L140/1.

[12] Council Directive 2002/90/EC of 28 November 2002 defining the facilitation of unauthorised entry, transit and residence [2002] O.J. L328/17.

[13] Council Framework Decision 2002/946/JHA of 28 November 2002 on the strengthening of the penal framework to prevent the facilitation of unauthorised entry, transit and residence [2003] O.J. L328/1.

[14] Directive 2005/35/EC of the European Parliament and of the Council of 7 September 2005 on ship-source pollution and on the introduction of penalties for infringements [2005] O.J. L255/1; Council Framework Decision 2005/667/JHA of 12 July 2005 to strengthen the criminal-law framework for the enforcement of the law against ship-source pollution [2005] O.J. L255/164.

[15] Case C-176/03 *Commission of the European Communities v. Council of the European Union* [2005] E.C.R. I-7879.   [16] Para. 33 of the judgment.

distinctive legal characters of both areas of integration. The first pillar, *modusoperandi*, reflects the supranational nature of the European Community, while the third pillar, law-making, is full of intergovernmental flavours. At the same time, however, a number of similarities between the two types of legal acts emerge.

A. Proposals for Legislation

Under the first pillar the right to propose legislation belongs primarily to the European Commission.[17] This does not change the fact that an inspiration may, in some cases, originate from the European Council, the Council of the European Union or the European Parliament.[18] When officially launched such proposals are made public in COM series and published in the Official Journal of the European Union.[19] In case of complex and far-reaching proposals their publication is preceded by White or Green Papers outlining key elements of the considered legislation. Responses received from the Member States and economic operators serve as a point of reference when it comes to drafting. The recent example of far-reaching reforms of EC law involving the beforehand publication of such papers is the revision of the anti-trust enforcement rules.[20]

In the framework of the third pillar the right to propose legislation is shared between the Member States and the European Commission. This is only so following the Treaty of Amsterdam which increased the powers of the latter. Such factor can be used to support the argument that following the recent revisions the third pillar is no longer the clear cut intergovernmental area of co-operation but rather the mixed zone, drifting slowly towards supranationalism. At the same time one could argue that the Member States' right to propose legislation make framework decisions more intergovernmental than supranational. Such argument may be dismissed on two grounds. First, there is no valid argument to make this kind of distinction based on the criterion of authority that proposed a particular piece of legislation. After all it is the adopting institution that matters most and in case of framework decisions it is always the Council of the European Union. Secondly, the Member States right to propose legislation is not totally unknown in the first pillar (albeit on a very limited scale) and does not lead to any distinctions between directives.

---

[17] Following the partial communautarisation of the third pillar the right to propose legislation based on Title IV EC had belonged for a period of five years to the European Commission and the Member States. Upon the expiry of the transitional period the first has the sole right of initiative, however it is clear that inspiration may also come from the Member States. See Article 67 EC.

[18] See for instance The Hague Programme: Strengthening Freedom, Security and Justice in the European Union [2005] O.J. C53/1.

[19] Article 13.1 Regulation (EC) No. 1049/2001 of the European Parliament and of the Council of 30 May 2001, regarding public access to European Parliament, Council and Commission documents [2001] O.J. L145/43.

[20] White Paper on Modernisation of the Rules Implementing Articles 85 and 86 of the EC Treaty [1999] O.J. C132/1; Council Regulation (EC) No. 1/2003 of 16 December 2002 on the implementation of the rules on competition laid down in Articles 81 and 82 of the Treaty [2003] O.J. L1/1.

As proved by the practice, both the Member States and the European Commission take the opportunity to propose legislation whenever desired.[21] The European Commission proposals for third pillar legal acts may, similarly to the first pillar, be preceded by consultation documents. It seems enough to mention, for example, a White Paper on exchanges of information on convictions[22] that is followed by a Proposal for a Council Framework decision published on 17 March 2005.[23]

B. Choice of Legal Basis and Source of Law

The choice of a legal basis and legal instrument is a much more complex and sophisticated exercise in the first pillar than in the third. When it comes to EC law the legislation must be based on a set of objective factors that include, *inter alia*, aims and content of proposed measures.[24] The choice of instrument may be determined by a legal basis as some provisions of the EC Treaty restrict the power of EC institutions. For example, Article 89 EC allows only adoption of regulations in the state aid area. At the same time, Article 52 EC on liberalization of national laws on services restricts the choice of instruments to directives only. There are several provisions that provide the EC institutions with several options. For instance, Article 40 EC on free movement of workers gives the choice between directives or regulations.

When it comes to the third pillar the choice of the legal basis and the instrument shall be determined by similar, objective factors. The choice, however, is restrained due to a limited number of provisions that may serve as legal basis and a clear cut distinction between the legal instruments available. With the diminishing role of common positions and conventions the third pillar *acquis* is dominated by framework decisions and decisions. Only the first may be used for approximation of laws hence the aims of legislation play a decisive role in the choice of the legal instrument. There seem to be no ground to contest the conclusion that the case law principle relating to objectivity of the legal basis shall not apply to the third pillar. This seems to be implicit in Case C-176/03 *Commission v. Council*.[25]

---

[21] See eg Proposal for a Council Framework Decision on the organisation and content of the exchange of information extracted from criminal records between Member States (presented by the Commission), COM (2005) 690 final; Initiative of the Republic of Austria, the Republic of Finland and the Kingdom of Sweden with a view to adopting a Council Framework Decision on the European enforcement order and the transfer of sentenced persons between the Member States of the European Union [2005] O.J. C150/1.

[22] White Paper on Exchange of information on convictions and the effect of such convictions in the European Union, COM (2005) 10 final.

[23] Proposal for a Council Framework Decision on taking account of convictions in the Member States of the European Union in the course of new criminal proceedings, COM (2005) 91 final.

[24] Case C-45/86 *Commission v. Council* [1987] 1493; C-300/89 *Commission v. Council* [1991] E.C.R. I-2867.   [25] See paras. 45–47 of the judgment.

The objectivity requirement has also an important cross-pillar dimension. Judging from the experiences so far one may conclude that the conflicts of legal basis between the first and the third pillar are inevitable. The mentioned ECJ judgment in Case C-176/03 *Commission v. Council* may serve as an excellent example in this respect. The ECJ agreed with the plaintiff that Council Framework Decision 2003/80/JHA on the protection of environment through criminal law should have been partly a directive adopted within the framework of the first pillar.[26] It was concluded the Council acted in breach of Article 47 EU. Bearing in mind the functional approach adopted by the European Court of Justice, the European Commission has recently requested the annulment of the Council Framework Decision 2005/667/JHA on strengthening of the criminal law framework against ship-source pollution.[27]

C. Law Drafting Technique

Similarities between framework decisions and directives are clearly visible when it comes to the drafting technique. There are no separate rules for the second and third pillars of the European Union. As proved by practice, the basic EC drafting standards are applicable *mutatis mutandis* to both areas. Interestingly enough such important issues touching the quality of EU legislation are regulated in non-binding interinstitutional agreements between the European Commission, the European Parliament and the Council.[28] As far as the first pillar legislation is concerned it shall be drafted clearly, simply and precisely. Moreover, the drafting shall be appropriate to the type of a legal act concerned. Its provisions shall be concise and homogenous as much as possible. Bearing in mind 23 official languages of the European Union, drafts shall be formulated in such a way as to respect the multilingual diversity of the Member States and EC legislation. Finally, legal acts shall follow a standard structure including title, preamble, provisions and annexes. The purpose of recitals is to 'set out concise reasons for the chief provisions of the enacted term, without reproducing or paraphrasing them'. Although all those rules are formally applicable to EC legislation only, the Council made it clear in its Statement that it is desirable that all those rules are applied to both, second and third pillar legislation.[29] This, as already noted, is the case in everyday practice of

---

[26] Council Framework Decision 2003/80/JHA of 27 January 2003 on the protection of the environment through criminal law [2003] O.J. L29/55.

[27] Action brought on 8 December 2005 by the Commission of the European Communities against the Council of the European Union (Case C-440/05) [2006] O.J. C22/10.

[28] Interinstitutional Agreement of 22 December 1998 on common guidelines for the quality of drafting of Community legislation [1999] O.J. C73/1; Interinstitutional Agreement of 28 November 2001 on a more structured use of the recasting technique for legal acts [2002] O.J. C77/1.

[29] 'The Council finds it desirable that the general principles of good drafting which may be drawn from the Common guidelines on the quality of drafting of Community legislation serve, where appropriate, as an inspiration for the drafting of acts adopted pursuant to Titles V and VI of the Treaty on European Union'.

the European Union. Framework decisions are drafted and structured equally to directives.[30]

Moreover, when drafting its proposals the European Commission is trying to follow the principles of proportionality and subsidiarity, enshrined in Article 5 EC. It is interesting to note, that although not formally obliged to do so, the European Commission follows both principles when drafting framework decisions. Council Framework Decision 2004/68/JHA on combating sexual exploitation of children[31] as well as Council Framework Decision 2005/222/JHA on attacks against information systems may serve as excellent examples.[32] Needless to say that such policy determines the contents and level of detail of framework decisions. Interestingly enough, there are hardly any references to the principles of proportionality and subsidiarity in framework decisions proposed by the Member States.

D. Decision-making Procedure

Significant differences between framework decisions and directives, reflecting the different legal natures of the first and third pillars come to the surface when decision-making procedures are considered. The first pillar arrangement is a direct result of five decades long evolution. The latter is characterized by an ever increasing role of the European Parliament as well as the replacement of unanimity by qualified majority voting in the Council of the EU. For the purposes of this analysis there is no need to go into details of those procedures, however, some general comparative conclusions are necessary.

When it comes to the first pillar of the EU there are different sets of the legislative procedures within the European Community and the European Atomic Energy Community. Following the recent revisions of the EC Treaty the co-decision procedure is the main *modus operandi*. The law-making tasks are equally divided between the European Parliament and the Council of the European Union acting as co-legislators.[33] The voting requirements in the latter have seen pivotal changes in the past two decades. The shift from the unanimity to qualified majority voting is at the heart of the matter. With every single revision of the treaty framework the qualified majority is being extended to more areas of EC law. At the same time the EAEC Treaty is dominated by the original consultation procedure that envisages limited involvement of the European Parliament. Moreover, decisions of the Council of the EU in most of cases require the unanimity among the Member States.

---

[30] See e.g. Council Framework Decision of 13 June 2002 on the European arrest warrant and the surrender procedures between Member States [2002] O.J. L190/1.

[31] Council Framework Decision 2004/68/JHA of 22 December 2003 on combating the sexual exploitation of children and child pornography [2004] O.J. L13/44. For a reference to the principles of subsidiarity and proportionality see recital 8 of the preamble.

[32] Council Framework Decision of 24 February 2005 on attacks against information systems [2005] O.J. L69/67. For a reference to the principles of subsidiarity and proportionality see recital 17 of the preamble.   [33] Article 251 EC.

The third pillar decision-making is dominated by intergovernmental features. However, following the Treaty of Amsterdam and the Treaty of Nice it has received a number of supranational flavours. First of all the powers of the European Parliament were strengthened considerably. On the basis of Article 39 EU it has powers to present opinions on proposed legislation. The Council has an obligation to ask for opinions. At the same time it may impose strict time limits that shall not be shorter than three months. As a matter of principle the adoption of the third pillar legislation requires unanimity in the Council. The qualified majority voting is available only exceptionally.

Decision-making procedures are one of the key elements differentiating the first and third pillars. They reflect different legal natures of both areas of integration. This has pivotal consequences for this analysis as the decision-making *modus operandi* draws one of the dividing lines between framework decisions and directives. This may be used to support the argument that both types of legal acts belong to the different species and should not be considered as two sides of the same coin.

There are lots of similarities between framework decisions and directives when it comes to publication in the Official Journal of the European Union. In both cases it is compulsory, however on different legal basis. As far as directives are concerned such obligation is explicit in Article 254 EC. Interestingly enough there is no obligation to publish directives adopted within the Euratom.[34] Compulsory publication of framework decisions is envisaged by a Council Regulation 1049/2001/EC on access to documents as well as Council Rules of Procedure.[35]

IV. Implementation of Directives and Framework Decisions: Separate or Concurrent Lines?

There is no doubt that there is a growing synergy between directives and framework decisions in the field of their implementation. There remain, however, certain differences. Now we would like to look closer at the two instruments and the ECJ case law concerning their implementation to national law.

A. Formal Requirements

We will start by examining what we call the formal implementation requirements. The latter comprise the requirements of:

- timely transposition;
- notification; and
- making references to Community instruments in national law.

---

[34] Article 163 EAEC.
[35] Council Decision of 22 March 2004 adopting the Council's Rules of Procedure (2004/338/EC, Euratom) [2004] O.J. L106/22 (as amended).

(i) The Obligation of Timely Implementation

As far as directives are concerned we can distinguish between different time limits.
The most important periods, which determine the consecutive implementation
stages, are:

(a) time of the *entry into force* of a directive;
(b) period prescribed for the completion of *the implementation* process; and
(c) period for the full application of the provisions of a directive, if different
     from the period prescribed for its implementation.

The same distinction can be applied to framework decisions, with some recogniz-
able differences with regard to point (c).

The first period—the time for a directive's entry into force is normally, in
accordance with Article 254 EC, specified in a directive. In case it is not provided
in a directive, the latter comes into force on the twentieth day after its publication
in the Official Journal of the European Union. If a directive is not addressed to all
Member States[36] and is not adopted in accordance with the procedure defined
in Article 254 EC, it comes into force with its notification to the addressees. In
accordance with the established practice, framework decisions enter into force on
the day of their publication in the Official Journal.

The second time limit (point (b)) is always stated in a directive. A Member
State generally has from six months to 2 years for its implementation.[37] This
fixed date cannot be modified unilaterally by a Member State and any going
beyond it would be recognized as belated implementation and could be sanctioned by the European Court of Justice in Article 226 EC procedure. The
prolongation of this period could be accepted by the European Court of Justice if
the Commission was informed and agreed to the prolongation of implementation
period. When it comes down to framework decisions, the fixed date is always
stated in a decision. The period given to the Member States for implementation
does not vary as much as in case of directives and amounts normally to two years.
Since for framework decisions there is no comparable judicial enforcement as it
is in case of directives, the period necessary to comply with the provisions of
framework decisions and the question of the prolongation of the period is of lesser
importance.

The last time-limit (point (c))—a separate period for the application of directives' provisions has to be also explicitly mentioned in a directive. It cannot be

---

[36] It is rare due to the principal nature of the directive as the harmonization instrument. See, for
instance, Commission Directive 65/330/EEC of 16 June 1965 setting the timetable for the phasing-
out of the tax applied by the Federal Republic of Germany to import of mutton sheep and sheepmeat
from the other Member States [1965] O.J. 120/2074; Council Directive 79/174/EEC of 6 February
1979 concerning the flood protection programme in the Hérault Valley [1979] O.J. L38/18.

[37] See D. Simon *La Directive Européenne* (Paris, Dalloz, 1997) pp. 44–45.

implied. Most often it is not, it is then assumed that all provisions do not only have to be transposed to national law, but are also fully applicable from the end of the implementation period. However, it sometimes happens that a directive provides a different time limit for taking legal steps which would guarantee achieving the envisaged result and a different time limit for achieving a practical compliance with its norms. Article 15 (1) and (2) of Directive 95/16/EC can serve as an example.[38] It assigns two different time limits: one concerns the adjustment of national law and the other concerns the actual application of the directive in the Member States. In case of this particular directive the difference between these two time limits is seven months. In case of Directive 76/760/EEC it is even shorter and is three months.[39]

Although framework decisions do not usually contain provisions limiting their applicability, there are clear exceptions. For instance, the framework decision on the application of the principle of mutual recognition to financial penalties[40] provides for a five-year-period in which only certain penalties on certain legal persons can be subject to the requirements of mutual recognition. It again resembles directives.

(ii) The Obligation to Notify Implementing Measures

We can distinguish between the three main types of notifications. They arise out of three different kinds of obligations:

(a) to inform *a priori*, i.e. before measures adopted by a Member State;
(b) to inform *a priori* and to get authorization before measures adopted by a Member state; and
(c) to inform *a posteriori*, i.e. after measures adopted by any Member State.

The obligation mentioned in point (c) is common to directives and framework decisions. However, its legal base and the follow-up of notification differ. The first two points are particular to the nature of directives as binding instruments.

In the case of directives, the obligation to notify the implementation measures to the Commission undertaken by a Member State in most cases results directly from directives' provisions.[41] Such an obligation normally consists of sending the

---

[38] European Parliament and Council Directive 95/16/EC of 29 June 1995 on the approximation of the laws of the Member States relating to lifts [1995] O.J. L213/1.

[39] See Article 11 of Council Directive 76/760/EEC of 27 July 1976 on the approximation of the laws of the Member States relating to the rear registration plate lamps for motor vehicles and their trailers [1976] O.J. L262/85.

[40] Council Framework Decision 2005/214/JHA of 24 February 2005 on the application of the principle of mutual recognition to financial penalties [2005] O.J. L76/16.

[41] See e.g. Article 12 of Council Directive 89/48/EEC of 21 December 1988 on a general system for the recognition of higher-education diplomas awarded on completion of professional education and training of at least three years' duration [1989] O.J. L19/16.

national implementing measures to the Commission, after having been adopted, for informative purposes. The dispatched documents serve the Commission as a source of information whether the country took appropriate steps in the implementation process.

The infringement of the notification obligation is a violation of loyal co-operation between the Community institutions and Member States.[42] The obligation does not cease to be valid even if, after legal proceedings under Article 226 EC have begun, the Commission decides to withdraw the complaint and it is removed from the register. Measures must be officially notified to the Commission notwithstanding whether the latter knew in reality about the existence of the implementation measures.[43] Some countries even decide to insert in their implementation measures an appropriate reference to the performed notification.[44] Moreover, the scrutiny done by the Commission of the obligation to notify has no bearing on the supervision of implementation instruments either by national courts or by the other institutions established with the same goal.[45]

The notification obligation concerning legal texts differs from the obligation to inform the Commission about the application of national implementing measures.[46]

In the case of framework decisions the notification is not transmitted only to the Commission, but also to to the General Secretariat of the Council. The Commission draws a report on the basis of the notification which allows for the assessment of Member States' compliance with the framework decision. It is interesting to note that the notification clause speaks only about the extent to which the *obligations imposed on the Member States (emphasis added)* were tranposed. Since according to Article 34 (2)(b) framework decisions do not entail direct effect, it seems the EU supervising institutions are not so much interested in potential rights arising out of this obligation. This question is left for national law.

Finally, it has to be noted that in the current legal setting there is no direct equivalent of Article 10 EC in the EU Treaty, therefore the necessary legal basis for providing the Commission with all other documents, which it would request from a Member State[47] does not exist for framework decisions.

---

[42] Case C-374/89 *Commission v. Belgium* [1991] E.C.R. I-367, para. 11.

[43] Case C-274/83 *Commission v. Italy* [1985] E.C.R. 1077, para. 42.

[44] See e.g. § 19 Austrian *Verordnung des Bundeskanzlers über elektronische Signaturen (Signaturverordnung—SigV)*, BGBl. II Nr. 30/2000.

[45] See Directive 95/46/EC of the European Parliament and of the Council of 24 October 1995 on the protection of individuals with regard to the processing of personal data and on the free movement of such data [1995] O.J. L281/31, which establishes the national supervision through the obligation to determine an institution responsible for monitoring of the application of this act. This authority is entitled to start proceedings in case of the infringement of national implementing provisions.

[46] See H. Jarass, *Grundfragen der innerstaatlichen Bedeutung des EG-Rechts: die Vorgaben des Rechts der Europäischen Gemeinschaft für die nationale Rechtsanwendung und die nationale Rechtssetzung nach Maastricht* (Cologne, Heymanns, 1994) p. 63.

[47] Case C-272/86 *Commission v. Greece* [1988] E.C.R. 4875, paras. 30–31.

(iii) The Obligation of Making References in
National Implementing Measures

Formally there is a clear difference between directives and framework decisions in this respect. In contrast to framework decisions, the obligation of making reference to directives in national implementing instruments results from the text of directives. From the 1990s the given clause is inserted in directives[48]:

> When Member States adopt [implementation] measures they shall contain a reference to the directive or be accompanied by such a reference on the occasion of their official publication. Member States shall determine how such reference is to be made.[49]

Certain scholars even claim that the lack of such a clause in a particular directive does not render this obligation inoperational. The obligation for a Member State to make references seems to be independent of the fact whether a particular directive contains clear provisions in this respect.[50] This is certainly not the case as far as framework decisions are concerned. They neither contain such obligation nor can it be inferred from the general duty of co-operation between the Community institutions and Member States. Moreover, in the present state of law there is no overriding *ratio legis* of creating the obligation to make reference to framework decisions in national law. Reasons are twofold. Although it would be very useful and would simplify the monitoring work done by the Commission, it is finally the Council that is accountable for the compliance score, and the jurisdiction of the European Court of Justice is limited to the interpretation or the application of framework decisions whenever a dispute in this regard between the Member States cannot be settled by the Council.[51] More importantly, such reference creates a clear and precise situation with regard to the assertion of individual rights based on EU law. It is fundamental for directives and much less for framework decisions. It makes possible to precisely identify the Community source of the particular national provision. In the case of abstaining from making such reference the position of individuals, who wish to invoke their rights resulting from the supremacy of Community law, is *de facto* considerably weakened due to the untraceable origin of national provision. Framework decisions do not create directly effective rights for individuals from an EU point of view.

---

[48] So D. Simon, loc. cit. n 37 at p. 46. More Ch. Timmermans, 'Rapport Communautaire' [in:] J. Temple Lang (ed.), *XVIII Congress FIDE* (Stockholm, FIDE 1998) p. 22.

[49] See Article 6 (1) of the Directive 2000/35/EC of the European Parliament and of the Council of 29 June 2000 on combating late payment in commercial transactions [2000] O.J. L200/35. See also D. Simon, loc. cit. n 37 at pp. 46–47. Directives also use the other wording having exactly the same meaning 'Member States shall determine how such reference is to be made'.

[50] So S. Heß, *Die Umsetzung von EG-Richtlinien im Privatrecht* (Frankfurt am. Main, Lang, 1999) p. 45.

[51] Subject to the declaration of the Member State, the ECJ can also rule indirectly on the correctness of the national implementing measures in the preliminary ruling procedure. See Article 35 (1) EU.

The style of making references to directives depends on a Member State and in this way the autonomy regarding 'implementation forms and methods' is also manifested. The only practical condition is that the reference should be inserted in the national official journal at the same time and together with the final version of the implementation measures.

The technical possibilities of making references are numerous; a reference may be made in a form of a footnote or in the act's preamble, in the title, in the text itself or as an explanatory note not formally a part of the text. It has to be admitted that the way the reference is made is a part of legal culture of the particular Member State. Nevertheless, it is submitted that they have to be effective, clear and concern all implementing measures. In many Member States private publishers of electronic databases of national legal acts implement this obligation thoroughly.

De lege ferenda, especially for the reasons of transparency, it would be advisable to prepare for framework decisions the so-called correlation tables (the tables of accordance) in which the national implementing measures would be compared with the corresponding provisions of framework decisions as it is already happening in case of directives. Moreover, the correlation tables should be available regardless of whether the reference is made in the preamble of national implementation acts or in their footnotes.[52] There should be a national database comprising these tables, brought up-to-date regularly and with no charge.

The role of the mentioned national database(s) with correlation tables is not to be underestimated in a situation when the norms of a new directive or framework decision would come across the norms already existing in national law and require their modification. The compliance with the requirements of *effective and clear reference* to EU instruments in national law would seem to be difficult without the existence of such database(s). It is not only about the process of following the changes of national regulations in force, but it is also about checking whether any modifications by later national regulations (*lex posterior*) did not alter the substance of implementation instruments to such a degree that they ceased to be adequate implementation means.

Material Requirements

Besides the implementation requirements that we called 'formal' there is a series of criteria against which the proper implementation is measured. We call them material implementation requirements as they relate to the substance of implementing measures. We are aware that this is not a perfect division. Nevertheless, it serves to illustrate the difference between technical obligations that have little to do with substance of national law and obligations relating to the way the EU rights and obligations are implemented to the national legal order. Moreover,

---

[52] The method of footnotes in various official publications is used in Germany; see S. Heß, loc. cit. n 50 at p. 46.

the formal requirements of timely implementation, *a posteriori* notification and making reference to EU law are, as far as directives are concerned, 'autonomous' and do not depend on the substance of the EU act. In both cases the required result is to be fully achieved at a certain point, before the time-limit expires at the latest. It is true both for directives and framework decisions. However, this does not mean that the obligation of fully achieving the result terminates at this point. It is then extended *ad infinitum* i.e. throughout the period of the EU instruments being in force.[53] As noted earlier the consequences of belated implementation differ for the two instruments.

Before looking in detail at how norms of EU law find their way to the national legal order, we would like to focus on the addressees of the obligation to reach the specified result. The addressee of both directives and framework decisions is a Member State. Not individuals but states are solely responsible for the final achievement of the result. It must create such a legal and factual situation in which the result is fully achieved. De facto implementation can be made both in case of directives and framework decisions by decentralized bodies and various organs of Member States. Directives refer indirectly by far more often, due to the subject of the regulation, to the achievement of results depending practically, to the great extent, on the co-operation with individuals.[54] Whereas in such a situation the European Court of Justice is not accepting any justification for the non-compliance with a directive other than *force majeure* or absolute practical impossibility,[55] framework decisions are sometimes phrased differently. Most of obligations imposed by framework decisions can be similarly described as taking 'the necessary measures to ensure' that the result is achieved. The same obligation can also be phrased as taking 'all measures possible to ensure'[56] the achievement of the result. This implies *obligation de résultat pas de moyen.*[57]

Both for directives and framework decisions achieving the desired result comprises of two kinds of obligations—'positive' and 'negative' ones.[58] While positive obligation requires a Member State to ensure that all necessary measures are taken in order to fulfil the obligation, negative obligation completes the positive one in a sense that a Member State is also obliged at the same time to abstain from taking any measures which could seriously endanger achieving the

---

[53] It can be called a 'permanent effectiveness', so M. Gellermann, *Beeinflussung des bundesdeutschen Rechts durch Richtlinien der EG* (Cologne, Heymanns, 1993) p. 31.

[54] See B. Kurcz, K. Zieleśkiewicz, 'Annotation to Case 60/01 of the European Court of Justice', 39 C.M.L. Rev. (2002) p. 1452. Nothing prevents the Member State from applying disciplinary sanctions, penal or administrative in nature, towards the entities or individuals responsible for the non-compliance with the result envisaged by the directive.

[55] See B. Kurcz, *Dyrektywy i ich implementacja do prawa krajowego* [Directives and their Implementation to National Law] (Kraków, Kantor Wydawniczy Zakamycze, 2004) pp. 426–28.

[56] See Article 9 (3) of the Council Framework Decision 2004/68/JHA of 22 December 2003 on combating the sexual exploitation of children and child pornography [2004] O.J. L13/44.

[57] See on this distinction in the context of obligations arising out of directives in the Opinion of Advocate General Lenz in Case C-265/95 *Commission v. France* [1997] E.C.R. I-06959, para. 45.

[58] See D. Simon, loc. cit. n. 37 at p. 36.

result.[59] Most often for the correct implementation of directives and framework decisions the fulfilment of both positive and negative obligations would be required. In cases of directives, in exceptional circumstances, the positive obligation may be reduced to zero when existing national law is in full conformity with the result envisaged by a directive.[60] This is highly unlikely to happen in the case of framework decisions, taking into account the regulation domain, though it is not excluded when the particular interpretation of existing law suffices.[61] In any event, in a case of implementation by existing law or an existing legal context, the statutory framework is essential since the European Court of Justice has repeatedly held that a directive should be implemented *in law and not only in fact*.[62]

(iv) Practical Effectiveness

The free choice of implementation form and methods implies that it is up to a Member State to decide whether there is a need for legislative, administrative and judicial activity. There is no reason to distinguish between directives and framework decisions in this respect. Again, due to the regulation field, it seems that in the latter case enacting laws and even changing national constitutions may be necessary. It is true both for directives and framework decisions that the implementation of a single directive or framework decision by means of several national legal acts is allowed and in many cases even required.[63] There is no theoretical obstacle, and many directives are actually implemented in this way, to transpose several directives or framework decisions by means of just one national act. Framework decisions obliging Member States to make certain types of conduct punishable make it also easier to implement them in one act. Nevertheless, there will be situations in which the regulation of confiscation[64] and taking all measures to protect the victim's family[65] would not be easily put in one act. In any case the

---

[59] Case C-129/96 *Inter-Environnement Wallonie* [1997] E.C.R. I-7411, para. 45. It is interesting to note that the test suggested by the ECJ is more restrictive to the Member States than the test put forward by Advocate General *Jacobs* in the same case. He suggested the prohibition of taking measures by the Member States which would make the achievement of the result *impossible or excessively difficult*. See also Case C-144/04 *Werner Mangold v. Rüdiger Helm* [2005] E.C.R. I-9981. For a critique see N. Reich, 'Zur Frage der Gemeinschaftsrechtswidrigkeit der sachgrundlosen Befristungsmöglichkeit bei Arbeitnehmern ab 52 Jahren', 17 EuZW 21 (2006) 17.

[60] There still remain formal implementation requirements.

[61] See, especially point 2.1.3. of the report from the Commission based on Article 11 of the Council Framework Decision of 13 June 2002 on combating terrorism, 8 June 2004, COM (2004) 409 final. This Framework Decision thus differs from those that do not require the incorporation of 'specific offences' as long as the conduct to be criminalized is already covered by a generic incrimination. In these cases, obligations regarding penalties can also be respected by applying the general rules on the matter.

[62] Case C-220/94 *Commission v. Luxembourg* [1995] E.C.R. I-1589, para. 10.

[63] It follows indirectly from Case C-339/87 *Commission v. the Netherlands* [1990] E.C.R. I-851.

[64] Council Framework Decision 2004/757/JHA of 25 October 2004 laying down minimum provisions on the constituent elements of criminal acts and penalties in the field of illicit drug trafficking [2004] O.J. L335/8.

[65] Council Framework Decision 2004/68/JHA of 22 December 2003 on combating the sexual exploitation of children and child pornography [2004] O.J. L13/44.

Member States are entitled to implement directives or framework decisions in stages as long as they are practically effective.[66]

It seems to us that the other requirements imposed by the European Court of Justice on Member States with regard to the material implementation of directives are very relevant to the implementation of framework decisions.[67] Member States should ensure legal certainty, completeness, clarity and precision of the implementing measures[68] and their binding force.[69] To which extent individuals should become 'fully aware of their rights'[70] and to have the practical possibility to invoke them before national courts[71] remains to be analysed in point 3.

With regard to legal certainty[72] the ECJ stated that '*Only the proper transposition of the directive will bring that state of uncertainty to an end and it is only upon that transposition that the legal certainty [...] is created*'.[73] Moreover, national implementing acts have to be universally binding that is to have external binding force or to be able to produce external effects (*Außenwirkungen*). The binding force of implementation acts is well connected with the other requirement which stipulates that implementation should be achieved by means of acts which have at least the same legal force (*la même force juridique*) as the provisions normally used in a given Member State in the fields within the substantive scope of the directive.[74]

By completeness of implementation we understand the creation of such a normative situation which would fully regulate the field harmonized by a directive or foreseen by a framework decision. In consequence, it will not be sufficient only to authorize the executive organs to undertake implementation steps or to pass a general law which designates the program to be realized in the future.[75]

National implementation means should contain clear and precise expressions, even in the case when certain provisions of the directive do not aim at granting rights or imposing obligations upon individuals.[76] The accuracy and clarity of

---

[66] Case C-129/96 *Inter-Environement Wallonie* [1997] E.C.R. I-7411, para. 49.

[67] See point 2.1.1. and 2.1.2 of the report from the Commission based on Article 11 of the Council Framework Decision of 13 June 2002 on combating terrorism, 8 June 2004, COM (2004) 409 final.

[68] See the criteria mentioned in the judgment, Case C-197/96 *Commission v. France* [1997] E.C.R. I-1489, para. 15.

[69] Case C-361/88 *Commission v. Germany* [1991] E.C.R. I-2567, para. 21.

[70] Case C-29/84 *Commission v. Germany* [1985] E.C.R. 1661, para. 23.   [71] *ibid.*

[72] In other language versions equivalent terms are used but with more emphasis on legal security— German *Rechtsicherheit*, French *sécurité juridique*, see, for instance, Case C-208/90 *Emmott* [1991] E.C.R. I-4269, para. 22, where an English version uses the term *legal certainty*, whereas the French version *sécurité juridique* and the German version *Rechtssicherheit*.

[73] *ibid.*, para. 22. Despite the later ECJ judgments, where it was clearly stated that the operative part of *Emmott* was confined to the facts of the case, it seems that arguments considering the implementation requirements are still valid.

[74] Case C-102/79 *Commission v. Belgium* [1980] E.C.R. 1473, para. 10 and also P. Gilliaux, *Les directives européennes et le droit belge* (Brussels, Bruylant, 1997) at p. 32. See also Case C-116/86 *Commission v. Italy* [1988] E.C.R. 1323, para. 14. See also M. Gellermann, loc. cit. n. 53 at p. 25.

[75] See Case C-255/93 *Commission v. France* [1994] E.C.R. I-4949.

[76] Case C-339/87 *Commission v. Netherlands* [1990] E.C.R. I-851, para. 25.

national implementation norms ought to be kept irrespective of whether, in a given country, the directive's norms may, in fact, be applied bearing in mind the geographical or specific cultural-political conditions.[77] The same applies to framework decisions, with the exception of Gibraltar which must be mentioned specifically.[78] Any sanctions cannot be presumed.[79]

In any event, the problem of sanctions is clearly different with regard to two instruments. The punishability of certain behaviour is of the essence for framework decisions, whereas for effective implementation of a directive, it might be necessary to lay down sanctions for non-compliance with Community norms even if the directive does not provide for any.[80] Then, if sanctions are considered indispensable, it must be determined whether they should be penal, administrative or civil, or maybe all of them combined. In principle, however, it seems that Community law cannot be considered as *lex imperfecta*.[81] Also in this context the principle of equivalence must be respected.[82] The formula is adopted both by directives and Community decisions: sanctions must be effective, proportional to the infringement and *dissuasive*.[83]

There remains a question to which extent the Member States can modify or introduce new requirements or sanctions not provided by EU acts. As far as directives are concerned the answer depends on the scope of harmonization provided by a directive.[84] The notions of total, alternative or minimum harmonization are very useful tools for such an analysis.[85] It seems that the approximation of legislation in criminal matters should also be analysed in these terms. As an example one could mention Article 4 of the framework decision concerning attacks against information systems[86] which shows typical features of minimum harmonization. The assessment whether additional mechanisms of administrative control should be created even if they are not envisaged by a directive or framework decision is to be made in

---

[77] *ibid.*, para. 25.

[78] See *expressis verbis* case of Gibraltar—Article 11 of Council Framework Decision 2003/80/JHA of 27 January 2003 on the protection of the environment through criminal law [2003] O.J. L29/55.

[79] See Case C-252/85 *Commission v. France* [1988] E.C.R. 2243.

[80] So S. Biernat, 'Zasada efektywności prawa wspólnotowego w orzecznictwie Europejskiego Trybunału Sprawiedliwości' [The Principle of Effectiveness of EC law in Jurisprudence of the European Court of Justice] in: S. Biernat (ed.), *Studia z Prawa Unii Europejskiej* [Esseys in Law of the European Union] (Kraków, Wydawnictwo Uniwersytetu Jagiellońskiego, 2000) p. 46.

[81] See C. Haguenau, *L'application effective du droit communautaire en droit interne—Analyse comparative des problèmes rencontrés en droit français, anglais et allemand* (Brussels, Bruylant, 1995), at p. 15.

[82] The ECJ held that the UK infringed Community law by not introducing sanctions in case when the infringements of national provisions, corresponding to Community norms, were sanctioned, Case C-382/92 *Commission v. United Kingdom* [1994] E.C.R. I-2435, para. 52.

[83] *ibid.*, para. 55 and the Council Resolution of 29 June 1995 on the effective uniform application of Community law and on the penalties applicable for breaches of Community law in the internal market [1995] O.J. C188/1.   [84] See B. Kurcz, loc. cit. n. 55 at pp. 72–107.

[85] *ibid.*

[86] See Council Framework Decision 2005/222/JHA of 24 February 2005 on attacks against information systems [2005] O.J. L69/67.

the light of the above.[87] On the top of that it seems self-evident that a Member State when implementing a given directive cannot infringe the other rules of primary or secondary Community law.[88] The implementation of a framework decision cannot infringe, in particular, Article 6 TEU.

V. The Application of Norms of Directives and Framework Decisions in National Law

Both directives and framework decisions operate by national provisions implementing them. Therefore, in principle, national administrative and judicial bodies should apply directly national law and not provisions of directives and framework decisions. Bearing this in mind there is no dogmatic reason why directives and framework decisions should be different in the possibility of creating norms directed at granting rights to individuals.[89] A different question, though, is the effectiveness of enforcement of these rights. The correct realization by a Member State of all Treaty obligations requires that rights (also claims and demands connected with them) should be realized by individuals predominantly through national implementing provisions or by existing national law, in case the latter is already in conformity with a directive or a framework decision.[90]

It is true, however, that the possible enforcement by individuals of their rights in case of belated or faulty implementation of framework decisions is less powerful than in the case of directives. The lack of direct effect of provisions of framework decisions inhibits the effectiveness of invoking rights by individuals before national courts when the implementation is incorrect.[91] In particular, the possibility of direct substitution by a national court of national law provisions by the corresponding provision of a framework decision is limited. One should remember, however, that even if it is possible to determine the content of a right

---

[87] Also in this case the question whether the harmonization of national laws envisaged by the directive is total or minimal plays an important role, Case C-304/88 *Commission v. Belgium* [1990] E.C.R. I-2801, paras. 18–21.

[88] Case C-173/83 *Commission v. France* [1985] E.C.R. 491, paras. 4 and 15.

[89] See how the ECJ mentions rights and obligations in directives e.g. Case C-131/88 *Commission v. Germany* [1991] E.C.R. I-825, para. 61: 'It must be observed that the procedural provisions of the directive lay down, in order to guarantee effective protection of groundwater, precise and detailed rules which are intended to create rights and obligations for individuals'.

[90] Similarly M. Gellermann, loc. cit. n. 53 at p. 10.

[91] The ECJ held that the right of a State to choose among several possible means of achieving the result required by a directive does not preclude the possibility for individuals of enforcing rights before the national courts. Nevertheless, despite the sufficiently precise determination of the beneficiaries and the right itself, the large implementation discretion as far as the indication of the persons/institutions liable to put this right into effect may make the direct reliance on the provisions of the directive impossible (*Francovich*). Often, however, the mere possibility of invoking Community provisions in proceedings before the national courts or administrative authorities is sometimes defined as 'a right'. See e.g. Case C-131/88 *Commission v. Germany* [1991] E.C.R. I-825.

on the basis of provisions of a directive, it may still be impossible to rely on the particular right before the national court. A directive may only give general 'instructions' on how to define in national law the addressees of particular obligations leaving a lot of leeway for a Member State and limiting thereby the scope of direct effect. It is therefore very important that the provisions of the directive aimed at granting rights and imposing obligations are correctly transposed into national law. The precision of the latter has to be at least such as to allow individuals to invoke their rights before national courts without any particular difficulty, in accordance with the material and procedural provisions of national law.

Moreover, there remain other ways to achieve a similar result. First, it is possible that national law provides a solid ground for the correct application of framework decisions treated internally as public international law acts. These acts could have supremacy over other provisions of national law in case of conflict.[92] Secondly, the European Court of Justice ruled in *Pupino* that individuals are entitled to invoke framework decisions in order to obtain a conforming interpretation of national law before the courts of Member States.[93] When applying national law, adopted before or after a framework decision, national courts must interpret it as far as possible in the light of the wording and purpose of a framework decision in order to attain the result which the framework decision pursues. Taking into consideration how far the Court stretched this obligation in the *Pfeiffer* case,[94] to almost the substitution of the provision of national law by the provision of the directive, it seems that the realization of rights based on the duty of conforming interpretation can be very effective.[95] It is even more so, bearing in mind that the Court reluctance to follow the Opinions of Advocate Generals in many cases,[96] but not necessarily in *Pfeiffer*,[97] was due to the horizontal nature of obligations created by the directives. Framework decisions tend to rather create vertical relationships between the rights of individuals and obligations of the state in the field of criminal justice. It was in this context that the judgment in *Pupino* establishing the obligation of conforming interpretation was rendered.

---

[92] See on this point Advocate General Kokott Case C-105/03 *Criminal Proceedings against Maria Pupino* [2005] E.C.R. I-5285 para. 37.   [93] *ibid.*, para. 38.

[94] Cases C-397/01 to C-403/01 *Pfeiffer and Others* [2004] E.C.R. I-8835, para. 116.

[95] The Court stresses that the principle of interpretation in conformity with Community law cannot serve as the basis for an interpretation of national law *contra legem*. It requires, however, that the national court considers the whole of national law in order to assess how far it can be applied in such a way as not to produce a result contrary to that envisaged by the framework decision. It should be remembered that a real conflict between the norms occurs if national and Community norms can be applicable to the same factual situation, but their simultaneous application would lead to completely different results.

[96] See Opinion of Advocate General Léger in Case C-287/98 *Linster* [2000] E.C.R. I-6917, para. 87 and others mentioned in paras. 56–57 of the Opinion of Advocate General Ruiz-Jarabo Colomer in Cases C-397/01 to C-403/01 *Pfeiffer and Others* [2004] E.C.R. I-8835.

[97] See Opinion Advocate General Ruiz-Jarabo Colomer in *Pfeiffer* para. 59. It should be stressed though that AG Colomer's final conclusion based on EC law conform interpretation of German law

Moreover, it is important to emphasize that the Court, following the Opinion of Advocate General Kokott, based the duty of loyal co-operation on Article 1 EU surmounting the obstacle of the lack of Article 10 in the EC Treaty. It stressed that police and judicial co-operation in criminal matters was entirely based on the co-operation between Member States and the institutions. Advocate General Kokott added that Article 3 EU obliged the Union to respect and build upon the *acquis communautaire*.

In any case, we have to admit that the biggest difference in the enforcement of individuals' rights between directives and framework decisions lies for the moment in the impossibility of state liability for the incorrect implementation of a framework decision. There is no equivalent *Frankovich/Köbler* liability for state actions concerning framework decisions. This limits substantially the state incentive to implement framework decisions in time. Following, however, the argumentation used in *Pupino* for the duty of conforming interpretation to arise out of Article 1 EU, it is not at all excluded that the Court would rule on such liability in case of framework decisions. Moreover, the lack of state liability based on EU law does not, obviously, exclude the possibility of such liability based on the relevant provisions of national law.

VI. Jurisdiction of the European Court of Justice

The differences between framework decisions and directives are very apparent when the jurisdiction of the European Court of Justice is taken into account. So far the Member States have been very reluctant to extend the powers of the court to the levels comparable to the first pillar. As long as the current treaty framework is in force the European Court of Justice's cognition in the third pillar is considerably limited.[98] For the purposes of this article it is necessary to have a closer look at the three types of procedures envisaged by the founding treaties.

A. Infraction Procedures

The starting point is the infraction procedure based on Article 226 EC (Article 141 EAEC). The *locus standi* belongs to the European Commission, which, whenever it finds that there are sufficient grounds, may initiate the procedure for breach

---

was only possible after the disapplication of one of its controversial provisions. Although the Court in its judgment did not mention the possibility of disapplication of national law following from the supremacy of EC law, it did not exclude it either. It is therefore arguable to which extent it resembles a well known debate about exclusionary/substitution distinction as far as the direct effect of directives is concerned. See 'Editorial Comments', 43 (2006) C.M.L. Rev. p. 1.

[98] This was meant to change with the adoption of the Treaty establishing a Constitution for Europe [2004] O.J. C310/1.

of EC law against a Member State. The non-implementation or partial implementation of directives is one of the most common types of infringements. The
judgments of the European Court of Justice, despite their declaratory character,
create the obligation for the Member States to take all necessary measures to
achieve the compliance. Failure to do so may lead to the follow-up infraction
procedure based on Article 228 EC (Article 143 EAEC).[99] The *locus standi*
belongs again to the European Commission; however, imposition of a financial
penalty may be requested.[100] Finally, both Treaties of Rome provide for a special
type of the infraction procedure that may be initiated by the Member States. It is
based on equally worded Articles 227 EC and 142 EAEC. For political reasons
this infraction procedure is hardly ever used. To this day the European Court of
Justice has delivered only three judgments in this framework.[101]

The basic infraction procedures based on Articles 226 and 228 EC (as well as
their equivalents in EAEC) are very strong tools in the hands of the European
Commission. Being assigned with the task of the guardian of the Treaties it is
equipped with a set of very strong weapons. It is certainly well empowered to
discipline the Member States in application of EC law. This is one of the key
factors determining the supranational character of the first pillar. Bearing this in
mind it doesn't come as a surprise that the Member States have so far not been very
keen on granting similar or equivalent powers to the European Commission
under the third pillar of the European Union.[102] The only infraction procedure
envisaged in Article 35(7) EU draws partly on the model known from Article 227
EC (Article 142 EAEC). The provision in question reads as follows:

The Court of Justice shall have jurisdiction to rule on any dispute between Member States
regarding the interpretation or the application of acts adopted under Article 34(2) whenever such dispute cannot be settled by the Council within six months of its being referred
to the Council by one of its member states.

It is notable that the submission of a dispute to the European Court of Justice shall
always be preceded by the recourse to the Council of the European Union. Under
the existing arrangements it will serve as a dispute settlement authority. This
differs considerably to the *modus operandi* of Article 227 EC (Article 141 EAEC).
In the latter case, prior to submission of a complaint to the European Court of
Justice, Member States have the obligation to inform the European Commission,

---

[99] Case C-387/97 *Commission v. Hellenic Republic* [2000] E.C.R. I-5047; Case C-278/01
Commission v. Spain [2003] E.C.R. I-14141; Case C-304/02 *Commission v. France* [2005] E.C.R.
I-6263; and Case C-177/04 *Commission v. France* [2006] E.C.R. I-2461.
[100] See the following documents of the European Commission: 'Memorandum on applying
Article 171 of the EC Treaty', [1996] O.J. C242/6; 'Method of Calculating the Penalty Payments
Provided for Pursuant to Article 171 of the EC Treaty', [1997] O.J. C63/2; and 'Application of
Article 228 of the EC Treaty', SEC (2005) 1658.
[101] Case 141/78 *France v. United Kingdom* [1979] E.C.R. 1925; Case C-338/95 *Belgium v. Spain*
[2000] E.C.R. I-3123; Case C-145/04 *Spain v. United Kingdom*, n.y.r.
[102] This was envisaged by the Treaty establishing a Constitution for Europe.

which eventually may take up the case. In this respect it certainly does not act in the capacity of a dispute settlement authority, but in its central role of the guardian of the treaties.

The scope and nature of the infringement procedures is one of the key factors differentiating framework decisions from directives. When it comes to the infringements of directives there is a set of enforcement channels that may be used by the European Commission, the Member States and the European Court of Justice in order to bring such infringements to an end. The extent to which Article 35 EU may be effectively used to sanction infringements of framework decisions is questionable. They certainly fall within the scope of the term 'application' used therein, however the political character of the entire procedure make its use rather unlikely. It must be stressed that the European Commission under no circumstances has powers to submit the actions for infringement in the third pillar. It may be argued that this very factor weakens the effectiveness of framework decisions and indirectly makes the Member States less disciplined to transpose and implement framework decisions on time.

There is also a degree of differentiation between the old and new Member States in this respect. Article 39 of the Act on Conditions of Accession annexed to the Treaty of Accession 2003[103] as well as Article 38 of the Act on Conditions of Accession annex to the Treaty of Accession 2005[104] contain safeguard clauses that may be applied in cases of shortcomings or risks associated with the transposition or implementation of framework decisions.[105] It does not apply to all framework decisions but only those dealing with the mutual recognition. It is argued that it

[103] Treaty between the Kingdom of Belgium, the Kingdom of Denmark, the Federal Republic of Germany, the Hellenic Republic, the Kingdom of Spain, the French Republic, Ireland, the Italian Republic, the Grand Duchy of Luxembourg, the Kingdom of the Netherlands, the Republic of Austria, the Portuguese Republic, the Republic of Finland, the Kingdom of Sweden, the United Kingdom of Great Britain and Northern Ireland (Member States of the European Union) and the Czech Republic, the Republic of Estonia, the Republic of Cyprus, the Republic of Latvia, the Republic of Lithuania, the Republic of Hungary, the Republic of Malta, the Republic of Poland, the Republic of Slovenia, the Slovak Republic, concerning the accession of the Czech Republic, the Republic of Estonia, the Republic of Cyprus, the Republic of Latvia, the Republic of Lithuania, the Republic of Hungary, the Republic of Malta, the Republic of Poland, the Republic of Slovenia and the Slovak Republic to the European Union, [2003] O.J. L236/17.

[104] Treaty between the Kingdom of Belgium, the Czech Republic, the Kingdom of Denmark, the Federal Republic of Germany, the Republic of Estonia, the Hellenic Republic, the Kingdom of Spain, the French Republic, Ireland, the Italian Republic, the Republic of Cyprus, the Republic of Latvia, the Republic of Lithuania, the Grand Duchy of Luxembourg, the Republic of Hungary, the Republic of Malta, the Kingdom of the Netherlands, the Republic of Austria, the Republic of Poland, the Portuguese Republic, the Republic of Slovenia, the Slovak Republic, the Republic of Finland, the Kingdom of Sweden, the United Kingdom of Great Britain and Northern Ireland (Member States of the European Union) and the Republic of Bulgaria and Romania, concerning the accession of the Republic of Bulgaria and Romania to the European Union, [2005] O.J. L157/11.

[105] See K. Inglis, 'The accession treaty and its transitional arrangements: A twilight zone for the' new Members of the Union' in Ch. Hillion (eds.), *EU Enlargement. A Legal Approach* (Oxford, Hart 2004) p. 77; A. Lazowski, 'And then they were Twenty-Seven.... A Legal Appraisal of the Sixth Accession Treaty', 44 C.M.L. Rev. (2007) p. 401.

could have been used to sanction the breach of the Council Framework Decision 2002/584/JHA on the European Arrest Warrant.[106] This theoretically could have been the case following a judgment of the Polish Constitutional Tribunal on conformity of national implementing legislation with a proviso of the Polish Constitution prohibiting extradition of its own nationals.[107] Similar actions could not have been taken in relation to Germany, where the Constitutional Court also annulled the domestic legislation implementing this Framework Decision.[108] The contested legislation would have lost force, had Poland failed to revise its Constitution.

B. Actions for Annulment

The next step is the actions for annulment. It is regulated in Article 230 EC (equally Article 146 EAEC) as well as in Article 35 EU. Drafters of the latter clearly took an inspiration from the first pillar arrangements. This part of the analysis will certainly demonstrate a number of similarities between those procedures and to this end indirectly between directives and framework decisions. The key elements of this procedure are taken on board in this paragraph. Those, *inter alia*, are *locus standi*, grounds for annulment as well as legal consequences of Court of First Instance/European Court of Justice judgments.

The *locus standi* in actions for annulment of directives belongs to various types of applicants. The first group contains so-called privileged applicants, which are the Member States, the European Commission, the Council of the European Union and, following the Treaty of Nice, the European Parliament. Moreover, the European Central Bank as well as the Court of Auditors may request annulment in order to protect their prerogatives. As a matter of principle, neither natural persons nor legal persons have the *locus standi* to submit actions for annulment of directives. However, as proved by the case law such actions shall not be excluded if pursued for annulment of directives, which in fact are decisions.[109]

The list of potential applicants in the third pillar actions for annulment of framework decisions is very short and only includes Member States and the European Commission. The lack of *locus standi* for individuals' follows the first pillar logic that such categories of applicants may only request annulment of administrative measures, not generally applicable legislation. It is surprising that

---

[106] A. Łazowski, 'Constitutional Tribunal on the Surrender of Polish Citizens under the European Arrest Warrant. Decision of 27 April 2005', 1 EuConst (2005) p. 569.
[107] Poland has recently revised its Constitution in order to accommodate fully the surrender procedure set forth in the framework decision; therefore the safeguard clause hasn't been used.
[108] J. Komàrek, *European Constitutionalism and the European Arrest Warrant: Contrapuntal Principles in Disharmony*, Jean Monnet Working Paper 10/05.
[109] Case C-298/89 *Government of Gibraltar v. Council of the European Communities* [1993] ECR I-3605.

the European Parliament has no standing at all. This only proves the democratic deficit of the third pillar and the very limited role of the only directly elected institution in this intergovernmental area of integration.

The grounds for annulment in the third pillar are just the same as in the first. Moreover, the relevant treaty provisions are equally worded in this respect. The grounds include lack of competence, infringement of an essential procedural requirement, infringement of the EC/EU Treaty or any rule relating to its application as well as misuse of powers.

Providing that actions based on Article 230 EC are well founded the Court of First Instance/the European Court of Justice shall declare a directive in question to be void. Thanks to a rather generous interpretation of Article 231 EC it seems clear that both courts may be willing to keep certain provisions of directives in force. As proved in practice there is no *per se rule* when it comes to an invalidation of directives. In other words, an invalidation of a directive does not automatically lead to an invalidation of domestic implementing legislation.[110] Depending on grounds for invalidation national authorities will take further steps at the domestic level. Due to a lack of treaty provisions and very limited case law there are no well established rules on the invalidation of framework decisions. So far the ECJ has done so only once in the well known case on the validity of the framework decision on the protection of environment by criminal law. However, there are no legal grounds precluding *mutatis mutandis* application of the first pillar principles to framework decisions.

C. Preliminary Ruling

The preliminary ruling procedure is one of the most important features of the EU legal system. It facilitates an everyday co-operation between national courts and the European Court of Justice. Over the decades it has proved to be an extremely successful tool allowing the European Court of Justice to assist national judiciaries on one hand and to develop key principles of EC law, on the other. The preliminary ruling may also serve as another very good example of the differences between the first and third pillars, reflecting the different characters of both areas of integration. Jurisdiction in the first pillar is compulsory and literally all national courts have the right (sometimes the obligation) to make references.[111] Under the special regime based on Article 35 EU, only courts from Member States what have recognized jurisdiction of the European Court of Justice may seek

---

[110] See T.A.J.A. Vandamme, *The Invalid Directive. The Legal Authority of a Union Act Requiring Domestic Law Making* (Europa Law Publishing, Groningen, 2005).

[111] There is an exception based on Article 68 EC. According to this special regime only courts from which there is no further remedy may seek the references from the European Court of Justice. See Case C-555/03 *Magali Warbecq v Ryanair Ltd.* [2004] E.C.R. I-6041.

preliminary references. Moreover, while accepting the jurisdiction Member States have the right to restrict the jurisdiction to courts from which there is no further remedy only.[112] This constitutes a major difference between the first and the third pillar and to this end between framework decisions and directives. However, when it comes to key elements of the preliminary ruling procedure the first pillar jurisprudence shall be applicable *mutatis mutandis* to the third pillar preliminary ruling regime. This is one of the conclusions stemming from the *Pupino* judgment.[113]

The jurisdiction of the European Court of Justice is one of the factors giving the strong intergovernmental flavors to the third pillar of the European Union. It has pivotal impact on framework decisions, their enforcement and interpretation at national level. To this end it also creates major differences between framework decisions and directives. This does not mean, however, that certain elements of the synergy are not visible in this respect. Quite to the contrary—the European Court of Justice has taken the opportunity in its recent jurisprudence to extend application of certain first pillar rules on the preliminary ruling procedure to the third pillar procedures. The full synergy between the pillars and to the same token both legal instruments in consideration would have been achieved with the European Constitution.

VII. Conclusions: Two Sides of the Same Coin?

Are framework decisions and directives two sides of the same coin? This analysis proves that the full unification of those legal acts has not yet taken place, however the path has been set and both acts are heading this way. Despite Member States' reservations this growing synergy is already visible in the practice of the European Court of Justice and the European Commission. The remaining differences between directives and framework decisions are more reflection of key factors underpinning the first and third pillars of the European Union than the characteristics of the legal acts themselves.

The very broad approach taken in this article allows us to see clearly the synergy appearing at different levels. It starts with the definitions of both types of legal acts and their legal character and aims. Directives as well as framework decisions are binding instruments for harmonization of national laws. They are always addressed to the Member States and require implementation to national orders. Looking at the drafting technique one may easily conclude that they both follow

---

[112] For a list of countries that have recognized the jurisdiction, see information concerning the declarations by the French Republic and the Republic of Hungary on their acceptance of the jurisdiction of the European Court of Justice to give preliminary rulings on the acts referred to in Article 35 of the Treaty on European Union, [2005] O.J. C318/1.

[113] See, *inter alia*, para. 19 of the judgment.

the same model. Directives and framework decisions are drafted and structured in one and the same way.

The decision-making procedures used in the first and third pillars are the pivotal differentiating factor. They clearly reflect the supranational and intergovernmental features of both those areas of integration. To this end the third pillar decision-making regime is dominated by the Council of the European Union, which in most of the cases takes decisions by unanimity. The roles of the European Commission and the European Parliament are fairly limited, though have been considerably increased in the course of the past decade. To this end they have initiated a step-by-step communautarization of the third pillar of the European Union.

Undoubtedly there is growing synergy between directives and framework decisions when it comes to their implementation to national law. The effectiveness of the two instruments requires legal certainty, completeness, clarity and the binding force of national law. There is no reason not to lay down references to framework decisions in national law as it is required in case of directives.

Enforcement at national level is yet another issue. The main difference between the first and third pillars is the treaty-based restriction precluding the direct effect of framework decisions. Moreover, so far the European Court of Justice has not extended application of the principles of supremacy and state liability to the third pillar legislation. Following the judgment in *Pupino* there are no doubts that the well established first pillar principle of indirect effect is applicable *mutatis mutandis* to framework decisions. Its scope is very broad. Undoubtedly this factor increases the synergy between framework decisions and directives.

Finally, considerable differences are appealing when enforcement of framework decisions is taken into account. Again, the limited jurisdiction of the European Court of Justice reflecting the intergovernmental character of the third pillar is the main differentiating factor. Infraction procedures brought by the European Commission against Member States are excluded; moreover, there are considerable limitations to the preliminary ruling procedure.

The judicial developments of the past years combined with the practice of the European Commission serve as the basis for the argument that the synergy between directives and framework decisions is not accidental. To the contrary it is a logical consequence of the changing nature of the EU legal system and the envisaged merger of both types of legal acts into European framework laws envisaged by the EU Constitution. As long as the latter is not in force framework decisions and directives are not two sides of the same coin, though very close to one another.

Economic Constitutionalism(s) in a Time of Uneasiness: Comparative Study on the Economic Constitutional Identities of Italy, the WTO and the EU

*Marco Dani**

I. From Abundance to Uneasiness—Re-Organization of Public Space and Challenges to the Monopoly of States on Constitutionalism

It may seem we live in a time of abundance in which the laws administered to citizens increasingly consist of blends of various ingredients. Such abundance is the outcome of a massive process of re-organization of the public space of government[1] whereby states outsource their functions to commonly established agencies which, for disparate reasons, are supposed to perform them more efficiently.[2] Hence, in almost all fields of substantive law[3] the monopoly of states on the business of

* Emile Noël Fellow 2004–05 at the Jean Monnet Center, NYU School of Law. Research Scholar of Comparative Public Law, Faculty of Law, University of Trento (Italy). Email: *dani@jus.unitn.it*. My sincere thanks to the Jean Monnet Center of the NYU School of Law and, particularly, to Professor Joseph Weiler, for his encouragement and critical support in writing this article. I want to thank also Professor Roberto Toniatti, Federico Ortino and Francesco Palermo for their valuable comments on draft versions of the article. The usual disclaimer applies.

[1] A synthetic description of the processes of re-organization of public space is provided in S. Cassese, *Lo spazio giuridico globale*, Roma-Bari, 2003, pp. 6–10.

[2] The post-national character of the issues they are called upon to deal with. In such cases, agencies are considered as performing better than states acting individually because of the trans-border indeed, uncoordinated initiatives by individual states are likely to generate negative externalities for their partners. The process of re-organization does not consist only in the empowerment of supranational or international agencies. It has been observed that a somewhat similar functional rationale underpins the allocation of political and administrative powers to sub-national and territorial authorities. In this regard, see M. Keating, *Europe's Changing Political Landscape: Territorial Restructuring and New Forms of Government*, in P. Beaumont, C. Lyons, N. Walker (eds.), *Convergence & Divergence in European Public Law*, Oxford-Portland Oregon, 2002 and the essays contained in R. Toniatti, F. Palermo, M. Dani (eds.), *An Ever More Complex Union—The Regional variable as a missing link in the EU constitution?*, Baden Baden, 2004.

[3] Depending upon the substantive fields, the extent and the nature of the delegations of course vary. There are cases where functions and procedure are completely outsourced to external authorities and, by contrast, cases where states retain parts of their powers and segments of procedures.

producing rules is being challenged by emerging non-state units potentially originating non-state legal regimes.[4]

Against this background, constitutional law is radically questioned. Assuming the legality of the delegation of functions to non-state legal orders, more serious concerns arise in respect to the impact of the re-organization of public space on the fundamental principles enshrined and enforced within national constitutions. Although in principle there is agreement on the idea of assisting the outsourcing of states' functions with comparable constitutional guarantees, scholarly debate is divided between those who maintain that non-state public units ought not to impair the standards of protection afforded in the national spheres and those who contend that, since the standards of protection depend upon the functional mandate of non-state units, a tolerable degree of difference ought to be accepted.[5]

Nevertheless, the most controversial issues emerge when newly established legal orders employ intensively the instruments and the language of constitutional law and, eventually, begin to invoke for themselves autonomous constitutional status. Predictably, also in this regard sharp divisions cross the doctrinal debate. On the one hand, those who cherish the integrity of traditional constitutionalism decline constitutional nature altogether for the non-state entities as not fulfilling its fundamental requirements. On the other hand, those who perceive the magnitude of the impact of the processes of re-organization on the traditional categories of constitutionalism seem more open to revisit their analytical tools by including post-national legal orders in their constitutional investigations.[6]

The choice between either of the alternatives has crucial implications for another thorny issue concerning the nature of the interactions among national and post-national legal orders. Here, those who vindicate the integrity of traditional constitutionalism advocate that, even when post-national legal orders are empowered with broad and vital competences, the constitutions of the states remain the ultimate and exclusive sources of legitimacy and authority and, therefore, the relationships between the national and post-national legal orders should reflect a simple 'principal-agent' scheme.[7] Hence, were the agents (post-national units) to stray from the desired results, they would be subject to the control and sanction by the principals (national authorities) overseeing their mandates. By contrast, to assume post-national legal orders as eligible to a constitutional status entails a more sophisticated theoretical framework. On the one hand, constitutional autonomy evokes for post-national units the possibility to evolve

---

[4] See J. Delbrück, *Transnational Federalism: Problems and Prospects of Allocating Public Authority Beyond the State*, in *IJGLS*, 2004, 11, p. 31, where it is argued the process of re-organization of public space creates forms of 'transnational federalism'.

[5] These alternatives emerge for instance in the debate on the Charter of Nice and, namely, on the degree of protection of fundamental rights in Europe. See below section III.B.

[6] See below section II.

[7] I tentatively apply to the relationships between national and post-national legal orders the 'principal-agent' and 'settler-trustee' (see below in the text) models, as defined in respect to the relationship between political institutions and administrative bureaucracies by A. La Spina, G. Majone, *Lo stato regolatore*, Bologna, 2000, pp. 218–25.

according to rationales different from and even colliding with the state benchmark; on the other hand, post-national constitutionalism remains inextricably entwined with the state paradigm.[8] The acknowledgement of constitutional autonomy for post-national legal orders,[9] thus, implies a significant deviation from the original principal-agent relationship. Arguably, with post-national units acquiring constitutional autonomy, the principal-agent scheme turns into a 'settler-trustee' relationship in which the power of control and sanction by states is remarkably marginalized. According to this template, the ultimate source of legitimacy and authority is still located in national constitutions. Yet, apart from the somewhat exceptional cases in which such an ultimate authority is effectively exercised,[10] post-national legal orders enjoy significant margins of constitutional autonomy to both develop their internal organization and compete externally with other legal orders (including national ones) for hegemony in the public space.

If this diagnosis is correct and, notably, if the monopoly on constitutions and constitutionalism by states undergoes the challenges by post-national units originally conceived for different and less ambitious purposes, it is not surprising that our time of abundance is rapidly turning into an age of constitutional uneasiness. The inclusion of post-national legal orders in constitutional investigations, indeed, obliges one not only to update the definition of constitution devised within the experience of state constitutionalism, but also to develop plausible guidelines for managing the frictions ensuing from the interactions among constitutional spheres of different nature.[11]

However, because of the extreme variety of the re-organization formulas of public space experimented in different policy areas, it is very difficult to provide a comprehensive solution to the latest issue put forward. Tentative answers may be given by adopting a more modest, but also more promising, sector-based approach. In this study, for instance, the constitutional tensions occurring in the European constitutional space in the field of economic and social regulation will be investigated.[12] In this substantive area, the regulatory principles expressed by post-national units, namely by the EU and the WTO, have been grafted onto the body of the national constitutional orders of their members. Whereas doctrinal orthodoxy

---

[8] See J. Shaw, *Postnational constitutionalism in the European Union*, in *JEPP*, 1999, 6, 4, p. 589, identifying the characters of post-nationalism as emerging and indissolubly linked to the states, but sustained by a separate logic.

[9] As it will be discussed below (section II), the acknowledgement of constitutional status to post-national legal orders is conditioned to specific requirements.

[10] This is particularly evident during the treaty-amending processes and in the controversial positions by those Constitutional and Supreme Courts which claim to have jurisdiction for reviewing EU law in case of breaches of the fundamental principles of the respective national constitutions.

[11] The same issue is similarly investigated, but rather in terms of identifying 'tertiary rules' to determine the allocation of authority between constitutions, in J. P. Trachtman, *The WTO Constitution: Tertiary Rules for Intertwined Elephants*, (September 1, 2005). *ExpressO Preprint Series*, Working Paper 753, <http://law.bepress.com/expresso/eps/753>.

[12] In dealing with the EU and WTO constitutional sphere, the article will focus more in detail on the substantive area of free movement of goods. Hence, although the methodology employed could be helpful also in the understanding of the constitutional identities of other substantive areas, the conclusions put forward are to be considered as limited to this sector.

considers national spheres as the only genuinely constitutional, in fact the principles endorsed by these post-national legal orders are gaining increasing momentum as providing clearer and, often, concurrent constitutional guidelines. As a consequence, a debate on the plausibility and characters of post-national constitutionalism has taken over, though with different emphasis and outcomes, both among the EU and WTO legal scholarships.[13]

This article intends to contribute constructively to this debate by arguing two quite provocative theses:

(1) The monopoly of states on constitutions and constitutionalism may be considered as an historical contingency. Constitutionalism in the last two centuries has been subject to various translations, depending upon the objectives pursued by states. Even in the current situation, the ideal inherent in constitutionalism—to achieve fundamental objectives by enabling and limiting institutions endowed with political powers—is susceptible to further developments also in non-state dimensions where it can originate autonomous constitutional spheres and doctrinal categories. As a result, both the EU and the WTO can be addressed as constitutional as far as the understanding of their specific constitutional nature (as well as that of the states) is construed in close connection with their foundational objectives and the characteristics of their legal frameworks.

(2) It is conceptually misleading to conceive of the interactions between the national, EU and WTO constitutional spheres on the basis of constitutional principles expressed within one of these legal regimes. It is argued that their relationships could be better managed by identifying guidelines for the behavior of judicial and political actors operating within these constitutional spheres. These criteria should be devised in order to profit from the diversity and the specific added value of each of the constitutional spheres and, at the same time, to promote among them a sufficient degree of substantive compatibility.

Such theses will be supported by arguments structured as follows. In section II, after questioning the exclusively state-centered approaches to constitutionalism, a core of constitutional elements shared by the Italian (as a sample of the EU member states), the WTO and EU legal orders will be singled out. On this basis, the concept of Economic Constitutional Identity (ECI) will be introduced as the most appropriate device to investigate, according to the methodology of comparative law, the attitudes towards economic issues by the legal orders considered. In section III, the ECIs of Italy, the WTO and the EU will be analyzed in detail by

---

[13] This article has been conceived in months when the process of ratification of the 'Treaty establishing a Constitution for Europe' was arduously taking place. In writing, I have decided not to deal explicitly with the solutions therein devised. Yet, the arguments proffered may be easily applied also to the economic constitutionalism enshrined in the constitutional treaty as far as it largely replicates the traditional regulatory principles of EC market integration (see articles III-42, III-43, III-65). A short comment on the Constitutional Treaty has been inserted in section IV (nt. 258) to express some critical remarks in the light of the conceptual framework developed in the article.

stressing in turn their divergent and convergent elements. Such understanding of the ECIs will be particularly helpful in sections IV and V, where criteria for interpreting their interactions and, arguably, the relationship among the whole constitutional spheres at hand will be put forward in order to safeguard their diverse natures and to benefit from the uneasiness engendered by their interactions.

II. State-centered Constitutionalism and its Discontents—The Economic Constitutional Identity (ECI) as an Instrument for Comparative Investigation of Economic Constitutionalism(s)

According to a traditional definition, a constitution is a legal document containing the fundamental rules of a community organized within a state.[14] Conversely, constitutionalism is the ideology advocating the constitution as the privileged means for the protection of individual freedoms from the abuses perpetrated in the exercise of public powers.[15] Because of this moral commitment, constitutionalism has been (and continues to be) a mobilizing ideology for generations of activists struggling within their national communities for individual freedoms and, at a later stage, democracy. Therefore, whereas all constitutions, by empowering (or acknowledging the power of) public authorities, establish limits to the exercise of political powers, only those which are grounded on the principles of separation of powers and judicial protection of fundamental rights belong to the realm of constitutionalism.[16] Nowadays, an ever increasing number of state constitutions fulfils these requirements and, thus, it can be argued that constitutionalism, at least within the western legal tradition, has attained a hegemonic position.

As a rule, when constitutionalism succeeds in national communities, constitutional activists turn into constitutional patriots. To their eyes, the stability of the values underpinning the constitution is normally equated with the stability of the constitution itself.[17] The momentum gained in the society and in the intellectual debate by constitutionalism is reflected in the legal doctrine as well. In states where a constitutionalist setting is consolidated, official legal scholarships celebrate the constitutions as inextricably entwined with the values these latter serve. By contrast, legal orders which deviate from constitutionalism are considered not only as

---

[14] G. de Vergottini, *Diritto costituzionale comparato*, I, Padova, 2004, p. 115; G. Morbidelli, L. Pegoraro, A. Reposo, M. Volpi, *Diritto pubblico comparato*, Torino, 2004, p. 27.

[15] G. de Vergottini, *Diritto costituzionale comparato*, I, Padova, 2004, p. 117. On the evolution of constitutionalism, see G. Rebuffa, *Costituzioni e costituzionalismi*, Torino, 1990.

[16] It is common to identify the requirements of liberal constitutionalism in article 16 of the *Déclaration des droits de l'Homme et du citoyen* (1789) providing that: 'toute société dans laquelle la garantie des droits n'est pas assurée ni la séparation des puoivoirs déterminée n'a point de Constitution'.

[17] In the approach of constitutional patriotism, therefore, the constitution acquires intrinsic value and loses its original instrumental role.

deserting its values but even as lacking a constitution at all.[18] In the western legal
tradition, indeed, constitutionalism dictates the mandatory requirements of legitimate government and, in this perspective, it is assumed as providing fundamental
guidelines of civilization.

The processes of re-organization of public space challenge the monopoly of
state constitutionalism on constitutions from an unusual standpoint. For a long
while, the hegemony of constitutionalism has spread in the sole direction of the
constitutional organization of states. It used to be within states, indeed, that the
main functions of government were carried out and, therefore, it used to be from
states that the most serious threats to fundamental rights could come. As mentioned, this reality undergoes considerable modifications. Public powers and
important policy areas are allotted to non-state units where, in some cases, legal
orders flourish to the extent that claims for emancipation from the sole paradigm
of state constitutionalism arise.[19]

As a result, particularly in respect to the EU and the WTO, legal scholarships
have engaged in debates on the plausibility and characters of post-national constitutionalism. The wide spectrum of opinions submitted in this regard oscillates
between two opposed, yet equally threatening, dangers. On the one hand, the most
orthodox positions, concerned with the need to preserve the integrity of state constitutionalism and the value of its traditional categories, refuse any constitutional
status to post-national legal orders. Yet, by stressing its alleged integrity,[20] constitutionalism is likely to end up as restricted to state units and significantly impaired
when the regulatory principles expressed by post-national entities prevail over some
of the vital aspects of national constitutions. On the other hand, serious concerns
arise also in respect to the most innovative opinions. As seen, there can be important and even compelling reasons to include (some of) the post-national legal orders
in the realm of constitutionalism and to re-define its categories accordingly. Yet, by
operating in this direction, the doctrine cannot dodge the demand of scientific
rigor animating the official legal scholarship. Even in the most flexible positions,
indeed, the attribution of constitutional status is to be conditioned to precise and
persuasive legal requirements so as to prevent constitutionalism (and its heuristic
value) from being emptied and, eventually, trivialized.

Predictably, the most common doctrinal responses to the stimuli determined
by this new legal reality have been driven by conditioned reflexes. This is the case
of authors who, although often inspired by opposite normative mindsets, assume
or define constitutionalism in traditional state-like terms. In respect to the EU, for

---

[18] This approach is of comparative law which, beside the 'constitutionalist constitutions', admits
the existence of other conceptions of constitutions (traditionalist, authoritarian rejected by the scholarship, Marxist). See G. de Vergottini, *Diritto costituzionale comparato*, pp. 119–27.

[19] See above section I.

[20] J. Shaw, *Postnational Constitutionalism in the EU*, p. 583, observes: 'Constitutionalism is [...] as
contested as it is closely studied. So, [...] it can be imbued with quite different meanings and functions depending upon the underlying world-view of the commentator'.

example, the use of the constitutional language is neglected in the works of those who stress the intergovernmental paradigm as the most adequate to explain the processes of transnational and international integration.[21] Quite similarly, constitutional Euro-sceptics argue that a European demos and, more broadly, the preconditions of democracy should mature before venturing into the road of constitutionalization of the supranational sphere.[22] Traditional constitutionalism is endorsed also by federalists as expressing the template the EU should comply with in order to gain full legitimacy.[23] Under this approach, indeed, constitutionalization arises out as a normative desideratum for its 'inducing effect' in respect to the social prerequisites of democracy, and as the most adequate answer to the challenges posed by economic globalization.[24]

The same arguments are employed also in respect to the WTO. Here, both the normative position favoring constitutionalization as enhancing the performances of the WTO in the protection of economic freedom[25] and the opposite opinion of those who dismiss constitutionalization as the correct answer to the legitimacy problems of the WTO,[26] share the uncontested assumption whereby constitutionalism can be translated exclusively in traditional terms.[27]

Other authors have elaborated these conditioned reflexes and admit that something called post-national constitutionalism may exist. These approaches acknowledge the existence of 'unfamiliar circumstances' in post-national units which prevent the application of the categories developed in the national sphere.[28] Yet, rather than dismissing constitutional language or advocating the idea of their normalization, these freak elements are, at least to some extent, enhanced by arguing for new and equally legitimate forms of constitutionalism.[29] Nonetheless, also among the discontents of the exclusivism of state constitutionalism the very nature of post-national constitutionalism is openly debated. In some cases, indeed, constitutional discourse is adopted for instrumental reasons. This is the case of certain decisions by the European Court of Justice in which constitutional language is used to

---

[21] A. Moravcsik, *Preferences and Powers in the European Community: A Liberal Intergovernmentalist Approach*, in *JCMS*, 1993, 31, 4, p. 473.

[22] D. Grimm, *Does Europe Need a Constitution?*, in *ELJ*, 1995, 3, 1, p. 282.

[23] Emblematic, in this regard, is the exchange between G. Ferrara, *La costituzione europea: un'ambizione frustrata*, in *Costituzionalismo.it*, fascicolo 2/2004 and G. Amato, *Il Trattato che istituisce la Costituzione dell'Unione Europea*, in *Costituzionalismo.it*, fascicolo 3/2004.

[24] J. Habermas, *Remarks on Dieter Grimm's 'Does Europe Need a Constitution?'*, in *ELJ*, 1995, 3, 1, p. 303.

[25] E-U. Petersmann, *The Transformation of the World Trading System through the 1994 Agreement establishing the World Trade Organization*, in *EJIL*, 1995, 6, 1, p. 1.

[26] R. Howse, K. Nicolaidis, *Enhancing WTO Legitimacy: Constitutionalization or Global Subsidiarity?*, in *Governance*, 2003, 16, 1, p. 73.

[27] Surprisingly enough, the debate on WTO constitutionalization adopts EU constitutionalism and, notably, the direct effect and supremacy doctrines, either as positive or negative normative benchmarks. This, arguably, strengthens the hypothesis here supported whereby the template of state constitutionalism is not exclusive.   [28] J. Shaw, *Postnational Constitutionalism in the EU*, p. 581.

[29] M. Poiares Maduro, *Europe and the constitution: what if this is as good as it gets?*, in J.H.H. Weiler, M. Wind (eds.), *European Constitutionalism Beyond the State*, Cambridge, 2003, p. 74.

reinforce the supremacy of supranational rules and obligations.[30] But instrumentality may be seen every time the constitutional frame is considered worth retaining as imparting legitimacy and some epistemological dividend.[31]

More interestingly, other works try to define post-national constitutionalism positively. For some, the specificity of European constitutionalism consists essentially in a conception of authority alternative to that of state federalism.[32] But, apart from this, it seems that EU constitutionalism conforms (or ought to conform) to the requirements of state constitutionalism. Other authors, instead, dig much deeper and identify in the characteristics progressively assumed by the process of formation of the European polity[33] or in the complementary relationship between many constitutive aspects of the post-national and national legal orders[34] the elements which distinguish and justify post-national constitutionalism.

Nevertheless, in these latest works the nature and the rationale of the processes prompting the upsurge of non-state public powers appear too easily left behind. Particularly the relationship between the functional concerns of post-national units and the inherent nature of their legal/constitutional frameworks is neglected.[35] Yet, this latest profile seems promising in the attempt to both re-define constitutionalism in the light of post-national realities and re-organize the interactions among the constitutional spheres.[36] Moreover, a similar functional perspective may respond to the scepticism of the most orthodox positions by stressing some traits of structural continuity between the constitutionalism evolved within the states and that possibly emerging in post-national spheres.

It was stated above how, in the perspective of constitutionalism, a society is considered as having a constitution only if the guarantee of the rights is ensured and the separation of powers is worked out. Nevertheless, guarantee of the rights and separation of powers are not invoked as self-referential elements. More specifically, these principles were considered as the most efficient means to perform the

---

[30] Case 294/83, *Parti Ecologiste Les Verts v. European Parliament* [1986] ECR I-1339; *Opinion 1/91* [1993] ECR I-6079.

[31] N. Walker, *Postnational Constitutionalism and the problem of translation*, in J.H.H. Weiler, M. Wind, *European Constitutionalism Beyond the State*, pp. 34–35.

[32] J.H.H. Weiler, *In defence of the status quo: Europe's constitutional* Sonderweg, in J.H.H. Weiler, M. Wind, *European Constitutionalism Beyond the State*, p. 7. Quite similarly, F. Palermo, *La Forma di stato dell'Unione Europea*, Padova, 2005, pp. 127–201, argues the specificity of the EU consists in the circular relationship between the ideological and axiological premises of the EU and those of its member states.

[33] J. Shaw, *Postnational Constitutionalism in the EU*, pp. 589–96, argues that the process of formation of the European polity departs from the assimilationist approach of traditional constitutionalism for its 'essentially contested' nature and commitment to intercultural dialogue.

[34] M. Poiares Maduro, *Europe and the constitution*, p. 98. This insight will be developed below in section V.

[35] Precious insights on the importance of a functional perspective in legal theory are provided by N. Bobbio, *Verso una concezione funzionalistica del diritto*, in N. Bobbio, *Dalla struttura alla funzione—Nuovi studi di teoria del diritto*, Milano, 1977, p. 63.

[36] Particular attention to the functional concerns in the comparative analysis of EU and national law is suggested in R. Dehousse, *Comparing National and EC Law: the Problem of the Level of Analysis*, in *AJCL*, 42, 4, pp. 778–80.

objectives demanded of the state by a liberal society. In other words, in the essence of constitutionalism, constitutions are not blindly venerated totems but instruments by which the tasks historically conferred on the state are accomplished.[37] This argument seems strengthened if one looks also at the following evolution of constitutionalism. The profound re-definition of objectives that occurred in the transition from the liberal to the social state has entailed huge modifications in the categories of state constitutionalism.[38] Thus, not only the theories of fundamental rights protection,[39] federalism[40] and form of government[41] have been reformulated, but even the very concept of constitution has undergone critical re-thinking in the light of the new functional concerns of the state.[42] As a result, a functional approach whereby constitutions serve (and are biased towards) the objectives inspiring their legal orders seems respectful of the historical role played by constitutionalism and, possibly, deserves consideration also in the debate on post-national constitutionalism.[43]

There is indeed a lesson to be drawn from this short excursus. Despite the attempts to depict it as monolithic, constitutionalism comes out as the historical product of the stratification of institutional solutions devised to respond to the functional concerns of the state form of government. At this point, it might well be maintained that the processes of re-organization of the public sphere which generate post-national legal orders do not amount to ruptures or paradigm shifts in the current phase of (state) constitutionalism. Coherently with this premise, it is correct to adopt the traditional categories as the benchmark to test and, consequently, to deny the constitutional nature of the post-national legal orders. Nevertheless, it might also be the case that the processes currently occurring in the organization of the public space resist the usual classifications and integrate a new episode in the evolution of constitutionalism, namely the stage in which constitutionalism is a

---

[37] The lost instrumental character of constitutionalism can be explained with the success of the structuralist approaches to law. Particularly in the theories of Kelsen, developed exclusively in respect to the state form of government, the functional perspective is mostly expunged from the legal analysis as contaminating the law with ideological or political elements. On the relationship between functional analysis and Kelsen's theories, see N. Bobbio, *Verso una concezione funzionalistica del diritto*, pp. 63–71.

[38] In this regard, I feel particularly indebted to the approach followed in G. Bognetti, *Federalismo*, in *Digesto delle discipline pubblicistiche*, VI, Torino, 1991, pp. 275–76, where the abstract classification of federal states is substituted by a more convincing classification of the federal systems depending upon their functional concerns (*forme di stato*).

[39] On the modifications that occurred in the forms of fundamental rights protection in the shift from liberal to social state, see A. Baldassarre, *Diritti inviolabili*, in *Enciclopedia Giuridica Treccani*, XI.

[40] G. Bognetti, *Federalismo*, p. 273.

[41] The implications of the shift from liberal to social state for the institutional architecture are well captured in G. Amato, *Forme di stato e forme di governo*, in G. Amato, A. Barbera (eds.), *Manuale di diritto pubblico*, I, Bologna, 1997, pp. 41–61.

[42] On the structural features of constitutional state, see A. Baldassarre, *Diritti sociali*, in *Enciclopedia Giuridica Treccani*, XI, 1989, pp. 7–9.

[43] This is not to say, against Kelsen, that the objectives underpinning the constitutions have automatically legal relevance. The analysis developed below (section III) will distinguish between the state constitutional sphere, where Kelsen's approach seems substantially adequate, and the legal orders of the EU and WTO, where functional elements may be acknowledged as having legal relevance.

tool employed for special purposes in non-state dimensions. On this premise, traditional categories constitute just one of the possible manifestations of constitutionalism and, therefore, they can hardly be invoked as the benchmark. More correctly, the benchmark might be identified in the seminal ideal of constitutionalism: the achievement of objectives of good government by empowering and limiting political institutions.[44] Since it does not seem ontological reasons exist to confine this ideal within the sole state borders, it might be productively introduced in other habitats and give birth to different historical epiphanies of constitutionalism shaped in the light of the functional concerns inspiring post-national legal orders.

In this unprecedented reality, the critical understanding of constitutionalism may profit from and enhance the role of the comparative law methodology. Whereas the comparative methodology is normally employed to classify states constitutions according to their respective political and ideological background,[45] an unexplored field of investigation could be envisioned in respect to the diverse interpretations of the constitutionalist ideal within states and post-national legal orders.[46]

A privileged field to test the validity of this functional and comparative approach to constitutionalism(s)[47] can be identified in the area of economic and social regulation within the European constitutional space. Legal orders operating in this field—namely, those of the member states, the EU and WTO—share a core of structural elements which articulate the above-mentioned seminal ideal of constitutionalism. Influenced by the principle of rule of law,[48] their foundations lay in constitutive and legally-binding documents establishing, *inter alia*, their respective fundamental objectives.[49] To accomplish these objectives, regulatory powers are allocated to political institutions.[50] Besides, the pursuit of fundamental objectives by political institutions must respect a plurality of constitutionally relevant interests. Finally, judicial or adjudicative bodies are empowered to enforce constitutional limits against the outcomes of the decision-making and, in this way, to prevent abuses by political institutions. From a functional perspective, the presence of these elements justifies the attribution of constitutional status to

[44] An alternative reconstruction of the core ideal of constitutionalism is submitted by N. Walker, *Constitutionalism and the problem of translation*, pp. 45–52, claiming that constitutionalism ought to develop '*the* great problem of modern political thought' consisting in 'the reconciliation of the three virtues of economic and material well-being, social cohesion and effective freedom'.

[45] See the classification presented in G. de Vergottini, *Diritto costituzionale comparato*, pp. 93–115.

[46] Comparative constitutional law has so far been conceived as an almost exclusively state-centric discipline. As state constitutionalism, therefore, also comparative methodology is under stress because of the processes of re-organization of public space. Nevertheless, constructive and comprehensive theoretical efforts in this respect are at the moment absent.

[47] In respect to national and post-national constitutionalism.

[48] Or its national equivalents. In the case of Italy, the principle of *legalità costituzionale* performs indeed functions equivalent to the principle of rule of law in the constitutional state.

[49] In this perspective, the sovereign or original nature of legal orders is an element that is extraneous to the analysis.

[50] In this study, 'regulatory autonomy' is used to address the forms of both legislative and secondary rule-making.

the considered post-national legal orders.[51] Nevertheless, their concrete developments remarkably differ depending upon the characteristics of the respective legal framework and, as a consequence, become susceptible to comparative analysis.

According to traditional constitutionalism, a comparative analysis on the attitude by the constitutions towards the economic issues is normally undertaken by pointing to the concept of economic constitution as comparator.[52] Despite its rigorous theoretical and normative foundations,[53] economic constitution is commonly employed to describe the economic regimes of states as disciplined by their constitutional provisions. In this approach, its definition is often neglected and its inherent structure poorly articulated. Thus, when employed in descriptive terms, economic constitution appears a scarcely useful and quite confusing device of investigation. In other doctrinal contributions, referring explicitly to its ordo-liberal origins, the concept is employed in more precise terms. Here, the economic constitution alludes to a specific model of constitution stipulating specific and binding guidelines of economic and social regulation which the political institutions and adjudicative bodies are expected to implement.[54] Nonetheless, even in this perspective, economic constitution reveals difficulties for our comparative investigation. Firstly, the analysis of national constitutions shows that a considerable discrepancy exists between concrete legal reality and the model suggested by this theory.[55] Secondly, economic constitution remains a largely unstructured device. Thirdly, the concept is historically state-centered and, notably, it does not take into account the possibility of constitutional regimes responding to diverse functional concerns. Finally, the normative potential of economic constitution is sometimes misused for ideological purposes in order to promote specific economic models and objectives and to assimilate constitutional spheres which articulate different solutions.[56]

Considering these difficulties, the analysis proposed in this study will reject the economic constitution as the device to compare the attitudes towards the

[51] Yet, even in the light of these requirements, the constitutional nature of the WTO remains considerably uncertain. See below section III.A.(i).

[52] Just to mention a few examples of the massive use of 'economic constitution' as a label or a tool of analysis in the constitutional spheres at issue, consider respectively M. Poiares Maduro, *We the Court: the European Court of Justice and the European Economic Constitution*, Oxford, 1998; E-U. Petersmann, *The Transformation of the World Trading System*, p. 1; and G. Bognetti, *La costituzione economica italiana*, Milano, 1995.

[53] The historical origins of economic constitution are depicted by D. J. Gerber, *Law and Competition in Twentieth Century Europe—Protecting Prometheus*, Oxford, 1998.

[54] D. J. Gerber, *Law and Competition*, p. 246, defines economic constitution according to the view of the ordo-liberals as 'a comprehensive decision concerning the nature and form of the process of socio-economic cooperation'.

[55] In this regard, the criticism expressed by M. Luciani, *Economia nel diritto costituzionale*, in *Digesto delle discipline pubblicistiche*, V, Torino, 1990, pp. 374–75, in respect to the adoption of economic constitution in the analysis of the Italian constitution seems appropriate.

[56] This is the case when economic constitution is adopted as heuristic (in reality, normative) tool for analyzing the WTO and when the EU regulatory principles are considered as having molded the economic constitution of the member states (see below section III.B).

economic issues by the Italian, WTO and EU constitutions. In the light of the functional approach previously suggested, the Economic Constitutional Identity (ECI) will be advocated as the alternative comparator to economic constitution. Its structure develops the general ideal of constitutionalism in the specific field of economic and social regulation. Moreover, such a device is capable of encompassing a broader range of solutions than those admitted by economic constitution, and permits their precise comparison through a grid of indicators concerning:

- the economic constitutional objectives of the legal orders and their scope/ramifications;
- the nature of their legal frameworks;
- the thickness of the constitutional constraints (i.e. standards of adjudication adopted in applying economic constitutional provisions); and
- the characters of regulatory autonomy/political deliberation in the pursuit of economic objectives.

The identity metaphor is succesful particularly also in conveying a more complex image of the constitutional aspects of the legal orders under consideration. As observed in the most sophisticated analyses, identities, rather than remaining stable and univocal, evolve and, as a rule, assume a multi-faceted character.[57] Arguably, the same occurs with the identities of constitutional orders. In this study, for instance, ECIs will be presented as products of processes of incremental stratification in which distinctive and convergent elements coexist.[58] In the analysis of the former, emphasis will be placed on the original identity of constitutional spheres and, therefore, on the elements which are more likely to create conflict and tension among them.[59] In the following stage of the analysis, the bias of the distinctive elements, though not obliterated, will be nuanced. In dealing with converging elements, thus, the similarities among the ECIs will be underlined by considering both their autonomous evolution and mutual interactions. Eventually, by stressing the idea of accretion inherent in the concept of stratification,[60] the complete images of the ECIs will result in a more sophisticated and less caricatural light than in the portraits normally depicted through static analyses.

---

[57] An extraordinary example, in this regard, is provided by the novel *Il visconte dimezzato* by I. Calvino.

[58] The metaphor of stratification is borrowed from J.H.H. Weiler, *The Geology of International Law—Governance, Democracy and Legitimacy*.

[59] The emphasis on the distinctive elements seems coherent with the comparative approach by L.J. Constantinesco, *Introduzione al diritto comparato*, Torino, 1996 (Italian edition by A. Procida Mirabelli di Lauro and R. Favale), pp. 224–31, where these are defined as those elements with more profound ideological and teleological connotations and in strict connection with the system of values underpinning the legal order.

[60] J.H.H. Weiler, *The Geology of International Law*, p. 3, observes that 'whereas the classical historical method tends to periodize, geology stratifies'.

III. Investigating Stratification—Comparative Analysis of the Economic Constitutional Identities of Italy, the WTO and the EU

A. Distinctive Elements

(i) Constitutional Objectives and Nature of the Legal Framework

Constitutionalism Serving Economic and Social Cohesion

Enacted in the aftermath of the Second World War (1947), the Italian constitution incorporates the typical elements of the continental model of social (or welfare) state.[61] Like other constitutions of this generation,[62] its adoption has followed a controversial process of constitutional transition. The new document, indeed, was expected to come to grips with a number of ticklish issues which, in the previous decade, had eventually degenerated into the war.[63] In this regard, the economic profile of the constitution was one of the thorniest problems. Although the economic models of previous constitutional regimes (liberalism, corporatism) were largely unpopular, deep ideological divisions existed, at least in principle, among the positions of the main political actors engaged in the constitutional transition.[64] Nonetheless, the constituent assembly eventually reached a general compromise whereby the constitution had to strike an appropriate balance between economic development and social protection and, therefore, to ensure conditions of economic and social cohesion. Nowadays, a similar objective directs the majority of the constitutions of EU member states. Thus, economic and social cohesion arises as one of the crucial elements which characterize, both ideologically and structurally, the European post-war constitutional panorama.[65]

As mentioned, in serving economic and social cohesion the Italian constitution embodies a compromise among the main political and social actors normally operating in a modern industrial society. Several constitutional provisions articulate that general objective by including a detailed list of social rights and, simultaneously, by

---

[61] A general description of the characters of social state is provided in G. Amato, *Forme di stato e forme di governo*, pp. 52–61. For a survey of the Italian model, see also A. Baldassarre, *Diritti sociali*, pp. 10–14.

[62] We can include in this generation the German *Grundgesetz* (1949) and the French Constitution of the Fourth Republic (1946).

[63] The intent of the new constitution, indeed, was not only to determine a break from the constitutional regime introduced during the Fascist period, but also to overcome the shortcomings of the previous liberal constitution (Statuto Albertino, 1848).

[64] For a survey of the main political and economic positions in the Italian post-war constitutional transition see G. Amato, *Il mercato nella costituzione*, in *QC*, 1992, 1, pp. 7–13.

[65] The principles inspiring the constitutions of social state are listed in G. Bognetti, *Costituzione economica e Corte costituzionale*, Milano, 1983, pp. 21–31.

ensuring the protection of economic freedom and the market.[66] Yet, because of the open-ended nature of the constitutional compromise, a precise hierarchy between economic development and social protection is not definitely struck.[67] Hence, the constitution is permeated by constant tension along the economic-social divide which surfaces quite clearly in the most conventional constitutional rhetoric. Traditionally, only the promotion of social objectives entails a proactive role for public authorities aimed at transforming social reality. By contrast, in dealing with economic objectives public powers are not expected to assume an equivalent attitude. The constitution, indeed, protects economic freedom against too intrusive pieces of legislation. Yet, the active pursuit of conditions of fair competition or economic efficiency does not come out as a positive constitutional obligation for public authorities.[68] As a result, it is difficult to deny that the constitution performs poorly in defining a detailed and prescriptive substantive economic model.[69] Taken by itself, the objective of economic and social cohesion neither drives regulation nor originates immediate solutions in the adjudication of economic conflicts. Nevertheless, it would be wrong to dismiss the potential of the Italian ECI by simply lamenting the scarce penetration of its substantive principles. At a closer analysis, its procedural dimension and the nature of its legal framework are equally eloquent traits that deserve careful consideration in this respect.

In the social state constitutions, the fulfilment of fundamental objectives is mainly conferred on political institutions which enjoy broad legislative powers.[70] In this regard, the Italian constitution gives legislation a role which is remarkably different from that played in the context of liberal constitutions. In the tradition of liberalism, indeed, legislation is a product of a single-class Parliament and serves essentially the objective of limiting public authorities in order to safeguard individual rights and, notably, economic freedom. With the institution of a democratically-elected Parliament and the shift from liberal to social state,[71] the character

---

[66] G. Amato, *Il mercato nella costituzione*, p. 12, observes that in the Italian constitutional language the concepts of market and economic freedom are normally matched.

[67] V. Onida, *Le Costituzioni. I principi fondamentali della costituzione italiana*, in G. Amato, A. Barbera (eds.), *Manuale di diritto pubblico*, p. 91.

[68] N. Irti, *L'ordine giuridico del mercato*, Roma-Bari, 1998, p. 18. In this regard, G. Amato, *Il mercato nella costituzione*, p. 10, has observed that in the ideological and cultural mindset of most of the members of the constituent assembly, the protection of economic freedoms was conceived for its beneficial contribution in terms of political freedom. By contrast, its contribution to the overall efficiency of the economic system was mostly neglected. A different opinion, whereby the protection of economic freedom implied also the protection of fair conditions of competition for the constituent assembly, is supported by F. Galgano, *Commento all'art. 41 Cost.*, in G. Branca (ed.), *Commentario della Costituzione. Rapporti economici*, II, Bologna, 1982, p. 11.

[69] In this respect, the Italian constitution appears to provide the fundamental principles for a transaction economy, see D.J. Gerber, *Law and Competition*, p. 248.

[70] Because of the vertical division of powers disciplined by article 117 Cost., in the Italian constitution the legislative power belongs to the state and to the regions. Both levels of government, though with different limits, have legislative competences in several specific areas of economic regulation.

[71] M.S. Giannini, *Diritto pubblico dell'economia*, Bologna, 1995, p. 31–32, has identified in these elements the major shift from the so-called *stato monoclasse* to the *stato pluriclasse*.

and function of legislation vary.[72] In the context of social state, the contents of legislative acts are determined by the competition (or the mediation) among political actors representing different parties and, often, different sectors of society. The legislation, therefore, abandons its original protective connotation and turns into an instrument of government of the economic and social reality. In conclusion, the constitutional compromise resonates in the inherent structures of the government by emphasizing representative democracy as the privileged means to achieve economic and social cohesion.

The protective role played in liberal constitutions by legislation is assumed in social state by the entrenched constitution.[73] Apart from allocating political powers, the constitution dictates also limits to the decision-making processes. Firstly, positive obligations are imposed on political institutions to pursue specific social objectives. Secondly, a number of constitutive principles are opposed to political institutions to avoid their possible abuses. In both of these dimensions, the binding and entrenched nature of the constitution is ensured by the Constitutional Court.[74] From its first decision,[75] the Court has enforced the constitutional provisions against the legislative acts submitted to its review. Nevertheless, substantive constitutional principles perform mostly as negative limits to legislation.[76] Once the essential content of fundamental rights is ensured, both the margins of economic freedom and the standards of protection of social rights remain largely in the hands of the political process.[77] As a result, depending on the outcomes of democratic deliberation, the market ends up being either an objective inspiring legislation or a generator of social exclusion to be constrained. The same applies to social objectives, either considered as goals for policy-making or obstacles to economic freedoms. In the backdrop of such divergent alternatives, the constitution establishes of course a minimum degree of substantive homogeneity. Nevertheless, its most visible contribution is its procedural frame. By delineating institutions and procedures for channeling political and social pluralism, the constitution contributes to the prevention of social conflicts and to the promotion of social integration. In this, it serves its ultimate objective of economic and social cohesion.[78]

---

[72] In this regard G. Zagrebelsky, *Il diritto mite*, Torino, 1992, p. 48, has observed that 'la legge, un tempo misura esclusiva di tutte le cose nel campo del diritto, cede così il passo alla Costituzione e diventa essa stessa oggetto di misurazione. Viene detronizzata a vantaggio di un'istanza più alta. E quest'istanza più alta assume ora il compito immane di reggere in unità e in pace intere società divise al loro interno e concorrenziali'.

[73] The introduction of a double circuit of legality within the systems with entrenched constitution is described in A. Baldassarre, *Diritti sociali*, pp. 8–9.

[74] It must be stressed that the positive constitutional obligations are mostly assisted by political guarantees.   [75] Corte Cost., sent. 5 June 1956, n. 1, in *GC*, 1956, p. 1.

[76] R. Bin, *Capire la costituzione*, Roma-Bari, 2002, p. 97 has described the negative role played by constitutional provisions through the following metaphor: 'A navigare è il 'politico', spesso nei panni del legislatore: è lui che decide da che parte si va e a quale velocità. La Corte costituzionale sta sulla nave per conto dell'armatore, nel cui interesse controlla come procede la navigazione, intervenendo quando ne vede infrante le regole'.   [77] In respect to economic freedom, see below section III.A.(ii).

[78] In this regard, V. Onida, *Le Costituzioni. I principi fondamentali della costituzione italiana*, p. 107, argues '... il conflitto sociale non è dunque ignorato né negato; nemmeno si ipotizza una sua soluzione

Legalism Serving Free Trade

The very objective of economic and social cohesion underlying domestic economic constitutionalism is reflected in the international dimension in a variety of distinct initiatives of cooperation among the states.[79] Against this background, the WTO, in its role as a special purpose organization,[80] plays a partial role. According to its preamble, economic and social welfare are pursued essentially by promoting economic growth through free trade.[81] Having embraced the latter as the most immediate objective and comparative advantage as the economic and ideological driving principle,[82] the WTO endorses an international trade regime unfettered by protectionist measures.[83] The fundamental objective of the WTO, therefore, consists in gradually reducing barriers and eliminating discriminations in international trade relations.[84]

Nevertheless, the scope of international trade regulation, far from remaining within clear-cut boundaries, is inevitably blurred. Originally, the reach of the GATT obligations was mainly underestimated. Merely treated as technical issues, the matters arising out of negotiations and adjudication have been for a long time insulated by neglecting the policy externalities of free trade.[85] Only recently this original attitude has changed and the WTO has started to cope with the problems related to its ramifications. In both negotiations and adjudication, the scope of the international trade obligations is currently managed by addressing a number of 'trade and ...' chapters.[86] Yet, although the legal protection of non trade interests

o scomparsa per la sola via politica; lo si riconduce e in un certo senso lo si garantisce nel suo concreto svolgersi, mentre alla politica (allo Stato) si affida il compito di regolare le condizioni fondamentali di sviluppo dell'assetto economico [...] La meta ultima è una società in cui la giustizia sociale sia assicurata. Ma i termini di tale 'giustizia' restano largamente indeterminati, e affidati da un lato alla dinamica dei rapporti sociali, dall'altro alle scelte politiche. *L'esito del processo è lasciato aperto*, pur indicandosene in termini generali gli obiettivi' (Italic in the original).

[79] In this regard, J.P. Trachtman, *WTO Constitution*, p. 19, observes that one could identify 'a kind of global functional federalism, in which the center is the general international legal system and the periphery is the functional organization.' A survey on the functional organizations operating in the international sphere is provided in B. Conforti, *Diritto internazionale*, Napoli, 2002, pp. 152–63.

[80] See article II.1 WTO, where the WTO is presented as providing 'the common institutional framework for the conduct of trade relations among its Members ...'.

[81] See R. Howse, K. Nicolaidis, *Constitutionalization or Global Subsidiarity*, pp. 76–77, addressing the GATT as an 'Embedded Liberalism Bargain'.

[82] A. Reich, *From Diplomacy to Law: The Juridicization of International Trade Relations*, in *NJILB*, 1996, 2/3, pp. 781–84.

[83] In this perspective, protectionism is considered as a political and economic failure by the governments following the regulatory capture by national firms and workers at detriment of consumers, see A. Reich, *From Diplomacy to Law*, p. 781; E-U. Petersmann, *The Transformation of the World Trading System*, p. 4.

[84] In the language of the preamble, the parties 'being desirous of contributing to these objectives [economic and social welfare] by entering into reciprocal and mutually advantageous arrangements directed to the substantial reduction of tariffs and other barriers to trade and to the elimination of discriminatory treatment in international trade relations'.

[85] J.H.H. Weiler, *The Rule of Lawyers and the Ethos of Diplomats: Reflections on the Internal and External Legitimacy of WTO Dispute Settlement*, in *JWT*, 2001, 35, 2, p. 191.

[86] This is particularly evident in the border between trade and environment. Here, a WTO Committee on Trade and Environment has been created in order to identify and study the problems

affected by the WTO obligations has been increasingly ensured, the WTO maintains its exclusive constitutional commitment to the objective of free trade.

Beside comparative advantage, the other ideological landmark of the GATT-WTO consists in its legal nature. History can witness to what extent an international trade regime based on rules rather than on powers, apart from serving general economic convenience, coincides with a profound choice of value.[87] A multilateral set of rules fosters negotiations rather than commercial wars and, at least purposively, reduces the inequalities among states. On these premises, the principle of rule of law has been employed from the very beginning in the achievement of GATT constitutional objectives.[88] Yet, the legal nature of the GATT has gone through several seasons. For a long time, because of a dispute settlement framework devised for negotiating rather than for adjudicating legal controversies, the binding nature of GATT obligations has relied largely on political guarantees.[89] Only with the entry into force of the Marrakech Agreement and the adoption of a new system of dispute settlement, the shift to legalism has been accomplished.[90] Like in the domestic sphere, also in the WTO the transformation of the constitutional framework has been certified by the judiciary.[91] In this regard, the extreme textualism employed by the Appellate Body from its first pronouncement is revealing of a change in the inherent structure of the legal framework.[92] The message sent by this decision is clear in stressing that the time when GATT obligations stood only as normative benchmarks for diplomacy is over. From now on, the treaties provides also compulsory yardsticks of adjudication and, arguably, constitutional constraints on members regulatory autonomy. The introduction of a judicial system of adjudication, indeed, strengthens the binding and supreme

emerging in the relationship between the WTO obligations and the environmental treaties. In other ambits, such as trade and labour relations, the WTO simply defers to the ILO (or, in other fields, to the relevant international agencies) the adoption of core labour standards.

[87] The reasons motivating the shift to legalism are discussed in A. Reich, *From Diplomacy to Law*, p. 775.

[88] Nevertheless, 'diplomacy v. legalism' is constantly a hot issue in the debate on international trade regulation. See M. J. Trebilcock, R. Howse, *The Regulation of International Trade*, New York, 1999, pp. 54–56; A. Reich, *From Diplomacy to Law*, pp. 830–39.

[89] In this regard J.H.H. Weiler, *The Rule of Lawyers and the Ethos of Diplomats*, p. 4, states that 'it is not inappropriate to think of that 'old' dispute settlement process as *diplomacy through other means*' (Italic in the original).

[90] It is common to identify in the article 6 DSU (right to have a panel) and articles 16.4 and 17.14 (right to have, respectively, a Panel or AB report adopted) the pillars of the juridification of the GATT. Arguably, even before the adoption of the DSU, the GATT was juridified, though its legal nature was considerably different.

[91] In this, it seems the WTO adjudicative bodies have simply fulfilled the role conferred to them by the treaties. A different opinion, whereby the Appellate Body ought to be regarded as 'the dynamic force behind constitution-building by virtue of its capacity to generate constitutional norms and structures during dispute resolution', is advocated by D.Z. Cass, *The 'Constitutionalization' of International Trade Law: Judicial Norm Generation as the Engine of Constitutional Development of International Trade*, in *EJIL*, 2001, 12, 1, pp. 41–42.

[92] See Report of the Appellate Body, *United States—Standards for Reformulated and Conventional Gasoline*, WT/DS2/AB/R, 29 April 1996.

nature of the WTO. As a consequence, its regulatory principles receive sufficient force to compete against the constitutional principles of the members in the definition of the relevant strategies of trade regulation. By playing this role, the WTO appears as taking its first steps along the road to constitutionalization.[93]

Yet, it would be misleading to affirm that the WTO, by employing the rule of law in the pursuit of its objectives, has deviated completely from its original legal roots. Despite the shift to legalism, the law of world trade still hinges on a legal framework which in many aspects reflects the ethos and the solutions of the purest international law. As a consequence, the injection in this context of the principle of rule of law originates a peculiar manifestation of constitutionalism which deviates remarkably from many of the distinctive elements of domestic constitutionalism. Arguably, the international law matrix of the WTO affects the scope of judicial review by its adjudicative bodies, the thickness of its constitutional principles and, eventually, the binding nature of its provisions.

From a certain perspective, the combination between rule of law and international legal framework amplifies the pervasiveness of constitutional constraints on the regulatory measures of the members. In the WTO, indeed, the definition of the acts subject to judicial review does not follow the formal categories normally employed by domestic constitutions.[94] As an international treaty, the WTO addresses its members in the entirety of their legal manifestations. Consequently, since the international trade obligations encompass all trade-related measures adopted by or imputable to the members, their reach is broader than that of domestic constitutional provisions.[95]

An increase in the degree of penetration of WTO obligations can be appreciated also from a different perspective. By ratifying this treaty, members have not simply declared their loyalty to a general economic model committed to economic growth through free trade. Members have indeed agreed also on a series of regulatory principles which articulate that general objective. Unlike the open-textured character of many provisions contained in domestic constitutions, the

---

[93] Admittedly, this presentation shows the WTO does not fulfill all the elements indicated above (section II) as necessary to be acknowledged with full constitutional status. In particular, it seems that the WTO misses the requirement concerning the allocation of regulatory powers to political institutions for the pursuit of its fundamental objectives. Yet, in the analysis of the elements of the ECI of the WTO converging towards those of the EU (see below section III.B), embryonic substantial positive integration powers will be identified in the WTO sphere and, as a consequence, the acknowledgement of full constitutional status to the WTO will become plausible.

[94] In the Italian constitution, for instance, only legislative acts are reviewed by the Constitutional Court (article 134 Cost.). By contrast, in the German Constitution also administrative and judicial acts are subject to review by the *Bundesverfassungsgericht* (articles 1.3 and 19.4 GG).

[95] Article XVI.4 WTO stipulates that the obligations provided by the annexed agreements act as yardsticks of 'conformity' in respect to the members' 'laws, regulations and administrative procedures.' Yet, in the adjudication the range of measures subject to review is often widened. A sophisticated test for identifying the minimal requirements for having a 'measure' is at the core of the decision issued by the Panel in *Japan Semi-Conductors* (Report of the Panel adopted on 4 May 1988, L/6309—35S/116, recital 109).

WTO enshrines more detailed regulatory principles which leave narrower room for interpretations based on alternative ideological options.[96]

Although these aspects emphasize the role of the WTO as a source of legal and judicial constraints, other traits of its legal framework lead to an opposite conclusion. In this perspective, the version of rule of law adopted by the WTO appears lighter than that developed within domestic constitutions.

The system of remedies is a first evident element impairing the stringency of the WTO provisions. Whereas in the domestic sphere an act infringing upon the constitution is normally annulled or disapplied, in the WTO the pronouncements of adjudicative bodies do not have *per se* legal effect on members measures. In case of nullification of the benefits accruing to the members from the WTO obligations, the best solution is always the withdrawal of the inconsistent measure by the wrongdoer. Without the cooperation of the latter, the WTO provides only a disciplined system of retaliation allowing for the suspension of concessions or other obligations.[97]

A further element influencing the reach of WTO provisions relates to the nature of its obligations. As demonstrated by the most accurate analyses,[98] the WTO is a multilateral treaty designed for purposes which do not transcend the individual interests of the contracting parties.[99] To be precise, the WTO consists of a compilation of state-to-state relations originating a bundle of detachable and bilateral obligations. A similar connotation entails a number of consequences that are particularly important for a proper understanding of the constitutional nature of the WTO.[100]

Because of the bilateral nature of obligations, world trade law operates according to the most classic patterns of public international law.[101] The WTO, indeed, rather than promoting autonomous and comprehensive strategies of economic regulation, is in the most modest business of setting a legal matrix for coexistence among its members in the field of trade relations.[102] Accordingly, no WTO

---

[96] D. J. Gerber, *Law and Competition*, pp. 248–49, distinguishes between constitutive principles, whose function is to establish the basic form of the economy, and regulatory principles which are more specific and serve to maintain the effectiveness of constitutive principles.

[97] In this regard, see articles 3.7, 19 and 22 DSU.

[98] J. Pauwelyn, *A Typology of Multilateral Treaty Obligations: Are WTO Obligations Bilateral or Collective in Nature?*, in *EJIL*, 2003, 14, 5, p. 907.

[99] For an analysis of the bilateral nature of the WTO obligations see J. Pauwelyn, *Are WTO Obligations Bilateral or Collective in Nature?*, pp. 930–41.

[100] The discipline of bilateral obligations under the law of the treaties and the law of state responsibility is summarized in J. Pauwelyn, *Are WTO Obligations Bilateral or Collective in Nature?*, pp. 923–24. In this respect, it is interesting to note that the AB, in *Japan—Taxes on Alcoholic Beverages* (Appellate Body Report, WT/DS8/AB/R, 4 October 1996, paragraph F), in defining the nature of WTO states that 'The WTO is a treaty, the international equivalent of a contract' . . . and not of a constitution!

[101] A survey on the different 'command' modes coexisting in international law making is presented in J.H.H. Weiler, *The Geology of International Law*, pp. 8–19.

[102] For this reason the WTO can be considered a 'member-driven organization', see J.P. Trachtman, *The WTO Constitution*, p. 23.

institution is entitled to represent and promote the collective interest of the community of the members. As a result, the effectiveness of the WTO obligations relies only upon the judicial initiatives brought by states.[103] Hence, serious concerns arise for all those cases in which members decide not to seek redress for the breaches suffered.[104]

A further element threatening the effectiveness of the WTO can be identified under public international law rules of conflict. According to the law of the treaties, parties maintain broad margins to contract out their previous bilateral obligations. As a result, the WTO members not only can dilute the application of treaty provisions by profiting from the several forms of dispute settlement alternative to adjudication,[105] but are even entitled to set them aside by concluding subsequent alternative arrangements.[106]

In conclusion, the bias of international law has profound effects on the ECI of the WTO. It has been shown that the stringency of constitutional provisions is intensified in the international legal framework. In the meantime, the same matrix also introduces a considerable degree of flexibility and, therefore, increases the uncertainty about the binding nature of WTO obligations. The paradoxical combination of these apparently opposite elements produces an original constitutional regime based on a flexible version of the principle of rule of law. A similar framework is coherent with the ambitions of the WTO undertaking. The existence of several safety nets is considered decisive in facilitating the achievement of consensus among the members on a comprehensive discipline of international trade. The flexibility of the regulatory principles, indeed, allows the tuning of trade arrangements to the diverse aspirations and priorities of members. In this, the legal framework seems to respond realistically to its functional concern of bringing international trade relations as close as possible to the objective of free trade.[107]

---

[103] The bilateral nature of the WTO obligations implies that only the member(s) detrimentally affected by a measure have standing to seek redress for this breach, J. Pauwelyn, *Are WTO Obligations Bilateral or Collective in Nature?*, p. 942.

[104] This possibility can occur especially in the case of infringements by big-consumer states which could not be challenged for fear of political consequences, but also in the case of breaches by small-consumer states which often are not challenged because of their scarce economic importance. Gaps in the application of the WTO regulatory principles occur also when states engage in collusive practices by omitting to react against their respective breaches.

[105] See articles 4 (consultations), 5 (Good Offices, Conciliation and Mediation) and even 12.7 DSU (entitling the Panel to submit a report only if 'the parties to the dispute have failed to develop a mutually satisfactory solution'). In all these cases the solution of the controversies only purposely complies with the WTO obligations (article 3.7 DSU). The flexible nature of the WTO obligations is evident also in the possibility of waiving an obligation according to article IX.3 WTO.

[106] According to article 34 of the Vienna Convention, later treaties among the WTO members must not affect the rights of other WTO members that are not party to this later treaty. In addition, later treaties derogating to WTO provisions are possible only if not prohibited by the WTO or a later treaty concluded among its members. See J. Pauwelyn, *Are WTO Obligations Bilateral or Collective in Nature?*, pp. 946–47.

[107] In this regard, J. Pauwelyn, *Are WTO Obligations Bilateral or Collective in Nature?* p. 949, has observed that 'permitting these alternatives to full compliance or specific performance would not be to the advantage of private economic operators concerning predictability, in particular traders [. . .].

Constitutional Law Serving Market Building

The EC pursues economic and social welfare by promoting economic integration among its member states and, namely, by establishing and ensuring the functioning of the common market.[108] In responding to this specific functional concern, the ECI of the EC diverges in many aspects from the templates provided by both the WTO and domestic constitutions.

There are of course many elements common to the EC and the WTO. Both of them are special purposes organizations, both of them support free trade and comparative advantage as means of fostering economic growth.[109] Despite these similarities, from its earlier stages the EC has served more ambitious objectives of economic integration than boosting free trade among its members. Market building, indeed, does not consist only in reducing (or dismantling) barriers to trade and phasing out discriminatory measures. In the design of the EC, the commitment to common market entails a more comprehensive regulatory strategy aiming at the establishment of an efficient framework of relations among economic and social actors belonging to different member states.

Meaningful discrepancies arise also in respect to the objectives pursued in the domestic sphere. In the language of the EC, indeed, the market is not only the pivotal means of integration, but springs up as the critical generator of economic and social welfare. Thus, in supporting the market as an implicit alternative to the state approach to economic and social cohesion, the EC constitutional strategy may easily sound like the conservative answer to the more socially-oriented national constitutions.[110] Yet, the design of economic integration purported by the EC seems more sophisticated and, although unequivocally centered on the market, it inherently departs also from the classic foundations of liberalism.[111]

In the tradition of liberal constitutionalism, the market is mostly conceived as synonym of economic freedom.[112] Such an approach, reminiscent of the theory of natural freedoms, is deeply rooted in the historical experience of liberalism. As

But this may be the price to pay for having legally enforceable WTO obligations in the first place, as well as a welcome democratic safety-net that may actually render WTO obligations more, rather than less, legitimate'.

[108]   Eloquent in this regard is article 2 EEC, especially in its original version.

[109]   These similarities emerge in the largely corresponding contents of their regulatory principles. For a comparative analysis of the regulatory principles of the GATT and EU see F. Ortino, *Basic Legal Instruments for the Liberalisation of Trade: a Comparative Analysis of the EC and WTO Law*, Oxford, 2003.

[110]   In considering economy, rather than politics, as the primary means for integrating society, the EC constitution appears coherent with the intellectual framework of ordoliberal thought (See D. J. Gerber, *Law and Competition*, p. 241). Arguably, this may have been one of the reasons which have brought some national Constitutional Courts to limit the pervasiveness of EC law in case of infringement of the fundamental principles of the national constitutions. On this issue see B. de Witte, *Community Law and National Constitutional Values*, in *LIEI*, 1991, 2, 1, p. 1; M.L. Fernandez Esteban, *Constitutional Values and Principles in the Community Legal Order*, in *MJECL*, 1995, 2, 2, p. 129.

[111]   In this regard, it could be argued that whereas in the tradition of liberalism market is a *locus naturalis*, in the EC common market it is conceived essentially as *locus artificialis*. On this distinction, see N. Irti, *L'ordine giuridico del mercato*, pp. 3–14.

[112]   As seen above, this cultural approach is largely shared by the mixed-economy constitutions.

widely known, the enfranchisement of economic actors from the constraints of the *ancien régime* has not been pursued through the law. More correctly, their emancipation has been essentially a result obtained by the national middle classes after fierce battles fought in the political arena. In this context, the law, by recognizing economic freedom and property rights as cornerstones of the liberal constitutions, has played the eminently defensive function of protecting these political achievements.

From this standpoint, the profile of the EC is totally different. In the EC Treaty, indeed, one does not merely find the endorsement of liberal claims for a broader protection of economic freedom. Its provisions, rather than reaffirming, presuppose the principles already recognized and protected by the national constitutions, and go further by devising an efficiency-oriented program of transformation of the economic and social reality.[113]

Unlike the WTO, the EC has pursued its goal by constantly expanding its substantive scope. The EC, rather than anesthetizing the potential ramifications of economic integration, has profited from them and, eventually, stretched the reach of its competences. Nevertheless, such an expansion has not diluted the EC original commitment to market-building.[114] On the contrary, by expanding its scope, the common market has subsumed within its circuits a number of policy areas traditionally perceived as distinct or even conflicting with the achievement of purely economic goals. Therefore, the configuration of the substantive domain of the EC, in maintaining a strategic link with the market, does not amount to the general vocation which, by contrast, marks domestic constitutions.[115]

The very objective of economic integration has played a key role also in shaping the specific constitutional nature of the EC. In this regard, other important differences with both the domestic and WTO legal frameworks can be underlined. The constitution of the common market, indeed, embodies neither the (international law) contractual intergovernmental matrix nor the (domestic constitutional) compromise between political actors supporting alternative projects of society. Market building is a different business, consisting of the implementation and enforcement of a comprehensive and autonomous constitutional programme made of clear-cut regulatory strategies. Arguably, the pursuit of these objectives cannot be performed only by building upon the flexible legal framework of international law. Therefore, already in their original versions, the treaties envisaged for the EC, a legal framework which, in many vital aspects, deviates from the classic matrix of international law.

---

[113] As a result, the economic integration pursued in the design of the common market encompasses a broader range of policy fields including, alongside the rules on free movement, competition law, state aids and approximation of laws.

[114] This emerges particularly in the words of article 308 EC. In entitling the EC institutions to adopt measures beyond the EC competences, this provision stipulates that these measures are 'necessary to attain, *in the course of the operation of the common market*, one of the objectives of the Community . . . ' (italics added).

[115] The limits to the EC domain determined by the persisting link with market integration are evident in the case *Kremzow* (Case 299/95, *Kremzow v. Austria* [1997] ECR I-269).

In this regard, a first innovation consists in the identification of a distinct interest of the community beside the individual interests of member states.[116] Integration, indeed, entails a more profound effort of cooperation than striking a balance among the members' individual interests. Implementation and enforcement of the market-building programme, therefore, could not been left entirely in the hands of the member states. An independent organ, such as the Commission, has been inserted in the EC institutional architecture in order to embody and pursue the Community's autonomous aspiration to integration. As a consequence, the EC legal framework has been enriched with institutional and procedural devices essentially aimed at the systematic and precise implementation of the constitutional programme.

A further innovative element introduced in the EC legal framework concerns the institutional architecture. The commitment to market integration could not rely on the sole application of treaty provisions by adjudicative or judicial bodies. As has been shown, market building is not simply about ensuring conditions for a peaceful coexistence among the member states in the field of trade. The limitation of the regulatory measures of the members, indeed, is only part of the strategy purported by the treaties. The achievement of the common market requires also the implementation and the articulation of the regulatory strategies stipulated by the treaties. In the EC, thus, the pursuit of constitutional objectives implies the allocation of regulatory powers on political institutions and, eventually, the introduction of a fully-fledged system of government.

Finally, it is broadly known that the deepest alteration of the international law framework has taken place in the judiciary of the EC. Also in this regard the approach of the Court of Justice remarkably differs from that of the Appellate Body. Whereas the Appellate Body has diligently certified the legal nature of GATT obligations, the Court of Justice has bravely molded the constitutional framework of its legal system in the light of its ultimate objective.[117] By adopting the doctrine of direct effect and, consequently, by empowering individuals as 'private attorney-generals',[118] the Court of Justice has strengthened the principle of rule of law and its judicial guarantees and, finally, transformed the original EC legal framework.[119] As a consequence, the effectiveness of EC law finds an additional

---

[116] Therefore, it could be argued that EC obligations, by pursuing an interest that transcends the individual interests of the contracting parties, are collective in nature. The existence of an EC constitutional interest distinct from the interests of the member states emerges, *inter alia*, in the constitutional regime of the Commission: see, for example, article 211 EC, where also the strict link with the objective of the common market is evident.

[117] Case C-26/62, *Van Gend en Loos v. Nederlande Administratie der Belastingen* [1963] ECR I-1. It is commonly acknowledged that in this case the Court of Justice, by adopting a radical teleological approach, has started to shape the constitutional nature of the EC.

[118] P. Craig, *Once Upon a Time in the West: Direct Effect and federalization of the EEC Law*, in *OJLS*, 1992, 12, 4, p. 453.

[119] Case 294/83, *Parti Ecologiste 'Les Verts' v. European Parliament*, [1986] ECR I-1339. In this regard, R. Toniatti, *Il principio di rule of law e la formazione giurisprudenziale del diritto costituzionale dell'Unione Europea*, in S. Gambino (ed.), *Costituzione italiana e diritto comunitario*, Milano, 2002, p. 503.

and more efficient means of enforcement openly developed on the basis of the domestic models of judicial review of legislation.

Yet, it would be superficial to conclude that the legal framework of the EC coincides perfectly with its domestic equivalents. Important distinctions need to be drawn in this sphere too. A first difference has already been pointed out. The national constitutions are not endowed with institutions and procedures—such as the Commission and the infringement procedure—specifically directed to the implementation of their regulatory strategies. In the domestic sphere, the achievement of constitutional objectives is largely left to the political-majoritarian circuits and the protection of constitutional principles relies only on the enforcement by the Constitutional Court.

Other differences concern the reach of the EC provisions. Despite efforts by the Court of Justice to handle the treaties as functional equivalents of domestic constitutions, several traits of the EC legal framework echo its roots in international law. Like in the WTO, for instance, treaties obligations address all the measures imputable to member states.[120] Like in the WTO, or better, more than in the WTO, treaties provisions operate as regulatory (rather than constitutive) principles and originate detailed constitutional strategies.

Finally, an important difference arises also in respect to the remedies for breaches of the treaties. In this regard, the sophisticated system of remedies elaborated by the Court of Justice is not even comparable with the primitive characters of its WTO equivalent. As seen, it is undeniable that national measures inconsistent with directly applicable EC law are to be set aside.[121] Yet, differences exist also in respect to the features of the national systems of judicial review of legislation. The pronouncements by the Court of Justice, indeed, do not have *per se* the effect of phasing out the inconsistent national measures.[122] More precisely, their effect (as for most of the EC acts) depends ultimately on the cooperation of national courts whose obedience draws upon their respective domestic constitutions.

In conclusion, the nature of constitutional objectives is decisive also for the connotation of the EC legal framework. By refining the classic framework of international law in the light of some of the typical traits of the state constitutions, the EC seems to have found the most appropriate instruments to serve the objective of market integration. Ultimately the very nature of supranational constitutionalism also consists of a such a complex combination.

---

[120] The breadth of the concept of measure in the EC is well represented by cases such as *Huenermund* (C-292/92, [1993] ECR I-6787) and *Commission v. France* (C-265/95, [1997] ECR I-6959). It must be remarked that the jurisdiction of the Court of Justice, differently from that of the WTO adjudicative bodies, is not confined to the measures of the member states but deals also with the legality of EC acts.

[121] It will be seen below (section III.A.(ii)) that national measures breaching the treaty provisions on free circulation of goods are not annulled but disapplied by national courts and administrations only in respect to imported products.

[122] B. de Witte, *Direct Effect, Supremacy, and the Nature of the Legal Order*, in P. Craig, G. de Bùrca (eds.), *The Evolution of the EU*, Oxford, 1999, p. 193.

(ii) Constitutional Constraints and Regulatory Autonomy
Judicial Review of Legislation Re-Enforcing Utilità Sociale

The pivotal provision of the Italian Constitution dealing with economic issues is article 41.[123] This article, by acknowledging both the liberal claims for economic freedom (*'l'iniziativa economica è libera'*) and the social demands for political regulation (*'non può svolgersi in contrasto con l'utilità sociale . . .'*), perfectly embodies the political compromise and the quest for economic and social cohesion inherent in the constitution.

Because of its central position, article 41 has constantly animated fierce political disputes concerning its interpretation and, namely, the substantive contents of the economic model enshrined in the constitution. Quite predictably, supporters of *laissez-faire* ideals passionately advocate the first paragraph of article 41 as their manifesto for a pure liberal economic model. Their political opponents, conversely, stress the passage on *utilità sociale* as an icon of social justice and, in some cases, even as the promise for an alternative economic system.

Apart from single opinions utterly biased by ideology,[124] the scholarship on constitutional law has largely refused such simplistic alternatives. Nonetheless, highly divisive doctrinal debates have arisen in respect to the meaning and the function of article 41. A first level of discussion translates in the more secular language of constitutional law the classic dialectic between economic freedom and public intervention. Although the existence of a model of mixed economy is normally admitted, a number of scholars present article 41 either stressing the room of maneuver granted to public authorities for the pursuit of social objectives or defending the necessity to protect economic freedom from excessively intrusive pieces of legislation.[125] Yet, in most of the cases these opinions add little to the critical understanding of the Italian ECI since their emphasis either on freedom or on its limits reflects more the authors' political preferences than the results of a rigorous scientific investigation.

Article 41 has occasioned a more interesting debate concerning the relationship between constitutional constraints and political decision-making in the field of economic regulation. In this regard, the doctrinal divide is subtler and the opinions offered in the discussion appear detached from the ideological divisions encountered in the political sphere.

---

[123] Article 41 Cost. reads as follows: 'L'iniziativa economica privata è libera. Non può svolgersi in contrasto con l'utilità sociale o in modo da recare danno alla sicurezza, alla libertà, alla dignità umana. La legge determina i programmi e i controlli opportuni perchè l'attività economica pubblica e privata possa essere indirizzata e coordinata a fini sociali'.

[124] C. Lavagna, *Costituzione e socialismo*, Bologna 1977, affirms the transitory character of the constitutional protection of economic freedom, to be overcome with the adoption of a more mature socialist regime.

[125] Broad margins of intervention for public authorities are acknowledged by C. Mortati, *Istituzioni di diritto pubblico*, II, Padova, 1976, p. 1114. A position more favorable to economic freedom is supported by M. Mazziotti, *Il diritto al lavoro*, Milano, 1956, p. 183 and, more recently, by A. Pace, *Problematica delle libertà costituzionali—parte speciale*, Padova, 1992, p. 487.

The starting point of this debate is the entrenched nature of the constitution as assisted by a system of judicial review of legislation, landmark innovations which have strengthened the binding nature of the fundamental rules after a long period of oblivion and defiance by political institutions. Prominent scholars have interpreted this turn into legalism with a pure civil law spirit. Textualism and direct effect have been addressed as the most coherent doctrines for granting supremacy to the constitution. Accordingly, constitutional provisions have been handled with the same hermeneutic instruments adopted in respect to legislation. Thus, the textual choices by the framers have resulted as the crucial elements in the identification of the prescriptive contents of the constitution.[126] Besides, the legal impact of constitutional provisions has been affirmed without hesitation. Considered as sources of regulatory principles, they considerably narrow the scope for legislation. In this perspective, therefore, the role of legislation and administration consists in the correct implementation of clear constitutional obligations. Similarly, courts are requested to apply constitutional principles directly and to set aside, according to the preliminary ruling procedure, the statutes in conflict with them.[127]

The outcomes of a similar approach to article 41 are quite disappointing. The morbid attention to its meagre textual elements has not kept the promise of providing a comprehensive constitutional discipline for economic issues. Even the most elegant of these interpretations[128] fail in devising appropriate standards of constitutional adjudication and, more importantly, in capturing the effective role played by article 41 in the legal reality.[129] Textualism, indeed, induces many authors to over-emphasize the semantic potential of constitutional principles and to misinterpret the relationship between constitutional constraints and political decision-making. By contrast, their works neglect the profound significance of the open-textured character of article 41, with the consequence of diminishing the

---

[126] For instance, M. Mazziotti, *Il diritto del lavoro*, pp. 158–59 has inferred from the use in article 41.3 of the plural form 'programmi' the impossibility of a single binding economic programme. The same Author (p. 154) has distinguished on mere textual bases the allegedly different intensity of the limits to economic freedom dictated in article 41.2. Whereas the contrast between economic freedom with *utilità sociale* is considered plainly unlawful, the conflict between economic freedom with the other explicit limits ('libertà', 'sicurezza' e 'dignità umana') would be banned only if amounting to a harmful event ('non deve recar danno . . .'). Several other examples emerge also in A. Pace, *Problematica delle libertà costituzionali*, pp. 490–96.

[127] This approach is particularly evident in C. Esposito, *I tre commi dell'art. 41 Cost.*, in *Giur. Cost.*, 1962, p. 33 and in A. Pace, *Problematica delle libertà costituzionali*, pp. 481–89.

[128] A. Baldassarre, *Iniziativa economica privata*, in *Enciclopedia del diritto*, XXI, pp. 594–95 interprets article 41 in the light of the contemporary processes of production and organization of economic activities. Hence, article 41.1 is considered as the provision regulating the right to invest which could not be constrained with binding limits by public authorities. Article 41.2, instead, contains the discipline for the organization of economic activities and the limits imposed to private initiatives could amount to binding constraints. Finally, article 41.3 calls into question the legislative to regulate the overall economic process and direct it towards the pursuit of social objectives. A similar approach is shared by M. Luciani, *Economia nel diritto costituzionale*, p. 380 and criticized by A. Pace, *Problematica delle libertà costituzionali*, pp. 461–62.

[129] A. Baldassarre, *Iniziativa economica privata*, p. 604, states that for instance the Constitutional Court could second-guess in the light of article 41 the policy objectives inspiring legislation.

potential of integration of a constitutional framework essentially directed at the promotion of economic and social cohesion.

These latest considerations motivate an alternative approach to article 41. An important part of the scholarship on constitutional law rejects textualism as the most appropriate methodology to deal with constitutional provisions.[130] Their inherent nature, indeed, does not seem compatible with the hermeneutic tools usually employed in the exegesis of legislative acts. A provision such as article 41 is anything but stringent and, therefore, attempts at inferring regulatory principles from its text are likely to be arbitrary. As a consequence, the binding nature of the constitution must also be conceived in a different way. Article 41 can be realistically treated as a source of negative limits to the legislative acts affecting economic freedoms. Its binding nature, therefore, manifests itself essentially in the scrutiny by the Constitutional Court directed to test whether, in the pursuit of social objectives, economic freedom has been adequately taken into consideration.[131]

In the case law by the Constitutional Court on article 41 examples of this more pragmatic approach abound. Despite the suggestions offered by the doctrinal debate, the Constitutional Court has discarded textualism together with the temptation of addressing (or opposing) to the legislation precise regulatory strategies. Constitutional adjudication, indeed, is not expected to devise autonomous political programmes, but to test according to legal criteria the political choices enshrined in legislation. Under this dispassionate approach, article 41 expresses constitutive principles (rather than rules) whose balance the Court is called to test according to a series of standards of review.[132]

A feature common to all the Constitutional Court decisions is the systematic acknowledgment of the policy objectives inspiring legislation. Coherently with the open-textured nature of article 41, the passage on *utilità sociale* has been construed on a case-by-case basis by admitting any goal of economic regulation.[133] After having identified the political objectives, in a first handful of cases the Court restrains from any sort of scrutiny and declares that a step further would determine the infringement of the constitutional prerogatives of the legislative power.[134] Yet, in the majority of the cases these further steps have been undertaken by testing the

---

[130] The following approach is suggested in R. Bin, *Diritti e argomenti*, Milano, 1992.

[131] See G. Morbidelli, *Iniziativa economica privata*, in *Enciclopedia Giuridica Treccani*, XVII, p. 3; G. Bognetti, *La costituzione economica italiana*, pp. 43–44.

[132] G. Zagrebelsky, *Il diritto mite*, pp. 147–73.

[133] As a consequence, in the language and practice of constitutional adjudication *utilità sociale* originates a quite picturesque list of meanings including, *inter alia*, the protection of the currency and the real value of salaries (Corte Cost., sent. 8 July 1957, n. 103, in *GC*, p. 976), the protection of plants against diseases (Corte Cost., sent. 9 March 1967, n. 24, in *GC*, p. 191), the defence of the balance between demand and offer in the peculiar market of bread (Corte Cost., sent. 28 January 1991, n. 63, in *GC*, p. 450), the necessary defence of the Italian production of hard wheat (Corte Cost., sent. 15 February 1980, n. 20), the support to the production of glassware in Murano (Corte cost., ord. 21 July 1988, n. 859, in *GC*, p. 4070).

[134] A clear example of this deferential approach emerges in Corte Cost., sent. 13 April 1957, n. 50, in *GC*, p. 621.

adequacy of the legislative means in respect to the objectives. Nonetheless, in many cases the Court appears still lenient in respect to legislation. Such deferential approach, normally justified in terms of respect of the autonomy of political decision-making, consists in a generic assessment of the instrumentality of the legislation to the achievement of the political objective. By contrast, any sort of analysis of the impact of the measures at issue, on their effective aptitude to achieve the prefixed goals and on the level of protection of the constitutional interests affected is avoided.[135] It comes as no surprise that most of the decisions end up in dismissing constitutional complaints. Only in a few cases, finally, the Court has scrutinized the legislation according to a less restrictive measure test.[136] But even here, the results have been mostly favorable to the legislative.[137]

In conclusion, it does not seem that the Constitutional Court has complied with uniform standards of review in the scrutiny under article 41. Nor it seems that the Court has provided explanations for the adoption of such diverse tests. Nonetheless, constitutional adjudication in the field of economic regulation reveals a stable character due to the mostly deferential attitude by the Court. Certainly, the case law on article 41 could be criticized for not clarifying the criteria which justify the adoption of different standards of adjudication or for being in certain cases too sympathetic with the outcomes of the political decision-making. Yet, it would be incorrect to blame the Court for its substantial self-restraint. Such a profile appears absolutely consistent with the ideological premises of a constitution conceived for serving the objectives of economic and social cohesion. On this premise, judicial review of legislation cannot be expected to drive the political decision-making towards defined objectives through thick constitutional guidelines.[138] The role of constitutional adjudication, indeed, is at most to correct the

---

[135] The Constitutional Court has observed that 'La Corte [...] nei casi in cui le leggi apportino limitazioni ai diritti di libertà economica, ha certamente il potere di giudicare in merito all'utilità sociale alla quale la Costituzione condiziona la possibilità di incidere su quei diritti. Ma tale potere concerne solo gli aspetti logici del problema e cioè la rilevabilità di un intento legislativo di perseguire quel fine e la generica idoneità dei mezzi predisposti per raggiungerlo'. For other cases in which a similar test has been adopted, see Corte Cost., sent. 10 June 1969, n. 97, in *GC*, p. 1239; Corte Cost., sent. 14 April 1988, n. 446, in *GC*, p. 2049; Corte Cost., sent. 12 December 1990, n. 548, in *GC*, p. 3147.

[136] In some cases the Court has denied the possibility of employing a less restrictive measure test. In Corte Cost., sent. 6 June 2001, n. 190, in *GC*, p. 1462, for instance, it was stated: 'Il legislatore regionale avrebbe certo potuto avvalersi di altri mezzi [...] ma esula dai poteri di questa Corte contrastare con una propria diversa valutazione la scelta discrezionale del legislatore circa il mezzo più adatto per conseguire un fine, dovendosi arrestare questo tipo di scrutinio alla verifica che il mezzo prescelto non sia palesemente sproporzionato'.

[137] Corte Cost., sent. 8 July 1957, n. 103, in *GC*, p. 976; Corte Cost., sent. 15 June 1960, n. 38, in *GC*, p. 629; Corte Cost., sent. 5 July 1961, n. 55, in *GC*, p. 1069; Corte Cost., sent. 12 July 2000, n. 379, in *GC*, p. 2708. In other cases, the application of the least restrictive test has helped identify breaches of article 41: see Corte Cost., sent. 30 December 1958, n. 78, in *GC*, p. 979; Corte Cost., sent. 26 July 1993, n. 356, in *GC*, p. 2801.

[138] See the considerations by G. Zagrebelsky, *La Corte in-politica*, in *QC*, 2005, 2, pp. 273–82, supporting the idea of a Constitutional Court mere custodian of the *pactum societatis* and, for this reason, not as part of the competition among political actors.

outcomes of the political process with the result, most of the time, of re-enforcing the decision-making.[139] As a consequence, the Italian ECI performs well in emphasizing the achievement of political objectives according to the patterns of representative democracy. At the same time, a decision-making shaped largely on the basis of political responsibility diminishes the scope for substantive constitutional judicial review and disregards the systematic pursuit of economic efficiency.

Judicial Review Enforcing National Treatment

The principle of national treatment (NT) is probably the most central of the GATT disciplines since it reflects the constitutional commitment by the members to preserve international trade from protectionism and discrimination. Consequently, the domain of NT emerges as a fertile ground for studying the relationship between constitutional constraints and members' regulatory autonomy in the context of the GATT and for catching further distinctive elements of the ECI of the WTO.

The underlying rationale of NT is that GATT members, though retaining the power to govern trade, cannot apply regulatory or fiscal measures to protect their internal economies. Accordingly, NT obliges the members to ensure equality of competitive conditions for imported products in relation to domestic products by sanctioning formal and material discriminations.[140] Imported products, therefore, do not receive a specific (absolute) level of treatment. Under NT their protection is relative, consisting in the guarantee against members affording to them less favorable treatment than that accorded to their domestic counterparts.[141]

Traditionally, the discipline of NT is construed upon the dichotomy between prohibition and justification. As mentioned, the main normative content of NT is to prohibit formal and material discriminations against imported products (article III GATT). Yet, the ban is not so straightforward, since those discriminatory measures which respond to compelling policy objectives can be covered under a list of general exceptions (article XX GATT).

In applying NT, the WTO adjudicative bodies mostly comply with this rule-exception scheme. The detection of nationality discriminations follows an 'objective approach' aimed at testing whether the complained measure is detrimental to

---

[139] R. Bin, *Diritti e argomenti*, p. 161 has observed that in these cases 'si tratta di [. . .] opporre al legislatore più che la linea estrema di difesa dei diritti di libertà, quella ben più flessibile e spezzata della considerazione equilibrata di tutti gli interessi in gioco, per evitare, più che la lesione eccezionale dei valori fondamentali, lo strisciante sopruso degli interessi privilegiati su quelli più deboli, delle maggioranze sulle minoranze, della morale corrente sulle devianze o sulle innovazioni'.

[140] In respect to fiscal measures, the principle has been expressed by the AB in *Japan—Taxes on Alcoholic Beverages*, with the following words: 'Article III obliges Members of the WTO to provide equality of competitive conditions for imported products in relation to domestic products [. . .] Article III protects expectations not of any particular trade volume but rather of the equal competitive relationship between imported and domestic products' (Paragraph F).

[141] The distinction between absolute and relative standard of treatment is explained in F. Ortino, *From 'non-discrimination' to 'reasonableness': a paradigm shift in international economic law?*, Jean Monnet Working Paper 1/05, <http://www.jeanmonnetprogram.org/papers/05/050101.html>, pp. 6–7.

imported products.[142] As a rule, NT entails a preliminary scrutiny on the likeness of the products involved by the measure at issue in order to gauge the degree of their actual or potential competitive relationship. Under the objective approach, likeness is assessed in the marketplace through a careful factual investigation of a number of relevant criteria concerning the physical characteristics of products, their end-uses, consumers' tastes and habits, and cross-price elasticity.[143] Only if the resulting competitive relationship is significant, there is ground for a further assessment on the adverse treatment of imported products. Also in this regard the scrutiny is eminently factual. In determining whether imported products receive less favorable treatment than domestic products, no consideration of the policy objective pursued by the measure at hand is involved. At this stage, the focus of the adjudicative bodies is totally on how the measure impacts on imported and domestic products. Objective approach, therefore, implies for the GATT constitutional constraints a more intrusive role than that played by national constitutional principles. Unlike article 41 Cost., Article III GATT is interpreted as addressing the members with specific rules of conduct, without any concession to the language and the practice of reasonableness. As a consequence, the role of the adjudicative bodies also ends up being remarkably different from that of their national equivalents. National measures are indeed tested in the light of more stringent standards of review in which their impact is privileged over their form, their discriminatory effect over their political intent.

The distance between the GATT patterns of adjudication and the deferential approach by the national Constitutional Court can be appreciated also when it comes to the justification of protectionist measures. As said, article XX and its list of general exceptions are the last resort for members' measures adversely affecting imported products. Nevertheless, precisely because the exceptions may be particularly appealing to members for sheltering camouflaged protectionist regulations, the adjudicative bodies have construed article XX strictly with the purpose of avoiding its abuse.[144] At a first glance, this interpretation of article XX consists apparently in an obsessive emphasis on its text. Textualism, indeed, is employed for establishing the exhaustiveness of the list of legitimate policy objectives justifying the exceptions. Textualism, in addition, is used for claiming that the intensity

---

[142] The characteristics of the 'objective approach' are expounded in H. Horn, J. H. H. Weiler, *European Communities—Measures Affecting Asbestos and Asbestos-Containing Products*, in H. Horn, P. C. Mavroidis (eds.), *The WTO Case Law of 2001: The American Law Institute Reporters' Studies*, Cambridge, 2004, pp. 17–22.

[143] These criteria have been indicated for the first time in the Report of the Working Party on *Border Tax Adjustements*, BISD 18S/97, recital 18.

[144] In *Reformulated and Conventional Gasoline*, the AB expounded the strict scrutiny on the article XX exceptions stating: 'the chapeau is animated by the principle that while the exceptions of Article XX may be invoked as a matter of legal right, they should not be so applied as to frustrate or defeat the legal obligations of the holder of the right under the substantive rules of the *General Agreement*. If those exceptions are not to be abused or misused, in other words, the measures falling within the particular exceptions must be applied reasonably, with due regard both to the legal duties of the party claiming the exception and the legal rights of the other parties concerned'.

of the means-ends relationship differs depending upon the wording of the exception at issue.

Nonetheless, behind the rhetoric of interpretation, the adjudicative bodies have applied a quite stable standard of review of the measures under article XX. Accordingly, the legitimacy of the policy objective at hand is firstly ascertained. Also in this regard, the scrutiny is more rigorous than the domestic standards employed to review the *utilità sociale*. The formal and substantial legitimacy of the measure is assessed by testing, respectively, whether the measure falls under one of the article XX exceptions and whether there are real and scientifically grounded concerns motivating the adoption of a discriminatory measure.[145] Besides, the relationship between measure and policy objective is scrutinized. Here, despite the textual differences in the list of exceptions, the adjudicative bodies have derived from the chapeau of article XX a substantially uniform least trade-restrictive measure test.[146] As a consequence, the overall regime of NT permits the adoption of those of the discriminatory regulatory solutions which are genuinely inspired to legitimate policy objectives and which happen to have the least impact on trade. In the light of a similar regulatory principle, both the pursuit of certain non-trade objectives and their level of protection as established by the members remain unaffected.[147] Yet, the least restrictive measure standard endorsed by the GATT entails for national regulators a duty to privilege the most trade-friendly solutions, to detriment sometimes of other concurring interests which, under domestic constitutionalism, would deserve equivalent consideration.[148]

More sound jurisprudential solutions have been suggested for tackling the legitimacy shortcomings inherent in the 'objective approach'. The rule-exception scheme marking NT case law does indeed give the impression that in the GATT sphere a hierarchy of values exists between trade liberalization, considered as the main value and default rule, and the pursuit of non-trade objectives, treated as ancillary values and exceptions.[149] Conscious of the symbolic distance between

---

[145] F. Ortino, *From 'non-discrimination' to 'reasonableness'*, p. 34.

[146] See *Reformulated and Conventional Gasoline*, paragraph IV.

[147] For an example, see *European Communities—Measures Affecting* Asbestos *and* Asbestos-Containing Products (Appellate Body Report, WT/DS135/AB/R, 12 March 2001), where the measure of the 'controlled use' of asbestos-containing products suggested by Canada has not been considered as an available alternative to the complete ban in force since it did not guarantee the level of health protection defined by France. It must be observed that, by preferring to safeguard the level of protection established by the members, the GATT, unlike the EC, does not adopt a principle of equivalence between members' regulatory solutions and, as a result, accepts a considerable degree of market fragmentations.

[148] In respect to the endorsement by the GATT of least trade restrictive measures, F. Ortino, *From 'non-discrimination' to 'reasonableness'*, pp. 34–35, observes: 'an important issue in this type of inquiry deals with how costs are defined. In the light of their principal function, the main relevant cost is usually determined taking into account the level of trade- or investment-restrictiveness of the measure at hand [. . .] While the adverse effects on trade or investment flows may be the main relevant cost at issue under a cost effectiveness test, it is evident that other costs, incurred by both public and private parties, may be brought into equation [. . .]. Thus, the scope of the costs brought into the analysis over the necessity of a measure will influence the outcome of the analysis itself'.

[149] In this regard, G. de Búrca, J. Scott, *The Impact of the WTO on EU Decision-making*, in G. de Búrca, J. Scott (eds.), *The EU and the WTO: Legal and Constitutional Issues*, Oxford, 2001, p. 4, have

this approach and the more pluralistic one by domestic constitutionalism, many commentators have argued in favour of interpretations of NT that are more in tune with the value of political autonomy. These alternative methodologies do not advocate for a reversal of the regulatory strategies so far enforced, but rather a hermeneutic attitude that is more open to the instances and the legal reasoning purported in the domestic sphere. With these approaches, indeed, the policy objective of the measures at issue is taken into account already in the scrutiny on discrimination. More in detail, the 'effect and purpose' approach shares the tests on likeness and adverse effect undertaken under the objective approach. Yet, a finding of violation of article III would be conditioned to an additional requirement concerning the protectionist purpose of measure at hand. Quite similarly, the 'alternative comparator' approach suggests the policy objectives could be relevant in the test on the competitive relationship between the products at stake. Likeness, indeed, should not be assessed in the marketplace but in the light of the alternative comparator construed upon the legitimate policy objective of the measure under scrutiny. On this same basis, the test on adverse effect should also be carried out.[150]

Despite their remarkable doctrinal support,[151] these alternative methodologies have been mostly rejected in the adjudication.[152] Objective approach and textualism have been preferred as the most natural answers to the shift to legalism by WTO and as the most responsive instruments for facing the legitimacy concerns of the newly established adjudicative bodies.[153] As a consequence, also in this regard there are several elements of conflict between the WTO and Italian ECIs. Differently from the domestic approach to constitutional provisions, in the GATT the rhetoric of interpretation has mostly succeeded and it can be rightly addressed as a characteristic element of the WTO foundational stage. More frictions arise out of the relationship between constitutional constraints and regulatory autonomy. It has been shown that NT is currently interpreted as expressing thicker regulatory principles than article 41 Cost. This higher constraining potential stems from the standard of review employed by the adjudicative bodies. Both the stringent scrutiny inherent in the objective approach and the strict construction of the general exceptions appear as evident deviations from the deferential attitude marking

observed: 'the centrality and the strength of the MFN, non-discrimination and other rules on trade effectively consign all other important policies [...] to the status of exceptions which must be argued for within relatively strict constraints, rather than important competing or even co-equal policies in their own right'.

[150] On the 'effect and purpose' and 'alternative comparator' approaches see H. Horn, J.H.H. Weiler, *European Communities—Measures Affecting* Asbestos, pp. 22–26.

[151] H. Horn, J.H.H. Weiler, *European Communities—Measures Affecting* Asbestos, p. 30. See also H. Horn, P. C. Mavroidis, *Still Hazy After All these Years: the Interpretation of National Treatment in GATT/WTO Case Law on Tax Discrimination*, in *EJIL*, 2004, 15, p. 39.

[152] Only in few cases, such as *Malted Beverages* (Report of the Panel adopted on 19 June 1992, DS23/R—39S/206), the purpose inspiring the measure has been taken into account to deny the protectionist nature of the measure under scrutiny.

[153] A critical analysis of the implications of the different approaches to NT is proffered in H. Horn, J.H.H. Weiler, *European Communities—Measures Affecting Asbestos*, pp. 27–31.

the Constitutional Court case law. On this ground lays also the most strident of the frictions. As seen, GATT obligations and members' regulatory autonomy can be harmoniously accommodated. Yet, the prevalent conceptual approach adopted in the adjudication too often seems to impact with the democratic ethos of domestic constitutionalism. It comes as no surprise that this generates a considerable degree of constitutional tension.

Judicial Review Promoting Access to Market

In the EC, a constitutional discipline equivalent to article III:4 GATT is absent. The very text of the treaty is laconic in this regard: whereas rules on taxation are explicitly laid down in article 90 EC, trade regulation of goods is not addressed by any specific provision. Hence, it has been up to the Court of Justice to fill the gap. There were two available alternatives. First, the GATT regime could have been replicated by extending to trade regulation the NT discipline of article 90. Second, regulatory measures could have been brought under the obstacle-based regime provided by article 28 for quantitative restrictions. As widely known, the last alternative was opted for in order to pursue a more ambitious design of economic integration than that promoted in the GATT.[154]

Coherently with the objective of building a common market, the Court of Justice has furthered a constitutional strategy centered on the idea of access to market. Its interest, indeed, was not simply about ensuring equality of competitive conditions for imported and domestic products. The common market design required the Court to tackle also the obstacles to trade resulting from the fragmentations of the market determined by the existence of different and non-protectionist national regulatory regimes. The obstacle-based regime of article 28 EC seemed the most suitable to this goal and, in *Dassonville*,[155] the Court of Justice addressed it as the relevant provision in dealing with the regulatory measures concerning the trade of goods. In deviating from the GATT, the Court has developed an original constitutional discipline which, arguably, constitutes the most central of the strategies of supranational integration.

Differently from article III:4, article 28 stipulates an outright prohibition for member states to apply quantitative restrictions and measures having equivalent effect.[156] No space is left to the language of non discrimination and no immediate relevance is recognized to the possible policy objectives underlying the measures at hand.[157] Access to market needs to be promoted by targeting all those measures

---

[154] The rationale for equating regulatory measures and quantitative restrictions can be appreciated by considering that regulatory measures dictating the conditions for the manufacturing and marketing of products bar the access to the domestic market to imported products not complying with such requirements exactly like a zero quota. From a market access perspective, therefore, it is nugatory to distinguish between regulatory measures and quantitative restrictions.

[155] Case 8/74, *Procureur du Roi v. Benoit and Gustave Dassonville* [1974] ECR 837.

[156] In this article 28 replicates the article XI GATT regime of quantitative restrictions.

[157] Yet, in *Dassonville* the Court established that, in the absence of a common community discipline, member states could adopt reasonable measures to prevent unfair practices (recitals 6, 7).

which have the effect of hindering the streams of intra-Community commerce. Article 28, therefore, not only tackles measures containing protectionist biases, but catches also the obstacles to trade engendered by the regulatory fragmentations of the market.

Although shaped according to the language of article 28, the EC discipline of national regulatory measures involving discriminations of imported products largely mirrors its GATT equivalent. The prohibition-justification structure is replicated and also the standard of review adopted attains those same outcomes. Direct[158] and indirect[159] discriminations are therefore carefully detected and also justifications are narrowly construed. Member states, indeed, can save their discriminatory measures only if they show that these measures fulfill one of the specific exceptions provided by article 30 EC[160] and result are the least trade restrictive.[161]

As anticipated, the core of the EC strategy of economic integration consists in tackling the application of different national regulatory regimes even where there is not a protectionist bias.[162] In this regard, the interpretation of article 28 provided in *Dassonville* has been developed by the Court of Justice in order to limit the distorting effect on access to market by the regulatory measures which resist a pure NT test. In *Cassis de Dijon*,[163] the Court affirmed that member states retain the power to adopt rules on the production and marketing of goods which normally result in fragmentations of the market. But precisely for this reason, article 28 prohibits in principle their application to the imported products lawfully marketed in the exporting country.[164] Market fragmentations, indeed, can be tolerated only if the national measures fulfill certain mandatory requirements.[165] In the other cases, foreign rules on manufacturing and marketing have to be accepted as the most proportionate.[166]

---

[158] Case 154/85, *Commission v. Italy* [1987] ECR 2717; Case 4/75, *Rewe-Zentralfinanz v. Landwirtschaftskammer* [1975] ECR 843.

[159] Case 82/77, *Openbaar Ministerie v. Van Tiggele* [1978] ECR 25; Case 45/87, *Commission v. Ireland* [1988] ECR 4929.

[160] The Court of Justice has always considered the list of article 30 as closed. In this regard, see Case 177/83, *Kohl v. Ringelhan* [1984] ECR 3651 and Case 21/88, *Du Pont de Nemours Italiana SpA v. Unità Sanitaria Locale 2 di Carrara* [1990] ECR I-889.

[161] In the language of the treaty, the discriminatory measure must not amount to an 'arbitrary discrimination' or a 'disguised restriction on trade'. For an application of the least trade restrictive test see Case 124/81, *Commission v. United Kingdom* [1983] ECR 203; Case 272/80, *Frans-Nederlands Maatschappij voor Biologische Producten* [1981] ECR 3277.

[162] Such a broad scope for the article 28 prohibition can be explained also by considering the substantial paralysis of the EC program of positive harmonization under the Luxembourg accord.

[163] Case 120/78, *Rewe-Zentrale AG v. Bundesmonopolverwaltung für Branntwein* [1979] ECR 649.

[164] Recital 14.

[165] Recital 8. In this respect, the *Cassis* decision can be seen as developing the rule of reason inherent in the *Dassonville* formula.

[166] For applications of the *Cassis* formula see Case 788/79, *Italian State v. Gilli and Andres* [1980] ECR 2071; Case 193/80, *Commission v. Italy* [1981] ECR 3019; Case 317/92, *Commission v. Germany* [1994] ECR I-2039.

A similar regime, conventionally labeled as 'functional parallelism' or 'mutual recognition', critically departs from that of the GATT. According to the *Cassis* formula, foreign products have access to the domestic market even if manufactured according to rules which do not meet the domestic standards of protection. As a consequence, functional parallelism entails a shift from the usual standard of review based on the necessity test (least trade restrictive measure) to a more intrusive proportionality test which has the effect of questioning the level of protection autonomously decided by member states.[167]

As mentioned, the *Cassis* formula also contains derogation to this general discipline. In the cases national measures do satisfy mandatory requirements, their application is also accepted in respect to imported products. Nonetheless, these measures are also subject to stringent scrutiny. Although the open list of mandatory requirements makes it easier to prove their formal legitimacy,[168] the Court normally tests their substantial legitimacy by investigating the effective existence of the concerns claimed in their support by member states.[169] Besides, the relationship of the measures with the policy objectives is variously assessed in order to avoid arbitrary discriminations or disguised restrictions on trade. Behind the constant recourse to the indistinctly defined category of proportionality, the Court has employed all the available standards of review, shifting from suitability[170] to necessity[171] and, even, to proportionality.[172]

The strategy of harmonization endorsed by the Court of Justice in the application of article 28 does not stand isolated in the overall design of market building. In the EC treaty, the promotion of the access to market and the removal of regulatory fragmentations can be pursued also through instruments of positive harmonization.[173] For a long time article 94 EC has been the only legal basis for the

[167] Yet, the difference between the standard of review introduced by the *Cassis* formula and that normally employed in the GATT is questioned by J.H.H. Weiler, *Epilogue: Towards a Common Law of International Trade*, in J.H.H. Weiler (ed.), *The EU, The WTO and the NAFTA—Towards a Common Law of International Trade*, Oxford, 2000, p. 231, who has addressed functional parallelism as a 'banal doctrinal manifestation of the principle of necessity'. According to the Author, indeed, 'for a member state to insist on a specific technical standard even if a different standard is functionally parallel in achieving the desired result, is to have adopted a measure which is not least restrictive possible' (p. 221).

[168] The Court has indeed accepted under the umbrella of mandatory requirements a wide number of policy objectives such as environmental protection (Case 302/86, *Commission v. Denmark* [1988] ECR 4607), promotion of cinematographic works (Cases 60 & 61/84, *Cinéthèque v. Fédération Nationale des Cinémas Français* [1985] ECR 2605), and maintenance of press diversity (Case 368/95, *Vereinigte Familiapress Zeitungsverlags- und vertriebs GmbH v. Heinrich Bauer Verlag* [1997] ECR I-3689).

[169] See Case 178/84, *Commission v. Germany* [1987] ECR 1227, recital 42.

[170] See, for instance, the test adopted in *Commission v. Denmark* (recital 13), or in *Cinéthèque* (recital 24), where the proportionality requirement is accomplished by the mere adequacy of the measure at issue with the claimed policy objectives.

[171] A least trade restrictive test is adopted in *Commision v. Germany* (recitals 44, 45, 53), *Familiapress* (recital 34).

[172] Arguably, the domestic level of environmental protection is questioned in the solution given in *Commission v. Denmark* (recitals 20–22).

[173] J.H.H. Weiler, *Towards a Common Law*, pp. 214–15, argues that this is the most distinctive element between the EC and GATT strategies of economic integration.

approximation of national measures directly affecting the establishment or the functioning of the common market.[174] With this instrument, EC institutions have been empowered to remove the obstacles to trade through the enactment of measures for the harmonization of the national regulatory regimes. In this, arguably, the margins of trade regulation domestically constrained have been regained in a broader and different dimension.

Nevertheless, the characteristics of the EC and domestic regulatory devices differ in a number of crucial aspects. A first clear distinctive element concerns the effect of the regulatory measures. Unlike national legislation, the instruments of positive integration do not have direct effect. Article 94, indeed, confers on the EC institutions only the power to adopt directives which, even though detailed, need to be incorporated into pieces of national legislation. Besides, the procedures leading to the adoption of, respectively, legislative acts and directives are crucially different. Legislation as a product of democratic deliberation was argued above. Looking at the EC regulatory measures, this character is absolutely marginal. The procedure set out in article 94, by favouring through the unanimity voting the intergovernmental bargaining in the Council, leaves the European Parliament and, with it, the spaces for democratic deliberation in an unquestionably ancillary position.[175] Finally, the very reach of the regulatory powers conferred on EC decision-making markedly differs from that enjoyed by domestic legislation. Article 94, indeed, rather than entitling the adoption of whatever piece of economic legislation, has been devised to enact directives coupled with the strategies of negative market integration. By profiting from its monopoly on the legislative initiative, the Commission has endorsed through article 94 a selective program of measures strategically aimed at harmonizing the market fragmentations surviving the application of the *Cassis* formula.[176]

In conclusion, also the ECI of the EC, at least if considered from the perspective of market integration, reveals a number of distinctive elements from both the WTO and domestic ECIs. The most evident divergence emerges at institutional level and, namely, in the role played by the Court of Justice. Unlike the deferential approach by the Italian Constitutional Court and the textualist attitude by the WTO adjudicative bodies, the Court has not only shaped the nature of the EC legal framework in the light of the constitutional objective of economic integration, but has embraced teleology for determining the very contents of that objective. Consequently, also the balance between constitutional constraints and regulatory autonomy has received from the activism of the Court of Justice a remarkable thrust. In the light of the EC regulatory principles, indeed, the margins of political regulation on trade by member states are considerably curtailed.

---

[174] The legal basis provided by article 95 EC will be dealt below in section III.B.
[175] Consider also that article 94 provides for the consultation of the European Parliament.
[176] Emblematic of this attitude is the constitutional strategy of regulation devised by the Commission in the Communication of 3 October 1980 [1980] OJ C256/2.

Whereas the regime of discriminatory regulations replicates the GATT standard, it is in the area of indistinctly applicable rules that the Court of Justice has promoted its more intrusive interventions by both constantly broadening the reach of article 28[177] and questioning, in some cases, the level of protection of non-trade objectives decided on a domestic level. It may be argued that, in the EC, regulatory autonomy is regained in the supranational sphere through the instruments of positive harmonization. But, as explained, also in this respect regulatory autonomy and, notably, its promise of political participation appear sacrificed by the thickness of constitutional strategies aimed at market efficiency and by the substantial leadership of the institutions embodying the community interest.

B. Convergent Elements

(i) Accommodating Utilità Sociale and Market Efficiency

The successful development of the common market undertaking has strongly influenced the evolution and general understanding of Italian ECI. To many commentators, also in the domestic sphere the commitment to market building and economic efficiency, rather than remaining an option for the political circuit, has rapidly achieved constitutional rank.[178]

Arguably, two interlinked key factors have contributed to this new economic constitutional sensitivity. The constitutionalization of the EC and, notably, the success of the direct effect and supremacy doctrines have played a major role in the process of re-definition of the Italian ECI. Because of their supposedly higher constitutional position, EC regulatory principles appear either as superseding[179] or as imparting a more definite meaning to the feeble substantive guidelines originally expressed by article 41 Cost.[180] Besides, the introduction of the EC principles of competition law within the national legislation on anti-trust is commonly considered as emblematic of the absorption of the culture of market within the Italian ECI.[181] In this regard, article 41 comes out as the crucial intersection between the domestic and supranational spheres. By stipulating that the anti-trust regime must be considered as an implementation of article 41[182] and by establishing that the domestic rules on competition law are to be interpreted in the light of the relevant

---

[177] The invasiveness of the article 28 jurisprudence on the jurisdiction of the member states must be considered also in the light of the strict connection between negative and positive harmonization. See below section III.B.

[178] The influence of EU regulatory principles on the interpretation of the Italian economic constitution is described G. Amato, *Il mercato nella costituzione*, p. 16.

[179] N. Irti, *L'ordine giuridico del mercato*, pp. 95–103 argues that article 41.3 Cost., because of the EC economic principles, would have lost legal effect.

[180] G. Bognetti, *La costituzione economica italiana*, pp. 36–49, stresses the necessity to interpret the economic provisions of the Italian Constitution more coherently with the principles developed in the EC sphere.

[181] Legge 10 Ottobre 1990, n. 287, *Norme per la tutela della concorrenza e del mercato*, in *Gazzetta Ufficiale*, 13 Ottobre 1990, n. 240.   [182] Article 1, paragraph 1.

EC principles,[183] this statute inevitably creates a sense of a progressive assimilation of the Italian ECI by that of the EU.[184]

Such an approach, biased as it is by a superficial understanding of the supremacy doctrine,[185] suggests that an incorporation doctrine of sort regulates the relationship between the EU and the Italian ECIs.[186] Accordingly, the constitutionalization of the EU would have spillover effects in the domestic sphere of economic regulation and, at the end, would imply a comprehensive overhaul of the national constitutional framework. Hence, imbued with the economic spirit of supranational constitutionalism both the substantive contents and structural aspects of the Italian ECI would be put under discussion. By incorporating in the domestic sphere the EC regulatory principles, the Italian ECI would be certainly endowed with more precise constitutional guidelines for regulation and adjudication. By contrast, the open-ended nature of the constitution as well as the role of constitutive principles played so far by its provisions would be impaired. The success of supranational constitutionalism, therefore, would affect from the roots the domestic legal framework and, eventually, would reshape the very nature of domestic constitutionalism.

The most recent outcomes in the constitutional adjudication under article 41 are a useful standpoint for assessing whether such modifications are effectively occurring and to what extent the Italian ECI converges towards that of the EU. At a first glance, also in the case law of the Constitutional Court the influence of the economic principles preached by the EU is unequivocal. The decisions on the regulatory regime of TV broadcasting are eloquent in this regard. Traditionally, the Italian legislation on TV broadcasting has been devised in order to guarantee pluralism of information. Correctly perceiving that in this delicate economic field a private monopoly is a serious threat to the quality of the democratic debate, the first pieces of legislation reserved for a single public economic actor the right to impart information on a national basis.[187] By contrast, the TV broadcasting market was opened to private actors only on a local level. Such a regime has lasted until the late 1980s, supported by the Constitutional Court which, in line with its deferential approach towards legislation, justified the different treatment between national and local markets on the ground of their technological disparities and

---

[183] Article 1, paragraph 4.

[184] Article 41 has therefore been susceptible to being interpreted consistently with the principles of fair competition, as already suggested by F. Galgano, *Commento all'art. 41*, p. 11, and G. Morbidelli, *Iniziativa economica privata*, p. 6.

[185] The supremacy doctrine, indeed, is arbitrarily considered as administering the relationship between the EU and the domestic constitutional spheres rather than as the criterion to solve conflicts between EU and national rules. See below section IV.

[186] This approach seems at the core of the considerations by S. Cassese, *La nuova costituzione economica*, pp. 287–93.

[187] This is one of the sectors where article 43 Cost., the constitutional provision allowing for the taking of public firms in the general interest, has been applied.

their different implications for the national political sphere.[188] Therefore, in the original spirit of the legislation on TV broadcasting, the relationship between pluralism and market freedom is one of antagonism.

In the early 1990s a comprehensive reform allowed private economic actors entitled by governmental concession to broadcast on a national level. According to the new legislation, the Constitutional Court revised the constitutional guidelines for the information market. Quite predictably, in the new interpretation of article 41 market competition and freedom of information cease to be perceived as clashing values. On the opposite, market competition, though under the guise of a system of governmental concession, starts to be understood as serving the pluralism of information.[189] In a later judgment, the Court apparently even turns to brave judicial activism in enforcing against legislation the principles of free market and freedom of expression. Invested by claims brought by economic actors excluded from the governmental system of concessions,[190] the Court has quashed the legislative limits to concentration as inappropriate for guaranteeing sufficient standards of media pluralism.[191] Thus, also the outcomes of constitutional adjudication seem to witness a clear move by the domestic ECI towards the typical substantive contents of market building. And, of course, it is difficult to deny that the principles which often inspire domestic regulation and adjudication evoke the regulatory strategies devised in the EU sphere.

Nevertheless, the same decisions by the Constitutional Court also reveal deep traits of continuity with the distinctive elements of the Italian ECI. To a large extent, the shift towards the principles of an open market economy ensues from a political and cultural change occurred in the legislative. On a closer inspection, the Constitutional Court has not modified its standards of adjudication on economic legislation. The discovery of free competition as a constitutional objective, for instance, has plainly followed the usual pattern of adjudication whereby *utilità sociale* consists in the political objective pursued by the legislative act under scrutiny. The traditional standards of review are respected even when the Court redefines the limits to concentrations in the TV broadcasting market. In this decision, the Court does not second-guess the political choices of the legislative in the light of constitutional guidelines derived from article 41. More cautiously, the Court employs a scrutiny based on the comparison between the limits on concentration adopted in the TV broadcasting market with the more severe limits existing in the comparable press market. It is only by drawing upon these disparities that the

---

[188] This emerges clearly in Corte Cost., sent. 21 July 1981, n. 148, in *GC*, p. 1379, where the Court affirms: 'da tutto quanto testè ricordato emerge pertanto la consolidata opinione della Corte che il servizio pubblico essenziale di radioteletrasmissione, su scala nazionale, di preminente interesse generale, può essere riservato allo Stato in vista del fine di utilità generale costituito dalla necessità di evitare l'accentramento dell'emittenza radiotelevisiva in monopolio od oligopolio privato'.

[189] Emblematical of this shift is Corte Cost., sent. 24 March 1993, n. 112, in *GC*, p. 939.

[190] Of course, through the preliminary ruling procedure.

[191] Corte Cost., sent. 5 December 1994, n. 420, in *GC*, p. 3716.

Court decides to strike down the least stringent rules on TV broadcasting. As a consequence, it seems incorrect to conclude that the domestic ECI overlaps completely with that of the EU. More appropriately it could be argued that the domestic legal framework can also serve the promotion of efficiency-driven regulatory strategies devised by legislation. But in this, the balance between constitutional constraints and political decision-making and, more broadly, the nature of the legal framework remain unaffected.

A further ground of convergence between the EU and Italian ECIs concerns the political decision-making process. Whereas the pivotal role of Parliament as the privileged seat of representative democracy is constantly celebrated in the constitutional rhetoric, there are clear signs that a large chunk of rule-making powers is progressively shifting to the Government.[192] As in other industrialized democracies and in the EU,[193] legislation is increasingly conceived as a source of rules which necessitate further articulation by additional instruments of delegated legislation or by subordinate regulations.[194] Such a process, determined by the diminishing capacity of the Parliament to integrate through the traditional channels of representative democracy the plurality of interests emerging in society,[195] accentuates the Government as the most apt institution in dealing with social demands of regulation.[196] The broader sources of expertise of the executive as well as its capacity to negotiate directly with social and territorial actors are increasingly addressed as justifications for its predominance and for suggesting reforms of the institutional architecture more responsive to this modified reality. Such changes, although tempered by parliamentary control on the processes of delegation,[197] radically questions the Italian ECI from its foundations. As seen, representative democracy and its aptitude for political integration are distinctive elements of a constitutional model aimed at the pursuit of economic and social cohesion. Hence, the constant ascent of the Government rule-making powers is in perspective a subversive element which cannot be ignored.

[192] Eloquent in this respect the figures published in Camera dei Deputati, *Osservatorio sulla legislazione. Rapporto 2004–2005 sullo stato della legislazione*, 11 luglio 2005, <http://testo.camera.it/files/servizi_cittadini/Rapporto_2004_5.pdf>, p. 293.

[193] S. Smismans, *Functional Participation in EU Delegated Regulation: Lessons from the United States at the EU's 'Constitutional Moment'*, in *IJGLS*, 2005, 12, 2, p. 599.

[194] The Constitution confers to the Government primary rule-making powers in the form *decreto legislativo* (art. 76) and *decreto-legge* (art. 77), and secondary rule-making powers in the form of subordinate regulations (*regolamento*, art. 117).

[195] F. Cortese, M. Dani, F. Palermo, *Back to Government? The Pluralistic Deficit in the Legislation, Administration and before the Courts*, in *IJGLS*, 12, 2, p. 409.

[196] A comprehensive analysis of the confused evolution of the Italian system of sources of law and, notably, of the increasing role played by the Government in the decision-making is provided in the essays contained in P. Caretti, A. Ruggeri (eds.), *Le deleghe legislative. Riflessioni sulla recente esperienza normative e giurisprudenziale*, Milano, 2003.

[197] On the role of the Parliament in respect to the implementation of delegated legislation, see G. Tarli Barbieri, *La grande espansione della delegazione legislativa*, in P. Caretti, A. Ruggeri, *Le deleghe legislative*, pp. 78–84.

In conclusion, the most visible element of convergence by the domestic ECI towards the EU consists in the pursuit by legislation of objectives of market efficiency. Despite this convergent move, the balance between constitutional constraints and legislation and, more broadly, the nature of domestic legal framework have remained unaffected. Deeper changes are occurring instead in political decision-making and in the channels employed to represent and govern the economic and social interests. The privileged role of legislation (together with the centrality of representative democracy) is being challenged by sources of law stemming from technocratic or neo-corporatist decision-making procedures hinging upon the apparatus of the executive. The stratification of the Italian ECI, therefore, is being enriched by a layer of convergence towards some of the distinctive elements of the ECI of the EU. Not only the substantive principles of market efficiency are being incorporated in the strategies of political regulation, but also some patterns of governance typical of the administrative state are mirrored. Yet, significant elements of distinction prevent convergence from resulting in assimilation. Both the incorporation of market efficiency objectives and the re-formulation of decision-making develop in a constitutional framework in which there are no precise constitutional strategies to pursue but, more modestly, constitutive principles to respect in order to safeguard the value of democratic pluralism.

(ii) Accommodating National Treatment and Market Efficiency

Arguably, also in the ECI of the WTO there are significant aspects witnessing a convergence towards the ECI of the EU. Whereas in the domestic sphere the most evident similarity concerns the teleology of economic regulation (incorporation of the objective of market efficiency in the political decision-making and, *per relationem*, in constitutional adjudication), in the WTO the analogies emerge directly in the contents and language of the regulatory strategies experimented within the common market. Although the WTO substantially upholds and unfolds the design of economic integration inherent in the GATT, fragmentations of the marketplace determined by indistinctly applicable rules have become a matter of concern also in international trade relations. On these grounds, at least to a certain extent, the ECI of the WTO can be seen as converging towards the distinctive elements of the ECI of the EU.

The clearest positions regarding market fragmentations arise out of the SPS and TBT agreements. Such agreements stand in the backdrop of the general exceptions provided by article XX GATT. SPS deals with the protection of human, animal or plant life or health in the field of sanitary and phytosanitary measures. Likewise, TBT, in dealing with technical regulations and standards concerning products and methods of productions, covers a broader range of policy objectives concerning, *inter alia*, national security requirements, prevention of deceptive practices, protection of human health or safety, animal or plant life or health, environment. In providing more detailed disciplines in these particularly problematic areas, these agreements aim at improving the members' standards of protection and, at the same time, at minimizing the negative impact of members' measures on trade.[198] The regulatory principles introduced by both the agreements in order to accomplish this twofold objective have nurtured the idea of a critical paradigm shift.[199] SPS and TBT, indeed, launch explicitly in the WTO sphere the language of reasonableness and harmonization and, meanwhile, downplay the traditional antidiscrimination ethos of the GATT.

As said, the epicentre of this convergent move is located in the indistinctly applicable measures interfering with the stream of commerce. In this regard, SPS and TBT introduce an absolute standard of treatment for imported products by stipulating the principle that members' measures must not be more trade-restrictive than necessary to fulfill their legitimate objectives.[200] Thus, an obstacle-based test enters the stage and even the language of equivalence (as synonym of mutual recognition and functional parallelism) finds its way into the realm of international trade.[201] Nevertheless, the major challenge to the GATT discrimination-based orthodoxy consists in complementing these regulatory principles with forms of positive integration. In both the agreements, the standards devised by competent international agencies are recognized as fulfilling the necessity requirements and, therefore, as complying with the GATT general obligations.[202] Hence, in adopting their measures, members are expected to rely on international standards,[203] even though they retain the power to decide autonomously the level of protection. Provided that their assessment is genuinely grounded on scientific evidence[204] and respects stringent requirements of necessity,[205] members are still entitled to establish higher standards of protection. Eventually, in SPS and TBT the NT matrix is superseded by a new science- and efficiency-driven legal frame. The most visible example of this irruption can be appreciated in the incorporation of the international standards in their regulatory measures by members. Here, it may be argued the bias of science on regulatory autonomy is internal. Quite similarly to the EC positive harmonization,[206] the political decision-making circuit

---

[198] See the preambles of both the treaties.

[199] See, for instance, H. Horn, J.H.H. Weiler, *European Communities—Trade Description of Sardines:* Textualism and its Discontents, in H. Horn, P.C. Mavroidis (eds.), *The WTO Case Law of 2002: The American Law Institute Reporters' Studies,* Cambridge, 2003. The shift has been emphasized in the first SPS decision *EC Measures Concerning Meat and Meat Products (Hormones),* Report of the Panel, WT/DS26/R/USA, 18 August 1997, recitals 8.39–8.41.

[200] Article 2.2 SPS, article 2.2 TBT.   [201] Article 4 SPS, article 2.7 TBT.

[202] See article 3.2 SPS and 2.5 TBT, where a presumption of consistency with, respectively, the SPS and TBT agreement and, in both cases, the GATT assists the measures conforming to the international standards.   [203] Article 3.1 SPS and 2.4 TBT.

[204] In the case of SPS, see article 3.3 and 5. In the TBT, see article 2.4 providing that members can depart from the international standards when these are ineffective or inappropriate means for fulfilling the legitimate objectives pursued.

[205] This is particularly evident in the SPS agreement. Whereas a classic least restrictive measure test is encapsulated in articles 5.4 and 5.6, article 5.5 requires the members departing from the international standards to respect also a certain degree of consistency in the levels of protection afforded in different situations. The issue of consistency is crucial in the *Hormones* case (See Panel report, recital 8.174; AB report, WT/DS48/AB/R, 16 January 1998, recitals 214–45).

[206] See below in the next sub-section.

is *de facto* pre-empted by sources of (soft) law stemming from institutions and procedures formally structured on an intergovernmental basis but substantially reflecting the technocratic paradigm.[207] In other cases, namely when the level of protection decided by members deviates from the international standard, science acts as an external constraint to regulatory autonomy. Here, political decision-making still enjoys important leeway of discretion in deciding among the several scientific options submitted by experts to regulators.[208] Nonetheless, the genuine pursuit of a higher level of protection is rigorously scrutinized in the light of constitutional yardsticks requiring scientifically grounded justifications.[209]

Also in the case of the WTO, it would be misleading to interpret the elements so far described as symptoms of a broader assimilation by the ECI of the EU. Beside unequivocal traits of convergence, the ECI of the WTO reveals a substantial continuity with its own distinctive elements. It is not just a matter concerning the teleology and nature of the legal framework, which assist without noticeable upgrading the newly introduced regulatory strategies. A complete analysis of the SPS and TBT agreements, indeed, shows that not only the language and the practice of NT have not been completely abandoned,[210] but that even the shift to reasonableness can hardly be considered revolutionary.[211] In defining the principle of equivalence, indeed, both the SPS and TBT provide only 'lighter versions' of functional parallelism. Here, unlike in the *Cassis* test, imported products are not admitted as merely complying with the parallel rules of the exporting country. The acceptance of other members' measures as equivalent is subject to a more stringent requirement consisting in the objective proof that the level of protection established by the exporting country meets the domestic standards.[212] Therefore, since the SPS and TBT

---

[207] See article 3.4 SPS and 2.6 TBT, where the members are expected 'to play a full part, within the limit of their resources, in the preparation of the appropriate international standardizing bodies of international standards for products . . . '. The issue of what can be correctly considered as an international standard is dealt in the *Sardines* case (*EC Measures—Trade Description of Sardines*, Report of the Appellate Body, WT/DS231/AB/R, 26 September 2002). Here, on the basis of the explanatory note to Annex 1.2 of the TBT agreement, it was found that, as a rule, standards are adopted by consensus, though also documents not adopted by consensus can be considered as such (recital 222).

[208] Important in this regard what the AB stated in *Hormones*: 'we do not believe that a risk assessment has to come to a monolithic conclusion that coincides with the scientific conclusion or view implicit in the SPS measure. The risk assessment could set out both the prevailing view representing the 'mainstream' of scientific opinion, as well as the opinions of scientists taking a divergent view. Article 5.1 does not require that the risk assessment must necessarily embody only the view of a majority of the relevant scientific community . . . ' (recital 194).

[209] The Panel in *Hormones* declared that the SPS obligation to base the measures on a risk assessment should have been interpreted both in procedural and substantive terms (recitals 8.114 and 8.117). This approach was somehow downplayed by the AB which established that the SPS agreement required only a substantive 'objective relationship' between the measure and the risk assessment (recital 189).

[210] See article 2.3 SPS and article 2.1 TBT.

[211] F. Ortino, *From 'non-discrimination' to 'reasonableness'*, p. 49, observes that 'despite the apparent widespread belief that the two norms under consideration—NT and reasonableness—represent two completely different legal paradigms, it is argued here that the overlap between non-discrimination and reasonableness is quite broad and may even be total. This is especially true with regard to the level of intrusiveness into national regulatory prerogatives of the two instruments at hand'.

[212] See article 4 SPS, article 2.7 TBT.

obligations do not affect the level of risk decided by members,[213] the WTO constitutional strategy of negative harmonization does not promote the same degree of integration reached by the common market. In the choice between economic interpenetration and safeguard of the levels of protection established by members, the WTO continues to opt for the latter with the result of confirming, notwithstanding the 'revolutionary' turn into reasonableness, the GATT approach to indistinctly applicable rules and market fragmentations.[214]

Elements of continuity can be identified also in the application of the GATT provisions. Also in this regard, the regulatory strategy underpinning the constitution of the common market has not been replicated by the WTO adjudicative bodies. The adoption of an obstacle-based approach *à la Dassonville* in article XI has been prevented by the strict textual margins of article III:4 and the Note Ad article III.[215] Hints of a more determined attitude towards the fragmentations of the market have emerged in the administration of the general exceptions by the adjudicative bodies. In *Korean Beef*,[216] the Appellate Body seemed to modify the consolidated interpretation of article XX consisting in the application of a least restrictive measure test. A more sophisticated 'weighing and balancing test' was experimented evoking a shift in the standard of review from necessity to proportionality.[217] Such an outcome has, however, been denied in *Asbestos*. Here, the same 'weighing and balancing' test turned out in the classic application of the necessity test, without any alteration of the level of protection established by the defendant state.[218]

In sum, it may be argued also for the WTO that its ECI is enriched by a layer of convergence towards the ECI of the EU. The principles of reasonableness and equivalence, though with peculiar characteristics, have become part of the WTO

---

[213] M. Matsushita, T. J. Schoenbaum, P.C. Mavroidis, *The World Trade Organization—Law, Practice, and Policy*, 2002, Oxford, p. 496.

[214] As mentioned in section III.A.(ii) this point is controversial (see above n. 167). In maintaining the validity of the distinction—only WTO equivalence seems to me as conforming with a pure necessity or least trade-restrictive test, while EC mutual recognition reflects a proportionality test in so far as it questions the level of protection of the importing state—it can be observed with F. Ortino, *From 'non-discrimination' to 'reasonableness'*, p. 43, that the determination of the level of protection of a measure is often a difficult task. As a consequence, it can be made the case of substantial modifications of the level of protection under the guise of the application of the necessity test.

[215] In *Asbestos*, Canada argued that the EC measure banning the importation of asbestos and asbestos containing products should have been scrutinized according to the obstacle-based regime of quantitative restrictions (article XI GATT). Quite predictably, on the basis of the Note Ad article III this argument was rejected by the AB. Nevertheless, a different and potentially ground-breaking approach seems to emerge under the GATS where the AB considered a domestic regulation banning the remote supply of gambling services as a *per se* prohibited market access restriction 'in the form of numerical quotas'. See Appellate Body Report on *US—Measures Affecting the Cross-Border Supply of Gambling and Betting Services*, WT/DS285/AB/R, 7 April 2005.

[216] *Korean Beef*, Report of the Appellate Body, WT/DS161/AB/R, 11 December 2000.

[217] Although camouflaged with the language of respect of the level for protection decided by the member, the AB obliged Korea to adopt alternative measures whose performances in achieving the policy objective of article XX(d) were arguably inferior to those of the measure under scrutiny (see recitals 178–179).   [218] See *Asbestos*, recitals 168, 172 and 174.

vocabulary and, in the perspective of legitimacy, they smoothen the symbolic frictions encountered in the analysis of the NT paradigm. Moreover, positive integration, though not vested with an institutional architecture and a political emphasis comparable to that of the EC, constitutes a crucial upgrading of the regulatory strategies and a further important step in the attainment of full constitutional status by the WTO.[219] Differently from the common market experience, these new elements have been only marginally devised in the adjudication. Convergence, indeed, results mostly from innovations in the treaties and, predictably, is simply acknowledged by the diligent adjudicative bodies.[220] The regulatory strategies of the WTO, therefore, and, underneath them, the most significant traits of its ECI appear as firmly belonging to the community of its members, with scarce chances of evolving autonomously within the institutional framework established by the treaties.

(iii) Re-Formulating Access to Market in the Light of National Treatment and Utilità Sociale

Compared with the ECIs previously dealt with, the EU appears as the constitutional sphere which is experiencing the deepest evolution as well as the most incisive convergence towards both the national and WTO constitutional tenets.[221]

The clearest ground of convergence consists in the expansion of the constitutional objectives and, notably, in their emancipation from the almost exclusive paradigm of market integration. It has been noted above that the ambition of widening its substantive domain is inbuilt in the original design of market building. Moreover, it has been stressed that in the EC the policy externalities of economic integration have been profited from in order to stretch the reach of the competences expressly attributed by the treaties. Yet, precisely because of this spillover evolution, the approach by the EC to certain non-economic—or, at least, non-immediately economic—constitutional objectives has been characterized by the filter of market integration.

In this regard, a remarkable convergent move has occurred ever since the entry into force of the Single European Act (SEA). With this treaty, a number of policy areas included in the process of supranational integration on the basis of far reaching interpretations of articles 94 and 308 EC have found autonomous discipline and enriched the list of the EC tasks. Yet, the most incisive changes have been brought about by the treaty of Maastricht. Here, the challenge to the consolidated

---

[219] At least in respect to the requirements of our definition. See above section II.

[220] In this regard, a consolidated distinctive element in the ECI of the WTO consists in the Appellate Body hermeneutic preference for textualism. Criticism, motivated by the legitimacy shortcomings of a similar approach, is expressed in this respect by H. Horn, J.H.H. Weiler, *Textualism and its Discontents.*

[221] This is mostly due to the several amendments to the treaties ever since the Single European Act. See B. de Witte, *The Closest Thing to a Constitutional Conversation in Europe: The Semi-Permanent Treaty Revision Process,* in P. Beaumont, C. Lyons and N. Walker (eds.), *Convergence and Divergence in European Public Law,* p. 39.

pattern of evolution of the EC has been twofold. Not only the introduction of the pillar structure has utterly subverted the incremental expansion through the community method, but, even within the EC, the newly established constitutional objectives have been conceived of as fully-fledged goals and policies rather than mere side-effects of market building. Economic integration, therefore, has ceased to be considered as the sole mean to promote economic and social progress, since further constitutional objectives and legal bases converging towards that same horizon were introduced.[222] Hence, the overall economic and social profile of the EC has undergone profound reconsideration.[223] By acknowledging that there are several elements and policy initiatives which concur in producing economic and social welfare, the exclusiveness of the market integration paradigm has been questioned. Although Maastricht has not overturned the original commitment to open economy and free competition,[224] the overall jurisdiction of the EU has become closer to that of the member states and to their commitment to economic and social cohesion, with the result of blurring the EC original functional nature.

In this process, elements of convergence with the ECI of the WTO can also be identified. On a closer inspection, the emancipation of economic and social cohesion from the market integration filter permits a more genuine approach to the regulation of the market itself. Relieved of the stress of its more distant ramifications, the regulation of the market, similarly to the WTO commitment to free trade, has returned to its core business, leaving to other and more attuned legal bases and procedures (as, in the international sphere, to more competent international agencies) the task of developing the respective policies.[225]

Nevertheless, also in the case of the EU, convergence is limited by significant aspects of continuity with the distinctive elements of the ECI. The EU approach to constitutional objectives and, notably, the intersection between the protection of fundamental rights and the distribution of powers between the EU and member states are clear examples in this regard. Surely, fundamental rights protection can be advocated as an example of the increasing convergence and even of the

---

[222] As usual, article 2 EC is emblematic in capturing this evolution when it states that the general objectives of the Community will be promoted 'by establishing a common market *and* an economic and monetary union *and* by implementing common policies or activities referred to in Articles 3 and 4' (italics added).

[223] This trend has been strengthened by the Treaty of Amsterdam in which more social objectives and policies have been introduced.

[224] See article 4 EC which stipulates 'for the purposes set out in article 2, the activities of the member States and the Community shall include [...] the adoption of an economic policy which is based on the close coordination of Member States' economic policies, on the internal market and on the definition of common objectives, and *conducted in accordance with the principle of an open market economy with free competition*' (italics added).

[225] It must be stressed that the most recent policies have been equipped with patterns of governance partially or totally alternative to the traditional 'community method' in order to graduate the level of intensity of integration and to benefit from the involvement of different economic and social actors. See J. Scott, D.M. Trubek, *Mind the Gap: Law and New Approaches to Governance in the European Union*, in *ELJ*, 2002, 8, 1, p. 1.

assimilation of the EU by domestic constitutionalism.[226] Such a position is largely acceptable in so far as it refers to the increasing convergence and compatibility between the axiological assumptions of both the EU and member states. It is indeed a trite to address the upsurge of sensibility for fundamental rights in the supranational sphere culminating in the adoption of article 6 EU and, later, in the Charter of Nice as well as to remember that the Court of Justice has developed a considerable jurisprudence in this regard in the attempt to silence the perplexities expressed by some Constitutional Courts in respect to the EU standards of fundamental rights protection.[227] Yet, it seems incorrect to identify in these elements a major change in the EU constitutional nature and, namely, to argue that the objective of fundamental rights protection has replaced the original commitment to market efficiency with a domestic-like attitude towards economic and social cohesion. Despite the abundant doses of rhetoric, it may be contended that the interpretation of article 6 and the contents of the Charter of Nice do not depart from the traditional understanding of the relationship between fundamental rights and EU competences as proffered by the Court of Justice in the *Opinion 2/94* on the accession by the EU to the ECHR.[228] Here, the Court defended a consolidated selective approach whereby fundamental rights do not influence the allocation of powers between the EU and member states.[229] As a consequence, the Court observed that fundamental rights could not be indiscriminately elevated to the level of objectives for the EU decision-making. In the EU sphere, fundamental rights play the defensive function of external limits to the exercise of EU powers. Therefore, only if coincident with the EU constitutional objectives they can be considered as sources of positive obligations for the EU institutions.[230] A similar view is endorsed also by the Charter of Nice in which a list of rights absolutely coherent with the tenets of national welfare state is accompanied by provisions such as articles 51.2 and 52.2 which totally exclude revolutionary consequence in this regard.[231] As a consequence, the functional commitment by the EU, though profoundly revisited in the light of the objective of economic and social cohesion,

---

[226] A. Manzella, *Dal mercato ai diritti*, in A. Manzella, P. Melograni, E. Paciotti, S. Rodotà (eds.), *Riscrivere i diritti in Europa*, 2001, Bologna, p. 29 and S. Rodotà, *La Carta come atto politico e come documento giuridico, ibid.*, p. 57.

[227] On this regard see the essays contained in R. Toniatti (ed.), *Diritto, diritti, giurisdizione—La Carta dei diritti fondamentali dell'Unione Europea*, Padova, 2002. See also F. Palermo, *La forma di stato dell'Unione Europea*, pp. 85–99.

[228] *Accession of the European Community to the European Convention for the Protection of Human Rights and Fundamental Freedoms*, Opinion 2/94, [1996] ECR I-1759.

[229] See recital 27 of the Opinion where the Court states 'no treaty provision confers on the Community institutions any general power to enact rules on human rights'.

[230] O. de Schutter, *The Implementation of the EU Charter of Fundamental Rights through the Open Method of Coordination*, Jean Monnet Working Paper 7/04, http://www.jeanmonnetprogram.org/papers/04/040701.html, pp. 4–5.

[231] Article 51.2 stresses that no provision of the Charter modifies the framework of the EU competences. Article 52.2 stipulates that the protection of the rights already established in the treaties is not affected by the Charter.

does not match completely with the domestic benchmark. As witnessed by the characters of fundamental rights protection, the EU approach is still partial, entwined as it is with the attributions of powers and regulatory strategies which constitute the very backbone of the EU legal framework.

The strategies of market integration may be considered as a further ground where the ECI of the EU converges towards the domestic and WTO benchmarks. In this regard, it may be argued that the discipline of NT has played as a model for a general relaxation of the constitutional constraints of article 28 and, as a consequence, for a more respectful attitude vis-à-vis the regulatory autonomy of member states. As mentioned above, the *Dassonville* and *Cassis* formulas proved to be far-reaching in catching all trade-related national regulatory measures. Under their application, not only obstacles to the stream of commerce were targeted but, more broadly, all measures potentially restricting the volume of trade were in principle considered as triggering article 28. A similar approach, largely determined by a certain conceptual confusion between access to market and economic freedom, revealed a number of regulatory as well as institutional shortcomings. Considering both the intrusiveness of the scrutiny of the Court of Justice and its implications in terms of positive harmonization, concern was expressed particularly for the impact of article 28 on the distribution of competences between the EC and the member states.[232] An attempt to redress this potentially disruptive situation was made in *Keck*.[233] In this pronouncement the Court employed a more selective standard of review of national regulatory measures in order to target the real obstacles to trade and, thus, to promote effectively the access to market of foreign products. According to *Keck*, trade rules concerning selling arrangements are subject to the article 28 regime only if discriminatory against imported products.[234] As a result selling arrangements, at least in principle, fall outside of article 28 and, therefore, do not require justification and harmonization, since their disparities are not considered as determining fragmentations of the market and as hindering the stream of commerce. By introducing a similar discipline, the Court of Justice mirrored in respect to selling arrangements the general NT regime of the GATT: for the law of prohibition to be triggered, a finding of discrimination of the measure at hand was preliminarily requested.

The *Keck* doctrine has considerably influenced the adjudication by the Court of Justice under article 28. Although the definition of selling arrangements sounds rather formalistic, its adoption in cases concerning static selling arrangements has not been particularly controversial.[235] By contrast, significant difficulties and

---

[232] These concerns have become particularly serious with the approval of the SEA and, notably, of article 95 EC which determined the shift to qualified majority vote in respect to the approximation of laws. Other difficulties emerged in respect to the application of the principle of proportionality in respect to the increasing number of mandatory requirements recognized by the Court and, last but not least, for the judicial workload connected with a broad interpretation of article 28.

[233] Cases 267/91 and 268/91, *Criminal proceedings against Bernard Keck and Daniel Mithouard* [1993] ECR I-6097.   [234] Recitals 16 and 17.

[235] Plain applications of the *Keck* formula can be appreciated in Cases 401 and 402/92, *Tankstation 't Heukste vof and J.B. E. Boermans* [1994] ECR I-2199; Cases 69 and 258/93, *Punto Casa*

disputes arise out of controversies concerning dynamic selling arrangements. In these cases, indeed, the category of selling arrangements is particularly inapt at dealing with restrictions on advertising or other forms of sales promotion which result in a double burden for the imported products and, therefore, in obstacles to their access to the domestic market.[236] For this reason, many commentators have suggested the *Keck* formula ought to be re-defined by switching from the formalism of selling arrangements to a more flexible solution directly centered on the idea of access to the market.[237] The wide doctrinal debate in this regard has also influenced to some extent the behavior of the Court of Justice. Although the reference to selling arrangements has not been abandoned, in cases such as *De Agostini, Gourmet* and *Heimdienst*, the Court has considerably refined its scrutiny on discrimination thereby re-vitalizing the potential of article 28 in respect to measures that in fact hinder the access to the domestic market. Hence, the *Keck* formula has substantially met the need to re-target the obstacle-based test introduced with *Dassonville* for national regulatory measures.[238] In the application of the NT regime to selling arrangements, one may identify a less stringent attitude in respect to national regulatory autonomy and a remarkable convergence towards the general GATT regime.[239] Yet, also in this case convergence does not go as far as to achieve assimilation. Notwithstanding *Keck*, in the EC national regulatory measures obey in principle to the *Dassonville* and *Cassis* formulas which, once relieved of the excessive stress of the pre-*Keck* legal practice, proffer the main regulatory principles for challenging the illegitimate partitions of market.[240]

SpA v. Sindaco del Comune di Capena [1994] ECR I-2355; Cases 418–421, 460–462 & 464/93, and Cases 9–11, 14–15, 23–24 & 322/94, *Semeraro Casa Uno Srl v. Sindaco del Comune di Erbusco* [1996] ECR I-2975.

[236] As observed in C. Barnard, *Fitting the remaining pieces into the goods and persons jigsaw?*, in *ELR*, 2001, 26, p. 43, this occurs notably in the case of new foreign products which need to gain foothold in the market and are prevented by domestic restrictions on advertising. In this regard see Case 412/93, *Société d'Importation Edouard Leclerc-Siplec v. TF1 Publicité SA and M6 Publicité* [1995] ECR I-179; Cases 34, 35 and 36/95, *Konsumentombudsmannen v. De Agostini Forlag AB and TV-Shop i Sverige AB* [1997] ECR I-3843; Case-254/98, *Schutzverband gegen unlauteren Wettbewerb v. TK-Heimdienst Sass GmbH* [2000] ECR I-151; and Case C-405/98, *Konsumentombudsmannen v. Gourmet International Products AB (GIP)* [2001] ECR I-1795.

[237] See S. Weatherill, *After Keck: Some Thoughts on how to Clarify the Clarification*, in *CMLRev*, 1996, 33, pp. 896–97, defining the following more attuned test: 'measures introduced by authorities in a Member State which apply equally in law and in fact to all goods or services without reference to origin and which impose no direct or substantial hindrance to the access of imported goods or services to the market of that Member State escape the scope of application of Articles 30 and 59.' A similar global test is suggested and critically discussed in C. Barnard, *Fitting the remaining pieces*, pp. 52–59.

[238] C. Barnard, *Fitting the remaining pieces*, p. 42, observes that '*Keck* has refocused the emphasis of the enquiry away from 'has there been an impact on trade in general' to whether there has been a sufficient impact on *cross-border* trade' (italics in the original).

[239] At the same time, it must be remembered that, as seen in the previous sub-section, the WTO is experiencing an analogous convergent move towards an obstacle-based regime for the regulatory measures falling under the SPS and TBT agreements.

[240] Case 470/93, *Verein gegen Unwesen in Handel und Gewerbe Köln v. Mars GmbH* [1995] ECR I-1923.

More profound developments have occurred in the field of positive harmonization. In this regard, the introduction of article 95 EC beside article 94 is probably the most important innovation. Like article 94, this additional legal basis has been devised as a means of phasing out the market fragmentations engendered by regulatory measures unilaterally adopted by member states in defense of non-trade interests. Yet, this new provision contains a number of elements which come closer to the forms of exercise of regulatory powers encountered in the domestic and, to some extent, even in the WTO constitutional spheres. Article 95, indeed, by entitling the Council to adopt regulatory measures by qualified majority, has mobilized EC decision-making and fueled the programmes of positive harmonization which had so far languished under the Luxembourg accord. In addition, the shift to qualified majority voting has opened the door to alternative forms of political deliberation to the mere intergovernmental bargaining of article 94. In particular, the amendments to article 95 introduced in turn by the treaties of Maastricht and Amsterdam have constantly strengthened the role of the European Parliament beside the Council, thereby conferring full political nature on EC decision-making.[241] The magnitude of these constitutional innovations, combined with further modifications intervened in the EU institutional architecture,[242] has gone as far as to suggest that the EU constitutional configuration is coming closer to that of the state forms of federalism and parliamentary government.[243]

Moreover, article 95 does not only nourish federal and state-like suggestions. A closer analysis of the provision reveals, for instance, many traits in common also with the SPS and TBT patterns of integration.[244] Also in this context, indeed, science plays a considerable role both as a source of inspiration for the regulatory initiatives and as a yardstick of control of the national measures maintained or adopted to pursue higher levels of protection of non-trade objectives.[245]

These latter considerations lead to a more cautious assessment of the alleged reconcilement of the ECI of the EU with the standards of domestic constitutionalism. The layer of convergence developed in respect to article 95 contains a number of aspects that are absolutely coherent with the original functional concerns of the EC. There are elements, for instance, to argue that the fate of article 95 is going to be different from that of the similar far-reaching provisions existing in

---

[241] The political nature of the EU decision-making on the basis of article 95 is acknowledged in Case 491/01, *R v. Secretary of State for Health, ex parte British American Tobacco (Investments) Ltd and Imperial Tobacco Ltd* [2002] ECR I-11453, recital 80.

[242] Significant in this regard is the introduction of a right for the Parliament to request the Commission to submit a legislative proposal (article 192 EC) as well as the powers of the Parliament to participate in the appointment of the Commission (article 214 EC), to censure it and to require its resignation (article 201 EC).

[243] The elements of the EU institutional architecture coherent with a parliamentary model are described in R. Dehousse, *European Institutional Architecture after Amsterdam: Parliamentary System or Regulatory Structure?*, in *CMLRev*, 1998, 35, pp. 603–12.

[244] See in particular paragraphs 3 to 8 of article 95.

[245] Illuminating in this regard the decision of Case 3/00, *Denmark v. Commission* [2003] ECR I-2643.

state federal systems. Recent case law shows that the Court of Justice, unlike many deferential Constitutional Courts and contrary to its traditional attitude, interprets rigorously its role of policing the excesses of the legislative.[246] In dealing with measures adopted on the basis of article 95, the Court has refused to pander to the centripetal dynamics which characterize many of the experiences of state federalism. By contrast, its constitutional leadership in market building has been maintained by promoting a more selective approach to positive harmonization which replicates the *Keck* rationale. The Court, indeed, has established that article 95 is not triggered by any discrepancy occurring between the national rules, but, more correctly, it serves essentially the objective of genuinely improving the conditions and functioning of the internal market.[247]

But also in respect to the contents and procedures employed in the adoption of EC regulatory measures, traces of the persisting commitment towards market efficiency are evident. The constitutional innovations introduced ever since the SEA have been accompanied by a parallel re-thinking of the techniques of harmonization which, in fact, downplay the turn to politicization of legislative decision-making. Particularly in the New Approach to Harmonization,[248] it has been made clear that political deliberation is limited to the adoption of legislative measures laying down essential requirements in the general interest. By contrast, the task of drawing up technical specifications and, therefore, of coping often with the most problematic issues is delegated to circuits of political administration, organized according to a technocratic and intergovernmental structure and operating through procedures remarkably different from the traditional patterns of representative democracy.[249] Here, both the Commission and the standardization bodies are engaged in efficiency-driven (rather than democracy-driven) processes of deliberation which, for the lack of transparency and for the difficulties in involving a balanced set of interests and actors, are at continuous risk of being captured.[250] From this standpoint and considering the increasing importance assumed by secondary rule-making,[251] the answers to the quest for legitimacy and democratic accountability inherent in the processes of convergence appear often misplaced or

---

[246] See Case 376/98, *Germany v. European Parliament and Council of the European Union* [2000] ECR I-8419, and the already quoted *British American Tobacco*.

[247] See recitals 83, 84 and 95. The same approach has been confirmed in the subsequent decision *British American Tobacco*, recitals 64, 65 and 75.

[248] See Council Resolution of 27 May 1985 on a New Approach to Technical Harmonization and Standards [1985] OJ C136/1 and White paper from the Comission to the European Council 'Completing the Internal Market', 14 June 1985, COM (85) 310 final.

[249] C. Joerges, J. Neyer, *From Intergovernamental Bargaining to Deliberative Political Process: The Constitutionalisation of Comitology*, in *ELJ*, 1997, 3, 3, p. 273.

[250] The risks of regulatory capture of the standardization bodies are signaled in A. McGee, S. Weatherill, *The Evolution of the Single Market—Harmonisation or Liberalisation*, in *MLR*, 1990, 53, p. 585.

[251] In this respect, see the figures reported in R. Dehousse, *Beyond representative democracy: constitutionalism in a polycentric polity*, in J.H.H. Weiler, M. Wind (eds.), *European Constitutionalism Beyond the State*, pp. 141–42.

unsatisfactory and call for a radical effort of construing efficiency through alternative patterns of governance conceived in the light of the traditional values of openness and participation.[252]

Put together, all the elements of which the layer of convergence of the ECI of the EU consists reveal how the incorporation of solutions adopted in the domestic sphere and in the WTO is firmly grafted on the still prevalent, though refined, paradigm of market integration. Of course, market integration does not occupy the pivotal position it used to have when it was the undisputed scenario of supranational integration. Yet, the most distinctive traits of the ECI of the EU have not been upset or impaired during their often tumultuous evolution. In particular, the pushes towards politicization have been skillfully embedded in comprehensively efficiency-oriented decision-making. Not only the leadership of the Court of Justice in establishing and renovating the constitutional strategies which ought to guide market integration has remained unaffected. Even when important spaces for regulatory autonomy have been recognized, legislation and representative democracy increasingly have left broad scope for forms of political administration marked again by the search of efficient solutions.

IV. Interpreting Stratification—A Comparative Survey on the ECIs

After having analyzed in detail the characteristics of the ECIs, it is now worth summarizing their main traits and to articulate some critical remarks on how economic constitutionalism(s) is developing alongside the processes of re-organization of public space also in post-national dimensions.[253]

The idea is often been advocated that each of the ECIs consists in a two layers-structure comprising respectively, distinctive and convergent elements. The most profound layer is made of the distinctive elements and points directly at the functional concerns of the constitutional spheres at issue. In this regard, it may be argued the ECIs serve different objectives which entail different approaches to the concept of integration. Economic constitutionalism of social state, for example, hinges upon a general idea of economic and social cohesion whereby the constitution establishes the principles and instruments to integrate through politics and representative democracy the interests of economic and social actors.[254] By contrast, in the WTO-GATT, integration is conceived in pure intergovernmental

---

[252] In this regard, R. Dehousse, *Beyond Representative Democracy*, p. 156, argues 'the input-oriented approach which has so far dominated discussions on the legitimacy of European institutions needs to be supplemented by a *process-oriented* one, in which interested citizens would be given a say in the post-legislative, bureaucratic phase'.

[253] A summary of the main traits of the ECIs is displayed in the table on stratification annexed to this article.

[254] In this regard, it may be argued that state economic constitutionalism is mostly input-oriented.

terms and relies on a contractual matrix directed at bringing international trade relations as close as possible to a free trade-oriented regime. In the EC, finally, a comprehensive idea of market plays as the pivotal factor of intergovernmental as well as social integration.[255]

In each of the ECIs, these teleological premises originate extremely different legal frameworks in nature. In the state dimension, economic constitutional provisions perform mostly as constitutive principles of a transaction economy which, on the one hand, leaves large room for political deliberation but, on the other, does not contain sufficient constitutional guarantees for market efficiency. In the GATT, constitutional provisions express more articulate regulatory principles, even though the bilateral nature of obligations accords still important margins of political-diplomatic maneuver for the members to accommodate their diversities in a comprehensive flexible scheme. It is in the EC, therefore, that constitutional provisions reveal their most aggressive profile. The regulatory principles which articulate the objective of market integration are indeed equipped with a double system of enforcement which, although crucially hinging upon the ultimate authority of member states, allows them to reduce significantly their scope for political decision-making. Here, it is important to underline that the nature of the legal framework appears as the only element in each of the ECIs which has not undergone alterations in the processes of convergence. Therefore, it seems that before venturing into any debate on the characters of economic constitutionalism(s), these elements of distinction should be adequately taken into consideration.

The functional concerns of the constitutional spheres and the nature of the legal frameworks resonate also in the remnant elements of the ECIs, namely the standards of review adopted by the adjudicative bodies and the characters of decision-making. In this regard, in the state dimension the emphasis on political decision-making matches with the deference by the Constitutional Court. By contrast, in the GATT/WTO, adjudicative bodies enforce NT regime against members' measures by employing a more intrusive pattern of decision made of 'objective approach' and textualism. In the EC, instead, access to market, as the key-concept of market integration, is promoted by the Court of Justice through incisive strategies of regulation resulting in an obstacle-based test and in the doctrine of functional parallelism. As seen, a similar regime is coupled by a legal basis of positive harmonization (article 94 EC) where regulatory autonomy, though under mostly intergovernmental guises, is to some extent regained. This latter element is critically absent in the distinctive layer of the ECI of the WTO and, for this reason, it constitutes a significant obstacle for the WTO to attain full constitutional status.

It has been argued, then, that the divergences between the distinctive elements of the ECIs may explain the generalized and mostly hidden uneasiness which is troubling the interactions among the legal orders operating in the European

---

[255] Supranational economic constitutionalism, therefore, may be considered as mostly output-oriented.

constitutional space. The frictions so determined are being faced in each of the constitutional spheres by alternating episodic moments of blunt conflict and prevalent processes of convergence whose achievements integrate the second layer of the ECIs. In the national (Italian) sphere, for instance, the objectives of market building and economic efficiency have entered in the constitutional discourse and inspired both legislative initiatives and constitutional adjudication. In the WTO, the SPS and TBT agreements have adopted the language of reasonableness and equivalence in dealing with market fragmentations. Moreover, minimal forms of intergovernmental decision-making have taken their first steps under these agreements replicating—although in a considerably different institutional background— the EC patterns of positive harmonization.

In the meantime, the distinctive elements of the ECI of the EU are perceived as benchmarks for the WTO and national ones, the EU itself starts to incorporate in its ECI some of the national and WTO tenets. Firstly, the expansion of constitutional objectives has been progressively enfranchised from the original and exclusive market frame. Thus, fully-fledged constitutional objectives have been conferred on the EU institutions and market-building itself has been relieved of the stress of coping with issues which, as a rule, are not dealt with from the economic standpoint. Secondly, NT and the language of anti-discrimination have been employed in the jurisprudence of the Court of Justice in order to promote a more selective approach to market access. Finally, the patterns of positive harmonization have been remarkably enriched by strengthening the role of political institutions according to the parliamentary model and by enhancing the contribution to decision-making by scientific expertise.

Although the processes of convergence appear in certain cases impressive, it must not be concluded that they automatically ensue from interactions among the ECIs. There are of course cases—such as the parliamentarization of the EU or the incorporation of the objective of market efficiency in the national spheres—in which there may be causation among the distinctive elements of an ECI and those convergent of another. Yet, this is not at all the rule, since in a number of other cases the adoption of regulatory solutions already developed in a different sphere is more the result of endogenous processes rather than of external influences.[256]

Furthermore, at many stages in the analysis of the convergent layer it has been alerted that convergence does not mean assimilation. For each convergent element, it has been repeatedly stressed, crucial traits of continuity with the original ECI exist and, hence, a proper understanding of the specificities of the ECIs requires them to be taken into account, even after (or during) their convergence. The ECIs, therefore, do not evolve simply by switching from one model to another. Inherent in the metaphor of stratification, indeed, is the idea that convergence does not

---

[256] Consider, for example, the adoption by the Court of Justice of the language of NT in *Keck*. As previously mentioned, this more selective approach to access to market goes back to the problems engendered by the too broad *Dassonville* formula rather than to an impact of the WTO on the EU.

mean dismissal of the original diversities but, more sophisticatedly, incorporation and re-elaboration of the principles or solutions devised in other ECIs within the original and unaltered legal frameworks.[257]

Precisely for this reason, it would be wrong to argue that convergence removes all the factors of uneasiness in the European constitutional space. Frictions may well be silenced and the sharpest elements may be rendered more palatable but the wheels of the ECIs appear to constantly require greasing. Most of the time, the usual shortcut to these problems is to advocate the rhetoric of assimilation and to neglect the instances of its discontents. An alternative and more radical approach, instead, is to try to devise a conceptual framework for the interactions among the ECIs in which, possibly, uneasiness is perceived more as a value generating stability rather than a matter to be concerned with.[258]

V. The Value of Uneasiness—A Conceptual Framework for the Interactions among the ECIs

The most common responses to the frictions among the ECIs are normally conceived with the aim of stifling uneasiness by concentrating constitutional authority. In this respect, the theoretical framework of state constitutionalism appears particularly suitable in so far as it draws upon the authoritative dividend of traditional concepts such as sovereignty or its corollaries (*pouvoir constituant, kompetenz-kompetenz* and so forth). Accordingly, in the most orthodox positions the interactions between states and post-national units are understood in terms of delegation of (quasi) sovereign rights by the states whose constitutions however retain ultimate authority and legitimacy. Nevertheless, a similar approach, although formally unquestionable, fails in capturing the more complex reality of the interactions among the ECIs. The emphasis on the ultimate authority of states evokes normally pathological or exceptional circumstances, such as serious infringements of the core principles of national constitutions or treaty amendments (with

---

[257] Just to remind of some examples from the above analysis, this has emerged quite clearly in the incorporation of the objective of market efficiency by the national ECI or in the 'lighter' version of functional parallelism developed in the SPS and TBT.

[258] The perils inherent in the rhetoric of assimilation have overtly emerged in process of ratification of the 'Treaty establishing a Constitution for Europe'. Arguably, this document has been devised to profit from the legitimacy dividend of state constitutionalism by camouflaging with its language and categories a legal framework and regulatory solutions mostly replicating—although with important innovations—the current EU legal framework. The discrepancy between the symbols invoked and the contents supplied was too strident not to be heard. Therefore, it is not surprising that the answers of the French and Dutch referenda to a similar offer were negative. Nowadays, when this kind of constitutional efforts seem chilled, the superficial enthusiasm at vesting the EU legal framework with the paraphernalia of state constitutionalism can also be considered more critically. It seems, indeed, that the current political circumstances suggest a more cautious and realistic attitude if European integration is to be re-vitalized. In this new stage, a more conscious and analytical approach to the constitutional identities involved in this process might be helpful.

subsequent ratifications), which do not seem the most eloquent or interesting factors for interpreting the legal reality of interactions. Moreover, the above analysis has shown not only that legal orders that flourished in post-national dimensions maintain several traits of discrepancy and even of collision in respect to national constitutional tenets, but also that processes of convergence follow trends which are very much more articulated than the unilateral principal-agent relationships underlying the traditional doctrinal categories.

Even more fallacious seem the conceptual frameworks embraced by those who, by drawing upon the doctrines of direct effect and supremacy, suggest that the ultimate authority (or the *Grundnorm*) has shifted to the EU or, even, WTO spheres. Unlike formalists, supporters of this approach capture the fact that in these post-national units there is more than obedient agents. Yet, in their approach, constitutional elements are superficially understood and, hence, over-emphasized forgetting, at the end, that no 'federal big-bang' has yet occurred.[259] Nonetheless, doctrines such as direct effect and supremacy, originally conceived to solve specific conflicts of norms, are (mis)used to nurture the perception of an incorporation of the constitutional spheres of the states by the EU (or the WTO) constitution.[260]

The shortcomings of these positions emerge even more clearly if one considers their implications in terms of understanding the single ECIs. The most orthodox positions, for example, by emphasizing the sovereign rights of the principals, stress the importance of delegations and, therefore, are likely to privilege the distinctive (over the convergent) elements of the ECIs. Yet, it is common experience that when orthodoxy and integrity are taken too seriously they rapidly turn in caricatures.

By contrast, the emphasis on supremacy unavoidably brings about assimilation. It has been repeated *ad nauseam* that this is not the most appropriate pattern of relations for identifying the nature of the interactions among the ECIs. Besides, it can be advocated that it is not even a desirable pattern: think only of the disasters which would follow institutional solutions such as a domestic Constitutional Court reviewing legislation according to Court of Justice-like standards of adjudication, a common market based on a legal framework made of bilateral obligations, a *Dassonville* formula introduced in the GATT ... Assimilation is not only legally unfounded, but also normatively dangerous as far as it entails an unacceptable impairment of the functional rationale underpinning the processes of re-organization of public space.

---

[259] R. Toniatti, *Federalismo e potere costituente*, in *Regionalismo e Federalismo in Europa*, Trento, 1997, p. 170.

[260] To appreciate the hegemony of such mindset, consider the following excerpt (taken from a genuinely pluralist writer such as J. Shaw, *Postnational constitutionalism in the EU*, p. 588): 'if legal orders can be overlapping and *do not stand in a hierarchy* or an arrangement which is either strict or fixed, it is possible to see the *EU as an entity of 'interlocking normative spheres'*; what is significant is that *no particular sphere is seen as privileged or predominant*' (Italics added). On a close reading, this is only apparently a pluralist image of the European constitutional space since the EU is not considered as one of the 'interlocking normative spheres' but, crucially, as 'an entity of interlocking normative spheres' and, therefore, is 'privileged and predominant'.

A more sound response to the conundrums arising out of the interactions among the ECIs could be envisaged by criticizing the assumption underlying state constitutionalism approaches. In these latter, indeed, the constant search for ultimate authorities seems motivated by deep concerns for the allegedly disruptive effects of uneasiness. Yet, the answers provided by the custodians of orthodoxy or by the supporters of assimilation do not seem to meet the theoretical and social expectations for an order in such a controversial context. It may be argued, therefore, that a more promising conceptual framework could be devised by focusing more on the physiognomy of interactions rather than on their pathology. In this perspective, uneasiness may be treated in more constructive terms. As noted, frictions among the ECIs have generated more convergence than conflict and, in some cases, more convergence through conflict. The diverse ECIs, indeed, respond to diverse and equally legitimate functional concerns[261] and, accordingly, their nature is essentially partial.[262] As a result, each ECI may be seen as producing assets as well as shortcomings which, at least in principle, compensate for (or are compensated by) the shortcomings and assets of the other ECIs.[263]

This is not to depict an idyllic and reconciled reality. Again, uneasiness is inherent in European constitutional space and, therefore, even the complementary nature of the ECIs is more an objective to pursue than an outcome attainable once and for all. More appropriately, uneasiness may be seen as the factor of equilibrium which engenders forms of mutual accommodation among constitutional spheres animated in principle by disparate and sometimes even colliding goals. It is clear now why all the conceptual frameworks which try to suppress uneasiness by concentrating an ordering principle for interactions within one of the ECIs appear legally and normatively inadequate.[264] If properly managed, uneasiness, rather than being a matter of concern, could be an answer to the concerns for the stability of the European constitutional space.

In this respect, a provocative (but also more realistic) conceptual framework for the interactions among the ECIs could be devised in the form of a 'code of conduct

---

[261] R. Dehousse, *Comparing National and EC law*, p. 779.

[262] N. Walker, *Constitutionalism and the problem of translation*, p. 54 observes: 'In terms of constitutional discourse, this development points to the increasing significance of the relational dimension generally within the post-Westphalian configuration. In this plural configuration, unlike the one-dimensional Westphalian configuration, the 'units' are no longer isolated, constitutionally self-sufficient monads. They do not purport to be comprehensive and exclusive polities [...] Indeed, it is artificial even to conceive of such sites as having separate internal and external dimensions, since their very identity and *raison d'être* as polities or putative polities rests at least in some measure on their orientation towards other sites'.

[263] In this respect, particularly interesting is the concept of 'counter-punctual law' suggested, although not in functional perspective, by M. Poiares Maduro, *Europe and the constitution*, p. 98.

[264] Observes M. Poiares Maduro, *Europe and the constitution*, p. 98, that 'in a world where problems and interests have no boundaries, it is a mistake to concentrate the ultimate authority and normative monopoly in a single source. Legal pluralism constitutes a form of checks and balances in the organization of power in the European and national polities and, in this sense, it is an expression of constitutionalism and its paradoxes'.

for managing uneasiness' directed at the judicial and political actors operating within them. Its contents might consist of two premises:

(1) ECIs respond to different and equally legitimate functional concerns. These consist in distinctive elements which are to be preserved in order to prevent disruptive phenomena of assimilation;

(2) The distinctive elements of the ECIs can be a source of conflicts among them. As a consequence, a sufficient degree of substantive compatibility ought to be pursued in order to facilitate their interactions;

and in a general recommendation:

Within each ECI, convergent interpretative and normative solutions should be endorsed as those which, while preserving diversity among the ECIs, achieve sufficient conditions of compatibility.

If assimilated, a similar recommendation might deliver more balance and order than those solutions devised by insisting on sovereignty and its substitutes. It seems, indeed, that after having endorsed for centuries the top-down authoritative (dis)order of the 'sovereigns'—being them alternatively the king, the state, the people, the constitution—in a time of constitutionalism(s) a bottom-up approach to stability, grounded on the legal consciousness and moral commitment by those who daily handle constitutions, could be attempted.

Principles of Reception of International Law in Community Law

Rass Holdgaard[*]

I. Introduction

As it is, the EC Treaty is virtually silent about whether and how international law can enter Community law and with which legal consequences.[1] Also the Constitutional Treaty, if it eventually enters into force, will maintain this state of affairs. Though several Articles in the Constitutional Treaty underline the importance of respecting and complying with international law and of fostering international co-operation, they do not spell out how (or whether) legal rules and principles should implement this general positive attitude to international co-operation.[2]

As a consequence of the political actors' persistent reticence,[3] the Court of Justice has been given the full responsibility for developing the principles of reception of international law in Community law. Needless to say, this area of Community law has significant practical and constitutional implications both within the Community and in the Community's relations with the outside world—The principles of reception function as a 'filter' between the Community

[*] The article is based on a chapter in the author's PhD thesis, 'Classic External Relations Law of the European Community-Doctrines and Discourses', University of Copenhagen, 2005. A rewritten and updated version of the thesis will be published by Kluwer Law International in 2007. E-mail: rho@kammeradv.dk.

[1] Articles 300(7) and 307 EC provide no precise guidance in this respect. E.g. Jacques H.J. Bourgeois, 'The European Court of Justice and the WTO: Problems and Challenges', in Weiler, ed. *The EU, the WTO, and the NAFTA: Towards a Common Law of International Trade?*, 2000, p. 77.

[2] E.g. Articles I-3(4) and III-292 (on the Union's external objectives). See also Article III-323(2) (now Article 300(7) EC). While Article I-6 codifies the principle of supremacy of Community law over national law, there is no mention in the Treaty of the hierarchical relationship between international law and Community law.

[3] A well-known exception is the preamble to Council Decision 94/800 [1994] OJ L336/1 concerning the conclusion of the WTO Agreements. In this Decision the Council explicitly states its view that the WTO Agreements are 'not susceptible to being directly invoked in Community or Member State courts'. See, moreover, the European Parliament's Resolution on the relationships between international law, Community law and the constitutional law of the Member States. Here, the European Parliament calls for a clear statement in the EC Treaty that the Community does not recognize the direct applicability of international law without any act of incorporation. [1997] OJ C325/26 (at paragraphs 14 and 15).

legal order (and thus the national legal orders) and international law. This filter allows some international legal obligations to play an important role within the Community area while barring other groups of international legal rules from doing the same. In this sense, the ECJ becomes a 'gatekeeper', guarding the admission of international law into the Community area.[4]

It is tradition in EC legal dogmatics to examine two essential characteristics of this 'international law filter'. The first concerns the size or the surface area of the filter: When (and to what extent) does a rule of international law fall within the domain of Community law; when is it *received* as an integrated part of Community law? The second issue concerns the nature of the grids in the filter: Given that a rule of international law is part of Community law, how is this rule given *effect* (notably direct effect) within the Community area?[5] While legal scholarship has always devoted most attention to the latter question, this article will analyse and propose a synthesis of the case law created legal principles that determine when and to what extent international law is integrated in Community law.

The structure will be thus: Section II will account for the general principles of reception of international law in Community law, established particularly in the *Haegeman, Kupferberg* and *Racke* cases. It is in the context of this case law that the corollary overarching requirement of uniform application of rules of international law was first developed by the Court. As we shall see, this well-known requirement has been informed by distinctive 'external relations' considerations, and these considerations have played a central role in the formulation of the principles of reception of international law. The requirement of uniform application of international law will be considered in some detail in Section III.

As it turned out, in practice, applying the above-mentioned general method of reception (hereinafter the Kupferberg principle) is problematic in relation to a relatively substantial amount of practically important international legal obligations, such as general principles of international law, mixed agreements, international human rights treaties, ILO Conventions UN Security Council resolutions etc. Against this backdrop, Section IV will consider whether and on what basis there are, or should be, alternative methods of reception. It will be

---

[4] Francis Snyder, *The Gatekeepers: The European Courts and WTO Law* (2003) 40 CML Rev 313–67. See also Nikolaos Lavranos, *Legal Interaction between Decisions of International Organizations and European Law*, 2004, p. 5.

[5] The literature and case law normally deals with these two issues in relation to the ECJ's jurisdiction over international agreements. Piet Eeckhout, *External Relations of the European Union: Legal and Constitutional Foundations*, 2004, p. 226, notes that the domestic effects of international agreements 'raises at least two kinds of questions. First, does the domestic court have jurisdiction to consider the agreement? Secondly, on the assumption that the reply to the first question is positive, what are the precise legal effects of the agreement in the domestic legal order?' See also e.g. Ilona Cheyne, 'International Instruments as a Source of Community Law', in Dashwood and Hillion, eds. *The General Law of E.C. External Relations*, 2000; Jacques H. J. Bourgeois, 'The European Court of Justice and the WTO: Problems and Challenges', in Weiler, ed. *The EU, the WTO, and the NAFTA: Towards a Common Law of International Trade?*, 2000.

shown that the inadequacies of the main principles for reception have made it necessary for the Court to develop alternative approaches—particularly in relation to international agreements to which the Community is not a party (Section IV.B) and in relation to mixed agreements (Section IV.C). After a relatively detailed account of the case law on these topics, Section V will summarize and conclude the analysis.

Before proceeding, however, a few terminological remarks are in order. First, it is generally accepted that to be formally applicable within and throughout the Community legal system, a provision of international law must be *received* by the Community legal order. To use a Hartian term, one of the Community legal system's 'rules of recognition' of international law must be satisfied.[6] (As the ECJ, I will use the following expressions interchangeably to denote that a provision of international law has been received as part of the Community legal system: The provision of international law may be referred to as 'an integral part of Community law',[7] 'an integral part of the Community legal system',[8] 'of a Community nature'[9] a 'part of the Community legal order',[10] a 'Community law obligation'[11] having 'entered the sphere of Community law'[12] or coming 'within the scope of Community law'.[13])

Second, to understand the many nuances in the case law in this area, it is important to maintain a relatively strict *distinction between the Community legal system and international law*. Even today—where legal pluralist theories are popular—the ECJ continues to insist on the separability (or autonomy) of Community law as a matter of principle: The Community legal system, on the one hand, and international law, on the other hand, are in principle separate (though interacting) legal systems with separate sources of law and separate methods of interpretation.[14] Therefore, it is necessary to distinguish between international law obligations, which are binding on the Community area *as a matter of international law*, and international law obligations, which are binding within the Community *as a matter of Community law*. These two legal systems have different criteria for determining whether a particular rule of international law is binding on and within the

---

[6] Ilona Cheyne, 'International Instruments as a Source of Community Law', in Dashwood and Hillion, eds. *The General Law of E.C. External Relations*, 2000. On rules of recognition, H.L.A. Hart, *The Concept of Law*, 1994 [1961], e.g. pp. 94.

[7] Case 181/73, *R. & V. Haegeman v State* [1974] ECR 0449; Case 188/91, *Deutsche Shell AG v Hamburg-Harburg* [1993] ECR I-363, paragraph 17.

[8] Case 104/81, *Hauptzollamt Mainz v a.A.* [1982] ECR 3641, paragraph 13.

[9] *Ibid.*, paragraph 14.

[10] Case 188/91, *Deutsche Shell AG v Hamburg-Harburg* [1993] ECR I-363, paragraphs 16 and 17; Case C-162/96, *Racke GmbH & Co. v Mainz* [1998] ECR I-3655, paragraph 46.

[11] Case C-13/00, *Commission v Ireland* [2002] ECR I-2943.

[12] Joined Cases C-392/98 and C-300/98, *Parfums Christian Dior SA v BV* [2000] ECR I-11307, paragraph 41. See also paragraphs 47 and 48.

[13] Case C-13/00, *Commission v Ireland* [2002] ECR I-2943, paragraph 13.

[14] See particularly the case law in Section II.B and, of course, Case 26/62, *van Gend en Loos v Administration* [1963] ECR 1 and Case C-53/96, *Hermès International v BV* [1998] ECR I-3603.

Community. Though the Community's position will normally be in line with international law, the potential difference between the two legal systems can be demonstrated by two practical examples. First, in situations where the Community institutions act in violation of primary Community law their actions may be invalid as a matter of Community law. Nevertheless, as a matter of international law, such actions may still bind the Community.[15] Second, if the Community and the Member States conclude a mixed agreement and in this connection submit to the contracting parties a declaration on allocation of competence between them, such a declaration may be binding as a matter of international law and may determine who has assumed and is responsible for which obligations. Nevertheless, the declaration submitted to the third parties may not necessarily depict which international obligations are binding as a matter of Community law and which are binding outside the Community legal framework.[16]

Third, a theoretical discussion of the hierarchical status of international law in Community law is beyond the scope of this article. Suffice it to note that, in the hierarchy of Community norms, the status of the 'external' sources of Community law has never been much disputed or discussed[17]: Community agreements, which are an integral part of Community law, have precedence over conflicting secondary Community law and, *qua* Community law, they have precedence over national law.[18] It is equally clear that, from the perspective of the Community legal order, these agreements do not have precedence over EC Treaty provisions or any other sources of primary Community law. International agreements are thus hierarchically situated somewhere between primary and secondary Community law. Also other sources of international law, which are an integral part of Community law, have precedence over secondary Community law.[19] It is still an open question whether some instruments of international law (of a particular

---

[15] Section II.B.

[16] Discrepancy exists also when the Community acts through the medium of the Member States cf. e.g. Case-439/01, *Libor Cipra et Vlastimil Kvasnicka* v *Mistelbach* [2003] ECR I-745.

[17] See e.g. C.D. Ehlermann and John Forman, *Case Law of the European Court of Justice 1972/73* (1973) 10 CML Rev 332–39, p. 337. Stefan A. Riesenfeld, *The Doctrine of Self-Executing Treaties and Community Law: A Pioneer Decision of the Court of Justice of the European Community* (1973) 67 AJIL 504–08, p. 506, Karl Meesen, *The Application of Rules of Public International Law within Community Law* (1976) 13 CML Rev 485–501; Gerhard Bebr, *Agreements Concluded by the Community and Their Possible Direct Effect: From International Fruit to Kupferberg* (1983) 20 CML Rev 35–73; Pierre Pescatore, 'Treaty-Making by the European Communities', in Jacobs and Roberts, eds. *The Effects of Treaties in Domestic Law*, 1987, pp. 181; Ilona Cheyne, *International Agreements and the European Community Legal System* (1994) 18 EL Rev 581–98, p. 586; Anne Peters, *The Position of International Law within the European Community Legal Order* (1997) GYIL 9–77, pp. 35; and Koen Lenaerts and Piet van Nuffel, *Constitutional Law of the European Union*, 1999, p. 552. Similarly, but critical: Steve Peers, *Constitutional Principles and International Trade* (1999) 24 EL Rev 185–95, p. 194.

[18] Most clearly: Case C-61/94, *Commission* v *Germany* [1996] ECR I-3989 (International Dairy Agreement). Early case law is also based on this assumption, e.g. Joined Cases 21–24/72, *International Fruit Company NV and others* v *Fruit* [1972] ECR 1219 and Case 9/73, *Carl Schlüter* v *Lörrach* [1973] ECR 1135. Case 40/72, *I. Schroeder KG* v *Germany* [1973] ECR 125.

[19] Case C-286/90, *Anklagemyndigheden* v *Corp.* [1992] ECR I-6019; Case C-162/96, *Racke GmbH & Co.* v *Mainz* [1998] ECR I-3655.

fundamental nature, for example) may have a status similar to or above general principles of Community law.[20] For the purpose of the present analysis, I will assume that all instruments of international law are hierarchically situated somewhere between primary and secondary Community law. Thus, customary international law, general principles of international law and international humanitarian law do not automatically have a status similar to or above primary Community law. This principled position ensures that international law does not threaten the autonomy of the Community legal order. A different question, which also falls outside the scope of this article, is whether the Court finds inspiration in these sources of law when it develops the general principles of Community law.

II. General Principles of Reception: Kupferberg and Racke

A. The Community's Responsibility under International Law

(i) International Agreements Concluded by the Community

In *Haegeman*, the Court held for the first time that provisions of an international agreement can form an integral part of Community law. A main issue was whether the Court had jurisdiction to interpret provisions in the Community's Association Agreement with Greece for the purpose of giving a preliminary ruling. The starting point for the Court was the text of Article 234(1)(b) according to which it had jurisdiction to give preliminary rulings concerning 'the interpretation of acts of the institutions': The Court noted that the Agreement was concluded by the Council (in the form of a decision) based on Articles 300 and 310 and was 'therefore, in so far as concerns the Community, an act of one of the institutions of the Community within the meaning of' Article 234(1)(b).[21] Therefore, 'The provisions of the Agreement, from the coming into force thereof, form an integral part of Community law' and, within the framework of this law, the Court had jurisdiction to give preliminary rulings.[22]

Kupferberg subsequently developed a substantive and more generally applicable rationale for the reception of international agreements concluded by the Community:

According to Article 228(2) [now Article 300(7)] these agreements [agreements concluded by the Community] are binding on the institutions of the Community and on the

---

[20] Some CFI judgments, e.g. Case T-306/01, *Ahmed Ali Yusuf* v *Commission* [2005] ECR II-3533 and Case T-115/94, *Opel Austria GmbH* v *Union* [1997] ECR II-39 may be interpreted to this effect. However, Case C-377/98, *Netherlands* v *Council* [2001] ECR I-7079 (biotechnology directive), paragraph 52 suggests that the Court does not distinguish between different sources of international law, but considers all 'instruments of international law' to have the same hierarchical status in Community law.

[21] Case 181/73, *R. & V. Haegeman* v *State* [1974] ECR 0449, paragraphs 3 and 4.

[22] Paragraphs 5 and 6. After *Haegeman*, the Court has preferred the term 'an integral part of the Community legal system', rather than 'an integral part of Community law'. E.g. Case 12/86, *Meryem Demirel* v *Gmund* [1987] ECR 3719, paragraph 7.

Member States. Consequently, it is incumbent upon the Community institutions, as well as upon the Member States, to ensure compliance with the obligations arising from such agreements.

(. . .)

In ensuring respect for commitments arising from an agreement concluded by the Community institutions the Member States fulfil an obligation not only in relation to the non-member country concerned but also and above all in relation to the Community which has assumed responsibility for the due performance of the agreement. *That is why* the provisions of such an agreement, as the Court has already stated in (. . .) Haegeman (. . .), form an integral part of the Community legal system.[23]

As Klabbers notes, in *Kupferberg* 'the Community nature of international agreements flowed not from any grand concerns about the position of individuals, nor from any theoretical notion of monism or dualism; it simply followed from the functional consideration that the Community ought to be enabled to make good on its word.'[24] In subsequent cases, preliminary rulings and direct actions alike, the Court has confirmed that *Haegeman*[25] and *Kupferberg*[26] set out why and how international agreements concluded by the Community form an integral part of the Community legal system. On the same grounds, the Court has also held that binding[27] and non-binding[28] measures emanating from bodies established by an agreement and entrusted with responsibility for the implementation of these agreements (such as association councils) are an integral part of the Community legal order, since these decisions are directly linked to the agreements.[29] *A contrario*, the Court has indicated that international obligations,

---

[23] Case 104/81, *Hauptzollamt Mainz* v *a.A.* [1982] ECR 3641, paragraphs 11 and 13, respectively (my emphasis).

[24] Jan Klabbers, *International Law and Community Law: The Law and Politics of Direct Effect* (2002) 21 YEL 263–98, p. 281.

[25] For example, in Case 30/88, *Hellenic Republic* v *Commission* [1989] ECR 3711, paragraph 12, (a direct action brought under Article 173 EC), the Court held that 'the provisions of an agreement concluded by the Council under Article 228 and 238 [now 300 and 310] of the Treaty form, as from the entry into force of the agreement, an integral part of the Community legal system.' (In a previous direct action concerning largely the same subject matter, the Court did not examine whether Decision 2/80 of the Association Council was an integral part of the Community legal order, Case 204/86, *Hellenic Republic* v *Council* [1988] ECR 5323.) More recently, Case C-13/00, *Commission* v *Ireland* [2002] ECR I-2943, paragraph 14.

[26] E.g. in Case 12/86, *Meryem Demirel* v *Gmund* [1987] ECR 3719, paragraph 11, and in Case C-13/00, *Commission* v *Ireland* [2002] ECR I-2943, paragraph 15.

[27] Case 30/88, *Hellenic Republic* v *Commission* [1989] ECR 3711, paragraph 13 (on Decision 2/80 of the Association Council set up under the Ankara Agreement); Case C-192/89, *Sevince* v *Justitie* [1990] ECR I-3461, paragraph 9 (on Decisions 2/76 and 1/80 of that Association Council).

[28] Case 188/91, *Deutsche Shell AG* v *Hamburg-Harburg* [1993] ECR I-363, paragraph 17 (on non-binding 'arrangements' concerning sealings of goods, adopted by the Joint Committee set up under the Convention on a Common Transit Procedure, concluded between the EC and the EFTA countries).

[29] E.g. Nikolaos Lavranos, *Legal Interaction between Decisions of International Organizations and European Law*, 2004; Armin von Bogdandy, *Legal Effects of World Trade Organization Decisions Within European Union Law: A Contribution to the Theory of the Legal Acts of International Organizations and the Action for Damages Under Article 288(2) EC* (2005) 39(1) JWT 45–66.

which the Community has not assumed responsibility for as a matter of international law, are generally not a part of Community law.[30]

Thus, *Haegeman* and *Kupferberg* offer two distinguishable reasons why agreements concluded by the Community are an integral part of the Community legal system. The first is textual and related to the wording of Article 234. The conclusion of an agreement (normally by a Council decision) is an act of a Community institution and therefore both that act and the agreement itself become an integral part of Community law over which the ECJ has jurisdiction.[31] This rather mechanical argument is supplemented by a second more substantive argument: By concluding agreements, the Community assumes responsibility vis-à-vis the third parties. In order for the Community to ensure due performance of these agreements, their provisions become binding within the Community, cf. Article 300(7) EC, and therefore an integral part of the Community legal system.[32] This latter reasoning has the broadest application and has subsequently been extended also to other instruments of international law.

(ii) Other Instruments of International Law

In light of the Court's case law, it may be useful, for the purpose of Community law, to make a general analytical distinction between sources of international law, which the Community has positively assumed in accordance with its conferred powers (either unilaterally or by agreement), and sources of international law, which apply to the Community's international activities, regardless of whether the Community assumes these obligations.[33] The latter rules—e.g. customary international law and general principles of international law—govern the Community's conduct of international relations in general and as a subject of international law, the Community is always bound by these rules.[34]

---

[30] In Case C-377/98, *Netherlands v Council* [2001] ECR I-7079, paragraph 52, the Court held that 'as a rule' the lawfulness of an internal Community measure cannot depend on its compatibility with an international agreement to which the Community is not a party. See also Section III.

[31] The internal procedure for conclusion and the international law act of conclusion are therefore the same in Community law. See e.g. Jacques H. J. Bourgeois, 'The European Court of Justice and the WTO: Problems and Challenges', in Weiler, ed. *The EU, the WTO, and the NAFTA: Towards a Common Law of International Trade?*, 2000, p. 77. Though it is now well-established, this textual approach has been criticized. One of the most criticized elements in the Court's reasoning is its failure to distinguish between the Council decision to conclude the agreement and the actual agreement itself. See notably T.C. Hartley, *International Agreements and the Community Legal System: Some Recent Developments* (1983) 8 EL Rev 383–92, pp. 390; T.C. Hartley, *The Foundations of European Community Law*, 2003, pp. 273. Similarly, Ilona Cheyne, 'International Instruments as a Source of Community Law', in Dashwood and Hillion, eds. *The General Law of E.C. External Relations*, 2000, p. 257. See, on the other hand, Piet Eeckhout, *External Relations of the European Union: Legal and Constitutional Foundations*, 2004, p. 234.

[32] Ilona Cheyne, 'International Instruments as a Source of Community Law', in Dashwood and Hillion, eds. *The General Law of E.C. External Relations*, 2000, pp. 257, 262.

[33] From an international law perspective, see Article 38 of the Statute of the International Court of Justice and e.g. Hugh Thirlway, 'The Sources of International Law', in Evans, ed. *International law*, 2003 (Chapter 4) and Malcolm N. Shaw, *International Law*, 2003 (Chapter 3).

[34] See Henry G. Schermers and Niels M. Blokker, *International Institutional Law*, 2001, §§ 1572.

As is apparent, the *Haegeman* reasoning set out above is not easily applicable to the latter sources of international law because there is no positive Community act that incorporates these rules. There was therefore for a long time uncertainty about the internal legal status of rules of international law, which are not contained in agreements concluded by the Community.[35] However, in *Racke*, the Court held that also those type of rules may be an integral part of the Community legal order. The main issue in that case was whether the fundamental customary international law rule of *pacta sunt servanda* could be relied on by individuals in order to challenge a Council decision suspending a Community agreement with Yugoslavia (based on the principle of *clausula rebus sic stantibus*). The Court held that:

45. (...) the European Community must respect international law in the exercise of its powers. It is therefore required to comply with the rules of customary international law when adopting a regulation suspending the trade concessions granted by, or by virtue of, an agreement which it has concluded with a non-member country.

46. It follows that the rules of customary international law concerning the termination and the suspension of treaty relations by reason of a fundamental change of circumstances are binding upon the Community institutions and form part of the Community legal order.[36]

This reasoning implicitly consolidates the *Kupferberg ratio* and extends it in a general manner to all sources of international law. Because the EC must comply with international law when it exercises its powers, rules of international law that apply to the Community's exercise of power are an integral part of EC law. Reception of such rules is necessary in order to ensure compliance. Analogous to the *Kupferberg* case, *Racke* links the Community's compliance with international law to the reception of international law as part of the Community legal order. Thus, as regards both international agreements concluded by the Community and other sources of international law, the Community's responsibility under international law determines the reception of international law in Community law.[37]

---

[35] Jan Wouters and Dries van Eeckhoutte, 'Giving Effect to Customary International Law Through European Community Law', in Prinssen and Schrauwen, eds. *Direct Effect: Rethinking a Classic of EC Legal Doctrine*, 2002, p. 185: 'the court has made numerous references to customary international law, even though the wording used often blurs the precise formal source of the rule.' See also e.g. Koen Lenaerts and Piet van Nuffel, *Constitutional Law of the European Union*, 1999, pp. 561; Karl Meesen, *The Application of Rules of Public International Law within Community Law* (1976) 13 CML Rev 485–501. See e.g. Cases 3, 4 and 6/76, *Cornelius Kramer and others* [1976] ECR 1279, paragraph 31; Case 41/74, *Yvonne van Duyn* v *Office* [1974] ECR 1337; Joined Cases C-89/85, C-104/85, C-114/85, C-116/85, C-117/85, C-125/85, C-126/85, C-127/85, C-128/85 and C-129/85, *A. Ahlström Osakeyhtiö and others* v *Commission* [1994] ECR I-99.

[36] Case C-162/96, *Racke GmbH & Co.* v *Mainz* [1998] ECR I-3655. The Court referred to Case C-286/90, *Anklagemyndigheden* v *Corp.* [1992] ECR I-6019, paragraph 9. Note that, in *Racke*, the Court finds the relevant customary international law to 'form part of the Community legal order' while international agreements concluded by the Community are normally said to 'form an integral part of the Community legal system'. This semantic difference does not signify different degrees of reception.

[37] In *Deutsche Shell*, the Court held that also instruments of international relations, which are not legally binding, can form an integral part of Community law. See *infra* note.

When Community law allows generally applicable rules of international law, such as *clausula rebus sic stantibus*, to be received as part of Community law, it is important to remember that *the scope of rules of international law and the scope of these rules in Community law* are not necessarily the same and therefore the same international obligation may apply sometimes in a Community context and sometimes in a purely national context. Generally, a rule of international law is an integral part of Community law only insofar as it applies within the scope of Community law. This is important to be aware of also when dealing with provisions in mixed agreements (See Section IV.C).

B. International Law Invalidated by Primary Community Law

The establishment of a Community responsibility under international law is not a sufficient condition for rules of international law to become a part of the Community legal order. Existing case law suggests that in order for international law to be an integral part of the Community legal order, the rules of international law must be valid according to Community law. This is a second general condition for the reception of international law.

The relatively few cases concerning the legality of *international agreements* assumed by the Community confirm this[38]: *France v Commission*, decided in 1994, was the first case in which the Court found an international agreement to be invalid as a matter of Community law. France had challenged the legality of the Commission's conclusion of an agreement with the US government regarding application of competition laws. The Court held that the agreement produced binding legal effects and, in case of non-performance, could give rise to liability at the international level.[39] Such an agreement should have been concluded by the Community (as such) according to the procedure in Article 300 EC and not by the Commission. The Commission had therefore acted *ultra vires* and the Court accordingly declared the Agreement invalid as a matter of Community law. This invalidity, obviously, does not affect the responsibility of the Community vis-à-vis third parties,[40] which is governed by principles of public international law.[41]

---

[38] In Opinion 1/75, *Understanding on a Local Cost Standard* [1975] ECR 1355, the Court held *obiter dictum* that the legality of an agreement was subject to review in annulment actions brought under Article 230. See also Case 165/87, *Commission v Council* [1988] ECR 5545, paragraphs 18–20. [39] Case C-327/91, *French Republic v Commission* [1994] ECR I-3641, paragraph 25.

[40] Similarly, Ilona Cheyne, 'International Instruments as a Source of Community Law', in Dashwood and Hillion, eds. *The General Law of E.C. External Relations*, 2000, p. 256, at note 11; paragraph 35 of AG Lenz's Opinion in Case 165/87, *Commission v Council* [1988] ECR 5545; Piet Eeckhout, *External Relations of the European Union: Legal and Constitutional Foundations*, 2004, p. 245.

[41] On international resonsibility for *ultra vires* acts, see in particular Article 46 of the 1969 Vienna Convention on the Law of Treaties and Article 46 of the 1986 Vienna Convention between States and International Organizations or Between Organizations. Generally, Malcolm N. Shaw, *International Law*, 2003, p. 1199 (and by analogy Chapter 14 on state responsibility); and Henry G. Schermers and Niels M. Blokker, *International Institutional Law*, 2001, §§ 1582–1590.

Therefore, the Community may be liable for the due performance of international obligations, which nevertheless do not, any more, have effects inside the Community. In practice, however, when the Court annuls a Council decision to conclude an international agreement, it can limit the effects of its judgment. In *Commission v Council* concerning transport agreements concluded by the Council with the wrong legal basis, the Court held that, 'in order to avoid any legal uncertainty as regards the applicability of the international commitments entered into by the Community within the Community legal order, the effect of the contested decisions must be maintained until the measures necessary to implement the present judgment have been adopted'.[42]

The *Energy Star Agreement* case (concerning conclusion of an agreement on the basis of the wrong power-conferring provision)[43] and *Germany v. Council* (Bananas II) (concerning conclusion of an agreement in violation of the primary Community law principle of non-discrimination)[44] likewise assume that Community law validity is a necessary condition for the reception of international agreements.

C. In Sum

Kupferberg, *Racke* and *France v Commission* together establish an external and internal substantive threshold for reception of international law in Community law. Generally, the Community legal order is based on the premise that the Community must, in the exercise of its powers, comply with international law. Therefore, *whenever the Community exercises its powers in international relations, rules of international law pertaining to the exercise of such powers are binding on the Community and will automatically also become an integral part of Community law.* However, in order to preserve the autonomy of (primary) Community law, *rules of international law are only part of Community law to the extent that they are valid*

---

[42] Case C-211/01, *Commission v Council* [2003] ECR I-8913, paragraph 57. Similarly, Case C-360/93, *European Parliament v Council* [1996] ECR I-1195: The Court annulled a Council decision to conclude a government procurement agreement with the US on the ground that it was adopted on the wrong legal basis. However, the Court found, relying on an analogy of Article 174 (2) (now Article 231 (2)) EC, for reasons of legal certainty that the effects of the Council Decision should be preserved (paragraphs 32 ff). See generally Christine Kaddous, *Le droit des relations extérieures dans la jurisprudence de la Cour de justice des Communautés européennes*, 1998, p. 51.

[43] Case C-281/01, *Commission v Council* [2002] ECR I-12049, paragraphs 48–49. The Court annulled the Energy Star Agreement concluded with the US because the Council had wrongfully based the Agreement on Article 175 EC instead of Article 133 EC. See also Case C-211/01, *Commission v Council* [2003] ECR I-8913, paragraphs 38 *et seq.* where the Court annulled transport agreements concluded with Bulgaria and Hungary.

[44] Case C-122/95, *Germany v Council* [1998] ECR I-973. The Court annulled Council Decision 94/800 concluding the WTO Agreements, to the extent that the Council thereby approved the conclusion of the Framework Agreement on Bananas with Costa Rica, Columbia, Nicaragua and Venezuela insofar as it violated a primary Community law principle of non-discrimination. At paragraph 43, the ECJ dismissed the argument that problems of reciprocity in international relations would arise as a consequence of partial (internal) annulment of the Community's international agreements.

according to primary Community law. In principle, only international law, which satisfies these two conditions, is an integral part of Community law. Section IV will consider possible alternatives and modifications to this general test for reception of international law.

III. The Requirement of Uniform Application

The requirement of uniform application is the core consequence of international law being an integral part of Community law, and these two issues are intimately linked: 'Certainly, when the Court takes cognisance of international agreements as part of Community law, it does so to protect the uniform application of Community law (. . .).'[45] This section will investigate the case law constructed meaning, the main limits and the rationales of the general requirement of uniform application of international agreements.

A. Establishing the Requirement of Uniform Application

The requirement that international agreements of a Community nature must receive uniform application was established by the Court in the 1970s and early 1980s. In *International Fruit*, the Court held that as a matter of principle provisions in international agreements can have direct effect, but as regards GATT 1947, individuals cannot rely directly on its provisions in order to challenge Community measures in national courts.[46] Since some national courts were willing to give direct effect to GATT law, it became necessary after *International Fruit* to clarify more precisely the division of tasks between Community and national legal systems. In the *Nederlandse Spoorwegen* case, the Court held that since the Community had replaced the Member States with respect to provisions in GATT,[47] the legal effects of these provisions must be determined solely by the Community legal system and not by the national legal systems.[48] In *Kupferberg*, the Court confirmed (in relation to a free trade agreement concluded with Portugal) that:

It follows from the Community nature of such provisions [i.e. provisions in Community agreements] that their effect in the Community may not be allowed to vary according to whether their application is in practice the responsibility of the Community institutions or

---

[45] L. Hancher, *Constitutionalism, the Community Court and International Law* (1994) XXV Netherlands Yearbook of International Law 259–98, p. 281. [46] See Section IV.B.(i).
[47] See Section IV.B.(i).
[48] Case 38/75, *Douaneagent der NV Nederlandse Spoorwegen v accijnzen* [1975] ECR 1439, paragraph 16. See the question of the Dutch court, paragraph 13. Henry G. Schermers, *Community Law and International Law* (1975) 12 CML Rev 77, pp. 88–89; Carlo Mastellone, *Case Law: Case 266/81, SIOT and Joined Cases 267–269/81, SPI and SAMI* (1983) 20 CML Rev 559–80, p. 579; Gerhard Bebr, *Agreements Concluded by the Community and Their Possible Direct Effect: From International Fruit to Kupferberg* (1983) 20 CML Rev 35–73, p. 41.

the Member States and, in the latter case, according to the effects in the internal legal order of each Member State which the law of that state assigns to international agreements concluded by it. Therefore it is for the Court, within the framework of its jurisdiction in interpreting theprovisions of agreements, to ensure their uniform application throughout the Community.[49]

Thus, whenever international agreements are an integral part of EC law they must receive uniform application.

In *SPI/SAMI*, the Court, again in the context of GATT 1947, explained what the requirement of uniform application of provisions in international agreements entails:

It follows that the jurisdiction conferred upon the Court in order to ensure the uniform interpretation of Community law must include a determination of the *scope and effect* of the rules of GATT within the Community and also of the effect of the tariff protocols concluded in the framework of GATT.[50]

It is immaterial, the Court said, whether the relevant provisions in the agreement are applied for the purpose of challenging the legality of a (conflicting) Community measure or the legality of a national measure.[51]

Thus, uniform application means a common approach to (at least) two facets of judicial application of provisions in international agreements. First, within the Community area, there should be one common Community approach to the interpretative 'scope' of application. A Member State cannot choose to give a more generous or a more restrictive interpretation to the scope of a provision in an agreement, which is an integral part of Community law. Secondly, the requirement of uniform application entails that provisions of international law must have the same 'effects' within the whole Community area. Thus, the judiciary of a monist-minded Member State cannot autonomously allow a provision in an agreement to invalidate a conflicting Community or national measure—if the Community legal system does not permit the provision to have such effects. Similarly, dualist-minded national courts cannot refuse to allow individuals to rely directly on provisions of international agreements if the Community legal order allows the provisions such effects. Exclusive ECJ jurisdiction is instrumental in order to ensure a uniform approach both to the scope and the effects of provisions in international agreements.

---

[49] Case 104/81, *Hauptzollamt Mainz* v *a.A.* [1982] ECR 3641, paragraph 14.
[50] Joined Cases 267/81, 268/81 and 269/81, *Amministrazione delle Finanze dello Stato* v *Italiana* [1983] ECR 801, paragraph 15 (my emphasis).
[51] *Ibid.*, paragraph 15. The Court had also in Case 104/81, *Hauptzollamt Mainz* v *a.A.* [1982] ECR 3641, paragraph 17, emphasized that the effects within the Community area of provisions of international agreements, which are of a Community nature, should be decided exclusively by the ECJ 'in the same manner as any question of interpretation'. Doubtless, the Court would also find that it has the sole jurisdiction to decide on the validity of the international obligations itself within the EC. For internal measures, see: Case 314/85, *Foto-Frost* v *Lübeck-Ost* [1987] ECR 4199.

Though these two aspects of application of provisions in international law are linked and may be difficult to separate in specific situations, the distinction is now generally used by the Court to structure most of its decisions involving provisions in international agreements.[52]

B. The (Vertical) Limits of the Requirement of Uniform Application

As a rule, uniform application of international law within the Community area can only be enforced against Member States to the extent that international law is an integral part of Community law. This seemingly trivial point has been tested before the Court on several occasions.

One of the earliest was the *Vandeweghe* case where the Court held that it has 'no jurisdiction under Article 177 [now Article 234] of the EEC Treaty to give a ruling on the interpretation of provisions of international law which bind the Member States outside the framework of Community law'.[53] The Court has upheld this rule even where it might lead to practical problems in particular cases. An illustration of this can be found in case law that deals with Member States' 'pre-Community agreements', cf. Article 307(1) EC. Pre-Community agreements are generally not an integral part of Community law. These agreements do not impose obligations on the Community institutions and Member States are, in principle, free to determine their scope and domestic effects subject to their general obligation to eliminate incompatibilities with Community law.[54] They are therefore also outside the ECJ's jurisdiction and not subject to the requirement of uniform application.

However, Member States' pre-Community agreements can at a later stage become binding also on the Community and thus an integral part of Community law. If this happens, the agreement must receive uniform application, regardless of whether Article 307(1) EC continues to apply. But even in such situations where the international agreement changes its status over time, the Court has been careful not to extend the requirement of uniform application to the period before the agreement became an integral part of Community law.

SPI/SAMI brought out this point clearly. In the earlier *International Fruit* case, the Court had found that the Community had substituted the Member States as regards fulfilment of GATT obligations as from 1 July 1968—the date of entry

---

[52] See e.g. the case law on the Europe Agreements and the Association Agreement with Turkey, Case C-162/00, *Land Nordrhein-Westfalen* v *Pokrzeptowicz-Meyer* [2002] ECR I-1049 and Case C-37/98, *The Queen* v *Secretary of State for Health* [2000] ECR I-2927. See also Section IV.C.(i) concerning Joined Cases C-392/98 and C-300/98, *Parfums Christian Dior SA* v *BV* [2000] ECR I-11307.

[53] Case 130/73, *Magdalena Vandeweghe and others v Berufsgenossenschaft für die chemische Industrie* [1973] ECR 1329, paragraph 2. The Court was asked to give a preliminary ruling on interpretation of provisions of a bilateral agreement between Germany and Belgium, which was concluded prior to the entering into force of the EC Treaty.

[54] Case 812/79, *Attorney General* v *Burgoa* [1980] ECR 2787.

into force of the Community's Common Customs Tariff.[55] After that date GATT law became binding on the Community and the Court had exclusive jurisdiction to determine how GATT provisions should be applied within the Community. One of the issues in *SPI/SAMI* was whether the ECJ had jurisdiction to interpret GATT rules that applied to situations occurring before 1 July 1968. The ECJ held that:

the provisions of GATT have since that date been amongst those which the Court of Justice has jurisdiction (...) to interpret by way of a preliminary ruling, regardless of the purpose of such interpretation. With regard to the period prior to that date, such interpretation is a matter exclusively for the courts of the Member States.[56]

The assumption in *SPI/SAMI* is that Community law cannot require uniform application of international agreements, which are not an integral part of Community law. This position has been confirmed in a line of subsequent cases, beginning with the *Andersson* case.[57]

The strict demarcation of Community and Member State spheres of international law, which is implicit in *SPI/SAMI*, *Andersson*, and similar cases may in specific situations result in complex and impractical overlaps of jurisdiction. Nevertheless, the rule is that outside the Community sphere, Member States preserve autonomy as regards the application of rules of international law.[58]

The point of this case law is neither banal nor a meaningless tautology:[59] The vertical limit of the requirement of uniform application of international law is an important specific manifestation of the general vertical division of tasks between the Community and the Member states, which runs as a recurring thread through EC external relations law. Maintaining this distinction between Community and Member State spheres is a necessary corollary of maintaining the principle of legality and the non-unitary external relations system established by the EC Treaty—even where the case for uniformity may be strong and obvious.[60]

---

[55] See Section IV.B.(i).

[56] Joined Cases 267/81, 268/81 and 269/81, *Amministrazione delle Finanze dello Stato* v *Italiana* [1983] ECR 801, paragraph 19.

[57] Case C-321/97, *Ulla-Brith Andersson and Susannne Wåkerås-Andersson* v *Sweden* [1999] ECR I-3551, paragraph 30–31; Case C-140/97, *Walter Rechberger, Renate Greindl, Hermann Hofmeister and Other* v *Österreich* [1999] ECR I-3499, paragraph 38; Case C-300/01, *Doris Salzmann* [2003] ECR I-4899, paragraphs 68–69. See also the case law on mixed agreements, Section IV.C.

[58] The Court has, however, developed a few specific exceptions, which allow it to extend its jurisdiction beyond the sphere of Community law, cf. Section IV.C on mixed agreements. See also the *Dzodzi-line* of cases. See Saulius Lukas Kaleda, *Extension of the preliminary ruling procedure outsie the scope of Community law: 'The Dzodzi line of cases'* (2000) 4 EIoP and Silvere Lefevre, *The Interpretation of Community Law by the Court of Justice in Areas of National Competence* (2004) 29 EL Rev 501–16.

[59] Neither is it uncontested. See e.g. Jacques H.J. Bourgeois, 'The European Court of Justice and the WTO: Problems and Challenges', in Weiler, ed. *The EU, the WTO, and the NAFTA: Towards a Common Law of International Trade?*, 2000, p. 89.

[60] See also Case 12/86, *Meryem Demirel* v *Gmund* [1987] ECR 3719, paragraph 28. Joined Cases 60 and 61/84, *Cinéthèque SA and others* v *français* [1985] ECR 2605, paragraph 24.

C. The Rationale for Uniform Application (I): The Two-fold Community Interest

Having recalled its (negative) limits, it is time to turn to the (positive) substantive reasons for requiring uniform application of international law that is an integral part of Community law.

It was also in the *SPI/SAMI* case that the ECJ for the first time explained in general terms why provisions of international agreements, which are of a Community nature, must always receive uniform application within and throughout the Community area:

(...) it is important that the provisions of GATT should, like the provisions of all other agreements binding the Community, receive uniform application throughout the Community. Any difference in the interpretation and application of provisions binding the Community as regards non-member countries would not only *jeopardize the unity of the commercial policy*, which according to Article 113 [now Article 133] of the Treaty must be based on uniform principles, but also create *distortions in trade within the Community*, as a result of the differences in the manner in which the agreements in force between the Community and non-member countries were applied in the various Member States.[61]

Here, the Court provides two substantive reasons for requiring uniform application of international agreements. The latter concerns internal Community relations. Disuniform application of GATT law within the Community area could jeopardize internal trade.[62] Though *SPI/SAMI* is specifically concerned with measures concerning internal trade in goods covered by the Community's CCP, the connection between the requirement of uniform application of international law and the proper functioning of internal Community law appears to have general application. Later cases concerning issues outside the scope of the CCP, such as *Demirel* and *Hermès*,[63] and *Ayaz*,[64] confirm this. Generally, to allow national variations in the application of provisions in international agreements that form an integral part of Community law could lead to distortions in intra-Community relations. As Hancher notes, 'it is unsurprising that the Court has emphasized the principle of uniform interpretation of international norms within the Community, sometimes even at the expense of effective judicial protection at

---

[61] Joined Cases 267/81, 268/81 and 269/81, *Amministrazione delle Finanze dello Stato v Italiana* [1983] ECR 801, paragraph 14 (my emphasis). Confirmed e.g. in Case C-192/89, *Sevince v Justitie* [1990] ECR I-3461, paragraphs 10–11.

[62] E.g. Marc Maresceau, 'The GATT in the Case law of the European Court of Justice', in Hilf, *et al.*, eds. *The European Community and GATT*, 1986, pp. 112.

[63] See particularly paragraphs 13–15 in AG Darmon's Opinion in Case 12/86, *Meryem Demirel v Gmund* [1987] ECR 3719 (concerning provisions on free movement of workers) and Case C-53/96, *Hermès International v BV* [1998] ECR I-3603, paragraph 32. See further Section IV.C.

[64] In Case C-275/02, *Engin Ayaz v Baden-Württemberg* [2004] ECR I-8765, paragraph 39, for example, the Court held that the concept of 'member of family' contained in Article 7 of Decision 1/80 of the Ankara Association Council must 'be construed in a uniform manner at Community level, in order to ensure consistent application in the Member States.'

the national level. This is crucial to the maintenance of the unity of the 'internal' Community legal order.'[65] This inward-looking Community interest is one reason for requiring uniform application of international agreements, which are an integral part of Community law.

The other reason offered by the Court in *SPI/SAMI* for requiring uniform application of all agreements binding on the Community (and *in casu* GATT 1947) concerns the Community's external relations. Uniform application of international agreements within the EC is necessary in order not to jeopardize the unity in the Community's commercial policy. Possibly, this reasoning is most compelling in relation to the *a priori* exclusive parts of the Community's commercial policy where Article 133(1) EC also provides that the CCP should be based on 'uniform principles'.[66] However, though the Court in *SPI/SAMI* bases its reasoning on Article 133, also this 'external' Community interest in unity is of a general nature and relevant also outside the sphere of the CCP.[67] In particular, the later *Dior* case implies a more general link between the requirement of uniformity in the (internal) application of international agreements and the (external) aspiration of unity in the international representation of the Community area. As will be shown in Section IV.C.(i), in *Dior* the Court held that the requirement of unity in the international representation of the Community necessitated uniform application of Article 50 of TRIPs within the Community area.[68] Thus, the general (external) Community interest in unitary international representation is another reason for requiring uniform application of provisions in an international agreement, which are an integral part of Community law.

In sum, the two Community interests expounded in *SPI/SAMI* have in later cases been given a more general application (beyond the CCP) and mutually reinforce the requirement of uniform application of all Community agreements.[69]

---

[65] L. Hancher, *Constitutionalism, the Community Court and International Law* (1994) XXV Netherlands Yearbook of International Law 259–98, p. 296.

[66] Case C-432/92, *The Queen* v *Minister of Agriculture* [1994] ECR I-3087, discussed below, confirms the external Community interest in uniform application.

[67] Compare Piet Eeckhout, *External Relations of the European Union: Legal and Constitutional Foundations*, 2004, p. 14.

[68] Joined Cases C-392/98 and C-300/98, *Parfums Christian Dior SA v BV* [2000] ECR I-11307, paragraph 36. The Court referred to Opinion 1/94, *Re WTO Agreement* [1994] ECR I-5267, paragraph 108.

[69] The dual Community interest in uniform application is also widely used by the literature and Advocates General as basic tools in analyses of the relationship between international law and Community law. See e.g. the Opinion of AG Cosmas, paragraph 52ff, in Joined Cases C-392/98 and C-300/98, *Parfums Christian Dior SA v BV* [2000] ECR I-11307. Paragraph 31 of AG Jacobs' Opinion in Case C-84/95, *Bosphorus Hava Yollari Turizm ve Ticaret AS* v *Minister for Transport* [1996] ECR I-3953 (concerning implementation of a UN Security Resolution); Pierre Pescatore, 'Conclusion', in Jacobs and Roberts, eds. *The Effects of Treaties in Domestic Law*, 1987; Piet Eeckhout, *The Domestic Legal Status of the WTO Agreement: Interconnecting Legal Systems* (1997) 34 CML Rev 11–58, p. 20; Marise Cremona, 'EC External Commercial Policy after Amsterdam: Authority and Interpretation within Interconnected Legal Orders', in Weiler, ed. *The EU, the WTO, and the NAFTA: Towards a Common Law of International Trade?*, 2000, p. 25.

D. The Rationale for Uniform Application (II): Proper Compliance with International Obligations

The *Anastasiou* case confirmed the above-mentioned two Community interests, but provided at the same time an additional reason for requiring uniform application of provisions in international agreements. The case concerned application of a Protocol regarding rules on products originating from Cyprus, which was annexed to the Association Agreement with Cyprus: Following the Turkish occupation of Northern Cyprus in 1974 and its subsequent proclamation of an independent 'Turkish Republic of Northern Cyprus', Northern Cypriot authorities began—without authorization from the Republic of Cyprus—to issue proofs of origin to producers exporting to the Community from Northern Cyprus. Producers and exporters of citrus fruits from the southern part of Cyprus brought action against the UK for accepting these certificates in violation of provisions in the Protocol and the Agreement. The Court first dealt with some of the general provisions of the Association Agreement, including notably Article 5, which provided that '[t]he rules governing trade between the Contracting Parties may not give rise to any discrimination between (. . .) nationals or companies of Cyprus'. The Court held that 'since Article 5 appears in an international agreement, the Community must take particular account of its partner to the Agreement when interpreting and applying it'.[70] In light of these considerations, the Court found that according to the provisions in the Agreement, the Community was not competent to accept proofs of origin from authorities not authorized by the Republic of Cyprus.

Next, the Court noted that, within the Community, the rules of origin contained in the Protocol were applied in a disuniform manner: After the Turkish occupation, the Court said, the official position of Cyprus as to how the Protocol should be applied clearly stood in contrast to the Commission's practice. Moreover, some Member States accepted certificates issued by authorities other than those of the Republic of Cyprus while others did not.[71] According to the Court:

> The existence of different practices among the Member States thus creates uncertainty of a kind likely to undermine the existence of a common commercial policy *and the performance by the Community of its obligations under the Association Agreement*[72]

On this ground, the Court found that the rules of the Protocol annexed to the Association Agreement should be interpreted strictly and in a uniform way within the Community. This meant that the UK authorities were under a Community law obligation not to accept certificates issued by North Cypriot authorities.[73]

---

[70] Case C-432/92, *The Queen v Minister of Agriculture* [1994] ECR I-3087, paragraph 46.
[71] Paragraphs 51- 52. See also AG Gulmann's Opinion, paragraph 62 and paragraphs 66–67.
[72] Paragraph 53 (my emphasis).
[73] See Marise Cremona, *Annotation to Case C-432/92, Anastasiou* (1996) 33 CML Rev 125–35.

The *Anastasiou* case thus provides an additional reason for requiring uniform application of provisions in international agreements. The Community must take into consideration its partners when applying an international agreement. This (international law) dimension of the requirement of uniform application also played a role in the *Dior* case. In that case, the Court held that Article 50 of TRIPs required to be applied in a uniform way within the Community. This, in turn, justified the Court's jurisdiction to determine the scope of that Article in a situation that was outside Community competence (see further Section IV.C.(i)).[74] A third rationale for the requirement of uniform application is that it enables the Community to comply with its international obligations and respect the position of its partners.[75]

E. In Sum

An analysis of the relatively few ECJ cases that have dealt with the meaning, limits and rationale(s) of the requirement of uniform application shows that four considerations have been particularly influential. First, the substantive scope of the requirement of uniform application of international law is restrained so as to respect the 'internal vertical' division between Community and Member State spheres in international relations (*SPI/SAMI* and *Andersson*). However, within the scope of Community law, when international law is of a Community nature, there are three positive substantive reasons for insisting on its uniform application within the Community. Two of these are distinctly Community interests (*SPI/SAMI*). First, uniform application preserves the undistorted functioning (*effet utile*) of internal relations. Second, uniform application of international agreements within strengthens external unity, i.e. uniform application facilitates the Community's general external aspiration to represent the Community area in a unitary way in international relations. Finally, the requirement of uniform application of international law within the Community is also a means to ensure proper compliance with this international law (*Anastasiou*).

Chronologically, the question of how to apply a rule of international law within the Community arises only after it has been determined whether this rule is an integral part of the Community legal system. The requirement of uniform

---

[74] Joined Cases C-392/98 and C-300/98, *Parfums Christian Dior SA* v *BV* [2000] ECR I-11307, paragraphs 37–38. In the case, the Commission had also made the point that disuniform application would be unacceptable from the perspective of third parties. See also AG Cosmas' Opinion, paragraphs 54 *et seq*.

[75] The legal literature confirms this international dimension of the requirement of uniform application. Fernando Castillo de la Torre, *The Status of GATT in EC Law, Revisited* (1995) JWT 53–68, p. 62, for example, identifies the connection between uniform application and the ECJ's 'Völkerrechtsfreundlichkeit'. See also Pierre Pescatore, 'Conclusion', in Jacobs and Roberts, eds. *The Effects of Treaties in Domestic Law*, 1987, p. 275; Jan Klabbers, *International Law and Community Law: The Law and Politics of Direct Effect* (2002) 21 YEL 263–98, p. 281; Nanette Neuwahl, 'Individuals and the GATT: Direct Effect and Indirect Effects of the General Agreement of Tariffs and Trade in Community Law', in Emiliou and O'Keeffe, eds. *The European Union and World Trade Law*, 1996.

application is thus the basic and overarching *consequence following* from the reception of international law in Community law. Yet, the need for uniform application is inextricably related to the substantive *reasons for receiving* international agreements as an integral part of Community law in the first place (cf. in particular the *Kupferberg* case). There is thus a close functional (even circular) relationship between the extent to which there is a need to apply international law in a uniform manner within the EC and the extent to which international law becomes an integral part of Community law.[76] Because of this linkage, it may be fruitful to use the considerations underlying the case law on uniform application as a basis for developing the principles of reception of international law in Community law. This will be explored and substantiated below.

IV. Alternative Principles of Reception of International Law

A. Introduction

It was established in Section II that the main criterion for Community's reception of international law in Community law is the Community's responsibility under international law (the *Kupferberg/Racke* principle). Hence, 'as a rule'[77] international agreements to which the Community is not a party are not an integral part of Community law since the EC is not responsible for their performance under international law. Yet, due in large part to the potential discrepancies between Community law and international law, the EC's responsibility under international law has in some situations proved unsuitable as a criterion for reception. To remedy the problems that arise in this respect, alternative methods of reception have been developed by the Court. To date, the Court of Justice has developed three such alternative methods of reception of international law: A doctrine of substitution (Section IV.B.(i)), a doctrine of delegation (Section IV.B.(ii)), and a set of special principles pertaining to mixed agreements (Section IV.C).

B. Substitution and Delegation

(i) International Fruit: The Doctrine of Substitution

The Establishment of a Doctrine of Substitution

GATT 1947 is the most prominent example of an international agreement, which for many years has been accepted as an integral part of Community law without the Community being a contracting party.[78] The only case in which the Court of

---

[76] See particularly Case 104/81, *Hauptzollamt Mainz* v *a.A.* [1982] ECR 3641, pargraph 14.

[77] Case C-377/98, *Netherlands* v *Council* [2001] ECR I-7079, paragraph 53.

[78] See, however, *infra* at note 94.

Justice has given extensive consideration to this issue is *International Fruit*. In that case the Court held that before a provision of international law can affect the validity of Community measures, 'the Community must first of all be bound by that measure'.[79] All six EC Member States were parties to the GATT when the EEC Treaty entered into force in 1958, but since the Community had never itself adhered to the Agreement, the possibility of relying on a reasoning similar to that in *Haegeman* (i.e. to consider GATT an act of Community institutions) was not available.[80] The Court, nevertheless, found that GATT 1947 was binding on the Community and therefore the Court had jurisdiction to determine its domestic effects within the Community. In order to justify this position, the Court first noted that the Member States could not escape their previously assumed obligations under GATT 1947 by entering into the EC Treaty. On the contrary, it was clear that the Member States, when concluding the EEC Treaty, had intended the to comply with their GATT obligations. This intention of the Member States was expressed both directly *to the GATT parties* (when the EEC Treaty was presented to them in accordance with Article XXIV of GATT 1947)[81] and in *provisions of the EC Treaty* (in Article 131 EC, which like GATT aims at international trade liberalization and in Article 307(1) EC, which provides that Member States' pre-Community agreements are not affected by the EC Treaty).[82] Next, the Court observed that by virtue of Article 111 (now repealed) and Article 133, the Community had 'assumed the functions inherent in the tariff and trade policy' progressively and in their entirety at the end of the transitional period, and that the Member States, by conferring these powers to the Community 'showed their wish to bind' also the Community by GATT law.[83] Third, the Court emphasized that since the entering into force of the EC Treaty and more particularly since the establishment of a Common Customs Tariff, the transfer of powers to the Community from the Member States had been 'put into concrete form' within the framework of GATT. The Court stressed that this transfer of powers had been 'recognized by the other Contracting Parties'. In particular, the Community had (since the setting up of a common external tariff) acted as a partner in tariff negotiations and concluded agreements within the framework of GATT.[84] Therefore, in so far as under the E(E)C Treaty the Community had assumed the powers previously exercised by the Member States in the area governed by GATT, the provisions of that Agreement had the effect of binding the Community.[85]

---

[79] Joined Cases 21–24/72, *International Fruit Company NV and others* v *Fruit* [1972] ECR 1219, paragraph 7.

[80] Contrast Ilona Cheyne, 'International Instruments as a Source of Community Law', in Dashwood and Hillion, eds. *The General Law of E.C. External Relations*, 2000, p. 257, who argues that the Court's reasoning in International Fruit 'appears to have been subsumed and extended by a different formulation in the later case of *Haegeman*'.

[81] Article XXIV of GATT provides an exception to the GATT general rules for regional economic integration in the form of customs unions, free trade areas and interim agreements leading to either of these. It requires, *inter alia*, notification to the other GATT parties.   [82] Paragraphs 10–13.

[83] Paragraphs 14–15.   [84] Paragraphs 16–17.   [85] Paragraph 18.

The CFI has recently used an analoguous reasoning in the *Yusuf* and *Kadi* cases.[86] A question in these cases was whether UN Security Council resolutions and the EC's implementing regulations violated fundamental rights in Community law. The CFI held that the EC is not directly bound by the UN Charter (paragraph 192 in *Kadi*), but drawing on the ECJ's reasoning in *International Fruit*, the CFI found that the EC Treaty nevertheless provided that the Community was bound by the Charter (paragraphs 193–204, *Kadi*). Hence,

it is not under general international law (. . .), but by virtue of the EC Treaty itself, that the Community was required to give effect to the Security Council resolutions, within the spheres of its powers. (paragraph 207, *Kadi*)

The CFI thus considered the relevant parts of the UN Charter and Security Council resolutions to be an integral part of Community law. The cases raise several important questions, which are beyond the scope of this article.[87] The decisions are appealed to the ECJ.[88]

The Doctrine of Substitution is an Independent Principle of Reception

The special circumstances surrounding the Community's relations to GATT 1947 makes it possible to argue that the Community was actually also responsible as a matter of international law for the performance of GATT obligations, and therefore the general Kupferberg principle would actually lead to the same result.[89] However, the Court's assessment in *International Fruit* of whether the Community had replaced the Member States was an (internal) EC law assessment—made for the purpose of clarifying internal legal issues. Though the perspective of third countries is taken into account, the reasoning is not dependent on international law responsibility. The Court's subsequent GATT case law clearly assumes that, in contrast to ordinary pre-Community agreements,[90] GATT 1947 became an integral part of the Community legal system.[91]

---

[86] Case T-306/01, *Ahmed Ali Yusuf* v *Commission* [2005] ECR II-0000, paragraphs 231–57 (judgment of 21 September 2005), and Case T-315/01, *Yassin Abdullah Kadi* v *Commission* [2005] ECR II-0000, paragraphs 176 ff (judgment of 21 September 2005).

[87] Having found that the relevant Security Council resolutions were an integral part of Community law, the CFI first denied to review the legality of these resolutions or the implementing regulations on the ground that they infringed general principles of Community law. Nevertheless, the CFI undertook 'to check, indirectly, the lawfulness of the resolutions of the Security Council in question with regard to *jus cogens*' (paragraph 226ff in *Kadi*). These two findings have, in my view, tremendous importance. The former concerns what kind of 'constitutional charter' the EC Treaty is, including to what extent EU fundamental rights are capable of protecting individuals, and how the EU's fundamental rights may differ from those enshrined in the Member States' constitutions. The second concerns the Court's willingness to check for compliance with *jus cogens*. This appears to be an important new way in which 'domestic' or regional courts can participate in developing the international rule of law. [88] C-415/05 P (*Yusuf*) and C-402/05 P (*Kadi*).

[89] See *infra* note 97. [90] E.g. Case 812/79, *Attorney General* v *Burgoa* [1980] ECR 2787.

[91] Similarly, e.g. Claus-Dieter Ehlermann, 'Application of GATT Rules in the European Community', in Hilf, *et al.*, eds. *The European Community and GATT*, 1986, p. 138; Ernst-Ulrich Petersmann, *International and European Foreign Trade Law: GATT Dispute Settlement Proceedings Against the EEC* (1985) 22 CML Rev 441, p. 456.

In *Nederlandse Spoorwegen* and *SPI/SAMI*, the Court confirmed that the Community was bound by provisions of GATT 1947, that it had 'replaced' the Member States as regards fulfilment of the commitments under GATT, and, as we saw above, that the Court had exclusive jurisdiction to interpret and determine the effects of GATT rules within the Community area.[92] Another relatively clear example is the *Nakajima* case where the Court held that the Community was 'under an obligation to ensure compliance with the General Agreement and its implementing measures'.[93] This implies that—from the Community's perspective—there was no legally relevant difference between the internal legal status of GATT 1947 (which the Community had not concluded) and its implementing agreements (*in casu* the Anti-Dumping Code to which the Community was a party).

The Scope of the Doctrine of Substitution: Two Approaches

The doctrine of substitution developed in *International Fruit* (and applied in *Yusuf* and *Kadi*) is therefore an alternative method of reception of an international agreement. However, the ECJ has so far offered no further clue as to the more precise scope of the doctrine. As a consequence, it remains uncertain whether and to what extent the *International Fruit* case could have been the beginning of the development of a practically important alternative procedure for reception of international law. As a matter of fact, the doctrine of substitution has hitherto been dormant and of very limited practical relevance (at least in litigation before the ECJ).[94] Yet, I submit, it is still possible to envisage two different directions for its future application.

On the one hand, the prevailing view seems to be that the circumstances surrounding GATT 1947 are extraordinary and so is the doctrine of substitution. According to this view, a set of cumulative criteria must be met before the doctrine of substitution can apply.[95] This also seems to be the assumption of the CFI

---

[92] Case 38/75, *Douaneagent der NV Nederlandse Spoorwegen* v *accijnzen* [1975] ECR 1439, paragraph 16; Joined Cases 267/81, 268/81 and 269/81, *Amministrazione delle Finanze dello Stato* v *Italiana* [1983] ECR 801, paragraph 14. See also e.g. Case 9/73, *Carl Schlüter* v *Lörrach* [1973] ECR 1135; Case C-280/93, *Germany* v *Council* [1994] ECR I-4973; Case C-61/94, *Commission* v *Germany* [1996] ECR I-3989.

[93] Case C-69/89, *Nakajima All Precision Co. Ltd* v *Council* [1991] ECR I-2069, paragraph 29. The Court referred to Case 104/81, *Hauptzollamt Mainz* v *a.A.* [1982] ECR 3641, paragraph 11 and Case 266/81, *Società Italiana per l'Oleodotto Transalpino (SIOT)* v *Ministère Italien des finances* [1983] ECR 731, paragraph 28.

[94] The ECJ has found only two other international agreements to be binding on the Community according to the principle of substitution. In Case 38/75, *Douaneagent der NV Nederlandse Spoorwegen* v *accijnzen* [1975] ECR 1439, paragraph 21, the Court held that, for the same reasons as those given in *International Fruit*, the Brussels Convention of 1950 on Nomenclature for the Classification of Goods in Customs Tariffs and the Convention of 1950 establishing a Customs Co-operation Council were binding on the Community.

[95] In his Opinions in Case 812/79, *Attorney General* v *Burgoa* [1980] ECR 2787, p. 2815, and Case 181/80, *Procureur général près la Cour d'Appel de Pau and others* v *Arbelaiz-Emazabel* [1981] ECR 2961, p. 2987, AG Caportorti derived (in effect) five cumulative criteria from the Court's

judges in the *Yusuf* and *Kadi* cases as regards the UN Charter and Security Council resolutions implemented by Community legislation.

On the other hand, there have been attempts in the literature to develop a more flexible approach to the doctrine of substitution applicable to contemporary external relations issues.[96] In this spirit, it is possible and plausible to see the reasoning in *International Fruit* as emphasizing three factors of particular relevance—rather than providing a set of cumulative criteria. In the first place, weight is accorded to the Member States' intention to bind both themselves and the Community by the international agreement. Particularly as regards GATT 1947, this intention had been expressed both to the GATT partners and in the EC Treaty. It is not clear, however, in which form and how qualified the Member States' intention must be expressed and whether the Community's objectives must also in some way be similar to the those of the international agreement. Second, *International Fruit* accords importance to the fact that (extensive) powers had been conferred to the Community in the area and that the Community had exercised these powers by setting up a common external tariff and by negotiating and concluding agreements within the framework of GATT. *International Fruit*, however, does not clarify whether the doctrine of substitution only applies in areas where Member States have given the Community (*a priori*) exclusive treaty-making competence. What is clear is that a second factor of importance to the issue of substitution is (the existence and nature of) the Community's external competence and the actual exercise of this competence in relation to the particular agreement. Third and finally, the position of Member States' contracting parties, (i.e. the perspective of 'the other side') is also accorded weight in *International Fruit*. The Court emphasizes that the Contracting Parties to GATT had approved the transfer of power from the Member States to the Community and the Community's exercise of this power, notably by accepting the Community as a negotiating partner within GATT and by entering into agreements with the Community.[97] Thus, the recognition, or at least interests, of third parties also

---

reasoning in *International Fruit*. To the same effect: Sebastian Bohr, *Sanctions by the United Nations Security Council and the European Community* (1993) 4 EJIL 256–68, p. 264, T.C. Hartley, *International Agreements and the Community Legal System: Some Recent Developments* (1983) 8 EL Rev 383–92; Jean Groux and Philippe Manin, *The European Communities in the International Order*, 1985, p. 108; Christine Kaddous, *Le droit des relations extérieures dans la jurisprudence de la Cour de justice des Communautés européennes*, 1998, pp. 276–81.

[96] E.g. Piet Eeckhout, *External Relations of the European Union: Legal and Constitutional Foundations*, 2004, p. 437 (also in the context of UN Security Council Resolutions). AG La Pergola attempts a more creative application of a principle of substitution in his Opinion (paragraph 18) in Case C-293/98, *Entidad de Gestión de Derechos de los Productores Audiovisuales (Egeda)* v *(Hoasa)* [2000] ECR I-629 (in the context of the Berne Convention and TRIPs).

[97] As Bourgeois puts it, 'the EC had over the years acquired the status to all intents and purposes of a contracting party'. Jacques H.J. Bourgeois, 'The European Court of Justice and the WTO: Problems and Challenges', in Weiler, ed. *The EU, the WTO, and the NAFTA: Towards a Common Law of International Trade?*, 2000, p. 71. In particular, GATT parties normally asserted their rights against the EC (and not the individual EC Member State) in dispute settlement proceedings under GATT.

seems to influence the question of whether the Community has substituted the Member States as regards a particular agreement.

This latter and more open approach suggests that particularly three factors carry weight in an assessment of whether the Community has substituted the Member States in relation to a particular agreement, but that their precise relationship and nature have not yet been worked out. The practical relevance of the doctrine of substitution in contemporary EC external relations law depends on whether it should be understood as consisting of a set of strictly cumulative criteria or as a more flexible assessment of three factors of relevance. Only in the latter scenario will the doctrine be able to function as a genuine practical alternative to the main principle of reception of international agreements, i.e. to the *Kupferberg* principle.

(ii) *Libor Cipra: The Doctrine of Delegation*

Another candidate for a practically important alternative to the general principles of reception of international law is the embryonic doctrine of delegation. The ECJ has indicated the existence of such a doctrine in only two cases.

In Opinion 2/91, the Court held that—when international law does not allow the Community to become a party to an international agreement—the Community can exercise its (exclusive or non-exclusive) treaty-making competence through the medium of the Member States.[98] According to the standard *Kupferberg* and *Racke* precedents, such international agreements would be wholly outside the sphere of Community law and there would therefore be no means of ensuring uniform application of their provisions within the Community. This would, however, lead to anomalous relationships since the Member States act only as agents of the Community and on the basis of a Community decision to exercise its own (perhaps exclusive) treaty-making competence. It may therefore be implicit already in Opinion 2/91 that when the Community exercises its treaty-making competence through the medium of the Member States, the international obligations assumed become an integral part of Community law.

A more recent case confirms this. In the *Libor Cipra* case, a question was whether the ECJ had jurisdiction under Article 234 to interpret provisions in the European Road Transport Agreement (called the AETR Agreement in the case). In order not to jeopardize the successful outcome of the AETR negotiations, the Court had accepted in the *AETR* case that—despite the Community's exclusive competence—Member States could conclude the Agreement.[99] Thus, the Community never became a party to the AETR Agreement. In his Opinion, AG Alber argued that as a consequence the *Kupferberg* principle was not applicable and therefore it would not be correct to consider the Agreement a part of Community law. Nevertheless, the Court had jurisdiction over the provisions

---

[98] Opinion 2/91, *re ILO Convention No. 170 on Safety in the Use of Chemicals at Work* [1993] ECR I-1061, paragraphs 36–38.   [99] Case 22/70, *Commission* v *Council* [1971] ECR 263.

of the Agreement because the Community had taken over Member States' competences within the scope of the Agreement.[100]

The Court (correctly) did not follow the AG. Instead, it emphasized that Council Regulation No 2829/77 had brought the Agreement into force in the Community and that according to the preamble to that Regulation, 'the Member States acted in the interest and on behalf of the Community' when they acceded to the AETR Agreement.[101] Moreover, the Court noted that, according to Article 2(2) of Council Regulation No 3820/85, as regards certain specified matters the AETR Agreement was to apply instead of the rules laid down in that Regulation. 'In the light of the foregoing, it must be held that the AETR Agreement forms part of Community law and that the Court has jurisdiction to interpret it.'[102]

Thus, international agreements may become a part of Community law when Member States enter into them in the interest and on behalf of the Community. However, as is the case with the doctrine of substitution, the scope of the doctrine of delegation is uncertain: Particularly pertinent issues are: Is the doctrine only applicable in areas where the Community has exclusive treaty-making competence? Must the Community's exercise of treaty-making competence through the Member States be explicitly stated in a Council decision or can it be implied? Does the doctrine require, in addition, that a Council decision explicitly states that the agreement is to enter into force within the Community?[103]

(iii) Concluding Remarks

Whether international agreements are an integral part of Community law or not is both theoretically and practically important. A determination of the scope of the

---

[100] Paragraph 31–35 of the Opinion. Thus, according to the AG, the Community had replaced the Member States as regards the Agreement because it had acquired exclusive treaty-making competence, but the Agreement nevertheless remained non-Community law.

[101] Council Regulation No 2829/77 on the bringing into force of the European Agreement covering the work of crews of vehicles engaged in international road transport. The fourth recital reads: 'Whereas, since the subject matter of the AETR Agreement falls within the scope of Regulation (EEC) No 543/69, from the date of entry into force of that Regulation the power to negotiate and conclude the Agreement has lain with the Community; whereas, however, the particular circumstances in which the AETR negotiations took place warrant, by way of exception, a procedure whereby the Member states of the Community individually deposit the instruments of ratification of accession in a concerted action but nonetheless act in the interest and on behalft of the Community'.

[102] Case-439/01, *Libor Cipra et Vlastimil Kvasnicka* v *Mistelbach* [2003] ECR I-745, paragraphs 23–24.

[103] The principle is immediately relevant in relation to some International Maritime Organization Conventions, cf. Council Decision 2002/762/EC (authorizing the Member States, in the interest of the Community, to sign, ratify or accede to the International Convention on Civil Liability for Bunker Oil Pollution Damage, 2001 (the Bunkers Convention) and Council Decision 2002/971/EC (authorizing the Member States, in the interest of the Community, to ratify or accede to the International Convention on Liability and Compensation for Damage in Connection with the Carriage of Hazardous and Noxious Substances by Sea, (the HNS Convention). Many thanks to Henrik Ringbom for drawing my attention to this. See Henrik Ringbom, *EU Regulation 44/2001 and its Implications for the International Maritime Liability Conventions* (2004) 35 JMLC 1–33, p. 9 and Henrik Ringbom, *Jurisdiction, Recognition and Enforcement of Maritime Judgments: The Dimension of EU External Relations Law* (2005) Marlus.

doctrines of substitution and delegation is therefore also important. The two key precedents are, however, capable of being interpreted in diametrically opposed ways. On the one hand, both *International Fruit* and *Libor Cipra* concerned international agreements, which have had a unique status in the history of EC external relations. The relevance of the two cases may therefore be limited to such peculiar types of international co-operation. On the other hand, a more flexible and dynamic interpretation of the cases is plausible. The open (i.e. vague) reasoning of the Court in both cases could form the basis for further development of distinct methods of reception of international law. A broader applicability of these alternative methods of reception could entail that some of the commitments flowing from weighty international organizations and conventions to which the Community cannot become a party may still be considered an integral part of Community law.[104] These include the UN, and in particular UN Security Council resolutions,[105] international human rights treaties,[106] ILO conventions,[107] intellectual property rights conventions,[108] international maritime conventions[109] etc.

C. Mixity Principles

Most of the ECJ's case law involving issues of international law has concerned provisions in mixed agreements. In the majority of these cases, this has caused no practical problems, mainly because it has been assumed that the relevant provisions were of a Community nature.[110] Yet, the Community and the Member States generally conclude mixed agreements *without* any clear decision about the

---

[104] Eileen Denza, 'The Community as a Member of International Organizations', in Emiliou and O'Keeffe, eds. *The European Union and World Trade Law*, 1996; I. Macleod *et al.*, *The External Relations of the European Communities*, 1996, pp. 169.; Rachel Frid, *The Relations Between the EC and International Organizations: Legal Theory and Practice*, 1995; Barbara Dutzler, 'The Representation of the EU and the Member States in International Organizations–General Aspects', in Griller and Weidel, eds. *External Economic Relations and Foreign Policy in the European Union*, 2002; Inge Govaere *et al.*, *In-Between Seats: The Participation of the European Union in International Organizations* (2004) 9 EFA Rev 155–87.

[105] In addition to the *Yusuf* and *Kadi* cases mentioned above, see e.g. Case C-124/95, *The Queen, ex parte Centro-Com* v *England* [1997] ECR I-81 and Sebastian Bohr, *Sanctions by the United Nations Security Council and the European Community* (1993) 4 EJIL 256–68; Iris Canor, 'Can Two Walk Together, Except They Be Agreed?' The Relationship Between International Law and European Law: The Incorporation of United Nations Sanctions Against Yugoslavia Into European Community Law Through the Perspective of the European Court of Justice* (1998) 35 CML Rev 137–87; Piet Eeckhout, *External Relations of the European Union: Legal and Constitutional Foundations*, 2004, p. 437.

[106] Presently, international human rights treaties, and in particular the ECHR, remain merely sources of 'inspiration' in Community law. They do not form part of the Community legal order. Case 4/73, *J. Nold, Kohlen- und Baustoffgroßhandlung* v *Commission* [1974] 491 and Paul Craig and Gráinne de Búrca, *EU Law: Text, Cases, and Materials*, 2003, p. 323. Howver, for practical purposes the ECHR is often treated as a part of (primary) Community law, which can be invoked both before the ECJ and national courts.

[107] See *supra* on Opinion 2/91, *re ILO Convention No. 170 on Safety in the Use of Chemicals at Work* [1993] ECR I-1061.   [108] E.g. the Berne Convention. See cases cited in Section IV.C.

[109] See *supra* note 103.

[110] E.g. Case 181/73, *R. & V. Haegeman* v *State* [1974] ECR 0449; Case 87–75, *Conceria Daniele Bresciani* v *Finanze* [1976] ECR 0129; Case 104/81, *Hauptzollamt Mainz* v *a.A.* [1982] ECR 3641.

extent to which the Community has assumed responsibility vis-à-vis third parties (an international law issue). In addition, mixed agreements never explicate to what extent the EC has exercised treaty-making competence (an internal Community law issue). Therefore, neither the *Kupferberg* principle nor any internal analogy of this principle can be applied easily.

Demarcation of the Community spheres of mixed agreements has in a few—but increasing—number of borderline cases required special attention. These cases show that to determine how much of a mixed agreement is Community law is intimately affixed to a Pandora's box of classic constitutional problems in EC external relations law. An analysis of the reasoning in the case law on mixed agreement shows that the Court centres around considerations similar to those that shaped the notion of uniform application, cf. Section III. Drawing on this insight, Section IV.C.(iii) will propose a general framework within which to develop more specific principles of demarcation of the Community sphere of mixed agreements.

(i) Preliminary Rulings

Demirel

The issue of vertical demarcation of provisions in mixed agreements was raised for the first time in the 1987 *Demirel* case.[111] The case concerned application of Articles 7 and 12 of the Association Agreement with Turkey and of Article 36 of a Protocol attached to this Agreement on the movement of workers.[112] The Agreement is a typical mixed association agreement in which competence has not been allocated internally between the Community and the Member States.

The Court's reasoning can be divided into three components. First, as a preliminary remark, the Court recalled the *Haegeman* case and pointed out that agreements concluded by the Community are acts of one of the institutions and an integral part of Community law.[113] This could *prima facie* be taken to mean that all provisions of mixed agreements are, like pure Community agreements, an integral part of the Community legal system. However, the subsequent reasoning shows that the reference to *Haegeman* is merely meant as an opening observation.

Next, in response to Germany's and the UK's interventions,[114] the Court then held:

8. (. . .) The German Government and the United Kingdom take the view that in the case of 'mixed' agreements (. . .), the Court's interpretative jurisdiction does not extend to

---

[111] Ruling 1/78, *Re Draft Convention of the International Atomic Energy Agency on the Physical Protection of Nuclear Materials, Facilities and Transports* [1978] ECR 2151, paragraphs 35–36, addressed in a very general manner the question of implementation of provisions in mixed agreements. See also John A. Usher, *International Competence of Euratom: European Court, Ruling 1/78* (1979) CML Rev 300–07, p. 306.

[112] Case 12/86, *Meryem Demirel* v *Gmund* [1987] ECR 3719.   [113] Paragraph 7.

[114] The arguments of the two Governments differed slightly. Germany argued mainly that the Community had not entered into the obligations concerning the free movement of workers (p. 3725), while the UK primarily stressed that the Community had no treaty-making competence to assume these commitments (p. 3729).

provisions whereby Member states have *entered into commitments* with regard to Turkey in the *exercise of* their own powers (. . .).

9. In that connection it is sufficient to state that that is precisely not the case in this instance. Since the Agreement in question is an association agreement creating special, privileged links with a non-member country which must, at least to a certain extent, take part in the Community system, Article 238 [now Article 310] must necessarily *empower* the Community to guarantee commitments towards non-member countries in all the fields covered by the Treaty. Since freedom of movement for workers is, by virtue of Article 48 [now Article 39] *et seq.* of the EEC Treaty, one of the fields covered by that Treaty, it follows that commitments regarding freedom of movement *fall within the powers conferred* on the Community by Article 238 [now Article 310]. Thus the question whether the Court has jurisdiction to rule on the interpretation of a provision in a mixed agreement containing commitments which only the Member States *could enter into* in the sphere of their own powers does not arise[115]

This reply is notoriously vague: A verbatim and isolated reading of paragraph 9 suggests that the Court here only dismisses the claim that the Community had *no competence* to assume the relevant international obligations.[116] The literature, however, has preferred to read paragraphs 8 and 9 together as implying that the Community (and not the Member States) had *assumed* the relevant provisions in the Agreements because they came within the scope of Article 310.[117] A third possibility is that the Court considered all provisions of mixed agreements, which are within the scope of the Community's treaty-making competence, to be an integral part of Community law.[118] Most likely, however, the Court simply did not seriously address any of these three important issues.

Finally, the Court added, the fact that, as Community law stood at the time, it was the Member States who in practice had to implement the obligations under the Agreement relating to free movement of workers did not affect the scope of the Court's jurisdiction. In other words, provisions of mixed agreements may be an

---

[115] My emphasis. On the discrepancy between the Member States' arguments and the Court's answers, J.H.H. Weiler, *Thou Shalt Not Oppress a Stranger: On the Judicial Protection of the Human Rights of Non-EC Nationals–A Critique* (1992) 65 EJIL 65–91, p. 74.

[116] Alan Dashwood, 'Preliminary Rulings on the Interpretation of Mixed Agreements', in O'Keeffe and Bavasso, eds. *Liber Amoricum in Honour of Lord Slynn of Hadley: Judicial Review in European Union Law,* 2000, p. 170. AG Tesauro goes further in paragraph 18 in his Opinion in Case C-53/96, *Hermès International* v *BV* [1998] ECR I-3603. He reads the passage as implying that the Court does not have jurisdiction beyond the Community's competence.

[117] J.H.H. Weiler, *Thou Shalt Not Oppress a Stranger: On the Judicial Protection of the Human Rights of Non-EC Nationals–A Critique* (1992) 65 EJIL 65–91, p. 76; Alan Dashwood, 'Preliminary Rulings on the Interpretation of Mixed Agreements', in O'Keeffe and Bavasso, eds. *Liber Amoricum in Honour of Lord Slynn of Hadley: Judicial Review in European Union Law,* 2000, p. 170. Panos Koutrakos, *The Interpretation of Mixed Agreements under the Preliminary Reference Procedure* (2002) 7 EFA Rev 25–52, p. 33. Joni Heliskoski, *The Jurisdiction of the European Court of Justice to Give Preliminary Rulings on the Interpretation of Mixed Agreements* (2000) 69 NJIL 395–412, p. 399. Contrast Philipp Gasparon, *The Transposition of the Principle of Member State Liability into the Context of External Relations* (1999) 10 EJIL 605–24, p. 612.

[118] Thus, AG Tesauro, paragraph 18 of his Opinion in Case C-53/96, *Hermès International* v *BV* [1998] ECR I-3603.

integral part of the Community legal system (and thus within the Court's jurisdiction) even if the Community is not, internally, responsible for their practical implementation. The Court referred in this respect to the *Kupferberg* case and Community's responsibility vis-à-vis Turkey.[119] This suggests that also the scope of the Community's responsibility under international law is a factor of relevance to the demarcation of Community and Member State spheres of mixed agreements. However, the Court does not investigate any further to what extent the Community is responsible vis-à-vis Turkey for the performance of the provisions on workers.

With this reasoning the Court concluded that it had jurisdiction to determine how the relevant provisions of the Agreement and the Protocol on freedom of movement for workers should be applied within the Community area.[120] The opaque reasoning invites the easy conclusion that the Court simply did not take the Member States' challenge seriously in the particular case.[121] In any event, few general guidelines can be derived from the *Demirel* case.

Hermès

A line of preliminary rulings concerning the TRIPs Agreement, which forms part of the WTO, have forced the ECJ to consider in a new context the extent to which provisions of mixed agreements are an integral part of the Community legal system and thus subject to the requirement of uniform application.[122]

---

[119] Paragraph 10.   [120] Paragraph 12.

[121] To the same effect, Marise Cremona, 'EC External Commercial Policy after Amsterdam: Authority and Interpretation within Interconnected Legal Orders', in Weiler, ed. *The EU, the WTO, and the NAFTA: Towards a Common Law of International Trade?*, 2000, p. 28; Nanette A. Neuwahl, *Joint Participation in International Treaties and the Exercise of Powers by the EEC and Its Member States: Mixed Agreements* (1991) 28 CML Rev 717–40, p. 736; Alan Dashwood, 'Preliminary Rulings on the Interpretation of Mixed Agreements', in O'Keeffe and Bavasso, eds. *Liber Amoricum in Honour of Lord Slynn of Hadley: Judicial Review in European Union Law*, 2000, p. 170. See also Case C-192/89, *Sevince* v *Justitie* [1990] ECR I-3461. In Case C-237/91, *Kazim Kus* v *Wiesbaden* [1992] ECR I-6781 (at p. 6786), Germany argued that Decision 1/80 of the Turkey Agreement Association Council was within the Member States' sphere of competence, but the Court dismissed the argument (paragraph 9) with reference to previous case law.

[122] For analyses Armin von Bogdandy, *Case Law: Case C-53/96, Hermès International v. FHT Marketing Choice BV* (1999) 36 CML Rev 663–72; Alan Dashwood, 'Preliminary Rulings on the Interpretation of Mixed Agreements', in O'Keeffe and Bavasso, eds. *Liber Amoricum in Honour of Lord Slynn of Hadley: Judicial Review in European Union Law*, 2000; Joni Heliskoski, *The Jurisdiction of the European Court of Justice to Give Preliminary Rulings on the Interpretation of Mixed Agreements* (2000) 69 NJIL 395–412; Andrea Filippo Gagliardi, *The Rights of Individuals to Invoke the Provisions of Mixed Agreements Before the National Courts: A New Message from Luxembourg* (1999) 24 EL Rev 276–92; Marise Cremona, 'EC External Commercial Policy after Amsterdam: Authority and Interpretation within Interconnected Legal Orders', in Weiler, ed. *The EU, the WTO, and the NAFTA: Towards a Common Law of International Trade?*, 2000; Jacques H.J. Bourgeois, 'The European Court of Justice and the WTO: Problems and Challenges', in Weiler, ed. *The EU, the WTO, and the NAFTA: Towards a Common Law of International Trade?*, 2000; Axel G. Desmedt, *European Court Rules on TRIPs Agreement* (1998) JIEL 679–82; Joni Heliskoski, *Joined Cases 300/98, Parfums Christian Dior SA v. Tuk Consultancy BV, and C-392/98, Assco Gerüste GmbH and R. van Dijk v. Wilhelm Layher GmbH & Co KG and Layher BV, judgment of 14 December, nyr* (2002) 39 CML Rev 159–74; Joni Heliskoski, *Mixed Agreements as a Technique for Organizing the International*

The first three of these cases concerned the ECJ's jurisdiction to determine the scope and effect of Article 50 of the TRIPS Agreement.[123] This Article is a detailed procedural provision that applies to all intellectual property rights falling within the ambit of the Agreement. It will be remembered that the Court in Opinion 1/94 found that the Community did not have exclusive competence to conclude the TRIPs Agreement. The WTO was subsequently concluded as a mixed agreement without any allocation of competence between the EC and the Member States.[124]

The problem of interest here is to what extent Article 50 of TRIPs is an integral part of the Community legal system. As a rule, the ECJ has (exclusive) jurisdiction to determine how Article 50 of TRIPs should be applied within the Community area only to the extent that the provision is an integral part of Community law.[125]

The *Hermès* case concerned an alleged violation of the Hermès trade mark, which was registered within the Benelux area.[126] Hermès had asked a Dutch court for an interim order, which would require FHT Marketing Choice BV to cease the illegal use of the trade mark. At the same time, Hermès asked the Dutch court to fix a period of three months within which revocation of the interim order was possible. Article 50(6) of the TRIPs Agreement provides that a decision by a court imposing protective measures against infringements, which has been adopted *inaudita altera partes* shall, if the defendant so requests, be revoked or otherwise cease to have effects if proceedings concerning the merits of the case are not initiated within a reasonable period. The Dutch court was in doubt as to the compatibility of the time limit asked for by Hermès with the requirements of Article 50(6) of TRIPs and referred a question to the ECJ concerning its interpretation.

Three intervening governments disputed the jurisdiction of the ECJ to interpret Article 50 of TRIPs, notably because the case concerned a Benelux trade mark and not a Community trade mark. They argued that the provision accordingly fell within the Member States' competence and that interpretation of the Article in such a situation is a matter solely within the jurisdiction of the Member States. The Commission, on the other hand, argued that a mixed agreement should generally be regarded as a single agreement, which should be interpreted and

---

Relations of the European Community and its Member States, 2001; Panos Koutrakos, *The Interpretation of Mixed Agreements under the Preliminary Reference Procedure* (2002) 7 EFA Rev 25–52; Gaëlle Bontinck, *The TRIPs Agreement and the ECJ: A New Dawn?–Some Comments About Joined Cases C-300/98 and C-392/98, Parfums Dior and Assco Gerüste* (2001) Jean Monnet Working Paper; Martha Pertegas Sender, *Case law: Parfums Christian Dior v. Tuk Consultancy* (2001) 7 Colum. J. Eur. L. 385; Francis Snyder, *The Gatekeepers: The European Courts and WTO Law* (2003) 40 CML Rev 313–67.

[123] Case C-53/96, *Hermès International* v *BV* [1998] ECR I-3603; Joined Cases C-392/98 and C-300/98, *Parfums Christian Dior SA* v *BV* [2000] ECR I-11307; C-89/99, *Schieving-Nijstad vof and Others* v *Groeneveld* [2001] ECR I-5851.   [124] Council Decision 94/800/EC.

[125] Gaëlle Bontinck, *The TRIPs Agreement and the ECJ: A New Dawn?–Some Comments About Joined Cases C-300/98 and C-392/98, Parfums Dior and Assco Gerüste* (2001) Jean Monnet Working Paper, p. 9: 'The possibility for the Court to answer the references implies that Article 50 of TRIPs is in some respect already part of Community law.'

[126] Case C-53/96, *Hermès International* v *BV* [1998] ECR I-3603.

applied in a uniform way. AG Tesauro provided an innovative and complex assessment of the scope of the Court's jurisdiction over mixed agreements.[127] His concluding observation is noteworthy:

Lastly, I should like to make a comment of a more general nature. The Community legal system is characterised by the simultaneous application of provisions of various origins, international, Community and national; but it nevertheless seeks to function and to represent itself to the outside world as a unified system. That is, one might say, the inherent nature of the system which, while guaranteeing the maintenance of the realities of States and of individual interests of all kinds, also seeks to achieve a unified modus operandi. Its steadfast adherence to that aim, which the Court itself has described as an obligation of solidarity, is certainly lent considerable weight by the judicial review mechanism which is defined in the Treaty and relies on the simultaneous support of the Community court and the national courts[128]

In effect, both the AG and the Commission argued backwards, so to speak, beginning with the need for a 'unified *modus operandi*' and uniform application, and ending with an exclusive ECJ jurisdiction (which entails that the relevant provision in the particular context is part of Community law).

The Court agreed that Article 50 of TRIPs should be interpreted in a uniform manner at Community level—even when it was applied to national trade mark rights. Its reasoning falls in three stages: First, the Court began by pointing out that the WTO was concluded as a mixed agreement without any allocation of competence between the Community and the Member States.

Equally, without there being any need to determine the extent of the obligations assumed by the Community in concluding the agreement, it should be noted that when the Final Act and the WTO Agreement were signed by the Community and its Member States on 15 April 1994, Regulation No 40/94 (on the Community Trade Mark) had been in force for one month[129]

It has been suggested that the Court in this way wished to emphasize the 'international law point of view', i.e. that the Community was responsible vis-à-vis third parties for any Member State violation of WTO law.[130] It is, however, not

---

[127] Paragraphs 10–21 of the Opinion. In short, (at paragraphs 19–21), the AG argued, first, that provisions of an international agreement may be 'interconnected' and different national interpretations could in these situations affect also Community law. Second, the Community was responsible as a matter of international law for all the WTO Agreements and thus the Court should be able to protect the Community from being liable vis-à-vis third parties for infringements committed by Member States. Third, he referred to the duty of close co-operation and the requirement of unity in the international representation and argued that different interpretations of provisions of a mixed agreement could undo the consensus (within the Community area) that may have been reached at the stage of negotiations and conclusion of the mixed agreement. For these reasons, the Court should ensure uniform application.   [128] Paragraph 21.

[129] Paragraphs 24–25.

[130] Allan Rosas, 'The European Union and Mixed Agreements', in Dashwood and Hillion, eds. *The General Law of E.C. External Relations*, 2000, p. 215; Piet Eeckhout, *External Relations of the European Union: Legal and Constitutional Foundations*, 2004, p. 240. See also AG Tesauro's Opinion in the case.

uncontested that the Community is responsible for all parts of the WTO Agreements vis-à-vis WTO Members, and it therefore seems unlikely that the Court would take a stance on this important issue in such a cursory manner without any further analysis of the Agreements. I submit, on the contrary, that the laconic introductory statement is meant to emphasize that determination of the scope of the Community's responsibility under international law is *not* necessary in order to decide on the (internal) issue of how much of the WTO Agreements are within the Court's jurisdiction.[131] By referring to internal legislation, the Court avoids expressing its view on the distribution between the Member States and the Community of responsibility vis-à-vis third parties—an issue over which the Court does not have final jurisdiction in relation to third parties. This is not an appropriate criterion with which to demarcate Community and Member State spheres of mixed agreements for Community law purposes. The Court thereby also preserves one of the main virtues of mixed agreements, which is to side-step contentious issues, such as who has exercised treaty-making competence (an internal question) and who has assumed responsibility vis-à-vis third parties (an international law question).[132] Such an approach, however, makes it impossible for the Court to use the *Kupferberg* principle, and therefore there is no mention of this principle in *Hermès* (or in any of the later TRIPs cases discussed below).

Next, the Court constructed a hypothetical situation involving a *Community* trade mark (though the actual case concerned a national (or regional) trade mark)[133]: *If* the legal dispute before the Dutch court had involved a Community trade mark, Article 99 of Regulation 40/94 would provide that the Community trade mark rights may be protected by national provisional safeguard measures. Like Article 50 of TRIPs, Article 99 of Regulation 40/94 concerned provisional safeguard measures for Community trade marks. Therefore, in (the hypothetical) situations where national courts deal with provisional protection of Community trade mark rights, national courts would in these situations be required to interpret Regulation 40/94 in light of Article 50 of TRIPs.[134] The ECJ would therefore also have jurisdiction over Article 50 of TRIPs in order to ensure that Community measures are consistent with TRIPs.

This excursion did not settle the problem since the actual case concerned the application of national procedural rules for the purpose of protecting *national* (Benelux) trade mark rights, and their relationship with Article 50 of TRIPs. In a

---

[131] In other words, in my submission, the Court here separates two questions, which by many have been considered inseparable. E.g. Marise Cremona, *The Doctrine of Exclusivity and the Position of Mixed Agreements in the External Relations of the European Community* (1982) 2 OJLS 393, p. 426: 'Should the Community be regarded as bound by the whole of a mixed agreement, or only by those parts of it which fall within its sphere of competence? This question would seem to be inseparable from the question of whether the whole agreement becomes part of Community law.'

[132] To the same effect, Ruling 1/78, *Re Draft Convention of the International Atomic Energy Agency on the Physical Protection of Nuclear Materials, Facilities and Transports* [1978] ECR 2151.

[133] Paragraphs 26–29.

[134] The Court referred to Case C-286/90, *Anklagemyndigheden* v *Corp.* [1992] ECR I-6019; Case C-61/94, *Commission* v *Germany* [1996] ECR I-3989.

third step, therefore, the Court provided two additional reasons why it should have jurisdiction to determine how Article 50 of TRIPs applies also in a situation involving national trade mark rights:

31 First, it is solely for the national court hearing the dispute, which must assume responsibility for the order to be made, to assess the need for a preliminary ruling so as to enable it to give its judgment. Consequently, where the question referred to it concerns a provision which it has jurisdiction to interpret, the Court of Justice is, in principle, bound to give a ruling (see, to that effect, Joined Cases C-297/88 and C-197/89 Dzodzi [1990] ECR I-3763, paragraphs 34 and 35, and Case C-231/89 Gmurzynska-Bscher [1990] ECR I-4003, paragraphs 19 and 20).

32 Second, where a provision can apply *both* to situations falling within the scope of national law and to situations falling within the scope of Community law, it is clearly in the Community interest that, in order to forestall future differences of interpretation, that provision should be interpreted uniformly, whatever the circumstances in which it is to apply (see, to that effect, Case C-130/95 Giloy (. . .) and Case C-28/95 Leur-Bloem (. . .))

The first argument relies on the principles in 'the *Dzodzi*-line of cases' and the general freedom of national courts to refer certain questions to the ECJ. In the *Dzodzi*-line of cases, the Court has held that it has jurisdiction to give an interpretation of Community law concepts even if these concepts are used in the Member States in a purely national context.[135] That reasoning seems unconvincing in this context, particularly because the ECJ's jurisdiction to interpret Article 50 of TRIPs in situations such as that in *Hermès* is not optional for national courts.[136] Later TRIPs cases make clear that, in the context of trade mark law, there is a Community law *obligation* on Member States, including on their courts, to apply Article 50 of TRIPs in a uniform manner throughout the Community.[137]

The second argument has more credibility and substance. Where the very same provision in a mixed agreement can apply both in a national and in a Community law context, there is a 'Community interest' in uniform interpretation—regardless of the specific context in which the provision applies. This 'Community interest' in uniform application of Article 50 of TRIPs seems to have been crucial for the Court.[138] In this sense, the reasoning in *Hermès* is in line with *SPI/SAMI* where the Court more explicitly identified two distinguishable Community

---

[135] See also Section III.B at note 58.

[136] Similarly Steve Peers, *Constitutional Principles and International Trade* (1999) 24 EL Rev 185–95, p. 191; Gaëlle Bontinck, *The TRIPs Agreement and the ECJ: A New Dawn?–Some Comments About Joined Cases C-300/98 and C-392/98, Parfums Dior and Assco Gerüste* (2001) Jean Monnet Working Paper, p. 15; Andrea Filippo Gagliardi, *The Rights of Individuals to Invoke the Provisions of Mixed Agreements Before the National Courts: A New Message from Luxembourg* (1999) 24 EL Rev 276–92, pp. 287. See also generally Saulius Lukas Kaleda, *Extension of the preliminary ruling procedure outsie the scope of Community law: 'The Dzodzi line of cases'* (2000) 4 EIoP.

[137] The Court has subsequently abandoned this argument. Compare e.g. Joined Cases C-392/98 and C-300/98, *Parfums Christian Dior SA v BV* [2000] ECR I-11307, paragraph 35.

[138] Similarly Philipp Gasparon, *The Transposition of the Principle of Member State Liability into the Context of External Relations* (1999) 10 EJIL 605–24, p. 613; Armin von Bogdandy, *Case Law: Case C-53/96, Hermès International v. FHT Marketing Choice BV* (1999) 36 CML Rev 663–72, p. 668.

interests in ensuring a uniform application of provisions of GATT 1947 within the Community. Uniform application is necessary, on the one hand, in order to avoid distortion of intra-Community relations and, on the other, in order not to jeopardize the unity in international representation (cf. Section III.C and the AG's conclusions quoted above). For these reasons, the Court had jurisdiction to determine how Article 50 of TRIPs should be interpreted even in a situation involving national trade mark rights.

Dior/Assco

The *Dior/Assco* case concerned two joined preliminary references, both referred by Dutch courts.[139] One related to a national trade mark on cosmetics (Dior) and the other to an industrial design right on a scaffolding system (Assco). Both courts found that their decisions would involve an interpretation of Article 50(6) of TRIPs and a determination of the domestic effects of that provision. In the *Assco* case, the Dutch Supreme Court had specifically asked the ECJ to consider whether it had jurisdiction to interpret Article 50 of TRIPs in a case that did not involve trade mark rights. As a novelty, in its reply the ECJ distinguished, (a) the question of interpretation of Article 50(6) of TRIPs from (b) the question of its domestic effect.

(a) Uniform Interpretation of the Scope of Article 50(6) of TRIPs As regards its jurisdiction to interpret Article 50 of TRIPs in a situation involving a national trade mark (the Dior situation), the Court could rely on *Hermès*. Therefore, the contentious issue was whether the Court had jurisdiction to interpret Article 50 of TRIPs also in a case involving a national design right. As opposed to the area of trade marks, there was no Community design right at the time or any other relevant Community legislation relating to the provisional protection of design rights. Therefore, the approach in *Hermès*—where the Court established a hypothetical case involving a Community trade mark—could not be transposed to design rights.

AG Cosmas provided a comprehensive assessment of the many issues linked to a determination of the scope of the Court's jurisdiction over mixed agreements. He focused in particular on the Court's jurisdiction to interpret provisions of mixed agreements when they apply in areas where the Community has not (yet) exercised its competence. As he pointed out, this is 'a complex question in which the general problem of the interrelationship of international, Community and national legal orders meets the regulation of institutional relations'.[140] He suggested that 'three fundamental aspects of the matter should be examined in order to decide that question: (aa) the institutional balance between Community

---

[139] Joined Cases C-392/98 and C-300/98, *Parfums Christian Dior SA* v *BV* [2000] ECR I-11307.
[140] Paragraph 31 of his Opinion.

and national authorities; (ab) the institutional balance between the Court and the other Community institutions; and (ac) the issue of the uniform application of TRIPs.'[141] Though legitimate, the need for uniformity could not, the AG argued, justify the reversal of the internal divisions of competence between the EC and the Member States and between the Community institutions.[142]

The Court's reasoning was less venturesome; again, it is useful to divide the Court's reasoning into three distinct parts. First, the Court noted that it always has jurisdiction to define the obligations assumed by the Community in a mixed agreement, and for this purpose to interpret TRIPs.[143] This type of jurisdiction is, however, not an exclusive jurisdiction to ensure uniform interpretation of Article 50 of TRIPs. If so, the Court could have ended its reasoning here. At this initial stage, the Court only and uncontroversially asserts its jurisdiction to determine which international obligations the Community has assumed in a mixed agreement.[144] Paradoxically, perhaps, the Court did not exercise this jurisdiction in relation to the provisions in TRIPs. Like in *Hermès*, the Court determined the scope of its own interpretative jurisdiction in the specific case without considering to what extent the Community had assumed the obligations contained in Article 50 of the TRIPs.

In the second and third steps of its reasoning, the Court turned to its jurisdiction to interpret the scope of Article 50 of TRIPs.

34 (...) the Court has jurisdiction to interpret Article 50 of TRIPs in order to meet the needs of the courts of the Member States when they are called upon to apply national rules with a view to ordering provisional measures for the protection of rights arising under Community legislation falling within the scope of TRIPs (see Hermès, paragraphs 28 and 29).

35 Likewise, where a provision such as Article 50 of TRIPs can apply both to situations falling within the scope of national law and to situations falling within that of Community law, as is the case in the field of trade marks, the Court has jurisdiction to interpret it in order to forestall future differences of interpretation (see Hermès, paragraphs 32 and 33).

36 In that regard, the Member States and the Community institutions have an obligation of close cooperation in fulfilling the commitments undertaken by them under joint competence when they concluded the WTO Agreement, including TRIPs (see, to that effect, Opinion 1/94, cited above, paragraph 108).

37 Since Article 50 of TRIPs constitutes a procedural provision which should be applied in the same way in every situation falling within its scope and is capable of applying both to situations covered by national law and to situations covered by Community law, that

---

[141] Paragraph 41.
[142] Paragraphs 52–69. The AG's analysis of the need for uniform application includes a wide array of considerations relating to the nature of the WTO Agreements themselves, the need for unity in external representation, the value of uniform interpretation and application within, the need to comply with international obligations etc.   [143] Paragraph 33.
[144] Contrast Panos Koutrakos, *The Interpretation of Mixed Agreements under the Preliminary Reference Procedure* (2002) 7 EFA Rev 25–52, p. 37.

obligation requires the judicial bodies of the Member States and the Community, for practical and legal reasons, to give it a uniform interpretation.

38 Only the Court of Justice acting in cooperation with the courts and tribunals of the Member States pursuant to Article 177 of the Treaty is in a position to ensure such uniform interpretation.

39 The jurisdiction of the Court of Justice to interpret Article 50 of TRIPs is thus not restricted solely to situations covered by trade-mark law.

While paragraphs 34 and 35 merely confirm the *Hermès* case, paragraphs 36–39 extend the Court's jurisdiction to interpret Article 50 of TRIPs to situations involving national design rights. This is done by a combination of two arguments.

First, in paragraph 36, the Court refers to the general 'duty of close co-operation'. In this way, the Court clarifies that this duty does not only apply to the Community's political institutions and to the Member State governments when they negotiate, conclude and implement a mixed agreement. It also applies to the judiciaries within the Community area when they perform their role in the implementation of mixed agreements. The duty of close co-operation is based on mainly two considerations. First, a general Community aspiration to present 'the Community area' to the outside world as a unitary actor, and, second, a need to ensure full compliance with the obligations assumed in a mixed agreement. *Dior/Assco* implies that these two considerations were particularly relevant to the scope of the Court's interpretative jurisdiction. (It will be recalled that the duty of close co-operation is a Community law obligation, which also applies in areas beyond Community competence.[145])

The second reason that justifies the Court's jurisdiction to interpret Article 50 of TRIPs when it applies to a national design right underlines the relationship between the requirement of uniform application and proper compliance with international obligations. In paragraph 37, the Court shifts perspective to the obligation contained in Article 50 of TRIPs itself; that Article is a procedural provision, which must be applied in the same way in every situation falling within its scope. Therefore, Article 50 of TRIPs obliges all Community courts, including the ECJ, for practical and legal reasons, to give it a uniform interpretation. Thus, the ECJ's jurisdiction and the requirement of uniform application of Article 50 of TRIPs is a matter of complying with international law.[146] These two considerations—the requirement of unity in international representation and the need to comply with the obligations flowing from the mixed agreement—justify that

[145] For criticism of the Court's use of the duty of close co-operation in this context, see Piet Eeckhout, *External Relations of the European Union: Legal and Constitutional Foundations*, 2004, p. 242.

[146] Prior to *Dior/Assco*, Bourgeois argued that 'if the EC, and in particular, in the absence of a determination by the EC political bodies, the ECJ fails to rule on whether and how GATS and TRIPS provisions are to be interpreted uniformly within the EC, a WTO panel or the WTO Appellate Body could very well be called upon to do so.' Jacques H. J. Bourgeois, 'The European Court of Justice and the WTO: Problems and Challenges', in Weiler, ed. *The EU, the WTO, and the NAFTA: Towards a Common Law of International Trade?*, 2000, p. 86.

Article 50 of TRIPs should be interpreted in a uniform manner within the Community also when it applies to a national design right.[147]

(b) The Effects of Article 50(6) In *Dior/Assco*, the ECJ was also asked, in its own words, 'to ascertain whether, and to what extent, the procedural requirements of Article 50(6) of TRIPs have entered the sphere of Community law so that, whether on application by the parties or of their own motion, the national courts are required to apply them.'[148]

The Court began by recalling that in *Portugal v Council* it had held that WTO rules could not, by virtue of Community law, be relied on in order to challenge the legality of Community acts and therefore they could not have direct effect.[149] However, since Article 50 of TRIPs could apply both to situations covered by Community law and to situations covered by national law, it was necessary to demarcate the Community sphere of Article 50 of TRIPs:

47. In a field to which TRIPs applies and in respect of which the Community has already legislated, as is the case with the field of trade marks, it follows from the judgment in *Hermès*, in particular paragraph 28 thereof, that the judicial authorities of the Member States are required *by virtue of Community law*, when called upon to apply national rules with a view to ordering provisional measures for the protection of rights falling within such a field, to do so as far as possible in the light of the wording and purpose of Article 50 of TRIPs.

48. On the other hand, in a field in respect of which the Community has not yet legis-lated and which consequently falls within the competence of the Member States, the protection of intellectual property rights, and measures adopted for that purpose by the judicial authorities, *do not fall within the scope of Community law*. Accordingly, Community law neither requires nor forbids that the legal order of a Member State should accord to individuals the right to rely directly on the rule laid down by Article 50(6) of TRIPs or that it should oblige the courts to apply that rule of their own motion.[150]

In the particular case, therefore, the Dutch court referring the *Dior* case (District Court, The Hague) was required to interpret Dutch trade mark law in light of Article 50 of TRIPs. The Dutch court referring the *Assco* case (the Dutch Supreme Court), by contrast, was, as a matter of EC law, free to decide which effects Article 50 should have in the context of Dutch design right law. (Both courts, however, were obliged to follow the ECJ's interpretation of the substantive scope of Article 50 of TRIPs.)

The approach in *Dior/Assco* raises numerous intricate problems. First of all, the very distinction by the Court between the interpretative scope of Article 50 of TRIPs and the domestic effects of that article is unusual. Previous case law clearly suggests that interpreting the substantive scope of a particular provision in an international agreement and determining its domestic effects are both questions

---

[147] Compare Section III.A.(iii) (on the external Community interest in uniform application) and Section III.A.(iv) (on the Community's capability of compliance with international commitments).

[148] Paragraph 41.

[149] Case C-149/96, *Portuguese Republic* v *Council* [1999] ECR I-8395, paragraph 46.

[150] Emphasis added.

of interpretation.[151] It would therefore have been more in line with earlier case law if the ECJ had connected the two issues. The approach raises the question of whether the 'Community area' is capable of managing the complexity that may follow in some situations. It has been questioned whether it is practically possible to operate with a distinction between these two closely related issues.[152] In any event, the distinction suggests that the Court's exclusive jurisdiction to *interpret* provisions in mixed agreements may cover some rules of international law, which are not an integral part of Community law; whereas the Court has exclusive jurisdiction to determine the *effects* of provisions in mixed agreements only in so far as these are an integral part of Community law.[153]

As regards the demarcation of Community and Member State spheres, in particular, it is unclear how the Court determine whether the Community has legislated within a 'field'. In *Dior/Assco*, it seems that trade mark law is one field and design right law is another.[154] What makes these two legal regimes distinct 'fields' is unclear. Moreover, the Court does not explain whether the 'fields' within which the Community determines the effects of provisions of mixed agreements are identical to those 'areas'[155] in which the AETR doctrine creates exclusive treaty-making competence for the Community.[156] Arguably, in light of the Court's current (narrow) application of the AETR doctrine, it would seem that the 'field' within which EC law determines the effects of provisions of mixed agreements is broader than the 'area' within which internal EC legislation creates exclusive external Community competence.[157]

Two subsequent cases have confirmed the principles in *Dior/Assco: Schieving-Nijstad* concerned the Route 66 trade mark, a Dutch trade mark used by

---

[151] E.g. Case 104/81, *Hauptzollamt Mainz* v *a.A.* [1982] ECR 3641, paragraph 17.

[152] The literature is generally sceptical: Panos Koutrakos, *The Interpretation of Mixed Agreements under the Preliminary Reference Procedure* (2002) 7 EFA Rev 25–52, p. 45; Joni Heliskoski, *Joined Cases 300/98, Parfums Christian Dior SA v. Tuk Consultancy BV, and C-392/98, Assco Gerüste GmbH and R. van Dijk v. Wilhelm Layher GmbH & Co KG and Layher BV, judgment of 14 December, nyr* (2002) 39 CML Rev 159–74, p. 173; Piet Eeckhout, *External Relations of the European Union: Legal and Constitutional Foundations*, 2004, pp. 242 and 273.

[153] See in particular paragraph 41 of the judgement, *supra* note 148.

[154] That 'trade marks' is a separate field in which the Community has legislated has been confirmed in C-89/99, *Schieving-Nijstad vof and Others* v *Groeneveld* [2001] ECR I-5851, paragraph 30 and Case C-245/02, *Anheuser-Busch Inc.* v *Budjovický Budvar* [2004] ECR I-10989, paragraph 55.

[155] E.g. Opinion 2/91, *Re ILO Convention No. 170 on Safety in the Use of Chemicals at Work* [1993] ECR I-1061, paragraph 25; Case C-476/98, *Commission* v *Germany* [2002] ECR I-9855 (Open Skies), paragraph 108.

[156] See e.g. Joni Heliskoski, *Joined Cases 300/98, Parfums Christian Dior SA v. Tuk Consultancy BV, and C-392/98, Assco Gerüste GmbH and R. van Dijk v. Wilhelm Layher GmbH & Co KG and Layher BV, judgment of 14 December, nyr* (2002) 39 CML Rev 159–74; Martha Pertegas Sender, *Case law: Parfums Christian Dior v. Tuk Consultancy* (2001) 7 Colum. J. Eur. L. 385, p. 389; Panos Koutrakos, *The Interpretation of Mixed Agreements under the Preliminary Reference Procedure* (2002) 7 EFA Rev 25–52, p. 45.

[157] Compare Case C-467/98, *Commission* v *Denmark* [2002] ECR I-9519 (*Open Skies*). (In French, the word 'domaine' is used both in *Dior/Assco* and in the *Open Skies* cases.)

Mr Groenveld in the marketing of alcoholic beverages and soft drinks.[158] *Anheuser-Busch* concerned the American Budweiser and the Czech Budvar trade marks used for beer.[159] In both cases, the Court confirmed its exclusive jurisdiction to determine the application of provisions of TRIPs when applied to trade mark rights, and in this way consolidated the method developed in *Dior/Assco*.[160]

From the TRIPs Agreement cases can be deduce the following principles:

1) When a provision in a mixed agreement is applied in a 'field' where the Community has legislated, the provision is a part of the Community legal order and must receive *uniform application* within the Community area. On the other hand, if the provision is applied in a field where the Community has not (yet) legislated, it is not an integral part of Community law and the Community will therefore not require uniform application in this context.[161]

2) When a provision in a mixed agreement is applied in a 'field' where there is no Community legislation, and when that provision could hypothetically apply also to a situation governed by internal Community legislation, the provision must have a *uniform interpretative scope*. In these situations, the Court has exclusive jurisdiction to interpret provisions of mixed agreements even in situations where they do not form part of the Community legal system.

(ii) Direct actions

In most situations, it is impossible to predict in which context a question of application of a rule of international law arises. The criteria for determining which spheres of mixed agreements are an integral part of Community law should therefore be the same, regardless of the particular context in which the issue arises. More specifically, the same criteria apply, regardless of whether a particular provision in a mixed agreement threatens the legality of a Community or a national measure, whether the issue arises in an indirect or a direct action etc. The only two direct actions in which it has been necessary for the Court to demarcate Community and Member State spheres of mixed agreements confirm this.

---

[158] C-89/99, *Schieving-Nijstad vof and Others* v *Groeneveld* [2001] ECR I-5851, particularly paragraphs 30–35 and 51–54. Nikolaos Lavranos, *European Court of Justice, 13 September 2001, Case C-89/99, Schieving-Nijstad vof et al. v. Robert Groenveld* (2002) 29 (3) LIEI 323–33. In this case, AG Jacobs expressed his bewilderment in relation to the prior case law. See paragraph 40 of his Opinion.

[159] Case C-245/02, *Anheuser-Busch Inc.* v *Budjovický Budvar* [2004] ECR I-10989, paragraphs 41–43 and 54–57.

[160] In the pending Case C-431/05, *Merck Genéricos-Produtos Farmacêuticos*, the Court has been asked whether it has jurisdiction to interpret Article 33 of the TRIPs Agreement.

[161] Compare Joni Heliskoski, *Joined Cases 300/98, Parfums Christian Dior SA v. Tuk Consultancy BV, and C-392/98, Assco Gerüste GmbH and R. van Dijk v. Wilhelm Layher GmbH & Co KG and Layher BV, judgment of 14 December, nyr* (2002) 39 CML Rev 159–74, p. 171.

The first case clearly demonstrates the (full) Court's difficulties with handling this problem. *Commission v Ireland* (the Irish Berne Convention case) concerned Ireland's failure to adhere to the Berne Convention.[162] Article 5 of Protocol 28 on Intellectual Property, annexed to the EEA Agreement, provides that the Contracting Parties, including the Member States of the Community, were required to adhere to the Convention by 1 January 1995 and to ensure that their national legislation conformed to the substantive provisions of the Convention by 1 January 1994.[163] The Commission brought action against Ireland under Article 226 for infringing Article 300(7) EC by failing to comply with the EEA Agreement's requirement to accede the Convention. Ireland readily admitted that it had breached its duty under the EEA Agreement. The main question in the case (not raised by Ireland itself, but by the UK) was whether Article 5 of Protocol 28 was in fact a Community law obligation. Alternatively, Ireland had breached (only) an international law obligation, which was undertaken directly vis-à-vis the EFTA Countries, and over which the ECJ did not have jurisdiction according to Article 226.[164]

The Court noted that the action brought by the Commission for failure to act could only concern whether Ireland complied with 'obligations under Community law'. Therefore, it was necessary, in order for the Court to proceed to the substance of the claim, to examine whether the obligation in Article 5 of the Protocol came 'within the scope of Community law'.[165] For the purpose of deciding whether the obligation was a Community law obligation, the Court first drew on the *Demirel* case and (in a rather woolly formulation in the English version) held that, generally, mixed agreements 'have the same status in the Community legal order as purely Community agreements, as these are provisions coming within the scope of Community competence'.[166] The (English) term 'as these are' could be understood as a general and sweeping statement to the effect that all parts of mixed agreements are like pure Community agreements. However, other language versions of this paragraph and the Court's reference to *Demirel*, paragraph 9, suggest that at this place the Court is (merely) asserting that mixed agreements have the same status as pure Community agreements *insofar* as their provisions come within Community competence.[167] However, even so, the

[162] Case C-13/00, *Commission v Ireland* [2002] ECR I-2943.
[163] The Berne Convention does not allow for international organizations, such as the EC, to become members.
[164] AG Mischo argued that Article 5 of the Protocol was in its entirety a Community law obligation because, (a) the Community had competence to assume the obligation (and its subject matter was within the scope of the Treaty), (b) internal Community legislation was capable of being affected by (at least parts of) the Berne Convention, and (c) the Berne Convention is indivisible and must be adhered to as a whole. Opinion of AG Mischo, paragraphs 7 *et seq.*   [165] Paragraph 13.
[166] Paragraph 14.
[167] According to the German version, mixed agreements have the same status as pure Community agreements 'soweit es um Bestimmung geht, die in die Zuständigkeit der Gemeinschaft fallen'. Similarly, in the French: '...s'aggisant des dispositions qui relèvent de la compétence de la Communauté...'; and Danish (as well as Swedish): 'blandede aftaler (...) har samme status

reasoning seems to suggest that all provisions of mixed agreements within the scope of the Community's treaty-making competence are part of Community law. This implies a general presumption that it is always the Community that has exercised treaty-making competence in areas where this competence is shared—a presumption which is not easy to reconcile with the principle of subsidiarity, cf. Article 5(2) EC.

Next, the Court reminded that in the *Demirel* case it had made clear (quoting *Kupferberg*) that the Member States have a Community law obligation to comply with international obligations for which the Community has assumed responsibility.[168] As in *Demirel*, it is difficult to ascertain whether the Court here intends to link the question of which provisions of mixed agreements are Community law obligations with the scope of the Community's international responsibility. However, if the Community's responsibility under international law was decisive, then the natural consequence would have been to examine whether and to what extent the Community, as a matter of international law, had assumed the obligation contained in Article 5 of the Protocol vis-à-vis the EFTA countries. As noted in the context of the *Hermès* case, this would inevitably force the Court into an analysis of the extent to which the Community is responsible for mixed agreements under international law.[169] This issue is not incontestable and the Court would have no judicial authority to decide on it with binding effects for third parties. Sensibly, therefore, the Court did use the *Kupferberg* principle to determine whether and to what extent Article 5 of the Protocol is a part of Community law.

Instead, in a third step, the Court turned to the (internal Community law) question of distribution of external competence between the EC and the Member States. It held that the Berne Convention came 'in large measure within the scope of Community competence' and that the subject matter of the Berne Convention is 'to a very great extent governed by Community legislation'.[170] The Court's emphasis on the amount of internal Community legislation brings to mind both the *Dior/Assco* case and the *AETR* case. The Court's cursory discussion of this matter suggests that it does not here consider the whole Berne Convention to be covered by exclusive external Community competence.[171] It is therefore more likely that the Court, without referring to it, uses the criterion introduced in *Dior/Assco*; i.e. whether the Community has legislated in the field. This is the most appropriate conclusion since both the *Irish Berne Convention* case and *Dior/Assco*

---

i fællesskabsretten som rent fællesskabsretlige aftaler, når der er tale om bestemmelser, der henhører under Fællesskabets kompetence').

[168] Paragraph 15. Contrast paragraphs 29 and 30 of the Opinion of the AG. It should also be noted that the Court in this case did not refer to the special nature of association agreements (unlike AG Mischo, paragraphs 33ff, and AG Darmon in the *Demirel* case, paragraphs 13–15).

[169] See *supra* at note 130.   [170] Paragraphs 16–17.

[171] Also implicitly assuming that the Berne Convention is not wholly within exclusive Community competence: Case C-293/98, *Entidad de Gestión de Derechos de los Productores Audiovisuales (Egeda)* v *(Hoasa)* [2000] ECR I-629; Case C-245/00, *Stichting ter Exploitatie van Naburige Rechten (SENA)* v *(NOS)* [2003] ECR I-1251.

are concerned with the extent to which a provision in a mixed agreement comes within the sphere of Community law—rather than with the extent to which the Community has exclusive treaty-making competence.

The fourth and final stage in the Court's analysis seems superfluous and bewildering. The Court added that, 'moreover', 'copyrights and related rights fall within the scope of application of the Treaty'.[172] Because the Berne Convention governs matters, which are 'covered by Community law', there is a 'Community interest' in ensuring that all EEA contracting parties adhered to the Berne Convention.[173] This addendum is puzzling. It is well-known that the *scope of application* of the EC Treaty differs significantly from *the scope of the Community's attributed competence*. Community law imposes obligations on the Member States in numerous areas in which the Community has no norm-setting competence. If 'the scope of application of the EC Treaty' is used as a new criterion to determine the Community sphere of a mixed agreement, this would have far-reaching consequences. In particular, it would make a number of provisions in mixed agreements, which are wholly outside EC competence capable of being an integral part of EC law. Therefore, since this fourth strand of reasoning seems to carry little weight in the overall reasoning in the judgment, it is probably best to regard it as a mishap.

On this basis, the Court finally concluded 'that the requirement of adherence to the Berne Convention which Article 5 of Protocol 28 to the EEA Agreement imposes on the Contracting Parties comes within the Community framework, given that it features in a mixed agreement concluded by the Community and its Member States and relates to an area covered in large measure by the Treaty.'[174] Thus, by failing to comply with Article 5 of the Protocol, Ireland was in breach of Community law.

The *Irish Berne Convention* case and the arguments presented provided the Court with an opportunity to develop the principles in *Dior/Assco*. Yet, the reasoning of the Court is regrettably confusing and offers little help in clarifying to what extent provisions in mixed agreements fall within the scope of the Community law. The Court uncritically accumulates various links between the Community legal order and Article 5 of the Protocol and concludes that these links together establish a sufficient 'Community interest' in ensuring that Ireland complies with the particular provision.

In the subsequent *Commission v France (Étang de Berre)* case, the Court was more precise in its reasoning.[175] Here, the Commisison claimed that France had

---

[172] Paragraph 18. The Court referred to Joined cases C-92/92 and C-326/92, *Phil Collins v GmbH* [1993] ECR I-5145, where the Court found that the Member States retained competence to regulate matters relating to copyrights, but that copyrights are within the scope of application a number of primary Community obligations, notably concerning the rules on free movement of goods and services and competition (paragraphs 22–28 of the judgment). See also Case C-360/00, *Land Hessen v GmbH* [2002] ECR I-5089, paragraph 24.   [173] Paragraph 19.

[174] Paragraph 20.

[175] Case C-239/03, *Commission v France* [2004] ECR I-9325 (*Étang de Berre*).

failed to fulfil its obligations under the Convention for the protection of the Mediterranean Sea against pollution by failing to prevent the discharge of fresh water into the aquatic environment of the Étang de Berre, a salt water mesh. France argued that the Convention was concluded as a mixed agreement and that no Community measure regulated the discharges of fresh water and alluvia. Therefore, the relevant provisions in the Convention were outside the scope of Community law and the Court did not have jurisdiction under Article 226.

The Court began by confirming that mixed agreements have the same legal status as pure Community agreements 'in so far as' the provisions of the mixed agreement fall within Community competence. The Court held that the provisions of the Convention covered 'a field which falls in large measure within Community competence' (paragraph 27). The Court noted that several directives concerned protection of the water against pollution and found that there was therefore a 'Community interest' in ensuring that both the Member States and the Commnuity complied with the Convention.

The fact that discharges of fresh water and alluvia into the marine environment, which are at issue in the present action, have not yet been the subject of Community legislation is not capable of calling that finding into question. (Paragraph 30.)

Both the *Irish Berne Convention* and the *Étang de Berre* cases provided the Court with an opportunity to develop the principles in *Dior/Assco*. Yet, the reasoning of the Court is regrettably confusing and offers little help in clarifying to what extent provisions in mixed agreements fall within the scope of the Community law. The Court appears to uncritically accumulate various links between the Community legal order and the relevant provision in the agreement and concludes o nthis basis that these links together establish a sufficient 'Community interest' in ensuring a uniform application of the particular provision within the Community.[176]

A point of particular interest is how a 'field' covered by Community legislation (or in which the Community has legislated) should be understood. The Court's emphasis on the amount of internal Community legislation brings to mind both the *Dior/Assco* and the *AETR* cases. If the facts of the *Irish Berne Convention* and *Étang de Berre* cases are juxtaposed to the *Open Skies* cases, it is clear that the principles by which mixed agreements are received as part of Community law are different from the principles by which external Community competence pre-empts Member State competence (the AETR principle). The Court's analysis in the *Irish Berne Convention* case suggests that it does not consider the Berne Convention to be covered by exclusive external Community competence.[177] It is

---

[176] The Court will have a third chance of clarifying this law in the pending Case 459/03, *Commission v Ireland*, (MOX plant).

[177] Also implicitly assuming that the Berne Convention is not wholly within exclusive Community competence: Case C-293/98, *Entidad de Gestión de Derechos de los Productores Audiovisuales (Egeda)* v *(Hoasa)* [2000] ECR I-629; Case C-245/00, *Stichting ter Exploitatie van Naburige Rechten (SENA)* v *(NOS)* [2003] ECR I-1251.

equally unlikely that the Court on the basis of the *Étang de Berre* case would conclude that the Member States had no competence to participate together with the Community in an agreement concerning disharge of fresh water into the marine environment. The *Irish Berne Convention* and *Étang de Berre* cases and *Dior/Assco* are concerned with the extent to which a provision in a mixed agreement comes within the sphere of Community law—rather than with the extent to which the Community has exclusive treaty-making competence. It remains to be clarified exactly how much legislation is required within a particular field before the Community acquires exclusive jurisdiction.[178]

Despite these uncertainties, *Irish Berne Convention* and *Étang de Berre* are important because they seem to trespass the vertical limits of the requirement of uniform application. The decisions entail that 'the EC may enforce international obligations across both [Member State and Community] domains'.[179] Judged from the general reasons for requiring uniform application of international agreements analysed in Section III), there may also be a good case for integrating these spheres of mixed agreements into Community law. In both cases, the Court refers to the two-fold Community interest discussed in Section III.C. Uniform application is, moreover, preferable in order to ensure compliance with the relevant obligation. As the Commission and AG Mischo pointed out, the Berne Convention itself (as well as Article 5 of the Protocol) does not allow for partial adherence but should be regarded as an indivisible whole.[180] Thus, (as the Court stressed with respect to Article 50 of TRIPs in *Dior*) the international legal obligation itself seems to require a uniform approach. In this respect, the *Irish Berne Convention* case also 'goes some way to meet the demands of third countries for greater transparency in the enforcement of international obligations'.[181] Similarly, the *Étang de Berre* case is best understood in light of both internal and external EC interests in uniform application as well as in light of the need to ensure France's full and correct compliance with the Convention in question.

(iii) Synthesis

Presently, it is difficult to detract from the case law a general legal method with which to determine to what extent provisions in mixed agreements are an integral part of the Community legal system. Nevertheless, the case law analysed in this section clearly illustrates that what may appear to be an abstract (and academic) question concerning vertical distribution of jurisdictional powers between Community and national courts may have a crucial impact on the legal position

---

[178] For a very Commission-friendly interpretation, which suggests that the *Étang de Berre* case should have implications for the AETR doctrine, see Pieter-Jan Kuijper, *Case C-239/03, Commission v. French Republic* (2005) 42 CML Rev 1491–1500, pp. 1497–8.

[179] Francis Snyder, *The Gatekeepers: The European Courts and WTO Law* (2003) 40 CML Rev 313–67, p. 352.   [180] Paragraphs 48 *et seq.* of his Opinion.

[181] Francis Snyder, *The Gatekeepers: The European Courts and WTO Law* (2003) 40 CML Rev 313–67, p. 353.

of individuals in particular cases. The issue determines how much of the agreement is an integral part of Community law and thus subject to the requirement of uniform application. This question will, in turn, determine whether a provision is capable of being directly invoked according to Community law or national law criteria. Hence, in the end, the question may have a decisive bearing on the legal position of individuals in particular cases. All this is nicely illustrated by the reasoning and outcome of the *Dior/Assco* case, which few could have predicted. In addition, as the *Irish Berne Convention* case illustrates, the extent to which mixed agreements are Community law determines how they can be enforced. More generally, the issue is closely related to questions concerning the scope, the nature and the exercise of Community and Member State external competences as well as to their liability under international law. All these issues deserve and require to be addressed—if they should be addressed in a particular case—in a systematic and coherent manner.

It is, nevertheless, possible to propose a tentative synthesis of the multiple strands of reasoning and distinctions that flow from the cases analysed in this Section. The synthesis is based on the premise that the extent to which provisions in mixed agreements are an integral part of Community law should be closely related to the extent to which uniform application is required, cf. Section III. On the basis of this key notion, it is possible to develop a framework approach to the question of when provisions of mixed agreements are an integral part of Community law; a framework which synthesises the case law on mixed agreements with the case law on uniform application of international agreements. The synthesis requires, first, an identification of the key considerations, which must be taken into account. On the basis of a balancing of these considerations, a number of general principles can then be proposed.

General Considerations *The dual 'Community interest' in uniform application*
As shown in section III.A.(iii), the Community interest in uniform application of international agreements has both an internal and an external element. There is, first, an *internal* Community interest in uniform application of provisions of international agreements within the Community area in order to avoid distortion of intra-Community affairs, and in particular of internal trade. This internal Community interest in uniform application is also reflected in the case law on mixed agreements. In *Hermès* (paragraph 32), the Court held that if a provision in a mixed agreement can apply both to situations covered by Community law and to situations covered by national law, uniform interpretation is necessary in order to forestall future differences of interpretation. *Dior/Assco* (paragraph 47) made clear that where a provision in a mixed agreement applies in a field where there is *internal* Community legislation, the Community legal system requires uniform application of that provision. In the *Berne Convention* case (paragraph 19), the Court held that because the Berne Convention concerned areas covered by

(internal) Community law there was a 'Community interest' in ensuring that all Contracting Parties to the EEA Agreement adhered to that Convention.[182] There is, in addition, a distinct *external* Community interest in uniform application: Disuniform application of provisions in international agreements *within* the Community area would jeopardize the Community's general aim of *external* unity. This external aspect of the requirement of uniform application played a role in *Dior/Assco* where the European Court of Justice held that the duty of close co-operation (which stems from a requirement of unity in international representation) compelled a uniform approach within the Community to the interpretation of Article 50 of TRIPs. Both internal and external Community interests in uniform application thus influence the extent to which provisions in mixed agreements form part of Community law.[183]

Compliance with International Law and Third Parties' Interests Third, in determining to what extent provisions in mixed agreements are an integral part of Community law, account must be taken of possible repercussions in international law. Section III.A.(iv) showed how the need to comply with international agreements is a third and distinct reason for requiring uniform application of these agreements within the 'Community area', cf. the *Anastasiou* case. In *Dior/Assco*, the Court emphasized in a similar manner the need to ensure compliance with the Community's obligations vis-à-vis third parties in the context of mixed agreements: The Court found that Article 50 of TRIPs itself required to be applied in a uniform manner within the Community.[184] The 'Community area' must comply correctly with all provisions in a mixed agreement and this is reflected in the extent to which provisions in mixed agreements form an integral part of Community law.

Vertical limits to uniformity The 'Community area' is not a single entity in international relations, but consists of both the Community and the Member States. As shown in Section III.A.(ii), this is reflected in the vertical limits to the general requirement for uniform application of provisions in international agreements, cf. e.g. the *SPI/SAMI* and *Andersson* cases. The phenomenon of mixity is a paradigmatic

---

[182] To the same effect, paragraph 40 of AG Jacobs' Opinion in C-89/99, *Schieving-Nijstad vof and Others* v *Groeneveld* [2001] ECR I-5851.

[183] Allan Rosas, 'The European Union and Mixed Agreements', in Dashwood and Hillion, eds. *The General Law of E.C. External Relations*, 2000, pp. 213–14: 'The need for unity of interpretation, including on such a fundamental question as to whether the agreement has direct effect or not, would certainly speak in favour of the competence of the Court over the whole range of issues covered by the agreement.'

[184] Joined Cases C-392/98 and C-300/98, *Parfums Christian Dior SA* v *BV* [2000] ECR I-11307, paragraph 37. See, to the same effect, Case C-13/00, *Commission* v *Ireland* [2002] ECR I-2943, paragraph 15. Similarly, AG Mischo in the *Berne Convention* case argued that Article 5 of Protocol 28 in the EEA Agreement was an indivisible obligation, and therefore it should be regarded as a Community law obligation in its entirety. See also Francis Snyder, *The Gatekeepers: The European Courts and WTO Law* (2003) 40 CML Rev 313–67, p. 353.

manifestation of the mixed nature of the EC area's external relations, and also in the application of mixed agreements, the vertical constitutional balances between the Community and the Member States must be safeguarded. In the context of mixed agreements, it is equally clear that 'part of the subject-matter of the agreement as a rule falls within national competence and may touch upon interests of the Member States which no concept of Community unity is capable of accommodating'.[185] To consider all provisions of mixed agreements a part of Community law (and thus subject to uniform application) would encroach upon Member States' remaining foreign affairs authority. This is why, in *Dior/Assco*, the Court accepted that the Member States could determine the effects of Article 50 of TRIPs in situations involving national design rights. The vertical constitutional balance between the Community and the Member States must be maintained and this fourth consideration also determines the extent to which provisions of mixed agreements are an integral part of Community law.[186]

General Principles

These considerations, derived from the Court's own reasoning, can be seen as the frame within which to develop more specific principles or criteria for determining when provisions of mixed agreements are within the sphere of Community law and thus subject to the requirement of uniform application. I submit that the following general principles pay due respect to these considerations.[187]

The starting point is always *the scope* of the Community's treaty-making competence. As a rule, in order for a provision in a mixed agreement to be an integral part of Community law, it is necessary that the Community has treaty-making competence to assume the commitments it contains.[188] Exceptional circumstances may lead to a modification to this rule due to a particularly strong need for uniform application, cf. below.

Secondly, provisions of mixed agreements falling within the scope of the Community's *exclusive* treaty-making competence are an integral part of Community law. As a rule, Member States cannot assume obligations in these areas.

Thirdly, when a provision *does not fall within the Community's exclusive competence*, the Community and the Member States can in principle *decide* who should exercise competence in relation to a mixed agreement. If such a decision exists, it will determine to what extent the provisions in the mixed agreement is an integral part of Community law. (In practice, however, such decisions do not exist.)

---

[185] Joni Heliskoski, *The Jurisdiction of the European Court of Justice to Give Preliminary Rulings on the Interpretation of Mixed Agreements* (2000) 69 NJIL 395–412, p. 409. See also Notably Nanette A. Neuwahl, *Joint Participation in International Treaties and the Exercise of Powers by the EEC and Its Member States: Mixed Agreements* (1991) 28 CML Rev 717–40, p. 736.

[186] Case C-13/00, *Commission v Ireland* [2002] ECR I-2943 is explicitly based on this assumption.

[187] For an alternative proposal, see Piet Eeckhout, *External Relations of the European Union: Legal and Constitutional Foundations*, 2004, p. 270.

[188] This is in line with Case 12/86, *Meryem Demirel v Gmund* [1987] ECR 3719, paragraph 9; Case C-13/00, *Commission v Ireland* [2002] ECR I-2943, paragraphs 14, 16 and 17.

It is predominantly the remaining situations in which Community spheres of mixed agreements have been difficult to demarcate. On the one hand, in areas where the Community holds non-exclusive external competence, it cannot automatically be assumed that provisions of mixed agreements are an integral part of Community law and subject to the requirement of uniform application.[189] If all provisions covered by non-exclusive external competence would be within exclusive ECJ jurisdiction and a part of the Community legal order, an important aspect of the distinction between exclusive and non-exclusive Community competences would be eradicated.[190] Member States would be deprived of the possibility of exercising their powers with respect to the application of the main parts of most of the existing mixed agreements.[191] The Court would therefore go too far if it assumed *a priori* exclusive jurisdiction over all parts of mixed agreements covered by non-exclusive Community competence. That would 'disregard the choice, ultimately made by the Council, not to exercise the non-exclusive Community competence'.[192] In addition, an assertion of exclusive Community jurisdiction in all areas of non-exclusive Community competence would seem to conflict with the principle of subsidiarity, which arguably supports the opposite assumption, cf. Article 5(2) EC.[193]

Therefore, fourthly, provisions of mixed agreements that fall within non-exclusive Community competence are only an integral part of Community law when they have a *'Community link'*, which makes it necessary to ensure their uniform application. Whether a sufficient 'Community link' can be established, it is submitted, depends on an assessment of the above-mentioned general considerations and their weight in the specific case. *Dior/Assco* makes clear that such a link exists when a provision in a mixed agreement applies in a 'field' where the Community has introduced internal legislation.[194] (Importantly, the establishment

---

[189] Similarly, Joni Heliskoski, *Mixed Agreements as a Technique for Organizing the International Relations of the European Community and its Member States*, 2001, p. 58. Contrast Piet Eeckhout, *External Relations of the European Union: Legal and Constitutional Foundations*, 2004, p. 272 (who appears to assume that the Community by default has concluded all parts of mixed agreements within the scope of its (exclusive and non-exclusive) competence) and Alan Dashwood, 'Preliminary Rulings on the Interpretation of Mixed Agreements', in O'Keeffe and Bavasso, eds. *Liber Amicorum in Honour of Lord Slynn of Hadley: Judicial Review in European Union Law*, 2000, p. 173.

[190] In a different context, the Court has accepted the close link between the judicial application of provisions in international agreements and the scope of political manoeuvre, cf. Case C-149/96, *Portuguese Republic* v *Council* [1999] ECR I-8395.

[191] Member States generally retain their external competence, e.g. to negotiate and make decisions in international organizations in areas of non-exclusive Community competence, e.g. Case C-25/94, *Commission* v *Council* [1996] ECR I-1469 (FAO).

[192] Joni Heliskoski, *The Jurisdiction of the European Court of Justice to Give Preliminary Rulings on the Interpretation of Mixed Agreements* (2000) 69 NJIL 395–412, p. 409.

[193] See Gráinne de Búrca, *The Principle of Subsidiarity and the Court of Justice as an Institutional Actor* (1998) 36 JCMS 217–35; Gráinne de Búrca, *Reappraising Subsidiarity's Significance after Amsterdam* (1999) No.7/99 Harvard Jean Monnet Working Paper. See also Antonio Estella, *The EU Principle of Subsidiarity and its Critique*, 2002, chapter V.

[194] Joined Cases C-392/98 and C-300/98, *Parfums Christian Dior SA* v *BV* [2000] ECR I-11307, paragraphs 47 and 48. To the same effect: Case C-13/00, *Commission* v *Ireland* [2002] ECR I-2943, paragraphs 17 and 20.

of a Community link with respect to a particular provision in a mixed agreement must not be confused with the establishment of exclusive external Community competence. [195]

There are at least two exceptions to these principles. First, the Community link to a particular provision in a mixed agreement may in exceptional circumstances require that that provision is an integral part of Community law—even if it is beyond Community competence. Again, this appears to require an assessment of whether there are qualified reasons for ensuring uniform application. An example of this may be a provision containing a general and indivisible obligation, such as Article 5 of Protocol 28 in the EEA Agreement, cf. the *Irish Berne Convention* case. Secondly, by way of exception, in special situations the requirement of uniform application will provide the Court with exclusive jurisdiction to *interpret* the scope of provisions in mixed agreements, which are otherwise not an integral part of Community law.[196] This is so, at least in situations 'where a provision such as Article 50 of TRIPs can apply both to situations falling within the scope of national law and to situations falling within that of Community law'.[197]

V. Conclusions

A bird's eye view on the case law on reception of international law in Community law suggests a manifest lack of clarity and coherence. Significant parts of international law have received only amorphous treatment in the Court's case law. Hitherto, the European Court of Justice has managed to avoid any categorization of the internal legal status of some of the heaviest legal vessels in international relations. Despite their relevance to many Community issues, UN law, including notably the UN Charter and Security Council resolutions, intellectual property rights conventions and ILO conventions remain in legal quicksand as a matter of Community law—while the European Convention on Human Rights is decidedly not an integral part of Community law. Moreover, given the prominence of mixity as a technique for EU international relations, the Court's reticence to disentangle pertinent issues is distressing. The lack of clear principles inevitably spills over and creates obfuscation in related areas of EC law. Notably, it blurs subsequent analysis

---

[195] When a provision in a mixed agreement 'affects' internal Community measures it falls within the Community's exclusive external competence, and the above-mentioned second principle provides that the particular provision is an integral part of Community law. Contrast Joni Heliskoski, *Mixed Agreements as a Technique for Organizing the International Relations of the European Community and its Member States*, 2001, p. 59.   [196] Similarly *ibid.*, p. 61.

[197] Joined Cases C-392/98 and C-300/98, *Parfums Christian Dior SA* v *BV* [2000] ECR I-11307, paragraph 35. Similarly Case C-53/96, *Hermès International* v *BV* [1998] ECR I-3603, paragraphs 32–33. Many provisions of international law can apply both in Community and national context. Important examples are the national and most-favoured-nation treatment principle in GATS, cf. Joni Heliskoski, *Joined Cases 300/98, Parfums Christian Dior SA v. Tuk Consultancy BV, and C-392/98, Assco Gerüste GmbH and R. van Dijk v. Wilhelm Layher GmbH & Co KG and Layher BV, judgment of 14 December, nyr* (2002) 39 CML Rev 159–74, p. 171.

of the scope and effects within the Community legal order of these rules of international law.

As cases such as *Dior* and *Kadi* and *Yusuf* show, the seemingly abstract topic of reception of international law in Community law may have significant practical consequences for individuals. These, in my view, are strong reasons for demanding coherent and structured legal reasoning and principles from the Court of Justice in this area of EC law.

In this article, I have proposed to reconstruct the existing case law on reception of international law in Community law.

Thus, if a rule of international law is received as part of Community law, a number of legal consequences follow. Most basically, the rule must receive *uniform application* throughout the Community area. From this key requirement flows a number of derived legal consequences. First of all, the ECJ will have exclusive jurisdiction to determine the interpretative scope and the effects of these rules of international law within the Community area. (On the contrary, when a provision of international law is not a part of the Community legal order [but only binding on the Member States], the Member States are in principle free to interpret it and determine its effects. Both the scope and effects of that provision may be construed differently in different Member States.[198])

This entails, in the first place, that when international law is part of Community law the Court is able to use the international legal obligation itself as the primary source of law. In consequence, the Court will *interpret* the provision directly in accordance with the relevant international law methodology.[199] If a rule of international law is not a part of Community law it may still be used in Community law as a source of inspiration or otherwise influence the legal position in a particular case. However, in these situations, the primary source of law is an internal Community measure and the method of interpretation is the Community law method. Thus, in principle, the 'genetic code' of the interpretative exercise differs depending on whether a rule of international law is part of Community law or not.

More practically important is the second main consequence that follows from the requirement of uniform application, namely that the Community legal order determines the *domestic effects*. When a provision of international law is part of Community law, the Community legal order determines: (a) *that* the provision has precedence over secondary Community law and national law; (b) *whether* the provision is capable of being invoked directly (and thus invalidating internal Community measures and rendering inapplicable national law); (c) *to what extent*

---

[198] See Section III. There is a modification to this in the context of mixed agreements, see Section IV.C.(iii).

[199] Jacques H. J. Bourgeois, 'The European Court of Justice and the WTO: Problems and Challenges', in Weiler, ed. *The EU, the WTO, and the NAFTA: Towards a Common Law of International Trade?*, 2000, p. 94, notes in particular the different methods of interpretation and hierarchical status of international law within the Community. See also Jacot-Guillarmod, *Droit communautaire et droit international public*, 1979, p. 104.

the provision can have various indirect effects in domestic law; (d) *to what extent* the provision can form the basis for an action for damage brought by individuals. Moreover, generally, when international law is part of Community law (e) the Community's judicial system can (and probably must)[200] be used to ensure compliance, notably through infringement proceedings: cf. Articles 226 and 227, preliminary rulings; cf. Article 234, and annulment actions; cf. Article 230. Conversely, if international law falls outside the Community's sphere, the Member States' legal systems determine how to apply, and ultimately whether to comply with, rules of international law. In short, the issue of reception of international law determines which legal system controls compliance.

As the role of judiciaries continuously grows within the Community into new areas of international relations, and perhaps eventually also into the field of foreign policy proper, there is a need for clarification of the basic doctrines of reception. I have proposed some building blocks with which to assist a development in this direction. The general idea was to construct these building blocks through interpretations of existing case law, i.e. to take as a starting point some of the already established and recurring themes and concerns of the Court and the legal community at large. This approach led to the conclusion that the principles of reception of international law and the requirement of uniform application have been particularly influenced by four recurring considerations (see notably Sections III and IV.C):

- Community interests in the functioning of intra-Community relations;
- Community interests in maintaining unity in international representation;
- Compliance with the Community area's international legal obligations; and
- Maintaining the principle of legality and the vertical divisions of Community and Member State spheres of international relations.

To return to the filter metaphor: The Court's construction of the size and shape of the Community's 'international law filter', in light of the above considerations, has resulted in four distinguishable methods of reception:

1) The *Kupferberg* principle. Rules of international law are an integral part of Community law to the extent that the Community can be held responsible for their performance under international law.

2) The *International Fruit* principle. An international agreement to which the Community is not a party is a part of Community law to the extent that the Community has subsequently replaced the Member States as regards their commitments under the agreement.

3) The *Libor Cipra* principle. An international agreement to which the Community is not a party is an integral part of Community law to the

---

[200] In the pending Case C-459/03, *Commission v Ireland* (MOX plant), the Court may clarify this question.

extent that Member States have concluded the agreement on behalf of and in the interest of the Community.

4) *Mixity principles.* The extent to which mixed agreements are an integral part of Community depends on a set of special mixity principles.

It remains to be seen whether this is an exhaustive list of the methods of reception of international law. Moreover, the content of the latter three methods are much in need of further clarification. In this development the four basic considerations, relatively firmly embedded in the case law that makes up the present law on reception of international law, could provide fruitful starting points.

Exploring the *Open Skies*: EC-Incompatible Treaties between Member States and Third Countries[1]

Christiana HJI Panayi[2]

I. Introduction

The interface of international and European law could be approached from many angles. It could be approached from the angle of human rights and how such rights are applied in the Community. It could also be approached from the angle of international organizations—the extent to which the European Union[3] acts like an international organization. In this article, the relationship between international law and European law is examined from the angle of international treaty law. The inspiration was the *Open Skies* line of cases.[4]

Arguably, the *Open Skies* could have been one of the most important cases decided, had the Court of Justice the courage to escape from the confines of its Ivory Tower and explore the full ramifications of an EC-incompatible treaty between a Member State and a third country (i.e. a non-Member State). Instead, the Court of Justice was limited to a finding of incompatibility. It found a breach

---

[1] An adapted version of this study was meant to be incorporated in the author's doctoral thesis, entitled 'Double Taxation, Tax Treaties, Treaty-Shopping and the European Community', to be published by Kluwer Law International, EUCOTAX Series 2007. In the end, however, the study was left out both from the thesis and the book. I would like to thank the editors of the Yearbook of European Law for giving me the opportunity to publish it in their journal. The author is responsible for all errors. For any comments, the author may be contacted by email at c.hji-panayi@qmul.ac.uk.

[2] Dr Christiana HJI Panayi; BA, BCL (Oxon), PhD (LSE); Lecturer in Tax Law, Centre of Commercial and Legal Studies, Queen Mary, University of London; Solicitor of England & Wales, Advocate of the Cyprus Supreme Court.

[3] A distinction should be made between the European Union and the European Communities. The European Communities are the European Coal and Steel Community (ECSC), the European Community (EC) and the European Atomic Energy Community (EAEC). ECSC ceased to exist in 2002. The European Union encompasses the European Communities. In fact, it is based on these three Communities. It also encompasses pillars two and three which deal with Common Foreign and Security Policy and with Justice and Home Affairs respectively. In this article, 'Community' or 'Community law' refer to the European Communities or the law of the European Communities.

[4] For full citations, see Part IV.

of the Community's external treaty-making competence and a breach of the Community's substantive Treaty provisions. In this article, the full possible ramifications of the *Open Skies* cases are considered; namely, the Community law but aslo the international law implications of an EC-incompatible treaty between a Member State and a third country. To an extent, this article is a suggested follow-up story of the *Open Skies* cases.

This article starts off by examining the general relationship between Community law and international law. There does not seem to be consensus as to the precise normative relation of the two and more specifically the dependence of Community law on international law. Whether the Community legal order, a creature of international law, has been emancipated from it, is a matter of intense debate both in academic and judicial circles. The practical implications of this debate are illustrated throughout this article.

Secondly, the system of attribution of powers in Community law is explained. This is to show the logic behind the rules governing the Community's and the Member States' external treaty-making powers. When the legal credentials of an international treaty between a Member State and a third country are assessed, questions on both the existence of the competence and the proper exercise of it are asked. Therefore, it is essential to answer the prior question of how the Community's treaty-making competence arises and when such competence is pre-emptive, preventing Member States from acting in the field. A cursory examination of the issues will show that the principles pertaining to treaty-making competences are anything but unequivocal.

The *Open Skies* cases are then analysed in greater detail. These are the main cases in which the Court of Justice dealt with EC-incompatible treaties between Member States and third countries. It will be made apparent that many important issues arising therein have been left unanswered.

An attempt is made first to consider the Community law repercussions of such treaties. Then, the emphasis shifts to some of the international law implications. The following questions are asked. Is an EC-incompatible treaty between a Member State and a third country automatically void? If not and the treaty is still valid in international law (even though disapproved under Community law) can it be terminated by the Member State and on what grounds?

It should be pointed out from the start that this article addresses issues of conflict and breach (or invalidity) but does not proceed to address questions of liability and reparation.[5] Neither is any reference made to dispute resolution

---

[5] Questions of international responsibility may also be relevant. For example, a Member State that has entered into a potentially invalid treaty with a third State might be responsible for this act under international law. Alternatively, a third country that has entered into a treaty with a Member State in full knowledge that this treaty conflicts with the Member State's obligations under a prior treaty might be held liable for assisting the Member State to breach its international law obligations. See draft articles on the Responsibility of States for Internationally Wrongful Acts, adopted by the International Law Commission at its fifty-third session (2001). *Official Records of the General*

mechanisms that might be encompassed in the treaty instrument itself. The issues are approached from the perspective of international treaty law and more specifically the Vienna Convention of the Law of Treaties.

II. Community Law and International Law: A Sub-System of International Law or a Separate Legal Order?

The relationship between Community law and international law is a topic of growing importance. There has been a lot of academic writing on the topic especially by international lawyers.[6] Furthermore, many cases with an international law element have been decided by the Court of Justice,[7] though not always coherently or satisfactorily.

Very early on in its jurisprudence, the Court of Justice emphasized the European Community's *sui generis* character perhaps in an attempt to detach it from its international law origins. In the much celebrated case of *Van Gend en Loos*, [8] the Court of Justice held that 'the Community constitutes a new legal order of international law, for the benefit of which states have limited their sovereign rights, albeit within limited fields, and the subject of which comprise not only Member States but also their nationals'.

In a similar vein, in *Costa v Enel*, the Court of Justice insisted on the integrity of the Community legal system and rejected dependency on international law. As the Court noted, '[b]y contrast with international treaties, the EEC Treaty has

---

Assembly, Fifty-sixth session, Supplement No. 10 (A/56/10), chapter IV.E.1. More specifically, see articles 1, 2, 16.

[6] See, for example, Max Sorensen, *Autonomous Legal Orders: Some Considerations relating to a System analysis of International Organisations in the World Legal Order*, 32 [1983] ICLQ 559; Andrea Ott, 'Thirty Years of Case-Law by the European Court of Justice on International Law: A Pragmatic Approach Towards its Integration', *The European Union and the International Legal Order: Discord or Harmony* (Vincent Kronenberger, TMC Asser Press), 95; Hartley, *European Union Law in a Global Context*, 134; Hartley, 'The Constitutional Foundations of the European Union', (2001) 117 LQR 225, 226; Hartley, 'International Law and the Law of the European Union—A Reassessment', [2001] 72 BYIL 1, 18

[7] Cases directly invoking international law principles: C-286/90, *Anklagemyndigheden v Poulson and Diva Navigation Corpn* [1992] ECR I-6019; Case T-115/94 *Opel Austria* [1997] ECR II-39; Case C-162/96 *Racke* [1998] ECR I-3655. Early on case law dealt with the direct effect of international agreements entered into between the Community and third countries or organizations. See, for example, Joined Cases 21–24/72 *International Fruit Company NV and others v Produktschap voor Groenten en Fruit*, 12.12.72; Case C-181/73 *Haegeman v Belgian State* [1974] ECR 449; Case 104/81 *Hauptzollamt Mainz v C.A. Kupferberg & Cie KG a.A.* [1982] ECR 3641; Case C-286/94 *Portugal v Council (India Agreement)* [1996] ECR I-6177; C-69/89, *Nakajima All Precision Co Ltd v EC Council* [1991] ECR I-2069; Joined Cases C-180 and 266/80, *José Crujeiras Tome v Procureur de la République and Procureur de la République v Anton Yurrita* [1981] ECR 2997; Case 181/80 *Procureur général près la Cour d'Appel de Pau and others v José Arbelaiz-Emazabel* [1981] ECR 2961.

[8] Case 26/62 *NV Algemene Transport- en Expeditie Onderneming van Gend & Loos v Netherlands Inland Revenue Administration* [1963] ECR 1.

created its own legal system which on the entry into force of the Treaty, became an integral part of the legal system of the Member States and which their courts are bound to apply'.[9]

One cannot help but wonder as to the reasons behind such approach. Why was it so important for the Court to emphasize the special nature of Community law? Why was it so important for Community law to be seen as an autonomous legal order and not a subset of international law?

Unsurprisingly, the Court of Justice never really explained its motives. A few reasons may, however, be suggested. It could be argued that the distinction was made with the aim of ensuring the exclusion of certain methods of general international law that were not conducive to European integration. The Court of Justice probably saw international law as a weak and ineffective system. Certainly, by distancing Community law from international law proper, it had become possible to develop doctrines, such as direct effect and supremacy, which made Community law more effective than international law had ever been.[10] Furthermore, the Court of Justice perhaps did not want to be bound by rules of international law.[11]

Overall, one could argue that the Court of Justice had instinctively emphasised the distinctness of the Community legal order from that of the international legal order, so as to let the former 'grow' rather than be subsumed by the latter. To an extent, by developing the notions of direct effect, supremacy, implied powers and state liability, the Court of Justice had imbued the Community Treaties with the character of a constitution.[12]

However, the fact that the Community Treaties were regarded as a constitutional charter[13] did not mean that they had 'broken free of international law and become independently valid in the way that the constitution of a State has'.[14] In other words, there was no complete de-linking between Community law and international law proper. Community treaties, as all treaties, were still dependent

---

[9] Case 6/64 [1964] ECR 585, 593.

[10] It was also thought that the methods of interpretation that the ECJ had followed could more easily be explicable if seen as part of a *sui generis* system rather than an expression of international law. See, T.C. Hartley, *Constitutional Problems of the European Union* (Oxford, 1999), 136–7.

[11] See Opinion 2/94. Arguably, in this case, the reason why the ECJ refused to find Community competence to accede to the European Convention of Human Rights was because it was unwilling to be bound by human rights legislation and international human rights tribunals.

[12] See Klabbers, 'Re-inventing the law of treaties: The Contribution of the EC Courts', [1999] NYIL 45–74, 53; L. Hancher, 'Constitutionalism, the Community Court and International Law', 25 [1994] NYIL 259–298; Jean-Clause Piris, 'Does the European Union have a Constitution? Does it need one?', [1999] ELR 557–585; Koen Lenaerts & Marlies Desomer, *Bricks for a Constitutional Treaty of the European Union: values, objectives and means*, (2002) EL Rev. 27(4), 377–407.

[13] See Case 294/83 *Les Verts v European Parliament* [1986] ECR 1339, para 23; Opinion 1/92 [1991] ECR I-6079, para 21: 'the EEC Treaty, albeit concluded in the form of an international agreement, none the less constitutes the constitutional charter of a Community based on the rule of law'.

[14] Hartley, *European Union law in a global context: text, cases and materials* (Cambridge: Cambridge University Press, 2004) 134.

on international law to derive their validity and regulate issues such as termination or amendment.

For example, some Member States referred back to domestic law when Community supremacy was considered. In other words, they considered that the Community derived its legitimacy and supremacy from express Member State stipulation (i.e. because of internal law), rather than because of the *sui generis* nature of Community law.[15] Therefore, it was argued, authorization actually came from the bottom-up and Community law was in fact a creature of internal law. It was empowered by internal law. As such, it was revocable. This re-conceptualization of the supremacy theory seems to have been adopted by several Member States,[16] even though it does not accord with earlier case law of the Court of Justice.[17]

It is this author's view that one should not easily surrender to either of these schools of thought; at least, not yet. Community law is not just a subset of international law. Nor are, however, principles of international law completely alien to the Community legal order. Although Community law seems to owe its existence to international law,[18] it is *gradually* becoming a distinct and self-contained legal order.[19] But Community law and international law have not yet become mutually exclusive. That is why, in this author's view, the implications of the one over the other should not be neglected. In recent case law, the Court of Justice has tried to tackle this overlap, though not always successfully.

In the *Poulsen and Diva Corporation* case, the Court of Justice paid some deference to international law principles, by stating that the 'European Community must respect international law in the exercise of its powers'.[20] The Court of

[15] See for example *Brunner v The European Union Treaty* [1994] 1 CMLRev. 57, decided by the German Constitutional Court (GCC) which held that it would 'review legal instruments of European institutions and agencies to see whether they remain within the limits of the sovereign rights conferred on them or transgress them' (para 49). The GCC insisted that the Community is 'a federation of States, the common authority of which is derived from the Member States and can only have binding effects within the German sovereign sphere by virtue of the German instruction that its law be applied'. (para 55)

[16] See Danish Supreme Court case: *Carlsen v Rasmussen* [1999] 3 CMLRev. 854. Also see UK, French and Italian case law analysed in Craig & de Burca, Chapter 6.

[17] See, for instance, Case 6/64 *Costa v Enel* [1964] ECR 585, where it has held that '[b]y creating a Community of unlimited duration, having its own institutions, its own personality, its own legal capacity, and capacity of representation on the international place, and more particularly, real powers stemming from a limitation of sovereignty or a transfer of powers from the States to the community, the Member States have limited their sovereign rights, albeit within limited fields, and have thus created a body of law which binds both their nationals and themselves.'

[18] If there was no international law, a group of countries could not have been bound internationally.

[19] Kristian Timmermans, 'The EU and Public International Law', 4 [1999] EFA 181–194; Hartley, *European Union Law in a Global Context*, 134; Hartley, 'The Constitutional Foundations of the European Union', (2001) 117 LQR 225, 226; Hartley, 'International Law and the Law of the European Union—A Reassessment', [2001] 72 BYIL 1, 18.

[20] See Case C-286/90 *Poulsen and Diva Corporation* [1992] ECR I-6019. The case involved a regulation adopted in the context on vessels of salmon caught in areas which were not under the sovereignty or jurisdiction of Member States. The Court of Justice held that it could take into account the relevant rules of the law of the sea in so far as these reflected or codified customary international law.

Justice insisted that it could take into account the relevant rules of international law in interpreting a Community instrument[21] in so far as these were reflected in customary[22] international law or were a codification of it. The rationale was that these principles, being customary law, were thought to be embedded in Community legal order anyway.

Whilst the *dicta* from the *Poulsen and Diva corporation* case were promising, they were largely qualified in subsequent cases. In *Opel Austria v Council* and in *Racke*, the Court of Justice and the Court of First Instance tried to 're-package' principles of customary law and present them as falling within the ambit of more traditional Community principles.

In *Opel Austria v Council*,[23] the Court of First Instance had to rule on the lawfulness of a Council regulation withdrawing tariff concessions granted to the Republic of Austria (before accession).[24] The regulation was adopted a few days before the Agreement on the European Economic Area (EEA Agreement) entered into force, and the applicant argued that it violated the provisions of that agreement.

The Court of First Instance held that the legality of the contested measure had to be assessed on the basis of the facts and the law as they stood at the time when the measure was adopted. It then referred to the principle of good faith, according to which, pending the entry into force of an international agreement, the signatories to an international agreement may not adopt measures which would defeat its object and purpose.[25] The Court of First Instance acknowledged that principle as a rule of customary international law. However, it considered this international law principle as a corollary of the principle of protection of legitimate expectations which formed part of the Community legal order.[26] Therefore, good faith was relevant because it fell within the ambit of legitimate expections. As Advocate General Jacobs commented in his opinion to the *Racke* case, in *Opel Austria v. Council* effectively, 'the international law principle of good faith was married to the Community law principle of protection of legitimate expectations'.[27]

The Court of Justice reached a similar conclusion in *Racke v Hauptzollamt Main*.[28] In this case, the Council had suspended and denounced the Co-operation

---

[21] In *Poulsen*, the relevant principles of international law were derived from the law of the sea. It involved the 1958 Geneva Conventions on the Territorial Sea and Contiguous zone, the UN Convention on the Law of the Sea 1982 etc. See para 9.

[22] Under Article 38(1)(b) of the Statue of the International Court of Justice, custom is included as one of the sources of law. International custom is referred to therein 'as evidence of a general practice accepted as law'. As Shaw, *International Law* (Cambridge, Cambridge University Press, 2003) p.69, notes, the existence of customary rules is deduced from the practice and behaviour of nations. It is not always easy to know when a certain practice has become custom, as custom is not a deliberate law-making process. The duration, consistency, repetition and generality of a practice are relevant factors proving the existence of custom.   [23] Case T-115/94 *Opel Austria v Council* [1997] ECR II-39.

[24] Council Regulation (EC) 3697/93 re-establishing duty on imports into the Community of gearboxes produced by the applying party in Austria.

[25] Case T-115/94 *Opel Austria v Council* [1997] ECR II-39 (paras 37–60).

[26] *Ibid.*, para 93.

[27] See Advocate General Jacobs' discussion of the *Opel Austria* case in his opinion to Case C-162/96 *Racke v Hauptzollamt Main* [1998] ECR I-3655, para 76.

[28] Case C-162/96 *Racke v Hauptzollamt Main* [1998] ECR I-3655.

Agreement between the Socialist Federal Republic of Yugoslavia and the Community following the outbreak of civil unrest,[29] on the basis of an alleged fundamental change of circumstances. One of the questions referred to the Court of Justice was whether this suspension was valid. The Court of Justice initially admitted that 'the rules of customary international law concerning the termination and the suspension of treaty relations by reason of a fundamental change of circumstances are binding upon the Community institutions and form part of the Community legal order.'[30]

However, again, what the Lord giveth, the Lord taketh away. In *Racke*, the Court of Justice proceeded with caution and held that 'because of the complexity of the rules in question and the imprecision of some of the concepts to which they refer, judicial review must necessarily [. . .] be limited to the question whether, by adopting the suspending regulation, the Council made manifest errors of assessment concerning the conditions for applying those rules'.[31] Therefore, the question of adherence to stand-alone principles of international law (here the rules on fundamental change of circumstances)[32] was rephrased as a question of manifest errors of assessment under Community law in the application of those principles.[33]

Nevertheless, it is obvious from these cases that, whilst the Community Courts have started to warm up to the idea of cross-fertilization of principles from the international law terrain, they are still reluctant to adopt principles of international law (codified or customary) on a stand-alone basis, especially if these principles are likely to limit or interfere with the scope of the Community Treaties.

In any case, in so far as *intra-Community matters* are concerned, international law principles may be of limited effect, especially if, as seen in the *Opel Austria* and *Racke* cases, Community principles can be used as 'surrogates' to classic principles of international law. However, when a third country is involved, 'surrogacy' might not be available; nor may it suffice. In other words, it may not always be possible to ignore the pure international law implications of Community and/or Member State actions and recharacterize the issues as being pure Community ones. A treaty relationship between the Community and a third country or a Member State(s) and a third country may potentially have *both* Community law and international law implications. From a Community law angle, an examination of this relationship usually focuses on whether the requisite competence for entering into the treaty existed, the nature of this competence and the implications of an infringement of this competence. From an international law angle, the examination

---

[29] Council Regulation (EEC) No 3300/91 of 11 November 1991 suspending the trade concessions provided for by the Co-operation Agreement between the European Economic Community and the Socialist Federal Republic of Yugoslavia (OJ 1991 L 315, p. 1)

[30] See *Racke*, para 46.   [31] See *Racke*, para 52.

[32] For an analysis of this ground of termination see Part V(A)(iii).

[33] For a criticism of the case, see Olufemi Elias, 'General International Law in the European Court of Justice: From Hypothesis to Reality?', 31 (2000) NYIL 3, 18. Also see Pieter-Jan Kuijper, 'From Dyestuffs to Kosovo Wine: From Avoidance to Acceptance by the European Community Courts of Customary International Law as Limit to Community Action', in *The Foundations and Sources of International Law*, (ed. Ige F. Dekker, Harry H.G. Post) 151, 170.

usually focuses on the legal credentials of the treaty, issues of international responsibility and reparation.

It is noteworthy that these international law issues have never really featured in the discussions of the Court of Justice, even though in some of its decisions, international issues were touched upon. This is, perhaps, a direct corollary of the *sui generis* rhetoric of the Court of Justice. It is this author's opinion that it is perhaps time that these international law principles be more readily acknowledged and explicitly examined in some areas of Community law such as that of treaty-making competences. Failure to address the international law perspectives of some arrangements sometimes may leave a legal vacuum; especially when something goes wrong in the arrangement.

In the next section, the Community system of attribution of competences is examined. In so far as external treaty-making is concerned, the question of competence is essential. To an extent, it is the Community's internal empowering process linking it to the outside world. It is therefore all the more necessary that its rules are succinct and precise. Is this the case? The following brief exposition of the case law seems to suggest otherwise.

III. The System of Attribution of Powers

It is the cornerstone of the European legal structure that the Communities and their institutions only have powers—or competences—[34] that the Member States have conferred upon them in the Community Treaties. This is the principle of attribution of powers,[35] previously implicit in the system of the Treaties and

---

[34] A distinction often made is that between capacity and authority (competence). Capacity relates to the legal power of the Community to enter into an agreement. It is an issue going to the legal personality of the Community and is ultimately a matter of international law. Authority, however, refers to the legality of the exercise of that power in the internal legal order and is a question of Community law. Even if there is general capacity, action must be referable on a specific legal basis (competence/authority) in order to be valid internally. See Maria Giavouneli, 'International Law Aspects of the European Union', [2000] 8 Tulane Journal of International and Comparative Law, 147, 158; MacLeod, Hendry & Hyett, *The External Relations of the European Communities* (OUP, 1996) 38–9. For the differences between competence, power and capacity in the federal context, see Weiler, *The external legal relations of non-unitary actors: mixity and the federal principle, in Mixed Agreements*, at 41.

[35] C.W.A Timmermans and E.L.M. Volker (Eds.) *Division of powers between the European communities and their member states in the field of external relations: colloquium, 30 and 31 May 1980* (Kluwer 1981); MacLeod, Hendry & Hyett, *The External Relations of the European Communities* (OUP, 1996), Chapters 1 and 3; Jean Groux & Philippe Manin, *The European Communities in the International Order* (The European Perspectives Series, Brussels, 1985), Part II; Arnull, Dashwood, Ross, Wyatt, *Wyatt & Dashwood's European Union Law* (Sweet & Maxwell, 2000), p. 153 *et seq.*; Alan Dashwood, 'External Relations Provisions of the Amsterdam Treaty', [1998] 35 CMLRev. 1019–1045; Alan Dashwood, *The attribution of External Relations Competence, Chapter 8 of The General Law of EC External Relations* (Sweet & Maxwell, 2000); Koen Lenaerts, Piet Van Nuffel and Robert Bray, *Constitutional Law of the European Union* (Sweet & Maxwell, 1999), 90–103; Dominic McGoldrick, *International Relations Law of the European Union* (Longman 1997, Harlow), Chapter 3; Udo di Fabio,

finally codified in Article 5 of the EC Treaty. The first paragraph of Article 5 EC provides:

The Community shall act within the limits of the powers conferred on it by this Treaty and of the objectives assigned to it therein.

Therefore, the Community order is not a self-authenticating or self-generating one.[36] It depends on the Member States having conferred powers to it and continuing to do so. For example, the European Union lacks the power to grant itself a constitution; the Member States have to approve this separately.

The principle of attribution of powers must be respected both in the internal and the external sphere of Community action. This means that every Community act must be based on a general or specific Treaty provision—a legal basis— empowering the Community, expressly or implicitly, to act.[37] Conversely, if a power is specifically attributed or simply left to Member States, then the allocation of this power must also be respected both internally and externally.[38] The Community cannot enact legislation in an area falling within the Member States' sphere of powers; nor can it enter into a treaty with third countries usurping such powers.

A. The Existence and Nature of Community Competence

It is important to emphasize from the outset the distinction between the existence of the Community's competence (i.e. whether competence arises from an express conferment of the Treaties or by implication) and the nature such competence (i.e. whether it is exclusive or shared).[39] The distinction is not always made clear in the Court of Justice's deliberations.[40] Logically, one examines the nature of a Community competence if such competence actually exists!

'Some Remarks on the Allocation of Competences between the European Union and its Member States', [2002] 39 CMLRev. 1289–1301; Pierre Pescatore, 'External Relations in the Case law of the Court of Justice of the European Communities' [1979] 16 CMLRev. 615–640, at 618.

[36] See, for example *Opinion 2/94 European Convention on Human Rights* [1996] ECR I-1759, at paragraph 23.

[37] *Ibid.*, paras 24–25. Also see KSC. Bradley, 'The European Court and the Legal Basis of Community Legislation' (1988) EL Rev. 379–402; Rene Barents, 'The Internal Market Unlimited: Some observations on the Legal basis of Community Legislation', [1993] 30 CMLR ev. 85–109.

[38] The Commission and Member States often have very different views on the scope of various powers conferred to the Community legislature, or whether an institution has used the correct legal basis for a legislative act. This is especially important if the disputed legal basis provides for less onerous voting requirements (e.g. qualified majority rather than unanimity) or less cumbersome procedural/consultation requirements. This is exacerbated by the fact that there is no dearth of legal bases on which to launch Community-wide initiatives. The analysis in this chapter proceeds on the basis that there is a clear allocation of power to Member States.

[39] Dashwood, 'Implied External Competence of the EC' in Martti Koskenniemi (Ed.), *International Law Aspects of the European Union* (Kluwer Law International, The Hague 1998) p.118.

[40] In some cases, court of justice made distinction between the existence of competence and the nature of it: e.g. Opinion 2/91, *Kramer*, Opinion 1/75. In other cases, the Court did not explicitly distinguish between the two issues (ERTA, Opinion 1/94, Opinion 2/92).

(i) The Existence of Community Competence

Community competence in external affairs may arise expressly or impliedly. External competence arises expressly where action by the Community is founded on a specific provision of the Treaty. The original EEC Treaty conferred very few express powers. For example, it empowered the Community to enter into agreements only as regards the common commercial policy[41] and association agreements,[42] and the development of co-operation with third states and international organizations.[43]

Subsequent Treaty amendments agreed by the Member States at successive intergovernmental conferences led to the inclusion of further express competences. The Community now has competence in monetary or foreign exchange regime matters,[44] research and development,[45] the environment,[46] and development co-operation.[47] The Community also has certain powers concerning the fostering of co-operation at international level. These powers are thought of[48] as empowering the Community to enter into international agreements in the areas of education, vocational training and youth,[49] culture,[50] and public health.[51]

Community competence may also arise by implication from provisions of the Treaty. It may also arise where measures have been adopted by the Community implying such competence. This is the doctrine of implied external competence.

The *locus classicus* of this doctrine is the *ERTA* judgment.[52] In this case, the Court of Justice held that external competence arises 'not only from an express conferment by the treaty [...] but *may equally flow from other provisions of the treaty and from measures adopted, within the framework of those provisions, by the Community institutions*'.[53]

The ERTA doctrine developed incrementally through case law. In the first two decades, the doctrine was interpreted rather widely.[54]

Opinion 1/76 extended the doctrine of implied external competence to encompass situations where internal powers to act existed but had not yet been exercised. In that case, the Court of Justice found that, the Community had authority to enter into an international agreement if this was necessary for the attainment of one of the objectives of the Community.[55] Therefore, the external powers could be derived from internal powers, regardless of whether measures had actually been adopted, if

---

[41] Formerly Article 113 EEC, now Article 133 EC Treaty.
[42] Formerly Article 238 EEC, now Article 310 EC Treaty.
[43] Formerly Articles 229–331 EEC, now Articles 302–304 EC Treaty.
[44] Article 113(3) EC Treaty. [45] Article 170 EC Treaty. [46] Article 174(4) EC Treaty.
[47] Article 181 EC. [48] See MacLeod, Hendry and Hyett, at p. 47.
[49] Articles 149(3) and 150(3) EC. [50] Article 151(3) EC. [51] Article 152 EC.
[52] Case 22–70 *Commission of the European Communities v Council of the European Communities (ERTA)* [1970] ECR 263. [53] Case 22–70, para 16. Author's emphasis.
[54] See, for example, Joined Cases 3, 4 and 6–76, *Cornelis Kramer and others* [1976] ECR 1279; *Opinion 1/76 (Re the Draft Agreement establishing a European laying-up fund for inland waterway vessels)* [1977] ECR 741; Opinion 2/91.
[55] *Opinion 1/76 (Re the Draft Agreement establishing a European laying-up fund for inland waterway vessels)* [1977] ECR 741, para 3.

the simultaneous exercise of external and internal competence or the prior exercise of the external power was *necessary* for the attainment of the objective. This was to be the necessity test. Similarly, in *Opinion 2/91*,[56] the Court of Justice held that external powers could be implied from powers in the internal system, whenever those internal powers existed *for the purpose of attaining a specific objective*.[57]

Subsequent cases interpreted the necessity test of *Opinion 1/76* in a more restrictive way. In *Opinion 1/94*,[58] the Court of Justice qualified the ambit of *Opinion 1/76*, in that the wide *dicta* therein related to a situation where the conclusion of an international agreement was necessary in order to achieve Treaty objectives *which could not have been attained by the adoption of autonomous rules*.[59]

The Court of Justice showed similar reticence in *Opinion 2/94*.[60] Whilst reiterating the classic authorities, it emphasized the principle of conferred powers enshrined in Article 5 EC and the need for 'a clear internal power, created for the purpose of attaining a specific objective, to form the basis of an implied external power necessary to attain that objective'.[61] Fundamental human rights were recognized as all-pervasive general principles of Community law, respect for which may be a condition of the lawfulness of Community acts.[62] However, general principles of law did not suffice in providing a basis on which to imply external powers.[63] Therefore, the Court of Justice rejected the argument that it had competence to accede to the European Convention for the Protection of Human Rights and Fundamental Freedoms (ECHR).[64]

The Court of Justice's reticence in this and subsequent cases should be considered in the background of the fierce constitutional debate over the autonomous legitimacy of Community law and its perceived hierarchical position in Member States' legal orders.[65] Overall, it would seem that the concept of implied external

---

[56] *Opinion 2/91 (Re ILO Convention 170)* [1993] ECR I-1061, [1993] CMLRev. 800. Also see Henry G. Schermers, 'Case Law (on Opinion 1/91, 1/92)', [1992] 29 CMLRev. 991–1009.

[57] See Opinion 2/91, para 3 of the Court's reasoning.

[58] *Opinion 1/94 (Re WTO Agreement)* [1994] ECR I-5267, [1995] 1 CMLRev. 205. The case will be analysed in more detail when the exclusivity question is addressed.

[59] *Opinion 1/94*, para 85.

[60] *Opinion 2/94 (Re Accession to the European Convention for the Protection of Human Rights and Fundamental Freedoms)* [1996] 2 CMLRev. 265.   [61] *Opinion 2/94*, paras 23–6

[62] *Ibid.*, para 34

[63] Neither could the default mechanism of Article 308 EC be used to fill in the legislative gap. Such use would in substance be to amend the Treaty without following the procedure which it provides for that purpose. This is because accession to the ECHR entails a substantial change to the Community system and as such change was of constitutional significance it required Treaty amendment (*Opinion 2/94*, paras 30, 34–5). See Inge Bernaerts, 'Opinion 2/94', [1996] Columbia Journal of European Law 372, at 381 discussing the political aspects of this case.

[64] *Opinion 1/94*.

[65] *Brunner* [1994] 1 CMLRev. 57; J. Weiler, 'Does Europe Need a Constitution? Demos, Telos and the German Maastricht Decision', [1995] 1 ELJ 219; G. de Burca, 'The Quest for legitimacy in the European Union', [1996] 59 MLR 349; T. Shilling, 'The Autonomy of the Community Legal Order: An Analysis of Possible Foundations', (1996) 37 Harvard ILJ 389; J. Weiler & U. Haltern, 'The Autonomy of the Community Legal Order: Through the Looking Glass', (1996) 37 Harvard ILJ 411.

powers is well established but within bounds. However, as shown below, the constant intermingling of the tests of implied external competence and implied exclusive external competence brings uncertainty to both.

(ii) Exclusive External Competence

Exclusive competence results from the complete transfer of competence from the Member States to the Community. When exclusive competence arises, the Member States are considered to have forfeited their legislative powers in that field. The mere existence of such competence prevents the Member States from acting in that field.

The exact boundaries of Community competences are not set out in the Community treaties, but it is 'generally accepted that Community powers are exclusive in so far as they cover areas which are strictly linked to the achievement of the essential objectives of European integration'.[66-67] A power is also exclusive where it appears from the wording or the context of the Treaty provisions in question that any action by the Member States would conflict with it.[68]

Exclusive external competence may arise expressly or by implication. There are very few examples of provisions in the Treaty or Acts of Association where there is explicit conferral of exclusivity. The most well-known provisions are Article 133 EC dealing with the Common Commercial Policy and Article 102 of the 1972 Act of Accession dealing with fisheries conservation.[69]

In order to avoid stagnation in the Community's exercise of external relations, the Court of Justice has developed, concurrently with the doctrine of *implied external* competence, the concept of *implied exclusive external* competence. With the caveat that any rigid categorization is somewhat incongruous with the Court of Justice's teleological approach, it would seem that the Court of Justice broadly acknowledges two circumstances under which implied exclusivity may arise.

First, the Community may acquire exclusive competence *as a result of internal measures adopted* by the Community.[70] Therefore, the nature of competence may

---

[66-67] Andrea Appella, 'Constitutional Aspects of Opinion 1/94 of the ECJ concerning the WTO Agreement', [1996] 45 ICLQ 440–462, at p. 442.

[68] *Opinion 1/75 Draft OECD Understanding on a Local Cost Standard* [1975] ECR 1355, at 1363–1364.

[69] Joined Cases 3–4/76 and 6/76 *Officier van Justitie v Kramer* [1976] ECR 1279; [1976] 2 CMLRev. 440, paras 39–41; Case 804/79 Re Fishery Conservation Measure (No. 2): *Commission v United Kingdom* [1981] ECR 1045; [1982] 1 CMLRev. 543, paras 17–18; *Opinion 2/91* [1993] ECR I-1061, para 8.

[70] Again, this principle is derived from the *ERTA* case where it was held that: 'Each time the Community, with a view to implementing a common policy envisaged by the Treaty, adopts provisions laying down common rules, whatever form these may take, the Member States no longer have the right, acting individually or even collectively, to undertake obligations with third countries which affect those rules. As and when such common rules come into being, the Community alone is in a position to assume and carry out contractual obligations towards third countries affecting the whole

vary according to the type and intensity of the common measures already adopted. A case-by-case assessment needs to be undertaken before a field is thought to have been pre-empted. This assessment is usually undertaken at the backdrop of national sensitivities and delicate political balances for which the Court of Justice is required to show political awareness and adopt a pragmatic approach. [71]

Secondly, pursuant to *Opinion 1/76*, exclusivity may arise without internal measures having been adopted if it is *necessary* in order to attain the objectives of the Treaty in an area and if *such objectives cannot be attained by introducing autonomous common rules.*

Both of these categories of exclusivity were given a restrictive interpretation in *Opinion 1/94*.[72] In this case, the Commission had requested from the Court of Justice under the procedure of Article 228(6) EC to confirm that the Community had exclusive competence pursuant to Article 133 EC to conclude the Agreement establishing the World Trade Organisation (WTO Agreement) which had been negotiated in the framework of the Uruguay Round negotiations.[73] The dispute

---

sphere of application of the Community legal system'. ERTA judgment, paras 17–18. In *Opinion 2/91*, the Court of Justice held that it sufficed if the area is merely one 'which is already covered to *a large extent* by Community rules ... adopted ... with a view to achieving an ever greater degree of harmonisation'. *Opinion 2/91 (Re ILO Convention 170)* [1993] ECR I-1061, [1993] CMLR 800, para 25

[71] See Tridimas & Eeckhout, 'The external competence of the Community and the case-law of the Court of Justice: principle versus pragmatism', 14 (1994) YEL 143–177,160. Also see Advocate General's arguments in *Open Skies* as to the difficulties of reviewing any *ex ante* decisions as to the exclusive nature of external competence in the abstract prior to any exercise of Community competence (paras 51–2).

[72] *Opinion 1/94 (Re WTO Agreement)*, [1994] ECR I-5267. For comments see Piet Eeckhout, 'The domestic legal status of the WTO Agreement: Interconnecting legal systems', [1997] 37 CMLRev. 11–58; Jacques Bourgeois, 'The EC in the WTO and Advisory Opinion 1/94: An Echternach Procession', [1995] 32 CMLRev. 763–787; Meinhard Hilf, 'The ECJ's Opinion 1/94 on the WTO—No surprise, but Wise?', 6 EJIL [1995] 245–259; Anonymous, 'The aftermath of Opinion 1/94 or how to ensure unity of representation for joint competences', [1995] 32 CMLRev. 385–390; Andrea Appella, 'Constitutional Aspects of Opinion 1/94 of the ECJ concerning the WTO Agreement', 45 [1996] ICLQ 440–462; Antti Maunu, 'The implied external competence of the European Community after the ECJ Opinion 1/94—towards coherence or diversity?', L.I.E.I. 1995, 2, 115–128; Pierre Pescatore, 'Opinion 1/94 on "Conclusion"' of the WTO Agreement: is there an escape from a programmed disaster?', [1999] 36(2) CMLRev. 387–405; Julio A. Baquero Cruz, 'Disintegration of the Law of Integration in the External Economic Relations of the European Community', [1997] 3 Columbia Journal of European Law, 257. For an explanation as to how the negative aspects of *Opinion 1/94* translated in the new Article 133 EC, see Horst Krenzler & Christian Pitschas, 'Progress or Stagnation?: The Common Commercial Policy After Nice', 6 [2001] EFA Rev. 291–313.

[73] The WTO Agreement embodied the results of the Uruguay Round multilateral trade negotiations launched by the Punta del Este Ministerial Declaration of 20 September 1986. With the approval of the Council and of the Member States, the Commission was to act as the sole negotiator on behalf of the Community and the Member States, but this was not intended to prejudice the question of competence of the Community or the Member States. See Council Decision of 22 December 1994 concerning the conclusion on behalf of the European Community, as regards matters within its competence, of the agreements reached in the Uruguay Round multilateral negotiations (1986–1994), OJ 1994, L336/1

centered on two agreements annexed to the WTO Agreement; namely, the General Agreement on Trade in Services (GATS)[74] and the Agreement on Trade Related aspects of Intellectual Property Rights (TRIPs).[75]

The Court of Justice found that the Community's competence to enter into these agreements, with the exception of some provisions dealing with cross-border supplies,[76] was non-exclusive. The Court said that the Community's exclusive external competence does not automatically flow from its power to lay down rules at internal level.[77]

The Member States, whether acting individually or collectively, *only* lose their right to assume obligations with non-member countries *as and when common rules which could be affected by those obligations come into being.* Only in so far as common rules have been established at internal level does the external competence of the Community become exclusive.[78]

For the Court of Justice, it was imperative that the Community had achieved *complete harmonization* of the rules in that area before a claim of exclusive competence could be acknowledged.[79] The task of finding whether an area has been completely or exhaustively occupied by the Community was itself subject to interpretation. '[R]egard must be had to the legal base of the internal Community measure [. . .], the reasons for adoption as set out in the preamble, and the subject-matter and scope of the measures themselves.'[80]

[74] The GATS is a framework agreement which subjects the supply of services to international rules akin to the GATT rules. The GATS covered trade in all services in all sectors, except services supplied in the exercise of governmental authority. Such trade in services would encompass cross-border supplies, consumption abroad, commercial presence and movement of persons.

[75] See Petersmann, 'The dispute settlement system of the World Trade Organisation and the evolution of the GATT dispute settlement system since 1948', [1994] 31 CMLRev. 1154–1244; Petersmann, 'Proposals for a new Constitution for the European Union: Building-blocks for a constitutional theory and constitutional law of the EU', [1995] 32 CMLRev. 1164–1172; Bronckers, 'The impact of TRIPS: intellectual property protection in developing countries', [1994] 31 CMLRev. 1245–1281; Weiss, 'The General Agreement on Trade in Services 1994', [1995] 32 CMLRev. 1177–1225; Lee and Kennedy, 'The potential direct effect of GATT 1994 in European Community Law', (1996/1) JWT, 67–89; Neuwahl, 'Individuals and the GATT: Direct Effect and Indirect Effects of the General Areement on Tariffs and Trade in Community Law', in Emiliou and O'Keeffe (Eds.), *The European Union and World Trade Law* (1996), pp. 313–328; Timmermans, 'The Implementation of the Uruguay Round by the EC', in Bourgeois, Berrod and Gippini Fournier (Eds.), *The Uruguay Round Results—A European Lawyers' Perspective* (European Interuniversity Press, 1995), p.509.

[76] The exceptions were the GATS provisions dealing with cross-border supplies and the TRIPs prohibitions of the release of goods into free circulation of counterfeit. The former were encompassed in the Common Commercial Policy. For the latter, internal Community legislation was in place. See Council Regulation (EEC) No 3842/86 of 1 December 1986 laying down measures to prohibit the release for free circulation of counterfeit goods (OJ 1986 L357, p.1). As for the rest of the areas of the TRIPs, harmonization was either partial or non-existent (*Opinion 1/94*, para 103).

[77] *Opinion 1/94*, para V 3, para 77.   [78] *Opinion 1/94*, para 77.

[79] *Opinion 1/94*, para 96. The Court in Opinion 2/92 and in the *Open Skies* cases reiterated the need for a complete harmonization as a pre-condition of exclusivity. See, for example, Case 467/98, para 84.

[80] See David O'Keeffe, 'Exclusive, Concurrent and Shared Competence', Chapter 12 of *The General Law of EC External Relations*, at 183. Also see Takis Tridimas, 'The WTO and OECD Opinions',

As the Court of Justice emphasized, a finding of (the existence of) implied external competence did not automatically mean that such competence was exclusive. If the Community had included in its internal legislative acts provisions relating to the treatment of nationals of non-member countries or expressly conferred on its institutions powers to negotiate with non-member countries, then the Community acquired exclusive external competence in the spheres covered by those acts.[81] This was not the case in *Opinion 1/94*.

Unlike the chapter on transport, the chapters on the right of establishment and on freedom to provide services do not contain any provision expressly extending the competence of the Community to 'relationships arising from international law'.[82]

The Court of Justice's disapproval of arguments based on general distortions in the flow of services in the internal market for allowing exclusive competence was seized upon in the *Open Skies* cases.[83] In those cases, the Court held that such distortions 'do not in themselves affect the common rules adopted in that area and thus are not capable of [justifying the establishment of] an external competence of the Community'.[84] In other words, one could not simply rely on the economic repercussions which the agreements may have generated on the functioning of the internal market to exclude the Member States' competence.[85] A more exacting analysis was necessary.[86]

Reverting to *Opinion 1/94*, the necessity doctrine of *Opinion 1/76* was distinguished to its own special facts.[87] For the Court of Justice, the starting point was that there must be prior exercise of internal powers for exclusivity to arise.[88] It, however, acknowledged that in exceptional circumstances, 'external powers may be exercised, and thus become exclusive, without any internal legislation having first been adopted'.[89] This would happen when an internal power was 'inextricably

---

Chapter 4 of *The General Law of EC External Relations*. MacLeod, 60–61, with the caveat that 'the precise terms of the power conferred on the Community institutions must be examined to determine whether the Community's competence is exclusive or not'.

[81] *Opinion 1/94*, para 95.   [82] *Ibid.*, para 81.

[83] Case C-267/98 *Open Skies*, para 81. Also see Opinion 2/92, para 33.

[84] *Open Skies*, para 85.   [85] See AG in *Open Skies*, para 77.

[86] Also see Advocate General Tizzano's more sophisticated analysis in *Open Skies* (paras 71–77). The Advocate General distinguished between cases where the international arrangements overlapped with the subject-matter of the common rules and those where there was no overlap with the exact subject-matter but common rules were affected ['concern agreements which are contiguous [...] to those governed by the common rules'] (paras 71 and 75 respectively). According to the Advocate General, whether or not the latter kind of international arrangements should be impugned depended on the circumstances of the case (paras 76–77).

[87] The purpose of that agreement was to rationalize the navigation in the inland waterways sector of the Rhine and Moselle basins. Because of the need to include Switzerland in those agreements, it was necessary to act by way of an international agreement. It was, therefore, understandable 'that external powers may be exercised, and thus become exclusive, without any internal legislation having first been adopted'.

[88] The Court seems to merge *ERTA* and *Opinion 1/76* as their distinguishing factor was the (absence of) prior exercise of internal powers.   [89] *Opinion 1/94*, para 85.

linked' with an external one and therefore both powers had to be simultaneously exercised.[90]

There has been some debate as to whether the *dicta* on 'inextricable link' are confined to the question of exclusivity, which was in fact the question that the ECJ was asked to opine upon, or whether it is also applied to the prior question of the existence of the competence. There seems to be some consensus among academics that the 'inextricable link' test only relates to questions of exclusivity.[91] In a way, confusion is unavoidable, as the tests for finding implied external competence and implied exclusive external competence are *prima facie* identical and referable to the same case law. The problem is also exacerbated by the Court of Justice's failure–deliberate or inadvertent—to distinguish in its analysis issues relating to the existence and issues relating to the nature of competence.

The cases are replete with contradictory *dicta*. At one juncture, in *Opinion 1/94*, the Court of Justice stated that 'external powers may be exercised, and thus *become* exclusive'.[92] This suggested that the mere exercise of the external powers rendered the competence exclusive; i.e. Community powers could be automatically exclusive regardless of any exercise of internal. At another juncture in the same case, the Court of Justice made comments to the contrary, in that 'save where internal powers can only be effectively exercised at the same time as external powers [. . .] internal competence can give rise to exclusive external competence *only if it is exercised*'.[93]

It is rather unfortunate that the Court of Justice failed to clarify matters in the *Open Skies* line of cases but rather perpetuated the confusion.[94] The *Open Skies* cases are discussed in more detail in Part IV. Suffice to note for now that in so far as the competence issues were concerned, the Court of Justice did not give any clear answers but rather perpetuated the confusion with contradictory dicta.

In the *Lugano* case decided in 2006,[95] the Court of Justice tried to rationalize its previous case law. Here, the Court was asked to give its opinion on whether the

---

[90] *ibid.* The possibility of exclusivity arising from Article 308 EC was left open, but phrased just as restrictively as the necessity principle in Opinion 1/76, in that 'save where internal powers can only be effectively exercised at the same time as external powers', internal competence can give rise to exclusive external competence only if it is exercised (para 89).

[91] McGoldrick, at p.61, thinks that the restrictive reading of the necessity test of *Opinion 1/76* applies only when the question relates to exclusivity of EC competence and not to the question of competence per se. Also see Dashwood & Heliskoski, 16; Tridimas & Eeckhout, 167.

[92] *Opinion 1/94*, para 85; *Opinion 2/92* para 32. This was also the view of the Commission in the *Open Skies* cases. See, for example, Case C-467/98 paras 45–49.   [93] *Opinion 1/94*, para 89.

[94] See for example Case C-467/98 *Commission v Denmark* [2002] ECR I-9519. In paragraph 45, whilst the title of a section was 'The alleged existence of an external competence of the Community within the meaning of Opinion 1/76' the Court concluded in paragraph 63 that in light of its discussion, 'the Community could not validly claim that there was an exclusive external competence . . .'. The same inconsistency appeared in its discussion of the *ERTA* principle (paragraph 65). See Liz Heffernan & Conor McAuliffe, 'External Relations in the Air Transport Sector: the Court of Justice and the Open Skies Agreements', E.R. Rev 2003, 28(5), 601–619. More inconsistencies are masterfully depicted by Raas Holdgaard, 'The European Community's Implied External Competence after the Open Skies Case', 8 [2003] EFA Review, 365–394, at 388 *et seq.*

[95] *Opinion 1/03*, Competence of the Community to conclude the new Lugano Convention on Jurisdiction and the recognition and enforcement of judgments in civil and commercial matters. The Opinion was given by a Full Court on 7 February 2006.

Community had exclusive or shared competence to conclude a new Lugano convention.[96] The Court decided that the Community did have such exclusive competence. In its analysis, the Court of Justice summarized the principles derived from its previous case law, in explaining the circumstances under which exclusive Community competence could arise.[97] First, where the conclusion of an agreement by the Member States is incompatible with the unity of the common market and the uniform application of Community law.[98] Secondly, where, given the nature of the existing Community provisions, such as legislative measures containing clauses relating to the treatment of nationals of non-member countries or to the complete harmonization of a particular issue, any agreement in that area would necessarily affect the Community rules.[99]

On the other hand, according to the Court of Justice, exclusive competence could not arise where the Community provisions merely laid down minimum standards. Nor could it arise where there was a chance that bilateral agreements would lead to distortions in the flow of services in the internal market.[100]

In deciding whether a given area was covered to a large extent by Community rules, thus precluding Member State action, the assessment was to be 'based not only on the scope of the rules in question but also on their *nature and content*'.[101] It was also 'necessary to take into account not only the current state of Community law in the area in question but also *its future development*, insofar as that is foreseeable at the time of [the] analysis'.[102] Arguably, the Court of Justice does not really draw a line as to what may and what may not be covered by exclusive Community competence. It leaves the question open: it all depends on the nature and content of the Community rules. Respectfully, this does not really take the discussion any further.

It is submitted that the question of the existence of competence should not be merged with that of its nature. Implied exclusive competence is not a case of the Community being able to act in the incumbent international field. It is a case of the Community being able to act in the incumbent international field *to the exclusion of the Member State(s)*. That is why, there is, or should be, some sort of gradation in terms of the severity of the tests that apply to establish it. Any attempt to elide the tests is, it is submitted, wrong and to a large extent, out of tune with the current trend of shared competences.[103] For, if the tests for implied external competence *simpliciter* and implied exclusive external competence are identical, this means you cannot have implied external competence that is not exclusive. It is an all or nothing approach. This author believes that the 'inextricable link' test referred to above only applies to exclusivity and not to the existence of competence.

---

[96] This new Lugano convention was meant to replace the existing Convention on jurisdiction and the recognition and enforcement of judgments in civil and commercial matters done at Lugano on 16 September 1988 (OJ 1988 L319, 9).   [97] See *Opinion 1/03*, para 122.

[98] *Ibid*. The Court cited the *ERTA* case, para 31.

[99] *Ibid*. The Court cited *Opinion 1/94*, paras 95–96 and the *Open Skies* case *Commission v Denmark*, paras 83–84.   [100] *Opinion 1/03*, para 123.

[101] *Ibid*., paragraph 126. Emphasis added.   [102] *Ibid*. Emphasis added.

[103] See Part III(A)(iii).

Let us not forget that both in *Opinion 1/94* and *Opinion 2/92*, whilst the Community did not satisfy the test of exclusiveness, nevertheless, it was still agreed that the community had some competence, albeit a shared one. If the strict test were applicable both to the existence and extent of the competence, then there would have been no Community competence at all. Therefore, it seems to be the case that the pre-requisite of prior exercise of internal powers for *Opinion 1/76* type of exclusivity is only relevant to the question of exclusivity and not competence.[104]

In any case, why is it so important to distinguish between exclusive and shared implied competence? That is because the repercussions of a finding of exclusivity are quite extensive. Once Community competence is identified as being exclusive, the Member States no longer have the right, acting individually or even collect-ively, to undertake obligations towards third countries.[105] This transfer of powers to the Community is thought to be conclusive and definitive.[106] This being the case, the Community is, in principle, allowed to exercise its powers with unfet-tered freedom. Such freedom is called into question, the argument goes, and the institutional balances are distorted if Member States retain the power to enter into agreements with third countries. Therefore, if the Member State acts in an area in which the Community enjoys exclusive competence, *it would be in breach of the Community laws on competence.*

ERTA and its successor cases suggest that the mere existence of the Community rules suffices to prevent the adoption of any measures in that field by the Member States, irrespective of the existence of an actual conflict.[107] In other words, the exercise of concurrent powers by the Member States in the area covered by the Community's exclusive competence is impossible.[108] Not only that, but also, if

---

[104] Also see Dashwood & Heliskoski, 16; Tridimas & Eeckhout, 167.

[105] Case 22/70 (*ERTA*), para 17. 'The exercise of concurrent powers by the Member States in this matters is impossible': *Opinion 1/75*, at para 1364.

[106] 'The power to adopt measures [...] has belonged fully and definitively to the Community. MS are therefore no longer entitled to exercise any power or their own in [these matters]. The adoption of [...] measures is a matter of Community law. The transfer to the Community of powers in this mat-ter being total and definitive, [...] a failure [of the Council] to act could not in any case restore to the MS the power and freedom to act unilaterally in this field' (Case 804/79, paras 17–20).

[107] See *Opinion 2/91*, paras 25–6: 'While there is no contradiction between [the] provisions of the [ILO] Convention and those of the directives mentioned, it must nevertheless be accepted that Part III of Convention No 170 is concerned with an area which is already covered to a large extent by Community rules progressively adopted since 1967 with a view to achieving an ever greater degree of harmonisation and designed, on the one hand, to remover barriers to trade resulting from differences in legislation from one Member State to another and, on the other hand, to provide, at the same time, protection for human health and the environmental.

In those circumstances, it must be considered that the commitments arising from Part III of Convention No 170, falling within the area covered by the directives [...] are of such a kind as to affect the Community rules laid down in those directives and that consequently Member States can-not undertake such commitments outside the framework of the Community institutions'.

[108] *Opinion 1/75*, para 1364. Also see *Ruling 1/78*, para 32: 'The Member States whether acting individually or collectively, are no longer able to impose on the Community obligations which impose conditions on the exercise of prerogatives which thenceforth belong to the Community and which therefore no longer fall within the field of national sovereignty'.

the substantive provisions of an international agreement fall within Community competence, 'the Community is also competent to undertake commitments for putting those provisions into effect'.[109]

Some scholars have urged for a common sense and pragmatic approach, limiting the prohibition to Member States measures 'which demonstrably have a negative effect on common rules'.[110] Others have argued that exclusivity arising as a result of a Treaty provision is different from exclusivity arising as a result of the exercise by the institutions of their internal powers.[111] In the first case, the Community occupies the field and pre-empts Member State action whether or not it conflicts with Community legislation and whether or not the Community has actually exercised its competence. There is no question of Member State competence continuing or being held in abeyance whilst the Community exercises its powers.[112] Exceptionally Member States may act pursuant to a specific authorization by the Community.[113] In the second case, there is no *ab initio* pre-emption. Member States may continue to act but should not adopt legislation which affects the Community rules or alters their scope. It would be a question of interpretation whether Community action has surpassed the threshold of peremptory pre-emption which precludes even consistent national measures.

As is shown in the following section on shared competences, the Court of Justice often adopts a common sense approach, even if it finds the Community exclusively competent. Older case law certainly seems to accord with this analysis.[114] It has been argued[115] that the Court of Justice has achieved a golden balance in that it is easy to find competence but difficult to characterize it as exclusive. The actual result might be further tempered by the pragmatic and political niceties of the situation, for the Court of Justice strives 'to effectively meet its Treaty

---

[109] *Opinion 2/91*, para 28.

[110] G.L. Close, 'Self-restraint by the EEC in the Exercise of its External Powers', 1 [1981] YEL 45, 64. Also see Tridimas & Eeckhout, 160. Cf with Heliskoski, in *Mixed Agreements*, p.40: 'In a field or matter falling within the exclusive competence of the Community, any concurrent authority on the part of the Member States is, by definition, excluded; legal acts are either performed by the Community or they are not performed at all'. Member States may only take measures if Community competence is non-exclusive.

[111] See Takis Tridimas, 'The WTO and OECD Opinions', in *The General Law of EC External Relations*, p. 58; Tridimas & Eeckhout, p.165.

[112] Case 804/79, para 20. Cf Armin von Bogdandy & Jürgen Bast, 'The European Union's Vertical Order of Competences: The Current Law and Proposals for its Reform', [2002] 39 CMLRev. 227–268, 237, who opine that when the Member States vest the Union with certain powers/competences the Member States do not necessarily lose 'ownership' of those competences.

[113] *Opinion 2/91*, para 30.

[114] For example, in *ERTA*, the Court did not impede the advanced and still on-going negotiation proceedings, as this would be very disruptive and would call into question the Member States' and the Communities credibility in the international scene. Contrast with *Opinion 1/94*, where the Court refused to sacrifice the correct legal analysis because of difficulties in implementing the WTO agreement (para 107).

[115] Tridimas & Eeckhout, 172; Charles Kotuby, 'External Competence of the European Community in the Hague Conference on Private International Law: Community Harmonisation and Worldwide Unification', 15 [2002] New York International Law Review 99.

objectives and exert a coherent external policy, yet ensure the mutual coexistence of functionally independent legal regimes'.[116]

A general re-assessment of the system of competences is certainly recommended. The tests for finding implied competence and implied exclusive competence need to be clearly delineated. It is important to clarify the areas in which and the extent to which a Member State, in its treaty-making dealings with third countries, is limited by Community law. It is also important to question the extent to which substantive Community provisions such as fundamental freedoms effectively circumscribe the treaty-making capacity of a Member State in a field in which the Member State retains, in principle, exclusive competence.

The mixing up of the legal test pertaining to each type of competence and the reformulation of some tests are not conducive to legal certainty. Nor do they enhance the credibility of the Community to the outside world. To an extent the concepts of shared competence and mixed agreements are a means of alleviating these difficulties.

(iii) Shared (or Non-Exclusive) Competence

Shared competence arises where this is implied in the Treaty Article conferring power on the Community. It can also arise where the Community has potential competence but has not exercised it,[117] or where an agreement includes provisions some of which fall within Community competence and some within Member State competence,[118] or where the Community's competence arises from the existence of internal 'minimum rules'.[119]

---

[116] Charles Kotuby, 'External Competence of the European Community in the Hague Conference on Private International Law: Community Harmonisation and Worldwide Unification', 15 [2002] New York International Law Review 99, 110.

[117] For example, with the common fisheries policy during the transitional period mentioned in Article 102. See Joined Cases 3, 4 and 6–76, *Cornelis Kramer and others* [1976] ECR 1279, para 12. Also see Case 61/77 *Commission v Ireland* [1978] ECR 417; Case 804/79 *Commission v UK* [1981] ECR 1045. See MacLeod, p. 65, 236. Costonis, Neuwahl, pp. 720–3. In so acting, Member States are perceived as acting on behalf of the Community as custodians or guardians or trustees of the Community interest (Case 804/79, para 28) in order to fill the legislative vacuum. They must not bind the Community in a way that is disruptive to its powers eventually coming into force. Kramer, paras 39–45; Freeman (1977) CLP at 167.

[118] *Rubber case*: *Opinion 1/78* [1979] ECR 2871; *Euratom* case: *Ruling 1/78 (Re the Draft Convention on the Physical Protection of Nuclear Materials, Facilities and Transports)* [1978] ECR 2151 at paras 13.

[119] *Opinion 2/91 (Re ILO Convention 170)* [1993] ECR I-1061. If the common rules are in fact 'minimum requirements' or standards, the Member States are not precluded from concluding international agreements which establish higher standards (*Opinion 2/91*, paras 18–21) so long as these international commitments are not an obstacle to the adoption of more stringent measures by the Community. It would seem, however, that as soon as a directive contains provisions which are more than minimum requirements, the Community would acquire exclusive competence and, therefore, an international agreement dealing with the same subject matter will necessarily 'affect' these rules. See MacLeod, p. 59; McGoldrick, p. 76; David O'Keeffe, 'Exclusive, Concurrent and Shared Competence', Chapter 12 of *The General Law of EC External Relations*, at 189.

Even if the Community's powers are unequivocally exclusive, Member State action is not always precluded. The Community might delegate powers back to the Member States, without necessarily conceding its competence or the exclusivity of it to the Member States.[120] Alternatively, or in addition to powers being delegated, Member States may be entrusted with the enforcement of Community obligations. This is the case with competition law,[121] all the more topical with the increased emphasis on decentralization. The Member States must generally exercise delegated powers in compliance with the terms under which such powers were delegated to them. Application of national law must not prejudice the full and uniform application of Community law or the effects of measures taken or to be taken to implement it.[122]

There seems to be a presumption that where the Community enjoys competence, competence is concurrent and not exclusive, unless there is a contrary indication from the text or context of the Treaty.[123] This is because Community powers are invariably of a general nature and pursue vague objectives. It is difficult to construe them as exclusive. In certain areas, Community and Member State competence can co-exist without either displacing the other—e.g. in the realm of Intellectual Property rights.[124]

The concept of shared competence should be distinguished from the case where the existence of an external legal or political impediment prevents the Community from becoming a party to a treaty even though it enjoys exclusive competence in the field. This could be the case, for example, if the EC is not recognised by the other party, or if the international instrument is only open to states.[125] In such

---

[120] See Freeman notes that this occurs frequently in the management of the customs union and of the Common Agricultural Policy (161). More generally, see Daniela Obradovic, 'Repatriation of Powers in the European Community', [1997] 34 CMLRev. 59–88.

[121] See Case 14/68 *Walt Wilhelm and other v Bundeskartellamt* [1969] ECR 1, re-affirmed in Case 7/72 *Boehringer v Commission* [1972] ECR 1281, para 3 and Case T-149/89 *Sotralentz SA v Commission* [1995] ECR II-1127.

[122] See Case 14/68 *Walt Wilhelm and other v Bundeskartellamt* [1969] ECR 1, para 9. See case notes by R.H. Lauwaars, [1969] CMLRev. 489–490, L. Michael, [1969] Texas International Law Forum 320–330, and Robert Walz, [1996] ELR 449–464.

[123] See Advocate General Jacobs in Case C-316/91 *European Parliament v European Union Council (EDF case)* [1994] ECR I-625, at I-639, para 40: 'In the absence of any indication to the contrary, it can be accepted that the Community and the Member States share competence in that field'. Also see Tridimas & Eeckhout, 154–5; Panos Koutrakos, 'The Interpretation of Mixed Agreements under the Preliminary Reference Procedure', [2002] EFA Review 7, pp. 25–72, at 30; Alan Dashwood, 'The relationship between the Member States and the European Union/European Community', [2004] 41 CMLRev. 355–381.

[124] See, for example, P. Demiray, 'Intellectual Property and the External Power of the European Community: The New Dimension', [1994] 16 Michigan Journal of International Law, 187–239.

[125] The ILO Convention is an example of this. It was possible for the agreement to fall within the exclusive competence of the Community but to be concluded by the Member States. In such circumstances, the Community's external competence may be exercised through the medium of the Member States acting jointly in the Community interests. See *Opinion 2/91 (Re ILO Convention 170)* [1993] ECR I-1061 at para 5; Case C-316/91, part IV. Also see Tridimas and Eeckhout, 148.

circumstances, it is thought that the Member States, in entering into the international agreement with third countries or international organisations[126] are effectively acting as trustees for the EC in relation to matters of Community competence or as put in Opinion 2/91, 'jointly in the Community's interest'.[127]

B. Mixed Agreements

The Court of Justice has clearly accepted the concept of mixed agreements.[128] Mixed agreements are agreements in which both the European Community and all or some of its Member States are parties and which fall partly within the competence of the Community and partly within the competence of the Member States.

Schermers defines mixed agreements as 'any treaty to which an international organization, some or all of its Member States and one or more third States are parties and for the execution of which neither the organization nor its Member States have full competence'.[129] This type of agreements was expressly recognized in Article 102 of the EURATOM Treaty.

Even though the legal credentials of this type of agreements have been questioned by various scholars,[130] it has become a well-established part of EC law,[131] recognized as a necessary evil. Mixed agreements are favoured by Member States as it allows them to preserve their presence and prestige in the international scene or their voting rights in an agreement.[132] They are also favoured by the Commission

---

[126] As to the relationship between the Community and international organizations, see Jörn Sack, 'The European Community's Membership of International Organisations', [1995] 32 CMLRev. 1227–1256.

[127] See *Opinion 2/91*, para 5. Also see *ERTA* para 80, and Case 804/79 *Commission v UK* [1981] ECR 1045.

[128] *Ruling 1/78* [1978] ECR 2151, *Opinion 1/78* [1979] ECR 2871, *Opinion 2/91 (ILO)*, and *Opinion 1/94*. Also see analysis of AG Jacobs in Case 316/91 *Parliament v Council* [1994] ECR I-625. Nanette A. Neuwahl, 'Shared Powers or Combined Incompetence? More on Mixity', [1996] 33 CMLRev. 667–687 at 668 refers to a 'benevolent' attitude towards mixity illustrated in the WTO Opinion.

[129] Henry G. Schermers, 'A Typology of Mixed Agreements', in O'Keeffe and Schermers, *Mixed Agreements*, 25–26. For a more minimalist definition, see Neuwahl (1996) at 671: '[I]t denotes the nature of the procedure which needs to be followed for decision-making: it has to involve a Community decision.'

[130] *Inter alios*, see J.J. Costonis, 'The Treaty Making Power of the EEC: The Perception of a Decade', (1967–68) 5 CMLRev. 421–57, p. 450; M. Cremona, 'The Doctrine of Exclusivity and the Position of Mixed Agreements in the External Relations of the European Community', [1982] 2 OJILS, 393–428; C.D. Ehlermann, 'Mixed Agreements: A List of Problems', in O'Keeffe and Schermers, *Mixed Agreements*; Nanette A. Neuwahl, 'Joint Participation in International Treaties and the Exercise of power by the EEC and its Member States: Mixed Agreements', [1991] 28 CMLRev. 717–740; Nanette A. Neuwahl, 'Shared Powers or Combined Incompetence? More on Mixity', [1996] 33 CMLRev. 667–687.   [131] MacLeod *et al.*, 143–4; Groux & Manin, 61–8.

[132] Ehlerman, 6–8; McGoldrick, 78; Nanette A. Neuwahl, 'Joint Participation in International Treaties and the Exercise of power by the EEC and its Member States: Mixed Agreements', [1991] 28 CMLRev. 717–740, 726.

for practical reasons. Mixed agreements are a useful device in avoiding or hiding inter-institutional tension since there is no need to agree on the exact delimitation of Community powers in relation to Member States' powers.[133] They cater for the constantly evolving nature of Community competences.[134] Therefore, the arduous task of agreeing the nature of some Community competences, which may in fact be evolving, is avoided. Politically, the Community also yields benefits, as its international presence is enhanced.

Mixed agreements are not always synonymous with shared competence between the Community and Member States. They could arise when the Community has exclusive competence but the legal personality of the Community is not recognized by the other party. For example, mixed agreements were used when countries of the former Soviet bloc refused to recognize the Community as having international personality or capacity to enter an international agreement.[135] Mixed agreements could also arise when the Community wishes to ensure and/or increase the responsibility of Member States in a given field, for example with environmental issues. It could also be the case that the Community is not able to fulfil a given objective

---

[133] Ehlerman, 8; Cremona, 411. As very vividly described by Weiler, they 'diffuse at a stroke the explosive issues of the scope of Community competences (and treaty-making power) and the parameters of the pre-emptive effect'. Weiler, 'The external legal relations of non-unitary actors: mixity and the federal principle', in O'Keeffe and Schermers, *Mixed Agreements*, 75

In fact, the ECJ is not particularly keen on express *ex ante* allocation of competences between the Member States and the Communities in an international agreement with third countries. As a matter of Community law, the Community and the Member States are under no obligation to provide how competences are divided in the agreement. This is a domestic question in which third States need not intervene. See, for example, *Ruling 1/78*, para 35. The inherent difficulty of delineating competences is obvious. Also, even the clearest division of powers is susceptible to change over time. See, for example, the Commission Communication to the Council on the participation by the Community in the Law of the Sea Convention, COM(81) 799 final p.3: '[S]uch requirements would be bound to lead to serious disputes, quite apart from the practical difficulty of their application in the case of the Community, given the essentially evolving nature of the responsibilities assigned to the latter by the Treaty of Rome'. Sometimes, a statement of the declaration of the respective competences of the Community and the Member States, what is called a 'declaration of competence', is insisted upon as a pre-condition for Community participation in an agreement. See, for example, the 3rd UN Convention on the Law of the Sea (Annex IX) (Misc 11(1983); Cmnd. 8941; (1982) 21 ILM 1261); the Vienna Convention on Illicit Trafficking in Narcotic Drugs and Psychotropic Substances (Art. 27(2), [1992] UKTS 26, Cm 1923); the Vienna Convention for the Protection of the Ozone Layer (Art 13 (3), [1988] OJ L297/8) etc. The declaration, which invariably describes the allocation of competences in general terms, is without prejudice to the allocation under the Treaties and contains caveats as to changes over time. The Community usually reserves the right to make further declarations of competence as its powers increase. The legal credentials of such declarations are also debatable as they cannot override the legal position under the Treaties.

[134] For example, see Case 25/94 *Commission v Council* [1996] ECR I-01469 (FAO Fisheries Agreement), the International Fruit line of cases etc.

[135] C.D. Ehlerman, 'Mixed Agreements: A list of Problems', in O'Keeffe and Schermers, *Mixed Agreements*, 4; Wellerstein, 'The relations of the European Communities with Eastern Europe', in O'Keeffe and Schermers (eds), *Essays in European Law and Integration* (Kluwer, 1982), pp. 197–208; Groux & Manin, 68–69.

independently, or as effectively as with the co-operation of a Member State, for example with humanitarian or development aid.[136]

C. Subsidiarity

A separate but related issue is the principle of subsidiarity. This principle is found in the second and third paragraphs of Article 5 EC. It reads as follows:

In areas which do not fall within its exclusive competence, the Community shall take action, in accordance with the principle of subsidiarity, only if and so far as the objectives of the proposed action cannot be sufficiently achieved by the Member States and can therefore, by reason of the scale or effects of the proposed action, be better achieved by the Community.

Any action by the Community shall not go beyond what is necessary to achieve the objectives of this Treaty.

Subsidiarity applies only in areas where the Community *does not* have exclusive competence. In such circumstances, Community action also has to be proportional and should not exceed what is necessary for the achievement of its objectives. In other words, the underlying rationale of the subsidiarity principle is that the Community is to take action only if the objectives of that action cannot be sufficiently achieved by the Member States and can be better achieved by the Community. Both limbs of the test must be satisfied, using 'qualitative or, wherever possible, quantitative indicators'.[137]

Whilst competence addresses the question of whether the Community has legal powers to act at all, the principle of subsidiarity takes the existence of such power as an assumption. It addresses the question of whether the Community should exercise this power or whether it should defer to Member State action.[138] Therefore, this principle does not affect the existence of Community competences, nor does it affect inter-institutional balances.[139] The Court of Justice has never annulled an act on the basis of a violation of the principle of subsidiarity,[140] even though the principle was analysed in some cases.[141]

D. Breach of Competence

There is no clear authority as to what happens when the Community enters into a treaty with a third country in breach of its competence. Even the *Open Skies* line of

---

[136] See, generally, Henry G. Schermers, 'A Typology of Mixed Agreements', in O'Keeffe and Schermers, *Mixed Agreements*.   [137] Subsidiarity Protocol, Arts 4–5.
[138] See Communication of the Commission to the Council, The principle of subsidiarity, SEC(92) 1990 final, 1.   [139] See SEC(92), 1, also Annex, p.2, para 4; Edinburgh Guidelines.
[140] See evidence given by Advocate General Jacobs to Working Group I on the Principle of subsidiarity, Summary of the meeting of 25 June 2002, Brussels 28 June 2002, (CONV 156/02 WGI 5).
[141] Cases dealt with this principle but were in the end decided on different grounds: Case C-84/94 *UK v Council (Working Time)* [1996] ECR I-5793; Case C-491/01 *BAT* [2002] ECR I-11453.

cases, to be examined below, which is the most high profile and recent precedent on the issue, avoided addressing this question.

It is submitted that the answer would depend on whether it is a breach of the existence or the nature of the competence.

If the Community has acted in breach of the *existence* of its competence,[142] *dicta* of the Court of Justice suggest that the international agreement will be deprived of any effect within the community legal order.[143] It is, however, unclear what the consequences of the annulment will be with respect to the international validity of the international agreement; and what consequences the Community expects there to be.

In *France v Commission*,[144] the Court of Justice found that although the Community had *no power* to enter into the anti-trust co-operation agreement with the USA (i.e. the Member States had exclusive competence), the agreement itself remained valid in international law and was binding on the Community. Non-performance of the international agreement could lead to liability at international level.[145] Maclead *et al.* conclude that the Community and Member States should ensure that the rights of third countries are respected. They should 'take steps to align the internal and external effects of the agreement by withdrawing from the agreement [. . .] by rectifying the defect of Community law or practice which had rendered the agreement invalid'.[146]

If the Community enters into the treaty in breach of its shared (non-exclusive) competence,[147] then similar reasoning should apply. Whilst the agreement may be annulled or impugned internally, there is no reason why this should affect the international validity of the instrument. In fact, the argument for invalidity is much weaker than where the bare existence of competence is in dispute, as in this case, there is some competence, albeit non-exclusive. Again, it would seem that Community and Member States must ensure that the rights of third countries are

---

[142] i.e., it had acted when it should not have acted at all because it had no competence in the field.

[143] See Case C-327/91 *France v Commission* [1994] ECR I-3641; Case C-122/95 *Germany v Council* [1998] ECR I-973; *Opinion 3/94 Framework Agreement on Bananas* [1996] ECR I-4577. MacLeod *et al.*, 131, opine that it is unlikely that such international agreements become an integral part of Community law. Also see Koen Lenaerts & Eddy de Smijter, *The European Union as an Actor under International Law*, 103.

[144] Case C-327/91 *France v Commission* [1994] ECR I-3641.

[145] Case C-327/91, para 25. Also see *Opinion 3/94*, para 22, where the Court said that consequences of decision of incompatibility 'might give rise to adverse consequences for all interested parties, including third countries'. In this case, whilst the Council decision to adopt the international instrument was annulled, the international instrument was not affected. Also see Case C-122/95 *Germany v Council* [1998] ECR I-973, paras 41, 45, where the Court found that the right of a Member State to bring an action for annulment of a Council decision concerning the conclusion of an international agreement, and to apply for interim relief at that time, is not undermined by the fact that that agreement was concluded by the Community without reservation, and that it binds the institutions and the Member States in both Community law and international law.

[146] MacLeod, 132.

[147] In this situation, the dispute in not over the existence of competence but over the nature of this competence, and whether Community action was in line with it.

respected. This could necessitate (increased) participation of the Member State in the international agreement.

Mutatis mutandis, when the Community's treaty-making exclusive competence is violated, that is if a Member State enters into a treaty with a third country for which it has no competence whatsoever, the international agreement should not automatically be considered invalid. This does not mean that the disputed agreement will remain in place indefinitely. It is in the nature of the principles of exclusive Community competence analysed above that the field is pre-empted. The treaty will eventually have to be streamlined with the Community laws on competence. If this means that the Member State should withdraw and/or denounce the treaty, stripped off its treaty-making capacity in the field, then so be it.

Arguably, matters are much more relaxed when the Community's competence is non-exclusive. If the Member State acts in such way as to encroach on the Community's non-exclusive competence, then the treaty remains valid as the area is not pre-empted. It just happens that the Member State may have to re-adjust its participation in the treaty. The third country contracting party need not be disturbed. It is an internal matter. Hence the attractiveness of mixed agreements.[148]

The Court of Justice's treatment (or better, non-treatment) of the question of repercussions from breach of competence in the *Open Skies* cases is analysed in greater detail in the next Part of this article.

IV. The *Open Skies* Saga[149]

Open Skies dealt with bilateral agreements on air transport made between the US and several European countries. The Commission brought actions under Article 226 EC before the Court of Justice against the United Kingdom, Denmark, Sweden, Finland, Belgium, Luxembourg, Austria and Germany.

The facts of these cases were similar. After World War II and before these countries acceded to the EU, they concluded bilateral agreements on air transport with the United States, the so-called Bermuda I agreements. These agreements were meant to facilitate alliances between US and European air carriers.

The Bermuda I agreements contained a nationality clause. Pursuant to this clause, each contracting party was empowered to revoke, suspend, limit or impose conditions on the traffic rights (operating authorizations and technical permissions) of airline operators acting in their territory where substantial ownership and

---

[148] See analysis in Part III(B).

[149] The eight ECJ *Open Skies* judgments are C-466/98 *Commission v. UK*; C-467/98 *Commission v Denmark*; C-468/98 *Commission v Suède*; C-469/98 *Commission v Finland*; C-471/98 *Commission v Belgium*; C-472/98 *Commission v Luxembourg*; C-475/98 *Commission v Austria*; and C-476/98 *Commission v Germany*.

effective control of that airline were not vested in the Contracting State or its nationals.[150]

In 1992, the United States began to make proposals to various Member States of the Community for the amendment of the existing bilateral air transport agreements in order to bring them into line with a specific, particularly liberal model agreement. These new agreements, the Bermuda II agreements, were to follow guidelines imposed by the US negotiator. The nationality clause was to continue to be applicable. By 1995, all the aforementioned Member States had amended their existing agreements in line with the US demands. In the late 1990s, the Bermuda II agreements came under attack by the Commission on the basis of lack of competence and incompatibility with Community law.[151] The Commission alleged, *inter alia*, that:

(1) Air transport fell within the Community's competence, as secondary law[152] had established a complete set of rules, which pre-empted the field.[153] Therefore, Member States had breached Community competence by entering into these agreements.

(2) Regardless of the findings as to competence, the nationality clauses of these agreements were incompatible with freedom of establishment. Such derogation was not justified under Article 46 as a public policy exception.

The Court of Justice found that indeed some of the secondary law enacted in this field (namely, Regulations 2409/92 and 2299/89) had a pre-emptive effect. Under Regulation 2409/92, the Community had prohibited air carriers of non-member countries which operated in the Community from introducing new products or

---

[150] See for example Article 5 of the Bermuda II between the UK–US (1977) replacing Article 6 of the Bermuda I Agreement (1946). It reads as follows:

'(1) Each Contracting Party shall have the right to revoke, suspend, limit or impose conditions on the operating authorisations or technical permissions of an airline designated by the other Contracting Party where:
    (a) substantial ownership and effective control of that airline are not vested in the Contracting Party designating the airline or in nationals of such Contracting Party; [. . .]
(2) . . . such rights shall be exercised only after consultation with the other Contracting Party.'

[151] The question of whether these agreements were protected by Article 307 EC will not be addressed here.

[152] Council Regulation (EEC) No 2407/92 of 23 July 1992 on licensing of air carriers, OJ 1992 L240, p. 1; Council Regulation (EEC) No 2408/92 of 23 July 1992 on access for Community air carriers to intra-Community air routes, OJ 1992 L240, p. 8; Council Regulation (EEC) No 2409/92 of 23 July 1992 on fares and rates for air services, which lays down the criteria and procedures to be applied for the establishment of fares and rates on air services for carriage wholly within the Community, OJ 1992 L240, p. 15; Council Regulation (EEC) No 2299/89 of 24 July 1989 on a code of conduct for computerised reservation systems, OJ 1989 L220, p. 1.

[153] A competence issue was not raised against the UK. This was because the Commission acknowledged that the agreement concluded by the United Kingdom with the United States administration in 1995 did not conform to the open skies format. Accordingly, the Commission did not charge the United Kingdom with infringement of the Community's external competence but only with breach of Article 43 EC.

fares lower than those existing for identical products. Under Regulation 2299/89, the Community had laid down rules on computerized reservation systems. Therefore, in those spheres, the Member States were precluded from undertaking international commitments.

In other words, the Community had acquired exclusive competence. Since the amended Bermuda II agreements contained clauses within those spheres, the Member States[154] were in breach of their obligations under Article 10 EC[155] and under Regulations 2409/92 and 2299/89.

The nationality clause of these agreements was impugned as being contrary to freedom of establishment. The Court of Justice found that these nationality clauses obliged the United States to grant the rights provided for in the agreements to carriers controlled by the Member State with which it had concluded the agreement. The Court of Justice also found that these clauses at the same time entitled the US to *refuse* those rights to carriers controlled by other Member States. The Court of Justice agreed with the Commission in that this was discrimination contrary to the freedom of establishment guaranteed by the Treaty, because it excluded Community airlines from the benefit of the treatment which the Member State concluding the agreement had reserved for its own airlines.

According to the Court of Justice, the breach consisted in the granting, for example, by the United Kingdom to the United States of America of the right contained in Article 5 of the Bermuda II Agreement[156] (which provision survived the amended Bermuda II agreement entered into by the UK in 1995). The direct source of the discrimination was not the conduct of the US–in fact the conduct of the US was irrelevant[157] but Article 5 of the Bermuda II agreement 'which specifically acknowledge[d] the right of the United States of America to act in that way'.[158] The Court of Justice declared that, *by concluding and applying* this agreement, it was the UK that had breached its Community obligations.[159]

The UK[160] tried to argue on the basis of *Saint Gobain* that freedom of establishment does not obligate the UK to amend agreements already concluded with non-member countries in order to impose new obligations upon them.[161] If, the argument goes, the Court of Justice were to interfere in the Bermuda II agreements, then new obligations would be imposed on the third country, in violation

---

[154] The UK was found to be in breach of freedom of establishment only, as no infringement of competence was alleged by the Commission.

[155] Pursuant to Article 10 EC, Member States are required to facilitate the achievement of the Community's tasks and to abstain from any measure which might jeopardize the attainment of the objectives of the Treaty.

[156] This was the Air Services Agreement signed on 23 July 1977. As it was based on the Bermuda I agreement, it was named Bermuda II.   [157] Case C-466/98 *Commission v UK*, para 33.

[158] Case C-466/98 *Commission v UK*, para 51.

[159] Case C-466/98 *Commission v UK*, para 52. The same point was made in the other cases. See, for example, Case C-467/98, para 131; Case C-468/98, para 123; Case C-469/98, para 128.

[160] Case C-466/98 *Commission v UK* [2002] ECR I-9427, [2003] 1 CMLR 143, para 36

[161] Case C-307/97 *Saint-Gobain v Finanzamt Aachen-Innenstadt* [1999] ECR I-6161, paras 59 and 60.

of the *Saint Gobain* safeguarding stipulation. The Court of Justice eschewed this point by simply noting that 'where the infringement of Community law results directly from a provision of a bilateral international agreement concluded by a Member State after its accession to the Community, the Court is [not] prevented from holding that that infringement exists so as not to compromise the rights which non-member countries derive from the very position which infringes Community law'.[162] Thus, its previous reservations vis-à-vis treaties with third countries were removed without much explanation.

The Court of Justice also found that the derogation from Community law was not justified by the public policy exception of Article 46 EC. The Member States had failed to prove such a direct link between the threat to public policy and the restriction of air traffic rights.[163]

The Member States[164] had tried to argue that as the Bermuda II agreements replaced the so-called Bermuda I agreements which had been entered into prior to the accession of the relevant Member States, then the Bermuda II agreements effectively constituted pre-accession agreements and were therefore covered by the subordination clause of Article 307 EC.[165] This was because, according to the Member States, the old agreements 'were amended only marginally and in any event in non-essential respects'.[166]

The Court's analysis (and rejection) of this argument was cursory. By looking into the preamble of the Bermuda II agreements, the Court of Justice concluded that the Bermuda II agreements were concluded for the purpose of replacing the Bermuda I agreements. Being post-accession agreements, Article 307 EC was inapplicable.

To sum up, essentially, in *Open Skies* cases, the Court of Justice found that when the relevant Member States entered into the Bermuda II agreements with the USA, they had acted in a field in which they had no competence. The Court

---

[162] Case C-466/98 *Commission v UK*, para 54.   [163] Case 467/98, para 137.

[164] The argument by the UK government was slightly different. The UK argued that the nationality clause which was carried over by the Bermuda I agreement to the Bermuda II agreement was covered by Article 307 EC. This was not accepted by the ECJ. See C-466/98 *Commission v UK* paras 17–21.

[165] The subordination clause is found in the first paragraph of Article 307 EC, which reads as follows: 'The rights and obligations arising from agreements concluded before 1 January 1958 or, for acceding States, before the date of their accession, between one or more Member States on the one hand, and one or more third countries on the other, shall not be affected by the provisions of this Treaty'.

The subordination clause is qualified by the second and third paragraphs of Article 307 EC which read as follows: 'To the extent that such agreements are not compatible with this Treaty, the Member State or States concerned shall take all appropriate steps to eliminate the incompatibilities established. Member States shall, where necessary, assist each other to this end and shall, where appropriate, adopt a common attitude. In applying the agreements referred to in the first paragraph, Member States shall take into account the fact that the advantages accorded under this Treaty by each Member State form an integral part of the establishment of the Community and are thereby inseparably linked with the creation of common institutions, the conferring of powers upon them and the granting of the same advantages by all the other Member States.'

[166] *Open Skies*, AG, para 110.

of Justice also found that freedom of establishment was infringed as a result of the nationality clause contained in those agreements. As these agreements were post-accession agreements, they were not covered by the subordination clause of Article 307 EC.

However, what was the Member State to do? What were the repercussions of the Court's decision? Were the Bermuda II agreements to be terminated? Were they to be renegotiated? The Court of Justice refrained from discussing this point.

Advocate General Tizzano also remained silent on this point. This is rather surprising, considering that in his Opinion, he went to great lengths to explain the duty of Member States to streamline their pre-accession agreements under the second paragraph of Article 307 EC, which was not even applicable on the facts of the case! According to the Advocate General, Member States had to try and renegotiate an incompatible pre-accession treaty with a third country. 'But if that did not happen, there is nothing the Member States could do, short of resorting (within the limits permitted by international law, obviously) to the extreme remedy of denouncing the earlier agreements [. . .].'[167]

In *Open Skies*, the Member States argued that although they had attempted to re-negotiate the clause in question with the United States authorities, they were met with a firm refusal from those authorities. To the Advocate General, this was not enough to exonerate the Member States from their obligation to streamline the pre-accession treaties, in accordance with Article 307(2) EC.[168]

[T]he Member States concerned must show that they made every effort to remove the incompatibility; and it does not seem to me that they have shown that they did so in this instance. It is, in particular, not in dispute that, notwithstanding the specific provision to that effect in [Article 307(2) EC], they did not adopt a common attitude *vis-à-vis* the United States, nor did they take steps to assist each other with a view to bringing the other contracting parties to agree to an amendment of the nationality clause so as to bring it into line with Community law. Furthermore, it does not appear that in the course of the negotiations the Member States concerned informed the United States of America that, if the nationality clause were not amended in the sense just indicated, they might ultimately find themselves in a situation in which it would be necessary to denounce the agreements.

Technically, these comments were *obiter*, as on the facts of the case, Article 307 EC was inapplicable. However, one could argue that if such an onerous duty is imposed on Member States to streamline *pre-accession* treaties with third countries which treaties are *expressly* protected under the first paragraph of Article 307 EC, then shouldn't just an onerous duty be imposed on post-accession treaties which are not so protected?

Arguably, if it is a question of incompatibility with a substantive provision of Community law, rather than Community competence, then the Member State may try to interpret or apply the incompatible provision in such a way so as to mitigate the incompatibility. This may not always be possible if, as in the *Open*

---

[167] *Ibid.*, para 115.   [168] *Ibid.*, paras 144–145.

Skies cases, the actual discriminatory treatment is a result of third country action, albeit empowered by the Member State's consent. Even if the Community breach can be removed through Member State action, this may be contrary to the objectives of the underlying treaty. As such, the third country contracting party may object to such change. If it is a question of incompatibility with the Community laws on competence, then, especially if it is a case of breach of the Community's *exclusive* competence, not much may be done. Withdrawal from the treaty may be the only way out.[169]

It is rather unfortunate that the Court of Justice refrained from clarifying these issues. However, in light of the previous discussion on the repercussions from breach of Community or Member State competences,[170] it would seem that renegotiation and/or termination are unavoidable. Failure to act in such way, especially since the Court of Justice openly allocates the blame to the Member State that has entered the treaty with the US, means that the Member State runs the risk of being found liable for the breach, under the *Francovich* principle of State liability.[171] It is noteworthy that the Community General Report for the year 2002, discussing this case, drew similar conclusions.[172]

However, what are the *international law* implications of a finding of breach of substantive Community law in a treaty with a third country? What are the implications of a finding of a breach of competence?

It should be reminded that in so far as Community law is concerned, there is nothing in the Court of Justice's jurisprudence that would seem to suggest that the international validity of treaties is impugned just because these treaties contain provisions which breach substantive Community law. As discussed in Part III(D), by analogy to the *France v Commission* case,[173] even when the Community's treaty-making competence is violated, the Court of Justice does not consider the international agreement invalid. However, the Community obligations imposed on the Member State (however vague they currently seem to be) may severely disturb the balance of the instrument to such an extent that invalidation or termination of it in *international law* will be sought by the Member State. In other words, the Member State party to the treaty might claim that due to the incompatibility with Community law, the treaty was in fact invalid and the Member State has no treaty obligations towards the third country. Alternatively, even if the Member State

---

[169] See fuller analysis in Part III(D).   [170] *Ibid.*

[171] See Joined Cases C-690 and C-9/90 *Francovich and Bonifaci v Italy* [1991] ECR I-5357 and C-46/93 *Brasserie du Pêcheur; Factortame III* [1996] ECR I-1029 paras 20, 22. For an exposition of the recent case law, see Takis Tridimas, 'Liability for breach of Community law: Growing Up and Mellowing Down?', [2001] CMLR 301–332.

[172] See <http://europa.eu.int/abc/doc/off/rg/en/2002/pt1070.htm>: 'Under international law the sections of the agreements which have been held to be contrary to Community law are not automatically invalid. But the Member States must accept the consequences of these judgments: they can no longer negotiate on matters which are within the Community's exclusive external competence, and must in any event rectify any incompatibilities arising out of the agreements, even if this makes it necessary to denounce the agreements.'

[173] Case C-327/91 *France v Commission* [1994] ECR I-3641.

concedes the validity of the treaty it might still try to terminate it—so as not to exacerbate its position in the Community—on grounds of supervening impossibility or fundamental change of circumstances. Or it might simply try to denounce the treaty.

Can the affected Member State pursue such courses of action? In other words, can the Member State ask that an EC-incompatible treaty be treated as invalid under international law? Can the Member State ask that an EC-incompatible treaty be terminated on the basis of the ensuing incompatibility?

These interesting issues are addressed in the remainder of this article.

V. International Law Implications of EC-Incompatible Treaties

A. Invalidity

When one talks of breach of a treaty, this carries the implication that the treaty was in fact valid but violated. Conversely, a claim of invalidity undermines the very legal roots of a treaty. Such claim 'compels attention to the moment of the conclusion of the treaty, for, at that very moment, something already must have existed which stood in the way of the validity of the treaty'.[174] The question of breach becomes irrelevant, for, how can you breach an instrument that does not exist?[175]

The Vienna Convention of the Law of Treaties (henceforth, VC)[176] which has largely codified customary law on the law of treaties, lays down the circumstances under which a treaty may be found invalid.[177] Section 2 (Articles 46 to 53) VC deals with invalidity of treaties and lays down the conditions for invalidity. These conditions are quite strict. As a safeguard for the stability of treaties, the validity and continuance in force of treaties is to be the normal state of things and may only be set aside on the grounds and under the conditions provided for in the VC. In any case, as a senior legal adviser to the Foreign and Commonwealth Office has noted, in practice, the question of invalidity of a treaty rarely arises, though this seems to be a topic of fascination for lawyers.[178]

---

[174] S.E. Nahlik, 'The Grounds of Invalidity and Termination of Treaties', 65 [1971] AJIL 736, 738.

[175] Issues of State responsibility in international law may become relevant but these are beyond the purview of this article.

[176] The VC entered into force on 27 January 1980. Customary law is still relevant for questions not dealt with under the VC or for treaties entered into with states that are not parties to the VC. See the Preamble to the VC. The full text of the treaty can be found in: <http://www.un.org/law/ilc/texts/treaties.htm>.

[177] In theory, an invalid treaty is void *ab initio*. In practice, the effects of an invalid treaty are curtailed, since the Vienna Convention lays down a compulsory procedure which has to be followed for a treaty to be invalidated.

[178] Anthony Aust, *Modern Treaty Law and Practice* (2000, Cambridge University Press), 252. Also see Reuter, P., *Introduction To The Law of Treaties* (Kegan Paul International, London and New York, 1989), 173–174: 'There is an almost total lack of practice in this field, which is just as well. [. . .] Cases

The analysis in this section will proceed on the basis that the given treaty is clearly in breach of Community law (whether the Community law of competence or substantive Community law). The question asked is whether such treaty is void in international law. As invalidity undermines the very legal roots of a treaty, such a finding would mean that, as a matter of law, the treaty is treated as if it had never existed. Thus, there would be no need to seek to terminate an inexistent instrument.

This question of invalidity is considered on the basis of Article 46 of the VC which deals with invalidity due to constitutional restrictions and on the basis of Article 53 VC which deals with invalidity due to conflict with *ius cogens*.

(i) *Invalidity Due to Constitutional Restrictions*[179]

It was generally accepted in customary law that a State could invoke its municipal law to justify failure to *perform* its (valid) treaty obligations.[180] This was replicated in Article 27 VC which states that '[a] party may not invoke the provisions of its internal law as justification for its failure to perform a treaty'.[181] However, when it came to non-performance of an allegedly invalid treaty, the situation was more complicated. The question here was not whether non-performance of a treaty was justified. Rather, it was whether the treaty itself had *ever* come into existence. Therefore, technically, non-performance was irrelevant as there was nothing there to perform.

Before the enactment of the VC, there were several views on the extent to which constitutional limitations affected the treaty-making power of a State and as a corollary the *validity* of the treaty. At one end of the spectrum there was outright refusal to allow any internal limitations to affect the treaty-making power of the State (the internationalist doctrine).[182] At the other end, there was an unequivocal

of invalidation are in practice settled by *ad hoc* conventions depending on the interests of the States concerned, which is hardly conducive to the elaboration of general rules.'

[179] See generally Blix, Hans, *Treaty-Making Power* (London: Stevens; New York: Praeger, 1960); P. Reuter, *Introduction To The Law of Treaties* (Kegan Paul International, London and New York, 1989), 173–185; Charles Fairman, 'Competence to Bind the State to an International Engagement', 30 (1936) AJIL 439; Fitzmaurice, 'Do Treaties Need Ratification?', 15 (1934) BYIL 130; Pitman B. Potter, 'Inhibitions Upon the Treaty-Making Power of the United States', 28 (1934) AJIL 456; Francis G. Jacobs, 'Innovation and Continuity in Law of Treaties', 33 (1970) MLR 510–517; Steward, 'International Responsibility for Commitments', 32 (1938) AJIL, 57–62.

[180] There seems to be 'remarkable unanimity on the issue of treaty performance'. Wildhaber, 'Provisions of Internal Law Regarding Competence to Conclude a Treaty', 8 (1967) Virginia Journal of International Law 94, 96. See *Exchange of Greek and Turkish Populations*, (1925) PCIJ ser B, No.10, at 20. *Case concerning the Factory of Chorzow (Merits)*, (1928) PCIJ, ser A, No. 17, at 33; *Jurisdiction of the Courts of Danzig*, (1928) PCIJ, ser B, No. 15, at 26–27; *Free Zones of Upper Savoy and the District of Gex*, (1930) PCIJ, ser A, No. 24, at 12; *Grego-Bulgarian 'Communities' Case*, (1930) PCIJ ser B, No. 17, at 32; *Treatment of Polish Nationals in Danzig*, (1932) PCIJ, ser A/B, No. 44, at 24.

[181] Article 27 VC deals with non-performance of a validly concluded treaty. Article 46 VC (effectively) deals with non-performance of a not validly created treaty. Article 27 VC is without prejudice to Article 46 VC. Similar provisions applies in regards to international organizations. See Arts 27 and 46 of the Vienna Convention on the Law of Treaties between States and International Organizations 1986.

[182] Fitzmaurice, 'Do Treaties Need Ratification?', 15 (1934) BYIL 130; Fitzmaurice, 'The Law and Procedure of the International Court of Justice, 1951–1954', 33 (1957) BYIL 203, 267–69; Read,

acceptance of the constitutional limitations as a determinant of the international validity of a treaty (the constitutionalist doctrine).[183] There was also the intermediary position, which depended on the degree of knowledge of the other treaty partner's constitutional arrangements to be imputed to States.[184]

The differences bring to the forum the doctrinal controversy between monist and dualist schools of international law. Pursuant to the monist school of thought, as municipal and international law are part of a unified legal order, a treaty concluded in contravention with municipal law is void not only in municipal law but also, *ipso facto*, in international law. By contrast, pursuant to the dualist school of thought, municipal and international law are separate systems of law. Therefore, a treaty may be valid in international law and invalid in municipal law.[185]

Arguably, both the internationalist and constitutionalist theories were extreme and untenable. It is not, therefore, surprising that the intermediary position was eventually codified in the VC and is to be found in Article 46 VC.[186] This provision reads as follows:

Provisions of internal law regarding competence to conclude treaties

1. A State may not invoke the fact that its consent to be bound by a treaty has been expressed in violation of a provision of its internal law regarding competence to

'International Agreements', 26 (1948) Canada Bar Review 520, 526; J. Henry, 'Treaties and Federal Constitutions' (Washington: Public Affairs Press, 1955) 153–158 (1955); Rice, 'Are Treaties and Agreements Which do not Conform with Nation's Constitution Nevertheless Internationally Binding?,' (1956) Wisconsin Law Review 187–192; J.E. Read, 'International Agreements', 26 (1948) Canada Bar Review 520.

[183] See, for example, Hienrich Triepel, *Volkerrecht und Landesrecht* (Scientia, Aalen, 1958), pp. 238–240 (1899); D. Anzilotti, *Cours de Droit International*, (Paris: Librairie de Recueil Sirey, 1929), p. 366, though he later changed his mind and fully espoused the internationalist doctrine. Also see Charles Fairman, 'Competence to Bind the State to an International Engagement', 30 (1936) AJIL 439, at 442–444.

[184] McNair, *Law of Treaties* (Oxford, Clarendon Press, 1961) 61 *et seq.*; John Mervyn Jones, *Full powers and ratification: a study in the development of treaty-making procedure* (Cambridge University Press, 1949), pp. 1–33; Northley, 'Constitutional Limitations as Affecting the Validity of Treaties', 11 University of Toronto Law Journal (1956) 175–176, 187, 193, 196–201; Rice, 'Are Treaties and Agreements Which do not Conform with the Nation's Constitution Nevertheless Internationally Binding?', (1956) Wisconsin Law Review 187–192.

[185] See T.O. Elias, *The Modern Law of Treaties* (A.W. Sijthoff International Publishing Company B.V., 1974), 144–145; Anthony Aust, *Modern Treaty Law and Practice* (2000, Cambridge University Press), pp. 143–161. J.E. Read, 'International Agreements', 26 (1948) Canada Bar Review 520. At 531: Municipal law is concerned with the rights and duties of individuals, association and corporations; and their relations inter se and with the state. International law, on the other hand, is concerned with the rights and duties of states inter se. Apart from exceptional and anomalous instances, an individual cannot have a right under international law and cannot be subject to a duty. International agreements are designed to create contractual obligations under international law. They do not give rise to rights vested in an individual against a foreign state, and they do not impose duties upon individuals as such. [. . .] International law is only concerned with the question whether an international obligation is brought into existence by an agreement. The question whether the courts can take cognizance of the obligation is, strictly, a matter of municipal law. It is always important to avoid confusion between the two questions.

[186] It also seems to be confirmed by international practice: H. Blix, *Treaty-Making Power* (London: Stevens, 1960). See R.D. Kearney, 'International limitations on external commitments, Article 46 of

conclude treaties as invalidating its consent unless that violation was manifest and concerned a rule of its internal law of fundamental importance.

2. A violation is manifest if it would be objectively evident to any State conducting itself in the matter in accordance with normal practice and in good faith.

The insertion of the concepts of manifest violation and good faith are indicative of an intermediary position. Article 46 VC reflects the philosophy that no internal provision below the level of a constitutional law could claim to be of fundamental importance.[187] It would not, for example, invalidate a treaty entered into by the duly appointed representative of a State contrary to a specific restriction on his authority to consent, unless the other contracting party was aware of the restriction prior to the expression of that consent.[188] This, however, does not mean that there is '[a] general legal obligation for states to keep themselves informed of legislative and constitutional developments in other states which are or may become important for the international relations of these states'.[189]

In any case, a treaty falling foul of Article 46 VC is not automatically void[190]; it is voidable. The State affected has the right to invoke this ground as a basis for attacking the validity of the treaty. Until the State does so and the treaty is terminated according to the provisions of the Vienna Convention,[191] the treaty remains valid. In practice, Article 46 VC is rarely raised by a State as a ground for reneging on its international obligations.[192]

Would a treaty entered into between a Member State and a third country be void (or better voidable) under Article 46 VC if this treaty was not within the Community's exclusive competence?[193]

It is this author's view that it is very unlikely. A Member State wishing to invoke this ground of invalidation would have to show first that there was a violation of internal law regarding competence to conclude treaties. In this context, if the Member State does not exercise its competence compatibly with Community

---

the Treaties Convention', The International Lawyer, [1969], vol. 4, p. 1; S. Rosenne, 'Problems of treaty-making competence', *Essays in Honor of Haim H. Cohn* (New York, 1971), p. 115; T. Meron, 'Article 46 of the Vienna Convention on the Law of Treaties (ultra vires treaties): some recent cases', 49 [1978] BYIL 175.

[187] Nahlik, p. 741.

[188] *Eastern Greenland case*, PCIJ, Series A/B, No. 53, 1933; *Qatar v Bahrain*, ICJ Reports [1994] 112.

[189] *Cameroon v Nigeria*, ICJ Reports 2002, para 266.

[190] Only if invalidity is due to breach of *jus cogens* or to coercion of the State by the threat or use of force is the treaty automatically void. See Arts 52–53 VC.   [191] Arts 65–66 VC.

[192] It is usually invoked after domestic political changes. Often, in the interim between conclusion of the treaty and invocation of invalidity, the treaty would have been partially performed and thus the State is often precluded by acquiescence. See Article 45: Loss of right to invoke a ground for invalidating, terminating, withdrawing from or suspending the operation of a treaty. Note that this article does not apply in cases where there is coercion of a representative of a State (Art 51), where there is coercion of a State by the threat or use of force (Art 52), and conflict with *jus cogens* (Art 53). For a discussion on this point, see, generally P. Reuter, *Introduction To The Law of Treaties* (London and New York: Kegan Paul International, 1989), 134–135.

[193] Either because the Community had exclusive competence or even if the Member State retained some competence, it did not exercise it appropriately.

law, this is not technically a violation of the *internal law* (i.e. of Member State law) regarding competence. It is actually a violation of the *Community law* on competences.

Even if Community law on competences is somehow internalized and considered as the internal law on competence, still, for Article 46 VC to apply, it must be shown that the internal law was one of fundamental importance and violation of it was manifest. Whilst clearly the principles of Community competence are of fundamental importance, as shown in Part III, the dividing line between exclusive and shared competence is not always clear. In fact, cases are frequently litigated either because a Member State's competence or the Community's exclusive competence are doubted. Therefore, it may be very difficult to prove that a violation of the Community's competence was manifest. If one day the external treaty-making powers of the Community are clearly delineated, then an argument of invalidity due to constitutional restrictions may be entertained. As matters currently stand, however, this is hardly a foreseeable eventuality.

Would the answer differ if the treaty was within the Member State's competence but in fact contained provisions which were contrary to Community law? Arguably, it is even more unlikely that the provision of Article 46 VC would be satisfied in such circumstances. If a Member State breaches substantive Community law in its treaties, this does not mean that it has violated its internal law on competences. The actual exercise of the treaty-making competence was consistent with Community law. Therefore, in this regard, the conditions of Article 46 VC would not be satisfied.

Is there any way in which breach of substantive Community law could render the treaty void or voidable? This is examined in the next section.

(ii) Invalidity Due to Incompatibility with Higher Law?[194]

Before the enactment of VC, scholars noted that a hierarchic principle was enshrined in the order of treaties.[195] According to this principle, some treaties had the character of international settlements, something akin to 'higher law'. 'Higher law' was not defined anywhere. It was thought of as encompassing fundamental and entrenched rules of international law,[196] international 'constitutions' such as

---

[194] See generally, Lauterpacht, 'The Covenant as the Higher Law,' 17 BYIL 54 (1936); Schwarzenberger, 'International 'Jus Cogens'?', 43 Texas Law Review 455 (1965); Verdross, 'Forbidden Treaties in International Law', 31 AJIL 571 (1937); Verdross, 'Jus Dipositivum and Jus Cogens in International Law', 60 AJIL 55 (1966); Hans Aufricht, 'Supersession of Treaties in International law', 37 (1951–1952) Cornell L. Q. 655; Christos Rozakis: *The Concept of jus cogens in the law of treaties* (Netherlands: North Holland Publishing Company, 1976); Jerzy Sztucki, *Jus Cogens and the Vienna Convention on the Law of Treaties: a critical appraisal*, (Wien, New York, Springer-Verlag, 1974).

[195] McNair, 'The Functions and Differing Legal Character of Treaties', 11 (1930) BYIL 100–118; Jenks: 436–7, p. 112; Oppenheim's International Law, p. 1212 *et seq.*; Hans Aufricht, 'Supersession of Treaties in International law', 37 (1951–1952) Cornell LQ 655, 682–683.

[196] Shaw, *International Law* (Cambridge: Cambridge University Press, 2003) 850.

the UN Charter and treaties which created 'a kind of public law transcending in kind and not merely in degree the ordinary agreements between States'.[197]

The term *jus cogens* was used interchangeably with higher law, again, without itself being defined and being just as 'controversial as to content and method of creation'.[198] *Jus cogens* was also predicated upon an acceptance of fundamental and superior values within the system. It was analogous to domestic notions of public order or public policy.[199] Prohibition of torture, prevention of slavery, the outlawing of genocide were thought to be examples of *jus cogens*.

No derogation was permitted from this concept as it was thought to have an *erga omnes* effect; that is, all States were perceived to have a legal interest and an obligation to protect it.[200] Treaties which were in conflict with higher law or *jus cogens* could be declared invalid.

The VC does not seem to recognize any general higher law, other than peremptory norms of general international law, deviations from which render a treaty invalid. Such peremptory norms of general international law are assimilated to *jus cogens* in the title to Article 53 VC. Pursuant to this Article:

Treaties conflicting with a peremptory norm of general international law (*jus cogens*)

A treaty is void if, at the time of its conclusion, it conflicts with a peremptory norm of general international law. For the purposes of the present Convention, a peremptory norm of general international law is a norm accepted and recognised by the international community of States as a whole as a norm from which no derogation is permitted[201] and which can be modified only by a subsequent norm of general international law having the same character.

Under the provisions of the VC, the possibility of invoking acquiescence is excluded.[202]

It is noteworthy to point out that McNair,[203] commenting long before the enactment of the VC, thought that higher law did not necessarily have to be *universally* accepted higher law. It could have also encompassed *regional, sectoral or self-imposed higher law*. Therefore, according to McNair, the validity of a later treaty could be impugned where an earlier treaty which binds at least one of the

---

[197] McNair, 'The Functions and Differing Legal Character of Treaties', 11 (1930) BYIL 100, 118.
[198] Shaw, *International Law* (Cambridge: Cambridge University Press, 2003) 850.
[199] *Ibid.*, 117.
[200] See, for example, the *Barcelona Traction case*, ICJ Reports [1970] 3 and *East Timor case*, ICJ Reports [1995] 90.
[201] The wording of this provision is obviously influenced by the ILC preliminary reports where it was stated that a treaty provision will not have the character of *jus cogens* just because the parties agree that no derogation from it is permissible. It has to be a peremptory norm of general international law. Obligations have primacy because they are *jus cogens* themselves rather than because they are embodied in a treaty. ILC Commentary (Treaties) Art 50, para (2); YBILC (1966), ii, pp. 247–8.
[202] See Art 45. This article does not apply in cases where there is coercion of a representative of a State (Art 51), where there is coercion of a State by the threat or use of force (Art 52), and conflict with jus cogens (Art 53).
[203] See McNair (1961), p. 220 *et seq*. See also Oppenheim's 9th edition by Jenks and Watts.

contracting States has *directly reduced the treaty-making capacity of that State*[204] either completely or in relation to a subject-matter if the later treaty is in excess of any such capacity.[205]

An instance of this was where State A surrendered its treaty-making capacity through an earlier Treaty I, either totally or in relation to some matters.[206] In such circumstances, McNair argued that Treaty I would have effectively 'produced a *capitis diminutio* in A (absolute or relative as the case may be) and the second treaty concluded by A in the absence, or in excess, of its treaty-making capacity [would be] null and void'.[207] This was the case for example when a State accepted by treaty the suzerainty or protection of another State. It could also have been the case with component States of a federation.

McNair also argued that if a prior treaty was a *multipartite law-making treaty clearly intended to create permanent rules akin to higher law* and containing no power of denunciation, a treaty made between two or more parties in derogation of this law-making treaty would probably be null and void.[208] A later treaty super-seded an earlier one if and only if it was on the same level as the earlier treaty or if it was on a higher lever than the treaty it superseded. A later treaty may not have abrogated an earlier treaty if it was on a lower level than the earlier treaty.[209]

In light of the actual wording of Article 53 VC, it would seem that McNair's broad definition of higher law does not sit easily with the language of the provision. Whilst it is true that certain other treaties such as the Community Treaties may be regarded, at least as between its Member States, as constituting 'higher law' or supreme law, as between those Member States and a third State, those treaties prob-ably have no greater legal significance than any other treaty.

The situations discussed by McNair might, if at all, fall within the ambit of Article 46 VC. In other words, these regional or sectoral self-imposed arrange-ments, even though they are not higher law in the sense intended by Article 53 VC, could be interpreted as imposing constitutional or treaty-making limitations on the States. Again, a State invoking this ground to attack the treaty would have to show that these supra-national arrangements have become internal law, breach of which was manifest. In the previous section, it was seen how difficult it was to satisfy this test.

It is noteworthy that in the discussions prior to the enactment of the VC, a draft article had been recommended to address the treaty-making capacity of compo-nent States of a federation. Pursuant to a draft Article 5(2), 'States members of a federal union may possess a capacity to conclude treaties if such capacity is admitted

---

[204] In McNair's words (1961) at p. 221 it has 'produced a *capitis diminutio*' absolute or relative.

[205] See McNair (1961), p. 221. See Oppenheim's *International Law*, p. 1215 who talks of a Contracting State 'surrender[ing] its treaty-making capacity, either totally or in relation to the kind of treaty of which the second treaty is an example'.

[206] McNair (1961), p. 221. See Oppenheim's *International Law*, p. 1215.

[207] McNair (1961), p. 221.   [208] McNair (1961), *ibid.*

[209] *Ibid.* Also see Aufricht, p. 683; M. Akehurst, 'The Hierarchy of the sources of International Law', (1974–75) BYIL 273.

by the federal constitution and within the limits there laid down'. Eventually, this article was voted down and deleted.[210] Thus, the correlation between sectoral 'higher' law and federal law was left unaddressed. As there are no specific provisions dealing with the treaty-making powers (and limitations) of component units of a federal state, the matter would seem to be subsumed by the general provisions of Article 46 VC. It would, therefore, still depend on the general constitutional provisions of the federation, whether the internal rules regarding competence are of fundamental importance and the breach is manifest. Quasi-federations such as the European Union would seem to be governed by the same regime.

Nevertheless, the VC does not preclude the possibility of a new peremptory norm of general international law emerging.[211] If it emerges, any existing treaty which is in conflict with that norm would become void. Therefore, if one day European law reaches the point where it becomes a peremptory norm of general international law (at universal level and not just in the Member States' legal orders), then treaties incompatible with Community law, whether because of lack of competence or breach of substantive law, may become void or voidable.

Until then, it would seem that, except where a treaty breaches a universally accepted peremptory norm of international law such as the UN Charter, a plain treaty entered into between a State, member of an organization, and a third country is valid, even if the treaty breaches the constitutive provisions of that organization. A treaty such as the *Open Skies* agreement is unlikely to breach such peremptory norms of international law so as to justify a finding of invalidity.

In any case, the International Court of Justice (ICJ)[212] which is the body that deals with international law disputes, is always reluctant to declare a treaty invalid on these grounds. It prefers to deal with a conflict by interpretative means or it limits its judgments to a finding of incompatibility without exploring the invalidity point.[213] This is because the consequences attendant on the invalidity of a treaty are very serious.

---

[210] See, generally, Luigi Di Marzo, *Component Units of Federal States and International Agreements,* (Sijthoff & Noordhoff, 1980), Chapter 2. [211] Article 64 VC.

[212] The International Court of Justice (known colloquially as the World Court or ICJ) is the principal judicial organ of the United Nations. It is located at The Hague, Netherlands. Established in 1945 by the Charter of the United Nations, the Court began work in 1946 as the successor to the Permanent Court of International Justice. Its main functions are to settle disputes submitted to it by States and to give advisory opinions on legal questions submitted to it by the General Assembly or Security Council, or by such specialized agencies as may be authorized to do so by the General Assembly in accordance with the United Nations Charter.

[213] See the *Oscar Chinn* case *(Series A/B, No. 63),* where the Permanent Court of International Justice had to deal with the compatibility of the Convention of St German of 1919 with the General Act of Berlin of 1885. The Court reached its decision without expressing an opinion as to the validity of the latter treaty. Also see *European Commission of the Danube* case, PCIJ, Series B, No. 14, in which the problem was dealt with by means of interpretation. Similarly, in its Advisory Opinion on the *Austro-German Customs Union* case, Series A/B, No. 41 (1931), The Permanent Court of Justice held that, by eight votes to seven, that the customs union to be set up pursuant the Austro-German Protocol of 19 March 1931 was incompatible with a Protocol of 4 October 1922 dealing with the independence of Austria. The PCIJ refrained from passing judgment upon the validity of the two conflicting treaties. It was sufficient to declare the incompatibility of the latter treaty.

It is, therefore, not surprising that the provisions of the VC on invalidity have been very stringently drafted. As such, the invalidity envisaged under Article 53 VC is not irremediable, automatic, invalidity.[214] Invalidity has to be established through the compulsory procedure of Article 65 VC.[215] Also, it is not an *erga omnes* invalidity as the power to initiate proceedings to invalidate the treaty is reserved solely for the parties to the illegal treaty.[216]

Besides, the State responsibility route is always open.[217] The point that the rules of the law of treaties are not meant to pre-empt the application of the rules of international responsibility and that both set of rules could apply simultaneously was reiterated in the Commentary to the Draft article on International Responsibility.[218] The fact that the international legal system enables the party to the conflicting instruments to extricate itself as well as it can (i.e. by paying damages without either treaty being invalidated) was not considered a deficiency.[219] As commented by a great scholar in international law '[s]uch restraint is congenial to the level of international integration on which it is meant to apply'.[220]

B. Termination of an Otherwise Valid Treaty

Even if all the conditions for the invalidation of treaties under the VC were satisfied, the political imperative of preserving the stability of treaties could prevent the application of these provisions. Alternatively, the contracting party trying to exit the treaty may prefer to treat it as valid but seek a way of terminating it.[221]

Following-up the *Open Skies* cases, the affected Member States might try to denounce the impugned treaties. If there is no right of denunciation, then the Member States could invoke the provisions of the VC and attempt to terminate the treaties on the basis of a fundamental change of circumstances or supervening impossibility.

(i) Denunciation

The first logical route for a Member State to explore is whether it has the right to denounce the treaty. Denunciation is withdrawal[222] from a bilateral treaty, usually

---

[214] See generally Rozakis, p. 109 *et seq.*   [215] Paras 1 and 2.

[216] Third parties extraneous to the treaty may take diplomatic steps and/or invoke the illegal character before a political organ such as the UN General Assembly, but the political organs of the UN are unable to invalidate an illegal treaty. They can only exert political pressure and issue recommendations or decisions condemning the violation of the jus cogens norm. See Rozakis, pp. 120–121, 137, ft 67.   [217] Article 73 VC.

[218] See Commentary of the ILC, in *Official Records of the General Assembly, Fifty-sixth session, Supplement No. 10* (A/56/10), chapter IV.E.2, para.4.   [219] *Ibid.*

[220] Schwarzenberger, p. 482.

[221] A treaty may also terminate if its purposes and objects have been fulfilled or if its lifeline was limited or subject to a period that had expired. See, for example, the *Rainbow* 82 (1990) ILR 499. It is assumed here that the treaty was to be valid for an indefinite period and its purposes and objects have not been fulfilled.

[222] Withdrawal *simpliciter* is a concept used in connection with a multilateral treaty. It does not normally put an end to the treaty but only to the withdrawing State's status as a party.

followed by its termination. Denunciation may be in pursuance of an express provision in the treaty instrument at hand. In the absence of an express provision, denunciation may only be admissible if both parties consent to it or if it is an implied provision of the treaty.[223]

A right of denunciation can be inferred from the intention of the contracting States, the circumstances in which the treaty was concluded and the nature of the subject-matter.[224] A right to denounce a treaty cannot be inferred by one party just because the other party attempted unlawfully to denounce it or if the other party is in breach of its obligations.[225] If that were the case, the substantive and procedural safeguards for allowing termination of a treaty as codified in the VC would be rendered ineffective. Therefore, an implied right to denunciation is not readily construed.

In any case, if the other contracting State disagrees, it is very unlikely that denunciation will be feasible. Unilateral renunciation by the Member State will probably be perceived by the third country as a material breach of the treaty (see Article 60 VC).[226] However, third country action is beyond the purview of this article. Only the legal courses of action that are available to the Member State to terminate the treaty are examined; namely, termination because of supervening impossibility of performance and termination because of fundamental change of circumstances.

These grounds are enshrined in Articles 61 and 62 VC.

(ii) Termination Because of Supervening Impossibility of Performance

Pursuant to Article 61(1) VC, a party 'may invoke the impossibility of performing a treaty as a ground for terminating it if the impossibility results from the permanent disappearance or destruction of an object indispensable for the execution of the treaty'.

Cases of physical disasters or impossibility arising from the total extinction of one of the parties to a bilateral treaty[227] are the most frequently cited examples of an event causing supervening impossibility of performance of treaty obligations. Cases of permanent[228] disappearance or destruction of an object indispensable to the execution of the treaty would seem to fall within the ambit of this provision.[229]

---

[223] See Starke, 433, McNair (1961), 510–511.

[224] If the treaty is in part executed and in part executory, then it is easier to imply a provision of denunciation.

[225] McNair (1961), 514. He concedes that the relevant authority on this point is diplomatic rather than judicial because governments are reluctant to submit such issues to adjudication.

[226] Article 60 VC deals with termination or suspension of the operation of a treaty as a consequence of its breach. If applicable because of the Member State's unilateral termination, Article 60 VC would presumably be invoked by the third country.

[227] See generally McNair (1961), pp. 685–688; Sinclair, *The Vienna Convention*, pp. 190–192.

[228] A temporary impossibility only warrants suspension of a treaty.

[229] Oppenheim's *International Law*, p. 1303.

It should be noted that a treaty is not automatically terminated if impossibility of performance arises. A party has to follow the procedure set out in the VC.[230]

However, Article 61(1) VC applies on very strict circumstances. It has to be proved that an object indispensable to the execution of the treaty has disappeared. Serious financial difficulties are not a sufficient ground for the invocation of this ground of termination.[231] Also, as explained in Article 61(2) VC, a party cannot invoke impossibility of performance if it results from its own breach of an obligation flowing from the treaty or of any international obligation owed to any other party to the *same* treaty.[232] *A fortiori*, impossibility of performance *may* be invoked when this impossibility is a result of a breach of international obligations owed to another party or parties under a *different* treaty.

Therefore, if a treaty between a Member State and a third country is found to be in breach of Community law (a different treaty), for example, after a decision of the Court of Justice as in the *Open Skies* cases,[233] could this be considered as a supervening impossibility of performance justifying the termination of the treaty by the Member State?

Arguably, this may depend on whether the breach is one of the Community's competence or of substantive Community law.

If it is a question of breach of competence, then to the extent that the Member State should not have entered *at all* into such a treaty with a third country, for instance if the Community enjoyed exclusive competence, then *prima facie* an argument of impossibility of performance may be entertained. Therefore, the general repercussions from breach of competence and the specific circumstances of the case would have to be taken into account, in examining whether there is in fact impossibility. Is the Member State required to renege on its treaty obligations immediately or is there a transitional period? Is the Member State actually able to perform its treaty obligations at least unilaterally? Given that mere financial difficulties do not suffice for the purposes of Article 61(1) VC, the Member State would need to show serious non-pecuniary difficulties in justifying impossibility of performance.

If it is a question of breach of substantive Community law, then again, similar issues should be considered. To what extent is the ability of the Member State to perform its obligations under the treaty constrained? Can the Member State remove the incompatibility (by, for example, compensating the affected parties) and still comply with its treaty obligations towards the third country?

---

[230] See section 4 of the VC and specifically Articles 65–67 VC.

[231] *Gabčikovo-Nagymaros Project*, para 102.

[232] Also see *Gabčikovo-Nagymaros Project* (Hungary/Slovakia), Judgment, ICJ Reports (1997), p. 7, 63–64. See Anthony Aust, *Modern Treaty Law and Practice*, (Cambridge University Press, 2000), pp. 239–240.

[233] Arguably, mere (academic) speculation of the possibility of breach of Community law would not suffice. Something determinative and authoritative is required. As seen further down, speculation may, however, be relevant in determining whether this impossibility was indeed supervening or whether it was within the contemplation of the contracting States.

Arguably, another relevant factor in both cases of breach is whether the Member State was aware of the possibility that its treaty was in breach of Community law. If at the time of entering into the treaty with the third country, it was widely believed that the Member State had no competence to do so or that the treaty contained discriminatory provisions, then perhaps this impossibility is not really 'supervening' as the likelihood of it existed all along. In other words, the potential of impossibility may have been within the contemplation of the contracting States when entering into the treaty. Conversely, if the speculation arose after the conclusion of the treaty, then the potential of impossibility may not have been within the contemplation of the contracting States.

Therefore, just because the Court of Justice finds a treaty incompatible with Community law, whether because of lack of competence or breach of a substantive provision, this does not necessarily mean that a supervening impossibility of performance within the ambit of Article 61 VC has arisen, enabling the Member State to terminate the treaty with the third country.

Is termination on the basis of a fundamental change of circumstances any easier to justify? This is examined next.

(iii) Termination Because of Fundamental Change of Circumstances[234]

Fundamental change of circumstances is another ground upon which the Member State party to the treaty may seek release from its obligations under the treaty. Arguably, this is the reverse scenario of the *Racke* case explained in Part II. In *Racke*, the question was whether principles of international treaty law, namely Article 62 VC, could be used by the Court of Justice as a ground for assessing the validity/lawfulness of acts of Community institutions *under Community law*. Here, the question is whether the application and enforcement of Community law could be grounds for terminating a treaty *under international (treaty) law*.

Fundamental change of circumstances is enshrined in Article 62 VC, which reads as follows:

Fundamental change of circumstances

1. A fundamental change of circumstances which has occurred with regard to those existing at the time of the conclusion of a treaty, and which was not foreseen by the parties, may not be invoked as a ground for terminating or withdrawing from the treaty unless:
    (a) the existence of those circumstances constituted an essential basis of the consent of the parties to be bound by the treaty; and
    (b) the effect of the change is radically to transform the extent of obligations still to be performed under the treaty.

[234] For an excellent illustration of scholarly and judicial treatment of the principle before the enactment of the Vienna Convention, see Oliver J. Lissitzyn, 'Treaties and Changed Circumstances (Rebus Sic Stantibus)', 61 (1967) AJIL 895. For an overview of some case law before and after the Vienna Convention and the representations during the Vienna Conference, see T.O. Elias, *The Modern Law of Treaties* (A.W. Sijthoff International Publishing Company B.V., 1974), 119–128.

2. A fundamental change of circumstances may not be invoked as a ground for terminating or withdrawing from a treaty:
   (a) if the treaty establishes a boundary; or
   (b) if the fundamental change is the result of a breach by the party invoking it either of an obligation under the treaty or of any other international obligation owed to any other party to the treaty.

3. If, under the foregoing paragraphs, a party may invoke a fundamental change of circumstances as a ground for terminating or withdrawing from a treaty it may also invoke the change as a ground for suspending the operation of the treaty.

This provision is thought of as codifying the *rebus sic standibus* principle of customary law. Pursuant to this principle, in an international agreement there is always an implied term to the effect that the obligations under the agreement would come to an end if there has been a change of circumstances. The modern view, however, as reflected in Article 62 VC, is that termination or suspension on the basis of fundamental change of circumstances is only applicable when certain strict conditions are satisfied.

There are no restrictions as to when a fundamental change may arise.[235] For the ground to be invoked, it must be established beyond doubt that at the time of concluding the treaty, the parties agreed that the presence of certain circumstances was an essential consideration—an essential basis of the consent of both parties to be bound by the agreement.

Fundamental change of circumstances is operative as a ground of termination if this change has resulted in a *radical transformation* of the extent of the obligations imposed by the treaty.[236] The change must be such as to have increased the burden of the obligations to be executed to the extent of rendering the performance *essentially different* from that originally undertaken.[237] Also, the changed circumstances must have been *unforeseen* at the time of concluding the treaty. This ground of termination, due to its negative and conditional wording is only applied in exceptional circumstances.[238]

As with supervening impossibility of performance, a party cannot invoke fundamental change of circumstances if it results from its own breach of an obligation under the *same* treaty[239] but *may* invoke it when it is a result of a breach of an international obligation owed to another party or parties under a *different* treaty.

Invocation of this principle does not automatically terminate the treaty, nor does it enable the party invoking it to denounce it unilaterally. As with the ground

---

[235] Starke, 432.
[236] See *Fisheries Jurisdiction case*, ICJ Rep (1973), para 36. See Herbert W. Briggs, 'Unilateral Denunciation of Treaties: The Vienna Convention and the International Court of Justice', 68 [1974] American Journal of International Law 51; R.B. Bilder, 'The Anglo-Icelandic Fisheries Dispute', 37 Wisconsin Law Review (1973), 37; S.R. Katz, 'Issues Arising in the Icelandic Fisheries Case', 22 ICLQ (1973), 83.   [237] *Fisheries Jurisdiction case*, ICJ Rep (1973), para 43.
[238] *Gabčikovo-Nagymaros Project* (Hungary/Slovakia), Judgment, ICJ Reports (1997), p. 7, paras 102–103. See Daniel Reichert-Facilides, 'Down the Danube: the Vienna Convention on the Law of Treaties and the Case Concerning the Gabcikovo-Nagymaros Project', 47(4) [1998] ICLQ 837–854.
[239] See Article 62(2)(b) VC.

of supervening impossibility of performance, it merely enables a party to the treaty to commence the mechanism for the termination of it.[240]

Fundamental change of circumstances has been invoked many times and no tribunal has ever denied its existence. However, in all cases that it was invoked, the ICJ construed its ambit very narrowly and found that on the facts of the case it was inapplicable.[241] Therefore, it seems that, far from endangering the stability of treaty relations, this system is meant to preserve and solidify them, as it does not allow any ground for disrupting the operation of a treaty to be presumed or sought for anywhere other than in the convention itself.[242]

Could the Member State claim that there is a fundamental change of circumstances justifying the termination of the treaty when its treaty with a third country breaches Community law? The arguments here are similar to the ones advanced in the previous section but not identical.

Here, the actual changed circumstances must be assessed. It must be shown that the existence of the 'unchanged' circumstances constituted an essential basis of the consent of the parties to be bound by the treaty. Was, for example, the existence of the nationality clause in the Bermuda II agreements so important to *both* contracting States to form the basis of their consent? Was the existence of competence of the Member States to enter into the Bermuda II agreements so important as to form the basis of the consent of *both* contracting States?

Even if the answer to the above questions is in the affirmative, how does a finding of breach of competence or breach of substantive Community law actually affect the third country? For this ground to be invoked succesfully, it must be shown that as a result of a finding of incompatibility the Member State's obligations were radically transformed. It must be shown that the obligations imposed on the Member State became essentially different from those originally undertaken towards the third country. If the Member State is forced to pay compensation to aggrieved EU nationals, does this radically transform its obligations? By contrast to Article 61 VC as interpreted by subsequent case law,[243] here, serious financial difficulties do not seem to be excluded from the equation in assessing whether one contracting State's obligations under the treaty were radically transformed.

Arguably, as with supervening impossibility of performance, an argument of fundamental change of circumstances cannot really be made until there is an authoritative judicial[244] statement that a given treaty is in breach of Community law–either because of lack of competence or on the basis of a substantive provision. Only such occurrence may, if at all, fundamentally change the circumstances of the case. A mere speculation as to the compatibility of the treaty with Community law is unlikely to trigger changes in the Member State's performance of the treaty.

---

240 See Articles 65–66 VC.
241 See, for example, *Fisheries Jurisdiction case and Gabčikovo-Nagymaros Project.*
242 S.E. Nahlik, 'The Grounds of Invalidity and Termination of Treaties', 65 [1971] AJIL 736, 740.
243 *Gabčikovo-Nagymaros Project*, para 102.
244 A mere Commission decision may not be enough, unless, of course, it is in a field where the Commission has definitive judicial powers (e.g. competition law).

However, such speculation may be relevant in considering whether the change was unforeseen. If the change was indeed foreseen at the time of the conclusion of the treaty, then the transformation of the treaty obligations could not have been so radical after all. Again, depending on whether the speculation arose before or after the conclusion of the treaty, the likelihood of breach might in fact have been contemplated by the contracting States to the treaty.

VI. Conclusion

This author drew her inspiration from the *Open Skies* cases in examining aspects of the relationship between Community law and international treaty law. The central issue was the following: what could be the Community law and international law repercussions of EC-incompatible treaties between Member States and third countries? Most of the questions posed had no definitive answers. Arguably, most of the suggested answers were in fact in a no-man's-land in so far as Community law and international treaty law scholarship was concerned. The analysis in this article should be read with that caveat in mind.

In a purely internal scenario, it was argued that the Community law principles tended to subsume the international ones. Some ad hoc techniques used by the Community Courts in dealing with international law issues were considered in the beginning of this article. The application of international law principles was not excluded, but it became unnecessary to consider them.

When a third country entered the equation, things were more complicated. It was shown how in principle, Community law did not have extra-territorial effect. The Court of Justice could, for example, find a Member State in breach of Community law. If there was a breach of the Community competences, the Court of Justice could also call for the invalidation of the treaty. In theory, the validity of the treaty in the outside world was not affected. In practice, it could be affected. This is because, as shown in this article, the treaty relationship between a Member State and the third country may have been affected not just by Community law but very possibly also by international law.

From a Community law perspective, the treaty relationship could have been affected by competence issues.

As seen from a brief exposition of the case law, there was limited authority on what action the Court of Justice expected from Member States when treaties were enacted with third countries in breach of Community competences. It was concluded that although the instrument remained valid, the Member State had to take action to rectify the breach, perhaps by denouncing or re-negotiating the treaty. State liability was also relevant. The same applied to treaties which complied with the Community law on competences but breached other Community provisions, though there was no authority on the precise question.[245]

---

[245] See arguments and analogies made in Part III(D).

From an international law perspective, the treaty relationship between a Member State and a third country could have been affected by issues of invalidity, lawful termination, international responsibility, and reparation. The latter two issues were not addressed in this article.

In Part V, it was questioned whether the Member State could seek to impugn an EC-incompatible treaty on the grounds of invalidity because of conflict with the internal law on competences or with higher law.

As to the first ground of invalidity, it was concluded that breach of substantive Community law did not suffice to prove all the constituent elements of Article 46 VC–an article dealing with breach of the internal rules on treaty-making competence. Neither was this ground of invalidity satisfied where there was breach of competence. This was because under Article 46 VC, the impugned internal rules on competences had to be manifest enough in objective terms and obvious to any State acting in good faith and in accordance with normal practice. As seen in Part III, the law of external competences of the Community was anything but clear to Member States, let alone third countries. The doctrines of implied competence and implied exclusive competence, often mixed up by the Court of Justice itself, were not manifest; the result of disputed cases was certainly not always predictable. Therefore, this ground of invalidation of the treaty could not have been sustained.

As for the other ground of invalidity considered in Part V, that of incompatibility with *jus cogens* or higher law, it was conceded that Community law did not constitute *jus cogens* or higher law. Only if these concepts were to be given a broader interpretation to catch federal or quasi-federal constitutional laws could an argument of breach of *jus cogens* or higher law be entertained. However, the concept of *jus cogens*, as portrayed in the Vienna Convention, seemed to preclude such broad interpretation. Therefore, it was concluded that it was not easy to satisfy the conditions under either of these grounds, but the conclusions could change with the passage of time.

What if the Member State conceded the validity of the treaty but sought to terminate it on the grounds of supervening impossibility of performance or fundamental change of circumstances? Would it be more successful? The preceding analysis suggested that the answer was not clear. The strict conditions of these two grounds of termination had to be satisfied by taking into account the specific facts of the case. For example, it had to be considered whether the treaty breached the Community law on competences and/or other Community principles. The degree of foreseeability of the breach and the actual effects on the treaty-partners relations were also highly relevant factors.

Arguably, the *Open Skies* cases represented a great opportunity for the Court of Justice to explore some of these interesting issues. Rightly or wrongly it chose not to. It chose to remain within the confines of its Ivory Tower, shielded behind its previous rhetoric of a *sui generis* legal order. This article tried to take the discussion a step further, by questioning the potential impact of the *Open Skies* decision in the Community and international law context. The overall aim was to show the necessity for addressing the repercussions of EC-incompatible instruments, both Community-wise and internationally.

The time is perhaps ripe to renew the debate on the relationship between Community and international law. The rhetoric of a *sui generis* legal order is appealing but it is not always a convincing carve-out, the efforts of the Court of Justice notwithstanding. The Community needs to clarify or re-encapsulate the basics of this relationship. What role do principles of customary international law and of international conventions really play in the acquis Communitaire? What role should they play and how should their incorporation in Community law be made?

It is suggested that the area of external Community competences is a useful starting point for (re-) examining the link between Community law and international law. This could prove to be a particularly enriching process to both legal orders—to the extent that they are distinct. Arguably, such examination may eventually betray some *de facto* or even *de jure* limitations to the Community legal order. It may, however, also lead to coherence and better integration of the European Union in the international legal order. In this author's view, the Community owes it to its forefathers to explore these possibilities, no matter the outcome.

Ivory Towers are no longer in fashion. Exploring the *Open Skies* is.

Judicial Control of CFSP in the Constitution: A Cherry Worth Picking?

*Alicia Hinarejos**

I. Introduction

The intergovernmental pillars of the European Union are areas in continuous evolution. Furthermore, this evolution seems to be towards a more institutionalized co-operation. This is especially obvious within the third pillar, where *Pupino*,[1] for example, seems to be part of a slow trend of approximation to the logic of the Community pillar. Although less pronounced, the same slow shift of perspective can be said to be taking place in the realm of the second pillar or Common Foreign and Security Policy (CFSP).

That is arguably why the governments of the Member States were ready to scrap the intergovernmental label, currently attached to both pillars, in the Constitutional Treaty. The necessary political will appears to be there for the CFSP, the main focus of this article, to move into the next phase: one which will necessarily entail less intergovernmentalism and 'more' community method—with judicial oversight as one of its central elements. It is therefore necessary to ask ourselves about the specific role the European Court of Justice should be given.

It is with this question in mind that we should approach the changes envisaged by the Constitutional Treaty (hereinafter CT). Even if this document is politically dead, it is the measure of how far the Member States were willing to go in changing the nature of the second pillar and its judicial control. It is foreseeable that a more or less obvious process of cherry-picking will take place in the future; the Member States and institutions, unable to see the CT ratified, will understandably seek to otherwise implement or bring about some of its reforms, if at all possible: those which allegedly deserve to be cherry-picked.

This article will consider the role that the ECJ was given within Common Foreign and Security Policy (CFSP) in the Constitution,[2] to decide whether it is

---

* University of Oxford. The author would like to thank Stephen Weatherill, Derrick Wyatt, Takis Tridimas, Paul Craig and Katja Ziegler for their comments. All errors remain, of course, her own.

[1] C-105/03 *Criminal Proceedings against Maria Pupino* [2005] ECR I-5285. For a full account of the significance of this judgment, see M Fletcher 'Extending 'Indirect Effect' to the Third Pillar: The Significance of Pupino' (2005) 30 ELR 862.

[2] For more general views on the jurisdiction of the Court in the CT, see A Arnull 'From bit part to starring role? The Court of Justice and Europe's Constitutional Treaty' (2005) 24 Yearbook of

good enough to be cherry-picked in the future. Is this the solution we want, or should we set out to find different, more suitable arrangements if the jurisdiction of the ECJ in matters of CFSP is to be reformed in the future?

With this in mind, I will examine the changes in the nature of the measures adopted under the CSFP envisaged by the CT (from intergovernmental to Union measures). Consequently, I will turn to the very restricted judicial control foreseen in this area. The jurisdiction of the ECJ is still excluded, save for some exceptions. This article will consider the scope of these exceptions to determine how far-reaching they are, and thus what kind of part they allow the ECJ to play.

Residual competences of the ECJ within the CFSP, such as policing the borders and upholding the primacy of Union law, will be considered in the first place. Secondly, we will find out whether there is a minimum control of measures adopted pursuant to the CFSP and their accordance to the Constitution. If there is no such control, the possibility of a conflict with national constitutional courts could arise, in the terms that we shall see below. Next, I will determine whether there is a judicial gap which endangers protection of the rights of individuals, caused by the cleavage that will necessarily appear between the transformed nature of CFSP measures (binding only under international law before, binding Union law after the Constitution) and the remedies granted to individuals against them. A very restricted protection offered by the ECJ could drive individuals to seek protection before the European Court of Human Rights (ECtHR). In this respect, I will look at how realistic the possibility of judicial control exercised by the ECtHR would be, as well as whether the Member States could be held responsible by this Court for the consequences of Union (CFSP) acts.

II. The Nature of CFSP Measures in the CT

A. Binding Force

Nowadays, any measures taken in the field of CFSP are either only binding under international law or are Community measures; i.e., to the extent that joint actions or common positions require the adoption of measures binding on third parties, these measures have to be taken by the States themselves or by the Community, normally under Articles 60 or 301 EC.[3] Since the Treaty of Maastricht, joint

European Law 1; T Tridimas 'The European Court of Justice and the Draft Constitution: A Supreme Court for the Union?' in P Nebbia and T Tridimas *EU Law for the 21st Century: Rethinking the New Legal Order Vol 1* (Hart, Oxford, 2004) 113. For a different perspective on this particular aspect of the jurisdiction of the Court, see MG Garbagnati-Ketvel 'The Jurisdiction of the European Court of Justice in Respect of the Common Foreign and Security Policy' (2006) 55 ICLQ 77.

[3] JA Usher 'Direct and Individual Concern—an effective Remedy or a conventional Solution?' (2003) 28 ELR 575, 593. Article 308 has also been used as a 'complementary' legal basis: see Cases T-315/01 *Yassin Abdullah Kadi v Council and Commission* [2005] ECR II-3649, paras 64–135; T-306/01 *Yusuf and Al Barakaat International Foundation v Council and Commission* [2005] ECR II-3533, paras 125–71.

actions and common positions, the instruments which are drawn up under the CFSP, have binding force under international law.[4] Because they are only binding under international law, they are not challengeable in the Community legal system; whereas if they are implemented by binding measures, those are Community measures and hence challengeable by normal communautaire means.

The formal disappearance of the pillars in the CT brings with it an important phenomenon: the difference between EU and EC law vanishes; thus we have no more, on the one hand, a corpus of measures adopted under the intergovernmental pillars which are, ultimately, measures of public international law and, on the other hand, measures of EC law which have 'stronger' features.

With regard to the legal instruments which will be used by the Union in the area of CFSP if the Constitution enters into force, Article I-40 (3) CT states that 'the European Council and the Council shall adopt the necessary European decisions'. A European decision is described elsewhere (Article I-33 CT) as 'a non-legislative act, binding in its entirety'. The measures taken by the European Council or the Council, when pursuing objectives of the CFSP, will thus be binding *under Union law* either generally or upon their addressees, both as regards aim and means to achieve it.

A major change is envisaged, judging from the differences between the pre- and post-Constitution situations. CFSP measures are binding in the first case under international law, whereas they are binding under Union law in the second. Let us not forget that 'Union law' ceases to have its current meaning (measures of international law adopted in the intergovernmental areas of the EU, and different from EC law). Everything, according to the CT, is Union law—which has the standard features of what nowadays is Community law: primacy over the law of the Member States, possible direct effect.[5]

Thus, it seems that the fact that CFSP measures will stop being binding only under international law to be binding also within the EU legal order implies a series of major changes in the nature and effects of such measures. The 'stronger' features of Community law, not applicable to international law, transform these measures and give them a different weight.[6]

B. Competent Courts

To what extent do national courts have jurisdiction at present to consider the legality of CFSP measures, binding under international law only? National courts

---

[4] cf E Denza *The Intergovernmental Pillars of the European Union* (OUP, Oxford, 2002) 311.

[5] Articles I-6 and I-33 CT, respectively.

[6] European decisions adopted pursuant to the CFSP shall have primacy (Article I-6 CT), but no direct effect, according to Article I-33 CT. It has been argued that primacy applies already to the current second pillar: see K Lenaerts, T Corthaut 'Of Birds and Hedges: The Role of Primacy in Invoking Norms of EU Law' (2003) 31(3) ELRev 287, 289. For the purposes of this article we will accept the orthodox view that a fully-fledged principle of supremacy applies only within the first pillar, at least for the time being.

may be competent to consider whether the national government acted legitimately when agreeing to the adoption of such measure; in that sense, they could analyse the measure itself in order to determine whether it is consistent with the national constitution and with fundamental rights standards. Whether—or which—national courts have this jurisdiction is a matter of pure domestic law.

These measures are excluded from the jurisdiction of the ECJ, given that they are not part of the legal system of the Community and the TEU does not bestow competence upon the Court.

But we have already seen that the Constitution envisages an important transformation. These measures become part of the Community (Union) legal order. Does this affect the picture presented above? As a matter of EU law it definitely does, since national courts are not competent to consider and rule invalid a measure emanating from such legal order. According to Article IV 4 (38) CT, the case law of the ECJ shall have continuity. This can surely only be interpreted to the effect that the principle emanating from *Foto-Frost*[7] would still be valid.

III. The Jurisdiction of the Court in CFSP: An Overview

The jurisdiction of the ECJ has been expanding throughout the years and the consecutive Treaty revisions. The Treaty of Amsterdam, for example, extended the jurisdiction of the Court to the third pillar, with exceptions.[8] The extension, however, did not affect the CFSP; the second pillar remained inevitably beyond the control of the ECJ.[9]

The Constitution envisages a merger of the former legal entities and the Treaties which leads to the creation of the European Union as an entity with full legal personality and the consequent disappearance, in theory, of the three-pillar structure.[10] The EC and EU treaties are thus subsumed in a single document, and European Community and European Union are merged into one entity with single legal personality.[11] Consequently, the third pillar has been included within the area of application of what we currently label the Community method, which results in the general extension of the jurisdiction of the Court (with, of course,

---

[7] Case 314/85 *Foto-Frost v Hauptzollamt Lübeck-Ost* [1987] ECR 04199.

[8] The restrictions are to be found in Articles 68 EC and 35 TEU. For a more detailed account of these changes, cf A Albors-Llorens 'Changes in the jurisdiction of the European Court of Justice under the Treaty of Amsterdam' (1998) 35 CML Rev 1273; AM Arnull *The European Union and its Court of Justice* (OUP, 2006) 131–37; P Craig and G De Búrca *EU Law. Text, Cases and Materials* (OUP, Oxford, 2003) 29–42.

[9] E Denza, *The Intergovernmental Pillars of the European Union* (Oxford: OUP, 2002) 311–22.

[10] Shaw rightly points out that the pillars do not disappear completely: J Shaw 'Europe's Constitutional Future' [2005] Spring PL 132, 139.

[11] For more details cf J Kokott and A Rüth 'The European Convention and its Draft Treaty establishing a Constitution for Europe: Appropriate Answers to the Laeken Questions?' (2003) 40 CML Rev 1315, 1322–1326.

some exceptions).[12] This is a considerable change, since the restrictions which currently curtail the jurisdiction of the Court within the third pillar would disappear.

The same, however, does not hold true for the provisions of the second pillar, given that their grouping with the correspondent provisions of the Community pillar does not result in a substantive fusion and hence general application of the Community method. Any control by the Court of Justice is generally excluded by way of Article III-376, with a few exceptions which I shall consider below:

The Court of Justice of the European Union shall not have jurisdiction with respect to Articles I-40 and I-41 and the provisions of Chapter II of Title V concerning the common foreign and security policy and Article III-293 insofar as it concerns the common foreign and security policy.

However, the Court shall have jurisdiction to monitor compliance with Article III-308 and to rule on proceedings, brought in accordance with the conditions laid down in Article III-365(4), reviewing the legality of European decisions providing for restrictive measures against natural or legal persons adopted by the Council on the basis of Chapter II of Title V.

This has been termed a 'rather unhappy compromise'[13] between those who wanted to exclude judicial control entirely and those who wished for an extension similar to the one applied to the third pillar. Of course, judicial control of matters of foreign policy is typically the subject of restriction even in national systems; it is hardly surprising that this shall be the case at the level of the Union. It is the chosen degree of restriction that can prompt a more useful debate. Albeit granting full legal personality to the Union, the Constitution does not make it a sovereign State in the sense of international law. The provisions of this pillar enhance co-operation and interdependence, but quite clearly do not aim at depriving Member States of their sovereignty as subjects of international law[14]; it would have been difficult, if not impossible, to imagine a different Constitutional Treaty, whereby matters arising under the second pillar fell within the Court's competence with no restraint, as if they were matters of the previous Community pillar.

Let us now examine those exceptional circumstances under which the Court can exercise jurisdiction over matters of CFSP. For organizational reasons, and in order to gain a quick overview of the competence of the Court, we can distinguish between the 'residual' competences of the Court (policing the borders, enforcing the primacy of Union law), 'abstract control of constitutionality' (that is, when the

---

[12] Article III-377 CT retains the limits of the Court's jurisdiction with regard to operations carried out by the police or other law enforcement services of the Member States and national measures to maintain law and order and to safeguard internal security. This restriction is currently found in Article 35(5) TEU.

[13] Written Evidence by AM Arnull in *The Future of the European Court of Justice. Report With Evidence. 6th Report of Session 2003–04* (HL Paper 47 2004) 55, 57.

[14] Written Evidence by J Priban in *The Future of the European Court of Justice. Report with Evidence. 6th Report of Session 2003–04* (HL Paper 47 2004) 90, 91.

conformity of a measure to higher law—the Constitution, in this case—is examined in the abstract), and 'protection of individuals' (when the measure is challenged by an aggrieved plaintiff).

IV. Primacy and Policing the Borders. Jurisdiction over Arts I-6 and III-308 CT

A. Primacy

We have already seen how primacy is arguably extended to the whole of Union law. On the other hand, the Constitutional Treaty does not explicitly exclude the competence of the Court when it comes to Article I-6 (Primacy of Union Law) in relation to CFSP measures.

This seems to entail that national courts can seek a preliminary ruling from the ECJ on the matter of primacy of CFSP measures over national law. Arnull has contended this,[15] arguing that it is unclear whether the possibility of a preliminary ruling will be open to national courts. The consequences of this assumption are disastrous: national courts know that primacy applies to CFSP measures, but if a doubt arises they are left to their own devices. Independently of their final decision, there is no possible way in which uniformity can be preserved across the Member States if national courts are forced to decide on a primacy issue without any guidance from the ECJ.

Some have argued that the solution to this problem is not to make the principle of supremacy apply to the former second pillar. Although there is no explicit allusion to this exception in the Constitution, their main claim, apart from the general assertion of the special nature of the CFSP, is that the ECJ would not be able to offer guidance to national courts whenever they had to refrain from applying a national measure which is contrary to a CFSP measure.[16]

I do not think this argument very forceful. It is true that some competence on the part of the ECJ is inexorably linked to the extension of supremacy to the second pillar. If, then, the Constitution explicitly extends supremacy to the second pillar and does not explicitly preclude the competence of the ECJ, surely it is more logical and faithful to the letter of the Treaty to believe that supremacy is extended and therefore competence exists, rather than to believe that there are implicit exceptions in both cases.

---

[15] *The Future Role of the European Court of Justice. Report with Evidence. 6th Report of Session 2003–04* (HL Paper 47 2004) 16.

[16] Editorial 'The CFSP under the EU Constitutional Treaty—Issues of Depillarization' (2005) 42 CML Rev 325, 326–327. On the contrary, Denza assumes that Article I-6 applies to CFSP: E Denza 'Common Foreign Policy and Single Foreign Policy' in T Tridimas and P Nebbia (eds) *European Union Law for the Twenty-First Century. Rethinking the New Legal Order* (Hart, Oxford, 2004), 267–268.

It is therefore submitted that the ECJ must be able to provide national courts with a preliminary ruling on the matter of primacy of CFSP measures. After all, Article III-376 CT lists exceptions, not a general rule whereby the ECJ shall have no jurisdiction to rule on any issue related to CFSP. It is difficult to imagine that such catalogue of exceptions can constitute an open list, since an exemption from the jurisdiction of the Court is serious enough to be necessarily embedded in the Constitution and properly delimited therein. An exception of this nature should be interpreted in a restrictive manner, consistent with the need to uphold legal certainty. The question seems to be, then, in how far the ECJ will be able to provide a preliminary ruling on the matter of supremacy of a CFSP measure over national law without thereby taking to itself a competence that it does not rightfully have, i.e., to substantially interpret and thus flesh out CFSP measures. This seems to be a very delicate and extremely difficult task; but this does not mean that we should abandon the idea altogether. The fact is that the strict wording of the Constitution does not exclude the principle of supremacy from applying to CFSP, and there are powerful arguments, outlined above, in favour of not accepting supremacy as a non-written exception from the outset. The same goes for the competence of the Court to rule on this matter: there is no explicit exception and, if we accept that primacy applies to CFSP, then some policing on the part of the Court is necessary. If we accept these premises (that Article I-6 CT applies to CFSP, and that such application falls within the ECJ's jurisdiction), the question of how this should be done without overstretching the Court's competence should be for the Court itself to decide.

B. Policing the Borders

Article III-376 CT explicitly says that, although CFSP is to be excluded from the jurisdiction of the Court, Article III-308 is an 'exception to the exception'.

Article III-308 CT reads as follows:

The implementation of the common foreign and security policy shall not affect the application of the procedures and the extent of the powers of the institutions laid down by the Constitution for the exercise of the Union competences referred to in Articles I-13 to I-15 and I-17.

Similarly, the implementation of the policies listed in those Articles shall not affect the application of the procedures and the extent of the powers of the institutions laid down by the Constitution for the exercise of the Union competences under this Chapter.

This provision is the successor of Article 47 TEU,[17] whereby the ECJ currently polices the borders between the intergovernmental pillars and the competences of the Community.[18] Several members of the Convention expressed their concern that, if a safeguard equivalent to that of Article 47 TEU was not included in the

---

[17] Which falls within the jurisdiction of the Court by means of Article 46 TEU.
[18] Case C-170/96 *Commission v Council (airport transit)* [1998] ECR I-02763.

Constitution, there would be 'a risk that acts relating to the former Community pillar would now be taken on the basis of procedures applicable to CFSP. Others expressed concern about "communatising" CFSP, i.e. that decisions on issues covered by CFSP would be taken by applying rules of former first pillar areas'.[19]

But what does exactly 'policing the borders' entail? It has been put forward in the literature that Article 47 TEU grants competence to the Court to review the accordance of CFSP measures with EC law, whenever the act in question falls within an area of EC competence.[20] This assumption seems to arise from drawing a parallel between the application of Article 47 TEU to police the borders and those cases where the ECJ reviewed the legality of national foreign policy measures.[21]

However, this is a false conclusion. Policing the boundaries between CFSP and EC competences cannot entail that the Court may examine the legality of those acts with regard to EC law (whenever the act is adopted in an area of Community competence). If the Court finds that the Union has adopted a measure pursuant to the CFSP when it should have been adopted under the first pillar, then the Union did not have the necessary competence to act. The principle of conferral of powers makes it impossible for this measure to be valid in any case, and no further review is necessary or legitimate. If an act has been enacted in an area where there was no competence to do so, the act is void—and a void act cannot display any effects, even if it does accord to EC law. This is also the interpretation to be given to the competence given to the Court by Article III-376(2) in relation to Article III-308 CT.

V. Abstract Control of Constitutionality

A. General Remarks

By 'abstract control' I refer to the competence of several national constitutional courts to check whether a challenged measure accords to higher law. This control is not triggered by an individual who considers his rights breached by such an act.

---

[19] The European Convention. Praesidium *Draft sections of Part Three with comments* (CONV 727/03 2003) 52. This view was shared by the Discussion Circle on the Court of Justice in its Complementary Report. The European Convention. Discussion Circle on the Court of Justice *Supplementary report on the question of judicial control relating to the common foreign and security policy* (CONV 689/1/03 REV 1 2003) 3. Hence, an explicit reference to the jurisdiction of the Court was included in the draft Treaty, albeit in a different location; it was part of what was then Article III-209 (now Article III-308 CT). It was during the works of the IGC that this reference was moved to Article III-376, 'for consistency's sake': Conference of the Representatives of the Governments of the Member States. IGC Secretariat *Editorial and legal comments on the draft Treaty establishing a Constitution for Europe–Basic Document* (CIG 4/03 2003) 371.

[20] M Koskenniemi 'International Law Aspects of the Common Foreign and Security Policy' in M Koskenniemi (ed) *International Law Aspects of the European Union* (Kluwer Law International, The Hague, 1998) 36–42.

[21] Case C-124/95 *The Queen, ex parte Centro-Com Srl v HM Treasury and Bank of England* [1997] ECR I-81; C-120/94 *Commission v Greece* [1996] ECR I-3037. But this comparison is flawed. In

It does not seek to protect the rights of (specific) aggrieved individuals, but to preserve the values and rules embedded in the Constitution, which often include a hard core of fundamental rights. This option is normally only open to privileged applicants. The mechanism that is closest to this is currently to be found in Article 230 EC.

This provision remains almost unchanged when included in the Constitution:

Article III-365 CT

1. The Court of Justice of the European Union shall review the legality of European laws and framework laws, of acts of the Council, of the Commission and of the European Central Bank, other than recommendations and opinions, and of acts of the European Parliament and of the European Council intended to produce legal effects vis-à-vis third parties. It shall also review the legality of acts of bodies, offices or agencies of the Union intended to produce legal effects vis-à-vis third parties.

2. For the purposes of paragraph 1, the Court of Justice of the European Union shall have jurisdiction in actions brought by a Member State, the European Parliament, the Council or the Commission on grounds of lack of competence, infringement of an essential procedural requirement, infringement of the Constitution or of any rule of law relating to its application, or misuse of powers.

[...]

This mechanism is similar to the national ones we can find in Germany, Spain or France, although at the national level this type of control is normally restricted to legislative acts, given that the control of non legislative acts can be carried out by lower courts. This is obviously not possible in the Union legal system.

This mechanism, however, cannot be applied to CFSP measures because the Court has no jurisdiction in this respect according to Article III-376. This entails that no review of such measures is possible, even if the act in question is in blatant violation of the Constitution.[22]

On the other hand, it is arguable that an abstract control of CFSP measures would be possible in the national constitutional courts at the moment, given that the EU has no legal personality and the measures taken pursuant to the second pillar are intergovernmental measures, which are ultimately measures of public international law. Hence the decision taken by the government to participate in such intergovernmental agreement or act could be theoretically challenged before the constitutional court, if national legislation so allows.

But this would no longer be possible after the ratification of the Constitution, for reasons already given above: CFSP measures would no longer be measures of

these cases, the Court is not competent by way of Article 47 TEU, and it is not policing the borders. Only EC law is at stake. Foreign and security policy is simply a national exception that the Member States claim in order to derogate from the law of the Common Market.

[22] Although we will consider them separately below, let us also point out now that international agreements adopted in the field of CFSP are nevertheless an exception to this exclusion: the procedure by which the Court can be asked to give an opinion on the conformity of an envisaged international agreement with the Constitution (Article III-325(11)) is not affected by Article III-376 CT.

public international law, but of Union law. This makes it impossible for national courts to rule them invalid, according to the *Foto-Frost*[23] principle.

The conclusion must therefore be that, in theory, CFSP measures (apart from international agreements, as we shall further explain below) would generally escape any kind of abstract judicial scrutiny, exercised either by the ECJ or by national constitutional courts. But there can be yet a further dimension to this problem.

B. A Possible Source of Conflict: National Constitutional Courts

It is possible to imagine that these constitutional provisions could place even more pressure on the not always peaceful relationship between the ECJ, on the one side, and several national constitutional courts, on the other. The latter courts generally count among their competences the capability to test the accordance of legislation with the national constitution they vow to preserve. Given that, as explained above, this will strictly speaking not be possible anymore in the field of CFSP measures, one can only discard the possibility of a conflict if this function is being effectively fulfilled by the ECJ. But is it?

National constitutional courts normally exercise two functions which could lead to conflict in the field of CFSP: verifying accordance with a hard core of fundamental rights embedded in the national constitution, and checking whether legislative measures are *ultra vires* due to a lack of competence.

Let us now consider these functions separately. The first of them relates to the accordance with a hard core of constitutionally encoded fundamental rights. A brief insight into the fundamental rights conflict between the ECJ and some national constitutional courts which took place in the past is necessary.

In practice, national constitutional courts have not recognized the unconditional supremacy of EC Law in the terms mapped out by the ECJ.[24] In some cases, the main worry of these courts was whether EC Law could impinge on fundamental rights enshrined in the hard core of the national constitution. The most famous case example is that of the German *Bundesverfassungsgericht*, which decided that the transfer of powers to the EC could not amend an essential feature of the *Grundgesetz*, such as the protection of fundamental rights. In the *Solange* case,[25] the court claimed that:

> [I]n the hypothetical case of a conflict between law and [...] the guarantees of fundamental rights in the Constitution, there arises the question of which system of law takes precedence, that is, ousts the other. In this conflict of norms, the guarantee of fundamental rights in the Constitution prevails as long as the competent organs of the Community have not removed the conflict of norms in accordance with the Treaty mechanism.[26]

---

[23] Case 314/85 *Foto-Frost v Hauptzollamt Lübeck-Ost* [1987] ECR 04199.

[24] For a general (non-exhaustive) account, cf S Weatherill *Cases and Materials on EU Law* (OUP, Oxford, 2007), 691–702; P Craig and G De Búrca *EU Law. Text, Cases and Materials* (OUP, Oxford, 2003), 285–315.

[25] *Internationale Handelsgesellschaft mbH v Einfuhr- und Vorratsstelle für Getreide und Futtermittel (2 BvL 52/71)* [1974] 2 Common Market L Rep 540.   [26] *ibid.* 551.

In its later judgment *Solange II*,[27] the Court nevertheless reconsidered the level of protection of fundamental rights within the legal system of the Community and decided that it was substantially similar to the one envisaged by the German constitution. It therefore claimed that it would 'no longer exercise its jurisdiction to decide on the applicability of secondary community legislation [. . .] and it will no longer review such legislation by the standard of the fundamental rights contained in the Constitution'.[28]

As it has been rightly pointed out,[29] the *Bundesverfassungsgericht* does not find in its judgment that it does not have jurisdiction to review EC law according to national standards when it comes to the protection of fundamental rights. It rather claims that, although such jurisdiction exists, it will not exercise it as long as it remains satisfied that there is an equivalent protection of fundamental rights overseen by the Community institutions. This view was further stressed in the *Maastricht*[30] judgment (as later explained by the German Court in the *Bananas*[31] decision). The latter decision indeed also stresses the improbability that the Court will exercise its jurisdiction to rule in favour of the disapplication of a Community measure in German territory; the burden placed on the plaintiff is extremely heavy.

The German one was not the only national constitutional court to voice such reservations with regard to the protection to fundamental rights.[32]

Considering now the situation as mapped out in the Constitution, it is easy to imagine a re-emergence of the old conflict if this aspect of abstract control is theoretically out of bounds for national constitutional courts, while also outside the ECJ's jurisdiction. Given that this is the case—the Court has no competence, as explained above, with the exception of international agreements—national constitutional courts may feel the need to reassert their self-perceived role again.

This, of course, has to be differentiated from—although taken into account with—the competence of the ECJ to review measures which affect the rights of a private plaintiff under Article III-376(2) CT, which we should examine in depth below. It could very well be that no conflict arises if the Court protects individuals consistently on a case-by-case basis, although it has no jurisdiction to monitor accordance of legislation with Part II of the Constitution *in abstracto*. This could be another incentive for the Court to interpret the wording of Article III-376(2)—both when determining whether it has competence, and whether the plaintiff has standing—in a non-excessively restrictive manner. A too narrow

---

[27] *Re Wünsche Handelsgesellschaft (Case 2 BvR 197/83)* [1987] 3 Common Market L Rep 225.

[28] *ibid.* 265.   [29] J Fröwein 'Solange II' (1988) 25 CML Rev 201, 203–204.

[30] *Manfred Brunner and Others v the European Union Treaty (Cases 2 BvR 2134/92 & 2159/92)* [1994] 1 Common Market L Rep 57.   [31] BVerfG Beschluss vom 7.6. 2000.

[32] Similar reservations had already been voiced by the Italian Constitutional Court, reaching the conclusion that: '[I]t should therefore be excluded that such limitations of sovereignty, concretely set out in the Rome Treaty [. . .] can nevertheless give the organs of the EEC an unacceptable power to violate the fundamental principles of our constitutional order or the inalienable rights of man. And it is obvious that if ever Article 189 had to be given such an aberrant interpretation, in such a case the

interpretation of *locus standi* as granted by Article III-365 CT could in theory lead to a re-awakening of the concerns of some national constitutional courts, and this does not apply solely to the CFSP, but to every field of Union competence. In this particular area, however, there is a further reason for concern: a broad interpretation of the competence of the Court and of standing, capable of guaranteeing thorough protection of individuals on a case-by-case basis, could be the only reason why constitutional courts accept the fact that neither they, nor the ECJ, can ensure the accordance of legislation with constitutionally encoded fundamental rights in the abstract. Otherwise, it is possible that the national court may choose to exercise the jurisdiction it has reserved to itself in order to review the validity of Union acts against national standards and ultimately may decide to rule in favour of the disapplication of such an act within its national territory.

Let us now consider the next aspect of an abstract control of legislation, i.e., ensuring the correct use of competences. National constitutional courts have also expressed concern in this respect in the past: the *Bundesverfassungsgericht* exposed clearly in the *Maastricht* judgment[33] its intention to monitor the exercise of the competences of the Community, making sure its institutions remained within their powers. Although the tone of the *Bananas*[34] decision is far more conciliatory, this 'subsidiary emergency jurisdiction'[35] remains. The Italian Constitutional Court, on its part, also signalled readiness to monitor correct use of competence in *Granital*[36] and *Fragd*.[37] The Danish Supreme Court came to a similar result in *Carlsen*.[38]

In the future, this could equally affect any competence of the Union. But are there any further particularities that make it necessary to take this sleeping threat into account in the field of CFSP especially? This would be so if the ECJ were less capable than in other areas to check that competence limits have been adhered to.

If this is the case, and the ECJ has less competence in the CFSP than in other fields with regard to the proper use of competence, then a special danger arises within this particular area, apart from the general and distant threat that applies to every other competence. Within the CFSP, national constitutional courts would

guarantee would always be assured that this Court would control the continuing compatibility of the Treaty with the above-mentioned fundamental principles'. *Frontini v Ministero delle Finanze (Case 183)* [1974] 2 Common Market L Rep 372, 389. This position was later on reinforced in *Fragd*. Corte Constituzionale, *21 Aprile 1989 n. 232—Pres. Conso; red. Ferri—S.p.a. Fragd c. Amministrazione delle finanze dello Stato* [1989] 72 Rivista di Diritto Internazionale 104.

[33] *Manfred Brunner and Others v the European Union Treaty (Cases 2 BvR 2134/92 & 2159/92)* [1994] 1 Common Market L Rep 57.   [34] BVerfG Beschluss vom 7.6.2000.

[35] A Peters 'The Bananas Decision 2000 of the German Federal Constitutional Court: Towards Reconciliation with the ECJ as regards Fundamental Rights Protection in Europe' (2000) 43 German Yearbook of International Law 276, 281.

[36] Unofficial translation in G Gaja 'Constitutional Court (Italy) Decision No. 170 of 8 June 1984, S.p.a. granital v Amministrazione delle Finanze dello Stato.' (1984) 21 CML Rev 756.

[37] *Corte Constituzionale, 21 Aprile 1989 n. 232—Pres. Conso; red. Ferri—S.p.a. Fragd c. Amministrazione delle finanze dello Stato* [1989] 72 Rivista di Diritto Internazionale 104.

[38] *Hanne Norup Carlsen and others v Prime Minister Poul Nyrup Rasmussen. Danish Supreme Court, 6 April 1998* [1999] 3 Common Market L Rep 854.

have more reasons to actively control whether the Union institutions have acted within their competences, given that the ECJ cannot do it, as least as efficiently or as widely as in other matters.

The Court is competent, according to Article III-308 CT, to police the borders between the CFSP and other competences of the Union. However, taking the case of the German Constitutional Court, the *Maastricht* judgment was concerned with 'alleged trespass beyond the outer limits of Treaty-conferred competence'.[39] This seems to be equivalent to the power the Court has outside CFSP under Article III-365 CT (the successor of Article 230 EC). But, as was pointed out above, this does not apply to CFSP; the only competence to police borders in this area is given to the Court under Article III-308 CT. This means that the Court has a more limited competence to check whether competence has been properly used, since it cannot consider the outer limits of the competence of the Union, but only the frontiers between this particular policy and others. It follows, then, that a specific danger arises in this area, in the terms and with the consequences pointed out above.

The UK debate on the jurisdiction of a future Supreme Court has also yielded results of interest to our discussion. According to Arden,[40] the creation of such court can be of particular importance within the CFSP, given the lack of ECJ jurisdiction. In her opinion, it is possible that national courts—and, among them the new UK Supreme Court—have jurisdiction to review such measures, if national legislation so provides. Although the author points out that this is merely a possibility to consider, it wonderfully conveys the rationale behind this section: if the ECJ cannot adjudicate within a particular field, it is very likely that national constitutional courts will feel more inclined to exercise judicial scrutiny themselves, in order to fill what they perceive to be a gap of constitutional authority.

Can it be the case that CFSP measures which escape the control of the ECJ and are perceived by a national constitutional court to run counter to the national constitution drive the latter court to strike a Union measure down? Could this be the spark that finally ignites the conflict?[41] The on-going disagreement on 'who decides who decides' between the ECJ and the national constitutional courts— considered by some as another form of check and balances[42]—could fulfil a beneficial function of control, whereby any potential shortcomings of the Constitutional Treaty with regards to the judicial control of foreign policy measures would be detected and reacted against. This is not to say, of course, that this

---

[39] S Weatherill *Cases and Materials on EU Law* (OUP, Oxford, 2007) 699.

[40] Lady Justice Arden 'Jurisdiction of the new United Kingdom Supreme Court' [2004] Winter PL 699, 700.

[41] Contrast *The Future Role of the European Court of Justice. Report with Evidence. 6th Report of Session 2003–04* (HL Paper 47, 2004) 25–27.

[42] M Poiares Maduro 'Europe and the Constitution: What if this is As Good As It Gets?' University of Manchester. Constitutionalism Web-Papers <http://les1.man.ac.uk/conweb/ConWEBNo.5/2000> (April 2005) 21–26. N Barber 'Constitutional Pluralism and the European Union' (2006) 12 ELJ 306.

form of control is preferable to others. If Union measures were to be ruled invalid by a national constitutional court in such circumstances, the long-standing principle of primacy of Union law (Article I-6) would fall. As would the uniformity of its application, which shall, in theory, ensure equality before the law for all citizens of the Union. In any case, the ignition of an open conflict would bring with it considerable damage; but it can very well be that the sole possibility of its existence presses the Court to take an interpretation of its jurisdiction that is as broad and generous as possible. The nature of legal reasoning is such that it is plainly impossible to prove a firm connection between the course selected by the European Court in interpreting EC law and the anxieties and preferences expressed by national courts, but, in particular in matters associated with the limits of competence and the protection of fundamental rights, it is very tempting to conclude from available rich evidence in the case law that practice in Luxembourg is influenced by the vital need to maintain the loyal support of national judiciaries, especially those in the superior constitutional courts of Europe, whose voice cannot therefore be lightly ignored in the shaping of EC law.[43]

C. Abstract Control of International Agreements within the CFSP

Article III-325 CT sets out the general procedure to conclude an agreement with third countries or international organizations:

A Member State, the European Parliament, the Council or the Commission may obtain the opinion of the Court of Justice as to whether an agreement envisaged is compatible with the Constitution. Where the opinion of the Court of Justice is adverse, the agreement envisaged may not enter into force unless it is amended or the Constitution is revised.

This article is not part of Chapter II of Title V concerning the common foreign and security policy, which is excluded from the Court's jurisdiction via Article III-376, nor is it included in this article as a further exception. On its face, this seems to imply that the ECJ can also decide on the legality of those international agreements concluded pursuant to the CFSP. It is true that Chapter II of Title V contains an article which relates exclusively to these agreements; this provision, however, only makes it plain that the Union will be able to conclude them. There is no *lex specialis* regarding procedure or control. It is therefore difficult to argue that, since *lex specialis* derogates *lex generalis*, Article III-325 (11) CT cannot apply to CFSP agreements.

This argument is reinforced by Article III-325 (1) CT, which acknowledges the existence of a special procedure for the conclusion of agreements pursuant to the

---

[43] A-M Slaughter, AS Sweet and JHH Weiler (eds) *The European Courts and National Courts: Doctrine and Jurisprudence* (Hart, Oxford, 1998); J Schwarze (ed) *The Birth of a European Constitutional Order: the Interaction of National and European Constitutional Law* (Nomos, Baden-Baden, 2000); S Weatherill 'Activism and Restraint in the European Court of Justice' in P Capps, M Evans and S Konstadinidis (eds) *Asserting Jurisdiction: International and European Legal Perspectives* (Hart, Oxford, 2003).

Common Commercial Policy (Article III-315). This hints towards the applicability of this general procedure to all other agreements, which would include those adopted pursuant to the CFSP. Otherwise, this exception from the general rule would have also been listed in Article III-325.

Furthermore, and as I have already argued, the catalogue of exceptions contained in Article III-376 CT should be considered a closed one, given that any other interpretation gravely conflicts with the need to uphold legal certainty. It follows that it is possible for the ECJ to examine the compatibility with the Constitution of international agreements concluded pursuant to the CFSP, if a Member State, the European Parliament, the Council or the Commission request the Court to issue an opinion on the matter. This conclusion is corroborated by several working documents of the Convention, where the inclusion of this legal safeguard was discussed.[44]

VI. Protection of Individuals Against CFSP Measures

The ECJ can protect the rights of specific individuals against restrictive CFSP measures in two different ways: it can review the validity of restrictive Union measures implementing a European decision adopted under Article III-322 CT (since

---

[44] The precedent of Article III-325(11) is Article 300(6) EC; hence the question during the Convention was whether the prior opinion procedure contained in Article 300(6) should also apply to international CFSP agreements. The Secretariat suggested to the Discussion Circle on the Court of Justice the inclusion of an allowance for the Court 'to examine whether a planned international CFSP agreement would be compatible with the provisions of the Constitution', should a Member State ask for such a ruling (The European Convention. Secretariat *Judicial control relating to the common foreign and security policy* (Working Document 10 2003) 6). The majority of members of the Discussion Circle came in favour of applying this prior opinion procedure to international CFSP agreements, although a general consensus could not be reached: The European Convention. Discussion Circle on the Court of Justice *Supplementary report on the question of judicial control relating to the common foreign and security policy* (CONV 689/1/03 REV 1 2003) 3.

The lack of consensus yield the wording of then Article 33(12) in an early draft of the articles on external action of the Constitution, which restricted the jurisdiction of the Court. According to this provision, the ECJ would be competent only to give a prior opinion on whether 'an agreement envisaged is compatible with the provisions of the Constitution *over which the Court of Justice has jurisdiction*' (The European Convention. Praesidium *Draft Articles on external action in the Constitutional Treaty* (CONV 685/03 2003) 68. Emphasis added).

Later on, however, the Praesidium reconsidered this restriction and decided that 'the Court must have jurisdiction to examine the compatibility of a proposed international agreement that comes within the CFSP with the provisions of the Constitution' (The European Convention. Praesidium *Articles on the Court of Justice and the High Court* (CONV 734/03 2003) 28).

Following this decision, a new draft of the provision appeared: the phrase 'over which the Court of Justice has jurisdiction' had disappeared. The Praesidium explained: 'As requested by some Convention members ... restriction of the Court of Justice's jurisdiction with regard to prior opinions as regards CFSP agreements has been deleted.' (The European Convention. Praesidium *Draft sections of Part Three with comments* (CONV 727/03 2003) 56).

The new wording of this provision found its way into the draft Treaty (Article III-227(12) draft CT) and later on into the definitive text of the Constitution (Article III-325(11) CT), suffering only slight changes along the way.

this provision is not excluded from the jurisdiction of the Court) or under the exception of Article III-376(2) CT (against a European decision itself, if it provides for restrictive measures against individuals).

When considering restrictive measures adopted against individuals, it is necessary to bear in mind that they may or may not be of an economic nature. The Constitution contains a legal basis for the adoption of both; this is the result of an evolution which I will consider first. Consequently, I will distinguish between the jurisdiction of the Court to review restrictive measures in the draft Treaty and in the Treaty, and depending on whether they are or not of an economic nature.

I will argue that the inadequate jurisdiction given to the Court in the draft Treaty created a judicial gap. The changes introduced afterwards and contained in the final version of the Treaty sought to put remedy to this gap; the result is an improvement, in any case, although the final outcome would depend on the attitude of the Court itself due to the considerable leeway left to it when interpreting the relevant provisions.

A. The Legal Basis for Restrictive Measures

(i) Restrictive Measures of an Economic Nature

Restrictive economic measures are nowadays adopted under Articles 60 and 301 EC. These articles have been interpreted broadly, so as to allow the adoption of restrictive measures against persons or associations which exercised control over a country. Article 308 EC has also been resorted to, whenever no other legal basis was at hand.[45]

The Convention had to decide whether to include in the new drafting of these provisions within the draft Constitution a specific legal basis for the adoption of such measures against individuals. This was suggested by the Secretariat to the Discussion Circle on the Court of Justice[46] and found general support within the latter.[47] The second paragraph of the then Article III-219 (later Article III-224 draft CT) was introduced in the draft Treaty.[48]

The process of elaboration of this provision confirms, in my view, that it was the intention of the legislator to make international CFSP treaties amenable to constitutional review. Contrast written evidence by G Gaja in *The Future of the European Court of Justice, Report with Evidence. 6th Report of Session 2003–04* (HL Paper 47 2004) 74, 75. For a broader perspective, cf M Cremona 'The Draft Constitutional Treaty: external relations and external action' (2003) 40 CML Rev 1347.

[45] The European Convention. Secretariat *Judicial control relating to the common foreign and security policy* (Working Document 10 2003) 2. See also cases *Kadi* and *Yusuf*, n 3.

[46] The European Convention. Discussion Circle on the Court of Justice *Supplementary report on the question of judicial control relating to the common foreign and security policy* (CONV 689/1/03 REV 1 2003) 2.   [47] *ibid.* 1.

[48] Appearing for the first time in: The European Convention. Praesidium *Draft sections of Part Three with comments* (CONV 727/03 2003) 73.

(ii) *Restrictive Measures of a Non-Economic Nature*

There was, however, a parallel discussion within the Convention that deserves our attention: whether a legal basis for the adoption of restrictive measures against individuals, other than those of an economic nature, should also be made explicit in the draft Treaty. The most apparent example of this kind of measure would be a visa ban.

The prevailing view in this respect considered the inclusion of an explicit basis unnecessary. The Praesidium 'felt that this would entail a complication of the procedures and undesirable delay in application: an act adopted under the provisions of Chapter II introducing visa restrictions is directly applicable by Member States'.[49] The reasoning underlying this statement seems to be that Article III-219 (later Article III-224 CT), the legal basis for restrictive economic measures against individuals, provided legal basis for implementing measures to be adopted by the Council following a European decision. The Praesidium considered that a European decision imposing, say, visa restrictions, would be directly applicable by the Member States, and thus the unnecessary adoption of implementing measures by the Council on the basis of Article III-219 would only lengthen the process. A specific legal basis for the adoption of (implementing) restrictive measures of a non-economic nature against individuals was therefore not included in the draft Treaty.

This changed, however, during the works of the IGC 2003. The Basic Document drafted by the Secretariat suggested that the wording of Article III-224(2) was too ambiguous; it allegedly made it:

[...] possible to take action in an undefined and therefore very wide-ranging fashion [...] against persons (relating only to their assets, property? Does it also relate to visas, the right to move freely? Does it solely relate to administrative measures?).[50]

The specific changes proposed in the Basic Document were not followed. Nevertheless, the Working Group of IGC Legal Experts suggested a new wording intended to settle the matter:

Where a European decision adopted on the basis of Chapter II of this Title so provides, the Council may adopt restrictive measures under the procedure referred to in paragraph 1 against natural or legal persons and non-State groups or bodies.[51]

As we can see, the scope of Article III-224(2) has been considerably widened. The draft provision produced by the Convention related only to restrictive measures of

---

[49] The European Convention. Praesidium *Draft sections of Part Three with comments* (CONV 727/03 2003) 55.

[50] Conference of the Representatives of the Governments of the Member States. IGC Secretariat *Editorial and legal comments on the draft Treaty establishing a Constitution for Europe—Basic Document* (CIG 4/03 2003) 393.

[51] Conference of the Representatives of the Governments of the Member States. *Draft Treaty establishing a Constitution for Europe (following editorial and legal adjustments by the Working Party of IGC Legal Experts)* (CIG 50/03 2003) 191.

an economic nature. It is difficult to see how this could be ambiguous, given that the paragraph allowed the adoption of such measures 'in the areas referred to in paragraph 1'. Paragraph 1, in turn, referred to the following scenario: 'Where a European decision on a Union position or action adopted in accordance with the provisions on the common foreign and security policy in Chapter II of this Title provides for the interruption or reduction, in part or completely, of economic and financial relations with one or more third countries'. The ambiguity found by the Secretariat arguably rested on the fact that the situations 'referred to in paragraph 1' could be understood to be any situation in which a European decision was adopted 'in accordance with the provisions of the common foreign and security policy in Chapter II of this Title', and that the fact that these decisions had to provide for the interruption or reduction of economic or financial relations with third countries (i.e., the economic nature of the measures) related only to paragraph 1 and not to paragraph 2.

Be it as it may, the wording of Article III-224 draft CT was changed following the suggestion of the Working Group of IGC Legal Experts, erasing any reference to paragraph 1 and deciding for the wider option when asked to define properly the scope of this provision. Thus, the implementing restrictive measures shall be based on a European decision adopted on the basis of Chapter II (CFSP), and any alleged ambiguity related to the economic nature of such decision has been removed. This is the wording, with slight changes, that found its way into the definitive text of the Treaty, this time as the second paragraph of Article III-322 CT.

As a result, restrictive implementing measures can be adopted by the Council against individuals, if a European decision adopted pursuant to the CFSP so provides. These measures need not be of an economic nature; this therefore includes visa bans and the like. Finally, a legal basis for the adoption of non-economic implementing measures of this kind has been included, contrary to the opinion expressed by the Convention—which found the inclusion of such a basis superfluous, because it would allegedly only lengthen the process of application unnecessarily.

B. Review of Restrictive Measures Against Individuals in the Draft Treaty: Article III-282 Draft CT

As pointed out above, there was an explicit legal basis in the draft Treaty for the adoption of restrictive economic measures against individuals (Article III-224 draft CT). There was also the presumption that adoption of non-economic restrictive measures against individuals was possible too, be it as a directly applicable European decision (the Presidium's conception),[52] or adopting a different,

---

[52] The European Convention. Praesidium *Draft sections of Part Three with comments* (CONV 727/03 2003) 55.

wider interpretation of Article III-224 (the opinion of the IGC legal experts).[53] It is difficult to see how an interpretation of Article III-224 draft CT which included non-economic restrictive measures could have been adopted; it is much more logical to assume that a directly applicable European decision would have been needed.

According to Article III-282 of the draft Constitution, the Court was only to be allowed to review the validity of restrictive measures against individuals adopted under Article III-224 draft CT. Thus, all restrictive measures not adopted under this heading would have been immune to review; most likely, all restrictive measures of a non-economic nature, given that Article III-224 does not seem to be a suitable legal basis for them.[54] In conclusion, the role of the ECJ was very restricted—so much, that a gap in the protection of individuals would have been almost inevitable.

With regard to what the Court could do—the review of measures adopted under Article III-224 draft CT—it is perhaps necessary to point out that in no case could this have been otherwise, i.e., that restrictive economic measures adopted against individuals could have gone unchecked by the ECJ, had it not been for the proviso of Article III-282. Such measures would have been within the jurisdiction of the Court in any case (just like their predecessors, based on Articles 60, 301 or 308 EC). The exception to the jurisdiction of the Court, set out in the first paragraph of Article III-282 draft CT, affected only 'Articles I-39 and I-40 and the provisions of Chapter II of Title V of Part III concerning the common foreign and security policy'. Article III-224 was not part of the mentioned chapter. It follows that the inclusion of the proviso in question in Article III-282 had a merely explanatory intention, and that this provision was not a real 'exception to the exception'.

C. Review of Restrictive Measures Against Individuals in the Constitution: Article III-376(2) CT

Restrictive measures against individuals could be adopted under Article III-322 CT (implementing measures) or could be provided for in a European decision. In the first case, review of implementing measures is unproblematic because Article III-322 CT is within the jurisdiction of the Court, just as its predecessor in the draft CT was: it does not fall within any of the exceptions of Article III-376 CT. What does fall within one of such exceptions is the review of other restrictive (non-implementing) measures, those not adopted under Article III-322 CT: the exception contained in Article III-376(2) CT.

---

[53] Conference of the Representatives of the Governments of the Member States. IGC Secretariat *Editorial and legal comments on the draft Treaty establishing a Constitution for Europe—Basic Document* (CIG 4/03 2003) 393.

[54] On the shortcomings of this exception, cf *The Future Role of the European Court of Justice. Report with Evidence. 6th Report of Session 2003–04* (HL Paper 47 2004) 30–34.

Article III-282 of the draft Constitution becomes Article III-376 of the Treaty, but further changes have also taken place. The Court can now review 'the legality of European decisions providing for restrictive measures against natural or legal persons adopted by the Council on the basis of Chapter II of Title V'. The reference to legal basis has changed; whereas before the role of the Court was reduced to monitoring restrictive measures based on an article which—allegedly—allowed for restrictive economic measures only, now the Court can monitor all restrictive measures adopted under any provision of the CFSP, be they of an economic or non-economic nature.

The restrictive measures mentioned in the earlier text (Article III-282 draft CT) were not adopted on the basis of the chapter relating to CFSP, but on an article which was to be found outside of it (Article III-224 draft Treaty).[55] Since the old legal base was not part of the CFSP chapter, it was also not excluded from the jurisdiction of the Court. So, whereas the proviso inserted in Article III-282 draft Treaty with regard to Article III-224 constituted no real exception, this is not the case for the one finally inserted in Article III-376 CT. On the contrary, the present inclusion within the jurisdiction of the Court of any restrictive measures against individuals adopted pursuant to the CFSP is a clear exception from the formula contained in the first paragraph of Article III-376 CT.

And finally, another change further adds significance to this 'exception to the exception': whereas Article III-282 draft CT allowed for the review of implementing measures adopted by the Council following a European decision, Article III-376 CT allows for the review of European decisions themselves.

What is the main consequence of all these textual changes? It is one of no little importance: whereas under the draft Treaty the ECJ could only review restrictive economic measures against individuals (a significant but nevertheless limited category), the Constitution now allows the ECJ to review the validity of European decisions which provide for restrictive measures against individuals. These measures do not have to be of an economic/financial nature any longer; there is no further requirement as to their content or intention. The European decisions referred to are reviewable by the ECJ, even though adopted pursuant to the CFSP, as long as they provide for restrictive measures against individuals.

It is remarkable that an alteration of this calibre did not find its way into the Constitution until a very late stage in the process. The Discussion Circle on the European Court of Justice could not reach an agreement on whether the Court should have jurisdiction to review restrictive measures which affect individuals other than from a economic point of view.[56] Accordingly, this was not included in

---

[55] The equivalent of this provision is, in the Constitution, Article III-322, which also falls outside the exception of Article III-376 and is therefore within the full jurisdiction of the Court without the need for an explicit indication.

[56] The European Convention. Discussion Circle on the Court of Justice *Supplementary report on the question of judicial control relating to the common foreign and security policy* (CONV 689/1/03 REV 1 2003) 3.

the draft Treaty submitted to the President of the European Council in Rome on 18 July 2003. It is in the Basic Document containing editorial and legal comments on the draft Treaty which the IGC Secretariat sends to the Working Party of IGC Legal Experts that the main change is introduced.[57] The Working Party changes the wording only slightly,[58] and this will be the final text of the new Article III-376(2) in the definitive version of the Treaty.

D. Standing for an Individual to Bring an Action for Annulment of a CFSP Restrictive Measure

Let us firstly focus on the conditions under which a person will be able to bring a direct action before the ECJ. Such conditions shall be the ones set out in Article III-365(4) CT:

Any natural or legal person may . . . institute proceedings against an act addressed to that person or which is of direct and individual concern to him or her, and against a regulatory act which is of direct concern to him or her and does not entail implementing measures.

This provision plays with the distinction between legislative and non-legislative (regulatory) acts. The general rule for acts of a general nature, be it legislative or regulatory, is that the plaintiff must prove direct and individual concern. However, there is an exception which only bites when the plaintiff seeks to challenge a regulatory act which does not entail implementing measures—in which case only direct concern is needed.

There are thus three different tests than can be applied to elucidate whether the individual has *locus standi*[59]:

(a) If the measure at stake is an act addressed to the individual in question, she need not prove direct or individual concern.

(b) If the measure is a legislative act, or a regulatory act with implementing measures, she must prove direct and individual concern.

(c) If, on the contrary, we are considering a regulatory act which does not entail implementing measures, then she must only prove direct concern and the fact that there are no implementing measures.

In order to find out what test shall be applied when facing an action for annulment of restrictive measures adopted against individuals within the CFSP, we have to make a distinction. As we have seen above, these measures can be adopted by

---

[57] Second paragraph of Article III-282 should read, according to the suggestions of the Secretariat: 'reviewing the legality of decisions providing for restrictive measures against natural or legal persons, adopted by the Council on the basis of Chapter II of Title V.' Conference of the Representatives of the Governments of the Member States. IGC Secretariat *Editorial and legal comments on the draft Treaty establishing a Constitution for Europe—Basic Document* (CIG 4/03 2003) 436.

[58] 'European decisions' instead of 'decisions'. CIG 50/03 (n 51) 213.

[59] On standing of individuals before the ECJ under the Constitution, see generally T Tridimas 'The European Court of Justice and the Draft Constitution: A Supreme Court for the Union?' in

the Council following a European decision on the basis of Article III-322(2) CT. But it is also possible that a European decision contains such measures and it is detailed enough not to need implementation at Union level by the Council (national implementation is, of course, another matter).

In the first case (measures adopted by the Council on the basis of Article III-322(2) CT), the ECJ is competent because this provision does not fall within the area over which the Court is bereft of jurisdiction.[60]

In the second case (a European decision adopted pursuant to the CFSP), the Court would not normally be competent, given that the measure in question falls within the excluded area: Chapter II of Title V, concerning CFSP. However, the second paragraph of Article III-376 exceptionally allows for judicial review in this case.

Let us now examine both situations separately.

(a) Annulment of a measure adopted under Article III-322(2) CT

In this case, the individual would be facing a restrictive measure adopted by the Council on the basis of a European decision. This type of measure is an implementing one, as provided for in Article I-37(2) CT.[61] The form these implementing measures shall take is that of European implementing regulations or European implementing decisions (Article I-37(4) CT).

What we should bear in mind after reading these provisions is that the measures adopted on the basis of Article III-322(2) will be of a regulatory (i.e., non-legislative) nature. The test to be applied will thus be either (b) or (c), depending on whether there are implementing measures at the national level (in which case direct and individual concern is necessary) or not (in which case direct concern shall suffice). In the first scenario, although it is more difficult for the individual to have *locus standi*, we should not forget that an indirect challenge remains possible. The Court is competent to give a preliminary ruling on a case referred by a national court.

(b) Annulment of a European decision which provides for restrictive measures against individuals (Article III-376(2) CT)

Although the Court should not normally be competent to exercise review in this case, Article III-376(2) CT allows the Court 'to rule on proceedings [...] reviewing the legality of European decisions providing for restrictive measures against natural or legal persons'.

P Nebbia and T Tridimas (eds) *European Union Law for the 21st Century: Rethinking the New Legal Order* Vol 1(Hart, Oxford, 2004) 113, 120–125; *The Future Role of the European Court of Justice. Report with Evidence. 6th Report of Session 2003–04* (HL Paper 47, 2004) 38–44.

[60] Articles I-40 and I-41; the provisions of Chapter II of Title V, concerning CFSP, and Article III-293, insofar as it concerns the CFSP (Article III-376(1) CT).

[61] 'Where uniform conditions for implementing legally binding Union acts are needed, those acts shall confer implementing powers on the Commission, or, in duly justified specific cases and in the cases provided for in Article I-40, on the Council.' Article I-40, in turn, refers to CFSP.

Article III-376(2) is an exception which enables the Court to have jurisdiction within set limits. It follows that it will firstly have to check whether it is competent against the requirements of the provision before going on to check whether the plaintiff has standing. I refer to this now because this first test could also determine *locus standi* later on; if 'restrictive measures against natural or legal persons' is taken to refer to measures formally addressed to the individual, then the competence of the Court is reduced to the direct and indirect review of those measures, and consequently this narrow interpretation of the provision will also determine the standing of individuals: the logical result would be for the formal addressee only to be granted standing.

It follows from this reasoning that if the Court adopts a restrictive view of its competence by claiming jurisdiction to review only measures formally addressed to an individual—reading which could be yielded by an interpretation *ad litera* of Article III-376(2)—only the first test to determine whether the plaintiff has standing, (a), would be effectively applied. Theoretically, the Court could interpret its competence narrowly (so as to include only measures formally addressed to the individual) and still allow for an applicant other than the formal addressee to challenge the measure directly, as long as that individual satisfies the requirements of either (b), direct and individual concern, or (c), direct concern. This, however, would be very surprising: what would have been the point, then, of interpreting competence so narrowly? Surely, if the Court desired to narrow down the scope of this exception it would be with a view to making it less likely for a Union measure to be struck down. This purpose would only be served if *locus standi* was accordingly reduced. Consequently, it is logical to assume that if the Court decided to consider only the validity of those measures formally addressed to an individual, the formal addressee would be the only person with standing to bring an action.

On the other hand, it would not be outrageous to suggest a more extensive and progressive interpretation of this provision, whereby measures need not have the potential plaintiff as their formal addressee; 'restrictive measures against natural or legal persons' could be taken by the Court to refer to any measure that happens to have a restrictive effect on an individual. A European decision is, according to Article I-33 CT, a 'non-legislative act'. The test to be applied in order to determine where the individual has standing would thus be either (b) or (c), depending on the existence of implementing measures.

In which sense shall 'implementing measures', as referred to by Article III-365(4), be interpreted? Is it to be taken to include implementing measures taken both at Union and national level? It is submitted that this provision refers to the existence of national implementing measures, given that its background points towards the will to liberalize access to the Court[62] and to avoid situations like

---

[62] The very restricted access granted by Article 230(4) EC has been the subject of a persisting discussion on the suitability of some changes in the Court's attitude towards individuals. Most scholars

those encountered in *UPA*[63] and *Jégo-Quéré*,[64] where individuals could not resort to indirect challenge because there was no national implementing measure they could challenge before national courts. The existence of implementing measures at Union level does not have any significance in this regard.

Now that we have reached the conclusion that the 'implementing measures' referred to in Article III-365(4) are different from those adopted by the Council under Article III-322(2), we can see that the reason to apply (b) or (c) is whether national implementing measures have been adopted, and it would be indifferent whether the Council has been called upon to implement this European decision at Union level.[65]

To sum up: the scope of the exception contained in Article III-376(2) shall be defined in the future by the Court. It is unlikely that it will take to itself, by way of interpreting extensively the wording of the examined provision, the competence to review measures of a general (regulatory) nature adopted pursuant to the CFSP, on the basis that the decision affects individuals' rights in a very vague fashion. The purpose of this article is not to suggest such thing. On the contrary, the ECJ has a long record of being extremely cautious when it comes to allow the challenge of a Community measure by non-privileged applicants—which has been shown in its strict reading of the conditions to grant standing to individuals—and one can also expect great awareness of the political delicacy of the field in question. It is more likely that the Court will interpret its competence to review European decisions in this case as a narrow exception. But there is a spectrum of possible interpretations, from the most restrictive to the most extensive one. Whether the interpretation taken by the Court will be so narrow so as to require the existence of a formal addressee remains to be seen; it is especially difficult to venture a prediction since we do not know how much the new post-enlargement composition of the Court may affect attitudes.

---

have argued for a relaxation of these requirements. For a non-exhaustive account of this discussion, compare A Albors-Llorens *Private parties in European Community Law. Challenging Community measures* (Clarendon Press, Oxford, 1996); A Albors-Llorens 'The standing of private parties to challenge Community measures: has the European Court missed the boat?' (2003) 62 CML Rev 72; P Craig 'Legality, standing and substantive review in Community Law' (1994) 14 OJLS 507; M Hedemann-Robinson 'Article 173 EC, General Community Measures and Locus Standi for Private Persons: Still a Cause for Individual Concern?' (1996) 2 European Public Law 127; P Nihoul 'La recevabilité des recours en annulation introduits par un particulier à l'encontre d'un acte communautaire de portée générale' (1994) 30 Revue Trimestrielle de Droit Européen 171; F Ragolle 'Access to Justice for private applicants in the Community legal order: recent (r)evolutions' (2003) 28 ELR 90; JA Usher 'Direct and Individual Concern- an effective Remedy or a conventional Solution?' (2003) 28 ELR 575; A Ward *Judicial Review and the rights of private parties in EC Law* (OUP, Oxford, 2000). A Arnull *The European Union and its Court of Justice* (Oxford, OUP, 2006) 69–94.

  [63] Case C-50/00 *Unión de Pequeños Agricultores v Council* [2002] ECR I-6677.
  [64] Case C-263/02 *Commission v Jégo-Quéré* [2004] ECR I-03425.
  [65] This would, of course, be all but indifferent on a separate point: if competence of the Court to review European decisions is interpreted in the most possibly strict terms, then challenging a measure adopted under Article III-322(2) CT would be easier for the applicant; as seen above, there is no restriction to the jurisdiction of the Court in that case.

E. Effects of Article III-376 CT on the Potential Judicial Gap

Is it possible to conclude, then, that Article III-376(2) effectively deals with the potential judicial gap in the protection of individuals which its predecessor in the draft Treaty seemed to create?

The answer to this question crucially, although unsurprisingly, depends on how this provision is interpreted by the Court. There are various possibilities:

(i) The wording of Article III-376(2) is taken to include restrictive measures formally addressed against natural or legal persons (regardless of whether they are of an economic nature). In this case, the possibility for an individual to challenge a measure would also be available under CFSP, but under more restricted conditions than within the Community pillar. Only the formal addressee would effectively be allowed to put forward such challenge.[66]

(ii) This exception would be much more significant if the Court interpreted that the wording of Article III-376(2) is not referring only to measures formally addressing an individual; in that case, a potential plaintiff would be allowed to bring an action against a regulatory measure taken in this field (a European decision), if direct concern and lack of implementing measures could be proved. This would cover cases such as *Racke*,[67] rightly pointed out by Schermers[68] as an occasion in which a measure of general nature substantially affects the rights of an individual. A breach that would, of course, go unchecked if the approach described in (a) were taken.

Let us now consider a different point: reluctance to allow individuals to challenge a general measure directly has often been put down to the fact that an indirect challenge remains possible, and it is a more appropriate channel for the individual in that case.[69] We shall not forget that, if the Court opts for a very strict interpretation of its competence under Article III-376(2), it also curtails its competence to give preliminary rulings on the same subject-matter. The jurisdiction of the Court includes both direct and indirect review. Thus, if the Court adopts a very narrow range of possible scenarios where it will be able to accept the direct challenge of an individual, it is also rejecting indirect review as an alternative in cases where the direct action is not possible. Once it adopts an interpretation of its competence, it will determine when the Court can act both with regard to direct actions and preliminary rulings, i.e. direct and indirect challenges. The individual, therefore,

---

[66] Examples of this kind of measure would be the 'lists' at stake in Cases T-315/01 *Yassin Abdullah Kadi v Council and Commission* [2005] ECR II-3649; T-306/01 *Yusuf and Al Barakaat International Foundation v Council and Commission* [2005] ECR II-3533; T228/02 *Organisation des Modjahedines du Peuple d'Iran v Council*, Judgment of 12.12.2006 (Not yet reported); Pending Case T-229/02 *PKK and KNK v Council*, Application OJ C233, 28.09.2002, p 32.

[67] C-162/96 *A. Racke GmbH & Co. v Hauptzollamt Mainz* [1998] ECR I-03655.

[68] Written evidence by HG Schermers in *The Future of the European Court of Justice. Report with Evidence. 6th Report of Session 2003–04* (HL Paper 47 2004) 94, 95–96.

[69] This seems to be the attitude of the Court in its landmark decisions on the matter. See e.g. Case 294/83 *Les Verts v Parliament* [1986] ECR 1339, para 23; Case C-50/00 *Union de Pequenos Agricultores v Council* [2002] ECR I-6677.

would not be refused direct access to the Court on the grounds that indirect action would be more suitable; indirect action would also be impossible, and the individual would be left defenceless.

A most restrictive interpretation of Article III-376(2)—in the terms outlined above, affecting only measures with a formal addressee—leads to a considerable reduction of the scope of this 'exception to the exception'. In fact, the reduction is so significant it can hardly be accepted: it would mean that a European decision which affects the rights of individuals (albeit not having a formal addressee) and which has no implementation at Union level (measures adopted under Article III-322(2) would fall within the jurisdiction of the Court) is beyond any judicial control. Neither a direct nor an indirect challenge would be possible, because the competence of the Court is symmetrically defined in both modalities by the same provision. Cases such as *Racke*[70] would still remain unchecked, and the Constitution and the careful considerations that led to its wording would have meant no improvement.

There are further factors—arising out of the unique context in which the Court has shaped and continues to shape the legal order over which it presides—which could, in the future, push the Court towards an approach that is not so restrictive. On the one hand, it may wish to avoid external scrutiny by the European Court of Human Rights, as we shall see below. On the other, it may also wish to avoid a rebellion of national constitutional courts, as pointed out above: a thorough case-by-case protection could be the only reason why national constitutional courts do not feel compelled to claim jurisdiction to control CFSP measures in the abstract. These factors are of sufficient importance so as to influence the interpretation the Court makes in the future of its competence within this area, pushing it towards a more active role.

F. Possible State Responsibility for CFSP Measures before the ECtHR

As we have just seen, the real scope of Article III-376(2) CT would have to be determined by the Court. There would doubtlessly be many occasions in which this provision could not bite because the Court is not competent, *locus standi* conditions are not satisfied, etc. In those situations, the only resort left to the individual would be to seek protection before the European Court of Human Rights (ECtHR). In this section I will examine the different possible results this path could lead to.

Whether a single Member State or the Union itself would be condemned by the ECtHR because of a human rights violation arising from a CFSP Union act depends on whether the Union has acceded to the European Convention on Human Rights (ECHR) and accepted the jurisdiction of its court. If this has occurred, the ECtHR could review the legality of the CFSP measure and condemn

---

[70] C-162/96 *A. Racke GmbH & Co. v Hauptzollamt Mainz* [1998] ECR I-03655.

the Union itself, should the court find a breach of fundamental rights. Indeed, the CT foresees the accession to the ECHR.[71] Whether and in which terms this takes place would have to be determined later, and would thus not be a direct and necessary effect of the ratification of the Constitution. That is why it is required to consider a different possibility: one where Member States are the ones who are held responsible for a Union measure in breach of the Convention. I will analyse this second scenario first, since it will also give us the key to understand what is likely to happen once accession has taken place.

In the second possible scenario, the accession has not taken place, even though the CT is in force, and therefore the Union cannot be directly accused in Strasbourg by an individual. Would a Member State be responsible for a measure taken by the Union as a whole, even though its free sovereign will is replaced in this case by the will of an entity with full legal personality? The answer to this question lies in the case law of the ECtHR relating to the relationship between Member States and the European Community. The conclusions are applicable to the case of the Union, since the premises are the same: individual State sovereignty replaced by the will of a supranational entity with full legal personality. This entity is, however, not signatory of the Convention and cannot be held directly responsible for its acts.[72]

In *M & Co v the Federal Republic of Germany*,[73] the ECtHR laid down the foundations of the 'equivalent protection' doctrine: State action taken in compliance with international obligations is justified as long as the relevant organization protects human rights in a manner equivalent to that provided by the Convention. In *Matthews v UK*,[74] this test was applied and the Community failed because there was no remedy left to the individual: the ECJ had no jurisdiction to review the measure in question, a measure of primary law. Finally, in *Bosphorus*,[75] the ECtHR further clarified the conditions under which an individual Member State will be held responsible for the actions of the Community (or the Union, we can assume).

The following picture emerges from this case law: the test of 'equivalent protection', a tool which enables the Court to determine whether its intervention is required, will be used when:

(a) EC law measures are at stake (*Matthews*).
(b) National implementation of EC law measures is at stake, if national authorities enjoyed no discretion in the matter (*Bosphorus*).[76]

---

[71] Article I-9(2): 'The Union shall accede to the European Convention for the Protection of Human Rights and Fundamental Freedoms. Such accession shall not affect the Union's competences as defined in the Constitution.'

[72] For a fuller account of the arguments contained in this section, see A Hinarejos 'Bosphorus v Ireland and the Protection of Fundamental Rights in Europe' (2006) 31 ELR 251.

[73] *M. & Co v the Federal Republic of Germany* (App no 13258/87) (1990) 64 DR 138.

[74] *Matthews v the United Kingdom* Series A 1999-I 251 (1999) 28 EHRR 361.

[75] *Bosphorus Hava Yolları Turizm ve Ticaret Anonim Şirketi v Ireland* (App no 45036/98) ECHR 30 June 2005 (2006) 42 EHRR 1.

[76] The existence of national discretion means that Member States are fully responsible ('It remains the case that a State would be fully responsible under the Convention for all acts falling outside its

The Community will fail this test if there is a manifest deficiency in its standard of protection of fundamental rights.

Very clarifying for the purposes of this article is the concurrent opinion of Judge Ress in *Bosphorus*, who sustains that the protection of fundamental rights within the Union will be considered manifestly deficient if 'there has, in procedural terms, been no adequate review in the particular case'.[77] Examples of this dysfunction are cases where the ECJ lacks competence or when it has been too strict in its interpretation of *locus standi*.

Note also that the case law on Member State responsibility for EC measures provides, too, the key to understand how the ECtHR would control the activity of the Union, should accession take place. The very same test (equivalent protection, manifest deficiency) would be applied in that case; the end result would only be altered to the extent that the Union, and not the Member States, would be held responsible.

It is then no longer an uncertain hypothesis that the ECtHR could step in to review the validity of Union measures adopted pursuant to the CFSP, if the ECJ lacks competence to do so in the particular case; this consequence derives from previous case law of the Strasbourg Court and has recently been confirmed by the above-described and consistent approach taken in *Bosphorus*.[78] This means that a gap in the protection of individuals against CFSP measures—due to a too restrictive interpretation of either the competence of the Court or the rules of standing (Article III-376(2)) CT—could prompt the intervention of the ECtHR, be it to condemn the Union, if accession has taken place, or to condemn individual Member States in its place.

VII. Conclusion

The, at least theoretical, fall of the pillars envisaged by the CT produces an important change in the nature of the measures adopted in the field of CFSP. The shift from public international law to Union law has the effect of endowing these

---

strict international legal obligations' *ibid.*, para 157). The Court relied on abundant case law on this point: *inter alia, Van de Hurk v the Netherlands* (App no 16034/90) (1994) Series A No 288 (1994) 18 EHRR 481; *Procola v Luxembourg* (App no 27/1994) (1996) Series A No 326 (1996) 22 EHRR 193; *Cantoni v France* (App no 17862/91) Series A 1996-V 1614; *Hornsby v Greece* (App no 18357/91) Series A 1997-II 495 (1997) 24 EHRR 250. It also pointed out that the ECJ's judgment in *Kondova* is consistent with this view: Case C-235/99 *R v Secretary of State for the Home Department, ex p Kondova* [2001] ECR I-6427.

[77] *ibid.*, concurring opinion of Judge Ress, para 3.

[78] There is yet another way in which it could be possible to hold the Union responsible indirectly for a breach of human rights; in this case it would not be necessary for a Member State to be implementing a Union measure. The potential context in which such situations may take place in the future is very well illustrated by the *Senator Lines* case: *Senator Lines v Austria, Belgium, Denmark, Finland, France, Germany, Greece, Ireland, Italy, Luxembourg, the Netherlands, Portugal, Spain, Sweden and the United Kingdom* App no 56672/00. Decision of the European Court of Human Rights,

measures with 'stronger' features and, at the same time, of preventing them as a matter of EU law from being ruled invalid by national courts.

In this context, it seems of critical importance to examine the jurisdiction of the ECJ over such measures, as well as to determine its limits.

Article III-376 CT excludes from the competence of the Court Articles I-40 and I-41, the provisions of Chapter II of Title V (CFSP), and Article III-293 (insofar as it concerns CFSP). I have thus argued that the Court would still be entrusted with the tasks of ensuring the primacy of Union law (Article I-6), as well as policing the borders within the CFSP and any other policies of the Union (Article III-308), and I have sought to define the scope of those competences.

For the purposes of this article, and following our study of the different facets of the competence of the Court, I have further distinguished between an abstract control of constitutionality (that is, when the conformity of a measure to higher law is examined in the abstract), and protection of specific individuals (when the measure is challenged by an aggrieved plaintiff).

Whereas the mechanism of abstract control of constitutionality can be applied in all other fields, this cannot be the case within the CFSP, since the Court generally bereft of jurisdiction in this area by means of Article III-376 CT. On the contrary, there is no reason why international agreements adopted in this field should be excluded from abstract control: they are concluded under Article III-325(11) CT, which does not fall within the set of provisions referred in Article III-376 CT.

Since, however, international agreements are the only measures which the ECJ is allowed to control in the abstract, the question arises whether this very restricted control of constitutionality could upset the precarious equilibrium between the ECJ and the national constitutional courts. The latter can, at present, control the conformity of intergovernmental CFSP measures with their national constitutions; given that this would become impossible if the shift towards Union law takes place, these national constitutional courts may rise against supremacy and *Foto-Frost*[79] if they are not assured that control of constitutionality will be exercised effectively by the ECJ. Since the latter cannot exercise the required abstract control of constitutionality, it may be that protecting the rights of specific individuals very thoroughly on a case-by-case basis is the only way to maintain the confidence of the national constitutional courts in the role of the ECJ.

With regard to the protection of specific individuals, the ECJ is competent to review the validity of restrictive measures adopted against individuals in the field of CFSP (Article III-376(2) CT), as well as their implementing measures (Article III-322 CT). I have mainly focused on Article III-376(2) because it is a real

---

10/03/2004. The same mechanism was used in *Segi and Gestoras pro-Amnistía*, where the applicants brought an action before the European Court of Human Rights against all States members of the European Council: *Segi and others and Gestoras pro-Amnistía and others v Germany, Austria, Belgium, Denmark, Spain, Finland, France, Greece, Ireland, Italy, Luxembourg, the Netherlands, Portugal, the United Kingdom and Sweden* Series A 2002-V 371.

[79] Case 314/85 *Foto-Frost v Hauptzollamt Lübeck-Ost* [1987] ECR 04199.

exception to the exclusion of jurisdiction of the Court. I have examined above the evolution this provision has undergone since it was first included in the draft Treaty, where only revision of restrictive measures of an economic nature was contemplated. The final article of the Treaty contains no reference to the mentioned economic nature, which widens significantly the scope of this exception and seeks to put remedy to the judicial gap that loomed over its predecessor.

To what extent this judicial gap has been effectively avoided will crucially depend, nevertheless, on the interpretation the Court makes of its own competence, as well as of the conditions to have standing. It has been argued that both points have to be decided on the basis of the same text within Article III-376(2) CT ('European decisions providing for restrictive measures against natural or legal persons'). This provision gives the measure of the competence of the Court, firstly, and of *locus standi*, secondly. It follows that if a very restrictive—or extensive—approach is followed on the first stage of the test, it should also be followed on the second.

In theory, it would be possible for the Court to restrict 'European decisions providing for restrictive measures against natural or legal persons' to measures formally addressed to the plaintiff. It is nevertheless submitted that this is not an acceptable interpretation of the competence of the Court, since many measures likely to impinge on the fundamental rights of individuals would remain immune to judicial scrutiny.

Independently of how wide the mentioned interpretation is, and of how many cases get to be heard by the ECJ, we should ask ourselves what will happen with those which do not get that far. In this spirit I have examined the possibility of external control being exercised by the European Court of Human Rights, and consequently argued that, according to recent case law, the Strasbourg Court is willing to scrutinize Union action and find that there has been a 'manifest deficiency' in those cases where the ECJ lacks the necessary competence to protect individuals, or where it has interpreted the standing rules too strictly. Thus, the ECtHR could feel obliged to step in against CFSP measures. The perspective of a control exercised by an external court may prompt the ECJ to interpret both competence and standing requirements (as set out in Article III-376(2)) in an extensive manner.

On the whole, we can maintain that the judicial control of CFSP measures foreseen in the Constitution is less satisfactory than at national level, even when taking into account the wide scope of discretion generally left to national governments in this area. The German Federal Constitutional Court, for instance, has explicitly rejected the political questions doctrine.[80] Similarly, the French case shows that, even in a system which traditionally accepts the doctrine of *acte de gouvernement*, the courts are willing to reduce as much as possible the area which they are not allowed to enter.[81]

---

[80] *Inter alia*: *Saarstatut* case, BVerfGE 4, 157; *Grundlagenvertrag* case, BVerfGE 36, 1; *Rudof Hess* case, BVerfGE 55, 349.

[81] The category of *actes détachables* has been constantly enlarged: for instance, military activities unconnected with warlike operations are considered reviewable. TC 9 June 1986, *Eucat*, AJDA 1986.

Do the changes proposed in the CT deserved to be cherry-picked in the future? Not totally. We have come to the conclusion that lack of competence to control the constitutionality of norms in the abstract is a serious shortcoming, which could lead to conflicts with national constitutional courts. On the other hand, a judicial gap in the protection of aggrieved individuals could appear, but the Court could avoid it by adopting an extensive interpretation of its competence. It would be desirable, if the changes in the jurisdiction of the Court were to be reconsidered, to extend abstract control of constitutionality to CFSP measures and to phrase the 'specific individuals exception' differently, so that it is not possible for the Court to adopt a too restrictive approach. The scope of the jurisdiction of the Court on this particular point needs to be sufficiently clear to preserve legal certainty. I would therefore argue for a reconsideration of these arrangements, for a wider extension and for more clarity; let us seize the opportunity that the apparent 'failure' of the Constitution gives us, and reflect on the possibility of a more careful extension of the jurisdiction of the Court to the second pillar.

One cannot help but think that, were it given the opportunity, the ECJ would act under the premise of judicial restraint, like its national counterparts. The ECJ has never shied away from considering the validity of measures which touch upon foreign policy when they fell within their competence.[82] The Opinion of AG Jacobs in *Commission v Greece*[83] deals at length with the question of justiciability, and freely acknowledges that the Court should not enter an area such that legal standards are not anymore at hand. In general, if we believe that AG Jacobs' Opinion shows the most likely attitude of the Court, we can assume that judicial restraint would certainly be a prominent feature of ECJ decisions in the area.

Finally, we should be aware of the fact that patterns of political (as opposed to judicial) oversight of executive action in the field of foreign policy differ widely between national legal systems, on the one hand, and the Union, on the other. In the first instance, judicial control is part of a system of checks and balances which includes political control, generally exercised by national parliaments (albeit that the dominance of the executive is a common feature of contemporary political practice). This is, however, not applicable to the Union, given that there is no effective parliamentary control in matters of CFSP.[84] What is a common thread in all systems is that the judicial role must be respectful of the political patterns of representation and accountability. The relative lack of these values in matters of CFSP means that a case can be made in favour of a more embracing role for the ECJ.

---

456. Other examples include CE 19 February 1988, *Societé Robatel*, AJDA 1988. 354; CE 22 December 1978, *Vo Thanh Nghia*, AJDA 1978. 4. 36.

[82] Case C-124/95 *The Queen, ex parte Centro-Com Srl v HM Treasury and Bank of England* [1997] ECR I-81; C-120/94 *Commission v Greece* [1996] ECR I-3037. [83] *Ibid.*

[84] Under the Constitution, the role of the Parliament in this area is negligible. Neither consent nor consultation is required, Article III-325(6) CT; the European Parliament must be merely informed, Article III-325(10) CT.

The Monitoring of the Application of Community Law: A Need to Improve the Current Tools and an Obligation to Innovate

Rodolphe Munoz*

I. Introduction

The European Community is at a key moment of its history because for the first time, it has accepted 10 new Member States. Accordingly, it launched a discussion process without precedent: the Convention on the Future of Europe.[1] The aim was to provide solutions to the problems encountered by the development of European integration. The intergovernmental Conference decided to broadly follow the main points developed by the Convention. However, the fate reserved for the draft Constitution by the French and Dutch citizens implies at the very least that this text will need to be modified, for these two states.[2]

In any case, even if the draft European Constitution rises from the ashes, aspects dealing with the Community judicial remedies are unfortunately insufficient. For instance, the important case of the individual applicant within the framework of the action for annulment is tackled,[3] but the even more important question to know what can be done regarding the increase of non-application of EC law by Member States remains unanswered. The need to find solutions concerning the control of the application of EC law is today more and more important.

The establishment of the internal market was a genuine success. The deadline of 1993[4] was respected and a vast majority of the 1985 White Paper

* Lecturer, University of Liège, IEJE. The present paper has benefited from financial support from the Interuniversity Attraction Poles (IAP) Program P5/32 Research Action P5 initiated by the Belgian State, Federal Office for Scientific, Technical and Cultural Affairs. The author would like to thank S. Lecrenier, Head of Unit at the European Commission and D Millerot, Administrator at the European Commission. The usual disclaimer applies. This article has been published as a Jean Monnet Working Paper n°4/2006.

[1] <http://european-convention.eu.int>.

[2] See the current discussions concerning the action to be taken on the text of the European Constitution, Agence Europe n°9035 of 27 September 2005, n°9036 of 28 September 2005 and n°9151 of 15 March 2006. See also plan D set up by the Commission aiming to reopen the debate <www.europa.eu.int>.   [3] Article III-365 of the draft constitutional treaty.

[4] The Community internal market: 1993 report, European Commission, Luxembourg: EC, 1994, 2v.

measures[5] were adopted at the appropriate time. Admittedly, all the sectors did not profit in the same way from the establishment of a single market without frontiers. The Commission and Member States[6] are aware of this fact. Indeed, the services and the freedom of establishment are the subject of a particularly ambitious programme aiming to bring back the service market at the same opening level as the market of the products.[7]

The Commission also set up a system of monitoring the progress of the internal market.[8] The aim is to follow constantly the development and ensure a periodical assessment. This monitoring of the internal market is a valuable instrument because it makes it possible to show the positive achievements but also the problems encountered.

However, an effective internal market must be above all an internal market which enables private applicants to profit from the rights which result from it.[9] The Treaty of Rome established a number of legal tools which makes it possible to ensure that EC law arising from the Treaty is respected. Each one of these tools is connected to the others and forms, in practice, a system of Community legal remedies.[10]

Within the framework of the monitoring of the application of Community law, the main tool is the infringement procedure, Article 226 (former Article 169). The Commission is the main actor of this procedure. As guardian of the Treaty, the Commission must ensure that the rights of the internal market are implemented correctly in all the Member States. But today, the Commission cannot fulfil its role properly, because available tools are no longer sufficient to remedy the current problems. Indeed, even if this sounds commonplace, it must be stressed that this legal system was set up at a time when the Community was composed of Six States. Today, there are 25 States and soon 27[11] or even more in the future. It is therefore normal that the old mechanisms are no longer adapted to the current challenges. Of course, it does not mean that the mechanisms for monitoring

  [5] The completion of the internal market: White Paper of the Commission for submission to the European Council (Milan, 28–29 June 1985), European Commission COM final 1985/310/EC.
  [6] European Council conclusions of Lisbon of 24 March 2000 which envisaged the drafting of a specific action concerning the field of services before the end of 2000.
  [7] Communication from the Commission to the Council and the European Parliament: an internal market strategy for services/UE, European (2000) 888 of 29 December 2000 p. 6, pursuant to the requests made by the States at the European Council of Lisbon.
  [8] Communication of the Commission of 21 January 2004, Report on the implementation of the Strategy for the internal market (2003–2006) COM (2004) 22 final.
  [9] For an analysis of the difficulty encountered for the application of the judgments in another Member State, see 'Les effets des jugements nationaux dans les autres Etats membres de l'Union Européenne, Colloque du 24 mars 2000, Université Jean Moulin Lyon 3 faculté de droit centre des Etudes Européennes, Bruylant 2001 Bruxelles', more particularly the excellent article of Judge J-P Puissochet.
  [10] Berrod F., *La systématique des voies de droit communautaire*, Paris: Dalloz, 2003.
  [11] The accession of Bulgaria and Romania is planned for 1 January 2007, see *inter alia* Communication from the Commission to the Council and to the European Parliament, of 13 November 2002, 'roadmaps for Bulgaria and Romania' [COM (2002) 624 final—Not published in the Official Journal].

the application of Community law have not evolved. New tools have been introduced,[12] but it seems that it did not enable to hold back the surge of cases related to the non-application of Community law, as shown by the increasing number of enforcement Actions against Member States. Indeed, the number of the infringement procedures did not cease growing progressively with the development of European integration.[13] This constant rise is logical because it is the result of several factors. First of all, better knowledge on the part of citizens and companies of their rights; secondly an increase in the number of Member States and finally an increase in the competences of the European Community implying more Community legislations.

Consequently, two possibilities are opened to the Commission. Firstly, to implement a filter in order to limit the number of infringement procedures; or secondly, to fight for a drastic reform of tools to control the application of Community law.[14]

The first option implies the setting up of a selectivity policy in the treatment of the infringement procedures. This option is certainly tempting prima facie because it makes it possible to solve instantaneously the problem of the increasing number of complaints. However, as any shock therapy, it will have serious side effects for the patient, here, citizens and companies. Indeed, this method raises numerous interrogations of a legal, factual and political nature which make it inapplicable.

First of all, the increasing number of complaints received by the Commission is related to the fact that citizens and companies consider the latter as more capable of settling the problems that they encounter in the implementation of Community law. Following that statement, we can already conclude on the general satisfaction of complaints handling and therefore the necessary intervention of the Commission on the matter.

Secondly, the debate on the differentiated treatment of the complaints raises the problem of the role of the Commission in general. According to Article 211 of the Treaty, the Commission takes care of the application of the provisions of this Treaty and of the provisions taken by the institutions under the terms of it (. . .). The Commission cannot suddenly decide to use its role of guardian of the treaties only for certain types of complaint.

Thirdly, the major problem of such a system is to find on the basis of what criteria one should decide on the selection of cases which will be done by the

[12] See as regards the application of this article: 'L'obscure clarté' de l'article 228 par. 2 TCE/Bénédicte Masson. Revue trimestrielle de droit européen 2004, v. 40, n. 4, October–December, p. 639–668.

[13] Turner C. et Munoz R. 'Revising the Judicial architecture of the European Union' 19 *Yearbook of European Law*, Oxford University Press, 2000, pp. 1–95.

[14] The author stresses the fact that any proposal which would involve an amendment of the treaty does not fall within the competence of the Commission because, within the framework of the intergovernmental Conference it depends on the willingness of the Member States, see the procedure of amendment of the treaty which is in Article 48 EU.

Commission. Would it for instance be that before starting any infringement procedure, one should check how often the complaint has occurred, for. e.g. several complaints on the same subject are necessary to launch a procedure. But such an approach has the inevitable consequence that the damage related to the incorrect or non-application of the Community law has created a larger number of obstacles before the Commission decides to tackle it.

Lastly, the same policy should be implemented at the level of the entire Commission. This would need to ensure that the Commission's various services develop similar criteria and avoid having more severe criteria in one sector and more flexible ones in another.

Consequently, even if the application of the principle of selectivity seems attractive at first sight, it raises numerous difficulties in its practical implementation and could ultimately imply the weakening of the Commission's role and by way of consequence of the protection of citizens and companies.

The other solution would be to re-examine in detail the tools which the Commission has to ensure the monitoring of the application of Community law. It can then be decided whether to reform these tools or to create new ones. An inventory of tools at the disposal of the Commission to ensure the application of Community law shows three types of instruments:

Firstly, *ex-ante* control tools, i.e. aiming to make sure that the measures that Member States intend to take are in conformity with Community law.[15] This type of tool has the advantage of acting before the obstacles produce negative effects. The major positive aspect is that operators do not have to undergo negative consequences. Moreover, it is easier and quicker to modify a national law, when it is at a draft stage. Logically, the Commission has more opportunity to see its requests satisfied at this stage than once they are adopted. Indeed, if the request of changes arises only after the entry into force of the law, even if the Member State agrees to change it following the arguments of the Commission or in relation with the decisions of the European Court of Justice, there will inevitably be an appreciable lapse of time before it is cancelled and replaced. This is of course due to the legal and political decisions necessary to make these changes.

Secondly, *a posteriori* control tools, consisting of checking the national measures once they are adopted in the legal order of the Member States. This involves the traditional control of the compatibility of national law in relation to Community law. This encompasses mainly enforcement actions (Articles 226–228). The Commission is the main actor of this procedure, with the exception of Article 227.[16] This procedure aims to force Member States to fulfil their obligation but to give as well a uniform interpretation of EC law. Indeed, it is not only a question of checking the transposition of a directive, or communicating the national

---

[15] The Notification Directive 83/189/EEC of 28 March 1983, [1983] OJ L109 8–12, codified by Directive 98/34/EC of 22 June 1998, [1998] OJ L204/37–48.

[16] Simon D., *Système juridique communautaire*, 2001, 3rd edition, sp. p. 631 and s.

implementation measures but also of applying correctly the obligations laid down in the Directive, therefore, this implies a checking of national measures. The action on preliminary reference in interpretation (Article 234) also fits, in certain cases, into this logic aiming at checking the interpretation of the Community law in order to make sure that EC law is uniformly applied.

Thirdly, besides these two types of controls, there have been different tools aiming at the establishment of a mechanism of resolving a dispute out of Court. The SOLVIT System[17] connects together directly the national administrations of each Member State in charge of a specific sector in order to find a solution to a precise and concrete problem encountered by citizens and companies. Another tool to mention is the fast track mechanism[18] known as 'the strawberry regulation' which deals with cases arising from repeated breaches of Community law.

This article intends to carry out the assessment of these procedures of monitoring of the application of Community law and to propose new ones in order to adapt to the developments of the European Community.[19] Certain changes can be envisaged by a simple modification of the secondary legislation. For others changes, amendments to the Treaty will be required.

II. The Monitoring of the Application of Community Law: the Various Forms of Control

A. Ex-ante Control: Directive 83/189/EEC[20]– 98/34/EC[21]

(i) Presentation

The main example[22] of this type of mechanism is the notification procedure of Directive 98/34/EC. This instrument deals with national measures which are

---

[17] Munoz R., Le système SOLVIT: résoudre en dix semaines certains obstacles au marché intérieur, Journal des Tribunaux de Droit Européen No.2. April 2003, pp. 97–100.

[18] Munoz R., Comment pallier les manquements du recours en manquement, Revue Europe, February, pp. 4–6.

[19] The case of the preliminary reference procedure will not be approached. National courts and the European Court of Justice: a public choice analysis of the preliminary reference procedure, George Tridimas, Takis Tridimas, *International Review of Law and Economics 2004*, v. 24, n. 2, June, pp. 125–145.

[20] Directive 83/189/EEC of 28 March 1983, [1983] OJ L109/8–12, codified by Directive 98/34/EC of 22 June 1998, [1998] OJ L204/37–48; Concerning this procedure see *inter alia*: Lecrenier S., Le contrôle des règles techniques des Etats et la sauvegarde des droits des particuliers, Journal des Tribunaux Droit européen Year 5, n°35, January 1997, pp. 1–9; and Weatherill S., Compulsory notification of technical draft regulations: the contribution of Directive 83/189 to the management of the Internal Market Yearbook of European Law, 1996, n°16, pp. 129–205.

[21] The author stresses that numerous ideas result from discussions during the time spent in DG ENTERPRISES and more particularly the numerous exchanges of view with Mrs S. Lecrenier, Head of Unit at the European Commission.

[22] There also exists in certain matters of the obligation to notify as within the framework, for example, of Directive 93/43/EEC on the hygiene of food products, [1993] OJ L175/93 and Regulation 315/93/EEC laying down Community procedures for contaminants in food, OJ L37/93.

outside the harmonized field of the Community legislation, i.e., when there is no Community legislation on the matter or when Community legislation regulates a sector only partially.

This Directive requires Member States to notify the Commission of national measures containing technical rules[23] at a draft stage. This procedure was initially set up in 1983 by Directive 1983/89/EEC and has seen its scope widened[24] over the years. It now includes all industrial products, fishing and agriculture products. Another Directive, namely Directive 98/48/EC,[25] was adopted in order to apply such notification procedure to information society services.

Once the national draft measures are notified to the Commission, it has three months to react. During this time lapse, these drafts are translated into all the official languages of the Community. Then, they are sent to the Commission services, to all the Member States and are put on a public website for comments.[26] The Commission and Member States can adopt observations and detailed opinion, the latter having the characteristic to involve blocking the measure for three additional months.

This instrument aims therefore to establish a dialogue between the Commission and the Member States but also between the Member States themselves in order to avoid future breaches of Community law. It must be noted that comments from the Member States are today definitely more numerous than those from the Commission.[27]

(ii) State of Play

The notification procedure has now existed for more than 20 years and has made it possible to check more than 10,000 draft national measures containing technical rules. The assessment of this procedure is particularly positive by establishing a genuine dialogue between the Commission and the Member States. Indeed, the Commission and Member States can discuss and exchange their points of view on each notified measures. The other advantage is that it allows companies to be informed of the draft measures containing technical rules which will enter into force in the forthcoming months in each Member State.

---

[23] Directive 98/34/EC of 22 June 1998 ([1998] OJ L204/37–48), Article 1 §9 'technical regulation', technical specifications and other requirements, including the relevant administrative provisions, the observance of which is compulsory, de jure or de facto, in the case of marketing or use in a Member State or a major part thereof, as well as laws, regulations or administrative provisions of Member States, except those provided for in Article 10, prohibiting the manufacture, importation, marketing or use of a product.

[24] The Commission drew up this Directive in order that Member States notify the national measures at the draft stage, with a view to analysing if the national measures containing technical regulations could generate obstacles to free movement of goods. This Directive was amended three times, twice in the sector of products (Directives 88/182/EEC of 22 March 1988 and 94/10/EC of 23 March 1994) in order to increase its scope of application, codified by Directive 98/34/EC of 22 June 1998 ([1998] OJ L204/37–48).

[25] Directive 98/48/EC of 20 July 1998, [1998] OJ L217/18–26.

[26] <http://europa.eu.int/comm/enterprise/tris/index_fr.htm>.   [27] *ibid.*

Thus, companies can be ready to fulfil national legal obligation but can also contact the authorities of the issuing Member State, or of their own Member State, and/or of the Commission, if they consider that the envisaged measure is likely to involve unjustified obstacles within the internal market.

It must, however, be stressed that one of the reasons which explains the success of this procedure is that the Court of Justice made a particularly important judgment[28] in which it indicated that if a Member State does not notify its measure at a draft stage, then the national text adopted without notification is regarded as never having existed and cannot therefore produce a legal effect. Vis-à-vis such a consequence, Member States prefer therefore notifying rather than incurring such a sanction.

The Commission publishes a report every three years on the application of this Directive.[29] In general, it appears that this procedure is particularly well tested and gives rise to a genuine exchange between the Member States and the Commission.

The development of the scope of the notification procedure since the first Directive of 1983 has been revealing regarding the interest that such a mechanism can have. Thus, if at the start it was envisaged that the Member States notify only certain draft technical measures, now, after the successive modifications, Member States have to notify all draft technical measures dealing with industrial, fishing and agricultural products. Moreover, since the introduction of this notification procedure in the field of information society in 1998, 70 draft regulations have been checked between the beginning of 1999 and February 2003,[30] now the last figure shows more than 171 notifications.

B. A Posteriori Control: The Procedure for Enforcement Action

(i) Article 226 Procedure

In 2001, there were 3,360 ongoing infringement files[31] compared to 3,541 in 2002. Obviously all these cases do not end up in front of the Court of Justice.

The procedure for enforcement action foresees an administrative (or precontentious) phase and only then, a contentious phase. At the time of the precontentious phase, the various stages of the procedure (letter pre-Article 226, letter of formal notice and reasoned opinion) make it possible to reduce considerably the number of infringement files. Indeed, the number of formal notices is definitely less high than the number of detailed opinions or than the number of referrals to the Court of Justice.

---

[28] Case C-194/94, CIA Security International of 30 April 1996, ECR I-2201; Simon D., Revue Europe, 1996 June, n° 245 p. 11–12.

[29] <http://europa.eu.int/comm/enterprise/tris/index_fr.htm>.

[30] XX° Commission Report, COM (2003) 669 final: <http://europa.eu.int/comm/enterprise/tris/reps_2002_1999_IS/COMM_PDF_COM_2003_0069_F_FR_ACTE.pdf>.

[31] <http://www.europa.eu.int/comm/secretariat_general/sgb/droit_com/pdf/dg_fr31-12-2001.pdf>.

As an indication, in 2001,[32] 1,050 letters of formal notice were sent, against 569 reasoned opinions. During the same period of time, 'only' 162 cases were submitted to the Court of Justice. It must be stressed that these figures are in constant increase from one year to another.[33] The total number of infringement procedures initiated by the Commission increased by 15 per cent (going from 2,356 in 2002 to 2,709 in 2003). Thus, on 31 December 2003,[34] there were 3,927 ongoing infringements cases: i.e. 1,855 cases in which a procedure was initiated, 999 cases where a reasoned opinion had been sent, and 411 cases referred to the Court of Justice.

More worrying: for 69 cases, the procedure of Article 228[35] had already been started. It is also interesting to consider the judgments of the Court in which Member States were condemned but had not yet carried out these judgments[36] as laid down in the XXI° Commission Report. Moreover, in 2002, 33.6 per cent of the cases of infringement had been opened for more than two years.[37] Lastly, in the majority of cases referred to the Court of Justice, the Member State is condemned. Thus, in 2004, on all the judgments for infringement procedure adopted by the Court of Justice, Member States had been condemned in more than 92 per cent of the cases.[38]

The Article 226 action is one of the cornerstones of the Community system. It appears as an exception within the framework of the international relations between the States not only for its nature but also because it is repeatedly used by them. However, even if the central role of this procedure in the establishment of the Community must not be underestimated, it has to be noted that it has numerous disadvantages which have increased after the deepening and widening of the Community.

First of all, it is an a posteriori approach, i.e. it acts only once the problem has caused damage, sometimes irreparable, to the citizens and/or to the companies such as, for example, the bankruptcy of a company. Consequently, Article 226 procedure has the disadvantage of acting, most of the time, too late.[39]

---

[32] <http://www.europa.eu.int/comm/secretariat_general/sgb/infringements/19report_2001_fr.htm>, Annex 2, p.19 Document 2.1.

[33] Decrease can be noticed for certain years but that is linked to artificial inflation the previous year due to specific litigation.

[34] XXI Commission Report on the monitoring of the application of Community law Brussels, 30 December 2004, COM (2004) 839 final, see sp. p. 4; <http://europa.eu.int/eur-lex/lex/LexUriServ/site/fr/com/2004/com2004_0839fr01.pdf>.

[35] XXI quoted Report note 35, annex II, table 2.3.; see also for a detailed presentation of new cases <http://europa.eu.int/eur-lex/fr/com/rpt/2003/act0669fr02/1.pdf> sp. p.9.

[36] <http://www.europa.eu.int/comm/secretariat_general/sgb/droit_com/pdf/rapport_annuel/annexe5_fr.pdf>.

[37] Annex I of the XXI Report sp. p.3 <http://www.europa.eu.int/comm/secretariat_general/sgb/droit_com/pdf/rapport_annuel/annexe1_fr.pdf>.

[38] The annual report 2004 of the Court of Justice indicates that of the 155 cases based under Article 226, Member States were condemned 144 times <http://curia.eu.int/fr/instit/presentationfr/rapport/stat/st04cr.pdf> sp. p. 179.

[39] Tomasevic D., L'usage du référé devant la Cour de justice à l'encontre des Etats membres de la Communauté européenne, RMUE, No. 4. 1999. pp. 25–43.

Secondly, the time of treatment of the complaints is the major problem of the procedure. Indeed, if, in comparison with disputes before national jurisdiction, the procedure cannot be considered as unreasonably long, it must be stressed that very often this period in front of the Community jurisdictions is added to the period in front of the national jurisdictions. Thus, when the Member State does not obey and decides to go before the Court of Justice, an infringement procedure lasts at least several years.

Moreover, this long procedure also applies in the case of an 'obvious' breach of Community law. It can be the case, for example, if the State does not communicate the national measures of implementation of a Community Directive.[40]

Thirdly, one must take account of the fact that the increasing number of referrals to the Court of Justice following an infringement procedure for breach of Community law takes a part in the obstruction of the European legal system, implying at the same time the slowing down of the treatment of other cases by the Court.

Fourthly, generally, once the infringement procedure is finished, the complainant will have to launch a national procedure for damages caused by the non-application of the Community law.[41] All this implies an even longer time for an effective treatment of the complaints and especially for the recovering of the damage suffered by the interested parties.

Fifthly, Article 226 procedure is less problematic for big companies than for SMEs which however account for 95 per cent of the Community industry.[42] Indeed, the biggest companies will have more financial facility to launch a procedure at Community level. It is economically still viable for a multinational to carry on complaints and to await the results of the Commission analysis and the judgment of the Court of Justice. Whereas an SME would have to close its doors if it has to wait until the end of the procedure. Consequently, it will have either to give up selling its product, or change its production and adapt it to the conditions imposed by the State of destination which at the same time means overbidding the price of the product.

Sixthly, States are also used to playing with the delays of this procedure. For instance, it is possible for a State to violate with impunity Community law for several months, or even several years, and then to comply just before the referral to the Court of Justice in order to avoid a condemnation. Article 226 does not make it possible to deal with this type of violation whilst it happens quite often and penalizes States which comply with EC law.

Lastly, for the Commission, the cost in terms of human resources of the current approach is very heavy. Indeed, it must initiate numerous Article 226 procedures and mobilize numerous civil servants in order to follow them.

---

[40] Even if in the case of non-communication of the transposition measures, the Commission does not proceed to send a pre-Article 226 letter.

[41] Takis Tridimas 'Liability for breach of Community law: growing up and mellowing down?' Common Market Law Review 2001, v. 38, n. 2, April, pp. 301–332.

[42] <http://epp.eurostat.cec.eu.int>.

It is therefore necessary to reform the current system of Article 226 procedure in order to create a genuine more reactive mechanism and thus meeting the citizens and company expectations. It is not a question of denying old mechanisms but more an opportunity to propose ways to adapt the current system in order to enable it to answer to the challenges of a Europe of 25.

(ii) The Specific and Worrying Case of the Transposition of the Directives

The Directive is one of the instruments at the disposal of the Community institutions pursuant to Article 249 TCE. It has as its specific character to envisage the aims of a measure and to leave to the Member States the choice of the means to achieve the goals defined in the Directive. However, Member States encounter several difficulties at the time of the Directive transposition and the Commission seems to be overwhelmed by the extent of the task it has to achieve.

Moreover, Directives which are not transposed or only partially so within the assigned time should be added and Directives which are badly transposed are also added to this list. Another particularly important point which must be underlined is the number of transposition of Community Directives within the time prescribed by the Directive and which are not subject to Article 226 procedure. Therefore, the number of Directives which give rise to an Article 226 procedure represents only the visible part of the iceberg.

Lastly, it must be stressed that 'problematic' Directives i.e., the Directives which were not transposed, differ from one State to another. This detail is of significance, indeed in a sector where a Directive is not transposed, the internal market is not harmonized and obstacles persist. But if, for example, each State does not transpose five different Directives, it is not 'just' in five sectors that there will be potential obstacles but probably in five X 25 sectors, i.e. 125 sectors.

Recent figures from the Commission show that, the average rate of communication of national measures of implementation on 7 September 2005[43] is 98.88 per cent (knowing that it does not prove in any way that the adopted measures are correct and are not likely to involve a procedure for bad transposition). This rate is in constant increase as a result of the repeated efforts of the Commission which decided to check systematically that States forwarded these documents.

However, vis-à-vis these good results, it must be known that if 'only' 1.12 per cent of non-communication of national implementation measures represents, due to the number of Directives (2601), almost 30 Directives by State. Applying the calculation that we made earlier, it gives us 25 X 30, i.e. 750 sectors where harmonization is not effective. However, the author is aware that in many cases it is the same Directive which is not transposed in more than one country.

Indeed, when reading the 19th annual report[44] on the monitoring of the application of Community law, it is clear that the main reason for launching

---

[43] <http://www.europa.eu.int/comm/secretariat_general/sgb/droit_com/pdf/mne_country_20050907_en.pdf> sp. p.2.   [44] See note 31.

infringement procedures is the non-communication by the Member States of the national measures of implementation of Directives. Regarding formal notices sent in 2001,[45] for 13 Member States, at least 50 per cent of the letters of formal notice concern cases of non-communication. Moreover, for nine Member States, the cases of non-communication account for 60 per cent or more of letters of formal notice. If one continues analysing the results for the following phase, which is the phase of the detailed opinion, figures remain high. For 10 Member States, 50 per cent of the detailed opinions sent by the Commission during 2001 concern cases of non-communication of the national measures of non-transposition.

Lastly, as regards the referral of the Court of Justice, figures remain high despite a slight decrease, because for Six States, the cases of non-communication account for 50 per cent or more of the cases brought to the Court of Justice. Furthermore, for four States, this type of cases concerns almost 70 per cent of the cases.

Figures of previous reports (1998, 1999 and 2000), support this analysis.[46] Indeed, for previous years also, the principal reason of letters of formal notice, of reasoned opinions and of referral of the Court of Justice is the non-communication of the national transposition measures. Consequently, it is clear that the cases of non-communication of national implementation measures represent a large majority of cases for which the Commission is responsible within the framework of Article 226 procedure.

All these figures are even more evocative when the other cases related to the transposition of Directives having involved the opening of an Article 226 procedure are added. Indeed, there are three hypothetical cases: first of all, the cases of non-communication that we have just approached, then, the cases of non-conformity and finally the cases of incorrect application. The cases of non-conformity are the ones where the Member State transposed a Directive in time and have communicated the national transposition measures but have wrongly transposed the obligations of this Directive. The cases of incorrect application concern cases where the Directive was transposed correctly but was badly implemented by the national authorities. These three cases cover 80 per cent or more of the letters of formal notice[47] and of the detailed opinions for all 15 Member States and 80 per cent or more referrals of the Court of Justice for 13 Member States, as laid down in the XIX° report.

These figures are confirmed by the following reports. Indeed, the very last report (XXI°) shows comparable results. It is even possible to note an increase of the impact of non-transposition and non-conformity on Article 226 actions. As regards the sending of the letters of formal notice, the non-communication of Directives accounts for 60 per cent of the cases for 14 States out of 15. It must be noted that it goes up to 70 per cent for 10 of these States and reaches more than 80 per cent for four of them.

---

[45] See note 31, specifically Table 2.2.1. Formal notices sent in 2001 by legal basis and Member State, page 20.
[46] See the site of the Secretariat General of the European Commission: <http://www.europa.eu.int/comm/secretariat_general/sgb>.   [47] See note 35.

Concerning reasoned opinions, the non-communication accounts for more than 50 per cent of the cases for 14 States out of 15 and this figure increases to more than 70 per cent for 4 States.

Lastly, the referrals account for more than 50 per cent for eight States. Moreover, if the cases of non-conformity are added, cases which could normally be avoided in the event of effective control of the transposition, they account for more than 50 per cent for 11 States.

It appears therefore necessary and important to take measures in order to sort out these types of dispute with other tools than Article 226. This would enable the institutions to tackle this constant increase of cases linked to the implementation of Directives obligations.

(iii) The Current Reactions vis-à-vis this situation

Member States

Firstly, Member States must interpret the obligations contained in the Directives. However, due to linguistic problems or following modifications of these Community texts during the legislative process, it appears sometimes difficult for the relevant ministries in the various Member States to understand clearly the obligations arising from the Directives. It means that the various experts in charge of the transposition have to carry out an interpretation of the content of the Directive in order to ensure its transposition.

But it should be noted that there is a solution to this problem of interpretation provided for in the Directives themselves and in the Treaty. First of all, most of the Directives have a clause which requires Member States to transmit national measures of transposition. It enables the Commission to know how far the Member State is in the implementation of the transposition measures and what are the problems it encountered. It is therefore an indicator because if the majority of States did not provide these intermediate measures, then the Commission can deduce that there is a problem.

Another possibility for the Member State is to inform the Commission of its interrogations concerning the interpretation of certain Articles of the Directive. Pursuant to Article 10 of the Treaty, Member States must do everything to co-operate in the implementation of the Community law. Consequently, the civil servant in charge of the file in the Member State which encounters difficulties in the interpretation of the Directive can contact the service in charge of the control of the transposition of the Directive at the European Commission in order to raise the difficulties encountered at the time of the drafting of the transposition measures.

If each Member State takes a different measure but which allows the Directive to be interpreted in the same way, it is not likely that this will create obstacles to freedom of movement. However, in the hypothetical case where Member States have divergent interpretations, then it becomes difficult to ensure the consistency of the Community system and obstacles to freedom of movement will appear whilst the aim of the harmonization measure was to avoid such obstacles. The solution is then to ask either via a preliminary reference or via an infringement procedure to the Court of Justice to interpret the Article of the Directive in question.

Secondly, some Directives require the involvement of several ministries inside the same Member State and the use of various legal tools. This can create certain difficulties of co-ordination in order to transpose the Directives. Consequently, it can happen that certain parts of the Directives are not transposed or are transposed very late due to the multiplication of the measures aiming at their transposition despite the various attempts by the Member States to rationalize the transposition of the Directives.[48]

Lastly, apart from certain exceptions, States do not monitor at all or only a little the application of the obligations arising from the Directives. This lack of follow-up makes the officials' work difficult because if there is a lack of political will to ensure a transposition on time, then it will be difficult, or even impossible, for the officials in charge of the file to force the other ministries to act.

The Commission

The Commission has a relatively passive role during the transposition phase. Its function becomes more active at the time of *a posteriori* control, once the date of transposition has passed. Moreover, at the time of the receipt of these intermediate measures, the Commission does not have sufficient means to analyse in detail these measures in a period of time sufficiently short as to ensure that comments arrive before the end of the period of transposition.

The Commission under a Communication[49] evokes possible solutions vis-à-vis the limits of the Article 226 procedure. This text, full of good wills, is only suggesting very good old solutions which have proven insufficient, as we demonstrated above.

The Commission knows that the infringement procedure is not adequate to deal with these types of cases, therefore it had fixed as a main goal the prevention of infringements. To this end, it developed three lines: greater transparency and knowledge of Community law, better co-operation between the Commission and the Member States and finally a larger communication of the transposition measures.

To improve this dialogue, the Commission proposes strengthening preventive co-operation between the Commission and the Member States. To this end, it recommends a broader use of the tools which have already proved their worth. It includes the interpretative Communications, the reporting obligation under Directive 98/34/EC, the regular publication of the statistics of the national

---

[48] See the case of France described in: Jean-Luc Sauron, L'administration française et l'Union européenne, 2000, La documentation française «Connaissance de l'administration française», sp. p. 127 à 167.

[49] Communication of the Commission on the improvement of the control of the application of the Community law, COM (2002) 725 final/3 of 20 December 2002.

measures of transposition of the Directives in the annual report on the monitoring of the application of Community law, the anticipation of certain major events, and finally a better exchange of information and of good practices. Moreover, the Commission proposes launching a specific Community law training programme for administrations, legal specialists, and national barristers.

The second objective put forward is the accompaniment and facilitation of a good transposition of Directives. Indeed, the transposition rate did not reach the levels recommended by the European Council of Stockholm. Several measures are therefore proposed. First of all, the Commission intends to increase the transparency level on the matter. Indeed, it is envisaged that a specific site gathering all the information concerning the national transposition measures is created. Moreover, the use of electronic means should encourage the sending of these measures in time and to the service concerned.

Then, the Commission wants to develop co-operation before the deadline of the transposition period. This approach aims to solve the problems before the non-transposition of the European Directives has produced negative consequences for private individuals and companies. There are three type of actions aimed at improving co-operation between the Commission and the Member States. The Commission intends initially to extend the practice of the 'package meetings'. Through these meetings, the Commission will try to encourage each Member State to set up unique 'co-ordination bodies' responsible for the application of Community law. Then, the Communication stipulates that the Commission services will contact the relevant Member States in the month of the adoption of the Directive and will propose their technical assistance. Moreover, the Commission commits itself to analyse certain preliminary drafts of national transposition measures in order to check their compatibility with Community law.

The other action, in this area, envisages the establishment of a contact point for discussion regarding transposition in co-ordination with the Member States. Its aim is to give interpretations and clarifications on the contents and the scope of the Community obligations.

Lastly, the Communication aims to improve the quality of the national transposition measures. Accordingly, the Commission has the intention to require Member States to provide a table of concordance showing clearly what measures have been taken in order to transpose each article of the Directive. Moreover, for this transmission, a standard electronic model will have to be used and the Secretariat-General of the Commission will become the central and single point of receipt of the national transposition measures. Lastly, the Commission wants to develop a network of databases with all the national transposition measures (known as the EULEX III project).

The third line aims to increase public information on Community law. To this end, the Commission intends to develop greater accessibility of Community law for citizens. To this end, the databases EUR-LEX and the gate mentioned previously should be put at the disposal of European citizens. Moreover, the

Commission is exploring how to develop specific means allowing a better participation of citizens as well as easier access to information. On this last point, the Commission takes the example of the Aarhus Convention[50] in the framework of the environmental policy.

The Court of Justice

On a preliminary basis, it should be noted that this article is not intended to deal with the current efforts made to improve the efficiency of the Community legal system with a single exception: it will briefly address the issue of enforcement actions for non-communication of the national transposition measures.

Today, the Court of Justice treats Article 226 actions for non-communication of the national implementation measures through a rapid and standardized procedure. The opinion of the Advocates General is thus also shortened and rationalized.[51]

The judgments of infringement were also standardized. This set of measures has shortened much if not nearly all the phases before the Court of Justice, such as, for example, translations.

The Court of Justice has thus gained valuable months in the treatment of Article 226 actions. The time of treatment of direct recourse is today 20 months.[52] However, even if this figure shows the will of the Court of Justice to quickly treat the cases of obvious failure, it remains considerably long in relation to the practical consequences of the judgment. Indeed, the judgment only recognizes the infringement and does not impose more to the State than the obligation to remedy this infringement within a reasonable time.

C. The Creation at the End of the 1990s of Alternative Mechanisms

Facing the challenges that the monitoring of the application of Community law represents, the Commission, due to the repeated refusals of the Member States to modify Article 226 procedure at the time of the various intergovernmental Conferences,[53] had to develop solutions without amending Article 226. Consequently, it adopted ad hoc mechanisms aiming at filling the gaps of the infringement procedure.

This does not involve at all amendments of Article 226 but complementary alternative mechanisms which deal with problems which are specific such as the incorrect application of Community law or the foreseeable breaches of Community law.

[50] <http://europa.eu.int/comm/environment/aarhus>.

[51] See, *inter alia*, the discussions concerning the approach of the Court of Justice: Francis G. Jacobs 'Recent and ongoing measures to improve the efficiency of the European Court of Justice', 2004, E.L.Rev., pp. 823–830.

[52] <http://www.curia.eu.int/fr/instit/presentationfr/index_cje.htm>.

[53] Mattera A., La procédure en manquement et la protection des droits des citoyens et des opérateurs lésés, RDUE, n°3, 1995 pp. 123–166.

Two mechanisms, which differ both by their objectives and by their respective scope, enter into this category: firstly, SOLVIT[54] which applies to the internal market, and secondly, the mechanism of Regulation 2679/98/EC,[55] which concerns only the free movement of goods.

The SOLVIT mechanism aims to solve the problems of the incorrect application of Community law by the national administrations. This involves therefore the cases where States transposed Community law but did not apply it correctly. This refusal can arise from several reasons like, for example, the simple fact that the administrations in charge of applying the specific piece of legislation have not been informed yet of the new Community legislation. Another reason could be the mechanical application of national measures without taking into account the existence of EC principles such as the prohibition of discrimination on the basis of nationality.

The second mechanism is Regulation 2679/98/EC, it aims to prevent foreseeable obstacles. It develops a fast warning mechanism between the Member States. For example, Member States could use it if they are informed of an imminent obstacle, like a strike which would block an important motorway axis, for instance.

(i) *The SOLVIT Mechanism*

Presentation
This system is based on three simple principles. Firstly, on the principle that the non-application or the incorrect application of the Community law arises most of the time because the national administrations are not informed of Community law. It might be enough therefore to inform these national administrations which automatically realize that they are contravening Community law.

The second principle is that when a problem arises, it is preferable to know how the national administration works so as to be able to know who to contact in order to end the breach of Community law. To this end, it is therefore preferable that the request emanates from a centre established in the State responsible for the breach, a centre composed of people who know very well their own national administration, than from an administration of another Member State or of a Community institution.

The last principle is that requests are dealt with in a diligent way if persons know each other. This involves therefore creating a centres' network in all the

---

[54] Communication from the Commission to the Council, to the European Parliament, to the Economic and Social Committee and to the Committee of the Regions of 27 November 2001, an effective system of resolution of the problems in the internal market (SOLVIT), COM (2001) 702 final; Recommendation of the Commission of 7 December 2001 'laying down the principles for the use of SOLVIT'—the network of resolution of the problems in the internal market, C (2001) 3901 final; Council Resolution 'Internal market, Consumers and Tourism' of 1 March 2002, see: <http://europa.eu.int/comm/internal_market/solvit/council-conclusions/conclusions_fr.pdf>.

[55] Council Regulation (EC) n°2679/98 of 7 December 1998, on the functioning of the internal market in relation to the free movement of goods among the Member States [1998] OJ L337/8.

Member States and ensuring that these centres know each other and communicate easily among themselves.

Consequently, each Member State must have a SOLVIT centre[56] and these centres are connected among themselves by a common database, the SOLVIT database. All the mails are sent electronically. The SOLVIT mechanism is therefore a network of contact points in the administrations of each Member State. These centres aim to solve the transnational cases related to the incorrect application of the Community law by a national administration.

Thus, if a citizen (or a company) of a Member State encounters a problem in another Member State in the application of the rights that he gains from Community law, he can contact by electronic mail, telephone, or fax the 'origin' co-ordination centre (it is the centre of the country from which the complainant is a national). An essential point for the success of the procedure is that the citizen or the company must formulate the encountered problem clearly. Indeed, the more the problem is identified clearly, the more it can easily be solved. The contacted 'origin' co-ordination centre becomes the centre responsible for informing the citizen or the company of the follow up given to their case.

The 'origin' co-ordination centre will then contact the State where the problem arises. The centre of this country becomes the 'leader' co-ordination centre. This centre will firstly have to indicate if it accepts the case. It has a week to take this decision. In the affirmative, it means that it commits itself to give an answer within the next 10 weeks.[57] The answer can be positive or negative. Consequently, a particularly important aspect is that the centre does not commit itself to solving the case, but it makes the commitment to ensure that everything possible is done to help find a solution to the encountered problem. Once the case is accepted, the 'leader' co-ordination centre will contact the services of the national administration of its country concerned regarding the case. It will question them and ask why Community law had not been applied correctly. Once the 10-week deadline is over or before, it will have to contact the 'origin' co-ordination centre to indicate the conclusions of its discussions with the national administrations and the possible solution which was found. In its turn, the 'origin' co-ordination centre will inform the citizen or the company of the consequences which were given to the request.

This mechanism can appear complex prima facie, but it proves simple in its implementation. The system is better understood by showing practical cases resolved concretely by the SOLVIT mechanism since its entry into force on 22 July 2002. For example, recently, a Czech citizen wanted to be established in Germany as an independent workman in the building sector. The German local authorities claimed that he must have a work permit to be able to provide services in the building sector, but refused to deliver it to him. The SOLVIT centre in Germany contacted the local authorities in order to specify to them that no work permit was

---

[56] <http://europa.eu.int/comm/internal_market/solvit/index_fr.htm>.
[57] This period can exceptionally be extended to four additional weeks.

required for self-employed workers. Following these contacts, the Czech worker received an authorization of establishment. This solution was found in four weeks.[58]

Inventory

The SOLVIT mechanism works very well. Indeed, as shown by the SOLVIT 2004 Report,[59] it appears that it makes it possible to solve concretely the cases of incorrect application of Community law in more than 75 per cent of the handled cases. Thus, without this system it would have been necessary for the individual or the company to fill in a complaint form, for the Commission to agree to take the case, and to start the Article 226 procedure. It is easy to see the advantage of such a system with so quick results compared to the time that the infringement procedure would have taken.

SOLVIT makes it possible therefore to find solutions to numerous cases which would have been handled by the Commission or possibly by the Court of Justice. It is even possible to say that SOLVIT makes it possible to deal with breaches of Community law which passed through the net of Article 226. Indeed, very often companies and citizens decided not to complain to the Commission and preferred giving up their rights rather than bear the cost of proceeding with the infringement procedure. Thus, thanks to this system, there is a better application of the Community law. SOLVIT has therefore filled in some gaps of the Article 226 action and should encourage citizens and companies to take advantage of their rights.

(ii) The Cases of Specific Breaches of Community Law: Regulation 2679/98/EC [60]

Presentation

This regulation aimed to supply a solution to a sensitive problem which is the multiplication of repeated cases of infringements limited in time. This regulation fell under the logic of the judgement of the Court of Justice judgment[61] which condemned the French government because of the destruction by French farmers of Spanish strawberries at the beginning of each season. Indeed, repeated and specific violations are a serious problem, and they must be treated in an urgent way. The multiplication of cases of repeated violations comes because Community law now applies to all sides of economic and political life. The mechanism set up by this regulation is intended to foresee certain breaches of Community law and to act before these produce negative effects.[62]

---

[58] This case is taken from the SOLVIT site where numerous other examples are listed <http://www.europa.eu.int/solvit/site/index_fr.htm>.

[59] See <http://ec.europa.eu/solvit/site/docs/news/2004-report_en.pdf> and a new report has been issued <http://ec.europa.eu/solvit/site/docs/news/2005-report_en.pdf>.

[60] Council Regulation (EC) n°2679/98 of 7 December 1998, on the functioning of the internal market in relation to the free movement of goods among the Member States [1998] OJ L337/8.

[61] Judgment of 9 December 1998, C-265/95 *Commission France*, I-6959 ECR.

[62] For more information on this mechanism see Mattera A., Un instrument d'intervention rapide pour sauvegarder l'unicité du Marché intérieur : le règlement 2679/98. RMUE 1999, N°2, p. 9–33

The purpose of the regulation is to set up a system of prevention, information and repression of actions of people that intended to disturb the internal market. But by rebound and because of Article 28, the responsibility for the existence of these obstacles comes back to the Member States. They have indeed the obligation not to adopt measures which represent obstacles to free movement of goods and they must also take all the measures necessary to facilitate this freedom of movement. Prima facie this system seems to want to answer to the principal deficiencies of Article 226 (namely the lack of transparency in the work of the Commission and the reduction of deadlines). However, a more careful look shows that it raises more questions than it answers problems of Article 226.

First of all, under this regulation the Commission can take a 'notification', but it intervenes only *a posteriori* i.e. when the obstacle is already carried out. Consequently, in relation to the system of the Article 226 action, it does not bring any added value. Moreover, it is only the Commission that considers that the obstacle occurred; the other Member States no longer intervene at this stage of the procedure. This is the same as the system of Article 226. Secondly, do the deadlines imposed by the Commission really bring changes or not compared to the procedure of Article 226? The question is to know what the links of this regulation with Article 226 are and, more precisely, what aspects of the procedure of Article 226 this notification wants to replace.

Thirdly, a careful reading of Article 5 of the Regulation shows that the notification includes a period of time in order 'to eliminate the obstacle' which is 'fixed according to the urgency'. Consequently, it is neither fixed nor limited in time. The five-working day deadline is applied 'only as from the reception of the text of the notification' and intends only to force the Member State to inform the Commission of the measures taken or to declare that there is no violation according to the State. Consequently, the full timing of the procedure might be comparable to Article 226 procedure. Lastly, the regulation does not say anything to regulate a case where the Member State does not comply with Community law within the time imposed by the regulation. That raises therefore the problem to know what is the legal strength of such 'Commission notification'.

Inventory

The Commission has made a report[63] on the procedure as required by the Regulation itself. It shows clearly that this mechanism did not have the expected success for two reasons.

---

et Carlos Gimeno Verdejo, La réponse communautaire aux blocages des réseaux de transport : application et perspectives d'avenir du règlement n° 2679/98 en vue de la protection du marché intérieur. CDE 2002, n°1–2, p. 45–93.

[63] COM (2001) Commission Report in the Council and in the European Parliament on the application of Regulation (EC) n°2679/98: <http://europa.eu.int/comm/internal_market/fr/goods/reg267998.htm>.

Firstly, the aim of this regulation at the time of its implementation was to find a solution to specific breaches of Community law. However, a careful look at the text shows rather that it involves a warning mechanism of potential violation for the Commission and the other Member States, but not a solving mechanism.

Secondly, the power of the Commission was considerably weakened compared to the original proposal of the Commission. Consequently, States have not really followed, in general, the obligations of this regulation. Indeed, certain States did not follow the obligation and have not warned other States of imminent obstacles to free movement of goods that they were informed of.

III. Proposals for Reform of the Current Systems and Development of New Methods

The monitoring of the application of Community law must remain in the hands of the Commission for two reasons. Firstly, the Commission is independent. Secondly, Article 226 has proven its effectiveness during more than 50 years. The actual failure of the infringement procedure is not linked to the Commission but rather to the tools available. This statement must be underlined before proposing alternative methods.

A. Reform of the Current Systems

(i) The Infringement Procedure

Before starting the analysis of the potential changes to be envisaged to reform the procedure of Article 226, one must emphasize an important point: each reform proposed in this part of the Article cannot, on its own, reverse the current tendency and solve all the problems that we raised above. Only the joint and simultaneous adoption of several measures could have a real impact.

Various ways of shortening the 'administrative' phase

We have already indicated the various stages of Article 226 procedure. One of these phases, the pre-contentious phase, is punctuated by three stages (pre-Article 226 letter, letter of formal notice, and detailed opinion). Admittedly, the delays between the different phases were considerably shortened by the Commission,[64] especially for cases of non-communication of the national implementation measures. However, it could be desirable to change in a more radical way the

---

[64] Commission Communication—Failure by a Member State to comply with Community law: standard form for complaints to be submitted to the European Commission [1999] OJ C119/5 and Commission communication to the European Parliament and the European ombudsman on relations with the complainant in respect of infringements of community law—COM (2002) 141 final, 10 October 2002, pp. 5–8.

enforcement action procedure. We will present these proposals for change while trying to put ahead the positive and negative effects that such choices could involve.

Firstly, the pre-Article 226 letter should be abandoned—it was not foreseen anyway in the original treaties. The pre-contentious phase is composed today of a three stages phase. This involves a long process of exchange of mails. The treaty stipulates that the State must be called on to make its comments, after which the Commission delivers a reasoned opinion. Article 226 never says that the Commission must send a warning to the relevant State of its intention to send a letter of formal notice before formally sending it. Moreover, there is no maximum time period to await the response of the Member State, even if the Commission applies the principle of reasonable time period.

It seems therefore that in practice additional stages have been added to a procedure which is already rather long. Admittedly, deleting this phase will not solve all the problems of the procedure. However, it will decrease the bureaucracy of the procedure and imply less administrative work for the Commission (the sending of all these letters is a heavy workload delaying the whole process).

Secondly, time limits for answers between each phase of Article 226 procedure should be applied in a stricter way. The infringement procedure is a succession of measures aiming to inform the State of the charges against it whilst providing the opportunity for it to present its argument against these allegations. It creates a kind of dialogue between the Member State and the Commission.

The succession of letters necessarily slows down the treatment of the files. Indeed, the Commission must first send a pre-Article 226 letter, then, as a result of the answer or in case of no answer, it must analyse the file more in-depth. Then a letter of formal notice is sent and it must wait for the response of the State or, if the State does not answer, it must send a reasoned opinion and again await the response of the State. If the answer is not satisfactory or if the State does not answer then it can refer the case to the Court of Justice.

To have a realistic view of the inherent slowness of this procedure, one must realize that the Commission has to translate the various documents at each stage of the procedure, and additionally, it must also consult the services concerned by the subject as well as the Legal Service.

Shorter deadlines between each phase are thus imperative. In the Communication related to the infringement procedure,[65] the Commission indicates that 'Commission departments will investigate complaints with a view to arriving at a decision to issue a formal notice or to close the case within not more than one year from the date of registration of the complaint by the Secretariat-General. Where this time limit is exceeded, the Commission department responsible for the case will inform the complainant in writing'. It still remains far too long. Indeed, it must always be borne in mind that an extra 20 months (on average) has

---

[65] See note 64.

to be added for the procedure before the Court of Justice. Once the State has received the letter of formal notice and that discussions have taken place, there should only be a very short time period for the rest of the procedure in cases where the Commission intends to prosecute the State. Indeed, the State is fully aware of the charges against it and has already had an exchange of views on the issue with the Commission.

Thirdly, a better information system should be set up for interested parties and the other Member States. The various documents concerning Article 226 cannot be revealed to the public. Persons carrying out the complaint are obviously kept informed; but on the whole, there is not enough publicity made about the procedure even if the policy of the Commission within the framework of the non-transmission of the national implementation measures has radically changed these last years with the publication of press releases.[66]

However, an interesting point is the non-information of the other Member States on the ongoing procedures. This aspect is interesting because if the other States were fully aware that the Commission is suspecting another country of contravening the law, they might support the Commission intervention very early in the procedure (e.g pre-contentious phase). In comparison, Directive 98/34/EC[67] is a good example of a procedure where States play an important role. Indeed, in this case, Member States know the position of the Commission as from the 'administrative' phase and indicate if they share the point of view of the Commission. Statistics[68] about this procedure show that most of the time cases considered as problematic by the Commission are also considered as such by Member States.

Fourthly, the Commission should produce an Act stating clearly during what time period the State has not complied with Community law in order to facilitate actions for damages before national jurisdictions. The aim of the infringement procedure is to put an end to the breaching of Community law. However, during the period that the failure is treated by the Commission, the breach of Community law entails financial consequences for citizens and economic operators. Moreover, as we have already underlined, once the procedures before the European Court of Justice are finished, actions before national jurisdictions still have to be launched in order to ensure that the State liability is possible for the violation of Community law.

Lastly, it is necessary to develop a faster mechanism to treat the cases of non-communication of national implementation measures. The Commission has decided to react in face of the increase of non-communication of national transposition measures. Indeed, it sends automatically the letter of formal notice if the State did not communicate these transposition measures in time. However, it

---

[66] See, for example, the following press releases: IP/05/1037 and IP/05/1007, <www.europa.eu.int>.

[67] See the procedure of the notification Directive, note 20, sp. Article 8 of the Directive.

[68] Report concerning the application Directive 98/34/EC, note 30.

works only if the State did not send any national implementation measures to the Commission. It can happen that a State sends only some implementing measures, and in this case, the Commission has to check all the documents received in order to identify which obligations contained in the Directive have been transposed and which have not. This automatic sending is already a noticeable improvement, but in this case, sending a letter of formal notice followed by a reasoned opinion seems to be useless. Indeed, the State knows what Community obligation it should have transposed and what contravening facts are in play. The Commission should thus have a specific tool to regulate the cases of non-communication. One could imagine Article 226 giving a specific power to the Commission in the event of non-communication (e.g. decision from the Commission condemning the incriminated State for not having respected its obligations).

The principal criticism which could be made to the first three proposals is that the pre-contentious procedure makes it possible at present to solve a large majority of cases.[69] However, it should not be forgotten that even if after some time the State ends up complying with Community law, the fact that this Community obligation was not applied correctly for some time has generated obstacles to the establishment of the internal market and has thus implied damages for companies and citizens.

Concerning the last aspect, it may happen that a State decides to notify 'all and anything' to fulfil their reporting obligation and avoid a 'Commission Decision'.

Proposals of amendment of Article 226
Consequently, the other possible solution is to develop new mechanisms and/or to improve the existing mechanisms in order to adapt them to the current challenges. As we underlined in the introduction, the system was not designed for a Europe of 25 members. It is therefore normal to change the system now to avoid having to do so in a hurry. Consequently, the question to be raised is: what are the possible alternatives?

Concerning Article 226 As within the ECSC framework[70] there should be a system enabling the Commission to take a decision against a Member State in cases where the State has not changed its position at the end of the administrative procedure (pre-Article 226 letter, letter of formal notice, and detailed opinion). The Member State would have the possibility of requesting its annulment within two months following the adoption of the decision by the Commission, pursuant to Article 230. This solution would have the advantage of considerably shortening the period of treatment of Article 226 cases. It should be mentioned that this proposal was the subject of considerable criticism on the part of the 'British Institute'.[71] We do not share this point of view and think that such a procedure

---

[69] See the figures of the XXI quoted report, note 35 and Simon, note 17, sp. pp. 656–657.
[70] Mattera, note 53 sp. p. 158 and Article 88 of the ECSC Treaty.
[71] British Institute of international and comparative law, 'The role and future of the European court of justice', *European Law Series*, British Institute, London, 1996.

could be put in place in the case of the non-communication of the national implementation measures. In such cases, the State had different opportunities to redress the situation but did not take them. Indeed, it could have complied within the deadline; the fact not to have complied on time is in itself a breach of Community law. Moreover, during the discussion phase, it could have accepted to communicate these measures but if it did not, then there is no doubt as to the deliberate will on the part of the State not to comply with a Community obligation known since a very long time.

Another possibility would be to give to the Commission the opportunity of requiring temporary measures to the Court of Justice before the end of the administrative period in order to avoid that States use in their favour the slowness of the administrative procedure.

Concerning Article 228 The condemnation of the State in relation to Article 228 should be automatic. Thus, if after the Court decision, the State did not take any measure in order to redress the fault within a specific time period; it should be automatically condemned to pay a periodic payment per day of delay. Indeed, at present, the infringement procedure and the fixing of a periodic payment is a very long procedure. One must add the average period of the Article 226 action and only then, if the Member State does not comply with the Court decision after a reasonable period, can the Commission start once again the whole process explained above (pre-contentious phase, contentious phase) in order to fix a periodic penalty payment to the incriminated State. Lastly, the mechanism referred to above could also apply to Article 228: namely that the 'Commission Decision' would intervene only in the second phase after an Article 226 decision of the Court.

Would modifying the role of the Commission, according to the stage of the procedure, be a solution?

The Commission has the opportunity to decide the proceedings within the framework of the infringement procedure. This means that it is the only one to decide to pursue a complaint or to end the procedure.

This is due to the specific role of the Commission in the institutional architecture of the Community. The Commission is the guardian of the treaties and thanks to its independence it has the possibility to check the problems encountered in the implementation of Community law for all the four freedoms.

Private operators have often requested that the Commission should no longer be able to decide on the opportunity of proceedings. This is understandable. Indeed, if a company encounters problems in the application of the rights which arise from Community law and that it is a real case of breach of Community law then it is difficult to understand why the Commission would not start an infringement procedure.

It should first be mentioned that in recent years, the Commission has already seen its power in the field of Article 226 framed by a specific procedure to follow in the field of the management of complaints. This framework has been set up following several complaints lodged by companies with the Ombudsman.[72] The Commission therefore decided to publish a Communication[73] aiming to make the procedure more transparent. The communication replaces and considerably amends a previous text.[74]

It seems essential to leave the Commission as the 'master' of the procedure of the infringement procedure. However, there should be a possibility of reopening a file if a private individual complains to the Ombudsman and if the latter decides in favour of the complainant. Such an approach can be tempting for companies but has negative aspects for the Commission. Indeed, it will likely mobilize numerous resources if the number of enquiries addressed to the Ombudsman increase, which is inevitable if such a system is set up. A solution could be to limit this appeal, for example, to the respect of certain specific rules of procedure.

(ii) Development of the Ad Hoc Mechanisms

The Development and the Strengthening of the SOLVIT System
SOLVIT is a tool which improves the application of Community law. Indeed, it is a real alternative to Article 226 procedure. It is therefore necessary to allow a greater development of this system. However, it cannot be done without three elements: better information, a greater implication of the Member States, and an increased control on the part of the Commission. In order to ensure its performance, this system should have strong financial and administrative support from the Member States. One should avoid falling into the traps experienced before.[75] There must be therefore a real political implication on the part of each State. Member States have already made a statement in the Council on the 'Internal market', stating that they would do everything possible to ensure the success of this system.[76] However, there are still considerable differences between States as shown by comparisons at the disposal of the SOLVIT centres and by the number of solved cases per country.[77]

---

[72] The case which started the adoption of this Commission Communication is the one dealing with the infringement of public procurement rules during the tender of the Thessaloniki underground. This case is developed in the 2001 report of the Ombudsman, <http://www.euro-ombudsman.eu.int/report01/pdf/fr/rap01_fr.pdf> pp. 119 *et seq.*

[73] This text showed the standard complaint form and gave certain general indications. Non-observance of Community law by a Member State: standard form for the complaints to be submitted to the Commission of the European Communities [1999] OJ C119/5–7.

[74] Communication from the Commission to the European Parliament and to the European Ombudsman concerning the relations with the complainant as regards infringements of Community law COM (2002) 141 final of 10 October 2002, pp. 5–8. For an analysis of the contents of this Communication: Munoz R., La participation du plaignant à la procédure d'infraction au droit communautaire diligentée par la Commission, Revue du Marché Commun, 2003, n. 472, October–November, pp. 610–616.

[75] Indeed, SOLVIT is based on a mechanism which had been set up several years ago but which had not succeeded, see <http://europa.eu.int/comm/internal_market/en/update/action/planfr.pdf>, see, *inter alia*, p. 7.   [76] <http://europa.eu.int/solvit/site/background/index_en.htm>.

[77] Commission Report on Development and Performance of the SOLVIT network in 2004 SEC (2005) 543 on 19 May 2005, sp. pp. 8–16.

However, in view of the overall good results of the system, the Commission should continue to develop it, but it should check the way the law is interpreted and it should also ensure a uniform application of Community law. Indeed, the decisions taken by the SOLVIT centres have to be taken in the framework of Community law, as stated in the SOLVIT Communication.[78] To ensure that this commitment is respected, the Commission must check in a very strict way the decisions taken by the various centres. Indeed, Community law is a very complex matter which requires real expertise and an approach different to that of a purely national approach. The Commission, as guardian of the treaties, must make sure that the decisions of these centres are in line with the Community position on the subject. Specific trainings will also have to be set up if the Commission realizes that a centre did not implement Community law correctly.

Lastly, the Commission must inform more widely all citizens and companies of the existence of this mechanism by publicity campaigns. In fact, SOLVIT is known for the moment only by some beneficiaries. However, this increased publicity must go together with a real development of the system so as to ensure that new cases could be treated exponentially. Indeed, if the system is known by the general public, the number of cases will undoubtedly increase.

The real development of the mechanism of Regulation 2679/98/EC
The idea of such a regulation must be taken up but its application should be made more flexible as the Member States had made the procedure too heavy. The Commission should have the power to penalize Member States for the non-observance of their obligations to inform each other. Indeed, the idea to have more information is very good because it makes it possible to limit the harmful consequences of an obstacle if this obstacle is foreseeable. But one must be able to force the States to give this type of information.

Moreover, we should come back to the original idea that the authors of this regulation had, namely, to prevent cases similar to the one of the Spanish strawberries which were systematically destroyed by French farmers. The purpose was thus to prevent a specific type of violation (repeated violations) and to ensure that the Commission could respond quickly on this repeated infringement.

In fact, Article 226 is not the tool to deal with such violations: due to its slowness and strict and long character of its procedure, it is not possible to cope with such violations. Consequently, there is still a need to develop an efficient mechanism aiming to deal specifically with repeated infringement within certain time limits.

(iii) Improvements of the Notification Procedure
This procedure works particularly well. It would thus be interesting to develop its scope *ratione materiae* and *personae*. Work has already started in this direction.

---

[78] Note 54.

Indeed, the Commission is exploring the possibility of implementing a notification procedure for services. DG Enterprises launched a study in order to analyse how many measures are adopted by states in the framework of the free movement of services.[79]

It should also be noted that the notification procedure was already imposed to the current new Member States before their adhesion in order to prepare them to apply it, but also in order to ensure the right application of the *acquis*.[80] It must also be stressed that this procedure applies with certain limits to Turkey.

Lastly, it is possible to mention that the experience of the notification procedure has inspired a very similar notification procedure at international level with the adoption of an International Convention under the Council of Europe.[81] This notification procedure might apply to all the Member States of the Council of Europe plus the States which are observers, such as the United States.

B. A General Recasting of the Approach vis-a-vis the Infringements of Community Law: Development of New Instruments

There might be three ways to reform in depth the monitoring of the application of Community law. The first way is to find a solution to the problem of the non-communication of the national implementing measures of Directives which, as we saw earlier, represent the large majority of cases of letters of formal notice and of reasoned opinion.

The second way is more general and aims at recasting the general approach of the monitoring of the application of Community law. A possibility would be to develop a platform aiming to manage the relations between the States and the Commission services.

Lastly, it would be possible to create a body whose aim would be to follow the transpositions or to make sure of the application of the Community law in general.

(i) *A New Ex-ante Mechanism to Deal with the Non-communication of the National Transposition Measures and Cases of Non-conformity*

The Ex-ante Notification of the National Implementing Measures[82]

The system allowing for *a priori* control of all the national implementing measures transposing the Community Directives could consist of the following.

Firstly, its scope should be limited, as it was for Directive 83/189/EEC at the time of its creation; the aim being, in the future, if the mechanism shows its effectiveness, to extend it to each new Directive referring to the internal market.

---

[79] Working document of DG ENTERPRISES <http://europa.eu.int/comm/enterprise/tris/rslt_svr_fr.pdf>.   [80] See note 2.

[81] Moscow Convention adopted within the Council of Europe at the conference 24° of the European Ministers for Justice in Moscow of 4–5 October 2001.

[82] *EU Law for the Twenty-First Century: Rethinking the New Legal Order*, Volume 1 (Co-editor with Nebbia P.), Oxford: Hart Publishing, 2004, 496, Chapter 7, Munoz R.

The fact of limiting it to some Directives will allow for the gradual introduction of this control.

The mechanism could work as follows: Directives should comprise of a legal obligation, such as a standard article in the final provisions, requiring Member States to notify to the Commission at the draft stage all the foreseen national measures which are aimed at implementing the obligations of a Directive before its adoption.

If the State does not have the draft measures yet, it could at least indicate the adoption timetable and as soon as the drafts are available, it should notify them to the Commission. Then, a 'rendez-vous clause' should make it compulsory for representatives from Member States to meet together with the Commission services in order to discuss the transposition at a specific moment. Thus, if the Directive should be transposed within 18 months, the Member States should have to meet 10 months following the publication of the Directive in the Official Journal of the European Communities, for instance.

The notified texts should then be analysed by the services in charge of the Directive in order to ensure that the national transposition measures are in accordance with the aims of the Directive. Member States should have access to each others draft measures so that if one country encounters a problem in the transposition of a measure, it could check how other Member States have dealt with it.

If the Member State notifies its national implementing measure, then the Commission services will be able to check the contents of these measures and, to ensure their conformity with the aims of the Directive and with general Community law. In that way, the Commission will be able to ensure that the transposition of Community law is effective and uniform in all the Member States. Therefore, such a system would make it possible to treat all the cases of non-communication and bad transposition.

Another added value would be that if it appears that many countries have problems interpreting the obligations of the Directive, the Commission will be able to take measures to make it more understandable.

Advantages and disadvantages

Advantages We will deal quickly with some of the advantages of such a mechanism because we will develop other elements in the following part, in answer to the potential criticisms of this mechanism.

The first advantage is that such mechanism will make it possible to solve the majority of cases of breach of Community law due to the non- (or bad) transposition of obligations before it creates concrete obstacles within the internal market. Consequently, companies and citizens will no longer have to wait for their rights to be violated and for not being allowed to sell their products to require the effective monitoring of the application of Community law. Furthermore, it must be recalled that if few cases go before the Court of Justice, most of them have to go through what is called 'the administrative phase'. This is the period of negotiation between the Commission and the Member States, and it can sometimes take more than two years during which the obstacles to the internal market remain.

The second advantage is related to the length of the enforcement actions procedure. Such a system would definitely shorten the procedures in cases related to the non- (or bad) transposition.[83] Thirdly, this mechanism will help rationalize the monitoring of transpositions and will also ensure access of citizens and companies to the national implementing measures. Lastly, the limitation of disputes in front of the Court of Justice will give it more time to deal with its other cases. It can then induce a quicker time of treatment of these other cases.

Criticisms We will in this part gather criticisms which can be made concerning the introduction of such a mechanism. We will try to give brief replies to these potential criticisms.

The first negative aspect might be that implementing such a mechanism might be very heavy if we consider the number of national implementing measures that States have to adopt for each Directive.

In answer to this comment, we can compare with the number of notifications which are made and treated each year by the Commission within the framework of the notification procedure. Indeed, in 2005, the Commission dealt with 700 notifications.[84] This number includes only the notified texts. It does not take into account all the mail sent for each notification (detailed opinion, comments, etc.). In fact, the Commission treats the sending of all these documents via a computer system which has now proven its worth. Therefore, the same approach can be developed for the *ex-ante* control of national transposition measures.

The second foreseeable criticism could be that these national implementing measures will need to be translated if the Commission wants to analyse its content and compare it to the original obligations of Directives.

Four answers can be given. Firstly, in any case these implementing measures will have to be read and compared to the original obligations. At some point, this translation will thus have to be made, at least partially. Secondly, translations in the framework of the Directive on notification are managed efficiently via a contract which requires high quality and sometimes very technical translations to be given in all the official languages of the Community with in a very short period of time. The third element is that the translations of these measures would not be used only for the Commission services, but they could also be placed at the disposal of all Member States and companies. This would give them access to the national implementing measures of each Directive translated into all the languages of the Community. Lastly, it is possible to impose limitations if the text

---

[83] The author underlines once again that quite obviously in 'political' cases, States will always prefer not to respect Directive obligations. However, these cases represent only a limited percentage of cases of non-transposition or of bad transposition of Directives.

[84] Statistics concerning technical regulations notified in 2004 within the framework of the Notification Directive 98/34/EC (2005/C 158/05).

exceeds e.g. 50 pages as is the case, for instance, under the Notification Directive 98/34/EC.[85]

The third criticism concerns the human resource necessary to develop such a mechanism. Indeed, the reception, management and analysis of these national implementing measures will certainly involve numerous people.

This comment is true, but has to be balanced. Indeed, if such a mechanism implies more human resource beforehand, it will require less resource later as there should then be less procedure under Article 226 which normally includes a very long administrative phase. Moreover, the monitoring of the application of Community law is in anyway compulsory. It is one of the main tasks of the Commission. Lastly, it will in any case involve a net gain for the internal market because the majority of problems will be solved before generating any obstacle and consequently, there will be no cost to bear by companies and citizens. Thus, the money currently lost by companies in cases of non- or bad transposition will be reinvested in the economy.

The fourth criticism could be that such a system will increase time limits for adoption of measures. Indeed, the transposition procedure is particularly long because in each State it implies several ministries and the adoption of numerous measures. Consequently, the fact of having to wait for the analysis of the Commission could further slow down the transposition periods. It is easy to answer such an argument by stating that within the framework of the notification procedure, the deadlines imposed on the Commission are particularly short and binding. Indeed, the Commission has only three months[86] to deliver its opinion on the text. It must be stressed that these three months also include all the translation periods. Lastly, on this aspect it should be noted that under the Directive on the services of the information society certain time limits were shortened.[87]

The fifth criticism is to stress that States can decide not to notify their national implementing measures. If Member States have not notified their draft national transposition measures within the prescribed time, the Commission could make contact directly with the State in order to ask for the notification of these measures. If despite that, a State still refuses to provide its draft measures, the Commission could begin a procedure for failure of non-observance of its notification duties even before the Directive enters into force.

The last criticism probably is the most difficult to counter argue. It is the natural reservation of the States to accept the establishment of such a mechanism. It is clear that politically, States are not likely to want such a mechanism to be implemented. However, they should be told that this mechanism does not have the objective to involve itself in their national sphere but rather to provide them

---

[85] The only limitation concerns the texts which make up of more than 50 pages, those are translated only in French, English and German but that represents a minority of the notifications.

[86] Article 9§1 of Directive 98/34/EC, note 20.

[87] Directive 98/48/EC of 20 July 1998, [1998] OJ L217/18–26, see specifically Article 9 §2 on the standstill period as a result of the sending of a detailed opinion.

with a system to better implement Community obligations. But what should mainly be stressed is that each State would ultimately benefit from the introduction of such a mechanism. Indeed, economically speaking, it can have positive impacts by producing an effective harmonization. For instance, companies from a State will no longer have to give up a market due to the non- or bad transposition of Community law.

(ii) The Development of a Platform

Presentation of such a system

Within the framework of the infringement procedure there are already mechanisms which allow for the targeting of controls and the development of specific contacts between the Commission and the Member States. They are called 'réunion paquet'. These meetings have existed for more than 15 years and enable the officials of the Commission to meet people in charge of the transposition files in each Member State, but also to meet people in charge of the treatment of the infringement files. This approach has made it possible to find numerous solutions before the implementation of the infringement procedure. Furthermore, these meetings also made it possible to close down infringement procedures which had been initiated.

This mechanism has already proved its worth today and is used in an extensive way. It would be interesting to wonder how this method could be developed more in-depth.

It should be added to this that if the Community keeps on growing, it will be increasingly difficult to manage the application of the Community law only from Brussels, even through 'package meetings'. A possible solution would be to have teams of officials who would make the tour of the capitals, 25 today, in order to ensure a proper application of Community law while other teams, in Brussels, would manage the legislative follow-up and fulfil the Commission initiative function.

An alternative could be the following: to set up platforms in each Member State which would be responsible in ensuring a proper application of Community law. This would not necessarily mean creating additional bodies but could work by setting up Community delegations in each European capital. By doing so, it would be possible first of all to make sure of effective and real control of all the legislation of the Member States, and secondly to have some kind of 'direct contacts' between the national administrations and the Commission within the framework of the transposition of the Directives. These 'contacts' would be useful not only within the framework of the procedure of the control of the application but also in order to build links with the socio-economic actors of each State whether companies or civil society interlocutors. These links could also be extended to other branches of State power and for instance could give rise to links strengthened with the national parliaments.

Such contacts could consist of a team of Commission civil servants operating in each State or, for smaller countries, of regional teams regrouping two to three countries. Commission representatives would be the interlocutors of the national administrations, companies, citizens etc. Their role would not be to sanction countries but to manage cases in a way which takes into account the reality of each country and help find solutions taking care of the country specificities. Moreover, concerning the cases of transposition of Directives, it will contribute to avoid non- or bad transposition. This mechanism can thus be put in parallel with the idea that we developed previously i.e. the notification of the draft national measures of transposition. Finally, such a mechanism would make it possible to develop several elements which are missing today: a direct link with the Member States, a forum of discussions and meetings and a relay with citizens.

Critical analysis

For the Commission A first obvious consequence is the splitting of the powers of the Commission as there will be several centres for discussion on the implementation of Community law.

However, as a matter of comparison, there are already delegations in third countries and the Community has decided to further develop such delegations for implementing specific tasks of the Community.[88] This approach was decided because it was obviously very difficult to follow the implementation of Community projects from a long distance. For the issue dealt with here, the problem is less the distance than the number of cases and the variety of subjects covered. For these reasons, we think that such an approach could be helpful. Lastly, the Community delegations in third countries are in constant contact with Brussels.

There are solutions to this issue of the splitting of the Commission's powers. One of them could be to set up a general follow-up mechanism of the discussions within the framework, either of the application of the Community law or of the monitoring of the complaints.

This would undoubtedly imply considerable co-ordination work. Once again previous experiences will be very useful such as the notification procedure which combines the necessity to work in a very co-ordinated way and a procedure for exchanging views within a very short time limit. The SOLVIT system can also be seen as a good example. SOLVIT envisaged from the very beginning to include the monitoring of complaints lodged by private individuals and companies so as to be able to take measures at Community level if a problem occurred in several States, or in order to make sure that the solutions proposed by the SOLVIT centres are in compliance with Community law.

Another undeniable consequence of such a mechanism might be its financial cost. But it should be compared to the economic cost of the non- or bad implementation of Community law for companies and citizens.

Lastly, from a human resource perspective, there will have to be at least some turnover of staff from one platform to another and back to Brussels, as it exists today for delegations in third countries.

---

[88] <http://europa.eu.int/comm/development/index_fr.htm>.

For the Member States Once again, the problem which is probably the most difficult to surmount will be the non-willingness of the Member States to develop such delegations because it might increase the effectiveness of the control of the Commission. They might also see such a system as a way to permanently control their national measures.

(iii) The Implication of the European Parliament in the Control of the Transpositions

The European Parliament should play a role in the implementation of Community law. Indeed, due to the increasing role of the European Parliament in the legislative sphere, it would be legitimate to give it more opportunity to monitor the adoption of Community acts, mainly Directives.

It will also make it possible to use contacts that the European Parliament has with the various national parliaments. These contacts will probably have to be developed more in depth. In practice, there is already a co-operation mechanism which could be used effectively; it is the COSAC (the Conference of bodies specialized in European Community Affairs of Parliaments of the European Union).[89] This body was created in Madrid in May 1989[90] in order to strengthen the role of the national parliaments in the Community process. This is a co-operation body which brings together, every two months, the members of the committees responsible for European affairs of each national parliament and the European Parliament.[91]

The COSAC was recognized formally at the time of the Amsterdam Treaty in 1997 with the introduction of a specific protocol on 'the role of the national parliaments'.[92] This protocol gives to the COSAC the opportunity of submitting to the European institutions any contribution that it will judge suitable.[93] It is therefore possible to use these meetings as a platform for tackling subjects related to the transposition of Community Directives. In fact, in a way, the COSAC has already began this work through its biannual reports[94] where it invites national parliaments to exchange their best practices about Community law. Therefore, this body could serve as a starting point to establish a more active monitoring of the national transposition measures.

---

[89] Houser Matthieu, La COSAC, une instance européenne à la croisée des chemins, RDUE, 2005, n°2, pp. 343–36. The website: <www.cosac.org>.

[90] The first meeting took place in Paris in November 1989.

[91] Candidate States have the right to send representatives.

[92] Protocol n°9 on the role of the national parliaments in the European Union 1997.

[93] Protocol n°9 item 4: The Conference of bodies specialized in Community Affairs (...) can submit any contribution that it considers suitable for the attention of the institutions of the European Union, in particular on the basis of measure projects that representatives of governments of the Member States can decide by mutual agreement to transmit it, in view of the nature of the question.

[94] <http://www.cosac.org/fr/documents/biannual>.

IV. Conclusions

The obstacles to the free movement of goods, capital, services and to the freedom of establishment are in themselves obstacles to the establishment of an effective internal market without frontiers. The multiplication of complaints of citizens and companies are certainly related to the fact that they are more informed of their rights and so more able to require their proper enforcement.

The battle to be fought is consequently even more important than it appears. It is the credibility of the Community system which is at stake. At present, Community citizens are not fully aware of the role that Community law has in their daily life. Although the Community is trying to raise this awareness through efforts like the action called 'Citizen first', if it is not to have the means to answer to the foreseeable increase of complaints, it will lose credibility. Indeed, if now, a citizen complains (rightly) that one of its rights has been denied by a Member State, and if the answer to him is that his case cannot be dealt with because it does not fit in with the priorities agreed by the Commission, all previous efforts will be lost.

It is true that for the moment, the entry of 10 new members did not result in an exponential increase of the number of infringements, on the contrary.[95] However, these States will surely also encounter at some point problems in the application of Community law.[96] To give an idea, the five States which have least communicated their national implementing measures are: Luxembourg, Italy, Greece, Portugal and France, i.e. five 'old' Member States. [97]

---

[95] <http://europa.eu.int/comm/secretariat_general/index_fr.htm>.

[96] <http://www.europa.eu.int/comm/secretariat_general/sgb/droit_com/pdf/mne_country_20050907_fr.pdf>.

[97] The term 'old' is taken here in opposition to the new States which joined the Community at the time of the last enlargement with the Athens Treaty.

National Courts in EU Judicial Structures

*Sacha Prechal**

I. Introduction

From the system of the EC Treaty it follows that the national courts are to a large extent responsible for the application and enforcement of EC law and for judicial protection in cases where EC law plays a role,[1] whether directly or 'in disguise', *i.e.* once it has been implemented in national law. They do not only enforce that law against Member State authorities or in disputes between individuals, but are also the first called upon when the validity of EC law is challenged. Yet, in the Treaty there is no explicit provision dealing with the role of national courts. The only exception is Article 234 TEC which was, not surprisingly, used by the ECJ as one of the arguments in favour of the direct effect of EC law.[2] For the rest, the role that national courts play within the judicial function of the EC is a matter of case law, the only basis for which is the catch-all Article 10 TEC.

The lack of explicit reference to national courts by no means restrained the ECJ from defining and, subsequently, refining and enhancing the role these courts play in the EC system of judicial protection and enforcement. The story is well known. Ever since *Van Gend en Loos* the Court has maintained that it is the task of the national court to protect the rights of individuals under Community law and to give full effect to Community law provisions. The national courts are therefore required to apply community law provisions when they are apt for such an application (direct effect), to set aside national law that is contrary to Community law (supremacy) and to give to domestic law provisions, as far as possible, an

---

* Professor of European Law, Europa Institute, Faculty of Law, Utrecht University. The present contribution was finalized in April 2006. It was written in the framework of an incentive of the Netherlands Organisation for Scientific Research, the so-called Revitalisation of Legal Research II (Saro II).

[1] This contribution focuses on EC law, as a part of a broader category of EU law, but which has to be distinguished from 'non-Community' Union law, *i.e.* the law which derives from the second and third pillars. As is well-known, the position of the national courts and the ECJ is different in these pillars due to the limited jurisdiction of the ECJ in the third pillar and no jurisdiction whatsoever in the second one.

[2] Indeed, in Case 26/62 *Van Gend & Loos* [1963] ECR 1. More recently, in Case C-105/03 *Pupino* [2005] ECR I-5285, the ECJ used the existence of the—curtailed—preliminary procedure provided for in Article 35 TEU as one of the arguments for recognizing an obligation of framework decision consistent interpretation.

interpretation which accords with the applicable Community law provisions (consistent interpretation).

In entrusting national courts with the responsibility for the enforcement of Community law and the protection of rights conferred upon individuals by Community law, it was assumed that national remedies and procedures were both sufficient and adequate. However, litigation involving Community law issues revealed that the national procedures and, in particular, the panoply of domestic remedies were sometimes deficient.

The ECJ therefore started to interfere with national procedures and remedies. These must satisfy the principles of equivalence and effectiveness and national courts are requested to provide effective judicial protection. Judicial review and, in certain circumstances, also interlocutory relief must be available to Community litigants; a remedy in restitution must allow the recovery of amounts of money paid in contravention of Community law; in case of loss sustained as a result of a breach of Community law individuals are entitled to an award of damages.

Although, as far as the national courts were concerned, the focus was essentially on the judicial protection of individuals against the Member States, the Court's case law went further. Relying, in particular, on the principle of the rule of law, the ECJ found that the EC Treaty intends to establish a complete and coherent system of judicial protection.[3] In an entity such as the EC, which is subject to the rule of law, the organization of the judicial function as a whole—thus including both levels of adjudication, Community and national—is guided by the idea that neither the Member States nor the national authorities can avoid a review of whether the measures they adopt are in conformity with the law, including Community law.[4] In brief: nothing escapes the courts' scrutiny.

The basic pattern of this system of judicial protection is one of 'communicating vessels'.[5] The jurisdiction of the national courts excludes the jurisdiction of the ECJ or the CFI and *vice versa*.[6] This system of communicating vessels comes

---

[3] This is obviously not the case in relation to the second and third pillar or, to an extent, in relation to Title IV of the EC Treaty. However, in the *Pupino*-case (Case C-105/03 [2005] ECR I-5285) certain constitutional and rule of law principles have been imported in the third pillar, which have also consequences for the scope of judicial protection.

[4] Cf. Case 294/83 *Les Verts* [1986] ECR 1339, Case C-2/88Imm. *Zwartveld I* [1990] ECR I-3365, Opinion 1/91 *EEA* [1991] ECR I-6079; for the coherence of the system see, for instance, already Case 112/83 *Société des produits de maïs* [1985] ECR 719 or Case 314/85 *Foto-Frost* [1987] ECR 4199.

[5] Cf. K. Lenaerts, 'The Legal Protection of Private Parties under the EC Treaty: a Coherent and Complete System of Judicial Review?', in *Scritti in onore Giuseppe Federico Mancini, Vol. II*, (Giuffrè editore, 1998), pp. 591–623.

[6] According to Nowak, for instance, this is '... ein ausgeprägtes Strukturprinzip des gemeinschaftlichen Rechtsschutzsystems ...'. Cf. C. Nowak, 'Das Verhältnis zwischen zentralem und dezentralem Individualrechtsschutz im Europäischen Gemeinschaftsrecht', (2000) EuR, p. 724, at p. 738. However, the mutual exclusion of jurisdiction is not absolute: cf., for instance, an Article 226 proceedings and proceedings concerning the same point before a national court. An important difference is indeed that the actions are then brought by two different parties, either with purposes of their own.

particularly to the fore in the context of an action for annulment. The possibility of redress in a national court is used as an argument against the admissibility of an application under Article 230.[7] And, conversely, the possibility to bring an action for annulment precludes the challenge of the validity of a Community act before the national courts (and before the ECJ in Article 234 proceedings).[8] Moreover, there exists also another pair of 'communicating vessels', namely within the context of the preliminary procedure. A poor EC-law performance by national judges has repercussions for the ECJ and *vice versa*.

The problem is indeed that the system of mutual complementarity is far from perfect in practice: the vessels are leaking and the system risks to be less complete and coherent than is often believed. Considered from the point of view of the role of national courts, the 'complete and coherent system' shows at least three weak points. First, the reality of the application of Community law by national courts shows a less positive picture than the one which serves as a basic assumption for the complete and coherent system of judicial protection in the Community. Although there is no point in advocating that theoretical designs always be adjusted to everyday practice, a system of judicial protection constituted in a way which does not sufficiently take reality into account is nothing more than a castle built in the sky.

Secondly, the preliminary procedure is permanently under pressure. Obviously, there is a close connection to the previous point. The role of the national court can hardly be considered separately from this unique method of co-operation between the national court and the ECJ. It is exactly through this procedure that national courts are assisted in matters of application and interpretation of Community law and, more importantly, that the unity and proper development of EC law are safeguarded.

Thirdly, the requirements that the ECJ imposes upon national courts in relation to the application of EC law raise various problems, in particular where the courts are asked to do something which is beyond their powers under national (constitutional) law.

The present contribution focuses on the role that national courts play within the Community system of judicial protection in relation to these three 'weak points'. It starts with a discussion of some of the main problems that national courts encounter when applying Community law and of some practical suggestions which have been made in order to improve this application. Next, since the preliminary procedure will continue to play an important role, it will briefly deal with the prospects for this procedure and discuss some aspects of the broader issue of how in the future to organize the co-operation between national and Community judges on preliminary references. Thirdly, it addresses the (in)sufficiency of the

---

[7] Cf. Case C-321/95P *Greenpeace* [1998] ECR I-1651 and Case C-50/00P *Union de Pequeños Agricultores* [2002] ECR I-6677.

[8] Cf. Case C-188/92 *TWD Textilwerke Deggendorf* [1994] ECR I-833 and subsequent case law, such as Case C-241/01 *National Farmers' Union* [2002] ECR I-9079.

theoretical basis for the Community law obligations of national courts. The final—concluding—part explores briefly what could be done to facilitate the task of the national courts.

The contribution seeks to combine two approaches: an academic approach and a more practical one, drawing upon the problems national courts seem to be facing in relation to the application of EC law.

II. National Courts: Still Struggling with EC Law

For its application and enforcement, Community law has always relied heavily on the quality and capacity of the national judiciary. This will not change in the future. On the contrary, the role of the national courts will be reinforced in this respect, last but not least due to the ongoing 'Europeanization' of major parts of national law.[9]

Since the creation of the EEC and the subsequent accession of certain Member States, considerable efforts have been invested in training the judiciary (and lawyers in general) in matters of EC law. Within the judiciary, certain expertise has been built up, in particular in those courts which come across EC law on a regular basis. Yet, on the basis of some scarce and stray publications—where often some cautious allusions are made on the matter— personal experience and contacts with the national judiciary, one comes to a somewhat perplexing conclusion, namely that the quality and capacity of the national courts to apply EC law and to do so correctly is a matter for serious concern.[10] It seems that after several decades

---

[9] In certain areas, like in EC competition law, a choice for decentralization was deliberately made. Arguably, also the re-nationalization of agricultural policy might lead to more and different involvement of national courts. On the other hand, there are also areas in which jurisdiction shifts to the European level, like in the field of trademark protection. Cf. for a more detailed discussion S. Prechal, R. H. van Ooik *et.al.*, 'Europeanisation' of the Law: Consequences for the Dutch Judiciary, report for the Raad voor de rechtspraak (Dutch Council for the Judiciary), The Hague 2005, in particular paras 2.1 and 4.2.

[10] The observations are mainly based on personal experience and contacts with other persons interested in the problems at issue. Moreover, the experience is inevitably and to an important extent 'Netherlands centred'. It is difficult to make statements which can be generalized, as there is, as far as I know, no systematic research that has been done in this area. From the scarce (and not entirely up-to-date) sources can be mentioned M. Fierstra, 'Nationale rechter en Europees recht; zorgen om een relatie, in Magistraten zonder grenzen—de invloed van het Europese recht op de Nederlandse recht-spleging', *Raio-congres* 2002, (Nijmegen 2002), M. Darmon & J-G. Huglo, 'La formation des juges en droit communautaire', in *Mélanges en hommage à Michel Waelbroeck*, (Bruxelles 1999), C. Naômé, 'Le Juge national et le droit communautaire: la pratique', in *De advocaat generaal gehoord. Essays over de totstandkoming van het Europees gemeenschapsrecht*, (Antwerpen—Apeldoorn, 1995), *Training of Judges in Community Law, European Institute of Public Administration*, (Maastricht, 1994), J. Baquero Cruz, 'La procédure préjudicielle suffit-il à garantir l'efficacité et l'uniformité du droit de l'Union Européenne?' in L. Azoulai & L. Burgorgue-Larsen, *L'autorité de l'Union Européenne*, (Bruxelles, 2006). Some concerns were also expressed at the FIDE Congress 2000, in Helsinki. See, for instance, the general report on 'The Duties of Cooperation of National Authorities and Courts and the Community Institutions under Article 10 EC Treaty', by John Temple Lang and the *Report by the Working Party on the Future of the European Communities' Court System* (report of the Due

of EC Membership national judges, even the 'younger' generation, are rather still struggling with EC law than smoothly applying it.

There are still—too many—judges unfamiliar with Community law. Under the current working conditions, they do not have much time to fill this gap in knowledge. The knowledge of EC law that students gain during their study is, on average, not very impressive either and, as a rule, it is not 'operational'. National courts still have difficulty in identifying the EC legal problem and, then, in coping with it. EC law is sometimes applied badly or avoided or circumvented. All this is usually not a matter of reluctance or laziness, but rather of limited knowledge or ignorance.

The role of the national judiciary in the Community system of judicial protection and EC law enforcement is furthermore complicated by the recent and the future enlargement. The application and enforcement of EC law poses specific problems in the new Member States and the accession countries, in addition to the particular problems the judges there are already facing.[11] Apart from the quite obvious point that judges in these States were never trained in EC law, it is necessary to realize that parts of EC law, like competition or public procurement are, by their very nature, new for them. Further, traditional attitudes, such as legal positivism, with a strong fixation on written law, make it difficult to cope with the approach of Community law, which is much more oriented to case law.

Good functioning of the Bench is intimately linked to the performance of the Bar. The point is, however, that the concerns just spelled out in relation to the judiciary also hold true—*mutatis mutandis*—for practising lawyers. While excellent and very knowledgeable EC law lawyers are concentrated in big law firms—dealing often with competition law mainly, an average 'advocate' finds him/herself in a comparable position as the national judge, as far as the knowledge, training and understanding of EU/EC law is concerned. Sometimes practising lawyers may even complicate the matter by grasping at European law as a last straw and submitting 'wild arguments' to the court which is supposed to make something meaningful out of it.

In brief, national courts must be better equipped to assume the role they have in the Community system of judicial protection. For that purpose, in the first place, much still has to be done in education and training of all those involved in the (possible) application of EC law, in order to improve national judges' awareness, knowledge and understanding of EC law. Much depends on the way such training

---

Committee), January 2000. Cf. also A.W.H.Meij, 'Guest Editorial: Architects or judges? Some comments in relation to the current debate', CMLRev. 2000, p. 1039, in particular at pp. 1044–1045.

[11] Cf. on this, for instance, D.M. Curtin & R.H. Van Ooik, 'Revamping the European Union's Enforcement Systems with a View to Eastern Enlargement', *WRR Working Document 110*, (The Hague, 2000). The Commission's Reports (at <http://www.europa.eu.int/comm/enlargement/candidate.htm>) on the candidate countries' progress towards accession included some information about the problems related to the 'judicial capacity'. See also E. Blankenburg, 'Legal Culture in Five Central European Countries', *WRR Working Document 111*, (The Hague, 2000) and Z. Kühn, 'The Application of European Law in the New Member States: Several (Early) Predictions', German Law Journal (2005) 563. For a very critical view, F. Emmert, 'Administrative and Court Reform in Central and Eastern Europe', ELJ 2003, pp. 288–315.

is organized. Short and incidental courses[12] often still focussing on a description of the Community institutions are obviously insufficient. EC law must be embedded in the permanent professional training of the judiciary. Apart from all the modalities of how EC law can be given effect and the system of judicial protection in the EU, such training must also address the most important parts of substantive EC law. Moreover, parallel to specific EU/EC law courses, EU/EC law should also be fully integrated into courses on national law.[13] Paradoxically, some comprehensive training programmes running in several Central and Eastern European countries seem more intensive and sometimes of a higher level compared to what the judges *in* the 'old' EU member States were ever taught.

It is also necessary to redefine the methods of education and training. European legal issues, EC law developments and their impact on day-to-day practice must be properly connected to the reality of that practice and fit within the frame of reference of the persons involved. This latter point is also closely linked with a rather peculiar phenomenon: it is striking how difficult it is for lawyers with a national law background to 'translate' the possible implications of EC law for national legal practice.[14] To this one may add that although there are perhaps already many manuals and specialized periodicals dealing with matters of EC law not often do these translate the implications of EC law for nationally-oriented lawyers.[15]

In relation to training, a complicating factor is that ordinary judges are not confronted with EC law on an everyday basis, or at least they don't think so. This may in some cases be a correct appraisal of the situation,[16] but sometimes the relevance of EC law does not occur to them because they just simply are unaware. Whatever the case may be, the fact is that there is not a naturally compelling drive for judges to acquaint themselves with EC law. Training which is not of immediate relevance to their daily work will not attract much attention.[17]

---

[12] This also holds true for programs like Schumann and Grotius, which have a limited impact only. Interestingly, quite some training initiatives are taken by the Commission in the area of Freedom, Security and Justice, prompted by the requirement of mutual trust and as a means of confidence-building, the two key notions governing this area. See, for instance, The Hague Programme: Strengthening Freedom, Security and Justice in the European Union, OJ 2005, C 53/1 and The Action Plan implementing the Hague Programme, OJ 2005, C 198/1. The problem here is, however, that these—somewhat monomaniac—initiatives focus on the FSJ mainly.

[13] This was, for long time, an issue that was ignored, partly because EC law was considered as some exotic specialization and its influence on national legal issues was rather under estimated. In some instances, where attention to EC law was paid, it was treated as an alien influence, which had to be approached with considerable suspicion. On the other hand it must be stressed that training in EC law solely through national law does not do justice to the unique system and method of EC law and its horizontal impact upon the often vertically stratified domains of national law.

[14] And there is a problem the other way round too: experts in EC law have difficulty in making this translation since they do not know enough of the national legal issues.

[15] Although, it must be noted that in The Netherlands, more and more general or even specialized periodicals do have regular reports on European developments in the domain concerned.

[16] In this respect it may be noted that, on the other hand, EC law protagonists tend to exaggerate the relevance of EC law for everyday practice.

[17] In The Netherlands, for instance, short introductory and compulsory courses are organized for trainee-judges. However, advanced level courses, which are not compulsory, are hardly

Finally, imparting or up-dating knowledge does not suffice. Training as to how to use the available sources is also necessary. This point is, in fact, closely linked to the next issue, namely the need to set up, within the Member States, an appropriate structure for assisting judges in the application of Community law.

From several sides,[18] pleas have been made for a powerful information system, safeguarding easy access to Community legislation and case law and for setting up national information or expertise centres on Community law, with the necessary computer links and staffed with experts, who may provide assistance and guidance to national judges.[19] After all, the experts know what to look for and where to search, while for others the information seems inaccessible. Another proposal is to appoint judges who are specialized in Community law, in order to assist in cases with an EC law dimension. They could either sit in these cases as a judge, or act as a special advisor or a kind of advocate general.

Although many of these proposals are valuable and may be helpful in several respects, to an extent they remain a palliative or, even worse, a dangerous recourse in the sense that they may produce perverse effects. Assistance to national courts can never replace the need for judges to have their own knowledge and understanding of EC law. It is primarily they who must be able to identify a problem of Community law. Or, put differently, they must develop a 'réflexe communautaire'.[20] Not every judge needs to know all the ins and outs of Community law (and who is able to know that nowadays, anyhow?) but they must have a sufficient awareness of

---

attended; unless there is a 'scandal', like sex-discrimination in social security, years ago, or the more recent '*Securitel* saga', sparked off by Case C-194/94 *CIA Security* [1996] ECR I-2201. Only more recently have a number of concrete and innovative steps been taken, like a broadly set up training for the judiciary, co-ordinated by the SSR (Stichting Studiecentrum Rechtspleging, the Dutch Training and Study Centre for the Judiciary), including more specialized courses like European social security law, European immigration law, European criminal law and European environmental law.

[18] Cf. several reports to the XIX FIDE Congress 2000, in Helsinki (e.g. the general report by John Temple Lang, 'The Duties of Co-operation of National Authorities and Courts and Community Institutions under Article 10 EC Treaty') and the *Report by the Working Party on the Future of the European Communities' Court System* (report of the 'Due Committee'), January 2000, at pp. 18–19. In the Netherlands, recently, specialists in EU law were appointed at all courts, who function as contact persons for EU law matters in their court. These specialists—who are already judges sitting in their court—meet regularly in the context of a network. The meetings and activities of this network overlap to a certain extent with the meetings and work of another, much older network, namely the Eurogroup. This group was established in 1995 in the context of the *Nederlandse Vereniging voor Rechtspraak* (Dutch Association for Judges and Public Prosecutors) with its main purpose to concentrate and study European law issues, in particular those which occur in everyday court practice.

[19] In this respect it could also be useful to create a system in which judges from other Member States could see how their colleagues are tackling a certain Community law problem. In fact, there is a hint in that direction in Case 283/81 *CILFIT* [1982] ECR 3415, where the ECJ observed, on the point of *acte clair*, that, before the national court comes to the conclusion that there is no reasonable doubt as to the manner in which a question of Community law has to be resolved, the court 'must be convinced that the matter is equally obvious to the courts of the other member States . . .' (point 16). An interesting initiative is, in this respect, an effort by the Association of Councils of State and Supreme Administrative Jurisdictions of the EU to publish important national cases, also involving European law, on their website: <www.raadvst-consetat.be>.

[20] Cf. Darmon en Huglo, 'La formation des juges en droit communautaire', in *Mélanges en hommage à Michel Waelbroeck*, (Brussel, 1999), at p. 306.

the EC law aspects in the cases they are dealing with. Assistance by specialists and experts may, at a certain point, be necessary, but the role the experts and specialist play must not lead to reinforcing the picture of EC law as a highly specialized area, which is inaccessible and perhaps even not directly relevant for the outside world. It is exactly this traditional approach of Community law as a specialization which is hampering its full integration into the basic 'tool kit' of the ordinary judge.

However, despite improvements in training and assisting national judges, it is not difficult to imagine that quite some interference will still be necessary by the ECJ, through the preliminary procedure, as courts will continue to need assistance. Arguably, the purpose of the preliminary procedure is not to inform courts about the state of development of Community law but to safeguard its unity and coherence.[21] However, the two issues are closely linked: even a well-equipped and well-trained national court, which is able to resolve several questions of EC law on its own, will at a certain point need guidance from the ECJ, which in turn is relevant for the unity and coherence of EC law. How soon and often this will occur depends on the 'EC law self-sufficiency' of the court in question.

III. Preliminary Procedure Under Pressure

The discussions about the ever increasing workload of the ECJ in general—and in preliminary cases in particular—and the risks this involves for the judicial function in the EU are well-known and certainly not new. In brief, the ECJ has backlog which is likely to increase as more and more cases are referred to Luxembourg. The preliminary procedure before the Court takes, on average, one and a half to two years and the workload puts the quality of the Court's work at risk. Although recently there was some improvement in the average duration of the preliminary procedure—23 months—this is probably only temporary.[22]

The 'problems in Luxembourg' obviously also have an impact on the application of EC law by national courts. Since the national system of judicial protection is, through the preliminary procedure, intimately linked with the procedure before the ECJ, sand in the Luxembourg machinery has direct consequences for the national judicial machinery. A lengthy preliminary procedure often means that many other (non-referred) cases have to wait and poorly reasoned preliminary rulings are not of much help to the national judge; these factors contribute to national courts avoiding EC law issues.

The prospects for the (near) future do not give rise to much optimism: more national judges find their way to Luxembourg and the areas in which the Court

---

[21] Cf. A.W.H. Meij, 'Guest Editorial: Architects or judges? Some comments in relation to the current debate', CMLRev. 2000, p. 1039, at p. 1044.

[22] The slight improvement is due to the measures taken to improve the efficiency of the working methods of the Court, the implementation of the amendments made by the Treaty of Nice and the arrival of 10 new judges. Cf. the Annual Report of the ECJ for 2004, at p. 12.

has or will have jurisdiction in the near future are increasing and increasingly varied.[23] Last but not least, not only will the accession of new Member States result in more cases,[24] more language problems, more translation problems and delays, but there will be more legal systems and cultures to bridge and probably also more difficulties in reaching agreement within the Court.[25] Finally, there are no prospects that—in the short term—the quality, complexity and what is called 'constructive ambiguity' of the Community legislative output will improve, despite several efforts of simplification and codification of Community legislation. Indeed, enlargement will complicate these matters rather than improve them.

Increasing workload on the one hand; the need to act within reasonable time limits while maintaining high quality of work, safeguarding adequate judicial protection and uniform and consistent interpretation, and application of the law on the other hand: is this not a dilemma for every mature legal system?

No doubt, there are specific features of EC law which complicate this already complex question of how to safeguard a certain level of uniformity of law and a high quality of adjudication. Although Community law has developed far beyond its initial objective—the establishment and operation of the Common market— the concept of the Common market is still important. Since a Common market is only common if the rules are uniformly interpreted and applied, the need for uniform interpretation and application seems obvious. Also the Court's task in the development of the law is different from the role that (highest) national courts play in this respect. The Community legislative process is slow and cumbersome; it is often lagging behind social needs and developments.[26] Legislation is often incomplete and sometimes also contradictory. There is still a relatively incomplete legal system and no mature common legal culture to provide well-defined methods and approaches to legal problems.[27] Apart from differences in legal approaches,[28] there are fewer common values and more ideological and sociological differences to set the background in which the law operates: views on the

[23] For instance the transfer of Schengen acquis from the third to the first pillar, the area of visa and asylum policy and other matters within Title IV EC-Treaty, decentralization of competition law, forthcoming European patents and possibly other industrial property rights, the (limited) jurisdiction in the third pillar .

[24] At least on the longer run; according to the statistics for 2004 there were only two references from the new Member States, namely from Hungary.

[25] It was argued that, since within the European courts, '25 legal traditions meet in 20 possible languages' the prospects for increasing drastically the processing capacity are rather limited. Cf. A. W. H. Meij, Effective preliminary cooperation: some eclectic notes, in *The Uncertain Future of the Preliminary Procedure*, Symposium Council of State, the Netherlands, 30 January 2004, The Hague 2004.   [26] Cf. for instance the saga of amending Regulation 1612/68.

[27] It is, however, to some extent arguable, that, little by little, things are changing. Cf. K. Mortelmans, 'Community Law: More than a Functional Area of Law, less than a Legal System', in LIEI, *Special Issue dedicated to Richard H. Lauwaars*, (1996) or J.Bell, 'Mechanisms for Cross-fertilisation of Administrative Law in Europe', in J. Beatson & T. Tridimas, *New Directions in European Public Law*, (Oxford, 1998).

[28] For instance, the French legalistic tradition versus the more flexible and result-oriented method of German lawyers with more scope for interpretation.

tasks of political institutions, on the one hand, and courts, on the other, opinions in moral and religious matters, conceptions of authority, the relevance and scope of general interest, differences in appreciation of the roles of public enterprises, all these—and many other—issues influence the way in which the law is understood, interpreted and applied. Not surprisingly, in such an incomplete and immanently pluralistic legal system, there often exists genuine uncertainty about the scope and meaning of EC law, which has to be resolved by a Community court. Seen from this perspective, uniform application was labelled by one author as a 'sort of existential problem of the Community legal order' and, therefore, the construction of the judiciary must be such as to limit the enhanced risk of divergence.[29]

However, do these special characteristics require that every single preliminary question be dealt with by the ECJ? The same author has also observed that the abstract focus on the importance of uniform application renders it almost impossible to work out an intelligible proposal of what preliminary questions should go to the Court.[30]

To this one may also add that, as in national legal orders, divergence has to be taken for granted to an extent. The question should perhaps rather be how much uniformity is required and, then, how to safeguard *a certain level* of uniformity?[31] The Community legal order already lives with consciously divergent rules, for instance, where options are left for the Member States in Community legislation or where it refers back to national law for the definition of legal concepts. However, in other respects as well, divergent interpretation and application of a Community rule may appear to be inherent to the Community legal system. This may happen, for instance, at the stage of appreciation of the requirement of necessity and proportionality in a free movement case. It may also happen where a substantive concept, as interpreted by the Court, is applied by the national judge. As is widely known, national procedural and remedial rules differ and, in addition to divergence in remedies and procedures, there is also divergence at the stage of translating Community law into national legal categories. In brief, wherever national law takes over, a kind of transformation takes place and the outcomes may differ. It is noticeable that, quite recently, some authors proposed that the ECJ should limit itself to setting standards for the doctrine of direct effect or the definition of the constitutive conditions of remedies and leave the modalities of application, in principle, to the national legal systems.[32] These proposals seem to draw on the idea that it is up to the Court to define the core, the main contours, or the skeleton of the rules at issue. These may then be 'fleshed out' by national

---

[29] P. Dyrberg, 'What should the Court of Justice be doing?', ELR 2001, p. 291, at p. 295.

[30] *ibid.*, p. 296.

[31] This is indeed closely linked to the question how much uniformity, in particular through harmonization, is needed.

[32] Cf. J.H. Jans & J.M. Prinssen, 'Direct Effect: Convergence or Divergence? A Comparative Perspective', in J.M. Prinssen and A. Schrauwen (eds), *Direct Effect. Rethinking a Classic of EC Legal Doctrine*, (Groningen, 2002), p. 107 and W. van Gerven, 'Of Rights, Remedies and Procedures', CMLRev. 2000, p. 501.

courts. In my view, it is worthwhile further to reflect on whether this approach could not be extrapolated to problems of interpretation of Community law in general, leaving only 'the core' for the ECJ to decide.

IV. What Should the National Courts be Doing?

The workload of the Court has been cause for concern ever since the 1970s and so has the preliminary procedure. The possible reforms to the judicial structure in the EU have generated a wealth of literature, reports, proposals and other documents, in particular the new and sometimes radical suggestions for reform made in the context of the IGC which ended with the adoption of the Treaty of Maastricht.[33] During the last decade several minor and mainly procedural changes have helped to reduce the workload of the Court and the length of the procedure in preliminary cases. However, in the course of the preparation of the 'Nice—IGC', attention to the European judicial system went beyond technical issues. Many documents and publications addressed much broader questions about the nature and role of the European judicial branch and the need for structural reform.[34]

The Nice Treaty itself introduced some important innovations, opening the door for possibly far-reaching reforms.[35] One of them is the possibility of conferring upon the CFI jurisdiction to give preliminary rulings in certain types of cases. Under Article 225(3) TEC the transfer of jurisdiction to the CFI in preliminary proceedings shall concern 'specific areas laid down by the Statute'. The crucial question is what type of cases will go to the CFI and according to what criteria will this be decided. In my opinion, from a long-term perspective, it would be unfortunate to stick to what is laid down in Article 225(3) TEC, namely giving the CFI a certain predefined category of cases. The major problem is that there are no appropriate criteria to be used for such a division of jurisdiction; neither the subject matter nor the status of the referring judge is a good guide as to the importance of the issues raised. From a short-term perspective, it would seem prudent to start the transfer of jurisdiction to the CFI 'in bits and pieces', preferably in areas in which it already has quite some expertise and which are closely linked with the

---

[33] The best known is probably that of J-P. Jacqué and J.H.H. Weiler, 'On the Road to European Union: A New Judicial Architecture', CMLRev. 1990, p. 185.

[34] For the sake of brevity, I mention only two vital documents: *The Future of the Judicial System of the European Union–Proposals and Reflections* (prepared by the ECJ/CFI), May 1999, and *Report by the Working Party on the Future of the European Communities' Court System* (report of the so-called Due Committee), January 2000, and one recent publication with many other references, M. Donny and E. Bribosia (eds.), *L'avenir du système juridictionnel de l'Union européenne*, (Bruxelles, 2002).

[35] According to Declaration 12 *et seq.* to the Nice Treaty, the Court and the Commission are supposed to submit proposals in order to make these novelties operational. For a brief discussion of these changes see, for instance, P. Eeckhout, 'The European Courts after Nice', in M. Andenas & J. Usher, *The Treaty of Nice and beyond: enlargement and constitutional reform*, (Oxford, 2003), p. 345.

direct actions brought to the CFI, such as competition and perhaps also intellectual property.[36]

However, at the end of the day, in my view, all preliminary references should go to the CFI.[37] The CFI should become the regular court for every action—direct actions and preliminary questions. Only cases of particular importance, novelty and complexity, which may seriously affect the unity and coherence of EU law or cases including important and new constitutional aspects should be dealt with by the ECJ. For this purpose, an appropriate mechanism should be put in place.[38]

It is striking that, as has been intensely observed,[39] in the discussions about the reform of the EU judicial function and in particular of the preliminary procedure, the focus is mainly on the Community courts' side of the problem, namely the management of the flood of references and the re-allocation of jurisdiction between the ECJ and the CFI. Although it is generally recognized that better training and assistance will help prevent premature, irrelevant or poorly prepared preliminary references, only few propose to enlarge the autonomous role of national courts in the application of EC law.

As I have already observed above, national courts will continue to require assistance from the ECJ, even if the ultimate purpose of the preliminary procedure is to safeguard the unity and coherence of Community law. In legal literature it has been proposed to abolish the preliminary procedure since only then would national courts be forced to treat Community law as an integral part of the national legal order. Both constitutional and more practical arguments have been put forward to underpin this proposition.[40] It is no doubt incongruous that national courts which are at least in functional terms a part of the EC judiciary, are called upon to apply EC law which, however, is still mainly considered as an alien law.[41] Although I have serious doubts that abolishing the preliminary procedure would make Community law more domestic than it is now, I will not speculate about any further effects of such a radical step. In any case, the fact remains that, as with any legal system, Community law needs a mechanism to safeguard its unity and coherence. For these purposes, the preliminary procedure is not doing that

[36] Until now, no agreement has been reached on a proposal.

[37] For a more detailed discussion of this proposal, see S. Prechal, 'Administration of Justice in the EU—who should do what?', in *La Cour de justice des Communautés européennes 1952–2002: bilan et perspectives*, Actes de la conférence organisée dans le cadre du cinquantième anniversaire de la Cour de justice, (Bruxelles, 2004). Cf. also, in the same vein, U. Everling, 'The Future of the European Judiciary within the Enlarged European Union', in *Mélanges en hommage à Michel Waelbroeck*, (Bruxelles, 1999) and P. Eeckhout, op. cit. note 35, at p. 363.

[38] Which is in fact already there, namely from the CFI to the ECJ provided for in Article 225(3) EC Treaty. In addition, the ECJ may be invited by an Advocate General to reconsider a case. Cf. Article 225(3) EC Treaty, in combination with Article 62 of the Statute for the Court of Justice.

[39] Cf. A.W.H.Meij, Guest Editorial, 'Architects or judges? Some comments in relation to the current debate', CMLRev. 2000, p. 1039, p. 1044.

[40] Cf. P. Allot, 'Preliminary rulings—another infant disease', ELR 2000, p. 538 and A.W.H. Meij, 'National Courts, European Law and Preliminary Co-operation', in R.H.M. Jansen *et al.* (eds), *European Ambitions of the National Judiciary*, (Deventer, 1997).

[41] On alienation, see also G. Davies, 'Abstractness and concreteness in the preliminary procedure' in Niamh Nic Shuibhne (ed.), *Regulating the internal market*, (Cheltenham, 2006).

badly at all. It is uncertain whether the alternatives, such as appeal or a sort of 'cassation' would do better.[42]

Moreover, as was already argued, there is a category of cases for which assistance from the ECJ is needed. These cases do not necessarily pertain to the basic principles of Community law, but stem from the uncertainty that Community law is still causing and from the new areas which are affected by Community law. Therefore, in terms of both assistance and development of the law the preliminary procedure must be maintained.

How large the category of the referred cases will remain, will depend for an important part on national judges. Arguably, we may ask more from the national courts, both in terms of better preparation of preliminary references and in terms of 'auto-limitation'.[43] On the one hand, 'auto-limitation' could turn out to be a means of educating national judges and stimulating them to take more responsibility in EC law matters. On the other hand, such 'auto-limitation' can only work properly if national courts are sufficiently acquainted with the principal features of EU law. It is submitted that only then will they be able to assess adequately the appropriateness of the reference, i.e. whether 'the question is one of general importance and the ruling is likely to promote the uniform application of the law throughout the European Union'.[44]

Another proposal, in which national courts play a crucial role, has been submitted by former ECJ Judge, P. Kapteyn[45]: courts of first instance should address their preliminary questions to specially established chambers of the courts at final instance. If this chamber of the supreme court considers that the issue is of general interest for the uniformity or development of Community law, the chamber should make a reference to the ECJ. In other situations, it should answer the preliminary question itself, in a non-binding opinion, on which the parties to the dispute may comment before the court of first instance. If the decision of the latter

---

[42] For a discussion see, for instance, P. Craig, 'The Jurisdiction of the Community Courts Reconsidered', in G. de Búrca and J.H.H. Weiler, *The European Court of Justice*, (Oxford, 2001), pp. 177–214, at pp. 201–204.

[43] Cf. F. Jacobs, 'The Role of National Courts and of the European Court of Justice in ensuring the Uniform Application of Community Law: Is a New Approach Needed?', in *Studi in onore de Francesco Capotorti, Vol. II.*, (Milano, 1999). A more active role for national courts is also advocated by the former ECJ Judge G. Hirsch, 'Das Vorabentscheidungsverfahren: Mehr Freiraum und mehr Verantwortung für die nationalen Gerichte', in N. Colneric *et. al.*, *Une communauté de droit, Festschrift für Gil Carlos Rodríguez Iglesias*, (Berliner Wissenschafts-Verlag, Berlin, 2003). For a critical discussion of 'auto-limitation' see, for instance, G. Vandersanden, 'La procédure préjudicielle: à la recherche d'une identité perdue', in *Mélanges en hommage à Michel Waelbroeck*, (Bruxelles, 1999) p. 619, in particular at pp. 634–641 and J. Baquero Cruz, op. cit. note 10.

[44] F. Jacobs, op.cit. note 43, at p. 180. Former ECJ Judge Kapteyn has proposed a comparable criterion to be taken into account by the lower courts when they consider making a reference: the general interest of the Community in avoiding divergent interpretation of basic Community rules by lower courts in various Member States must be at stake and an authoritative ruling by the ECJ may be of more general importance for similar cases. Cf. P.J.G.Kapteyn, 'Europe's Expectation of its Judges', in R.H.M. Jansen *et al.* (eds), *European Ambitions of the National Judiciary*, (Deventer, 1997), at p. 185. There is also a certain analogy to the 'core' issues of EU law, mentioned above, in Section III.

[45] Cf. P.J.G. Kapteyn, 'Reflections on the Future of the Judicial System of the European Union after Nice', YEL 2001, p. 123, in particular at pp. 183–185.

court is appealed, the appeal court will still be empowered to make a reference to the ECJ. Such a procedure is believed to encourage national judges themselves to resolve problems of interpretation and application of EU law.

A more active role for national courts is also inherent to the so-called 'green-light procedure', proposed by the Dutch CFI Judge A. Meij. He points to the artificial distinction between interpretation and application of the law, which is inherent to the preliminary reference procedure as it functions at present. In his view, the national court should complete the entire process of judicial decision-making in the case at hand and it should make a complete draft judgment, including an interpretation of the provisions of EU law that are at stake. The preliminary question should then be accompanied by this draft judgment. Next, it will be up to the ECJ to decide whether full proceedings are necessary in respect of the unity or consistent development of EC law. In cases where, in the light of the solution envisaged by the referring court, there are no issues of unity and further development of EU law, the case may be sent back to the national court. In this way, the latter will get a 'green light' to proceed with the case.[46]

The various proposals, which aim at shifting the responsibility for the interpretation of Community law to national courts, will require an adjustment of the *Cilfit* criteria.[47] However, in the first place, they imply that national courts should be better placed to give informed decisions in cases involving Community law and to decide whether a case is of sufficient importance to be referred to the Community court for preliminary decision. The need for better training, facilities and technical assistance which is indispensable in this respect was discussed above. Moreover, as was also pointed out above, the approach and policy in these matters must be such that Community law is regarded and treated not as a sort of exotic specialization, but as a field of law that can occur in every legal context. Yet there remains another issue to be addressed in relation to the national courts' role. Even if the courts are well-trained, familiar with and experienced in Community law, the fact remains that in their function of 'Community judiciary' they may be required to do something which is beyond the powers they have under national (constitutional) law. This is the topic of the next Section.

V. Duties v. Powers

The very fact that the national courts have been made accomplices in the enforcement of Community law has led to a situation in which the *formal* source of their power stems from the national legal order, while the *substance* of their function

---

[46] Cf. A.W.H. Meij, op. cit. note 25. Same concerns about the artificial division of law application and law interpretation have been voiced by G. Davies, op. cit. note 41, who favours an appeal structure instead of the preliminary reference. See also J. Baquero Cruz, op. cit. note 10 and G. Hirsch, op. cit. note 43.

[47] Case 283/81 *CILFIT* [1982] ECR 3415. See, however, the reserved position of the ECJ in Case C-461/03 *Schul* [2005] ECR I-10513.

may originate in Community law. In other words, they remain national judges but they have a Community law mission. This mission may imply certain duties for which, in order to accomplish them successfully, the courts do not always have the necessary powers or are even straightforwardly prohibited from taking a certain course of action. The most obvious example of this is indeed the doctrine of supremacy of EC law, as expounded in the *Simmenthal* case.[48] This case made clear that even those courts which are not allowed to do so in national law must review national (primary) legislation and this review must, at least, result in setting aside the national rules which conflict with Community law. It other words, it also extends to national procedural or constitutional rules which would prevent the courts from giving effect to EC law.[49]

The duty of the national court to give effect and precedence to Community law stems from the system of the Treaty as interpreted by the ECJ—*i.e.* Community law is considered as an integral part of the legal systems of the Member States 'which their Courts are bound to apply' and which cannot be overridden by domestic legal provisions[50]—as well as from Article 10 EC.[51] A second, national basis for these duties is explicitly or implicitly (and not always perfectly) provided either in national constitutions or in Acts regulating the accession of a Member State to the EC. As is well known, the acceptance of direct effect and supremacy, in terms of national constitutional law as well, has resulted in changing the traditional subordination of the judiciary to the legislature which was, in different degrees, the common model in many Member States.

In 1976, the Court started to develop another line of case law in the *Comet* and *Rewe* judgments which made explicit the basis of the national court's duty or task of protecting the rights which individuals derive from Community law, namely Article 10. Another argument may also be drawn from the rule of law. The control required by the rule of law necessarily involves the application of Community law by the national courts. Similarly, the principle of the '*Rechtsstaat*' requires that the rights of individuals be effectively protected. In the absence of protection provided directly by the Court of Justice at national level, this task must be assumed by the national courts.

The subsequent development was and still is not very easy to grasp. Over the years, the case law relating to the problems of enforcement of Community law through national procedural and remedial mechanisms has grown increasingly complex and, not surprisingly, it has generated a wealth of literature. The appreciation of the case law ranges from critical comments—blaming the Court for unnecessary interference with national procedural and remedial law in favour of

---

[48] Case 106/77 *Simmenthal* [1978] ECR 585.

[49] This duty of the courts may be considered as a procedural aspect of supremacy, in addition to the 'normal' effect of supremacy, namely that provisions of Community law have precedence over national rules.   [50] Case 6/64 *Costa v. ENEL* [1964] ECR 585, at. p. 593.

[51] Cf. for instance Case C-213/89 *Factortame* [1990] ECR I-2433, Case 190/87 *Moormann* [1988] ECR 4689.

effectiveness of Community law—to pleas for further uniformity to be introduced, preferably by harmonizing certain aspects of national procedures and remedies.[52] In some cases, the ECJ seems to respect entirely the notion of national procedural autonomy and requires that only the two—rather minimal—principles of equivalence and effectiveness be met. In other cases it seems to be the principle of effective judicial protection, 'discovered' some 10 years after *Comet* and *Rewe*,[53] which is relied upon as a source of the national courts' duties. This latter principle proved to be capable of having a considerable—if not disruptive—impact on the national systems of judicial protection and it developed into a powerful source of various duties of national courts, including, arguably, the creation of new remedies. The principle of effective judicial protection culminated, *inter alia*, in the acceptance of State liability for breaches of Community law, as laid down for the first time in *Francovich*[54] and developed since then.

An additional difficulty is that it is not clear how the approach along the line of effectiveness/effective judicial protection relates to the far-reaching dicta of *Simmenthal* and later also of *Factortame*.[55] These two cases may be explained by the fact that the national rules at issue, which hindered the effective application of Community law, were of a constitutional nature.[56] However, the acceptance of State liability for legislative wrongs of the primary legislature is also in many countries barred by constitutional principles. Yet here the ECJ does not rely on a *Simmenthal/Factortame*-type solution, since those two cases gave the impression that supremacy and the duty of setting aside may immunize the most fundamental (constitutional) rules and principles.

An example of the difficulties that national courts are facing in this uncertain context is found in the *Waterpakt* case, decided relatively recently by the Dutch Hoge Raad.[57] In that case several environmental organizations sought, *inter alia*,

[52] See, for instance, A. Biondi, 'The European Court of Justice and Certain National Procedural Limitations: Not Such a Thorough Relationship', CMLRev. 1999, p. 1271; M. Hoskins, 'Tilting the balance: Supremacy and national procedural rules', (1996) EL Rev., p. 365; G. De Búrca, 'National procedural rules and remedies: The changing approach of the Court of Justice' in J. Lonbay and A. Biondi (eds.), *Remedies for Breach of EC Law* (Chichester, 1997); p. 37, W. Van Gerven, 'Of rights, remedies and procedures', CMLRev. 2000, p. 501; S. Prechal, 'Judge-made harmonisation of national procedural rules: a bridging perspective', in J. Wouters and J. Stuyck (eds.), *Principles of Proper Conduct for Supranational, State and Private Actors in the European Union: Towards a Ius Commune, Essays in Honour of Walter van Gerven*, (Antwerpen, Groningen, Oxford, 2001), p. 39; M. Dougan, 'Enforcing the Single Market: The Judicial Harmonisation of National Remedies and Procedural Rules', in C. Barnard and J. Scott (eds.), *The Law of the Single European Market*, (Oxford, 2002), p. 153 and P. Girerd, 'Les principes d'équivalence et effectivité: encadrement ou désencadrement de l'autonomie procédurale des Etats membres?', RTDE 2002, p.75.

[53] Namely in Case 222/84 *Johnston* [1986] ECR 1651.

[54] Joined Cases C-6/90 and C-9/90 [1991] ECR I-5357.

[55] The *Factortame* judgment is in fact based on both: the supremacy argument from *Simmenthal* and the need for effective judicial protection.

[56] For an effort to find an explanation see, for instance, S. Prechal, *Directives in EC Law*, (Oxford, 2005), in particular pp. 137–142 and the Opinion of A-G Jacobs in Joined Cases C-430/93 and C-431/93 *Van Schijndel* [1995] ECR I-4705.

[57] Judgment of 21 March 2003, JB 2003, nr. 120. For a discussion of this case in English, see CMLRev. 2004, p.1429 (by Besselink).

an order to legislate, before a certain deadline, directed at the State. The substance concerned the non-implementation of Directive 91/676 ('nitrates directive'). In 'cassation', the Hoge Raad held, *inter alia*, that, under Dutch constitutional law, the making of primary legislation is a political process in which the Government and the parliament act together and balance all the interests involved. It is not for the courts to interfere in this process. Even when the legislation has to be adopted in order to comply with a directive, that does not change the matter. According to the Hoge Raad, the courts still lack jurisdiction in this respect because the question as to whether legislation should be adopted and, then, what the content of the legislation would be, remains a matter for the political branch. It is also up to that branch to choose for non-implementation and consequently risk an action under Article 226 TEC. As to the specific point, namely whether Community law dictates a different solution, the Hoge Raad referred to the duty of national courts to ensure the full effect of Community law and to protect the rights which individuals may derive from that law. However, it followed from *Van Schijndel* that this duty exists only within the scope of competences and jurisdiction as defined under national law. In Dutch law the limit prescribed was exactly that the courts have no jurisdiction to order the adoption of primary legislation.

From a Community law perspective, this decision is certainly debatable, in particular because the Hoge Raad did not make a preliminary reference, against the Advocate General's suggestion. Equally, arguments about the political choice of the legislator—to implement or not—leave a Community law minded reader somewhat perplexed.[58] However, the case also illustrates the difficult position of a national court which is told, on the one hand, that jurisdiction as defined by national law is decisive, provided that the minimum requirements of equivalence and effectiveness are satisfied and on the other hand, in cases such as *Simmenthal*, *Factortame* and the State liability case law, that the constitutional rules have to yield to the effective application of Community law and that if the courts do not have jurisdiction, they have to assume it.

The national—constitutional or other, for instance, procedural—rules, principles, notions and doctrines under discussion here often reflect the position of the national courts within that national constitutional context, i.e. *vis-à-vis* the other State organs. The arguments against far-reaching intrusion by the courts in the process of effective application of Community law often relate to the separation of powers and the limits of the judicial function in the constitutional setting. However, this is not necessarily so. There are also other principles which may restrain national courts' actions. For instance in case of *Nimz*,[59] the problem was rather in how far a court may interfere in collective agreements, therefore with what both sides of the industry have agreed. Similarly, in *Van Schijndel*,[60] it was

---

[58] For instance, how to reconcile it with the ECJ's finding that non-implementation constitutes *per se* a sufficiently serious breach?

[59] Case C-184/89 [1991] ECR I-292. Cf. also the more recent case, Case C-187/00 *Kutz-Bauer* [2003] ECR I-2741.   [60] Joined Cases C-430/93 and C-431/93, [1995] ECR I-4705.

one the most essential features of civil law that was at stake, namely the parties' freedom of disposition. According to this principle, in civil proceedings, the initiative as to the extent to and manner in which the parties should proceed lies in their hands. They determine the issues to be ruled on by the court; it is in principle up to them to choose the cause of action or defence, as well as the remedy they are seeking. The parties' freedom of disposition implies that Community law is not to be applied when the parties—intentionally or by negligence—do not rely on Community law provisions. The central issue to the *Van Schijndel* case was whether Community law has a special status in this respect and whether the requirement of its full and effective application may change this situation, thus, in fact, limiting the procedural freedom of the parties.

In this case the ECJ upheld the procedural equivalent of this freedom of disposition, namely the principle of judicial passivity in civil matters, that the national court should not go beyond the ambit of the dispute and asserted facts as presented by the parties. According to the ECJ, this principle 'reflects conceptions prevailing in most of the Member States as to the relations between the State and the individual; it safeguards the rights of defence; and it ensures proper conduct of the proceedings by, in particular, protecting them from delays inherent to examination of new pleas'.[61]

The complex case law just briefly sketched above relates, as a rule, to situations in which the protection of individuals against Member State authorities or against other individuals[62] is at stake. However, after some hesitation in previous cases, the ECJ has fully imported this case law into the 'second limb' of the 'complete system of judicial protection'. In its judgment in the case of *Union de Pequeños Agricultores*[63] it decided, somewhat in contrast to its earlier case law, that standing in an Article 230 TEC action cannot depend on whether an individual can bring an action in the national courts. But it also pointed out that 'national courts are required, as far as possible, to interpret and apply national procedural rules governing the exercise of rights of action in a way that enables natural and legal persons to challenge before the courts the legality of any decision or other national measure relative to the application to them of a Community act of general application, by pleading the invalidity of such act.'[64] Apparently, the national courts are expected to stretch the provisions of their own legal system, perhaps sometimes even of what is reasonably possible and, moreover, this seems to be based on the erroneous assumption that national courts are perfectly able to deal adequately with Community law matters.[65]

---

[61] Point 21 of the judgment.   [62] Cf. Case C-453/99 *Courage* [2001] ECR I-6297.

[63] Case C-50/00P *Union de Pequeños Agricultores* [2002] ECR I-6677.

[64] Point 42 of the judgment.

[65] Some authors seem to be very optimistic about what the courts may do. Cf. J. Temple Lang, 'Actions for declarations that Community regulations are invalid: the duties of national courts under Article 10 EC', ELRev. 2003, p. 102. Others take a more cautious position and point out what type of difficulties this approach may cause. Cf. P. Cassia, 'Le juge administratif français et la validité des actes communautaires', RTDeur 1999, p. 409.

In general, national courts have a considerable scope for manoeuvre (and imagination and creativity!) to satisfy the requirements of the ECJ. From a national law perspective, national constitutional, legislative or other rules and principles often provide, also in this respect, the necessary basis for adjusting the procedures and remedies in order to ensure effective judicial protection of individuals and full enforcement of Community law. However, as was already pointed out above, the limit is reached where a court is required to do something which is beyond its competence, i.e. beyond the rules—constitutional or otherwise—defining its powers. This is a particularly pressing question in situations where the national court should depart from the relevant rules defining its powers without it being possible to indicate an explicit Community law provision serving as a basis for the power to do this.

It is argued that the jurisprudential developments amount to a *direct empowerment* of national courts. These should, where necessary, extend their existing powers or assume, on the basis of Community law alone, new powers which do not exist under national law in order to fulfil effectively the task assigned to them by the Court of Justice. In my view, an assignment of tasks to the national courts, entrusting them with a Community law *mission* or giving them a *function* in the enforcement of Community law, cannot as such create the necessary *powers*. The same holds true for catchwords, like '*juge national en sa qualité de juge communautaire*' or the Community law mandate of the national judge. These do not create the necessary powers. The first merely describes the function of the national court; the second connotes the development brought about by the Court's case law which started to define the national courts' powers. The very problem is exactly that the basis for such a mandate is lacking. National courts are (still) organs of the national legal order. They still derive their authority from the State; as was already observed, the *formal* source of their power is national law.[66]

This state of affairs is in accordance with the principle of institutional autonomy: it is a matter for the Member States to decide which bodies will be entrusted with the fulfillment of obligations resulting from Community law and to give them the necessary powers for this purpose. Specifically in relation to courts this means that it is for the Member States to decide which court will have jurisdiction in matters involving Community law and to invest it with the necessary powers, enabling it to provide effective judicial protection. Due in particular to the Court's jurisprudence, the professed non-intervention in the internal organization of the Member States (the organization of the judiciary included) is under pressure and the case law is on some points rather ambiguous.[67] However, it is certainly not abolished as yet. It is therefore submitted that the national courts' Community law mission is in need of a more solid basis. The bases in Community law which have an *empowering effect* (i.e. which arguably create the necessary

---

[66] Cf. also the Opinion of A-G Léger in Case C-224/01 *Köbler* [2003] ECR I-10239, at point 66.

[67] By referring, for instance, to the jurisdiction of national courts and thereby suggesting that they are still acting within their competence, the Court is concealing the real scope of its case law. Cf. what happened in this respect in the *Waterpakt* case, briefly discussed above.

powers for the national courts) and on which the Court sometimes seem to rely,—in particular the principle of effective judicial protection,[68] the full force and effect of Community law and the useful effect of Article 234 respectively, are rather tenuous and certainly debatable.

VI. Facilitating the National Courts' Mission: Some Suggestions

Many of the matters discussed in this contribution, in particular in Section II, are of a practical nature and, as such, they do not need any legislative, let alone constitutional or Treaty, provisions.[69] These include the rethinking educational methods, developing adequate training and devise new structures to assist national judges. After all, the requirement of a good knowledge and understanding of the basic tenets of European Union law on the part of all national judges and their ability to handle that law is fundamental. To this one may add other practical matters, such as smooth *exchange of information* between courts on how EU law is applied and interpreted. European liaisons and networks may facilitate this task. Mutual information, co-operation and networks where judges (from different Member States) can consult each other may also become increasingly important if the preliminary reference procedure does no longer function properly.

The recent reform of the EU judicial system and the methods of work of the Luxembourg courts has taken place after the new 'openings' in the Nice Treaty. However, it is questionable whether these changes will suffice. Further reform may be necessary in the middle to longer term. In this respect it should be re-emphasized that, if such steps will be taken, when reforming the system of judicial protection laid down in the Treaty and, in particular, the preliminary procedure, proper account must be taken of the 'reality' that national courts are facing. A system built on theoretical assumptions alone will not work. The small excursion into the reality of the national judge *'en sa qualité de juge communautaire'* made above indicates that any change to the co-operation between the national and the Community courts must be prepared with utmost caution, paying sufficient attention to this reality. Otherwise an important part of the Community system of judicial protection will again be based on a false assumption about the 'capacity' of the national courts. It is suggested that national judiciaries, for instance through their organizations, should be actively involved in possible upcoming changes to the EU judicial system and in particular to any future changes to the preliminary reference procedure. They should be able to make their views and concerns known and to anticipate what is going to happen.

---

[68] According to some authors (Temple Lang, *inter alia*) this principle boils down to the application of Article 10. Thus also Article 10 is assumed to have such an investitive power. For reasons set out above I cannot agree with this view.

[69] Cf. on these suggestions also S. Prechal, R.H. van Ooik *et al.*, op. cit. note 9 , in particular para. 4.2 and A.W.H. Meij, op. cit. note 25, para IV.

Finally, there are certain issues which could and should be addressed in—preferably—the EU Treaty, not primarily in order to change the state of affairs, but rather to make the role and function of the national courts more visible. The relevant provisions should be worded in such a way that they help national courts to assume more responsibility for the application of Community law in the exercise of their jurisdiction, and provide them with a useful and explicit tool for fulfilling their role in the Community law system of judicial protection. Particularly (but not only) with a view to the recent accession of many new Member States more explicit provisions are, in my opinion, of great importance.

In the build-up to the EU Constitutional Treaty, some suggestions have been made to that effect. For instance, Jacques Ziller and Jaroslaw Lotarski have proposed that in the Constitutional Treaty a provision should be included stating that national courts are 'associates' of the ECJ and that they are obliged to apply European Union law.[70] While the second obligation might, in my opinion, be included in a Treaty text, for instance as a specification of the obligations resulting from Article 10, I have difficulty with the first limb of their proposal. Ziller and Lotarski argue that national courts are *de facto* '*des juridictions de droit commun de l'Union*'. The Constitutional Treaty should not be silent on their role. However, it is not easy to understand why there should be such a provision on national courts and not on other national organs, like the legislator and in particular the national administration. All these are, in their respective roles, called upon to implement, apply, enforce or otherwise give effect to Community law.[71] This is the consequence of the quasi-federal structure of the EC and the mainly decentralized system of implementing legislation, administration and enforcement (with, indeed, as one of the consequences, adjudication of disputes involving community law by national courts). The role of national administrative authorities and even the national legislator may also be conceived as one of an 'associate'.[72] The role of national courts, in collaboration with the ECJ through the preliminary procedure, has been perhaps—not least due to 'vigilant individuals'—more spectacular, but that does not as such justify a specific provision in the Treaty.

If ever the Constitutional Treaty is going to be revitalized or another round of EU Treaty revision will take place, it seems more appropriate to emphasize the national courts' role in the context of the preliminary procedure. This could take shape in the form of an explicit mention of this mission, as proposed by the Due Committee, namely that national courts have full authority to deal with questions of Community law which they encounter in the exercise of their

---

[70] Cf. J. Ziller and J. Lotarski, 'Institutions et organes judiciaires', in B. de Witte (ed.), *Ten Reflections on the Constitutional Treaty for Europe* (Florence, EUI, 2003).

[71] For a brief account, with further references to national reports, see J. Dutheil de la Rochère & I.Pernice, 'European Union Law and National Constitutions', General Report, FIDE 2002, London.

[72] Cf., for instance, the role of national authorities in the administration of the European Social Fund or in the context of the placing on the market of products containing GMOs. Another illustration of how intertwined the EC and national administrations are and the complications this may give rise to in the context of (State) liability is provided in Case C-275/00 *Franex* [2002] ECR I-10943.

national jurisdiction.[73] Second, the 'immanent' duty of the courts to give effect and precedence to Community law should be reinforced by codifying the Court's case law in the Treaty, thus by inserting a provision about the relationship between national and Community law, provided that the formulation leaves enough scope for further development.[74] Third, the national courts' role in relation to providing effective judicial protection should be facilitated. This could be done by stating in general terms what is increasingly commonly provided for in secondary legislation,[75] namely that the Member States must provide for remedies and procedures in national courts which ensure effective judicial protection for the rights guaranteed by Union law.[76] These type of provisions may be used as a stepping stone when interpreting their own powers and may therefore help national courts to give effect to their obligations to provide effective judicial protection.

The reference to a general obligation of the Member Sates to provide for effective remedies and procedures brings me to another vital point. Not only at Community or European Union level but also at national level the necessary—parallel—provisions should be enacted in national constitutional or other relevant texts, in order to improve the 'interconnection' between Community/Union and national legal orders, facilitating the national courts' role.[77] The national courts may, with the creativity they have already shown, often find the necessary solutions. However, it is submitted that with a view to minimizing the possibility of conflict and for reasons of clarity, there is also an important role for those ultimately responsible for the relevant national (constitutional) provisions to ensure that there is a certain harmony between the European and national levels. The gap which the national courts are regularly asked to bridge and which stems from the tension between the formal and substantive mandates, should be kept as narrow as possible.

---

[73] *Report by the Working Party on the Future of the European Communities' Court System*, January 2000, at p. 14. The proposed text of Article III-362 (old Article 234 TEC) does not address this matter, neither does any other provision of the Constitutional Treaty.

[74] Cf. the principle of supremacy, as it was laid down in Article I-6 of the Constitutional Treaty.

[75] See, for instance, Article 12 of Directive 96/9 (protection of databases), Article 7 of Directive 93/13 (unfair terms in consumer contracts) and Article 7 of Directive 2000/43 (race/ethnic origin discrimination). Obviously, these provisions relate only to the subject matter of the Directive at issue.

[76] A provision to such effect was included in the Constitutional Treaty in Article I-29.

[77] A good example of mutual reinforcement is, for instance, the German case law of the BverG, according to which the ECJ is to be considered as the 'gesetzliche Richter'. Under certain circumstances, not making a preliminary reference does not amount only to a violation of Community law but also of Article 101(1) of the German Constitution. Cf. on this C.D. Classen, 'German *Bundesverfassungsgericht*: Medical training, Decision of 9 January 2001', CMLRev. 2002, p. 641–652. See also Case C-25/02 *Rinke* [2003] ECR I-8349.

The Action for Annulment, the Preliminary Reference on Validity and the Plea of Illegality: Complementary or Alternative Means?

*Carmen Martínez Capdevila**

I. The Issue Raised

It is well known that the EC Treaty includes three mechanisms addressed at controlling the lawfulness of acts adopted by Community institutions: the action for annulment (Article 230), the preliminary reference on validity (Article 234), and the plea of illegality (Article 241).[1] These are not only the means specifically established in the EC Treaty for this purpose but, according to the *Fotofrost* ruling,[2] they are the only means possible.

An action for annulment is to be filed within two months and may refer to any binding act of secondary law. It can be brought by: the Council, the Commission, the European Parliament and the Member States, all of which are 'privileged claimants'; by the ECB and the Court of Auditors, which can only act to defend their prerogatives; and, by private individuals, who may only seek the annulment of decisions of which they are the addressees, and of any other binding act that may directly and individually concern them.

The preliminary reference on validity can only be raised to the ECJ by the courts of Member States. It may refer to any EC act, whether binding or

* PhD in Law. Professor of International Public Law (Universidad Autónoma de Madrid). This article is a version of the article published in the Revista de Derecho Comunitario Europeo, iss. 20 (2005), entitled 'El recurso de anulaci ón, la cuestión prejudicial de validez y la excepci ón de ilegalidad: vías complementarias o alternativas?'. The author wishes to express her acknowledgment to Professor Javier Díez-Hochleitner (Universidad Autónoma de Madrid) for his comments and to Fernando Bergasa Cáceres for his help with the translation.

[1] The action for damages (Article 235 EC) could be added to these three mechanisms, because although it is not specifically intended to control the lawfulness of secondary law—but rather to declare the institutions liability for the damages they have caused, insofar as the concurrence of that liability is subject to the unlawful nature of the Community measure from which the damage arose—the grounds of all judgments in which this is upheld will necessarily contain considerations on the unlawfulness of the conduct of the respondent institution.

[2] Case 314/85, [1987] E.C.R. 4199.

non-binding, that the referring court must apply when resolving on a pending case.[3] The preliminary reference is said to be non time-barred, because the validity of a measure can be monitored in this way, irrespective of when it became public knowledge.

With regard to the plea of illegality, Article 241 EC sets forth that this may be raised by 'any party in proceedings in which a regulation (...) is at issue'. Despite the literal content of this provision, the ECJ has extended its material scope of application to all general acts.[4] In the same way as with the preliminary reference, the plea of illegality is not time-barred.

The grounds of unlawfulness, common to the three means described, are listed in Article 230 EC: infringement of the Treaty, lack of competence, infringement of an essential procedural requirement, and misuse of powers.

The considerations made so far demonstrate that the material scopes of the three procedures can overlap: a binding act can be subject to an action for annulment and to a preliminary reference and if, furthermore, it has a general scope, it can also be subject to a plea of illegality. In this exposé, we will analyse the relationship that exists between, on the one hand, the action for annulment (as a means that enable a direct verification of legality) and, on the other, the preliminary reference on validity and the plea of illegality (as indirect means of performing the same verification).

The relevant question is whether these are complementary or alternative means. In other words, does the fact that a particular party can file an action for annulment against a certain act prevent it from incidentally contesting its lawfulness at the ECJ (plea of illegality) or in national courts (preliminary reference on validity)?

The EC Treaty does not provide a clear response to this question. Therefore, the ECJ has been at liberty to construct its own doctrine, which we will now describe and comment.

II. The Response From The ECJ

The Court's position regarding the relation between direct and indirect mechanisms for reviewing the legality of binding acts in EC secondary law is not unambiguous.

---

[3] In relation to the different scope of the action for annulment and the preliminary reference on validity with regard to acts reviewable under one or the other procedure (the first covers only the binding acts, while the second also extends to non-binding ones), the ECJ has maintained: 'unlike Article 173 of the EEC Treaty [now Article 230 EC], which excludes review by the Court of acts in the nature of recommendations, Article 177 [now Article 234] confers on the Court jurisdiction to give a preliminary ruling on the validity and interpretation of all acts of the institutions of the Community without exception' (Case C-322/88, *Grimaldi* [1989] E.C.R. I-4407, para. 8).

[4] Case 92/78, *Simmenthal IV* [1979] E.C.R. 777, paras. 40–41.

A. Complementary Nature of Direct and Indirect Means of Controlling Lawfulness: Parallel Application

In the *Rau* case, the Court held that 'the possibility of bringing a direct action under the second paragraph of Article 173 of the EEC Treaty [now Article 230 EC] against a decision adopted by a Community institution does not preclude the possibility of bringing an action in a national court against a measure adopted by a national authority for the implementation of that decision on the ground that the latter decision is unlawful'.[5]

The ECJ affirmation seems to imply that, irrespective of whether it is exercised, mere legal standing within the context of an action for annulment at no time precludes use of the preliminary reference procedure. The Court has subsequently been compelled to clarify its pronouncement to respond to those who—citing the *Rau* judgment—claimed entitlement, at expiry of the two months established in Article 230 EC, to invoke in national courts the unlawfulness of Community acts whose annulment could have requested to the Court of Justice. In the *TWD* and *Wiljo* cases, the ECJ ascertained that the report for the hearing in the *Rau* case evidenced that the claimants in the principal proceeding had brought an action before the ECJ for the annulment of the decision to which the preliminary reference referred. This meant that in that judgment: 'the Court did not therefore rule, and did not have to rule, (…) on the time-barring effects of the expiry of time-limits'.[6]

The only thing that the ECJ would have accepted in *Rau* is that the fact that a particular party had exercised the right of appeal acknowledged under Article 230 EC against a particular act, does not preclude it from initiating parallel proceedings to query its validity in national courts.

The action for annulment and the preliminary reference can, therefore, be consolidated and exercised in tandem. In this respect, they are perfectly complementary mechanisms.[7]

---

[5] Joined Cases 133–136/85, [1987] E.C.R. 2289, para. 12. For a comment on this pronouncement, see Bebr, 'The Reinforcement of the Constitutional Review of Community Acts under Article 177 EEC Treaty', 26 CML Rev. (1989), 667–691, 684–691.

[6] Case C-188/92, *TWD* [1994] E.C.R. I-833, para. 20; Case C-178/95, *Wiljo* [1997] E.C.R. I-585, para. 22.

[7] Given the short time-limit established in the EC Treaty to file an action for annulment, the usual way to proceed for the party concerned is to address itself firstly to the ECJ and subsequently, insofar as the proceeding is still pending and the Court has not ordered that application of the contested act be suspended as an interim measure, to incidentally query its validity in national courts. In any event, if the Community act were to be implemented promptly, it could also occur that an entity queries its lawfulness in national courts and then (because, for example, it wishes to obtain the suspension of its application in the territory of all Member States) decides to file an action for annulment.

B. Alternative Nature of the Direct and Indirect Means of Controlling Lawfulness: The Party that Refrained from Bringing an Annulment Action Against a Certain Act, cannot Incidentally Query its Validity Later On

According to settled case law of the Court of Justice, decisions whose legality is not called into question by their addressees within the two months laid down in Article 230 EC, shall become definitive as against those parties.

In accordance with this principle, the Court has systematically declared that, within the framework of an infringement action, a Member State cannot properly plead the unlawfulness of a decision addressed to it when it has allowed the period in which an action for annulment could have been filed to expire. There have been numerous pronouncements in this respect; for example, we can mention the judgment of 12 October 1978 in the *Commission v. Belgium* case, the judgment of 10 June 1993 in the *Commission v. Greece* case, and the judgment of 26 June 2003 in the *Commission v. Spain* case.[8]

The Court refusal to allow Member States to incidentally invoke the unlawfulness of decisions of which they are the addressees at the ECJ extends to procedural spheres other than infringement actions. In the context of an action for annulment brought by Spain against two Commission decisions, the ECJ raised the matter of whether it was possible to accept that the first of these two decisions was subject to a plea of illegality that would arise as the foundation of an action for annulment brought against the second decision. The Court replied categorically:

to accept that an applicant could, in an action for annulment of a decision, raise a plea of unlawfulness against an earlier act of the same kind, annulment of which he could have sought directly, would make it possible indirectly to challenge earlier decisions which were not contested within the period for bringing proceedings prescribed in Article 173 [now Article 230] of the Treaty, thereby circumventing that time-limit.[9]

In the same way as with States, individuals cannot contest the validity of decisions of which they are addressees by means of Article 241 EC. In its judgment on the *Macchiorlati Dalmas* case, the Court stated that a different construction 'would conflict with the fundamental principle established by Article 33 [of the ECSC Treaty, concerning the action for annulment]. In fact the strict time-limit for instituting proceedings laid down by this provision is in keeping with the necessity to prevent the lawfulness of administrative decisions being called in question indefinitely'.[10]

---

[8] Case 156/77, *Commission v. Belgium* [1978] E.C.R. 1881, para. 20; Case C-183/91, *Commission v. Greece* [1993] E.C.R. I-3131, para. 10; Case C-404/00, *Commission v. Spain* [2003] E.C.R. I-6695, para. 40. Other pronouncements are: Case 52/83, *Commission v. France* [1983] E.C.R. 3707, para. 10; Case 52/84, *Commission v. Belgium* [1986] E.C.R. 89, para. 13; Case 226/87, *Commission v. Greece* [1988] E.C.R. 3611, para. 14; Case C-404/97, *Commission v. Portugal* [2000] E.C.R. I-4897, para. 34.

[9] Case C-135/93, *Spain v. Commission* [1995] E.C.R. I-1651, para. 17.

[10] Case 21/64, [1965] E.C.R. 227, 244.

Similarly, the ECJ rejects that, once the time-limit under Article 230 CE has expired, the State and individuals who are the addressees of a decision can query the validity of the latter (this time) in national courts when they have not appealed directly. In the *National Farmers' Union* judgment, the Court was particularly explicit:

a Member State which is an addressee of Decisions (. . .) and which has not challenged the lawfulness of those decisions within the time-limit laid down by the fifth paragraph of Article 230 EC does not have standing subsequently before a national court to invoke their unlawfulness in order to dispute the merits of an action brought against it.[11]

With regard to individuals, in the *Wiljo* judgment, the Court did not accept that this company, the addressee of a Commission decision for which annulment had not been requested beforehand, could subsequently contest its legality in support of an action lodged at an Antwerp court against the implementing act issued by the Belgian authorities.[12]

Bearing in mind that both Member States and individuals have legal standing to bring an action for annulment against decisions addressed against them, the quoted case law supports the idea that, at least in the case of decisions, the Court believes that those entitled to bring an action for annulment, but who fail to do so within the term established in the EC Treaty, cannot subsequently contest the validity of the decision in question.

What about acts other than decisions addressed to States or individuals? In these cases, does the Court also establish a link between the conditions for admissibility of Article 230 EC, on the one hand, and of Articles 234 and 241 EC, on the other, thus leading to excluding results? In most cases, it would seem that this is indeed the case.

Starting with directives, in the judgment of 27 October 1992, in the *Commission v. Germany* case, the ECJ denied this country the possibility to plead as a defence the unlawfulness of the provision of the Sixth Directive that it was accused of infringing.[13]

The Court has not been that clear with respect to regulations. In fact, its *modus operandi* in the *Commission v. Germany* case, resolved in a judgment of 18 September 1986, in which it examined (and finally dismissed) the plea of illegality raised by the German government in the context of the appeal filed against it for an alleged infringement of Regulation 1698/70, offers a certain degree of support to the idea that, in the case of regulations, there would be no time-bar for a State to query its validity.[14] In all events, this is not a position of principle.

Regarding individuals and, more specifically, their authority to challenge in national courts the legality of regulations, directives or decisions addressed to a third party, the Court of Justice case law enables us to conclude that the action for

11 Case C-241/01, [2002] E.C.R. I-9079, para. 39.
12 Case C-178/95, n. 6 above, para. 24.   13 Case C-74/91, [1992] E.C.R. I-5437, para. 10.
14 Case 116/82, [1986] E.C.R. 2519.

annulment and the preliminary reference also have an alternative nature. With a slight difference: in order for legal and natural persons to forfeit their capacity to query the validity of this kind of measures in national courts, the ECJ does not exclusively assess whether they do have legal standing to approach the CFI directly or not, but requires that this *jus standi*, in addition to existing, must be beyond doubt. Only when there is no doubt that an individual could have filed an action for annulment against any of such measures, will the Court deny the possibility to allege its invalidity in national courts; only then will what N. Moloney calls the 'guillotine effect' occur.[15]

Thus, in the *University of Hamburg* case, the ECJ accepted that this institution could question the validity of a Commission decision addressed to all Member States in a German court. This was so because, however much it was directly and individually concerned by the decision, given the circumstances of the case, the University had no reason to be aware of the effects of the decision on itself.[16]

On the contrary, in the *TWD* case, the Court challenged the right of this company to contest the validity of a Commission decision addressed to the German government in a national court, inasmuch as that company was not only immediately made aware of it but, in addition, had been informed by the national Administration of the possibility to file an action for annulment against it.[17]

In the *Accrington Beef*,[18] *Eurotunnel*[19] and *Nachi*[20] cases, the ECJ seems to accept that the principle established for decisions addressed to a third party also applies when a directive (*Eurotunnel*) or a regulation (*Accrington Beef* and *Nachi*) is involved. We can deduce from its preliminary rulings in these cases that, for the Court, unambiguous legal standing under Article 230 EC (undoubted legal standing that applied to *Nachi*, but not to *Accrington Beef* or *Eurotunnel*) deprives an individual of the possibility to invoke the invalidity of such measures in national courts, once the time-limit set down in that Article has expired. With regard to an individual who could have applied for annulment, the regulation or directive will then become definitive.[21]

---

[15] 39 CML Rev. (2002), 393–405, at 396.

[16] Case 216/82, [1983] E.C.R. 2771. For a comment on this pronouncement, see Usher, 'Preliminary References on Individual Decisions: The Undecided Question or a Plea of Unlawfulness?', 9 ELR (1984), 106–108.

[17] Case C-188/92, n. 6 above. For a comment on this pronouncement, see Hoskins, 31 CML Rev. (1994), 1399–1408; Ross, 'Limits on Using Article 177 EC', 19 ELR (1994), 640–644; Simon, 1995 JDI, 438–440; Turner, 'Challenging EC Law before a National Court: a Further Restriction of the Rights of Natural and Legal Persons?', 1 Irish Journal of European Law (1995), 68–87; Wyatt, 'The Relationship between Actions for Annulment and References on Validity after *TWD Deggendorf*', in Lonbay and Biondi (Eds.), *Remedies for Breach of EC Law* (Chichester, 1997), 55–66.

[18] Case C-241/95, [1996] E.C.R. I-6699.

[19] Case C-408/95, [1997] E.C.R. I-6315. For a comment see Stanley, 35 CML Rev. (1998), 1205–1213.

[20] Case C-239/99, [2001] E.C.R. I-1197. This pronouncement is commented by Moloney, n. 15 above.

[21] L. Danieli summarizes the Court of Justice case law as follows: 'la competenza del giudice comunitario e quella dei giudici nazionali si configurano come alternative, con prevalenza della

Pending deeper analysis, it seems understandable that individuals are deprived of their faculty to query the validity of an act other than decisions adopted against them in national courts only when their right to seek annulment from the CFI was undoubted. As we have said, the legal standing of individuals to directly challenge these measures depends on whether they are directly and individually concerned. Although direct concern can easily be assessed (it is merely a matter of establishing that the act *per se* deprives the individual of a right or imposes an obligation upon him),[22] assessing individual concern (which means that the act affects him by reason of certain attributes which are peculiar to him or by reason of circumstances in which he is differentiated from all other persons)[23] is not so simple. Given the uncertainty surrounding an individual's right to bring an action for annulment against regulations, directives or decisions addressed to a third party, it would be too severe to establish a connection between the admissibility of an action for annulment on the one hand, and the preliminary reference on the other, thus denying an individual access to the latter procedure because, albeit unaware of the fact, he could have filed an action for annulment.[24] Moreover, the right to effective judicial protection would be in peril.

Also, the unambiguous nature of the *locus standi* of individuals required by the Court to exclude the means of incidental control avoids that individuals must ascertain, at the adoption of acts not addressed to them, whether they can bring an action for annulment against them.[25] In addition, it overlooks 'precautionary annulment actions', as called by G. Bebr.[26] Furthermore, it significantly reduces the complexity of the preliminary judgment to be made by national courts prior to filing the request for a preliminary reference,[27] since it is no longer a matter of determining whether an individual was entitled to a right of appeal pursuant to

---

prima sulla seconda, soltanto nei casi in cui l'interessato possa 'senza alcun dubbio' proporre un ricorso ai sensi dell'ar. 173 [now Article 230], quarto comma. Negli altri, invece, cioé quando la rice-vibilitá di un ricorso di annullamento é probabile ma non certa, le due competenze saranno tra di loro concorrenti' ('Brevi osservazioni in merito ad alcuni casi di interferenza tra competenza diretta del giudice comunitario e competenza dei giudici nazionali', in Nascimbene and Danieli, Eds., *Il ricorso di annullamento nel Trattato istitutivo della Comunitá europea*, Milan, 1998, 15–24, at 20).

[22] Case 112/77, *Töpfer* [1978] E.C.R. 1019.

[23] Case 25/62, *Plaumann* [1963] E.C.R. 197.

[24] AG Jacobs considers that the approach of the Court of Justice 'is (. . .) commended by the con-sideration that the rights of individuals should not be prejudiced as a result of uncertainty in the law' (Case C-188/92, *TWD*, n. 6 above, para. 26 of his Opinion).

[25] Carrera Hernández, *La excepción de la ilegalidad en el sistema jurisdiccional comunitario*, McGraw Hill, Madrid, 1997, 62.

[26] See n. 5 above, at 690. Similarly, P. Stanley states that '[o]ne is not to be penalized for declining to try one's luck in a doubtful case before the Court of First Instance' (n. 19 above, at 1211).

[27] Regarding this criticism to the ECJ case law, see Bebr, n. 5 above, at 689–690; *id.*, 'Direct and Indirect Judicial Control of Community Acts in Practice: The Relation between Articles 173 and 177 of the EEC Treaty', in *The Art of Governance. Festschrift zu Ehren von Eric Stein* (Baden-Baden, 1987), 91–111, at 96; Tesauro, 'The Effectiveness of Judicial Protection and Co-operation between the Court of Justice and the National Courts', 13 YEL (1993), 1–17, at 16; Ross, n. 17 above, at 643–644; Turner, n. 17 above, at 86.

Article 230 EC, but rather, in the words of P. Stanley, 'it is sufficient that his position was not obvious'.[28]

When considering whether an individual did have an indubitable right (which he failed to use) to appeal to the CFI to obtain the annulment of an act other than a decision addressed to him, the ECJ not only takes account of the factual circumstances of the case, but also bears in mind strictly legal considerations. In this regard, in the *Nachi* case, the Court abided by its case law whereby regulations imposing an anti-dumping duty are liable to be of direct and individual concern to those importers whose retail prices for the products in question formed the basis of the constructed export price, in order to conclude that Nachi, a company that fulfilled those conditions, could 'undoubtedly' have availed itself of Article 230 EC (and could not therefore subsequently invoke the invalidity of the anti-dumping duty in a national court).[29]

Leaving aside the *Commission v. Germany* judgment, in which, as we have already said, the Court of Justice does not adopt a position of principle regarding the capacity of Member States to call into question a regulation by means of Article 241 EC, the remaining case law can be explained by the ECJ intention to safeguard legal certainty. 'The periods within which legal proceedings must be brought', states the ECJ, 'are intended to ensure legal certainty by preventing Community acts which produce legal effects from being called in question indefinitely'.[30]

Along with this premise, the ECJ has also sometimes advocated the respect of the deadline for appeal set forth in Article 230[31] and 'the requirements of good administration of justice and procedural economy'.[32]

The arguments above and pure consistency would lead us to believe that the Luxembourg Court would not accept that, at expiry of the time-limit laid down in

---

[28] See Stanley n. 19 above, at 1213. In this respect, see the Opinion of AG Jacobs in the *TWD* case (para. 26) and Tridimas, *The General Principles of EC Law* (Oxford, 1999), at 168. Nevertheless, J.A. Usher observes that 'even to distinguish between cases where there is no doubt and cases where there may be difficulties requires a preliminary investigation of the same sort, particularly since the relevant case law has not been marked by total consistency' ('Direct and Individual Concern: An Effective Remedy or a Conventional Solution?', 28 ELR (2003), 575–600, at 590).

[29] Case C-239/99, n. 20 above, para. 40.

[30] Case C-188/92, *TWD*, n. 6 above, para. 16; Case C-178/95, *Wiljo*, n. 6 above, para. 19; Case C-310/97 P, *Commission v. AssiiDomän Kraft Products* [1999] E.C.R. I-5363, para. 61; Case C-239/99, *Nachi*, n. 20 above, para. 29; Case C-241/01, *National Farmers' Union*, n. 11 above, para. 34.

As regards the protection of legal certainty as the reason why the ECJ prohibits access to the incidental means of controlling the lawfulness of EC secondary law to those who could have directly applied for annulment of a certain act, it is interesting to underline that, in many cases in which the Court has refused that, within the context of an infringement proceeding, a State could defend itself arguing that the individual decision it was accused of infringing was unlawful (Case 156/77, *Commission v. Belgium*; Case 52/83, *Commission v. France*; Case 52/84, *Commission v. Belgium*; Case 226/87, *Commission v. Greece*; Case C-183/91, *Commission v. Greece*; Case C-404/97, *Commission v. Portugal*; Case C-404/00, *Commission v. Spain*; all cited in n. 8 above), the Court, far from referring to the literal content of Article 241 EC, which only considers regulations as the possible object of a plea of illegality, has repeatedly invoked, often as its only argument, the principle of legal certainty and the very system of appeals established by the Treaty.

[31] Case C-135/93, *Spain v. Commission*, n. 9 above, para. 17.

[32] Case C-310/97 P, *AssiDomän Kraft Products*, n. 30 above, para. 61.

Article 230, the ECB and the Court of Auditors could use the plea of illegality in order to denounce possible irregularities of an act associated with the defence of their prerogatives, as these could have been raised within the framework of an action for annulment.[33]

Surprisingly, the ECJ did not adopt this approach in its judgment of 10 July 2003 in the *Commission v. ECB* case.[34]

When seeking to clarify whether the plea of illegality raised by the ECB against Regulation 1073/1999 was admissible, the Court referred to the considerations made in *Nachi*, whereby 'a regulation becom[es] definitive as against an individual in regard to whom it must be considered to be an individual decision and who could undoubtedly have sought its annulment under Article 230 EC' and concluded that, as in the *Commission v. ECB* case, 'the legislative nature of Regulation 1073/1999 has not been challenged by any of the parties and that, more particularly, it has not been claimed that the regulation should be treated as a decision or that the ECB would, in such a case, be the addressee thereof', it was therefore not possible to deny the ECB the right to invoke the possible unlawfulness of Regulation 1073/1999 by means of Article 241 EC.

Thus, the Court extended the doctrine established in *Nachi* with regard to private individuals to the ECB: as the Regulation did not directly or individually concern the Bank, expiry of the time-limit under Article 230 EC did not make the right of the ECB to challenge its validity disappear.

In this application of the *Nachi* judgment to the ECB, the Court of Justice overlooked the fact that the *jus standi* of individuals and of the ECB in an action for annulment is based on different postulates. The consequence was that the Court reached a conclusion that betrayed the main inspirational principle of its doctrine on the relationship between direct and indirect means of controlling the lawfulness of EC secondary law.

While the legal standing of individuals depends on the kind of the contested act and eventually on how this act may concern them, the legal standing of the ECB depends on the defect alleged. In the specific case of regulations, individuals may directly query their lawfulness if they are directly and individually concerned by them, whereas the ECB could do it when the enactment of such acts has violated any of its attributions. The statement whereby, being the Regulation 1073/1999 a true regulation, the ECB should be acknowledged the right to approach the ECJ

---

[33] Since the legal standing of the ECB and the Court of Auditors is subject to the defence of their prerogatives, their appeals can only be based on grounds that refer to infringement of the latter (see Case C-70/88, *European Parliament v. Council* [1990] E.C.R. I-2041).

[34] Case C-11/00, [2003] E.C.R. I-7147. This ruling has been widely commented for reasons different from those that concern us here; thus: Lavranos, 'The Limited, Functional Independence of the ECB', 29 ELR (2004), 115–123; Santos Vara, 'La independencia del Banco Central Europea y del Banco Europeo de Inversiones frente a la Oficina Europea de Lucha contra el Fraude (OLAF) (Comentario a las sentencias del TJCE de 10 julio de 2003, Comisión c. BCE y Comisión c. BEI)', 17 RDCE (2004), 237–257; Sucameli, 'L'indipendenza della Banca centrale europea fra separazione ed equilibrio istituzionale', 2004 Riv.it.dir.pubbl.comunitario, 694–705.

with no time-limit on the irregularities that can be invoked, would enable the Bank to allow the time-limit laid down in Article 230 EC to expire and still incidentally contest the legality of the regulation in question on the basis of its attributions. This approach would, however, go against what seems to be the *leitmotiv* of ECJ case law, which is to prevent a party that could have brought an action for annulment (against a specific act or on particular grounds), and who failed to do so, from disputing the validity of the act in question beyond the term provided in the Treaty for that purpose.

For the sake of consistency, it would have been reasonable to expect that the ECJ would have permitted the ECB to avail itself of Article 241 EC only in order to substantiate those defects which, insofar as they were not connected with its prerogatives, could not have been invoked within the context of Article 230 EC. In this respect, far from examining whether the enactment of Regulation 1073/1999 incurred in an infringement of an essential procedural requirement deriving from the fact that the requirement to consult the ECB beforehand not had not been observed, the Court should have directly denied this invocation from the Bank *ex* Article 241 EC.

Whilst waiting to see whether the Court will confirm or rectify the doctrine established in the *Commission v. ECB* ruling, we will now focus on the case in which the ECJ has accepted that expiry of the time-limit under Article 230 EC does not deprive the parties with a right to appeal (not exercised) of their possibility to subsequently invoke the unlawfulness of a specific act either at the ECJ or in national courts.

C. The 'Theory of Acts Non-existent' as Grounds for Access to the Means of Incidental Control by those having Legal Standing Under Article 230 EC

Early on, the Luxembourg Court has acknowledged that there are certain defects that render the acts of EC law not simply unlawful but, more radically, non-existent.[35] In his study on the 'theory of acts non-existent' in the EC legal system, A. Kalogeropoulos states: 'si l'acte juridique inexistant constitue l'opposé logique de l'acte juridique existant, il n'est pas moins opposé, aussi, à la notion de l'acte juridique simplement illégal, c'est-à-dire à l'acte juridique qui, tout en ne remplissant pas les conditions d'une légalité parfaite, en raison des vices dont il est atteint, doit, cependant, être considéré comme juridique existant, c'est-à-dire intégré, même provisoirement, dans l'ordre juridique concerné'.[36]

---

[35] On the 'theory of acts non-existent' in EC law see Van Empel, 'L'acte public inexistant et le droit communautaire', (1971) CDE, 251–283, at 269–283; Bergeres, 'La théorie de l'inexistence en droit communautaire', (1989) RTDE, 393–437 and 647–683; Kalogeropoulos, 'Eléments de l'application de la théorie de l'inexistence des actes juridiques en droit communautaire', in *Etat-Loi-Administration. Mélanges en l'honneur d'Epaminondas P. Spiliotopoulos* (Athens, 1998), 181–201.

[36] Kalogeropoulos, *ibid.*, at 181.

The first reference to acts non-existent can be found in the judgment of 10 December 1957 in the *Société des usines à tubes de la Sarre v. High Authority* case.[37] In this pronouncement the Court held that the statement of reasons 'is an essential, indeed constituent element of (. . .) an act, with the result that in the absence of a statement of reasons the act cannot exist'.[38]

As regards which faults will render an act non-existent, the Court has declared that 'for reasons of legal certainty which are evident, that classification must (. . .) be restricted under Community law, as under the national legal systems which provide for it, to acts which exhibit particularly serious and manifest defects'.[39]

'For an act to be (. . .) deprived of the presumption of validity which the Treaties attach, for obvious reasons of legal certainty, even to irregular acts of the institutions, the irregularity must be so gross and so obvious that it goes far beyond a 'normal' irregularity resulting from an erroneous assessment of the facts or from a breach of the law'.[40]

Severity and evidence of the defect are two conditions that must concur.[41] In this respect, in some judgments the ECJ has denied that a particular act could be regarded as being non-existent merely on observing that the defect alleged was not self-evident, since it could not be detected from a reading of the act.[42]

In any event, the Court has understood that, because of the gravity of the consequences attaching to a finding that an act of a Community institution is non-existent, such a finding must be reserved for 'quite extreme situations'.[43]

We address here the 'theory of acts non-existent', because it represents an exception to the case law analysed in the preceding section. To quote the Court, 'if a measure is deemed to be non-existent, the finding may be made, even after the period for instituting proceedings has expired, that the measure has not produced any legal effects'.[44] In other words, when addressing acts non-existent, expiry of the time-limit of Article 230 EC does not produce the usual closure; accordingly,

---

[37] Joined Cases 1 and 14/57, [1957] E.C.R. 201.

[38] *ibid.*, at 220. It is necessary to point out that this statement is substantiated by the circumstances of the case; indeed, in pronouncements immediately subsequent to this one, the Court will conclude that the absence or insufficiency of the statement of reasons does not render an act non-existent, but simply unlawful (Case 18/57, *Nold I* [1959] E.C.R. 89; Case 8-11/66, *Société anonyme Cimenterie set al.* [1967] E.C.R. 93).

[39] Case 15/85, *Consorzio cooperative d'Abruzzo v. Commission* [1987] E.C.R. 1005, para. 10; Case 226/87, *Commission v. Greece*, n. 8 above, para. 16; Case T-156/89, *Valverde Mordt v. European Court of Justice* [1991] E.C.R. II-407, para. 84. For a comment on the first of these pronouncements, see Letemendia, 'Le retrait d'un acte illegal', (1989) CDE, 627–645.

[40] Case T-156/89, *ibid.*, para. 84.

[41] Although the ECJ generally mentions the 'severity' and the 'evidence' of the irregularity as being two different conditions, it seems that on some occasions it wished to reduce these to one single condition: that of the 'evidence of the severity' (Case C-137/92 P, *BASF* [1994] E.C.R. I-2555, paras. 49 and 52; Case C-200/92 P, *ICI* [1999] E.C.R. I-4399, paras. 70 and 72).

[42] Case 15/85, *Consorzio cooperative d'Abruzzo*, n. 39 above, para. 11.

[43] Joined Cases T-79, 84–86, 89, 91, 92, 94, 96, 98, 102 and 104/89, *BASF* [1992] E.C.R. II-315, para. 50; Case C-200/92 P, *ICI*, n. 41 above, para. 71.

[44] Case 15/85, *Consorzio cooperative d'Abruzzo*, n. 39 above, para. 10.

even the party having *jus standi* under that provision could, in all events, benefit from the mechanisms described in Articles 234 and 241 EC.

It is worth remarking that, according to ECJ doctrine, it is not possible to file an action for annulment against an act non-existent, as, by definition, it would have no subject matter. In the *Société des usines à tubes de la Sarre* and *BASF* judgments, the ECJ and the CFI, respectively, declared for this reason that both proceedings were inadmissible.[45] Albeit logical, the solution could nonetheless seem strange: how can the Court annul acts that entail lesser irregularities and yet be unable to do the same with acts that incur in serious and obvious irregularities? T.C. Hartley downgrades the importance of this paradox: 'in practice (. . .) this is not as serious a drawback as it might appear since, if the Court gives a judgment stating that the case is inadmissible because the 'act' is non-existent, the practical effect will be the same as a declaration of invalidity (and costs may even be granted to the applicant -who is technically the losing party- if he can show that the defendant was at fault in leading him to believe that the 'act' was in fact legally effective)'.[46] J. García Luengo believes that, in any event, it is advisable for the Court to judge these acts non-existent and to issue a judgment that puts an end to any semblance of validity that may have arisen.[47]

Thus, we cannot deduce from the Luxembourg Court case law that, when an act non-existent is involved, the direct and indirect means of controlling the lawfulness of the EC secondary law become complementary or cumulative. What happens instead is that expiry of the time-limit under Article 230 EC does not produce the usual preclusive effect for the parties to which this provision acknowledges *jus standi*.

The CFI judgment in the *BASF* case whereby 'non-existent measures may be challenged without regard to time-limits'[48] could be completed, for our purposes, with 'and without considering the role that a determined party is acknowledged in the context of Article 230 EC'.

With regard those cases in which there are significant irregularities, the ECJ priority is to eliminate the acts from the legal system. Accordingly, it facilitates their suppression by accepting that any party can incidentally query their lawfulness at the ECJ or in national courts, even after expiry of the two months provided to file

---

[45] Joined Cases 1 and 14/57, *Société des usines à tubes de la Sarre*, n. 37 above, 220; Joined Cases T-79, 84–86, 89, 91, 92, 94, 96, 98, 102 and 104/89, *BASF*, n. 43 above, para. 101. In the first case, the finding that the act was non-existent arose when examining the admissibility of the appeal; in the second, although this was not expressly stated, the examination of admissibility was combined with that of the merits of the case.

The CFI ruling in the *BASF* case was later quashed by the ECJ, which did not uphold the argument that the irregularities of the Commission decision had sufficient entity to render it non-existent (Case C-137/92 P, n. 41 above). For a comment on the two judgments issued in the *BASF* case, that of the CFI and that of the ECJ, see Toth, 32 CML Rev. (1995), 271–304.

As regards the existence of an act as a preliminary condition for the admissibility of an action for annulment, see Schepisi, 'La nozione di atto impugnabile ai sensi dell'art. 173 del trattato CE', en Nascimbene and Danieli (Eds.), *Il ricorso di annullamento.*, n. 21 above, 109–140, at 111–114.

[46] *The Foundations of European Community Law* (Oxford, 2003), at 348.

[47] *El recurso comunitario de anulación: objeto y admisibilidad* (Madrid, 2004), at 123.

[48] Joined Cases T-79, 84–86, 89, 91, 92, 94, 96, 98, 102 and 104/89, *BASF*, n. 43 above, para. 101.

the action for annulment. In these cases, the Court sacrifices the valued legal certainty (which, as we have said, supports maintaining those acts which, albeit with defects, were not challenged after a certain time) in order to safeguard the legality of the system. This is a principle which, unlike legal certainty, supports the elimination of irregular acts. As the ECJ has declared, the Community legal system 'cannot tolerate' patently and obviously invalid measures.[49]

To conclude, let us add a final idea in relation to the acts non-existent: that States can always argue that an act is non-existent as a defence to avoid a conviction for its infringement.[50]

III. Consequences of the ECJ Response

The case law analysed in the preceding section, particularly in points B and C, has several implications.

A. Ranking of Irregularities Under Article 230 EC

From a theoretical perspective, ECJ case law acknowledges that the grounds of illegality listed in Article 230 EC can arise in either an attenuated or a serious manner. In their 'decaffeinated' version, they can be invoked by those with legal standing in the action for annulment only within the two-month term established in the EC Treaty. In their 'strong' version, they can be invoked by them at any time ('theory of acts non-existent').

This ranking of causes of unlawfulness is present in many national legal systems. In the case of Spain, it enables us to differentiate between void and voidable acts.

As regards the conceptual equivalence between acts 'non-existent' and acts 'void', we must mention that in the *Valverde Mordt* judgment, the CFI accepted that the second of these concepts, invoked by the appellant, 'corresponds in substance to the provision, recognised in the case law of the Court of Justice, according to which, in exceptional circumstances, a measure may be deemed to be non-existent if it exhibits particularly serious and manifest defects'.[51] T.C. Hartley uses the terms 'void' and 'voidable', when he states that 'in Community law the general provision is that invalid acts are voidable, not void' or that 'for some

---

[49] C-135/93, *Spain v. Commission*, n. 9 above, para. 18.

[50] Case 226/87, *Commission v. Greece*, n. 8 above, para. 16; Case C-74/91, *Commission v. Germany*, n. 13 above, para. 11; Case C-404/97, *Commission v. Portugal*, n. 8 above, para. 35; Case C-404/00, *Commission v. Spain*, n. 8 above, para. 41; the idea was already implied, in a somewhat veiled form, in Joined Cases 6 and 11/69, *Commission v. France* [1969] E.C.R. 523. In 1972, P. Mathijsen called this a 'plea of nullity' ('Nullité et annulabilité des actes des institutions européennes', in *Miscellanea W.J. Ganshof van der Meersch. Studia ab discipulis amicisque edita*, Brussels, 1972, vol. II, 271–283, at 282), but, in light of the terminology used by the ECJ, it would today be perhaps more suitable to speak of a 'plea of non-existence'.

[51] Case T-156/89, n. 39 above, para. 84. The distinction between void acts and voidable acts appears in an early ECJ judgment, of July 12, 1957, whereby: 'In the opinion of the Court, the

purposes a voidable act which has not been annulled within the time-limit has the same effect as a valid one'.[52]

B. Member States cannot Challenge the Validity of Binding Acts in National Courts

Additionally, we can deduce from the stand taken by the ECJ that, in principle, unless there are particularly serious and manifest irregularities that render the act in question non-existent or unless they have lodged an action for annulment that is still pending a decision, States would be unable to challenge the validity of a regulation, a directive or a decision addressed against a third party in national courts after the two-month period laid down in Article 230 EC. We have just seen that the Luxembourg Court denies this possibility to individuals when their right to appeal pursuant to Article 230 EC is beyond all doubt. Since the legal standing of Member States to petition the Court for annulment of the three kinds of measures considered is always beyond doubt, the conclusion would be that the former could never call into question their lawfulness in national courts. If we add to this the fact that the Court has expressly refuted that Member States can query the validity of decisions of which they are addressees in those same courts (*National Farmers' Union* judgment), the final conclusion must be that Member States cannot call into question in national courts the lawfulness of any binding act adopted by Community institutions.

Those who see parallel mechanisms for controlling the lawfulness of EC secondary law in the preliminary reference on validity and in the plea of illegality would furthermore conclude that Member States can never use the plea of illegality, unless against an act non-existent. They would then criticize the action of the ECJ in the *Commission v. Germany* case, because, instead of dismissing *a limine* the German government's allegation that the Commission regulation purportedly violated by that country was unlawful, the Court examined whether it did indeed incur in the irregularities denounced.

C. Extension of the Legal Standing of Individuals in the Action for Annulment may have a Price . . .

A further implication of the ECJ case law is that proposals to extend the *jus standi* of individuals under Article 230 EC (partially enacted by the Constitutional

---

unlawful nature of an individual administrative measure entails its complete nullity only in certain circumstances (. . .). Apart from those exceptional cases, the theoretical writing and the case law of the Member States allow only of voidability and revocability' (Joined Cases 7/56 and 3–7/57, *Algera* [1957] E.C.R. 39).

With regard to whether 'nullity' and 'non-existence' are interchangeable expressions or, on the contrary, they reflect two different legal realities, see Van Empel 'L'acte public inexistant . . .', n. 35 above, at 252–253.

[52] See n. 46 above, at 347–348.

Treaty) should be assessed carefully.[53] We should not overlook the fact that, until the Court changes its position, if the content of Article 230 EC is amended to extend the right to appeal of individuals, this would entail a reduction of their role within Articles 234 and 241 EC. It would then be necessary to ascertain which one is most suitable from the perspective of legal protection of private individuals: to have access to an action for annulment or to have the possibility to incidentally query the lawfulness of Community acts in the national courts and at the ECJ.

In his opinion on the *UPA* case, AG Jacobs expounds, with remarkable brilliance, the reasons which, in his opinion, make Article 230 EC preferable to Article 234 EC.[54] Among other things, the Advocate General emphasizes that the preliminary reference is a tool to be used at the discretion of the national courts, that in order for individuals to challenge a Community act in national courts, it is necessary for measures of implementation to have been enacted in national law, and that proceedings in the national courts, with the additional stage of a reference to the ECJ, are likely to involve substantial additional costs and delays. On the other side, proceedings before the CFI under Article 230 EC are more appropriate for determining issues of validity than reference proceedings under Article 234 EC because: (a) the institution that adopted the impugned measure is a party to the proceeding from beginning to end, (b) a direct action involves a full exchange of pleadings, and (c) it is possible for third parties to intervene. Following AG Jacobs there are additional advantages: the interim measures that may be adopted by the Court, in accordance with Articles 242 and 243 EC, will be effective in all Member States, and direct actions are the most satisfactory from the perspective of legal certainty, since they must be brought within the time-limit of two months, whereas the validity of Community measures may be questioned before the national courts at any point in time.

Without questioning the essence of AG Jacobs' reasoning, we would like to point out that some of his arguments are irrelevant from the perspective of judicial protection of private individuals. Specifically, the fact that the action for annulment enables a more complete examination of the lawfulness of Community acts, as long as the institutions that approved them are a party in the proceedings from the beginning and the intervention of third parties is possible, is irrelevant for private individuals, who do not act as agents of Community legality but are guided by their own personal interests.

At the same time, submitting an action for annulment within a limit of two months could be, as AG Jacobs states, an advantage in terms of legal certainty, but this may also be unsuitable for individuals. One advantage of both the preliminary reference and the plea of illegality is that they both make it possible to query

---

[53] Article III-365 of the Constitutional Treaty extends the *locus standi* of private individuals, insofar as, in order to acknowledge the possibility to challenge regulatory acts that do not entail implementing measures, the only condition required is that these acts must be of direct concern to them (the condition of individual concern is thus eliminated).

[54] Case C-50/00 P, [2002] E.C.R. I-6677, paras. 36 *et seq.* of his Opinion.

the lawfulness of a Community act without regard to when it was published or notified. Bearing in mind that, in general, individuals do not usually read the *Official Journal of the European Union*, the possibility to challenge the validity of a regulation, a directive or a decision addressed to a third party with no time-limit would be extremely attractive. In the particular case of directives, the absence of a time-bar adds an advantage for private individuals, namely that they can wait to be fully aware of the national measures of implementation, and thus consider the provisions applicable as a whole and in detail, before deciding to challenge them.[55]

These reflections should not be misunderstood. We are not defending that it is preferable for individuals to have access to incidental means of control rather than to an action for annulment. We seek no more than to draw attention to the fact that, given the case law of the Court of Justice, extension of the right to appeal of an individual under Article 230 EC would have a price: the reduction in his possibilities of an indirect challenge. We must therefore examine closely whether it is worth paying it.

The same considerations are valid in the event that the Court, without altering its present position on the relationship between mechanisms for controlling the lawfulness of EC secondary law, should decide to apply a definition of 'individual concern', concurrence of which could be more easily observed than that applied since 1963.[56] If, for example, the Court accepted a definition along the lines of that suggested by the CFI in the *Jégo-Quéré* judgment, then the legal standing of individuals to challenge acts other than the decisions of which they are addressees would be greatly clarified.[57] In this situation, we can assume that the Court would cease to maintain its present reservations when depriving natural and legal persons of the right to query the validity of such acts. Since it would be easy to determine whether 'individual concern' does concur, its mere legal standing under Article 230 EC would suffice to deprive them of the possibility to incidentally query the lawfulness of a regulation, a directive or a decision addressed to a third party.[58]

---

[55] With respect to this point, see the pleadings of the Council made in the Case T-167/02, *Etablissement Toulorge v. European Parliament and Council* [2003] E.C.R. II-1111, para. 31.

[56] Case 25/62, *Plaumann*, n. 23 above.

[57] Let us recall that, in order to favour the access of individuals to Article 230 EC, and thus to increase the right to an effective judicial protection, the CFI defended that 'a natural or legal person is to be regarded as individually concerned by a Community measure of general application that concerns him directly if the measure in question affects his legal position, in a manner which is both definite and immediate, by restricting his rights or by imposing obligations on him' (Case T-177/01, [2002] E.C.R. II-2365, para. 51). In our opinion, such interpretation of the notion of 'individual concern' comes very close to that of 'direct concern' considered by the ECJ, and it is true that appreciation of the concurrence of the latter does not usually cause problems.

As is well known, the CFI proposal was not accepted by the ECJ which, in the *UPA* judgment, issued a few months later, re-affirmed its traditional definition of individual concern (Case C-50/00 P, n. 54 above). Accordingly, it was foreseeable that the ECJ would find well grounded the appeal brought by the Commission against the CFI judgment in *Jégo-Quéré* and quash it (C-263/02 P, *Commission v. Jégo-Quéré* [2004] E.C.R. I-3425).

[58] In this respect, see the allegation made by the Commission in the Case C-263/02 P, *Commission v. Jégo-Quéré*, [2004] E.C.R. I-3435, para. 25.

In our view, these are the most noteworthy consequences of the position adopted on the matter by the Court of Justice. Nevertheless, we must question whether is accurate the conception of the legal institutes described in Articles 234 and 241 EC as mechanisms subordinated to the action for annulment, which would operate only when it was impossible, for lack of a clear legal standing, to use Article 230 EC.

IV. Evaluation of the ECJ Response

A. In Favour of the Alternative Nature of the Action for Annulment and of the Preliminary Reference in the Case of Individual Decisions

In the case of decisions having an individual scope, we agree with the Court of Justice that the addressee cannot let the time period under Article 230 EC expire and subsequently seek to contest its validity in the national courts. The administrative 'doctrine of the consented act' operates here: by not challenging the act within the legally established period, it is considered that the addressee has accepted it. The decision becomes then incontestable, unless the 'theory of acts non-existent' applies.[59]

The right to judicial protection of the party in question is safeguarded by offering the latter a channel, the action for annulment, that enables him to query the lawfulness of the decision addressed to him. Once the period to use that channel has expired, safeguarding of legal certainty becomes paramount, whereby it becomes impossible to contest the decision lawfulness any longer.[60]

Indeed, not only does it occur that the addressee cannot contest the validity of the decision in the national courts but, in addition, neither can the national courts query that validity *ex officio* or at the instance of another party in the proceedings. Accordingly, it would not be possible to submit a request for a preliminary ruling to the ECJ. The Court states that the definitive character acquired by a decision for its addressee 'binds the national court'.[61]

This construction can be extended, as the Court has done, to individuals other than the addressee of the decision when their legal standing to file an action for

[59] In relation to the 'doctrine of the consented act' in EC law, see Alonso García, *Derecho comunitario. Sistema constitucional y administrativo de la Comunidad Europea* (Madrid, 1994), at 386–387.

[60] We would like to emphasize that it is the principle of legal certainty (which lays behind the establishment of a deadline to file an action for annulment) and not observance of the deadline as such, what impedes the challenge of acts at all times. G. Vandersanden does not seem to see it in this way; he considers that the case law analysed 'équivaut à faire prévaloir le respect d'une règle de procédure—en l'occurrence un délai—sur la question plus fondamentale de l'illégalité d'un acte et des conséquences qui peuvent s'en suivre' ('La protection juridictionnelle effective: une justice ouverte et rapide?', in Dony and Bribosia, Eds., *L'avenir du système juridictionnel de l'Union européenne*, Brussels, 2002, 119–154, at 126).

[61] Case C-188/92, *TWD*, n. 6 above, para. 25; Case C-178/95, *Wiljo*, n. 6 above, para. 24; Case C-239/99, *Nachi*, n. 20 above, para. 40.

annulment is beyond all doubt. Their right to judicial protection is safeguarded by the obvious access they had to annulment proceedings. Thereafter, it is legal certainty that must be protected.[62]

Only when legal standing of a third party under Article 230 EC has not existed or has simply not been evident can that party invoke the unlawfulness of a Community decision in national courts, and these, insofar as they doubt the validity of such measure, set in motion the mechanism of Article 234 EC to consult the ECJ on the matter. Assuming that the addressee of a decision challenged by a third party and the subject of a preliminary reference is a Member State, the question is whether it can, by means of Article 23 of the Statute of the Court of Justice, submit written observations to the Court defending the unlawfulness of the decision or whether the fact that it did not file an action for annulment at the pertinent time also deprives it of this ability. Here, we agree with D. Anderson, who believes that such an intervention should be accepted, because, on the one hand, 'the alternative would be to impose a remarkable restriction on (. . .) the right of Member States (. . .) to comment upon the issues raised by a preliminary reference' and, on the other, 'where the challenge has already been legitimately brought by a person not directly and individually concerned, the damage to legal certainty has already been done and cannot be worsened by the intervention of a party which did have standing to commence a direct action'.[63]

From this construction it would follow that, with respect to individual acts, the preliminary reference procedure would only be justified in order to protect the right to judicial protection. If this right has already been protected, the request for a preliminary reference is not admissible.

So far, we have no objections to the Court of Justice approach. The situation changes when we move on from individual to general acts.

B. In Favour of the Complementary Nature of the Action for Annulment and of the Preliminary Reference in the Case of General Acts

The Court did not distinguish, when drawing up its case law, whether it was dealing with general or individual acts in each case, thus creating a single doctrine. It is not that the Court failed to realize the distinct legal nature that the measures emanating from Community institutions can have, but rather that it deliberately avoided adapting its response to the matter of relations between the direct and indirect mechanisms of controlling the lawfulness of EC secondary law in the light of this. In its written observations in the *National Farmers' Union* case, the French government expressly alleged the normative nature of the two Commission

---

[62] Logically, preservation of the right to effective judicial protection will require a very strict appreciation of the unquestionable character of the *locus standi* of these third persons in the action for annulment (see, in this respect, Tridimas, n. 28 above, at 168).

[63] *References to the European Court* (London, 1995), at 119.

decisions against which it had failed to file an action for annulment at the appropriate time and whose legality it challenged before the national courts. The Court did not amend its case law because of this, rather it re-affirmed the definitive nature of decisions as against the addressees who failed to challenge them by means of Article 230 EC.[64]

ECJ case law, impeccable when it refers to individual acts, is open to criticism when applied to measures of general application.[65] In our opinion, a party must be able to query the validity of a normative measure in national courts, regardless of the fact that it could have brought an action for annulment and failed to do so. Similarly, and on sounder foundations, since the preliminary reference does not cease to be a tool that Article 234 EC places at the disposal of national judges, a Member State court should be able to submit a request for a preliminary reference to the ECJ in order to raise its doubts on the validity of that normative measure.

It must be remembered that, in the case of general acts, precisely because of their general scope of application, it is especially important that should they present any irregularity, they be eliminated from the legal system. In the case of norms, it is important that the principle of legality prevails. With regard to general acts, R. Alonso García states that: 'inasmuch as they do not merely implement the legal system, but are an integral part of it, unlawful provisions cannot be maintained, because this would leave the way open to equally unlawful individual implementation acts'.[66] Defence of the legality of the system and of the legal order requires admitting a permanent control of the lawfulness of general acts. J. García Luengo talks of the 'impossibility of an invalid normative measure to become definitive' and states that 'an unlawful normative measure cannot avoid a declaration of annulment for the mere fact that the periods for direct challenge have expired'.[67]

---

[64] In his Opinion on the *TWD* case, AG Jacobs seems to introduce a distinction depending on whether we are dealing with individual or general acts; the British Advocate General thus justifies the different solution he proposes to the ECJ in this case with respect to that adopted by the Court in the *University of Hamburg* case. This line of argument disappears however from the AG Jacobs' discourse in subsequent Opinions.

[65] J. García Luengo also distinguishes between administrative and normative acts and while in the case of the former maintains the inadmissibility of any challenge outside the period laid down in Article 230 EC by those who could have sought their annulment, in the case of general acts, he favours the contrary (*El recurso comunitario de anulación* . . . ., n. 47 above, at 85–96 and 118–128). This approach is exceptional. Authors usually criticize the position of the ECJ in a general manner, without distinguishing whether it refers to individual or general acts; their objections are based on the attack presumed to be made against the prerogatives of national judges and on the weakening of the positon of individuals in the EC system (thus, Usher, 'Preliminary references . . .', n. 16 above, at 108; Bebr, 'Direct and Indirect Judicial Control . . .', n. 27 above, at 96; Tesauro, 'The Effectiveness of Judicial Protection . . .', n. 27 above, at 16; Simon, n. 17 above, at 440; Turner, 'Challenging EC Law . . .', n. 17 above, at 78 and 86; Waelbroeck, 'Le contrôle incident de la légalité des actes communautaires', in *La tutela giurisdizionale dei diritti nel sistema comunitario*, (Brussels, 1997), 135–141, at 139; Barav, 'Le juge et le justiciable', in *Scritti in onore di Giuseppe Federico Mancini*, (Milan, 1998), vol. II, Diritto dell'Unione europea), 1–74, at 37; Mancini and Curti Gialdino, 'Brevi note in tema di abuso del processo comunitario', 1998 RDE, 245–253, at 251; and, Vandersanden, 'La protection juridictionnelle . . .', n. 60 above, at 126).

[66] *Derecho comunitario* . . . , n. 59 above, at 387 (the translation is ours).

[67] *El recurso comunitario de anulación* . . . , n. 47 above, at 93–94 (the translation is ours).

If in the case of individual acts the preliminary reference guarantees judicial protection (so that it cannot be used when this asset has already been protected by other means), in the case of general acts, the preliminary reference should have a second function. We believe that, in the case of general acts, the preliminary reference should operate as a permanent mechanism for controlling their lawfulness.[68] This is why, for general acts, national courts should be able to raise a preliminary reference (an instrument, we repeat, at their service), whenever doubts arise as to the validity of an act of this nature, without considering whether one of the parties in the proceedings could or could not have filed an action for annulment, or any other issue (such as whether it was the party that could have used Article 230 EC that casted doubt on the lawfulness of the act in question before the national court or whether that party will be the one that will benefit from a possible declaration of invalidity thereof by the ECJ).

Indeed, it is not only that negligence of a party should not affect the faculty of the judge *a quo* to use Article 234 EC, but, in addition, we also believe that the fact of having been able to directly petition the Court of Justice for the annulment of a general act does not prevent the party in question from invoking its unlawfulness in national courts.

We would like to add three arguments in support of our position in favour of autonomy of the action for annulment and the preliminary reference on validity when general acts are involved.

Firstly, Article 241 EC, which permits an incidental challenge of general acts, with no time-bar, supports the idea that, with regard to these kinds of measures, it is particularly important to ensure the lawfulness of the legal system.

Secondly, we must point out that our position in favour of the principle of legality does not necessarily involve sacrificing the principle of legal certainty. As we are all aware, the Court has the means to preserve this asset, by limiting the retroactive effects of its preliminary rulings.[69]

Thirdly, we would like to draw attention to the circumstance that, while in the case of decisions, the ECJ states that, once these become definitive due to the absence of a challenge *ex* Article 230 EC, they 'bind' the national courts, the Court makes no similar affirmation when referring to regulations or directives attributed with a definitive character as against the party who could undoubtedly have brought an action for annulment there against. In other words, the Court affirms that a regulation or a directive becomes definitive in respect of a certain party and that party cannot query its lawfulness in national courts, but it has never declared that this deprives those courts, of the possibility to question by themselves the lawfulness of that measure or dispossess them of the authority they are attributed by Article 234 EC to approach the ECJ.

---

[68] The *erga omnes* effect of the preliminary rulings declaring the invalidity of a Community measure demonstrates the reality of this second function that we attribute to the preliminary reference.

[69] See, in this respect, Bebr, 'Direct and Indirect Judicial Control … ', n. 27 above, 96.

Moving on from the preliminary reference to the plea of illegality, what can we say about the relationship between the action for annulment and the plea of illegality, a figure that covers only general acts?

C. Dismissal of the Subsidiary Nature of the Plea of Illegality vis-à-vis the Action for Annulment

The answer to the question asked at the end of the preceding point depends on the function acknowledged to the plea of illegality in the Community procedural system. If the plea of illegality is configured as a mechanism solely intended to safeguard judicial protection, then we must agree that those parties who could have filed an action for annulment against a regulation or a general act should not be able to make use of Article 241 EC, inasmuch as they had Article 230 EC at their disposal. The conclusion will therefore be that the relationship between an action for annulment and the plea of illegality is one of exclusion. On the ontrary, if we consider that the purpose of the plea of illegality is also to protect the lawfulness of the Community legal order, then we can conceive that the action for annulment and the plea of illegality are autonomous means and we will accept that even the party that could have sought the annulment of a certain general act, but failed to do so, can subsequently incidentally query its validity at the ECJ.

We are aware of the intense ongoing doctrinal debate regarding the purpose of the figure described in Article 241 EC, and, closely linked to this issue, on who can make use of this Article and, therefore, on its relationship with the action for annulment. We are also aware of the ambiguity displayed by the Court of Justice with regard to all these aspects. Having to take a stand on this point, the considerations made already on the advisability of safeguarding the lawfulness of the legal system when general acts are involved incline us to defend the autonomous nature of the mechanisms of Articles 230 and 241 EC, and to accept that even the privileged claimants under the former provision can avail themselves of the latter. This core argument could be accompanied by others discussed in doctrine, such as: the wording of Article 241 EC which, when referring to the parties who are allowed to use it, mentions 'any party in proceedings'; the fact that the irregularities in a general act often do not appear until it is applied to specific cases; the principle whereby Treaty provisions relating to the right to appeal cannot be interpreted restrictively; or the fact that if States were obliged to act against a general act within the short period laid down in Article 230 EC, whereas individuals can plead their unlawfulness with no time-bar, this would lead to the acknowledgement to the latter of rights that are more extensive than those of the former, which is contrary to the system established in the Treaty.

Those who attribute to the plea of illegality the exclusive function of protecting the right to judicial protection (thus denying those with legal standing under

Article 230 EC the possibility to use this instrument) usually see a confirmation of their thesis in the *inter partes* effect of a successful plea of illegality.

It is true that, in accordance with the ECJ case law and as the Treaty infers when speaking of the 'inapplicability' of the regulation challenged incidentally, the effect of a successful plea of illegality is not annulment of the general act, but rather its non-application in the proceeding in which it is raised. However, in our view, it is also true that the effect of the pronouncement transcends the specific case. Thus, if a Member State court were to raise a preliminary reference on the validity of a general act which the Court had previously deemed unlawful *ex* Article 241 EC, the ECJ will more than likely give its decision by a reasoned order that refers to its previous pronouncement.

Indeed, the effect of a successful plea of illegality is the same as that of a preliminary ruling of invalidity, in respect of which nobody doubts that it can be attributed *erga omnes* effects. Formally, the preliminary ruling is binding only on the referring court. What happens is that, as the ECJ has proclaimed, a ruling declaring the invalidity of a certain act 'is sufficient reason for any other national court to regard that act as void for the purposes of a judgment which it has to give'.[70] We believe that the pronouncements issued by virtue of Article 241 EC have this same *vis expansiva*; to limit their effect to the case pending at the ECJ in which the plea of illegality was raised is a purely formal approach, which overlooks the reality we have mentioned.

In another order of considerations, doubts arise on whether the complementary nature with which we tend to conceive the action for annulment and the plea of illegality implies that a State can allege the illegality of the general act it is accused of infringing in order to evade a conviction from the Court. We know that, in general, authors who defend the access of States to Article 241 EC admit this possibility. However, there is an idea appealing to us: given the presumption of validity enjoyed by acts adopted by EC institutions (and which will be maintained until the ECJ decides otherwise), Member States are obliged to respect such acts. In this regard, despite the fact that an act may entail some of the irregularities of Article 230 EC, EU countries should act in accordance with it and would not avoid a conviction for infringement, however much they allege that the act in question is unlawful and however well-founded this allegation may be.

These considerations (and not the affirmation—which we contest—of the subsidiary nature of the plea of lawfulness vis-à-vis the action for annulment) would, eventually, lead us to applaud the declaration of the ECJ that a State cannot 'plead the unlawfulness of a directive which the Commission criticizes it for not having implemented'[71] and to criticize its action in the case of *Commission v. Germany* that we have often cited, in which the Court analysed whether the regulation this country was accused of infringing did entail the defects it denounced.

---

[70] Case 66/80, *International Chemical Corporation* [1981] E.C.R. 1191, para. 13.
[71] C-74/91, *Commission v. Germany*, n. 13 above.

D. Conclusions

To summarize, the direct and indirect means to challenge the lawfulness of EC secondary law must be deemed to be complementary mechanisms, so that the possibility (not exercised) to file an action for annulment does not preclude the preliminary reference on validity or the plea of illegality. This cumulative character disappears when the 'doctrine of the consented act' comes into play, which means that individual decisions that were not directly appealed at the Court of Justice by their addressee or by the party who undoubtedly had *ius standi* under Article 230 EC, 'bind' national courts. Furthermore, although we have our doubts here, it has not been said that this cumulative nature implies that a State can query the validity of a measure it is accused of infringing in order to evade a judgement of conviction from the Court.

Denial of the subsidiary nature of the mechanisms of Article 234 and of Article 241 EC with respect to the action for annulment implies that, however much their 'privileged claimants' condition in the context of Article 230 EC, States could challenge the validity of regulations, directives or general decisions in national courts and at the ECJ after the time-limit laid down in that provision.

At the same time, the extension of *jus standi* of individuals in the action for annulment with respect to general acts, either by reviewing the Treaty or by relaxing the criteria of 'individual concern', should not give rise to any negative feeling because it would in no way diminish the effectiveness of Articles 234 or 241 EC.

Finally, we must emphasize that proclamation of the complementary nature of the direct and indirect means of controlling the lawfulness of EC secondary law does not render the distinction between 'unlawful' and 'non-existent' acts meaningless. This classification remains valid inasmuch as, when faced with an individual decision that, due to its defects, merits the consideration of 'non-existent', it would be possible for the addressee to query its lawfulness in national courts and for the latter to raise the pertinent preliminary reference (the 'doctrine of consented act' thus ceases to operate). On the other hand, it is clear that States can always argue successfully that an act is non-existent in the context of an infringement action (the possible obstacle represented by the presumption of validity of Community acts would thus vanish).

Waves between Strasbourg and Luxembourg: The Right of Access to a Court to Contest the Validity of Legislative or Administrative Measures

*Tim Corthaut and Frédéric Vanneste**

I. Introduction

The European Court of Human Rights (hereafter the ECtHR) and the European Court of Justice (hereafter ECJ) have a fascinating relationship. The existence of two supranational judicial bodies with overlapping jurisdiction—at least in certain human rights matters—could have created a 'battle of the judges'. Fortunately, the opposite seems to be true.[1] The spirit of mutual trust between the two Courts is paving the way for a remarkable jurisprudential cross-fertilization, whereby the two Courts contribute significantly to the creation of a European Public Order,[2] with at its centre International Human Rights Law. A striking example of such a 'jurisprudential dialogue' between the two Courts can be found in cases concerning the right of access to a tribunal to contest legislative or administrative acts. It suffices to refer to two noticed judgments of both Courts. In the case of *Posti and Rakho* of 24 September 2002 the ECtHR refers to, and even quotes, European Community law in order to strengthen the authority of its reasoning.[3] In turn the ECJ has reversed a previous judgment of the Court of

---

* The authors are assistants and PhD-candidates at the Institute for European Law and at the Institute for Human Rights of the KU Leuven, respectively. The authors wish to thank Professor Paul Lemmens, Professor Koen Lenaerts, Frederik Naert and Peter Schollen for their invaluable comments during the drafting of this article. Errors and omissions are of course entirely due to the authors. The opinions expressed herein only bind the authors.

[1] See in this respect most recently *Bosphorus v. Ireland*, ECtHR (2005), <www.echr.coe.int>. For more on this judgment, see *infra*.

[2] *Louzidou v. Turkey*, ECtHR (1993), *Series A* No. 310, § 93; See also Harlow, ' Access to Justice as a Human Right: The European Convention and the European Union', in P. Alston (ed), *The EU and Human Rights* (1999) 187–214.

[3] *Posti and Rakho v. Finland*, (2002), *Reports* 2002-VII, § 53. In this case the ECtHR refers to Article 230 of the EC Treaty and to Case C-358/89 *Extramet Industrie v. Council* [1991] ECR I 2501, § 13.

First Instance (CFI) in the case of *Jégo-Quéré* in which the latter Court had invoked Articles 6 and 13 of the European Convention of Human Rights (hereafter ECHR) to reinterpret Article 230(4) of the EC Treaty (hereafter TEC).[4] We will analyze below whether those mutual references were opportune and correct.

This article aims at describing and evaluating the right of access to a court[5] as the two main supranational European Courts understand it today. The focus will be on the situations in which the individual claims the possibility to contest the validity of legislative and administrative acts with a general scope.[6] In a first and second part we address the scope of the right of access to a court according to the case law of the ECtHR and the significance of this right for the ECJ. This will allow us to deal in a third part with the question whether or not a new approach is warranted. A possible accession of the European Union (hereafter EU) to the European Convention on Human Rights makes this question all the more relevant.[7] It is our submission that a more demanding approach as to access to court is a necessary corollary of the deference to the European Union shown by the ECtHR in *Bosphorus*.[8] As the Treaty establishing a Constitution for Europe would enhance the right to an effective remedy in the EU context it remains in our view important to highlight those improvements, even at a time when the ratification process appears to have come to a grinding halt.

---

[4] Case T-177/01 *Jégo-Quéré v. Commission* [2002] ECR II-2365 [hereafter *Jégo-Quéré*]; Case C-263/02 P *Commission v. Jégo-Quéré* [2004] ECR I-3425.

[5] It must be kept in mind that 'the right of access is only one aspect of the right to a court'. *Golder v. United Kingdom*, ECtHR (1975), *Series A* No. 18, § 3.

[6] For the purposes of this article we will define '*administrative acts*' as 'the acts taken by the executive' and '*legislative acts*' as the 'laws in the formal sense of the term, i.e. provisions enacted by the legislator'. In the context of the European Union a formal distinction between legislative and executive acts is lacking, at least as long as the new Constitution is not adopted. Therefore the terms 'administrative' or 'executive' acts and 'legislative acts' will in the EU-context be used in line with the distinctions made by the ECJ in Case C-16/88 *Commission v. Council* [1989] ECR 3457. There the Court considered legislative acts as an act of general scope and content taken by an institution on the basis of the Treaties. This implies that the EU does not have a single 'formal' legislative procedure. Implementation on the other hand 'comprises both the drawing up of implementing rules and the application of rules to specific cases by means of acts of individual application'. As a result there may be administrative decisions containing an application of the rule on (a) individual case(s) and administrative implementing acts setting out further specified rules. Both types of administrative acts may, in accordance with Article 211 TEC, be taken by either the Commission or the Council. For more on the distinctions between legislative and executive acts, see K. Lenaerts and M. Desomer, 'Towards a Hierarchy of Legal Acts in the European Union? Simplification of Legal Instruments and Procedures', 11 *European Law Journal* (2005) 744.

[7] Cf. Article I-9(2) Treaty establishing a Constitution for Europe (2004) OJ C310/1 [hereafter the European Constitution] provides that 'The Union shall accede to the European Convention for the Protection of Human Rights and Fundamental Freedoms. Such accession shall not affect the Union's competences as defined in the Constitution'.

[8] *Bosphorus v. Ireland*, ECtHR judgment of 30 June 2005.

II. The Right of Access as Developed by the European Court of Human Rights

In 1975 the ECtHR decided in the *Golder* case that the right to a fair trial under Article 6 ECHR implies a right of access to a court for every person wishing to commence an action in order to have his civil rights and obligations determined.[9] Although this right has not been laid down in express terms in Article 6, the ECtHR established it 'as an inherent aspect of the safeguards enshrined in Article 6, referring to the principles of the rule of law and the avoidance of arbitrary power which underlie much of the Convention'.[10] The ECtHR based its reasoning on two legal principles: the principle whereby a civil claim must be capable of being submitted to a judge, as one of the universally recognized fundamental principles of law, and the principle of international law which forbids denial of justice.[11] Since *Golder* the ECtHR has had the opportunity to elaborate this reasoning in its case law. Usually the ECtHR proceeds in two steps to investigate if the applicant has a right of access to a tribunal as secured by Article 6. It first ascertains whether Article 6 is applicable, and next whether the State complies with the requirements of an effective access to the courts.

A. The Applicability of Article 6 with Respect to Disputes Relating to Administrative or Legislative Acts

The ECtHR has developed in its vested case law some criteria concerning the applicability of Article 6 that—at first sight—seem to exclude or at least to limit the right of access to contest legislative or administrative acts with a general scope. The ECtHR usually recalls the principles developed in its case law as to the applicability of Article 6 as follows: it must be ascertained 'whether there is a dispute (contestation) over a 'right' which can be said, at least on arguable grounds, to be recognised under domestic law. This dispute must be genuine and serious; it may relate not only to the actual existence of a right but also to its scope and the manner of its exercise; and the result of the proceedings must be directly decisive for the right in question. Finally the right must be of a 'civil character.'[12]

First there must thus be a *dispute*. In the *Le Compte* case the ECtHR for the first time tackled explicitly the question whether a dispute was characterised by the

---

[9] *Golder v. the United Kingdom, supra,* fn. 5 §§ 25 *et seq.*

[10] *Z and Others v. the United Kingdom* ECtHR (2001), *Reports* 2001-V, § 91; *Golder, supra,* fn. 5, § 36.

[11] *Ibid.,* § 35. See also P. van Dijk & G. van Hoof, *Theory and Practice of the European Convention on Human Rights* (1998) 418–419; C. Ovey, W. Robin & G. Jacobs, *Jacobs & White. European Convention on Human Rights* (2002) 150–154.

[12] See, for example, *Zander v. Sweden,* ECtHR (1993), *Series A* no. 279-B, § 22; *Z and others v. the United Kingdom, supra,* fn. 10, § 87.

existence of two conflicting claims or applications'.[13] The ECtHR emphasized in this landmark judgment that 'this word [dispute] should not be construed too technically and that it should be given a substantive rather than a formal meaning.'[14] The interpretation of the French equivalent for dispute ('contestation') implies above all the existence of a disagreement, and not necessarily a conflict between two different claims.[15] This disagreement must be of a legal character: it must concern the violation of a right and the alleged illegality of that violation.[16] It is thus absolutely crucial that the matter lends itself to a judicial decision,[17] although the dispute may deal with both 'questions of fact' and 'questions of law'.[18] Moreover, it is of no importance that the proceedings concern a dispute between an individual and a public authority acting in its sovereign capacity; the character 'of the legislation which governs how the matter is to be determined' and of the 'authority' which is invested with jurisdiction in the matter are of little consequence.[19]

If the dispute concerns an application for judicial review of an *administrative act*, it is essential to bear in mind that the illegality of that action (understood as the contravention of objective law) must be at stake.[20] If the citizen only invokes policy objections Article 6 will not be applicable.

In respect of the possibility of contesting *a legislative act*, the ECtHR admits that the safeguards of Article 6 ECHR are in principle also applicable to constitutional appeals, which are remedies enabling anyone to challenge a law directly, provided that the domestic law offers that kind of remedy[21] and provided that the outcome of the proceedings is decisive for the determination of the applicant's civil rights and obligations.[22] The ECtHR thus recognizes that proceedings in a constitutional court can form a 'dispute' within the meaning of Article 6 ECHR[23]

[13] *Le Compte, Van Leuven and De Meyere v. Belgium*, ECtHR (1981), *Series A* no. 43, § 45 *et seq.*
[14] *Ibid.*   [15] *Ibid.*
[16] See i.a. *Le Compte, Van Leuven and De Meyere v. Belgium, supra*, fn. 13, § 44; P. Vandijk en G. Van Hoof, *supra*, fn. 11, 396.
[17] *Van Marle v. the Netherlands*, ECtHR (1986), *Series A* No. 101, § 35; P. Lemmens, Ge*schillen over burgerlijke rechten en verplichtingen*, (1989) 36–37.
[18] *Van Marle* v. *the Netherlands, supra*, fn. 17, § 32; *Albert and Le Compte*, ECtHR (1983), *Series A* No. 58, § 29 and § 36.   [19] *Ringeisen v. Austria*, ECtHR (1971), *Series A* No. 13, § 94.
[20] See i.a. *Le Compte, Van Leuven en De Meyere, supra*, fn. 13, § 44; *Procola v. Luxembourg*, judgment of 28 September 1995, *Series A* no. 326, §§ 36–37; M. Viering *Het toepassingsgebied van artikel 6 EVRM*, (1994) 77; P. Lemmens, *supra*, fn. 17, 41.
[21] *Voggenreiter v. Germany*, ECtHR (2004), §§ 31–33, *unpublished*. The original French text reads as follows: 'La Cour rappelle aussi que [...] une procédure peut relever de l'article 6 même si elle se déroule devant une juridiction constitutionnelle. A cet égard, peu importe que la procédure devant la juridiction constitutionnelle s'inscrive dans le cadre d'un renvoi préjudiciel ou dans celui d'un recours constitutionnel dirigé contre des décisions judiciaires. Il en va, en principe, de même lorsque la juridiction constitutionnelle est saisie d'un recours dirigé directement contre une loi si la législation interne prévoit un tel recours.' See also *Süssman v. Germany*, ECtHR (1996), *Reports* 1996-IV, § 40; *Hesse-Anger v. Germany*, ECtHR (2001), 3, *unpublished*; *Wendenburg v. Germany*, ECtHR (2003), § 3, unpublished.
[22] See for example *Süssman v. Germany*, ECtHR (1996), *Reports* 1996-IV, § 41.
[23] This conclusion can also be drawn from the case law in which the ECtHR concedes that the procedural safeguards of Article 6, such as for example the reasonable time requirement, may apply to

and that in principle they do not fall outside the scope of Article 6.[24] However, the first additional requirement leads to the strange conclusion that the right of access to a court, which is enshrined in Article 6, is not applicable to constitutional proceedings when there are no such proceedings in domestic law. This approach is confusing and it would appear more logical to assess whether the absence of a constitutional appeal is a legitimate restriction of the right of access to a court (*infra* under heading B).

Another crucial requirement for the applicability of Article 6 (and thus also the right of access), concerns the fact that the (claimed) judicial proceedings must lead to a *determination* of civil rights or obligations.[25] This means that it must be shown that the 'dispute' relates to 'civil rights and obligations', in other words that the 'result of the proceedings' will be '*directly* decisive' for such a right.[26] If someone thus claims a right of access to a judge he will have to prove that the judgment by this judge will be 'directly decisive' for a civil right or obligation.

When the ECtHR deals with complaints concerning the lack of possibility to contest *administrative acts* before a tribunal it will often evaluate the impact of the challenged administrative decision on the civil rights and obligations of the individual.[27] This evaluation will be important in order to decide whether the outcome of the claimed proceedings could be directly decisive for those rights and obligations.[28] In other words, everyone who considers the intervention of the public authority in her civil rights or obligations illegal has a right of access to a judge,[29] provided that she is 'personally affected by the measure in a way that is not only

proceedings in constitutional courts. The relevant test in determining whether constitutional proceedings come within the scope of Article 6 § 1 is whether their outcome is decisive for the determination of the applicant's civil rights and obligations. See for example *Kraska v. Switzerland*, ECtHR (1993), *Series A* No. 254-B, § 26, *Ruiz-Mateos and Others v. Spain*, ECtHR (1993), *Series A* No. 262, *Pierre-Bloch v France*, ECtHR (1997), *Recueil* 1997-VI, § 48, *Diaz Aparicio v Spain*, ECtHR (2001), unpublished, *Soto Sanchez v. Spain*, ECtHR (2003), unpublished and *Voggenreiter v. Germany*, ECtHR (2004), § 31, unpublished.

[24] For example, *Trickovic v. Slovenia*, ECtHR (2001), § 37.

[25] *Ringeisen v. Austria, supra*, fn. 19.

[26] *Le Compte, Van Leuven and De Meyere, supra*, fn. 13, § 46–47.

[27] P. Lemmens *supra*, fn. 17, 73 *et seq*. Lemmens refers, *inter alia*, to *König* where the ECtHR mentions the 'rights affected by the withdrawal decisions'. The judgment in *Posti and Rakho v. Finland* confirms this view. In this case the ECtHR has limited 'its examination to the direct effect which the 1996 and the 1998 decrees—issued on the basis of a law—had on the applicant's livelihood.' The ECtHR even omits to refer to the direct effect of the outcome of the proceedings.

[28] See *Balmer-Schafroth and Others v. Switzerland*, ECtHR (1997), *Reports* 1997-IV, § 40: '[The applicants] did not [. . .] establish a direct link between the operating conditions of the power station which were contested by them and their right to protection of their physical integrity, [. . .] Therefore the effects on the population of the measures which the Federal Council [the Federal Council's decision were according to the majority of the ECtHR more akin to a judicial act than to a general policy decision] could have ordered to be taken in the instant case remained hypothetical'. In the same line, *Athanassoglou v. Switzerland* ECtHR (2000), *Reports* 2000-IV, in which the Court assesses the impact of the extension of a licence for a nuclear power plant on civil rights.

[29] In order to be able to claim a violation of Article 6 before the Court, the applicant will first have to prove that she has exhausted all her domestic remedies (Article 35 of the Convention). The applicant will thus have to prove that no judicial decision was possible at the domestic level.

serious but also specific and, above all, imminent'.[30] Some judges wonder whether all of those three last criteria, which seem to give content to the 'direct' requirement in cases concerning administrative acts, are appropriate.[31] Moreover, the *Posti and Rakho* judgment of 24 September 2002 has added to the confusion. According to this judgment the individual should also prove that her civil rights are affected 'by reason of certain attributes peculiar to [her] or by reason of a factual situation which differentiates [her] from all other persons'.[32] As the ECtHR had never mentioned this requirement before, it is unclear whether the ECtHR wanted to introduce a new criterion, namely that the individual has to be individually affected in the sense of the current interpretation by the ECJ of Article 230(4) TEC, or whether this is a 'slip of the pen' of the ECtHR. At least it can be ascertained that the ECtHR will closely verify whether the individual is *personally* affected. Still, previous cases have shown that the application of this requirement often results in unsatisfactory judgments. The Grand Chamber of the ECtHR stated in the *Athanassoglou* judgment that the connection between a decision by the Federal Council, the Swiss government, to extend the operating licence of a nuclear power plant and the domestic-law rights invoked by the applicants in that case was too tenuous and remote to assess that they were personally affected.[33] Hence, the ECtHR decided that the outcome of the procedure before the Federal Council was indeed decisive for the general question whether the operating licence of the nuclear power plant should be extended, but not for the 'determination' of any 'civil right', such as the rights to life, to physical integrity and of property, which Swiss law conferred on the applicants in their individual capacity. In our opinion this ruling was rightly criticized by the five dissenting judges.[34] But

---

[30] *Balmer-Schafroth and Others v. Switzerland, supra,* fn. 28; *Athanassoglou (GC) v. Switzerland supra,* fn. 28 § 51. See also, Recommendation Rec (2004)20 of the Committee of Ministers to Member States on judicial review of administrative acts and the explanatory Memorandum CM (2004)214, available at <http://www.coe.int>. In § 39 of the Explanatory Memorandum it is said that 'such acts must therefore adversely affect the applicant and have the effect of altering his/her legal situation. This precludes certain categories of administrative acts from a judicial remedy, such as preliminary measures.'

[31] *Athanassoglou v. Switzerland, supra,* fn. 28, Joint dissenting opinion of Judges Costa, Tulkens, Fischbach, Casadevall and Maruste: 'One might of course question whether it is possible to establish that the danger exists to the requisite degree. For example, it is virtually impossible to prove imminent danger in the case of inherently dangerous installations: the catastrophes that have happened in a number of countries were obviously unforeseeable or, in any event, unforeseen.'

[32] *Posti and Rakho v. Finland, supra,* fn. 3, § 53. Notice that the ECtHR is quoting literally the case law of the ECJ (cf. *infra*).   [33] *Athanassoglou v. Switzerland, supra,* fn. 28, § 51.

[34] *Athanassoglou v. Switzerland, supra,* fn. 28, Joint dissenting opinion of Judges Costa, Tulkens, Fischbach, Casadevall and Maruste. There was first a disagreement on the nature of the Federal Council's decision. Whereas the majority believed that this decision was more akin to a judicial act than to a general policy decision, the minority stressed the executive character of the decision. Accordingly, they argued that no domestic court had been able to assess whether the applicants had established a sufficiently close link between the operation of the power plant and their rights, in particular to life and to physical integrity. In their view it would be in accordance with the, in most European states, well-established general principle of law that executive acts must be judicially reviewable by a court which is able to ensure that the law has been properly applied and the procedural rules followed. That principle was unambiguously recognized, admittedly in an EU context, by the ECJ in the *Johnston* case (Case 222/84 *Johnston* [1986] ECR 1651).

even if *Athanassoglou* has enumerated the basic conditions for the determination requirement, there is now uncertainty whether individuals should be 'personally' or 'individually' affected. The present authors would welcome it if the ECtHR were to stick to the concept of 'personally affected' and clarify its content.[35]

The ECtHR also stresses the crucial importance of the 'determination' requirement in cases concerning the applicability to *constitutional proceedings* of Article 6: 'the relevant test in determining whether constitutional proceedings come within the scope of Article 6 § 1 is whether their outcome is decisive for the determination of the applicant's civil rights and obligations'.[36] For this to be the case it is not necessary that the finding of unconstitutionality amounts to the civil liability of the state.[37] It suffices that this conclusion can have consequences for the civil rights of the individual.[38] One could think of the situation in which a constitutional court can quash an impugned judicial decision in a civil case and remit the case for re-trial[39] or the situation in which a lower (civil) court asks the constitutional court to give a ruling on the constitutionality of legislative provisions that affect the legal position of the individual.[40] But even without a link with a civil proceeding before a lower court, the constitutional proceedings can have a direct effect on civil rights. Some constitutional courts can for example in certain situations oblige the legislator to provide for an indemnification or for a transitional period. Moreover, some constitutional courts have the possibility to order provisional measures.[41]

In practice, it seems that the ECtHR will assess whether a legislative act (or its presumed unconstitutionality) has a 'direct effect' on the civil rights and obligations of the applicant. However, it will only do so when the domestic system allows national laws to be challenged (cf. *supra*). It has already been pointed at: even if a law affects directly the civil rights and obligations of an individual and clearly appears to be unconstitutional, no right of access to a court will thus exist under the ECHR, unless the domestic system provides for one.

The ECtHR must also ascertain whether 'the dispute concerns *a right*, which can be said, at least on arguable grounds, to be recognised *under domestic law*'.[42]

---

[35] Compare with *Hatton v. United Kingdom*, ECtHR 2003, *Reports* 2003 VIII, § 127. In the context of the right to privacy it states that 'where a limited number of people in an area (2 to 3% of the affected population) are particularly affected by a general measure, the fact that they can, if they choose, move elsewhere without financial loss must be significant to the overall reasonableness of the general measure'. In this case, the ECtHR underlined that applicants 'could have challenged subsequent decisions, or the scheme itself, in the courts'. Hence, the right of access was as such not at stake.

[36] See for example *Kraska v. Switzerland*, ECtHR (1993), *Series A*, No. 254-B, § 26, *Ruiz-Mateos and Others v. Spain*, *supra*, fn. 23, § 57–59; *Pauger v. Austria*, ECtHR (1997), *Reports* 1997-III, § 46; *Pammel v. Germany*, ECtHR (1997), *Reports* 1997-IV, § 53; *Jankovic v. Croatia*, ECtHR (2000), *Reports* 2000-X, 2; *Soto Sanchez v. Spain*, ECtHR (2003), *unpublished* and *Voggenreiter v. Germany*, *supra*, fn. 21, § 31.   [37] *Voggenreiter v. Germany*, *supra*, fn. 21, §§ 31–33.

[38] *Voggenreiter v. Germany*, *supra*, fn. 21, § 41.

[39] See for example, *Jankovic v. Croatia*, *supra*, fn. 36.

[40] See for example, *Ruiz-Mateos and Others v. Spain*, *supra*, fn. 23, § 15, *Pammel v. Germany*, judgment of 1 July 1997, *Reports* 1997- V, § 52.   [41] *Ibid.*

[42] See, for example, *Zander v. Sweden*, ECTHR (1993), *Series A* No. 279-B, § 22, emphasis added.

This is an important feature because it distinguishes Article 6 from Article 13 of the Convention, which states that 'everyone whose rights and freedoms *as set forth in this Convention* are violated, shall have an effective remedy before a national authority'.[43] Article 6 thus can not guarantee any particular content for (civil) 'rights and obligations' in the substantive law of the Contracting States, nor can the ECtHR create, by way of interpretation of Article 6, a substantive civil right which has no legal basis in the State concerned.[44] This reasoning can lead to some confusion, especially when the ECtHR states that Article 6 is also applicable to the dispute about the *existence* of the right under the domestic law.[45] In our view this only underlines the distinction between substance and procedure in Convention jurisprudence.[46] Article 6 only requires that a domestic judge can determine whether there is a legal claim under domestic law. If there is no such legal claim, it is sufficient that the judge can establish this. He does not need to ascertain whether this is reasonable, at least not in the light of Article 6.[47] Conversely, if a right is recognized by the national legal order, the national judge must offer the guarantees of Article 6. Of course, if a right is at stake that is protected by the Convention itself, it is almost self-evident that it should also be protected under national law and thus fall within the scope of Article 6. However, the fact that a right, recognized by the domestic legal order does not appear in the Convention does not exclude its procedural protection under Article 6. In this respect it is also important to underline that the fact that authorities enjoy discretion in their decision-making and that the person concerned can thus not claim a specific outcome, does not mean that no right is involved.[48] Indeed, discretion is not unrestricted, and must at least be exercised in conformity with generally recognized legal and administrative principles.[49] Finally it is to be said that a person

[43] Emphasis added. The right under Article 13 arises not when the applicant's civil rights and obligations are in question, but where there is an 'arguable complaint' that a substantive Convention right has been violated (*Silver v. United Kingdom*, Series A No. 61, § 113). Moreover, Article 13 is less demanding for the States because it only requires an effective remedy before a national *authority*, meanwhile Article 6 requires a *judge*. However, the ECtHR sometimes finds a violation of Article 13 because 'the scope of review by the domestic *courts* was not sufficient' (cf. *Hatton v. the United Kingdom*, ECtHR (8 July 2003), unpublished, emphasis added).

[44] *James and Others v. the United Kingdom*, ECtHR (1986), Series A No. 98, § 81; *Z and Others v. the United Kingdom*, supra, fn. 10, § 98 and 101.

[45] *Osman v. the United Kingdom*, ECtHR (1998), Reports 1998-VIII; *Z. and Others*, supra, fn. 10, § 89. See also, Lidbetter & George, 'Negligent Public Authorities and Convention Rights—The Legacy of Osman', 6 *E.H.R.L.R.* (2001) 599–615.

[46] See, for example, *Al-Adsani v. the United Kingdom*, ECtHR (2001), Reports 2001-XI, § 47.

[47] P. Lemmens, *supra*, fn. 17, 52. The claimant still can invoke Article 13, which states that everyone whose rights and freedoms as set forth in the Convention are violated should have an effective remedy before a national authority.

[48] *Zander v. Sweden*, supra, fn. 42, § 25 'Any discretion enjoyed by the competent administrative authorities in this regard was limited by both the terms of section 5 [...] and by the generally recognised principles of administrative law that such discretion is not unfettered.' See also P. van Dijk & G. van Hoof, *supra*, fn. 11, 395.

[49] M. Viering, *supra*, fn. 20, 77. Concerning Article 13 the ECtHR concludes also that judicial review is not an effective remedy when the domestic courts define policy issues so broadly that it is not possible for the applicants to make their Convention points in the domestic courts (*Smith and*

can only invoke the guarantees of Article 6, § 1 if the dispute concerns 'his' rights and obligations.[50] But, and this will be important for further reasoning in this article, the fact that the person concerned is in an identical legal position as many others should not impede the conclusion that he or she has a civil right that ought to be protected by Article 6(1) ECHR.[51]

The fourth and most debated, but for the purposes of this article less important criterion is the *civil* character of the right or obligation in question.[52] The ECtHR has never defined exactly what is to be understood under 'civil', although some important general features have been identified in its case law. First, according to the ECtHR, the concept of 'civil rights and obligations' cannot be interpreted solely by reference to the domestic law of the respondent State. This has led the ECtHR to find that procedures classified under national law as being part of 'public law' could come within the purview of Article 6 under its 'civil' head if the outcome was decisive for private rights and obligations, *inter alia*, in regard of such matters as the sale of land, the running of a private clinic, property interests and the granting of administrative authorizations relating to the conditions of professional practice or of a licence to serve alcoholic beverages.[53] Secondly, it is not in itself sufficient to show that a dispute is 'pecuniary' in nature to attract the applicability of Article 6 § 1 under its 'civil' head.[54] As the ECtHR has held, 'there may exist 'pecuniary' obligations *vis-à-vis* the State or its subordinate authorities which, for the purpose of Article 6 § 1, are to be considered as belonging exclusively to the realm of public law and are accordingly not covered by the notion of 'civil rights and obligations'. Apart from fines imposed by way of 'criminal sanction', this will be the case, in particular, where an obligation which is pecuniary in nature derives from tax legislation or is otherwise part of normal civic duties in a democratic society.'[55] In sum, the State's increasing intervention in the individual's day-to-day life requires the ECtHR to evaluate features of public law and

Grady v. the United Kingdom, ECtHR (1999)), *Reports* 1999-VII, §§ 135–139. *Mats Jacobsson v. Sweden*, ECtHR (1988), § 32, unpublished.

[50] P. Lemmens, *supra*, fn. 17, 55.

[51] See, for example, *Allan Jacobsson v. Sweden (No. 1)*, ECtHR (1989), *Series A* No. 163, § 72: 'In the circumstances of the present case, the applicant's disputed 'right' to build on his land is of a 'civil nature' for the purposes of Article 6 § 1. This is not affected by the general character of the building prohibitions, nor by the facts that the planning procedure, as was submitted by the Government, is part of public law and that a building prohibition is a necessary element in urban planning.' See also P. van Dijk & G. van Hoof , *supra*, fn. 11, 397–398. *Mats Jacobsson v. Sweden*, ECtHR (1988), § 33, unpublished.

[52] Access to a court can also be invoked in criminal cases, but as those cases are not especially essential for the purposes of this article we will not deal further with these sort of cases.

[53] See, among other authorities, *Ringeisen v. Austria*, *supra*, fn. 17, § 94; *König*, *supra*, §§ 94–95; *Sporrong and Lönnroth v. Sweden*, ECtHR (1982), *Series A* No. 52, § 79; *Benthem v. the Netherlands*, ECtHR (1985), *Series A* No. 97, § 36; and *Tre Traktörer AB v. Sweden*, ECtHR (1989), *Series A* No. 159, § 43; *Allan Jacobsson v. Sweden (No. 1)*, *supra*, fn. 51, § 73.

[54] See *Editions Périscope v. France*, ECtHR (1992), *Series A* No. 234-B, § 40; *Schouten and Meldrum v. the Netherlands*, ECtHR (1994), *Series A* No. 304, § 50; *Pierre-Bloch v. France*, ECtHR (1997), *Reports* 1997-VI, p. 2223, § 51 and *Pellegrin v. France*, ECtHR (1999), *Reports* 1999-VIII, § 60.

[55] See, among other authorities, *Ferrazzini v. Italy* ECtHR (2001), *Reports* 2001-VII, § 25.

private law before concluding that the asserted right could be classified as 'civil'.[56] The ECtHR considered for example, as mentioned above, that tax matters still form part of the hard core of public-authority prerogatives, with the public nature of the relationship between the taxpayer and the community remaining predominant.[57] Many authors and dissenting judges have rightly criticized this approach, for among other things, the lack of legal certainty.[58] But it would exceed the purpose of this article to examine this matter in greater depth.

B. The Right of Access to a Court in Order to Contest Administrative or Legislative Acts

The ECtHR held in *Golder* that the procedural guarantees laid down in Article 6 concerning fairness, publicity and expeditiousness would be meaningless if there were no protection of the pre-condition for the enjoyment of those guarantees, namely, access to a court.[59] This means that the right of access not only guarantees that the person concerned has a right to apply to a court for the determination of his right or obligations and to present his case properly and satisfactory, but also that he or she has a right to an independent and impartial court to make this determination.[60] Moreover, the right to a court also protects the implementation of final, binding judicial decisions, which cannot remain inoperative to the detriment of one party. Accordingly, the execution of a judicial decision cannot be unduly delayed.[61] However, the right of access is not absolute.[62] It may be subject to legitimate restrictions such as statutory limitation periods, security for costs orders, regulations concerning minors and persons of unsound mind, and finally immunities.[63] 'Where the individual's access is limited either by operation of law

---

[56] *See*, among other authorities, *Feldbrugge v. the Netherlands*, ECtHR (1986), *Series A* No. 99, § 40; *Deumeland v. Germany*, ECtHR (1986), *Series A* No. 100, § 74.

[57] *Ferrazzini v. Italy, supra*, fn. 55.

[58] This is especially so since the ECtHR acknowledges that the individual rights and obligations of an individual are not necessarily always civil in nature. For example, political rights and obligations, such as the right to stand for election to the National Assembly, are not civil in nature (see *Pierre-Bloch, supra*, fn. 54, § 50), even though in those proceedings the applicant's pecuniary interests may be at stake (*ibid.*, § 51). Article 6 does also not apply under its civil head to disputes between administrative authorities and those of their employees who occupy posts involving participation in the exercise of powers conferred by public law (see *Pellegrin v. France, supra*, fn. 54). Similarly, the expulsion of aliens does not give rise to disputes (contestations) over civil rights for the purposes of Article 6 § 1 of the Convention, which accordingly does not apply (see *Maaouia v. France*, judgment of 5 October 2000, *Reports* 2000-X, §§ 37–38). See i.a. P. van Dijk & G. van Hoof, *supra*, fn. 11, 404 and *Pellegrin v. France, supra*, fn. 54, joint dissenting opinion of Judges Tulkens, Fischbach, Casadevall and Thomassen.

[59] *Golder v. the United Kingdom, supra*, fn. 5, §§ 28–36; *Z and Others v. the United Kingdom, supra*, fn. 10, § 91.

[60] See, for example, *Sporrong and Lönnroth, supra*, fn. 53, § 81, *Tre Traktorer, supra*, fn. 53, § 40.

[61] *Immobiliare Saffi*, ECtHR (1999), *Reports* 1999-V, § 66.

[62] *Z and Others v. the United Kingdom, supra*, fn. 10, § 93.

[63] See among other authorities *Al Adsani v. The United Kingdom, supra*, fn. 46; *Stubbings and Others v. the United Kingdom*, ECtHR (1996), *Reports* 1996-IV, §§ 51–52; *Tolstoy Miloslavsky v. the*

or in fact, the ECtHR will examine whether the limitation imposed impaired the essence of the rights and in particular, whether it pursued a legitimate aim and whether there was a reasonable relationship of proportionality between the means employed and the aim sought to be achieved'.[64] If the restriction is compatible with these principles, no violation of Article 6 will arise.

In the context of this contribution, assuming that Article 6 is applicable, the question arises whether either the impossibility in the domestic system to contest the legality of an administrative act (with a general scope), or the impossibility to claim the unconstitutionality of a legislative act before a court, could be a *legitimate restriction* of the right of access to a court.

Concerning the impossibility to contest the legality of an *administrative act* (with a general scope) which has a direct effect on the rights of the individual, it seems, according to the ECtHR case law, that the party concerned ought to have a right of access to a court.[65] Indeed the right of access should not be dependent on whether the domestic legal system in question provides for a judicial procedure to contest administrative acts.[66] The specificity of the domestic system is thus not a legitimate restriction here. This is in line with the assertion that it is a general principle of law that executive acts must be judicially reviewable by a court which is able to ensure that the law has been properly applied and the procedural rules followed.

As far as it concerns the possibility to contest a *legislative act*, the ECtHR is more reluctant to grant a right of access to a court. When examining whether the individual should have a right of access to proceedings in which the constitutionality of a legislative act can be assessed, the ECtHR will bear in mind that it should not impose a constitutional structure.[67] This also explains why States are not under an obligation to grant a right of individual petition to protect at national

---

United Kingdom, ECtHR (1995), *Series A* No. 316-B, §§ 62–67; and *Golder v. the United Kingdom*, *supra*, fn. 5, § 39.

[64] See for example: *Ashingdane v. the United Kingdom*, ECtHR (1985), *Series A* No. 39, § 57; *Waite and Kennedy v. Germany*, judgment of 18 February 1999, *Reports* 1999-I, § 59; *Hans- Adam II of Liechtenstein*, ECtHR (2001), *Reports* 2001-VIII, § 44; *Z and Others v. the United Kingdom*, *supra*, fn. 10, § 93; *Kutic v. Croatia*, ECtHR (2002), *Reports* 2002-II.

[65] See, for example, *Posti and Rakho*, *supra*, fn. 3, § 65: 'The Court concludes that, for the purposes of Article 6 § 1, no such recourse was available to the applicants whereby they would have obtained a court determination of the effect which the [. . .] decrees had on the contractual terms of their leases of State-owned fishing-waters.' This is confirmed by Recommendation Rec (2004)20 of the Committee of Ministers to Member States on judicial review of administrative acts, available at <http://www.coe.int>. Principle 2a is phrased as follows: 'Judicial review should be available at least to natural and legal persons in respect of administrative acts that directly affect their rights or interests. Members states are encouraged to examine whether access to judicial review should not also be opened to associations or other persons and bodies empowered to protect collective or community interests.' [66] P. van Dijk & G. van Hoof, *supra*, fn. 11, 426.

[67] Cf. For example *Kleyn and others v. the Netherlands*, ECtHR (2003), § 193, unpublished: '[. . .], neither Article 6 nor any other provision of the Convention requires States to comply with any theoretical constitutional concepts regarding the permissible limits of the powers' interaction. The question is always, whether in a given case, the requirements of the Convention are met.'

level the fundamental rights guaranteed in their respective Constitutions.[68] In line with this case law the impossibility to contest a law seems also to be a legitimate restriction for the ECtHR. Notice, however, that at our knowledge the ECtHR has never explicitly tackled the impossibility to contest a law from the perspective of a legitimate restriction, but has always stated that Article 6 does only apply to constitutional proceedings that do exist under domestic law. Nevertheless, whether the problem is tackled under the applicability of Article 6 or under the right of access to a court, the result is always the same: Article 6 does not as such guarantee a right of access to a court with competence to invalidate or override a law.[69]

The right of access in order to contest a law is thus, unlike the right of access in order to contest an administrative act, dependent on whether the domestic legal system in question provides for a constitutional procedure. It is disappointing that the ECtHR has never duly explained why Article 6 does not guarantee a right to invalidate or override a law. Admittedly, one can argue that respect for constitutional traditions and the parliamentary power may play a role. Nevertheless, it would be interesting to learn why the ECtHR finds it more important to respect the constitutional traditions of the States than to impose on States the possibility for individuals to ask for a constitutional review (provided that there is a constitution) when their civil rights are directly affected by a legislative act. In fact, the ECtHR seems to place more trust in legislative acts than in administrative acts. This should at least be questioned. While the creation of legislative acts, admittedly, used to be accompanied by more democratic guarantees, it seems that in most countries parliamentary power is nowadays eroding with the consequence of legislative acts being the emanation of the executives (the governments) will. In those circumstances a distinction between legislative and administrative acts may well be unwarranted.

In the context of EU law, where the distinction between legislative and administrative acts are blurred[70] and where democratic input in the legislative process is at times highly limited, shielding legislative acts from judicial review seems even more problematic.[71] However, the ECtHR seems even less inclined to impose a right of access to contest general (legislative) acts of the EU. Indeed, in the *Bosphorus* case it found that the protection of fundamental rights by EC law can

---

[68] See for example *Süssman v. Germany, supra*, fn. 21, § 37: 'The Court is fully aware of the special role and status of a Constitutional Court , whose task is to ensure that the legislative, executive and judicial authorities comply with the Constitution, and which, *in those States that have made provision for a right of individual petition*, affords additional legal protection to citizens at national level in respect of their fundamental rights guaranteed in the Constitution.' Emphasis added. We could deduce from this that there is no obligation for states to provide for a right of individual (constitutional) petition. Notice, however, that Art. 13 ECHR requires that the individual should have an effective remedy before a national authority (not necessarily a court) to protect the rights *enshrined in the Convention.*   [69] See *Ruiz-Mateos and Others v. Spain*, ECtHR (19 April 1991), *DR* 69.
[70] See fn. 6.
[71] For more on this, see Lenaerts & Corthaut, 'Judicial Review as a contribution to the development of European constitutionalism' 22 *YEL* (2003) (1) 16.

be considered to be 'equivalent' to that of the Convention system.[72] It is thus for the applicant before the ECtHR to rebut this presumption of 'equal protection' of human rights and to prove that there is a dysfunction of the mechanisms of control of the observance of Convention rights. Only once this presumption has been rebutted, the applicant will be able to bring his complaint about a violation of a fundamental human right by a legal obligation flowing from the EU-system before the ECtHR.[73] Applied to the right of access to contest general obligations imposed by the EU, this means that one must first prove that the EU does not provide for sufficient procedural mechanisms to control the observance of the right of access to court within the EU-system. In light of the *Bosphorus* case, it is unlikely that the ECtHR will come to such conclusion in the near future.[74]

III. The Right of Access to a Court as Relevant for the Court of Justice

A. Article 6 and EU law

As discussed above, the right of access to a court derives from Article 6 ECHR and plays a vital role within the judicial system of the EU. As is well known, the EU is not a party to this Convention, though its Member States are and can be held responsible for the acts they use to implement acts of the institutions which may violate the ECHR[75] or for deficiencies of the EU legal order as a whole[76]; yet we will not elaborate on this.[77] Moreover up to now, practical[78] and

---

[72] *Bosphorus v. Ireland*, ECtHR (2005), unpublished, §§ 149–166.

[73] It is to be noted that this presumption is limited to the situations in which a State does no more than implement legal obligations flowing from its membership of the EU. A State remains fully responsible under the Convention for all acts falling outside its strict international legal obligations. If a State still has some discretion the ECtHR will be able to fully review the exercise of this discretion.

[74] In which the ECtHR refers to Case C-50/00 P *Unión de Pequeños Agricultores v. Council* [2002] ECR I-6677. For more on the EU rules on *locus standi*, see *infra*.

[75] *Cantoni v. France*, ECtHR (1996), *Reports* 1996-V where the applicant complained that he had been prosecuted in France under a vague criminal norm. Although the measure was formally a French act, in practice the case boiled down to an analysis of the underlying directive, as the contested provision was in essence copied from this EC measure.

[76] *Matthews v. the United Kingdom*, ECtHR (1999), *Reports* 1999-I where the UK was condemned for having agreed to an act of primary EU law that deprived the inhabitants of Gibraltar from voting during elections for the European Parliament.

[77] For more see, *inter alia*, Cohen-Jonathan & Flauss, 'A propos de l'arrêt Matthews c/Royaume-Uni' 35 *Rev.trim.d.h.* (1999) 637–657; Tulkens, 'L'Union européenne devant la Cour européenne des droits de l'homme', *RUDH* (2000) 50–57; Lhoest & De Schutter, 'La cour européenne des droits de l'homme juge de droit communautaire: Gibraltar, l'Union européenne, et la Convention européenne des droits de l'homme', *CDE* (2000) 141–214.

[78] The main practical obstacle is the fact that Article 59 only allows Members of the Council of Europe to become a party to the ECHR. Admittedly, the 14th Protocol provides for the insertion of an additional paragraph enabling accession of the EU, but this Protocol, though only open for signature since 13 May 2004, has not yet entered into force. Moreover, nothing is said how this should be organized. The EU for its part has on the occasion of the adoption of the European Constitution

constitutional[79] problems still prevent the EU from acceding to the Convention.[80] However, since the early 1970s the fundamental rights have been incorporated into the constitutional law of the EU through the case law of the ECJ.[81] The prime source of inspiration for the ECJ was the text of the ECHR, the case law of the ECtHR[82] and the constitutional traditions of the Member States[83] or a combination of those sources[84] and other international instruments.[85] The Maastricht Treaty has made this link between the EU and the ECHR all the more visible in Article 6(2) of the EU Treaty (hereafter TEU) by providing that 'The Union shall respect fundamental rights, as guaranteed by the European Convention for the Protection of Human Rights and Fundamental Freedoms signed in Rome on 4 November 1950 and as they result from the constitutional traditions common to the Member States, as general principles of Community law'. Admittedly, no reference is made to the case law of the ECtHR. In practice, though, the ECJ usually takes the case law of the Strasbourg court duly into account[86] and at times even offers protection where little[87] or

already indicated its wishes as to the conditions for accession in the Protocol relating to Article I-9(2) on the accession of the European Union to the European Convention on human rights and the Declaration *re* Article I-9(2) annexed to the Final Act of the Intergovernmental Conference.

[79] Opinion 2/94 *Accession of the Community to the ECHR* [1996] ECR I-1759. On the future relation between the ECJ and the ECtHR, see also the Declaration on Article I-9(2) annexed to the Final Act of the Intergovernmental Conference.

[80] On the side of the EU the problems will disappear if and when the Draft Treaty establishing a Constitution for Europe is adopted and enters into force. Its Article I-9(2) provides: 'The Union shall seek accession to the European Convention on Human Rights and fundamental Freedoms. Accession to that Convention shall not affect the Union's competences as defined in this Constitution.' As a result the EU will have a legal basis for accession and even the positive obligation to seek an agreement with the other parties to the ECHR on amending the Convention itself to facilitate the accession of the EU.

[81] Case 29/69 *Stauder* [1969] ECR 419 and in particular Case 11/70 *Internationale Handelsgesellschaft* [1970] ECR 1125.

[82] Case 222/84 *Johnston* [1986] ECR 1651; Case C-185/97 *Coote* [1998] ECR I-5199 (both moreover on Article 6 and 13 ECHR).

[83] Case 11/70 *Internationale Handelsgesellschaft* [1970] ECR 1125; Case 4/73 *Nold v. Commission* [1974] ECR 491.   [84] Case 44/79 *Hauer* [1979] 3727.

[85] Case 149/77 *Defrenne* [1978] 1365 (European Social Charter and the ILO Convention N° 111 concerning discrimination in respect of employment and occupation).

[86] See, for a recent example, Case C-117/01 *K.B.* [2004] ECR I-541, in which the ECJ reconsiders its case law in the light of the ECHR's judgments of 11 July 2002 in *Goodwin v United Kingdom* and *I.* v *United Kingdom*, published in the *Reports* 2002-VI. Remarkably the ECHR had itself based its judgment in that case in part on the new formulation of the right to marry enshrined in Article 9 of the Charter of Fundamental rights of the European Union. Ironically, the ECJ does not invoke that same Article in its judgment in *K.B.* See in this respect also the absence of a reference to the case law of the ECtHR in Article 52 of the Charter, though a reference is made to the case law of the ECtHR in the preamble of the Charter.

[87] Case C-60/00 *Carpenter* [2002] ECR I-6279, annotated by Jadoul and Vanneste in *ColJEL* (2003) 447–455. See also Acierno, 'The Carpenter judgment: fundamental rights and the limits of the Community legal order' 28 *E.L.Rev.* (2003) 398–407. The fact that her expulsion would have prevented Ms. Carpenter from looking after the children of Mr. Carpenter while the latter is on a business trip to the Continent was held to be a (rather remote) restriction on the free movement of services, which could then only be justified by the UK to the extent that the restriction did not violate

no[88] connection with EU law exists. This principled respect for the ECHR is in turn recognized in the rather deferential approach taken by the ECtHR in *Bosphorus* in respect of cases involving EU law.[89]

As far as, more in particular, the right to an effective remedy is concerned, the ECJ has on numerous occasions referred to the Articles 6 and 13 ECHR. The ECJ regularly confirms that individuals are entitled to effective judicial protection of the rights they derive from the Community legal order, and that the right to such protection is one of the general principles of law stemming from the constitutional traditions common to the Member States.[90] However, an attentive reader will have noticed that none of those cases concern access to the ECJ, but rather the effectiveness of the remedies available in the legal orders of the Member States for enforcing Community law. The ECHR is seemingly used as additional, but highly compelling support for the obligations of the Member States to ensure the effectiveness of Community law under Article 10 TEC. The right to an effective remedy is also laid down in Article 47 of the Charter on Fundamental Rights,[91] which was held by one chamber of the Court of First Instance to reflect the common traditions of the Member States[92] and thus—implicitly but certainly—to be binding on the Union through Article 6(2) TEU.[93] It is, however, only in recent years that before both the Court of First Instance and the Court of Justice Articles 6 and 13 ECHR have been raised in order to obtain modifications to the Community system of contesting legislative acts and administrative acts of the EU institutions.[94]

Article 8 ECHR. Not every Advocate General seems to be convinced by the approach taken by the Court in *Carpenter*, see Opinion of AG Geelhoed of 27 April 2006 in Case C-1/05 *Jia*, [2007] ECR I-0000.

[88] Case C-71/02 *Karner* [2004] ECR I-3025. The ECJ manages to decide on the application of Article 10 ECHR in a purely internal situation, with no restrictions on any of the four freedoms. Ironically, the ECJ bases itself on (but in practice ignores) Case C-255/95 *Kremzow* [1997] ECR I-2629, which had previously put limits to the possibility of relying on EC law in order to enforce fundamental rights.   [89] *Bosphorus v. Ireland*, ECtHR (GC) 2005, §§ 149–166.

[90] Case 222/84 *Johnston* [1986] ECR 1651, § 18; Case 222/86 *Heylens* [1987] ECR 4097, § 14; Case C-185/97 *Coote* [1998] ECR I-5199, § 21; Case C-424/99 *Commission v. Austria* [2001] ECR I-9285, § 45.

[91] [2000] OJ C 364/1. The Charter is, subject to minor adjustments, also integrated in Part II of the Constitution, where the corresponding Article is II-107.

[92] Case T-54/99 *Max.mobil Telekommunikation Service v. Commission* [2002] ECR II-313, § 48 and 57; Case T-177/01, *Jégo-Quéré v. Commission* [2002] ECR II-2365, § 42.

[93] See, however, *contra*: Joined Cases T-377/00, T-379/00, T-380/00, T-260/01 and T-272/01 *Philip Morris International and others v. Commission* [2003] ECR II-1, § 122, where a different chamber of the CFI somewhat ambiguously stated that 'although this document does not have legally binding force, it does show the importance of the rights it sets out in the Community legal order', and thus continued to analyse the submissions by the applicants on that point.

[94] See most notably, Case T-172/98, T-175/98 and T-177/98 *Salamander and others v. European Parliament and Council* [2000] ECR II-2487, § 72–78; Case T-177/01, *Jégo-Quéré v. Commission* [2002] ECR II-2365, § 42.

B. Contesting Legislative Acts and Administrative Decisions of the EU Institutions

The constitutional importance of judicial review of Community acts has always been stressed by the ECJ,[95] most notably in *Les Verts*.[96] However, the ECJ has always been highly reluctant to give individuals *locus standi* before the Community courts to obtain such a review under Article 230(4) TEC. This approach could mainly be justified because of the numerous indirect ways of action to obtain the review of a Community act. Yet, despite the fact that recent cases demonstrate that these indirect routes do not always suffice, the ECJ does not appear willing to lower criteria for standing of private applicants. In addition, it should be noticed that the limited jurisdiction of the ECJ in the third pillar and the virtually non-existent jurisdiction of the ECJ in the second pillar greatly hamper any attempt of individuals to obtain judicial review of non-Community EU acts.[97] In the following we will focus on judicial protection against acts of the EC institutions. It is obvious that in the absence of direct actions for individuals to challenge EU-acts, both of an individual and a legislative nature in the third pillar[98] and of any judicial protection, whether directly or indirectly in the second pillar,[99] the EU is currently showing major deficiencies in the light of Article 6 ECHR in those fields.

(i) The Classical System of Judicial Protection before the ECJ or CFI

The classical system of judicial protection against the Community institutions is well documented.[100] At the heart of the debate lies the interpretation of Article

---

[95] Lenaerts & Corthaut, *supra*, fn. 71 (1) 2.

[96] Case 294/83 *Parti Ecologiste 'Les Verts' v. European Parliament* [1986] ECR 1339, § 23.

[97] See in this respect most notably the Order in Case T-338/02 *SEGI and others v. Council* [2004] ECR I-1647, § 38, where the CFI held that 'Concerning the absence of an effective remedy invoked by the applicants, it must be noted that indeed probably no effective judicial remedy is available to them, whether before the Community Courts or national courts, with regard to the inclusion of Segi on the list of persons, groups or entities involved in terrorist acts.' The Order has been appealed and this appeal is currently pending before the ECJ. The Advocate General rejects the blunt conclusion reached by the CFI, but for this he needs to impose an unprecedented series of requirements as to effective judicial protection on the Member State legal systems to compensate for the lack of effective judicial protection at the level of the Community Courts, see Opinion of AG Mengozzi in Joined Cases C-354/04 P and C-355/04 P *SEGI and others v Council*, not yet reported. This in turn raises major concerns as to national procedural autonomy and subsidiarity, similar to those expressed in Lenaerts & Corthaut, *supra*, n. 71, (l) 16–19. However, this approach may be in line with the option taken in Article I-29(1), second paragraph, of the European Constitution. See in that respect, Corthaut, *infra*, fn. 145 (110) 113 *et seq*.

[98] For the available courses of action in the third pillar and their restrictions, see Article 35 TEU.

[99] See Article 46 and 47 TEU. Admittedly, it can be argued that the level of judicial protection can be considerably raised if one accepts that Member State courts can watch over the validity of EU law. This is however highly controversial. Nonetheless, in our opinion this is the only way to avoid the conclusion that the Member States, despite the judgment of the ECtHR in *Matthews v. UK* and *Waite and Kennedy v. Germany*, would have transferred competences to a supranational body without complementing this transfer with sufficient guarantees as to the judicial protection.

[100] For thorough examinations, see K. Lenaerts, D. Arts, I. Maselis & R. Bray (eds), *Procedural Law of the European Union* (2006); H.G. Schermers & D.F. Waelbroeck, *Judicial Protection in the*

230(4) TEC. This Article allows private parties to challenge the validity of a Community act directly before the Court of First Instance in only three circumstances, depending on the nature and the addressee of the act.

The simplest situation arises when the Community had adopted a decision addressed to the applicant. In those circumstances the addressee always has the right to bring a direct action for annulment within the time limits set in Article 230(5) TEC. Moreover, after that period no other route, direct or indirect, exists to obtain judicial review of the decision.[101]

The second situation is the adoption of an individual administrative act addressed to another person, but which is of 'direct and individual concern' to the applicant, who moreover must have an interest in the annulment. The other person can basically be anyone, including a Member State.[102] Classic examples are the decisions by the Commission to impose a fine on an undertaking or to order a Member State to recover unduly paid State aid. The problem of course is the phrase 'direct an individual concern'. The 'direct concern' is relatively easy, but should not be confused with the 'direct link' within ECtHR jurisprudence.[103] It depends on the question whether or not the consequences for the legal situation of the applicant are really the result of the contested act, or are the result of an intervening act by an authority with a certain margin of appreciation. An action for annulment can only be brought if the consequences for the applicant of the act are the immediate result of the contested act.[104]

The main problem, however, is the issue of 'individual concern'. In *Plaumann* the ECJ, despite starting its reasoning by stating that 'provisions of the Treaty regarding the right of interested parties to bring an action must not be interpreted restrictively',[105] has given a very strict reading of the condition of individual concern. According to the classic definition, 'persons other than those to whom a decision is addressed may only claim to be individually concerned if that decision affects them by reason of certain attributes which are peculiar to them or by reason of circumstances in which they are differentiated from all other persons and by virtue of these factors distinguishes them individually just as in the case of the

---

European Union (2001). For a summary of the spirit of the vested case law, see Ward, 'Locus Standi under Article 230(4) of the EC Treaty: Crafting a Coherent Test for a 'Wobbly Polity', 22 *YEL* (2003) (45) 52–53. For an interesting comparison between the courses of action and the procedures before the ECJ and the ECtHR, see Krenc, 'La comparaison des systèmes de procédure communautaire avec ceux de la Convention Européenne des Droits de l' Homme', 57 *Rev. trim dr. h.* (2004) 111–140.

[101] Case C-188/92 *TWD Textilwerke Deggendorf* [1994] ECR I-833; Case C-178/95 1997 *Wiljo* [1997] ECR I-585. [102] Case 25/62 *Plaumann v. Commission* [1963] ECR 95.

[103] In ECtHR case law the 'direct link' refers to the *outcome of the proceedings* on the civil rights of the individual, while in the Community context 'direct concern' alludes to the *consequences of the contested act*. However, concerning administrative decisions and legislative acts, the ECtHR seems to focus more and more on the impact of the acts or decisions on the rights of the individual, and not on the outcome of the proceedings. Cf. *supra*, fns. 27–28 and accompanying text.

[104] For a recent extensive analysis of the requirement of 'direct concern', see Case C-486/01 P *Front National v. European Parliament* [2004] ECR I-6289.

[105] Case 25/62 *Plaumann v. Commission* [1963] ECR 95.

person addressed.'[106] An example of the former would be the special role that was assigned to the applicant in the decision-making process.[107] The latter instance may occur if a decision has retroactive effects on a closed, well-defined group of private parties, including the applicant.[108] Basically the definition indicates that the decision, though not addressed to the applicant, produces similar effects as if it were addressed to the applicant. But that is not enough. It must do so in a manner that makes the applicant particularly affected in a manner that others, who are also concerned by the decision, are not. The deadly blow for the case of most private parties, however, results from the application of the test. The applicant in *Plaumann* was an importer of clementines. In a decision addressed to Germany, the Commission had decided not to allow the suspension of the collection of import duties for clementines. At the time of the contested decision, only a limited number of companies imported clementines. So one could have expected the ECJ to find that Plaumann, being one of few importers of clementines in Germany, had peculiar attributes (namely being actively involved at all relevant times in the relatively exclusive business of importing clementines into Germany) if compared to virtually everyone else so as to distinguish him individually from all other persons. However, the ECJ ruled that Plaumann was 'affected by the disputed decision as an importer of clementines, that is to say, by reason of a commercial activity which may at any time be practised by any person and is not therefore such as to distinguish the applicant in relation to the contested decision as in the case of the addressee.'[109] This is not only harsh, it is conceptually wrong, as *locus standi* does consequently not depend on the actual situation at the time of the adoption of the act or the time of the judgment (even if the exact number of persons affected is known, this is not deemed decisive[110]), but only on the virtual reality issue whether it is conceivable that there will ever be someone who may also be affected by the contested act besides the applicant.[111] In such a scenario, the applicant does not belong to a closed category and cannot be distinguished enough of all past, present and future persons to be allowed *locus standi*.

---

[106] Case 25/62 *Plaumann v. Commission* [1963] ECR 95. A slightly more readable definition can be found in Case T-266/94 *Foreningen af Jernskibs- og Maskinbyggerier i Danmark, Skibsværftsforeningen and others v. Commission* [1996] ECR II-1399: 'It is settled case law that persons other than those to whom a decision is addressed may claim to be individually concerned only if that decision affects them by reason of attributes peculiar to them or by reason of factual circumstances differentiating them from all other persons and, as a result, distinguishing them individually in like manner to the person addressed.'

[107] This is for instance the case with competitors who have made submissions to the Commission during the administrative procedure in competition cases, see Case 75/84 *Metro v. Commission* [1986] ECR 3021.

[108] See for instance Joined Cases 106 and 107/63 *Toepfer v. Commission* [1965] ECR 405, where a Commission decision of 3 October 1963 only affected undertakings that had requested import licences for maize on 1 October 1963.

[109] Case 25/62 *Plaumann v. Commission* [1963] ECR 95.

[110] Joined Cases 789 and 790/79 *Calpak v. Commission* [1980] ECR 1949, § 9; Case C-131/92 *Arnaud v. Council* [1993] ECR I-2573, § 13.

[111] P. Craig and G. De Búrca, *EU Law, Text, Cases and Materials*, (OUP, 2003), 488–491.

The third situation is a more complicated variation on the previous theme. The basic idea behind Article 230 TEC is that individuals should only be able to bring actions for annulment against individual decisions. However, it cannot be excluded that the institutions try to immunize a decision from legal challenge by giving it the name of another legal instrument, such as 'regulation' (or even—though not explicitly mentioned in Article 230(4) TEC—'directive'[112]), effectively suggesting that the contested act is a piece of legislation or an administrative act of a general scope and application while in fact it is not. In order to close this potential avenue for abuse, applicants are allowed to demonstrate that an act, though bearing another name, is in reality a decision. Once this is established, the *Plaumann* test comes back into play, as an applicant will only be giving standing if the unmasked decision is of direct and individual concern to the applicant. In practice, the question whether a regulation is in reality a decision and the issue of direct and individual concern are often mixed up and treated together. The ECJ does not hesitate to consider that a regulation is in reality a decision, because it is of direct and individual concern to the applicant.[113]

(ii) Exceptions

All this seems to effectively rule out the possibility of a direct action brought by an individual against *real* acts of a general scope and application, irrespective of whether they are legislative or administrative in nature.[114] Nonetheless two exceptions can be found in the case law.

A first group of cases concern anti-dumping regulations. Formally, anti-dumping regulations are legislative measures with a general scope. However, the ECJ has accepted that producers and exporters who are able to establish that they were identified in the measures adopted by the Commission or the Council or were concerned by the preliminary measures can consider the act to constitute a decision.[115] For all others, however, including in principle the Community importers of goods subject of an anti-dumping measure, the anti-dumping regulation is regarded to be of a legislative nature.[116]

[112] Joined Cases T-172/98, T-175/98 and T-177/98 *Salamander v. European Parliament and Council* [2000] ECR II-2487, § 55–69; Case C-298/89 *Gibraltar v. Council* [1993] ECR I-3605 and the accompanying opinion of Advocate General LENZ. For more, see Corthaut, case note under Case T-177/01 *Jégo-Quéré v. Commission* and Case C-50/00 P *Unión de Pequeños Agricultores v. Council, ColJEL* (2002) 141 at 146.

[113] Case C-358/89 *Extramet Industrie v. Council* [1991] ECR I-2501; Case C-309/89 *Codorníu SA v. Council* [1994] ECR I-1853.

[114] The main distinction behind Article 230(4) TEC is thus not between legislative and administrative acts. The system is based on the distinction between individual decisions addressed to the applicant and other acts, namely individual decisions addressed to a third party or acts of a general scope and application, irrespective whether they set out basic policy choices, have been adopted following legislative procedures and find their legal basis in the Treaty or are administrative acts of general scope and application.

[115] Joined Cases 239 and 275/82 *Allied Corporation and others v. Commission* [1984] ECR 1005, § 12; Joined Cases C-133 and 150/87 *Nashua Corporation v. Commission and Council* [1990] ECR I-719 and Case C-156/87 *Gestetner Holdings v. Council and Commission* [1990] ECR I-781.

[116] Case 307/81 *Alusuisse v. Council and Commission* [1982] ECR 3463; Case 301/86 *Frimodt Pederson v. Commission* [1987] ECR 3123. An exception is made for the importers whose retail prices

The second category is formed by highly exceptional hardship cases in which the rules were bended to bail out the applicant. Firstly, in *Extramet*,[117] one importer was allowed to challenge an anti-dumping regulation because the applicant had 'established the existence of a set of factors constituting such a situation which is peculiar to the applicant and which differentiates it, as regards the measure in question, from all other traders'.[118] At first sight this is fully an application of the *Plaumann* test. However, the situation of the importer also concerned a commercial activity, the import of calcium, which in theory at any time could be exercised by any other person. Nonetheless, the accumulation of a series of other features[119] made him meet the test. Moreover, it is not explained whether this regulation really was a disguised decision vis-à-vis the applicant, except for the fact that he was in any event directly and individually concerned. A second case is *Codorniu*,[120] in which the holder of the Spanish graphic trademark 'Gran Cremant de Codorniu' was allowed to challenge the validity of a regulation reserving the term 'crémant' for sparkling wines produced by fermentation in the bottle following the traditional method in certain parts of France and Luxembourg. For any other person, even other producers of crémant, this regulation was an ordinary piece of legislation against which no direct course of action was available, as the production of sparkling wines is a commercial activity which at any time can be exercised by any other person.[121] In the case of Codorniu, though, the regulation would effectively deprive the company of an intellectual property right it had acquired long before the regulation came into being. In this way Codorniu had 'established the existence of a situation which from the point of view of the contested provision differentiates it from all other traders'.[122] Again, the ECJ does not make clear whether the regulation should be equated with a decision vis-à-vis Codorniu (because it amounts to an individual expropriation order) or that it is sufficient that this regulation turns out to be of direct and individual concern to

---

for the goods in question have been used as a basis for establishing the export prices, see Case C-304/86 *Enital v. Commission and Council* [1990] ECR I-2939, Case C-305/86 *Neotype Techmashexport v. Commission and Council* [1990] ECR I-2945, and Case C-157/87 *Electroimpex v. Council* [1990] ECR I-3021. For more, see K. Lenaerts, D. Arts & I. Maselis; R. Bray (ed.), *Procedural Law of the European Union*, (2006) 7–106 to 7–110; Vanginderachter, 'Recevabilité des recours en matière de dumping' *CDE* (1987) 623–666.

117   Case C-358/89 *Extramet Industrie v. Council* [1991] ECR I-2501.   118   *ibid.*, § 17.

119   Extramet was the largest importer of the product forming the subject-matter of the anti-dumping measure and, at the same time, the end-user of the product. In addition, its business activities depended to a very large extent on those imports and were seriously affected by the contested regulation in view of the limited number of manufacturers of the product concerned and of the difficulties which it encountered in obtaining supplies from the sole Community producer, which, moreover, was its main competitor for the processed product. See Case C-358/89 *Extramet Industrie v. Council* [1991] ECR I-2501, § 17.

120   Case C-309/89 *Codorníu SA v. Council* [1994] ECR I-1853.

121   See the very similar case, but resulting in the opposite decision as to admissibility, of wine producers working according to the 'méthode champenoise' outside the Champagne region, Case 26/86 *Deutz und Geldermann v. Council* [1987] ECR 941.

122   Case C-309/89 *Codorníu SA v. Council* [1994] ECR I-1853, § 22.

the applicant. The latter rationale seems to prevail; though, this would be a departure from the text of Article 230(4) TEC.[123]

(iii) Judicial Protection before Domestic Courts

In ordinary circumstances, however, the normal way of contesting the validity of Community acts of a general scope and application goes through the national courts. The ordinary judge of Community law is the national judge. In a majority of cases this works excellent.[124] Most disputes arise in a national context and often involve both issues of national and European law. If the national judge cannot solve a problem of Community law, he can refer the issue to the ECJ. This may take time,[125] but helps to ensure the uniform interpretation and application of Community law. During the national procedure also issues of validity of Community law can be raised. Unlike for direct actions, there is no limitation on the types of act that can be contested. In this sense both individual acts and acts of a general scope and application, irrespective of their legislative or implementing character can be challenged. However, the contested act must have a bearing on the case before the national court and the applicant may not have been in a position to challenge the validity of the act directly.[126]

At first sight the EU system of judicial protection thus seems to go further than the requirements of the ECHR as identified at the end of Section II. By combining the action for annulment and the preliminary reference procedure it thus is often possible to challenge administrative and even legislative acts, though the latter

---

[123] Recently the ECJ has indicated that if a regulation is of direct and individual concern to an applicant it is 'thus' a decision. See Case C-50/00 P *Unión de Pequeños Agricultores v. Council* [2002] ECR I-6677, § 36. For a slightly different reading, see Ward, *supra*, fn. 100 (45) 63.

[124] Some authors go even that far that this is always the case and that no gap in judicial protection exists, see Temple-Lang, 'Actions for Declarations that Community Regulations are Invalid: The Duties of National Courts under Article 10 TEC', *E.L.Rev.* (2003) 102–111; Groussot, 'The EC System of Legal Remedies and Effective Judicial Protection: Does the System Really Need Reform?' 30 *L.I.E.I.* (2003) (221) 243–248.

[125] The average duration for answering a preliminary ruling is around 20.4 months; see the statistics section of the 2005 Annual Report of the ECJ, which can be consulted on <http://www.curia.europa.eu./en/instit/presentationfr/rapport/stat/stoscr.pdf>, p. 198. To this must be added the duration of the procedure before the national judge. The latter can be protracted as well, especially because a lower judge has no obligation to refer the case to the ECJ if he himself does not doubt the validity of the act—only judges against whose decisions no further appeal is possible or lower courts judges questioning the validity are under an obligation to refer—see Case 314/85 *Foto-Frost* [1987] ECR 4199, § 12–20. Exceeding the reasonable time may by itself constitute a breach of a fundamental right recognized by the Community legal order, see Joined Cases T-213/95 and T-18/96 *SCK and FNK v. Commission* [1997] ECR II-1739, § 53–64 and Case C-185/95 P *Baustahlgewebe v. Commission* [1998] ECR I-8417, § 20–22 and 26–48. However, the ECtHR has held that the duration of the preliminary rulings procedure before the ECJ should not be included while considering whether the reasonable delays have been exceeded by the State Party, see *Pafitis and others v. Greece*, Judgment of 26 February 1998, *Report of Judgments and decisions*, 1998-I, § 95.

[126] Case C-188/92 *TWD Textilwerke Deggendorf* [1994] ECR I-833; Case C-178/95 1997 *Wiljo* [1997] ECR I-585. See in particular, Case C-239/99 *Nachi Europe* [2001] ECR I-1197, where this reasoning was applied in a case involving an anti-dumping regulation, which is formally a legislative measure but falls within the exception mentioned above.

possibility does not seem to be demanded by the ECtHR. The system of judicial protection through the national courts, though, is not entirely satisfactory.

Firstly, the parties are not in control of the preliminary questions. In *Foto-Frost*,[127] the ECJ has explained that national judges who doubt the validity of a Community act must refer the case to the Court. However, if the judge does not share the doubts of the parties he does not have to refer, unless there is no further appeal possible against his judgment. This means that someone who wants to challenge the validity of a Community act may first have to go through long and expensive appeal procedures. Moreover, the reference procedure can be protracted as well. Furthermore, the national judge, if and when he makes an order for reference, decides autonomously on the wording of the reference. If the national judge misstates the arguments of the applicant against the contested act, the case may be presented to the ECJ in a way the party contesting the validity did never intend.

Moreover, all this implies that a national court case can be brought in the first place. This is not self-evident, though. Often it is indeed impossible to bring a case as an applicant before a national court. If for instance a licence to plant a vineyard is refused by the national authorities on the basis of a Community regulation, the validity of this national decision can be challenged before a national administrative court, which in turn can query the ECJ about the validity of the underlying Community regulation.[128] However, if a prohibitive regulation does not need any implementing acts at all, the only way to provoke a court case may consist of breaking the regulation. An individual who disagrees with the prohibition is then placed before the dilemma of giving up an activity which he claims should be lawful or breaking the law. If he takes the former option, he will lose his income and cannot go to court anyway, as there is no further act to challenge. If he decides to take the risk of breaching the law, he may get his day in court if and when the national authorities are willing to prosecute him, but if his arguments are rejected he may immediately also be confronted with considerable sanctions. Either way, a safe way of testing the validity of the regulation, seems lacking.

This is precisely what happened in *Jégo-Quéré*,[129] where a French fishing company, the only company that regularly catches hake in the waters south of Ireland while fishing for whiting, tried to contest the validity of a Commission regulation[130] preventing it from fishing for hake in that area. The regulation at stake was a measure of a general scope and application implementing the Common Fisheries Policy and thus of an administrative nature. As fishing is an economic activity that can at any times be exercised by any person, the company did not meet the *Plaumann* test for bringing a direct action. Yet, the fishing company tried to convince the CFI that if they were not allowed to bring their case, they would

---

127 Case 314/85 *Foto-Frost* [1987] ECR 4199, § 12–20.
128 Case 44/79 *Hauer* [1979] ECR 3727.
129 Case T-177/01 *Jégo-Quéré v. Commission* [2002] ECR II-2365.
130 Commission Regulation (EC) No 1162/2001 of 14 June 2001 establishing measures for the recovery of the stock of hake in ICES sub-areas III, IV, V, VI and VII and ICES divisions VIII a, b, d, e and associated conditions for the control of activities of fishing vessels (2001) OJ L 159/4.

have nowhere to turn to. The CFI accepted that the preliminary reference procedure did not offer sufficient protection, because '[i]ndividuals cannot be required to breach the law in order to gain access to justice'.[131] In order to ensure effective judicial protection for individuals, which in the opinion of the CFI could also not be guaranteed using the action for damages,[132] the CFI, inspired by Articles 6 and 13 ECHR and 47 of the Charter of Fundamental Rights,[133] then proceeded with introducing a new definition of individual concern,[134] which resulted in declaring the action admissible.

Unfortunately, the ECJ has soon afterwards made clear that it did not appreciate the new approach to *locus standi* as developed by the CFI. In a series of judgments starting with *Unión de Pequeños Agricultores*,[135] the ECJ has reaffirmed the classical system, which may be summarized as follows. Individuals are entitled to effective judicial protection of the rights they derive from the Community legal order, and the right to such protection is one of the general principles of law stemming from the constitutional traditions common to the Member States.[136] However, this protection should not necessarily be offered uniquely through direct actions before the ECJ. It is the combination of Article 230 (action for annulment) and Article 241 TEC (plea of illegality) on the one hand, and the preliminary reference procedure of Article 234 TEC that ensures sufficient protection.[137] This list of courses of action should presumably be completed with the action for damages.[138] If a gap in the protection arises, the conditions of Article 230 TEC cannot be altered to bail out the applicant. The *Plaumann* test is deemed to be the only way the condition of individual concern can correctly be

---

[131] Case T-177/01 *Jégo-Quéré v. Commission* [2002] ECR II-2365, § 45. See also Opinion of Advocate General F. Jacobs in Case C-50/00 P *Unión de Pequeños Agricultores v. Council* [2002] ECR I-6677, § 41.

[132] Case T-177/01 *Jégo-Quéré v. Commission* [2002] ECR II-2365, § 46. The action for damages had been earmarked as a cornerstone of the Community system of judicial protection in Joined Cases T-172/98, T-175/98 and T-177/98 *Salamander v. European Parliament and Council* [2000] ECR II-2487, § 78.

[133] Case T-177/01 *Jégo-Quéré v. Commission* [2002] ECR II-2365, § 47.

[134] Case T-177/01 *Jégo-Quéré v. Commission* [2002] ECR II-2365, § 51: '[A] natural or legal person is to be regarded as individually concerned by a Community measure of general application that concerns him directly if the measure in question affects his legal position, in a manner which is both definite and immediate, by restricting his rights or by imposing obligations on him. The number and position of other persons who are likewise affected by the measure, or who may be so, are of no relevance in that regard.'

[135] Case C-50/00 P *Unión de Pequeños Agricultores v. Council* [2002] ECR I-6677.

[136] Case C-50/00 P *Unión de Pequeños Agricultores v. Council* [2002] ECR I-6677, §§ 38–39. However, the cases cited (Case 222/84 *Johnston* [1986] ECR 1651, § 18 and Case C-424/99 *Commission v. Austria* [2001] ECR I-9285, § 45) all concern instances where the *national* legal order did not offer sufficient judicial protection, see Corthaut, *supra*, fn. 112, 141 at 162.

[137] Case C-50/00 P *Unión de Pequeños Agricultores v. Council* [2002] ECR I-6677, § 40. This is fully in line with earlier case law, see Case 294/83 *Parti Ecologiste 'Les Verts' v. European Parliament* [1986] ECR 1339, § 23 and Case 314/85 *Foto-Frost* [1987] ECR 4199, § 20.

[138] The ECJ does not mention the action for damages, however the action for damages featured prominently in Case T-177/98 *Salamander v. European Parliament and Council* [2000] ECR II-2487, which does not seem to be overruled. For a more subtle approach, see Opinion of AG Sharpston in Case C-131/03 P *R.J. Reynolds Tobacco Holdings v. Commission*, [2006] ECR I-000, nyp §§ 74–76.

interpreted. In those circumstances it is for the national judge, despite the national procedural autonomy, to provide for an effective remedy under national law,[139] or at least to try to do so.[140] The condition of individual concern must nevertheless be interpreted in the light of the principle of effective judicial protection and thus take into account all relevant factual elements,[141] even if the ECJ is at times very restrictive in applying this principle.[142] A real adjustment of the conditions for admissibility can only be made, however, by the Member States in their capacity of Masters of the Treaty.[143]

(iv) The Right of Access in the Draft Treaty Establishing a Constitution

An attempt in this respect has been made in the Treaty establishing a Constitution for Europe,[144] which will not only apply in the sphere of the current EC-competences,

---

[139] Case C-50/00 P *Unión de Pequeños Agricultores v. Council* [2002] ECR I-6677, § 42; Case C-491/01 *British American Tobacco (Investments) Ltd. and Imperial Tobacco Ltd.* [2002] ECR I-11453, § 39–40. Some authors read into those paragraphs an obligation for national judges to provide for effective remedies enabling individuals to contest the validity of Community acts in circumstances where a direct action for annulment does not otherwise appear to be available, either in the Community courts or in the national courts, see Nihoul, 'Le recours des particuliers contres les actes communautaires de portée générale. Nouveaux développements dans la jurisprudence' 11 *JTDE* (2003) 38 at 39. See also Köngeter, 'Erweiterte Klageberechtigung bei Individualnichtigkeitsklagen gegen EG-Verordnungen?' 55 *NJW* (2002), 2216 at 2217; Gundel, 'Die Tabakprodukt-Richtlinie vor dem EuGH: Zur Zulässigkeit der Nutzung doppelter Rechtsgrundlagen im Rechtssetzungsverfahren der Gemeinschaft', 38 *EuR*, (2003) at 100–101. However, this approach has also been vigorously contested as it seems to be based on wrong assumptions, needlessly curtails the national procedural autonomy and cannot effectively be enforced, see Lenaerts & Corthaut, *supra*, fn. 71, 12–19.

[140] Case C-50/00 P *Unión de Pequeños Agricultores v. Council* [2002] ECR I-6677, § 42. The ECJ indicates that 'national courts are required, *so far as possible*, to interpret and apply national procedural rules governing the exercise of rights of action in a way that enables natural and legal persons to challenge before the courts the legality of any decision or other *national measure* relative to the application to them of a Community act of general application, by pleading the invalidity of such an act' (emphasis added). This approach, however, misses the point. On the one hand, no judicial protection is guaranteed if the national judge happens to be less creative. Moreover, on the other hand, the main problem precisely concerns those situations where there are no national implementing measures—the issue is not whether the legality of a national measure can be examined, but whether the legality of a Community act that does not need further implementing measures can be challenged. See in this sense also Hanf, 'Talking with the "*pouvoir constituant*" in Times of Constitutional Reform', (2003) 10 *MJ* (265) 280–281 and Usher, 'Direct and individual concern—an effective remedy or a conventional solution?', 28 *E.L.Rev.* (2003) (575) 584–585.

[141] Case C-50/00 P *Unión de Pequeños Agricultores v. Council* [2002] ECR I-6677, § 44; Case C-312/00 P *Commission v. Camar and Tico* [2002] ECR I-11355. See also D. Waelbrouck, 'Le droit au recours juridictionnel effectif du particulier trois pas en avant, deux pas en arrière' 38 *CDE* (2002) 3 at 7; and Van den Brouck, 'A Long Hot Summer for Individual Concern? The European Court's Recent Case Law on Direct Actions by Private Parties ... and a Plea for a Foreign Affairs Exception' 30 *LIEI* (2003) 61 at 73–74.

[142] See Case C-142/00 P *Commission v. Nederlandse Antillen* [2003] ECR I-3483. Nonetheless, the CFI does not seem to be deterred, see Case T-243/01 *Sony Computer Entertainment Europe Ltd v. Commission* [2003] ECR II-4189, § 56–78.

[143] Case C-50/00 P *Unión de Pequeños Agricultores v. Council* [2002] ECR I-6677, § 45. On this remarkable example of judicial restraint, see Hanf, *supra*, fn. 140, 265–290.

[144] [2004] OJ C310/1.

but also to all issues of the current third pillar.[145] In Article III-365(4), the new formula reads as follows 'Any natural or legal person may, under the same conditions, institute proceedings against an act addressed to that person or which is of direct and individual concern to him or her, and against a regulatory act which is of direct concern to him or her and does not entail implementing measures.' This compromise solves only part of the problem: it will be possible for individuals to contest the validity of acts of general scope and application, which are of an executive nature and do not entail an intervening act. However, it will still not be possible to bring a direct action against a legislative act in the sense of Article I-33,[146] unless it can be demonstrated that this act is of both direct and individual concern in the classic sense.[147] In the case of legislative measures, individuals may still have to breach the act first, before being given an opportunity to obtain sufficient judicial protection.

Furthermore, the drafting of this Article is rather unfortunate. Firstly, the term 'regulatory act' is not properly defined and may wrongfully suggest that legislative acts are covered as well.[148] A tentative definition may be that 'regulatory acts' are all non-legislative acts of general scope and application or with regulating effects for an open class of legal subjects beyond the addressee. The term 'regulatory act' thus definitely covers every type of non-legislative act with a general scope and application. This encompasses all implementing regulations (Article I-37) and in our view also the delegated European regulations (Article I-36).[149] It also comprises the

---

[145] This is the logical consequence of the disappearance of the three pillar structure. However, in respect of issues that fall under the CFSP an express exception is made in Article III-376. In this sense the internal logic of the Constitution has not been followed to the end. Nonetheless, even in respect of the CFSP some progress has been made with the exception in Article III-376, second paragraph allowing for an action for annulment for individuals against restrictive measures against individuals adopted under the CFSP. For more on the impact of the Constitution on the judicial protection in the sphere of the CFSP, see Corthaut, 'An Effective Remedy for All? Paradoxes and Controversies in Respect of Judicial Protection in the Field of the CFSP under the European Constitution', (2005) 12 Tilburg Foreign Law Review, 110–144.

[146] The Constitution introduces a distinction between legislative, further elaborated in Article I-34 and non-legislative acts, further explained in Article I-35 and encompassing individual decisions and implementing regulations (Article I-37). A third category of non-legislative acts is created in Article I-36 with so-called delegated European regulations, which are non-legislative acts that can be used to alter the non-essential parts of legislative acts, if that act so provides.

[147] In this respect the current exceptions, such as anti-dumping regulations and cases like Case C-309/89 *Codorníu SA v. Council* [1994] ECR I-1853 and Case C-358/89 *Extramet Industrie v. Council* [1991] ECR I-2501, will presumably continue to apply.

[148] The legal experts group of the IGC had suggested to change the term 'regulatory act' into 'regulation or decision having no addressees', see document CIG 4/1/03 REV1. This option would have brought some clarity as to which acts are covered and which acts are not. However, in the final draft this suggestion was apparently abandoned again.

[149] As delegated regulations are also non-legislative acts with a general scope and application, an action for annulment will thus also be available for individuals under the looser criteria against delegated regulations (Article I-36), even if they are meant to alter legislation. Apparently, those acts— and despite the special procedure enabling both the Council and the European Parliament to intervene—do not enjoy the democratic legitimacy European laws and European framework laws enjoy. This can result in a reverse discrimination if—as often happens—the legislator annexes to the original legislative act a list (for instance with dangerous substances to which the European law

decisions without addressee (Article I-33(1), fifth indent). In our view, and perhaps more controversially, it should also cover decisions addressed to Member States, but effectively hiding a measure of a general scope and application. The prime example of the latter is the type of act which was at stake in *Plaumann*: formally it was a decision addressed to Germany, but behind it was the (confirmation) of a rule that all German importers of clementines had to pay the full amount of import duties.[150] Not covered by the term 'regulatory act' are thus 'true' individual decisions and legislative acts in the sense of Article I-34. For those acts the old regime as outlined above continues to apply. This means that it is still possible that in the case of prohibitive legislative acts an individual will only be able to obtain judicial protection by breaking the law first. Similarly, it cannot be excluded that in the case of a legislative act abolishing certain advantages[151] problems may still arise because of the absence of national implementing measures which could be challenged in a national court in order to trigger the indirect route for judicial review through the preliminary reference procedure. This exclusion of legislative acts from judicial review was apparently inspired by a similar respect for the democratic legislator, which has lead the ECtHR to accept that Member States are not under an obligation to provide for mechanisms for review of legislative acts. However, as indicated above, this approach is questionable. Moreover, as also indicated by Advocate General Jacobs, this approach is particularly unfortunate in the context of the EU where there is not always firm democratic control.[152]

---

applies) which is amenable for review by the Commission through a delegated regulation. Those directly concerned by the annex will not be able to bring an action for annulment unless they can also demonstrate that they are individually concerned, while those directly concerned by a later amendment of the annex introduced by a delegated regulation will be able to bring an action for annulment. On the other hand, it has been observed that a clear distinction between executive and legislative acts as to the conditions for judicial review may well be an incentive for the Commission and the Council to 'elaborate measures that are truly normative in nature via the procedures laid down for basic acts' with moreover greater involvement of the Parliament in making the basic policy choices, as the Council in particular and the Commission have no interest in basic policy choices made in executive acts that are much more vulnerable, see Ward, *supra*, fn.100 (45) 50–51.

150 In this sense there is an obvious link between the lack of individual concern and the scope of the measure. Formally qualified as a decision with a clear addressee, it was held not to be of individual concern to an importer of clementines, because he was 'affected by the disputed decision as an importer of clementines, that is to say, by reason of a commercial activity which may at any time be practised by any person and is not therefore such as to distinguish the applicant in relation to the contested decision as in the case of the addressee'. It is precisely the fact that Germany thus had to apply the decision in an undefined number of cases to all present and future importers that on the one hand precludes the individual concern, but on the other hand leads us to conclude that this type of acts are actually regulating market conditions for an open class of legal subjects, making it fall under the qualification of a 'regulatory act' in the sense of Article III-365(4). Moreover, as indicated in fn. 148, the term regulatory acts was preferred over the phrase 'regulation or decision having no addressees'. This seems to suggest that in certain circumstances also decisions with an addressee can qualify as a 'regulatory act'.

151 This was for instance at issue in Case C-50/00 P *Unión de Pequeños Agricultores v. Council* [2002] ECR I-6677.

152 Opinion of Advocate General F. Jacobs in Case C-50/00 P *Unión de Pequeños Agricultores v. Council* [2002] ECR I-6677, § 89–90. For a further analysis in this sense, see Lenaerts & Corthaut, *supra*, fn. 71 (1) 20, 14–16.

Secondly, the requirement that no further implementing measures are needed, at first sight hardly adds anything to the condition of direct concern.[153] Direct concern already means that the contested act and not some further implementing act regulates the legal position of the applicant. The drafters of this Article were presumably mainly preoccupied with *Jégo-Quéré* like situations[154] where an executive act of general scope and application affects the legal position of the applicant by imposing obligations on the applicant or restricting his rights in a manner that is both immediate and definite. In such a situation the requirement of direct concern and the condition that no further implementing acts are needed should best be considered as meaning exactly the same, and this will almost always be the case when regulatory acts not needing further implementing measures are at stake.[155] However, if we stick to this pleonastic reading no limits exist on bringing a direct action against those 'regulatory acts', except for the general requirement that one must have an interest[156] in the annulment of the contested act[157] and in the pleas put forward.[158] As it has been argued that also under the CFI's *Jégo-Quéré* test 'interest' and 'individual concern' have both a distinct meaning with the latter being more restrictive than the former,[159] the result may well be that in respect of

[153] It is important to indicate in this respect that even if European framework laws fall outside the scope of the 'regulatory acts', there may still be plenty of cases where the absence of any further implementing acts is also an issue: the terms 'regulatory act' or 'regulation or decision having no addressees' also cover the equivalent of the present day implementing directives. Article I-33 indicates that a regulation may either be binding in its entirety and directly applicable in all Member States, or be binding, as regards the result to be achieved, on all Member States to which it is addressed, but leaving the national authorities entirely free to choose the form and means of achieving that result. The latter regulations fall within the scope of Article III-365(4), yet in all but the rarest of cases a direct action will fail because of the requirement that there should be no need for further implementing measures.

[154] In this sense the formula was proposed as a compromise between those who wanted to expand the possibility of direct standing and those attached to the current system. See the final report of the Discussion Circle on the Court of Justice, CONV 636/03, 6–10.

[155] The only situation in which this does not seem to be the case would be a decision having no addressees or a regulation adopted by the Commission authorizing a Member State to take certain measures the Member State had announced to take once authorized to do so. In those circumstances there still are implementing measures needed, even if the act containing the authorization should be deemed to be of direct concern, in line with Case 92/70 *Bock v. Commission* [1971] ECR 897, § 6–8.

[156] The interest requirement is, however, not expressly stated in the current Article 230(4), nor in the future Article III-365(4). For a full analysis of the concept of interest, see M. Canedo, 'L'intérêt à agir dans le recours en annulation du droit communautaire' 36 *RTDE* (2000) 451–510.

[157] This means that the annulment of the act must eliminate the negative repercussions the act has on the legal position of the applicant. For more, see K. Lenaerts, D. Arts & I. Maselis; R. Bray (ed.), *Procedural Law of the European Union* (2006) 7–113 to 7–120.

[158] Case 90/74 *Deboeck v. Commission* [1975] ECR 1123; Joined Cases 209–215 and 218/78 *Van Landewyck v. Commission* [1980] ECR 3125; Case 85/82 *Sloh* [1983] ECR 2105; K. Lenaerts, D. Arts & I. Maselis; R. Bray (ed.), *Procedural Law of the European Union* (2006) 7–113 to 7–120; Usher, *supra*, fn. 140 (575) 600.

[159] Lenaerts & Corthaut, *supra*, fn. 71. Calliess even considers that the formula of the CFI would actually have had a positive effect on *locus standi* in only a very limited number of cases, see Callies, 'Kohärenz und Konvergenz beim europäischen Individualrechtsschutz' 49 *NJW* (2002) (3577) 3582.

those 'regulatory acts' soon even more cases will reach the ECJ than if the ECJ had simply accepted the formula proposed by the CFI.[160]

Alternatively, if this were not the case, then 'direct concern' in the second part of Article III-365(4) may not mean 'direct concern' at all, but rather the new version of individual concern as proposed in *Jégo-Quéré*. Not much changes then. The old condition of 'direct concern' would then be replaced by 'does not entail implementing measures' and the condition of individual concern would be replaced by something that is called 'direct concern', but actually refers to the interpretation of individual concern by the CFI in *Jégo-Quéré*. Fascinatingly, 'direct concern' would then come close to 'direct link' as understood in the *Athanassoglou* case before the ECtHR, which was discussed above in Section II. Though, this would then in turn result in the absurd situation that the word direct concern has two meanings in one and the same sentence—the first time its classic meaning and the second time actually meaning individual concern, but not the individual concern of earlier in the sentence but the individual concern as defined in *Jégo-Quéré*.

Therefore we defend a third option in which direct concern means something more than that no further implementing measures are needed, without amounting to individual concern. Direct concern may indeed, in line with recent case law under Article 230(4) TEC, stress the effective impact the act must have on the legal position of the applicant, or in the words of the ECJ: 'the measure complained of to affect[s] directly the legal situation of the individual and leave[s] no discretion to the addressees of that measure, who are entrusted with the task of implementing it, such implementation being purely automatic and resulting from Community rules without the application of other intermediate rules'.[161] Direct concern thus not only demands that no further implementing acts are needed, but primarily deals with the immediate impact the act has on the legal position of the applicant. This approach gives a separate meaning to all the terms of Article III-365(4), while closing the avenue of the *actio popularis*.

An example may clarify the differences. Suppose the Commission adopts a directly applicable delegated regulation adding a newly discovered pesticide to a list annexed to a European law on dangerous chemicals, which prohibits the

---

[160] Neither AG Jacobs, nor the CFI advocated an *actio popularis* at EU level, see Hanf, *supra*, fn. 140 (265) 280 and Malvasio, 'Débat sur l'accès des particuliers au prétoire communautaire', *AJDA* (2002) (867) 872. As the latter remarks this is in line with the current practice of the majority of the Member States. See also, Usher, *supra*, fn. 140 (575) 585, who observes that public interest litigation, such as Case C-321/98 P *Greenpeace v. Commission* [1998] ECR I-1651, still seems to be excluded.

[161] Case C-404/96 P *Glencore Grain v. Commission* [1998] ECR I-2435, § 41. Indeed, as is demonstrated by the judgment in Case C-486/01 P *Front National v. European Parliament* [2004] ECR I-6289, § 29, it may occur that an act does not need further implementing measures but only has the negative consequences by proxy. As the ECJ stated: 'Although it cannot be denied that no implementing measure is necessary for the act to produce effects, there is also no question that, pursuant to the actual wording of Rule 29, the act can produce effects only on the legal situation of Members of the Parliament and not on that of national political parties from whose lists those Members were elected and which, in some cases, have played a part in securing the election of those Members. Contrary to the requirements laid down by the case law referred to in paragraph 34 of this judgment, such an act therefore does not directly produce effects on the legal situation of the Front National.'

production, distribution and use of the listed dangerous substances. Firstly, several groups in society may have an interest in its annulment: farmers, environmental groups, producers of the pesticide, the chemical industry in general, trade unions and so on. The next step is to determine whether the act is a 'regulatory act'. As indicated above delegated regulations are 'regulatory acts' as they are non-legislative acts of general scope and application. Thirdly, it needs to be determined that no further implementing acts are necessary. In the case of delegated regulations changing the annex to a prohibitive regulation this seems to be the case. One could of course argue that the real consequences for the producer will stem from the prosecution lodged by the Member State if he fails to comply with the legal regime, but that would make judicial protection again dependent on people having to breach the law first—something the drafters of the Constitution definitely wanted to avoid bearing in mind the *Jégo-Quéré* case. We can thus reasonably say the prohibition as such is the mere result of the delegated regulation.[162] Finally, we still have to determine direct concern. The act will be of direct concern to the extent that the measure complained of directly affects the legal situation of the individual (and leaves no discretion to the addressees of that measure, who are entrusted with the task of implementing it, such implementation being purely automatic and resulting from Community rules without the application of other intermediate rules). Accordingly, we can distinguish between those persons who are able to effectively challenge this legislation and those persons who, even if no further implementing measures are needed against them either, only feel the consequences by proxy and can therefore not challenge the regulation directly for lack of direct concern. In our example the persons whose legal position is directly affected by the measure are the producers who are prevented from producing the pesticide concerned. One could also argue that the same applies to the distributors who have to dispose of their stocks but cannot sell them. The position of farmers seems borderline, as the impact of the measure may be fairly limited, unless they too still have large stocks of a now prohibited product. At first sight these are exactly the same persons as those who have an interest in the case. Yet, this is not the case. The financial position of a bank, which has invested heavily in a producer of the prohibited agent, may well be affected by the regulation; however, the legal position of the bank will not be altered, so it will not be able to bring an action for annulment. Only those applicants who can demonstrate that the regulation effectively affected their legal position by imposing an obligation of limiting their

---

[162] While this requirement will usually be fulfilled in respect of regulations mirroring the current regulations, it will usually not be the case for certain executive measures to the extent that the Commission is currently adopting highly detailed directives while implementing Community law and may continue to do this under the Draft Constitution by adopting non-directly applicable regulations which need to be implemented further in the national legal order. For an extensive analysis of the problems that arise for the *locus standi* of individuals under Article 230 TEC when the Commission, often through the Comitology procedure, adopts highly detailed directives, see Ward, *supra*, fn. 100 at 60–61 and 67–69. Ward therefore argues that in such cases the criteria for determining 'direct concern' are too stringent.

rights should and will get a course of action. Presumably only the producers and wholesalers facing civil or even penal sanctions if they continue to produce or market the product will be in this position. Bankers, shareholders, and trade unions may all be affected by the measure, but only indirectly. Their fate is the indirect result of the impact the matter has on the companies that are directly concerned. Also the position of consumer and environmental groups is rather remotely affected, as the measure in all likelihood does not affect their legal position as none of their rights are restricted, nor does the measure impose a prohibition on them—only their policy view may not have been taken up by the Commission. They too will thus not be able to claim direct concern. In this way a good balance can be struck between the legitimate desire to avoid that the system could be stemmed because of the introduction of an *actio popularis* and the effective judicial protection of those private parties, which are most affected.

IV. The right of Access to a Court Revisited

The right of access to a court is a relatively new right and it seems both the ECtHR and the ECJ are still looking for its exact significance. Further reflection is thus required on the scope of and the need for an effective right of access to a court within the European legal order. It must be noticed that both supranational courts have (re)opened the discussion through their 'jurisprudential dialogue'. Still it should only be the beginning of a vast debate. Questions remain as to the significance of Article 6 ECHR for the EU, especially because the EU is considering acceding to the ECHR, or the opportunity for the ECtHR to refer to ECJ jurisprudence concerning the right of access to a court. Moreover, at a time when the EU is trying to adopt its own constitution, the opportunity should not be missed to give full weight to the right of access to a court.

A. The Right of Access within the EU Viewed from the Perspective of the ECtHR

If the EU were to adhere to the ECHR two questions concerning the right of access should be answered: first whether Article 6 ECHR is applicable to the judicial system of the EU and, if this appears to be the case, whether the substantial criteria are met. The CFI stated that 'the procedures provided in, on the one hand, Article 234 TEC and on the other hand, Article 235 TEC and the second paragraph of Article 288 TEC can no longer be regarded, in the light of Articles 6 and 13 ECHR, as guaranteeing persons the right to an effective remedy enabling them to contest the legality of Community measures of general application which directly affect their legal situation'.[163] In other words, the CFI suggests that

---

[163] Case T-177/01 *Jégo-Quéré v. Commission* [2002] ECR II-2365, § 47.

Article 6 ECHR, and the right of access to a court enshrined in it, could be applicable to Community measures of general application, which directly affect the legal situation of the individual and are of a legislative nature. Moreover, the CFI is thus of the opinion that indirect routes for challenging the validity of such acts may not always suffice to comply with Articles 6 and 13 ECHR. It is not sure whether the ECtHR would conclude the same, especially when we take into account the judgments in *Ruiz-Mateos, Athanassoglou, Posti and Rakho* and *Voggenreiter* discussed above. In our opinion, however, the CFI has rightly given a strong signal that the right of access might enshrine more than what the ECtHR has admitted up until now. We will elaborate this in the final section below.

The issue of compliance with Article 6 § 1 ECHR also merits examination from an EU perspective, even if a lot of the cases arising under EU law may well fall outside the scope of Article 6 ECHR. However, if the ECtHR were to return to a more lenient applicability test, as defended below by the present authors, the EU system may not meet the substantial criteria set out for domestic systems. The restricted approach to *locus standi* before the CFI is, as stated above, usually defended by reference to the existence of two compensation mechanisms which expand the possibilities to test the validity of Community acts: on the one hand the possibility to bring an action for damages against the Community[164] and on the other hand the possibilities to challenge Community measures indirectly—usually before the national court. Both approaches are doubtful in the light of the case law of the ECtHR.

The first compensation mechanism, based on the action for damages, becomes doubtful in the light of the ECtHR's assessment of the Finnish plea in *Posti and Rahko* that the applicants were capable of bringing an action for damages against the Finnish State.[165] Indeed, in most cases involving EC law it cannot be 'convincingly demonstrated that the applicants could have expected with any reasonable degree of likelihood to obtain damages from the State [or the Community] on the basis of its liability for such mistakes or omissions in the use of public authority'.[166] As has been admitted by the CFI in *Jégo-Quéré* with ample references to the case law of the ECJ and the CFI[167]: 'The procedural route of an action for damages based on the non-contractual liability of the Community does not, in a case such as the present, provide a solution that satisfactorily protects the interests of the individual affected. Such an action cannot result in the removal from the Community legal order of a measure which is nevertheless necessarily held to be illegal. Given that it presupposes that damage has been directly occasioned by the application of the measure in issue, such an action is subject to criteria of admissibility and

[164] Case T-177/98 *Salamander v. European Parliament and Council* [2000] ECR II-2487.
[165] *Posti and Rahko v. Finland, supra*, fn. 3, § 61–62.
[166] Compare *Posti and Rahko v. Finland, supra*, fn. 3, § 61.
[167] Case C-352/98 P *Bergaderm and Goupil v. Commission* [2000] ECR I-5291, §§ 41 to 43; Case T-155/99 *Dieckmann & Hansen v. Commission* [2001] ECR II-3143, §§ 42 and 43; Joined Cases C-104/89 and C-37/90 *Mulder and Others v. Council and Commission* [1992] ECR I-3061, §§ 18 and 19; and Case T-196/99 *Area Cova and Others v. Council and Commission* [2001] ECR II-3597, § 43.

substance which are different from those governing actions for annulment, and does not therefore place the Community judicature in a position whereby it can carry out the comprehensive judicial review which it is its task to perform. In particular, where a measure of general application, such as the provisions contested in the present case, is challenged in the context of such an action, the review carried out by the Community judicature does not cover all the factors which may affect the legality of that measure, being limited instead to the censuring of sufficiently serious infringements of rules of law intended to confer rights on individuals'.[168] The main problem is thus that while any infringement of higher rules of EC law may result in the annulment of the act, the requirements for a successful action for damages are far more difficult to fulfil, despite the lower admissibility criteria. In particular, under the so-called *Bergaderm* criteria, in an action for damage one has to indicate that there was a sufficiently serious breach of a rule intended to confer rights on individuals resulting in damage.[169] In practice, there have already been cases where the claim was dismissed because, despite there being a breach which could have resulted in annulment, the breach was either not sufficiently serious[170] or the rule breached was not intended to confer rights on the individual.[171]

Also the trust placed in the preliminary rulings procedure may be unfounded. As explained above, where the EC enacts legislation containing a prohibition, which does not need any further implementation by the Member States, the only way to obtain judicial review is by breaching the law. The ECtHR in *Posti and Rahko* fully sided with the—in our opinion almost self-evident[172]—position expressed by both Advocate General Jacobs[173] and the CFI,[174] that individuals cannot be required to breach the law in order to gain access to justice and have a 'civil right' determined in accordance with Article 6 §1.[175]

---

[168] Case T-177/01 *Jégo-Quéré* [2002] ECR II-2365, § 46. Compare also with respect to the notion of 'victim', which allows a person to bring a complaint before the ECtHR, in cases where an act contains a prohibition. See fn. 175.

[169] Case C-352/98 P *Bergaderm and Goupil v. Commission* [2000] ECR I-5291, §§ 41 to 43.

[170] Joined Cases C-104/89 and C-37/90 *Mulder and Others v. Council and Commission* [1992] ECR I-3061, §§ 18 and 19.

[171] Case T-196/99 *Area Cova and Others v. Council and Commission* [2001] ECR II-3597, § 43. Admittedly, the ECtHR would probably dismiss most of those cases by arguing that the dispute is not genuine and serious and thus not applicable to article 6 ECHR (see *supra*, fn. 30 and accompanying text). In this interpretation, the *Begaderm* case law is in full compliance with the jurisprudence of the ECtHR under Article 6 ECHR.

[172] See, however, Barents, 'Een midzomernachtdroom op de Kirchberg' 51 *SEW* (2003) 2 at 7.

[173] See point 43 of the Opinion of AG Jacobs delivered on 21 March 2002 in Case C-50/00 P *Unión de Pequeños Agricultores v. Council* [2002] ECR I-6677.

[174] Case T-177/01 *Jégo-Quéré* [2002] ECR II-2365, § 45. See in this sense also the pending Case C-432/05 *Unibet* (2006) OJ C 36/47.

[175] *Posti and Rahko v. Finland, supra,* fn. 3, § 64. Compare also with respect to the notion of 'victim', which allows a person to bring a complaint before the ECtHR, in cases where an act contains a prohibition. *Dudgeon v. Ireland,* judgment of 22 October 1981, *Series A* n°45, § 41: 'In the personal circumstances of the applicant, the very existence of this legislation continuously and directly affects his private life: either he respects the law and refrains from engaging—even in private with consenting male partners—in prohibited sexual acts to which he is disposed by reason of his homosexual tendencies, or he commits such acts and thereby becomes liable to criminal prosecution.'

It is, however, important to notice in this respect the presence in the Constitution of Article I-29(1), second sentence which reads as follows: 'Member States shall provide rights of appeal sufficient to ensure effective legal protection in the fields covered by Union law.' Building on the appeals judgment of 1 April 2004 in *Jégo-Quéré*,[176] this Article could be construed as demanding that Member States, even artificially, create ways for individuals to challenge every piece of EU law—even legislative acts—as applicants before the national courts by challenging *ad hoc* national acts, such as a 'decision' by the government confirming a prohibition in a European measure. This indirect approach for judicial review may well prove a time consuming procedural detour which will not limit the workload of the EU courts, as those national courts are all under an obligation to refer questions to the ECJ once they doubt the validity of an EU act.[177] The better option would therefore have been to lower the threshold for direct actions before the CFI.

B. The Influence of the Case Law of the ECJ on the Right to Access in the Case Law of the ECtHR

If the EU is influenced by the ECHR in cases concerning the right to access, it can also be ascertained that the ECtHR refers to EU jurisprudence in this matter. This is remarkable because references to the case law of the ECJ are a rarity in the case law of the Strasbourg Court. Especially the *Posti and Rakho* case attracts our attention: the context in which the reference to the *Extramet* case was made is rather peculiar, as the ECJ was absolutely not concerned with the ECHR in that case. Nor is the ECtHR in *Posti and Rahko* dealing with an issue of EU law.[178] Moreover, the choice for the *Extramet* case is quite peculiar. As we have explained above, the *Extramet* case is considered to be an exceptional case in which the ECJ proved willing to slightly bend the rules on admissibility to *increase the scope of judicial protection offered by the ECJ*. Things are becoming more obvious if we have

---

[176] Case C-263/02 P *Commission v. Jégo-Quéré* [2004] ECR I-3425 § 31–33.

[177] Case 314/85 *Foto-Frost* [1987] ECR 4199, §§ 12–20. The drafters of the Constitution have missed the opportunity to codify this case law into the successor of Article 234 TEC, Article III-369. This also clarifies the previous point: only in respect of CFSP-measures, which fall outside the competence of the ECJ, can the national courts offer added value as they alone will be able to rule on their legality without the delays inherent in the preliminary reference procedure. On the duration of the preliminary reference procedure, see, *supra*, fn. 125.

[178] Even when the ECtHR is dealing with EU matters, it does not always have a sufficiently clear view on the issues at stake. In the SEGI case (*SEGI and Gestoras pro-amnistia*, Judgment of 23 May 2002, <www.echr.coe.int>), the ECtHR suddenly refers to the judgment in Case T-177/01 *Jégo-Quéré* [2002] ECR II-2365, dealing with EC law while dealing with a case relating to third pillar EU law—for which the system of judicial protection is rather limited. While the ECtHR does not go into the matter, the ECtHR unfortunately seems to give the impression that there may be some relevance in *Jégo-Quéré* for the position of the applicants, if the circumstances were slightly different—*quod non*. The applicants in SEGI moreover appeared to prove the ECtHR wrong when the CFI rejected their action for damages, while admitting that neither EU law nor national law provides an alternative remedy, see, Case T-338/02 *SEGI and Others v. Council* [2004] ECR II-1647, § 38. See also, *supra*, fn. 98. On appeal the ECJ suggested, however, an alternative route for review through the national courts, see Joined Cases C-354/04 P and C-355/04 P *SEGI and others v. Council* [2007] ECR I-0000, § 49–57.

a look at the quote itself.[179] The cited passage is nothing else but the classic *Plaumann* test. In fact the ECtHR is just using this test to assess the '*direct effect* which the 1996 and the 1998 decrees—issued on the basis of a law—had on the applicants' livelihood'.[180] Ironically, by implementing this test the *ECtHR is restricting the scope of application of Article 6* instead of expanding it: besides the direct effect requirement, the ECtHR adds via the *Plaumann* test the requirement of being individually concerned as understood by the ECJ—or at least the ECtHR is suggesting this by using exactly the same wording. In our view this approach is unwarranted and even highly undesirable. The ECtHR should have held on to its earlier wordings where it required 'the individual to be personally affected by the measure in a way that is not only serious but also specific and, above all, imminent.'[181] This, combined with the requirement that the individual should have an interest in the outcome of the (claimed) proceedings, would have been sufficient for several reasons.

First, the *Plaumann* test results from Article 230 TEC, which explicitly mentions the requirement of the applicant being individually concerned, while Article 6 ECHR does not mention this requirement. Adding new requirements as to the admissibility of cases under Article 6 ECHR can but negatively affect overall judicial protection. Secondly, the application of the *Plaumann* test has proven to be subject of controversy within the EU, and the same could be true within the ECtHR. As demonstrated above, there is already enough confusion as to the scope of application of Article 6 without this test. Finally, the earlier wording is far more in line with the findings of the CFI in *Jégo-Quéré*, which moreover inspired the drafters of the Constitution, where it appeared that an applicant could be individually concerned if the measure in question affects his legal position, in a manner which is both definite and immediate, by restricting his rights or by imposing obligations on him. So if the ECtHR considered it necessary to adapt its jurisprudence in this field in line with EC law, the judgment of the CFI in *Jégo-Quéré* could have been a better source of inspiration than the quoted *Extramet* case.[182] Of course words like 'personally', 'specific' and 'imminent' also need further clarification; nevertheless this wording would avoid confusion between the scope of

---

[179] *Posti and Rahko v. Finland, supra*, fn. 3 § 53: 'Where a decree, decision or other measure, albeit not formally addressed to any individual natural or legal person, in substance does affect the 'civil rights or obligations' of such a person or of a group of persons in a similar situation, whether by reason of certain attributes peculiar to them or by reason of a factual situation which differentiates them from all other persons, Article 6, § 1 may require that the substance of the decision or measure in question is capable of being challenged by that person or group before a "tribunal" meeting the requirements of that provision.'

[180] *Posti and Rakho v. Finland, supra*, fn. 3, § 52, emphasis added.

[181] *Athanassoglou v. Switzerland, supra*, fn. 28, § 51.

[182] Admittedly, the judgment of the ECtHR was delivered after the ECJ had indicated its discontent with the approach of the CFI (see Case C-50/00 P *Unión de Pequeños Agricultores v. Council* [2002] ECR I-6677). However, as this judgment does not effectively addresses all problems of the Community system revealed by the CFI, the ECtHR could have intervened in order to support the most liberal interpretation of its case law.

application of Article 6 and the scope of application of Article 230 TEC. After *Posti and Rakho*, though, individuals whose legal position is affected by a legislative or administrative act which restricts his or her rights or imposes obligations on him or her in a manner which is both definite and immediate, face even greater difficulties to invoke a right of access to a court than before. However, the importance of *Posti and Rakho* is still unclear: no other judgment of the ECtHR has up until now reproduced the motivation of this judgment. Perhaps it is just as 'slip of the pen'. Perhaps we should remember more the positive result (Article 6 was applicable to a decree—issued on the basis of a law) than the concrete motivation of the judgment.

To sum up, the criteria which have been developed through the years by the ECtHR as to the admissibility and the scope of the right of access are not only rather complex but also seem to allow a lack of judicial protection of the individual.[183] This entices us to propose another approach and interpretation as to the scope of the right of access to a court. First we will point at what this right should entail, and subsequently we will draw the consequences for the interpretation of the applicability of Article 6. In order to understand the following arguments it is important to bear in mind that the right of access is an expression of the profound belief of the States in the rule of law and the importance to avoid arbitrary power.[184] The possibility of judicial review is a vital tool for upholding the rule of law.[185]

C. A New, More Coherent, Approach?

First there seems to be unfortunate case law which does not give the individual the possibility to contest all administrative acts.[186] However, the tendency is clear: both the ECtHR and the ECJ admit in most cases that executive acts must be judicially reviewable by a court which is able to ensure that the law has been properly applied and the procedural rules followed. In this context and, for the sake of legal certainty, we may hope that the case law that is inconsistent with this principle will be overruled. The new EU constitution is in any event an important step in the right direction. Considerably more administrative acts could be made subject to judicial review if our broad definition of 'regulatory' acts were to be taken over by the ECJ.

Second, we could even widen the debate by pushing the argument to its logic, yet controversial conclusion. The right of access to a court does still not give the

---

[183] Which is not good for legal certainty. Concerning administrative decisions, see for example *Athanassoglou v. Switzerland*, *supra*, fn. 28. Concerning legislative acts, see for example *Ruiz-Mateos and Others v. Spain*, Commission decision of 19 April 1991, *supra*, fn. 69.

[184] *Golder v. UK*, *supra*, fn. 5, § 34.

[185] Case 294/83 *Parti Ecologiste 'Les Verts' v. European Parliament* [1986] ECR 1339, § 23; illustrated with numerous examples in the fields of transparency, accountability and democracy in Lenaerts & Corthaut, *supra*, fn. 71, 1–43. See also Cygan, 'Protecting the interest of civil society in Community decision-making—The limits of Article 230 EC' 52 ICLQ (2003) (995) 997–1000, with references to the ECJ and Member State courts, in particular from the UK.

[186] See for example *Athanassoglou v. Switzerland*, *supra*, fn. 28.

individual the right to contest the constitutionality of legislative acts that have a direct effect on his civil and political rights. One could wonder why. The national constitution contains in most States the fundamental rights and rules that have been established by a special majority of the people (Constituent Assembly). It thus offers special guarantees. When a law, which does not require the same majority and guarantees, seems to violate those fundamental rights and guarantees proclaimed by the State itself, the individual should be able to turn to an impartial and independent party to assess whether a violation of the constitution effectively exists. The parliament, who did not want to or succeed in changing the constitution, is already involved and can thus not be asked for a ruling on that matter (*'nemo iudex in causa sua'*). Judges offer the best guarantees. In fact, the right of access to a court to contest the constitutionality of a law should be made dependent on the existence of a constitution and not on the existence of constitutional proceedings. Of course this should not result in the possibility to bring an *actio popularis*. Therefore it is also necessary that the individual can prove that his (civil) rights or obligations are directly affected and that he has an interest. In other words, if one disagrees with a legislative act, but one can argue that his rights or obligations are directly affected by it and can establish a *prima facie* case that the act is unconstitutional, one should be able to ask a (domestic) court to review the constitutionality of the act, on condition that the conclusion of unconstitutionality can affect his civil rights. The refusal by the ECtHR to advocate for such a system can only be understood as the result of an unwarranted double fear: on the one hand, the fear that this would place too much of a burden upon States by requiring them to provide for a fully-fledged system of judicial review,[187] and on the other hand the fear that this would interfere too much with the constitutional order of the States. As to the first objection the practice of European States shows that it is not an insurmountable burden to give the individual, provided he has a legal interest,[188] the possibility to contest legal acts. In several European States, like Belgium and

---

[187] In *Kudla v. Poland*, ECtHR (2000), *Reports* 2000-XI, § 151, the ECtHR stated the following: 'Article 13 does not go so far as to guarantee a remedy allowing a Contracting State's laws to be challenged before a national authority on the ground of being contrary to the Convention' [...]. Thus, Article 13 cannot be read as requiring the provision of an effective remedy that would enable the individual to complain about the absence in domestic law of access to a court as secured by Article 6§ 1. As regards an alleged failure to ensure trial within a reasonable time, however, no such inherent qualification on the scope of Article 13 can be discerned'. It is difficult to understand this reasoning, as article 13 deals with 'the rights and freedoms as set forth in this Convention', save if you take into account the reluctance of the ECtHR to give the right of access its full weight.

[188] In Belgium, for example, the Constitutional Court (Arbitragehof) and the Supreme Administrative Court (Raad van State) admit that everyone who 'could be affected in a direct and disadvantageous way by a contested norm' has an interest to lodge a complaint about the constitutionality or legality of a decision or act. See A. Alen, *Handboek van het Belgisch staatsrecht*, (1997), 218. This criterion has also a lot of similarities with the 'victim' criterion of Article 34 of the Convention and the fact that the applicant before the Court must be 'personally affected', which is not the same as being 'individually' affected. The first means that the person should be directly affected by the act or omission at issue, meanwhile the second implies 'peculiar attributes or a factual situation which differentiates the applicant from all others'.

Austria, anyone can for example bring an action for annulment of regulations with force of law for violation of certain constitutional requirements, provided they can demonstrate an interest.[189] The second objection is also unfounded. The constitutional traditions of the States are not endangered: the States are free to decide whether they want a (written) constitution. But once they have decided to have one, they should give the individual the opportunity to protect his civil rights which are affected by a law which seems to be unconstitutional. That is exactly what the right of access to a court is about. If you have a constitution, it is not an excuse to state that you do not have any constitutional proceedings. Ever since *Marbury v. Madison*[190] it is clear that a written Constitution only offers effective protection if it is coupled with constitutional review of the acts of the other branches of government. Moreover, especially in the case of the EU Member States, (at least incidental) judicial review of legislative acts is common day practice. Ever since the judgment in *Van Gend & Loos*,[191] national judges are required to set aside conflicting rules of national law (and even the national constitutions[192]). If States are willing, and they have just for the first time openly confirmed the primacy of EU law in the Constitution,[193] to subject their legislation to judicial review in the light of even the least important details of EU law then it is hard to understand why the same should not apply to judicial review in the light of the fundamental rules enshrined in their own constitution. Of course the subsidiarity principle must be respected.[194] It is 'not the task of the ECtHR to take the place of the domestic courts or to express a view on the appropriateness of the domestic courts' choice of policy as regards case law; its task is confined to determining whether the consequences of that choice are in conformity with the Convention'.[195] The ECtHR should neither impose a constitutional structure, as it is for the States to decide the way in which the constitutionality supervision is organized.[196]

---

[189] Alen & Melchior; 'The relations between the Constitutional Courts and the other national courts, including the interference in this area of the action of the European courts', General report at Conference of European Constitutional Courts (XIIth Congress), <www.arbitrage.be> (21 September 2003).   [190] *Marbury v. Madison*, 5 U.S. 137, 2 L.Ed. 60 (1803).

[191] Case C-26/62 *Van Gend & Loos* [1963] ECR 1.

[192] Case C-106/77 *Simmenthal* [1978] ECR 629.

[193] See Article I-6. In this sense it can be argued that the Member States have finally 'consummated' what has been called the 'revolution' or even 'coup d'état' introduced by *Van Gend & Loos*, see Schilling, 'The Court of Justice's revolution: its effects and the conditions for its consummation. What Europe can learn from Fiji', 27 *E.L.Rev.* (2002) 445–463.

[194] See in this respect also the critical analysis of the ECJ judgment in *Unión de Pequeños Agricultores* in Lenaerts & Corthaut, *supra*, fn. 71, 16–18, where the argument is made that demanding from the Member States that they provide procedures during which not only national legislation can be reviewed, but also—albeit subject to the obligation stemming from the *Foto-Frost* case to refer issues of validity to the ECJ—EC legislation is contrary to the principle of national procedural autonomy and the subsidiarity principle. For more on the difficulties in applying the principle of subsidiarity in the context of judicial protection after *Unión de Pequeños Agricultores*, see Gilliaux, 'L'arrêt Unión de Pequeños Agricultores: entre subsidiarité juridictionnelle et effectivité', CDE (2003) 177–202.

[195] *Brualla Gomez de la Torre*, judgment of 19 December 1997, § 31, <www.echr.coe.int>.

[196] Of course the domestic courts should still be able to ascertain that no civil rights of the applicant are directly affected. Member states can still exclude an undesirable *actio popularis*: without legal interest there should be no standing.

Finally, in the context of the EU there is an additional reason why the ECtHR should take a somewhat bolder approach. The ECtHR has in *Bosphorus* decided to continue showing great deference to the EU, on the basis of the rebuttable[197] presumption of equivalent protection. However, crucial to the justification of this systemic approach is the procedural guarantees that the EU system offers for the protection of fundamental rights. Several observations need to be made in this respect. Firstly, in *Bosphorus* there was no reason to doubt at all that there had been sufficient procedural tools for the applicant company to effectively challenge the contested EU regulation through the national courts. However, this should not blind us from the fact that others may not be so well protected. The ECtHR seems to be aware of this, but does not appear too concerned by it.[198] This optimism may be misplaced in light of the observations made above and is even fully indefensible when it comes to EU acts that would fall in the second or third pillar. Secondly, it is important to avoid circular reasoning whereby the presumption of equivalent protection of substantive fundamental rights (such as the right to property at stake in *Bosphorus*) that in turn is premised on a presumption of there being sufficient 'mechanisms of control in place',[199] is extended to a presumption of compliance with Articles 6 and 13 ECHR. This would effectively immunize the EU system of fundamental rights protection from all criticism (as the EU would always be deemed to offer equivalent protection because it has sufficient judicial protection mechanism in place because it offers equivalent protection ...) and undercut the necessary control the ECtHR must still carry out as to whether the rebuttable presumption is still warranted. In our view, the ECtHR may well be on the right track when it looks at the EU system of judicial protection in justifying a rebuttable presumption of equivalence. However, the ECtHR should also have the courage of addressing the gaps in the system. If the ECtHR is of the opinion that such a presumption is the best way of ensuring a harmonious co-existence with the ECJ, it is in its own interest to make sure that the preconditions for it are effectively fulfilled. Being more demanding as to the possibilities for individuals to challenge normative acts that directly concern them may go a long way in this respect. Ultimately, this will also force the Member States to seriously consider options for effective judicial protection in respect of the second and third pillar. Again, if the aim of the presumption of equivalence is to enable the ECtHR to steer away from the controversial issues of foreign policy, the ECtHR will only be credible in doing so if there indeed is a sufficiently high level of judicial protection within the EU.

Admittedly our approach includes a new interpretation of the scope of Article 6. We submit that Article 6 can be read as guaranteeing the right of access to a

---

[197] *Bosphorus v. Ireland*, fn. 1, §§ 154–158. The ECtHR holds indeed one ace up its sleeve allowing it to carry out an examination *in concreto* of the equivalence of protection offered by the EU and the ECtHR However, the actual examination in *Bosphorus* did not seem to add more to make much of a difference.   [198] *ibid.*, §§ 162–163.

[199] *ibid.*, § 160.

court whenever one is directly affected by a legislative or administrative act in a sense that it imposes obligations on the individual or restricts his rights and one has a legal interest to lodge a complaint.[200] The current interpretation as to the applicability of Article 6 does not even need to change radically. As the ECtHR states, the requirement that there must be a 'dispute' (French *contestation*) should be given a substantive rather than a formal meaning, bearing in mind that there is no mention of this requirement in the English text of Article 6 par. 1.[201] It should thus suffice that there is a disagreement between two parties (in the case of judicial review one of the parties being a state body) concerning the legality or constitutionality of an administrative or a legislative act. As to the required 'determination' of civil rights or obligations it appears that civil rights can be determined by an administrative or a legislative act. An individual solely has to demonstrate that he is personally affected in a way that is definite and immediate. The ECtHR should thus drop the 'individually affected' requirement it seems to have introduced in *Posti and Rakho*. An *actio popularis* can already be avoided sufficiently by requiring that the outcome of the proceedings be directly decisive for the civil rights the individual wants to protect. In other words the applicant must show that there is some legal interest at stake for him or her in the proceedings complained of [or the proceedings he wants to access].[202] Besides that, the dispute should still concern a 'right', 'which can be said, at least on arguable grounds, to be recognised under domestic law'.[203] Concerning the right of access, however, this should be understood in a way that allows the individual to lodge a complaint with a judge whenever his rights are restricted or an obligation is imposed by a legislative or administrative act. The judge should then be able to ascertain the legality or constitutionality of this act, not its opportunity.

Once it is admitted that Article 6 (and thus the right of access to a court) is always applicable to legislative or administrative acts that directly affect the civil right or obligations of the individual, the ECtHR will have to explain whether the absence of a right to contest such acts can ever be a legitimate restriction on the right of access. It will only be able to do so if it manages to weaken the arguments in favour of a judicial constitutional control. Whatever the outcome, the reasoning by the ECtHR can only contribute to a better understanding of the right of access to a court.

---

[200] The Committee of Ministers already recognized the principle that 'all administrative acts should be subject to judicial review' and that 'judicial review should be available at least to natural and legal persons in respect of administrative acts that directly affect their rights or interests'. See, Recommendation Rec (2004)20 of the Committee of Ministers to Member States on judicial review of administrative acts and the explanatory Memorandum CM (2004)214, available at <http://www.coe.int>. Notice, however, that the ECtHR itself does not always grant access when only a legal interest is at stake: 'In principle, it does not suffice for an individual applicant to claim that the mere existence of a law violates his rights under the Convention; it is necessary that the law should have been applied to his detriment.' (*The Christian Federation of Jehovah's witnesses in France v. France*, decision of 6 November 2001, Reports 2001-XI.)

[201] *Le Compte, Van Leuven and De Meyere v. Belgium, supra*, fn. 11, § 45.

[202] *Kienast v. Austria*, judgment of 23 January 2003, § 39, <www.echr.coe.int>.

[203] See for example *Zander v. Sweden*, fn. 41, *supra*, § 22.

In our view the time has come for this interpretation of the scope of Article 6 ECHR, even if the ECtHR is still hesitant. Admittedly, this could mean an important change for most European countries, but we are convinced that it would be a huge step in the building of European public legal order. As the ECtHR itself has stated on several occasions: the situation within and outside the Contracting State must be assessed 'in the light of present-day conditions' in order to know what is now the appropriate interpretation and application of the Convention.[204] Therefore the importance of the discussions at EU level on the scope of the right of access cannot be underestimated. As indicated, the debate at EU level has not ended with the ECJ's rejection of looser *locus standi* requirements in *Unión de Pequeños Agricultores*.[205] Since then, the EU Heads of State and Government have agreed on a Constitution, which amends the rules on standing, precisely because of concerns on its congruence with Article 6 ECHR. In this way another hurdle for the envisaged accession of the European Union to the ECHR is cleared. Ironically, if the *Posti and Rahko* approach were to be confirmed, the worries expressed by the CFI and the members of the Convention may have been unwarranted. However, in our view, a correct reading of the ECHR does imply a major reform of the criteria for standing.[206] Even if, as indicated, the end result is far from perfect, and the fate of the Constitution itself is highly uncertain, the dominant current in the EU States and candidate States, which form a majority among the Contracting Parties of the ECHR, seems to go in the direction of wider courses of action for individuals in challenging acts of a general scope and application. The ECtHR will sooner or later be invited to join the wave.[207]

---

[204] See amongst others the *Tyrer v. the United Kingdom* ECtHR (1978), *Series A* No. 26, § 31; *Christine Goodwin v. the United Kingdom*, ECtHR (2002), *Reports* 2002-VI, § 75.

[205] Case C-50/00 P *Unión de Pequeños Agricultores v. Council* [2002] ECR I-6677.

[206] Moreover, even if the problems in the current first pillar fall outside the scope of Article 6 ECHR, even greater problems as to judicial protection exist in respect of the current second and third pillar, see Usher, *supra*, fn. 140 (575) 592–595. Furthermore, with the EU getting more and more involved in areas such as family law and criminal justice (an evolution which is further sanctioned by the Constitution) imposing strict requirements on standing for individuals who want to challenge the validity of acts in those fields may effectively undermine the chances of those legal instruments being swiftly reviewed in the light of some of the core rights of the ECHR such as the right to family life or basic guarantees in criminal matters. On a positive note, though, the current third pillar issues and the matters falling under visa, asylum and immigration will in the future at least be subject to the same, albeit imperfect, new regime of judicial review as the traditional EC matters. For matters falling within the sphere of the Common Foreign and Security Policy, however, judicial review is still hardly available, despite the introduction in Article III-376 of a direct action for annulment against restrictive measures against natural or legal persons. For more on judicial protection under the Constitution for CFSP-matters, see Corthaut, fn. 145, 110–144.

[207] In light of the recent judgment of the ECJ in Case C-432/05 *Unibet* [2007] ECR I-0000, this have may soon become a tidal wave. For more, see the postscript at the end of this volume.

EU-Fundamental Rights in the National Legal Order: The Obligations of Member States Revisited

*Alexander Egger**

The Court's jurisdiction in the field of fundamental rights has acquired more importance in recent years. During the last four years, the ECJ has had to deal with a large variety[1] of fundamental rights: respect for human dignity,[2] the right to property,[3] the right to respect for family life,[4] the right to respect for private life,[5] procedural rights enshrined in Articles 6 and 13 of the European Convention on Human Rights (ECHR),[6] the principle of retroactive application of the more lenient penalty,[7] freedom of expression,[8] freedom of

* Dr.iur. Dr.phil., Universitätsdozent, Europainstitut (Jean Monnet-Center of Excellence) at the University of Economics and Business Administration, Vienna, and former Référendaire at the Court of Justice, Luxembourg.

[1] According to J. Schwarze, 'Der Schutz der Grundrechte durch den EuGH' Neue Juristische Wochenschrift (2005) 3459 (3460), the case law is not concentrated any more on economic rights. For the right to vote see Case C-300104 *Eman and Sevinger*, judgment of 12 September 2006.

[2] Case C-36/02 *Omega* [2004] ECR I-9609.

[3] Joined Cases C-20/00 and C-64/00 *Booker Aquacultur Ltd (C-20/00) and Hydro Seafood GSP Ltd (C-64/00) v The Scottish Ministers* [2003] ECR I-7411.

[4] Case C-60/00 *Mary Carpenter v Secretary of State for the Home Department* [2002] ECR I-6279; Case C-459/99 *Mouvement contre le racisme, l'antisémitisme et la xénophobie ASBL (MRAX) v Belgian State* [2002] ECR I-6591; Case C-109/01 *Secretary of State for the Home Department v Hacene Akrich* [2003] ECR I-9607; Joined Cases C-482/01 and C-493/01 *Georgios Orfanopoulos and Others v Land Baden-Württemberg (C-482/01) and Raffaele Oliveri and Others v Land Baden-Württemberg (C-493/01)* [2003] ECR I-5257; Case C-441/02 *Commission v Germany*, judgment of 27 April 2006.

[5] Joined Cases C-465/00, C-138/01 and C-139/01 *Rechnungshof (C-465/00) v Österreichischer Rundfunk and Others and Christa Neukomm (C-138/01) and Joseph Lauermann (C-139/01) v Österreichischer Rundfunk* [2003] ECR I-4989.

[6] Case C-7/98 *Dieter Krombach v André Bamberski* [2000] ECR I-1935; *MRAX, supra* n. 4; Case C-276/01 *Joachim Steffensen* [2003] ECR I-3735; Case C-105/03 *Maria Pupino*, [2005] ECR I-5285; Case C-283/05 *ASML*, judgment of 14 December 2006.
The wide application of Article 6 is criticized by G.Britz, 'Bedeutung der EMRK für nationale Verwaltungsgerichte und Behörden—Erweiterte Bindungswirkung nach EuGH, Slg. 2002, I-6279—Carpenter?' Neue Zeitschrift für Verwaltungsrecht 2004, 173 (175), who rejects the assessment of judicial proceedings in the light of Community fundamental rights.

[7] Joined Cases C-387/02, C-391/02 and C-403/02 *Silvio Berlusconi (C-387/02), Sergio Adelchi (C-391/02) and Marcello Dell'Utri and Others (C-403/02)*, [2005] ECR I-3565.

[8] Case C-245/01 *RTL Television GmbH v Niedersächsische Landesmedienanstalt für privaten Rundfunk* [2003] ECR I-12489; Case C-101/01, *Bodil Lindqvist* [2003] ECR I-12971; Case C-71/02, *Herbert Karner Industrie-Auktionen GmbH v Troostwijk GmbH* [2004] ECR I-3025.

assembly[9] and the right to marry under Article 12 of the ECHR.[10] Recent trends in
ECJ's case law confirm that the question 'To what extent are Community fundamental rights also binding on the authorities of the Member States?'[11] remains significant.
This is an appropriate time for a review of the Court's case law and for a systematic
analysis. Aside form the case law, another important factor in the development of fundamental rights is the so-called 'Treaty establishing a Constitution for Europe' which
incorporates in its Part Two the former 'Charter of Fundamental Rights'. For the first
time, fundamental rights would be codified in EU law. The analysis of both the incorporation of the Charter into primary law and of recent judgments shall be focussed on
the effect on Member States of having to fulfil fundamental rights obligations under
EU law. This article outlines those many essential elements of obligations. It will be
seen that a general theory on protection of EU fundamental rights may be deduced
from the cases under review. This article is structured as follows. After identifying
ways in which the scope of EU fundamental rights within the national legal order
may be determined, it deals with how they are applied not only as a result of their
transposition into national law but also in the process of legislative interpretation.
The subsequent section highlights the role played by fundamental rights in the context of Member States' obligations also under EU law, explores the various interests at
play, in particular when fundamental freedoms are invoked, and assesses the effects of
protecting fundamental rights on Member States and on individuals. The article then
examines different aspects of judicial protection by different courts. It then questions
whether the modifications introduced by the 'Charter of Fundamental Rights' and
the 'Treaty establishing a Constitution for Europe' have an impact on Member States'
obligations.[12] This part is followed by some concluding remarks.

I. Determining the Scope of EU Fundamental Rights in the National Legal Order

One condition for the application of EU fundamental rights to measures taken
by a Member State is that the measures concerned come within the scope
ratione materiæ of those rights. To determine this scope, two approaches may be

---

[9] Case C-112/00 *Eugen Schmidberger, Internationale Transporte und Planzüge v Republic of Austria*
[2003] ECR I-5659.
   On the legal foundations and the scope of this fundamental right, see T. Mann and S. Ripke,
'Überlegungen zur Existenz und Reichweite eines Gemeinschaftsgrundrechts der Versammlungsfreiheit'
EuGRZ (2004) 125 (127 *et seq.*)

[10] Case C-117/01 *K.B. v The National Health Service Pensions Agency and The Secretary of State for
Health* [2004] ECR I-541.

[11] O. Due and C. Gulmann, 'Community fundamental rights as part of national law' in Scritti in
onore di Giuseppe Mancini, vol. II, 1998, 405 (407). According to these authors Community fundamental rights are part of national law and not of a separate legal order, *viz.* Community law, which has
to be applied by all Member States' organs.

[12] On this issue, see St. Griller, 'Der Anwendungsbereich der Grundrechtscharta und das Verhältnis zu
sonstigen Gemeinschaftsrechten, Rechten aus der EMRK und zu verfassungsgesetzlich gewährleisteten
Rechten' in A. Duschanek and St. Griller (eds.), *Grundrechte für Europa* (Springer 2002), 131 (182).

taken: the traditional approach consisting of several categories and a new approach, consisting of a single formula.

A. The Traditional Approach: Division into Categories

The Court's case law on protection of fundamental rights has been clarified in several different ways by academic commentators. Traditionally, two types of situations are distinguished: on the one hand, the so-called agency-situation, on the other hand, the so-called ERT-situation, named after the ERT-judgment.[13] This approach is adopted e.g. by Schilling[14] and Weiler.[15]

For a better understanding of what is meant by 'agency-type review' or 'agency-situation', it is necessary to go back to its origins, i.e. to the *Wachauf*-case. There, the Member State had to apply a Community regulation in the field of agriculture to a farmer who requested compensation.[16] In such a situation, Member States act as the executive branch[17] of the Community. Thus, there is an agency-situation wherever Member States 'execute'[18] EC law, i.e. *Wachauf stricto sensu*. In a broad sense, Member States could be termed agents whenever they take 'measures on behalf of the Community'.[19]

ERT-type cases are characterized by a Member State derogating from Community law,[20] especially from the fundamental freedoms. Recent case law illustrates that such cases still occur, in particular where Member States invoke reasons of public interest to justify a national measure, e.g. a decision to deport,[21] a decision not to revoke a deportation order[22] or the prohibition on the commercial exploitation of games involving the simulation of acts of violence against persons.[23] In another judgment, the Court held that provisions of a directive must be interpreted in the light of fundamental rights in so far as they infringe

---

[13] Case 5/88 *Hubert Wachauf v Bundesamt für Ernährung und Forstwirtschaft* [1989] ECR 2609; Case C-260/89 *Elliniki Radiophonia Tiléorassi AE (ERT) and Panellinia Omospondia Syllogon Prossopikou v Dimotiki Etairia Pliroforissis and Sotirios Kouvelas and Nicolaos Avdellas and others* [1991] ECR I-2925.

[14] Th. Schilling, 'Bestand und allgemeine Lehren der bürgerschützenden allgemeinen Rechtsgrundsätze des Gemeinschaftsrechts' EuGRZ (2000) 3 (8 *et seq.*).

[15] J.H.H. Weiler, *The Constitution of Europe* (1999) 120 *et seq.*

[16] See *Wachauf*, *supra* n. 13, para. 22, where the Court speaks explicitly about applying the regulations. Besides, there was a national law based on a power contained in a regulation, which contained further rules for compensation.

[17] J.H.H. Weiler and N. Lockhart, ' "Taking rights seriously" seriously: The European Court and its Fundamental rights jurisprudence' 32 CML Rev. 51 (74).

[18] 'Vollzug' as it is called by U. Mager, Juristenzeitung (2003) 204 (205).

[19] This corresponds to the third category identified by J.Temple Lang, 'The Sphere in which Member States are Obliged to Comply with the General Principles of Law and Community Fundamental Rights Principles', LIEI (1991/2) 23 (30).

[20] On this wide sense, i.e. without limiting this category to the derogation of fundamental freedoms, see M. Demetriou, 'Using Human Rights through European Community Law', E.H.R.L.R. (1999) 484 (488).   [21] *Carpenter*, *supra* n. 4, para. 40.

[22] *Akrich*, *supra* n. 4, paras. 58 *et seq.*   [23] *Omega*, *supra* n. 2, paras. 28 *et seq.*

fundamental freedoms.[24] *Carpenter* and *K.B.* illustrate that the ECJ examines fundamental rights issues in cases concerning restrictions on the fundamental freedoms, especially but not only[25] where they are connected with the derogation.

Recent case law could bring an end to all criticisms normally made of the ECJ's application of fundamental rights to national rules which derogate from one of the fundamental freedoms. Those criticisms derive from a misunderstanding of the ERT-case law. In the ERT-situation, fundamental rights are presumed to apply only within the scope of Community law. *Stricto sensu*, the ECJ does not apply fundamental rights to national rules falling outside the scope of Community law. The Court simply applies fundamental rights in relation to the Community rule which provides for the derogation, such as Article 30 EC, or contains a mandatory requirement, such as Article 28 EC. Fundamental rights simply serve to assist interpretation of those provisions, *viz.* to define the conditions under which a Member State may derogate, which is simply a question of competence. The Court examines whether the Member State has fulfilled the requirements set out in Community law, in line with the rule that the scope and the conditions for applying derogations are 'creatures' of Community law.[26]

Thus, the ECJ has jurisdiction to examine national provisions which restrict fundamental freedoms.[27] For it is precisely applying a derogation or invoking a justification which brings the national rule within the scope of Community law. In essence, the ECJ is, as would be expected, interpreting primary law in the light of fundamental rights.[28] Conversely, where the Court concludes that an act adopted by a Member State is outside the scope of Community law, it will not, or rather should not, be the subject of further examination,[29] particularly as regards compliance with fundamental rights.

Finally, recent case law, e.g. *Carpenter* and *Schmidberger*, confirms the view that fundamental rights may be invoked in connection with both an express derogation and with a mandatory requirement.[30] If one intends to continue to speak of

[24] Joined Cases C-465/00, C-138/01 and C-139/01, *supra* n. 5, para. 68.
[25] Cf. P. Eeckhout, 'The EU Charter of fundamental rights and the federal question' 39 CML Rev. 945 (978), who expects the ECJ to respect that limit.
[26] Eeckhout, *supra* n. 25, 977; Weiler, *supra* n. 15, 122. Cf. K. Korinek, 'Zur Bedeutung des gemeinschaftsrechtlichen Grundrechtsschutzes im System des nationalen und europäischen Schutzes der Grund- und Menschenrechte' in Brenn, Huber and Möstl (eds.), Der Staat des Grundgesetzes (2004) 1099 (1105); Ch. Ranacher, 'Die Bindung der Mitgliedstaaten an die Gemeinschaftsgrundrechte' 58 Zeitschrift für öffentliches Recht (2003) 21 (55 and 59); H.-W. Rengeling and P. Szczekalla, *Grundrechte in der Europäischen Union* (2004) 166 *et seq.*
[27] The opposite position is taken by M. Ruffert, 'Die Mitgliedstaaten der Europäischen Gemeinschaft als Verpflichtete der Gemeinschaftsgrundrechte', EuGRZ (1995) 518 (529). See the criticism by F. Jacobs, 'Human rights in the European Union: the role of the Court of Justice' 26 EL Rev (2001) 330 (338).
[28] Cf. Eeckhout, *supra* n. 25, 978; J. Kühling, 'Grundrechte' in Bogdandy (ed.), Europäisches Verfassungsrecht (2003) 583 (609).
[29] Jacobs, *supra* n. 27, 336. For the opposite approach, see the judgment in *Karner*.
[30] According to A. Alemanno, 'À la recherche d'un juste équilibre entre libertés fondamentales et droits fondamentaux dans le cadre du marché intérieur' Revue du Droit de l'Union Européenne

the ERT-situation, one can extend it, in a sense even broader, to all provisions containing derogations or restrictions on fundamental freedoms (i.e. those limits which are inherent in the system).[31]

Analysing the case law, it is easy to identify cases which do not enter the two traditional categories *stricto sensu*. This is largely so in cases which concern the transposition of directives, the application of directly effective rules of primary law and the application of transposing provisions. *Akrich* in particular demonstrates that there are circumstances additional to the agency—sand the ERT-situations in which Member States have to respect fundamental rights. In that case, the ECJ obliged national immigration authorities to have regard to the right to respect for family life under Article 8 ECHR in assessing an application to enter and remain in the Member State in a situation in which the applicant could not rely on a Community regulation.[32]

The judgment in *Steffensen* also illustrates that the Court applies fundamental rights outside the two traditional categories, namely in assessing national rules of procedure. The circumstances at issue, which called into question the Member State's autonomy in setting procedural rules,[33] came within the scope of Community law because the Community law in question gave rise to a substantive right.[34]

In academic writing, two methods are used to classify cases which strictly fall outside the traditional two categories. On the one hand, the two categories—each broadly construed—are applied. On the other hand, a third, residual category is used to classify cases which do not fit into the traditional two categories.

Some authors, e.g. Holoubek and Kotroni, follow in essence the agency-ERT dichotomy but distinguish between cases concerning the application of regulations, the transposition of directives and the restriction of fundamental freedoms.[35] They simply divide implementation into application and transposition of Community rules. It is worth noting that this approach defines 'implementation'.

Conversely, Tridimas enumerates three situations: implementation of Community law, interference with fundamental freedoms, and other measures which fall within the scope of Community law.[36] Young adopts another approach, identifying as a third category the application of Community law which is based

---

(2004) 709 (736), the ECJ does not determine the type of justification in *Schmidberger*; T. Tridimas, *The general principles of EC law* (OUP, 1999) 230. On the different conditions of application, see Frenz, 'Freiheitsbeschränkungen durch Grundrechte' Europäisches Wirtschafts- und Steuerrecht 2005, 15 (18).

[31] Cf. Mager, *supra* n. 18, 205.   [32] *Supra* n. 4, para. 61.

[33] For some agricultural cases, see Eeckhout, *supra* n. 25, 963 *et seq.*; cf. W. Schaller, EuZW (2003) 671 (672), with regard to *Steffensen*.   [34] Cf. Schaller, *supra* n. 33, 672.

[35] M. Holoubek, 'Grundrechtsschutz durch Gemeinschaftsgrundrechte', in St. Griller and H.P. Rill (eds.), Verfassungsrechtliche Grundfragen der EU-Mitgliedschaft (1997) 73 (82 *et seq.*); L. Kotroni, *Grundrechtliche Verpflichtungen der Mitgliedstaaten der Europäischen Union* (2004) 213 *et seq.*; I. Pernice, 'Multilevel constitutionalism and the Treaty of Amsterdam' 36 CML Rev. 703 (724).

[36] Tridimas, *supra* n. 30, 225.

upon the protection of a particular human right.[37] Schaller and Scheuing suggest creating a third category covering cases concerning the compatibility of national rules of procedure. [38]

Thus, some suggest adopting a new category. Such an approach could have the disadvantage that categories must be supplemented each time new case law does not fit those in use. Another approach might be to use a new concept which covers all cases on the basis of a single criterion.

B. The New Approach: One Single Formula

Whereas the traditional approach is characterized by a system consisting of several categories, a new approach consists of a single *formula*.[39] The purpose of this section is to develop this *formula*, on the basis of the Court's recent case law.

The point of departure for determining the scope of application of EU fundamental rights in the Member States is the relationship between EU law and national law. Thus, the first step consists in identifying the different situations where Member States are bound by EU law, in particular Community law, and developing a precise terminology with regard to Member States' obligations under each type of situation. Under the second step, the scope of fundamental rights is determined in the light of several sources, in particular Treaty provisions.

The first clarification to be made is that EU fundamental rights are applicable to Member States' measures regardless of their status.[40] What matters is the legal nature of the corresponding EU rules and their relationship with national law.

Clearly it is helpful to use precise rather than ambiguous terms for the *formula*. 'Implementation' could be understood as a generic term covering the application of regulations as well as the transposition of directives.[41] To avoid confusion, one should use more specific terms. To begin with, it is worth analyzing the institutional practice. As far as the legislature[42] is concerned, the institutions use the expression 'implementation of directives' with regard to the transposition of directives. This is not precise enough because it could also refer to the application of directly applicable provisions. In fact, this kind of 'implementation' appears in standard provisions in the final part of directives in the following terms: 'Member States shall bring into force' or 'shall adopt and publish'.

---

[37] A. Young, 'The Charter, Constitution and Human Rights: is this the Beginning or the End for Human Rights Protections by Community law?' 11 European Public Law 219 (221). See N. Napoletano, 'La nozione di "campo di applicazione del diritto comunitario" nell'ambito delle competenze della Corte di giustizia in tema di tutela dei diritti fondamentali' IX Il diritto dell'Unione europea (2004) 679 (705), who arrives at five categories.

[38] Advocated by Schaller, *supra* n. 33, 671, and D. Scheuing, 'Zur Grundrechtsbindung der EU-Mitgliedstaaten' EuR (2005) 162 (169).

[39] For a critical position towards any *formula*, see Weiler and Lockhart, *supra* n. 17, 66 *et seq.*

[40] Cf. Weiler and Lockhart, *supra* n. 17, 74.

[41] Holoubek, *supra* n. 35, 83 *et seq.*; T. Kingreen, Comment on Article 6 EUT, in C. Calliess and M. Ruffert, Kommentar zum EU-/EG-Vertrag (2002) paras. 57 *et seq.*; Kühling, *supra* n. 28, 607.

[42] Joint Practical Guide of the European Parliament, the Council and the Commission (2003) 69.

The terminology used by the ECJ is slightly better.[43] In the Court's case law, we find the term 'transposition' used in infringement proceedings were there has been no transposition at all[44] or, occasionally, in preliminary rulings, even in the operative part of the judgment.[45] But in most cases the ECJ uses the term 'implementation'. A clear distinction between the different phenomena is important here too. This is demonstrated by the somewhat misleading wording of a recent judgment on fundamental rights where the Court refers to the application of a directive by Member States without examining the direct effect of certain provisions and without limiting application of the directive to those provisions.[46] Since application of the directive is qualified by the ECJ as a sub-category of implementation (*la mise en œuvre*), it is not surprising that the Court refers to the *Wachauf* case law on regulations in order to underline the parallelism between the application of directives and the application of regulations. Nonetheless, in the same judgment implementation is used in a narrow sense meaning the adoption of measures by the Member State concerned.[47]

In the literature, other terms are used, e.g. 'legislative execution' of Community law in place of its 'application'.[48] The first term is misleading insofar as it covers only measures adopted by the legislator but excludes acts adopted by administrative authorities which, depending on the national legal order, could also be transposing acts which fulfil the criteria laid down by Community law. Another view is taken by Besselink. According to this commentator, as a rule of reason, measures implementing Community law fall within the scope of application of fundamental rights where there is an explicit derogation to EC law.[49]

Inspirations for a new single *formula* may be found in recent judgments where the ECJ simply states that fundamental rights 'are protected in the Community legal order'[50] or, similarly, 'in Community law'.[51] For several years, the Court has assessed whether national rules of procedure comply with fundamental rights with regard to the scope of Community law. It has ruled that it had no jurisdiction with regard to national legislation 'which falls outside the scope of Community law'[52] or which is 'lying outside the scope of Community law'.[53] In *Pupino*, a case concerning the Italian Code of Criminal Procedure, the ECJ applied for the first

---

[43] According to Eeckhout, *supra* n. 25, 969, the notion applied by the ECJ does not encompass all types of linkage with EC legislation.

[44] Case C-381/92 *Commission v Ireland* [1994] ECR I-215; Case C-441/00 *Commission of the European Communities v United Kingdom of Great Britain and Northern Ireland* [2002] ECR I-4699.

[45] Case C-392/93 *The Queen v H. M. Treasury, ex parte British Telecommunications plc* [1996] ECR I-1631.

[46] *Booker, supra* n. 3, para. 88. This wording corresponds to the French version which is not formulated in a better style.   [47] *Booker, supra* n. 3, paras. 90 and 92.

[48] W. Schaller, *Die EU-Mitgliedstaaten als Verpflichtungsadressaten der Gemeinschaftsgrundrechte* (Nomos, 2003) 36.

[49] L.F.M. Besselink, 'The Member States, the national constitutions and the scope of the Charter', 8 MJ 68 (76).   [50] *Akrich, supra* n. 4, para. 58.

[51] *Carpenter, supra* n. 4, para. 41.

[52] Case C-144/95 *Maurin* [1996] ECR I-2929, para. 13.

[53] Case C-177/94 *Perfili* [1996] ECR I-161, para. 20.

time an equivalent test in connection with a framework decision reminding the Member States to comply with their obligations with regard to national rules of procedure applicable in criminal proceedings.[54]

In the literature as well as in recent case law of the Court, we find formulations such as 'within the field of application of Community law',[55] 'in the fields covered by the EC Treaty',[56] 'within the scope of Community law',[57] 'within the scope of application of the Treaty'[58] or as far as the Member States are determined by Community law.[59] In some judgments the ECJ uses the opposite approach, i.e. comes to the conclusion that a situation lies[60] or falls[61] outside the scope of Community law or, in a quite different way, examines the case from the Member State's point of view, stating that the national legislative has competence in the matter.[62] It is suggested that the latter approach is confined to pre ERT-cases.

From a normative point, all of those *formulae* may be used interchangeably since they all refer to the field of application. Thus, whether to speak about the scope, area or field of application of Community law is simply a stylistic matter.

To sum up, Member States must respect EU fundamental rights in applying primary law, including derogations, and regulations, in transposing directives and framework decisions, the adopting national rules which supplement regulations, and in applying national law which falls within the scope of Community law.

C. Determining the Scope: Possible Points of Reference

There are several points of reference to determine the scope of application of fundamental rights, such as the so-called 'link with Community law', the competence of the EU, Article 12 EC, and Article 18 EC.

The term 'link with Community law' should first be clarified. In general, it refers to a condition required by the ECJ for applying primary law in a specific case, the opposite being characterized as a purely internal situation. This criterion is of crucial importance with regard to the application of fundamental freedoms, as *Carpenter* illustrates.

In *Carpenter*, the ECJ was asked to give an interpretation, *inter alia*, of Article 49 EC. As the freedom to provide services is not applicable to situations which do not have a link with Community law, the Court had to examine this condition

---

[54] *Pupino, supra* n. 6.

[55] *Steffensen, supra* n. 6, para. 70; *Karner, supra* n. 8, para. 49; Case C-328/04 *Attila Vajnai*, order of 6 October 2005, para. 12.   [56] Jacobs, *supra* n. 27, 338.

[57] *Schmidberger, supra* n. 9, para. 75; Opinion of A.G. Stix-Hackl in *Carpenter, supra* n. 4, para. 83; Tridimas, *supra* n. 30, 231.   [58] Due and Gulmann, *supra* n. 11, 416.

[59] W. Cremer, 'Der programmierte Verfassungskonflikt: Zur Bindung der Mitgliedstaaten an die Charta der Grundrechte der Europäischen Union nach dem Konventionsentwurf für eine Europäische Verfassung' Neue Zeitschrift für Verwaltungsrecht (2003) 1452 (1453).

[60] Case 12/86 *Demirel v Stadt Schwäbisch Gmünd* [1987] ECR 3719, para. 28; Opinion of A.G. Stix-Hackl in *Carpenter, supra* n. 4, para. 82.   [61] *Maurin, supra* n. 52, para. 13.

[62] Joined Cases 60 and 61/84 *Cinéthèque v Fédération Nationale des Cinémas Français* [1985] ECR 2605. On the differences between those *formulæ*, see Tridimas, *supra* n. 30, 229.

first. As the application of fundamental rights depends on whether the situation falls within the scope of Community law, the ECJ usually has to examine whether this condition is fulfilled. Only after concluding that Mr. Carpenter was exercising the right to provide services freely could the ECJ examine the case in the light of fundamental rights. In *Carpenter*, the ECJ had, according to usual practice, established that the situation was one in which a fundamental freedom applied. As far as the substance was concerned, the ECJ did not examine separately whether the situation fell under Community law. At first sight, it could be argued that once there is a link with Community law, fundamental rights are automatically applicable. In my view, this is not the case, and was not the case in *Carpenter*.[63] Certainly, it is correct to say that once a fundamental freedom is applicable, the necessary link exists to apply also fundamental rights. The slight but important difference lies in the fact that a link with Community is not the only criterion for the applicability of fundamental rights. Equally, a fundamental right can not in itself establish a link with Community law.[64]

In *Vajnai*, where the ECJ had to deal with a purely internal situation, the Court ruled it had no jurisdiction, following *Kremzow*.[65] Using different wording than in *Carpenter* and in *Karner*, the ECJ proceeded on the basis that it had no 'jurisdiction with regard to national provisions outside the scope of Community law and when the subject-matter of the dispute is not connected in any way with any of the situations contemplated by the treaties'.[66] Conversely, in *Karner* the ECJ, first, denied that the fundamental freedom in question applied but, nonetheless, continued scrutinizing the national legislation, although referring explicitly to *Kremzow*.[67] This approach which stands in sharp contrast to established case law could be understood either as using fundamental rights as a separate, independent set of rules for assessing compatibility of national law with Community law or as a wide interpretation of 'link with Community law'.[68]

The interplay of 'link with Community law' and the scope of fundamental rights is as follows: where fundamental rights are at stake alongside fundamental freedoms,

---

[63] On a critique as regards the indirect use of the ECHR by the ECJ, see N. Reich, 'Citizenship and family on trial: A fairly optimistic overview of recent court practice with regard to free movement of persons' 40 CML Rev. 615 (631); According to Britz, *supra* n. 6, 176, the ECHR should not be applied in all cases where fundamental freedoms apply.

[64] Mager, *supra* n. 18, 206, argues that according to the Court the Community link in *Carpenter* lies in the fundamental right itself and not in the way in which Mr. Carpenter exercised his fundamental freedom.   [65] Case C-299/95 *Kremzow* [1997] ECR I-2629.

[66] *Vajnai*, *supra* n. 55, para. 13.   [67] *Karner*, *supra* n. 8, paras. 47 *et seq*.

[68] J. Stuyck, Comment on *Karner* 41 CML Rev. 1683 (1695 *et seq*.). H.Weyer, 'Gemeinschaftsrechtliche Überprüfbarkeit mitgliedstaatlicher Regelungen der Verkaufsmodalitäten', EuZW (2004) 455 (457), argues that affecting trade or a directive containing a minimum harmonization could be sufficent to establish a 'Community link'. The first approach was mostly rejected: W.Schaller, Comment on *Karner*, Juristenzeitung (2005) 193 (194 *et seq*.); Scheuing, *supra* n. 38, 174 *et seq*.; E. Spaventa, Comment on *Akrich*, 42 CML Rev. 225 (236). See in contrast, F. de Cecco, 'Room to move? Minimum harmonization and fundamental rights' 43 CMLRev. (2006) 9 (13 *et seq*.).

it has to be examined, first, whether one of the fundamental freedoms is applicable which depends, *inter alia*, but not exclusively on the 'link with Community law'.

Using the field-of-application concept needs clarification in so far as it could be confused with other key issues of Community law for which similar *formulae* are used, namely the competence of the '*dimension communautaire*'.[69] The fact that the latter plays a role even in the context of fundamental rights does not facilitate the task of defining the particularities of each concept and explain the differences between those concepts.

Some define the field of application of Community fundamental rights by referring to the Community's competence.[70] It is submitted that this test has its merits when Community measures are to be examined in the light of fundamental rights. There, the competence to take the measures corresponds to the scope of fundamental rights as they have to be respected wherever the Community has power to act. The two spheres are congruent. With regard to measures adopted by Member States, defining the scope of fundamental rights should not be seen as a matter of competence. Certainly, there are also competence issues, e.g. the question whether and to what extent the ECJ is entitled to scrutinize Member State measures[71] directly or, indirectly, as in preliminary rulings.[72] To start from the Community's competence is an approach which provides many more questions than answers. In particular, there are *formulae* which entail the risk that the scope of fundamental rights would be limited to areas where the Community has exercised legislative competence. This is the case with the following criterion: 'a field "occupied" by the Community'.[73] As 'occupation' is usually understood as adoption of Community acts in certain fields, this would exclude the application of fundamental rights to measures which are to be examined in the light of primary law, e.g. the fundamental freedoms. To avoid this limitation and to cover both situations, it was suggested to apply fundamental rights to 'measures affecting rights given or protected by Community law or in areas specifically regulated by Community law'.[74] As every *formula* based on division of competence needs further precision, such an approach is not very helpful.

With regard to determining the scope of fundamental rights, mention should also be made of Article 12 EC where the wording 'scope of application of this Treaty' is used. At first sight, this criterion could be relevant as it refers to one field of application of fundamental rights, i.e. the scope of Community law. Besides,

---

[69] G. Dellis, 'Le Droit au juge comme élément de la problématique sur la protection des droits fondamentaux au sein de l'ordre juridique communautaire' 13 ERPL (2001) 279 (284). See Kotroni, *supra* n. 35, 188 and 211, who rejects Article 12 EC as relevant reference.

[70] Th. Jürgensen and I. Schlünder, 'EG-Grundrechtsschutz gegenüber Maßnahmen der Mitgliedstaaten', 121 Archiv des öffentlichen Rechts (1996) 200 (222 *et seq.*); Temple Lang, *supra* n. 19, 31. See the critique expressed by Rengeling and Szczekalla, *supra* n. 26, 188 and 201.

[71] This concerns in particular the meaning of Article 46(d) EU.

[72] See e.g. *Vajnai*, *supra* n. 55, para. 13.   [73] This *formula* is used by Jacobs, *supra* n. 27, 337.

[74] Temple Lang, *supra* n. 19, 30.

both the term 'Treaty' in Article 12 EC and the scope of fundamental rights is to be construed widely.

The two sets of rules, i.e. fundamental rights and Article 12 EC, apply where and whenever a situation falls under Community law. Limiting the applicability of fundamental rights so that their scope is narrower than the scope of Article 12 EC would have an absurd consequence: the general principle of equal treatment, one of the most important fundamental rights, would, in essence, have a narrower scope of application than the specific principle of non-discrimination laid down in Article 12 EC.[75] To highlight the extent to which those principles overlap, one could use the same *formula* in applying both—that a rule of Community law applies.[76] Thus, it is correct to state that the field of application of Community fundamental rights is not static.[77] Proceeding on the basis that the two principles overlap,[78] this becomes clear from analysing the development of the case law on Article 12 EC. This seems to be the approach taken e.g. by Griller who refers to the *Bickel* case concerning the interpretation of Article 12 EC when examining the scope of application of fundamental rights.[79]

On this point, it is necessary to recall another prevailing view in the literature: the scope of application of Article 12 EC is wider than the scope of general principles, including fundamental rights,[80] and broader than the condition for applying fundamental rights, i.e. the 'field of application of Community law'.[81]

Another possible point of reference for determining the scope of fundamental rights could be Article 18 EC and cases before the Court in which the rights provided for in Article 18 EC, i.e. the right to move and reside freely within the territory of the Member States were invoked. As recent case law demonstrates, the ECJ has not interpreted those rights generously for all citizens.[82] Thus, the Court distinguishes citizens of the Union in a situation which has a link with Community law from those whose circumstances have no such link.[83] It could be argued that in the light of *Baumbast* things have changed: persons falling under Article 18(1) EC are no longer required to fulfil the 'Community link' requirement. As the Court states that limitations and conditions referred to in Article 18 EC are to be 'applied in compliance with the general principles of Community law and, in

---

[75] This does not mean overlooking the precedence specific non-discrimination clauses take over Article 12 EC.

[76] As far as the scope of fundamental rights is concerned, Temple Lang, *supra* n. 19, 33, requires the application of a substantive rule.   [77] Weiler and Lockhart, *supra* n. 17, 64.

[78] See Eeckhout, *supra* n. 20, 959 *et seq.*, who analyzes the case law on Article 12 EC in the context of interpreting the scope of the Charter on fundamental rights.

[79] Griller, *supra* n. 12, 140 *et seq.*   [80] See the discussion by Demetriou, *supra* n. 20, 491.

[81] Eeckhout, *supra* n. 20, 961 and 963.

[82] As to such an approach see Eeckhout, *supra* n. 20, 970 *et seq.*; E. Spaventa, 'From *Gebhard* to *Carpenter*: Towards a (non-)economic European Constitution' 41 CML Rev. 743 (770 *et seq.*); Kotroni, *supra* n. 35, 201 *et seq.*, who rejects Article 18 EC as relevant reference; Ranacher, *supra* n. 26, 73 *et seq.*

[83] F. Zampini, 'La Cour de justice des Communautés européennes, gardienne des droits fondamentaux «dans le cadre du droit communautaire»' RTDE (1999) 659 (672).

particular, the principle of proportionality',[84] the latter principle can be replaced by other general principles, namely fundamental rights, such as the right to respect for family life. Thus, a joint application of Article 18 EC and the right to respect for family life could confer a right of residence.[85]

In addition, it should be recalled that the scope of Community fundamental rights is not fulfilled by Article 18 EC when applied in isolation.

II. A Multifunctional Instrument: Different Ways of Applying Fundamental Rights

Although all the case law reviewed above derived from preliminary references, recent case law shows a large variety of ways in which the Court deals with fundamental rights and clearly illustrates that their application serves different purposes. On the one hand, at times the ECJ limits itself to interpreting provisions of Community law in the light of fundamental rights. On the other hand, at others the ECJ focuses on transposition or even on application.

A. Interpretation in the Light of Fundamental Rights

In most of the cases under review, the Court simply construes provisions of Community law in the light of a fundamental right. In *MRAX*,[86] the Court was called to construe many provisions in secondary legislation[87] but, unlike the Advocate General,[88] referred to fundamental rights only when interpreting the procedural aspects of one of several provisions[89] listed in the preliminary reference. Further cases concerning the interpretation of directives were *Steffensen*, the

---

[84] *Baumbast*, Case C-413/99, [2002] ECRI-7091, para. 94.
[85] M. Dougan and E. Spaventa, 'Educating Rudy and the (non-)English Patient: A double-bill on residency rights under Article 18 EC' 28 EL Rev (2003) 699 (710 *et seq.*). See Case C-200/02 *Zhu and Chen v Secretary of State for the Home Department* [2004] ECR I-9925, where the ECJ recognized Article 18 EC and a directive on the free movement of persons as legal bases for a right to reside. See also Case C-209/03 *Bidar* [2005] ECR I-2119.   [86] *MRAX, supra* n. 4, para. 101.
[87] Council Directive 68/360/EEC of 15 October 1968 on the abolition of restrictions on movement and residence within the Community for workers of Member States and their families (OJ, English Special Edition 1968 (II), 485); Council Directive 73/148/EEC of 21 May 1973 on the abolition of restrictions on movement and residence within the Community for nationals of Member States with regard to establishment and the provision of services (OJ 1973 L 172/14), Council Regulation (EC) No 2317/95 of 25 September 1995 determining the third countries whose nationals must be in possession of visas when crossing the external borders of the Member States (OJ 1995 L 234/1).   [88] Opinion of A.G. Stix-Hackl in *MRAX, supra* n. 4.
[89] Article 9(2) of Council Directive 64/221/EEC of 25 February 1964 on the co-ordination of special measures concerning the movement and residence of foreign nationals which are justified on grounds of public policy, public security or public (OJ, English Special Edition 1963–1964, 117).

Austrian data protection cases,[90] *Lindqvist*,[91] *RTL*[92] and *Berlusconi*,[93] and in *Baumbast*[94] and *Akrich*[95] the ECJ was asked to interpret a regulation.[96]

An opportunity to refer to fundamental rights in connection with the Brussels Convention arose in *Krombach*[97] where the ECJ had to construe a provision[98] in the light of the right to a fair hearing.

It should be noted that there was criticism of the Court's method of interpretation which has deemed to go beyond the wording of Community law provisions, to reduce their meaning[99] and to interpret those provisions *contra legem*.[100] It is suggested that this ambitious approach taken by the ECJ illustrates the importance the ECJ attaches to fundamental rights and highlights the influence fundamental rights can have on the interpretation of other Community law provisions.

In *Pupino*, where the ECJ was for the first time called upon to give a ruling on fundamental rights in the Third Pillar, the ECJ, first, ruled that framework decisions must be interpreted in such a way that fundamental rights are respected, in particular the right to a fair trial as set out in Article 6 of the ECHR and interpreted by the ECtHR.[101] Second, the ECJ went a step further and transposed the principle of interpretation in conformity with Community law to framework decisions, i.e. it recognized an obligation to construe national law in conformity with EU law.

B. The Level of Transposition

One may deduce from the case law that Member States must respect fundamental rights in transposing directives. Thus, fundamental rights limit the autonomy Member States have in deciding how a directive should be transposed. As in ERT-situations, Member States must respect the limits imposed by fundamental rights.

[90] Joined Cases C-465/00, C-138/01 and C-139/01, *supra* n. 5, para. 68. Directive 95/46/EC of the European Parliament and of the Council of 24 October 1995 on the protection of individuals with regard to the processing of personal data and on the free movement of such data (OJ 1995 L 281/31). Scheuing, *supra* n. 38, 173. [91] *Lindqvist, supra* n. 8, para. 87.
[92] *RTL, supra* n. 8, paras. 68 *et seq.* Article 11(3) of Council Directive 89/552/EEC of 3 October 1989 on the coordination of certain provisions laid down by law, regulation or administrative action in Member States concerning the pursuit of television broadcasting activities (OJ 1989 L 298/23, as amended by Directive 97/36/EC of the European Parliament and of the Council of 30 June 1997, OJ 1997 L 202/60). [93] *Berlusconi, supra* n. 7.
[94] *Baumbast, supra* n. 84, para. 72. [95] *Akrich, supra* n. 4, para. 61.
[96] Regulation (EEC) No 1612/68 of the Council of 15 October 1968 on freedom of movement for workers within the Community (OJ, English Special Edition 1968 II, 475). For Regulation (EC) No 44/2001 see *ASML, supra* n. 6. [97] *Krombach, supra* n. 6.
[98] Article 27, point 1, which states that a judgment shall not be recognized if such recognition is contrary to public policy in the State in which recognition is sought (OJ 1978 L 304/36, several times amended).
[99] Y. Donzallaz, 'Le renouveau de l'ordre public dans la CB/CL au regard des ACJCE *Krombach* et *Renault* et de la révision de ces traités' Aktuelle juristische Praxis (2001) 160 (165 *et seq.*); F. Matscher, 'Der verfahrensrechtliche ordre public im Spannungsfeld von EMRK und Gemeinschaftsrecht' Praxis des internationalen Privat—und Verfahrensrechts (2001) 428 (433).
[100] H. Muir Watt, Revue critique de droit international privé 2000, 489.
[101] *Pupino, supra* n. 6, para. 59; for an analysis, see A. Egger, 'Die Bindung der Mitgliedstaaten an die Grundrechte in der III. Säule' EuZW (2005) 652 (654).

As far as the transposition of directives[102] is concerned, it is suggested that Member States cannot, as in *Wachauf*, be termed as 'agents' when transposing directives. Member States should be termed as agents only when applying regulations. In such a situation, they act in place of the Commission. When Member States transpose directives or when they apply national measures adopted in view of transposition, they do not act as agents in the *Wachauf* sense.

In relation to regulations, the situation is similar: Member States are confronted with an obligation distinct from the requirement to apply regulations. To guarantee their correct application and effectiveness,[103] Member States have to adopt supplementary national rules to ensure their implementation and must in particular provide for establishing organization of institutions, for procedural rules and for sanctions. It was only reasonable for the ECJ to insist on the respect of fundamental rights in such a context.[104]

An obligation similar to the requirement to transpose directives may arise even under the Third Pillar, i.e. the Judicial and Police Cooperation in Criminal Matters. *Pupino* concerned the requirement to transpose a framework decision. The ECJ ruled that the national court must be able to authorize certain persons to give evidence in accordance with certain arrangements.[105] This wording and the distinction made by the ECJ between that obligation and the obligation to construe and to apply national law in conformity with fundamental rights[106] may lead to the conclusion that the ECJ also requires Member States to transpose framework decisions in conformity with fundamental rights.

C. The Level of Application

Furthermore, recent case law runs counter the view[107] that fundamental rights do not play a role at the level of applying Community law, in particular the application of national law which transposes directives[108] or framework decisions. With regard to directives, the ECJ recalled such an obligation in *Booker*, the Swedish and Austrian data protection cases, *Steffensen*, *Berlusconi* and *Commission v. Germany*.[109] In *Pupino*, the ECJ continued to look to the protection of individuals and extended

---

102 Demetriou, *supra* n. 20, 487.
103 Case C-177/95 *Ebony Maritime SA, Loten Navigation Co. Ltd v. Prefetto della Provincia di Brindisi and Others* [1997] ECR I-1111.
104 Case 72/85 *Commission v. Netherlands* [1986] ECR 1219; Due and Gulmann, *supra* n. 11, at 418.
105 *Pupino*, *supra* n. 6, para. 61.
106 *Pupino*, *supra* n. 6, para. 43 *et seq.* and 60. On the distinction between different obligations in *Pupino*, see Egger, *supra* n. 101, at 653.
107 T. Kingreen and R. Störmer, 'Die subjektiv-öffentlichen Rechte des primären Gemeinschaftsrechts', EuR (1998) 263 (281).
108 On a wide interpretation of 'implementation', see: W. Hummer, *Der Status der 'EU-Grundrechtecharta': politische Erklärung oder Kern einer europäischen Verfassung?* (2002) 77; H. D. Jarass, EU-Grundrechte (2005) 38 *et seq.*; Jürgensen and Schlünder, *supra* n. 70, 224; Rengeling and Szczekalla, *supra* n. 26, 162 *et seq.*; Ruffert, *supra* n. 27, 527 *et seq.*; Schaller, *supra* n. 48, 44 *et seq.*
109 *Booker*, *supra* n. 3, para. 88; *Lindqvist*, *supra* n. 8, para. 87; Joined Cases C-465/00, C-138/01 and C-139/01, *supra* n. 5, para. 80; *Steffensen*, *supra* n. 6, para. 80; *Berlusconi*, *supra* n. 7, para. 69; *Commission v Germany*, *supra* n. 4, para. 108.

the obligation to apply national law in conformity with Community law to the Third Pillar.[110]

Yet, there is another situation which falls outside the traditional two categories, in which Member States have to apply provisions which are directly applicable.[111] Such a situation typically concerns primary legislation but also arises in case of regulations and provisions of directives having direct effect.

As far as regulations are concerned, guidance may be found in recent case law. In *Baumbast*, where the ECJ had to construe a provision of a regulation,[112] it simply recalled its case law[113] on the obligation to interpret legislation in the light of the ECHR.[114]

That approach is somewhat controversial if adopted for the application of primary legislation. On the one hand, some commentators take the view that individuals may rely on Community fundamental rights where primary legislation confers rights on individuals.[115] On the other hand, others argue that Member States are bound by Community fundamental rights when applying primary legislation only where they have discretion[116] or that they have to respect Community fundamental rights only to the extent that a national measure interferes with fundamental freedoms.[117]

With regard to primary law, not all cases correspond to the ERT-situation. Certainly, Member States may only restrict fundamental freedoms as provided. But they are also bound by many more obligations flowing from primary law, e.g. Article 10 EC read together with Article 81 or Article 82 EC. The existence of the latter type of obligation under primary law is confirmed by the judgment in *K.B.*, where the ECJ interpreted Article 141 EC in the light of Article 12 of the ECHR.[118]

In this context, it is worth drawing attention to *Carpenter*. Here, the ECJ had to construe a Treaty provision with direct effect, *viz.* the freedom to provide services guaranteed by Article 49 EC. The terms used by the Court are: '... Article 49 EC, read in the light of the fundamental right to respect for family life, is to be interpreted as ...'.[119] Leaving aside other parts of this heavily criticized ruling, it as well as the judgment in *K.B.* confirm again that fundamental rights come into play even when Member States have to apply primary law. In view of the restrictive effect of the national measure on a fundamental freedom, it is not surprising that this case is presented by the ECJ as an ERT-situation. It has been argued[120]

---

[110] *Pupino, supra* n. 6, para. 60.   [111] *Carpenter, supra* n. 4.

[112] Article 12 of Regulation (EEC) No 1612/68 of the Council of 15 October 1968 on freedom of movement for workers within the Community (OJ, English Special Edition 1968 (II), 475).

[113] Case 249/86 *Commission v Germany* [1989] ECR 1263, para. 10.

[114] *Baumbast, supra* n. 84, para. 72.

[115] See the discussion by Jürgensen and Schlünder, *supra* n. 70, 211.

[116] See e.g. Schaller, *supra* n. 48, 43.

[117] See e.g. Schaller, *supra* n. 48, 45 *et seq.*, who denies that the Member States are bound in such a context. Schaller achieves this result by applying the *Wachauf-formula* which is, to my mind, not the correct test.   [118] *K.B., supra* n. 10, paras. 33 *et seq.*

[119] *Carpenter, supra* n. 4, para. 46.   [120] Reich, *supra* n. 63, 635.

that the Court includes respect for family life as one of the conditions under which an economic activity may be restricted. Thus, it is not totally correct to classify *Carpenter* outside the two traditional categories.[121] Without doubt, the facts, the legal issues and the Court's findings concerning the freedom to provide services were unusual.

III. Functions and Effects of Fundamental Rights: Member States and Individuals

This section concerns the relationship between Member States and individuals. It starts by identifying the different functions of EU fundamental rights in national judicial protection. It then outlines Member States' obligations with regard to fundamental rights, continues by highlighting the interests and relations involved and by examining the relationship between fundamental rights and fundamental freedoms. It concludes by assessing the effects of protecting fundamental rights on individuals' and on Member States' competences.

A. The Objective and the Subjective Function of Fundamental Rights

Fundamental rights may have two different functions in national judicial protection. On the one hand, fundamental rights serve to protect an individual's right, i.e. they have a so-called subjective function. On the other hand, they can be applied in an objective way, i.e. in serving as a measure to assess the compatibility of national law with Community law.

This section provides an analysis of the Court's recent case law in order to determine the function the ECJ attributes to fundamental rights. No single approach is used by the Court, but rather a scale with subjective application at one end and objective application at the other.

The case in which the subjective function of fundamental rights is undoubtedly most apparent is *Carpenter*.[122] In that judgment, the Court focussed on the personal situation of the family concerned under the decision to deport and emphasized that the effects of such an order were not confined to the spouse whose deportation was to be decided. The assessment made by the ECJ and the result achieved in that case, i.e. that the decision to deport Mrs Carpenter constitutes an infringement, illustrate that the Court, implicitly, recognized Mrs Carpenter's right to stay[123] as a consequence of the right to respect for family life.

---

[121] See the qualification made by Mager, *supra* n. 18, 205.

[122] *Carpenter*, *supra* n. 4, paras. 40 *et seq*. According to G. Nicolaysen, 'Die gemeinschaftsrechtliche Begründung von Grundrechten' EuR (2003) 719 (739), the individual position is not taken into account.

[123] On the ECHR, see in general M. Holoubek, *Grundrechtliche Gewährleistungspflichten* (Springer, 1997) 61.

In some judgments, the ECJ examines the case from an objective perspective but refers in some points to the position of the individual concerned. This kind of reasoning appeared in the Austrian cases on data protection relating to information on personal income where the ECJ, in the course of examining whether the national law was compatible with the directive interpreted in the light of a fundamental right, stated that persons may suffer harm as a result of negative effects of publicising their income.[124] A similar approach was taken in *Akrich* where the Court examined the case mainly in the light of the objective function of the right to respect for family life[125] and held, in abstract terms, that removal of a person from a country where close members of his family were living may amount to an infringement.

As far as procedural rights are concerned, *Krombach*[126] illustrates that the ECJ acknowledges the right to a fair hearing as recognized by the ECHR. In *Steffensen*, where that right was invoked, the ECJ focussed on its objective function. It highlighted the need to apply national procedural rules correctly, in particular the obligation to exclude the results of analyses in order that the admission of those results as evidence did not give rise to an infringement of the right to a fair hearing.[127] A similar approach was taken in *Pupino*.[128]

A more objective approach was taken in *RTL* where the ECJ had to construe a provision of a directive in the light of the freedom of expression. The same is true as regards the interpretation of principles on state liability in the light of Article 41 of the ECHR in *Köbler*.[129]

In *Booker*, where fish farmers' right to property was examined, the ECJ stated that national measures did not constitute a disproportionate and intolerable interference impairing the very substance of the right to property.[130] The ECJ simply transposed the result of examining similar Community measures to Member States' measures. Although the ECJ referred to the effects on the undertakings' right to property, the subjective function of the fundamental right played a minor role in that analysis.

In some cases, the ECJ has based its analysis on the objective function of fundamental rights, as in *K.B.*,[131] where the ECJ simply examined the compatibility of the applicable legislation in the main proceedings, i.e. underlined the objective function of Article 12 of the ECHR. In *Karner*,[132] the Court assessed the compatibility of national law with the principle of freedom of expression as laid down in Article 10 of the ECHR. In *Berlusconi*,[133] in which the ECJ analysed the effect of the principle of retroactive application of the more lenient penalty in criminal proceedings, it examined the case merely in an abstract way without taking account of the specific facts of the case.

---

[124] Joined Cases C-465/00, C-138/01 and C-139/01, *supra* n. 5, para. 89.
[125] *Akrich*, *supra* n. 4, paras. 58 and 61.   [126] *Krombach*, *supra* n. 6, para. 44.
[127] *Steffensen*, *supra* n. 6, paras. 78 *et seq.*   [128] *Pupino*, *supra* n. 6, para. 60.
[129] *Köbler*, *supra* n. 20, para. 49.   [130] *Booker*, *supra* n. 3, paras. 90, 92 and 93.
[131] *K.B.*, *supra* n. 10, para. 34.   [132] *Karner*, *supra* n. 8, paras. 49 *et seq.*
[133] *Berlusconi*, *supra* n. 7, paras. 70 *et seq.*

Even where the Court focuses on the objective function of fundamental rights, the result has an impact on rights of the individual. The cases considered above clearly demonstrate that examining national measures in the light of fundamental rights favours principally individuals rather than the Community and its interests. The ECJ is nothing less than an another forum to protect individuals against unlawful measures taken by public authorities in the Member States.[134]

In preliminary rulings, a fundamental right has often been invoked by one of the parties before the referring court. This was not the case in *Schmidberger*, as the individuals invoking fundamental rights were parties to the administrative proceedings concerning the demonstration whereas the main proceedings concerned an action brought by an individual, viz. a transport undertaking seeking damages against Austria, i.e. they concerned about state liability.

Whether the Court takes an objective or a subjective approach in preliminary references, depends mainly on the wording of the preliminary question. In infringement proceedings, it is influenced by the wording of the Commission's request. Conversely, whether the case is about the interpretation of a Community provision in the light of a fundamental right or about the compatibility of a national measure with fundamental rights does not seem to be the decisive factor.

B. Member States' Negative and Positive Obligations

Recent case law confirms that the ECJ acknowledges that Member States have positive obligations regarding fundamental rights. As opposed to negative obligations, i.e. the obligation to refrain from interfering with fundamental rights, Member States must actively protect fundamental rights.

The distinction between positive and negative obligations should not be confused with the distinction between positive action and omission. The latter distinction is made in *Schmidberger* where a demonstration was not banned by an administrative authority. On the one hand,[135] not banning the demonstration could be regarded as an omission, but on the other hand, especially in the specific circumstances of the case, it could also be regarded as a positive action.[136] The order issued by an administrative authority to its subordinate authority was appositive action which could be considered as interference.

Another case which illustrates that fundamental rights have more than a mere defensive function[137] and give rise to rights going beyond simply procedural

---

134 Weiler and Lockhart, *supra* n. 17, at 621.

135 B. Koch, EuZW (2003) 598. According to F. Ronkes Agerbeek, 'Freedom of expression and free movement in the Brenner corridor: the Schmidberger case', 29 EL Rev (2004) 255 (263), there was a collusion of a positive obligation under the EC Treaty and a negative obligation under the rights to freedom of expression.

136 R. Krist, 'Rechtliche Aspekte der Brennerblockade—Versammlungsfreiheit contra Freiheit des Warenverkehrs' Österreichische Juristenzeitung (1999) 241 (249).

137 On individuals' rights flowing from the defensive function, see in general L. Jaeckel, 'The duty to protect fundamental rights in the European Community' 28 EL Rev (2003) 508 (521).

rights, is *Steffensen*. It has been argued that fundamental rights may, in certain cases, give rise to an obligation on the Member States to take measures benefiting on individuals, including legislative measures.[138] In some judgments, e.g. in *Pupino* and in *Berlusconi*, in which the ECJ ruled national courts must respect fundamental rights in criminal proceedings, the ECJ found that fundamental rights impose even positive obligations on the national legislature. Certainly, it should be stressed that fundamental rights never oblige a Member State to take a specific measure.[139]

These positive obligations have been drawn from two different sources: First, there are those deriving from the fundamental freedoms[140] and related case law.[141] The second source is the ECHR and the case law of the ECtHR. As the EHCR is a source of EU fundamental rights, the ECJ should generally follow the ECtHR which recognizes positive obligations.[142] In this respect, one can say: What is considered good law in Strasbourg[143] should be taken into account in Luxembourg.

In legal academic writing, positive obligations are usually identified as playing three different roles: a protective role, providing institutional guarantees, and ensuring the rights of the individual to participate in a national regime.

The protective role of Member States includes the duty to protect the rights of the individual.[144] The counterpart of this duty is the individual's right vis-à-vis Member States to be protected against interferences by entities other than the state,[145] such as environmental pollution, especially emissions, or actions taken by other individuals.

The Court has recently confirmed earlier case law[146] stating that the ECJ recognizes the protective role of Member States.[147] This was made clear in the Austrian

---

[138] Cf. Holoubek, *supra* n. 123, 55; L. Jaeckel, *Schutzpflichten im deutschen und im europäischen Recht* (2001) 265.

[139] Cf. J. Suerbaum, 'Die Schutzpflichtdimension der Gemeinschaftsgrundrechte' EuR (2003) 390 (414).

[140] D. Schindler, *Die Kollision von Grundfreiheiten und Gemeinschaftsgrundrechten* (2001) 156 *et seq.* Cf. Schilling, *supra* n. 14, 36; P. Szczekalla, *Die sogenannten grundrechtlichen Schutzpflichten im deutschen und europäischen Recht* (2002) 640 *et seq.*

[141] Case C-265/95 *Commission v France* [1997] ECR I-6959. As there was no fundamental right at stake, the view taken by Jaeckel, *supra* n. 137, 518, 522 and 526 *et seq.*, is not correct. This author refers to that case with regard to the duty to protect fundamental rights.

[142] An obligation to recognize positive obligations is acknowledged by Suerbaum, *supra* n. 139, 404 *et seq.*

[143] Apart from the case law on Article 10, see the following recent cases: *Tepe v Turkey*, judgment of 9 May 2003, § 177, concerning Article 2 § 1 and the obligation to provide a framework of law which prohibits the taking of life; *Hatton and others v The United Kingdom*, judgment of 8 July 2003, § 119, concerning a failure to regulate private industry in a manner securing proper respects for the rights enshrined in Article 8.

[144] In German they are also called 'Schutzgewährrechte'. Cf. C. Dröge, *Positive Verpflichtungen der Staaten in der Europäischen Menschenrechtskonvention* (2003) 223.

[145] Suerbaum, *supra* n. 139, 405 and 409.

[146] D. Ehlers, § 14 Allgemeine Lehren, in Ehlers and Becker (eds.), *Europäische Grundrechte und Grundfreiheiten*, 2nd Edition (2005) at para. 24; Jaeckel, *supra* n. 138, 215.

[147] For the opposite view, see T. Schmitz, 'Die EU-Grundrechtecharta aus grundrechtsdogmatischer und grundrechtstheoretischer Sicht' 56 Juristenzeitung (2001) 833 (839).

data protection cases[148] where the ECJ identified the interference with the fundamental right to respect for private life as enshrined in Article 8 ECHR by referring
to different infringing actions. In para. 74, the ECJ qualified the communication
of the data on personal income as interference. But, in considering whether the
interference was justified, the ECJ identified disclosure of the names of the persons concerned as interference, in paras. 79 and 90, as well as publication of the
names by the Austrian Court of Auditors (para. 86). The difference is not insignifi-
cant: communication of the data is an act of the employer whereas drawing up
and communicating the report is an action of the Court of Auditors.

If the action of the Court of Auditors rather than that of the employer constitutes interference with the fundamental right, then the case rides on the defensive
role of fundamental rights, *viz.* the Member State's obligation to refrain from
interfering with the right to respect for private life by drawing up and communicating a report.

At first sight, *Schmidberger* could be regarded as a typical case in which the
rights to freedom of assembly was opposed to the exercise of another right, and as
a case in which a Member State had to protect the freedom of assembly from
interference by other individuals. On further examination, it is true that in
Schmidberger some citizens were exercising fundamental rights, i.e. the freedom of
assembly and the freedom of expression.[149] But the interference can be attributed
to an individual exercising a fundamental freedom. In this respect, it is argued that
the liberal and social dimensions were intermingled.[150] From the perspective of
the individual, i.e. the transport undertaking, invoking a fundamental freedom it
was the defensive and not the protective role of the fundamental freedom which
was at stake. From the perspective of the individuals invoking their right to freedom of assembly, it could hardly be argued that the Member State was required to
take measures flowing solely from the defensive role of the fundamental right.[151]

The second category of positive obligations includes institutional guarantees,
especially regarding freedom of assembly and the freedom of expression, *inter alia*,
the Member States' obligation to ensure pluralism of mass media. This dimension
of fundamental rights was already recognized in older case law[152] and can be identified in *Schmidberger*. This judgment demonstrates the growing importance of
positive obligations and indicates that, in future, the ECJ will be confronted with
many more cases about the duty on Member States to take measures to protect
individuals' fundamental rights.

The third category includes so-called rights to participate in a national regime.[153]
Within this category, a distinction can be made between derived rights to participate

---

[148] Joined Cases C-465/00, C-138/01 and C-139/01, *supra* n. 5.
[149] *Schmidberger*, *supra* n. 9, para. 86.   [150] Dröge, *supra* n. 144, 218.
[151] Cf. Szczekalla, *supra* n. 140, 641 *et seq.*
[152] Case C-288/89 *Stichting Collectieve Antennevoorziening Gouda and others v Commissariaat voor de Media* [1991] ECR I-4007; Case C-368/95 *Vereinigte Familiapress Zeitungsverlags— und ver-triebs GmbH v Heinrich Bauer Verlag* [1997] ECR I-3689.
[153] Schwarze, *supra* n. 1, 3463.

and original rights to benefits. The difference lies in the fact that derived rights cover rights to participate in an existing regime, i.e. the extension of a right to a group of persons not hitherto entitled to those rights, e.g. social advantages. The judgment in *K.B.*, although focusing on the right to marry under Article 12 of the ECHR, concerns in essence K.B.'s right to nominate her partner as the beneficiary of a survivor's pension. Conversely, original rights concern rights to benefit from a regime which does not yet exist and which, first of all, has to be created.

C. Protecting Fundamental Rights: Diverging Interests and Plurality of Relations

In an action that raises issues of fundamental rights several parties will have differing interests: the Member State, the individual relying on a fundamental right, and, the Community defending its interests. In a case in which another individual infringes the fundamental rights, the source of interference is another individual, that individual represents a further point of reference transforming the 'triangle' into a square.[154]

This section concentrates on such 'horizontal' cases,[155] and in particular on the relationship between the individuals, whether private persons or undertakings, where one individual is relying on a specific fundamental right which is infringed by another individual. It will be shown that account must be taken of the Member State and their obligations even in such a context.

Here, it is of assistance to distinguish between two relationships: a vertical relationship between the Member State and the individual, and a horizontal relationship between the two individuals.

In horizontal cases, the solution to the fundamental rights problem may either be found by weighing the interests of the individual and the interest of the Member State, or by balancing the interests of the two individuals involved,[156] e.g. of consumers against undertakings as in *Karner* and *RTL*. Such cases could be termed triangular situations in which the interests of an individual and of a Member State are opposed and in which the outcome of proceedings has an influence on the position of another individual, e.g. in company law, labour law, media law, public procurement law and environmental law.

As shown above, Member States must respect negative as well as positive obligations. With regard to the relationship between an individual and the Member State, the latter has to refrain from interfering with individuals' fundamental rights and to protect their interests from interferences by another individual. The second duty entails an obligation to intervene in the relationship between two

---

[154] Cf. Jaeckel, *supra* n. 138, 266; B. Koch, *Die Gewährleistungspflicht der Mitgliedstaaten zur Aufrechterhaltung des Binnenmarktes* (2003) 75.

[155] Cf. P. Chr. Müller-Graff, 'Grundfreiheiten und Gemeinschaftsgrundrechte', in *Tradition und Weltoffenheit des Rechts* (2002) 1281 (1296).

[156] Such a distinction is made by Schindler, *supra* n. 140, 173 *et seq.*

individuals.[157] This is an essential aspect of the indirect horizontal effect of fundamental rights and demonstrates their protective role.[158]

If fundamental rights were attributed direct horizontal effect, an individual, and not the Member State would be obliged to respect any such right, so that an individual would be entitled to invoke that fundamental right against another individual.

In typical horizontal cases, such as *Schmidberger*, *Krombach* and *Karner*, one group of individuals relies on a fundamental right, another relies on a fundamental freedom. The relationship between fundamental rights and fundamental freedoms shall be dealt with in the following section.

D. Fundamental Rights v. Fundamental Freedoms

Before examining the ECJ's case law on the relationship between fundamental rights and fundamental freedoms, it is worth outlining their common characteristics. As far as their position in the Community legal order is concerned, it should be noted that they are of equal normative rank,[159] fundamental rights being at the apex, along with other general principles, of the normative pyramid of Community law norms.[160] Although there is no difference as regards their legal value,[161] fundamental rights may prevail over fundamental freedoms in a particular case. As a guideline, fundamental rights need not be ranked higher. Finally, there is no indication in the Court's case law that fundamental freedoms are *leges speciales*[162] in the context of fundamental rights.

Another similarity between fundamental rights and fundamental freedoms is the test used to assess the compatibility of a national measure. As both govern the limits of Member States' actions, in assessing their compatibility, the Court will examine whether the national measure pursues a legitimate objective and will then apply the proportionality test,[163] usually consisting of several steps which may differ from case to case.

---

[157] Th. Ackermann, Comment on *Omega*, 42 CML Rev. 1107 (1115 *et seq.*).

[158] On this issue, see H. Gersdorf, 'Funktionen der Gemeinschaftsgrundrechte im Lichte des Solange II-Beschlusses des Bundesverfassungsgerichts' Archiv des öffentlichen Rechts (1994) 400 (421).

[159] A. Alemanno, *supra* n. 30, 723; Th. Georgopoulos, 'Libertés fondamentales communautaires et droits fondamentaux européens: Le conflit n'aura pas lieu' Petites affiches (2004) 8 (13); Kingreen and Störmer, *supra* n. 50, 283; Schindler, *supra* n. 140, 163 *et seq.*; T. Tridimas, 'The European Court of Justice and the Draft Constitution: A Supreme Court for the Union?' in T. Tridimas and P. Nebbia (eds.) *European Union Law for the Twenty-First Century* (2004) 113 (139).
According to G. Gonzales, 'EC Fundamental Freedoms v. Human Rights in the Case C-112/00 Eugen Schmidberger v. Austria [2003] ECR I-5659' 31 LIEI 219 (226), giving priority to fundamental rights indicates their higher rank. This aspect is called 'normative relationship' by Weiler and Lockhart, *supra* n. 17, 579, 595.

[160] Dellis, *supra* n. 69, 283.

[161] Cf. Schilling, *supra* n. 14, 34. Alemanno, *supra* n. 30, 744 and 750, advocates attributing a stronger legal force to fundamental rights.

[162] This idea is put forward by Müller-Graff, *supra* n. 155, 1295.

[163] Alemanno, *supra* n. 30, 738 *et seq.*; Frenz, *supra* n. 30, 18 *et seq.*; Schaller, *supra* n. 48, 97; cf. F. Kessler, 'L'actualité de la jurisprudence communautaire et internationale' Revue de jurisprudence sociale (2003) 751 (752), with regard to *Schmidberger*.

Recent judgments, in particular *Schmidberger*,[164] *Familiapress* and *Omega*, demonstrate that fundamental rights as well as fundamental freedoms protect specific interests or goods. On the one hand, rights to 'freedom of expression' and 'freedom of assembly' were relied on. On the other hand, the free movement of goods and the freedom to provide services were invoked.

Apart from the relationship between different fundamental rights,[165] a topic which is outside the scope of this article, recent case law reveals differing relationships between fundamental rights and fundamental freedoms. In abstract terms, two types of relationship may be identified.[166] On the one hand, fundamental rights may justify restrictions on fundamental freedoms[167]; on the other hand, fundamental rights may limit Member States' discretion to restrict fundamental freedoms.[168] Whereas in some cases fundamental rights may serve to enforce fundamental freedoms, they may collide with fundamental freedoms in others.[169]

If a case brought before the ECJ entails the opposition of principles with the same legal value, the solution must be found by balancing the principles involved.[170] The ECJ must weigh the interests of one individual against the interests of another. In contrast to a situation in which each principle is applied alone, this balancing act limits the normative effects of principles. Thus, balancing may have the effect that fundamental rights restrict the obligations flowing from fundamental freedoms, or *vice versa*, e.g. freedom of expression or freedom of assembly may restrict the rights flowing from the free movement of goods.[171]

The balancing method[172] was adopted in *Schmidberger* where the Court stated that 'the interest involved must be weighed . . . in order to determine whether a fair balance was struck between those interests'[173] by the national authorities whose actions were to be examined.

As regards assessment of national measures, it may be distinguished by two methods: the 'Luxembourg approach' and the 'Strasbourg approach'.[174] The first

---

[164] On certain aspects of *Schmidberger*, see Schindler, *supra* n. 140, 177 *et seq*.

[165] According to Weiler and Lockhart, *supra* n. 17, 602 *et seq*., the basic normative conflict in Case C-159/90 *SPUC v Grogan* [1991] ECR I-4685, was rather between the human right to life invoked by Ireland and the freedom of expression than between a human right and a fundamental freedom.

[166] See Szczekalla, *supra* n. 140, 1105; Alemanno, *supra* n. 30, 736 *et seq*.

[167] Müller-Graff, *supra* n. 155, 1299.

[168] Cf. Kingreen, *supra* n. 41, paras. 78 *et seq*.; Müller-Graff, *supra* n. 155, 1299.

[169] Ehlers, *supra* n. 146, para. 13; Schindler, *supra* n. 140, 143. As Weiler and Lockhart, *supra* n. 17, at 593, rightly point out the term 'fundamental' is of no relevance for the substance.

[170] Frenz, *supra* n. 30, 18 *et seq*; Georgopoulos, *supra* n. 159, 13 *et seq*.; Schindler, *supra* n. 140, 162 *et seq*.; Weiler and Lockhart, *supra* n. 17, 592.

[171] Cf. Schilling, *supra* n. 14, 40, who refers only to positive obligations. Schindler, *supra* n. 140, 170.

[172] This does not seem to be the view taken by Agerbeek, *supra* n. 135, 262, who argues that the Court did not devote attention to reconciling the principle of free movement and the right to freedom of expression.   [173] *Supra* n. 9, para. 81.

[174] Those approaches are called 'styles' by C. Brown, 'Comment on *Schmidberger*' 40 CML Rev. 1499 (1507 *et seq*.).

difference lies in the standard applied rather than in the object examined. Under the Luxembourg approach, the national measure will first be examined in the light of a fundamental freedom, whereas the Strasbourg approach starts by analysing compatibility with a fundamental right. The second step is always an examination of whether the measure is justified *stricto sensu*, i.e. whether it satisfies the proportionality test. Under the Luxembourg approach, the justification is examined in the light of the fundamental right. For all these reasons, it is of no assistance to recognize a third category of justifications or a third approach.[175]

A good example to demonstrate the use of both approaches,[176] in the Court's practice is *Schmidberger*. The case concerned a demonstration that an environmental group was allowed to organize on the Brenner motorway. Since this main transit route between Germany and Italy was closed for more than one day, a German transport undertaking alleged Austria was liable for damage caused by permitting the demonstration. In its judgment, first, the ECJ, qualified the failure to ban the demonstration as a measure having equivalent effect. Then, the ECJ weighed the interests involved, i.e. the two fundamental rights invoked by the demonstrators as well as the freedom of goods. The Court came to the conclusion that the protection of fundamental rights is a legitimate interest which justifies a restriction on the free movement of goods by the Austrian authorities who struck the correct balance.

In *Schmidberger*, the ECJ does not treat both approaches in the same manner; there are not two equal tests. In essence, the Court gives precedence to the traditional Luxembourg approach. This can easily be deduced from the fact that one part of the judgment is entitled: 'Whether there is a restriction of the free movement of goods', that the following part is entitled 'Whether the restriction may be justified' and that the paragraph preceding that second heading, para. 64, states that the national measure, *viz.* the decision not to ban the demonstration, is incompatible with the 'obligations arising from Articles 30 and 34 of the Treaty ... unless that failure to ban can objectively be justified'. That structure runs parallel to the one used by AG Jacobs in his Opinion.[177] The Strasbourg approach is used in para. 79 *et seq.* in which the Court refers to two specific fundamental rights and to the possibility of restricting their exercise. In para. 82, the ECJ returns to the Luxembourg approach. To explain why the Court chose to adopt its traditional approach, one has to bear in mind that the judgment in *Schmidberger* was a preliminary ruling. In such proceedings, the starting point is the questions referred by the national court except where there is a need to reformulate them. It is only of theoretical interest to ask whether the ECJ would have applied the same test if the national court had not phrased its reference in terms of the free movement of goods but of a fundamental right.

---

[175] Schaller, *supra* n. 48, 112. The existence of such a third category is denied by Alemanno, *supra* n. 30, 736.   [176] Also called 'styles'; see Brown, *supra* n. 174, 1507 *et seq.*
[177] Opinion of AG Jacobs in *Schmidberger*, *supra* n. 9, paras. 85 *et seq.*

The approach taken in *Schmidberger* is not totally new since traces of it may be found in previous case law, in particular in *Familiapress*.[178] In both cases, Austria relied on overriding requirements to justify rules which were likely to obstruct the exercise of free movement of goods. In *Familiapress*, a national prohibition on selling publications which offered the chance to take part in prize competitions was to be examined in the light of the freedom of expression.[179] But in contrast to *Schmidberger*, the ECJ initially applied the Strasbourg approach and went on to combine it with the Luxembourg approach, holding that 'it must therefore be determined whether a national prohibition ... is proportionate to the aim of maintaining press diversity and whether that objective might not be attained by measures less restrictive of both intra-Community trade *and* freedom of expression.'[180] A similar approach was adopted in *RTL*[181] and *Karner*[182] where the Court examined whether the national restriction was justified under Article 10(2) of the ECHR.

As the structure of the Luxembourg approach differs from the Strasbourg test, it is worth examining whether the choice of approach has, or may have, an influence on the outcome of a case.[183] On this point, it is important to identify a second difference between the two approaches, namely the burden of proof. This element is more significant than usually given credit for, as it can be the decisive factor in assessing whether a national measure is compatible with Community law. Where the Luxembourg approach is applied, Member States must demonstrate that a measure does not infringe a fundamental freedom. Whereas Member States must justify that the measure does not infringe a fundamental right under the Strasbourg approach. Moreover, the difference, in effect, becomes clearer when comparing the burden of proof from the perspective of the individual relying on a fundamental right (situation A) or a fundamental freedom (situation B). If one starts from the Member State's defence that the measure is compatible with the fundamental freedoms, it is up to the individual to demonstrate that the measure infringes a fundamental right (situation A). If one starts from the Member State's defence that the measure is compatible with fundamental rights, it is up to the individual to demonstrate that the measure infringes a fundamental freedom (situation B).

A third difference between the test applied by the ECJ with regard to fundamental rights and the test applied with regard to fundamental freedoms may be deduced from recent case law. *Carpenter* and *Schmidberger* in particular, illustrate that Member States enjoy less discretion where they intended to interfere with fundamental rights and more discretion where they intended to protect them.[184]

---

[178] Cf. Jacobs, *supra* n. 27, 336 *et seq.*, referring to a case where a Member State tries to justify a restriction in the interest of human rights.   [179] *Familiapress, supra* n. 152, para. 26.

[180] *ibid.*, para. 27 (emphasis added).   [181] *RTL, supra* n. 8, paras. 69 *et seq.*

[182] *Karner, supra* n. 8, paras. 49 *et seq.*

[183] See Schaller, *supra* n. 48, 103, who rather denies an influence on the result.

[184] For the comparison, see Schindler, *supra* n. 140, 186.

E. Effects on Member States' Competences and on Individuals

Another important point which becomes apparent in recent case law, are the effects Community fundamental rights have on Member States as well on individuals. On the one hand, fundamental rights may have a restrictive effect on Member States' competences; on the other hand, some cases demonstrate that fundamental rights may also be used by Member States as an instrument to defend their competences.

The restrictive effect becomes particularly evident in cases concerning national procedural rules (*Steffensen, Köbler, Pupino*) or immigration law (*Akrich, Carpenter*).[185] Fundamental rights may restrict Member States' margin of discretion either when they transpose Community law or when they apply national law, e.g. immigration rules for third country nationals who are married to EU-citizens.

Defence of national competences due to the enforcement of fundamental rights was the outcome in *Schmidberger* and *Omega*. The novel aspect of those cases, in particular the protection of fundamental rights to justify restriction of a fundamental freedom, is in line with former case law.[186] For the ECJ had already held that national measures taken to safeguard objectives connected with a specific fundamental right enshrined in the ECHR could justify restriction of fundamental freedoms. Certainly, it should not be overlooked that the Court presents its findings in *Schmidberger*, at least in some paragraphs,[187] in a different way, i.e. as a case in which a national measure is to be examined in the light of a fundamental right.

IV. Judicial Protection of Fundamental Rights by the Court of Justice—Some General Remarks

Recent case law shows that the ECJ when interpreting and applying fundamental rights in connection with national law is not constrained by Article 46(d) EUT although this article refers only to 'actions of the institutions' and not to national

---

[185] Gonzales, *supra* n. 159, 228; Spaventa, *supra* n. 82, 768.

[186] *Gouda, supra* n. 152, para. 23, concerning the freedom of expression as protected by Article 10 ECHR. On former case law and on fundamental rights as justification, see Ranacher, *supra* n. 26, 57 and 62 *et seq.* See Kotroni, *supra* n. 35, 228 *et seq.*, who also distinguishes between a restrictive and a pro-national effect of fundamental rights. Tridimas, *supra* n. 159, 138, underlines the differences between *Schmidberger* and former case law, especially C-62/90 *Commission v Germany* [1992] ECR I-2575, where the ECJ attached more importance to the free movement. On this issue, see V. Skouris, 'Koordination des Grundrechtsschutzes in Europa—die Perspektive des Gerichtshofes der Europäischen Gemeinschaften' 124 Zeitschrift für Schweizerisches Recht (2005) 31 (41). For a comparison, see M.K. Bulterman/H.R. Kranenborg, 'What if rules on free movement and human rights collide? About laser games and human dignity: the Omega case' 31 ELRev. (2006) 93 (98).

[187] *Schmidberger, supra* n. 9, paras. 79 *et seq.*

measures as being within the scope of fundamental rights.[188] This approach appears correct as the restriction in Article 46(d) refers only to Article 6(2) EUT and not to Community law as such. As the source of fundamental rights is not solely Article 6(2) but general principles of Community law as separate source of law, the Court's competence to oversee respect of fundamental rights by Member States does not depend on an explicit provision of the law of the EU.

Yet there is no light without shade. It has been argued in academic writings that the ECJ did not examine all cases in the light of fundamental rights where such an analysis was required. In particular, the ECJ has been criticized for not referring to freedom of expression and the right to the free exercise of one's business activities in actions concerning advertising.[189] There are cases in which the Court did not refer to fundamental rights even when relied on by the parties and/or mentioned in the reference.[190] Conversely, many judgments, e.g. *Carpenter, Baumbast, RTL, K.B.* as well as *Karner* and, to a limited extent, *Akrich, Köbler* and *Pupino*, illustrate that it is possible for the parties in the main proceedings to raise a fundamental rights issue before the ECJ although the questions referred contained no reference to fundamental rights.

This section examines different aspects of judicial protection which highlight the degree of protection afforded to EU fundamental rights: first, applying fundamental rights in a specific case before the ECJ, second, assessment by the ECJ of the compatibility of national law with fundamental rights, third, the question whether national fundamental rights are recognized, and, fourth, the protection of fundamental rights by different judicial systems.

A. The Application of Fundamental Rights to the Facts

In some preliminary ruling the ECJ has gone beyond mere interpretation of Community law and has explicitly applied the provisions construed to the facts in the main proceedings. Although this is a frequent occurrence and is not limited to cases dealing with fundamental rights, applying Community law to specific facts in preliminary proceedings is an unorthodox technique in the case law. Ordinarily, it is for the ECJ to give an abstract answer and for the referring national judge to progress the main proceedings in the light of the preliminary ruling. It is the national judge who must apply the provision as construed by the ECJ in the specific case. Orthodox drafting consistent with that case law is, for example: 'Article ... must be interpreted ... ' or 'Article ... is to be construed as meaning ... '.

---

[188] Griller, *supra* n. 12, 142, argues that Article 46(d) EUT may not be construed in a way to restrict the Court's competence; similarly, A. O'Neill, 'The Protection of Fundamental Rights in Scotland as a General Principle of Community Law—the case of *Booker Aquiculture*' E.H.R.L.R. (2000) 18 (25), doubts whether the Court will feel restricted by that provision; U. Wölker, 'Grundrechtsschutz durch den Gerichtshof der Europäischen Gemeinschaften und nationale Gerichte nach Amsterdam' EuR, Beiheft 1 (1999) 99 (111); Scheuing, *supra* n. 38, 178.
[189] Schaller, *supra* n. 48, 74 *et seq.*   [190] *Chen, supra* n. 85.

It should be noted that *Carpenter, Omega, Karner* and *Berlusconi*,[191] in which the ECJ applied Community law to the specific facts, are in sharp contrast to that orthodox approach. In some cases, the Court, moreover, left no margin of discretion to the referring judge. The ECJ did not use *formulæ* such as 'it is for the national court to assess whether, in the light of all the factual and legal evidence', as it did in *Steffensen* and in *Pupino*.[192] Such an approach would have been in line with the approach adopted in examining whether an interference is justified, as in the Austrian data protection cases.[193] For the sake of completeness, it should be pointed out that the opposite approach—delivering rather abstract judgments— may risk the development of divergent case law in the Member States.[194]

Criticism has been made of the adoption of a case-by-case approach, e.g. in *Schmidberger*,[195] and it has been argued that the scope of judgments is therefore unclear.[196] It is suggested here that the Court's approach, which is, in principle, correct, may be explained by two factors.

First, fundamental rights cases often require a proportionality assessment. This is especially true of the respect for private and family life, freedom of expression and freedom of assembly, enshrined in Articles 8, 10, and 11 of the ECHR respectively. In such cases, it must be ascertained whether the conditions of the second paragraph are fulfilled, i.e. whether the interference is necessary in a democratic society to achieve the legitimate aim pursued. As this depends on the specific circumstances, this requires a case-by-case assessment as performed by the ECtHR in Strasbourg. The second factor concerns the type of proceedings before the ECJ. Although preliminary rulings should be drafted in an abstract manner, the judgments are to a certain degree confined to the legal and factual situation in the main proceedings.

B. The Compatibility of National Law with Community Fundamental Rights

Recent case law also confirms the existence of another way of protecting fundamental rights. In some cases, the Court has gone a step further even in preliminary rulings and decided explicitly on the compatibility of a national measure.

---

[191] *Carpenter, supra* n. 4, para. 41; *Omega, supra* n. 2, paras. 39 *et seq.*; *Karner, supra* n. 8, para. 52; *Berlusconi, supra* n. 7, para. 78. The other options, which the ECJ had, are discussed by C. Smith and Th. Fetzer, 'The uncertain limits of the European Court of Justice's authority: Economic freedom versus human dignity' 10 Columbia Journal of European Law 445 (480 *et seq.*).

[192] *Steffensen, supra* n. 6, para. 78; *Pupino, supra* n. 6, para. 60.

[193] Joined Cases C-465/00, C-138/01 and C-139/01, *supra* n. 5, para. 88.

[194] Young, *supra* n. 37, 236. It has to be pointed out that this is true not even for all preliminary rulings. For positive aspects see Bulterman/H.R. Kranenborg, *supra* n. 186, 101.

[195] For such a criticism, see Kessler, *supra* n. 163, 753; Koch, *supra* n. 135, 599.

[196] Criticized by Brown, *supra* n. 174, 1509 *et seq.*; P. Cavicchi, 'Preambolo e disposizioni generali della Carta dei diritti: una riaffermazione della specificità dell'ordinamento comunitario' Riv. ital. di diritto pubblico comunitario XII (2002) 599 (613).

However, it should be noted that it was necessary to make such an assessment of compatibility. But as the ECJ held in *Steffensen*[197] and in the Austrian data protection cases,[198] it is for the national court to assess the compatibility of the national measure with Community fundamental rights.

Some recent judgments give good examples of cases in which the Court examined the compatibility of a national measure either with a provision of the Treaty, as in *Schmidberger* and *K.B.*,[199] or directly with the fundamental right, as in *Carpenter*, *Steffensen*, *Booker*, *RTL*, and *Karner*.[200]

In *Carpenter*, the ECJ came to the conclusion that 'the decision to deport Mrs Carpenter constitutes an infringement',[201] i.e. the Court did not leave the application of the proportionality test to the national court. That approach was taken again in *RTL*,[202] *Karner*[203] and *Omega*[204] and is in contrast to that taken in the Austrian data protection cases.[205] Some favour an approach whereby it is up to the national courts to define the precise content and standard of enforcement of fundamental rights.[206] Such an approach goes beyond the ECJ's method of setting the standard and leaving to the national judge merely its application to the specific facts. Above all, the above-mentioned approach would jeopardize the uniformity of Community law by resulting in case law which differs not only from Member State to Member State but from national court to court.

In some cases, the Court rules explicitly on the (in)compatibility of national law even in the operative part of the judgment. In *Booker*[207] that technique may be explained by the fact that the Court also had to examine the compatibility of Community measures which were similar to the national measures.[208] In *Schmidberger*, the ECJ did not limit itself to construing several Treaty provisions but explicitly stated that a specific measure 'is not incompatible' with those provisions.[209]

Whereas in the operative part of *Schmidberger*, the Court referred only to compatibility with Treaty provisions, the Court explicitly stated in *Booker* that the national law was not incompatible with fundamental rights as such. It has even been argued that in *Steffensen* the ECJ added a third principle to the principles of

---

[197] *Steffensen*, *supra* n. 6, para. 70.

[198] Joined Cases C-465/00, C-138/01 and C-139/01, *supra* n. 5, para. 91.

[199] *K.B.*, *supra* n. 10, para. 34.

[200] *Carpenter*, *supra* n. 4, para. 40; *Steffensen*, *supra* n. 6, para. 70; *Booker*, *supra* n. 3, para. 93; *RTL*, *supra* n. 8, para. 69, and *Karner*, *supra* n. 8, para. 49. On this issue, see R. Kanitz and Ph. Steinberg, 'Grenzenloses Gemeinschaftsrecht? Die Rechtsprechung des EuGH zu Grundfreiheiten, Unionsbürgerschaft und Grundrechten als Kompetenzproblem' EuR (2003) 1013 (1022 *et seq.*).

[201] *Carpenter*, *supra* n. 4, para. 45.   [202] *RTL*, *supra* n. 8, para. 72.

[203] *Karner*, *supra* n. 8, para. 52.   [204] *Omega*, *supra* n. 2, para. 40.

[205] Joined Cases C-465/00, C-138/01 and C-139/01, *supra* n. 5, para. 88.

[206] This idea is advocated by O'Neill, *supra* n. 188, 28. For a more traditional approach as regards the competence of national courts under Article 234 EC, see C. D. Classen, Comment on *Österreichischer Rundfunk* 41 CML Rev. 1377 (1384 *et seq.*).   [207] *Booker*, *supra* n. 3.

[208] That approach is criticized by O'Neill, *supra* n. 188, 28.

[209] *Schmidberger*, *supra* n. 9, para. 94.

equivalence and effective protection, namely the principle of compatibility with fundamental rights.[210]

C. The Recognition of Purely National Fundamental Rights

It is questionable whether the ECJ requires that fundamental rights are recognized by Community law. In *Schmidberger*, the Austrian authorities based their decision on freedom of expression and freedom of assembly enshrined in and guaranteed by the ECHR and the Austrian Constitution. Although the second question explicitly referred to 'national provisions on freedom of assembly', for the Court[211] as well as for its Advocate General[212] recognition by Community law was decisive.

The importance of rights being recognized by Community law is underlined by the Court's reference to 'fundamental rights the observance of which the Court ensures'.[213] As may be deduced from another part of *Schmidberger*,[214] and as confirmed in *Berlusconi*, the ECJ recognizes both the constitutional traditions common to the Member States and guidelines under international treaties as points of reference. As the ECJ requires something additional to mere national recognition, *Schmidberger* is not authority for the Court accepting of fundamental rights provided for only in national law.

Omega could be seen as going in a different direction, since the ECJ ruled that it 'is not indispensable in that respect for the restrictive measure issued by the authorities of a Member State to correspond to a conception shared by all Member States as regards the precise way in which the fundamental right or legitimate interest in question is to be protected.'[215] Further, in another part of the judgment the ECJ underlined the fact that 'the Community legal order undeniably strives to ensure respect for human dignity as a general principle of law. There can therefore be no doubt that the objective of protecting human dignity is compatible with Community law, it being immaterial in that respect that, in Germany, the principle of respect for human dignity has a particular status as an independent fundamental right.'[216] In essence, the ECJ qualified the protection of fundamental rights as 'a legitimate interest which, in principle, justifies a restriction of the obligations imposed by Community law, even under a fundamental freedom guaranteed by the Treaty such as the freedom to provide services.'[217] Thus, there was no further need to enter into a discussion about principles concerning

---

[210] Schaller, *supra* n. 33, 672, and Schaller, *supra* n. 68, 194.

[211] *Supra* n. 9, para. 73 (emphasis added).

[212] Opinion of AG Jacobs in *Schmidberger*, *supra* n. 9, para. 102.   [213] *Supra* n. 9, para. 75

[214] *Supra* n. 9, para. 71.

[215] *Supra* n. 9, para. 37. Skouris, *supra* n. 186, 41, underlines the recognition of national fundamental rights. The recognition of national fundamental rights as part of the public policy clause is criticized by Alemanno, *supra* n. 30, 737. See the positive evaluation by Bulterman/H.R. Kranenborg, *supra* n. 186, 97 *et seq.*

For a criticism of the concept of 'Human Dignity', see G. Chun, ' "Playing at Killing" Freedom of Movement' 33 LIEI (2006) 85 (91 *et seq.*).

[216] *Supra* n. 9, para. 34.   [217] *Supra* n. 9, para. 35.

recognition of national fundamental rights and to develop general conditions for protecting national fundamental rights. Nonetheless, it may be deduced from *Omega* that the Court recognizes national fundamental rights as a legitimate interest justifying restriction of fundamental freedoms.

D. Multiple Control of National Measures

Protection of fundamental rights against Member State infringements is ensured by three different legal systems, i.e. EU law, the ECHR, and national law.[218] Consequently, Member States are under the scrutiny of three different (categories) of courts.[219] First, the ECJ interprets fundamental rights in the field of Community law. Second, the ECtHR in Strasbourg oversees the compatibility of measures taken by the Member States. Third, national measures are, depending on the national legal order, subject to review by national courts which must guarantee the respect of fundamental rights. This *triumvirate* has been termed as a Bermuda triangle[220] in which the protection of fundamental rights disappears. It is submitted that in reality the opposite is the norm, with all the courts involved creating a safety net. Certainly, this requires more than peaceful co-existence, rather a fertile cooperation between the courts showing mutual respect,[221] which might even result in competition between them to the advantage of individuals seeking protection of fundamental rights.[222]

One point of criticism concerns adjudication under several legal systems. In this context, it should be recalled that the oversight of Community fundamental rights is the responsibility of all national authorities applying Community law. This is true even in Member States where the oversight of fundamental rights is conferred upon one single court, e.g. a Constitutional Court.

According to the 'double standard' principle, which is the norm in many Member States, national measures must be compatible with national as well as with Community fundamental rights.[223] National courts run into difficulties

---

[218] M. Holoubek, 'OGH, EMRK und Gemeinschaftsrecht' Zeitschrift für Verwaltung (1996) 28 (35), refers to three different courts.

[219] J. Bergmann, 'Diener dreier Herren?—Der Instanzrichter zwischen BVerfG, EuGH and EGMR', EuR (2006) 101.

S. Broß, 'Grundrechte und Grundwerte in Europa' 58 Juristenzeitung (2003) 429 (431); Korinek, *supra* n. 26, 1106 *et seq.*; Napoletano, *supra* n. 37, 714; Skouris, *supra* n. 186, 31; Suerbaum, *supra* n. 139, 408.

[220] C. Lenz, 'Comments on Matthews v United Kingdom, judgment of 18 February 1999' EuZW (1999) 308 (312).

[221] A. Berramdane, 'Les droits fondamentaux dans la Constitution européenne' Revue du Droit de l'Union Européenne (2003) 613 (638); Schwarze, *supra* n. 1, 3462 *et seq.*

[222] Cf. Schwarze, *supra* n. 1, 3460 *et seq.* ; S. Douglas-Scott, 'A tale of two Courts: Luxembourg, Strasbourg and the growing European human rights *Acquis*' 43 CMLRev. (2006) 629 (665).

[223] Korinek, *supra* n. 26, 1108 *et seq.*; Napoletano, *supra* n. 37, 720; Ranacher, *supra* n. 26, 78 *et seq.*; V Skouris, 'Zum Verhältnis nationaler und europäischer Grundrechte aus europäischer Sicht' in Soziale Grundrechte in der Europäischen Union (2001) 47 (54).

particularly where Strasbourg and Luxembourg apply different standards.[224] Some fear that the ECJ could exert pressure on the constitutional courts to apply its standards rather than enhancing cooperation, as it did in *Schmidberger*[225] and *Omega*.

Another criticism concerns an alleged difference between the different systems on substantive issues and on judicial protection.[226] In principle, different courts tend to apply different standards. Although the core of rules is identical, *viz.* the ECHR, each judicial system develops its own case law, which may produce differing standards. To minimize the risk of conflict, Luxembourg takes its cue from Strasbourg and regularly refers to the latter's case law.[227] Sometimes, it is Strasbourg which follows and reaches the same conclusion as the ECJ, as in *Krombach*.[228] Despite differing standards, it may well be Luxembourg which applies a standard more favourable to individuals, e.g. with regard to deportation.[229]

More attention should be given to the criticism that national courts may apply another standard to 'purely national' measures than that which is applied to measures implementing Community law.[230]

Comparing standards of judicial protection in the two systems does not see losing the contest. First, the ECJ can assess the compatibility of national measures with fundamental rights not only in infringement proceedings under Article 226 EC but even, albeit indirectly, in preliminary rulings. As all the cases under review clearly demonstrate, it is generally through preliminary rulings that the ECJ ensures fundamental rights are observed in the Member States.[231] Thus, the ECJ acts mainly at the behest of national courts in order to enhance judicial cooperation and not *ex officio* with the intention of intervening in legal disputes, let alone in conflicts of purely national law. Second, judicial protection under the Community framework is not *per se* less efficient than under the ECHR system: a case may be brought to Strasbourg only once national legal remedies have been exhausted.

It is worth mentioning the advantages of enforcement under Community law,[232] in particular the obligation of certain courts to refer to the ECJ. Using remedies under Community law for breaches of fundamental rights benefits

[224] Bergmann, *supra* n. 219, 111 *et seq.*); Young, *supra* n. 37, 227.

[225] Tridimas, *supra* n. 159, 139.

[226] See in general Schaller, *supra* n. 48, 114 *et seq.* and 138 *et seq.*; Schwarze, *supra* n. 1, 3461; for *Carpenter*, see H. Toner, 'Comments on *Carpenter* v. *Secretary of State*', European Journal of Migration and Law (2003) 163 (170 *et seq.*).

[227] Douglas-Scott, *supra* n. 222, 640 *et seq.*; Schwarze, *supra* n. 1, 3461; Young, *supra* n. 37, 232.

[228] *Krombach v France*, judgment of 13 February 2001.

[229] Dougan and Spaventa, *supra* n. 85, 711 and n. 51.

[230] Cf. Griller, *supra* n. 12, 166; T. Stein, ' "Gut gemeint": Bemerkungen zur Charta der Grundrechte der Europäischen Union' in *Tradition und Weltoffenheit des Rechts* (2002) 1425 (1435).

[231] Schwarze, *supra* n. 1, 3460.Suerbaum, *supra* n. 139, 415, in contrast, refers only to the infringement procedure.

[232] Due and Gulmann, *supra* n. 11, 421; Demetriou, *supra* n. 20, 493; Smith and Fetzer, *supra* n. 191, 465.

enforcement of Community law in general.[233] Other advantages are that Community fundamental rights enjoy supremacy and, depending on the relevant provision of Community law, direct effect.[234] In addition, the ECJ's rulings have direct effect.[235] Besides, including human rights in Community law gives greater legitimacy to the EU.[236]

Review by Luxembourg does not preclude individuals from taking their case to Strasbourg. Judicial protection in that court has its advantages, e.g. due to the generous *locus standi* for individuals and the possibility of applying for damages. Besides, the chances of success in the case itself may be greater. Finally, national courts, except for Constitutional courts, gain in their review powers as they are also required to apply Community fundamental rights, under the authority of the ECJ.[237]

V. Amendments by the 'Charter of Fundamental Rights' and the 'Treaty Establishing a Constitution for Europe'

Another recent development, concerns the incorporation of the 'Charter of Fundamental Rights' in the proposed 'Treaty establishing a Constitution for Europe' as Part Two. This gives rise to the question whether those amendments, if they enter into force, have an effect on the scope of fundamental rights or on the content of Member States' obligations.

The starting point in this context is Article II-111. The first sentence of Article II-111(1) reads as follows: 'The provisions of the Charter are addressed ... to the Member States only when they are implementing Union law.' As has rightly been pointed out, this provision refers explicitly only to 'implementation'[238] and replaces the traditional *formula* used by the Court,[239] leaving aside circumstances in which the ECJ recognizes the application of Community fundamental rights in the Member States, e.g. as a justifiable restriction of fundamental freedoms[240] or in circumstances akin to *Steffensen*.[241]

---

[233] Schaller, *supra* n. 48, 147.

[234] Napoletano, *supra* n. 37, 697, 713 and 719; Scheuing, *supra* n. 38, 180; Smith and Fetzer, *supra* n. 191, 465; Zampini, *supra* n. 83, 679.

[235] Demetriou, *supra* n. 20, 494; R. Lawson, 'Human Rights: The Best is Yet to Come' 1 European Constitutional Law Review (2005) 27 (34), points at the exhaustion of domestic remedies.

[236] Tridimas, *supra* n. 159, 135 *et seq.*; Young, *supra* n. 37, 238 *et seq.* For an opposite view, see A. Arnull, 'Protecting Fundamental Rights in Europe's New Constitutional Order' in T. Tridimas and P. Nebbia (eds.) *European Union Law for the Twenty-First Century* (2004) 95 (101).

[237] Napoletano, *supra* n. 37, 707; Weiler, *supra* n. 15, 124; Zampini, *supra* n. 83, 706 *et seq.*

[238] Eeckhout, *supra* n. 20, 977.

[239] C. Calliess, '§ 20 Die Europäische Grundrechts-Charta' in Ehlers and Becker, *Europäische Grundrechte und Grundfreiheiten*, 2nd Edition (2005) paras. 26 *et seq.*; C. Grabenwarter, 'Die Charta der Grundrechte für die Europäische Union' 116 Deutsches Verwaltungsblatt (2001) 1 (2); F. C. Mayer, 'La Charte européenne des droits fondamentaux et la Constitution européenne' RTDE (2003) 175 (186).   [240] Griller, *supra* n. 12, 139.

[241] Schaller, *supra* n. 33, 672.

It is widely accepted that the wording of that provision points towards restricting the field of application of fundamental rights.[242] Thus, it should be examined whether this interpretation tallies with alternative methods of interpretation and other parts of the Constitutional Treaty.

One widely recognized interpretation method is to analyse the intention of the authors of the Charter and its legislative history.[243] The texts which served as the basis for the final version were amended several times. In an early version, the applicability of fundamental rights was limited to cases in which the Member States had no jurisdiction.[244] In a later document, Member States were to apply fundamental rights wherever their actions fell within the field of Community law.[245] In essence, the legislative history supports an extensive approach.[246]

But regard should also be held to the 'Explanations' which are considered to be a valuable tool of interpretation.[247] There are the explanations of the Charter-Convention and the explanations of the Constitution-Convention.

The Final explanations of the Præsidium of the Convention that drafted the Charter[248] which referred to *Wachauf* and ERT favour a wide interpretation.[249] In the Explanations updated by the Præsidium of the European Convention[250] reference is made to *Annibaldi*[251] concerning a situation not falling within the scope of Community law, i.e. a case not fitting into one of the traditional categories. In addition, the explanations refer to *Karlsson*[252] where the Court follows a rather puzzling terminology using 'implementing' in a broad sense as in *Bostock*.[253] There, the Court had to deal with supplementing provisions, i.e. neither with the direct application of Community law nor with the transposition of directives, but, nonetheless, referred to *Wachauf* and, more surprisingly, to *ERT*. All these references in the Explanations point towards a broad interpretation.

---

[242] J.-P. Jacqué, 'La Charte des Droits Fondamentaux de l'Union Européenne: Aspects juridiques généraux' 14 ERPL No. 1 (2002) 107 (111); E. Vranes, 'Die Grundrechtscharta der Union: Grundsätzliche Fragen und sich abzeichnende Detailprobleme' in W. Mantl, S. Puntscher Rieckmann and M. Schweitzer (eds.), *Der Konvent zur Zukunft der Europäischen Union* (2004).

[243] St. Barriga, *Die Entstehung der Charta der Grundrechte der Europäischen Union* (2003) 61 and 151 *et seq.*; Schaller, *supra* n. 48, 213 *et seq.*   [244] CHARTE 4123/1/00 REV 1.

[245] CHARTE 4235/00.

[246] Ehlers, *supra* n. 146, para. 35; C. Grabenwarter, 'Auf dem Weg in die Grundrechtsgemeinschaft?' EuGRZ (2004) 563 (565 *et seq.*); Scheuing, *supra* n. 38, 183.

[247] Conversely, B. Bercusson, 'The Contribution of the EU Fundamental Rights Agency to the Realization of Workers' Rights' in Monitoring Fundamental Rights in the EU (2005) 189 (204), regards the Explanations as an inadequate instrument.   [248] CHARTE 4473/00 REV 1.

[249] See e.g. Griller, *supra* n. 12, at 139. For a different opinion see F. Turpin, *L'intégration de la Charte des droits fondamentaux dans la Constitution européenne* (2004) 615 (622).

[250] CONV 828/1/03 REV 1.

[251] Case C-309/96 *Daniele Annibaldi v Sindaco del Comune di Guidonia and Presidente Regione Lazio* [1997] ECR I-7493.

[252] Case C-292/97 *Kjell Karlsson and Others* [2002] ECR I-2737, para. 37.

[253] Case C-2/92 *The Queen v Ministry of Agriculture, Fisheries and Food, ex parte Dennis Clifford Bostock* [1994] ECR I-955, para. 16.

The legal value of these Explanations is defined in Article II-112(7) which states that the 'explanations ... shall be given due regard by the courts of the Union and of the Member States'.[254]

Moreover, the Explanations are referred to in the fifth paragraph of the Preamble to the Charter, i.e. to Part Two of the proposed Constitutional Treaty and in a 'Declaration for incorporation in the Final Act concerning the explanations relating to the Charter of Fundamental Rights' which reproduces the explanations cited above.[255] The relevant part of the Preamble reads as follows: '... the Charter will be interpreted ... with due regard to the explanations prepared under the authority of the Præsidium of the Convention that drafted the Charter and updated under the responsibility of the Præsidium of the European Convention'.

A comparison of Article II-112(7) and the Preamble reveals a slight difference. Whereas the Preamble states that 'the Charter *will be interpreted* by the courts of the Union and the Member States with due regard to the explanations', Article II-112(7) merely qualifies 'the explanations drawn up *as a way of providing guidance* in the interpretation of the Charter'.[256] This illustrates that the Preamble attaches a slightly higher degree of obligation to the explanations. As Article II-112 enjoys greater binding force than the Preamble, it outweighs an interpretation solely based on the latter.[257] For these reasons, the Explanations support an extensive interpretation of the scope of fundamental rights,[258] i.e. including at least derogations from fundamental freedoms.

In addition to those arguments, there are two other provisions in the proposed Constitutional Treaty which corroborate a wide interpretation.[259] First, Article I-9(3) which corresponds to Article 6(2) EUT states that 'Fundamental rights, as guaranteed by the European Convention for the Protection of Human Rights and Fundamental Freedoms and as they result from the constitutional traditions common to the Member States, shall constitute general principles of the Union's law'. Second, Article II-113 provides: 'Nothing in this Charter shall be interpreted as restricting ... human rights ... as recognised, ... , by Union law and ... by international agreements ... , including the European Convention for the Protection of Human Rights and Fundamental Freedoms, ... '.

In addition, a broad interpretation of Article II-111 is supported by a recital in the preamble of the Charter (Part Two) stating: 'This Charter reaffirms, ... , the rights as they result, ... from the case law of the Court of Justice ... '.

---

[254] On the legal value, see L. Burgorgue-Larsen, 'Ombres et lumières de la constitutionalisation de la Charte des droits fondamentaux de l'Union européenne' CDE (2004) 663 (671 *et seq.*).

[255] CIG 87/04.   [256] Emphasis added.

[257] This difference is made evident by Bercusson, *supra* n. 247, 204.

[258] R. Alonso García, 'Le clausole orizzontali della Carta dei diritti fondamentali dell'Unione Europea' Riv. ital. di diritto pubblico comunitario XII (2002) 1 (4); F. Benoît-Rohmer, 'Valeurs et droits fondamentaux dans la Constitution' 41 RTDE (2005) 261 (272); Besselink, *supra* n. 49, 76 *et seq.*; Griller, *supra* n. 12, 139; Jarass, *supra* n. 108, 40 *et seq.*; Ranacher, *supra* n. 26, 98; Scheuing, *supra* n. 38, 186; E. Vranes, 'Der Status der Grundrechtscharta der Europäischen Union' 124 Juristische Blätter (2002) 630 (635).   [259] See Mayer, *supra* n. 239, 186 *et seq.*

Furthermore, the long list of rights and principles as well as the enhanced Union citizenship support such a wide interpretation. These demonstrate that the IGC wanted to enhance fundamental rights.[260] For these reasons, the argument that explanations may not override the explicit wording of Article II-111(1)[261] fails.

As a result, a wide interpretation[262] should be maintained, i.e. that Article II-111 does not change the scope of fundamental rights with regard to Member States.[263] Thus, 'implementation' covers transposition, including the adoption of supplementing provisions, as well as direct and indirect application of Community law.[264]

Therefore, Article II-111 is not to be construed as a signal to the Court to reverse its case law.[265] The ECJ will continue to adopt an open-ended approach and to adjudicate on the basis of its existing case law, referring to general principles of law and internationally protected rights.[266] Even if the Constitutional Treaty is construed in a restrictive way, some commentators expect that the ECJ will not feel itself bound by such restrictions and will construe 'implementation' in a wide manner, in particular in view of Article IV-438 (4).[267] It is suggested that this provision is of no assistance here, as it is of a prospective nature merely stating that '[t]he case law of the Court of Justice … shall remain, mutatis mutandis, the source of interpretation of Union law' and referring in particular to 'the comparable provisions of the Constitution'. Consequently, that provision cannot 'entrench' old case law which refers to provisions of the Treaties in so far as those provisions have been amended.

---

[260] Alonso García, *supra* n. 258, 6 *et seq.*

[261] This argument is put forward by Kingreen, *supra* n. 41, para. 61. On a restrictive interpretation, see: M. Borowsky, in J. Meyer (ed.), *Kommentar zur Charta der Grundrechte der Europäischen Union* (2003) 570; Cremer, *supra* n. 59, 1455 *et seq.*; Th. Kingreen, 'Theorie und Dogmatik der Grundrechte im europäischen Verfassungsrecht' EuGRZ (2004) 570 (576).

[262] Eeckhout, *supra* n. 20, 993; A. Menéndez, 'Rights to solidarity: balancing solidarity and economic freedoms' in The chartering of Europe (2003) 179 (195).

[263] Griller, *supra* n. 12, 142; A. Williams, 'EU human rights policy and the Convention on the Future of Europe: a failure of design?' 28 E.L.Rev (2003) 794 (808).

[264] Borowsky, *supra* n. 261, 569 *et seq.*

[265] R. Barents, *Een grondwet voor Europa* (2005) paras. 1103 *et seq.*; Ehlers, *supra* n. 146, para. 35; Grabenwarter, *supra* n. 246, 565; M. Ruffert, 'Die künftige Rolle des EuGH im europäischen Grundrechtsschutzsystem' EuGRZ (2004) 466 (467 *et seq.*). Cf. Besselink, *supra* n. 49, 79, who qualifies Article II-51 (which corresponds to Article II-111) as such a signal.

[266] G. De Búrca, 'Fundamental rights and Citizenship' in De Witte, Ten Reflections on the Constitutional Treaty for Europe (2003) 11 (15); U. Haltern, *Europarecht* (2005) 460; in similar terms Mayer, *supra* n. 239, at 186.

[267] M. Cartabia, 'Articolo 51' in R. Bifalco, M. Cartabia and A. Celotto (eds.) *L'Europa dei diritti. Commento alla Carta dei diritti fondamentali dell'Unione* (2001) 349; S. Koukoulis-Spiliotopoulos, 'Which Charter of Fundamental Rights Was Incorporated in the Draft European Constitution?' REDP (2004) 295 (300 *et seq.*); R. Lawson, 'The Contribution of the Agency to the Implementation in the EU of International and European Human Rights Instruments' in Monitoring Fundamental Rights in the EU (2005) 229 (248); Napoletano, *supra* n. 37, 710; Ranacher, *supra* n. 26, 99; Scheuing, *supra* n. 38, 187, argues that there is room for a wide interpretation.

VI. Concluding Remarks

Protecting human rights constitutes an important factor in the development of a Political Union. This highlights the constitutional role played by the Court[268] and its role together with national courts as guarantor of individuals' rights.

This article has shown that the Court's case law extends into the legislative, administrative and judicial activities of Member States. In recent years, the ECJ has had to examine general as well as individual national measures. In addition, recent judgments show that fundamental rights are not confined to particular policies, but relate to various fields, i.e. state liability,[269] labour and social law,[270] advertising in connection with unfair competition and consumer protection,[271] public order,[272] aquaculture,[273] data protection,[274] food law,[275] immigration law, in particular that of the UK,[276] as well as civil[277] and criminal proceedings.[278]

Recent case law has shown further development rather than revolutionary change. Certainly, some rulings are irreconcilable or are regarded as aberrations, such as *Karner*. As this article has shown, the traditional approach to determine the scope of fundamental rights, i.e. the division into agency-type and ERT-type cases, does not cover all cases. This is confirmed by the case law under review in which the Court does not limit itself to those two categories.[279] This is especially true where the ECJ interprets a provision in the light of fundamental rights. Determining the scope of fundamental rights by referring to the 'Community link', to the EU competence or to specific articles of the Treaty, has, with the exception of Article 12 EC, proved to be inadequate. The most promising approach, therefore, consists in a single formula focusing on the scope of Community law as such. As we have also seen, fundamental rights may serve as a multifunctional instrument, not only in theory but also in practice. Frequently, the Court has recognized an obligation to construe provisions in the light of fundamental rights derived from Community law, EU law, in particular framework decisions, and even national law. Such a wide approach to interpretation is also adopted by the Court with regard to the level of transposition, including Member States' obligations under regulations and framework decisions. The Court also demands the respect of fundamental rights when the Member States apply

---

[268] Berramdane, *supra* n. 3, 636 *et seq.*; Dellis, *supra* n. 69, 284; Douglas-Scott, *supra* n. 222, 661; Tridimas, *supra* n. 159, 135 *et seq.*; Young, *supra* n. 37, 234 *et seq.*

[269] Case C-224/01 *Gerhard Köbler v Republic of Austria* [2003] ECR I-10239.

[270] *K.B., supra* n. 10.   [271] *Karner, supra* n. 8; *RTL, supra* n. 8.

[272] *Omega, supra* n. 2; *Schmidberger, supra* n. 9.   [273] *Booker, supra* n. 3.

[274] Joined Cases C-465/00, C-138/01 and C-139/01, *supra* n. 5; *Lindqvist, supra* n. 8.

[275] *Steffensen, supra* n. 6.

[276] *Akrich, supra* n. 4; Case C-413/99 *Baumbast and R v Secretary of State for the Home Department* [2002] ECR I-7091; *Carpenter, supra* n. 4.   [277] *Krombach, supra* n. 6.

[278] *Berlusconi, supra* n. 7; *Lindqvist, supra* n. 8; *Pupino, supra* n. 6; *Vajnai,* supra n. 55.

[279] Cf. Besselink, *supra* n. 49, 78.

national law, EU law, i.e. framework decisions, and Community law, especially provisions of primary law which have direct effect, so that the Court does not limit itself to derogations from fundamental freedoms. As far as the different functions of fundamental rights are concerned, the article has shown that the ECJ has not always applied the same test, using fundamental rights as a means of protecting individuals (subjective function of fundamental rights) or as an instrument to assess the compatibility of national measures (objective function). Nonetheless, even case law following the latter approach has effects on individuals. It has been shown that the Court recognizes negative as well as positive obligations. As to their legal source, reference should be made of ECJ's case law on fundamental freedoms and the case law of the ECtHR. With regard to positive obligations, the case law contains examples of three varieties: the protective role, providing institutional guarantees, and protecting rights to participate. Protecting fundamental rights illustrates that there are diverging interests at play, and a series of relationships between the parties involved which may include the Member State, two individuals with opposed interests, and the Community. This article has shown how the Court deals with horizontal cases and that it recognizes the indirect horizontal effect of fundamental rights. As far as the relationship of fundamental rights to fundamental freedoms is concerned, this article has outlined their main common characteristics, such as their legal value, the application of the principle of proportionality, and their role in protecting interests or values. It has been shown that where fundamental freedoms and fundamental rights are opposed, the Court gives both due consideration. In the case law, two different approaches, the Luxembourg and the Strasbourg approach, may be identified. These tests differ with respect to the standard of protection, the burden of proof, and the degree of discretion Member States enjoy. This article further has shown that fundamental rights may in some cases restrict Member States' competences, in others they may defend such competences. The Court takes its task of protecting human rights seriously. Thus, the ECJ has applied provisions to the specific facts of the case, effectively preventing national courts from coming to another conclusion, and has assessed the compatibility of national measures with fundamental rights in preliminary rulings. With regard to national fundamental rights, we have seen that the Court recognizes national fundamental rights as a legitimate interest. The article has provided a careful analysis of substantive as well as procedural differences between the judicial systems of the EU, the ECHR and national legal orders, and outlined the advantages of an additional judicial protection by Luxembourg not without pointing at the resistance that this development faces. One should not forget that Strasbourg requires that the EU protects human rights in a manner equivalent to the ECHR.[280] If a Member State does no more than implement requirements flowing from its membership, the presumption will be that it has

---

[280] See the judgment delivered by the ECtHR *Bosphorus v Ireland*, judgment of 30 June 2005, para. 155; Napoletano, *supra* n. 37, 713 *et seq.*; Scheuing, *supra* n. 38, 180; Skouris, *supra* n. 186, 37.

not departed from its obligations under the ECHR.[281] If the new model of governance materializes, the new Fundamental Rights Agency would supplement the Court's role in monitoring human rights, albeit in a different way.[282] Whereas the ECJ 'ensures a post hoc judicial protection',[283] the agency could operate ex ante[284] as well as ex post.[285] As the agency's remit will be limited, it is doubtful whether an individual complaints procedure should be provided for.[286] Finally, this article provides an analysis of Member States' obligations under the 'Charter of fundamental rights' and the 'Treaty establishing a Constitution for Europe'. As we have seen, it is unfortunate that the authors of the Charter and the Treaty opted for unclear wording, and that strong arguments favour a wide interpretation of the scope of fundamental rights with respect to national measures. In general, as one commentator has said, it is doubtful whether the Charter will help to develop a more structured and coherent theory of fundamental rights.[287] Recent case law suggests that the Court will continue to enhance protection of human rights even without the Constitutional Treaty and will remain the 'moteur d'intégration'.[288]

---

[281] *Bosphorus v Ireland*, judgment of 30 June 2005, para. 156.

[282] G. de Búrca, 'New Models of Governance and the Protection of Human Rights' in Monitoring Fundamental Rights in the EU (2005) 25 (31).

[283] O. De Schutter, 'Mainstreaming Human Rights in the European Union' in Monitoring Fundamental Rights in the EU (2005) 37 (40).   [284] De Schutter, *supra* n. 283, 44.

[285] Lawson, *supra* n. 267, 249; St. Peers, 'The Contribution of the EU Fundamental Rights Agency to Civil and Political Rights' in Monitoring Fundamental Rights in the EU (2005) 111 (126 *et seq.*).

[286] M. Nowak, 'The Agency and National institutions for the Promotion and Protection of Human Rights' in Monitoring Fundamental Rights in the EU (2005) 91 (100 *et seq.*)

[287] This development was expected by M. Poiares Maduro, 'The double constitutional life of the Charter of Fundamental Rights' in The chartering of Europe (2003) 199 (210 *et seq.*)

[288] On the risk for the future development of the case law, see Mayer, *supra* n. 239, 182 *et seq.*

EC Competition Law and the Right to a Fair Trial

Ólafur Jóhannes Einarsson *

I. Introduction

Article 6(1) ECHR[1] provides that, 'in the determination of his civil rights and obligations or of any criminal charge against him, everyone is entitled to a fair and public hearing within a reasonable time by an *independent and impartial tribunal* established by law' (emphasis added). Article 6(1) ECHR is a central provision of the Convention and the ECtHR has said that in a democratic society within the meaning of the Convention, the right to a fair administration of justice holds such a prominent place that a restrictive interpretation of Article 6(1) would not correspond to the aim and the purpose of that provision.[2]

The European Commission has a multi-faceted role in infringement proceedings in EC competition law, combining investigative, prosecutorial and adjudicative functions. The article will examine whether the procedure in EC competition law is in conformity with the requirement of Article 6(1) ECHR of a trial before an independent and impartial tribunal.

The first chapter of the article begins with a brief summary of the origins of fundamental rights in EU law and the influence of the ECHR on the ECJ's jurisprudence. Then the focus will turn to oft-mentioned conflicts in the case law of the ECtHR and the Community Courts, which closer examination shows are far from clear cut. Finally, responsibility for EU acts in Strasbourg will be briefly examined as well as the possible effects of the Charter of Fundamental Rights.

The next chapter will start by analysing the concept of *'criminal charge'* within the autonomous meaning of Article 6(1) ECHR, focusing in particular on the criteria employed by the ECtHR. Following that will be an account of the case law of the ECtHR that is of significance for the classification of the fines levied by the Commission under Article 23 of Regulation 1/2003. The jurisprudence of the Community Courts regarding this issue will also be examined.

---

* Officer, EFTA Surveillance Authority. This article is a revised version of the author's MPhil thesis written at the University of Oxford under the supervision of Professor Stephen Weatherill.
[1] The full title is Convention for the Protection of Human Rights and Fundamental Freedoms usually referred to as European Convention on Human Rights.
[2] *Delcourt v Belgium* (1970) 1 EHRR 355, para 25.

The third chapter examines the requirements of Article 6(1) ECHR to the effect that everyone is entitled to a trial before an independent and impartial tribunal established by law. After having analysed what constitutes a tribunal according to the Article and having had a brief look at independence and impartiality, the focus will turn to the main feature of the chapter: to what extent judicial review can cure breaches of Article 6(1) in case the primary decision-maker does not meet the requirements as regards independence and impartiality. Finally, it will be examined whether corporate entities enjoy the same right to a trial before an independent and impartial tribunal as natural persons.

The final and central chapter of the article focuses on judicial review of Commission decisions finding infringement of the competition rules of the Treaty. This is the key issue, as previous chapters will have established, because it is the extent of judicial review that determines whether competition proceedings are Convention compliant. First the roles of the CFI and the ECJ in judicial review of competition decisions will be briefly dealt with. Following that discussion will be an examination of the jurisprudence of the Community Courts regarding the question whether the procedure is in accordance with Article 6(1) ECHR. Attention will then turn to judicial review under Articles 229 and 230 EC. The extent of the review under each article will be examined in turn but review under both must satisfy the requirements of the ECHR.

II. EU and ECHR

A. Introduction

It hardly bears repetition to mention that the original Treaty of Rome contained no chapter on fundamental rights.[3] The ECJ initially resisted attempts to develop a doctrine of fundamental rights; however, it soon changed its tune, at least partially in order to stave off a threat to the supremacy of Community law. *Internationale Handelsgesellschaft*[4] is perhaps the most note-worthy example of this early case law regarding fundamental rights.[5] There the ECJ stated that respect for fundamental rights formed an integral part of the general principles of law protected by the Court of Justice. The protection of such rights, whilst inspired by the constitutional traditions common to the Member States, must be ensured within the framework of the structure and objectives of the

---

[3] The terms fundamental rights and human rights will be used interchangeably in the article. On the terminology in EC law: B de Witte 'The Past and Future Role of the European Court of Justice in the Protection of Human Rights' in P Alston (ed) *The EU and Human Rights* (OUP Oxford 1999) 859, 860–861.

[4] Case 11/70 *Internationale Handelsgesellschaft GmbH v Einfuhr and Vorratsstelle für Getreide und Futtermittel* [1970] ECR 1125.

[5] For a good overview of these early cases see eg: S Douglas-Scott *Constitutional Law of the European Union* (Longman Harlow 2002) 437–441.

Community.[6] Along with the common constitutional traditions the ECJ soon recognized that international treaties for the protection of human rights of which the Member States were signatories, also constituted a source for protection of human rights within the Community. The first explicit reference to the ECHR was made in *Rutili*.[7]

Under the ECJ's case law fundamental rights form a part of what is called the general principles of Community law. Tridimas uses the term fundamental principles to signify both principles which derive from the rule of law and systematic principles which underlie the constitutional structure of the Community.[8] As regards the first category Tridimas considers those principles to have constitutional status and states that a measure, legislative or administrative, which infringes them, is illegal and might by annulled by the Community Courts.[9] Douglas-Scott is less unequivocal about the status of the principles and poses the question how the principles operate within the EC; as binding rules or something vaguer. The protection of rights can differ depending on the answer and according to her the ECJ has, unfortunately, given no clear indications on this issue.[10]

When referring to fundamental rights as general principles of law, the Community Courts have by now adopted a fairly standard formula which is almost invariably cited. As an example of the formula the following citation from *ERT*[11] can be given:

> [. . .], it must first be pointed out that, as the Court has consistently held, fundamental rights form an integral part of the general principles of law, the observance of which it ensures. For that purpose the Court draws inspiration from the constitutional traditions common to the Member States and from the guidelines supplied by international treaties for the protection of human rights on which the Member States have collaborated or of which they are signatories (see, in particular, the judgment in Case C-4/73 Nold v Commission [1974] ECR 491, paragraph 13). *The European Convention on Human Rights has special significance in that respect* (see in particular Case C-222/84 Johnston v Chief Constable of the Royal Ulster Constabulary [1986] ECR 1651, paragraph 18). It follows that, as the Court held in its judgment in Case C-5/88 Wachauf v Federal Republic of Germany [1989] ECR 2609, paragraph 19, *the Community cannot accept measures which are incompatible with observance of the human rights thus recognized and guaranteed.* (emphasis added)

As noted by the Council of Europe observers[12]: 'Applying the ECHR "as general principles of Community law" must probably be distinguished from applying it

---

[6] Case 11/70 *Internationale Handelsgesellschaft GmbH v Einfuhr and Vorratsstelle für Getreide und Futtermittel* [1970] ECR 1125, para 4.

[7] Case 36/75 *Roland Rutili v Ministre de l'intérieur* [1975] ECR 1219, para 32; P Craig and G de Búrca *EU Law Text, Cases, and Materials* (3rd edn OUP Oxford 2003) 323–327.

[8] T Tridimas *The General Principles of EC Law* (2nd edn OUP Oxford 2006) 4.   [9] *Ibid.*, 6.

[10] S Douglas-Scott *Constitutional Law of the European Union* (Longman Harlow 2002) 452.

[11] Case C-260/89 *Elliniki Radiophonia Tileorassi AE and others v Dimotiki Etairia Pliroforissis and others* [1991] ECR-I 2925, para 41.

[12] Attending the proceedings where the Charter of Fundamental Rights was being drafted.

per se; otherwise the question would arise why the substantive provisions of the ECHR had not already been integrated as such into the Treaties.'[13] This question of the status of fundamental rights as general principles of Community law is obviously significant. The answer given to it, *inter alia*, has impact on the importance one attaches to the inclusion of the Charter of Fundamental Rights in the Constitutional Treaty.[14] For the purposes of this article it is; however, not necessary to reach a definite conclusion on the issue. The case law of the Community Courts has made it clear that measures infringing the general principles of law can be annulled.[15] Another issue is whether using the ECHR as a source for the general principles of Community law results in an equivalent standard of human rights protection. Potential conflicts in the case law within the field of competition law will be briefly analysed here below.

From the outset it should be noted that the case law of the Community Courts shows that a mere reference to their standard formula does not tell the whole story. The application of the Convention and the case law of the ECtHR has differed, as the following examples demonstrate. In *Orkem*,[16] discussed below, the ECJ stated that Article 6 ECHR may be relied upon by an undertaking subject to an investigation relating to competition law. In *Emesa Sugar*[17] regarding the question whether the fact that the parties were not permitted to respond to the opinion of the AG constituted an infringement of Article 6(1) ECHR, the ECJ was at pains in distinguishing the case from the ECtHR judgment in *Vermeulen*.[18] In *Baustahlgewebe*[19] the ECJ cited cases from the ECtHR and used the criteria derived from them when evaluating whether the procedure before the CFI had been conducted within a reasonable time in accordance with the requirements of Article 6(1) ECHR. The CFI did the same in *SCK*[20] where the Court was examining the duration of the procedure before the Commission. By contrast, in *Mannesmannröhren*[21] the CFI disregarded ECtHR cases regarding the privilege against self-incrimination, neither applying them nor trying to distinguish them even though they were specifically mentioned in the pleadings of the applicant.

---

[13] Here cited after: S Douglas-Scott *Constitutional Law of the European Union* (Longman Harlow 2002) 453.

[14] At the time of writing it is unclear whether the Treaty will ever enter into force.

[15] For an, admittedly rare, example of legislation being (partially) struck down: Cases C-364/95 and C-365/95 *Firma T. Port GmbH v Hauptzollamt Hamburg Jonas* [1998] ECR I-1023. Case T-30/91 *Solvay v Commission* [1995] ECR II-1775 is a good example of an administrative measure being annulled. There the CFI struck down a decision because the Commission had infringed the general principle of equality of arms.

[16] Case 374/87 *Orkem SA v Commission* [1989] ECR 3283, para 30.

[17] Case C-17/98 *Emesa Sugar (Free Zone) NV v Aruba* [2000] ECR I-665, paras 13–17.

[18] *Vermeulen v Belgium* (2001) 32 EHRR 15; there is a difference of opinion as to whether the distinguishing made was convincing: Lord Goldsmith 'Charter of Rights' (2001) 38 CML Rev 1201, 1206.

[19] Case C-185/95P *Baustahlgewebe GmbH v Commission* [1998] ECR I-8417, para 29.

[20] Cases T-213/95 and T-18/96 *Stichting Certificatie Kraanverhuurbedrijf and others v Commission* [1997] ECR II-1739, para 57.

[21] Case T-112/98 *Mannesmannröhren Werke AG v Commission* [2001] ECR-II 729.

Looking at these examples, it is perhaps not surprising that Toth has termed the lack of clarity as to whether the Community Courts consider themselves bound by the interpretation of the ECtHR as one the of major drawbacks of the present status of the Convention in Community law.[22] In this context it might also be noted that the Community Courts have been inconsistent when it comes to applying standards on the limitation of rights. Sometimes the test as laid down by the ECHR is applied, whereas, in other cases a more specific EC standard is used.[23]

Finally, it is worth recalling that the ECJ received political approval for its activity in the sphere of human rights with the joint declaration on fundamental rights by the European Parliament, the Council and the Commission of 5 April 1977.[24] The declaration stated that the institutions stressed the prime importance they attached to the protection of fundamental rights, as derived from the sources mentioned above. Furthermore, it was stated that in the exercise of their powers and in pursuance of the aims of the European Communities they respected and would continue to respect these rights. Proper approval by way of Treaty amendments came with Article 6(2) (ex Article F(2)) of the TEU. The Article provided that the Union should respect fundamental rights as guaranteed by the ECHR and as they resulted from common constitutional traditions as general principles of Community law. The Amsterdam Treaty also added Article 49 TEU which requires that applicant states respect the principles contained in Article 6(1) TEU. This effectively means that being a signatory to the ECHR is a prerequisite for joining the Union.[25] It should be mentioned that all the Member States have signed up to the ECHR and recognized the right of individuals to submit applications to the ECtHR.[26] The Member States are therefore, unlike the EU itself, subject to external control by the ECtHR for their compliance with the rights protected under the ECHR.

B. Potential Conflicts in the Case Law

Two issues related to the enforcement of Community competition law are often cited as examples of diverging standards of human rights protection offered by the ECtHR on the one hand and the ECJ on the other. They are the right to silence as protected by Article 6 ECHR and the applicability of the right to privacy under

---

[22] AG Toth 'Human Rights as General Principles of Law, Past and Future' in U Bernitz and J Nergelius (eds) *General Principles of European Community Law* (Kluwer Law International The Hague 2000) 73, 82.

[23] S Peers 'Taking Rights Away? Limitations and Derogations' in S Peers and A Ward (eds) *The European Union Charter of Fundamental Rights* (Hart Publishing Oxford 2004) 141, 149–152.

[24] [1977] OJ C 103/1.

[25] H Schermers and DF Waelbroeck *Judicial Protection in the European Union* (6th edn Kluwer Law International The Hague 2001) 312.

[26] K Lenaerts and P van Nuffel R Brady (ed) *Constitutional Law of the European Union* (2nd edn Sweet and Maxwell London 2005) 25–26.

Article 8 ECHR to business premises and business activities.[27] Both these topics are complicated and worthy of a detailed discussion in their own right. The purpose here is merely to emphasize that things are perhaps not quite as straightforward as they might seem.

Scope of the Right to Privacy

In *Höchst*[28] which concerned dawn raids conducted by the Commission, the ECJ, at the time not guided by any precedents from the ECtHR, said that the right to privacy under Article 8 ECHR did not extend to business premises. The Court; however, recognized the protection against arbitrary and disproportionate intervention as a general principle of Community law. In the instant case the ECJ considered that the principle had been complied with.

The ECtHR reached the opposite conclusion on the scope of Article 8 ECHR in *Niemietz*.[29] The Court held that to interpret the words '*private life*' and '*home*' as including certain professional or business activities or premises would be consonant with the essential object and purpose of Article 8, namely to protect the individual against arbitrary interference by the public authorities. The Court; however, left open the possibility of paragraph 2 of the Article permitting interference with the right to a greater extent when involving business activities.

Comparing the scope of protection under the general principle outlined by the ECJ with the interpretation of the ECtHR in *Niemietz*, Lawson submits that it is at least doubtful that the former one meets the standards applied by the ECtHR.[30] A recent judgment of the ECtHR *Stés Colas*[31] has cast further doubts on whether the principle is compatible with the protection offered under the Convention. The case concerned a dawn raid conducted by the French competition authority and the ECtHR found that there had been an infringement of Article 8 ECHR. In reaching that conclusion the Court noted, *inter alia*, that the inspections took place without any prior warrant being issued by a judge and without a senior police officer being present.[32] Community law does not require the Commission

---

[27] See eg: S Douglas-Scott *Constitutional Law of the European Union* (Longman Harlow 2002) 467; AG Toth 'Human Rights as General Principles of Law, Past and Future' in U Bernitz and J Nergelius (eds) *General Principles of European Community Law* (Kluwer Law International The Hague 2000) 73, 82.

[28] Cases 46/87 and 227/88 *Höchst AG v Commission* [1989] ECR 2859, paras 18–19.

[29] *Niemietz v Germany* Series A No 251 (1993) 16 EHRR 97, paras 30–31. It is worth adding that recent case law of the ECJ regarding Article 8 ECHR has added another twist in the tale. In *Carpenter* (Case C-60/00 *Carpenter v Secretary of State for the Home Department* [2002] ECR I-6279) the ECJ, albeit implicitly, went beyond the jurisprudence of the ECtHR by holding that the Article prevented the deportation of an illegally resident spouse. For a critical appraisal of this case: P Oliver and WH Roth 'The Internal Market and the Four Freedoms' (2004) 41 CML Rev 407, 432–433.

[30] R Lawson 'Confusion and Conflict? Diverging Interpretations of the European Convention on Human Rights in Strasbourg and Luxembourg' in R Lawson and M de Blois (eds) *The Dynamics of the Protection of Human Rights in Europe Essays in Honour of Henry G Schermers Volume* III (Martinus Nijhoff Publishers Dordrecht 1994) 219, 244–247.

[31] *Stés Colas Est and others v France* Application 37971/97 judgment of 16 April 2002.

[32] *Ibid.*, para 49.

to obtain a judicial warrant before conducting an inspection. In the event of an inspection carried out with the assistance of national authorities, the relevant national procedural requirement must be complied with. Commenting on this in *Höchst* the ECJ remarked that the national body could not substitute its own assessment of the need for the investigations ordered for that of the Commission. The lawfulness of whose assessment of fact and law is subject only to review by the Court. On the other hand it fell to the national body to consider whether the measure was excessive or arbitrary having regard to the subject-matter of the investigation and ensure compliance with national law.[33]

In *Roquette Frères*,[34] an Article 234 reference from the *Cour de Cassation* in France, the ECJ was effectively asked to overrule *Höchst*, in particular as regards the limited power given to national courts ruling on whether a search warrant should be granted. Significantly the ECJ was willing to depart from *Höchst* saying that, in determining the scope of protection offered to business premises under the principle of protection against arbitrary or disproportionate intervention, regard must be had to the case law of the ECtHR subsequent to *Höchst*. In that respect the Court cited the two above-mentioned judgments of ECtHR, *Niemietz* and *Ste Colas*.[35] Despite that the ECJ essentially confirmed the division of powers between the national and the Community Courts; however, greater requirements were placed on the Commission to provide the national courts with evidence and reasons for the request. Furthermore, the Court elaborated on the competence of the national body when ruling on whether to grant a warrant.[36]

Despite these refinements to *Höchst* and the willingness to recognize the evolution in the jurisprudence of the ECtHR, the standard of protection applied by the ECJ is still open to criticism. As was outlined above, the ECtHR required a prior judicial warrant without the limitations placed on the national court by the ECJ, and the presence of a police officer. On the other hand allowing the national court to examine the decision substantively would in effect give it the power to rule on the validity of a Commission decision ordering an investigation. That would be contrary to the principle established by the ECJ in *Foto-Frost* that only the Community Courts may annul a measure of the Community institutions. Underlying that finding is of course the fundamental issue of the supremacy of Community law. In *Foto-Frost* the Court, *inter alia*, remarked that: 'since Article 173 [230] gives the court the exclusive jurisdiction to declare void an act of a community institution, the coherence of the system requires that where the validity of a community act is challenged before a national court the power to declare the act

---

[33] Cases 46/87 and 227/88 *Höchst AG v Commission* [1989] ECR 2859, para 35.

[34] Case C-94/00 *Roquette Frères v Directeur général de la concurrence, de la consommation et de la répression des fraudes* [2002] ECR I-9011. [35] *Ibid.*, para 29.

[36] *Ibid.*, paras 54–94. M Lienemeyer and D Waelbroeck 'Annotation on case: Roquette Freres SA v Directeur General de la Concurrence de la Consommation et de la Repression des Fraudes' (2003) 40 CML Rev 1481, 1485–1491. The judgment had an effect on the wording of Article 20(8) of Regulation 1/2003, *Ibid.*, 1493–1494.

invalid must also be reserved to the Court of Justice.'[37] This problem could be side-stepped by granting the Community Courts the power to grant a prior judicial authorization for inspections carried out by the Commission. Giving the Community Courts such powers would require legislation.[38]

The Right to Silence

Turning to the issue of the right to silence, the ECJ denied in *Orkem* that Article 6 ECHR conferred a privilege against self-incrimination but held that the Commission may not compel an undertaking to provide it with answers which might involve an admission on its part of the existence of an infringement which is incumbent on the Commission to prove.[39] This principle has been reaffirmed several times by the Community Courts with *Mannesmannröhren* providing the most detailed treatment.[40] There is a consensus that the protection offered by the Orkem principle is limited and in practice merely hinders the Commission from asking leading questions.[41]

The ECtHR on the other hand concluded in *Funke*[42] that a right to silence was implicit in the fair trial guarantees of Article 6 ECHR. Admittedly, the judgment is rather opaque on the rationale behind the right and the extent of it according to the Strasbourg case law is not quite clear. *Funke* appeared to be in part overruled by *Saunders*.[43] Later developments in the Court's jurisprudence; however, suggest a shift back to the position adopted in *Funke*; cf eg *JB v Switzerland*.[44] In any event

---

[37] Case 314/85 *Foto-Frost v Hauptzollamt Lübeck-Ost* [1987] ECR 4199, paras 16–20.

[38] Opinion of AG Mischo in *Höchst*: Cases 46/87 and 227/88 *Höchst AG v Commission* [1989] ECR 2859, paras 146–147.

[39] Case 374/87 *Orkem SA v Commission* [1989] ECR 3283, para 35; K Dekeyser and C Gauer 'The New Enforcement System for Articles 81 and 82 and the Rights of Defence' in BE Hawk (ed) *Annual Proceedings of the Fordham Corporate Law Institute* (Juris Publishing Inc New York 2005) 549, 558–559.

[40] Case T-112/98 *Mannesmannröhren Werke AG v Commission* [2001] ECR II-729, paras 59–79. See also: Cases C-238/99P, C-244/99P, C-245/99P, C-247/99P, C-250/99P-C-252/99P, C-254/99P, *Limburgse Vinyl Maatschappij and others v Commission* [2002] ECR I-8375, paras 273–280; Cases T-236/01, T-239/01, T-244-246/01, T-251/01 and T-252/01 *Tokai Carbon Co Ltd and others v Commission* [2004] ECR II-1181, paras 401–406. It should be noted that the application of the principle in the last judgment might be regarded as differing somewhat from the previous case law, analysis of that; however, falls outside the scope of the discussion here: CS Kerse and N Kahn *EC Antitrust Procedure* (5th edn Sweet and Maxwell London 2005) 142–143; B Vesterdorf 'Legal Professional Privilege and the Privilege against Self-incrimination in EC Law: Recent Developments and Current Issues in BE Hawk (ed) *Annual Proceedings of the Fordham Corporate Law Institute* (Juris Publishing Inc New York 2005) 701, 717–718. On appeal the ECJ concluded that the findings of the CFI were vitiated by an error of law. Consequently, it appears that the Orkem principle is alive and well: Case C-301/04P *Commission v SGL Carbon* [2006] ECR I-5915 paras 38–50.

[41] CS Kerse and N Kahn *EC Antitrust Procedure* (5th edn Sweet and Maxwell London 2005) 139.

[42] *Funke and others v France* Series A No 256-A (1993) 16 EHRR 297, para 44.

[43] *Saunders v United Kingdom* (1997) 23 EHRR 313.

[44] *JB v Switzerland* Application 31827/96 judgment of 3 May 2001. For an attempt to reconcile the case law of the ECtHR: T Ward and P Gardner 'The Privilege Against Self-Incrimination: In Search of Legal Certainty' [2003] Eur Human Rights L Rev 388, 394–398.

it has been maintained that the protection offered under Article 6 ECHR is more extensive than according to the Orkem principle irrespectively of whether *Saunders or Funke* is applied.[45]

Here it is submitted that those assertions are correct, if it is accepted that the privilege against self-incrimination as established by the ECtHR applies equally to natural and legal persons. As will be discussed in chapter IV it is clear that legal entities, in general, may avail themselves of the protection of Article 6 ECHR. However, with regard to the right to silence things are by no means clear and all the judgments of the ECtHR relating to the right to silence have so far been concerned with the rights of individuals. The only observations from Strasbourg on the issue can be found in an admissibility decision of the now defunct European Commission of Human Rights. There the Commission recalled that some of the applicants were companies which in their own legal capacity were found guilty of the charges brought against them. Then the Commission stated: '*the question arises therefore whether or to what extent these companies can incriminate themselves through statements made by their employees.*'[46] The application was considered inadmissible and it is very difficult to draw any conclusion as regards the scope of the privilege from it.

The reason for doubting whether the right to silence is the same in relation to undertakings lies in the rationale underlying the right. The ECtHR did not elaborate on it in *Funke* but stated in *Saunders*: 'the right not to incriminate oneself, in particular, presupposes that the prosecution in a criminal case seek to prove their case against the accused without resort to evidence obtained *through methods of coercion or oppression in defiance of the will of the accused.*' (emphasis added).[47] The Court also added that the right did not extend to materials obtained through the use of compulsory powers which have an existence independent of the will of the suspect.[48] It has been maintained that these arguments underpinning the right to silence are less relevant when dealing with the rights of corporation.[49] In light of the case law of the ECtHR on the protection of legal persons, which will be briefly elaborated on below, it has to be considered rather unlikely that the Court will adopt the same attitude as the US Supreme Court, which rejected that corporations could rely on the privilege

---

[45] PR Willis ' "You have the Right to Remain Silent [. . .]", Or do You? The Privilege against Self-incrimination Following Mannesmannröhren-Werke and Other Recent Decisions' (2001) 22 ECLR 313, 314–317; A Riley 'Saunders and the power to obtain information in Community and United Kingdom competition law' 25 ELR 264, 275–277.

[46] *Peterson Sarpsborg AS and others v Norway* Application 25944/94 decision of 27 November 1996.

[47] *Saunders v United Kingdom* (1997) 23 EHRR 313, para 68. The Court's use of this term has been inconsistent: A Ashworth 'Commentary on JB v Switzerland' [2001] Crim LR 749, 750.

[48] *Ibid.*, para 69.

[49] Janet Dine 'Criminal Law and the Privilege Against Self-Incrimination' in S Peers and A Ward (eds) *The EU Charter of Fundamental Rights* (Hart Publishing Oxford 2004) 269, 276–286.

against self-incrimination.[50] On the other hand it must be considered quite plausible that the extent of the protection offered to corporations would be more limited in scope. That would be in line with the jurisprudence of the ECtHR in other areas, eg with regard to Article 8 of the Convention as outlined above. As another example it might be mentioned that greater limitations are permitted to the commercial freedom of expression than to expressions related to items of general interest.[51]

C. Responsibility for EU Acts in Strasbourg

As will be mentioned below, it is stated in the Constitutional Treaty that the Union shall accede to the ECHR. Even if the Community were not to accede to the ECHR it does not follow, that it is thereby excluded that Community acts could come under scrutiny before the ECtHR, though presently applications cannot be lodged against the EU itself. Some decisions of the European Commission of Human Rights have dealt with the compatibility of the signatories of the Convention transferring power to inter/supranational organizations. In *M & Co v Germany*[52] the Commission said that the transfer of powers to an international organization is not incompatible with the Convention provided that within that organization fundamental rights will receive an equivalent protection. The Commission noted the joint declaration of the Parliament, Council and Commission mentioned above. Furthermore, it was stated that the ECJ had developed case law according to which it was called upon to control Community acts on the basis of fundamental rights, including those enshrined in the Convention. With specific reference to the complaint the Commission noted that the ECJ had recognized the right to a fair hearing as a fundamental principle of Community law.[53] The review of compatibility of fundamental rights protection conducted in this case is fairly superficial and in general terms without any in-depth analysis of the content of the right.

---

[50] *Hale v Henkel* 201 US 43 (1906). AG Geelhoed in his opinion in *SGL Carbon* drew attention to the state of the law in the US: Case C-301/04P *Commission v SGL Carbon* opinion of AG Geelhoed [2006] ECR I-5915, para 63.

[51] *Casado Coca v Spain*, (1994) 18 EHRR 1, paras 50–51; N Holst-Christensen and others *Den Europæiske Menneskerettighedskonvention Artikel 1–10 med kommentarer* (2nd edn Jurist—og Økonomforbundets Forlag København 2003) 474-476. For a difference of opinion on the extent of the right to silence as regards corporations: BE Hawk (ed) *Annual Proceedings of the Fordham Corporate Law Institute* (Juris Publishing Inc New York 2005) 756–758.

[52] *M & Co v Germany* Application 13284/87 (1990) 64 DR 138. The case concerned the compliance of competition procedures with Article 6 ECHR and the applicant was one of the firms fined in *Pioneer*, Cases 100–103/80 *Musique Diffusion Française SA and others v Commission* [1983] ECR 1825.

[53] For an overview of these decisions of the European Commission of Human Rights and the criticism they received: R Harmsen 'National Responsibility for European Community Acts Under the European Convention on Human Rights: Recasting the Accession Debate' (2001) 7 Eur Public L 625, 628–632.

The ECtHR gave a signal of stricter scrutiny in *Cantoni*[54] holding it irrelevant with regard to state responsibility under the Convention that the legal provision in question was an implementation of Community legislation. That conclusion was far from surprising but a more interesting development followed with *Matthews*.[55] There the ECtHR held that the exclusion of Gibraltar from European Parliament election by virtue of a provision enjoying Treaty status in the EU was an infringement of Article 3 of Protocol 1 to the Convention (right to free election) and, more importantly, that the UK was liable for the violation.

It had been anticipated that further elaboration on responsibility for EU acts would be forthcoming when the ECtHR would pronounce judgment on the application of Senator Lines against the EU Member States. However, that did not turn out to be the case.[56] The application was also of particular interest for the purposes of this article. The applicant alleged that an enforcement of a Commission decision imposing a fine for infringing the competition rules would lead to a winding-up of the firm before the company could have its case heard by a court. The applicant claimed this infringed his right to the presumption of innocence and right to a judicial recourse, cf Article 6(2) and Article 6(1) ECHR. However, before the ECtHR decided the case, the CFI partially annulled the Commission decision and quashed the fine.[57] In light of that the ECtHR reached the conclusion that the company could not claim to be a victim of a violation in the meaning of Article 34 ECHR. The Court therefore declared the application inadmissible and did not rule on the merits of the case.[58]

In *Bosphorus*[59] the applicant company alleged that the impounding of an aircraft infringed the company's right to property according to Article 1 of Protocol 1 to the Convention. The statutory basis relied on by the Irish government was an EC Regulation and the ECtHR concluded that the Irish Government had no discretion when complying with its obligations under EC law.[60] The Court held that action pursuant to such an obligation was justified, provided that the organization protected fundamental rights, both as regards substantive guarantees and the mechanism controlling their observance, in a manner at least equivalent of the Convention. If those conditions are satisfied there exists a presumption that the Convention has been complied with, which may be rebutted on a case-by-case basis if it is considered that the protection of Convention rights was manifestly deficient.[61] Several judges delivered concurring opinions, criticizing the abstract

[54] *Cantoni v France* Application 17862/91 judgment of 15 November 1996 (Reports 1996 V-20 1614), para 30.
[55] *Matthews v United Kingdom* (1999) 28 EHRR 361, especially paras 33–35.
[56] The application can be found in: Human Rights Law Journal (2000) 18, 112.
[57] Cases T-191/98 and T-212-214/98 *Atlantic Container Line and others v Commission* [2003] ECR II-3275.
[58] *Senator Lines GmbH v Austria and others* Application 56672/2000 decision of 10 March 2004.
[59] *Bosphorus Hava Yollari Turizm ve Ticaret AS v Ireland* Application 45036/98 judgment of 30 June 2005.   [60] *Ibid.*, para 148.
[61] *Ibid.*, para 155–156.

analysis of fundamental rights protection in the EU undertaken by the majority, yet noting that the judgment left the approach applied in *M & Co* far behind.[62]

D. Possible Effects of the Constitutional Treaty

Before signing off on this chapter of the article, a few words on the Constitutional Treaty and its possible effects, one first comes across paragraph 2 of Article I-9 of where it is stated that the Union shall accede to ECHR. Were an accession to take place it would strengthen the credibility of the Union in the field of human rights as it would just as the Member States be subject to the supervision of the ECtHR.[63] In the event of accession, potential conflicts in the case law should also cease to be of any significance as those who consider the standard of protection as applied by the Community Courts to fall beneath the Convention minimum could take their case to the ECtHR. There are other provisions of interest to the relationship between the EU and the ECHR: Articles 52(3) and 53. However, in light of the uncertain situation regarding the Treaty they will not be examined in this article.

E. Summary

Summing up this brief overview of the relationship between the EU and ECHR it may clearly be stated that the ECHR has had a major influence on the protection of fundamental rights in the EU. There is still some uncertainty as regards the status of fundamental rights as general principles of EU law and potential conflicts may possibly be identified between the Community Courts' case law and that of the ECtHR; however, the influence of the Convention is increasingly pervasive in Community law.[64] The remainder of this article is based on the premises that the EU is bound to observe at least the same standard of protection of human rights as secured by the ECHR.

III. Article 6 ECHR and Fines Under Regulation 1/2003

A. Introduction

When deciding whether a penalty is considered criminal under Article 6(1) of the Convention, the ECtHR usually applies the following three criteria: (a) the domestic classification, (b) the nature of the offence, and (c) the severity of the

---

[62] See eg para 1 of the concurring opinion of Judge Ress.

[63] Hans Christian Krüger 'The European Union of Fundamental Rights' in S Peers and A Ward (eds) *The European Union Charter of Fundamental Rights* (Hart Publishing Oxford 2004) xvii, xxv.

[64] B Vesterdorf 'Legal Professional Privilege and the Privilege against Self-incrimination in EC Law: Recent Developments and Current Issues' in BE Hawk (ed) *Annual Proceedings of the Fordham Corporate Law Institute* (Juris Publishing Inc New York 2005) 701, 709.

potential penalty.[65] It should be emphasized from the outset that the ECtHR has on numerous occasions stated that the concept of a *'criminal charge'* is an autonomous one. The Court will look beyond formal classification and scrutinize the substance of the case.[66] In this respect reference can be made to *Öztürk* where the Court remarked as follows:

[I]f the Contracting States were able at their discretion, by classifying an offence as 'regulatory' instead of criminal, to exclude the operation of the fundamental clauses of Articles 6 and 7 (art. 6 art. 7), the application of these provisions would be subordinated to their sovereign will. A latitude extending thus far might lead to results incompatible with the object and purpose of the Convention.[67]

When it comes to examining whether a criminal charge is at stake, the starting point is the domestic (for present purposes the EC) classification of the fines. If the domestic legislation classifies the offence as a criminal one, Article 6(1) ECHR applies under its criminal head.[68] On the other hand it should be noted that the ECtHR has underlined that 'this factor is of a relative weight and serves only as a starting point'.[69] Trechsel goes far in downplaying the importance of this criteria, saying that it is not a factor at all and that the Court has never attached any weight to it.[70]

As far as Community law is concerned, Article 23 of Regulation 1/2003[71] concerns the fines the Commission can levy on undertakings, and in paragraph 5 it is stated that decisions taken pursuant to paragraphs 1 and 2 shall not be of a criminal law nature. Therefore it is quite clear that the legislation does not classify the fines as criminal. Article 23(5) echoes what was previously said in Article 15(4) of Regulation 17/62.[72] The reasons behind the enactment of Article 15(4) of Regulation 17/62 were not in any way related to the ECHR classification. The provision was probably inserted to alleviate concerns of the Member States that

[65] This test was first used in Engel: *Engel and others v Netherlands* Series A No 22 (1979–80) 1 EHRR 647, para 82. For a general discussion see eg: P van Dijk and GJH van Hoof *Theory and Practice of the European Convention on Human Rights* (3rd edn Kluwer Law International The Hague 1998) 407–418. *Han & Yau v Commission of Customs and Excise* [2001] HRLR 54 also contains a good overview of the case law of the ECtHR.

[66] The ECJ employs similar methodology, eg when determining whether a measure constitutes an impediment to the free movement of goods under Article 28 EC and when defining state aid under Article 87: S Weatherill and P Beaumont *EU Law* (3rd edn Penguin London 1999) 504, 1019. For an example from the case law: Case 173/73 *Italy v Commission* [1974] ECR 709, para 13. The ECJ said: 'Article 92 [87] does not distinguish between the measures of state intervention concerned by reference to their causes or aims but defines them in relation to their effects.'

[67] *Öztürk v Germany* Series A No 73 (1984) 6 EHRR 409, para 49.

[68] P van Dijk and GJH van Hoof *Theory and Practice of the European Convention on Human Rights* (3rd edn Kluwer Law International The Hague 1998) 410.

[69] *Weber v Switzerland* Series A No 177 (1990) 12 EHRR 508, para 31.

[70] S Trechsel *Human Rights in Criminal Proceedings* (OUP Oxford 2005) 18.

[71] Regulation on the Implementation of the Rules of Competition Laid Down in Articles 81 and 82 of the Treaty [2003] OJ L 1/1.

[72] First Council Regulation implementing Articles 85 and 86 of the EC Treaty, [1962] OJ Spec Ed 204/62 87, as amended by Regulation (EC) No 1216/1999 of 10 June 1999 [1999] OJ L148/5.

they were not seen to be relinquishing any sovereignty in criminal law matters.[73] Interestingly enough in the light of the case law and the arguments outlined below, the preamble of Regulation 1/2003 offers no reasoning for the insertion of Article 23(5).

The second criterion of the test applied by the ECtHR when determining whether a penalty constitutes a criminal charge is the nature of the offence. The ECtHR examines whether the relevant legal provision is addressed to a specially defined group or has a general application; whether the executing authority is a public law body acting under statutory powers; whether the imposition of a penalty is conditioned on a finding of culpability and whether there is a punitive and deterrent element to the process.[74] Examining the fines levied under Article 23(5) of Regulation 1/2003 in light of the mentioned criteria it should first be noted that they are of a general nature, applicable to every person or legal entity that falls under the scope of the definition of undertaking in Articles 81 and 82 of the Treaty.[75] The Commission is a public law body (see Section 3 of Part 5 of the Treaty), which in this case bases its powers on the relevant provisions of Regulation 1/2003.

According to Article 23(3) of Regulation 1/2003, in fixing the amount of the fines regard shall be had both to the gravity and duration of the infringement. This demonstrates that the fines are supposed to have a punitive and deterrent effect. In paragraph 4 of the Commission's Guidelines on the method of setting fines[76] it is, *inter alia,* stated that fines should have a sufficiently deterrent effect, not only in order to sanction the undertakings concerned but also in order to deter other undertakings.

The Community Courts have referred to this twofold element of the fines, ie punishing for violations and providing a deterrent. As an example the ECJ said in *Chemiefarma*[77] that the fines have as their objective to punish illegal conduct as well as to prevent it being repeated. In *Pioneer*[78] the ECJ upheld the Commission's decision to increase the level of fines from previous practice. The Court remarked that the power of the Commission to impose fines on undertakings that intentionally or negligently commit infringements of Articles 81(1) and 82 was one of the means conferred on the Commission to carry out its task of supervision. That task included the duty to investigate and punish individual infringements and also the duty to pursue a general policy designed to apply to competition matters.

[73] CS Kerse *EC Antitrust Procedure* (4th edn Sweet and Maxwell London 1998) 287–288.

[74] B Emmerson and A Ashworth *Human Rights and Criminal Justice* (Sweet and Maxwell London 2001) 151.

[75] On what constitutes an undertaking see eg: R Whish *Competition Law* (5th edn Lexis Nexis London 2003) 80–87. It is worth noting that individuals can constitute an undertaking, an opera singer being a classic example, *Ibid.* 82–83.

[76] Guidelines on the method of setting fines imposed pursuant to Article 23(2)(a) of Regulation No 1/2003, [2006] OJ C210/2.

[77] Case 41/69 *ACF Chemiefarma NV v Commission* [1970] ECR 661, para 173. Translation of W Wils *The Optimal Enforcement of EC Antitrust Law* (Kluwer Law International The Hague 2002) 206.

[78] Cases 100–103/80 *Musique Diffusion Française SA and others v Commission* [1983] ECR 1825.

Therefore the Commission must take into consideration not only the particular circumstances of the case but also the context in which it occurs and ensure that its actions have the necessary deterrent effect especially as regards infringements which are particularly harmful to the attainment of the objectives of the Community.[79] The CFI has also made similar remarks, eg in *Cartonboard* where it remarked that 'when assessing the general level of fines the Commission is entitled to take account of the fact that clear infringements of the Community competition rules are still relatively frequent and that, accordingly, it may raise the level of fines in order to strengthen their deterrent effect.'[80]

The third criterion, the severity of the penalty, has sometimes been regarded as decisive by the ECtHR especially if there is a possibility of imprisonment.[81] Significant financial penalties can also suffice and even minor ones where they clearly have a punitive and deterrent purpose.[82] The ECtHR has consistently held that in every case it is the potential penalty which is examined and not the actual penalty incurred.[83] The fines levied by the Commission on the basis of Article 23(2) of Regulation 1/2003 can be substantial, up to 10 per cent of the turnover of the preceding business year. As an example of heavy fines issued by the Commission, the *Vitamins*[84] case may be mentioned where the total amount of the fines issued on the participants in the cartel was € 855,230,000.

Finally, worth mentioning is the relationship between the three criteria employed by the ECtHR. The Court has held that the criteria used are alternative.[85] However, there are instances when a cumulative approach is applied in cases where the use of each criterion does not lead to a clear conclusion.[86]

B. Case Law of the ECtHR

The ECtHR has never had to rule on whether the fines imposed under Regulation 1/2003 or 17/62 fall under the concept of a '*criminal charge*' according to Article

---

[79] *Ibid.*, paras 105–106. These remarks have often been cited, for a recent example: Cases C-189/02P, C-202/02P, C-205/02-C-208/02 P and C-213/02 P *Dansk Rørindustri and others v Commisssion* [2005] ECR I-5425, paras 169–170.

[80] Case T-354/94 *Stora Kopparbergs Bergslags AB v Commission* [1998] ECR II-2111, para 167.

[81] S Trechsel *Human Rights in Criminal Proceedings* (OUP Oxford 2005) 22.

[82] *Öztürk v Germany* Series A No 73 (1984) 6 EHRR 409, para 53.

[83] *Campbell and Fell v UK* Series A No 80 (1985) 7 EHRR 165, para 72 and *Weber v Switzerland* Series A No 177 (1990) 12 EHRR 508, para 34; B Emmerson and A Ashworth *Human Rights and Criminal Justice* (Sweet and Maxwell London 2001) 151–152.

[84] *Vitamins* OJ [2003] L 6/1, [2003] 4 CMLR 1030. This decision was appealed to the CFI: Case T-15/02 *BASF AG v Commission* [2006] ECR II-197 and T-26/02 *Daiichi Pharmaceutical Co. Ltd. v Commission* [2006] ECR II-713. For a discussion of the fines levied by the Commission in 2001 and 2002: R Whish *Competition Law* (5th edn Lexis Nexis London 2003) 456–460.

[85] See eg: *Garyfallou AEBE v Greece* (1999) 28 EHRR 344, para 33; *Janosevic v Sweden* (2004) 38 EHRR 473, para 67; R Clayton and H Tomlinson *Fair Trial Rights* (OUP Oxford 2001) 84; S Trechsel *Human Rights in Criminal Proceedings* (OUP Oxford 2005) 27–28.

[86] Campbell and Fell v UK, Series A No 80 (1985) 7 EHRR 165, para 72; *Bendenoun v France* Series A No 284 (1994) 18 EHRR 54, para 47.

6(1) of the Convention. However, decisions of the European Commission of Human Rights are of interest. In the previously mentioned decision *M & Co*[87] the Commission cited *Öztürk* and said that it could have been assumed that the anti-trust proceedings in question would have fallen under Article 6 ECHR if they had been conducted by the German and not the European judicial authorities. More significantly, in the case of *Société Stenuit*,[88] the European Commission of Human Rights unanimously held that the fines imposed under French competition law constituted a *'criminal charge'*. The Commission observed that the aim of the act was to maintain free competition in France. The law therefore affected the general interests of society normally protected by criminal law. The Minister could as an alternative to imposing a fine submit the case to the prosecuting authorities. Under the provisions of the act the Minister of Finance was permitted to impose a fine which could be up to 5 per cent of a firm's annual turnover and 5,000,000 FRF for other *contrevenants*. In the opinion of the Commission this showed quite clearly that the penalty was supposed to be deterrent. Therefore the European Commission of Human Rights concluded that the criminal aspect of the case was revealed unambiguously by the combination of the factors noted.[89]

This approach of the European Commission of Human Rights is consistent with the case law of the ECtHR, cf eg *Bendenoun*.[90] In this case the Court reached the conclusion that tax surcharges imposed under French law were to be regarded as a *'criminal charge'*. Firstly, the court pointed out that the relevant legal rule covered all citizens in their capacity as taxpayers. Secondly, the tax surcharges were not intended as pecuniary compensation for damage but as a punishment to deter re-offending. Thirdly, they were imposed under a general rule, the purpose of which was both deterrent and punitive. Lastly, the court remarked that the fines in the instant case were very substantial (422,534 FRF for Mr. Bendenoun personally and 570,398 FRF for his company) and that in the event of non-payment imprisonment could follow. The Court did not find these criteria decisive on their own but taken together and cumulatively they made the charge a criminal one.[91]

Comparing this with the fines levied according to Article 23(2) of Regulation 1/2003 it would seem that the same conclusion should be reached as regards those fines.[92] The only factor which could be regarded as distinguishing is the fact that the fines issued under Regulation 1/2003 do not carry with them the possibility of imprisonment. According to case law subsequent to *Bendenoun* this factor is not crucial when it comes to examining whether Article 6(1) ECHR is applicable under its criminal head.[93] In *Janosevic*, a case which also was concerned with tax

---

[87] *M & Co v Germany* Application 13284/87 (1990) 64 DR 138, 145.
[88] *Société Stenuit v France* Series A No 232-A (1992) 14 EHRR 509. The case was, however, settled before the ECtHR and therefore the Court did not rule on its merits.   [89] *Ibid.*, paras 62–65.
[90] *Bendenoun v France* Series A No 284 (1994) 18 EHRR 54.   [91] *Ibid.*, para 47.
[92] D Waelbroeck and D Fosselard 'Should the Decision-Making Power in EC Antitrust Procedure be Left to an Independent Judge?—The Impact of the European Convention of Human Rights on EC Antitrust Procedures' [1994] Ybk of Eur L 111, 123.
[93] *Lauko v Slovakia* (2001) 33 EHRR 40, para 58.

surcharges, the Court said: '*It is true that surcharges cannot be converted into a prison sentence in the event of non-payment; however, this is not decisive for the classification of an offence as 'criminal' under Article 6.*'[94] Here, reflecting on UK practice, it might be added that in *Napp Pharmaceutical*[95] the parties agreed that the penalties levied by the Office of Fair Trading (OFT) under Section 36 of the Competition Act 1998 (CA) involved a '*criminal charge*' for the purposes of Article 6 ECHR. The Competition Appeals Tribunal (CAT) held that there was not a relevant difference, within the meaning of Section 60 of the CA, between Section 36(3) of the Act and Article 15(2) of Regulation 17/62, the predecessor of Article 23(2) of Regulation 1/2003.

On the basis of the foregoing it seems clear that the imposition of a fine pursuant to Article 23(2) of Regulation 1/2003 constitutes a '*criminal charge*' under Article 6(1) of the Convention. This is a conclusion that is widely supported in the academic literature.[96] However, it has been maintained that a fairly recent admissibility decision of the ECtHR in *OOO Neste*[97] has thrown that finding into doubt.[98] There the applicant companies were found guilty of a breach of the law on competition and the restriction of monopolies in the commodity markets and were ordered to repay the profits they had obtained as a result of the infringement. They complained of a violation of Article 6(1) ECHR but the ECtHR found their application inadmissible as they were not charged with a criminal offence for the purposes of the Article. As a preliminary point it should be remarked that the Court rejected the applicants' assertion that competition law offences should be regarded as criminal within the meaning of Article 6 ECHR. That is a logical conclusion, as competition laws differ and therefore it is more appropriate to analyse each case on the basis of the criteria habitually applied by the Court.

The 'financial penalties' at stake in this case appear to differ from the fines levied under Regulation 1/2003. Firstly, it might be pointed out that they were based on a law that only concerned competition in the commodity markets.[99] Therefore they only had a limited as opposed to a universal application. Secondly, the ECtHR held that the main goal of the process was the prevention of

---

[94] *Janosevic v Sweden* (2004) 38 EHRR 473, para 69.

[95] *Napp Pharmaceutical Holdings Ltd v Director General of Fair Trading* [2002] ECC 13, para 93; see also the interim decision in: *Napp Pharmaceutical Holdings Ltd v Director General of Fair Trading*, [2002] ECC 3, para 71.

[96] A Riley 'Saunders and the Power to obtain Information in Community and United Kingdom Competition Law' (2000) 25 ELR 264, 270–272; D Waelbroeck and D Fosselard 'Should the Decision-Making Power in EC Antitrust Procedure be Left to an Independent Judge?-The Impact of the European Convention of Human Rights on EC Antitrust Procedures' [1994] Ybk of Eur L 111, 121–123; IS Forrester 'Modernisation of EC Competition Law' in BE Hawk (ed) *Annual Proceedings of the Fordham Corporate Law Institute* (Juris Publishing Inc New York 2000) 181, 218–222.

[97] *OOO Neste St. Petersburg and others v Russia* Application 69042/01 decision of 3 June 2004.

[98] E Paulis & C Gauer 'Le règlement n∞1/2003 et le principe du *ne bis in idem*' (2005) 1 Concurrences 32, 37.

[99] This fact is disputed by Ortiz Blanco, one of the applicants' lawyers: 'Rights, Privileges, and Ethics in Competition Cases Roundtable' in BE Hawk (ed) *Annual Proceedings of the Fordham Corporate Law Institute* (Juris Publishing Inc New York 2005) 777.

disturbances of competition and restoration in the case of disturbances, not to punish or deter offenders. It was noted that the authorities were only competent to issue fines for interference with their investigation, not for substantive infringements. Thirdly, the companies were ordered to pay back the profit they had reaped, which the Court considered confiscation of unlawfully gained profit. Accordingly, it was a pecuniary compensation for damage rather than a punishment to deter re-offending. With reference to these differences between the penalties under scrutiny in the decision the ones levied for breaches of Community competition law it is submitted that this decision does not affect the conclusion reached above.

Furthermore, it might be noted that Harding and Joshua, discussing the nature of the procedure, maintain that it is still possible to argue that prosecuting under the EC competition rules is different in some important respects from the usual type of criminal proceedings at national level.[100] That might very well be the case but as the preceding discussion reveals, it is not decisive when it comes to classifying the offence in accordance with the ECHR. Offences domestically classified as administrative, which are distinct from the usual criminal proceedings, may fall under the criminal head of Article 6(1) ECHR, cf for example *Bendenoun* and *Janosevic*. Furthermore, it is worth underlining that a finding to the effect that the Article 6(1) applies is not synonymous with concluding that the general principles of national criminal law are applicable.[101]

C. Case Law of the Community Courts

Although not necessary for the purposes of classifying the fines under Article 6(1) ECHR, it is nevertheless interesting to look at the relevant case law of the Community Courts. For one thing it may offer insights into whether the Courts are alert to the underlying ECHR dimension when it comes to judicial review of the fines issued for breaches of the competition rules of the Treaty. The Community Courts have never explicitly stated that they consider Article 6(1) applicable under its criminal head. There are; however, strong indications in the case law to the effect that the Courts are of that opinion. In *Polypropylene*[102] AG Vesterdorf said that the fines had a criminal law character (citing *Öztürk*) and that it was vitally important that the Court should seek to bring about a state of legal affairs not susceptible to any justified criticism with regard to the ECHR.

In *Hüls*[103] the ECJ strongly signalled that it considered the fines to constitute a criminal charge; the Court referred to Article 6(2) ECHR (the presumption of innocence) and Article 6(2) TEU. Then the Court said that it accepted, given the

---

[100] C Harding and J Joshua *Regulating Cartels in Europe* (OUP Oxford 2003) 190.
[101] *Napp Pharmaceutical Holdings Ltd v Director General of Fair Trading* [2002] ECC 13, para 101.
[102] Opinion of AG Vesterdorf in Cases T-1-4/89, T-6-15/89, *Rhone Poulenc SA and others v Commission* [1991] ECR II-867, 885–886; [1992] 4 CMLR 84, 101.
[103] Case C-199/92P *Hüls v Commission* [1999] ECR I-4287.

nature of the infringements in question and the nature and degree of severity of the ensuing penalties, that the principle of the presumption of innocence applied to the procedures relating to infringements of the competition rules applicable to undertakings that may result in the imposition of fines or periodic penalty payments.[104] In that respect the ECJ cited the *Öztürk* and *Lutz* cases of the ECtHR. Having regard to the fact, that the presumption of innocence according to Article 6(2) ECHR is only applicable in cases concerning a criminal charge, and to the reasoning of the ECJ quoted above regarding the nature of the penalty where the Court refers explicitly to two ECtHR cases regarding the concept of a criminal charge, it seems clear the ECJ is in fact endorsing the view that the fines do constitute a criminal charge within the meaning of the ECHR.

In *PVC II*[105] the ECJ, albeit *sub silentio*, reaffirmed the findings of *Hüls*. Two factors may be listed in support of that assertion. Firstly, the Court evaluated whether the proceedings had been conducted within a reasonable time with reference to the investigatory and administrative proceedings, which is only required in cases involving a criminal charge.[106] Secondly, the ECJ referred to the case law of the ECtHR regarding the privilege against self-incrimination, cases which are not relevant unless a criminal charge is at stake.[107]

Without making any attempt to list exhaustively the relevant judgments of the Community judicature, two AG opinions are worth a mention in this context. In his opinion in *Woodpulp*[108] AG Darmon considered that a Commission decision in the field of competition ordering a trader to pay a fine was manifestly of a penal nature. AG Leger was even more forthright in his opinion in *Baustahlgewebe* where he said:

It cannot be disputed—and the Commission does not dispute—that, in the light of the case law of the European Court of Human Rights and the opinions of the European Commission of Human Rights, the present case involves a criminal charge.[109]

Finally, it might be conceded that the case law of the Community Courts is not quite consistent in this respect and in *LRAF 1998*[110] the CFI, surprisingly considering the above, referred to Article 15(4) of Regulation 17/62 and said that the fines were not of a criminal law nature. The Court then remarked that the Commission nonetheless was required to observe the general principles of

---

[104] *Ibid.*, paras 149–150.

[105] Cases C-238/99P, C-244/99P, C-245/99P, C-247/99P, C-250/99P-C-252/99P, C-254/99P, *Limburgse Vinyl Maatschappij and others v Commission* [2002] ECR I-8375.

[106] *Ibid.*, paras 180–200. The ECJ adopted the same approach in: Case C-194/99P *Thyssen Stahl AG v Commission* [2003] ECR I-10821, paras 154–168. In her opinion in the case AG Stix-Hackl explicitly referred to cases from the ECtHR regarding the criminal head of Article 6(1) ECHR, para 235. See also: Cases T-67/00, T-68/00, T-71/00, T-78/00, *JFE Engineering Corp. and others v Commission* [2004] ECR II-2501, para 178.

[107] Cases C-238/99P, C-244/99P, C-245/99P, C-247/99P, C-250/99P-C-252/99P, C-254/99P, *Limburgse Vinyl Maatschappij and others v Commission* [2002] ECR I-8375, paras 274–275.

[108] Opinion of AG Darmon in Cases C-89/85, C-104/85, C-114/85, C-116/85, C-117/85 and C-125/85-129/85 *A. Ahlström Osakeyhitö and others v Commission* [1993] ECR I-1307, para 451.

[109] Opinion of AG Leger in Case C-185/95P *Baustahlgewebe v Commission* [1998] ECR I-8417, para 31.   [110] Case T-23/99 *LRAF 1998 v Commission* [2002] ECR II-1705, para 220.

Community law. The Court referred to Article 6(2) TEU and considered Article 7 ECHR (non-retroactivity of penalties) to be one of the general principles of law the Commission was bound to observe.[111] Accordingly, it would appear that this inconsistency is of little significance. On appeal the ECJ did not explicitly address the issue of the classification of the fines; however, there appears little doubt that the Court bases its ruling on the premises that there is a criminal charge at stake.[112] Firstly, as regards the issue of whether the applicants should have been permitted to hear witnesses before the CFI, the ECJ referred to case law from the ECtHR on the interpretation of Article 6(3)(d).[113] Secondly, the ECJ also referred to precedents from Strasbourg when dealing with the question whether the fines levied by the Commission were in breach of the principle of non-retroactivity of penalties.[114]

In *Volkswagen*[115] the applicant maintained that to establish an intentional infringement it would have been necessary to identify the persons responsible. The ECJ, in rejecting this ground of appeal, said that the view of the undertaking could have no application in Community competition law and in that respect referred to Article 15(2) of Regulation 17/62. Moreover, the Court also cited Article 15(4) saying that the fines were not of a criminal law nature. Finally the ECJ added that if the applicant's view were upheld it would seriously impinge the effectiveness of competition law.[116] The judgment is very vague on this issue and it is far from clear what the citation to Article 15(4) of Regulation 17/62 is supposed to mean. The Court does not make any reference to the relevance of Article 6(1) ECHR nor does it attempt to outline why it is of significance that the fines are not of a criminal law nature. If the Court is merely referring to the fact that, the procedure is not within the context of a classic criminal trial, and that therefore it considered unnecessary to identify the persons responsible there is probably not much cause for concern. If on the other hand Court is maintaining that Article 15(4) (now Article 23(5) of Regulation 1/2003) has an effect on the classification of the procedure, other than confirming the obvious that it is not a classic criminal trial, then the Court is on a slippery slope. In light of the cases referred to above the former hypothesis must be regarded as the more likely one.

IV. Independent and Impartial Tribunal

A. Introduction

The ECtHR has ruled on quite a few occasions that the word *'tribunal'* in Article 6(1) ECHR has a wider scope than merely referring to a court of law in the classic

---

[111] *Ibid.*, paras 217–219.
[112] Cases C-189/02P, C-202/02P, C-205/02-C-208/02P and C-213/02P *Dansk Rørindustri and others v Commisssion* [2005] ECR I-5425.   [113] *Ibid.*, paras 70–71.
[114] *Ibid.*, paras 215–219.
[115] Case 338/00P *Volkswagen AG v Commission* [2003] ECR I-9189.
[116] *Ibid.*, paras 95–97.

sense.[117] According to the case law a tribunal is characterized in the substantive sense of the term by its judicial function, that is to say determining matters within its competence on the basis of rules of law and after proceedings conducted in a prescribed manner.[118]

The Court has held that administrative authorities cannot be classified as tribunals. In *Benthem*[119] the Court said that the word tribunal denotes bodies which exhibit common fundamental features of which the most important are independence and impartiality and the guarantees of judicial procedure. In the instant case the Crown, the head of the executive, had taken a decision, which from a formal point of view constituted an administrative act, emanating from a Minister responsible to Parliament. The decision was thereby made by a body which did not constitute a tribunal within the meaning of Article 6(1) ECHR. The famous case of *Bryan*,[120] *inter alia*, addressed whether a planning inspector could be considered an independent and impartial tribunal. The ECtHR held that the requirements were not fulfilled since the Secretary of State could at any time, even during proceedings in progress, issue a direction to revoke the power of an inspector to decide a case.[121] This case also shows that deciding whether an organ constitutes a tribunal can in some cases not easily be dislodged from ruling on its independence and impartiality.[122] That is also apparent from the oft-used dictum of the ECtHR that only an institution that has full jurisdiction and satisfies a number of requirements, such as independence of the executive and also of the parties, merits the description '*tribunal*' within the meaning of Article 6(1).[123] On the basis of the above it is clear that the Commission cannot be regarded as an independent and impartial tribunal within the meaning of Article 6(1) ECHR. The ECJ has also held that the Commission does not constitute a tribunal within the meaning of the Article.[124]

In order to fulfil the requirement of independence a tribunal needs to be independent both of the parties and the executive. Several factors are relevant in this regard:

[T]he manner of appointment of its members and the duration of their term of office . . . , the existence of guarantees against outside pressures . . . and the question whether the body presents an appearance of independence.[125]

The test of impartiality is usually divided into a subjective and an objective one.[126] The subjective test requires a proof of actual bias, whereas the objective needs a

---

[117] See eg: *Campell and Fell v UK* Series A No 80 (1985) 7 EHRR 165, para 76; N Holst-Christensen and others *Den Europæiske Menneskerettighedskonvention Artikel 1–10 med kommentarer* (2nd edn Jurist-og Økonomforbundets Forlag København 2003) 280.

[118] See eg: *H v Belgium* Series A No 127 (1988) 10 EHRR 339, para 50.

[119] *Benthem v Netherlands* Series A No 97 (1986) 8 EHRR 1, para 43.

[120] *Bryan v UK* Series A No 335-A (1995) 21 EHRR 342.   [121] *Ibid.*, para 38.

[122] G Jörundsson 'Um rétt manna samkvæmt 6. gr. Mannréttindasáttmála Evrópu til að leggja mál fyrir óháðan og hlutlausan dómstól' in *Ármannsbók* (Sögufélagið Reykjavík 1989) 165, 172.

[123] See eg: *Vasilescu v Romania* (1999) 28 EHRR 241, para 41.

[124] Cases 209–215/78 *Heintz van Landewyck Sarl and others v Commission* [1980] ECR 3125, para 81.   [125] *Campbell and Fell v UK* Series A No 80 (1985) 7 EHRR 165, para 78.

[126] *Piersack v Belgium* Series A No 53 (1983) 5 EHRR 169, para 30.

finding of a legitimate doubt as to the impartiality of the members of the tribunal, which is capable of being objectively justified.[127] The ECtHR has held that judges adjudicating a case are not impartial if they have previously acted as investigating judges in the case.[128] However, where the judge has only played a minor role in the investigation, bias has not been found to exist.[129] As mentioned above the Commission cannot be considered to constitute a tribunal in the meaning of Article 6(1) ECHR. On the other hand it is equally clear that the CFI fulfils all the requisite requirements save in the unlikely scenario that a subjective bias would be established. Therefore an assessment of these criteria is not necessary for present purposes.[130]

Article 6(1) ECHR does not explicitly guarantee a right of access to court. However, in the seminal *Golder*[131] the Court held such a right to be inherent in the Article. Subsequently, in *Le Compte*[132] (concerning access after an administrative decision) the ECtHR qualified the previous finding by holding that disputes over civil rights and obligations need not be conducted at every stage before a tribunal meeting the requirements of Article 6(1). As regards criminal charges the ECtHR concluded in *Öztürk*[133] that conferring the task of prosecution and punishment of minor offences on administrative authorities is not inconsistent with the Convention. In order to avoid infringing Article 6(1) it is necessary to have available recourse to a judicial determination before a court with full jurisdiction.[134] What this entails is different depending on the subject-matter at hand. For our purposes it is useful to distinguish between three different categories:

- Decisions under the head of *'civil rights and obligations'*. How strict a scrutiny is required by the court performing judicial review differs depending on the subject-matter, eg policy decisions involving exercise of administrative discretion *contra* decisions interfering with important rights.[135]

- Decisions under the head of *'criminal charge'* within the autonomous meaning of Article 6(1) ECHR, classified as disciplinary or administrative according to national law.

- Decisions under the head of *'criminal charge'* both under the Convention and national law.

---

[127] R Clayton and H Tomlinson *Fair Trial Rights* (OUP Oxford 2001) 109.
[128] *Pfeifer and Planck v Austria* Series A No 297 B (1994) 14 EHRR 692, paras 35–39.
[129] N Holst-Christensen and others *Den Europæiske Menneskerettighedskonvention Artikel 1–10 med kommentarer* (2nd edn Jurist- og Økonomforbundets Forlag København 2003) 292.
[130] N Holst-Christensen and others *Den Europæiske Menneskerettighedskonvention Artikel 1–10 med kommentarer* (2nd edn Jurist- og Økonomforbundets Forlag København 2003) 286–298.
[131] *Golder v UK* Series A No 18 (1979–80) 1 EHRR 524, para 36.
[132] *Le Compte and others v Belgium* Series A No 43 (1982) 4 EHRR 1, para 51.
[133] *Öztürk v Germany* Series A No 73 (1984) 6 EHRR 409, para 56.
[134] S Grosz J Beatson and P Duffy *Human Rights The 1998 Act and the European Convention* (Sweet and Maxwell London 2000) 126–129.
[135] The use of the term *'full jurisdiction'*, see for example *Albert and Le Compte v Belgium* Series A No 58 (1983) 5 EHRR 533, para 29, has caused some confusion, see the following observation of Lord Clyde in Alconbury: 'At first sight the expression might seem to require in every case an exhaus-

B. Civil Rights and Obligations

Two well-known ECtHR cases can be mentioned as examples where the ECtHR has accepted limited review. In *Zumtobel*,[136] concerning an expropriation order for the construction of a highway, the ECtHR considered, having regard to the respect which must be accorded to administrative decisions on the grounds of expediency and to the nature of the complaints, that the review fulfilled the requirements of Article 6(1) ECHR. The case is; however, to be narrowly interpreted because the ECtHR notes that the applicant's submissions were examined without the Administrative Court ever declining jurisdiction in replying to them or ascertaining the facts. In the above-mentioned *Bryan*[137] case (demolition of buildings built without planning permission), the review by the High Court was considered to be sufficient. In assessing this, the ECtHR said it was necessary to have regard to matters such as the subject-matter of the decision appealed against, the manner in which that decision was arrived at and the content of the dispute.[138] In finding no infringement the Court relied on the quasi-judicial nature of the proceedings, that there was no dispute as to the primary facts and the case concerned a specialized area of law.[139] However, the above should not give the impression that the ECtHR always considers cases in this category subject to sufficient judicial review.[140] It should be mentioned that after the entry into force of the Human Rights Act 1998 the House of Lords has had to grapple with these issues in a number of high profile cases, most notably *Alconbury*[141] and *Runa Begum*.[142] It is worth noting that there is a divergent opinion as to whether and to what extent safeguards in the administrative process are necessary to ensure compliance with Article 6(1) ECHR and the above-mentioned House of Lords decisions, *inter alia*, dealt with that issue.[143] Since these issues are not determinative where criminal charges are at stake it will not be discussed further here.

---

tive and comprehensive review of the decision including a thorough review of the facts as well as the law. If that were so a remedy by way of a statutory appeal or an application to the supervisory jurisdiction of the courts in judicial review would be inadequate. But it is evident that this is not a correct understanding of the expression. Full jurisdiction means a full jurisdiction in the context of the case .... The nature and circumstances of the case have accordingly to be considered before one can determine what may comprise ' "full jurisdiction".' R (on the application of Holding & Barnes Plc) v Secretary of State for the Environment, Transport and the Regions [2003] 2 AC 295, para 154.

[136] *Zumtobel v Austria* Series A No 268-A (1994) 17 EHRR 116, para 32.

[137] *Bryan v UK* Series A No 335-A (1995) 21 EHRR 342.   [138] *Ibid.*, para 45.

[139] *Ibid.*, paras 46–47.

[140] See for example *Kingsley* which concerned the revocation of a licence to run a casino: *Kingsley v UK* (2002) 35 EHRR 10, para 34; *Kingsley v UK* (2001) 33 EHRR 13, paras 57–59.

[141] *R (on the application of Holding & Barnes Plc) v Secretary of State for the Environment, Transport and the Regions* [2003] 2 AC 295.

[142] *Begum (Runa) v Tower Hamlets LBC* [2003] 2 AC 430. For an appraisal of the relevant case law: P Craig 'The HRA, Article 6 and Procedural Rights' [2003] PL 753, 762–766.

[143] On the approach of the ECtHR: R Clayton and H Tomlinson *Fair Trial Rights* (OUP Oxford 2001) 97–98; the varying opinions of the Lords in *Alconbury*: D Elvin and J Maurici 'The Alconbury Litigation: Principle and Pragmatism' [2001] JPEL 883, 895–899; the approach in *Runa Begum*: R Clayton and V Sachdeva 'The Role of Judicial Review in Curing Breaches of Article 6' [2003] Judicial Rev 90, 95–96.

W v UK[144] is a good example of a case where the ECtHR has required stricter judicial review. The matter at hand was parental access to children, protected by Article 8 ECHR. The case was initially decided by a local authority and on application for a judicial review the courts would not review the merits of the decision but confined themselves to ensuring, in brief, that the authority did not act illegally, unreasonably or unfairly. The ECtHR found an infringement of Article 6(1) of the Convention. The Court required in a case of this kind that the local authority's decision could be reviewed by a tribunal having jurisdiction to examine the merits of the matter.[145] It might be noted that the control of administrative discretion held to be insufficient was Wednesbury unreasonableness. In its original meaning the test required for an administrative decision to be struck down that it was so unreasonable that no reasonable authority could have come to it.[146] Cases which have been considered to fall into this category, demanding a more rigorous review, have for example concerned a dismissal and professional disciplinary proceedings involving employment and livelihood issues.[147]

C. Criminal Charge—Autonomous Meaning

The second category concerning judicial review of criminal charges within the autonomous meaning of Article 6(1) ECHR is the most important one for our purposes since the fines levied by the Commission according to Article 23(2) of Regulation 1/2003 fall within that category. It is unequivocal that where a criminal charge is at stake a more rigorous judicial control is necessary to comply with Article 6(1) ECHR. In that respect reference can be made to the following observation of the European Commission of Human Rights in *Umlauft*:

> The Commission finds that whilst in civil matters a somewhat limited review of the decisions of administrative authorities may, in certain circumstances, satisfy the requirements of Article 6 of the Convention ... criminal cases may require a different approach. In particular, they involve rules directed towards all citizens in their capacity as road users, which prescribe conduct of a certain kind and create sanctions for non-compliance. Where a defendant *desires a court to determine a criminal charge against him, there is no room for limitation on the scope of review required of the decisions of administrative authorities.* Accordingly, the Commission finds that the applicant in the present case was entitled to, but did not have the benefit of, a court *which could consider all the facts of the case.*[148] (emphasis added)

It is appropriate to recall the above-mentioned *Öztürk*[149] which concerned an administrative imposition of a fine for a minor traffic offence. After having

---

[144] *W v UK* Series A No 121 A (1988) 10 EHRR 29.   [145] *Ibid.*, para 82.

[146] *Associate Picture Houses Ltd v Wednesbury Corporation* [1948] 1 KB 223, 230. On the past and present of Wednesbury unreasonableness: PP Craig *Administrative Law* (5th edn Thomson Sweet and Maxwell London 2003) 610–617.

[147] M Poutsie 'The Rule of Law or the Rule of Lawyers ? Alconbury, Article 6(1) and the Role of Courts in Administrative Decision-Making' (2001) 6 Eur Human Rights L Rev 657, 668–669.

[148] *Umlauft v Austria* Series A No 328-B (1996) 22 EHRR 76, para 48 of the Commission's opinion.

[149] *Öztürk v Germany* Series A No 73 (1984) 6 EHRR 409.

reached the conclusion that the offence constituted a *'criminal charge'* the ECtHR remarked that, having regard to the large number of minor offences, notably in the sphere of road traffic, a Contracting State may have good cause for relieving its courts of the task of their prosecution and punishment. Conferring the prosecution and punishment of minor offences on administrative authorities is not inconsistent with the Convention provided that the person concerned is enabled to take any decision thus made against him before a tribunal that does offer the guarantees of Article 6.[150] The majority of the case law on administrative prosecution of minor offences has involved traffic offences[151] but it has been confirmed that the same legal arguments are equally applicable with regard to other minor offences, see for example *Belilos*[152] (participation in unauthorised demonstration) and *Lauko*[153] (nuisance towards neighbours).

The ECtHR has also held in cases regarding tax surcharges that an administrative imposition of fines is Convention compliant even though the fines were substantial. In *Bendenoun*[154] the Court considered, having regard to the large number of offences of the kind that was at stake (somewhat simplified, the offence consisted of submitting incorrect information to tax authorities in bad faith), that Contracting States must be free to empower the Revenue to prosecute and punish them, even if the surcharges imposed as a penalty were large ones. This conclusion as regards tax surcharges was confirmed in *Janosevic*.[155]

The key question is what is required in terms of judicial review after an administrative imposition of a penalty. As has been mentioned, the European Commission of Human Rights said in *Umlauft* that there was no room for limitation on the scope of review and the court needed to be competent to consider all the facts.[156] In *Janosevic*[157] the ECtHR remarked that the applicant had to be able to: '[B]ring any such decision affecting him before a judicial body that has full jurisdiction, including the power to quash in all respects, on questions of fact and law, the challenged decision'. The ECtHR considered the review of the Swedish Administrative Courts to be sufficient for the purposes of Article 6(1) ECHR. In reaching that conclusion the ECtHR noted that the courts had jurisdiction to examine all aspects of the matter before them. Their examination was not limited to points of law but might also extend to factual issues, including the assessment of evidence. If the courts disagreed with findings of the Tax Authority, they had the power to quash the decisions appealed against.[158]

---

[150] *Ibid.*, para 56.
[151] See eg: *Umlauft v Austria* Series A No 328-B (1996) 22 EHRR 76; *Schmautzer v Austria* Series A No 328-A (1996) 21 EHRR 511.
[152] *Belilos v Switzerland* Series A No 132 (1988) 10 EHRR 466, para 68.
[153] *Lauko v Slovakia* (2001) 33 EHRR 40, para 64.
[154] *Bendenoun v France* Series A No 284 (1994) 18 EHRR 54, para 46.
[155] *Janosevic v Sweden* (2004) 38 EHRR 473, para 81.
[156] *Umlauft v Austria* Series A No 328-B (1996) 22 EHRR 76, para 48 of the Commission's opinion.
[157] *Janosevic v Sweden* (2004) 38 EHRR 473, para 81. See also *Bendenoun v France* Series A No 284 (1994) 18 EHRR 54, para 46. [158] *Janosevic v Sweden* (2004) 38 EHRR 473, para 82.

To meet the requirements of Article 6(1) ECHR it is not sufficient for it to be theoretically possible to bring a case before a court with full jurisdiction; the court must exercise its review functions in the instant case. This is demonstrated by the decision of the European Commission of Human Rights in *Société Stenuit*.[159] The applicant company had, *inter alia*, argued that the penalties were contrary to the ECHR but the *Conseil d'Etat* held that the company could not pursue that line of argument. The Commission remarked that although it seemed that under domestic law the court's supervision of the fines could have taken the form of full judicial review, in the instant case the *Conseil d'Etat* did not examine the appeal lodged by the applicant. Consequently, it did not rule on the merits and the Commission therefore found an infringement of Article 6(1) ECHR.[160] The ECtHR adopted the same approach in *Terra Woningen*,[161] a case under the civil head of Article 6(1). At the time the case was decided by a district court in the Netherlands there existed uncertainty as to whether the courts could themselves rule on whether the criteria for the application of a particular provision were fulfilled or were bound by the findings of the administration. The ECtHR held that the district court had just accepted the conclusion of the administration and in doing so had deprived itself of jurisdiction to examine facts which were crucial for the determination of the dispute.[162]

Article 6(1) ECHR does not merely guarantee an access to court but also that the right is effective. The ECtHR has in a number of cases said that the Convention is to guarantee not rights that are theoretical or illusory but rights that are practical and effective. This is sometimes referred to as the principle of effectiveness.[163] In *Janosevic* the ECtHR held that the applicant's right to an effective access to court had been infringed. He had requested the tax authority to reconsider its tax assessment, a necessary prerequisite for instigating judicial proceedings; soon thereafter enforcement measures commenced and were not suspended since the applicant could not supply the required bank guarantee. The enforcement actions resulted in the applicant being declared bankrupt. The ECtHR considered that the situation in which the applicant was placed made it indispensable that the reassessment be conducted promptly if he was to have effective access to court. The very essence of the right would otherwise be impaired.[164] The Court held that the three years which the process took without the facts revealing any particular justification constituted a failure to act with the urgency the circumstances required and therefore the Court found a violation of Article 6(1) ECHR.[165]

---

[159] *Société Stenuit v France* Series A No 232-A (1992) 14 EHRR 509.   [160] *Ibid.*, para 72.
[161] *Terra Woningen v Netherlands* (1997) 24 EHRR 456.   [162] *Ibid.*, paras 53–54.
[163] Jacobs and White *European Convention on Human Rights* (3rd edn C Ovey and RCA White OUP Oxford 2002) 36. One of the most striking examples of application of this principle, *Airey* concerned the right of access to court, *Airey v Ireland* Series A No 32 (1979–80) 2 EHRR 305, para 24; R Clayton and H Tomlinson *Fair Trial Rights* (OUP Oxford 2001) 90–91.
[164] *Janosevic v Sweden* (2004) 38 EHRR 473, para 88.
[165] This case has interesting parallels with the application in *Senator Lines*. There the applicant claimed that the enforcement of a Commission decision would lead to a winding-up of the company,

D. Criminal Charge

The third category is the most straightforward one. In *De Cubber*,[166] after bias had been established at the first instance, the Belgian government relied, *inter alia*, on *Öztürk* and maintained that the defect had been cured on appeal. The ECtHR pointed out that the cases cited by the government involved a criminal charge within the autonomous meaning of Article 6(1). The same line of argument could not be extended to a case which not only under the Convention but also under Belgian law was a criminal one. The Court concluded by saying that the reasoning of the judgments could not justify reducing the requirements of Article 6(1) in its traditional and natural sphere of application. A restrictive interpretation of this kind would not be consonant with the object and purpose of Article 6(1).[167] The ECtHR has confirmed this approach in later judgments.[168] There is no doubt therefore that in a classic criminal trial the requirements of independence and impartiality have to be complied with at every stage of the proceedings.

E. Protection of Legal Entities

The final issue to be examined in this chapter is whether corporate entities enjoy like natural persons the right to a fair trial before an independent and impartial tribunal according to Article 6(1) ECHR. Article 34 ECHR provides that the Court may receive applications from any person, non-governmental organization or group of individuals claiming to be a victim of a violation of the Convention rights.[169] The most detailed observations on the subject under scrutiny are to be found in the opinion of the European Commission of Human Rights in *Société Stenuit*. In that case the French government maintained that corporate bodies could not be liable under criminal law. The Commission noted that the Convention contained no provision to that effect and in the instant case the applicant had faced a criminal charge. The Commission held that corporations could avail themselves of the protection of Article 6 when a criminal charge was made against them. The Commission relied on the fact that the ECtHR had already recognized that corporate bodies could exercise a number of rights under the Convention such as the ones set out in Articles 9 and 10.[170] Reliance was also

which would infringe his right to presumption of innocence and right to judicial recourse, see paras 62–77 of the application to the ECtHR: Human Rights Law Journal (2000) 18 112, 121–123.

[166] *De Cubber v Belgium* Series A No 86 (1985) 7 EHRR 236, para 31.

[167] *Ibid.*, para 32.

[168] *Findlay v UK* (1997) 24 EHRR 221, para 79; *Riepan v Austria* application 35115/97 judgment of 14 November 2000, para 40; N Holst-Christensen and others *Den Europæiske Menneskerettighedskonvention Artikel 1–10 med kommentarer* (2nd edn Jurist- og Økonomforbundets Forlag København 2003) 282.

[169] On the protection of legal entities: P van Dijk and GJH van Hoof *Theory and Practice of the European Convention on Human Rights* (3rd edn Kluwer Law International The Hague 1998) 45–46.

[170] As regards Article 10 it is worth drawing attention to the following remarks of the ECtHR in *Autronic*: 'In the Court's view, neither Autronic AG's legal status as limited company nor the fact that

placed on the oft-repeated dictum that Article 6 reflects the fundamental principle of the rule of law and that a restrictive interpretation would not be consonant with the object and purpose of the provision.[171] To this reasoning of the European Commission of Human Rights it might be added that the ECtHR has subsequently held that the rights guaranteed by Article 8 ECHR can also encompass the right to respect for a company's registered office, branches or other business premises.[172]

The ECtHR has never commented directly on this issue but there are no indications that it does not share the view of the Commission. Quite the contrary; the Court has decided some cases where Article 6 has been considered applicable under its criminal head to corporate bodies facing criminal charges and apparently the applicability of the provision was not contested before the Court.[173] Equally the ECtHR has on numerous occasions examined complaints from legal persons under the civil head of Article 6(1) ECHR without any doubt being cast on that they could exercise the rights guaranteed by the Article.[174] Even more significantly the Court has held that legal persons can be awarded non-pecuniary damages according to Article 41 ECHR if their right to a trial within a reasonable time had not been respected.[175] The Portuguese government disputed that legal entities could enjoy that right and referred to the fact that the compensation was to provide reparation for anxiety, mental stress, uncertainty, etc., which did not apply to legal persons. The ECtHR rejected the argument relying, *inter alia*, on its case law regarding non-pecuniary damages for breaches of other Articles of the Convention (Articles 10, 11 and 13) and the principle of effectiveness, noting that if the right guaranteed by Article 6 was to be effective it must be empowered to award non-pecuniary damages to companies.[176]

On the basis of the above it appears quite clear that legal persons enjoy the fair trial guarantees recognized under Article 6(1) ECHR. There is also nothing that

---

its activities were commercial nor the intrinsic nature of the freedom of expression can deprive Autronic AG of the protection of Article 10 (art. 10). The Article (art. 10) applies to "everyone", whether natural or legal persons. The Court has, moreover, already held on three occasions that it is applicable to profit-making corporate bodies . . .' *Autronic AG v Switzerland* Series A No 178 (1990) 12 EHRR 485, para 47. It should be mentioned that regarding Article 9 it has been held that legal entities can exercise the freedom of religion but not the freedom of conscience, *Kontakt-Information-Therapie and Hagen v Austria* Application 11921/86 (1988) 57 DR 241; Jacobs and White *European Convention on Human Rights* (3rd edn C Ovey and RCA White OUP Oxford 2002) 273.

[171] *Société Stenuit v France* Series A No 232-A (1992) 14 EHRR 509, para 66.

[172] *Niemietz v Germany* Series A No 251-B (1993) 16 EHRR 97, para 30; *Stés Colas Est and others v France* Application 37971/97 judgment of 16 April 2002, paras 41 and 49.

[173] *Garyfallou AEBE v Greece* (1999) 28 EHRR 344, paras 31–35; *Vastberga Taxibolag and Vulic v Sweden* application 36985/97 judgment of 23 July 2002, paras 76–82.

[174] See eg: *Tre Traktörer AB v Sweden* Series A 159 (1991) 13 EHRR 309; *Dombo Beheer BV v Netherlands* Series A No 274-A (1994) 18 EHRR 213; *Canea Catholic Church v Greece* (1999) 27 EHRR 521. In the last case the ECtHR held that the failure to acknowlegde the applicant's legal personality, which lead to cases it had brought before the Greek courts being dismissed, impaired the very substance of the applicant's right to court, para 40–42.

[175] *Comingersoll SA v Portugal* (2001) 31 EHRR 31.   [176] *Ibid.*, paras 32–36.

suggests that the standard of protection varies when the right to a trial before an independent and impartial tribunal is at stake. On the other hand it is possible, that in a few instances the standard could vary depending on whether the rights of a corporation or an individual are at issue. The prime example is the right to silence as recognized by the ECtHR, where as outlined above it is unclear, when regard is had to the rationale underlying the right as protected by Article 6 ECHR, to what extent it applies to legal entities.[177]

V. Judicial Review in Competition Cases

A. Introduction

This central chapter of the article focuses on judicial review of Commission decisions, which as previously has been established, determines whether the competition proceedings are Convention compliant. Considering how important judicial control of Commission decisions is, it is a bit surprising that in the wealth of literature regarding competition law, there is rather little to be found regarding judicial review. Although following high-profile cases such as *Airtours* and *Tetra-Laval*,[178] several articles have appeared regarding the review of merger decisions. Quite a bit of the writing that does exist is characterized by partisanship. On one side of the fence are practitioners lamenting the lack of judicial control and on the other Commission officials decrying the requirements the Community Courts impose on the Commission and their interventionist stance. The following remarks of Van Bael are a good illustration of the former viewpoint:

Thus, from the Court's pronouncements in *Grundig* and *Remia*, it is clear that it is only inclined to intervene when the Commission's findings would appear to be wrong on the surface or totally lacking in support. In other words, the Court, rather than doublechecking the findings made by the Commission, will tend to give them full credit, unless, prima facie, there would be something grossly wrong.[179]

Joshua on the other hand captures well the latter stance:

The Courts have also shown themselves increasingly ready to undertake an extensive review of the facts in any case and in some examples one might ask whether they have

---

[177] In his opinion in *SGL Carbon* AG Geelhoed observed that ECtHR case law regarding the right to silence concerned natural persons in the context of classical criminal proceedings and it was not possible, without more, to transpose those findings to legal persons or undertakings: Case C-301/04P *Commission v SGL Carbon* opinion of AG Geelhoed [2006] ECR I-5915, paras 63–67. See also: WPJ Wils 'Self-Incrimination in EC Antitrust Enforcement: A Legal and Economic Analysis' (2003) 26 World Competition 567, 577.

[178] Case T-342/99 *Airtours plc v Commission* [2002] ECR II-2585; Case T-80/02 *Tetra Laval BV v Commission* [2002] ECR II-4519.

[179] I van Bael 'Insufficient Judicial Control of EC Competition Law Enforcement' in BE Hawk (ed) *Annual Proceedings of the Fordham Corporate Law Institute* (Transnational Juris Publications Kluwer Law & Taxation Publishers New York 1993) 733, 741.

exceeded the normal limits of judicial review in carrying out de novo their own investigation of the facts found in the decisions.[180]

Since the inception of the CFI in 1989 judicial review against Commission decisions has been brought before the CFI. The competence of the CFI to hear these cases is now provided for in Article 225(1) EC. The Article also states that judgments given by the CFI under the paragraph may be subject to a right of appeal to the ECJ on points of law only. Further guidance is offered by Article 58 of the Statute of the Court of Justice[181] which says that the appeal shall lie on the grounds of lack of competence of the CFI, a breach of procedure before it which adversely affects the interests of the appellant as well as the infringement of Community law by the CFI.

The ECJ has held that the appraisal of the evidence by the CFI does not constitute a point of law, which is subject to review by the ECJ, save where there is a clear sense that the evidence has been distorted.[182] As regards a review of the facts the ECJ said in *John Deere*:

When the Court of First Instance has established or assessed the facts, the Court of Justice has jurisdiction under Article [225] of the Treaty to review the legal characterisation of those facts by the Court of First Instance and the legal conclusions it has drawn from them .... The Court of Justice thus has no jurisdiction to establish the facts or, in principle, to examine the evidence which the Court of First Instance accepted in support of those facts.[183]

According to the case law of the ECtHR, an appeal to a higher or a supreme court on a point of law or on the constitutional validity of a decision is insufficient to rectify a breach of Article 6(1) ECHR by the primary decision-maker.[184] One of the reasons for this conclusion is that the higher court does not have jurisdiction to examine the relevant facts.[185] The significance of this case law is that for our purposes the appellate role of the ECJ is irrelevant, since the review undertaken by the Court is inadequate for the purposes of Article 6(1) ECHR. In other words, it is the extent of judicial review by the CFI, which resolves whether competition proceedings are compatible with the Convention. However, Case law of the ECJ prior to the inception of the CFI, when the ECJ adjudicated competition cases as a court of first and last instance, will be examined to determine whether the review conducted then by the ECJ was in compliance with requirements of the Convention. Subsequently the attention will turn to the jurisprudence of the CFI.

---

[180] JM Joshua 'Attitudes to Antitrust Enforcement in the EU and United States: Dodging the Traffic Warden or Respecting the Law?' in BE Hawk (ed) *Annual Proceedings of the Fordham Corporate Law Institute* (Juris Publishing Inc Sweet and Maxwell New York 1996) 101, 102–103.

[181] Protocol on the Statute of the Court of Justice [2002] OJ C325/167.

[182] Case C-53/92P *Hilti v Commission* [1994] ECR I-666, para 42.

[183] Case C-7/95P *John Deere v Commission* [1998] ECR I-3111, paras 21–22. For an overview of the scope of appeal: A Jones and B Sufrin *EC Competition Law Text, Cases, and Materials* (2nd edn OUP Oxford 2001) 1155–1158.

[184] *Zumtobel v Austria* Series A No 268-A (1994) 17 EHRR 116, paras 29–30; *Belilos v Switzerland* Series A No 132 (1988) 10 EHRR 466, paras 70–72.

[185] *Zumtobel v Austria* Series A No 268 (1994) 17 EHRR 116, para 30.

B. The Case Law of the Community Courts

The first time the ECJ was confronted with a question regarding the application of Article 6(1) ECHR to competition proceedings was in *Fedetab*.[186] It is interesting to note that the applicants claimed the Commission decision affected their civil rights and obligations rather than constituting a criminal charge.[187] The reason is probably that no fine was imposed by the Commission and perhaps also that the case law of the ECtHR as regards the classification of a criminal charge was less developed. The ECJ held that the reference to Article 6(1) ECHR was irrelevant and that the Commission could not be classified as a tribunal within the meaning of the Article. The Court also stated that the Commission was bound to respect the procedural guarantees provided for in Community law.[188] In *Pioneer*[189] one of the applicants maintained that the decision was unlawful since the Commission combined the functions of prosecutor and judge in contravention of Article 6(1) ECHR. The ECJ rejected the argument and confirmed *Fedetab*. The Court added that the argument was based on a misunderstanding of the nature of the procedure before the Commission.[190] In his opinion AG Slynn said that the procedure before the Commission was not judicial but administrative and that the Commission could not be classified as a tribunal. He stressed that this did not mean that the Commission was exempt from behaving fairly, however, it meant that there was no substance in the argument that the procedure did not comply with Article 6(1) ECHR.[191] This approach has been applied in subsequent cases, for example *Shell*[192] *(Polypropylene)* and *Enso Española*[193] *(Cartonboard)* which will be dealt with in detail below.

Although as previously mentioned the conclusion that the Commission does not constitute a tribunal is in accordance with the case law of the ECtHR, it is submitted that this jurisprudence of the Community Courts is misconceived and avoids tackling the issue at stake. The crucial question when ruling on the applicability of Article 6 ECHR is whether the case involves a determination of a criminal charge or civil rights and obligations. In other words, the decisive element is the nature of the dispute not the constituent elements of the decision-maker.[194] Were it the other way around the scope of Article 6 ECHR could be side-stepped by

---

[186] Cases 209–215/78 *Heintz van Landewyck Sarl and others v Commission* [1980] ECR 3125. For an early criticism of this case: S Ghandi 'Interaction Between the Protection of Fundamental Rights in the European Economic Community and under the European Convention on Human Rights' [1981] Legal Issues of European Integration 9, 11–12.   [187] *Ibid.*, para 79.

[188] *Ibid.*, para 81.

[189] Cases 100–103/80 *Musique Diffusion Française SA and other v Commission* [1983] ECR 1825, paras 6–7.   [190] *Ibid.*, para 11.

[191] Cases 100–103/80 *Musique Diffusion Française SA and other v Commission* [1983] ECR 1825, 1920; [1983] CMLR 221, 277–278.

[192] Case T-11/89 *Shell v Commission* [1992] ECR II-757, para 39.

[193] Case T-348/94 *Enso Española v Commission* [1998] ECR II-1875, para 56.

[194] D Waelbroeck and D Fosselard 'Should the Decision-Making Power in EC Antitrust Procedure be Left to an Independent Judge?-The Impact of the European Convention of Human

entrusting the matter to a body which would not be classified as tribunal and therewith deprive those concerned of the protection of the Article.

By far the most detailed treatment of the Community Courts as to whether competition proceedings are in conformity with the requirement of a trial before an independent and impartial tribunal is to be found in *Enso Española*. There the applicant alleged that the dual role of the Commission infringed his right to an independent and impartial tribunal according to Article 6(1) ECHR and that the review of the CFI was not sufficient to meet the requirements of the ECtHR of a review by a court with full jurisdiction.[195] The CFI started by repeating the oft-cited formula about fundamental rights forming a part of the general principles of Community law and the special significance of the ECHR in that respect. Then as mentioned the Court followed the case law outlined above.[196] Regarding the applicant's assertion that judicial review had not been adequate, the CFI said that the requirement of effective judicial review of any Commission decision that finds and punishes an infringement of the competition rules was a general principle of Community law which followed from the common constitutional traditions of the Member States.[197] The CFI found on three grounds that the principle had not been breached. First, it was stated that the CFI was an independent and impartial tribunal, which as mentioned in the previous chapter is not open to debate. Interestingly the Court also referred to the third recital of the preamble of the Council Decision establishing the CFI. The recital said that the establishment of the CFI was particularly to improve the judicial protection of individuals in respect of actions requiring close examination of complex facts.[198] Second, the Court said that a review of legality under Article 230 EC must be regarded as effective judicial review. The pleas which might be relied on in an application of annulment were of such a nature to allow the Court to assess the correctness in law and in fact of any accusation made by the Commission in competition proceedings.[199] Third, the CFI referred to the unlimited jurisdiction, see Article 229 EC, exercised under Article 17 of Regulation 17/62 (Article 31 of Regulation 1/2003) and said that it followed that the Court had jurisdiction to assess whether the fine or penalty payment imposed was proportionate to the seriousness of the infringement.[200] In *Cement*,[201] the CFI also dealt with questions regarding the limits of its judicial review, saying that when reviewing the legality of a decision finding an infringement of Article 81(1) and/or Article 82 the applicants may call upon the

---

Rights on EC Antitrust Procedures' [1994] Ybk of Eur L 111, 115; IS Forrester 'Modernisation of EC Competition Law' in BE Hawk (ed) *Annual Proceedings of the Fordham Corporate Law Institute* (Juris Publishing Inc New York 2000) 181, 218.

[195] Case T-348/94 *Enso Española v Commission* [1998] ECR II-1875, paras 33–44. This issue was not dealt with on appeal: Case C-282/98P *Enso Española v Commission* [2000] ECR I-9817.

[196] *Ibid.*, paras 55–56.   [197] *Ibid.*, para 60.   [198] *Ibid.*, para 62.

[199] *Ibid.*, para 63.   [200] *Ibid.*, para 64.

[201] Cases T-25/95, T-26/95, T-30-32/95, T-34-39/95, T-42-46/95, T-48/95, T-50-65/95, T-68–71/95, T-87/95, T-88/95, T-103/95 and T-104/95 *Cimenteries CBR and others v Commission* [2000] ECR II-491, para 719.

Court to undertake an exhaustive review of both the Commission's substantive findings of fact and its legal appraisal of those facts, as well as citing the reasons given above in *Enso Española*.

Without making any comment at this stage as to whether the CFI reached the correct conclusion, the judgment in *Enso Española* is open to criticism in some respects. As outlined above the case law saying that the Commission does not constitute a tribunal is far from convincing and does not deal with the issue posed. Also and perhaps most tellingly the CFI makes no attempt to classify the fines levied by the Commission according to Article 6(1) ECHR and in fact does not even refer to the Article. The characteristics of the decision are essential when evaluating whether judicial review meets the requirements of the ECHR. It would additionally have been most welcome had the Court quoted the jurisprudence of the ECtHR because, as Lenaerts remarked, that is essential for a credible application of the ECHR by the Community Courts.[202] Related to this criticism it might be mentioned that the Court made no attempt to explain whether or how the application of the general principle of effective judicial review would differ depending on the issues at stake. Finally, the CFI does not use examples from the case law of the Community Courts to elucidate how the judicial review plays out in practice. As will be recalled the ECtHR requires not only that the courts have the necessary competence but also that the review undertaken in the instant case is sufficient.

These observations do not of course overlook the fact, that it would have been difficult, as well as unusual, for the CFI to disregard the judgments of the ECJ. The judgment of the CFI also, at least in some respect, shows the limitations posed by the requirements of unanimous rulings.[203] One of the judges in the *Enso Española* was Bo Vesterdorf, whose opinion in *Polypropylene* in many ways set the scene for the judicial review function of the CFI. There he, as mentioned before, stated that it was vitally important the Court should seek to bring about a state of legal affairs not susceptible to any justified criticism with regard to the ECHR.[204] Judging by those remarks it is tempting to speculate whether Vesterdorf would not have been willing to be more explicit in dealing with the issues raised by the applicants.

These issues were also addressed in the UK in an interim decision of the CAT in *Napp Pharmaceutical*.[205] As will be recalled the Director General of Fair Trading (DGFT) did not dispute the submission of the applicant that the proceedings under the CA were criminal for the purposes of Article 6(1) ECHR.[206] The CAT

[202] K Lenaerts 'Fundamental Rights in the European Union' (2000) 25 ELR 575, 580.

[203] AL Young 'The Charter, Constitution and Human Rights: is this the Beginning or the End for Human Rights Protections by Community Law' Eur Public L (2005) 11 219, 235. The article states that the compromises needed are more likely to be reached as to a minimal as opposed to a maximal protection and lead to vague language.

[204] Opinion of AG Vesterdorf, Cases T-1-4/89, T-6-15/89, *Rhone Poulenc SA and others v Commission* [1991] ECR II-867, 1019; [1992] 4 CMLR 84, 101

[205] *Napp Pharmaceutical Holdings Ltd v Director General of Fair Trading* [2002] ECC 3.

[206] *Ibid.*, para 71.

said that the administrative procedure before the DGFT might not itself comply with Article 6(1) but that did not constitute a breach of the Article provided that the DGFT were subject to control by a judicial body with full jurisdiction. In that respect the CAT cited two judgments previously mentioned, *Albert and Le Compte v Belgium*[207] and the House of Lords judgment in *Alconbury*.[208] The CAT concluded by saying that the CA looks to the judicial stage of the process before the Tribunal to satisfy the requirements of Article 6 ECHR.[209] It should be added that, as mentioned in the ruling of the CAT, the jurisdiction of the CAT differs from that of the CFI when the Court rules on appeals against Commission decisions. An examination of this difference is; however, not necessary for the purposes of this article.[210] The approach taken by the Tribunal is preferable to the one applied by the CFI since it fits the framework of analysis undertaken by the ECtHR when confronted with questions of this kind. There is, however, one shortcoming in the reasoning of the CAT, ie it refers to cases which concerned the civil head of Article 6(1) and as has been repeatedly mentioned the requisite standard of judicial review differs depending on the subject-matter at hand.[211]

C. Unlimited Jurisdiction

Article 229 EC provides that regulations may give the Court of Justice unlimited jurisdiction with regard to the penalties provided for in such regulations. That has been the case in competition proceedings ever since the adoption of Regulation 17/62, cf Article 17 of the Regulation, and is now provided for in Article 31 of Regulation 1/2003.[212] It should be underlined that the unlimited jurisdiction extends only to the imposition of the penalties, cf the wording *'in regard to the penalties'*, not the underlying infringement decision, which is subject to an action for annulment under Article 230.[213] However, in practice the courses for action are closely intertwined with applicants making use of them both.[214] The Community

---

[207] *Albert and Le Compte v Belgium* Series A No 58 (1983) 5 EHRR 533.

[208] *R (on the application of Holding & Barnes Plc) v Secretary of State for the Environment, Transport and the Regions* [2003] 2 AC 295.

[209] *Napp Pharmaceutical Holdings Ltd v Director General of Fair Trading* [2002] ECC 3, para 76.

[210] Appeal to the CAT is an appeal on the merits not just appeal by way of judicial review: R Whish *Competition Law* (5th edn Lexis Nexis London 2003) 402–403.

[211] In the final decision of this case (*Napp Pharmaceutical Holdings Ltd v Director General of Fair Trading* [2002] ECC 13, para 137) the CAT added one case to its list of authorities (*Magill v Porter* [2002] 2 WLR 37) which also regarded civil rights and obligations.

[212] For clarification it might be added that since its creation the CFI has exercised this unlimited jurisdiction, cf the discussion above regarding the ECJ's appellate role.

[213] Cases C-89/85, C-104/85, C-114/85, C-116-117/85 and C-125-129/85 A. *Ahlström Oy and others v Commission* [1993] ECR I-1307, opinion of AG Darmon, para 462; Case C-291/98P *Sarrio SA v Commission* [2000] ECR I-9991, paras 69–71; J Usher 'Exercise of the European Court of its Jurisdiction to Annul Competition Decisions' [1980] ELR 287, 299–300. See also the comment of F Mancini 'Judicial Review of EEC Competition Cases Panel Discussion' in BE Hawk (ed) *Annual Proceedings of the Fordham Corporate Law Institute* (Matthew Bender Times Mirror Books New York 1988) 629, 632.

[214] M Smith *Competition Law-Enforcement and Procedure* (Butterworths London 2001) 215; C Harding and J Joshua *Regulating Cartels in Europe* (OUP Oxford 2003) 172.

Courts have also treated an application under eg Article 17 of Regulation 17/62 as an action for annulment in the sense that their point of departure is not the alleged infringement but the Commission decision.[215]

Toth describes the Community Courts' power in an action falling under unlimited jurisdiction as follows:

Following the theory of *recours de pleine juridiction* as known in French administrative law, in these proceedings the Court's powers are not limited to reviewing the objective legality of the acts or omissions of the institutions. Rather, the Court is free to deal with all aspects of the case, factual or legal. Thus, it can assess and interpret the facts, it can evaluate the appropriateness or expediency of the act in question in the light of the underlying economic, monetary, etc. considerations, taking into account all relevant circumstances. In annulling the act, the Court is not restricted to the four grounds of action. Moreover, the Court has the power not only to annul but also to vary the challenged act by reducing or even increasing the fine or penalty imposed, and to award any appropriate damages acting, if necessary, of its own motion.[216]

If this view of unlimited jurisdiction is the prevailing one it appears fairly clear that, in principle, there is every possibility of judicial review which would satisfy the requirements of Article 6(1) ECHR. However, not everyone signs up to this opinion of the Community Courts' power when exercising unlimited jurisdiction. Joshua says that it does not confer on the Court *carte blanche* simply to substitute its own opinion on the facts for that of the Commission. It allows the Court to cancel, reduce or increase the fine imposed but it does not give it any greater powers to intervene on the facts than under Article 230.[217] This is; however, clearly a minority view among commentators, eg neither Bebr nor Schermers and Waelbroeck mention any limitations in the Court's review of the facts.[218] Kerse and Kahn state that when looking at the fine imposed by the Commission, the Court can consider all aspects of the case and all relevant questions of law and fact.[219]

Lenaerts and Arts say that scholarly writing has distinguished between two views of unlimited jurisdiction, the broad and the narrow one. That differentiation does; however, not correspond to the difference of opinion outlined above. On the broad view of unlimited jurisdiction, the Court is permitted to evaluate the reasonableness of a sanction irrespective of whether the act is tainted with illegality.

---

[215] HG Schermers and DF Waelbroeck *Judicial Protection in the European Union* (6th edn Kluwer Law International The Hague 2001) 579.

[216] AG Toth *The Oxford Encyclopaedia of European Community Law Volume 1 Institutional Law* (Clarendon Press Oxford 1990) 539.

[217] JM Joshua 'Attitudes to Antitrust Enforcement in the EU and United States: Dodging the Traffic Warden or Respecting the Law?' in BE Hawk (ed) *Annual Proceedings of the Fordham Corporate Law Institute* (Juris Publishing Inc Sweet and Maxwell New York 1996) 101, 109.

[218] G Bebr *Development of Judicial Control of the European Communities* (Martinus Nijhoff Publishers The Hague 1981) 130–131; HG Schermers and DF Waelbroeck *Judicial Protection in the European Union* (6th edn Kluwer Law International The Hague 2001) 579–580.

[219] CS Kerse and N Khan *EC Antitrust Procedure* (5th edn Sweet and Maxwell London 2005) 461.

On the narrow view the Court on the other hand is only permitted to interfere when the act is tainted with illegality.[220] Probably both these views are capable of allowing the Community Courts to exercise judicial review sufficient in scope for the purposes of the ECHR. However, as will be shown when analysing the case law there is little doubt that the Community Courts have endorsed the broad view. As will be described below, Article 230 EC does not contain any limitations, which in principle preclude judicial review from being in conformity with Article 6(1) ECHR, the same considerations would seem to apply *a fortiori* to Article 229 EC.

A note-worthy early case regarding the exercise of judicial review in the context of unlimited jurisdiction is *Alma*[221] which was concerned with the application of Article 36 ECSC. The ECJ noted that the action was one in which it had unlimited jurisdiction and was therefore empowered not only to annul but also to amend the decision which had been adopted.[222] The Court considered that the amount of the fine imposed had not been excessive. After having commented on the gravity of the offence and the financial situation of the applicant the ECJ said that no manifest injustice had been established and the Court did not intend to substitute its assessment for that of the High Authority.[223] It is highly unlikely that a review of this type would be deemed to be in accordance with the requirements of Article 6(1) ECHR. The reference of the ECJ to *'manifest injustice'* has undoubted similarities with Wednesbury unreasonableness. In that context it will be recalled that in *W v UK*,[224] the ECtHR held that to be insufficient control of administrative discretion. Since the review was considered inadequate for the purposes of the civil head of Article 6(1) ECHR (albeit an interference with a right protected under Article 8 ECHR) a similarly lax type of review would almost certainly be condemned as well when concerned with a criminal charge. The review has; however, developed considerably as will be shown. Another old case worthy of mention is *Niederrheinische*,[225] where AG Lagrange said that unlimited jurisdiction was traditionally characterized by two factors:

> [O]n the one hand, the *powers of the court* which consist not only in the power of annulment but also of amendment and in certain cases powers of injunction and of imposition of pecuniary penalties and, on the other hand, the *subject matter of the proceedings* which concerns subjective rights and not the objective legality of an administrative measure.[226]

Lenaerts and Arts cite this opinion as a source for saying that the Court may take into account matters to which it would not be entitled to have regard to in judicial

---

[220] K Lenaerts and D Arts R Brady (ed) *Procedural Law of the European Union* (2nd edn Sweet and Maxwell London 2006) 308–309.

[221] Case 8/56 *Acciaierie Laminatoi Magliano Alpi v High Authority* [1957] ECR 95. This case was referred to by the applicant in *Enso Española* (p 48–50).   [222] *Ibid.*, 99.

[223] *Ibid.*, 100.   [224] *W v UK* Series A No 121 A (1988) 10 EHRR 29.

[225] Cases 2–3/60 *Niederrheinische Bergwerks-Aktiengesellschaft and others v High Authority* [1961] ECR 133.   [226] *Ibid.*, 152.

review proceedings concerning the legality of the act.[227] Waelbroeck and Fosselard on the other hand say that on the basis of the definition of the AG the jurisdiction involved in judicial review by the Community Courts could only be described as being of a limited character.[228]

Commercial Solvents[229] is a good example of a stricter type of judicial review in relation to the amount of fine imposed. The ECJ upheld the Commission's decision substantively but decided nevertheless to reduce the fine by half. In doing so the Court observed that the duration of the infringement, which was calculated at two years, might have been shorter had the Commission intervened more quickly after receiving a complaint. Also the ill-effects of the abuse had been limited. The ECJ makes no explicit reference to the standard of review but there can be no doubt that the Court is applying a more stringent standard than in *Alma* and does not require the establishing of a manifest injustice on behalf of the Commission. In this context it is worth mentioning the following statement of AG Warner:

> At all events, Article 17 of Regulation No 17 confers on the Court an unlimited jurisdiction to review a decision of the Commission imposing a fine: the Court may cancel, reduce or increase the fine as it thinks fit. I do not doubt that in exercising that jurisdiction the Court is entitled to take into account considerations of common justice.[230]

In *BMW Belgium* we come across another interesting comment from AG Warner. After having referred to Article 17 of Regulation 17/62 and the competence it bestows on the Court the AG said:

> That does not, however, in my opinion, mean that the Court should, in every case brought before it, substitute its own assessment of the appropriate fine for the Commission's. The Court should, in my opinion, alter the amount of a fine imposed by the Commission only if persuaded that the Commission has, in fixing the fine, made a material error of fact or of law. Such an error may of course be either implicit or explicit in the relevant decision of the Commission.[231]

On the basis of this it appears that the AG considers that, in principle, the Court could always substitute its own judgment for that of the Commission. His reference to material error does not seem to be linked with what was above termed as the narrow view of unlimited jurisdiction, which, *inter alia*, can be inferred from that he refers to material error in '*fixing the fine*', whereas, the narrow view required the illegality of the decision to permit the Court to interfere with the

---

[227] K Lenaerts and D Arts R Brady (ed) *Procedural Law of the European Union* (2nd edn Sweet and Maxwell London 2006) 448.

[228] D Waelbroeck and D Fosselard 'Should the Decision-Making Power in EC Antitrust Procedure be Left to an Independent Judge?-The Impact of the European Convention of Human Rights on EC Antitrust Procedures' [1994] Ybk of Eur L 111, 128.

[229] Cases 6–7/73 *Istituto Chemioterapico Italiano SpA and Commercial Solvents v Commission* [1974] ECR 223, paras 51–52.

[230] Cases 6–7/73 *Istituto Chemioterapico Italiano SpA and Commercial Solvents v Commission* [1974] ECR 223, 274; [1974] 1 CMLR 309, 334.

[231] Cases 32/78 and 36–82/78 *BMW Belgium and others v Commission* [1979] ECR 2435, 2494.

amount of the fine. It is difficult to discern whether the ECJ signed up to this view of the AG, since it dismissed the application for reduction of the fines and dealt only briefly with it.[232]

In *Michelin*,[233] we find an observation of the ECJ regarding unlimited jurisdiction, saying that it was for the Court exercising its powers of unlimited jurisdiction to assess for itself the circumstances of the case and the nature of the infringement in question in order to determine the amount of the fine. This statement shows that the Court considers itself competent to substitute its own judgment on what is the appropriate fine, see the above-mentioned opinion of AG Warner. The wording '*the circumstances of the case*' also clearly implies that the Court is competent to evaluate all the facts. However, it is not certain whether the Court agrees with AG Warner, ie that there needs to be an error in fixing the fine before the Court decides to exercise its competence. In the instant case two aspects of the Commission's decision regarding the abuse committed by the company were considered not to have been proven, which led to a reduction in the fine.

The view of AG Warner in *BMW Belgium* is endorsed by AG Vesterdorf in *Polypropylene*[234] who quotes the opinion after having stated his view that in normal circumstances the Community Courts should not pursue their own penalties policy but, within the limits of Regulation 17/62, leave it to the Commission to set the general level of the fines. He added that he considered there was only reason to intervene where the Commission without giving reasons departed from a relatively well-established level of fines in a single case and thus acted contrary to the principle of equal treatment. These statements in the opinions of the AG's probably do not give rise to concerns over whether the review is sufficient. If the Court has reviewed the case both in law and in fact and concluded that the Commission had not erred in levying the fine it would not be required under the case law of the ECtHR to use its competence to substitute judgment on the amount, see *Janosevic*.

There is; however, another comment in the opinion of AG Vesterdorf in *Polypropylene*, which is apt to give doubts as to whether the type of review of the fines he envisages would satisfy the requirements of Article 6(1) ECHR. When discussing whether the Commission should draw up a catalogue of fines, the AG says that it must be acknowledged that the Commission should have a broad discretion to determine the fines according to its assessment of all the circumstances of the case. The problem is no different from other areas of law where the administration has more or less a broad discretion. As he points out there is; however, a difference in that in Community law the Court has unlimited jurisdiction with regard to the fines and can therefore substitute its own assessment for that of the

---

[232] *Ibid.*, paras 54–55.
[233] Case 322/81 *Nederlandsche Banden-Industrie Michelin NV v Commission* [1983] ECR 3461, para 111.
[234] Cases T-1-4/89, T-6-15/89, *Rhone Poulenc SA and others v Commission* [1991] ECR II-867, 1019; [1992] 4 CMLR 84, 239.

Commission. The AG believes that the Court should display some caution in that regard and only step in when it comes to the conclusion that the Commission has been guilty of a clear error of assessment. That might for example be thought to be the case where it appeared that the Commission had taken incorrect turnover or sales figures as a basis for its assessment.[235]

This view of AG Vesterdorf seems to be shared by Schermers and Waelbroeck, who say that it is only if the amount is manifestly disproportionate and based on a manifest error that the Court will review the amount.[236] However, the later cases cited by them do not seem to warrant that assertion. In these cases the ECJ remarked that *'the amount of the fine is appropriate to the gravity of the infringements'*.[237] The review of the amount of the fine is admittedly superfluous compared to the detailed review now conducted by the CFI, see below. On the other hand it is submitted here that the text does not support the view that the ECJ requires a manifest error, especially when regard is had to the fact the Court says that the fine is appropriate. That would appear to suggest that the ECJ assessed the amount and would have been prepared to interfere had it found the fine inappropriate.

The CFI did not subscribe to this observation of AG Vesterdorf, which is best demonstrated by the judgment in *ICI*.[238] There the CFI exercised its unlimited jurisdiction by reducing the fine levied on ICI by 1,000,000 ECU since it considered that the Commission had not given enough weight to the co-operation of the firm when determining the fine. The Court said, *inter alia*, that it would have been more difficult for the Commission to establish the existence of the infringement and bring it to an end if it had not had the benefit of the company's reply to the request for information.[239] There is no reference to a clear error of assessment and the CFI substitutes its own judgment as to the utility of the information supplied by ICI to the investigation of the Commission. Interestingly, van der Woude maintains that the CFI held that the Commission made a manifest error in regard to the co-operative attitude of ICI. The wording used by the Court does not support that assertion; however, it is possible that the Court implicitly regarded the way in which the extent of the ICI's co-operation was reflected in the fine imposed as a manifest error.[240] Finally, worth noting this case has been given

---

[235] Cases T-1-4/89, T-6-15/89, *Rhone Poulenc SA and others v Commission* [1991] ECR II-867 1027–1028; [1992] 4 CMLR 84, 247.

[236] HG Schermers and DF Waelbroeck *Judicial Protection in the European Union* (6th edn Kluwer Law International The Hague 2001) 580.

[237] See eg: Case 48/69 *ICI v Commission (Dyestuffs)* [1972] ECR 619, para 147. The remarks of the ECJ as regards the fine are as follows: 'In view of the frequency and extent of the applicant's participation in the prohibited practices, and taking into account the consequences thereof in relation to the creation of a common market in the products in question, the amount of the fine is appropriate to the gravity of the infringement of the Community rules on competition.'

[238] Case T-13/89 *ICI v Commission (Polypropylene)* [1992] ECR II-1021.

[239] *Ibid.*, paras 392–394.

[240] M van der Woude 'The Court of First Instance: The First Three Years' in B Hawk (ed) *Annual Proceedings of the Fordham Corporate Law Institute* (Transnational Juris Publications Kluwer Law & Taxation Publishers New York 1993) 621, 667.

as an example of a reduction of a fine even though the Commission decision was not vitiated with illegality, ie endorsing the broad view of unlimited jurisdiction as outlined above.[241]

The CFI

The CFI has devoted much more attention to the question of the amount of the fines than the ECJ was accustomed to. As will be recalled one of the reasons for the establishment of the CFI was to provide for a more detailed examination of complex facts. The founding of the CFI has also coincided with a considerable rise in the fines levied by the Commission, which inevitably has meant that the focus of judicial control has become more centered on the amount of the fines.[242] As a good early example of the CFI checking meticulously the criteria governing the level of the fine, *Dunlop Slazenger*[243] may be mentioned. There the Court examined, *inter alia*, the gravity of the infringement and whether the alleged lack of precedent had any effect on the imposition of the fine, the duration of the infringement, the conduct of the firm during the investigation and the turnover to be taken into consideration. The CFI held that the Commission had not proved the existence of infringements for the entire period alleged in the decision.[244] When deciding on the reduction the Court said that it did not necessarily have to be proportionate to the amount by which the Court reduced the duration of the infringements, given the Commission's findings as to the gravity and cumulative nature of the infringements. The CFI therefore, exercising its unlimited jurisdiction, lowered the fine from 5,000,000 ECU to 3,000,000 ECU saying it represented a fair assessment of the circumstances.[245]

Another case worth noting is *Parker Pen*[246] which reinforces that the CFI endorses the broad view of what constitutes unlimited jurisdiction. The Commission decision was upheld in its entirety; however, the Court was of the opinion that the Commission had not taken into consideration the fact that the turnover accounted for by the products in question was relatively low in comparison with the applicant's total sales. In light of that and related considerations the CFI thought the fine imposed to be inappropriate and lowered it considerably.[247] However, the CFI has lately not applied its power to reduce fine without annulling any parts of a decision and *Parker Pen* is the last example of that taking place.[248]

---

[241] K Lenaerts 'Procedures and Sanctions in Economic Administrative Law' in J Schwarze (ed) in *17 FIDE Kongress Conclusions and Perspectives* (Internationale Föderation für Europarecht Berlin 1996) 101, 172; K Lenaerts and D Arts R Brady (ed) *Procedural Law of the European Union* (2nd edn Sweet and Maxwell London 2006) 450.

[242] On the recent developments as regards appeals of the fines: R Whish *Competition Law* (5th edn Lexis Nexis London 2003) 459.

[243] Case T-43/92 *Dunlop Slazenger v Commission* [1994] ECR II-441.

[244] *Ibid.*, paras 153–157.   [245] *Ibid.*, paras 178–179.

[246] Case T-77/92 *Parker Pen Ltd v Commission* [1994] ECR II-549.

[247] *Ibid.*, paras 94–95.

[248] CS Kerse and N Khan *EC Antitrust Procedure* (5th edn Sweet and Maxwell London 2005) 463. Although note *Compagnie Generale Maritime*, mentioned below.

For a more recent example of the CFI's review of the fines levied by the Commission, *Volkswagen*[249] is a fine one. The Commission had imposed what was then an unprecedented fine, €103,000,000, on Volkswagen. With regard to the substance of the case, the CFI upheld the Commission's decision except that it considered that the Commission had not proved the duration of the infringement to the extent alleged in the decision. The Court held that the breach was committed intentionally and that the Commission had not erred by not reducing the fine on grounds put forward by the undertaking.[250] On the other hand the CFI considered that the Commission was not permitted to regard a certain agreement as a factor justifying an increase in the amount of the fine since it had previously been brought to the Commission's notice.[251] In the light of the above it fell to the CFI in the exercise of its unlimited jurisdiction to vary the decision and reduce the amount of the fine. As in *Dunlop Slazenger* the Court remarked that the reduction in the fine did not necessarily have to be proportionate to the reduction in time. The Court then cited *Michelin* saying that the Court must carry out its own assessment of the case in order to determine the amount of the fine. All things considered the CFI reduced the fine to €90,000,000.[252]

CMA CGM[253] contains a very extensive examination by the CFI of the amount of the fines levied on the firms subject to the decision by the Commission. An important development occurred in 1998, the Commission published Guidelines on the method of setting the fine, the objective of which was according to the preamble to ensure the transparency and impartiality of Commission decisions.[254] The CFI held that the Commission had not erred in law by classifying the infringement as serious according to Section 1A of the Guidelines.[255] The Commission had stated in the decision that the basic level of the fine should be set at the very lowest end of the scale appropriate for a serious infringement, ie €1,000,000. The Commission, however, imposed a fine of €1,300,000 on the largest undertaking and proportionally on the other undertakings. The CFI

---

[249] Case T-62/98 *Volkswagen AG v Commission* [2000] ECR II-2707.

[250] *Ibid.*, paras 332–341.   [251] *Ibid.*, para 343.

[252] *Ibid.*, paras 346–348, the judgment was upheld on appeal: Case C-338/00P *Volkswagen AG v Commission* [2003] ECR I-9189.

[253] Case T-213/00 *CMA CGM and others v Commission* [2003] ECR II-913.

[254] Guidelines on the method of setting fines imposed pursuant to Article 15(2) of Regulation No 17 and Article 65(5) of the ECSC Treaty [1998] OJ C9/3. These guidelines have now been replaced by: Guidelines on the method of setting fines imposed pursuant to Article 23(2)(a) of Regulation No 1/2003 [2006] OJ C210/2. The wide discretion enjoyed by the Commission and the alleged lack of transparency and consistency came under criticism from the practitioners' camp: I van Bael 'Fining A La Carte: The Lottery of EU Competition Law' (1995) 16 ECLR 237, 237 etc. Predictably this view was opposed by the advocates of the Commission. For an overview of the debate: A Jones and B Sufrin *EC Competition Law Text, Cases, and Materials* (OUP Oxford 2001) 907–910. Since the adoption of the guidelines the CFI has shown a tendency to follow the approach outlined there when deciding on reductions in fines: CS Kerse and N Khan *EC Antitrust Procedure* (5th edn Sweet and Maxwell London) 461.

[255] Case T-213/00 *CMA CGM and others v Commission* [2003] ECR II-913, paras 265–267. The appeal of the Commission was dismissed by an order of the ECJ dated 28 October 2004.

considered that the Commission's decision was vitiated by an inadequate statement of reasons for imposing a fine higher than the basic amount according to the
Guidelines.[256] The Court then thoroughly examined the applicants' submissions
regarding the amount of the fine which, *inter alia*, related to a failure on behalf of
the Commission to take account of mitigating circumstances, the entitlement to
additional reduction on grounds of co-operation with the Commission, the fact
that the Commission had failed to assess that no financial advantage derived
from the infringement and that the Commission breached the principle of non-
discrimination. The CFI rejected all the arguments except that it found that the
Commission had infringed the principle of non-discrimination when dividing
the undertakings into four groups for the purposes of calculating the fine.[257] The
CFI did not decide on the appropriate fine in this case because it considered that
the Commission was time-barred from imposing fines, see Regulation 2988/74.[258]

One of the best examples from the recent case law of the CFI demonstrating the
Court's competence when exercising unlimited jurisdiction is *Compagnie
Generale Maritime*.[259] The case concerned both the application of Article 81 EC
and the specific rules relating to maritime transport, in particular, Regulation
4056/86.[260] The Court upheld the Commission's findings that the applicants had
acted in breach of the competition rules and did not fulfil the conditions for an
individual exemption under Article 81(3). The Commission had imposed a fine
of only 10,000 ECU on each undertaking saying that given the existence of mitigating circumstances the level of the fines was set a symbolic level.[261] The Court
disagreed with the Commission on this point and thought the imposition of fines
not justified. The CFI referred amongst other things to the tariffs in question
being a matter of public knowledge; it took the Commission some time to define
its view on the subject; even though a horizontal price-fixing agreement was at
stake the case raised complex issues of both an economic and legal nature; numerous factors led the applicants to believe that the agreement was lawful.[262] The
Court summed up by saying: 'In light of all those circumstances, the [CFI] considers, in the exercise of its unlimited jurisdiction, that there is justification for not
imposing a fine in the present case.'[263] This is interesting to compare with the

---

256 *Ibid.*, paras 272–275.   257 *Ibid.*, para 426.
258 Council Regulation concerning limitation periods in proceedings and the enforcement of
sanctions under the rules of the European Economic Community relating to transport and competition [1974] OJ L319/1.
259 Case T-86/95 *Compagnie Generale Maritime v Commission* [2002] ECR II-1011.
260 Council Regulation No 4056/86 of 22 December laying down detailed rules for the application of Articles 85 and 86 of the Treaty to maritime transport [1986] OJ L378/4. This Regulation has
been repealed by Council Regulation (EC) No 1419/2006 of 25 September 2006 repealing
Regulation (EEC) No 4056/86 laying down detailed rules for the application of Articles 85 and 86 of
the Treaty to maritime transport, and amending Regulation (EC) No 1/2003 as regards the extension
of its scope to include cabotage and international tramp services [2006] OJ L269/1.
261 *Far Eastern Freight Conference* [1994] OJ L378/17, paras 158–159.
262 Case T-86/95 *Compagnie Generale Maritime v Commission* [2002] ECR II-1011, paras 481–487.
263 *Ibid.*, para 488.

statements of AG Warner in his opinion in *Miller*[264] where he said that in a case where the Commission had fixed the fine at the lowest end (around 0.73 per cent of the turnover) of the scale: '[I]t would show scant respect for the exercise by the Commission of its discretion if the Court were to reduce the fine still further on the mere ground that the infringement was trivial.'[265] The CFI is probably going a bit further than AG Warner though it is not quite clear since he only speaks of the infringement being trivial, whereas there were several grounds which led to the conclusion of the CFI. In any event possible discrepancy in this respect, would in all probability not be of significance for our purposes and it is worth remembering that AG Warner said in *Commercial Solvents* that the Court could take considerations of common justice into account.[266]

Even in recent judgments from the CFI examples can be found where the Court refers to the standard of '*manifest error*'. On close examination these examples do; however, not give rise to any concerns regarding the way in which the Court carries out its reviewing functions. In *Tokai Carbon I* the CFI stated, that claiming a reduction in fine was insufficient in comparison to what was granted to other firms was not sufficient to establish a manifest error of assessment on behalf of the Commission.[267] On the other hand the Court analysed the applicant's submissions thoroughly and concluded that the Commission had, on various points, failed to appreciate the importance of the co-operation provided by the applicant and granted a further 10 per cent reduction of the fine.[268] Nothing in the Court's reasoning appears to suggest that a standard of '*manifest error*' was applied when reaching this conclusion. In *Tokai Carbon II* the CFI concluded that the Commission had committed a manifest error of assessment.[269] The explanation for that reference seems to be quite simply, the Commission had indeed committed a manifest error of assessment, when in determining the turnover in the relevant products, took into figures which included other products as well, despite express statements to the contrary.[270]

On the basis of the above it seems safe to conclude that the CFI in the exercise of its unlimited jurisdiction is conducting judicial review which satisfies the requirements of Article 6(1) ECHR. The Court reviews all issues of both law and facts regarding the imposition of penalties and can substitute its own judgment for that of the Commission. Linking this to the scholarly writing mentioned above, the Court endorses the broad view of unlimited jurisdiction and considers itself competent to evaluate all the facts. As we have seen the review as applied by

---

[264] Case 19/77 *Miller International Schallplatten GmbH v Commission* [1978] ECR 131.

[265] Case 19/77 *Miller International Schallplatten GmbH v Commission* [1978] ECR 131, 161; [1978] 2 CMLR 334, 346.

[266] Cases 6–7/73 *Istituto Chemioterapico Italiano SpA and Commercial Solvents v Commission* [1974] ECR 223, 274; [1974] 1 CMLR 309, 334.

[267] Cases T-236/01, T-239/01, T-244/01-T-246/01, T-251/01 and T-252/01 *Tokai Carbon and others v Commission* [2004] ECR II-1181, para 428.   [268] *Ibid.*, para 440.

[269] Cases T-71/03, T-74/03, T-87/03 and T-91/03 *Tokai Carbon and others v Commission* [2005] ECR II-10, para 251.   [270] *Ibid.*, para 242–250.

the ECJ in the early years would not have been in accordance with the requirements of the ECHR. Without wishing to state precisely when the review of the Community Courts came into line with the requirements of Article 6(1) ECHR it is likely that a review like the one performed in *Commercial Solvents* would have sufficed even though it is far less exacting than the review now undertaken by the CFI.

D. Judicial Review under Article 230 EC

Article 230(2) EC provides for four heads of review: lack of competence, infringement of an essential procedural requirement, infringement of the Treaty or any rule of law relating to its applications, and misuse of powers.[271] There is no question over the CFI's jurisdiction over points of law under the Article.[272] Also worth noting is that the Community Courts accord the Commission no deference over legal interpretation.[273] The case law has also established that error of fact plays an important role in annulment proceedings in competition law.[274] Bellamy has even characterized three additional grounds of review added by the case law: error of fact, error of appreciation and absence of reasoning.[275] It should be made clear from the outset that proceedings under Article 230 are not an appeal by a way of rehearing. In the words of AG Warner: '*[T]he Court is empowered to set aside the act complained of only if it finds that that act was unlawful on one (or more) of the grounds mentioned in the Article.*'[276] The Community Courts have jurisdiction to annul a Commission decision wholly or partially; however, they do not have jurisdiction to remake the decision under appeal. In *Italian Flat Glass* the CFI stated that the assumption of such a jurisdiction could disturb the inter-institutional balance established by the Treaty and would risk prejudicing the rights of defence.[277] As regards the inter-institutional balance it is clear, that the Commission has a power

---

[271] The European Commission of Human Rights referred to Article 230, formerly Article 173, in *Kaplan* (*Kaplan v UK* (1982) 4 EHRR 64, para 160) saying: 'It [the Commission] notes further that the limited scope of judicial review in many contracting States is also reflected in the scope of the jurisdiction afforded to the European Court of Justice under Article 173 of the Treaty ... Under that provision the Court has jurisdiction to review the legality of acts of the Council and Commission of the European Communities only on grounds of .... These limited grounds of action appear fairly typical of those existing in a number of Contracting States.' This case was referred to the Commission in *Enso Española* (Case T-348/94 *Enso Española v Commission* [1998] ECR II-1875, para 53) that reference is; however, misplaced because *Kaplan* arose under the civil head of Article 6(1) ECHR.

[272] FG Jacobs 'Court of Justice Review of Competition Cases' in BE Hawk (ed) *Annual Proceedings of the Fordham Corporate Law Institute* (Matthew Bender Times Mirror Books New York 1988) 541, 544.

[273] C Bellamy 'Antitrust and the Courts' panel discussion in BE Hawk (ed) *Annual Proceedings of the Fordham Corporate Law Institute* (Juris Publishing Inc New York 1999) 369, 416.

[274] KPE Lasok 'Judicial Review of Issues of Fact in Competition Cases' (1983) 4 ECLR 85, 86.

[275] C Bellamy 'Antitrust and the Courts' panel discussion in BE Hawk (ed) *Annual Proceedings of the Fordham Corporate Law Institute* (Juris Publishing Inc New York 1999) 369, 389.

[276] Cases 19–20/74 *Kali und Salz and others v Commission* [1975] ECR 499, 527; [1975] CMLR 154, 165.

[277] Case T-68/89 and T-77-78/89 *Societa Italiano Vero Spa and others v Commission* [1992] ECR II-1403, para 319.

of appraisal (*pouvoir d'appreciation*) when applying Articles 81 and 82. That in itself says nothing about the intensity of judicial review of a decision taken on the basis of such a power.[278] On the other hand the Commission sometimes has a margin of discretion when making those decisions, in particular, where something that may loosely be termed as a policy decision are at stake.[279]

Before moving on to examining the case law it needs to be ascertained whether there are any reasons, in principle, which preclude review under Article 230 from being sufficient for the purposes of Article 6(1) ECHR. Duffy captures well what is required of the review saying that the Community Courts will only provide the judicial redress required if all issues are fully considered and no discretionary reserve is shown in relation to the Commission's findings of fact and/or economic evidence.[280]

Toth states that when the Council or the Commission are exercising wide discretionary powers for formulating and implementing economic policies the Community Courts are restricted, when reviewing legality, to examine whether there was a manifest error or the institution clearly exceeded its competence.[281] On this view Article 230 places some limitations on the review function of the Community Courts, however, the restrictions as outlined by Toth could not be said to apply when the Courts are reviewing a decision imposing fines for infringement of the competition rules. Jacobs says that in those cases the Court has gone well beyond the apparent confines of Article 230, which can be said to reflect the recognition of a fundamental legal principle that every executive decision must be subject to judicial review on both law and fact.[282] Implicit in these remarks of Jacobs is that Article 230 places no limitations on judicial review which would preclude the review from being sufficient with regard to the ECHR. In this respect the observations of AG Cosmas in *Masterfoods*[283] are also of interest. He remarks that the assessment of the legality of a Community legislative measure is principally confined to pure judicial review. On the other hand: '[I]n the case of individual administrative measures such as that before the Court, the exercise of full

---

[278] V Tiili and J Vanhamme 'The 'Power of Appraisal' (*Pouvoir d'Appreciation*) of the Commission of the European Communities vis-à-vis the Powers of Judicial Review of the Communities' Court of Justice and Court of First Instance' (1999) 22 Fordham International Law Journal 885, 899.

[279] D Bailey 'Scope of Judicial Review under Article 81 EC' (2004) 41 CML Rev 1327, 1337–1339.

[280] House of Lords Select Committee on the European Communities *Enforcement of Community Competition Rules* (London HMSO 1993) memorandum of Peter Duffy, 196.

[281] AG Toth *The Oxford Encyclopaedia of European Community Law Volume 1 Institutional Law* (Clarendon Press Oxford 1990) 339. For recent examples from the case law: Case C-434/02 *Arnold André & Co v Commission* [2004] ECR I-11825, para 46; Case C-380/03 *Germany v Parliament and Council*, judgment of 12 December 2006 nyr, para 145.

[282] FG Jacobs 'Court of Justice Review of Competition Cases' in BE Hawk (ed) *Annual Proceedings of the Fordham Corporate Law Institute* (Matthew Bender Times Mirror Books New York 1988) 541, 543.

[283] Case C-344/98 *Masterfoods Ltd v HB Ice Cream Ltd* [2000] ECR I-11369, opinion of AG Cosmas.

review of substance is capital for the effective provision of judicial protection.'[284] This does, however, not mean that the appropriate standard of review is uniform when legislative measures are at stake. In *Tobacco Advertising* AG Fennelly advocated for a stricter standard of review when legislation restricts fundamental personal rights such as freedom of expression.[285] The above demonstrates that Article 230 is flexible enough to allow for different degrees of judicial scrutiny depending on the subject-matter at hand.[286]

Review in competition cases should also be variable in degrees of scrutiny depending on the context, as the different requirements the ECtHR has made with regard to judicial review bear out. Merger decisions and decisions taken pursuant to Article 81(3) EC would not fall under the criminal head of Article 6(1) ECHR but under the Article's civil head.[287] The intensity of review can of course differ within that category of decisions but an examination of that falls outside the scope of the article.[288]

---

[284] *Ibid.*, para 53. It should be noted that the word *'capital'* appears to be an incorrect translation. The German version refers to *'wesentlich'* and the Swedish one to *'väsentligt'* whereas the original Spanish says *'crucial'*.

[285] Case C-376/98 *Germany v Parliament and Council* [2000] ECR I-8419, paras 157–161 of the opinion of AG Fennelly. Since the ECJ annulled the directive for being adopted without sufficient legal basis the Court did not examine the other pleas of the applicant, *Ibid.*, para 118.

[286] See also: P Craig and G de Búrca *EU Law Text, Cases, and Materials* (3rd edn OUP Oxford 2003) 537–540. In his opinion in *Ladbroke* (Case C-83/98P *French Republic v Ladbroke Racing and Commission* [2000] ECR I-3271, para 16) AG Cosmas stated: 'It should be noted that the breadth of a court's jurisdiction when it reviews the legality of an administrative measure—such as the measure challenged at first instance—cannot be defined in an absolute and static manner. Apart from the need to adjust the breadth to the facts of each case, a need which exists beyond all doubt, a tendency may be observed in the case law of the Court of Justice towards a dynamic broadening of judicial review and a strengthening of jurisdiction even in instances where it is necessary to solve complex legal problems with a strong economic flavour such as problems related to competition law. That tendency reflects the basic endeavour of every judicial body—such as the Court of Justice—to ensure that judicial review is carried out as comprehensively as possible in the interests of observing the principle of legality and protecting the rights of the litigants. In conclusion, a comprehensive review as to the substance in cases such as the present one does not, of course, supplant the administrative work of the Commission but constitutes a correct exercise of judicial tasks in a legal order—like the Community legal order—governed by the principle of legality and the rule of law.'

[287] D Waelbroeck and D Fosselard 'Should the Decision-Making Power in EC Antitrust Procedure be Left to an Independent Judge?-The Impact of the European Convention of Human Rights on EC Antitrust Procedures' [1994] Ybk of Eur L 111, 124–125.

[288] The review has intensified in recent years, see for example: Cases T-374-375/94 and T-388/94 *European Night Services and others v Commission* [1998] ECR II-3141. C Bellamy 'Antitrust and the Courts' panel discussion in BE Hawk (ed) *Annual Proceedings of the Fordham Corporate Law Institute* (Juris Publishing Inc New York 1999) 369, 390–392; D Bailey 'Scope of Judicial Review under Article 81 EC' CML Rev (2004) 41 1327, 1346–1353. As regards merger cases, the Commission appealed the judgment of the CFI in *Tetra Laval* (Case T-05/02 *Tetra Laval BV v Commission* [2002] ECR II-4381) alleging, *inter alia*, that the standard of judicial review was inconsistent with Article 230 EC. The ECJ did not subscribe to that remarking: 'Whilst the Court recognises that the Commission has a margin of discretion with regard to economic matters that does not mean that the Community Courts must refrain from reviewing the Commission's interpretation of information of economic nature. Not only must the Community Courts, inter alia, establish whether the evidence relied on is factually accurate, reliable and consistent but also whether the evidence contains all the information which must be taken into account in order to assess a complex situation and whether it is capable of of substantiating the conclusions drawn from it. Such a review is all the more necessary in the case of a prospective analysis required when examining a planned merger with conglomerate

The Early Years

The first pronouncement of the ECJ regarding the standard of judicial review in competition law is to be found in the seminal *Consten-Grundig*.[289] There the ECJ famously remarked that:

[T]he exercise of the Commission's powers necessarily implies complex evaluations on economic matters. A judicial review of these evaluations must take account of their nature by confining itself to an examination of the relevance of the facts and the legal consequences which the Commission deduces therefrom.[290]

Judicial review of this kind would not be considered Convention compliant in the context of a criminal charge and in that respect reference can be made to the discussion above.[291] However, it should be stressed that the Court was speaking in the context of Article 81(3) so the comments cannot automatically be transposed to review of infringement decisions.

The first cartel cases dealt with by the ECJ reveal a pattern of judicial review which is light, especially when compared to the scrutiny Commission decisions are now subject to by the CFI. As an example *Boehringer Mannheim*[292] can be cited. The way in which the ECJ dealt with whether the parties to the cartel had jointly fixed sales prices was quite superficial. It can at least be questioned whether this aspect of the Commission decision would have been upheld today by the CFI.[293] It should though be conceded that the ECJ held that part of the infringement had not been sufficiently proven.[294] Another example in the same vein is *Dyestuffs*[295] where the ECJ with relative ease found that the parties had concerted as regards certain price increases.[296] The Commission, though far from rigorous in its fact-finding, had uncovered some evidence which could point to concerted

---

effect.' Case C-12/03 *Commission v Tetra Laval* [2005] ECR I-987, para 39. The CFI has referred to this statement of the ECJ see e.g. Case T-63/01 *General Electric Company v Commissio*: judgment of 14 December 2005, not yet reproted, para 63; Case T-464/04 *Independent Music Publishers and Labels Association v Commission*, judgment of 13 July 2006, not yet reported, paras 327–328. On review of merger decisions: B Vesterdorf 'Standard of Proof in Merger Cases' European Competition Journal (2005) 1 3, 8–19; M Nicholson, S Cardell and B Mckenna 'The Scope of Review of Merger Decisions under Community Law' European Competition Journal (2005) 1 123, 126–149.

[289] Cases 56 and 58/64 *Consten and Grundig v Commission* [1966] ECR 299. Incidentally this was the first case where judicial review proceedings were brought against a Commission decision.

[290] *Ibid.*, 347.

[291] In his opinion in *Distillers* (Case 30/78 *Distillers Company Ltd v Commission* [1980] ECR 2229, 2286–2287; [1980] 3 CMLR 121, 150), AG Warner made the following interesting observation regarding the scope of review according to *Consten-Grundig*: 'Secondly, the Commission relies on the Consten and Grundig case for the proposition that, where the Commission is required to make a complex assessment of economic factors, the Court's jurisdiction to interfere with the Commission's judgment is limited. No doubt it is, but the Commission went on to argue as if the Court's jurisdiction in such circumstances was virtually non-existent. The judgment in the Consten and Grundig case is clearly not authority for that.'

[292] Case 45/69 *Boehringer Mannheim GmbH v Commission* [1970] ECR 769.

[293] *Ibid.*, paras 36–38.   [294] *Ibid.*, paras 39–40.

[295] Case 48/69 *ICI v Commission (Dyestuffs)* [1972] ECR 619.

[296] *Ibid.*, paras 83–119. For a criticism of the case: V Korah 'Concerted Practices' (1973) 36 MLR 220, 220 *et seq.*

practices.[297] For example, the firms had held meetings, which afforded opportunities to discuss prices; some undertakings had sent their subsidiaries telexes
with instructions sometime within the same hour and the language of these
instructions contained some identical phrases. The ECJ did not even mention this
evidence in its judgment let alone analyse whether it constituted sufficient proof
of concerted practices. The manner in which the Court examined the evidence
and questions of parallel behaviour cannot be reconciled with later case law, cf for
example *Woodpulp*.[298] It is difficult to assert with certainty that the review undertaken in these cases is not compliant with the requirements of Article 6(1) ECHR
but at least they are vulnerable to criticism in that respect. This is not meant to
imply that the ECJ always rubber-stamped Commission decisions. Even as early
as *Continental Can*[299] we come across a judgment where the Court rejected the
economic assessment of the Commission.[300]

As mentioned previously, around 1980 the Commission increased the level of
fines levied on undertakings for infringing Articles 81(1) and 82, which in many
respects coincided with the ECJ taking a tougher stance as regards judicial review.
Jacobs uses a trio of judgments handed down in 1983, *AEG, Michelin* and *Pioneer*
to maintain that they suggest that if a convincing attack is made on the
Commission's findings of fact, the ECJ will be prepared to investigate the facts
anew.[301] In *Pioneer*[302] the ECJ heard oral evidence to be better placed to resolve
the factual dispute between the applicants and the Commission. The case also
bears out that the Court carefully examined both the oral and the documentary
evidence. The case, *inter alia*, concerned concerted practices between Pioneer and
some of its distributors to prevent parallel imports into France. One of the
elements of those practices was the alleged refusal by Melchers (the German
distributor) to sell products without a guarantee not to resell abroad. The ECJ
said, after reviewing various correspondences between the firms, that in view of
the opposing arguments of the parties and the contradictory statements of an
employee of Grunoer (German wholesaler) it was necessary to examine the other
evidence.[303] The Court held that it was evident that representatives of Gruoner
and Melchers had discussed the subject of exports and the information supplied
by the employees of the latter was such as to indicate the refusal to sell goods destined for France.[304] Melchers explained its failure to deliver the goods by citing
low levels of stock. The ECJ did not accept that explanation and said it failed to

---

[297] *Re Cartel in Aniline Dyes* [1969] OJ L195/11, [1969] CMLR D23.

[298] Cases C-89/85, C-104/85, C-114/85, C-116-117/85 and C-125-129/85 *A. Ahlström Oy and others v Commission* [1993] ECR I-1307.

[299] Case 6/72 *Euroemballage Corporation and others v Commission* [1973] ECR 216.

[300] FG Jacobs 'Court of Justice Review of Competition Cases' in BE Hawk (ed) *Annual Proceedings of the Fordham Corporate Law Institute* (Matthew Bender Times Mirror Books New York 1988) 541, 560.   [301] *Ibid.*, 570.

[302] Cases 100–103/1980 *Musique Diffusion Française SA and others v Commission* [1983] ECR 1825, paras 37–80.   [303] *Ibid.*, para 51.

[304] *Ibid.*, para 54.

understand why the firm made no offer to make partial deliveries and did not contact Pioneer to obtain further supplies.[305] The ECJ also held it impossible to disregard the chronological sequence of events or the fact that they were contemporaneous with those relating to parallel imports from the UK.[306] The Court therefore concluded that the Commission had satisfactorily shown that Melchers had refused to sell the goods on account of their destination.[307] The review conducted by the ECJ is far more rigorous than the one undertaken in *Dyestuffs*. Judicial review of this kind would in all probability be regarded as Convention compliant. However, it may be questioned whether the evidentiary requirements placed on the Commission are quite as strict as now are made by the CFI.

A case decided shortly afterwards, *Remia*,[308] is very important for our purposes. The case concerned the applicability of Article 81(1) and 81(3) to non-competition clauses in an agreement for the sale of an enterprise. Importantly no fine was at issue.[309] The ECJ remarked as follows on the standard of judicial review:

> *Although as a general rule the court undertakes a comprehensive review of the question whether or not the conditions for the application of Article 85(1) are met*, it is clear that in determining the permissible duration of a non-competition clause incorporated in an agreement for the transfer of an undertaking the Commission has to appraise complex economic matters. The court must therefore limit its review of such an appraisal to verifying whether the relevant procedural rules have been complied with, whether the statement of the reasons for the Decision is adequate, whether the facts have been accurately stated and whether there has been any manifest error of appraisal or a misuse of powers.[310] (emphasis added)

From this statement we can deduce that the ECJ considers comprehensive review to be the general standard when examining Article 81(1) cases. It is perhaps not surprising that the ECJ first makes this statement regarding the standard of review shortly after having handed down the judgments mentioned above. However,

---

[305] *Ibid.*, para 56.   [306] *Ibid.*, para 58.   [307] *Ibid.*, para 60.

[308] Case 42/84 *Remia BV and others v Commission* [1985] ECR 2545.

[309] The agreement had been notified to the Commission and the parties therefore enjoyed immunity from fines, see Article 15(5)(a) of Regulation 17/62.

[310] Case 42/84 *Remia BV and others v Commission* [1985] ECR 2545, para 34. It is possible to construe what marginal review entails in different ways. In *Florimex* (Case C-265/97P *VBA v Florimex BV and others* [2000] ECR I-2061, para 33 of the AG's opinion), AG Saggio interpreted narrowly the constraints marginal review places on the Community Courts by saying: 'Any error in the application of the competition rules which may result from incorrect reconstruction and characterisation of the facts must therefore be for the Court to ascertain, even when the appraisals of their appropriateness from a technical-economic viewpoint are based on criteria not open to review by the Court.' This is interesting to compare with the following comment of AG Tizzano from his opinion in *Tetra Laval* (Case C-12/03P *Commission v Tetra Laval BV* [2005] ECR I-987, para 86): 'With regard to the findings of fact, the review is clearly more intense, in that the issue is to verify objectively and materially the accuracy of certain facts and the correctness of the conclusions drawn in order to establish whether certain known facts make it possible to prove the existence of other facts to be ascertained. By contrast, with regard to the complex economic assessments made by the Commission, review by the Community judicature is necessarily more limited, since the latter has to respect the broad discretion inherent in that kind of assessment and may not substitute its own point of view for that of the body which is institutionally responsible for making those assessments.'

when assessing complex economic matters it exercises what can be termed as marginal review. It is though not the complexity of the issues that should determine whether comprehensive or marginal review is applied. Cooke perceptively points out that the economic factors raised by Articles 81(1) and 82 can be just as complex as the ones under Article 81(3). He says that judicial deference is a recognition of the fact that when deciding on exemptions the Commission is exercising a policy function and the Court will not substitute a different policy choice for one reached on a sound basis. He considers *Remia* to be a case regarding a policy decision albeit within the context of Article 81(1).[311] It is submitted that the distinction between infringement and policy decisions is an appropriate one when discussing judicial review of competition decisions in the context of Article 6(1) ECHR.[312] Lenaerts mentions *Remia* as an exceptional case as far as concerns review of Article 81(1) issues and stresses that the imposition of a sanction was not at stake.[313] It is quite possible to interpret his comments as meaning that he is implicitly aware of the ECHR dimension when it comes to judicial review of Commission decisions. On the other hand Van Bael seems to regard *Consten-Grundig* and *Remia* as dictating the general standard of review in competition cases, see the extract quoted at the beginning of this chapter.[314] On the basis of the above it is submitted that the assertion is mistaken and not based on a correct reading of the cases. Finally worth mentioning is that the ECJ followed *Remia* in *BAT-Reynolds* and has subsequently done so on a number of occasions.[315]

The CFI

The CFI, as already stated, was founded to improve the judicial protection of individuals in respect of actions requiring close examination of complex facts. Another reason mentioned in the preamble to the Council Decision was to maintain the quality and effectiveness of judicial review in the Community legal

---

[311] JD Cooke 'Changing Responsibilities and Relationships for Community and National Courts: The Implications of the White Paper' in *The Modernisation of European Competition Law: The Next Ten Years* (University of Cambridge Centre for European Legal Studies Occasional Paper No 4 Cambridge 2000) 58, 62–63; V Tiili and J Vanhamme 'The 'Power of Appraisal' (*Pouvoir d'Appreciation*) of the Commission of the European Communities vis-à-vis the Powers of Judicial Review of the Communities' Court of Justice and Court of First Instance' (1999) 22 Fordham International Law Journal 885, 889–890.

[312] If an infringement decision were subject to marginal review by the Community Courts that would not be Convention compliant, whereas the ECtHR considers that a more limited type of review can be adequate when dealing with the exercise of administrative discretion under the civil head of Article 6(1) ECHR, see for example *Bryan v UK* Series A No 335-A (1995) 21 EHRR 342, para 47.

[313] K Lenaerts 'Report on the Proceedings of Working Group 3' in J Schwarze (ed) in *17 FIDE Kongress Conclusions and Perspectives* (Internationale Föderation für Europarecht Berlin 1996) 173, 179.

[314] I van Bael 'Insufficient Judicial Control of EC Competition Law Enforcement' in BE Hawk (ed) *Annual Proceedings of the Fordham Corporate Law Institute* (Transnational Juris Publications Kluwer Law & Taxation Publishers New York 1993) 733, 741.

[315] See eg Cases 142 and 156/84 *British American Tobacco Company Ltd and others v Commission* [1987] ECR 4487, para 62; T-168/01 *GlaxoSmithKline v Commission*, judgment of 27 September 2006, nyr, para 57.

order.[316] The alleged lack of rigour of the ECJ when conducting judicial review had received some criticism from practitioners.[317] However, as we have seen, at least some of this criticism was not fully justified. It might though be mentioned that in the context of so-called rule of reason cases under Article 81(1) the ECJ sometimes let the Commission get away with opaque decisions.[318]

Any discussion on the role of the CFI in judicial review of competition cases should start with the opinion of AG Vesterdorf in *Polypropylene*.[319] The first item of interest is that the AG refers to the preamble of the Council Decision outlined above. From that he concludes:

[T]he very creation of the Court of First Instance as a court of both first and last instance for the examination of the facts in the cases brought before it is an invitation to undertake an intensive review in order to ascertain whether the evidence on which the Commission relies in adopting a contested decision is sound.[320]

AG Vesterdorf also outlines the principle of unfettered evaluation of the evidence saying:

It is important first to point out that the activity of the Court of Justice and thus also that of the Court of First Instance is governed by the principle of the unfettered evaluation of evidence, unconstrained by the various rules laid down in national legal systems.[321]

Later he continues by saying that conclusions drawn from the evidence must of course never develop into ill-founded speculation. There must be a sufficient basis for the decision and any reasonable doubt must be for the benefit of the applicants according to the principle in *dubio pro reo*.[322] The CFI did not explicitly mention these issues but there can be little doubt that in essence the Court agreed with the AG. In support of that assertion reference can be made to Lenaerts and Vanhamme who convincingly cite *Polypropylene* as an example of comprehensive review of all the inferences drawn by the Commission from the evidence on which it relies.[323]

The most famous example of rigorous review from the early years of the CFI is *Italian Flat Glass*.[324] There the CFI examined in great detail the evidence used by the Commission and exposed some flaws in the Commission's handling of it.[325]

---

[316] Council Decision (ECSC, EEC, Euratom) 88/591 establishing a Court of First Instance of the European Communities [1988] OJ L319/1.

[317] See eg: N Green 'Evidence and Proof in E.C. Competition Cases' in PJ Slot and A McDonnel (eds) *Procedure and Enforcement in E.C. and U.S. Competition Law* (Sweet and Maxwell London 1993) 127, 127.

[318] S Weatherill and P Beaumont *EU Law* (3rd edn Penguin London 1999) 917.

[319] Cases T-1-4/89, T-6-15/89, *Rhone Poulenc SA and others v Commission* [1991] ECR II-867; [1992] 4 CMLR 84.   [320] *Ibid.*, ECR II-908.

[321] *Ibid.*, ECR II-954.   [322] *Ibid.*

[323] K Lenaerts and J Vanhamme 'Procedural Rights of Private Parties in the Community Administrative Process' (1997) 34 CML Rev 531, 562.

[324] Cases T-68/89 and T-77-78/89 *Societa Italiano Vetro SpA and others v Commission* [1992] ECR II-1403.

[325] *Ibid.*, paras 172–313. See also: M van der Woude 'The Court of First Instance: The First Three Years' in B Hawk (ed) *Annual Proceedings of the Fordham Corporate Law Institute* (Transnational Juris Publications Kluwer Law & Taxation Publishers New York 1993) 621, 634–635.

One of the infringements was that the applicants were alleged to have communicated identical prices to their customers. The CFI said after a meticulous analysis of the evidence that annex 3 to the Commission decision gave only a partial and sometimes inaccurate account of the timing and of the surrounding circumstances of price changes. Consequently, the Court held that the Commission had not proved to the requisite legal standard that the applicants had communicated identical price lists to their customers on dates which were close to one another and in some cases on the same days.[326] It is interesting to contrast the CFI's examination of this issue with the ECJ's review of the question of price increases in *Dyestuffs* mentioned above.[327]

Ehlermann takes *Italian Flat Glass* and *Woodpulp* as authority for saying that when fines are imposed the Courts do not accord the Commission a margin of economic discretion of any significance whatsoever.[328] Van der Woude remarks that the CFI is a jurisdiction deciding in adversarial proceedings and it may not carry out an active investigation on its own initiative. He wonders whether this principle of judicial restraint was completely respected in *PVC I* and *Italian Flat Glass*.[329] As outlined above, the Community Courts have sometimes considered that judicial restraint was called for when reviewing Commission decisions, mainly when faced with reviewing policy decisions made by the Commission. As regards infringement decisions the review takes place within the context of a criminal charge within the autonomous meaning of Article 6(1) ECHR. Therefore, there is hardly any place for judicial restraint, which if applied could easily lead to the proceedings not being in compliance with the requirements of the ECHR. There is also no reason, in principle, which excludes the CFI from being more inquisitorial than the ECJ had been. Indeed it had been accurately predicted that the CFI would need to be more inquisitorial and activist because the applicants would place greater emphasis on factual issues.[330]

In *Italian Flat Glass* the CFI makes numerous references to the *'requisite legal standard'*.[331] That is the standard of proof the Court has applied when examining whether the Commission has proved its case.[332] The CFI has never directly stated

---

[326] *Ibid.*, para 192.   [327] Case 48/69 *ICI v Commission (Dyestuffs)* [1972] ECR 619.

[328] CD Ehlermann 'Community Competition Law Procedures' in Lord Slynn of Hadley and SA Pappas (eds) *Procedural Aspects of EC Competition Law* (European Institute of Public Administration Maastricht 1995) 9, 17–18.

[329] M van der Woude 'The Court of First Instance: The First Three Years' in B Hawk (ed) *Annual Proceedings of the Fordham Corporate Law Institute* (Transnational Juris Publications Kluwer Law & Taxation Publishers New York 1993) 621, 661.

[330] JT Lang 'The Impact of the New Court of First Instance in EEC Antitrust and Trade Cases' in BE Hawk (ed) *Annual Proceedings of the Fordham Corporate Law Institute* (Matthew Bender Times Mirror Books New York 1988) 579, 590.

[331] Cases T-68/89 and T-77-78/89 *Societa Italiano Vetro SpA and others v Commission* [1992] ECR II-1403, paras 202, 250, 275, 281, 303, 313.

[332] For recent examples see: Case T-368/00 *General Motors BV and others v Commission* [2003] ECR II-4491, paras 78–89; Cases T-5-6/00 *Nederlandse Federative Vereniging voor de Groothandel op Elektrotechnisch Gebied and other v Commission* [2003] ECR II-5761, paras 333–339.

what precisely this standard entails though there can be little doubt that the Court requires strong evidence in infringement cases. Bellamy (a former judge at the CFI) speaking extra-judicially has remarked that in practice the standard was something quite close to *'proof beyond reasonable doubt'*. The Court therefore tends to look very closely at what elements of proof the Commission had before it.[333] Bellamy summarized the methodology of the CFI by saying that the Court checked whether the facts were established; the economic appreciation supported by the evidence; the important arguments answered in a credible way. Adding that of course the Court examined whether all relevant procedures had been fairly followed and all questions of law correctly addressed.[334] In this context it might be noted that there is theoretically a difference between 'standard of proof' on the one hand and 'standard of judicial review' on the other. However, in practice these two standards are so closely related as to become indivisible.[335]

The CFI has on occasion referred to the standard of review it applies in judicial review of competition cases. As will be recalled the Court said in *Cement* that as regards infringement decisions the applicants may call upon it to undertake an exhaustive review of both the Commission's substantive findings of fact and its legal appraisal of those facts.[336] In *Bayer*[337] the CFI said it was settled case law (citing *Remia* and *BAT-Reynolds*) that it must undertake a comprehensive review of the question whether or not the conditions for applying Article 81(1) are met. Both these cases also demonstrate that the CFI certainly does more than just pay lip-service to undertaking comprehensive review. To illustrate, the following example from *Bayer* may be used. In the case one of the central elements was whether the Commission had proved that the applicant had imposed an export ban on wholesalers in France and Spain. Among the evidence relied on by the Commission was an internal document from Bayer, which according to the Commission described how the applicant monitored which of its customers were exporting. The CFI said after having analysed the document that it did not contain any indication of an intention by the applicant to prohibit exports or to monitor the quantities actually exported by the wholesalers. The Court therefore concluded that the document could not be regarded as demonstrating that the applicant had based its strategy on monitoring the final destination of the products

---

[333] C Bellamy 'Antitrust and the Courts' panel discussion in BE Hawk (ed) *Annual Proceedings of the Fordham Corporate Law Institute* (Juris Publishing Inc New York 1999) 369, 389. The CAT examined the standard and burden of proof in *Napp Pharmaceutical* (*Napp Pharmaceutical Holdings Ltd v Director General of Fair Trading* [2002] ECC 13, para 112) and said the following on the position in EC law: '[T]here is no doubt that, in general, those Courts require convincing proof that the alleged infringements have been committed in the form of a "firm, precise and consistent body of evidence".'

[334] *Ibid.*, 392.

[335] B Vesterdorf 'Standard of Proof in Merger Cases' (2005) 1 European Competition Journal 3, 6–8.

[336] Cases T-25/95, T-26/95, T-30-32/95, T-34-39/95, T-42-46/95, T-48/95, T-50-65/95, T-68-71/95, T-87/95, T-88/95, T-103/95 and T-104/95 *Cimenteries CBR and others v Commission* [2000] ECR II-491, para 719.

[337] Case T-41/96 *Bayer AG v Commission* [2000] ECR II-3383. The judgment of the CFI was upheld on appeal, Cases C-2-3/01P *Commission and others v Bayer AG* [2004] ECR I-23.

and the penalization of exporting wholesalers.[338] Then the CFI scrutinized the evidence relating to individual wholesalers where it also found the Commission's assessment of the evidence lacking. As an example, the Commission had used minutes one of the wholesalers had kept from a meeting with Bayer where the company had tried to persuade Bayer to give it further supplies. The Court said that the document did not contain any reference to an export ban imposed by the applicant or to a policy of systematic monitoring *a posteriori* of products supplied. Therefore, contrary to what the Commission claimed, nothing in the document proved the alleged need for the wholesaler to convince Bayer that it would not engage in exports.[339] These are good examples of the point that the CFI carefully examines the evidence relied on by the Commission and whether an infringement has been proven to the requisite legal standard. The Court also shows no hesitation in interpreting the evidence differently from the Commission.

Cement is a voluminous judgment, in all 5,134 paragraphs, and it abounds with examples of detailed factual analysis. To name but one, the Court's treatment of the question whether the existence of the so-called Cembureau agreement had been proven can be mentioned.[340] The CFI examined, *inter alia*, the documentary evidence relied on by the Commission and also the alternative explanations of the documents in question put forward by the applicant.[341]

The Court annulled the Commission's decision (Article 5 of the decision) as regards one of the applicants, who subsequently brought an action for damages against the Commission under Article 288 EC.[342] When deciding on whether non-contractual liability exists, one of the factors involved is the measure of discretion accorded to the relevant Community institution.[343] Therefore, the CFI had to examine the extent of the Commission's discretion in the context of the *Cement* decision. The Court referred to the paragraphs of the judgment, which set out the grounds for the annulment of Article 5 of the decision, and stated that it followed from them that the CFI had undertaken a comprehensive review of application of the defendant. Furthermore, it was noted that no reference was made to economic appraisals or discretion that might limit the scope of review. The question as to whether there had been an infringement of Article 81(1) fell within the scope of the simple application of the law on the basis of the elements of fact available to the Commission. On the basis of these factors the Court concluded that the Commission's discretion had been reduced.[344]

---

[338] Case T-41/96 *Bayer AG v Commission* [2000] ECR II-3383, paras 88–89.
[339] *Ibid.*, paras 99–100.
[340] Cases T-25/95, T-26/95, T-30-32/95, T-34-39/95, T-42-46/95, T-48/95, T-50-65/95, T-68-71/95, T-87/95, T-88/95, T-103/95 and T-104/95 *Cimenteries CBR and others v Commission* [2000] ECR II-491, paras 861–1095.
[341] *Ibid.*, para 863. See for example paras 1004–1027, regarding the confirmation of the Cembureau agreement at a meeting on 19 March 1984.
[342] Case T-28/03 *Holcim (Deutschland) AG v Commission* [2005] ECR II-1357.
[343] P Craig and G de Búrca *EU Law Text, Cases, and, Materials* (3rd edn OUP Oxford) 555.
[344] Case T-28/03 *Holcim (Deutschland) AG v Commission* [2005] ECR II-1357, para 97–100.

Michelin II[345] and *Ventouris Group*[346] can be cited as two relatively recent examples of comprehensive review by the CFI, though neither case refers to the standard of review being neither comprehensive nor exhaustive. In the former case one of the abuses of Article 82 of which the Commission considered the applicant guilty of was the use of the Michelin club as an instrument for rigidifying and improving the applicant's position on the market. The Court examined thoroughly the documentary evidence the Commission had used to establish of temperature obligation (refers to observing Michelin market shares and carrying sufficient stock of Michelin tyres) on the members of the club.[347] The CFI scrutinized each document and finally concluded that they established the existence of a temperature obligation.[348] The latter case concerned the applicant's involvement in a cartel and one of the pleas for annulment related to whether that had been proven. The CFI said that the plea called for a detailed analysis of the various pieces of documentary evidence on which the Commission based its conclusion.[349] The Court then proceeded to do just that.[350] As an example one can refer to the Court's analysis of a facsimile of 8 December 1989 where the applicant and seven other companies had signed a table of tariffs. The CFI found the document to establish an agreement to fix prices and rejected the applicants argument that the company had already decided on its prices and that the prices mentioned in the document were merely indicative.[351]

Having regard to the above discussion on judicial review under Article 230 one must conclude that the CFI reviews all aspects of Commission decisions finding an infringement of the competition rules of the Treaty. The review encompasses both question of law and fact and fulfils the requirement of Article 6(1) ECHR. A line of cases regarding information exchange agreements though needs to be examined further, as will be done below. There it appears that the review is more limited than customarily. The review undertaken by the ECJ in cases like *Pioneer* and *Michelin* should be regarded as being compliant with the Convention. However, as mentioned, some of the early cases can justifiably be criticized for the lack of rigour in judicial review and it can be questioned whether review of that kind would have satisfied the ECtHR. Whether, and then to what extent, the underlying ECHR dimension has played a role in the intensifying of the review to difficult to state with any certainty. It is though worth recalling the remarks of Vesterdorf regarding the Convention, cited above, and that Lenaerts (a former judge at the CFI now at the ECJ) is apparently fully attentive to this issue.[352]

---

[345] Case T-203/01 *Manufacture française des pneumatiques Michelin v Commission* [2003] ECR II-4071.

[346] Case T-59/99 *Ventouris Group Enterprises SA v Commission* [2003] ECR II-5257.

[347] Case T-203/01 *Manufacture française des pneumatiques Michelin v Commission* [2003] ECR II-4071, paras 182–194. [348] *Ibid.*, para 196.

[349] Case T-59/99 *Ventouris Group Enterprises SA v Commission* [2003] ECR II-5257, para 34.

[350] *Ibid.*, paras 35–106. [351] *Ibid.*, paras 35–54, see in particular paras 45–51.

[352] K Lenaerts 'Report on the Proceedings of Working Group 3' in J Schwarze (ed) in *17 FIDE Kongress Conclusions and Perspectives* (Internationale Föderation für Europarecht Berlin 1996) 173, 177 and 179.

The conclusion as regards the extent of judicial review conducted by the CFI is in this respect consistent with the findings of Harding and Joshua.[353] The tenor of their writing is though implicitly critical of the approach of the CFI. They note that the CFI has in cartel cases during the 1990s mostly upheld the Commission's findings of fact, which they say raises questions regarding the claimed necessity of intensive judicial review.[354] The fact that the CFI, to a significant extent, upheld the decisions of the Commission shows that some of the criticism levied at the Commission and quoted by Harding and Joshua were not justified. However, their view overlooks that review undertaken by the CFI must be sensitive to the requirements of the ECHR. In this context it is worth bearing in mind that they, as previously mentioned, consider the nature of the Commission's procedure to be opaque.[355]

Bailey's conclusions are also very much in the same vein, *inter alia*, saying that the CFI has usually taken particular care to verify the facts considered by the Commission to constitute an infringement of Article 81.[356] Interestingly, Bailey speculates whether the experience of the CFI in competition cases and the demands of effective judicial protection might eventually require the case law on limited review to be reconsidered.[357] Such an extension would not be required in order for the proceedings to be in compliance with Article 6(1) ECHR, the requirements of the Convention are on the other hand only a minimum and nothing that prevents Community law from providing better protection in this respect.

Information Exchange Agreements

Information exchange agreements between competitors can infringe Article 81(1).[358] In *John Deere*,[359] one of the first cases to deal with this type of infringement, the CFI said that the Commission had not made a manifest error of assessment when concluding that the agreement in question made it possible to identify the sales of each competitor. On appeal the ECJ upheld this finding of the CFI and cited in that respect *Remia* and *BAT-Reynolds* and then remarked: '[T]he setting of the criterion preventing exact identification of competitors' sales is based on a complex economic appraisal of the market. The Court of First Instance therefore rightly undertook only a limited review of that aspect.'[360] This analysis was conducted under Article 81(1) but did not involve any element of a policy decision of the type that for instance was at stake in *Remia*. One possible justification for this limited review is that the Commission had not imposed a fine.

---

[353] C Harding and J Joshua *Regulating Cartels in Europe* (OUP Oxford 2003) 178–181.
[354] *Ibid.*, 179–180.
[355] C Harding and J Joshua *Regulating Cartels in Europe* (OUP Oxford 2003) 189.
[356] D Bailey 'Scope of Judicial Review under Article 81 EC' CML Rev (2004) 41 1327, 1359–1360.   [357] *Ibid.*
[358] R Whish *Competition Law* (5th edn Lexis Nexis London 2003) 486–496.
[359] Case T-35/92 *John Deere Ltd v Commission* [1994] ECR II-957, para 92.
[360] Case C-7/95P *John Deere Ltd v Commission* [1998] ECR I-3111, paras 34–35.

However, the ECtHR has maintained that it is the potential penalty that is decisive, not the actual penalty imposed.[361] Due to subsequent case law of the ECJ where fines have been levied it is not necessary to examine this issue further.

In *Thyssen Stahl*,[362] the ECJ reiterated that the standard of review when reviewing information exchange agreements was one of a manifest error of assessment. It should be noted that the case was decided on the basis of Article 65 ECSC and therefore the standard of review had a Treaty basis in Article 33 ECSC. However, in light of that the Court treated the standard of review under both the EC and ECSC Treaty as being the same and cited the traditional case law (*Remia* and *BAT-Reynolds*) as authority and apparently referred to Article 33 ECSC as additional support, it is submitted that this was not determinative. That seems also to be confirmed by the ECJ's judgment in *Cement* where the Court repeated its previous statements.[363] It is worth noting that the ECJ does not refer specifically to information exchange agreements; rather the Court uses the usual criterion of 'complex economic assessment'.

It is interesting to examine the judgments of the CFI in the above-mentioned cases. As will be recalled the CFI said in *Cement* that in cases of that kind it undertook exhaustive review. Nothing in the Court's detailed treatment of the information exchange agreements points to the Court employing less stringent review than generally.[364] Somewhat paradoxically the ECJ said, when commenting on the implementation of Cembureau agreement by the exchange of price information, that after carefully examining the evidence before it, the CFI found no error in the Commission's conclusion.[365] This wording can hardly be said to be demonstrative of the use of a standard of manifest error. In *Thyssen Stahl*,[366] the CFI made no explicit reference to the standard of review. Reading the judgment though leaves one in little doubt that the CFI reviewed the case comprehensively. As regards the information exchange agreement the Court analysed in detail both the legal and factual issues. First, the Court confirmed the Commission's finding that the information had been broken down for each undertaking and that it had been distributed among the participants. Then the Court analysed the legal questions in light of the facts and held that the information exchange agreement constituted a separate infringement.[367] Nothing in this analysis of the CFI gives reason to deduce that the Court departed from its usual standard of review.

---

[361] See also: Case T-65/98 *Van den Bergh v Commission* [2003] ECR II-4653, para 80. In this case the Commission had concluded that the applicant had infringed Articles 81 and 82 EC but not imposed a fine. With regard to the question of whether market foreclosure was high enough to constitute an infringement of Article 81 the CFI said it would only undertake marginal review.

[362] Case C-194/99P *Thyssen Stahl AG v Commission* [2003] ECR I-10821, para 78.

[363] Cases C-204/00P, C-205/00P, C-211/00P, C-213/00P, C-217/00P and C-219/00P *Aalborg Portland and others v Commission* [2004] ECR I-123, para 279.

[364] Cases T-25/95, T-26/95, T-30-32/95, T-34-39/95, T-42-46/95, T-48/95, T-50-65/95, T-68-71/95, T-87/95, T-88/95, T-103/95 and T-104/95 *Cimenteries CBR and others v Commission* [2000] ECR II-491, paras 1467–1647.   [365] *Ibid.*, para 287.

[366] Case T-141/94 *Thyssen Stahl AG v Commission* [1999] ECR II-347.

[367] *Ibid.*, paras 374–378, 385–412.

As mentioned earlier, judicial review involving a standard of manifest error of assessment would not be in compliance with Article 6(1) ECHR. Therefore the ECJ is not correct in applying the standard when analysing whether information exchange agreements infringe Article 81(1). It should though be conceded that it would be possible to maintain, that these statements of the ECJ were irrelevant when evaluating whether the proceedings were Convention compliant, since it is the review of the CFI that matters and in these cases it was not found lacking. The ECJ is; however, undoubtedly sending out the wrong signals to the CFI and should the CFI follow this case law it would lead to the proceedings violating Article 6(1) ECHR. Finally, it is worth noting that the ECJ offers no reasons why this particular type of infringement of Article 81(1) should be subject to more limited review than others. Even though it may be maintained in some cases that the economic considerations might be regarded as unusually complex, that would not in any way legitimize limited review under the circumstances.

VI. Conclusion

On the basis of the criteria employed by the ECtHR when examining the applicability of Article 6(1) ECHR under its criminal head as well as the Court's case law, it is impossible but to conclude that the fines levied by the Commission under Article 23 of Regulation 1/2003 form a *'criminal charge'* within the autonomous meaning of Article 6(1) ECHR. That has never been expressly endorsed by the ECJ; however, the Court has implicitly acknowledged that conclusion. There is some inconsistency in the jurisprudence of the Community Courts, but it does not appear to be of much significance.

As the fines levied by the Commission constitute a criminal charge within the autonomous meaning of the Article, it is clear according to the case law of the ECtHR that administrative imposition of the fines is not precluded. What is required by the Strasbourg jurisprudence is, to quote *Janosevic*, recourse to a: '[J]udicial body that has full jurisdiction, including the power to quash in all respects, on questions of fact and law, the challenged decision'.[368] It is worth emphasizing that if a decision concerns 'civil rights and obligations' within the meaning of Article 6(1) ECHR, less intensive judicial review is required to satisfy the requirements of the Convention. In that context it should be borne in mind that decisions made under Article 81(3) and merger decisions fall under the civil head of Article 6(1) ECHR. Therefore pronouncements of the Community Courts on the standard of review in those cases cannot automatically be equated with the standard employed in infringement cases.

The case law of the Community Courts on the question whether the procedure affords a trial before an independent and impartial tribunal is unsatisfactory. Old

---

[368] *Janosevic v Sweden* (2004) 38 EHRR 473, para 81.

cases of the ECJ, *Fedetab* and *Pioneer*, decided the issue merely by saying that the Commission is not a tribunal, which *per se* is undoubtedly correct. However, this approach is inadequate because it avoids tackling what is at stake. The applicability of Article 6(1) ECHR is determined by the subject-matter of the decision, not the constituent elements of the decision-maker. The judgment of the CFI in *Enso Española* is a distinct improvement on earlier case law although there are elements in the judgment that are not exempt from criticism.

What determines whether the procedure in EC competition law is compliant with Article 6(1) ECHR is whether the Community Courts exercise sufficiently rigorous judicial review both under Articles, 229 and 230 EC. Examination of the case law reveals that initially the review was not strict enough to satisfy the conditions of the ECtHR. That finding is unequivocal with regard to Article 229, see for example *Alma*. It is, however, not quite as clear in relation to Article 230; it is though very probable that a review of the type exercised in *Dyestuffs* would have been found lacking. It is difficult to pinpoint precisely when judicial review was brought in line with the requirements of Article 6(1) ECHR. *Commercial Solvents* indicates sufficient review under the head of Article 229 and a trio of cases decided in 1983, *Pioneer, Michelin* and *AEG* point to the same conclusion concerning Article 230.

The CFI was founded, *inter alia,* to improve judicial protection in respect of actions requiring close examination of complex facts. It can safely be concluded that the Court has been successful in improving the quality of judicial review in competition cases. There can be no doubt that the review undertaken by the Court is in accordance with Article 6(1) both as regards Articles 229 and 230, see for example *Compagnie Générale Maritime* and *Bayer*. It is worth mentioning that the ECJ has been sending out worrying signals regarding the standard of judicial review in cases concerning information exchange agreements. If the CFI were to adhere to that standard, the review would fall short of the requirements of the ECHR.

Suggestions of reform of the current set-up of enforcement in EC competition law have been put forward, independently of whether the current one is compliant with Article 6(1) ECHR, with some commentators suggesting that the decision-making powers of the Commission should be vested in an independent court (the CFI). Joshua says that such a change would alter the emphasis of the judicial process portraying the Commission as an officer of justice instead of putting it on the defensive.[369] Montag on the other hand maintains that it would noticeably strengthen the granting and effectiveness of the rights of the defence in infringement proceedings.[370] Interestingly, Harding and Joshua have said that de facto

---

[369] JM Joshua 'Attitudes to Antitrust Enforcement in the EU and United States: Dodging the Traffic Warden or Respecting the Law?' in BE Hawk (ed) *Annual Proceedings of the Fordham Corporate Law Institute* (Juris Publishing Inc Sweet and Maxwell New York 1996) 101, 135.

[370] F Montag 'The Case for a Radical Reform of the Infringement Procedure under Regulation 17' (1996) 17 ECLR 428, 435–436.

there has been a separation of functions and if the CFI were formally given the role of trial court in competition proceedings little would change regarding its substantive role.[371] It is submitted that this statement is going too far. The tenor of the proceedings would be altered were it to take place in the context of a criminal trial with the Commission acting as a prosecutor. Despite the CFI undertaking exhaustive review the focus is still on whether an administrative decision can withstand judicial scrutiny, ie has it complied with the relevant substantive and procedural rules. That would inevitably change if the Commission would not have decision-making powers and the trial be more or less like a classic criminal trial.

Finally, it is worth mentioning that the requirements of the ECHR are minimum requirements. The French courts, both the *Cour de Cassation* and the *Conseil d'Etat*, have, at least arguably, interpreted Article 6(1) more strictly than the ECtHR and placed limitations on the involvement of the *rapporteur* in administrative proceedings leading to imposition of fines.[372] It is of course possible that this line of case law could provide an inspiration for the ECtHR or even the Community Courts, which might prompt a re-assessment of the issues dealt with in this article.

---

[371] C Harding and J Joshua *Regulating Cartels in Europe* (OUP Oxford 2003), 201.

[372] D Waelbroeck and M Griffiths 'Annotation on case: Cour de Cassation: T.G.V. Nord et Pont Normandie judgment of 5 October 1999' (2000) 37 CML Rev 1465, 1465–1467, 1470–1471.

Survey

Environmental Law 2004–2005

*Nicola Notaro and Martina Doppelhammer**

I. Introduction

This survey aims at highlighting the main developments in EC environmental legislation and case law between 2004 and 2005.[1]

We have structured our article, roughly, around the main priorities identified in the Sixth Environmental Action Programme (6th EAP)[2] as described in previous surveys.[3] Therefore, we focus first on Air Pollution and Climate Change (Section II.), Environment and Health (Section III.), Nature and Biodiversity (Section IV.), and Natural Resources and Waste (Section V.). Following these four thematic sections are three additional ones covering Horizontal Instruments (Section VI.), Citizens' Rights (Section VII.) and the Case Law of the European Court of Justice (ECJ) (Section VIII.).

The current dominance of competitiveness concerns in the political debate throughout Europe has made the conditions under which environmental policy-makers operate more difficult in the biennium under review here. This has happened even despite that the European Council renewed 'Lisbon agenda', aimed at making the EU the most competitive economy in the world by 2010, explicitly acknowledges the role of environmental policy action in reaching its objective.[4]

---

* Nicola Notaro (LLM Bruges, PhD London) and Martina Doppelhammer (LLM Bruges) are civil servants in the Environment Directorate General of the European Commission. The views expressed here are personal to the authors and by no means reflect the point of view of the European Commission.
[1] EC legislation in which environmental protection is only an ancillary objective will not be accounted for. Only major Commission proposals will be described. The present survey is updated to the end of 2005. Only occasionally, events in 2006 have been taken into consideration.
[2] Decision No 1600/2002/EC laying down the Sixth Community Environment Action Programme, [2002] OJ L 242/1.
[3] *Yearbook of European Law*, Vol. 21, Oxford University Press, 493–495.
[4] Communication to the Spring European Council: 'Working together for Growth and Jobs: A new Start for the Lisbon Strategy', COM(2005) 24.

Only a few new legislative initiatives have been taken while a number of new policy and 'strategic' papers have been put forward by the Commission. The recently adopted Thematic Strategies seek to present a consistent framework for certain policy areas. They vary significantly, however, in their impact on their respective sectors.

At the same time, the European Court of Justice (ECJ) has rendered a number of important judgments that provide the Commission with new tools to boost Member States' implementation of EC environmental law. In difficult times for the European project with a Constitution that may never enter into force, the Court confirms its role of essential engine to further European integration.

II. Air Pollution and Climate Change

A. Air Pollution

In September 2005, the Commission proposed a Thematic Strategy on air pollution.[5] It is one of the seven thematic strategies foreseen in the 6th EAP and based on the Clean Air for Europe (CAFE) programme launched in 2001.[6]

The Thematic Strategy aims to cut by 2020 the number of premature deaths from air pollution related diseases by almost 40 per cent from 2000 levels. It also aims to substantially reduce the area of forests and other ecosystems suffering damage from airborne pollutants. It proposes a number of measures to attain these objectives, including streamlining existing legislation on air quality, introducing limit values for PM 2.5 (dust particles in the range of 2.5 to 10 μm in diameter) and measures in related sectors such as energy and transport.

Together with the Thematic Strategy, the Commission adopted a legislative proposal for a new Directive on Ambient Air Quality and Cleaner Air for Europe.[7] The proposal aims to revise and merge the current Air Framework Directive 1996/62/EC,[8] its first three Daughter Directives 1999/30/EC,[9] 2000/69/EC,[10] and 2002/3/EC,[11] and the Exchange of Information Decision 97/101/EC[12] into a single legal instrument.

The proposal introduces limit values for PM 2.5, which are not covered in the current legislation. According to new scientific evidence, PM 2.5 are even more

---

[5] COM(2005) 446.   [6] COM(2001) 245.   [7] COM(2005) 447.

[8] Council Directive 96/62/EC on ambient air quality assessment and management, [1996] OJ L 296/5.

[9] Council Directive 1999/30/EC relating to limit values for sulphur dioxide, nitrogen dioxide and oxides of nitrogen, particulate matter and lead in ambient air, [1999] OJ L 163/41.

[10] Directive 2000/69/EC relating to limit values for benzene and carbon monoxide in ambient air, [2000] OJ L 313/12.

[11] Directive 2002/3/EC relating to ozone in ambient air, [2002] OJ L 67/14.

[12] Council Decision 97/101/EC establishing a reciprocal exchange of information and data from networks and individual stations measuring ambient air pollution within the Member States, [1997] OJ L 35/14.

dangerous for human health than PM 10 and therefore need to be regulated. The proposal foresees a cap on the average concentration for PM 2.5 of 25 μg per calendar year to be attained by 2010. This is coupled by a non-binding target to reduce human exposure to PM 2.5 generally between 2010 and 2020 in each Member State.

At the same time, the proposal foresees that Member States may delay compliance with limit values for certain pollutants in certain zones for a maximum of five years, if specific criteria are met. For nitrogen dioxide, benzene and PM 2.5, Member States have to establish and communicate to the Commission an air quality plan or programme for the zone in question designed to achieve the speci-fied limit values. Moreover, they have to establish and communicate to the Commission an air pollution abatement programme for the period of intended postponement, which demonstrates that conformity with the limit values in question will be reached before the expiry of the extended deadline. For sulphur dioxide, carbon monoxide, lead and PM 10, any exemption in addition requires that the limit values cannot be reached because of site-specific dispersion charac-teristics, adverse climatic conditions or transboundary contributions.

Limit values may never be exceeded by more than the maximum margin of tolerance specified for each of the pollutants in the Annexes to the draft Directive. Member States have to notify the Commission of any intended delay in compli-ance with specified limit values. If the Commission does not raise objections within nine months of receipt of the notification, the requirements for the extension will be deemed to be met.

Whilst the planned inclusion of PM 2.5 in the draft Directive is undoubtedly positive from an environmental point of view, the extension possibility for the Member States seems, at first sight, a drawback, in particular given the increasingly worrying studies on the health risks of particles and other substances. On the other hand, the experience with the PM 10 limit values that have entered into force on 1 January 2005 has shown that the limit values and deadlines laid down at present are probably unrealistic. It is expected that the same holds true with regard to limit values for other substances that still have to enter into force. It is probably more realistic to grant the Member States the extension possibility, but at the same time oblige them to elaborate long-term plans and programmes to meet the limit values before the end of the extension deadline. It will be very important that the Commission carefully monitors the establishment of these plans and pro-grammes, their implementation and the development of the emissions over time.

Further measures to reduce air pollution are taken in related sectors such as energy and transport. Directive 2005/33/EC on sulphur content of marine fuels was adopted in July 2005.[13] It aims at reducing sulphur dioxide emissions from seagoing ships. A Proposal for a 'Euro 5'—Regulation was tabled in December 2005.[14] It

---

[13] Directive 2005/33/EC amending Directive 1999/32/EC, [2005] OJ L 191/59.

[14] Proposal for a Regulation of the European Parliament and of the Council on type approval of motor vehicles with respect to emissions and on access to vehicle repair information, COM(2005) 683.

establishes requirements for the type approval of motor vehicles and replacement parts with regard to their emissions and aims at laying down harmonized rules on the construction of motor vehicles with a view to ensuring the functioning of the internal market whilst at the same time achieving reductions in atmospheric emissions from those vehicles.

B. Climate Change

In January 2005 the European Union Greenhouse Gas Emission Trading Scheme (EU ETS) commenced operation as the largest gas emission trading scheme world-wide. The scheme is based on Directive 2003/87/EC,[15] which entered into force on 25 October 2003. This is a cornerstone of EU climate change policy aiming at implementing the Kyoto Protocol.[16] It is the first international trading system for CO_2 emissions in the world. It covers over 11.500 energy-intensive installations across the EU, which represent close to half of Europe's emissions of CO_2. These installations include combustion plants, oil refineries, coke ovens, iron and steel plants, and factories making cement, glass, lime, brick, ceramics, pulp and paper.

The scheme is based on National Allocation Plans (NAPs) which determine the total quantity of CO_2 emissions that Member States grant to their companies and which can then be sold or bought by the companies themselves. This means each Member State must ex-ante decide how many allowances to allocate in total for a trading period and how many each plant covered by the Emissions Trading Scheme will receive. The first trading period runs from 2005 to 2007, the second one from 2008 to 2012, and the third one will start in 2013.

Emissions trading allows for cheaper compliance with existing targets under the Kyoto Protocol by letting participating companies buy or sell emission allowances at least cost. Member States limit CO_2 emissions from the energy and industrial sectors through the allocation of allowances, thereby creating scarcity, so that a functioning market can develop and overall emissions are reduced.

Allowances traded in the EU ETS will be held in accounts in electronic registries set up by Member States. All of these registries will be overseen by a Central Administrator at EU level who, through the Community independent transaction log, will check each transaction for any irregularities.

NAPs have to be drawn up periodically. Each Member State had to prepare and publish a first NAP for the 2005–2007 trading period by 31 March 2004 (1 May

---

[15] Directive 87/2003 establishing a scheme for greenhouse gas emission allowance trading within the Community and amending Council Directive 61/1996, [2003] OJ L 275/32; See also Decision 280/2004 concerning a mechanism for monitoring Community greenhouse gas emissions and for implementing the Kyoto Protocol, [2004] OJ L 49/1.

[16] Council Decision 2002/358 concerning the approval, on behalf of the European Community, of the Kyoto Protocol to the United Nations Framework Convention on Climate Change and the joint fulfilment of commitments there under [2002] OJ L 130/1.

2004 for the 10 new Member States). The NAPs for the second 2008–2012 trading period had to be prepared and published by 30 June 2006. The NAPs have to be approved by the Commission that will assess, in particular, three aspects: 1) if there is an over allocation that jeopardizes the achievement of the Kyoto target; 2) if the allocation is consistent with the projected emissions; and 3) if a Member State intends to make so-called 'ex-post adjustments' to allocations i.e. to intervene in the market after the allocation is done.

Many questions have been raised about the cost of climate change policy in general and of the ETS in particular. However, if Europe wants to develop as a low-carbon economy, the ETS certainly represents an opportunity, e.g. to become a world leader and exporter of low-carbon technologies, especially if seen in the medium/long-term perspective.

Another opportunity to reduce compliance costs with the Kyoto Protocol is given by the 'Linking Directive'.[17] The latter creates a link between the Flexible Mechanisms of the Kyoto Protocol—Joint Implementation (JI) and the Clean Development Mechanism (CDM)—and the EU emissions trading scheme. Companies which carry out emission reduction projects outside the EU through JI or CDM can convert the credits they earn from those projects into allowances under the EU Emissions Trading Scheme. The Linking Directive therefore offers more options for complying with the requirements of the Emissions Trading Scheme.

The Commission monitors the functioning of the EU ETS. In Autumn 2006, it will present a report to the Council and the European Parliament, considering the items listed in Article 30 of the Directive (e.g. inclusion of other sectors and gases, allocation method, level of the excess emissions penalty). It may propose amendments to the scheme but any amendments to the Directive would most likely only have an effect as from the third trading period beginning in 2013.

Shortly after the start of the EU ETS, the Commission, on 9 February 2005, adopted the Communication on 'Winning the Battle Against Climate Change'[18] and a more detailed Staff Working Paper. The Communication outlines key elements for the EU's post-2012 strategy. It highlights the need for broader participation by countries and sectors not already subject to emissions reductions, the development of low-carbon technologies, the continued and expanded use of market mechanisms, and the need to adapt to the inevitable impacts of climate change.

This paper comes as a response to the European Council request for an analysis of benefits and costs of action against climate change, which takes account both of environmental and competitiveness considerations.

---

[17] Directive 2004/101/EC, amending Directive 2003/87/EC, establishing a scheme for greenhouse gas emission allowance trading within the Community, in respect of the Kyoto Protocol's project mechanisms, [2004] OJ L 338/18.   [18] COM(2005) 35.

III. Environment and Health

A. The Environment and Health Action Plan

In June 2004, the Commission adopted an Environment and Health Action Plan, covering the period 2004–2010.[19] It is based on the Commission's European Environment and Health Strategy launched in June 2003.

The Action Plan suggests an integrated approach involving closer co-operation between the health, environment and research areas. It envisages the development of a Community System integrating information on the state of the environment, the ecosystem and human health to render the assessment of the environmental impacts on human health more efficient.

The Action Plan identifies a number of actions focusing on developing integrated environment and health information; strengthening research on environment and health and identifying emerging issues; and reviewing and adjusting risk reduction policy and improving communication.

B. Reach

The co-decision procedure on the Commission's proposal for a new framework on chemicals (REACH = Registration, Evaluation and Authorisation of Chemicals)[20] is ongoing. After the European Parliament's first reading, the Council reached a Common Position on June 27, 2006.

Further amendments are likely to follow at the second reading and the final adoption of the proposal is expected by the end of 2006. Therefore, the final text of REACH will be commented in the next survey.

C. Persistent Organic Pollutants

The Community ratified the Protocol on Persistent Organic Pollutants (POPs) to the Convention on Long-Range Transboundary Air Pollution[21] in April 2004[22] and the Stockholm Convention on POPs[23] in November 2004.[24]

The two instruments establish international rules on the handling of initial lists of POPs (16 in the Protocol, 12 in the Convention; additional chemicals may be added in both cases). They include the prohibition or severe restriction of the

---

[19] COM(2004) 416.　　　[20] COM(2003) 644.

[21] Protocol to the United Nations Economic Commission for Europe (UNECE) Convention on Long-Range Transboundary Air Pollution (CLRTAP) on POPs, opened for signature in June 1989 and entered into force on 23 October 2003; <http://www.unece.org/env/lrtap/pops_h1.htm>.

[22] Decision 259/2004/EC, [2004] OJ L 81/35.

[23] Stockholm Convention on POPs, opened for signature in May 2001 and entered into force on 17 May 2004; <http://www.pops.int>.

[24] Ratification on 16 November 2004, following a Council Decision of 14 October 2004, not yet published.

production and use of intentionally produced POPs, restrictions on export and import of such POPs, provisions on the safe handling of stockpiles, on the environmentally sound disposal of waste containing POPs and on the reduction of emissions of unintentionally produced POPs such as dioxins and furans.

Regulation (EC) No 850/2004 was adopted on 29 April 2004 to align Community legislation with the requirements of the above two instruments.[25] It entered into force on 20 May 2004. The Commission has also tabled a proposal for a Council Decision concerning proposals to add further substances to the lists of POPs in both international instruments.[26]

D. Genetically Modified Organisms

In early 2004, the Commission adopted a Decision laying down detailed arrangements for the operation of registers for recording information on genetic modifications in genetically modified organisms (GMOs),[27] as provided for in Directive 2001/18/EC on the deliberate release into the environment of GMOs.[28]

Also in 2004, the Commission adopted a Regulation establishing a system for the development and assignment of unique identifiers for GMOs[29] and a Recommendation on technical guidance for sampling and detection of genetically modified organisms and material produced from GMOs.[30]

At the same time, the implementation of the regulatory framework continues to pose problems, in particular with regard to the placing on the market of GMOs. The individual bans imposed between 1997 and 2000 by Austria, France, Germany and Luxemburg on GM crops authorized to be placed on the market have still not been lifted.

The bans were imposed on a temporary basis using a so-called 'national safeguard clause' in Directive 90/220/EEC that Member States can invoke when they have doubts about a product's safety for human health or the environment. The Scientific Committees of the European Community examined the scientific evidence provided by the Member States concerned, but considered there was no new evidence to overturn the authorization decision. Nevertheless, a so-called

---

[25] Regulation (EC) No 850/2004 on persistent organic pollutants and amending Directive 79/117/EC, [2004] OJ L 158/7.

[26] Proposal for a Council Decision concerning proposals, on behalf of the European Community and the Member States, for amendments to Annexes I-III of the 1998 Protocol to the 1979 Convention on Long Range Transboundary Air Pollution on Persistent Organic Pollutants and to Annexes A-C of the Stockholm Convention on Persistent Organic Pollutants, COM(2004) 537.

[27] Commission Decision 2004/204/EC laying down detailed arrangements for the operation of the registers for recording information on genetic modifications in GMOs, provided for in Directive 2001/18/EC, [2004] OJ L 65/20.

[28] Directive 2001/18/EC on the deliberate release into the environment of genetically modified organisms and repealing Council Directive 90/220/EEC, [2001] OJ L 106/1.

[29] Commission Regulation (EC) No 65/2004 establishing a system for the development and assignment of unique identifiers for genetically modified organisms [2004] OJ L 10/5.

[30] Commission Recommendation 2004/787/EC, [2004] OJ L 348/18.

de facto moratorium on GM crops approvals existed in the EU from 1999 to 2003, that is no further products were authorized.

Even, following the repeal of Directive 90/220/EEC and the implementation of Directive 2001/18/EC in October 2002, eight of the nine bans originally imposed remained in place as Directive 2001/18/EC contains a similar safeguard clause to that of Directive 90/220/EEC. However, product approval has restarted in 2004 when the Commission used its power under EC comitology procedure to break the deadlock in the Council.

It is interesting to note in this respect that a WTO dispute panel, in a dispute brought by the United States, Argentina and Canada in 2003 against the above-referenced *de facto* moratorium of the EU, issued in February 2006 a preliminary report, according to which there existed a moratorium that was in breach of WTO rules. The final WTO report[31] confirms the finding of the preliminary report and also condemns the individual bans by the Member States. This might be an incentive for the Member States concerned to eventually lift them.

Should the publication of the final WTO dispute panel report confirm the reported criticism of the individual bans, this might be an incentive for the Member States concerned to eventually lift them.

IV. Nature and Biodiversity

A. Natura 2000 Network

Considerable progress was made in 2004 and 2005 with regard to the completion of the Natura 2000 network. The Commission has adopted lists of sites of Community interest pursuant to Directive 92/43/EEC (Habitats Directive)[32] for the Alpine,[33] Atlantic,[34] Continental,[35] and Boreal[36] biogeographic regions. Since the list for the Macaronesian region had already been adopted in 2001,[37] only the Mediterranean list is missing for the EU old 15 Member States.[38] At present, a total of 20,587 sites and 545,815 km² are covered.

Progress has also been made in the designation of special protection areas pursuant to Directive 79/409/EEC (Birds Directive).[39] A total of 4,212 sites covering 386,547 km² have so far been designated as special protection areas and have been notified to the Commission.

---

[31] Published at <http://www.wto.org/english/news_e/news06_e/291r_e.htm>.

[32] Council Directive 92/43/EEC on the conservation of natural habitats and of wild fauna and flora, [1992] OJ L 206/7.   [33] Commission Decision 2004/69/EC, [2004] OJ L 14/21.

[34] Commission Decision 2004/813/EC, [2004] OJ L 387/1.

[35] Commission Decision 2004/798/EC, [2004] OJ L 382/1.

[36] Commission Decision 2005/101/EC, [2004] OJ L 40/1.

[37] Commission Decision 2002/11/EC, [2004] OJ L 5/16.

[38] For an overview of the biogeographic regions and the Member States covered see <http://dataservice.eea.europa.eu/atlas/viewdata/viewpub.asp?id=155>.

[39] Council Directive 79/409/EEC on the conservation of wild birds, [1979] OJ L 103/1.

Infringement procedures are pursued against those Member States lagging behind in their designation of Natura 2000 sites. At the same time, the designation of sites in the new Member States as well as of marine areas is under preparation.

In addition, a Commission Communication on financing Natura 2000 has been published.[40] Substantial new co-financing opportunities have also been included in the proposals for the Rural Development and Structural Fund Regulations for 2007–2013.

B. The Biodiversity Communication

The Commission Communication Halting the loss of biodiversity by 2010—and beyond was scheduled for 2005 and finally adopted in early 2006.[41] The objective to halt the loss of biodiversity by 2010 had been laid down in the 6th EAP. In addition, the EU Heads of State and Government had committed the EU to this goal at the Gothenburg European Summit in 2001.[42]

The Communication follows the EC Biodiversity Strategy of 1998[43] and its related Action Plans of 2001[44] and builds upon the recommendations from the Malahide and Bergen-op-Zoom Conferences on biodiversity held in 2004.

The Communication elaborates on the key reasons for biodiversity loss, takes stock of the progress made within the EU and at the international level. It identifies needs for further action and proposes an EU Action Plan to 2010 and beyond.

The Action Plan identifies four key policy areas and 10 priority objectives to be met in these areas. The four key policy areas are biodiversity in the EU, the EU and global biodiversity, biodiversity and climate change and the knowledge base. The priority objectives focus on addressing most important habitats and species; actions in the wider countryside and the marine environment; making regional development more compatible with nature; reducing impacts of invasive alien species; effective international governance; supporting biodiversity in international development; reducing negative impacts of international trade; adaptation to climate change; and strengthening the knowledge base. In addition, four key supporting measures are mentioned: ensuring adequate financing, strengthening EU decision-making, building partnerships, and building public education, awareness and participation.

The Action Plan also foresees regular monitoring, evaluation and review of the progress and the measures taken. It is also proposed that the implementation of the Action Plan is overseen by the existing Biodiversity Expert Group (BEG). The latter should ensure coordination and complementarity between actions at EU and at Member State level.

The Communication sets out an ambitious approach to halting the loss of biodiversity and, with the Action Plan, provides a rather detailed instrument to

---

[40] COM(2004) 431.   [41] COM(2006) 216.
[42] Presidency Conclusions, Gothenburg European Summit, 15 and 16 June 2001.
[43] COM(1998) 42 final.   [44] COM(2001) 162 final.

achieve this goal. Its success will depend on the implementation of the suggested measures both at the Member States and at EU level. Given the delay in the adoption of the Communication, however, time now seems rather short to reach the targets until 2010.

C. Life III

In September 2004, Regulation (EC) No 1682/2004[45] extended the LIFE III program for a further two years (2005 and 2006), with an additional budget of €317 million. This extension avoids a legal gap from the end of LIFE III in 2004, and the new Community Financial Perspectives in 2007. The Commission also adopted a proposal for a new LIFE, called LIFE+, for the period 2007–2013.[46] It proposes a budget of €2,190 million in total, and a simplified structure with two components: LIFE+ implementation and governance, and LIFE+ information and communication.

At present, there are a few environmental funding programmes and LIFE is the biggest one (LIFE Nature, LIFE Environment, and LIFE Third Countries). LIFE+ will be the EU single financial instrument exclusively devoted to the environment and supporting the priorities of the 6th EAP. Third country actions will no longer be financed under LIFE, but instead will be financed under the EU external assistance programmes.

The final budget for LIFE+ will depend on the figure that will be agreed by the European Parliament and the Council for the overall EU Financial Perspectives for the 2007–2013 period.

D. Flegt

In 2003, the Commission adopted a Communication on an Action Plan on Forest Law Enforcement, Governance and Trade (FLEGT). A key component of the Action Plan was a proposal to establish voluntary FLEGT Partnerships between the EU and countries with serious illegal logging problems. Through the FLEGT Partnerships exports of timber products from these countries would be accompanied by a legality licence providing an assurance that the timber has been legally harvested. The FLEGT Partnerships would require substantial capacity building through development cooperation in order to develop timber tracking systems and audit/monitoring capabilities.

In order to implement the FLEGT Partnerships, legislation was needed allowing for EU customs to prevent the entry of relevant timber products from FLEGT partner countries in the case that they were not accompanied by a 'legality license'.

---

[45] Regulation (EC) No 1682/2004 amending Regulation (EC) No. 1655/2000 concerning the Financial Instrument for the Environment (LIFE), [2004] OJ L 308/1.

[46] Proposal for a Regulation of the European Parliament and of the Council concerning the Financial Instrument for the Environment (LIFE+), COM(2004) 621.

This legislation was proposed by the Commission in 2004 and adopted by the Council in 2005—the FLEGT Regulation.[47]

Negotiations with potential partner countries are expected to start in 2006. However, the public debate between the Commission and NGOs has already started on additional legislative options to exclude illegal timber from the European market. These options aim at addressing the fact that a number of important wood producing countries may not sign up to partnership agreements therefore leaving a big loophole in the system. NGOs have been advocating new European legislation to make the importation of illegally logged timber in the EU illegal.[48]

E. The Marine Strategy

Another strategy planned in accordance with the 6th EAP and proposed by the Commission aims at protecting the European marine environment. The Thematic Strategy on the Protection and Conservation of the Marine Environment[49] sets the double goal of achieving good environmental status of the EU's marine waters by 2021 and of protecting the resource base for marine-related economic and social activities. In parallel, the Commission is developing an EU maritime policy to achieve the economic potential of oceans and seas and the Marine Strategy should be the green pillar of that policy.

The Marine Strategy is accompanied by a Directive[50] that will establish European Marine Regions on the basis of geographical and environmental criteria. Each Member State, in close cooperation with the neighboring countries within a Marine Region, will have to develop Marine Strategies for its marine waters. These Marine Strategies assess the marine environment at the regional level, try to define 'good environmental status' and provide for targets and monitoring measures. Emphasis is put on the *ex ante* evaluation of the costs and benefits of such measures to be conducted by the Member States

The Marine Strategy takes into account the Water Framework Directive from 2000[51] and should help fulfilling its objectives i.e. the achievement, by 2015, of good ecological status for surface freshwater and ground water bodies.

A more strategic approach to the protection of the European marine environment is warranted especially if one considers the steady increase of people leaving on European coastlines paralleled by the degradation of the latter and of the adjacent waters. However, the proposed Strategy contains no binding targets itself but rather delays their setting to cooperation among Member States in the framework of more strategies at regional level. This approach may lead to inconsistent and delayed protection of the marine environment throughout the EU.

---

[47] Regulation (EC) No. 2173/2005 on the establishment of a FLEGT licensing scheme for imports of timber into the European Community, [2005] OJ L 347/1.
[48] See <www.illegal-logging.info/papers/EU_Civil_Society_Initiative.pdf>.
[49] COM(2005) 504.   [50] COM(2005) 505.
[51] Directive 2000/60/EC establishing a framework for the Community action in the field of water policy, [2000] OJ L 327/1.

V. Natural Resources and Waste

A. The Strategy on Sustainable Use of Natural Resources

The Thematic Strategy on Sustainable Use of Natural Resources[52] tackles environmental aspects of resource use in an overarching fashion. Its objective is to de-couple environmental impacts from economic growth. To achieve a stable de-coupling the Strategy identifies three factors: creating more value with fewer resources (increasing 'resource productivity'); reducing the overall environmental impact per unit of resources used (increasing 'eco-efficiency'); and substituting presently used resources with better alternatives.

The strategy applies a life-cycle approach; it has a time span of 25 years and focuses on: improving understanding of resource use and its environmental impacts; developing tools to monitor and report progress; and initiating actions to achieve its goals while building on existing policies and legislation.

Some specific measures are identified. A European Data Centre on natural resources will be established to gather all the available information in order to monitor and analyse it and to provide information to decision-makers. Indicators will be developed by 2008 to measure progress in resource productivity and eco-efficiency. Member States are expected to develop national measures and programmes to achieve a stable de-coupling trend for the next 25 years by focusing on the resource use that has the most significant environmental impacts in its area.

A High-Level Forum composed of senior Member States' officials; the Commission and stakeholders will facilitate the development of the national measures and programmes.

In the context of the EU Strategy for Growth and Jobs, the life-cycle thinking will be applied to assess the most significant negative environmental impacts and to identify concrete actions to reduce them. Greater eco-efficiency is expected to be a driver for innovation, competitiveness and growth.

At the international level, the Strategy envisages the establishment of an International Panel on the sustainable use of natural resources in cooperation with the United Nations Environment Programme (UNEP). The Panel aims at providing independent scientific advice about key environmental impacts of resource use. This is expected to contribute to the development of strategies to reduce environmental impacts by changing unsustainable patterns of consumption and production and via capacity building in developing countries.

The strategy contains an annex that provides examples of measures that Member States could take. They include mapping resource use and projecting it

---

[52] COM(2005) 670. In 2005, the Commission also adopted a Communication on the Review of the Sustainable Development Strategy—A Platform for Action, COM(2005) 658. This proposal is under discussion in the Council and the outcome of the review (expected for mid-2006) will be commented in the next survey.

for the future; encouraging the development of clean products and the change of production and consumption patterns; developing import measures to reduce the environmental impacts in exporting countries; and developing a timetable towards de-coupling their economy.

While it is impossible to predict what effect this Strategy will have by the end of its long-term time span, the paper is not very innovative. The focus of the measures it envisages is essentially related to information gathering and it is doubtful if this would have not happened anyway without the Strategy on the basis of existing private/civil society or UNEP initiatives. Also, Member States have no obligation to develop national measures, as this Strategy is not accompanied by any proposal for the adoption of a legislative instrument. Some of the measures suggested in the annex could have already been the subject of EC legislation in the short/medium term. One can, however, hope that the Strategy will indeed spark initiatives and a new focus in some, if not all, Member States, to de-couple economic growth from environmental impacts.

B. The Waste Strategy

The Waste Strategy's[53] main objective is to make Europe a recycling society that seeks to prevent waste and, where waste cannot be prevented, uses it as a resource.

As a first concrete step in this direction, the Commission proposes a revision of the Waste Framework Directive to:

1. Shift the attention of waste policy on the key environmental impacts and on improving the natural resources management by introducing the life-cycle approach;

2. Oblige Member States to develop waste prevention programmes within three years of the entry into force of the revised Waste Framework Directive;

3. Set environmental standards to be fulfilled by recycled wastes for them to be considered high-quality secondary materials.

4. Foster the use of market-based instruments by Member States, such as landfill taxes.

5. Simplify waste legislation by clarifying definitions and consolidating into one text several directives in the waste field.

More actions are envisaged for the coming years but their content will only be developed gradually over time building on the experience gathered with the implementation of the first measures put in place.

Other, non-legislative measures will facilitate the achievement of the objectives of the Strategy, e.g. the implementation of the EU Environmental Technologies

---

[53] A Thematic Strategy on the prevention and recycling of waste, COM(2005) 666.

Action Plan (ETAP) and the use of European funds for research and development of waste technology to tackle the key environmental impacts of waste. The review of the guidelines on state aid for environmental protection will provide an opportunity to clarify when state aids may be granted to support waste recycling.

The Thematic Strategy on waste will be reviewed in 2010 when the necessity of additional measures to achieve its goals will be assessed.

While overall the Strategy is likely to bring about a modernization of and more efficient approach to EC waste legislations, some concerns may be raised with respect to the suggested simplification of waste legislation. In the current political debate focused on competitiveness, the temptation will be strong for Member States to use 'simplification' as a de-regulation tool in a field like waste whose economic importance is quite high.

VI. Horizontal Instruments

A. ETAP

Early in 2004, the Commission adopted a Communication on an Environmental Technology Action Plan (ETAP).[54] The plan has three main axes.

The first is 'Getting from Research to Markets' and focuses on attracting more private and public investment for the development and demonstration of environmental technologies in line with the EU objective of 3 per cent of GDP for research. It also emphasizes the role of technology platforms, public/private partnerships on a specific topic bringing together interested stakeholders to develop and promote a specific technology. Environmental Technology Verification is also fostered using Community research funding for the establishment of networks of testing centres, in order to develop common or co-ordinated protocols and practices of technology assessment in the water, soil or land use.

The second axe aims at 'Improving Markets Conditions'. To this end, it stresses the role of performance targets as one way to encourage industry to develop and take up environmental technologies. These targets need to be based on best environmental performance, while being realistic from an economic viewpoint. A number of existing EC policy and legislative instruments are relevant in this respect including the Integrated Product Policy, the Energy-using Products Directive, the IPPC Directive (Integrated Pollution Prevention Control), the EU Eco-Label, and EMAS (Environmental Management and Auditing Scheme).

---

[54] Stimulating Technologies for Sustainable Development: An Environmental Technologies Action Plan for the European Union, COM(2004) 38. In relation to horizontal instruments in the survey period, it is also worth noting that the EC became a Party to the Aarhus Convention in 2005. See Council Decision on the conclusion, on behalf of the European Community, of the Convention on access to information, public participation in decision-making and access to justice in environmental matters [2005] OJ L 124/1.

In addition, the plan identifies potential sources of funding for environmental technologies through a range of financial instruments. Together with the Framework-Programme on Research and Development and the demonstration programmes, such as LIFE-Environment; the Structural Funds and the Cohesion Fund remain the main EU source of grants in eligible geographic areas. A new Competitiveness and Innovation Programme (CIP) is under preparation by the Commission. This programme will also address eco-innovation.

Furthermore, the Plan highlights the central role of market-based instruments. In this regard, success stories exist in the promotion of energy efficiency investments in households and for investing in renewable energy. These instruments can take various forms, for example, they can be tradeable permits or tax incentives.

The second axe also stresses the role of green public procurement as a potentially powerful tool for the promotion of environmental technologies[55] and promotes awareness raising and training activities in conjunction with the development and take-up of environmentally friendly technologies.

The third axe of ETAP focuses on 'Acting Globally' i.e. on supporting eco-technologies in developing countries, and fostering foreign investment to promote sustainable development at the global level.

ETAP, with its focus on technology is one of the few areas of EC environment policy that has been promoted rather than questioned by competitiveness concerns. It has a good chance of helping the EC Member States keeping or even consolidating their world lead in the development of 'green technologies'.

B. The Liability Directive

Directive 2004/35/EC on environmental liability with regard to the prevention and remedying of environmental damage was adopted on 21 April 2004.[56] It aims at establishing a framework for environmental liability, based on the polluter-pays-principle, to prevent and remedy environmental damage.

Environmental damage is defined so as to cover damage to protected species or habitats pursuant to the Birds and the Habitats Directives, waters covered by Directive 2000/60/EC (Water Framework Directive),[57] and land contamination that risks harming human health.

The Directive establishes two distinct, but complementary liability regimes for environmental damage: The first applies to operators who professionally conduct

---

[55] See 'Buying green! A handbook on environmental public procurement' SEC(2004) 1050. In 2004, the Commission developed a Handbook on Environmental Public Procurement to explain how public authorities can integrate environmental considerations into public procurement procedures. It clarifies the possibilities created by the existing public procurement legislation which allow for environmental considerations in technical specifications, selection and award criteria and contract performance clauses. It also takes into account the most recent jurisprudence of the Court of Justice in this field. It is worth recalling that public contracting authorities annually spend between 14 and 16 per cent of EU GDP.   [56] [2004] OJ L 56/56.

[57] See n. 51 above.

risky or potentially risky activities listed in Annex III of the Directive such as industrial activities, waste management operations, the release of pollutants into water or into the air, the production, storage, use and release of dangerous chemicals, and the transport, use and release of GMOs. In these cases, strict liability applies in principle, although the operators may under certain conditions be exempted from liability. The second regime applies to activities other than those listed in Annex III, which cause damage to protected species or habitats, if the operator is at fault or negligent.

The Directive does not apply to cases where environmental damage or an imminent threat of such damage is caused by an act of armed conflict, hostilities, civil war or insurrection, or a natural phenomenon of exceptional, inevitable and irresistible character. The same is true, *inter alia*, with regard to damage caused by nuclear risks, national defence activities and incidents, such as oil pollution by sea-going ships, in respect of which liability and compensation falls within the scope of certain international conventions (listed in Annexes IV and V of the Directive).

Finally, the Directive does not apply to damage to persons, private property or economic losses. These continue to be covered by national civil liability regimes.

Where environmental damage has not yet occurred, but there is an imminent threat of such damage, the operator shall, without delay, take the necessary preventive measures and, in certain cases, inform the competent authority of all relevant aspects of the situation, as soon as possible.

Where environmental damage has occurred, the operator shall, without delay, inform the competent authority of all relevant aspects of the situation, take all practicable steps to immediately control, contain, remove or otherwise manage the relevant contaminants and/or any other damage factors in order to limit or to prevent further environmental damage and adverse effects on human health, in accordance with the relevant provisions of the Directive (in particular Annex II).

The operator has to bear the costs of remedial action, unless he can prove that the damage or the imminent threat of the damage have occurred due to activities by a third person or due to the implementation of instructions by authorities. Member States may also provide that the operator does not have to bear the costs of remedial activities, if he can prove that he has not acted with fault or negligence and that the damage resulted from a permitted emission or activity or an emission or activity, which, according to the state of the art, was not likely to cause damage.

The operator liable under the Directive bears the costs of the preventive and remedial measures. Where a competent authority has acted in place of the liable operator, it shall recover the costs incurred from the operator. In the case of various liable operators, the Directive leaves it to the Member States to allocate individual responsibilities and costs.

Natural or legal persons affected or likely to be affected by environmental damage or having a sufficient interest or whose rights have been impaired may request the competent authority to take action under the Directive. Those persons shall have access to a court or other independent and impartial public body who is competent to review the procedural and substantive legality of the decisions, acts or failure to act of the competent authority.

The Directive does not provide for an obligation to introduce financial security instruments. Member States are however encouraged to develop such instruments and markets with the aim of enabling operators to use financial guarantees to cover their responsibilities under the Directive. The Commission will report, by 30 April 2010, on the availability and affordability of financial security products. In the light of this report, the Commission will, if appropriate, submit proposals for a system of harmonized mandatory financial security.

The Directive has to be transposed by 30 April 2007. It will not have retroactive effect, that is it will only apply to activities and damage occurring after this time.

The obligations under the Directive complement other Community environmental legislation, in particular as regards nature conservation. While most other instruments apply during authorization procedures or require sanctions for certain damaging acts, under the environmental liability Directive for the first time specific obligations are being created to take preventive and/or restorative action.

C. Protection of the Environment Through Criminal Law

In a landmark judgment of September 2005,[58] the ECJ annulled Council Framework Decision 2003/80 on the protection of the environment through criminal law.[59] The Decision, which had been adopted in the framework of Title VI of the Treaty on the European Union (TEU),[60] required Member States to prescribe criminal penalties for a number of environmental offences. The Commission had brought an action for annulment against this Decision to the ECJ in 2003, because it considered that the Decision should have been adopted on the basis of Article 175 of the Treaty establishing the European Community (TEC).

The ECJ agreed with the position taken by the Commission and held that the measures in question had as their main purpose the protection of the environment. Whilst the Community in principle had no competence with regard to criminal law and procedures, it could take measures in the field of criminal law, which were necessary to ensure the full effectiveness of EC environmental rules. Therefore, the rules in question should have been adopted on the basis of Article 175 EC. The Court also recalled that Article 47 TEU stated that nothing in the TEU was to affect the EC Treaty. Since the Framework Decision could not be divided, it was annulled.

---

[58] Case C-176/03, *Commission v. Council*, [2005] ECR I-7879. For the sake of clarity, the judgment is discussed here and not under Chapter VIII.
[59] Council Framework Decision 2003/80/JHA on the Protection of the Environment through Criminal Law, [2003] OJ L 29/55.   [60] In particular Articles 29, 31(e) and 34 (2)(b).

This is a very important ruling, because the ECJ for the first time has to some extent broken the taboo of criminal law being the exclusive prerogative of the Member States. It did so by recognizing the possibility of partial harmonization of Member States' criminal laws in the environmental field: The Member States have to criminalize certain conducts, which are particularly detrimental to the environment, but remain free in the choice of the penalty to apply, although the penalty has to be effective, proportionate and dissuasive.

The content of the Framework Decision now has to be transformed into an EC instrument. This is positive from a Community integration as well as from an environmental point of view, since it will entail substantial European Parliament involvement in the legislative process as well as Commission control and ECJ jurisdiction on the instrument following its adoption.

The Commission is currently considering how to proceed. A proposal for a directive on environmental criminal law had already been made in 2001,[61] but had not found a majority in the Council. In November 2005, the Commission has issued a Communication to the European Parliament and the Council on the implications of the judgment on existing and pending legislation relating to criminal matters[62] suggesting various possible ways forward. A decision has not yet been taken.

VII. Citizens's Rights

A. The Aarhus Package

(i) Overview and Ratification

Further progress has been made in aligning Community legislation with the requirements of the Aarhus Convention on Access to Information, Public Participation in Decision-Making and Access to Justice in Environmental Matters.[63]

The first two pillars of the Convention (access to information, and public participation in environmental decision-making) have been transposed at Community level by Directives 2003/4/EC on access to environmental information[64] and 2003/35/EC on public participation in environmental decision-making.[65] The transposition deadlines of both directives expired in 2005.

[61] Proposal for a Directive of the European Parliament and the Council on the Protection of the Environment through Criminal Law, COM(2001) 139, [2001] OJ C 180E/238.

[62] COM(2005) 583.

[63] United Nations Economic Commission for Europe (UNECE) Convention on Access to Information, Public Participation in Decision-Making and Access to Justice in Environmental Matters of 25 June 1998; entered into force on 30 October 2001; <http://www.unece.org/env/pp/documents/cep43e.pdf>.

[64] Directive 2003/4/EC on public access to environmental information and repealing Council Directive 90/313/EEC, [2003] OJ L 41/26.

[65] Directive 2003/35/EC providing for public participation in respect of the drawing up of certain plans and programmes relating to the environment and amending with regard to public participation and access to justice Council Directives 85/337/EEC and 96/61/EC, [2003] OJ L 156/17.

In October 2003, the Commission proposed a draft third Directive on access to Justice in environmental matters[66] (third pillar of the Convention) as well as a draft Regulation on the application of the provisions of the Convention to EC institutions and bodies[67] covering all three pillars of the Convention. At the same time, a draft decision to ratify the Convention was tabled.[68]

Following difficult negotiations both in the European Parliament and in Council, a political agreement on the draft Regulation as well as on the draft Decision to ratify the Convention was reached at the Environment Council in December 2004.

The Decision to ratify the Convention was formally adopted on 17 February 2005.[69] The Regulation was adopted on 6 September 2006.[70] It is doubtful whether the proposed Directive on Access to Justice will ever become law due to the lack of political will of the Member States which see this area as beyond Community competence.

(ii) Draft Directive on Access to Justice

The draft Directive on Access to Justice grants legal standing in environmental proceedings to challenge the procedural and substantive legality of administrative acts and omissions in breach of environmental law to members of the public, if they have a sufficient interest in the related act or omission or maintain the impairment of a right, where the administrative procedural law of a Member State requires this as a precondition. With the incorporation of these criteria, the Commission opted not to introduce a general right of legal standing for every natural person (*actio popularis*). This is in line with the Aarhus Convention, which leaves the possibility to lay down criteria in national law.

While it does not introduce an *actio popularis*, the draft Directive does expand the standing of members of the public by granting standing to 'qualified entities'. These entities have to meet certain criteria (for instance, they have to be independent and non-profit making legal persons which have the objective to protect the environment) and be recognized under national law following a specific procedure. The draft Directive also foresees transboundary legal standing for these entities.

The draft Directive also obliges Member States to ensure that the above-referenced entities may request an internal review prior to having access to environmental proceedings. It is for the Member States to determine the competent authority for such review.

The Proposal is still pending at the Council in first reading.

---

[66] COM(2003) 624.   [67] COM(2003) 622.   [68] COM(2003) 625.

[69] Decision 2005/370/EC, [2005] OJ L 124/1.

[70] Regulation (EC) No 1367/2006 of the European Parliament and of the Council of 6 September 2006 on the application of the provisions of the Aarhus Convention on Access to Information, Public Participation in Decision-making and Access to Justice in Environmental Matters to Community institutions and bodies, OJ (2006) L 264/13.

(iii) Regulation on the Application of the Provisions of the Convention to EC Institutions and Bodies

The Regulation lays down rules aiming to apply the principles of the Aarhus Convention to Community institutions and bodies, in particular by:

(a) guaranteeing the right of public access to environmental information held by or for Community institutions and bodies;

(b) ensuring that environmental information progressively becomes available in electronic databases that are easily accessible to the public through public telecommunications networks;

(c) providing for public participation in respect of the preparation by Community institutions and bodies of plans and programmes relating to the environment; and

(d) granting access to justice in environmental matters at Community level under the conditions laid down by the Regulation.

The provisions contained in the Regulation on the three pillars of the Aarhus Convention are largely similar to those contained in the (draft) Directive.

As the draft Directive on Access to Justice, the Regulation introduces an internal review procedure for administrative acts and omissions. An 'administrative act' is thereby defined as any administrative measures taken under environmental law by a Community institution or body having legally-binding and external effect. Administrative acts and omissions shall not include measures taken by a Community institution in its capacity as an administrative review body such as under Articles 226 and 228 EC (infringement proceedings).

Decisions taken by the Commission in infringement proceedings are therefore excluded both from internal review and also from the provisions on standing before the ECJ. It is questionable how decisions by the Commission to close complaints files, which have not become infringements, will be dealt with in this light. Clearly, they do not fall under the exception for measures taken in infringement proceedings. On the other hand, given the informal nature of the Commission complaint procedure, they can hardly be considered to have legally-binding and external effect. Therefore, decisions to close complaints will probably also remain outside the scope of application of the Regulation.

This is regrettable, since complaint procedures in environmental matters are an important tool to improve implementation and enforcement of Community environmental law. Formalizing this procedure and as a result granting standing at least with regard to decisions to close complaint files in internal review and possibly also Court proceedings would not only foster citizens' rights, but also considerably enhance importance and effects of these procedures. Whilst the Commission's discretion in deciding whether or not and how far to pursue a case in an infringement procedure certainly needs to be preserved, that does not mean that the factual basis of such decisions, as well as possible mistakes in exercising this discretion, could or should not be reviewed. Administrative review procedures in many Member States show that this is possible and how.

This would also allow for a review of decisions in complaint procedures within the judicial architecture of the Community. The present situation, where a growing number of complainants is turning to the Ombudsman for a review of substance of such decisions due to the lack of any administrative review within the Commission, is not satisfactory, *inter alia*, because the Ombudsman's competences under the Treaty are limited to investigating possible instances of maladministration on the part of the Community institutions and because there is no possibility of a review of the Ombudsman's decision by the ECJ (this will not change on the basis of the Regulation).

B. EPER

The European Pollutant Emission Register (EPER) was opened to the public by the European Commission and by the European Environmental Agency (EEA) in February 2004.

EPER was established by a Commission Decision of 17 July 2000,[71] which in turn was based on Article 15(3) of Directive 96/61/EC on integrated pollution prevention and control (IPPC-Directive).[72] According to the EPER Decision, Member States have to report to the Commission every three years on emissions from all individual facilities with one or more activities listed in Annex I of the IPPC-Directive. They have to report the emissions into air and water of all pollutants for which certain threshold values are exceeded. Both pollutants and threshold values are listed in Annex A1 of the Decision. The Decision also establishes certain criteria for the format in which the information has to be provided.

The first reporting year was 2001. Information was reported to the Commission in June 2003 and published on the internet in February 2004. The website,[73] which is managed by the European Environment Agency (EEA), gives interested citizens access to information on the emissions of about 9,200 industrial installations in the 15 old Member States as well as in Norway and Hungary. The information can be obtained in various different ways, such as searching a pollutant, an activity (sector), a facility (individual installation), the medium concerned (air or water) or an EU Member State. The second reporting year is 2004. Data from the new Member States will be included. The information will be published in late autumn 2006.

---

[71] Commission Decision 2000/479/EC on the implementation of a European pollutant emission register (EPER) according to Article 15 of Council Directive 96/61/EC concerning integrated pollution prevention and control (IPPC), [2000] OJ L 192/36.
[72] Council Directive 96/61/EC concerning integrated pollution prevention and control, [1996] OJ L 257/26.   [73] <http://eper.ec.europa.eu/>.

EPER will be succeeded by the European Pollutant Release and Transfer Register (E-PRTR). This is based on Regulation (EC) No 166/2006[74] and is intended to fully implement the Community's obligations under the Kiev PRTR Protocol to the UNECE Aarhus Convention.[75] The obligations under the Regulation go beyond the scope of EPER mainly because more facilities and substances as well as releases to land will be included. Reporting will take place on an annual basis. The Commission shall disseminate the E-PRTR free of charge on the internet. The Regulation also foresees public participation in the further development of the E-PRTR. The first reporting year under E-PRTR will be 2007. Reports will have to be provided to the Commission by 2009.

The opening of EPER to the public is an important step towards an enhanced public access to information on industrial emissions not only in individual Member States but all over Europe. It may also be hoped that the publication of the data on the internet will contribute to encourage covered operators to decrease pollution levels as much as possible.

VIII. ECJ Case Law[76]

A selection of the most significant cases decided by the ECJ and by the Court of First Instance (CFI) in the field of environment in the biennium of reference is briefly addressed below.

A. Air Pollution and Climate Change

In 2005, in *United Kingdom v. Commission*,[77] the CFI annulled a Commission decision refusing to consider an upward revision of the amount of carbon allowances that the UK wanted to give to its national industry in the first phase of the EC emission trading scheme (2005–2007).[78] The Court recognized the right of Member States to amend National Allocation Plans (NAPs) including the total emissions allowance when, for instance, new elements have emerged after stakeholders consultation or new data have become available. A different approach would render stakeholders consultation redundant or would neglect the real situation on the ground, e.g. when material errors have occurred or when there has

---

[74] Regulation (EC) No 166/2006 concerning the establishment of a European Pollutant Release and Transfer Register and amending Council Directives 91/689/EEC and 96/61/EC, [2006] OJ L 33/1.

[75] Kiev Protocol on Pollutant Release and Transfer Registers to the UNECE Aarhus Convention, adopted at an extra-ordinary meeting of the Parties to the Convention on 21 May 2003; signed by 36 states and the European Community; <http://www.unece.org/env/pp/prtr/docs/PRTR%20Protocol%20English.pdf>.

[76] Parts A, C and D of this sections draw heavily upon N. Notaro, 'Case Law of the European Court of Justice' (survey) in *yearbook of European Environmental Law*, Vols 5 and 6, Oxford University Press.

[77] Case T-178/05, *United Kingdom v. Commission*, not yet reported.

[78] See n. 15 above.

been an underestimation of the allowances allocated to an individual installation. While the Commission cannot restrict the Member States' right to propose amendments, these amendments will still have to be approved by the Commission after their compatibility with the emission-trading directive has been checked. In other words, the Commission still holds the power to check that the environmental objectives of the directive are respected.

In the Court's view, the Commission's fear that allowing a change in the total emissions allowance would have destabilized the market was not properly substantiated and certainly 'exaggerated'. The amendment sought by the UK was relatively limited and of minor importance compared to the overall EU scheme whose functioning was yet to start at the time the amendment was sought.

It is possible that the Commission was resisting any amendment to the UK NAP with a view not to create a 'bad precedent' rather than for the specific circumstances of the case. Indeed, this case could provide an incentive to Member States to revise their national allocations time and again, e.g. when they come under pressure by some sectors of national industry or when other national political circumstances push them to do so. This could stretch the already very limited Commission's resources over a multiplication of assessments of NAPs and could indeed cause delays in the functioning of the scheme. On the other hand, there are limits to this negative incentive as the Commission will still need to approve any amendment suggested by a Member State and will reject them when they are unsubstantiated.

More strikingly, in our view, is the fact that the Court, while recognizing that the UK request for an amendment to the NAP was submitted after 30 September 2004 and therefore in violation of Article 11(1) of the emission trading directive,[79] did not attach any particular consequence to this clear violation of EC law. The CFI should have, in our mind, recognized that the UK request was indeed inadmissible as decided by the Commission but on the basis of the non-fulfilment of the above-mentioned imperative deadline rather than on the basis of the Commission's argumentation. One can understand that the Commission did not put much emphasis on Article 11(1) because by so doing it would have *a contrario* recognized that Member States are entitled to ask for amendments. However, the CFI should have highlighted such a self-evident violation of EC law and drawn consequences from it in order to ensure the fulfilment of the time limits set by EC law.

B. Environment and Health

Cases T-366/03 and T-235/04, *Land Oberösterreich and Austria v. Commission*,[80] concerned an action for annulment against a Commission decision rejecting a

---

[79] Article 11(1) of the Directive (above n. 3) states that Member State' decisions on the allocation of allowances 'shall be taken' at least three months before 1 January 2005, i.e. by 30 September 2004. The UK request for a revision of its NAP was sent to the Commission only on 23 December 2004 (see paras. 14–15 of the case).   [80] Judgment of 5 October 2005, not yet reported.

request for derogation, made by Austria under Article 95(5) TEC, with regard to a draft law of the Land Oberösterreich banning GMOs within its territory.[81]

In its judgment of 5 October 2005, the CFI dismissed the actions as unfounded and upheld the challenged decision. The Tribunal supported the Commission's position that Austria had failed to prove that the conditions for a derogation pursuant to Article 95(5) TEC had been met, in particular, since Austria had failed to demonstrate that a *specific problem* had arisen in the Land Oberösterreich following the adoption of Directive 2001/18/EC.

C. Nature and Biodiversity

In 2004, in Case C-127/02, *Landelijke Vereniging tot Behoud van de Waddenzee, also acting on behalf of Nederlandse Vereniging tot Bescherming van Vogels v. Staatssecretaris van Landbouw, Natuurbeheer en Visserij*,[82] the Court provided a preliminary ruling on a number of questions relating to Article 6 of the Habitats Directive[83] raised by a Dutch court. The questions concerned mechanical cockle fishing in the Dutch Waddenzee, a Special Protection Area classified under Article 4 of the Birds Directive.[84] The ECJ explained that this activity falls within the concept of 'plan or project' under Article 6(3) of the Habitats Directive. A plan or project not directly connected with or necessary to the management of a site is to be subject to an appropriate assessment of its implications if it cannot be excluded that it will have a significant effect on that site. On the basis of the precautionary principle, the risk of such an effect exists if it cannot be excluded on the basis of objective information. The ECJ also clarified that 'likely to have significant effects' means 'likely to undermine the site's conservation objectives'. In the remarkable paragraph 61, the ECJ provided guidance on the notion of an 'appropriate assessment' by offering a rather wide interpretation of the concept and, more importantly, applied a very strong notion of the precautionary principle by ruling that an activity that has implications for a protected site can be authorized only if it is 'certain that it will not adversely affect the integrity of that site. That is the case where no reasonable scientific doubt remains as to the absence of such effects'.

The ECJ also ruled that a national court can determine the lawfulness of an authorized plan or project by assessing whether the national authorities have observed the limits of the discretion as set out in Article 6(3), even when this provision has not been transposed into national legislation despite the expiry of the time limit.

The adoption by the ECJ of a very strong notion of the precautionary principle is not new, but its explicit use in the context of Article 6 of the Habitats Directive

---

[81] The background and arguments by the parties have been discussed in detail in the last survey, cf. *Yearbook of European Law*, Vol. 23, Oxford University Press, 385–391.
[82] [2004] ECR I-7405.   [83] See n. 32 above.   [84] See n. 39 above.

is very welcome as it calls for strong caution at Member States level when authorizing activities that could render vain the objectives of the European network of protected areas (Natura 2000), one of the key instruments to protect biodiversity in Europe.

In Case C-117/03, *Dragaggi*,[85] also a preliminary ruling, it concerned the question whether or not Article 6(3) and (4) of the Habitats Directive should be applied to sites that had been included in national lists, but not yet in the Community list of sites pursuant to Article 4(2) of the Directive.

In its judgment of 13 January 2005, the ECJ held that Articles 6(2) to (4) of the Directive only applied to sites that had been included in the Community list of sites. Nevertheless, according to the ECJ, for sites eligible to be included in the Community list, which are included in the national lists of sites transmitted to the Commission, in particular when they are hosting priority habitats and species, Member States are required to take appropriate protection measures for the purpose of safeguarding the relevant ecological interest which the sites have at national level by virtue of the Directive itself.

In concrete terms, this means that, whilst Member States for instance are under no obligation to follow the procedural requirements laid down in Article 6(3) and (4) of the Habitats Directive, for instance they do not have to carry out impact assessments with regard to planned projects, *de facto*, they will have to assess the impacts of planned projects in order to take the appropriate protection measures for the sites concerned.

Further clarifications on nature and scope of the protection regime applicable to sites before their inclusion in the Community list of sites have been requested from the ECJ in a further preliminary ruling procedure referred by a German court.[86]

Also in relation to nature protection—although in the fisheries sector, one case decided in 2005 stands out for its particular importance: *Commission v. France*.[87] France has been condemned on the basis of Article 228 TEC for its failure to comply with an earlier judgment decided in 1991[88] on the implementation of fisheries legislation aimed to protect juvenile fish in order to re-establish fish stocks. The ECJ considered that France failed to carry out adequate controls on the implementation of EC legislation and to take action to stop infringements. It ordered France to pay both a penalty of over €57 million on a half year basis as long as the previous judgment is not fully complied with, and a lump sum of €20 million.

Previously, the court already imposed periodical penalty payments twice,[89] but never a lump sum. The Commission had only asked for the payment of daily

---

[85] [2005] ECR I-167.   [86] Case C-244/05, *Bund Naturschutz in Bayern u.a.*

[87] Case C-304/02, *Commission v. France* [2005] ECR I-6263.

[88] Case C-64/88, *Commission v. France* [1991] ECR I-2727.

[89] Case C-387/97, *Commission v. Greece* [2000] ECR I-5047; and Case C-278/01, *Commission v. Spain* [2003] ECR I-14141.

penalty payments but the Court felt that, in light of the particular features of the breach it had established, a lump sum was also warranted. Most of the 16 Member States intervening before the Court spoke, predictably, against the cumulating of a penalty payment with a lump sum. The Commission and a few other Member States supported it. The Court stated that a combination of the two measures is one and the same means of achieving the objective of Article 228 of the Treaty i.e. to induce a Member State to comply and to reduce the possibility of similar infringements to be committed again in the future. The use of the word 'or' in Article 228(2) to link the financial penalties that can be imposed may, linguistically, have an alternative or a cumulative sense and, in the light of the objective of Article 228, must be understood in a cumulative sense.

The Court reinforced this conclusion by rebutting all sort of shaky legal arguments that Member States had put forward in a desperate attempt to reduce the future penalties they may incur. All kind of defences had been raised from the violation of the *ne bis in idem*, to the disrespect of the principles of legal certainty, predictability, transparency and equal treatment. More strikingly, Germany openly questioned the political legitimacy of the Court to impose a penalty not suggested by the Commission. The ECJ replied very clearly by stating that the matter of whether or not a Member State has complied with a previous judgment is subject to a legal procedure and political considerations are irrelevant.

This case marks a very welcome development that could turn out to be a cornerstone in strengthening the implementation of EC law in general. The imposition of penalty payments to which the Court resorted in the past only starts producing its effects too late. Member States need to be condemned by the Court twice and only then can they incur fines that increase on the basis of the time during which they remain in non-compliance after the second judgment. It is true that the amount of this kind of fine is calculated on the basis of the Member State's ability to pay, on the seriousness and also on the *duration* of the infringement but penalty payments are not, as such, retrospective. In particular, the duration criterion is the less important as it has a co-efficient that is far lower than the other two and therefore much less influential on the determination of the total amount of the fine.[90] Therefore, Member States are not required adequately to account for (sometimes many) years of non-compliance preceding the Court's rulings. On the other hand, the cumulating of a lump sum with a penalty payment also punishes Member States for 'the effects on public and private interests of the failure of the Member State concerned to comply with its obligations'[91] and provides a greater deterrent against persistent cases of non-compliance.

The Court was also wise in imposing a penalty payment on a half-yearly rather than daily basis as this leaves some margins to the Member States to actually get

---

[90] The duration criterion has a co-efficient that can vary on a scale from 1 to 3; a scale of 1 to 10 is applicable to the seriousness criterion while the ability to pay has, in the case of France, a co-efficient of 21.1 which is based on the gross domestic product of the country and on the number of votes it has in the Council.   [91] Para. 81 of the judgment.

their acts together and work seriously on implementation. The amount of €20 millions for the lump sum is clearly very low if one considers that for many years French fishermen have profited economically from illegal fishing tolerated by the national authorities. It is, however, understandable that the Court showed some self-restraint in order not to spark too strong a reaction by the Member States to its decision. If the approach taken by the Court in this decision is appropriately used by the Commission and is routinely applied to a growing number of Article 228 judgments, it could determine a shift in the mentality of Member States' administrations in relation to compliance with EC law.

In Case C-239/03, *Commission* v. *France*,[92] the ECJ built on a previous ruling[93] in which it had confirmed that Article 6 of the Protocol for the Protection of the Mediterranean Sea against Pollution from Land Based Sources,[94] has direct effect and can be relied upon by interested persons before national jurisdictions. In the currently reviewed Case C-239/03,[95] the ECJ stated that the environment is an area largely regulated by EC law, and the EC has an interest in that Member States respect commitments taken under international environmental agreements, even in the absence of specific EC law implementing them. Therefore, the Court declared itself competent to judge on the action brought by the Commission against France for violation of the above-mentioned Article 6. This case is remarkable in that it states very clearly that environmental protection is an area largely covered by EC law, and on this basis the Community is competent even in areas not yet regulated. Thus, despite the fact that international environmental agreements are the subject of mixed competence, EC competence should be interpreted as having a wide scope. This ruling could be used by the Commission to claim an even more important role in the negotiations of international environmental agreements, comparable to its competencies in areas of exclusive competence, such as trade and agriculture.

D. Natural Resources and Waste

In Case C-1/03, *Van de Walle*,[96] the ECJ provided further clarification on the definition of waste pursuant to Directive 75/442/EEC (the 'Waste Directive').[97] In its judgment of 5 September 2004 in the preliminary ruling case referred by a Belgian court, the ECJ held that the holder of hydrocarbons which are *accidentally*

---

[92] [2004] ECR I-9325.

[93] Case C-213/03, *Syndicat professionnel coordination des pêcheurs de l'Etang de Berre et de la région v. Electricité de France (EDF)* [2004] ECR I-7357.

[94] Athens (Greece), 17 May 1980, entered into force 17 June 1983, amended in Syracusa (Italy), 6–7 March 1996, published on the Internet at: <http://sedac.ciesin.org/entri/texts/mediterranean. pollution.1976.html>. The Protocol was concluded by the EC through Decision 83/101/EEC [1983] OJ L 67/1.   [95] See n. 92 above.

[96] [2004] ECR I-7613.

[97] Council Directive 75/442/EEC on Waste [1975] OJ L 194/39, as amended by Council Directive 91/156/EEC [1991] L 78/32.

spilled and which contaminate soil and groundwater 'discards' those substances, which must as a result be classified as waste within the meaning of Article 1(a) of Directive 75/442/EEC. The ECJ, moreover, clarified that even if the contaminated soil was not excavated, that did not change its quality as waste.

In *Commission v. Ireland*,[98] the ECJ condemned the latter for its general and persistent failure to implement the Waste Directive. The judgment demonstrates that Ireland had been in non-compliance for some 20 years. Breaches included municipal landfills operating without a licence and long delays (years!) before decisions were taken on granting or refusing a licence. Authorities implemented the waste legislation at issue in an extremely belated fashion; they systematically refrained from requiring existing unauthorized activities to cease and did not take appropriate measures to ensure that municipal landfills were promptly made subject to the domestic system eventually set up. Ireland was found in breach of eight Articles of the Waste Directive. There was in fact in the country a large-scale administrative problem that generated a practice of the national authorities not ensuring a correct implementation of the Waste Directive. Finally, Ireland was also found in violation of the duty of loyal co-operation enshrined in Article 10 of the TEC having 'forgotten' to answer to a Commission letter seeking observations on a complaint it had received.

This case is quite striking. Firstly, it is remarkable how persistent national authorities can be in openly disrespecting the obligations they have entered into under EC law. Obviously, in the EU this is not only the case of the Irish authorities and reflects a mentality of laissez faire on which basis Member States consider that they can get away with their lack of implementation of EC law for many years if not for ever. It is also quite surprising that the case was brought to the Court so late. Clearly, the Commission enjoys discretion under the Treaty in choosing which infringements to pursue and when, and its resources are far too limited compared to the number of violations of EC environmental law by the Member States. Still, one would have expected that a general and persistent failure as the one in question would have been given a higher priority also in order to give a clear political signal to the Irish authorities.

This decision of the Court does provide the Commission with a new possibility to step up its efforts to ensure better compliance with EC environmental legislation. In the past, the Court avoided extrapolating a general failure from specific, proved cases of non-compliance. The Commission must satisfy the burden of proof for each and every allegation of non-compliance against Member States. However, in this case the Court stated that nothing prevents the Commission from seeking in parallel a more general finding that breaches are linked to a general practice adopted by national authorities. This new approach, especially if combined with the effects of the decision on fines against France commented

---

[98] Case C-494/01, *Commission v. Ireland* [2005] ECR I-3331.

above could indeed give a boost to the Commission's action on implementation provided that adequate resources are allocated to the pursuit of infringements of EC environmental law.

E. Citizens' Rights

An interesting case on access to documents, Case T-168/02, *IFAW Internationaler Tierschutz-Fonds GmbH v. Commission*, was decided in the reference period.[99] The IFAW had requested access, based on Regulation 2001/1049/EC on public access to European Parliament, Council and Commission documents,[100] to a number of documents in the hands of the Commission related to the extension of the Mühlenberger Loch in Hamburg and the Commission Opinion pursuant to Article 6(4) of the Habitats Directive in this context. The documents included an exchange of correspondence between the German authorities and the Commission. The Commission had denied access to this correspondence, since the German authorities had asked the Commission not to disclose them pursuant to Article 4(5) of the Regulation. The plaintiff brought an action for annulment against this decision to the Tribunal arguing that a Member State, in the context of Article 4(5), had no right to veto the disclosure of a document, and that the final decision concerning disclosure had to remain with the Commission.

The CFI, in its judgment of 30 November 2004, rejected this argument and upheld the position taken by the Commission. The CFI held that, whilst the Commission's duty to consult third parties under Article 4(4) of the Regulation did not affect its power to decide whether one of the exceptions provided for in Article 4(1) and (2) of the Regulation was applicable, Member States were subject to a special treatment pursuant to Article 4(5) of the Regulation. The provision did grant the right to a Member State to veto the disclosure by the Community institutions of a document originating from that Member State. This could be explained by the fact that it was neither the object nor the effect of the Regulation to amend national legislation on access to documents. The Member State did not have to state reasons for a veto. Once a Member State had expressed a veto, it was no longer for the Community institution concerned to assess whether the non-disclosure of the document was justified.

As the CFI explained, the Community does not intend to interfere with Member States' national legislation on access to documents on a case-by-case basis. Where a Member State refuses access to a particular document on the basis of its national legislation, it is according to the Tribunal not for the Community to grant access to this document through the back door and against the Member States' will. This is in line with Declaration No 35 annexed to the Treaty of

---

[99] [2004] ECR II-4135.
[100] Regulation (EC) No 1049/2001 regarding public access to European Parliament, Council and Commission documents, [2001] OJ L 145/43.

Amsterdam, by which the Conference agreed that the principles and conditions set out in Article 255 EC would allow a Member State to request the Commission or the Council not to communicate to third parties a document originating from that State without its prior agreement. It is also wise in view of maintaining co-operative and trusting working relations between the Community institutions and the Member States. Finally, should the Member State's rules on which the refusal is based turn out to be in conflict with the Community Directive 2003/4/EC on access to environmental information, this could be addressed by the Commission at a more general level by means of an infringement procedure pursuant to Article 226 EC.

Reviews of Books

The European Employment Strategy: Labour Market Regulation and New Governance by Diamond Ashiagbor (Oxford: Oxford University Press, 2005), 380 pages, hardback, £69.95, ISBN 978–0–19–927904–7.

Since the foundational period and the minimalist and non-interventionist approach of the Community in the social field, EU labour law and policy has undergone different paths of evolution and involution which highlight its fragmented structure.

With regard to the study of EU social law it has become customary among labour lawyers to systematize its paroxysmal development into various phases. Following this hermeneutic approach we may argue that the social dimension of the European Union has entered a new distinctive sixth phase which started with the Amsterdam European Council, further reinforced by the Lisbon Strategy and, more recently, by the Barcelona European Council. This phase is characterized by a new typology of acts, new institutions, actors, processes and outcomes and—as Ashiagbor takes pains to stress in the course of her investigation—by the displacement of other discourses by employment and economic discourses over social policy and social law.

The new scenario also explains why at European level the focus has shifted from 'government' to the broader notion of 'governance' encompassing economic, technological and knowledge-based processes as well as the political and legal. The latter includes both formal and institutionalized procedures and informal and non-institutionalized ones. The shift towards experimentation with new methodologies in European socio-economic regulation is, at the same time, a means *for* and a consequence *of* the furthering of the Europeanization process.

The book by Ashiagbor effectively captures all of these multi-faceted changes that have taken place in the context of EU labour law and policy and provides a highly original and fresh account of recent developments in EU labour regulation through the lens of the European Employment Strategy (EES) and, more broadly, of new modes of policy-making which form part of what has been commonly termed 'New Governance'. The book, which is well written and very thoroughly referenced, presents itself as a contextual study of law and regulatory policy. By drawing on economic theory and socio-legal methodologies, the book provides a 'synthesis of detailed policy analysis with an interpretative study of the ideological setting in which policy is developed' (p. 3). Such approach is employed in order to unravel how economic theory has construed the legal regulation of the labour market.

The book starts by analysing the law and economics of EU labour market regulation and, in particular, the labour market flexibility debate which also informs the EES and, more broadly, the role of employment law in job creation. The main purpose of this analysis is twofold. First, it provides a strong theoretical framework for subsequently assessing both the legal and economic rationales underpinning the launch and evolution of the EES and its principal regulatory mode of governance, the OMC. Second, it enables us to better understand the 'processes by which particular conceptions of the way in which the economy functions can lead to certain policy recommendations, goals or 'guidelines', which in turn have implications for law in its regulatory role' (p. 3). In particular, Ashiagbor explains how the choices over regulation or deregulation and the differing conceptions of a European social model are dependant on our understanding of notions such as, for instance, flexibility and liberalization. The deregulatory impetus of the EES is assessed in the light of the efficiency reasons for labour market regulation offered by new institutional economics although the book itself presents a normative argument for labour market institutions and regulation based on the goals of social justice. The analysis of economic theories of labour market regulation and of the interaction between law and economics is further enriched with a comparison of economic, labour market and employment performance between the EU and the US models also with regard to policy choices underpinning labour law.

In her book, Ashiagbor presents a thorough theoretical discussion of the promises and limitations of the EES for EU social law and policy and for the safeguard of social rights and illuminates the reasons for the co-existence *of* and interaction *between* the two main (opposing) discourses central to the strategy, that is to say, an economic policy discourse and a social policy one. In particular, Ashiagbor shows how this interaction has led to the development of an employment policy discourse which merges the objectives of the above discourses. However, the attempt to have recourse to the combined use of two different policy objectives brings with it internal contradictions which, inevitably, impact upon policy outcomes. One of the key dilemmas of the EES, which the book brings to the fore, is that it pursues a job creation agenda whilst attempting, at the same time, to provide the grounds for the realization of fundamental social rights. Ashiagbor questions whether—in the context of an explicitly 'hard' economic policy coordination backed by sanctions—there can be a form of governance which, while departing from centralized social policy norms, can adequately ensure a core of social rights below which no member state can fall.

Whilst the procedural innovations introduced by the EES, as 'the' paradigm example of the OMC, provide important regulatory tools for the use of the OMC in other social policy areas and thus for the wider Europeanization process, the dominance of the economic policy discourse which informs the EES concerning social justice and solidarity brings with it the danger that the OMC might end up coalescing exclusively around an economic criterion. Ashiagbor rightly points out that whatever the definition or label of regulatory tools like the OMC and 'soft' law strategies such as the EES, it is necessary to ensure that these forms of EU governance are underpinned by a European-level core of fundamental rights and principles. The OMC and the EES, therefore, should not only provide new regulatory techniques but enable European social policy to reconstruct its own architecture on the basis of social citizenship, rights and quality of jobs.

The key argument of the book is that social rights and labour standards need to be built into the EES in order to counterbalance economic discourse but in such a way as to preserve a space for national diversity and experimentation. The EES, as a form of 'soft harmonization' has the potential to forge a middle course through the means of hard law and within the regulatory choices facing the EU, between full harmonization, on the one hand, and mutual recognition or regulatory competition, on the other. The peculiarity of the EES is that it eschews the well-established individual rights-based model and, in particular, rather than providing for specific rights, such as, for instance, the right to work, it is proactive and collective as it places a positive duty on public authorities to identify the causes of unemployment and to remedy them. Hence, even though it does not provide for enforceable individual rights it may nevertheless be said to produce normative effects in that it creates a duty to act which the state and, more broadly, all public authorities must undertake. However, the multiplicity and variety of objectives do not come without problems and the book effectively shows how the problem with strategies pursuing different political and socio-economic objectives (neo-liberal *versus* social democratic; social justice and social protection *versus* flexibility) such as, for instance, the EES is that they have inherent paradoxes that may be difficult to overcome and which might, ultimately, undermine the effectiveness of the overall process.

Another strength of the book is its elaboration of the constitutional framework within which questions over the effectiveness of the EES are set. This in turn provides a better understanding of the implications that 'soft' law strategies such as the EES have on the constitutional structures of the member states and for social regulation at both national and European levels. One of the most disquieting shortcomings of 'soft law' instruments, which represents a challenge for legal scholars, is the difficulty in evaluating compliance with 'soft law' measures and, linked to this, in establishing whether there has been policy transfer. A very interesting and original part of the book is Ashiagbor's analysis of the meaning of compliance in the context of the EES, first, followed by her assessment of the ways of measuring compliance with the 'soft law' requirements of the EES. 'Rather than attempting to trace direct causal links between the EES and member states' employment policies, regulatory strategies and labour law, the aim of the book instead is to identify the influence of the EES on the *discourse* within member states over employment and labour market policy choices' (p. 242).

In the more comprehensive and substantive chapters of the book Ashiagbor also explains how the EES is the result of a combination of both economic realism and political requirement and how it exemplifies the continuous tension between *inter-governmentalism* and *supranationalism* and, therefore, how it illustrates writ large the complexities of the process of Europeanization. The investigation also focuses on the Economic and Monetary Union (EMU) and the Lisbon Strategy which have acted as catalysts for an emphasis on regulatory approaches to social policy. This analysis is important because it helps us to understand to what extent the EES represents an alternative to the Community Method and, if so, in what way. Second, this study is necessary because the genesis and further implementation of the EES must also be understood against the backdrop of economic processes taking place in the EU, particularly the economic policy co-ordination process in the context of which the Council, through the formulation of Broad Economic Policy Guidelines (BEPGs), establishes specific policy objectives that aim at achieving an adequate policy mix for the member states. The relevance of this examination is confirmed by the decision at EU level to streamline the employment and economic policy co-ordination processes and, more recently, by the adoption of 'Integrated Guidelines.'

Hence, in the broader context of the economic agenda of the EU and, chiefly, by placing the analysis of the EES and of the OMC within the pursuit of the Internal Market agenda and EMU and within the interaction between the Cardiff, Cologne and Luxembourg processes, Ashiagbor leads the reader to her conceptualization of the EES as a form of 'soft harmonization' through the means of 'hard law.' Indeed, all of these processes at European level which originated from political realism and pragmatism, but chiefly economic in nature, together establish a rigid macroeconomic framework that severely limits the decision-making power of the states and also of non-state actors. The overall outcome, therefore, as aptly argued by Ashiagbor, is that the 'soft' coordination of the OMC does have a 'hard' impact and that rather than focusing the debate on the nature of EU strategies such as the EES either on a rigid dichotomy between soft and hard law or between the intergovernmental or supranational, it would be more appropriate to contextualize it within the conceptual framework of an 'organized form of decentralization'.

The reviewer would have found of interest an empirical study of the operation of the EES and its regulatory tool, the OMC, also based on a comparative case study of those EU member states' which find it difficult to 'comply' with the 'soft law' requirements of the EES and, more broadly, with the goals set out in the Lisbon Agenda, rather than concentrating solely on the experience of two countries such as the UK and the Netherlands that have domestic policy agendas presenting similarities with the employment policy discourse of the EES. However, this comparative empirical analysis may have gone beyond the scope of the book.

This reflection aside, the book is a truly invaluable contribution to the study of EU social governance for any scholar engaging in an interdisciplinary study of the social dimension of the European integration process.

Samantha Velluti

The Mechanics and Regulation of Market Abuse: A Legal and Economic Analysis by Emilios Avgouleas (Oxford: Oxford University Press, 2005), i–lv + 517 pp including index, hardback, £110, ISBN 978–0–19–924452–2.

This book provides an exhaustive and systematic analysis of the practice and regulation of market abuse in the financial sector. The choice of such a research *topic* is not surprising: market abuse is the generic name referring to a variety of economic practices the common denominator of which is the creation of false impressions about the economic value of issuers in financial markets and the instruments that depict this value. Evidently, this affects the heart of the functioning of financial markets as an efficient allocation of funds mechanism and is indeed considered the pathology of the financial sector. While this is an old phenomenon, its *topicality* is immense. Not only is there a general trend in the financial sector of increasingly shifting the focus of attention towards the securities markets as the preferred and more efficient method for the allocation of resources, rather than the (traditional for some markets) banking financing. There are also specific reasons for the renewed interest in the topic of market abuse in particular: new insights on market abuse following the recent corporate crises in the US (like Enron), plus new data on the basis of how these practices are carried out in the modern more integrated global financial markets, requires analysis anew in an interdisciplinary, modern and systematic fashion. It is to this conceptual and academic need that Dr. Avgouleas' book responds. Within the EU context, in particular, the topicality of the theme becomes even more accentuated by another shift of focus, this time from the pre-occupation with setting in place a framework for creating a single European financial market (the so-called 'integrating' measures) to the establishment of rules that seek to regulate problems of an integrated single market (i.e. 'post-integration' or 'post-harmonization' measures). This distinction is taken up by the author, at p. 240 (as well as by other researchers in this field, e.g. see Niamh Moloney, *New Frontiers in EC Capital Markets Law: From Market Construction to Market Regulation*, 40 Common Market Law Review, 809–843 (2003)) and serves to demonstrate the novel EU interest in post-harmonization matters such as market abuse, that are considered as the 'core' of securities regulation in the US.

The main *aim of the work* is to seek to contribute to the 'deterrence and punishment of market abuse, as well as enhance the efficient function of contemporary financial markets' (at p. 21). In order to respond to such a demanding research question, the author makes use of inter-disciplinary *tools*, by applying both economic and legal analysis to his topic, as the sub-title of the book also suggests. In other words, a twin concern of the book is to: firstly, examine what and how market abuse operates in financial markets (an economic analysis); secondly, given the insights from the former analysis, explore the efficiency of the current regulatory strategy on market abuse and how this can be improved to provide optimal results in terms of decreased occurrence of the phenomenon (a legal analysis).

As concerns now the *scope of the work*, on the one hand, the concept of market abuse is examined in its two main expressions: insider dealing and market manipulation. On the other hand, the regulatory environment used as a framework of reference upon which to apply the findings of the economic analysis is the EU legal framework, complete with an extensive review of its implementation in a country with probably the deepest and oldest financial markets in the world, i.e. the UK. Despite the discussion of the matter within the particular EU and UK legal orders, the usefulness of the research cannot be underestimated: given the (in)famous inter-dependence of economies and markets of our times, it is not only the economic analysis of market abuse that can have universal application; indeed, also legal approaches and regulatory solutions tend to cross-fertilize and possibly even converge. This inter-dependence is to be found, for example, behind the apparently 'proactive' EU regulation of market abuse (i.e. not as a reaction to any particular crisis, as is often the case in financial regulation), which is, in reality, also 'reactive' in character, if one considers the recent US corporate scandals owed also to instances of market abuse. In this respect, the incorporation of examples and research insights from the US context renders this study truly comprehensive and global in its appreciation and usefulness.

In the economic analysis of market abuse the *framework of analysis* employed is finance theory, while traditional legal analysis is the tool used in the second part of the work. Finally, in the intersection of the two analyses, i.e. the application of the findings of the economic analysis to the legal framework of the prohibition and punishment of market abuse in the EU and the UK, the author employs the methodological tool of economic analysis of law, justified by the fact that, more so in securities law than in other legal disciplines, the main rationales of regulation are economic considerations of efficiency that make the case for a 'law and economics' approach stronger, if not imperative. The core *findings and related proposals* of the book can be summarized in the following: firstly, a redefinition of the concept of market manipulation so as to provide increased certainty as to the practice that can be held to constitute such an offence. Secondly, the establishment of a general right of action for insider trading and market manipulation; and thirdly, the resolution of the insider dealing debate by resort to the 'social norms' theory, which would help highlight societal preferences on the issue' (at p. 16), in addition to investor protection and efficiency considerations, which combined, call for a prohibition of the practice.

If now one wanted to sketch an *outline* of the main body of the work, one would find that this is also based on the dual approach of economic and legal analysis, in that order. Thus, chapters 2–5 (inclusive) are dedicated to the former, while chapters 6–9 (inclusive) to the latter. The first part of *chapter 2* provides a bird's eye view of the financial markets world. This includes a survey of the possible ways of classifying the various types of financial markets; an exploration of the role and functioning of stock exchanges; market composition and the growth of institutional investors particularly through collective investment schemes; financial innovation and its results (new products such as derivatives, and new trading practices such as program trading or portfolio insurance etc.). The second part of this chapter, instead, deals with the theoretical framework behind the functioning of financial markets. The most established (in terms of 'solid empirical evidence', p. 48) theoretical view for explaining and understanding them is the Efficient Capital Market Hypothesis (ECMH) which can be essentially described as holding that the price of a security reflects the information available on that security. In that sense ECMH is based on rationality expectations on the part of the investors. Nevertheless, recently developing theories such as 'behavioural finance' and 'chaos theory' have come to show 'that investor behaviour is much more complex and perhaps much more repetitive and predictable than the rationality assumption of the ECMH would have us believe' (at p. 73). But adhering to the explanations of one over the other economic theory has repercussions on the regulatory approach to be followed: indeed, behavioural finance and chaos theories have provided the basis of calls for deregulation in the securities markets and the redundancy of e.g. the insider trading prohibition. The author's finding in this respect is that these theories (which he calls post-modern) contribute to and refine the ECMH theory but do not seem to offer conclusive and solid evidence that would suffice to discard it completely, therefore their importance lies in focusing our (scarce so far) attention on market institutions and market microstructure, instead.

One such aspect of market microstructure is market abuse, the two facets of which (insider trading and market manipulation), are taken up in chapters 3 and 4, respectively. *Chapter 3* firstly provides an overview of the literature on the impact of insider trading on market efficiency. The author's conclusion is that there is ultimately a stronger case for considering insider dealing harmful to market efficiency, which serves to provide a rationale for requiring disclosure in a legal and regulatory framework. A final section of this chapter is then dedicated to exploring the relationship between various inter-related concepts: the author finds that corporate fraud exacerbates occurrences of market abuse by contributing to the creation of a favourable environment for its perpetration; market abuse and market 'bubbles', even though not entailing any element of deception, are 'mutually facilitating factors' since the latter create opportunities for concealing insider dealing practices, while market abuse can perpetuate, although not create, a 'bubble'; weak corporate governance can again facilitate the occurrence of market abuse practices; finally, insider trading and market manipulation are two closely related concepts, as they both constitute market abuse, with the sole difference that the former is information-based manipulation, while the latter trade-based manipulation.

The second of the twin concepts of market abuse, i.e. market manipulation, is taken up in *chapter 4*. A first part of it is concerned with the basic problem of defining market manipulation, since difficulties in accurately describing it gives rise to problems of applying it in a legal and regulatory context. The author reviews the various definitions that have been suggested thus far and comes up with an, arguably, more workable definition of the concept of market manipulation that presents it in a more synthetic manner, taking also into account the characteristics of modern financial markets. In the third and final part of this chapter, the author then applies the new definition to case-studies, thereby coming up with a new classification (albeit not exclusive, as he notes, p. 154) of market manipulation practices. He roughly distinguishes them in, (a) information-based manipulations, (b) manipulations based on artificial transactions and (c) price manipulations (which, in turn, are further elaborated in other distinctions). He then concludes that (a) and (b) above 'are probably a species of fraud' (p. 154) but that they should still constitute a separate offence, given their adverse influence on the market's price formation mechanism, while as concerns cases falling under (c), since they seem to not be very straightforward, with possibility of abuse e.g. 'of one price effect in order to influence the profitability of positions held on another market' (p. 155), it would be perhaps prudent to require the examination of the simultaneous existence of different cross-market positions or open contracts held, or, in other cases of 'suspicious' trading to establish 'a refutable presumption of intent to manipulate the market'.

Chapter 5 examines the rationale and welfare effects of prohibiting insider dealing and market manipulation. It does so by firstly surveying general theories of regulation and applying them to financial markets regulation (including the emerging 'behavioural' theory of regulation, whose merits are also explored). In a second section of the chapter, the specific regulatory tool of mandatory disclosure and the literature on its pros and cons are examined. The analysis at this point is dense and exhausting and the summary provided here does not do justice to its convincing power, but due to space restrictions it should suffice here to note that the author ultimately argues in favour of using mandatory disclosure, on the basis that a liberalized regulatory setting might be optimal but much more vulnerable to the occurrence of abuse. While he recognizes the problematic aspects of mandatory disclosure, i.e. costs of compliance and lack of flexibility, he proposes to mitigate them by shifting to a mixed system of implementation of mandatory disclosure standards through self-regulatory rules. As concerns now market transparency, the author finds that the discussion on its welfare effects on liquidity is similar to the preceding one on mandatory disclosure and that the conclusion is again that 'arguments against high standards of market transparency contain a number of loopholes' (at p. 192) on which he then elaborates. An exploration of the merits and problems with insider dealing is then presented, with reference to the US jurisprudence. The result advocates again in favour of regulating insider dealing, with the main rationale being that legalizing insider dealing would reduce the availability of public information in the market, 'a necessary condition of market efficiency' (at p. 205). Additional rationale for this proposition is the suggested use of a purely sociological approach to the matter, dictating the replication in legal rules of social norms on the unfairness of insider trading, as can be shown by the strong social reaction to the recent US corporate scandals that led to the enactment of the Sarbanes-Oxley Act. Finally, the prohibition of market manipulation is analyzed both from a purely economic efficiency point of view, i.e. as to the economic and compliance costs it entails, as well as from a behavioural viewpoint. The author concludes that fraud should probably be prohibited and then enforced through self-regulation and private litigation rights, while 'deregulating other forms of 'suspicious' trading as liquidity-enhancing speculation' (p. 234) would lead to efficiency gains.

Having completed the economic analysis of market abuse practices in the previous four chapters, the book then embarks upon the *legal analysis* of the topic in *chapter 6*. It begins with a brief excursus of the evolution of EU financial services law (from original ECJ case law on the 'general good', to the mutual harmonization principle, to the FSAP—Financial Services Action Plan—reform of EC financial markets legislation, and the adoption of the Lamfalussy framework regarding financial decision-making). Then, a detailed examination of the provisions of the main legislative tool, the Market Abuse directive, and its level 2 implementing measures follows: these include both substantial provisions (such as the prohibition of insider trading and market manipulation or issuers' continuing disclosure obligations etc.) as well as more procedural questions (e.g. supervisory powers and provisions relating to regulatory cooperation in the market abuse regime). But the picture of the EU law on market abuse is not complete unless provisions of other EU directives are included: the conflicts of interest, licensing and conduct rules for investment firms, included in the MiFID (Market in Financial Instruments Directive); and the rules for continuous disclosure of information by issuers of financial instruments contained in the Prospectus and Transparency Directives. The author finds that the definition of insider trading within this legislative framework is rather confusing, while the multiple legislative texts make compliance a daunting and costly exercise. Also, he points at what he sees as a large problem in the institutional side of the regime: the enforcement of the largely 'self-standing regulatory [market abuse] regime . . . by at least twenty-five—and probably many more . . . —country regulators' (at p. 305). Therefore he calls for the establishment of a pan-European authority with both regulatory and enforcement powers, to be observed across the EU.

Chapter 7 examines the details of implementation of the EU directives in the UK. A historical survey of the evolution of the regime is provided, from which the author concludes that while the UK framework (the Financial Services and

Markets Act 2000 (FSMA)) precedes the EU one, its approach and the guidance provided by the Financial Services Authority (FSA), were rather confusing and restrictive. Thus, the reforms that the adoption of the EU Market Abuse Directive dictated were actually a welcome change that allowed for a more flexible system and increased compliance. But in addition to regulatory prohibitions, also criminal law provisions characterize the UK market abuse regime; these the author finds largely untouched by the EU Market Abuse Directive reform. The final section of this chapter is devoted to the impressive enforcement arsenal of the regime that includes: regulatory investigations; regulatory remedies and criminal prosecution; exchanges' rules on market abuse; ECHR (European Convention of Human Rights) implications; and the role of the financial services tribunal. The author finds that the UK institutional edifice for enforcing its market abuse regime, through a combination of criminal law provisions with increased FSA powers, 'such as the issue of restitution orders and public statements and the ability to impose (unlimited) financial penalties' (at p. 387) probably makes for one of the most comprehensive market abuse deterrence systems available in developed countries. Nevertheless, he also finds that focusing on the FSA as the almost exclusive arbiter of the regime might be an unfortunate choice, which he suggests to cure by opening up the system to private enforcement in order to enhance its deterrent force.

This matter he takes up more in detail in *chapter 8* where he examines all possible means of redress in a market abuse scenario on the part of investors themselves, directly, and not through the FSA. Topics covered here include: the FSMA framework; claims in tort; claims for breach of contract; liability in equity and equitable remedies; unjust enrichment; and restitution. The analysis concludes that statutory, common law or equitable rights of action alike are burdened with limitations in their potential use by investors that have suffered loss, therefore what is suggested as a solution is the creation of a general right of action in damages for insider dealing and market manipulation through the establishment of a 'statutory tort for all breaches of section 118' (at p. 445).

Chapter 9, engages in a more general discussion of the use of civil liability regimes as tools for deterring market abuse, using economic analysis as a benchmark for judging the efficiency of such tools. Thus, an overview and comparison of the effectiveness of criminal law sanctions and civil penalties on the one side, with the deterrent force and economic efficiency of civil remedies on the other side is provided. The question of over-deterrence and the choice between civil sanctions or civil remedies is then also examined, while resort to the US regime on civil remedies is also made. The author's proposal mentioned above regarding the creation of a private right of action for market abuse is further explained and details are provided in order to render this a calibrated tool, able to provide relief only where there is identifiable loss to the plaintiff, thereby avoiding the dangers of vexatious litigation. The problem of loss evaluation the author proposes to solve through event-based studies. Thus, the panorama of the author's views on the optimal use of the various enforcement options becomes clear: criminal law tools would be better used in case of widespread financial frauds where there is a 'strong public demand for the criminal punishment of the engineers of such abuses' (at p. 495), complemented by civil penalties and private enforcement; while the aforementioned properly calibrated civil rights of action and civil penalties should be used in cases of smaller abuses. Proper levels of retribution and deterrence would then be possible, with higher chances for the attainment of enhanced legitimacy of financial market regulation in general.

In sum, this is an excellent work, whose many virtues include simplicity and clarity in the description of complex, sophisticated economic concepts without the resort to mathematical formulae. Indeed, what this lawyer reviewer found extremely helpful is that while finance theory bases its findings on rigorous mathematical models, this book manages to give the kernel of their conclusions in a very jurist-friendly fashion! An additional contribution of the book is depth of analysis; a thorough literature survey is provided of all competing views and theories on each sub-topic treated, thereby allowing even the un-initiated to get a complete picture of the main concerns and trade-offs involved. Nevertheless, breadth of the research is also there, not sacrificed in the name of depth of analysis: the book exhausts all aspects of the market abuse phenomenon, from an economics and legal viewpoint, in the context of the EU and the UK, but with lessons from the US experience, examining both the regulatory, criminal (in the UK context) and civil enforcement of a regime. One theme that could have been developed slightly more extensively is perhaps the section on the impact of the institutional organization for the EU financial sector, especially since the author finds that it creates potential problems in the correct and efficient application of the market abuse provisions, and since the Market Abuse Directive was one of the first to be produced according to the Lamfalussy process. Despite this minor point, Dr. Avgouleas' book not only contributes immensely to our understanding of the phenomenon of market abuse, thereby clarifying the optimal ambit of the related prohibitions, but with its comprehensive coverage of all features and related facets of market abuse stands up to the challenge of any 'checklist' of future developments to look out for in this area.

DESPINA CHATZIMANOLI

The Politics of Judicial Co-operation in the EU: Sunday Trading, Equal Treatment and Good Faith by Hans-W. Micklitz (Cambridge: Cambridge University Press, 2005), 572 pp, hardback, ISBN 978–0–52–182510–0.

Today, practitioners and scholars alike agree that the European Court of Justice (ECJ) and processes of legal integration have greatly shaped what we today understand as the politics of European unification. Legal scholars and political scientists continue to point to the long reach of the law when explaining new political developments in European integration. Yet there remains much contention over exactly how, when and with what cross-national effects the law matters for everyday politics in Europe. In particular, the effects of EU legal integration on ordinary citizens and public interests have only recently gained scholarly recognition. Micklitz's *The Politics of Judicial Co-operation in the EU* makes a solid contribution to this exciting and rich new research agenda—and is a study that is a must read for lawyers and political scientists alike.

The book takes as its central question *how* far the law reaches into EU political developments and answers this through an examination of the interaction between the ECJ, national courts, private litigants and organized public interests. In particular, Micklitz unpacks this larger query by examining three connected questions: what explains variation in judicial co-operation between national courts and the ECJ; how and why do private litigants and organized public interests invoke their rights; and importantly, exactly how both the supranational and national courts politically and legally legitimate their decisions? At its core, this book provides a unique perspective on EU constitutionalism from the bottom up. A particularly insightful strategy—given that complementary top down processes have recently led to a constitutional crisis and halt on new developments.

Theoretically, Micklitz weaves these empirical questions into an intellectually rich critical discussion of the three main premises underlying the ECJ's establishment of the European legal order: (1) co-operation between national and supranational courts through the Article 234 preliminary reference procedure; (2) organized law enforcement; and (3) the political and legal acceptance of ECJ led integration (legitimacy). Thus, the theoretical framework subsequently provides the foundation on which Micklitz can test when and how these widely held premises regarding judicial co-operation, organized law enforcement and political legitimacy do in fact hold true. The theoretical approach is quite broad adopting a perspective that considers how the European legal order comes to operate *across* fields of law, forcing us to think not only empirically but theoretically about how EU law in action might vary across substantive areas of law. Micklitz theorizes how these three main premises may come to operate in very different ways across three legal domains which also represent three categories of the EU legal order: EU trade law (common market), EU labour law (internal market), and EU private law (private legal order).

The book's theoretical assumptions are particularly provocative and salient, invoking key values that are both controversial and at the heart of EU legal reforms: freedom, equality and justice. Scholars assert that the ECJ has played a dominant role in the protection of market freedoms often at the expense of labour equality and grants only narrow access to justice. Micklitz provides a different and more nuanced picture, laying out a set of theoretical assumptions explaining how the ECJ's establishment of the legal order through judicial co-operation, organized law enforcement and political legitimacy is critically connected to the values of freedom, equality and justice and how this may vary across the categories of EU law (common market, internal market and private legal order).

First, out of the three values, market freedoms, are most easily developed by the ECJ through the tripartite dynamic of the EU legal order. How will the ECJ balance this market driven legal order in the future? Micklitz hypothesizes that as the ECJ narrows down the scope of EU free trade law (such as Article 30) it in effect will allow EU citizens greater access and voice in obtaining market freedoms (p. 31). Second, the ECJ also plays a defining, albeit somewhat more complex, and at times quite fragile in terms of political legitimacy, role in the development of EU equality law, particularly in regards to equal treatment between men and women. This development is characterized by judicial co-operation between the ECJ and in particular German and UK courts and a steady stream of litigation fueled by trade unions and women's organizations. Micklitz thus argues that the ECJ in collaboration with national courts has provided the foundations for EU labour law that may serve as a 'precedent' for other social policy domains (p. 31). Finally, Micklitz hypothesizes about justice in terms of the ECJ's role in developing the private legal order. On all fronts—judicial co-operation, organized law enforcement and legal-political legitimacy—EU private consumer law remains in its infancy. Drawing from the lessons learned in the other EU legal domains, Micklitz hypothesizes that legitimacy in the private legal order will hinge on a 'new pattern of justice' one that is grounded in access to justice in private law rather than distributive justice as seen in the labour law field (p. 32).

This rich theoretical framework guides the equally in-depth empirical case studies. The book includes three case study chapters examining substantive areas of EU litigation that are selected from the three general areas of EU law discussed above (trade law, labour law and private law): Sunday trading litigation, gender equal treatment litigation and 'good faith' in consumer law litigation. While the case studies are cross-sectoral, they focus on this evolving dynamic of EU law in a single country, the United Kingdom (UK). Micklitz applies a legal-sociological approach moving beyond mere data collection and instead a rigorous examination of how meaning is structured throughout the development of the EU legal order. The reader is provided with a detailed 'reconstruction' that includes analysis of legal documents from written to oral, as well as interviews with and analysis of all parties involved in the litigation, from the judges to the disputing parties.

The findings are succinct: judicial communication is in disorder, organized law enforcement is imbalanced and beyond the case of market freedoms, the legal-political legitimacy gap is extremely fragile. However, Micklitz does not leave us high and dry with this negative forecast, but instead, utilizes the variation found across his three case studies to propose a rubric for a successful and democratic future expansion of the EU legal order.

First, while many scholars tout a successful history of co-operation between the ECJ and national courts, Micklitz argues that in fact this is not sufficient, and what is greatly needed is 'mutual communication'. The case studies reveal a handful of maladies. One example is the disconnect between a *vertical* style of national problem-solving used by national courts and *horizontal* decision-making that characterized the ECJ's construction of the EU legal order. He calls for a 'redefinition' of judicial co-operation between the ECJ and national courts—a reality that is achievable by transforming the ECJ's capacity to engage in dialogue with these referring courts (p.425). Second, Micklitz reveals a great disparity in litigation success across organized interests. His cases demonstrate that trade groups are the best equipped with resources, organization and legal skills to utilize litigation strategies followed by the equality and employment organizations with public interest groups least likely to succeed. Given this finding, Micklitz suggests an important new area of research that might identify exactly how public interest groups can improve through an acquisition of litigation skills that are both compatible with their interests and provide the necessary tools to participate in the EU law enforcement process. Finally, Micklitz argues that closing the legitimacy gap is critically linked to individuals successfully asserting and attaining their EU political rights and political remedies through litigation. The case studies illustrate how the ECJ has facilitated this fragile balance by focusing on the content of the EU legal order, by emphasizing the importance of subjective rights, and insisting on real remedies to enforce EU law (p. 479). Micklitz ties this three-pronged strategy to the ECJ's continued success at maintaining a dominant role in the development of the EU legal order.

The book does suffer a common aliment of single country case studies. We are not given the broader perspective to know whether this interaction between UK courts and the ECJ does in fact represent a generalizable trend. While the importance of UK courts in referring cases to the ECJ is known, Micklitz helps us understand the details of this effect, however, his analysis still leaves us wondering why some countries such as Portugal have low reference rates regardless of legal domain. If Micklitz's findings are correct, the Article 234 preliminary reference process will continue to play a critical role in the evolution of EU law, and thus recent studies which take on the issue of cross-national variation in preliminary reference rates become increasingly important. Likewise, the author's assertion that qualitative methods are the 'best suited' for analyzing this legal process (p. 39), may be shortsighted, again for the achievement of greater explanation and testing of trends across time, country and policy area. Qualitative research is both invaluable and necessary for providing the real empirical information behind the general quantitative trends, and thus using multi-methods, both quantitative and qualitative, may bring us the greatest insights to the complexity and nuances of EU legal integration.

Despite these minor setbacks, *The Politics of Judicial Co-operation in the EU* provides a wealth of empirical information that moves us closer to explaining how the ECJ has come to define the EU legal order in the past and the starring role it will continue to play in the future. While the book will find its main readership amongst lawyers, political scientists who continue to privilege the role of EU law and judicial politics in explaining integration, will find this book equally of interest. Perhaps an unintended consequence of the study, this book does contribute to an important agenda of narrowing the gap that once existed between law and politics in EU studies. Understanding the dynamics of EU legal integration will take the skills and insights of both lawyers and political scientists, who increasingly have come to equally appreciate both the legal and political dimensions of this evolving legal order.

RACHEL A. CICHOWSKI

Handbook on the European Arrest Warrant by Rob Blekxtoon (T.M.C Asser Press, 2005), xiv + 283 pp + index 6pp, hardback, £55.00, ISBN 978–90–6704–181–2.

The European Arrest Warrant (EAW) is now widely used to secure the arrest and surrender of persons across the European Union (EU) and, as a recent European Commission's report indicates, has largely overtaken traditional extradition procedures as between Member States. Therefore, a 'handbook' on the EAW, purporting to serve '*as a guide to the judiciary and other interested parties*' (p. 6), is undeniably a welcome prospect, particularly when supported and updated by a website, <http://www.eurowarrant.net>, which serves as the vehicle of a collective research project launched by the Asser Institute around a pan-European consortium of public and private bodies.

Nonetheless, this is not a 'handbook' in the practical sense of the term. Although the Framework Decision is reproduced at the end with annotations and with the standard form to be used by the courts involved in the procedure, the corresponding provision-by-provision comments are rather brief. The main part of the book is a collection of academic papers divided into three parts: a first one that sets out a general framework, which includes a short history of extradition as a legal system, compares the EAW with the old system and makes a short overview of the EAW procedure as well as the role to be played by the Eurojust body; a second one in which specific principles regarding the implementation of the EAW are dealt with; and a third one on the relation between the EAW and human rights instruments.

In this regard, some of the specific contributions are particularly interesting. Professor van der Wilt's chapter on *Ne Bis in Idem* is especially helpful with regard to, (i) the problems arising from the differences between the civil and common law concepts of *ne bis in idem* v double jeopardy and (ii) the corresponding proposed mechanisms for dispute resolution between Member States in the event of discrepancy on the scope of this principle. Also interesting is Professor Lagodny's consideration of the concept of surrender (as distinct from traditional extradition). But these materials appear to be more directly relevant to the academic and international lawyer than the criminal law practitioner.

Other contributions are, despite the interest of the topic, of more doubtful value due to the way they are developed. It is, for example, disappointing that Paul Garlick's chapter on the EAW and the European Convention of Human Rights (ECHR) focuses much more on English case law than on that of the European Court of Human Rights (EctHR). The same holds for other chapters, such as Krapac's and Keijzer's, in which a very narrow scope—Croatian and Dutch standpoints—seems too specific for a book that is intended to have a broader nature.

In addition, from a substantial viewpoint, Selma de Groot points out, on the basis of the mutual trust principle enshrined by the EAW, that the refusal to surrender on the basis of an *ex ante* review '*can possibly not be fulfilled to the same scale than before*' (p. 97). Although her chapter is very well structured, this conclusion is somehow contested by recent episodes: the EAW has come under attack in a number of national courts and significant problems have arisen in some Member States where their constitutions provide protection against extradition of their own nationals. As a direct consequence, the mutual trust principle has suffered and has given rise to a revival of the reciprocity principle between Member States. In this regard, in response to the German Constitutional Court's ruling on the insufficient fundamental rights protection contained in the German implementing legislation, the Spanish authorities rejected several EAW requests from Germany because under Spanish Constitutional law extradition is permitted only on the basis of reciprocity.

Furthermore, there is some lack of consistency in Garlick's chapter regarding its treatment of Article 6 of the ECHR, since he points out as a given that the fair trial rights in Article 6 '*are engaged in the process of executing the EAW*' (pp. 167–168) but does not clarify sufficiently that the bar is extremely high: as recognized by Keijzer in its chapter, in the *Mamatkulov case* (*Mamatkulov v Turkey* (46827/99 and 46951/99, Chamber judgment, 6 February 2003; Grand Chamber, 4 February 2005), the EctHR did accept that a country proposing to surrender a fugitive must give proper consideration to the possibility of a breach of article 6 of the ECHR only when there would be a '*flagrant denial of justice*'. Caroline Morgan, in her otherwise useful and wide-ranging chapter on defendants' rights, faces the same problem. Taking into account the notion used by the EctHR together with the mutual trust principle at the basis of the EAW, it is, therefore, difficult to see the ground for Garlick's expressed hope that in this regard UK courts '*will give section 21 of the Extradition Act 2003* [judge at extradition hearing must consider ECHR compatibility] *a wide interpretation*' (p. 181).

Also, since the EAW was, in its last preparation stage at least, deemed to be a response to 9/11, the reader may regret that terrorism as such is not dealt with in the Handbook. It seems quite disappointing, taking into account that the Framework Decision mentions 'terrorism' as one of the offences to which the EAW applies without verification of double criminality, that Nico Keijzer's chapter dealing with this requirement only dedicates two lines to the issue. Besides, the category of murder, referred to as '*clear enough*' (p. 156), is far from being clear. As noted by the Commission in its recent Report, some Member States have indicated a wish to review the double criminality list because of concerns in relation to abortion, euthanasia and possession of drugs: there are circumstances where abortion and euthanasia may not be unlawful and their categorization raises difficult questions of fundamental rights and morality. Moreover, questions relating to the legality of the double criminality in the EAW are also pending before the European Court of Justice (ECJ). In July 2005 the Belgian Court of Arbitration made a reference to the ECJ in a case challenging, *inter alia*, the legality of the partial abolition of dual criminality. Although the Advocate General has rejected the claim, it remains to be seen what the ECJ rules on this matter.

These comments notwithstanding, the Handbook serves as a good starting point for understanding the issues which underlie the EAW. The overall structure of the book is quite coherent—which is not always the case with collections of academic papers. In this respect, it goes in certain matters beyond introduction and is of great interest even for those readers already more familiar with this field of research or expertise. Nevertheless, it needs to be read critically in some respects, as noted above. In any event, taking into account that the book is part of a general ongoing project with an on-line expression, it is to be expected that some of the shortcomings mentioned above will be dealt with more in depth in the updates posted in the website.

TONY FERNÁNDEZ

The National Courts' Mandate in the European Constitution by Monica Claes (Oxford: Hart Publishing, 2006), xlvi + 771 pp, hardback, £72.50, ISBN 10: 1–84113–476–7.

It has become a norm of the European legal scholarship to conceive of the judicial system of the European Union as comprising not only 'Community courts', located in Luxembourg, but also all courts of the (at present) 25 Member States. More importantly, although not so widely accepted, the views of the national courts on the European legal order are no longer (at least by some) treated as deviations from the single 'right' perspective given by the Luxembourg oracle, but as legitimate moderations of the supranational construction of the European legal order, expressing European legal pluralism.[1] Still little, however, has been so

---

[1] See particularly Maduro, 'Contrapunctual Law: Europe's Constitutional Pluralism in Action', in: N. Walker (ed), *Sovereignty in Transition* (Hart Publishing, 2003) and Kumm, 'The Jurisprudence of Constitutional Conflict: Constitutional Supremacy in Europe before and after the Constitutional Treaty', (2005) 11 *European Law Journal* 262.

far written on how the national courts actually coped with *all* the doctrines formulated by the Court of Justice in its endeavour to create a functioning and effective legal order of the European Union. *The National Courts' Mandate in the European Constitution*, written by Monica Claes (originally as her PhD thesis in Maastricht) therefore promises to fill in the gap and to help us 'to gain a better understanding of the involvement of national courts in the European Union judicial system, and its impact on the national constitutional position of courts' (p. 16).

As we can infer from this book's 'mission statement', it does not intend to look at the national courts as mere agents of European Union law within the Member States' legal systems. Her focus (or perspective) is dual: the first may be labelled as supranational, examining how faithfully the national courts have accomplished their mission of being the 'Community courts of general jurisdiction'.[2] Secondly, she looks at the courts from an internal perspective of national legal systems. As Claes puts it: 'what the Court asked [the national courts] to do had a vital impact on many deeply rooted constitutional principles, including the limits of their own mandate' (p. 5). This concerns the other side of European legal integration: its effects beyond positive law, its influence on the national legal systems' constitutional and institutional structures.

Corresponding to this dual perspective is Claes' concept of a 'judicial mandate'. She draws inspiration from the work of a Dutch internationalist, H.F. van Panhuys, who examined how legal norms originating from different legal orders (municipal and international law) were to be applied by various actors at different levels. Claes cites an example given by van Panhuys: a Dutch play celebrating the 400th birthday of William the Silent, where the audience watched a stage divided into two sub-stages. Each of these sub-stages presented the story of the Netherlands' fight for independence from different angles: William's cobelligerents' on one sub-stage and his Spanish opponents' on the other. Thus, the audience could follow the story from different perspectives and gained a more complete picture of what happened then. Claes takes on the role of the audience and observes from a neutral perspective a drama of mutual interaction of the supranational and national legal orders, a play of application of European Union law by courts at different levels. If we transpose the example of the Dutch drama to the world of legal norms, courts become actors playing on stages construed by their respective legal orders. They are attributed roles—judicial mandates. According to Claes, whereas in some cases courts may apply rules originating in different legal systems than their own, their mandate always comes from their own stage—the national legal order, the Constitution (p. 29). In relation to the European judicial system, she says at p. 27: 'the formal source of [the national courts'] judicial power remains within the national legal order, the content of their function as Community law courts is defined by Community law'. This seems to contest the traditional view

---

[2] Court of First Instance in Case T-51/89 *Tetra Pak v Commission* [1990] ECR II-309, paragraph 42, cited at p. 3.

of a national judge, 'wearing a Community law wig' (in Lord Slynn of Hadley's words quoted at p. 33) whenever he or she applies Community law and thereby becoming a veritable, full Community court.

The 'mandate model' is very useful, since it always reminds us that although the national court may change its wig, it cannot transform its core identity anchored within the context of the national legal system. The national court remains part of the national institutional structure, subjected to limitations imposed by the national Constitution—and at the same time called on by the Court of Justice to overcome these limitations in the name of the effective application of Community law. As Claes notes, this model is attractive as 'it allows the spectator to gain a good view of reality, as he is allowed to retain his seat in the audience'. She explains that it was why she had opted for this attitude 'of a neutral observer, who does not choose a particular perspective, but is at liberty to alter perspectives and angles' (p. 32). However, as we will see below, this 'neutral approach' has its inherent limitations, as it does not allow for offering normative solutions to the conflicts arising from occasional clashes of different perspectives. In other words, the neutral approach binds those who adopt it to remain a passive audience although there is a role for legal academics to play in the drama of the European legal integration.

With these different perspectives Claes approaches the three main topics related to the judicial mandate of the national courts: first, the role of ordinary courts, second, a more problematic involvement of national constitutional courts and third, the future role of courts in European constitutionalism. The following will briefly present them in turn, while considering some shortcomings of the 'neutral-observer approach', which stand in opposition to its advantages mentioned above.

In the first, and perhaps the most significant, part, the book focuses on ordinary courts and their Community mandates: the 'Simmenthal mandate'—the duty to set aside national legislation conflicting with Community law, and the 'Francovich mandate', which requires national courts to award damages in cases where individuals are harmed by Member State's violations of Community law. Starting with the 'Simmenthal mandate', Claes firstly digs into the depths of the European legal integration history and focuses on the question of the extent to which the constitutions of the six original Member States allowed their courts to examine national legislation in light of international obligations entered into by these States. She comes to the conclusion that in spite of different constructions adopted by national constitutions in their relationship to international law (Italy and Germany dualist, the rest, with a certain simplification, monist), these differences did not lead to great variations in practice: the courts (perhaps with the exception of Luxembourg) rather declined to apply international law directly in preference to conflicting national legislation. Indeed, this was not a very fortunate starting-position for the Court of Justice in the sixties. In accordance with the dual-perspective approach, the book subsequently inquires into the Court's of Justice definition of the Simmenthal mandate and provides the readers with a very interesting discussion of the notions of direct effect and supremacy, where it goes beyond the existing caselaw of the Court and considers the possibilities of extending these doctrines to 'Non-Community Union law'.

The following discussion of the principle of supremacy provides very useful categories. It firstly distinguishes *substantive and structural supremacy*, the former concerning the substantive rules of national law, which are to be set aside because of their conflict with Community law, the latter procedural rules. The second distinction concerns the position of national rules in the hierarchy of the national legal system. *Ordinary supremacy* applies to ordinary rules, while *ultimate supremacy* covers national rules of a constitutional nature. As Claes notes, this distinction has explanatory value when we look at the effect of different categories of supremacy on the national judicial structure. E.g., while ordinary supremacy comes in play primarily before ordinary courts, which are thus empowered to exercise judicial review, ultimate supremacy concerns supreme or constitutional courts, whose position as ultimate guardians of the constitutional and legal order is threatened by Community law, where the Court of Justice claims for itself the last word.

After supremacy the book addresses problems sometimes called 'second generation issues'. They relate to national procedural laws and the way in which national courts must protect individual rights, stemming from directly effective Community law provisions. These may be considered as mere technical problems, whose resolution does not touch highly praised national constitutional principles. However, these questions concern *law* and its functions as such. As Claes notes, the key word for the Court of Justice is effectiveness (p. 142). Alas, it sometimes seems that the Court is so much obsessed with the effectiveness of Community law, that its doctrines destroy principles preserving the functions and effectiveness of law, law meaning a system of institutionalized social governance regardless from which source it stems (be it the Community or its Member States). Law, among other things, should provide certainty and predictability for those who are governed by it, so that they may plan their actions in accordance with it. Here comes the problem with the neutral-observer approach. The book is able to change the perspectives and to tell us the story of national courts' involvement in creating the functioning legal order of the European Union, but after a time, this play with different perspectives ends in describing what each of the sides (supranational and national) says without providing a normative evaluation of these positions, an evaluation which could move us closer to the different-perspectives conundrum.

This relates to the book's definition of a judicial mandate. As Claes puts it, the mandate stems from the national Constitution and is transformed by Community law. However, the judicial mandate of *European courts* (Luxembourg together with national) may be viewed at one level of abstraction higher. Claes touches on this when she states that '[a] judge's mandate consists, in general terms, in applying the law' (p. 29). This is too general a characterization. The executive also applies the law, although in a different manner than the judiciary. But we can reformulate this characterization of the courts' role and say that *the courts' principal mission is to ascertain that the rule of law is observed.* Because the rule of law is not bound to a particular legal order, neither the supranational nor that of the Member States, the importance of their different perspectives diminishes. Instead, we are provided with a tool to evaluate each of the perspectives in light of principles, common to both of them, which express the finality of European legal integration, the rule of law being its indispensable part.[3] It would allow lawyers studying the role of courts in European legal integration to leave their comfortable seat in the audience and become actors at the stage where the drama of European legal integration takes place (which they are in any case if we understand legal discourse as reaching beyond institutions). An example of such a case, where the effectiveness of Community law struggles with the effectiveness and functionality of law as such, is the Court's treatment of the principle of *res judicata* in *Larsy*,[4] discussed by Claes at pp. 133–135 and only briefly evaluated as '[drawing] extreme conclusions from the basic principles of Community law' or the 'Constanzo mandate'—the duty to set aside conflicting legislation imposed on national administrations, which Claes discusses in an 'excursion'.

However, this criticism does not undermine the great contribution the book makes. With all its inquiry into 'national answers', as Claes calls parts of the book describing how national courts embraced (or failed to) the Court of Justice's appeals, Claes shows that the reality of European law is much more colourful than that regarded exclusively from Luxembourg. The book explores national constructions of the relationships between the legal orders as well as constraints on exercising the 'Simmenthal mandate' due to the constitutional limitations of the judicial function of the national courts. Still, it may be understood as a call for further attention to go beyond these descriptions and to analyse critically whether some of the limitations would not make sense in the name of law. This is somewhat lacking in a concluding chapter to the part dealing with the 'Simmenthal mandate', which otherwise provides an overview of possible reasons which have led national courts to its acceptance.

The second part of the book is called 'La guerre des Juges?' and deals with the far more problematic relationship, which the Court of Justice has had with national constitutional courts. 'Hailed as protectors of the national sovereignty, national fundamental rights or the Nation State by some, they have been accused by others of interfering with European integration, of jeopardising the uniform application of Community law and of provoking the Court of Justice' (p. 388). As elsewhere in the book, in this part the constitutionalization of the European Union is perceived from different angles. When examining the Union perspective,

---

[3] Along these lines M. Kumm made his analysis of constitutional conflicts and proposed that the courts should be led by principles underlying both national and supranational legal order (he called this the principle of best fit). M. Maduro designed a similar approach, aiming at an every-day practice of courts, applying 'contrapunctual law principles'. Cf. supra n 1.

[4] Case C-118/00 *Larsy* [2001] ECR I-5063.

Claes does not limit herself to the 'constitutional rhetoric of the Court of Justice' (p. 408 *et seq.*), but equally explores the 'constitutional language in legal writing' (p. 404 *et seq.*), showing the importance of the European academic discourse. Is the Court of Justice a constitutional court? Partly, due to its jurisdiction, the methods it employs and its role as guardian of fundamental rights as well as the important part it played in the completion of the Common Market, Claes concludes that it is. However, the Court's constitutional role creates tensions with national constitutional courts, so well known from their 'strenuous dialogue', although some of them are reluctant to enter the conversation with the Court of Justice, as Claes shows in her examination of how these courts view their obligation to submit preliminary references to the Court.

After briefly examining the 'Simmenthal Mandate' of the constitutional courts, where Claes pleads for their duty to annul conflicting national rules due to their conflict with Community law if they are empowered to do so in cases of conflict with national constitution, Claes defines four kinds of conflicts between national constitutions and supranational law, where constitutional courts may or actually do play a role. Firstly, when they have power of a prior, preventive, international treaty review as to its compatibility with the national constitution. Claes sees this 'at the time of a major Treaty amendment, after all a "constitutional moment", [...] a logical step', although she admits that it 'does not offer a guarantee that constitutional issues will not emerge once the Treaties have been ratified and are operational' (p. 494).

A posteriori constitutional review of the Treaties, the second kind of a conflict which may arise before a constitutional court, is much more problematic. Of course prohibited by the supranational perspective, it is still practised by national courts, each of them formulating its own version, fitting its own constitution. Another critical objection could be made here, as in this part Claes repeats a great deal of material that was contained in the first part, where she examined the relationship between the Community and national legal orders. Moreover, the book quite often does so without cross-referencing these again-emerging issues, which makes it less coherent than would have been desirable, especially when taken into account its extent. What is interesting, on an example of Ireland and its 'abortion problem', the Constitution of which has an express provision giving precedence to Community law even before the Constitution, Claes shows that in case of a direct conflict between the most sensitive provisions of a national constitution and Community law, even this express provision does not avert serious problems.

Thirdly, Claes examines possibilities for preventive constitutional review of secondary law. There she finds that courts having procedural avenues to take such review show great restraint towards governments, which act in their capacity as the Union legislative body—the Council.

Perhaps most problematic seems the last type of conflict, the judicial review of secondary Union law by national courts. There, when analysing 'the banana saga' of the German courts and the Court of Justice, Claes makes a remark, which should be heard cautiously by authors of EU law textbooks and EU law teachers: 'an entire course on Community law could be built on [the saga]' (p. 611). Here, the 'neutral approach', changing the perspectives, appears again problematic, and some normative evaluation is lacking, as the chapter more or less only depicts practices in the Member States and does not offer some unifying perspective on them. Claes concludes the part by saying that '[a]s long as the protection offered by the national Constitution is not substituted, in the European context, with comparable protection at that level, the national courts will not fully retreat' (p. 650), but her reasons for them to step back before the supranational constitution are put somewhat simplistically as she merely states that it would be 'inconvenient, impracticable and simply unfair for national courts to exercise review powers over Community legislation' (p. 650). The desire for a more normative evaluation advocated above is fully applicable here.

This leads us to the very last part of Claes' book devoted to the future of courts in the European constitutionalism. Although written before the referenda in France and the Netherlands, it does not limit the discussion to the Constitutional Treaty, whose future seems to be uncertain today. The book discusses the primacy clause in the Constitutional Treaty, the role of the codified Charter of Fundamental Rights and finally, possibilities of resolving the Kompetenz-Kompetenz issue. Taking the principle of primacy, Claes observes the tacit agreement between the Court of Justice and its national counterparts to avoid conflicts as far as possible as an expression of European legal pluralism, which 'is not a solution which lawyers, especially those educated in systems based on clear-cut Kelsenian hierarchy of norms and straightforward rules of conflict, will find particularly satisfying' (p. 670). This is an exact diagnosis, however, in the next part we may engage in a suspicion with Claes that she did not fully escape this 'Kelsenian disease' of European lawyers. She firstly rejects the codification of the principle on a basis that it would not be possible to include all 'the footnotes to the principles, the subtleties and niceties' now existing to the principle at a national level and which are desirable given the fact that this 'two-dimensional' principle of primacy '[adds] to the legitimacy of Community law in the domestic legal order: the mere possibility that in exceptional cases, Community law may not be supreme before the national courts, contributes to its acceptance in all other cases' (p. 675). But then Claes says that '[i]t is commendable, in order to make the provision on primacy fully effective [...] to complete any primacy provision in the Treaty with a provision to the same effect in the national Constitutions' (p. 676). It is true that Claes is not very clear whether it is desirable to have a formally codified principle of primacy or not, and qualifies this recommendation: '*if it must be incorporated*, it should be incorporated at both levels' (p. 678, emphasis added). However, if one believes in pluralism and its importance for the European constitutionalism, one should also be clear that the absence of clear hierarchies is one of its fundamental components, which should be preserved not only in order to enhance legitimacy and acceptance of supranational law in national legal orders but because the permanent tension between the supranational and national constitution produces real engagement of both levels which may produce a constitution which would unite these levels while leaving them diverse, to paraphrase the European Union's motto. However, this involves not the neutral-observer approach chosen by Claes for her book, but some kind of normative pluralism, normative in a sense that it sees some value in the persisting diversity of the European constitutional order.

This last remark confirms the impression the book leaves with its reader: for anyone interested in the legal side of European constitutionalism, it is essential reading. Perhaps its weaknesses are at the same time its strengths: it invites to further thinking, in more conceptual and normative terms, about the proper role of courts in European legal integration and its constitution-building while it provides many insights into still unexplored national legal contexts.

Jan Komárek

Human Rights Conditionality in the EU's International Agreements by Lorand Bartels (Oxford: Oxford University Press, 2005), 326 pp, hardback, £49.95, ISBN 978–0–19–927719–3.

Enforcement has always been a vital concern in the realization of human rights. For all the arcane debate concerning their definition and content the practical question is: how can we ensure that abuse is prevented, punished, or impeded, remains the priority? What else would provoke and capture public support for the conceit that 'we' can interfere with the affairs of 'them'?

The question of enforcement outside its borders has indeed troubled the EU in its external affairs for 30 years or more. One technique that has found particular favour is the inclusion and application of human rights clauses in aid and trade agreements with third (mostly developing) states. These *contractual* terms, for that is what they are, are recognized by the EU as providing it 'with a basis for positive engagement on human rights and democracy issues with third countries'.[1] They are viewed as an effective part of an incentive-based strategy as well as a potential means for demonstrating the Union's determination to address human rights violations wherever necessary. That is the official line.

Lorand Bartels has produced a book that analyses the development and legality of these clauses. He tells the story of their creation with commendable clarity and draws attention to their location within the EU's external human rights policies as a whole. This form of review is generally descriptive but useful for all that. It is certainly important to appreciate the history of the EU's approach to this particular strategy as it provides important clues when it comes to critique, an issue I will return to later.

---

[1] Council of the EU, *EU Annual Report on Human Rights 2005* at <http://consilium.europa.eu/uedocs/cmsUpload/HR2005EN.pdf>.

In the first part of his book, Bartels therefore usefully offers an analysis of the key moments and processes that emerged and demonstrates how the clauses really 'came of age' with the end of the Cold War, specifically with the prospect of a mass enlargement eastwards. Hopeful candidates for accession suddenly became amenable to the prospect of an intrusive involvement in their human rights affairs, if only to stand a chance of accessing the bounty that membership offered. The developing world had no prospect of resistance in this new environment, in contrast to the defiance that was possible whilst the USSR remained a global influence. Including human rights clauses in agreements thus gathered a momentum that proceeds to the present. But of course, as with so many external policies of the EU, the story is fractured in the particular. By providing in his second part a detailed examination of the actual clauses placed into agreements, Bartels demonstrates the variety in drafting that presents interpretative chaos. His legal analysis is admirably exact and comprehensive, dealing with the procedural and composition aspects that emphasize the tangled web characterizing this contractual attempt to address human rights. In essence the message is that we have a confused and confusing approach that provokes differing legal responses depending upon the particular clause concerned. Is the EU under an obligation to apply these clauses? Does it even have the authority to enact them? These are the questions that Bartels poses.

Much of the remainder of the book then considers the 'implications under EU law of the conclusion that in most cases human rights impose positive obligations on the Community to secure respect for human rights' (p. 3). The EU's competences lie at the heart of this enquiry. But again incoherence reigns. Bartels concludes that the 'Community's pure agreements, the Cotonou Agreement, and those of its other mixed agreements subject to binding dispute settlement, appear to be *ultra vires* insofar as these agreements have the effect of binding the Community to perform obligations in areas of exclusive Member State competence, enforceable by way of suspension of the agreement' (pp. 226–227). In other words, the legal bases for certain clauses are suspect.

Throughout the final section of the book, Bartels in effect explores the difference between rights and obligations with regard to action under the clauses. The legal problem arises for him when the 'Community' has 'an obligation to take measures to ensure respect for human rights and democratic principles in areas of exclusive Member State legislative competence' (p. 228). He concludes that where this is the case (and this depends on the specific clause in question) Member States would be obliged to act.

So far so good, and up to this point Bartels has treated us to a thorough examination of the technical aspects of these human rights clauses. The depth and scope of legal analysis is noteworthy and probably of great interest to Community officials intent on improving the composition of these clauses. But what is missing is perhaps a reflection of the underlying approach to this form of human rights strategy adopted by the EU. In short, a hard, critical, contextual edge is absent.

Not only is the policy of conditionality left uncritiqued but so too is the context within which it has been applied. There is little, if any, consideration of the power relations at play and, in many cases, the adopted neo-colonial thinking that echoes Livingstone's mantra of Christianity, Commerce, and Civilization. The very real problem of 'double-victimization', the question of the impact on people who have already suffered abuse through action under the clauses, also fails to draw meaningful attention. The whole convoluted matter of what is meant by human rights when considering the 'obligation to take measures to ensure respect' is left untouched. Perhaps the failure to delve beneath the surface attraction of conditionality through legal agreement is the reason why we have such an incoherent approach to the drafting and implementation of these clauses. The incremental and ad hoc approach adopted to date suggests a complete failure to grasp key questions. What are the principles that govern these clauses? How are they determined? Who decides? How do they reflect on the EU's approach to its Member States with regard to human rights violations?

Bartels to his credit does call for greater coherence. However, one wonders whether he missed an opportunity to provide critical reflection on the problems of these clauses rather than treat them as, in theory, an unqualified good in terms of human rights. Surely the problems of human rights enforcement using this method are not captured by 'drafting weaknesses' (p. 237) technically resolvable by clever EU lawyers. This ignores the political environment that has always dominated the EU's external human rights policy. The problems also relate to legitimating a policy through a reasoned and principled approach that is both defensible and workable. The legal dimension, vital as it is, demands an appreciation of that wider context to transform action away from the arbitrary and towards the principled. At least, that is something that the promotion of the value of respect for human rights, advocated by the Treaty Establishing a Constitution for Europe, would suggest.

Although one must respect the parameters of any work, determined as they must be by the author, some acknowledgement of the wider context, intellectual as well as political, would not have been out of place. Bartels claims to provide 'an analysis of the EU's human rights clauses, and of their implications for the EU legal order' (p. 2) and he achieves the latter. But the former is underdone. In this respect, the work of Katarina Tomasevski, Upendra Baxi, and Martin Holland for instance, could and perhaps should have been considered. Their omission is surprising.

This book, although valuable and meticulous in highlighting the legal confusion in operation, therefore leaves one asking more questions than it answers. By consolidating the technical at the expense of the critical it may even contribute to a myth that the EU's human rights external policy is achieving coherence.

ANDREW WILLLIAMS

Addendum

Postscript to *Waves between Strasbourg and Luxembourg: The Right of Access to a Court to Contest the Validity of Legislative or Administrative Measures*

Tim Corthaut and Frédéric Vanneste

On 13 March 2007 the Grand Chamber of the ECJ delivered its judgment in Case C-432/05 *Unibet*. In this case the ECJ was essentially asked 'whether the principle of effective judicial protection of an individual's rights under Community law must be interpreted as requiring it to be possible in the legal order of a Member State to bring a free-standing action for an examination as to whether national provisions are compatible with Article 49 EC if other legal remedies permit the question of compatibility to be determined as a preliminary issue'.[1] This of course goes to the heart of the matter discussed above. The ECJ responded in a rather nuanced manner, which goes a long way to meet the criticism expressed in our contribution on p. 475 onwards of the prior case law. The ECJ decided that 'the principle of effective judicial protection of an individual's rights under Community law must be interpreted as meaning that it does not require the national legal order of a Member State to provide for a free-standing action for an examination of whether national provisions are compatible with Article 49 EC, provided that other effective legal remedies, which are no less favourable than those governing similar domestic actions, make it possible for such a question of compatibility to be determined as a preliminary issue, which is a task that falls to the national court'.[2] This means that in practice every Member State must have a procedure in place during which, as a preliminary matter, the validity of national law in the light of EC law can be tested in a risk free manner, i.e. without having to break the law first and face a penalty, even if no specific

---

[1] Case C-432/05 *Unibet* [2007] ECR I-0000, paragraph 36.
[2] *Ibid*, paragraph 65.

procedure must be created for that purpose. Indeed, in the preceding paragraph, the ECJ points out that 'if [. . .] [the applicant] was forced to be subject to administrative or criminal proceedings and to any penalties that may result as the sole form of legal remedy for disputing the compatibility of the national provision at issue with Community law, that would not be sufficient to secure for it such effective judicial protection'.[3] Accordingly, while incidental review in the context of an action for damages against the government may suffice, the ECJ now recognizes that one should not have to break the law first before having access to a court to contest the validity of a national law in the light of EC law.

This is not the place to give a full assessment of the impact of this landmark judgment. Suffice it to say that it is to be welcomed and that it may have a profound impact on the way judicial protection is ensured in the Community. In particular, attention should be drawn to the obvious tension that exists between this judgment and the 'as far as possible' approach of the appeals cases in *Jégo-Quéré* and *UPA*,[4] so that it now seems inevitable that a similar protection should also be awarded through the mediation of national courts in cases involving the validity of EU law.[5]

---

[3] Case C-432/05 *Unibet* [2007] ECR I-0000, paragraph 64.

[4] Contrast Case C-263/02 P *Commission v. Jégo-Quéré* [2004] ECR I-3425, paragraphs 31-33 and Case C50/00 P *Unión de Pequeños Agricultores v. Council* [2002] ECR I-6677, paragraph 42 with Case C-432/05 *Unibet* [2007] ECR I-0000, paragraphs 42 and 64.

[5] See in this respect also Case C-355/04 P *Segi* [2007] ECR I-0000.

Table of Cases

ALPHABETICAL TABLE OF CASES

OTHER CASES

ICJ Reports

PCIJ

Other

Tables of Legislation

Conventions

Agreements

Index